The Wiley International Handbook of Clinical Supervision

The Wiley International Handbook of Clinical Supervision

Edited by C. Edward Watkins, Jr.
and Derek L. Milne

WILEY Blackwell

This edition first published 2014

Registered Office
John Wiley & Sons Ltd, The Atrium, Southern Gate, Chichester, West Sussex, PO19 8SQ, UK

Editorial Offices
350 Main Street, Malden, MA 02148-5020, USA
9600 Garsington Road, Oxford, OX4 2DQ, UK
The Atrium, Southern Gate, Chichester, West Sussex, PO19 8SQ, UK

For details of our global editorial offices, for customer services, and for information about how to apply for permission to reuse the copyright material in this book please see our website at www.wiley.com/wiley-blackwell.

Library of Congress Cataloging-in-Publication Data

The Wiley international handbook of clinical supervision / edited by C. Edward Watkins, Jr., and Derek L. Milne.
pages cm
Includes bibliographical references and index.
ISBN 978-1-119-94332-7 (cloth)
1. Clinical psychologists–Supervision of. 2. Psychotherapists–Supervision of. 3. Counselors–Supervision of. I. Watkins, C. Edward, Jr., editor of compilation. II. Milne, Derek, 1949– editor of compilation. III. Title: International handbook of clinical supervision.
RC480.5.W453 2014
616.89'14–dc23

2013051202

A catalogue record for this book is available from the British Library.

Cover image: World map made of real rust © costasss/iStockphoto

Set in 10/12.5 pt GalliardStd by Toppan Best-set Premedia Limited

1 2014

To Our Respective Children and Grandchildren
Amelia, Grant, and Milo
and
Kirsty and Martha

Contents

Contributors

Gellisse Bagnall, Ph.D., Educational Development Manager (retired), NHS Education for Scotland (United Kingdom)

Kenneth C. Bailey, M.Ed., Department of Educational Psychology, University of Oklahoma (United States)

Matthew Bambling, Ph.D., School of Medicine, University of Queensland (Australia)

Michael Barkham, Ph.D., Centre for Psychological Services Research, University of Sheffield (United Kingdom)

Helen Beinart, Ph.D., Oxford Institute of Clinical Psychology Training, Harris Manchester College, University of Oxford (United Kingdom)

Siv Boalt Boëthius, Ph.D., Department of Education, Stockholm University, Sweden

Craigery B. Cruzan, M.Ed., Department of Educational Psychology, University of Oklahoma (United States)

Lavanya Devdas, M.S.W., Department of Education and Human Services, Lehigh University (United States)

Gillian Eagle, Ph.D., Department of Psychology, University of the Witwatersrand (South Africa)

Michael V. Ellis, Ph.D., Division of Counseling Psychology, University at Albany (United States)

Eugene W. Farber, Ph.D., Department of Psychiatry and Behavioral Sciences, Emory University School of Medicine (United States)

Craig J. Gonsalvez, Ph.D., School of Social Sciences and Psychology, University of Western Sydney (Australia)

Görel Hansebo, Ph.D., Department of Health Care Sciences, ErstaSköndal University College, Sweden

Jonathan T. Hart, M.S., Department of Educational Psychology, University of Oklahoma (United States)

Clara E. Hill, Ph.D., Department of Psychology, University of Maryland (United States)

Elizabeth L. Holloway, Ph.D., Leadership and Change Doctoral Program, Antioch University (United States)

Heidi Hutman, M.A., Division of Counseling Psychology, University at Albany (United States)

Arpana G. Inman, Ph.D., Department of Education and Human Services, Lehigh University (United States)

David J. Kavanagh, Ph.D., Institute of Health and Biomedical Innovation, Queensland University of Technology (Australia)

Mona Kihlgren, Ph.D., Centre of Caring Sciences, Örebro University Hospital, Sweden

Carol Long, Ph.D., Department of Psychology, University of the Witwatersrand (South Africa)

Linh Luu, M.S., Department of Education and Human Services, Lehigh University (United States)

Derek L. Milne, Ph.D., School of Psychology, Newcastle University (United Kingdom)

Mary Lee Nelson, Ph.D., Department of Counseling and Family Therapy, University of Missouri, St. Louis (United States)

Agnes K. T. Ng, M.S.W., Department of Applied Social Sciences, Hong Kong Polytechnic University (People's Republic of China)

Kieran O'Donoghue, Ph.D., School of Health and Social Services, Massey University (New Zealand)

Analise O'Donovan, Ph.D., School of Applied Psychology and Griffith Health Institute, Griffith University (Australia)

Marie-Louise Ögren, Ph.D., Department of Psychology, Stockholm University, Sweden

Asmita Pendse, M.A., Department of Education and Human Services, Lehigh University (United States)

Stephen Pilling, Ph.D., Research Department of Clinical, Educational, and Health Psychology, University College London (United Kingdom)

Robert P. Reiser, Ph.D., School of Nursing and Health Professions (PsyD Program), University of San Francisco (United States)

David A. Richards, Ph.D., University of Exeter Medical School, University of Exeter (United Kingdom)

Sandra A. Rigazio-DiGilio, Ph.D., Department of Human Development and Family Studies, University of Connecticut (United States)

Anthony D. Roth, Ph.D., Research Department of Clinical, Educational, and Health Psychology, University College London (United Kingdom)

Tony Rousmaniere, Psy.D., Student Center for Health and Counseling, University of Alaska, Fairbanks (United States)

Mikko Saarikoski, PhD., Department of Nursing Science, University of Turku, Finland

Douglas J. Scaturo, Ph.D., Syracuse Vet Center, Syracuse VA Medical Center (United States)

Graham Sloan, Ph.D., Psychological Services, NHS Ayrshire and Arran (United Kingdom)

Cal D. Stoltenberg, Ph.D., Department of Educational Psychology, University of Oklahoma (United States)

Eva Sundin, Ph.D., Division of Psychology, Nottingham Trent University (United Kingdom)

Janet T. Thomas, Psy. D., Independent Practice, Saint Paul, Minnesota (United States)

Ming-sum Tsui, Ph.D., Department of Applied Social Sciences, Hong Kong Polytechnic University (People's Republic of China)

Uchechi Ukuku, Department of Educational Psychology, University of Oklahoma (United States)

Tanja Rupnik Vec, Ph.D., National Education Institute, Slovenia

Tomaž Vec, Ph.D., Faculty of Education, University of Ljubljana (Slovenia)

Chiachih DC Wang, Ph.D., Department of Psychology, University of North Texas (United States)

C. Edward Watkins, Jr., Ph.D., Department of Psychology, University of North Texas (United States)

Sue Wheeler, Ph.D., Vaughan Centre for Lifelong Learning, University of Leicester (United Kingdom)

Edward White, Ph.D., Osman Consulting Pty Ltd (Australia)

Julie Winstanley, Ph.D., Osman Consulting Pty Ltd (Australia)

Sonja Žorga, Ph.D., Faculty of Education, University of Ljubljana (Slovenia)

Preface

In the pages that follow, we wish to explore the ever-evolving, fascinating, dynamic, generative, and multifaceted endeavor of clinical supervision, an essential ingredient in modern mental health services and in the development of high-quality therapists. While supervision is a wide-ranging activity, the specific focus of this handbook will be on the supervision of psychotherapy and counseling services. To enhance that focus, we have put forth a definition of supervision at the outset to guide our effort (see beginning portion of Chapter 1). The book's preeminent purpose will be to consider the nature of clinical supervision from an international perspective and, thereby, enhance our grasp of its scope and application, especially the role played by context. From this perspective, we also aim to enable greater mutual awareness of recent international developments, assisting researchers, supervisors, and supervisees to extend and refine their involvement in clinical supervision. This handbook therefore celebrates the way that supervision has increasingly become recognized internationally as a vital component of psychological education and therapy/counseling monitoring – a chief means by which we strive to develop and enhance supervisee competence so that the provision of safe, effective client care is ensured (Milne, 2009; Milne & Reiser, 2012; Watkins, 2012, 2013a, 2013b). Bernard and Goodyear (2014) have rightly noted that supervision research, though most often a product of the United States and the United Kingdom, has ever more become a global effort: all indications suggest that this will continue to be the case, and a growing number of supervision contributions from an ever-growing number of countries can be expected in the years and decades ahead.

While supervision's expanding reach and relevance has been widely recognized, we have lacked for a text that captures the increasingly international flavor and diversity of clinical supervision today. With this handbook, our hope is to begin to fill that void. Toward that end, we have attempted to bring together some vibrant supervision voices and stimulating perspectives from diverse contexts around the globe. Although many of the subsequent contributors hail from the United Kingdom or the United States (because those countries remain the dominant centers of supervision research activity), you will also find vital contributions from Australia, Finland, Hong Kong, New Zealand, Slovenia, South Africa, and Sweden. In our view, this reference resource – admittedly by no means comprehensive with regard to the growing international nature of clinical supervision – is a good start: (a) it presents a cultural immersion experience that allows readers and contributors to become more aware of supervision research and practice from around the world, while seeking to make supervision a more culturally informed topic; and (b) it provides an inclusive, globally applicable foundation on which future research/practice efforts can continue to build (van de Vijver, 2013). In turn, we have treated the *Handbook of Psychotherapy Supervision* (Watkins, 1997) as a foundation for the present volume.

As you would expect from that heritage, a mixture of supervision theory, research, and practice is reflected throughout the book, although some chapters will give primary emphasis to one area or the other. To maximize the international dimension within this handbook, each author or set of authors was asked to highlight their particular supervision context and to identify and present the potential international relevance or implications of the supervision topic being addressed. We hoped that such an approach might ultimately promote collegial interaction, cooperation, and collaboration beyond borders and beyond this handbook.

The handbook is divided into six parts. In Part I, Conceptual and Research Foundations, attention is given to defining and presenting a model of clinical supervision, considering matters of competence and evidence-based practice, examining the available research, and discussing methodological and design issues. In Part II, Practice Foundations, the focus is on ethical and diversity-sensitive supervision practice, organizational factors, and the training of supervisors. With Part III, Core Skills in Clinical Supervision, the supervision alliance, contracting, supervision formats, and skill training are emphasized. With Part IV, Measuring Competence (a marked development since Watkins, 1997), various supervision measures of practical utility are described; supervision outcomes are reviewed; possible developments are considered; and the invaluable skill of providing feedback is evaluated. In Part V, Supervising Psychotherapies, theory-specific, developmental, and social role perspectives on supervision are presented. And in Part VI, we provide a wrap-up, attempting to offer some integrative thoughts about supervision as an eminently global enterprise at the crossroads of a major advance in research and practice. All of these themes are consistent with those earlier reflected in the *Handbook of Psychotherapy Supervision* (Watkins, 1997), but supplement them with some explicit practice focus.

This handbook is designed to create an opportunity for the broadening, deepening, and strengthening of clinical supervision understanding and application. We view the text as being particularly useful for (a) practicing supervisors who want to enhance their professional development and get a good, up-to-date read about the many and varied areas that form contemporary clinical supervision; (b) supervisors in training who are being introduced to supervision and are preparing themselves for its practice; (c) supervisees who are curious about their optimal involvement in supervision; and (d) supervision scholars (e.g., researchers and trainers) who want a relatively comprehensive, diversity-rich, authoritative, inspirational, and eminently current source book on which to draw. While there are certainly limits to this handbook's coverage, it does from our perspective provide a pragmatic yet uplifting guide and rare state-of-the-art overview of much of the international scope of clinical supervision as we now know it.

In putting this handbook together, we have a host of people to thank. Any such work is a product of many voices and ours is no exception. First, we would like to express our deepest appreciation to the chapter contributors whose wise words fill this book. In the case of each and every chapter, authors collaborated with us energetically and thoughtfully, and their studious and successful efforts are beautifully on display in the pages that follow. Together we formed a formidable team of 51 authors, committed to enhancing our collective understanding of supervision. Second, at Wiley Blackwell, we thank Andy Peart, who first proposed the idea for an international handbook. He was committed to seeing such a supervision handbook in print, and he has faithfully stood by us from beginning to end, trusting us to make that original idea become reality. We are much indebted to project manager Kathy Syplywczak for her incredible energy and professionalism, which made the final editing phase of this large venture a pleasure. Last, and certainly not least, we thank our families for the continued and unfailing support that they provided to us throughout the life of this project.

Happy reading and supervising!

C. Edward Watkins, Jr. and Derek L. Milne

References

Bernard, J. M., & Goodyear, R. (2014). *Fundamentals of clinical supervision* (5th ed.). Boston, MA: Allyn & Bacon.

Milne, D., & Reiser, R. P. (2012). A rationale for evidence-based clinical supervision. *Journal of Contemporary Psychotherapy*, *42*, 139–149.

Milne, D. L. (2009). *Evidence-based clinical supervision: Principles and practice.* Malden, MA: BPS/Blackwell.

van de Vijver, F. J. R. (2013). Contributions of internationalization to psychology: Toward a global and inclusive discipline. *American Psychologist*, *68*, 761–770.

Watkins, C. E., Jr. (Ed.). (1997). *Handbook of psychotherapy supervision.* New York, NY: Wiley.

Watkins, C. E., Jr. (2012). Psychotherapy supervision in Poland and beyond. *Archives of Psychiatry and Psychotherapy*, *5*, 48.

Watkins, C. E., Jr. (2013a). On psychotherapy supervision competencies in an international perspective: A short report. *International Journal of Psychotherapy*, *17*(1), 78–83.

Watkins, C. E., Jr. (2013b). What matters in psychotherapy supervision? Some crucial features of international import. *International Journal of Psychotherapy*, *17*(2), 63–73.

Part I

Conceptual and Research Foundations

1

Defining and Understanding Clinical Supervision
A Functional Approach

Derek L. Milne and C. Edward Watkins, Jr.

Introduction

Definition of clinical supervision

In this book, we use the term "supervision" synonymously with "clinical supervision" and "psychotherapy supervision." However, what is meant by these terms requires some consideration, as there has been a wide range of practices across the mental health professions (e.g., "management" supervision, clinical "case" supervision), with the use of correspondingly different definitions. There are also differences of emphasis internationally. A popular definition in the United States regards supervision as

> . . . an intervention provided by a more senior member of a profession to a more junior colleague or colleagues who typically (but not always) are members of that same profession. This relationship is evaluative and hierarchical, extends over time, and has the simultaneous purposes of enhancing the professional functioning of the more junior person(s), monitoring the quality of professional services offered to the clients, she, he, or they see, and serving as a gatekeeper for the particular profession the supervisee seeks to enter. (Bernard & Goodyear 2014)

In the United Kingdom, supervision has been defined within the National Health Service (NHS) as "A formal process of professional support and learning which enables practitioners to develop knowledge and competence, assume responsibility for their own practice, and enhance consumer protection and safety of care in complex situations" (Department of Health, 1993, p. 1). However, prior reviews suggest that these definitions of supervision are problematic (e.g., Hansebo & Kihlgren, 2004; Lyth, 2000). For example, the popular Bernard and Goodyear (2014) definition does not specify the nature of the "intervention." Additionally, surveys

The Wiley International Handbook of Clinical Supervision, First Edition. Edited by C. Edward Watkins, Jr. and Derek L. Milne.

indicate that practitioners are unclear over the nature and purposes of supervision (e.g., Lister & Crisp, 2005).

To develop an improved, empirical definition of clinical supervision, a systematic review of 24 empirical studies was reported by Milne (2007). The first part of that review was "logical," clarifying the criteria for such an improved definition. This indicates that a definition needs to state the precise, essential meaning of a word or a concept in a way that makes it distinct (*COED*, 2004), the "precision" criterion. This requires comparisons and examples to distinguish related concepts (e.g., therapy, coaching, or consultancy). Second, a sound definition also needs "specification," namely a detailed description of the elements that make up the concept of supervision (*COED*, 2004). The next task is to operationalize the key relationships in supervision, so that appropriate forms of measurement are indicated, and so that we know what it means to manipulate supervision with fidelity (e.g., to prepare a manual or guideline). The fourth and final logical condition for an empirical definition of supervision is that it has research support: it is corroborated by the available evidence. Milne then applied these logical criteria to the available definitions, building on Bernard and Goodyear, to offer a definition that synthesized those available: "The formal provision, by approved supervisors, of a relationship-based education and training that is work-focussed and which manages, supports, develops and evaluates the work of colleague/s. It therefore differs from related activities, such as mentoring and therapy, by incorporating an evaluative component and by being obligatory. The main methods that supervisors use are corrective feedback on the supervisees' performance, teaching, and collaborative goal-setting. The objectives of supervision are "normative" (e.g., case management and quality control issues), "restorative" (e.g., encouraging emotional experiencing and processing, to aid coping and recovery), and "formative" (e.g., maintaining and facilitating the supervisees' competence, capability, and general effectiveness). These objectives could be measured by current instruments (e.g., Teachers' PETS; Milne, James, Keegan, & Dudley, 2002)." This definition was then tested through a systematic review, to assess whether it was consistent with and supported by the findings of the most relevant supervision research (a sample of 24 studies). Overall, the systematic review indicated that the definition was valid. We have shared this definition with the contributors to this handbook, with the aim of working from a clear and shared definition.

Functions of Psychotherapy Supervision

Milne's (2007) definition identified three broad objectives of supervision: normative, restorative, and formative. This follows Proctor (1988) and is consistent with the one used by the NHS in the United Kingdom (Department of Health, 1993). Bernard and Goodyear's (2014) definition also identifies three purposes of supervision, two of which overlap with the normative (i.e., monitoring the quality of professional services and serving as a gatekeeper) and one with the formative objective (i.e., enhancing professional functioning). As will be indicated shortly, there are additional functions that supervision can serve, although the terms that are used by different authors can obscure the distinctions that they make. To provide a more complete specification of what supervision can achieve and to clarify how these functions relate, we distinguish between what supervisors do (i.e., the methods or techniques that they use, such as the different approaches to teaching), the functions that these methods serve (e.g., normative, formative, and restorative), and the outcomes or goals that normally result (i.e., competencies, capability, a sense of professional identity, and the obtaining of a professional qualification or award). Figure 1.1 provides a graphic display of those distinctions. It indicates that the ultimate purpose of all this integrated activity is safe and effective psychotherapy.

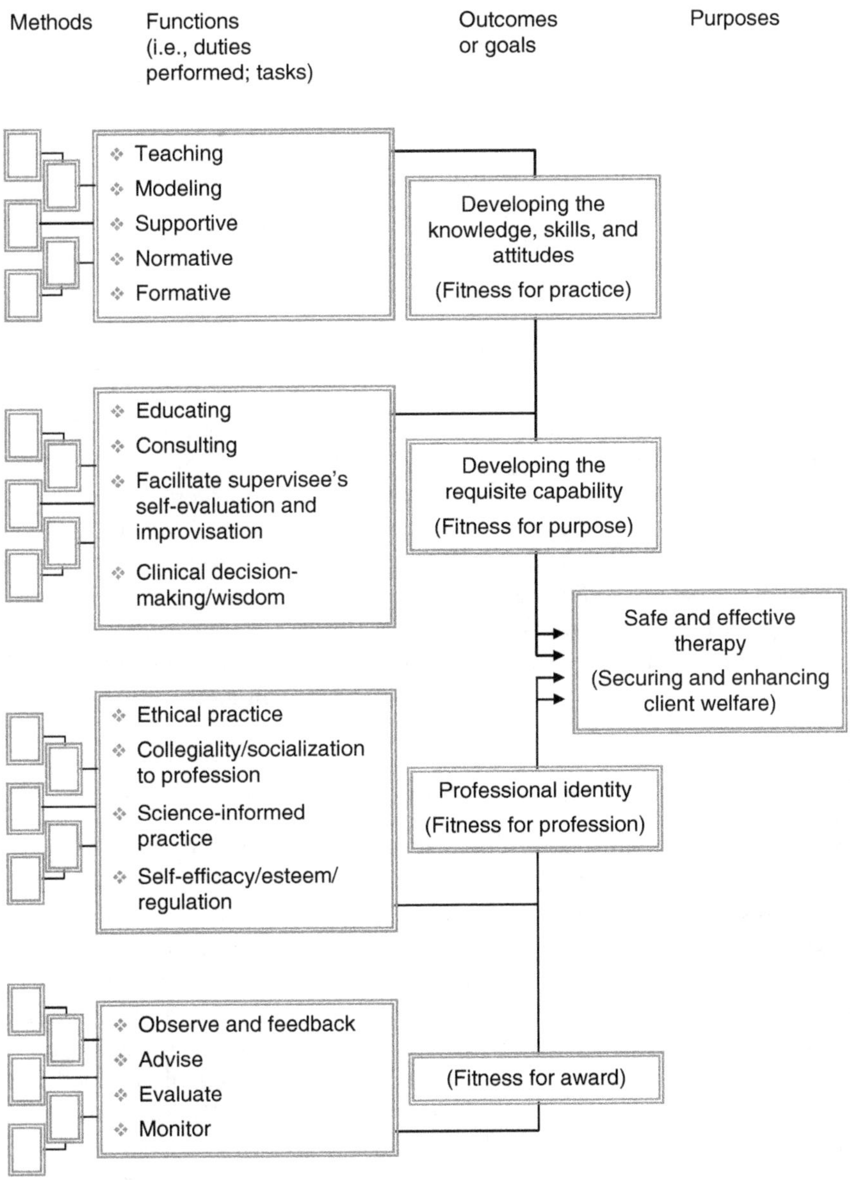

Figure 1.1 How the different functions of supervision combine to foster safe and effective clinical practice. *Source:* Milne (2009). Reproduced with permission of Wiley.

Developing competent therapists

Perhaps the best-recognized function of supervision is to enable supervisees to become competent as psychotherapists. It also appears to be supervision's key contribution: "Supervision has been identified as perhaps the most important mechanism for developing competencies in therapists in training" (Callahan, Almstrom, Swift, Borja, & Heath, 2009, p. 72), something that has been recognized by others previously (Falender & Shafranske, 2004; Holloway & Poulin, 1995; Watkins, 1997a). This endorsement also comes from both parties: a UK survey suggested that supervision was the main influence on clinical practice, as perceived by supervisors and their supervisees (Lucock, Hall, & Noble, 2006). As indicated by Figure 1.1, supervisors utilize interventions such as teaching and modeling to assist supervisees in becoming competent therapists, but it is also noted there that supervisors need to provide a supportive environment (Ladany & Inman, 2012; Russell & Petrie, 1994; Watkins & Scaturo, 2013), one that acknowledges the requirements for competent practice (e.g., recognizing any service standards that apply, such as those that specify how clinical reports should be completed).

Developing capable therapists

Of course, it has also been recognized that no amount of expert supervision prepares novice therapists for their whole careers. This is why there are systems of continuing professional development (Golding & Gray, 2006; Grant & Schofield, 2007). But one of the vital building blocks that a supervisor can help to cultivate during initial professional training is the capacity for future development. A term that is used in the United Kingdom to capture the distinction between such current and future competence is "capability." This refers to those problem-solving, creative features of a rounded practitioner (Fraser & Greenhalgh, 2001). In pursuing this function, Figure 1.1 notes that a supervisor may emphasize education rather than training so as to facilitate career-fostering qualities such as critical thinking and self-evaluation.

Creating a professional identity

Alongside competence and capability, the supervisee needs to develop an ethical approach (Thomas, 2010) and so the supervisor will encourage suitable reflection (and similar methods, such as guided reading) to foster cultural competence, related awareness of sound practice, and therapist identity development (cf. Leszcz, 2011; Watkins, 2012b). Linked to ethical awareness is socialization to the supervisee's profession, as in developing collegial attitudes and practices, and in highlighting distinctive features of one's own profession. This is captured in Figure 1.1 as the third broad goal of supervision, one that is concerned with enabling practitioners to fulfill the expectations (purpose) of their own profession. To illustrate, a capable clinical psychologist has research skills in order to work as a scientist-practitioner, drawing on research competencies to tackle clinical problems. Over time and once internalized, these should afford the novice therapist with a means of self-monitoring and self-regulation. In such ways, supervision enhances clinical accountability (Milne

& Reiser, 2012; Watkins, 2012c) and can afford an accepted defense against litigation (Thomas, 2010).

Enabling supervisees to obtain their qualifications

Since we have been emphasizing the novice supervisee, it is appropriate to add that a key function of supervision is to assist supervisees who are in initial professional training to secure the necessary qualifications to continue their careers. This implies that supervisors will use methods that support systematic observation of their supervisees, so that corrective feedback (formative evaluation) can be provided during the process of supervision, but also so that formal (summative) evaluation can be carried out at the close, as in recommending a grade or an action. In turn, this may lead to advice to address a failure to demonstrate competence, and related methods that support suitable monitoring arrangements. A case in point is a supervisee who has not yet demonstrated the correct application of particular therapeutic skills, who lacks the necessary treatment fidelity. Within England's innovative program, Improving Access to Psychological Therapies (IAPT; Department of Health, 2008), "supervision is a key activity which has a number of functions, not least to ensure that workers deliver treatments which replicate . . . the procedures developed in those trials that underpin the evidence-base: treatment fidelity" (Richards & Whyte, 2008, p. 102). Once supervisees can demonstrate the necessary fidelity, then supervisors are normally empowered (by the university that grants the degrees) to recommend that supervisees pass that element of their training.

Safe and effective therapy (clinical benefits)

The aforementioned four supervisory objectives or functions can be viewed as providing the necessary conditions for supervision's overriding purpose, which is to promote safe and effective clinical practice (Falender & Shafranske, 2004; Kilminster, Cottrell, Grant, & Jolly, 2007). In being effective, supervision should improve the outcomes for clients (Holloway & Neufeldt, 1995; Krasner, Howard, & Brown, 1998; Lichtenberg, 2007) – the long-standing "acid test" of supervision (e.g., Ellis & Ladany, 1997; Lambert & Arnold, 1987). Due to complex causal relationships and associated methodological challenges (Wampold & Holloway, 1997), that supervision–client outcome link has been minimally studied (Hill & Knox, 2013; Watkins, 2011). But those few outcome studies that do exist suggest that supervision can indeed contribute to client gains (e.g., Bambling, King, Raue, Schweitzer, & Lambert, 2006; Callahan et al., 2009; Wrape, Callahan, Ruggero, & Watkins, in press).

Context

While in Figure 1.1 we have depicted the supervisee as nested within supervision, it is also appropriate to think of the supervisor in turn as nested within a wider system, one with very similar parameters. For instance, the supervisor should also be competent, capable, and ethical. This begs the question of whether suitable arrangements are in place to support and develop the supervisor. For instance, do patients provide feedback on the supervisees, their therapists (e.g., client satisfaction data)? Do supervisees provide feedback on their supervisors (e.g., fidelity to the training programs specification for supervision)? Are supervisors supported by training and other forms of continuing professional development? How is the overall system managed? In relation to the final question, the supervision system normally includes relevant policy guidance, whether from professional bodies (who approve training programs for therapists, issue practice guidelines, etc.), public governance (national or state legislation, funding, etc.), or other sources. For instance, the UK government has increasingly supported supervisor development (e.g., Department of Health, 1998), with "dramatic changes," such as the IAPT initiative (Turpin, 2012, p. 24).

In summary, we realize that we have not done justice to all the functions that can be served by supervision (e.g., during the post-qualification period, through improving the recruitment and retention of therapists, raising job satisfaction, or aiding workload management), but it is clear that supervision serves several vital functions, ones that have increasingly received recognition within research, as well as through some professional bodies and government policies. We next ask how supervision has developed latterly, selecting the competencies movement as our example.

Developments in Clinical Supervision

As an educative process, clinical supervision is designed to foster the development and enhancement of therapeutic competence in supervisees. But what are the specific supervision competencies that make achieving that objective increasingly likely? What are the specific supervision competencies that guide and provide direction for the entirety of the supervision process? While those questions have always been of supervisory concern, the matter of competencies has received unparalleled attention in the supervision arena over the last approximate 15-year period. Substantive supervision competency initiatives have emerged from Australia, the United Kingdom, and the United States (see Falender & Shafranske, 2004, 2012b; Falender et al., 2004; O'Donovan, Slattery, Kavanagh, & Dooley, 2008; Psychology Board of Australia, 2013; A. Roth & Pilling, 2008; Turpin & Wheeler, 2011). In each of those efforts, a host of core competencies – deemed *sine qua non* to the effective practice of clinical supervision – has been identified and explicated. Although those initiatives continue to evolve, they seemingly provide a useful blueprint for competency considerations in other countries as well (e.g., Bang & Park, 2009). Indeed, the international zeitgeist within the supervision field has become dominated by the competency-based training of supervisors (Holloway, 2012), and all indications suggest that that trend will continue its ascendance in the decades ahead.

But with all of this attention being directed toward competencies, what do we mean specifically by the more focused term of "competency" and the broader term of "competence"? Professional competence can be defined as being qualified, knowledgeable, and able to act in a consistently appropriate and effective manner – reflecting critical thinking, judgment, and decision making – that is in accordance with standards, guidelines, and ethics of the particular profession being practiced (Rodolfa et al., 2005). It involves, to use the often quoted words of Epstein and Hundert (2002), "the habitual and judicious use of communication, knowledge . . .

[and] technical skills, clinical reasoning, emotions, values, and reflection in daily practice for the benefit of the individual and the community being served" (p. 226). In Figure 1.1, competence is synonymous with "capability."

The more focused term, competency, could be defined as "the combination of skills, abilities, and knowledge needed to perform a specific task" (U.S. Department of Education, National Center for Education Statistics, 2002, p. 7). This supervisory goal – the development of the requisite knowledge, skills, and attitudes for clinical practice – is also noted within Figure 1.1. Across supervision competency frameworks developed thus far, skills, knowledge, and values have been repeatedly accentuated as being the core, requisite components of competencies, and it is their amalgamation and integration that then bring competencies to life. For example, where the competency of "establish effective supervision alliance" is concerned, some of the skills and knowledge that would be needed to make that reality include understanding what an alliance is, having understanding about what is involved in its formation and repair, possessing the interpersonal skills to develop and maintain such an alliance, and being able to effectively implement those alliance-fostering skills during supervision (Falender & Shafranske, 2004; Watkins, 2013b, 2013c). A competency, then, first entails the necessary bundling of the required knowledge, skills, and values, and once that particular set has been satisfactorily integrated, only then does realization of the competency begin to occur within the practice setting, guided by a value base.

On contemporary competency frameworks

Let us look more specifically at the three supervision competency frameworks developed thus far and consider the primary guidance that we can accordingly extract from each of them (see Watkins, 2012a).

1. *The North American approach* In 2002, the Association of Psychology Postdoctoral and Internship Centers Competencies Conference, in conjunction with 34 professional groups or associations, sponsored the Competencies Conference in Scottsdale, Arizona. Professionals were included from the United States, Canada, and Mexico. The primary purposes of the conference were to identify core psychology practice competencies, formulate competency models for guiding future training, and develop means by which competencies could be assessed and evaluated (Kaslow et al., 2004). Some of the principal contributions to either emerge from that conference or that have since been stimulated by its deliberations include the following: the proposal of the cube model of competency development in professional psychology (Rodolfa et al., 2005); adaptation of that model to clinical supervision (Bernard & Goodyear, 2014); identification of competency benchmarks across different developmental levels (American Psychological Association, 2011, 2012; Fouad et al., 2009); fashioning of an assessment toolkit for competency evaluation purposes (Kaslow et al., 2009); and engagement in continuing efforts to revise, refine, and render the culture of competence increasingly practical and user-friendly (e.g., Association of State and Provincial Psychology Board's competency-based practice framework; Hatcher et al., 2013; Rodolfa et al., 2013; Schaffer, Rodolfa, Hatcher, & Fouad, 2013).

At the 2002 Competencies Conference, its supervision work group (composed of both academicians and practitioners with supervision expertise) was specifically charged with identifying the core components of competence in supervision, the most critical educational and training experiences that facilitate development of supervision competence, and various strategies for assessing supervision competence (Falender et al., 2004). The supervision work group developed a supervision competencies framework that (a) utilized three variables – knowledge, skills, and values – in understanding and defining the various competencies of supervision; (b) was guided by an appreciation of developmental and diversity considerations; and (c) embraced the view that being and becoming a competent supervisor was a lifelong process that required ongoing reflection, self-assessment, practice, and education. Some of the knowledge, skills and values competencies that their expert consensus work group identified as important included knowledge of models and research on supervision, awareness, and knowledge of diversity in all of its forms, relationship skills, commitment to lifelong learning and professional growth, and commitment to knowing one's own limitations (Falender et al., 2004). This assembly of competencies was considered to provide a somewhat comprehensive framework or blueprint that could then be used accordingly to guide and inform the supervision process; that continues to be the case today (Falender & Shafranske, 2007, 2012a, 2012b; Fouad et al., 2009).

2. *The UK approach* In the United Kingdom's IAPT program, the construct of competencies has also been and continues to be central to the defining of supervision practice (A. Roth & Pilling, 2008; Turpin, 2012; Turpin & Wheeler, 2011). The IAPT initiative, which began in 2006, is designed to offer approved interventions for individuals suffering from depression and anxiety. Shortly after the program's initiation and in an attempt to increase the probability of competent therapeutic practice being provided, attention understandably turned to the importance of delivering competent supervisory services, and a group of experts was subsequently convened to identify the competencies that were deemed necessary for the provision of effective supervisory functioning.

   Based on that expert reference group's deliberations, four sets of supervisor competencies were identified and elaborated on: generic supervision competencies, specific supervision competencies, specific models/contexts, and metacompetencies. Those competencies were designed primarily with the practicing professional in mind. Some of the IAPT generic supervision competencies include ability to enable ethical practice; ability to foster competence in working with difference; ability to form and maintain a supervisory alliance; and ability for supervisor to reflect (and act) on limitations in own knowledge and experience (A. Roth & Pilling, 2008). The overall group of IAPT competencies shares much in common with, and nicely corresponds with, the earlier work of Falender et al. (2004). Like the US supervision competence framework, the IAPT supervision competence framework provides a somewhat comprehensive blueprint that can be used to guide and inform the supervision process (A. Roth & Pilling, 2008). Furthermore, as of this writing, more specific competency frameworks that give focus to particular forms of treatment supervision (e.g., cognitive-behavioral, psychodynamic) have been developed and detailed (http://ucl.ac.uk/clinical-psychology/CORE/supervision_framework.htm).

3. *The Australian approach* In Australia, a competency-based system to guide supervisory practice and evaluation has also been recently established. While mandatory supervisor training programs have been in place in Queensland, Tasmania, and New South Wales, the Psychology Board of Australia has worked to establish a national system for the training of clinical supervisors and has now successfully done so; that work builds on, and is informed by, the earlier supervision competence frameworks that have emerged from the United States and United Kingdom (Gonsalvez & Milne, 2010; O'Donovan et al., 2008; Psychology Board of Australia, 2013). Thus, a competency-based approach to supervision – "which includes an explicit framework and method of supervision practice, and a consistent evaluative and outcome approach to supervision training" (Psychology Board of Australia, 2011, p. 5) – has been vigorously advocated, pursued, and now achieved.

The board has identified seven competencies that supervisors must demonstrate: Knowledge and understanding of the profession, knowledge of and skills in effective supervision practices, knowledge of and ability to develop and manage the supervisory alliance, ability to assess the psychological competencies of the supervisee, capacity to evaluate supervisory process, awareness and attention to diversity, and ability to address the legal and ethical considerations related to professional practice (Psychology Board of Australia, 2013). More detailed specification of what is involved in each particular competency has been clearly provided by Australia's Psychology Board (see *Guidelines for Supervisors and Supervisor Training Providers*). Like its predecessors, the Australian supervision competence framework provides a nice blueprint that informs supervisory conceptualization and conduct, and the supervision process ideally should be conducted with those competencies foremost in mind.

On consistency across frameworks

In surveying these three frameworks, what might be their binding similarities of which we should take note? What consistencies in supervision competencies are in evidence from Australia, the United Kingdom, the United States, and perhaps even beyond? In considering how those competency blueprints might apply to the treatment/supervision situation in other countries (cf. Atieno Okech & Kimemia, 2012; Bang & Park, 2009; Malikiosi-Loizos & Ivey, 2012; Palmer, Palmer, & Payne-Borden, 2012; Richards, Zivave, Govere, Mphande, & Dupwa, 2012; Stupart, Rehfuss, & Parks-Savage, 2010; Vera, 2011), six fundamental areas of supervision competency appear to be identifiable across cultures and countries: (a) knowledge about and understanding of supervision models, methods, and intervention; (b) knowledge about and skill in attending to matters of ethical, legal, and professional concern; (c) knowledge about and skill in managing supervision relationship processes; (d) knowledge about and skill in conducting supervisory assessment and evaluation; (e) knowledge about and skill in fostering attention to difference and diversity; and (f) openness to and utilization of a self-reflective, self-assessment stance in supervision (Watkins, 2013a). While not necessarily exhaustive, those six areas of focus appear (to at least some degree) to be universally important for supervisory practice wherever it may be conducted. The crucial, differentiating variable within this international mix, however, would seemingly be the ways in which those areas of focus are particularized and indigenized across cultures (cf. Moir-Bussy & Sun, 2008). That indigenization will be informatively communicated and displayed in the many instructive chapters that follow. We have wished to provide a forum here where (a) the richness and beauty of supervision's international diversity could be accentuated and appreciated, and (b) cultural incommensurability (Kozuki & Kennedy, 2004) – the inappropriate, indiscriminate, and ethnocentric application of a culture-bound way of thinking to other cultures – would be avoided. In our view, the contributors to this handbook have indeed fulfilled these wishes.

What Can We Expect of an "International" Handbook?

Bernard and Goodyear (2009) have stated, "Clinical supervision is of interest to mental health professionals in a number of countries. . .. supervision research is becoming increasingly global" (p. 300). Despite this, we lack a book that takes a truly global perspective. To illustrate, the 52 contributors to the *Handbook of Psychotherapy Supervision* (Watkins, 1997b) were all based in North America, as were the 48 contributors to *Psychotherapy Supervision* (Hess, Hess, & Hess, 2008). The handbook by Cutcliffe, Hyrkas, and Fowler (2011) adopts a similarly narrow perspective, restricted this time by profession (nursing). Therefore, in the present handbook one of our goals is to give voice to the increasingly international, multidisciplinary nature of clinical supervision. But what does it mean to take an international perspective, and what is the rationale?

Mutual awareness

At one level, an international perspective means acknowledging that the national context matters by giving researchers from around the globe a chance to present their perspectives, concerns, and related work. As a result of this internationalization effort (van de Vijver, 2013), we hope to offer a more culturally informed, inclusive, and globally applicable account of supervision. This effort facilitates dialogue and surely aids the dissemination of research and practice between countries, fostering the exchange of ideas between a worldwide cast of authors (and readers). This is surely a readily achievable but nonetheless valuable goal, because it better acknowledges what is deemed important within supervision research and practice in different national contexts, helping to raise awareness and deepen our understanding (through accessing multiple, culturally diverse perspectives: Nilsson & Wang, 2008).

In this sense, we hope that the handbook will be a bit like a "cultural immersion experience," allowing readers and contributors to become more aware of the diversity of research and practice across countries (Wood & Atkins, 2006). Benefits to such heightened awareness include recognition of our respective cultural biases, such as the dominant Western value of "individualism" (i.e., stressing autonomy and competition) in contrast to the kind of "collectivist" value base (i.e., stressing interdependency and collaboration) associated more commonly with Asia and Africa (Brislin,

2000). In practical terms, this means that Western interventions, such as cognitive-behavioral therapy (CBT) supervision, may be relatively unacceptable or ineffective in some other cultures, due (for instance) to locating problems within the individual instead of the system. A further example of international diversity is the status accorded to people within a hierarchy: by comparison with Western cultures, in Asian cultures a person in authority (like a supervisor) might be accorded greater respect and authority, and expected to provide more protection and guidance. Reiser and Milne (2012) cite an example:

> In initial meetings, discussions with an Asian American immigrant trainee included a review of cultural differences and her sense of willingness to accept challenges in supervision versus the level of support she felt she needed. She also noted that her cultural heritage involved high levels of respect for elders and teachers; and a sense that it might be impolite to ask questions, reveal private emotions (might be viewed as weakness) or unnecessarily 'bother' her supervisors. The trainee and the supervisor noted how this cultural predisposition might prevent the student from fully participating in supervision and feeling free to disclose difficult emotions associated with being in supervision-normative experiences as a therapist in training. (p. 14)

On this awareness-raising rationale, we are delighted to have recruited a truly international cast of authors, including those from many countries that have perhaps been overlooked in previous handbooks. Consolidating this "awareness-raising" aim, one of our contributors, Professor Tsui (Chapter 10), will explore international perspectives explicitly, giving attention to how variables such as personal characteristics (e.g., race and religion), social roles, and contextual factors (cultural and political) influence supervision.

Providing assistance

In addition, we think that an international perspective means assisting researchers in other countries through promoting collegial interaction, cooperation, and collaboration, to pool resources. For instance, supervision researchers in Australia (e.g., Gonsalvez & Milne, 2010) have drawn on British guidelines on clinical supervision (A. Roth & Pilling, 2008). As a result of such assistance, we are in a position to consider the global implications arising from research in one particular country. A case in point is supervisor training, something close to our hearts (see Chapter 8).

Mutual development

A final major way we see an international perspective paying dividends is through mutual development. In this sense, if this book is truly international we would hope to see authors from around the globe drawing on it to trade supervisory practices and exchange research findings in ways that help to strengthen the discipline. This might include drawing on concepts or techniques that help to accelerate progress, or which highlight unwise options or empirical blind alleys. Fostering such collaboration is our most ambitious goal because of obstacles such as the inherent cross-cultural challenges: just as there are challenges in working in a culturally competent way in a clinical or supervisory capacity, so there are challenges in doing so between culturally divergent systems or states. That is, the individual differences that rightly interest us in our one-to-one work are mirrored by "international differences." In both instances we surely need cultural competence: the ability to work effectively with people with distinctive qualities, including their country, ethnicity and culture. Few would question that "culture matters in psychotherapy and supervision" (Lopez, 1997, p. 586), and we hope to illuminate some of the important ways that it also matters internationally, so as to help researchers to address these obstacles.

In summary, we believe that the rationale for "an international perspective" is to promote mutual awareness-raising, mutual help, and mutual development. The intellectual origins of supervision are truly international, drawing initially on European philosophy, alongside Russian physiology and neuropsychology. Although the field has developed most rapidly within the United States, supervision has progressed differently in the rest of the world, representing different things to different people at different times (for an illustration from psychology, see Baker, 2012). The cross-cultural emphasis in the international handbook is intended to make research and its applications more globally accessible, acceptable, and effective while valuing diversity in understandings, perspectives, and methods.

Conclusion

Supervision is now recognized as essential to high-quality clinical practice and to the development of mental health clinicians, a status that appears to be shared internationally. "From Sweden to Slovenia, from north Texas to Northumberland, supervision has. . . become or is fast becoming an increasingly internationalized, globalized, and (ideally) indigenized area of practice and inquiry . . ." (Watkins, 2012a, p. 301). In some countries, it has progressed from relying on the opinions of a few enthusiastic experts to a situation where governments, professional bodies, and others now firmly acknowledge the necessity of supervision. Therefore, now is a very good time to try and to ensure its continued development. We believe that this development is likely to be accelerated through continued collaboration between experts, as per the illustration of the consensus over the supervision competencies. Further, we hope that the international dimension within this volume will contribute direction and collegiality to the collaborative effort.

References

American Psychological Association. (2011). *Revised competency benchmarks in professional psychology.* Retrieved from http://apa.org/ed/graduate/benchmarks-evaluation-system.aspx

American Psychological Association. (2012). *A practical guidebook for the competency benchmarks.* Retrieved from http://apa.org/ed/graduate/benchmarks-guide.aspx

Atieno Okech, J. E., & Kimemia, M. (2012). Professional counselling in Kenya: History, current status, and future trends. *Journal of Counseling and Development, 90*, 107–112.

Baker, D. B. (2012). *Oxford handbook of the history of psychology.* Oxford, UK: Oxford University Press.

Bambling, M., King, R., Raue, P., Schweitzer, R., & Lambert, W. (2006). Clinical supervision: Its influence on client-rated working alliance and client symptom reduction in the brief treatment of major depression. *Psychotherapy Research, 16*, 317–331.

Bang, K., & Park, J. (2009). Korean supervisors' experiences in clinical supervision. *The Counseling Psychologist, 37*, 1042–1075.

Bernard, J. M., & Goodyear, R. (2009). *Fundamentals of clinical supervision* (4th ed.). Boston, MA: Allyn & Bacon.

Bernard, J. M., & Goodyear, R. (2014). *Fundamentals of clinical supervision* (5th ed.). Boston, MA: Allyn & Bacon.

Brislin, R. (2000). *Understanding culture's influence on behaviour* (2nd ed.). San Diego, CA: Hardcourt College Publishers.

Callahan, J. L., Almstrom, C. M., Swift, J. K., Borja, S. E., & Heath, C. J. (2009). Exploring the contribution of supervisors to intervention outcomes. *Training and Education in Professional Psychology, 3*, 72–77.

Concise Oxford English Dictionary (COED). (2004). Oxford: Oxford University Press.

Cutcliffe, J. R., Hyrkas, K., & Fowler, J. (2011). *Routledge handbook of clinical supervision: Fundamental international themes.* London, UK: Routledge.

Department of Health. (1993). *A vision for the future.* London, UK: Department of Health.

Department of Health. (1998). *A first-class service: Quality in the new NHS.* London, UK: Department of Health.

Department of Health. (2008). *Supervision: The key to successful patient outcomes by delivering IAPT interventions of proven high quality and fidelity.* London, UK: Department of Health.

Ellis, M. V., & Ladany, N. (1997). Inferences concerning supervisees and clients in clinical supervision: An integrative review. In C. E. Watkins, Jr. (Ed.), *Handbook of psychotherapy supervision* (pp. 447–507). New York, NY: Wiley.

Epstein, R. M., & Hundert, E. M. (2002). Defining and assessing professional competence. *Journal of the American Medical Association, 287*, 226–235.

Falender, C. A., Cornish, J. A. E., Goodyear, R. K., Hatcher, R., Kaslow, N. J., Leventhal, G., & Grus, C. (2004). Defining competencies in psychology supervision: A consensus statement. *Journal of Clinical Psychology, 60*, 771–785.

Falender, C. A., & Shafranske, E. P. (2004). *Clinical supervision: A competency-based approach.* Washington, DC: American Psychological Association.

Falender, C. A., & Shafranske, E. P. (2007). Competence in competency-based supervision practice: Construct and application. *Professional Psychology, Research and Practice, 38*, 232–240.

Falender, C. A., & Shafranske, E. P. (2012a). *Getting the most out of clinical training and supervision: A guide for practicum students and interns.* Washington, DC: American Psychological Association.

Falender, C. A., & Shafranske, E. P. (2012b). The importance of competency-based clinical supervision and training in the 21st century: Why bother? *Journal of Contemporary Psychotherapy, 42*, 5–13.

Fouad, N. A., Grus, C. L., Hatcher, R. L., Kaslow, N. J., Hutchings, P. S., Madson, M., & Crossman, R. E. (2009). Competency benchmarks: A model for the understanding and measuring of competence in professional psychology across training levels. *Training and Education in Professional Psychology, 3*(4 Suppl.), S5–S26.

Fraser, S. W., & Greenhalgh, T. (2001). Complexity science: Coping with complexity: Educating for capability. *British Medical Journal, 323*, 799–803.

Golding, L., & Gray, I. (2006). *Continuing professional development for clinical psychologists.* Leicester, UK: BPS Blackwell.

Gonsalvez, C. J., & Milne, D. L. (2010). Clinical supervisor training in Australia: A review of current problems and possible solutions. *Australian Psychologist*, *45*, 233–242.

Grant, J., & Schofield, M. (2007). Career-long supervision: Patterns and perspectives. *Counselling and Psychotherapy Research*, *7*, 3–11.

Hansebo, G., & Kihlgren, M. (2004). Nursing home care: Changes after supervisions. *Journal of Advanced Nursing*, *45*, 269–279.

Hatcher, R., Fouad, N., Grus, C., McCutcheon, S., Campbell, L., & Leahy, K. (2013). Competency benchmarks: Practical steps toward a culture of competence. *Training and Education in Professional Psychology*, *7*, 84–91.

Hess, A. K., Hess, K. D., & Hess, T. H. (Eds.). (2008). *Psychotherapy supervision: Theory, research and practice* (2nd ed.). New York, NY: Wiley.

Hill, C. E., & Knox, S. (2013). Training and supervision in psychotherapy. In M. J. Lambert (Ed.), *Bergin and Garfield's handbook of psychotherapy and behavior change* (6th ed., pp. 775–811). Hoboken, NJ: Wiley.

Holloway, E. L. (2012). Professional competence in supervision. In J. N. Fuertes, A. Spokane, & E. L. Holloway (Eds.), *Specialty competencies in counseling psychology* (pp. 165–181). New York, NY: Oxford University Press.

Holloway, E. L., & Neufeldt, S. A. (1995). Supervision: Its contribution to treatment efficacy. *Journal of Consulting and Clinical Psychology*, *63*, 207–213.

Holloway, E. L., & Poulin, K. L. (1995). Discourse in supervision. In J. Siegfried (Ed.), *Therapeutic and everyday discourse in behaviour change: Towards micro-analysis in psychotherapy process research* (pp. 245–273). Norwood, UK: Ablex.

Kaslow, N. J., Borden, K. A., Collins, F. L., Jr., Forrest, L., Illfelder-Kaye, J., Nelson, P., & Rallo, J. S. (2004). Competencies Conference: Future directions in educationand credentialing in professional psychology. *Journal of Clinical Psychology*, *60*, 699–712.

Kaslow, N. J., Grus, C. L., Campbell, L. F., Fouad, N. A., Hatcher, R. L., & Rodolfa, E. R. (2009). Competency assessment toolkit for professional psychology. *Training and Education in Professional Psychology*, *3*(4 Suppl.), S27–S45.

Kilminster, S., Cottrell, D., Grant, J., & Jolly, B. (2007). AMEE Guide No. 27: Effective educational and clinical supervision. *Medical Teacher*, *29*, 2–19.

Kozuki, Y., & Kennedy, M. G. (2004). Cultural incommensurability in psychodynamic psychotherapy in Western and Japanese traditions. *Journal of Nursing Scholarship*, *36*, 30–38.

Krasner, R. F., Howard, K. I., & Brown, A. S. (1998). The acquisition of psychotherapeutic skills: An empirical study. *Journal of Clinical Psychology*, *54*, 895–903.

Ladany, N., & Inman, A. G. (2012). Training and supervision. In E. Altmaier & J. C. Hansen (Eds.), *Oxford handbook of counseling psychology* (pp. 179–207). New York, NY: Oxford University Press.

Lambert, M. J., & Arnold, R. C. (1987). Research and the supervisory process. *Professional Psychology, Research and Practice*, *18*, 217–224.

Leszcz, M. (2011). Psychotherapy supervision and the development of the psychotherapist. In R. H. Klein, H. S. Bernard, & V. L. Schermer (Eds.), *On becoming a psychotherapist: The personal and professional journey* (pp. 114–143). New York, NY: Oxford University Press.

Lichtenberg, J. W. (2007). What makes for effective supervision? In search of clinical outcomes. *Professional Psychology, Research and Practice*, *38*, 27–28.

Lister, P. G., & Crisp, B. R. (2005). Clinical supervision in child protection for community nurses. *Child Abuse Review*, *14*, 57–72.

Lopez, S. R. (1997). Cultural competence in psychotherapy: A guide for clinicians. In C. E. Watkins, Jr. (Ed.), *Handbook of psychotherapy supervision* (pp. 570–588). New York, NY: Wiley.

Lucock, M. P., Hall, P., & Noble, R. (2006). A survey of influences on the practice of psychotherapists and clinical psychologists in training in the UK. *Clinical Psychology and Psychotherapy, 13*, 123–130.

Lyth, G. M. (2000). Clinical supervision: A concept analysis. *Journal of Advanced Nursing, 31*, 722–729.

Malikiosi-Loizos, M., & Ivey, A. E. (2012). Counseling in Greece. *Journal of Counseling and Development, 90*, 113–118.

Milne, D., & Reiser, R. P. (2012). A rationale for evidence-based clinical supervision. *Journal of Contemporary Psychotherapy, 42*, 139–150.

Milne, D. L. (2007). An empirical definition of clinical supervision. *British Journal of Clinical Psychology, 46*, 437–447.

Milne, D. L. (2009). *Evidence-based clinical supervision: Principles and practice.* Malden, MA: BPS/Blackwell.

Milne, D. L., James, I. A., Keegan, D., & Dudley, M. (2002). Teachers PETS: A new observational measure of experiential training interactions. *Clinical Psychology and Psychotherapy, 9*, 187–199.

Moir-Bussy, A., & Sun, C. (2008). From didactic to dialectic – Intercultural exchanges in contemporary counsellor education. *International Journal for the Advancement of Counselling, 30*, 202–212.

Nilsson, J. E., & Wang, C.-C. (2008). Supervising international students in counseling and psychology training. In A. K. Hess, K. D. Hess, & T. H. Hess (Eds.), *Psychotherapy supervision: Theory, research and practice* (2nd ed., pp. 70–81). New York, NY: Wiley.

O'Donovan, A., Slattery, L., Kavanagh, D., & Dooley, R. (2008). Opinions of Australian Psychological Society College Chairs about process and content in supervision training: Preliminary investigation in Queensland. *Australian Psychologist, 43*, 114–120.

Palmer, G. J., Palmer, R. W., & Payne-Borden, J. (2012). Evolution of counseling in Jamaica: Past, present, and future trends. *Journal of Counseling and Development, 90*, 97–101.

Proctor, B. (1988). A cooperative exercise in accountability. In M. Marken & M. Payne (Eds.), *Enabling and ensuring* (pp. 21–34). Leicester, UK: Leicester National Youth Bureau and Council for Education and Training in Youth and Community Work.

Psychology Board of Australia. (2011). *Exposure draft: Guideline for supervisors and supervisor training providers.* Retrieved from http://www.psychologyboard.gov.au/Registration/Supervision.aspx (see Past Consultations).

Psychology Board of Australia. (2013). *Guidelines for supervisors and supervisor training providers.* Retrieved from http://www.psychologyboard.gov.au/Registration/Supervision.aspx

Reiser, R., & Milne, D. L. (2012). CBT supervision in a University-based training clinic: A case study in bridging the gap between rigor and relevance. *Journal of Cognitive Psychotherapy, 27*, 30–41.

Richards, D., & Whyte, M. (2008). *Reach Out: National programme educator materials to support the delivery of training for practitioners delivering low intensity interventions.* York, UK: University of York.

Richards, K. A. M., Zivave, A. T., Govere, S. M., Mphande, J., & Dupwa, B. (2012). Counseling in Zimbabwe: History, current status, and future trends. *Journal of Counseling and Development, 90*, 102–106.

Rodolfa, E., Bent, R., Eisman, E., Nelson, P., Rehm, L., & Ritchie, P. (2005). A cube model for competency development: Implications for psychology educators and regulators. *Professional Psychology, Research and Practice, 36*, 347–354.

Rodolfa, E., Greenberg, S., Hunsley, J., Smith-Zoeller, M., Cox, D., Sammons, M., & Spivak, H. (2013). A competency model for the practice of psychology. *Training and Education in Professional Psychology, 7*, 71–83.

Roth, A., & Pilling, S. (2008). *A competence framework for the supervision of psychological therapies.* Retrieved from http://www.ucl.ac.uk/clinical-psychology/CORE/supervision_framework.htm

Roth, A. D., & Pilling, S. (2008). Using an evidence-based methodology to identify the competences required to deliver effective cognitive and behavioural therapy for depression and anxiety disorders. *Behavioural and Cognitive Psychotherapy, 36*, 129–147.

Russell, R. K., & Petrie, T. (1994). Issues in training effective supervisors. *Applied and Preventive Psychology, 3*, 27–42.

Schaffer, J. B., Rodolfa, E. R., Hatcher, R. L., & Fouad, N. A. (2013). Professional psychology competency initiatives: Reflections, contrasts, and recommendations for next steps. *Training and Education in Professional Psychology, 7*, 92–98.

Stupart, Y., Rehfuss, M., & Parks-Savage, A. (2010). Counselor supervision in Jamaica: An initial exploration. *Journal of International Counselor Education, 2*, 74–95.

Thomas, J. (2010). *Ethical and legal issues in supervision and consultation.* Washington, DC: American Psychological Association.

Turpin, G. (2012). The impact of recent NHS policy on supervision in clinical psychology. In I. Fleming & L. Steen (Eds.), *Supervision and clinical psychology: Theory, practice and perspectives* (pp. 23–46). London, UK: Wiley.

Turpin, G., & Wheeler, S. (2011). *IAPT supervision guidance.* Retrieved from http://www.iapt.nhs.uk/silo/files/iapt-supervision-guidance-revised-march-2011.pdf

U.S. Department of Education, National Center for Education Statistics. (2002). *Defining and assessing learning: Exploring competency-based initiatives*, NCES 2002-159, prepared by E. A. Jones & R. A. Voorhees, with K. Paulson, for the Council of the Postsecondary Education Cooperative Working group on Competency-Based Initiatives. Washington, DC: Author.

Vera, G. D. (2011). Venezuelan counseling: Advancement and current challenges. *The Professional Counselor: Research and Practice, 1*, 5–9.

van de Vijver, F. J. R. (2013). Contributions of internationalization to psychology: Toward a global and inclusive discipline. *American Psychologist, 68*, 761–770.

Wampold, B. E., & Holloway, E. L. (1997). Methodology, design and evaluation in psychotherapy supervision research. In C. E. Watkins (Ed.), *Handbook of psychotherapy supervision* (pp. 11–30). New York, NY: Wiley.

Watkins, C. E., Jr. (1997a). Defining psychotherapy supervision and understanding supervisor functioning. In C. E. Watkins, Jr. (Ed.), *Handbook of psychotherapy supervision* (pp. 3–10). New York, NY: Wiley.

Watkins, C. E., Jr. (Ed.). (1997b). *Handbook of psychotherapy supervision.* New York, NY: Wiley.

Watkins, C. E., Jr. (2011). Does psychotherapy supervision contribute to patient outcomes? Considering 30 years of research. *The Clinical Supervisor, 30*, 235–256.

Watkins, C. E., Jr. (2012a). Educating psychotherapy supervisors. *American Journal of Psychotherapy, 66*, 279–307.

Watkins, C. E., Jr. (2012b). On demoralization, therapist identity development, and persuasion and healing in psychotherapy supervision. *Journal of Psychotherapy Integration, 22*, 187–205.

Watkins, C. E., Jr. (2012c). Psychotherapy supervision in the new millennium: Competency-based, evidence-based, particularized, and energized. *Journal of Contemporary Psychotherapy, 42*, 193–203.

Watkins, C. E., Jr. (2013a). On psychotherapy supervision competencies in an international perspective: A short report. *International Journal of Psychotherapy, 17*(1), 78–83.

Watkins, C. E., Jr. (2013b). The contemporary practice of effective psychoanalytic supervision. *Psychoanalytic Psychology, 30*, 300–328.

Watkins, C. E., Jr. (2013c). On psychoanalytic supervisor competencies, the persistent paradox without parallel in psychoanalytic education, and dreaming of an evidence-based psychoanalytic supervision. *The Psychoanalytic Review*, *100*, 609–646.

Watkins, C. E., Jr., & Scaturo, D. J. (2013). Toward an integrative, learning-based model of psychotherapy supervision: Supervisory alliance, educational interventions, and supervisee learning/relearning. *Journal of Psychotherapy Integration*, *23*, 75–95.

Wood, M. J., & Atkins, M. (2006). Immersion in another culture: One strategy for increasing cultural competency. *Journal of Cultural Diversity*, *13*, 50–54.

Wrape, E. R., Callahan, J. L., Ruggero, C. J., & Watkins, C. E., Jr. (in press). An exploration of faculty supervisor variables and their impact on client outcomes. *Training and Education in Professional Psychology*.

2

The Competent Clinical Supervisor

Stephen Pilling and Anthony D. Roth

Introduction

Psychological interventions are increasingly accepted as an important element of health care. They can form the principal component of an intervention (e.g., a stand-alone course of psychological therapy) or an important element of many health care interventions (e.g., the psychological treatment component of a cardiac rehabilitation program). This increasingly diverse role is reflected in the increasing number of practitioners providing psychological interventions. For example, the number of clinically trained psychologists in the United States in the early 1950s was around 1,000; in 2012 it was 93,000. A similar situation obtains in the United Kingdom where fewer than 100 clinical psychologists were employed in the health care or related services in the early 1950s, but over 15,000 in 2012. This expansion is not confined to psychologists, psychiatrists or psychotherapist; psychological interventions are provided by a range of health professionals and paraprofessionals operating in a wide range of health and social care settings. Moreover, the range of psychological interventions has expanded enormously in the past 60 years, with an increasing variety in the mode and context of delivery (e.g., computerized or face to face; individual or group therapy), and the emergence of many condition-specific interventions (e.g., trauma-focused cognitive-behavioral therapy [CBT] for post-traumatic stress disorder [PTSD]; interpersonal psychotherapy [IPT] for depression; and parenting interventions for conduct disorder; Roth & Fonagy, 2004). This raises some important questions and challenges in ensuring best practice. What is it that these practitioners should be doing? Are they providing a safe therapeutic environment? Where the evidence supports their use, are they effectively using condition-specific techniques to facilitate change in particular symptoms?

The Wiley International Handbook of Clinical Supervision, First Edition. Edited by C. Edward Watkins, Jr. and Derek L. Milne.

Concern about the effective delivery of psychological therapies is not restricted to those who develop, practice, or evaluate psychological therapists; it also extends to those who fund clinical services, and those who are the recipients of therapy. The past 30 years has seen an expansion of the theory and practice of evidence-based medicine (EBM; Sackett, Rosenberg, Gray, & Haynes 1996), which has become the dominant paradigm for filtering the expanding evidence base on the process and outcome of psychotherapy into routine clinical practice. Many countries have agencies whose task is to interpret the evidence base (e.g., National Institute for Health and Care Excellence in the United kingdom and the Agency for Healthcare Research and Quality in the United States), although these need to be accompanied by some means of promoting evidence-based practice which guides not only the work of an individual practitioner, but increasingly is used to inform services delivery systems, health care policy, funding arrangements, and also clients about the appropriate use, likely content, and expected outcomes of a particular treatment. The best developed form of EBM in this area is the clinical guideline (Pilling, 2008), and a number of organizations now exist to both develop and disseminate this information. Increasingly these are concerned not just with recommendations for best practice but also with the reduction of harm. This can be challenging in the case of a complex intervention such as a psychological treatment, in which multiple factors (both internal and external to the intervention) can contribute to change, but it need not be an insurmountable problem (see Pilling, 2008; Roth & Fonagy, 2004 for a fuller discussion of these issues).

Obviously a number of factors are associated with successful implementation of evidence-based psychological interventions in routine practice: in this chapter the focus is on the performance of the therapist and, specifically, on what role supervision competence frameworks may have in improving clinical outcomes. While the relative contribution of nonspecific, specific, and extra-therapeutic factors to the outcome of treatment still attracts considerable controversy (Beutler, 2002; Wampold et al., 1997), there is good evidence that differences in therapist performance are a source of considerable variation in treatment outcomes (especially outside the special conditions that pertain in clinical trials). Two studies from Mike Lambert's group illustrate this. Brown, Lambert, Jones, and Minami (2005) reported on the outcome of 281 individual therapists providing a range of different psychological interventions in a large cohort study (over 10,000 participants) and showed that the best-performing 25% achieved 53% greater improvement than the other 75% of their colleagues. This is perhaps not surprising but what the study demonstrated was that a range of factors including diagnosis, age, sex, severity, treatment history, length of treatment, or, most interestingly from the perspective of this chapter, therapist training or experience, could not account for these marked differences in outcome. In a similar, but somewhat smaller, study (149 therapists and over 7,500 participants), Okiishi et al. (2006) reported that the best-performing therapist not only had significantly better outcomes (by a factor of around 100%) but that the situation also held for deterioration in patients' outcomes; that is the worst-performing therapist had deterioration rates over double that of their most able colleagues. This raises two important issues: how can supervision be used to address the issues of potential harm and what might this mean for the conduct of supervision?

The Development of the UCL Supervision Competence Framework

The context for development of the competence framework was the initiation of the Improving Access to Psychological Therapies (IAPT) program, launched by the English Department of Health in 2007. This is the largest psychological therapies implementation program in the world. Initially, the program focused on adults, but more recently it has been expanded to cover children and young people (Layard & Dunn, 2009). By 2015 the IAPT program will have trained an additional 7,200 psychological therapists, and the estimate is that these new therapists will have treated an additional 1,800,000 patients at a cost of £720 million (approximately $1,120 million in 2012).[1] IAPT services provide National Institute for Clinical Excellence (NICE)-supported treatments within a stepped-care framework, initially offering "low-intensity" interventions (such as guided self-help, computerized cognitive behavioral therapy, and psycho-educational groups) provided by specifically trained and recruited paraprofessional staff. Clients who are stepped-up receive "high-intensity" interventions (formal psychological therapies such as CBT, IPT, counseling, and short-term psychodynamic therapy) provided by psychological therapists trained at master's and doctoral levels. The majority of clients are first seen and assessed by a low-intensity worker, and (for example, if they do not seem appropriate, or fail to respond to a low-intensity intervention) may then be referred on for high-intensity treatment. This initial assessment process is closely monitored and supervised and referral is determined by a number of factors, including the nature and severity of the disorder.

There are specifically designed training courses for both high- and low-intensity staff, and there is also a strong emphasis on careful supervision in the workplace. There are nationally agreed curricula based on a suite of competence frameworks developed specifically for the IAPT program (Roth & Pilling, 2007; as discussed later in this chapter (and detailed in http://www.iapt.nhs.uk and http://www.ucl.ac.uk/CORE/).

In the context of the IAPT program the need to develop a supervision competence framework was clear. A major virtue of the program is its recognition that training and supervision are the bedrock of effective service delivery, and this implies the need to specify the content and structure of supervision in a way that effectively encompasses the range of interventions provided in the program. Our challenge, then, was to arrive at a framework that would be generic, but also capable of supporting supervision of specific therapeutic interventions.

Our methodology for constructing competence frameworks is detailed in Roth and Pilling (2007) and was initially applied to a series of single modality frameworks (for CBT, IPT, humanistic, systemic, and psychodynamic approaches, respectively). Subsequently, it has been applied to the specification of competences for client groups (children and adolescents, people with personality disorder, people with psychosis and bipolar disorder), and so the approach has broadened to allow for the specification of a multiple modalities.

[1] Full details of the IAPT program can be found at http://www.iapt.nhs.uk.

It is based on a set of principles and procedures that underpin all the frameworks:

An evidence-based approach: Any framework faces the challenge of narrowing down the competences associated with a therapeutic approach and identifying those that are relevant to the tasks of therapy from those that are peripheral or irrelevant. There are many ways of approaching this problem, one of which would be to be focused on practitioners, examining what therapists actually do when delivering a particular intervention, complementing observation with some form of commentary from the therapists in order to identify their intentions as well as their actions (e.g., Skills for Health). The strength of this method – it is based on what people do when putting their competences into action – is also its weakness. In routine practice "pure" forms of therapy are often modified as therapists exercise their judgment in relation to their assessment of a client's need. Sometimes these modifications are appropriate, fully justified, and congruent with the model, but sometimes they are erroneous and distracting, and if incorporated into a competence framework they would be misleading.

To avoid this problem, a decision was made to stay as close to the evidence base as possible, delineating competences as those that have been used by therapists in research trials, and where the approach taken has shown evidence for efficacy; the assumption is that the manual used in the trial can be used to specify best practice. This approach also carries a risk; trial manuals are packages of interventions/techniques that alone or in combination may be beneficial but the effectiveness of individual components or competences is usually unknown. Specifying the competences in a rigorous manner does also provide a basis for the empirical work, which can help determine which competence or combinations thereof are associated with effective therapy and those which are not.

Oversight and guidance by experts in the field: Each framework is overseen by an Expert Reference Group (ERG) comprising individuals with nationally recognized expertise in relation to clinical application, research, and training. The ERG ensures that decisions about the scope of the framework are rooted in an appropriate interpretation of the evidence base and that clinical and professional judgment is available to guide those areas of the framework where a formal evidence base is limited or unavailable. In this sense the ERG operates in a similar manner to the expert groups convened to construct NICE guidance (NICE, 2012).

Organizing competence lists into an "architecture": One way to ensure that competence frameworks have utility is to structure them in a way that is user-friendly and intuitive, in that the structure reflects the way clinicians think about the skills they are deploying. As such, all the frameworks are represented by a "map" of competences that sets out the skills in a series of domains; within each domain the map displays a series of higher order descriptors (such as "the ability to engage the client"). These maps are displayed on the Web, and a full list of the pertinent competences is accessed by "clicking" on whichever area of the map is of interest.

Frameworks as clinical support tools: The frameworks are intended to be indicative rather than prescriptive, indicating the range of relevant competences, but assuming that clinical judgment will be needed to decide when, whether and how a specific competence is deployed. As such they are best seen as tools that support the work of clinicians and allow them to retain choice about their actions.

The procedure for arriving at a competence framework follows a series of steps. The first of which is to *identify relevant clinical trials*. Usually, this is achieved by identifying high-quality reviews (such as the NICE or Scottish Intercollegiate Guidelines Network [SIGN] guidelines, or recent high-quality reviews of relevant literature), and commissioning scoping reviews where this seems appropriate (for example, where the coverage of guidelines is not sufficiently comprehensive or the guidance is somewhat out of date). The second step involves *identifying descriptions of practice*, usually achieved by locating the manuals used by trials to describe the treatment model and associated interventions. The third step involves *extracting the competences* from the manual, a process of translating the manual into a set of behaviorally specific statements that identify and encompass both the knowledge and skills that are expected of the clinician. This involves a careful review of the manual by an experienced clinician with knowledge of the intervention. This leads to the development of the map of competences. Figure 2.1 shows this schematically; from left to right the maps specify the core or generic skills needed to carry out an intervention, followed by assessment and formulation skills, followed by the specific "packages" of interventions for which there is evidence of efficacy. The final domain is a set of meta-competences, a set of competences or procedures that guide practice, across all levels of the interventions. They represent procedural knowledge and the exercise of judgment about when and how to adapt, titrate, and apply the skills denoted in the rest of the framework and are a necessary inclusion because while the actions guided by the exercise of competences are often observable, the intentionality of the therapist is not, reflecting as this does the use of procedural knowledge (e.g., Bennett-Levy, 2005).

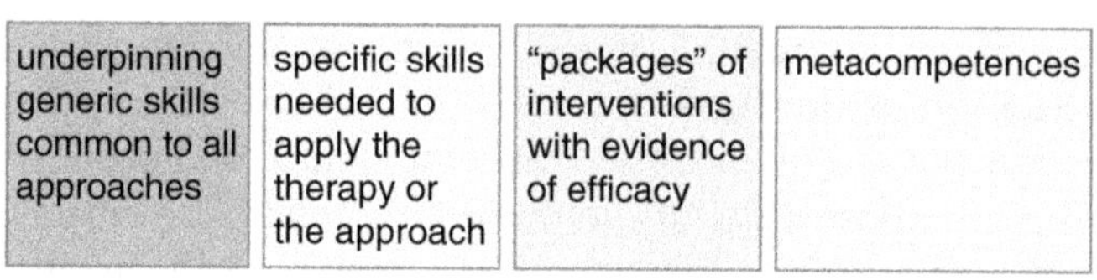

Figure 2.1 Basic structure of competence maps.

The final step in framework development is a process of peer review, in part conducted by the ERG, but also through detailed scrutiny from experts with national and international recognition as proponents or developers of the interventions being described.

The Supervision Competence Framework

The development of the supervision competence framework drew on the method just described. Our intent was to generate a set of evidence-based supervision competences applicable across a broad range of therapeutic modalities, based on the assumption that supervision has a central strand of common elements that are independent of any particular modality.

Achieving this aim required us to overcome two challenges. The first was to arrive at a common definition of supervision that could encompass the variation of practice across professional groupings, therapeutic orientations, and clinical contexts. In common with the approach taken by Milne and Watkins in Chapter 1 of this volume, the framework drew on a number of sources (e.g., Bernard & Goodyear, 2004; Falender & Shafranske, 2004; Scaife, 2001) to arrive at a conceptualization of supervision as a formal but collaborative relationship that takes place in an organizational context, which forms part of the overall development and training of practitioners, and which is guided by some form of contract between supervisors and supervisees. The expectation is that the supervisees offer an honest and open account of their work, and that the supervisors offer feedback and guidance, which has the primary aim of facilitating the development of the supervisees' therapeutic competences, ensures that they practice in a manner that conforms to current ethical and professional standards, and thereby supports the effective delivery of care to patients.

The second challenge concerned the location of the best available evidence regarding supervision. Several systematic reviews (Ellis & Ladany, 1997; Freitas, 2002; Kilminster & Jolly, 2000; Lambert & Ogles, 1997; Milne & James, 2000; Wheeler & Richards, 2007) were available at the time of development of the supervision framework, but these yielded very limited evidence on the *outcomes* associated with supervision either in terms of the impact of supervision on the supervisee's competence, or in relation to the benefit of supervision on client outcomes, which can be seen as the ultimate test of effective supervision (Ellis & Ladany, 1997). Most research focused on the *process* of supervision, possibly reflecting the methodological challenges of undertaking outcome research. Whatever the reason, this means that professional assumptions regarding the inherent virtue of supervision are untested in the face of a weak evidence base in support of this contention (e.g., Cape and Barkham, 2002; Milne and Watkins, this book).

A number of themes emerged from our scoping review (Roth & Pilling, 2008), foremost among them being the modest link between training and client outcome, although with some evidence of specific benefits associated with improvements in supervisee interviewing skills, interpersonal skills, and technical skills, and a focus on changing supervisee values and attitudes, and promoting their personal growth. As noted earlier most studies address a range of process issues, but one theme emerged as particularly significant: attempts to identify supervisor behaviors which enhance learning, and particularly those behaviors that impact on the "supervisory alliance" (a phrasing deliberately chosen to echo the notion of the therapeutic alliance This can be seen as a basic building block of successful supervision (e.g., Ladany, 2004), with an affirming, supportive, structured and interpersonally sensitive approach to supervision playing a central role in reducing unhelpful supervisee behaviors, especially the nondisclosure of important clinical information. Proper attention to the supervisory relationship may also help address the problems that arise when interpersonal issues become entangled in the assessment process. For example, both Carey, Williams, and Wells (1988) and Dodenhoff (1981) found evidence of a "halo" effect whereby the fit between supervisee and supervisor seemed to play a major part in the supervisor's evaluation of supervisee competence, and also in the supervisee's evaluation of the quality of supervision. Accurate evaluation is clearly not a straightforward process, not only because of interpersonal biases, but also because supervisors need to be able to separate out the influence of context and complexity from the capacity of the trainee.

As may be apparent from this brief summary, reliance on empirical data alone would have led to a fairly limited competence list. As a consequence, it was accepted that framework development would need to include whatever empirical findings were available, and supplement these through professional consensus drawing on publications on supervision that were viewed as authoritative by the ERG. These sources were included based on the following criteria:

- There was a clear consensus that they represented basic and authoritative texts.
- They contained a clear description of supervision techniques or process issues.
- They were used by more than one professional group.

To supplement these texts, we also identified "consensus" statements on supervision from a wide range of professional bodies; these set out supervision competences, usually on the basis of research evidence and professional consensus. As noted earlier, the ERG also took a more active role than is usual in our framework development: it included representatives of a wide range of professional groups and professional training programs, along with prominent clinicians and researchers with specific expertise in supervision.

The Map of Supervisor Competences

As shown in Figure 2.2, the map has four domains: generic supervision competences, specific supervision competences, the application of supervision to specific models or contexts, and metacompetences. A summary of the key components of these domains follows; full details can be found at http://www.ucl.ac.uk/CORE/.

Generic supervision competences

These are a suite of competences that, taken together, underpin the supervision of all therapeutic interventions; they comprise the following:

- The **ability to employ educational principles that enhance learning** and that can be employed in supervision recognizes that supervision is an educational process and, as such, benefits from using well-established principles that are known (from other contexts) to improve the likelihood of learning.
- The **ability to foster ethical practice** is essential, and supervisors need to be able to ensure that supervisees are aware of a broad range of ethical principles and professional codes of conduct, making sure that these are embodied in their clinical practice.

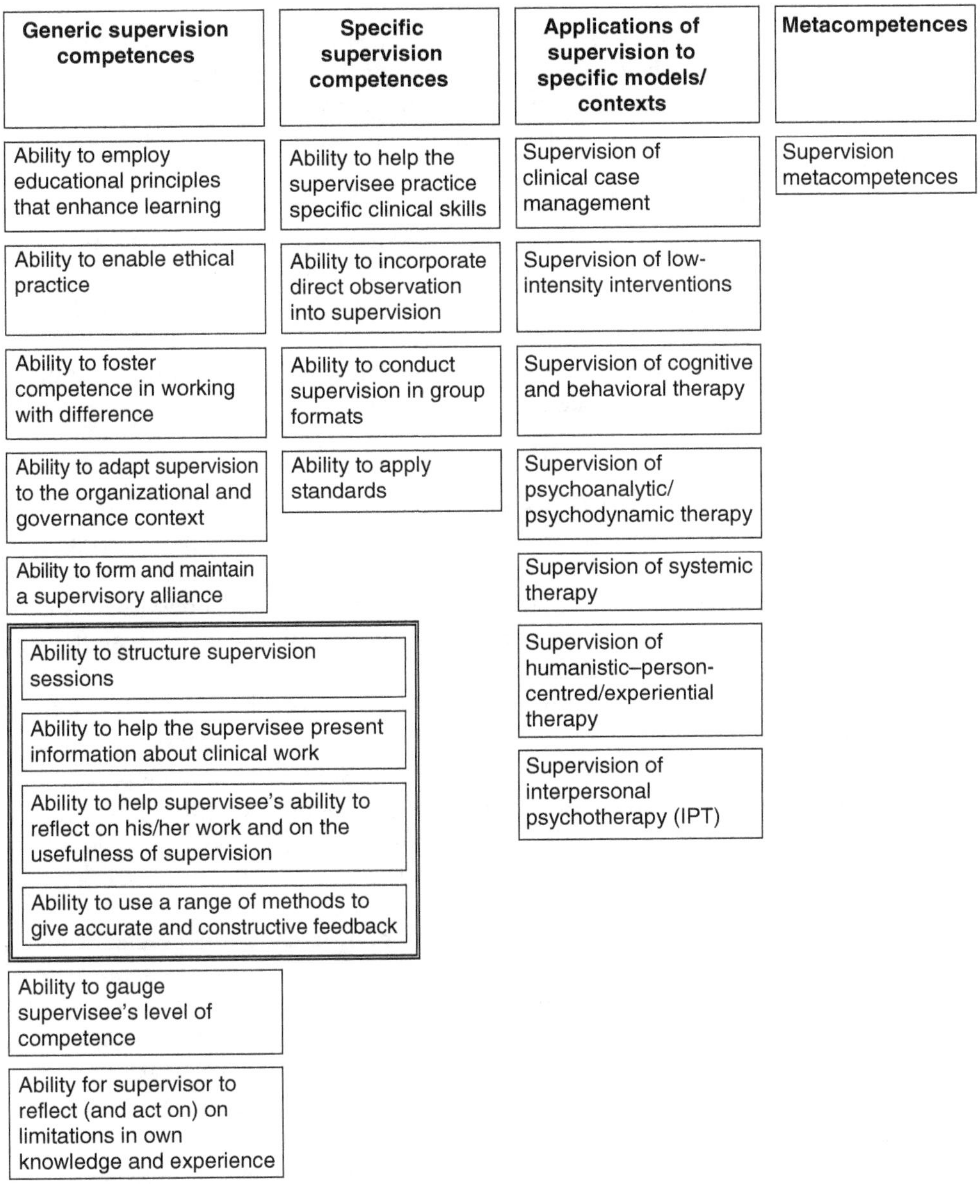

Figure 2.2 Map of supervisor competences.

- The **ability to work with "difference"** refers to a capacity to work effectively with clients across a broad spectrum of cultural and demographic variation, especially where "difference" is linked to the experience of discrimination and disadvantage.
- The **ability to adapt supervision to the organizational and governance context** refers to the need to ensure that the processes of supervision reflect the setting within which the supervisee practices, and within which supervision takes place.

- The **ability to form and maintain a good supervisory alliance** is generally accepted as crucial to the delivery of good supervision; indeed there is evidence that a poor alliance can have a negative impact on the effectiveness of supervision (Ramos-Sánchez et al., 2002). There are four further areas that are subsumed under this header because each of them contributes to the likelihood that a good alliance will be evident:
  - The **ability to structure supervision** involves establishing the professional framework for supervision, establishing and maintaining appropriate personal and professional boundaries, and ensuring that there is a contract for supervision which covers both concrete issues (such as timing and duration) as well agreements about supervision content.
  - The **ability to help the supervisee present clinical information** is an important, if somewhat overlooked, skill; it is important to help supervisees to identify content that is relevant and also to consider how best to present this information.
  - The **ability to help supervisee's "reflect"** and to undertake accurate self-appraisal is critical for adult learning. This requires a capacity to be open to experience and to learn from experience after it has occurred. Developing these skills is important as it facilitates development of a supervisee's ability to learn for themselves; without this skill they will find it hard to shift from a position of being dependent on others.
  - The **ability to use a range of methods to give accurate and constructive feedback** is one of the more challenging aspects of supervision since it requires considerable skill to detect what should be focused on and how the feedback should be delivered. Although supervisors can often detect aspects of the supervisee's behavior that need improving, unless feedback is delivered in a way that can be utilized by the supervisee it will not be "heard," and hence it will not be acted on.
- The ability **to gauge a supervisee's level of competence** can be challenging, given what is known about the impact of supervisor biases on the assessment of supervisee competence. Clear criteria and the use of a range of methods to appraise competence are two ways in which this issue can be addressed. Included here is the **ability to use objective "measures" to gauge progress** (defining "measures" as any systematic form of data collection). This requires the supervisor to have and to convey knowledge of the measures and their interpretation and to help the supervisee make use of information from them within supervision. It is worth observing that supervisors probably make less use of objective measures than might be expected, despite the fact that these are one of the few ways of reliably gauging the supervisee's clinical impact.

Specific supervision competences

This domain includes a range of specific skills that seem, on the basis of the evidence, to be associated with improved therapist competence. In contrast to the generic competences, which would be expected to be employed by all supervisors (and supervisees) in most supervision sessions, the use of specific supervision competences may vary, depending both on the therapeutic modality of the therapist and on the setting in which the treatment and supervision take place:

- The **ability to help the supervisee practice specific clinical skills** could be seen as critical since this forms a direct bridge between theory and practice. One way of doing this is for the supervisor to model skills, providing a behavioral demonstration for the supervisee, either in the supervision session or in vivo with clients; in both instances the expectation is that the supervisee is given the opportunity to implement the skills themselves and appropriate feedback is given.
- The **ability to incorporate direct observation into supervision** is important, especially because there is good evidence that it is difficult to assess a supervisee's clinical work without doing this – reliance only on self-report can be misleading. Direct observation, with a client's consent, can be carried out using audio or video recordings, or by being present in the therapy room. In general, evidence suggests that recordings should be listened to in an active manner, stopping and starting the recording and asking supervisees to reflect on the reasons for their actions. An alternative way of directly observing supervisees is through co-working – for example, the supervisor could act as an observer or the work could be shared (giving the supervisor an opportunity to model skills). Where this occurs it is important that the supervisee and supervisor are clear about the manner in which they will intervene during sessions since there is a risk that they can inadvertently undermine the supervisee.
- The ability to **conduct supervision in group formats** is an important skill because this can be an efficient way of using supervisory resources; it also helps supervisees to learn from each other. However, it does require supervisors to prepare and support group members by helping them to think about how to present their work, by managing and structuring the group, and by being responsive to group dynamics, especially if these are such that learning is being inhibited.
- The **ability to apply standards** is a demanding and important area since the interests of clients are poorly served by failing to act on evidence of poor or incompetent practice. Many supervisors find it hard to be appropriately critical or to fail supervisees, perhaps because the supportive nature of supervision can make it harder to make such decisions. Within the framework standard setting applies dirrently to trainees and to qualified practitioners. For trainees this amounts to "gatekeeping," making decisions that relate to allowing the practitioner to qualify. This process is usually facilitated by training programs, who act as external consultants to support what can often be a difficult process of decision-making. This support can be lacking when the supervisee is an autonomous practitioner whose practice is revealed by supervision to be deficient in some way. For this reason systems of governance around supervision need to be clear and explicit, and specify how concerns about practice will be managed and communicated.

Supervision of specific models

The framework includes a specification of supervision of both high- and low-intensity CBT, psychoanalytic psychotherapy, systemic therapy, humanistic/

experiential therapy, and IPT. Good-quality supervision of specific therapy modalities rests on the set of competences described earlier; these form the context and the underpinning for the supervision of specific skills associated with particular therapies. What follows is a brief summary of the model-specific competences.

Supervision of cognitive and behavioral therapies – These competences include a focus on adapting the content of supervision to the supervisee's understanding and experience of the CBT model, for example, encouraging them to use CBT techniques on themselves to promote their own learning (e.g., by completing thought records or undertaking behavioral experiments). This section also identifies ways of structuring supervision in a manner that is consonant with a CBT approach (for example, agreeing collaborative supervision agendas or reviewing "practice assignments" related to trying out therapeutic techniques), and ensuring that supervisees are active participants (for example, encouraging them to use "capsule" summaries to convey their understanding of what has been discussed in supervision). Finally, it encourages direct monitoring of the supervisee's work, using session-by-session outcome monitoring to guide the supervision agenda.

Supervision of low intensity cognitive and behavioral interventions – The low-intensity (LI) model is part of a stepped-care approach within the IAPT program, and focuses on encouraging the use of self-help materials rather than directly delivering a therapeutic intervention. Those delivering the interventions are likely to be paraprofessionals rather than specialists in mental health. As a consequence, the emphasis in this area is on providing knowledge regarding the rationale for LI interventions, the supervisee's ability to assess a client's appropriateness for an LI intervention, their ability to work within agreed protocols for the delivery of the interventions, the use of outcome monitoring, and an ability to determine when an LI intervention is not appropriate or (after a trial of the intervention) the client requires "stepping-up" to more intensive interventions.

Supervision of psychoanalytic/psychodynamic therapy – An important starting point is the ability of the supervisor to reflect on and monitor the emotional and interpersonal process in the supervisor–supervisee relationship, linking supervision not only with the supervisee's training needs but also with their personal development. There is a specific focus on a number of clinical areas, such as balancing supportive and expressive interventions and the supervisee's ability to observe and explore patterns in the clinical material, especially as they relate to unconscious dynamics and how these may relate to the supervisee's experience of therapy. There is also a recognition of the "parallel process," which allows for an exploration of processes that may be played out both in therapy and in supervision, and any implications of these for the supervisee.

Supervision of systemic therapy – Central to the effective delivery of systemic supervision is an ability to hold in mind the multiple levels that may be pertinent, including relationships in the family, between the family and the therapist, and the therapist and the supervisor and also the relevance of these for the relationship between supervisor and supervisee; as such, supervision includes a focus on helping the supervisee understand the connections between systemic theory and their personal and professional lives. One distinct area of activity is the use of live supervision, both as part of training and development, but also central to the effective delivery of systemic interventions.

Supervision of humanistic psychological therapies – The key competences of humanistic therapy mirror those of the therapy itself. As such, there is a strong emphasis on active listening and on helping the supervisee to increase his or her capacity to focus on the client's experiences and to respond in a flexible and spontaneous manner to the client. This also involves the supervisor modeling the humanistic approach in supervision, for example, by being congruent and transparent in response to material presented by the supervisee. As with psychodynamic supervision, there is an emphasis on the "parallel process," whereby the supervisor draws attention to overlaps in dynamics between the supervisory and therapeutic dyad.

Supervision of IPT – A central strand of IPT is its focus on detecting interpersonal themes that are pertinent to the client's presentation and distress, and central to supervision is helping the supervisee derive a formulation, using this to identify and implement the most appropriate IPT strategies. Given its interpersonal focus, supervision includes attention to the relationship between the supervisee and the client. There is also an emphasis both on self-assessment and on the use of recordings to monitor the supervisee's competence.

Finally, in some settings supervision will focus on the management of clinical caseload. Intentionally, this has a more managerial approach than other areas of competence described in the framework, focusing as it does on arrangements for overviewing and tracking progress across the supervisee's complete caseload, and gauging the supervisee's capacity to manage their work.

Metacompetences

Most of the metacompetences focus on the need to make appropriate adaptations in order to maximize the supervisee's ability to learn. For example, supervisors need to balance an educational focus against the need to ensure that the supervisee feels appropriately supported, "titrating" supervision to support the supervisee's development. A further example would be finding ways to give feedback in a manner that accurately reflects any concerns, but that will be received as is enabling rather than critical. As such, the exercise of professional judgment is a recurrent theme.

Defining Supervision and Applying the Competence Framework

In the introduction to this handbook, Milne and Watkins (Chapter 1) provide a definition of supervision, along with their sense of its key objectives and functions. Supervision is defined as a relationship-based education and training that is work focused and which manages, supports, develops, and evaluates the work of supervisees; the evaluative component is obligatory. Its functions include corrective feedback on the supervisees' performance, teaching, and collaborative goal-setting. Supervision operates through a number of processes, which can be "normative" (e.g., case management and quality control issues), “restorative” (e.g., encouraging emotional experiencing and processing), and “formative” (e.g., maintaining and facilitating the supervisees’ competence, capability, and general effectiveness). The functions of supervision are subsumed under four headings of skills development, namely developing capacity, professional identity, and fitness to practice, and all are seen as promoting safe and effective practice. Work by Milne (e.g., Milne, 2009) suggests there is reasonable consensus in the field with regard to this characterization.

Although these broad aims and objectives have much in common with the structure and content of the supervision framework, it is worth drawing attention to some differences of emphasis and their implications.

The use of routine outcome monitoring in supervision

Outcome monitoring is central in the IAPT program, supporting the evaluation of individual patient progress, individual therapist performance as well as the overall performance of IAPT services at the local and national levels through the use of a standardized set of patient-completed outcome measures. An emphasis on outcome monitoring in the UCL frameworks in part reflects their origins in this program, but it also helps draw attention to an important potential challenge, that is, balancing the interest of ensuring the best outcome for the patient with the need to develop the competence of the therapist.

This suggests that one priority for supervision, particularly when this is focused on post-qualification practice in routine settings, is to obtain the best possible outcomes for the client, making the client’s progression a central concern in supervision. This has implications for the performance of both supervisor and supervisee and would be demonstrated through the use of routine outcome measurement to identify clients on whom supervision should focus (e.g., those who are not improving) or to indicate where the focus of an intervention should lie (e.g., where outcome measures indicate an improvement on rituals but not on ruminations in a client with obsessive compulsive disorder [OCD]).

Another important function of supervision is *the prevention of harm*. This is reflected not only in the competences concerned with knowledge of the evidence base for effective interventions, ethical practice, and outcome monitoring, but also in the use of direct observation (e.g., the routine use of audio and video recordings in supervision). Even in the best conducted research trials some patients will deteriorate and harm may arise despite the fact that therapists are acting with the best of intentions and with high levels of support and training, In routine clinical settings harms could arise from inappropriate treatment choices (e.g., critical incident debriefing for PTSD), suboptimal treatments (e.g., failure to address the key concerns or complaints of a client in a session), or administrative or technical errors, which may undermine the alliance or result in no benefit from a specific intervention. Effective supervision can help identify and correct these problems.

A considerable body of evidence (e.g., Roth & Fonagy, 2004) now exists *on the effective delivery of treatment* and so a central function of supervision is concerned with ensuring that the correct treatments are offered to those patients who are likely to benefit from them. This requires that supervisees have a good understanding of the evidence base underpinning their work and that supervisors are aware of supervisees' level of knowledge and current training and professional development, and adjust the focus of supervision to take this into account.

Of course none of the above functions could be achieved if supervision did not have as a key function *the improvement and development of therapist skills*. This may require the development of competences in a range of different therapeutic modalities, patient populations and clinical settings. It also highlights the close relationship between supervision and training, which is discussed later.

Uses of the Supervision Competence Framework

The IAPT program had a number of expectations of the UCL competence frameworks, which applied both to the frameworks specifying the competences required to deliver different modalities and to the supervision framework. These concerned primarily the use of the frameworks to support the implementation of the program and in particular the following:

a. **The development of training programs** – Because of their structure and the level of behaviorally specific detail, the frameworks naturally specify the syllabus for training programs, and within IAPT form the basis both for training in several modalities and for training in supervision, which is mandatory for all supervisors working in IAPT services.
b. **The development of measures of therapist performance** – Because the frameworks identify the competences that should be present in a skilled practitioner, there should be a natural link to the development of measures of therapist performance. However, finding ways systematically to compress the level of detail in the framework into a workable and reliable measure presents a challenge. Nonetheless, work to address this has been initiated, with the development of a measures of therapist and supervisor adherence that is being applied in trials of contingency management in substance misuse services (Pilling, Mictheson, Little, Weaver, and Metrebian (2012), and through the development of a protocol for deriving modality-specific competence rating systems from the competence frameworks (with two "prototype" rating scales, for generic therapeutic competences and for CBT, currently being piloted; Roth, 2013a, 2013b).

Supervision and Its Relationship to Training

There is a close association between training (in any modality) and supervision; within the competence frameworks these activities are seen as complementary aspects of the learning process. Training provides the knowledge needed to institute an intervention to the general clinical context, whereas supervision builds on an individual's clinical work and experience in order to help them apply this knowledge to specific clients and contexts, consolidate and maintain skills and promote further learning. There are good reasons to strengthen this link as there is substantial evidence that training needs to be linked to organizational change (where necessary) and to the subsequent provision of supervision if it is to have a substantive impact on therapist skills and competence (Herschell, Kolko, Baumann, & Davis, 2010). Indeed, failure to mirror the results of randomized clinical trials in routine practice (Chambless & Ollendick, 2001) may well come as a result of the failure to replicate the high levels of training and supervision found in clinical trials. Exemplifying this, Roth, Pilling, and Turner (2010), in a review of 27 high-quality trials that underpinned the CBT competence framework, found that these studies consistently provided specific training for the therapy modality under test, regular (weekly or fortnightly) supervision, routine outcome monitoring and monitoring adherence to the protocol.

This has implications for the implementation of the supervision framework. Much writing and research on supervision has focused on its role in supporting and developing psychological therapists in some type of formal training (Goodyear & Guzzardo, 2000) with an understandable emphasis on the development of competence and, as noted above, less emphasis on the impact of supervision on client outcomes. Supervision for qualified staff has also tended to stress the need to support and sustain psychological therapists in what is often perceived to be a difficult and challenging task, again with a considerable emphasis on the relationship between therapist and client). This may in part reflect the fact that much of the early developmental work on supervision was undertaken by therapists from psychodynamic and humanistic traditions where the relationship is seen as a central element of the effective delivery of any intervention (Ladany, Friedlander, & Nelson, 2005). The increasing interest in supervision from other modalities, such as CBT, which have a strong emphasis on the use of specific techniques (such as homework or behavioral experiments) and on outcome monitoring in routine practice has contributed to an increased focus on these issues which in turn is reflected in the competence framework. In addition to taking into account this shift of emphasis, the framework was also designed to meet the needs of individuals at different stages of their professional development as well as those whose primary training may not be in the delivery of psychological interventions, for example:

- supervision for trainees aiming to become competent, independent practitioners, where supervision is often closely linked to an accredited professional training program;
- supervision for experienced practitioners who wish to develop their skills in a modality in which they have no previous training;
- supervision of a qualified practitioner's routine clinical practice; and
- supervision for paraprofessional practitioners (e.g., providers of low intensity IAPT interventions) or practitioners (such as nurses in primary care) gaining experience of mental health interventions

Summary and Conclusion

The supervision competence framework described in this chapter was developed to support the implementation of the IAPT program in the United Kingdom, and in particular to support supervision and training across a number of different modalities. As such, most of its content is pantheoretical (bringing together supervision competences pertinent to all modalities), as well as identifying activities more or less unique to particular orientations. We have highlighted some of the ways in which the framework challenges "traditional" assumptions about the aims and content of supervision. However, what became clear during its development was that there was much that experts from all orientations could agree on, despite the inclusion of elements that may not represent current practice in their fields. Indeed this commonality of view among experts in the United Kingdom is also reflected in the emerging consensus internationally on competence-based approaches to the development of supervision (see Chapter 1 of this volume). We look forward to increased international collaboration not only in methodological developments of the competence frameworks but also in methods to better support their dissemination and uptake.

As with psychological therapies, identifying mutative processes is a significant challenge – we cannot be sure which particular supervision activities or techniques actually result in improved therapist performance or better client outcomes. Although we can be reasonably confident of the benefits of the supervision framework as a whole, the efficacy of supervision would be much enhanced if we knew which components require our attention. Hopefully the framework can contribute to researching this question, and in turn be modified by the conclusions reached.

References

Bennett-Levy, J. (2005). What role does the "person of the therapist" play in therapist skill development? Empirical and theoretical perspectives. In M. Jackson & G. Murphy (Eds.), *Theory and practice in contemporary Australian cognitive and behaviour therapy: Proceedings of the 28th National AACBT Conference* (pp. 32–37). Melbourne, Australia: Australian Association for Cognitive and Behaviour Therapy.

Bernard, J. M., & Goodyear, R. K. (2004). *Fundamentals of clinical supervision* (3rd ed.). Boston, MA: Pearson Education.

Beutler, L. (2002). The dodo bird is extinct. *Clinical Psychology: Science and Practice*, *9*, 30–34.

Brown, G. S., Lambert, M. J., Jones, E. R., & Minami, T. (2005). Identifying highly effective psychotherapists in a managed care environment. *American Journal of Managed Care*, *11*, 513–520.

Cape, J., & Barkham, M. (2002). Practice improvement methods: Conceptual base, evidence-based research, and practice-based recommendations. *British Journal of Clinical Psychology*, *41*, 285–307.

Carey, J. C., Williams, K. S., & Wells, M. (1988). Relationship s between dimensions of supervisors' influence and counselor trainee's performance. *Counselor Education and Supervision*, *28*, 130–139.

Chambless, D. L., & Ollendick, T. H. (2001). Empirically supported psychological, interventions: Controversies and evidence. *Annual Review of Psychology*, *52*, 685–716.

Dodenhoff, J. T. (1981). Interpersonal attraction and direct-indirect supervisor influence as predictors of counselor trainee effectiveness. *Journal of Counseling Psychology*, *28*, 47–52.

Ellis, M. V., & Ladany, N. (1997). Inferences concerning supervisees and clients in clnical supervision: An integrative review. In C. E. Watkins (Ed.), *Handbook of psychotherapy supervision* (pp. 447–507). New York, NY: John Wiley and Sons.

Falender, C. A., & Shafranske, E. P. (2004). *Clinical supervision: A competency-based approach.* Washington, DC: American Psychological Association.

Freitas, G. J. (2002). The impact of psychotherapy supervision on client outcome: A critical examination of two decades of research. *Psychotherapy: Theory, Practice, Training, 39*, 354–367.

Goodyear, R. K., & Guzzardo, C. R. (2000). Psychotherapy supervision and training. In S. D. Brown & R. W. Lent (Eds.), *Handbook of counseling psychology* (3rd ed., pp. 83–108). Hoboken, NJ: John Wiley & Sons.

Herschell, A. D., Kolko, D. J., Baumann, S. L., & Davis, A. C. (2010). The role of therapist training in the implementation of psychosocial treatments: A review and critique with recommendations. *Clinical Psychology Review, 30*, 448–486.

Kilminster, S. M., & Jolly, B. C. (2000). Effective supervision in clinical practice settings: A literature review. *Medical Education, 34*, 827–840.

Ladany, N. (2004). Psychotherapy supervision: What lies beneath. *Psychotherapy Research, 14*, 1–19.

Lambert, M. J., & Ogles, B. M. (1997). The effectiveness of psychotherapy supervision. In E. Watkins (Ed.), *Handbook of psychotherapy supervision* (pp. 421–446). New York, NY: John Wiley and Sons.

Layard, R., & Dunn, J. (2009). *A good childhood: Searching for values in a competitive age.* London, UK: Penguin Publishing.

Ladany, N., Friedlander, M.L., & Nelson, M.L. (2005) *Critical events in psychotherapy supervision: An interpersonal approach.* Washington, DC: American Psychological Association.

Milne, D. L. (2009). *Evidence-based clinical supervision: Principles and practice.* Oxford, UK: Blackwell Publishing Ltd.

Milne, D. L., & James, I. (2000). A systematic review of effective cognitive behavioural supervision. *British Journal of Clinical Psychology, 39*, 111–127.

NICE. (2012). *Guideline technical manual.* London, UK: National Institute of Health and Care Excellence.

Okiishi, J. C., Lambert, M. J., Egget, D., Nielsen, L., Dayton, D. D., & Vermeersch, D. A. (2006). An analysis of therapist treatment effects: Toward providing feedback to individual therapists on their clients' psychotherapy outcome. *Journal of Clinical Psychology, 62*, 1157–1172.

Pilling, S. (2008). History, context, process and rationale for the development of clinical guidelines. *Psychology and Psychotherapy: Theory, Research and Practice, 81*, 331–350.

Pilling, S., Mictheson, L., Little, N., Weaver, T., & Metrebian, N. (2012). Supervision for psychological interventions evaluation scale – Contingency management unpublished scale and manual UCL.

Ramos-Sánchez, L., Esnil, E., Goodwin, A., Riggs, S., Touster, L. O., Wright, L. K., . . . Rodolfa, E. (2002). Negative supervisory events: Effects on supervision and supervisory alliance. *Professional Psychology, Research and Practice, 33*, 197–202.

Roth, A. D. (2013a). *UCL rating scale for competence in CBT.* Unpublished manuscript.

Roth, A. D. (2013b). *UCL rating scale for core and generic therapeutic competences.* Unpublished manuscript.

Roth, A. D., & Fonagy, P. (2004). *What works for whom? A critical review of psychotherapy research* (2nd ed.). New York, NY: Guilford Publications.

Roth, A. D., & Pilling, S. (2007). *The competences required to deliver effective cognitive and behavioural therapy for people with depression and anxiety disorders.* London, UK: Department of Health.

Roth, A. D., & Pilling, S. (2008). Using an evidence-based methodology to identify the competences required to deliver effective cognitive and behavioural therapy for depression and anxiety disorders. *Behavioural and Cognitive Psychotherapy, 36*, 129–147.

Roth, A. D., Pilling, S., & Turner, J. (2010). Therapist training and supervision in clinical trials: Implications for clinical practice. *Behavioural and Cognitive Psychotherapy, 38*, 291–302.

Sackett, D. L., Rosenberg, W. M. C., Gray, J. A. M., & Haynes, R. B. (1996). Evidence-based medicine: What is and what isn't. *British Medical Journal, 312*, 71–72.

Scaife, J. (2001). *Supervision in the mental health professions: A practitioner's guide*. Hove, UK: Brunner-Routledge.

Wampold, B. E., Mondin, G. W., Moody, M., Stich, F., Benson, K., & Ahn, H. (1997). A meta-analysis of outcome studies comparing bona fide psychotherapies: Empirically, "all must have prizes." *Psychological Bulletin, 122*, 203–215.

Wheeler, S., & Richards, K. (2007). The impact of clinical supervision on counsellors and therapists, their practice and their clients: A systematic review of the literature. *Counselling and Psychotherapy Research, 7*, 54–65.

3

Toward an Evidence-Based Approach to Clinical Supervision

Derek L. Milne

Introduction

Supervision takes place in a political and social context, including the prevailing policies of national governments and the pressing priorities within local clinical services. This makes an awareness of context vital for the successful development of supervision. Over the past two or three decades, evidence-based practice (EBP) has become a prominent feature of the work environment, at least for Western countries like the United Kingdom and the United States. As will be detailed later, EBP combines a number of related activities to emphasize how professional judgment can draw on the best-available evidence and the clinician's expertise in order to guide decision-making and optimize client safety and clinical effectiveness, in the light of contextual considerations, client preferences, and individual characteristics.

In the United Kingdom and the United States, supervisors have experienced economic pressures in their role as clinicians, such as implementing stepped care and operating within managed care (Bower & Gilbody, 2010). There has also been pressure to guide their supervisees in EBP, in accordance with regulatory mandates (McHugh & Barlow, 2010), and to respond to current thinking about supervision as a science-informed activity (Falender & Shafranske, 2004). EBP also represents a modern, consumer-oriented approach, assisting accessibility and accountability. Seen from the supervisor's perspective, EBP helps ensure "fitness-for-practice" (i.e., achieving the standards expected by others, such as service commissioners, highlighting quackery, guiding training, and enabling professional registration). EBP also supports the supervisor by providing guidelines (a form of protection from legal and other challenges) that can encourage reflective practice, aid decision-making, boost confidence, and encourage empirical thinking (e.g., theoretically informed observation, objective measurement, and reasoning about causal connections; Milne, 2012).

The Wiley International Handbook of Clinical Supervision, First Edition. Edited by C. Edward Watkins, Jr. and Derek L. Milne.

Taken together, it becomes apparent how EBP enables supervisors to make better professional judgments. For those with a research bent, EBP has a pluralistic orientation to scientific methodology and flexibility in clinical application, such that the best-available evidence may be judged to derive from practice-based (effectiveness) research, as well as from the most rigorous, efficacy research that is available (e.g., the randomized controlled trial [RCT]). This promotes its appeal to managers, administrators, and others who support clinicians and supervisors. EBP's relatively brief procedures, an intrinsic interest in cost-effectiveness, and demonstrable results boost such appeal.

These reasons also make EBP appealing to governments, internationally. In the United States there has been a $2 billion public and private health investment, intended to disseminate evidence-based psychological treatments "with a marked sense of urgency" (McHugh & Barlow, 2010, p. 73). The aims are to raise standards of care and improve clinical outcomes while rectifying the gulf between research and practice. This gulf, which predates EBP (Barlow, Hayes, & Nelson, 1984), highlights the existence of significant barriers to the implementation of EBP. These barriers can be characterized as "personal" and "situational," and both require attention if we are to move toward EBP within supervision. Some of the personal barriers will be discussed in the next section, alongside a summary of EBP and its variants. I will then note some of the situational barriers, to afford a preliminary formulation of EBP implementation, before drawing out the implications for moving clinical supervision toward EBP. The heart of this chapter is an illustration, indicating how we can move toward EBP within supervision, given this formulation. Conclusions are drawn for an EBP approach to clinical supervision.

Definition and Personal Barriers to EBP

Definitions provide the focus for mental health policy (e.g., what is prioritized), practice (e.g., what is reimbursed), training (e.g., what is taught), and research (e.g., what is funded; Norcross, Beutler, & Levant, 2005). Partly because such weighty matters hinge on what we mean by EBP, definitions can also trigger dissent from the professionals involved in these activities, making an impartial and balanced overview somewhat challenging. Therefore, to aid my summary, I will focus on the core issues, with the relatively straightforward aim of drawing out the implications for an evidence-based approach to supervision.

Evidence is something that provides proof of something or which enables conclusions to be drawn, as in proof of guilt in a legal situation. As this basic dictionary definition implies, in law several different sources of information are acceptable as evidence, although their trustworthiness or truth value varies (ranging from dubious eye-witness reports to compelling forensic data). This definition also applies within the behavioral sciences, as does a shared emphasis on conforming to accepted principles and procedures in the accumulation of evidence. An example is systematically applying established instruments in order to collect reliable and valid data.

However, when it comes to applied sciences (such as clinical psychology) and related practices (such as psychotherapy) the situation is far less straightforward, due to practitioners' diverse assumptions, divergent theoretical orientations, and discrepant belief systems. At one end of the continuum is the "scientist-practitioner" (Barlow et al., 1984), for whom evidence corresponds to the assumptions and conventions of applied science and for whom EBP is a natural and welcome move toward a system-wide development of this approach. At the other end of this continuum are clinicians for whom "evidence-based psychotherapy is a myth" (Marzillier, 2004, p. 395), a myth based on the misguided and simplistic emphasis on evidence as a foundation for therapy. For therapists with this position on evidence, research is no guide to practice: "In over 30 years of psychotherapeutic work, not one outcome study has influenced my practice to any significant degree" (Marzillier, 2004, p. 394). Such therapists are irked by the dominance of traditional research methods (e.g., the RCT), by the related dismissal of clinical wisdom as "anecdotal evidence," and by the pressure to utilize laboratory-derived interventions that bear little resemblance to what experienced therapists routinely practice in their community clinics (Greene, 2012). In some ways we are fortunate to live at a time when such divergent beliefs can coexist, providing a pluralistic, vibrant context for activities like supervision. But it does carry with it a need to define and develop respective stances with unusual care. So, in relation to dictionary definitions of evidence these divergent beliefs are equally acceptable, as evidence is the basis for a belief in a particular intervention, a belief that in mental health is based on a number of sources, particularly clinical experience and scientific research.

Within EBP, evidence is a more restricted term, appealing to traditional research concepts such as objectivity and replicable findings. Although the EBP approach endorses a wide variety of research methods, there is nonetheless a hierarchy regarding the trustworthiness of this evidence, with the RCT at the top (Bower & Gilbody, 2010). This is because EBP is an extension of evidence-based medicine. According to the most cited definition, this is

> The conscientious, explicit and judicious use of current best evidence in making decisions about the care of individual patients. The practice of evidence-based medicine means integrating individual clinical expertise with the best available external clinical evidence from systematic research. By individual clinical expertise we mean the proficiency and judgement that individual clinicians acquire through clinical experience and clinical practice . . . By best available external clinical evidence we mean clinically relevant research, often from the basic sciences of medicine, but especially from patient-centred clinical research into the accuracy and precision of diagnostic tests. . .external clinical evidence both invalidates previously accepted diagnostic tests and treatments, and replaces them with new ones that are more powerful, more accurate, more efficacious and safer. (Sackett, Rosenberg, Gray, Haynes, & Richardson, 1996, pp. 71–72)

This definition has been widely cited and frequently extended to the different mental health disciplines. For example, the American Psychological Association (APA, 2006, p. 273) defined EBP in psychology as "the integration of the best available research with clinical expertise . . .," adding an emphasis on "the context of patient characteristics, culture, and preferences." This definition highlights individual differences as a consideration. The definition used within the United Kingdom is similar (Parry, Roth, & Fonagy, 2005) but embeds EBP within a range of supportive influences, service considerations, and overlapping sources of evidence, including continuing professional development, expert-generated clinical guidelines, and outcome monitoring (each such element is discussed in detail later). These definitions share the objective of linking clinical judgments about individual patients to the best available research evidence. This UK emphasis on EBP is both psychologically attuned (in the sense that psychologists stress the interdependence of activities and context) and pragmatically helpful, as it itemizes the different factors requiring attention. For these reasons, this broader UK definition will be assumed in what follows, rather than purely the judgments made in relation to these factors.

The extension of evidence-based medicine to other disciplines is straightforward because it represents a problem-solving process that is content-free, rather than referring to a particular discipline, intervention, or technology. This means that it can be applied readily to clinical supervision. I will be discussing EBP in relation to supervision shortly, but for now will continue to summarize the situation regarding EBP in the general mental health field, particularly with reference to clinical psychology (simply as it is the discipline which I know best).

The Variants of EBP

In addition to the multiple applications of the basic EBP model, there are multiple variants of EBP. These variants give differential emphasis to one or more of the EBP elements, particularly to the different types of research evidence (including practice-based evidence [PBE] and a wide spectrum of methodologies). It may help implementation to note that the EBP variants map onto some of the variants of the scientist-practitioner, such as the clinical scientist, evaluative clinical scientist, and empirical clinician, representing different emphases on producing, utilizing, or consuming research, respectively (Milne & Paxton, 1998). In this sense, there already exists what we might regard as a helpful hierarchy of positions on EBP implementation, ones that might help the individual practitioner to cope with EBP. For instance, while EBP focuses on the interplay between the clinician, the best available research evidence, and the individual patient, other approaches stress the potency of the intervention, as in "well-established treatments," "probably efficacious treatments," and (latterly) "empirically validated therapies" (EVTs; Chambless et al., 1998). These are interventions that have "produced therapeutic change in controlled trials" (i.e., in RCTs: Kazdin, 2008, p. 147), and which are entered on a list of approved therapies for specific problems. Such variants are most naturally associated with clinical scientists, as a corollary of their interest in evaluating treatment effectiveness from their base within university research centers, where a reductionist approach is prized (e.g., minimizing the emphasis on common factors, such as the therapeutic alliance, or on patient factors). This emphasis on scientific rigor (i.e., internal validity or "efficacy" research) can be contrasted with PBE (Barkham, Hardy, & Mellor-Clark, 2010), which prizes clinician-led "effectiveness" research, conducted within routine service settings (i.e., high external validity), but as part of a research cycle that is recognized as complementary to, and interdependent with, efficacy research: "Practice-based evidence means integrating both individual clinical expertise and service-level parameters with the best-available evidence drawn from rigorous research activity, carried out in routine clinical settings" (Barkham et al., 2010, p. 23). Therefore, while EVT and PBE can be caricatured as representing two poles of influence on therapists (rigor vs. relevance; clinical scientists vs. empirical clinicians), both approaches actually acknowledge the importance of both influences, and recognize both styles of research.

A further variant is "empirically grounded clinical interventions," a UK term that refers to a broader approach to evidence than EVT or PBE as it embraces theory, phenomenology, and clinical observation while eschewing controlled trials as the paramount source of proof (EGCI; Salkovskis, 2002). For instance, Salkovskis argued that cognitive-behavioral therapy (CBT) had developed largely because it drew on $n = 1$ and related experimental studies, and because it considered the critical processes and mechanisms that explained effective therapy (e.g., the misinterpretation of bodily sensations in panic disorder). Similar arguments against controlled research and in favor of PBE have been developed in advocating "case-based research" (CBR) in the United States (Edwards, Dattilio, & Bromley, 2004). These variants start from the perspective of the clinician, although they acknowledge the complementary nature of the evidence that emerges, so they advocate collaboration with university-based researchers.

An extension of these clinician-based approaches to EBP is to place the onus on the therapeutic relationship while retaining a commitment to the scientific enterprise. This prizes the therapeutic relationship as the primary vehicle for clinical improvement, also recognizing the great diversity in clients (including the resources that they bring to therapy). On these premises an APA Task Force identified the empirical support for elements of therapeutic relationship (such as the alliance, empathy, and client feedback), using a series of meta-analytic reviews of the empirical literature filtered by expert consensus (see summary in Norcross & Wampold, 2011). Emphasizing the centrality of the therapeutic relationship also reduces a personal barrier to EBP for many clinicians.

In summary, while there appears to be no consensus among mental health professionals and researchers as to the most relevant criteria by which to define EBP, they all seem to recognize that a national policy of EBP requires a constructive response, particularly one that is based on greater collaboration between researchers and clinicians (Barkham et al., 2010; Goldfried & Wolfe, 1998). This is reflected in the explicit recruitment of scientists and practitioners to collaborate on the development of therapy guidelines within The APA (Kurtzman & Bufka, 2011). The traditional gulf between scientists and practitioners may finally be narrowing, thanks to some mutual accommodation, for example, replacing rigid manuals with guidelines that invite clinical judgment (Greene, 2012). This brings us back to the interface between the individual clinician and the work context.

Situational Barriers to EBP Implementation

Whichever EBP variant one considers, implementation is necessary if the anticipated benefits of EBP are to be achieved. Putting EBP into action represents a further significant challenge, comparable in complexity to the challenge of building a consensus on EBP, but with a much longer history (Rotheram-Borus, Swendeman, & Chorpita, 2012). Known by such terms as "innovation" (Georgiades & Phillimore, 1975), "organizational development" (West & Farr, 1989), or "implementation science" (Tansella & Thornicroft, 2009), this literature consistently highlights the surprising difficulty of fostering positive changes within health care systems. This is why it is important, for instance, to construct task forces so that the proponents of different variants of EBP can engage in a collaborative process that builds a consensus and so reduces some of the personal barriers to EBP.

All of these considerations apply to supervision as one kind of intervention within EBP. It follows that any attempt to move toward an evidence-based approach to supervision needs to take account of the implementation challenge. What do we know about implementing such a change? Which implications follow for an EBP approach to supervision? Systematic reviews conducted on both sides of the Atlantic (i.e., Fixsen, Blase, Duda, Naoom, & van Dyke, 2010; Greenhalgh, Robert, Macfarlane, Bate, & Kyriakidou, 2004) agree broadly that innovations are fostered by features such as organizational support (including training and supervision), effective leadership (e.g., fostering collaboration among the stakeholders), operationally defined interventions that target challenging goals, and the capacity to experiment with and adapt the intervention, based on corrective feedback (including improving compatibility with the values, norms, and needs of the stakeholders). Based on this knowledge, it seems that the most promising variants of EBP are those that incorporate such guidelines, encouraging collaboration between scientists and practitioners, that is, "implementation science" (Tansella & Thornicroft, 2009), and drawing reflexively on psychology to formulate the inevitable challenges in implementing EBP (Michie et al., 2005).

Implications of an EBP approach

Which implications follow for moving toward an EBP approach to supervision? Of the points just made (some of which will be illustrated shortly), I would in particular emphasize the importance of adopting a reflexive process. On this view, EBP is both an inclusive attitude to evidence and a problem-solving strategy, one that is guided by an empirical approach. In this sense, EBP is more than the use of particular tools (e.g., guidelines or instruments) or reference to the extant literature, and more like an attitude to basic scientific principles and methods (e.g., openness to objective evaluation; empiricism). In practice, this means treating the extant tools and the most pertinent research as building blocks toward progressively better theories, research and implementation. This constructive strategy can be pursued individually, as per a supervisor who is a scientist-practitioner, and/or collectively, as per PBE within a clinical service. In the following section I will outline a combination of these emphases, drawing extensively on my own program of EBP (see Milne, 2009).

A Case Study in Moving toward Evidence-Based Clinical Supervision (EBCS)

The examples that follow address the EBP elements, starting with theory development then moving through research to the practical by-products (including guidelines and a supervisor training manual). This leads into a summary of their influence on supervision practice, concluding with audit. I will cite publications extensively to provide a complete summary of this UK/US program of research and development, and so that the reader can better judge the status of this aspect of the evidence base. As will become clear from references to the numerous co-authors and to our consensus-building work, this research program depended on extensive collaboration with key stakeholders throughout the United Kingdom and the United States (see the Acknowledgments).

Theory development

The convention within the clinical supervision literature is to borrow minimally from the neighboring literatures, most commonly to acknowledge the relevance of the developmental model in relation to the supervisee and to incorporate the therapeutic alliance as a pillar of good professional practice. My own stance has consistently been to extend this approach where appropriate, within a basic "reasoning-by-analogy" strategy, particularly by incorporating concepts from the literature on experiential learning, for example, the role of emotions; staff development, for example, the place of educational needs assessment; and psychotherapy, for example, the value of micro process-outcome analyses (Milne, 2006).

As an integrative approach, reasoning-by-analogy imports promising concepts and methods, adapting them as necessary to develop supervision. This has been especially helpful where the supervision literature is limited, affording a working solution to pressing problems such as how to train supervisors or to evaluate their effectiveness. Complementing this "borrowing" strategy has been a "burrowing" approach: conducting highly selective, in-depth systematic (meta-analytic) reviews of the available supervision literature. Together, these defined the focus for supervision research, developed more specific theory, and suggested pragmatic ways forward. To illustrate, an early review developed an empirical definition of what is meant by "clinical supervision" by conducting a logical analysis, tested against a systematic review of 24 empirical successful manipulations of supervision (Milne, 2007). The logical analysis applied four criteria for an empirical definition to existing definitions, especially the most widely cited one by Bernard and Goodyear (2004). These were the precision, specification, operationalization, and corroboration of a definition. Unfortunately, Bernard and Goodyear's definition was judged to have failed all four of these tests, but to merit refinement. Next, the review aspect tested a refined, working definition against the explicit or implicit definition of supervision within 24 carefully selected experimental studies (we used the "best-evidence synthesis" [BES] method for our systematic reviews, which meant selecting studies where the manipulation of supervision was effective and where inferences were plausible; Petticrew & Roberts, 2006). This analysis suggested an empirical definition of supervision: "The formal provision, by senior/qualified health practitioners, of an intensive, relationship-based education and training that is case-focused and which supports, directs and guides the work of colleagues" (Milne, 2007, p. 440). The paper by Milne (2007) was an example of how a review can serve to focus research. Related reviews (systematic, theoretical, and integrative) helped to develop how we theorized about supervision (particularly CBT supervision), including a basic model (Milne, Aylott, Fitzpatrick, & Ellis, 2008), the methods and micro-methods used in supervision (James, Milne, Blackburn, &

Armstrong, 2006; James, Milne, & Morse, 2008; Milne & James, 2000), and the role of emotions (Lombardo, Milne, & Proctor, 2009). Other reviews built a bridge from theory to practice, including an enhancement of CBT supervision based on the reported effectiveness of different methods, for example, use of tapes; corrective feedback (Milne et al., 2010); how best to train supervisors (Milne, Sheikh, Pattison, & Wilkinson, 2011); measurement options (Milne & Reiser, 2011); and two meta-reviews that synthesized this theoretical effort and suggested ways in which supervision might be enhanced (Milne, 2008, 2009). Some of these reviews contributed directly to other parts of EBP, as in highlighting methods that could be considered for guidelines. An account of the related research activity now follows.

Range of research activity

EBP includes an "hourglass" of research methods, denoting the cycle from exploratory studies (including instrument development) to rigorous experiments (the "pinch" in the hourglass, indicating "tighter" research, i.e., emphasizing internal validity) to dissemination work (i.e., high external validity). The exploratory studies underpinning EBCS included qualitative analyses of the content of supervision (Milne, Pilkington, Gracie, & James, 2003); interpersonal processes, for example, collusion (Milne, Leck, & Choudhri, 2009); and the "episodes" that indicate progress (Breese, Boon, & Milne, 2012). Other preliminary work is noted later, in relation to issues such as consensus-building and supervisor training.

The qualitative content analyses have been based largely on in-depth examinations of naturalistic videotape recordings of supervision but include interview-based approaches. One such study attempted to develop theory by using the constructivist revision of grounded theory methodology (Johnston & Milne, 2012). Seven trainee clinical psychologists participated in interviews with the first author, focusing on their receipt of supervision to date (i.e., during their doctoral training up to that point: at least four different supervisors). The conceptual model that emerged indicated that these supervisees perceived their receipt of supervision to have two developmental dimensions, concerned with competence and awareness. A cluster of supervisory methods facilitated their progression along these two dimensions, including reflection, Socratic information exchange, scaffolding, and a sound alliance.

Turning to the use of videotape recordings to develop theory via qualitative research, one study entailed the transcription of eight naturalistic recordings of a range of supervision approaches, conducted with supervisees who differed significantly in their clinical experience (in order to examine a popular theory of leadership). In support of this "situational leadership" theory, we found that supervisor speech decreased with supervisee experience, but conversely that many of the other predictions arising from this theory were not supported, for example, higher frequencies of questioning, explanation, and feedback with increased experience (Papworth, Milne, & Boak, 2009). In a second content analysis we scrutinized 10 consecutive sessions led by one supervisor, linked to the 10 subsequent therapy sessions, as led by the supervisee (Milne et al., 2003). This enabled us to conduct a thematic analysis of the supervision, which corresponded closely to a CBT approach, and to assess the degree to which supervision transferred (generalized) to therapy. We found considerable transfer, most frequently the provision of factual information (100%), followed by specific ways of agenda-setting and managing the sessions (90%). We thought that this small study suggested that CBT supervision could be effective in encouraging appropriate changes in therapy.

Latterly we have focused on the episode approach, which Ladany, Friedlander, and Nelson (2005) developed from the Gestalt therapy research by Greenberg (1984). An episode consists of the identification of a supervisee problem or need; working through this problem, using a variety of supervision methods within an "interaction sequence"; and the "resolution" of the need/problem (see Figure 3.1 for an example). Having established that this method was preferable to a similar approach that used a longer time frame (Breese et al., 2012), we identified 31 episodes within the $n = 1$ study noted earlier, that is, from all 37 supervision sessions that were taped, over the

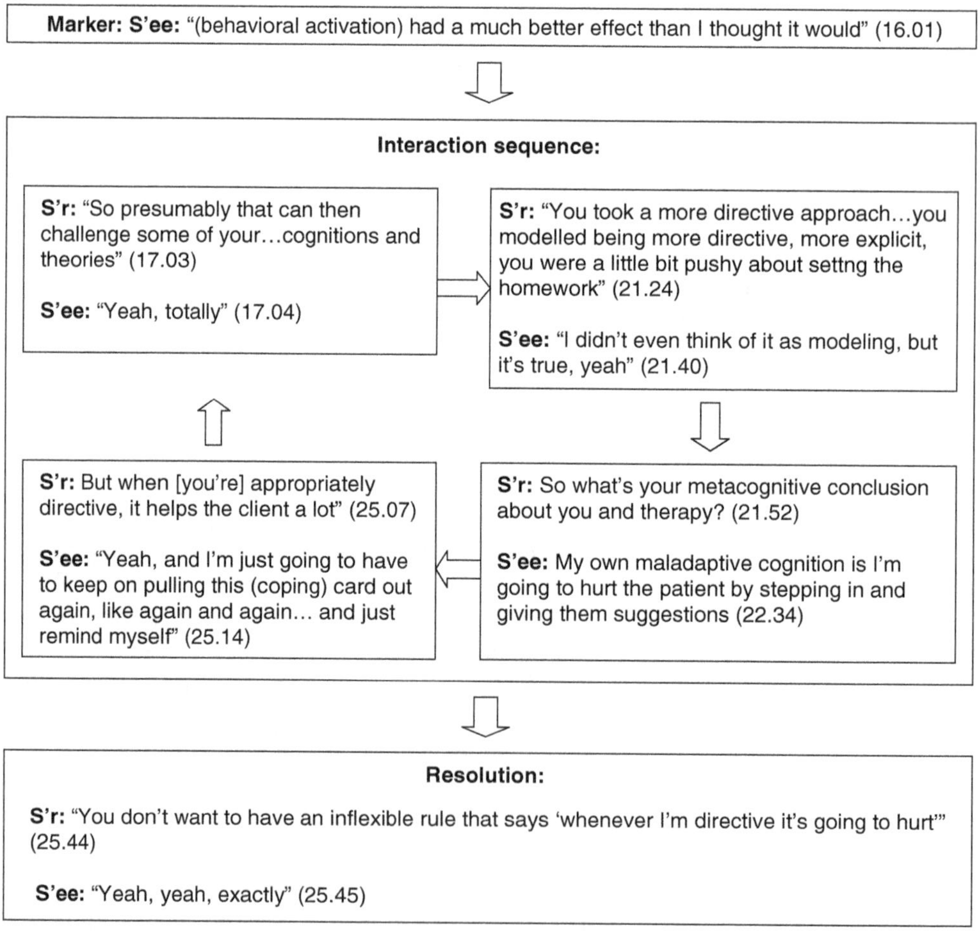

Figure 3.1 An episode within supervision, indicating decision-making that is based on evidence from within CBT concerning what is likely to benefit the patient (e.g., behavioral activation, modeling, homework). S'r = supervisor; S'ee = supervisee; figures in brackets denote elapsed minutes and seconds. Milne et al., 2011. Reproduced with permission of Cambridge University Press.

11-month study period (Milne, Reiser, & Cliffe, 2013). These 31 episodes were first analyzed qualitatively for markers, interaction sequences, and resolutions (Milne, Reiser, Cliffe, Breese, et al., 2011). We then compared the CBT supervision phases (i.e., supervision-as-usual) with the EBCS phases of the $n = 1$ design. This indicated that both approaches were similar in terms of both the number and types of episodes that occurred: in 28 of the episodes the markers were concerned with the supervisee's need for guidance or corrective feedback; the interaction sequence usually focused on skill or therapeutic process; and the dominant resolutions were skill enhancement and improved self-awareness. Next, to assess the fidelity of supervision to these two approaches (CBT and EBCS), we also analyzed the kind of utterances made by the supervisor. These were found to include appropriate high fidelity utterances, such as structuring statements, modeling and identifying specific cognitions in CBT; and discussing feeling reactions, challenging, and role-plays in EBCS. But we also found a high frequency (i.e., 35 instances) of inappropriate, low-fidelity utterances in the CBT phases, most being consistent with a counseling focus (e.g., exploring feelings and being nondirective). This counseling focus also appeared during the EBCS phases but was only observed on five occasions. We concluded that this qualitative methodology had helped to clarify the comparative fidelity and effectiveness of these two approaches to supervision, complementing the similarly detailed $n = 1$ evaluation, as outlined next.

Building on this exploratory qualitative work, the most rigorous (i.e., internally valid) EBCS research to date has utilized the $n = 1$ methodology, within a series of naturalistic studies where attempts were made to enhance supervision-as-usual among experienced CBT supervisors by drawing on evidence-based methods (e.g., providing the supervisor with corrective feedback, based on quantitatively coded recordings of their supervision). These entailed close collaboration with colleagues from backgrounds in mental health nursing and clinical psychology, individuals with a keen interest in developing the supervision skills that were part of their routine work (in the United Kingdom and the United States). The first of these presented the EBCS rationale, with an $n = 1$ study as an illustration (Milne & Westerman, 2001). I acted as the consultant, guiding the supervisor (i.e., "supervision-of-supervision"). This was enabled by videotape recordings of supervision, which were made over an eight-month period. Three supervisees were included, within a multiple-baseline design. During the baseline phases, supervision was dominated by listening to and supporting the supervisees (seen individually), which was associated with high levels of reflecting by the supervisees. However, during the intervention and maintenance phases the supervisor gradually utilized slightly more experiential methods (e.g., educational role-play), resulting in a better balance across the supervisees' learning modes (i.e., increased frequencies in their "experimenting," "experiencing," "conceptualizing," and "planning"). This basic methodology was repeated in three further $n = 1$ studies, with different supervisors and supervisees (Milne & James, 2002; Milne, Kennedy, et al., 2008; Milne et al., 2013). These served to replicate the finding of modest but valuable improvements in supervision, which appeared to improve the supervisees' learning. Some methodological refinements were also made, as in adding comparisons using inferential statistics, a manual to guide supervision, and improved measurement. These developments are detailed next.

In summary, in this research and development (R&D) program of pluralistic research, EBCS has been shaped by a range of qualitative and quantitative methodologies, ones that might be referred to as "upstream" (due to their exploratory, small-sample emphasis). Instrument development and measurement refinement were further features of this initial phase of research activity. Clearly, larger sample studies and further improvements to measurement are desirable to complement this part of the research hourglass and to test the findings from this preliminary research more vigorously (including independent replications). Some further methodological illustrations from the R&D followed behind EBCS, many using larger samples while remaining exploratory in style. The main conclusion is that a diverse range of exploratory research methods have been utilized within the EBCS program, corresponding with the EBP model. Of course, as clearly shown by the reference list within my summary of EBCS (Milne, 2009), the EBCS approach was also hugely influenced by other "downstream" research work, including relevant literature on staff training (e.g., Colquitt, LePine, & Noe, 2000), instrument development (e.g., Palomo, Beinart, & Cooper, 2010), RCTs (e.g., Bambling, King, Raue, Schweitzer, & Lambert, 2006; Heaven, Clegg, & Maguire, 2006), and other rigorous, large-sample studies of direct relevance to EBCS (e.g., Gilbody, Bower, Fletcher, Richards, & Sutton, 2006; Henggeler, Schoenwald, Liao, Letourneau, & Edwards, 2002).

Consensus-building

Within the EBCS research and development program we have adopted formal consensus-building methods to develop supervision guidelines (see next section) and to consider how we should train supervisors (Milne, Scaife, & Cliffe, 2009). Prior consensus-building work on this topic conducted within the United States had suggested several helpful pointers, such as using a developmental approach and drawing on the research literature (Falender et al., 2004; Kaslow et al., 2004). Would a British sample of supervisors and their trainers agree? We held a brief workshop with 36 experienced supervisors and trainers, using the nominal group technique (NGT) (Delbecq & Van de Ven, 1972) to try and capture their wisdom regarding the facilitation of experiential learning. The resulting consensus statement included 16 factors, with the greatest support for "safe space" (a learning alliance), followed by setting suitable tasks, enabling reflection, and addressing practicalities (e.g., keeping to time). These factors overlapped strongly with the US consensus statements noted earlier (and with conventional thinking on what makes for good supervision), except for excluding a developmental approach and reference to relevant research or other features of EBP. These differences may be confounded by the different methods used to build a consensus, or it may be that there are indeed international differences in what works best during experiential learning. Either way, engaging in such a process is consistent with EBP and is likely to enhance implementation.

Supervision guidelines

One popular way to try and bridge the research–practice gulf that bedevils EBP is to develop evidence-based guidelines (Watkins, 1997). The APA defined these as "a set of statements that recommend specific professional conduct" (APA, 2002, p. 1048) and emphasized that these guidelines were not mandatory, nor intended to take priority over professional judgment. Rather, they should provide a tool for assisting practitioners in reaching well-informed judgments. Good guidelines grade the quality of the best-available evidence, by reference to a hierarchy of evidence (e.g., NICE, 2003). Crucially for bridging the perspectives of researchers and clinicians (Bower & Gilbody, 2010), this evidence should be appraised by a guideline development group, including practitioners, policy-makers, researchers, and service users.

We therefore took three steps in developing the present EBCS guidelines, based on the NICE advice (NICE, 2003) and Parry (2000). First, we conducted a systematic review of the evidence for clinical supervision; second, we developed a model of clinical supervision that was broad enough to be acceptable to most mental health practitioners within the National Health Service (Milne, Aylott et al., 2008); and third, we sought professional consensus and evaluation at every stage of the guideline development process (Milne & Dunkerley, 2010). Four guidelines were developed in this way, addressing the main elements of the "supervision cycle": alliance development; assessing learning needs and collaborative agenda-setting; facilitating learning; and evaluation (Milne, 2009). Each guideline broadly followed the same NICE format (NICE, 2003), including an introduction that covers the context and scope of the guideline; key practice recommendations; the principles for these recommendations; practice suggestions; a review of the evidence base; and a rating for the strength of the evidence on which the guideline is built.

Reactions to the guidelines, in terms of their acceptability (including readability, factual accuracy, and likely value), were obtained from the 13 members of the guideline development group, 30 supervisors, 49 clinical tutors (the people who supervise and train the supervisors within clinical psychology programs in the United Kingdom), and four UK experts in supervision. The overall rating for all four guidelines was in the "acceptable" range, mid-way to the best available rating of "good," and all guidelines were rated as factually accurate, readable, and valuable in promoting competent supervision (copies are available free from the author. This project was supported by the Higher Education Academy, Psychology Network).

Training supervisors

Spence, Wilson, Kavanagh, Strong, and Worrall (2001) noted that "we have little information to guide us as to the most effective ways of training supervisors" (p. 135). To contribute information, we conducted a systematic review of the extant controlled evaluations of supervisor training (Milne, Sheikh, et al., 2011) and I developed a supervisor training manual, reflecting EBCS (Milne, 2010). This manual was piloted UK-wide by 25 trainers (i.e., tutors from clinical psychology programs in the United Kingdom) and their workshop delegates ($n = 256$ clinical psychology practicum/placement supervisors). To strengthen the acceptability evaluation, the trainers were allocated randomly to either a manual alone or to a manual plus consultancy condition. After trying out at least one session from the three-day workshop outlined within the manual, all trainers then rated the manual, while delegates rated the workshop. Trainers rated the manual and the EBCS approach favorably (mean endorsement: 78%), and the supervisors within the consultancy group rated the sessions significantly more favorably than their counterparts. I concluded that this pilot study indicated that this manual-based training was acceptable to clinical psychology trainers and supervisors in the United Kingdom.

In a subsequent local evaluation of the manual (Culloty, Milne, & Sheikh, 2010) my group adopted the "fidelity framework" (Bellg et al., 2004) to assess how the trainer followed the manual and to ascertain how her 17 delegates (drawn from two consecutive workshops for mental health professionals) rated the acceptability of the approaches taken to both the delivery of the workshop and EBCS. In an uncontrolled design, a combination of direct observation and delegates' ratings indicated that the trainer had delivered the three-day workshop with high fidelity and that this was related to excellent acceptability feedback (89% endorsement of the EBCS approach; 88% endorsement of the trainer's workshop delivery). However, the more challenging evaluation of whether this was transferred to the professionals' subsequent supervision indicated that, up to 12 weeks post workshop, only six of them reported any transfer and that this was minimal (e.g., collaborative agenda-setting).

This degree of fidelity to a manual is promising, as adherence to EBP is generally problematic (Waller, 2009). It was not clear whether this also applied to trainers using our EBCS manual. Therefore, a further local evaluation (Evans & Milne, 2012) was conducted, drawing on a large-scale dissemination of EBCS to multi-professional staff within the NHS of which I was a member (i.e., some 1,000 supervisors and supervisees received a one-day version of the workshop described earlier). This training effort required a team of trainers, and 10 of them participated in semi-structured interviews with a third-party interviewer. According to the trainers' replies to an open-ended question on fidelity to the EBCS manual, there were six influential factors, including the physical context, the participants' reactions, their own training styles and preferred methods, and the materials available to support their training. In discussing these replies, the researchers thought that these 10 trainers indicated a judicious application of the manual, rather than a problematic drift away from EBP: the six identified themes were wide-ranging but coherent, reflecting the trainers' judgment in applying EBP (e.g., considering participant characteristics, culture, and preferences).

In summary, these three studies indicate how some small steps were taken toward an evidence-based approach to supervisor training, particularly regarding the detailed scrutiny of the best available research evidence and consensus-building, important steps in developing a trainer's manual. According to Beidas and Kendall (2010), the gold standard for quality training in EBP is a workshop, plus manual, plus supervision. On this logic, we should next give attention to systematically supporting and guiding the supervisor trainers, something that only took place informally within the discussed studies.

Judgments made by supervisors

The foregoing supports for EBP should facilitate good decision-making by the supervisor, as in developing theoretically informed formulations about the clinical presentations facing the supervisee, together with research-informed judgments about the best course of action. What is meant by "good" is indicated by the definition of EBP:

"The conscientious, explicit and judicious use of current best evidence in making decisions about the care of individual patients . . ." (Sackett et al., 1996, p. 71). In relation to supervision, all the usual clinical decisions have to be made through the supervisee (unless there is some form of co-therapy), which adds a need to make judgments about care through the relatively inexperienced and biased eyes of the supervisee (at least in prequalification supervision). In such a training situation there is also the distinctive task of forming judgments about the supervisee's competence. For instance, novices appear to overestimate their competence (Kruger & Dunning, 1999), a general finding that might influence a supervisor to emphasize observation or other forms of monitoring.

We have not studied supervisors' judgments directly within the R&D program underpinning EBCS. The closest work has been the episodes method, as described earlier. Relevant aspects of decision-making have also been assessed with our main supervisory competence tool, SAGE (see Chapter 18), such as formulating, listening, and observing. However, this does not afford a direct way of studying supervisory judgments. Therefore, I will simply outline here how the episode approach illuminated examples of the supervisor's decision-making process within our most recent $n = 1$ study (Breese et al., 2012; Milne, Reiser, Cliffe, Breese, et al., 2011). Within the illustrative episode above (see Figure 3.1), reference to "the conscientious, explicit, and judicious use of current best evidence" in making the decision that follows (i.e., that the supervisee needs to be more directive with the patient) is indicated by the supervisor's use of evidence-based CBT techniques (e.g., behavioral activation, modeling, homework).

Supervision practice

By comparison with the "judgments made by supervisors" aspect of EBP, the EBCS research program has paid significant attention to analyzing and developing what the supervisor does, based on such judgments. This has already been illustrated qualitatively by the episode approach (Figure 3.1) and by the grounded theory examination of how supervisors enable supervisees to acquire competence (Johnston & Milne, 2012). Therefore, I will next outline briefly how my group studied supervision quantitatively, through the use of our competence rating tool, SAGE (Supervision: Adherence and Guidance Evaluation ; Milne, Reiser, Cliffe, & Raine, 2011), and through supervisee feedback. As SAGE is detailed in another chapter, here I will only note how it can be used. After viewing a tape of a supervision session, each of the 23 items is rated by an observer, using a 7-point competence rating scale. SAGE can therefore provide a summary rating of competence, or a supervision practice profile. The final five items can also provide an indication of how supervision is initially impacting on the supervisee.

Complementing the use of SAGE and direct observation, we have used supervisees' feedback as a way to foster supervision practice and EBP. This has included semi-structured interviews and brief questionnaires. The best-developed questionnaire within the EBCS program has been REACTS (Rating of Experiential learning And Components of Teaching & Supervision), an 11-item, supervisee-completed rating of supervision. These items assess EBCS by reference to Proctor's (1988) "normative" and "restorative" aspects of supervision (e.g., items on the frequency of the supervision sessions and the provision of emotional support). However, REACTS mainly focuses on the "formative" aspect of supervision (i.e., educative function), listing Kolb's (1984) learning modes (i.e., experiencing, reflecting, conceptualizing, experimenting, and planning). An example item (number 5) is "I was able to recognize relevant feelings, becoming more self-aware (e.g., role-play helped me to express emotion)." The 5-point rating scale ranges from *strongly agree* to *strongly disagree* (with a *not applicable* option), giving a score range of 8–40 (there are eight rated items), where higher scores represent greater supervisee satisfaction and learning. REACTS also includes a "Helpful aspects" item, to collect qualitative data, and a final item inviting any further comments. It can be completed by the supervisee within 5 min. REACTS has demonstrated good psychometric properties (e.g., test–retest reliability: $r = .96$; internal consistency: Cronbach's alpha = .94). Further psychometric findings are reported in Milne et al. (2012).

Supervisee development

The supervisee's response to supervision has been the primary criterion of effectiveness within the EBCS program, by contrast with clinical outcomes, the criterion advocated by many (e.g., Ellis & Ladany, 1997). As touched on earlier, this reflects our "upstream" attention to the variables that first need to be understood, measured, and manipulated with fidelity as causal precursors to clinical outcomes. That is, before we can infer that such outcomes are attributable to supervision, we need to be able to show a causal chain that starts with supervision (e.g., as measured by SAGE items 1–18), leads to predicted changes in the supervisee ("receipts," e.g., learning and action planning, as measured by SAGE items 19–23), which can then be shown to transfer to the therapy situation ("enactment") and which similarly impacts on the patient (e.g., learning new coping strategies and achieving related clinical outcomes). This account and terminology is based on the fidelity framework (Bellg et al., 2004) but extends it to cover the clinical outcome.

Improved patient care

Within the EBCS program we have not studied in a systematic way the improved clinical outcomes that should follow from high-fidelity supervision, having taken more interest in the supervisor–supervisee interaction, which is perhaps closer to the notion of "patient care". However, there have been two minor reports. Following the Milne et al. (2003) $n = 1$ study, we undertook a retrospective, longitudinal comparison for the relevant patients (two adults, one presenting with anxiety, one with depression). This was based on the symptom questionnaires that the therapist used in his routine work (including The Beck Depression Inventory [BDI], used only pre–post therapy). This uncontrolled comparison indicated that these patients' self-reported symptoms reduced significantly during therapy, reaching the normal range for the patient with anxiety, and dropping down to the "moderate" level for the depressed patient (for details, see Milne, 2008b).

In the second such study we conducted (Milne et al., 2003) there was a content analysis (qualitative and quantitative) of the transfer of impacts from supervision to therapy: did CBT supervision improve patient care? To ascertain the strength of this link, we studied 20 tape recordings, being alternating supervision and therapy sessions over 10 iterations (i.e., we studied tape one from supervision in order to identify any material that might transfer to the first therapy session, etc., successively). We reported good transfer and, of most relevance here, found that this was appropriate (i.e., high fidelity) in over 90% of observed occasions. This suggests that supervision clearly and repeatedly improved patient care, albeit within an uncontrolled $n = 1$ design.

Large-sample RCTs in Australia and the United Kingdom have also reported significant clinical benefits, such as symptom reduction (Bambling et al., 2006; Bradshaw, Butterworth, & Mairs, 2007), which is consistent with an earlier systematic review of such impacts within 28 controlled studies (Milne & James, 2000) and a more recent systematic review of the effectiveness of collaborative care for depression in primary care (Bower, Gilbody, Richards, Fletcher, & Sutton, 2006). This latter study used a regression design across 34 studies to conclude that regular specialist supervision predicted good clinical outcomes. Therefore, there is reason to believe that supervision is associated with improved patient care and in turn with clinical benefits. However, caution in inferring a causal link is appropriate: these studies fail to demonstrate this link, there being no data concerning what exactly was done within supervision, nor whether it was done with fidelity.

Some believe that such clinical outcomes are the acid test of supervision (e.g., Ellis & Ladany, 1997), but even if one accepts this criterion as paramount, there remain complex challenges in modeling and measuring the supervisory process (Ellis, D'luso, & Ladany, 2008). My own view is that the ideal evaluation of supervision would demonstrate objectively that clinical outcomes were linked causally to the relevant moderators, mediators, and change mechanisms (Milne, Kennedy et al., 2008), in the same way that we would seek to demonstrate the effectiveness of any similar intervention (e.g., staff training). Although it is tempting to assume that supervision benefits patients, a considerable body of evidence within the staff training literature bears out the need for caution in inferring causal links and the need for a stepwise evaluation strategy (e.g., Beidas & Kendall, 2010; Rakovshik & McManus, 2010).

Audit

Audit entails an evaluation of whether agreed standards have been met, as in surveying a group of supervisors to determine their adherence to criteria that have been defined within a clinical service. This can be based on the criteria that exist within published instruments, allowing comparative profiles to be created, contrasting the findings from the survey with published norms. To illustrate, Edwards et al. (2006) surveyed 260 mental health nurses in Wales by means of the Manchester Clinical Supervision Scale (MCSS; Winstanley, 2000; and see Chapter 17). They found that three of the MCSS subscales were favorable (trust/rapport; support/advice; improving care/skills) but that the survey data for the remaining four scales fell below the normative data. Alternatively, audit can be based on locally defined standards, as in developing a supervision policy within one service. This can clarify adherence to such a policy, across departments and professions (e.g., Webb, 1997). Our own use of audit has been similar, focusing on the extent to which a local supervision policy (incorporating EBCS) was being implemented (Milne & Choudhri, 2007), and on trainee clinical psychologists' use of their program's recommended methods of supervision (Milne & Gracie, 2001). The latter drew on the trainees' written records of their supervision during one calendar year, indicating that key standards were satisfied (e.g., that there was direct observation and that the supervisees' were active collaborators).

Summary and Conclusions

In this chapter I have summarized EBP and its variants, adding some implications and a note on the implementation challenge. To paraphrase Machiavelli, there are few tougher challenges than innovation, and innovation is perhaps particularly fraught when (as in supervision) there are entrenched personal positions in a context of increasing pressure to implement EBP. The kinds of barriers and boosters to EBP already noted represent a huge challenge, one that requires pro-innovation reasoning. In this chapter, I have offered a sketched force-field analysis (Lewin, 1951) or formulation of this challenge, consistent with one of the innovation guidelines (i.e., draw reflexively on psychology to formulate the challenges in implementing EBP; Michie et al., 2005). Linked to this preliminary understanding, the examples of EBCS at the heart of this chapter indicated how we can move toward EBP within the supervision field. Specifically, the strategies outlined earlier included a flexible approach (i.e., fitting the EBP variant or activity to the local situation), building expert consensus, and collaboration within programmatic but methodologically inclusive research. These examples and strategies contributed to the aims of the chapter, which were to respond constructively to a changing public context, including growing governmental pressure to implement EBP, as well as chronic problems in spanning the science–practice divide.

Many have lamented the weak status of the research literature within clinical supervision (e.g., Ellis & Ladany, 1997), and there is absolutely no doubt that much remains to be done. The issue is how we respond to such adversity. In place of the familiar pessimistic general overviews of this literature, the EBCS program has responded by borrowing, burrowing, and bolstering. In borrowing from outside the supervision field, it has recognized parallel literatures as a valid source of ideas, extending these to supervision through reasoned analogies, methods, and findings. In burrowing within the field, EBCS has adopted the BES approach to the systematic (meta-analytic) review, providing a method for defining and mining seams of relatively high-quality research. This forms a much firmer foundation for statements about what we know and what we have yet to find out about supervision. Similarly, in conducting research we have worked in an exploratory, fine-grained way (e.g., qualitative analyses), and zoomed in on micro-processes and outcomes utilizing rigorous $n = 1$ studies. In bolstering the field, the EBCS program has used these appeals to parallel literatures and to detailed analyses to guide a program of research and development, guided by the EBP model. I believe that this move toward EBP represents a more systematic and coherent way to develop clinical supervision, as hopefully illustrated by the EBCS program.

In essence, this is an empirical problem-solving strategy, as EBP is more than the use of particular tools, signifying an ongoing commitment to moving the field forward through basic scientific attitudes, principles and methods (e.g., scholarly attention to the literature, empiricism, objective evaluation). In turn, this means treating examples such as EBCS and the elements detailed here as building blocks toward progressively better theories and more sophisticated research. This constructive strategy can be pursued individually (e.g., by a supervisor who is a scientist-practitioner) or collectively (as in PBE within a clinical service) and should of course be responsive to the cultural context (including national policies and priorities). Suitable next steps toward an EBP approach within the United Kingdom include broadening the theoretical arena (EBCS is currently CBT-centric), deepening some of the key research activity (e.g., improving the measurement options; large-N designs), extending the focus to include group supervision (and other formats), and developing the approaches to implementation. I hope that this chapter facilitates such progress, ideally pursued internationally.

Acknowledgments

I am grateful to many British colleagues for their interest, support and direct collaboration over some 20 years of research on clinical supervision. They include Roger Paxton, Colin Westerman, Tonia Culloty, Ian A. James, Caroline Leck, Nasim Choudhri, Alia Sheikh, John Ormrod, Peter Armstrong, Mark Freeston, Joyce Scaife, Graham Sloan, Dave Green and his DROSS group (i.e., the Development and Recognition of Supervisory Skills initiative, based in Northern England, later rechristened STAR), and by my Clinical Tutor colleagues within the Group of Trainers in Clinical Psychology (GTiCP). But the greatest recent impetus has been the stimulating research collaboration with my international colleague, Californian Dr. Robert Reiser. This included one of his supervisees, Andrea Feit (i.e., the supervisee during the training phase of Milne et al., 2013). The EBCS program has benefitted enormously from their input. As far as this chapter is concerned, I am grateful to Ed Watkins for his generous feedback on a draft, and to Ros Raine for her help in preparing the chapter.

References

American Psychological Association. (APA: 2002). *Guidelines on multicultural education, training, research, practice, and organizational change for psychologists*. Washington, DC: Author.

American Psychological Association. (APA: 2006). Evidence-based practice in psychology: APA presidential task force on evidence-based practice. *American Psychologist, 61*, 475–476.

Bambling, M., King, R., Raue, P., Schweitzer, R., & Lambert, W. (2006). Clinical supervision: Its influence on client-rated working alliance and client symptom reduction in the brief treatment of major depression. *Psychotherapy Research, 16*, 317–331.

Barkham, M., Hardy, G. E., & Mellor-Clark, J. (Eds.). (2010). *Developing and delivering practice-based evidence*. Chichester, UK: Wiley.

Barlow, D. H., Hayes, S. C., & Nelson, R. O. (1984). *The scientist-practitioner*. London, UK: Pergamon.

Beidas, R. S., & Kendall, P. C. (2010). Training therapists in evidence-based practice: A critical review of studies from a systems-contextual perspective. *Clinical Psychology: Science and Practice*, *17*, 1–30.

Bellg, A. J., Borrelli, B., Resnick, B., Hecht, J., Minicucci, D. S., Ory, M.,. . .Czajkowski, S. (2004). Enhancing treatment fidelity in health behaviour change studies: Best practises and recommendations from the NIH Behaviour Change Consortium. *Health Psychology*, *23*, 443–451.

Bernard, J. M., & Goodyear, R. K. (2004). *Fundamentals of clinical supervision* (3rd ed.). London, UK: Pearson.

Bower, P., & Gilbody, S. (2010). The current view of evidence and evidence-based practice. In M. Barkham, G. E. Hardy, & J. Mellor-Clark (Eds.), *Developing and delivering practice-based evidence* (pp. 1–20). Chichester, UK: Wiley.

Bower, P., Gilbody, S., Richards, D., Fletcher, J., & Sutton, A. (2006). Collaborative care for depression in primary care. *British Journal of Psychiatry*, *189*, 484–493.

Bradshaw, T., Butterworth, A., & Mairs, H. (2007). Does structured clinical supervision during psychosocial intervention education enhance outcome for mental health nurses and the service users they work with? *Journal of Psychiatric and Mental Health Nursing*, *14*, 4–12.

Breese, L., Boon, A., & Milne, D. L. (2012). Detecting excellent episodes in clinical supervision: A case-study, comparing two approaches. *The Clinical Supervisor*, *31*, 121–137.

Chambless, D. L., Baker, M. J., Baucom, D. H., Beutler, L. E., Calhoun, K. S., Crits-Cristoph, P., et al. (1998). Update on empirically-validated therapies, II. *The Clinical Psychologist*, *51*, 3–16.

Colquitt, J. A., LePine, J. A., & Noe, R. A. (2000). Toward an integrative theory of training motivation: A meta-analytic path analysis of twenty years of research. *Journal of Applied Psychology*, *85*, 678–707.

Culloty, T., Milne, D. L., & Sheikh, A. I. (2010). Evaluating the training of clinical supervisors: A pilot study, using the fidelity framework. *The Cognitive Behaviour Therapist*, *3*, 132–144.

Delbecq, A., & Van de Ven, A. (1972). The Nominal Group as a research instrument for exploratory health studies. *American Journal of Public Health*, *62*, 337–342.

Edwards, D. J. A., Dattilio, F. M., & Bromley, D. B. (2004). Developing evidence-based practice: The role of case-based research. *Professional Psychology, Research and Practice*, *35*, 589–597.

Edwards, E., Bernard, P., Hamigan, B., Cooper, L., Adams, J., & Juggessur, T. (2006). Clinical supervision and burn out: The influence of clinical supervision for community mental health nurses. *Journal of Clinical Nursing*, *15*, 1007–1015.

Ellis, M. V., D'luso, N., & Ladany, N. (2008). State of the art in the assessment, measurement, and evaluation of clinical supervision. In A. K. Hess, K. D. Hess, & T. H. Hess (Eds.), *Psychotherapy supervision: Theory, research, and practice* (2nd ed., pp. 473–499). New York, NY: Wiley.

Ellis, M. V., & Ladany, N. (1997). Inferences concerning supervisees and clients in clinical supervision: An integrative review. In C. E. Watkins (Ed.), *Handbook of psychotherapy supervision* (pp. 447–507). New York, NY: Wiley.

Evans, N., & Milne, D. L. (2012). Puzzling over professionals' application of evidence-based practice: An exploratory study from supervisor training. *Clinical Psychology Forum*, *237*, 10–15.

Falender, C., Cornish, J. A. E., Goodyear, R., Hatcher, R., Kaslow, N. J., Leventhal, G., et al. (2004). Defining competencies in psychology supervision: A consensus statement. *Journal of Clinical Psychology*, *60*, 771–785.

Falender, C. A., & Shafranske, E. (2004). *Clinical supervision: A competency-based approach*. Washington, DC: APA.

Fixsen, D. L., Blase, K. A., Duda, M. A., Naoom, S. F., & van Dyke, M. (2010). Implementation of evidence-based treatments for children and adolescents. In J. R. Weisz & A. E. Kazdin (Eds.), *Evidence-based psychotherapies for children and adolescents* (pp. 435–450). New York, NY: Guilford Press.

Georgiades, N. J., & Phillimore, L. (1975). The myth of the hero innovator and alternative strategies for organizational change. In C. C. Kiernan & F. P. Woodford (Eds.), *Behaviour modification with the severely retarded* (pp. 313–319). New York, NY: Associated Scientific.

Gilbody, S., Bower, P., Fletcher, J., Richards, D., & Sutton, A. J. (2006). Collaborative care for depression: A meta analysis and review of longer-term outcomes. *Archives of Internal Medicine, 166*, 2314–2320.

Goldfried, M. R., & Wolfe, B. E. (1998). Toward a more clinically valid approach to therapy research. *Journal of Consulting and Clinical Psychology, 66*, 143–150. doi:10.1037/0022-006X.66.1.143

Greenberg, L. (1984). Task analysis: The general approach. In L. N. Rice & L. S. Greenberg (Eds.), *Patterns of change: Intensive analysis of psychotherapy process* (pp. 67–123). New York, NY: Guilford.

Greene, L. R. (2012). Group therapist as social scientist, with special reference to the psychodynamically oriented psychotherapist. *American Psychologist, 67*, 477–489.

Greenhalgh, T., Robert, G., Macfarlane, F., Bate, P., & Kyriakidou, O. (2004). Diffusion of innovations in service organizations: Systematic review and recommendations. *Milbank Quarterly, 82*, 581–629.

Heaven, C., Clegg, J., & Maguire, P. (2006). Transfer of communication skills training from workshop to workplace: The impact of clinical supervision. *Patient Education and Counselling, 60*, 313–325.

Henggeler, S. W., Schoenwald, S. K., Liao, J. G., Letourneau, E. J., & Edwards, D. L. (2002). Transporting efficacious treatments to field settings: The link between supervisory practices and therapist fidelity in MST programmes. *Journal of Clinical Child Psychology, 31*, 155–167.

James, I. A., Blackburn, I.-M., Milne, D. L., Freeston, M., & Armstrong, P. (2005). Supervision training and assessment rating scale for cognitive therapy (STARS – CT).Unpublished instrument. Available from Ian James (ianjamesncht@yahoo.com); The Centre for the Health of the Elderly, Newcastle General Hospital, England, NE4 6BE.

James, I. A., Milne, D. L., Blackburn, I.-M., & Armstrong, P. (2006). Conducting successful supervision: Novel elements towards an integrative approach. *Behavioural and Cognitive Psychotherapy, 35*, 191–200.

James, I. A., Milne, D. L., & Morse, R. (2008). Microskills of clinical supervision: Scaffolding skills. *Journal of Cognitive Psychotherapy: An International Quarterly, 22*, 29–36.

Johnston, L. H., & Milne, D. L. (2012). How do supervisee's learn during supervision? A grounded theory study of the perceived developmental process. *The Cognitive Behaviour Therapist, 5*, 1–23.

Kaslow, N. J., Borden, K. A., Collins, F. L., Forrest, L., Illfelder-Kaye, J., Nelson, P. D., et al. (2004). Competencies conference: Future directions in education and credentialing in professional psychology. *Journal of Clinical Psychology, 60*, 699–712.

Kazdin, A. E. (2008). Evidence-based treatment and practice: New opportunities to bridge clinical research and practice, enhance the knowledge-base, and improve patient care. *American Psychologist, 63*, 146–159.

Kolb, D. A. (1984). *Experiential learning: Experience as the source of learning and development*. Englewood Cliffs, NJ: Prentice-Hall.

Kruger, J., & Dunning, D. (1999). Unskilled and unaware of it: How difficulties in recognizing one's own competence lead to inflated self-assessments. *Journal of Personality and Social Psychology*, *77*, 1121–1134.

Kurtzman, H., & Bufka, L. (2011). APA moves forward on developing clinical treatment guidelines. *Practice Update*, July 14, 2011.

Ladany, N., Friedlander, M., & Nelson, M. (2005). *Critical events in psychotherapy supervision. An interpersonal approach.* Washington, DC: American Psychological Association.

Lewin, K. (1951). *Field theory in social science.* New York, NY: Harper.

Lombardo, C., Milne, D. L., & Proctor, R. (2009). Getting to the heart of clinical supervision: A theoretical review of the role of emotions in professional development. *Behavioural and Cognitive Psychotherapy*, *37*, 207–219.

Marzillier, J. (2004). The myth of evidence-based psychotherapy. *The Psychologist*, *17*, 392–395.

McHugh, R. K., & Barlow, D. H. (2010). The dissemination and implementation of evidence-based psychological treatments. *American Psychologist*, *65*, 73–84.

Michie, S., Johnston, M., Abraham, C., Lawton, R., Parker, D., & Walker, A. (2005). Making psychological theory useful for implementing evidence-based practice: A consensus approach. *Quality and Safety in HealthCare*, *14*, 26–33.

Milne, D., & James, I. (2000). A systematic review of effective cognitive-behavioural supervision. *British Journal of Clinical Psychology*, *39*, 111–127.

Milne, D. L. (2006). Developing clinical supervision through reasoned analogies with therapy. *Clinical Psychology and Psychotherapy*, *13*, 215–222.

Milne, D. L. (2007). An empirical definition of clinical supervision. *British Journal of Clinical Psychology*, *46*, 437–447.

Milne, D. L. (2008). Evaluating and enhancing supervision: An experiential model. In C. Falender & E. Shafranske (Eds.), *Casebook for clinical supervision: A competency-based approach* (pp.211–233). Washington, DC: American Psychological Association.

Milne, D. L. (2009). *Evidence-based clinical supervision: Principles and practice.* Malden, MA: BPS/Blackwell.

Milne, D. L. (2010). Can we enhance the training of clinical supervisors? A national pilot study of an evidence-based approach. *Clinical Psychology & Psychotherapy*, *17*, 321–328.

Milne, D. L. (2012). A rationale for evidence-based clinical supervision. *Journal of Contemporary Psychotherapy*, *42*, 139–149.

Milne, D. L., Aylott, H., Fitzpatrick, H., & Ellis, M. V. (2008). How does clinical supervision work? Using a Best Evidence Synthesis approach to construct a basic model of supervision. *The Clinical Supervisor*, *27*, 170–190.

Milne, D. L., & Choudhri, N. (2007). Recognising and developing clinical supervision. Internal report, available from derek.milne@ncl.ac.uk.

Milne, D. L., & Dunkerley, C. (2010). Towards evidence-based clinical supervision: The development and evaluation of four CBT guidelines. *The Cognitive Behaviour Therapist*, *3*, 43–57.

Milne, D. L., & Gracie, J. (2001). The role of the supervisee: 20 ways to facilitate clinical supervision. *Clinical Psychology Forum*, *5*, 13–15.

Milne, D. L., & James, I. A. (2002). The observed impact of training on competence in clinical supervision. *British Journal of Clinical Psychology*, *41*, 55–72.

Milne, D. L., Kennedy, E., Todd, H., Lombardo, C., Freeston, M., & Day, A. (2008). Zooming in on clinical supervision: A comparison of two levels of effectiveness evaluation. *Behavioural and Cognitive Psychotherapy*, *36*, 619–624.

Milne, D. L., Leck, C., & Choudhri, N. Z. (2009). Collusion in clinical supervision: Literature review and case study in self-reflection. *The Cognitive Behaviour Therapist*, *2*, 106–114.

Milne, D. L., Leck, C., James, I., Wilson, M., Procter, R., Ramm, L., et al. (2012). High fidelity in clinical supervision research. In I. Fleming & L. Steen (Eds.), *Supervision and clinical psychology* (pp. 142–158). London, UK: Routledge.

Milne, D. L., & Paxton, R. (1998). A psychological re-analysis of the scientist-practitioner model. *Clinical Psychology and Psychotherapy, 5*, 216–230.

Milne, D. L., Pilkington, J., Gracie, J., & James, I. A. (2003). Transferring skills from supervision to therapy: A qualitative N=1 analysis. *Behavioural and Cognitive Psychotherapy, 31*, 193–202.

Milne, D. L., & Reiser, R. (2011). Observing competence in CBT supervision: A systematic review of the available instruments. *The Cognitive Behaviour Therapist, 4*, 89–100.

Milne, D. L., Reiser, R., Aylott, H., Dunkerley, C., Fitzpatrick, H., & Wharton, S. (2010). The systematic review as an empirical approach to improving CBT supervision. *International Journal of Cognitive Therapy, 3*, 278–294.

Milne, D. L., Reiser, R., & Cliffe, T. (2013). An N=1 evaluation of enhanced CBT supervision. *Behavioural and Cognitive Psychotherapy, 41*, 210–220. doi:10.1017/S1352465812000434

Milne, D. L., Reiser, R., Cliffe, T., Breese, L., Boon, A., Raine, R., & Scarratt, P. (2011). A qualitative comparison of cognitive-behavioural and evidence-based clinical supervision. *The Cognitive Behaviour Therapist, 4*, 152–166.

Milne, D. L., Reiser, R., Cliffe, T., & Raine, R. (2011). SAGE: Preliminary evaluation of an instrument for observing competence in CBT supervision. *The Cognitive Behaviour Therapist, 4*, 123–138.

Milne, D. L., Scaife, J., & Cliffe, T. (2009). How should we train effective supervisors? A British consensus on facilitating experiential learning. *Clinical Psychology Forum, 203*, 7–12.

Milne, D. L., Sheikh, A. I., Pattison, S., & Wilkinson, A. (2011). Evidence-based training for clinical supervisors: A systematic review of 11 controlled studies. *The Clinical Supervisor, 30*, 53–71.

Milne, D. L., & Westerman, C. (2001). Evidence-based clinical supervision: Rationale and illustration. *Clinical Psychology and Psychotherapy, 8*, 444–445.

NICE. (2003). *Guideline development methods: Information for national collaborating centres and guideline developers.* London, UK: National Institute for Clinical Excellence.

Norcross, J. C., Beutler, L. E., & Levant, R. F. (2005). *Evidence-based practices in mental health: Debate and dialogue on the fundamental questions.* Washington, DC: American Psychological Association.

Norcross, J. C., & Wampold, B. E. (2011). Evidence-based therapy relationships: Research conclusions and clinical practices. *Psychotherapy, 48*, 98–102.

Palomo, M., Beinart, H., & Cooper, M. J. (2010). Development and validation of a questionnaire measure of the supervisory relationship. *British Journal of Clinical Psychology, 49*, 131–149.

Papworth, M. A., Milne, D. L., & Boak, G. (2009). An exploratory content analysis of situational leadership. *Journal of Management Development, 28*, 593–606.

Parry, G. (2000). Developing treatment choice guidelines in psychotherapy. *Journal of Mental Health, 9*, 273–281.

Parry, G., Roth, A., & Fonagy, P. (2005). Psychotherapy research, funding, and evidence-based practice. In A. Roth & P. Fonagy (Eds.), *What works for whom? A critical review of psychotherapy research* (pp. 37–56). New York, NY: Guilford Press.

Petticrew, M., & Roberts, H. (2006). *Systematic reviews in the social sciences: A practical guide.* Oxford, UK: Blackwell.

Proctor, B. (1988). Supervision: A cooperative exercise in accountability. In M. Marken & M. Payne (Eds.), *Enabling and ensuring* (pp. 21–34). Leicester, UK: Leicester

National Youth Bureau and Council for Education and Training in Youth and Community Work.

Rakovshik, S. G., & McManus, F. (2010). Establishing evidence-based training in cognitive-behavioral therapy: A review of current empirical findings and theoretical guidance. *Clinical Psychology Review*, *30*, 496–516.

Rotheram-Borus, M. J., Swendeman, D., & Chorpita, B. F. (2012). Disruptive innovations for designing and diffusing evidence-based interventions. *American Psychologist*, *67*, 463–476.

Sackett, D. L., Rosenberg, W. M. C., Gray, J. A. M., Haynes, R. B., & Richardson, W. S. (1996). Evidence-based medicine: What it is and what it isn't. *British Medical Journal*, *312*, 71–72.

Salkovskis, P. M. (2002). Empirically-grounded clinical interventions: Cognitive-behavioural therapy progresses through a multi-dimensional approach to clinical science. *Behavioural and Cognitive Psychotherapy*, *30*, 3–9.

Spence, S. H., Wilson, J., Kavanagh, D., Strong, J., & Worrall, L. (2001). Clinical supervision in four mental health professions: A review of the evidence. *Behaviour Change*, *18*, 135–155.

Tansella, M., & Thornicroft, G. (2009). Implementation science: Understanding the translation of evidence into practice. *British Journal of Psychiatry*, *195*, 283–285.

Waller, G. (2009). Evidence-based treatment and drift. *Behaviour Research and Therapy*, *47*, 119–127.

Watkins, C. E. (Ed.). (1997). *Handbook of psychotherapy supervision*. New York, NY: Wiley.

Webb, B. (1997). Auditing a clinical supervision training programme. *Nursing Standard*, *11*, 34–39.

West, M. A., & Farr, J. L. (1989). Innovation at work: Psychological perspectives. *Social Behaviour*, *4*, 15–30.

Winstanley, J. (2000). Manchester clinical supervision scale. *Nursing Standard*, *14*, 31–32.

Worthen, V. E., & Lambert, M. J. (2007). Outcome-oriented supervision: Advantages of adding systematic client tracking to supportive consultations. *Counselling and Psychotherapy Research*, *7*, 48–53.

4

Current Trends Concerning Supervisors, Supervisees, and Clients in Clinical Supervision

Arpana G. Inman, Heidi Hutman, Asmita Pendse, Lavanya Devdas, Linh Luu, and Michael V. Ellis

Given the significance of the gate-keeping role of supervisors (Bernard & Goodyear, 2014), arguably, supervision is the most important activity informing the development of therapeutic competence and the provision of effective clinical practice (Ladany & Inman, 2012). As such, clinical supervision has been deemed essential to mental health professionals across all mental health disciplines (Watkins, 2011) and in a number of countries, making supervision research and practice increasingly global (Bernard & Goodyear, 2014). Despite the increased emphasis, in our review of the literature, there seems to be limited information regarding the kinds of systematic empirical research conducted in the area of clinical supervision across the globe, preventing us from understanding the current international issues salient to supervisors, supervisees, and their clients in clinical supervision. In an effort to better understand the trends, make inferences, and identify gaps in the existing research, this chapter provides a review of the past 18 years (i.e., 1994–2012 inclusively; i.e., since Ellis & Ladany, 1997) of empirical work and a critical and integrative analysis of the published research in clinical supervision across multiple disciplines globally.

In identifying articles, we used search engines such as PsycINFO, PsycARTICLES, Google Scholar, ERIC, EBSCOhost, and Social Sciences Citation Index. In addition, to further ensure adequate representation, the authors reached out to colleagues working outside of the United States to identify international journals and publications. To obtain all relevant results, the authors used key search terms such as supervision and supervisee, supervisor, clinical training, client, multicultural supervision, supervisor and supervisee development and training, working alliance, conflict, parallel process, evaluation, satisfaction, countertransference, disclosure, sexual attraction, and harmful supervision. The preliminary search results identified 312 possible publications. Subsequently, we refined the search to only include peer-reviewed journal articles. Our inclusion criteria were focused on identifying articles from within a

The Wiley International Handbook of Clinical Supervision, First Edition. Edited by C. Edward Watkins, Jr. and Derek L. Milne.

mental health/counseling discipline. As such, our review reflects studies conducted in the discipline of counseling psychology, clinical psychology, school psychology, marriage and family therapy (MFT), social work, counselor education, rehabilitation counseling, school counseling, and addictions/substance abuse counseling. Articles from speech pathology, occupational or physical therapy, nursing, and psychiatry were excluded as they pertained to the medical profession. In addition, we restricted the scope of the review to include only studies pertaining to individual supervision, excluding articles on peer and group supervision. A total of 233 articles (112 quantitative, 94 qualitative, and 27 mixed methods) across 61 journals satisfied the criteria to be included in the present review. These articles were international, encompassing research conducted in Australia (8%), Canada (2%), Denmark (0.5%), Germany (1%), Ireland (1%), the Netherlands (0.5%), New Zealand (2%), Norway (1%), the United Kingdom (12%), Sweden (0.5%), and the United States (71.5%). Modeling it on Inman and Ladany's (2008) review, we clustered studies into seven broad themes: relevance and access to supervision, supervisee–supervisor development, relationship issues in supervision, multicultural issues in supervision, role of supervision in therapy and client outcome, evaluations in supervision, and specialization areas in supervision.

Relevance of and Access to Supervision

A small subgroup of researchers has examined the importance of supervision as well as access to supervision in clinical practice. Some studies have examined access to supervision in relation to demographic variables. Gabbay, Kiemle, and Maguire (1999) examined the role of specific demographic variables (gender, seniority, specialty, and clinical approach) on access to supervision among clinical psychologists in the United Kingdom. Their findings revealed that women, those with less seniority and those practicing psychodynamically, were more likely to access supervision. Grant and Schofield (2007) surveyed members of the Psychotherapy and Counseling Federation of Australia (PACFA) with regard to amount and type of supervision, reasons for supervision, reasons for not pursuing supervision, and levels of satisfaction with supervision in relation to their age, gender, qualifications, years of practice as a psychotherapist, work sector, amount of personal therapy, and professional development. Similar to Gabbay et al.'s study, these authors found that female therapists had access to more supervision per month. In addition, Grant and Schofield's findings also revealed that therapists with higher client contact hours, higher rates of personal therapy, and undergraduate training compared to vocational training received more hours of supervision per month. The emphasis on supervision in general is consistent with the requirement that post-training, members of the Register of Practitioners receive 10 hr of supervision every year to maintain their registration (Grant & Schofield, 2007). Similarly, Townend, Iannetta, and Freeston (2002) surveyed a sample of accredited British Association of Behavioural and Cognitive Psychotherapists (BABCP) about supervision practices (i.e., organization of supervision, content, techniques, models, interdisciplinary work, satisfaction, and supervision of others). Findings revealed that 90% of accredited therapists received supervision with the mean amount of supervision being higher (1 hr for every 26 hr of client work) than set by the BABCP (i.e., 1 hr/month). While different modalities of supervision were used (e.g., individual, group), supervision was often less structured, with little use of audio-video tapes of therapy sessions in supervision. Interestingly, although cognitive-behavioral therapy (CBT) supervision training varied across supervisors, satisfaction with supervision was high among these therapists.

Relatedly, research has examined supervision in the context of licensure regulations and ethical guidelines. Borders and Cashwell (1995) surveyed the supervisors of counselors who were applying for licensure across various disciplines (e.g., clinical psychology, psychiatry, schoolwork, pastoral care, and MFT) in two states (South Carolina and Missouri) regarding the nature of supervision being provided to applicants, as well as the impact of regulations on the conduct of supervision. The authors found that the state board's supervision regulations had some impact on the practice of supervision. Specifically, supervisors in South Carolina (identified as the regulated state) seemed to adhere more to the requirements (e.g., attend professional workshops, review audiotapes and videotapes of sessions rather than rely on self-reports, discuss parallel process and supervisor–counselor relationships, and engage in formal evaluations), perceiving licensure and supervision as a way to enhance job opportunities and status, as well as to add variety to their work. Participants from South Carolina were also more likely to report greater benefits of supervision with regard to increased awareness of supervision process, the supervision field, and professional identity. In a related study, McMahon and Patton (2001) surveyed the importance of and the need for clinical supervision between two groups of school counselors in Australia: those that received supervision and those that did not. Benefits of supervision were reflected in receiving support, new ideas and strategies, feedback on their work, personal growth, and opportunities to debrief. Both McMahon and Patton's and Gabbay et al.'s (1999) studies, however, found that a majority of their participants perceived supervision to be less than ideal, with a significant portion of participants having no access to or not receiving supervision despite professional practice regulations requiring them to do so.

Chiller and Crisp (2012) surveyed the challenges of retaining social workers in the work force in Australia and found that supervision served an important role in reinforcing their stay in the field by facilitating learning, providing support, and helping participants develop critical awareness and growth from challenging experiences. In a similar vein, Pettifer and Clouder's (2008) exploration of the value of academic staff supervising practitioners in the United Kingdom revealed that supervision was seen as an extension of their professional work, making them better academics. Supervision allowed them to feel connected to the practice of psychotherapy and to assist practitioners in keeping abreast of the research in the field. Participants also felt rewarded by conducting supervision as it had mutual benefits for the supervisor and supervisee. These findings are consistent with Sherr, Bergenstrom, and McCann's study (1997) on school counselors where supervision was seen as an important avenue for growth. Availability of and access to regular supervision were identified as instrumental in providing emotional support, theoretical insights, interpretations on issues, and the ability to share case histories. They also identified some unhelpful aspects of supervision related to rigidity in instructions, pathologizing of issues, difference in theoretical viewpoints, condescending attitudes, and difficulties inherent to traveling to supervision.

In summary, these findings reveal that supervision is considered to be an important tool for professional development that offers several advantages in delivering and receiving supervision. Further, the finding that women have more access to supervision is interesting and merits investigation regarding gender differences. Conversely, it is disconcerting to see that several supervisees seem to have inadequate to no supervision despite regulations and ethical mandates. Additional research is warranted in this area.

Supervisee–Supervisor Development

Supervisee development

The professional development of supervisees has gained considerable attention in both supervision theory and research. In particular, empirical studies on supervisee development have focused on the three areas of supervisee attributes (Vespia, Heckman-Stone, & Delworth, 2002; Wilcoxon, Norem, & Magnuson, 2005), supervision methods (Dennin & Ellis, 2003; Gonsalvez, Oades, & Freestone, 2002), and supervision structure (Clarkson & Aviram, 1995; Lochner & Melchert, 1997; Wark, 1995b) as factors that play an integral role in supervisees' professional development.

Supervisee attributes A review of the empirical literature suggests that a developmental theoretical paradigm has dominated the examination of supervisee functioning (Johnston & Milne, 2012; O'Donoghue, 2012). In particular, the bulk of the studies have conceptualized supervisee development as a progressive journey wherein supervisees become increasingly clinically competent with experience and training (Johnston & Milne, 2012; Krasner, Howard, & Brown, 1998; Lovell, 2002; O'Donoghue, 2012; Wulf & Nelson, 2001). For instance, for beginning therapists, formal supervision rather than direct client experience has been noted to have more influence on supervisee development (Ronnestad & Skovholt, 2003).

Relatedly, one of the important facets of clinical training is the supervisee's ability to make use of his or her supervision experiences (Reichelt & Skjerve, 2000). Research suggests that supervisees with greater cognitive complexity and self-awareness or reflectivity more readily develop specific clinical skills and utilize supervision effectively (Geller, Farber, & Schaffer, 2010; Haarhoff, 2006; Neufeldt, Karno, & Nelson, 1996). Learning within a supervisory setting is often dependent on the supervisees' ability to model themselves after their supervisors, as well as to draw on internalized representations of the roles and functions performed in the supervisory relationship (Geller et al., 2010; Nye, 2003). A study by Geller et al. (2010) provided evidence for such modeling where therapists-in-training tended to elicit representations of their supervisors' words and vocal qualities in order to help guide challenging clinical interventions. Relatedly, research has also highlighted supervisee attributes that contribute to outstanding professional growth (e.g., maturity, autonomy, perspicacity, motivation, self-awareness, and openness to experience; Norem, Magnuson, Wilcoxon, & Arbel, 2006), as well as supervisee qualities that interfere with professional growth (e.g., inability to conceptualize, unresolved personal issues, social limitations, unwillingness to accept feedback, limited motivation; Wilcoxon et al., 2005). Despite the emphasis on specific attributes as influential in supervisee professional advancement, trainees often do not get any formal training to orient them to the supervisee role. Accordingly, Vespia et al. (2002) attempted to create a Supervision Utilization Rating Form (SURF) that illustrates supervisee characteristics (e.g., demonstrates respect and appreciation for individual differences, willingness to grow, takes responsibility for consequences of behavior) that can be used to inform supervisee role induction. The authors asserted that this scale would not only help supervisors as a teaching tool but would also assist supervisees in understanding different role expectations at different developmental levels.

Supervision methods Research has also shown that supervisees need and utilize different types of supervision methods (e.g., discussion, observation, role-playing, modeling, reflection). Talen and Schindler (1994) found that supervisees preferred direct, concrete, and observable strategies to help achieve their stated goals and needs in supervision. Skill modeling, skill shaping, and skill generalization methods such as role-playing, video modeling, and co-therapy have also been considered to be important elements for supervisee skill advancement (Gonsalvez et al., 2002; Talen & Schindler, 1994). Further, Johnston and Milne (2012) suggested that supervisee development could be a function of the interplay among the supervisory working alliance, scaffolding, Socratic information exchange, and reflection. An attitude of trust and positive regard from the supervisor can further help supervisees to overcome fears and anxieties experienced during clinical training (Talen & Schindler, 1994). Interestingly, although supervision is an integral part of trainees' development, it is not always readily available. Several authors have identified self-supervision as a potential way to maintain competence and to promote autonomous development (e.g., Littrell, Lee-Borden, & Lorenz, 1976; Morrissette, 1999). In response to these propositions, Dennin and Ellis (2003) presented self-regulation training as a way to promote self-supervision in counseling. Their findings revealed that while such training increases supervisees' ability to use metaphors, it does not affect use of empathy.

Structure of supervision A third area of focus in supervisee development has been on the structure of supervision. There is some evidence that suggests that supervisees at different developmental levels and of different theoretical orientations prefer different structures of supervision. For instance, Lochner and Melchert (1997) investigated the effects of trainees' theoretical orientations on their preference for supervisory style. Their findings revealed that more behaviorally oriented supervisees preferred task-oriented supervision, whereas those with interpersonal orientations preferred relationship-oriented supervision. On a similar note, some attention has been given to the role of live supervision in supervisee skill development in family therapy training (Wark, 1995b). Preliminary evidence suggests that perceived support, encouragement, and the autonomous nature of live supervision have been found to be helpful in trainee skill development.

In summary, our review of the literature revealed that supervisee development is considered to be an important concept globally (i.e., Australia, Norway, United Kingdom, and United States). Unfortunately, it appears that much of the research in this area, while focused on developmental trends, continues to lack longitudinal methodology and, thus, an assessment of trainee changes in development over time is wanting (Ellis & Ladany, 1997). Additionally, while formal supervisee role induction and structured supervision seem to be salient factors in supervisee development, systematic empirical research is needed to determine the effectiveness of supervision role induction procedures. Finally, for a holistic understanding of the complexities involved in supervisee developmental processes, inclusion of both supervisee and supervisor perspectives appears necessary.

Supervisor development

The role of the supervisor is indisputably critical to the supervisory process. As such, the development of a supervisory identity is considered a core competency for professional psychologists (American Psychological Association, 2012; Falender et al., 2004). In recent years, scholars from various mental health disciplines have shown an increased interest in supervisor development as evidenced by the growth of empirical studies in this area. Similar to supervisee development, supervisor development is viewed as a developmental process, with supervisors gradually acquiring the required skills with structured training (Borders & Fong, 1994). Specifically, studies have focused significant attention to the effects of training on supervisor development (e.g., Borders, Rainey, Crutchfield, & Martin, 1996; Kavanagh et al., 2008; Ybrandt & Armelius, 2009), factors that facilitate supervisor training (e.g., McMahon & Simons, 2004; Milne, 2010), supervisor competencies (e.g., Owen-Pugh & Symons, 2012; Zarbrock, Drews, Bodansky, & Dahme, 2009), doctoral students' journey from supervisees to supervisors (e.g., Majcher & Daniluk, 2009; Rapisarda, Desmond, & Nelson, 2011), and the status of supervision training across disciplines (e.g., Crook-Lyon, Presnell, Silva, Suyama, & Stickney, 2011; Scott, Ingram, Vitanza, & Smith, 2000).

Together, formal training and supervised supervision experience have been associated with the development of a supervisor identity. Effects of training on the supervisor's development of self-image were examined in two studies. Ybrandt and Armelius (2009) used structural analysis of social behavior (SASB; Benjamin, 1974, 1996) to assess the self-image of psychotherapists in Sweden. When compared with experienced supervisors, post-training supervisor trainees rated themselves as equally autonomous in their role as supervisors. After training, trainees' self-image was also found to be more positive, consisting of more self-acceptance, self-reliance, and self-caring. Similarly, Borders and Fong (1994) found that supervision training courses had a significant impact on beginning supervisors' self-appraisals of their supervisory abilities, as well as their conceptualization skills. However, they also found that training did not have any effect on supervisors' style and perceptions of supervisory focus in session.

Training strategies that facilitate supervisor development were also investigated to some extent. Baker, Exum, and Tyler (2002) examined the developmental process of clinical supervisors by using Watkins's (1993) supervisor complexity model. Their findings revealed that supervisory skills not only mature over time, but they also strengthen when combined with didactic and experiential training components.

Along similar lines, a systematic review by Milne, Sheikh, Pattison, and Wilkinson (2011) provided empirical support for the combined use of experiential and didactic components in training activities. Further, McMahon and Simons (2004) developed a short-term intensive supervisor training workshop for counselors from various disciplines throughout Australia. The training program had a significant positive impact on supervision competence (knowledge, awareness, and skills) for both supervisors and supervisees, and the effects persisted over time. Milne's (2010) pilot study using an evidence-based supervisor training manual for clinical psychology supervisors in the United Kingdom draws attention to the potential for manualized and standardized training in delivering continuing professional development of supervisors (see also Milne & Dunkerley, 2010). Finally, Manzanares et al. (2004) evaluated the effectiveness of a supervisor CD-ROM approach for educating and supporting prepracticum, practicum, and internship site supervisors. The CD-ROM contained video clips of faculty discussions and document resources that focused on topics related to prepracticum, practicum and internship expectations, supervision issues, challenges and benefits of supervision, professional behavior, and faculty support. Focus groups held with site supervisors revealed that the content of the CD-ROM was perceived as extremely beneficial to the participants. The CD-ROM format of the training, however, proved to be challenging for several of the participants.

Consideration has also been given to identifying the supervisory competencies needed to provide effective supervision. Owen-Pugh and Symons (2012) examined the extent to which Roth and Pilling's (2009) competency framework, commissioned as a training resource by the UK government's project on "improving access to psychological therapies," captured current supervisory practices. The model incorporates four domains: generic competencies (e.g., ability to facilitate ethical practice and to employ educational principles to enhance learning), specific competencies (e.g., ability to help supervisees practice specific clinical skills and to conduct supervision in group format), application to specific models (e.g., cognitive/behavioral, psychoanalytic/psychodynamic, systemic, and humanistic/person centered/experiential), and metacompetencies (e.g., giving feedback, managing serious concerns about practice) that cut across therapeutic modalities. The findings revealed a significant overlap in competencies identified by supervisors regardless of their theoretical orientation. However, CBT Supervisors stood out in that they rated themselves as significantly more confident that they incorporated elements pertaining to the competency of helping supervisees practice specific clinical skills. Wallace, Wilcoxon, and Satcher (2010), on the other hand, developed and validated an instrument focusing on three domains of lousy supervision (e.g., administrative/organizational, cognitive/technical, and relational/affective). The authors were interested in understanding the factor structure of worst and best supervision experiences and how demographic variables may influence participant responses. Participants were members of the American Counseling Association. Consistent with other research, a major recurring theme suggested that productive supervision was typically associated with effectively managing the multiple functions and foci of supervision (e.g., administrative and relational tasks). Additionally, participants who had served as both supervisees and supervisors had more negative views of their worst supervision experience when compared with those who had only functioned in the supervisee role. A study conducted in Germany (Zarbrock et al., 2009) tested the psychometric properties of a measure of supervisory process using Grawe's (1999) model of psychotherapy, which included three dimensions: clarifying, problem-solving, and relationship. Although there was some support for the three-factor solution for both the supervisor and supervisee measures, the best predictors of supervision satisfaction were the relationship and clarifying subscales, highlighting these aspects as important competencies for supervisors.

Recent research has highlighted doctoral students' perspectives on their transition from being supervisees to becoming supervisors. Rapisarda et al. (2011) interviewed counselor supervisor trainees who described two key factors in their transition from supervisee to supervisor – establishing a safe environment for supervisees and developing supervisory skill sets. The participants reflected on their role as supervisees to utilize their past experiences in their new role as supervisors. They also identified challenges associated with this transition. Specifically, supervisor trainees identified as challenging giving evaluative feedback, providing interpersonal support, managing preparation, and allotting time for evaluation. A similar study by Majcher and Daniluk (2009) shed some light on counseling psychology supervisor trainees' needs and learning experiences in their early stages of supervisor development. Their findings supported several supervisor development models – the participants transitioned from a sense of role ambiguity to a sense of confidence and competence. Moreover, beginning supervisors' needs appeared to parallel those of counselors trainees; similar to counselor trainees, the supervisors needed support, structure, and encouragement. These findings correspond with other studies that highlight the importance of skill growth over time (Nelson, Oliver, & Capps, 2006) and the role of being a supervisee as catalysts for supervisor development (Urdang, 1999).

For the past couple of decades, mental health professionals have recognized the importance of supervisory training and attempts have been made to develop rigorous programs, guidelines, and models (Borders, 2005). Despite these efforts, there seems to be a discrepancy in its application in various fields. For instance, Scott et al. (2000) found that counseling psychology programs and counseling center internship sites provided more extensive supervision training when compared with clinical psychology programs. Similarly, Crook-Lyon et al. (2011) noted that counseling center interns reported receiving more supervision training activities, more supervisees, and more supervision of supervision when compared with interns at other sites. Moreover, Lyon, Heppler, Leavitt, and Fisher (2008) investigated the quality and extent of supervision training received by 233 predoctoral interns. Their results revealed that about 72% of their sample had supervised at least one trainee, yet only 39% had received supervision training. Their findings drew attention to the ethical guidelines of the American Psychological Association and accompanying implications of supervising trainees without prior training, competence, or supervised supervision.

Supervision of supervision has deemed to be an important aspect of supervisors' competence development and has gained some attention over the past two decades; however, the empirical literature is still scant (Watkins, 2010). Given the mandatory requirements of supervision of supervision by the British Association for Counselling and Psychotherapy (BACP) and PACFA, research has slowly but systematically started investigating this phenomenon. For instance, Wheeler and King (2000) empirically addressed the status of supervision of supervision in the United Kingdom. Their findings revealed that more than half of the supervisors received supervision, reiterating the importance of supervision of supervision. However, it also pointed to ethical concerns in terms of adhering to BACP guidelines; namely, a majority of the participants seemed to engage in dual roles, such that the same supervisor supervised them for both their clinical work and their supervision of supervisees. Similarly, Townend et al. (2002) and Atkinson and Woods (2007) have highlighted the dual relationship concern in their survey study; however, =the former authors' investigations yielded some promising data regarding supervision of supervision, where more than 50% of their respondents had received some form of supervision of supervision. Furthermore, using a single subject methodology, Milne and Westerman (2001) studied the effects of fortnightly supervision of supervision (also referred to as consultation) on the clinical supervision of supervisees over an eight-month period. Their results indicated that consultancy improved the supervisor's use of intended techniques and also positively affected supervisee development. In a similar vein, Milne and James (2002) and Milne, Reiser, and Cliffe (2012), in their single-subject studies, successfully showed the impact of consultancy (when based on systematic feedback and supportive didactic training, respectively) on the improvement of supervisor competence in using CBT.

Interestingly, despite some discrepancies in how supervision has been incorporated in different disciplines, O'Donovan, Slattery, Kavanagh, and Dooley's (2008) study highlights the similarity in the salience of supervisory activities across disciplines. These authors investigated the impact of a supervision training workshop on the perceived importance of process and content issues in supervision across a range of psychological specialties. Participants were chairs of the Australian Psychological Society specialization colleges. Findings revealed a great deal of overlap across specializations regarding their views on the process of supervision, characteristics of effective supervisors and supervisees, and concerns about supervision. Participants believed that supervision should maintain professional standards and serve as a gatekeeper to the profession, enhance the knowledge and skills of supervisees, assist with the development of reflective practice, expose supervisees to the workings of the profession, provide opportunities for networking, and model real-world experiences. Regardless of specialization, a generic scientist-practitioner model incorporating assessment/diagnosis, intervention, conceptualization, and evaluation/outcome measurement was advocated with a specific focus on the integration of theory and practice. Supervisee development was perceived as significantly influencing the direction, pace, and foci of clinical supervision.

In summary, it is reassuring to find an increased attention to supervisor development given the critical role supervisors play in trainees' professional development. It may be helpful to focus research on the challenges faced by supervisor trainees in developing their supervisor identities, to examine the structure and role of established supervision training courses, to compare the effects of supervisor training for supervisors at various developmental levels, to investigate the influence of supervision training on diversity issues, and to examine in greater detail the role of supervision of supervision in supervisor development. Finally, given that most of these studies were conducted in the United States, a greater multinational/international presence would aid in understanding the state of supervision training within and across different disciplines, countries, and cultures.

Relationship Issues in Supervision

The supervisory relationship has been deemed as foundational to effective supervisory practice (Bernard & Goodyear, 2014; Ladany, Friedlander, & Nelson, 2005). Due to the influential role of the working alliance in supervisory processes, we have chosen to highlight not only the critical factors related to the supervisory working alliance but also specific relational variables that are subsumed within the overarching construct of the working alliance. In this section, we highlight research conducted on the supervisory working alliance, countertransference, conflict, parallel process, sexual attraction, and disclosures in supervision.

Critical factors related to the supervisory working alliance

Because supervision is inextricable from the relational context in which it unfolds, many studies have investigated the construct of the supervisory working alliance and its relation to other important supervisory processes and outcomes (e.g., Carless, Robertson, Willy, Hart, & Chea, 2012; Dickson, Moberly, Marshall, & Reilly, 2011; Fernando & Hulse-Killack, 2005; Ladany & Friedlander, 1995). Specifically, studies have highlighted the role of a strong supervisory working alliance in enhancing supervisee satisfaction with supervision (Cheon, Blumer, Shih, Murphy, & Sato, 2009; Worthen & McNeill, 1996), trainees' perceived self-efficacy (Fernando & Hulse-Killacky, 2005; Gibson, Grey, & Hastings, 2009), supervisee stress levels and coping resources (Gnilka, Chang, & Dew, 2012), and effective practicum experiences (Henderson, Cawyer, & Watkins, 1999; Trepal, Bailie, & Leeth, 2010). Overall, the findings from these studies suggest that supervisory alliances that consist of care, concern, and a safe environment (Jordan, 2006), complemented with offering supportive feedback, normalizing mistakes, and providing opportunities to observe supervisors, facilitate trainees' early professional development. Other studies have suggested that supervisors and supervisees with higher levels of emotional intelligence jointly perceive the working alliance more positively than dyads in which the supervisor, supervisee, or both score lower on emotionally adeptness (Cooper & Ng, 2009). Supervisees also appear to experience less role difficulties when supervisors explicitly discuss trainees' roles and responsibilities within the context of a positive supervisory working alliance (Friedlander, Keller, Peca-Baker, & Olk, 1986; Olk & Friedlander, 1992). Relatedly, a weaker working alliance has been associated with greater role ambiguity and conflict among supervisees in two studies (i.e., Ladany & Friedlander, 1995; Protivnak & Davis, 2008), suggesting that supervisors need to articulate clearly their expectations of supervisees and to establish mutually agreed upon supervision goals.

Moreover, the working alliance has also been investigated from an attachment theory perspective (Bennett, Mohr, BrintzenhofeSzoc, & Saks, 2008; Dickson et al., 2011; Foster, Lichtenberg, & Peyton, 2007). According to Foster et al. (2007), supervisees exhibit attachment styles to their supervisors that are similar to their attachment patterns in other close relationships. Additionally, supervisees who had insecure attachments to their supervisors perceived themselves as being at lower levels of professional development, relative to their securely attached counterparts. Similarly, Bennett, BrintzenhofeSzoc, Mohr, and Saks (2008) found that for social work supervisees, a supervision-specific attachment strongly predicted perceptions of supervisory working alliance and supervisory style. In a similar vein, Dickson et al. (2011) found that trainees' perceptions of their supervisors' attachment style were related to their perceptions of the working alliance, with trainees reporting lower ratings of the working alliance when they perceived their supervisors to be insecurely attached. The results of one study on collusion in supervisory relationships suggested that using self-reflection was an effective tool for understanding this dysfunctional supervision process and for strengthening the relationship (Milne, Leck, & Choudhri, 2009).

Countertransference

In spite of its popularity in the psychotherapy process literature, very little research has been conducted on countertransference within the supervisory relationship. Williams, Judge, Hill, and Hoffman (1997) studied changes in prepracticum trainees' management of countertransference reactions and found support for the notion that trainees become better at coping with countertransference as they progress in their training. Further, Ladany, Constantine, Miller, Erickson, and Muse-Burke's (2000) qualitative investigation found that manifestations of countertransference included behavioral, emotional, and cognitive aspects that were triggered in response to the intern's interpersonal approach and by the supervisor's unresolved problems in his or her personal life. Although supervisors often sought out the support and assistance of trusted colleagues to cope with such reactions, most of the supervisors noted that they had received little or no training to address and manage countertransference issues in supervision. Because supervisors are responsible for modeling appropriate and ethical professional behavior, the extent to which they feel ill-equipped to manage their personal reactions effectively could have significant implications for supervision outcomes and trainee development (Ladany et al., 2000).

Conflict

Although clinical supervision has the potential to be a productive and positive experience, the evaluative nature and disproportionate power inherent in the supervisory relationship make conflict in supervision a common reality (Nelson, Barnes, Evans, & Triggiano, 2008). Several studies have contributed to a better understanding of conflictual experiences in supervision from the supervisee's perspective (i.e., Gray, Ladany, Walker, & Ancis, 2001; Magnuson, Wilcoxon, & Norem, 2000; Martinez, Davis, & Dahl, 2000; Nelson & Friedlander, 2001; Ratliff, Wampler, & Morris, 2000). Across these investigations, findings indicate that conflictual experiences in clinical supervision are characterized by a tenuous relationship, frequent miscommunications (e.g., disagreements concerning the tasks and goals of supervision), a perceived lack of commitment, availability, and support from the supervisor, and supervisor inappropriateness and disrespectful behavior (e.g., lack of respect and mutuality, misuse of power). In response to these circumstances, trainees have reported a range of negative affective reactions, including feelings of incompetence, anxiety, and anger, and have coped by withdrawing emotionally from supervision and relying on the support of peers instead (e.g., Nelson & Friedlander, 2001). Typically, issues have gone unresolved and participants have reported an inability to recover from the conflictual event (e.g., Gray et al., 2001). Despite their desire to speak up, vulnerabilities related to relying on their supervisors for positive evaluations and future recommendation letters seem to prevent supervisees from addressing their concerns. Relatedly, research (Nelson et al., 2008) has revealed that supervisors' responses to conflict can serve to strengthen the relationship if supervisors convey openness to working through conflict by assuming an empathic and nondefensive stance, demonstrating awareness of their own limitations, and modeling vulnerability and transparency. In so doing, supervisees can feel more comfortable and safe to address their concerns as they arise.

Parallel process

Parallel processes (also referred to as isomorphism) refer to aspects of the relationship between therapists and clients that are reflected or mirrored in the relationship between therapists and supervisors, and vice versa (Caldwell, Becvar, Bertolino, & Diamond, 1997; McNeil & Worthen, 1989; Searles, 1955). The concept of parallel process has occupied an important place in psychoanalytic literature (Gediman & Wolkenfeld, 1980) and has also been considered an important and expected part of the supervisory relationship (Ekstein & Wallerstein, 1972). Despite its theoretical significance, the empirical literature is fairly underdeveloped. In our review, we were only able to locate four studies that systematically investigated the concept of parallel processes in supervision (i.e., Jacobsen, 2007; Raichelson, Herron, Primavera, & Ramirez, 1997; Tracey, Bludworth, & Glidden-Tracey, 2012; White & Russell, 1997).

Raichelson et al. (1997) investigated the presence of parallel processes in supervision, its impact on supervisors and supervisees, in addition to its utilization in different theoretical orientations. Their findings revealed that participants of psychoanalytic orientations presented with greater awareness and more frequent use of interventions to address parallel processes, compared with supervisors of nonpsychoanalytic orientations. Tracey et al.'s (2012) rigorous study of interaction patterns among different supervision triads (client, therapist, supervisor) provided convincing evidence for the existence of parallel process. Their study also provided strong evidence for the bidirectional nature of parallel processes; that is, interactions in the supervisory relationship are mirrored in the therapeutic relationship as much as the other way around. On the other hand, Jacobsen's (2007) qualitative case study calls into question the adequacy of the bidirectional representation of parallel processes. Instead, he proposed a kaleidoscopic nature of parallel processes, wherein the supervisory relationship oscillates along many axes, the rotation of which depends on the unique combination of the supervisor's, supervisee's, and client's defense mechanisms and the ways in which they are manifested. In proposing this alternative conceptualization, Jacobsen argued that parallel processes not only can be described in terms of their direction but can also be shaped by the relational dynamics, interactions, and accompanying reactions of each person involved. Additionally, there is some evidence for the presence of parallel processes (*isomorphism*) in the MFT supervision models (White & Russell, 1997). Some preliminary empirical work suggests that parallel processes impact MFT supervision and practice. It is noteworthy that in the MFT literature, this construct lacks conceptual clarity and further research is warranted.

Sexual attraction

Supervisees' feelings of sexual attraction toward clients appear to be a taboo topic that rarely gets discussed in clinical training or supervision, even though research suggests that such feelings are common (Ladany, Melincoff, et al., 1997). For instance, preliminary findings from Ladany et al.'s qualitative study suggested that half of the trainee participants brought up their sexual feelings toward their clients in supervision and that supervisors seldom initiated discussions about sexual attraction. Relatedly, McMurtery, Webb, and Arnold's (2011) quantitative study suggested that supervisors might be hesitant to address these issues due to concerns about being accused of ethical violations, and the blurring of professional and personal boundaries. Unfortunately, because feelings of attraction toward clients appear to influence the therapeutic process and outcome, supervisors miss an important opportunity to normalize their supervisees' feelings and equip them with the tools and resources needed to manage them effectively and to avoid ethical violations (Ladany, Melincoff, et al., 1997).

Disclosures in supervision

One of the most central, yet often implicit, assumptions of supervision is that supervisees must disclose information about themselves, the client, and the therapy and supervision process for the supervisor to facilitate supervisee development and to ensure optimal client care (Heru, Strong, Price, & Recupero, 2004; Ladany, Hill, Corbett, & Nutt, 1996). Similarly, supervisor disclosure is important in facilitating a supportive environment (Knox, Burkard, Edwards, Smith, & Schlosser, 2008; Knox, Edwards, Hess, & Hill, 2011). As such, researchers have begun to investigate the frequency and nature of supervisee and supervisor nondisclosures.

For example, Ladany et al. (1996) and Yourman and Farber (1996) found that more than 90% of supervisees intentionally withheld information from their supervisors. Negative reactions to the supervisor were the most frequent type of nondisclosure. Collectively, researchers (i.e., Hess et al., 2008; Mehr, Ladany, & Caskie, 2010; Webb & Wheeler, 1998; Yourman, 2003) have consistently found that supervisee nondisclosures are especially common in the context of a problematic supervisory relationship. Supervisees have cited feelings of shame and anxiety, and fears of being negatively evaluated and criticized, as motivations for nondisclosures. Because withholding information from supervisors can be detrimental to both the supervisee's ability to intervene competently with clients (e.g., Hess et al., 2008) and his or her overall satisfaction with supervision (e.g., Ladany et al., 1996), additional research is needed to determine the ways in which supervisors can more effectively promote supervisee disclosure.

Much like the area of supervisee nondisclosures, researchers are increasingly beginning to attend to the influences of supervisor disclosure in supervision. For instance, Knox et al. (2008) found that supervisors perceived their self-disclosures positively, stating that it helped to normalize supervisees' struggles and to enhance their learning by providing them with real-life clinical examples. In a follow-up study of supervisees, Knox et al. (2011) found that some supervisees perceived that their supervisors used self-disclosure positively, with intentions to assuage concerns, to enhance rapport, and to facilitate clinical skill development. Contrary to supervisor perceptions, however, supervisees also discussed inappropriate uses of supervisor self-disclosure (e.g., supervisors discussing their mental health issues), which resulted in a perceived loss of supervisor credibility and expertise. Thus, supervisor self-disclosure has the potential to serve as a powerful supervisory intervention when used judiciously and directed at the supervisee's needs. In light of Knox et al.'s mixed findings though, supervisor self-disclosure merits further study to determine which types of supervisor disclosures are most helpful and for whom.

In summary, a critical aspect of effective supervisory process and outcome is the establishment of a productive supervisory working alliance (Ladany et al., 2005). The supervisory working alliance not only has been the subject of numerous studies but also appears to be foundational to effective supervision. In fact, the supervisory working alliance is important to several relational variables, specifically, countertransference, conflict, parallel process, sexual attraction, and self-disclosures. Our review revealed that despite the salience of these variables, research is lacking, with some exceptions. Specifically, recent attention to nondisclosures in supervision highlights the importance of the supervisory working alliance and its connection to other outcomes in supervision. While countertransference, conflict, parallel process, and sexual attraction have been identified as important factors influencing the process and outcome of supervision, additional research is warranted. Investigators could work to develop a more comprehensive understanding of countertransference influences in supervision and to determine how supervisors can facilitate more effectively discussions of conflict, sexual attraction, and concerns and reactions to and about clients, therapy, and supervision; and identify parallel processes among the therapeutic and supervisory relationships, especially from the perspective of nonpsychodynamic theoretical orientations.

Multicultural Issues in Supervision

In light of the increasingly diverse trainee and clinical populations entering into graduate programs and treatment, respectively, effective multicultural clinical supervision and practice are more paramount than ever before (Gardner, 2002; Inman, 2006). Reflecting its recognized importance, the literature on multicultural issues in supervision has expanded considerably over the last 20 years, contributing to a better understanding of the current state of multicultural training and supervision, and the limitations therein (Falender, Burnes, & Ellis, 2013).

Early research on the intersection between cultural variables and clinical supervision tended to focus exclusively on supervisory dyads in which the supervisor and supervisee differed racially. For example, Fukuyama (1994) found that minority trainees perceived positive experiences in multicultural supervision as consisting of the supervisor being willing to address cultural issues in supervision, conveying an attitude of openness and support, and providing culturally relevant clinical guidance and resources. Negative experiences in multicultural supervision included supervisees discussing a lack of cultural awareness on the supervisor's part, as well as a questioning of abilities when supervisees made an effort to address cultural factors as they pertained to their training or clinical work, thereby communicating that such issues were of minimal importance. These findings are highly congruent with Dressel, Consoli, Kim, and Atkinson's (2007) more recent study on successful and unsuccessful behaviors in multicultural supervision. It is interesting to note that both of these investigations highlighted a lack of supervisor cultural awareness. Without an awareness of and sensitivity to their own identities, biases and worldviews, supervisors are at risk for engaging in microaggressions and other acts of racism and discrimination in relation to their culturally different supervisees, or their supervisees' clients (e.g., stereotyping and pathologizing trainee/client behaviors, and providing culturally insensitive treatment recommendations; Constantine & Sue, 2007).

These studies and others (e.g., Burkard et al., 2006; Duan & Roehlke, 2001; Gatmon et al., 2001; Hernandez, Taylor, & McDowell, 2009) suggested that negative experiences in multicultural supervision are unfortunately quite common and may be attributed to several factors. In particular, some scholars (e.g., Burkard et al., 2006) have argued that a generational training gap exists whereby the overwhelming majority of professionals currently serving in a supervisory capacity were educated prior to the introduction of culturally focused curricula, and thus, they may lack the training and resources needed to provide culturally competent supervision. Researchers (e.g., Burkard et al., 2006; Duan & Roehlke, 2001; Hird, Tao, & Gloria, 2004) have consistently found that trainees perceive discussions concerning cultural differences as occurring infrequently in supervision. Further, findings suggest that when such conversations do occur, supervisors rarely initiate them (Gardner, 2002). These dialogues have been found to be particularly challenging for White supervisors, as they may struggle to be aware of the ways in which their memberships in the dominant racial group confer additional social power beyond that inherent in their supervisory roles (Constantine & Sue, 2007; Estrada, 2005; Gloria, Hird, & Tao, 2008; Maidment & Cooper, 2002; Nilsson & Duan, 2007).

In an illuminating study that compared the perspectives of supervisees and supervisors in cross-racial dyads, Duan and Roehlke (2001) found that minority supervisees perceived themselves as being significantly more sensitive to cultural issues relative to their White supervisors. Furthermore, they experienced their supervisors as making fewer efforts to initiate conversations about cultural factors than reported by the supervisors themselves, indicating that supervisors are genuinely unaware of how they are perceived by their trainees and that the efforts they make to address cultural variables in cross-racial supervision are largely ineffective. Because research has also found that supervisees value discussions concerning multicultural issues (Burkard et al., 2006; Dressel et al., 2007; Duan & Roehlke, 2001; Fukuyama, 1994; Hird, Cavaleri, Dulko, Felice, & Ho, 2001; Lawless, Gale, & Bacigalupe, 2001), they may find themselves frustrated by their supervisors' ignorance and may experience supervision as inadequately contributing to their development as therapists. Indeed, supervisees who perceive their supervisors as lacking in multicultural competence and, in turn, failing to engage in discussions concerning cultural factors have been found to rate their supervisory working alliances and satisfaction with supervision more poorly than trainees who experience their supervisors as possessing competence in this realm (Gatmon et al., 2001; Inman, 2006; Toporek, Ortega-Villalobos, & Pope-Davis,

2004). Moreover, although both European American and supervisees of color have been found to experience culturally unresponsive supervision events negatively, minority supervisees appear to be more profoundly impacted, reporting more intense emotional reactions (Burkard et al., 2006).

Race

Due to the complex and multifaceted nature of racial issues in supervision, researchers have also have examined the influence of racial matching in clinical supervision. However, these studies have yielded inconclusive results, with some suggesting that racial matching can lead to more frequent and lengthy discussions about cultural factors in supervision (Hird et al., 2004), as well as a sense of kinship among racially matched dyads (Goode-Cross, 2011), and others failing to find significant effects in terms of supervisory working alliance and supervision satisfaction ratings (Gatmon et al., 2001). Such mixed conclusions have led researchers to turn their attention away from racial matching and, instead, to focus on the influence of racial identity development in supervision. Overall, these studies suggest that racial identity development is a more viable construct for understanding the complex processes underlying multicultural issues in clinical supervision.

Specifically, supervisors with racial consciousness that is higher than (i.e., progressive) or on par with (i.e., parallel) their supervisees' stage of racial identity development tend to be more effective at creating supervisory climates in which racial issues can be discussed, supervisee multicultural competency development can be fostered, and stronger working alliances can be established (Bhat & Davis, 2007; Constantine, Warren, & Miville, 2005; Ladany, Brittan-Powell, & Pannu, 1997; Ladany, Inman, Constantine, & Hofheinz, 1997). Alternatively, when supervisees surpass their supervisors regarding racial identity development status (i.e., regressive dyads), a range of negative affective responses ensues, hindering the overall effectiveness of supervision. As Jernigan, Green, Helms, Perez-Gualdron, and Henze (2010) astutely note, supervisors of color are not inherently experts on race and culture, as the ability to be multicultural competent is contingent upon one's beliefs and life experiences rather than merely being a member of a minority group.

Gender

Another area that has received some consideration in the clinical supervision literature is the role of gender and, in particular, gender matching. Analogous to the research on racial matching, results have been mixed. Specifically, several studies have failed to find that gender matching influences the structure of supervision, supervisee skill development, or working alliance ratings (e.g., Sells, Goodyear, Lichtenberg, & Polkinghorne, 1997). However, Hicks and Cornille's (1999) qualitative study revealed that when female trainees are supervised by female supervisors, they tend to experience supervision as more collaborative and relationally focused. Additionally, Wester, Vogel, and Archer (2004) studied male interns' restricted emotionality (RE) in relation to gender matching and the supervisory alliance. Although no significant differences emerged in terms of the association between supervisees' reported levels of RE and supervisor sex, male interns were found to rate the supervisory working alliance significantly lower when they were matched with male supervisors.

More recently, researchers have shifted away from classifying gender as a categorical and biologically determined variable, moving toward a more postmodern stance of viewing gender as socially constructed and inextricably related to societal attitudes, values, and belief systems (e.g., Rarick & Ladany, 2012). For instance, several studies have looked at how feminist principles are enacted in supervision practice. Overall, these studies have found that feminist supervision is a collaborative endeavor which consists of opposing sexism and rejecting essentialist notions of gender, fostering a sense of commitment to women's issues and activism, and making central the ways in which sexism and other forms of oppression inform clinical training and practice (Green & Dekkers, 2010; Martinez et al., 2000; Prouty, 2001; Prouty, Thomas, Johnson, & Long, 2001; Szymanski, 2005). Moreover, Walker, Ladany, and Pate-Carolan (2007) investigated female supervisees' perceptions of gender-related events in supervision. Gender-related events were operationalized as supervision incidents that pertained to either the trainee's or the client's sex, gender, or stereotypes and assumptions concerning gender roles and expectations. Supportive gender-related events were reported by roughly half of the participants and consisted of supervisors assisting the supervisee in integrating gender into their clinical work, processing feelings related to gender, and considering gender expectations and roles during discussions related to professional development and growth. Alternatively, nonsupportive events were identified by approximately half of the participants and included comments based on gender stereotypes, inappropriate behavior, and a dismissal of trainees' efforts to discuss gender, in relation either to themselves or to their clients. In sum, gender issues continue to pervade the supervisory context, and approaching gender as socially constructed, rather than biologically determined, represents a necessary paradigm shift toward further illuminating gender-related processes in supervision.

Sexual orientation

Unfortunately, the influence of sexual orientation in clinical supervision has not received the same empirical attention as race and gender. For instance, in Taylor, Hernández, Deri, Rankin, and Siegel's (2006) qualitative study on the ways in which supervisors integrate diversity dimensions into clinical supervision, supervisor participants described dialogues concerning ethnicity, race, and gender as common occurrences, whereas issues related to sexual orientation were notably absent from supervision discussions. These findings are especially concerning when considered alongside Harbin, Leach, and Eells's (2008) study, which found that manifestations of supervisors' homophobic beliefs were associated with deleterious effects on trainees' satisfaction with supervision, regardless of supervisee sexual orientation. The few studies that have been conducted in this area highlight the importance of supervisors being open to and comfortable with addressing sexual orientation in supervision and modeling sensitive and affirmative clinical practice, as well as supporting their lesbian, gay, bisexual, transgendered, and queer (LGBTQ) supervisees in navigating institutional or agency homophobia, and helping them to integrate their sexual minority statuses with their professional identities (Burkard, Knox, Hess, & Schultz, 2009; Messinger, 2007; Satterly & Dyson, 2008).

Spirituality and religion

Another area that has been neglected in multicultural supervision literature is spirituality and religion. The fact that very little has been written on this topic is not surprising given the current zeitgeist of secularity. However, the research that has been done in this area suggests that issues surrounding spirituality are relevant for clinical training and practice (Aten, Boyer, & Tucker, 2007; Miller & Ivey, 2006; Miller, Korinek, & Ivey, 2006), in spite of how infrequently such issues are discussed in supervision (Gilliam & Armstrong, 2012). As the findings of Gubi's (2007) study indicate, counselors are often reticent to discuss the use of prayer in supervision due to fears of being misunderstood, judged, dismissed, and pathologized for their religious and/or spiritual beliefs.

International cross-cultural supervision

Finally, in light of the increasing numbers of international students being trained and immigrant clients being served, a small but burgeoning area of research has focused on international supervisees' experiences in supervision and related factors, such as acculturation and language issues. Specifically, research has found that international trainees are more apt to feel self-efficacious in their role as therapists and satisfied with their supervision experiences when supervisors initiate supportive discussions concerning their cultural differences and backgrounds (Ng & Smith, 2012; Nilsson, 2007). Moreover, such conversations appear to be particularly important for trainees who are less acculturated (Mori, Inman, & Caskie, 2009; Nilsson & Dodds, 2006) and have language barriers (Verdinelli & Biever, 2009). When supervisors fail to be sensitive to supervisees' cultural backgrounds and are not open to discussing their adjustment struggles, supervisees may experience feelings of frustration, disappointment, and isolation, as well as a pressure to conform to foreign norms and to accept derogatory comments (Sangganjanavanich & Black, 2009). Clearly, more research is essential for informing the development of supportive supervision practices that consider the unique needs and hardships of international trainees.

In summary, although the investigations reviewed here constitute important advancements, much work remains to be done to ensure a holistic understanding of the complex processes undergirding multicultural supervision. As noted, although researchers have increasingly begun to attend to racial and gender issues, much less is known about the influences of sexual orientation, religion and spirituality, and international student status in supervision and training. Moreover, our search failed to yield any studies that explicitly attended to the role of disability or socioeconomic status (SES) in clinical supervision. Thus, disproportionate attention appears to be given to some cultural variables over others, limiting the field's ability to account for the full scope of identities that feature into the supervisory context (Sangganjanavanich & Black, 2011). In addition, researchers continue to examine these variables in isolation, resulting in a fragmented and unidimensional understanding of cultural issues in supervision. As each person is composed of multiple and intersecting identities, the ways in which such identities interact and inform supervision experiences represent a crucial consideration for researchers moving forward (e.g., Inman, 2006; Toporek et al., 2004).

Impact of Supervision on Therapy and Client Outcome

A few studies have examined the influence of supervision on client outcome and therapy. Callahan, Almstrom, Swift, Borja, and Heath (2009) used archival data from 76 discharged clients in a training clinic located in South Central United States. Changes in scores on the Beck Depression Inventory (BDI) from intake to termination revealed that supervisors accounted for 16% of the variance in client outcome, beyond that accounted for by clients' initial severity and the treating therapists' attributes. Nyman, Nafziger, and Smith (2010) examined client outcome data to assess the impact of a multitiered supervision training model (i.e., predoctoral interns who supervised second semester practicum students and obtained supervision from licensed professionals) at a college counseling center. Scores on the College Adjustment Scale (CAS) and the Outcome Questionnaire (OQ-45) were examined over a three-year period. Findings revealed that although clients' symptoms improved over time, there were no significant differences across counseling levels. Similarly, Bambling, King, Raue, Schweitzer, and Lambert (2006) evaluated the influence of clinical supervision on the therapeutic working alliance and client symptom reduction in the brief treatment of major depression among 127 clients. Supervisors were trained in alliance skill-focused or alliance process-focused supervision whereas therapists were trained in problem-solving therapy. Findings revealed that regardless of the supervision conditions, supervision had a significant influence on the working alliance when compared to ratings from the first therapy session, as well as symptom reduction, and treatment retention and evaluation. Further, working alliance scores were significantly related to the BDI changes; however, the relation was stronger for supervised conditions. Thus, alliance-focused supervision seems to be an important variable in therapy outcomes for depression, and supervision appears to bolster treatment effectiveness.

Two qualitative studies conducted by Vallance (2004, 2005) explored counselor experiences and perceptions of the role of supervision on client work. The findings revealed that exploring client–counselor dynamics and raising counselor self-awareness, and having an egalitarian relationship (Vallance, 2004), directive styles of working, and confidence in the supervisory relationship (Vallance, 2005) were associated with increased perceptions of counselors' confidence in themselves and in the counseling relationship, greater focus, higher levels of counselor congruence, safety, and freedom and effective work with clients. Reese et al. (2009), in their quasi-experimental repeated measures study, examined the effects of continuous feedback in counseling on client outcome over one academic year for trainees in MFT and counseling-clinical psychology programs. Outcome data from 110 clients presenting with a variety of mental health concerns were assessed using the Outcome Rating Scale (ORS), a four-item measure of client progress given at each session, whereas counselors completed multiple measures (i.e., therapeutic and supervisory working alliance, supervisory outcomes, and counselor self-efficacy). Findings revealed that although clients in both conditions (feedback and no-feedback conditions) showed overall improvement, clients in the feedback condition showed greater improvement than clients in the no-feedback condition – counselors in the feedback condition exhibited higher outcome effect sizes for each client in their caseload. Further, there was no difference between trainees on measures of the supervisory alliance and supervisory outcomes in the two groups, suggesting that client feedback does not influence supervisory process. However, the supervisory working alliance was strongly related to the therapeutic working alliance. Interestingly, Crocket et al.'s (2009) qualitative study found that the link between supervision and clinical practice is more about the practitioner's reflections and how supervision may inform the questions or discussions shared with clients rather than on a particular outcome.

Empirically supported treatments

In keeping with the recent focus on empirically supported treatments, studies have examined the role of supervision on therapy and empirically supported treatments. Slavin-Mulford, Hilsenroth, Blagys, and Blais (2011) examined the relation between supervisors' years of experience working within a particular theoretical orientation (cognitive-behavioral [CB] or psychodynamic-interpersonal [PI]) and their endorsement of therapy techniques. As would be expected, supervisors who had more experience in a given theoretical orientation were more likely to endorse techniques consistent with their theoretical orientation. Thus, these results highlight the interplay between theoretical orientation in supervisory and therapeutic efforts.

Schoenwald, Sheidow, and Chapman (2009) examined the relations among supervisors' adherence to supervision and therapy protocols (multisystemic therapy [MST], an empirical supported treatment) and changes in client outcomes (i.e., behavior and function of youth with serious antisocial behavior). Supervisors' adherence to treatment principles predicted therapist adherence. Supervisors' adherence to the structure and process of supervision and a focus on supervisee development predicted changes in youth behavior. Similarly, Accurso, Taylor, and Garland (2011) examined the perspectives of both supervisors and supervisees regarding the role of supervision in the implementation of evidence-based practices (EBPs) with children displaying behavioral disturbances. Supervisor–supervisees dyads completed a supervision process questionnaire assessing the different supervisory functions and a treatment strategy questionnaire, assessing the degree to which supervision focused on EBPs. Supervisor and supervisee ratings were moderately to substantially consistent for supervision functions in all areas except case conceptualization and the supervisory working alliance. The supervisory dyads tended to disagree on the degree of focus on evidence-based treatments. EBP was discussed during supervision to some extent but not in depth. Finally, Carlson, Rapp, and Eichler (2012) sought to identify the supervisory behaviors that contribute to successful implementation of EBP in adult mental health treatment. Supervisors across three modalities were compared: assertive community treatment, integrated dual diagnosis treatment, and supported employment. Enhancing staff skills, monitoring and using outcomes, and implementing continuous quality improvement activities were highly rated. Additional favorably rated supervisory behaviors included supervisors' own professional development and supervision, incorporating EBP into the team's supervisory style and practice, supervisors' development and maintenance of effective relationships with external stakeholders (see also Henderson, 2010), and helping staff with non-EBP activities (e.g., preventing burnout, organizing workload).

In summary, our review suggests that supervision has a significant influence on the therapeutic working alliance, client symptom reduction, and client treatment retention. Working alliance-focused supervision was more effective than problem-focused supervision in terms of client outcome irrespective of whether client data were discussed or not in supervision. And although client feedback may not influence the supervisory process, it is essential and should be paired with routinely tracking client outcomes. Further, to the extent possible, supervision research should be inclusive of client perspectives and therapeutic variables so that a more comprehensive understanding of the supervisory triad (supervisor, supervisee, and client) can ensue. Relatedly, it may be helpful to investigate the links between supervision and the therapist's language, interventions, and interactions with clients. The research seems to suggest that supervision plays an important role in adherence to empirically supported treatments and that supervisor support and encouragement may increase the clarity, focus and congruence in counselor–client work. However, further research in needed in this area.

Assessment/Evaluation/Feedback and Ethical Issues in Supervision

Central to the gate-keeping role, assessment (i.e., systematic gathering of data), evaluation (i.e., determining the extent to which expected supervisee performance is congruent with actual performance), and feedback (i.e., communicating the assessment and evaluation effectively) are not only critical to promoting supervisee growth and development but also paramount to ethical practice (Bernard & Goodyear, 2014). As such, some empirical attention has been given to this important supervisory function. In our review, four themes emerged from studies focusing on evaluation: validity of assessment/evaluation (e.g., Ellis, Krengel, & Beck, 2002; Gonsalvez & Freestone, 2007; McManus, Rakovshik, Kennerley, Fennell, & Westbrook, 2012), supervisee and supervisor perspectives on the nature and importance of the evaluation process (e.g., Heckman-Stone, 2003; Lehrman-Waterman & Ladany, 2001; Sherr et al., 1997), effective modalities of evaluation and feedback (e.g., Amerikaner & Rose, 2012; Heppner et al., 1994; Hunt & Sharpe, 2008; Saltzburg, Greene, & Drew, 2010), and the influence of evaluative feedback on supervisee outcomes (e.g., Britt & Gleaves, 2011; Lehrman-Waterman & Ladany, 2001).

Assessment

Investigators have examined the validity and consistency of supervisory assessment (Fitch, Gillam, & Baltimore, 2004; Gonsalvez & Freestone, 2007; McManus et al., 2012). Fitch et al. (2004) explored variations in supervisor assessment of a counselor's video role-play session based on gender, theoretical orientation, age, and years of supervision experience. While a majority of the supervisors were consistent in how they rated the skills, female supervisors rated the session more favorably than their male counterparts. Further, although theoretical orientation was not a significant factor, age and number of years of supervision were both negatively related to skill rating. Conversely, Gonsalvez and Freestone (2007) found that supervisory ratings may be influenced by a leniency bias such that earlier ratings may be poor predictors of later ratings by different supervisors. On the other hand, McManus et al. (2012) compared supervisees' self-ratings of their CBT competence with their supervisors' ratings. They found that less competent trainees' low self-ratings were similar to their supervisors' ratings; however, more competent trainees seemed to underestimate their competence in comparison to their supervisors' ratings.

The evaluation process

Studies on supervisees' perspectives on the nature and importance of evaluation (Heckman-Stone, 2003; Lehrman-Waterman & Ladany, 2001; Tromski-Klingshirn & Davis, 2007) have converged to emphasize the benefits of key aspects of evaluative feedback. Specifically, feedback that is clear, goal-directed, timely, systematic, consistent and balanced (positive and negative), and based on supervisees' performance, seems to facilitate supervisees' positive experiences of evaluation (Heckman-Stone, 2003; Talen & Schindler, 1994; Tromski-Klingshirn & Davis, 2007). Supervisors' perspectives on the provision of evaluative feedback corroborate these findings; namely, the manner or style of communication and appropriate timing of feedback have been identified as potential factors that may increase supervisee receptivity to challenging feedback (Hoffman, Hill, Holmes, & Freitas, 2005).

Interestingly, studies on the supervisor's perspective of the evaluation process (Gonsalvez & Freestone, 2007; Hoffman et al., 2005; Rapisarda & Britton, 2007) have focused on specific challenges and difficulties that supervisors experienced in providing feedback. Hoffman et al. (2005) found that supervisors encountered difficulties when the feedback was about the supervisee's personal and professional issues, was provided indirectly, and was accompanied by the supervisee's lack of receptivity to feedback. Similarly, Gonsalvez and Freestone (2007) noted that supervisors tended to be more lenient in addressing the supervisee's interpersonal and professional development, and assessment and intervention skills. Other difficulties identified by supervisors have included conflicting interests, such as providing direct feedback to a supervisee who pays for supervision, lacking adequate skills and training to deal with supervisees with problems in professional competence and remediation thereof, lacking specific objective criteria and assessment tools for competency evaluations (Magnuson & Wilcoxon, 1998; Nelson & Graves, 2011; Rapisarda & Britton, 2007), and inconsistencies in providing feedback (Gonsalvez & Freestone, 2007). Other factors influencing evaluation included supervisor impressions of both the therapist's experience and the client's progress. For instance, Dohrenbusch and Lipka (2006) found that more experienced supervisees were held to higher evaluation standards, thereby receiving less positive evaluative ratings. Collectively, these studies highlight the need for supervisors to attend strategically to the evaluation process by reducing supervisee anxiety, clarifying evaluation criteria, and focusing on supervisees' professional development and competencies.

Feedback

A third common theme that emerged across studies was related to effective methods of providing feedback in supervision. Specifically, researchers (Amerikaner & Rose, 2012; DeRoma, Hickey, & Stanek, 2007; Hunt & Sharpe, 2008; Saltzburg et al., 2010) have examined supervisees' perspectives of the effectiveness of didactic and live supervision. Although DeRoma et al. (2007) offered direct observation, progress notes review, and verbal reports of feedback (didactic supervision) as the preferred methods of supervisory feedback, others (Amerikaner & Rose, 2012; Heppner et al., 1994; Saltzburg et al., 2010) have delineated the benefits of direct observation via live/recorded clinical work on supervisee skill development (Wark, 1995a). Specifically, across different disciplines (counseling, MFT), authors (e.g., DeRoma et al., 2007; Heppner et al., 1994) have identified immediacy of feedback, the ability to apply theory *in vivo* to clinical practice, and directive feedback as important unique benefits of live supervision. Further, supervisees indicated that a structured directive approach that challenged their therapeutic style tended to promote their self-efficacy and to strengthen their clinical skill repertoire (Wark, 1995a).

A related study (Hunt & Sharpe, 2008) conducted in Sydney moved beyond supervisee reports to include patient perspectives of treatment that incorporated live supervision. The patients and clinical psychology interns' ratings of their supervisors' approach (walking into or calling in via a phone during a therapy session) suggested that most participants (interns and patients) were amenable to both methods of live supervision feedback. Only a few patients and interns rated the live supervision methods as intrusive. These data also suggested that relatively few supervisors (24%) observe their supervisees' clinical work on a regular and direct basis (Amerikaner & Rose, 2012; DeRoma et al., 2007; Ladany, Lehrman-Waterman, Molinaro, & Wolgast, 1999).

Supervision outcomes

Another area that has garnered attention is the influence of evaluation on supervision outcomes. Studies have linked evaluative practices to supervisee satisfaction (Britt & Gleaves, 2011) and the supervisory working alliance (Lehrman-Waterman & Ladany, 2001). For instance, goal-setting and feedback have been significantly associated with a stronger supervisory working alliance, increased supervisee satisfaction with supervision, and enhanced perceptions of the supervisor playing a role in increasing supervisee self-efficacy (Lehrman-Waterman & Ladany, 2001). Additionally, supervisees' satisfaction with supervision has also been associated with the extent to which supervisors provide ongoing feedback, check in with supervisees regarding their overall supervision experience, and elicit feedback from supervisees on supervision (Britt & Gleaves, 2011).

On the other hand, concerns about evaluations have been associated with supervisee nondisclosure (Worthington, Tan, & Poulin, 2002) and supervisor ethical violations (Amerikaner & Rose, 2012; Ladany et al., 1999; Martinez et al., 2000). For instance, inadequate and inconsistent evaluative practices and the lack of direct observation of trainees' clinical work have been shown to negatively influence supervisee satisfaction, supervisee self-disclosure, and the supervisory working alliance (Ladany et al., 1999). Further, misuse of power in supervision has also been identified as an ethical dilemma for supervisees in their relationship with their supervisors (Martinez et al., 2000). Specifically, supervisees reported fearing repercussions from evaluating their supervisors and felt that the evaluation process was more inclined to accommodate supervisors' rather than supervisees' professional developmental needs. These studies highlight the salience of effective evaluative practices in the context of a hierarchical supervisory relationship where the supervisee is vulnerable.

In summary, research continues to emphasize supervisee and supervisor preferences for systematic, consistent, and collaborative feedback as beneficial to the trainee's overall professional development. The use of empirically validated evaluation instruments that assess professional competencies may help to ensure that criteria for effective feedback are articulated clearly to the supervisee and implemented on an ongoing basis. The use of a variety of methods for providing feedback may contribute further to the knowledge base on evaluative processes in supervision and individual differences among supervisors. Furthermore, while some attention has been given to supervisee characteristics and supervisee outcomes, researchers could pursue the role of the interactional styles of the supervisor and supervisee, and reciprocal feedback. In this regard, the data suggested the importance of empowering supervisees through safety and assurance if feedback is to be implemented reciprocally. Moreover, the studies reviewed underscore the importance of supervisors delineating fully the criteria for evaluation. Examining the moment-by-moment experiences of supervisory dyads during interactions involving feedback and evaluation may unlock the nuances of contextual, supervisee, supervisor, and relational variables affecting feedback in supervision.

Areas of Specialization

Though limited, a number of articles have focused on specialized forms or areas of supervision. Interestingly, the majority of the articles in this category were published within the last decade. Specialized supervision methods and approaches (e.g., Chapman, Baker, Nassar-McMillan, & Gerler, 2011; Coker, Jones, Staples, & Harbach, 2002; Graham & Pehrsson, 2008; Sommer, Ward, & Scofield, 2010; Young & Borders, 1998, 1999), supervising specialized populations or addressing specific client concerns (e.g., Culbreth & Borders, 1998; Fazio-Griffith & Curry, 2009; Sommer & Cox, 2005; West, 2010), and supervision of specialized fields (e.g., Cearley, 2004; Collins-Camargo & Millar, 2010; McMahon, 2003; Reid, 2007) have been the primary areas of focus.

Cybersupervision is one method that has received significant attention (Chapman et al., 2011; Coker et al., 2002; Luke & Gordon, 2011). Specifically, these researchers have examined the effectiveness of cybersupervision with master's level counselor education trainees and counseling interns. Not only has cybersupervision been demonstrated to be as effective as individual face-to-face supervision, but the findings have also revealed no difference in supervisor and supervisee perceptions of the supervisory working alliance. Live supervision is another specialized method of supervision that has been a topic of interest for researchers (Mauzey & Erdman, 1997; Moorhouse & Carr, 1999). Live supervision or phone-ins are particularly common in family therapy, relative to other types of counseling. Mauzey and Erdman (1997) and Moorhouse and Carr (1999) both found that phone-ins could be perceived positively or negatively depending on the content of the call, the way suggestions were delivered, and the supervisor's personality. Most supervisees found live supervision to be helpful yet anxiety provoking. Another specialized method of supervision – triadic supervision (i.e., supervisory relationship is between one supervisor and two counseling trainees) – is primarily found in the counselor education literature (Hein & Lawson, 2008, 2009; Newgent, Davis, & Farley, 2004). Overall, researchers (Hein & Lawson, 2008, 2009; Newgent et al., 2004) found that perceptions of the supervisory working alliance did not differ between triadic supervision and individual supervision. Understandably, managing relationship dynamics of the supervisors–supervisees triangle seemed to be the most salient concern in this type of supervision.

In addition to cybersupervision, live supervision, and triadic supervision, a number of other specialized supervision methods and approaches have been studied, including bibliosupervision (i.e., an approach that blends fiction, storytelling, and narrative ways of knowing the world with counseling processes; Graham & Pehrsson, 2008), the use of metaphors in supervision (Sommer et al., 2010; Young & Borders, 1998, 1999), specific social work supervision models in hospital settings (i.e., supervisors not only supervise the clinical work of supervisees but also assume administrative responsibility to prepare and maintain supervisees' effectiveness and efficiency; Kadushin, Berger, Gilbert, & de St. Aubin, 2009), mindfulness-based role-play supervision (i.e., the integration of role-playing using empty chair techniques and dialogical mindfulness as main foci of supervision; Andersson, King, & Lalande, 2010), wellness model of supervision (i.e., supervision focuses on ensuring trainees' well-being by introducing models of wellness to trainees, continuously using wellness assessments, and facilitating trainees' development of personal wellness plans; Lenz, Sangganjanavanich, Balkin, Oliver, & Smith, 2012), interprofessional supervision (supervision teams consisting of professionals from multiple disciplines such as nursing, social work, occupational therapy, and recreational therapy; Bogo, Paterson, Tufford, & King, 2011), and creative supervision (a supervision group directed by supervisees with some facilitation by a supervisor; Neswald-McCalip, Sather, Strati, & Dineen, 2003). All the aforementioned specialized methods and approaches of supervision have been found effective and received positive feedback from the studies' participants.

Supervising therapists working with specific client concerns/specialized populations has been another area of focus. In particular, attention has been given to supervising therapists working with high-risk populations such as clients with trauma (Sommer & Cox, 2005; West, 2010), clients with borderline personality disorder (Fazio-Griffith & Curry, 2009), and clients with substance abuse issues (Culbreth & Borders, 1998; Culbreth & Cooper, 2008). A number of studies have also explored supervision with professionals from different disciplines. Some researchers have focused on the supervision of welfare workers and, in particular, child welfare workers (Cearley, 2004; Collins-Camargo & Millar, 2010; Rushton & Nathan, 1996), whereas others have explored the experiences of school psychologists and counselors (Harvey & Pearrow, 2010; Luke, Ellis, & Bernard, 2011; Peace & Sprinthall, 1998) and psychosexual therapists (Lawrence, 2001) as they relate to supervision. Career counseling is perhaps the most researched topic in this area. McMahon and Patton (2000), McMahon (2003), and Reid (2007) examined the experiences and needs of career counselors in Australia and England. These researchers reached similar conclusions – while career counselors believed in the importance of supervision, there was minimal support for and provision of supervision for these professionals. Supervision of family and couples counseling (Denton, Nakonezny, & Burwell, 2011), play therapy (Ceballos, Parikh, & Post, 2012; VanderGast, Culbreth, & Flowers, 2010), emotionally focused counseling (Palmer-Olsen, Gold, & Woolley, 2011), and applied behavioral analysis (Gibson et al., 2009) were also examined, though the literature on these specific approaches and modalities continues to be sparse, thus limiting the ability to draw conclusions. In summary, many of the studies seem exploratory in nature. Further, although a recent focus, these studies reflect a fragmented emphasis on specialized topics in supervision. Additional research is warranted across disciplines, methods, and client populations within a global context.

Conclusion

Our intent was to review the international published empirical literature in clinical supervision in mental health disciplines since 1994 (i.e., since Ellis & Ladany, 1997). The articles also had to be published or translated into English. So what can be concluded from the 233 articles reviewed here? To answer this question, it is important to bear in mind some of the limitations of this review. As noted, we excluded published articles from the medical and allied professions in part because our initial search identified over 300 potential articles, thus potentially constituting a herculean task beyond that which we could accomplish in the allotted time frame. The majority of these nonreviewed articles reported research conducted outside the United States and published in nursing journals. Hence, the conclusions reached in our review are not fully comprehensive. Moreover, unpublished studies are not reflected in our review.

Second, due to the large number of articles reviewed, we took a more flexible approach in reviewing articles and the studies reported therein. For example, for the majority of our review, we did not distinguish the results from quantitative and qualitative research designs as a methodological critique of the studies was deemed beyond the scope of this chapter. Instead, we focused on the "what" of the clinical supervision literature rather than the "how." Thus, readers should be cautious in drawing any firm methodological conclusions from the findings reported.

Perhaps one of the most apparent conclusions is the sheer number of published articles in clinical supervision in the past 18 years. The field has proliferated – the number of published research articles in clinical supervision has increased exponentially since Watkins (1997; see Bernard & Goodyear, 2014). This is a welcome observation, evidence that clinical supervision is becoming a recognized and distinctive discipline. As is also evident here, although our knowledge and understanding of supervision has burgeoned (Watkins, 2012), that which we do not understand or understand well continues to be vast.

In terms of the seven broad themes, a few observations merit comment. Four themes garnered the bulk of the studies reviewed. Perhaps not surprising, investigations of the supervisory working alliance encompassed the theme most researched (50 articles), followed closely by multicultural issues in supervision (48 articles), supervisee–supervisor development (47 articles or 18 and 29 articles, respectively), and specialization areas in supervision (42 articles). These are the areas of focus that the majority of researchers in clinical supervision deem worthy of study. Although there has been an increase in the research on clinical supervision since Ellis and Ladany (1997), the impact of supervision on therapy and client outcome has clearly lagged behind the other themes with a mere 11 articles. Because studies that include supervision, therapy, and client outcomes are the acid test for supervision, this very difficult to study theme clamors for empirical attention. The evidence continues to support the supervisory relationship as the most important and central component of effective clinical supervision. We encourage researchers to seek a more nuanced understanding of why and how supervisor, supervisee, and interactional processes shape the relationship over time (e.g., Ellis, 2006). Indeed, there remains a clear lack of longitudinal data about why and how supervisees develop professionally and personally during graduate training and over the course of their careers. This unfortunate state has persisted and remained essentially unchanged since Watkins (1997). Multisite, multicohort longitudinal research is sorely needed.

The review suggests that clinical supervision in non-US countries has, in some cases, outpaced supervision research in the United States. Consider, for instance, the first randomized clinical trial investigating supervision of therapists (Bambling et al., 2006). Hence, one can conclude that clinical supervision is truly international and interdisciplinary, with investigators from multiple countries and disciplines continuing to pursue research and cross-national empirical endeavors (e.g., Bambling et al., 2006; Davys & Bedoe, 2009). We hope this international and interdisciplinary trend continues (e.g., the annual International Interdisciplinary Conference on Clinical Supervision; see http://socialwork.adelphi.edu/academics/continuing-education-professional-development/international-interdisciplinary-conference-on-clinical-supervision/). The research reviewed here only serves to beckon more questions and invite further empirical inquiry. We also hope that new investigators join in the pursuit to understand and increase the efficacy of clinical supervision. To this end, Watkins and Milne (2014) may serve to stimulate further interest and inquiry.

Acknowledgments

The authors would like to acknowledge and thank Maria Lauer-Larrimore, Carin Molenaar, Bethany Perkins, Candice Presseau, Valeriya Spektor, Lehigh University, and Alexa Hanus, Abigail Nicolas, Lauren Dasen, University at Albany, for their assistance with the literature review and coding of the articles.

References

Accurso, E. C., Taylor, R. M., & Garland, A. F. (2011). Evidence-based practices addressed in community-based children's mental health clinical supervision. *Training and Education in Professional Psychology*, *5*, 88–96. doi:10.1037/a0023537

American Psychological Association. (2012). *Benchmarks clusters and core competencies.* Retrieved from http://www.apa.org/ed/graduate/benchmarks-clusters-competencies.pdf

Amerikaner, M., & Rose, T. (2012). Direct observation of psychology supervisees' clinical work: A snapshot of current practice. *The Clinical Supervisor, 31*, 61–80. doi:10.1080/07325223.2012.671721f10.1080/07325223.2012.671721

Andersson, L., King, R., & Lalande, L. (2010). Dialogical mindfulness in supervision role-play. *Counselling and Psychotherapy Research, 10*, 287–294. doi:10.1080/14733141003599500

Aten, J. D., Boyer, M. C., & Tucker, B. T. (2007). Christian integration in clinical supervision: A conceptual framework. *Journal of Psychology and Christianity, 26*, 313–320.

Atkinson, C., & Woods, K. (2007). A model of effective fieldwork supervision for trainee educational psychologists. *Educational Psychology in Practice, 23*, 299–316. doi:10.1080/02667360701660902

Baker, S. B., Exum, H. A., & Tyler, R. E. (2002). The developmental process of clinical supervisors in training: An investigation of the supervisor complexity model. *Counselor Education and Supervision, 42*, 15–30. doi:10.1002/j.1556-6978.2002.tb01300.x

Bambling, M., King, R., Raue, P., Schweitzer, R., & Lambert, W. (2006). Clinical supervision: Its influence on client-rated working alliance and client symptom reduction in the brief treatment of major depression. *Psychotherapy Research, 16*, 317–331. doi:10.1080/10503300500268524

Benjamin, L. (1974). Structural analysis of social behavior. *Psychological Review, 81*(5), 392–425.

Benjamin, L. S. (1996). A clinician-friendly version of the interpersonal circumplex: Structural analysis of social behavior (SASB). *Journal of Personality Assessment, 66*(2), 248–266.

Bennett, S., BrintzenhofeSzoc, K., Mohr, J., & Saks, L. (2008). General and supervision-specific attachment styles: Relations to student perceptions of field supervisors. *Journal of Social Work Education, 44*(2), 75–94. Retrieved from http://search.ebscohost.com.libproxy.albany.edu/login.aspx?direct=true&db=a9h&AN=35566884&site=ehost-live

Bennett, B., Mohr, J., BrintzenhofeSzoc, K., & Saks, L. V. (2008). General and supervision-specific attachment styles: Relations to student perceptions of field supervisors. *Journal of Social Work Education, 44*(2), 75–94.

Bernard, J. M., & Goodyear, R. K. (2014). *Fundamentals of clinical supervision* (5th ed.). Boston, MA: Allyn & Bacon.

Bhat, C. S., & Davis, T. E. (2007). Counseling supervisors' assessment of race, racial identity, and working alliance in supervisory dyads. *Journal of Multicultural Counseling & Development, 35*, 80–91. Retrieved from http://search.ebscohost.com.libproxy.albany.edu/login.aspx?direct=true&db=a9h&AN=4752076&site=ehost-live

Bogo, M., Paterson, J., Tufford, L., & King, R. (2011). Interprofessional clinical supervision in mental health and addiction: Toward identifying common elements. *The Clinical Supervisor, 30*, 124–140. doi:10.1080/07325223.2011.564961

Borders, D. L., Rainey, L. M., Crutchfield, L. B., & Martin, D. W. (1996). Impact of a counseling supervision course on doctoral students' cognitions. *Counselor Education and Supervision, 35*, 204–228. doi:10.1002/j.1556-6978.1996.tb00224.x

Borders, L. D. (2005). Snapshot of clinical supervision in counseling and counselor education: A five-year review. *The Clinical Supervisor, 24*, 69–113. doi:10.1300/J001v24n01_05

Borders, L. D., & Cashwell, C. S. (1995). Supervision of counselor licensure applicants: A comparative study. *Counselor Education and Supervision, 35*, 220–233. doi:10.1002/j.1556-6978.1995.tb00209.x

Borders, L. D., & Fong, M. L. (1994). Cognitions of supervisors-in-training: An exploratory study. *Counselor Education and Supervision, 33*, 280–293. doi:10.1002/j.1556-6978.1994.tb00294.x

Britt, E., & Gleaves, D. H. (2011). Measurement and prediction of clinical psychology students' satisfaction with clinical supervision. *The Clinical Supervisor, 30*, 172–182. doi:10.1080/07325223.2011.604274

Burkard, A., Knox, S., Hess, S. A., & Schultz, J. (2009). Lesbian, gay, and bisexual supervisee's experience of LGB-affirmative and nonaffirmative supervision. *Journal of Counseling Psychology, 56*, 176–188. doi:10.1037/0022-0167.56.1.176

Burkard, A., Johnson, A. J., Madson, M. B., Pruitt, N., Contreras-Tadych, D. A., Kozlowski, J. M., . . . Knox, S. (2006). Supervisor cultural responsiveness and unresponsiveness in cross-cultural supervision. *Journal of Counseling Psychology, 53*, 288–301. doi:10.1037/0022-0167.53.3.288

Caldwell, K., Becvar, D. S., Bertolino, R., & Diamond, D. (1997). A postmodern analysis of a course on clinical supervision. *Contemporary Family Therapy, 19*, 269–287. Retrieved from http://link.springer.com/article/10.1023%2FA%3A1026175320634?LI=true#page-1

Callahan, J. L., Almstrom, C. M., Swift, J. K., Borja, S. E., & Heath, C. J. (2009). Exploring the contribution of supervisors to intervention outcomes. *Training and Education in Professional Psychology, 3*, 72–77. doi:http://dx.doi.org/10.1037/a0014294

Carless, S. A., Robertson, K., Willy, J., Hart, M., & Chea, S. (2012). Successful postgraduate placement experiences: What is the influence of job and supervisor characteristics? *Australian Psychologist, 47*, 156–164. doi:10.1111/j.1742-9544.2012.00085.x

Carlson, L., Rapp, C. A., & Eichler, M. S. (2012). The experts rate: Supervisory behaviors that impact the implementation of evidence-based practices. *Community Mental Health Journal, 48*, 179–186. doi:10.1007/s10597-010-9367-4

Cearley, S. (2004). The power of supervision in child welfare services. *Child and Youth Care Forum, 33*, 313–327. doi:10.1023/B:CCAR.0000043038.97882.2f

Ceballos, P. L., Parikh, S., & Post, P. B. (2012). Examining social justice attitudes among play therapists: Implications for multicultural supervision and training. *International Journal of Play Therapy* [Advance online publication]. doi:10.1037/a0028540

Chapman, R. A., Baker, S. B., Nassar-McMillan, S. C., & Gerler, E. R. (2011). Cybersupervision: Further examination of synchronous and asynchronous modalities in counseling practicum supervision. *Counselor Education and Supervision, 50*, 298–313. Retrieved from http://onlinelibrary.wiley.com/journal/10.1002/%28ISSN%291556-6978

Cheon, H., Blumer, M. L. C., Shih, A., Murphy, M. J., & Sato, M. (2009). The influence of supervisor and supervisee matching, role conflict, and supervisory relationship on supervisee satisfaction. *Contemporary Family Therapy, 31*, 52–67. doi:10.1007/s10591-008-9078-y

Chiller, P., & Crisp, B. R. (2012). Professional Supervision: A workforce retention strategy for social work? *Australian Social Work, 65*, 232–242. doi:http://dx.doi.org/10.1080/0312407X.2011.625036

Clarkson, P., & Aviram, O. (1995). Phenomenological research on supervision: Supervisors reflect on "being a supervisor." *Counselling Psychology Quarterly, 8*, 63–80. doi:10.1080/09515079508258698

Coker, J. K., Jones, W. P., Staples, P. A., & Harbach, R. L. (2002). Cyber-supervision in the first practicum: Implications for research and practice. *Guidance & Counseling, 18*, 33–38. Retrieved from http://connection.ebscohost.com/c/articles/9989271/cybersupervision-first-practicum-implications-research-practice

Collins-Camargo, C., & Millar, K. (2010). The potential for a more clinical approach to child welfare supervision to promote practice and case outcomes: A qualitative study in four states. *The Clinical Supervisor, 29*, 164–187. doi:10.1080/07325223.2010.517491

Constantine, M. G., & Sue, D. W. (2007). Perceptions of racial microaggressions among black supervisees in cross-racial dyads. *Journal of Counseling Psychology, 54*, 142–153. doi:10.1037/0022-0167.54.2.142

Constantine, M. G., Warren, A. K., & Miville, M. L. (2005). White racial identity dyadic interactions in supervision: Implications for supervisees' multicultural counseling competence. *Journal of Counseling Psychology, 52*, 490–496. doi:10.1037/00220167.52.4.490

Cooper, J. B., & Ng, K. (2009). Trait emotional intelligence and perceived supervisory working alliance of counseling trainees and their supervisors in agency settings. *International Journal for the Advancement of Counselling, 31*, 145–157. doi:10.1007/s10447-009-9074-4

Crocket, K., Pentecost, M., Cresswell, R., Paice, C., Tollestrup, D., DeVries, M., & Wolfe, R. (2009). Informing supervision practice through research: A narrative inquiry. *Counselling and Psychotherapy Research, 9*, 101–107. doi:10.1080/14733140802688936

Crook-Lyon, R. E., Presnell, J., Silva, L., Suyama, M., & Stickney, J. (2011). Emergent supervisors: Comparing counseling center and non-counseling center interns' supervisory training experiences. *Journal of College Counseling, 14*, 34–49. doi:10.1002/j.2161-1882.2011.tb00062.x

Culbreth, J. R., & Borders, L. D. (1998). Perceptions of the supervisory relationship: A preliminary qualitative study of recovering and nonrecovering substance abuse counselors. *Journal of Substance Abuse Treatment, 15*, 345–352. doi:10.1016/S0740-5472(97)00254-7

Culbreth, J. R., & Cooper, J. B. (2008). Factors impacting the development of substance abuse counseling supervisors. *Journal of Addictions & Offender Counseling, 29*, 22–35. Retrieved from http://search.ebscohost.com.libproxy.albany.edu/login.aspx?direct=true&db=a9h&AN=35001856&site=ehost-live

Davys, A. M., & Bedoe, L. (2009). Interprofessional learning for supervision: "Taking the blinkers off." *Learning in Health and Social Care, 8*, 58–69. doi:10.1111/j.1473-6861.2008.00197.x

Dennin, M. K., & Ellis, M. V. (2003). Effects of a method of self-supervision for counselor trainees. *Journal of Counseling Psychology, 50*, 69–83. doi:10.1037/0022-0167.50.1.69

Denton, W. H., Nakonezny, P. A., & Burwell, S. R. (2011). The effects of meeting a family therapy supervision team on client satisfaction in an initial session. *Journal of Family Therapy, 33*, 85–97. doi:10.1111/j.1467-6427.2010.00518.x

DeRoma, V. M., Hickey, D. A., & Stanek, K. M. (2007). Methods of supervision in marriage and family therapist training: A brief report. *North American Journal of Psychology, 9*, 415–422. Retrieved from http://psycnet.apa.org/psycinfo/2007-19659-001

Dickson, J. M., Moberly, N. J., Marshall, Y., & Reilly, J. (2011). Attachment style and its relationship to working alliance in the supervision of British clinical psychology trainees. *Clinical Psychology & Psychotherapy, 18*, 322–330. doi:10.1002/cpp.715

Dohrenbusch, R., & Lipka, S. (2006). Assessing and predicting supervisors' evaluations of psychotherapists – An empirical study. *Counselling Psychology Quarterly, 19*, 395–414. doi:10.1080/09515070601106737

Dressel, J. L., Consoli, A. J., Kim, B. S. K., & Atkinson, D. R. (2007). Successful and unsuccessful multicultural supervisory behaviors: A Delphi poll. *Journal of Multicultural Counseling & Development, 35*, 51–64. doi:10.1002/j.2161-1912.2007.tb00049.x

Duan, C., & Roehlke, H. (2001). A descriptive "snapshot" of cross-racial supervision in university counseling center internships. *Journal of Multicultural Counseling & Development, 29*, 131–146. doi:10.1002/j.2161-1912.2001.tb00510.x

Ekstein, R., & Wallerstein, R. S. (1972). *The teaching and learning of psychotherapy* (2nd ed.). New York, NY: International Universities Press.

Ellis, M. V. (2006). Critical incidents in clinical supervision and in supervisor supervision: Assessing supervisory issues. *Training and Education in Professional Psychology, S*(2) 122–132. doi:10.1037/1931-3918.S.2.122

Ellis, M. V., Krengel, M., & Beck, M. (2002). Testing self-focused attention theory in clinical supervision: Effects on supervisee anxiety and performance. *Journal of Counseling Psychology, 49*, 101–116. doi:10.1037//0022-0167.49.1.101

Ellis, M. V., & Ladany, N. (1997). Inferences concerning supervisees and clients in clinical supervision: An integrative review. In C. E. Watkins, Jr. (Ed.), *Handbook of psychotherapy supervision* (pp. 447–507). New York, NY: Wiley.

Estrada, D. (2005). Multicultural conversations in supervision: The impact of the supervisor's racial/ethnic background. *Guidance & Counseling, 21*, 14–20. Retrieved from http://www.utpress.utoronto.ca/GCentre/07784guidco.html

Falender, C. A., Burnes, T. R., & Ellis, M. V. (2013). Multicultural clinical supervision and benchmarks: Empirical support informing practice and supervisor training. *The Counseling Psychologist, 41*, 1–20. doi:10.1177/0011000012438417

Falender, C. A., Cornish, J. A., Goodyear, R., Hatcher, R., Kaslow, N. J., Leventhal, G., . . . Grus, C. (2004). Defining competencies in psychology supervision: A consensus statement. *Journal of Clinical Psychology, 60*, 771–787. doi:10.1002/jclp.20013

Fazio-Griffith, L., & Curry, J. R. (2009). Supervising trainees who counsel clients with borderline personality characteristics: Implications for training and practice. *Journal of Mental Health Counseling, 31*, 234–248. Retrieved from http://connection.ebscohost.com/c/articles/44087984/supervising-trainees-who-counsel-clients-borderline-personality-characteristics-implications-training-practice

Fernando, D. M., & Hulse-Killacky, D. (2005). The relationship of supervisory styles to satisfaction with supervision and the perceived self-efficacy of master's-level counseling students. *Counselor Education and Supervision, 44*, 293–304. doi:10.1002/j.1556-6978.2005.tb01757.x

Fitch, T., Gillam, L., & Baltimore, M. (2004). Consistency of clinical skills assessment among supervisors. *The Clinical Supervisor, 23*, 71–81. doi:10.1300/J001v23n01_05

Foster, J. T., Lichtenberg, J. W., & Peyton, V. (2007). The supervisory attachment relationship as a predictor of the professional development of the supervisee. *Psychotherapy Research, 17*, 353–361. doi:10.1080/10503300600823202

Friedlander, M. L., Keller, K. E., Peca-Baker, T. A., & Olk, M. E. (1986). Effects of role conflict on counselor-trainees' self-statements, anxiety level, and performance. *Journal of Counseling Psychology, 33*, 73–77. doi:10.1037/0022-0167.33.1.73

Fukuyama, M. A. (1994). Critical incidents in multicultural supervision: A phenomenological approach to supervision research. *Counselor Education and Supervision, 34*, 142–151. doi:10.1002/j.1556-6978.1994.tb00321.x

Gabbay, M. B., Kiemle, G., & Maguire, C. (1999). Clinical supervision for clinical psychologists: Existing provision and unmet needs. *Clinical Psychology and Psychotherapy, 6*, 404–412. doi:10.1002/(SICI)1099-0879(199911)6:5<404::AID-CPP209>3.0.CO;2-B

Gardner, R. D. (2002). Cross-cultural perspectives in supervision. *Western Journal of Black Studies, 26*, 98–106. Retrieved from http://psycnet.apa.org/psycinfo/2003-08513-002

Gatmon, D., Jackson, D., Koshkarian, L., Martos-Perry, N., Molina, A., Patel, N., & Rodolfa, E. (2001). Exploring ethnic, gender, and sexual orientation variables in supervision: Do they really matter? *Journal of Multicultural Counseling and Development, 29*, 102–113. doi:10.1002/j.2161-1912.2001.tb00508.x

Gediman, H., & Wolkenfeld, F. (1980). The parallelism phenomenon in psychoanalysis supervision: Its reconsideration as a triadic system. *Psychoanalytic Quarterly, 49*, 234–255.

Geller, J. D., Farber, B. A., & Schaffer, C. E. (2010). Representations of the supervisory dialogue and the development of psychotherapists. *Psychotherapy, 47*, 211–220. doi:10.1037/a0019785

Gibson, J. A., Grey, I. M., & Hastings, R. P. (2009). Supervisor support as a predictor of burnout and therapeutic self-efficacy in therapists working in ABA schools. *Journal of Autism and Developmental Disorders, 39*, 1024–1030. doi:10.1007/s10803-009-0709-4

Gilliam, T. H., & Armstrong, S. A. (2012). Spirituality and counseling supervision: Current practices of board-approved supervisors. *The Clinical Supervisor, 31*, 25–41. doi:10.1080/07325223.2012.671718

Gloria, A. M., Hird, J. S., & Tao, K. W. (2008). Self-reported multicultural supervision competence of White predoctoral intern supervisors. *Training and Education in Professional Psychology, 2*, 129–136. doi:10.1037/1931-3918.2.3.129

Gnilka, P. B., Chang, C. Y., & Dew, B. J. (2012). The relationship between supervisee stress, coping resources, the working alliance, and the supervisory working alliance. *Journal of Counseling and Development, 90*, 63–70. doi:10.1111/j.1556-6676.2012.00009.x

Gonsalvez, C. J., & Freestone, J. (2007). Field supervisors' assessments of trainee performance: Are they reliable and valid? *Australian Psychologist, 42*, 23–32. doi:10.1080/00050060600827615

Gonsalvez, C. J., Oades, L. G., & Freestone, J. (2002). The objectives approach to clinical supervision: Towards integration and empirical evaluation. *Australian Psychologist, 37*, 68–77. doi:10.1080/00050060210001706706

Goode-Cross, D. T. (2011). "Those who learn have a responsibility to teach": Black therapists' experiences supervising Black therapist trainees. *Training and Education in Professional Psychology, 5*, 73–80. doi:10.1037/a0023187

Graham, M. A., & Pehrsson, D. (2008). Bibliosupervision: A multiple-baseline study using literature in supervision settings. *Journal of Creativity and Supervision, 3*, 428–440. doi:10.1080/15401380802531052

Grant, J., & Schofield, M. (2007). Career-long supervision: Patterns and perspectives. *Counselling and Psychotherapy Research, 7*, 3–11. doi:10.1080/14733140601140899

Grawe, K. (1999). *Psychologische therapie [Psychological therapy]*. Bern, Germany: Hans Huber.

Gray, L. A., Ladany, N., Walker, J. A., & Ancis, J. R. (2001). Psychotherapy trainees' experience of counterproductive events in supervision. *Journal of Counseling Psychology, 48*, 371–383. doi:10.1037/0022-0167.48.4.371

Green, M. S., & Dekkers, T. D. (2010). Attending to power and diversity in supervision: An exploration of supervisee learning outcomes and satisfaction with supervision. *Journal of Feminist Family Therapy, 22*, 293–312. doi:10.1080/08952833.2010.528703

Gubi, P. (2007). Exploring the supervision experience of some mainstream counsellors who integrate prayer in counselling. *Counselling and Psychotherapy Research, 7*, 114–121. doi:10.1080/14733140701342544

Haarhoff, B. A. (2006). The importance of identifying and understanding therapist schema in cognitive therapy training and supervision. *New Zealand Journal of Psychology, 35*, 126–131. Retrieved from http://www.biomedsearch.com/article/importance-identifying-understanding-therapist-schema/158523017.html

Harbin, J. J., Leach, M. M., & Eells, G. T. (2008). Homonegativism and sexual orientation matching in counseling supervision. *Counselling Psychology Quarterly, 21*, 61–73. doi:10.1080/09515070801913569

Harvey, V., & Pearrow, M. (2010). Identifying challenges in supervising school psychologists. *Psychology in the Schools, 47*, 567–581. doi:10.1002/pits.20491

Heckman-Stone, C. (2003). Trainee preferences for feedback and evaluation in clinical supervision. *The Clinical Supervisor, 22*, 21–33. doi:10.1300/J001v22n01_03

Hein, S., & Lawson, G. (2008). Triadic supervision and its impact on the role of the supervisor: A qualitative examination of supervisors' perspectives. *Counselor Education and Supervision, 48*, 16–31. doi:10.1002/j.1556-6978.2008.tb00059.x

Hein, S. F., & Lawson, G. (2009). A qualitative examination of supervisors' experiences of the process of triadic supervision. *The Clinical Supervisor*, *28*, 91–108. doi:10.1080/07325220902832630

Henderson, C. E., Cawyer, C. S., & Watkins, C. E., Jr. (1999). A comparison of student and supervisor perceptions of effective practicum. *The Clinical Supervisor*, *18*, 47–74. doi:10.1300/J001v18n01_04

Henderson, K. (2010). Work-based supervisors: The neglected partners in practice learning. *Social Work Education*, *29*, 490–502. doi:10.1080/02615470903156352

Heppner, P. P., Kivlighan, D. M., Burnett, J. W., Berry, T. R., Goedinghaus, M., Doxsee, D. J., . . . Wallace, D. L. (1994). Dimensions that characterize supervisor interventions delivered in the context of live supervision of practicum counselors. *Journal of Counseling Psychology*, *41*, 227–235. doi:10.1037/0022-0167.41.2.227

Hernandez, P., Taylor, B., & McDowell, T. (2009). Listening to ethnic minority AAMFT approved supervisors: Reflections on their experiences as supervisors. *Journal of Systemic Therapies*, *28*, 88–100. doi:10.1521/jsyt.2009.28.1.88

Heru, A. M., Strong, D. R., Price, M., & Recupero, P. R. (2004). Boundaries in psychotherapy supervision. *American Journal of Psychotherapy*, *58*, 76–89. Retrieved from http://psycnet.apa.org/?fa=main.doiLanding&uid=2004-13324-007

Hess, S. A., Knox, S., Schultz, J. M., Hill, C. E., Sloan, L., Brandt, S., . . . Hoffman, M. A. (2008). Predoctoral interns' nondisclosure in supervision. *Psychotherapy Research*, *18*, 400–411. doi:10.1080/10503300701697505

Hicks, M. W., & Cornille, T. A. (1999). Gender, power and relationship ethics in family therapy education. *Contemporary Family Therapy*, *21*, 45–56. Retrieved from http://link.springer.com/article/10.1023%2FA%3A1021910620587?LI=true

Hird, J. S., Cavaleri, C. E., Dulko, J. P., Felice, A. A. D., & Ho, T. A. (2001). Visions and realities: Supervisee perspectives of multicultural supervision. *Journal of Multicultural Counseling and Development*, *29*, 114–130.

Hird, J. S., Tao, K. W., & Gloria, A. M. (2004). Examining supervisors' multicultural competence in racially similar and different supervision dyads. *The Clinical Supervisor*, *23*, 107–123. doi:10.1300/J001v23n02_07

Hoffman, M. A., Hill, C. E., Holmes, S. E., & Freitas, G. F. (2005). Supervisor perspective on the process and outcome of giving easy, difficult, or no feedback to supervisees. *Journal of Counseling Psychology*, *52*, 3–13. doi:10.1037/0022-0167.52.1.3

Hunt, C., & Sharpe, L. (2008). Within-session supervision communication in the training of clinical psychologists. *Australian Psychologist*, *43*(2), 121–126. doi:10.1080/00050060801933402

Inman, A. G. (2006). Supervisor multicultural competence and its relation to supervisory process and outcome. *Journal of Marital and Family Therapy*, *32*, 73–85. doi:10.1111/j.1752-0606.2006.tb01589.x

Inman, A. G., & Ladany, N. (2008). Research: The state of the field. In A. K. Hess, K. D. Hess, & T. H. Hess (Eds.), *Psychotherapy supervision: Theory, research, and practice* (2nd ed., pp. 500–517). New York, NY: John Wiley & Sons.

Jacobsen, C. (2007). A qualitative single case study of parallel processes. *Counselling and Psychotherapy Research*, *7*, 26–33. doi:10.1080/14733140601140410

Jernigan, M. M., Green, C. E., Helms, J. E., Perez-Gualdron, L., & Henze, K. (2010). An examination of people of color supervision dyads: Racial identity matters as much as race. *Training and Education in Professional Psychology*, *4*, 62–73. doi:10.1037/a0018110

Johnston, L., & Milne, D. (2012). How do supervisees learn during supervision? A grounded theory study of the perceived developmental process. *The Cognitive Behaviour Therapist*, *5*, 1–23. doi:10.1017/S1754470X12000013

Jordan, K. (2006). Beginning supervisees' identity: The importance of relationship variables and experience versus gender matches in the supervisee/supervisor interplay. *The Clinical Supervisor, 25*, 43–52. doi:10.1300/J001v25n01_04

Kadushin, G., Berger, C., Gilbert, C., & de St. Aubin, M. (2009). Models and methods in hospital social work supervision. *The Clinical Supervisor, 28*, 180–199. doi:10.1080/07325220903324660

Kavanagh, D. J., Spence, S., Sturk, H., Strong, J., Wilson, J., Worrall, L., . . . Skerrett, R. (2008). Outcomes of training in supervision: Randomised controlled trial. *Australian Psychologist, 43*, 96–104. doi:10.1080/00050060802056534

Knox, S., Burkard, A. W., Edwards, L. M., Smith, J. J., & Schlosser, L. Z. (2008). Supervisors' reports of the effects of supervisor self-disclosure on supervisees. *Psychotherapy Research, 18*, 543–559. doi:10.1080/10503300801982781

Knox, S., Edwards, L. M., Hess, S. A., & Hill, C. E. (2011). Supervisor self-disclosure: Supervisees' experiences and perspectives. *Psychotherapy, 48*, 336–341. doi:10.1037/a0022067

Krasner, R. F., Howard, K. I., & Brown, A. S. (1998). The acquisition of psychotherapeutic skill: An empirical study. *Journal of Clinical Psychology, 54*, 895–903. doi:10.1002/(SICI)1097-4679(199811)54:7<895::AID-JCLP4>3.3.CO;2-Y

Ladany, N., Brittan-Powell, C. S., & Pannu, R. K. (1997). The influence of supervisory racial identity interaction and racial matching on the supervisory working alliance and supervisee multicultural competence. *Counselor Education and Supervision, 36*, 284–304. doi:10.1002/j.1556-6978.1997.tb00396.x

Ladany, N., Constantine, M. G., Miller, K., Erickson, C. D., & Muse-Burke, J. L. (2000). Supervisor countertransference: A qualitative investigation into its identification and description. *Journal of Counseling Psychology, 47*, 102–115. doi:10.1037//00220167.47.1.102

Ladany, N., & Friedlander, M. L. (1995). The relationship between the supervisory working alliance and trainees' experience of role conflict and role ambiguity. *Counselor Education and Supervision, 34*, 220–231. doi:10.1002/j.1556-6978.1995.tb00244.x

Ladany, N., Friedlander, M. L., & Nelson, M. L. (2005). *Critical events in psychotherapy supervision: An interpersonal approach.* Washington, DC: American Psychological Association.

Ladany, N., Hill, C. E., Corbett, M. M., & Nutt, E. A. (1996). Nature, extent, and importance of what psychotherapy trainees do not disclose to their supervisors. *Journal of Counseling Psychology, 43*, 10–24. doi:10.1037/0022-0167.43.1.10

Ladany, N., & Inman, A. G. (2012). Training and supervision. In E. Altamaier & J. Hansen (Eds.), *The Oxford handbook of counseling psychology* (pp. 179–207). New York, NY: Oxford University Press.

Ladany, N., Inman, A. G., Constantine, M. G., & Hofheinz, E. W. (1997). Supervisee multicultural case conceptualization ability and self-reported multicultural competence as functions of supervisee racial identity and supervisor focus. *Journal of Counseling Psychology, 44*, 284–293. doi:10.1037/0022-0167.44.3.284

Ladany, N., Lehrman-Waterman, D., Molinaro, M., & Wolgast, B. (1999). Psychotherapy supervisor ethical practices: Adherence to guidelines, supervisory working alliance, and supervisee satisfaction. *The Counseling Psychologist, 27*, 443–475. doi:10.1177/0011000099273008

Ladany, N., Melincoff, D. S., O'Brien, K. M., Hill, C. E., Knox, S., & Petersen, D. A. (1997). Sexual attraction towards clients, use of supervision, and prior training: A qualitative study of predoctoral psychology interns. *Journal of Counseling Psychology, 44*, 413–424. doi:10.1037/0022-0167.44.4.413

Lawless, J. J., Gale, J. E., & Bacigalupe, G. (2001). The discourse of race and culture in family therapy supervision: A conversation analysis. *Contemporary Family Therapy, 23*, 181–197. doi:10.1023/A:1011198219209

Lawrence, E. (2001). The nature of supervision with trainee psychosexual therapists. *Sexual and Relationship Therapy, 16*, 127–143. doi:10.1080/14681990120040069

Lehrman-Waterman, D., & Ladany, N. (2001). Development and validation of the evaluation process within supervision inventory. *Journal of Counseling Psychology, 48*, 168–177. doi:10.1037/0022-0167.48.2.168

Lenz, A. S., Sangganjanavanich, V. F., Balkin, R. S., Oliver, M., & Smith, R. L. (2012). Wellness model of supervision: A comparative analysis. *Counselor Education and Supervision, 51*, 207–221. doi:10.1002/j.1556-6978.2012.00015.x

Littrell, J. M., Lee-Borden, N., & Lorenz, J. (1976). A developmental framework for counseling supervision. *Counselor Education and Supervision, 19*, 129–136. doi:10.1002/j.1556-6978.1976.tb02021.x

Lochner, B. T., & Melchert, T. P. (1997). Relationship of cognitive style and theoretical orientation to psychology interns' preferences for supervision. *Journal of Counseling Psychology, 44*, 256–260. doi:10.1037//0022-0167.44.2.256

Lovell, C. W. (2002). Development and disequilibration: Predicting counselor trainee gain and loss scores on the supervisee levels questionnaire. *Journal of Adult Development, 9*, 235–240. doi:10.1023/A:1016060328253

Luke, M., Ellis, M. V., & Bernard, J. M. (2011). School counselor supervisors' perceptions of the discrimination model of supervision. *Counselor Education and Supervision, 50*, 328–343. doi:10.1002/j.1556-6978.2011.tb01919.x

Luke, M., & Gordon, C. (2011). A discourse analysis of school counseling supervisory e-mail. *Counselor Education and Supervision, 50*, 274–291. doi:10.1002/j.1556-6978.2011.tb00124.x

Lyon, R. C., Heppler, A., Leavitt, L., & Fisher, L. (2008). Supervisory training experiences and overall supervisory development in predoctoral interns. *The Clinical Supervisor, 27*, 268–284. doi:10.1080/07325220802490877

Magnuson, S., & Wilcoxon, A. (1998). Successful clinical supervision of prelicensed counselors. *The Clinical Supervisor, 17*, 33–47. doi:10.1300/J001v17n01_03

Magnuson, S., Wilcoxon, S. A., & Norem, K. (2000). A profile of lousy supervision: Experienced counselors' perspectives. *Counselor Education and Supervision, 39*, 189–202. doi:10.1002/j.1556-6978.2000.tb01231.x

Maidment, J., & Cooper, L. (2002). Acknowledgement of client diversity and oppression in social work student supervision. *Social Work Education, 21*, 399–407. doi:10.1080/02615470220150366

Majcher, J., & Daniluk, J. C. (2009). The process of becoming a supervisor for students in a doctoral supervision training course. *Training and Education in Professional Psychology, 3*, 63–71. doi:10.1037/a0014470

Manzanares, M. G., O'Halloran, T. M., McCartney, T. J., Filer, R. D., Varhely, S. C., & Calhoun, K. (2004). CD-ROM technology for education and support of site supervisors. *Counselor Education and Supervision, 43*, 220–231. doi:10.1002/j.1556-6978.2004.tb01844.x

Martinez, L. J., Davis, K. C., & Dahl, B. (2000). Feminist ethical challenges in supervision. *Women & Therapy, 22*, 35–54. doi:10.1300/J015v22n04_03

Mauzey, E., & Erdman, P. (1997). Trainee perceptions of live supervision phone-ins. *The Clinical Supervisor, 15*(2), 115–128. doi.org/10.1300/J001v15n02_09

McMahon, A., & Patton, W. (2000). Conversations on clinical supervision: Benefits perceived by school counselors. *British Journal of Guidance and Counselling, 28*, 339–351. doi:10.1080/713652301

McMahon, M. (2003). Supervision and career counsellors: A little-explored practice with an uncertain future. *British Journal of Guidance & Counselling*, *31*, 177–187. doi:10.1080/030698803100010235

McMahon, M., & Patton, W. (2001). Clinical supervision: The perceptions and experiences of school counsellors in Australia. *International Journal for the Advancement of Counseling*, *23*, 201–214. doi:10.1023/A:1013170011770

McMahon, M., & Simons, R. (2004). Supervision training for professional counselors: An exploratory study. *Counselor Education and Supervision*, *43*, 301–309. doi:10.1002/j.1556-6978.2004.tb01854.x

McManus, F., Rakovshik, S., Kennerley, H., Fennell, M., & Westbrook, D. (2012). An investigation of the accuracy of therapists' self-assessment of cognitive-behaviour therapy skills. *British Journal of Clinical Psychology*, *51*, 292–306. doi:10.1111/j.2044-8260.2011.02028.x

McMurtery, R. F., Webb, T. T., & Arnold, R. D. (2011). Assessing perceptions and attitudes of intimate behaviors in clinical supervision among licensed professional counselors, licensed social workers, and licensed psychologists. *The Researcher: An Interdisciplinary Journal*, *24*(2), 57–78. Retrieved from http://connection.ebscohost.com/c/articles/67298447/assessing-perceptions-attitudes-intimate-behaviors-clinical-supervision-among-licensed-professional-counselors-licensed-social-workers-licensed-psychologists

McNeill, B. W., & Worthen, V. (1989). The parallel process in psychotherapy supervision. *Professional Psychology: Research and Practice*, *20*, 329–333. doi:10.1037/0735-7028.20.5.329

Mehr, K. E., Ladany, N., & Caskie, G. I. L. (2010). Trainee nondisclosure in supervision: What are they not telling you? *Counselling & Psychotherapy Research*, *10*(2), 103–113.

Messinger, L. (2007). Supervision of lesbian, gay, and bisexual social work students by heterosexual field instructors: A qualitative dyad analysis. *The Clinical Supervisor*, *26*, 195–222. doi:10.1300/J001v26n01.13

Miller, M., Korinek, A. W., & Ivey, D. C. (2006). Integrating spirituality into training: The spiritual issues in supervision scale. *American Journal of Family Therapy*, *34*, 355–372. doi:10.1080/01926180600553811

Miller, M., & Ivey, D. (2006). Spirituality, gender, and supervisory style in supervision. *Contemporary Family Therapy: An International Journal*, *28*, 323–337. doi:10.1007/s10591-006-9012-0

Milne, D. (2010). Can we enhance the training of clinical supervisors? A national pilot study of an evidence-based approach. *Clinical Psychology & Psychotherapy*, *17*, 321–328. doi:10.1002/cpp.657

Milne, D., & Dunkerley, C. (2010). Towards evidence-based clinical supervision: The development and evaluation of four CBT guidelines. *The Cognitive Behaviour Therapist*, *3*, 43–57. doi:10.1017/S1754470X10000048

Milne, D. L., & James, I. A. (2002). The observed impact of training on competence in clinical supervision. *British Journal of Clinical Psychology*, *41*, 55–72.

Milne, D. L., Leck, C., & Choudhri, N. Z. (2009). Collusion in clinical supervision: Literature review and case study in self-reflection. *The Cognitive Behaviour Therapist*, *2*, 106–114. doi:10.1017/S1754470X0900018X

Milne, D. L., Reiser, R. P., & Cliffe, T. (2012). An N = 1 evaluation of enhanced CBT supervision. *Behavioural and Cognitive Psychotherapy*, *41*, 210–220.

Milne, D. L., Sheikh, A. I., Pattison, S., & Wilkinson, A. (2011). Evidence-based training for clinical supervisors: A systematic review of 11 controlled studies. *The Clinical Supervisor*, *30*, 53–71. doi:10.1080/07325223.2011.564955

Milne, D., & Westerman, C. (2001). Evidence-based clinical supervision: Rationale and illustration. *Clinical Psychology & Psychotherapy*, *8*, 444–457. doi:10.1002/cpp.297

Moorhouse, A., & Carr, A. (1999). The correlates of phone-in frequency, duration, and the number of suggestions made in live supervision. *Journal of Family Therapy, 21*, 407–418. doi:10.1111/1467-6427.00128

Mori, Y., Inman, A. G., & Caskie, G. I. L. (2009). Supervising international students: Relationship between acculturation, supervisor multicultural competence, cultural discussions, and supervision satisfaction. *Training and Education in Professional Psychology, 3*, 10–18. doi:10.1037/a0013072

Morrissette, P. J. (1999). Family therapist self-supervision: Toward a preliminary conceptualization. *The Clinical Supervisor, 18*(2), 165–183.

Nelson, K. W., Oliver, M., & Capps, F. (2006). Becoming a supervisor: Doctoral student perceptions of the training experience. *Counselor Education and Supervision, 46*, 17–31. doi:10.1002/j.1556-6978.2006.tb00009.x

Nelson, M. L., Barnes, K. L., Evans, A. L., & Triggiano, P. J. (2008). Working with conflict in clinical supervision: Wise supervisors' perspectives. *Journal of Counseling Psychology, 55*, 172–184. doi:10.1037/0022-0167.55.2.172

Nelson, M. L., & Friedlander, M. L. (2001). A close look at conflictual supervisory relationships: The trainee's perspective. *Journal of Counseling Psychology, 48*, 384–395. doi:10.1037/0022-0167.48.4.384

Nelson, T. S., & Graves, T. (2011). Core competencies in advanced training: What supervisors say about graduate training. *Journal of Marital and Family Therapy, 37*, 429–451. doi:10.1111/j.1752-0606.2010.00216.x

Neswald-McCalip, R., Sather, J., Strati, J., & Dineen, J. (2003). Exploring the process of creative supervision: Initial findings regarding the regenerative model. *Journal of Humanistic Counseling, Education & Development, 42*, 223. doi:10.1002/j.2164-490X.2003.tb00008.x

Neufeldt, S. A., Karno, M. P., & Nelson, M. L. (1996). A qualitative study of experts' conceptualization of supervisee reflectivity. *Journal of Counseling Psychology, 43*, 3–9. doi:10.1037/0022-0167.43.1.3

Newgent, R. A., Davis, H., Jr., & Farley, R. C. (2004). Perceptions of individual, triadic, and group models of supervision: A pilot study. *The Clinical Supervisor, 23*, 65–80. doi:10.1300/J001v23n02_05

Ng, K. M., & Smith, S. D. (2012). Training level, acculturation, role ambiguity, and multicultural discussions in training and supervising international counseling students in the United States. *International Journal for the Advancement of Counselling, 34*, 72–86. doi:10.1007/s10447-011-9130-8

Nilsson, J. E. (2007). International students in supervision: Course self-efficacy, stress, and cultural discussions in supervision. *The Clinical Supervisor, 26*, 35–47. doi:10.1300/J001v26n01_04

Nilsson, J. E., & Dodds, A. K. (2006). A pilot phase in the development of the international student supervision scale. *Journal of Multicultural Counseling & Development, 34*, 50–62. doi:10.1002/j.2161-1912.2006.tb00026.x

Nilsson, J. E., & Duan, C. (2007). Experiences of prejudice, role difficulties, and counseling self efficacy among U.S. racial and ethnic minority supervisees working with white supervisors. *Journal of Multicultural Counseling & Development, 53*, 219–229. doi:10.1002/j.2161-1912.2007.tb00062.x

Norem, K., Magnuson, S., Wilcoxon, S., & Arbel, O. (2006). Supervisees' contributions to stellar supervision outcomes. *Journal of Professional Counseling: Practice, Theory, and Research, 34*(1/2), 33–48. Retrieved from http://search.proquest.com/docview/212436846?accountid=12043

Nye, C. H. (2003). Using developmental processes in supervision: A psychodynamic approach. *The Clinical Supervisor, 21*, 39–53. doi: 10.1300/J001v21n02_03

Nyman, S. J., Nafziger, M. A., & Smith, T. B. (2010). Client outcomes across counselor training level within a multitiered supervision model. *Journal of Counseling & Development*, *88*, 204–209. doi:10.1002/j.1556-6678.2010.tb00010.x

O'Donoghue, K. (2012). Windows on the supervisee experience: An exploration of supervisees' supervision histories. *Australian Social Work*, *65*, 214–231. doi:http://dx.doi.org/10.1080/0312407X.2012.667816

O'Donovan, A., Slattery, L., Kavanagh, D., & Dooley, R. (2008). Opinions of Australian Psychological Society college chairs about process and content in supervision training: Preliminary investigation in Queensland. *Australian Psychologist*, *43*, 114–120. doi:10.1080/00050060801978654

Olk, M. E., & Friedlander, M. L. (1992). Trainees' experiences of role conflict and role ambiguity in supervisory relationships. *Journal of Counseling Psychology*, *39*, 389–397. doi:10.1037/0022-0167.39.3.389

Owen-Pugh, V., & Symons, C. (2012). Roth and Pilling's competence framework for clinical supervision: How generalisable is it? *Counselling and Psychotherapy Research: Linking Research with Practice*, *13*, 126–135. doi:10.1080/14733145.2012.707218

Palmer-Olsen, L., Gold, L. L., & Woolley, S. R. (2011). Supervising emotionally focused therapists: A systematic research-based model. *Journal of Marital & Family Therapy*, *37*, 411–426. doi:10.1111/j.1752-0606.2011.00253.x

Peace, S. D., & Sprinthall, N. A. (1998). Training school counselors to supervise beginning counselors: Theory, research, and practice. *Professional School Counseling*, *1*(5), 2–8. Retrieved from http://web.ebscohost.com.ezproxy.lib.lehigh.edu/ehost/detail?sid=86477414-5daf-4f59a2bf51622c9d02f7%40sessionmgr110&vid=2&hid=127&bdata=JnNpdGU9ZWhvc3QtbGl2ZQ%3d%3d#db=ehh&AN=747258

Pettifer, A., & Clouder, L. (2008). Clinical supervision: A means of promoting reciprocity between practitioners and academics. *Learning in Health and Social Care*, *7*, 168–177. doi:10.1111/j.1473-6861.2008.00186.x

Protivnak, J. J., & Davis, T. E. (2008). The impact of the supervision relationship on the behaviors of school counseling interns. *Journal of School Counseling*, *6*(19), 1–22. Retrieved from http://www.eric.ed.gov/contentdelivery/servlet/ERICServlet?accno=EJ894790

Prouty, A. (2001). Experiencing feminist family therapy supervision. *Journal of Feminist Family Therapy*, *12*, 171–203. doi:10.1300/J086v12n04_01

Prouty, A. M., Thomas, V., Johnson, S., & Long, J. K. (2001). Methods of feminist family therapy supervision. *Journal of Marital and Family Therapy*, *27*, 85–97. doi:10.1111/j.1752-0606.2001.tb01141.x

Raichelson, S. H., Herron, W. G., Primavera, L. H., & Ramirez, S. M. (1997). Incidence and effects of parallel process in psychotherapy supervision. *The Clinical Supervisor*, *15*, 37–48. doi:10.1300/J001v15n02_03

Rapisarda, C. A., & Britton, P. J. (2007). Sanctioned supervision: Voices from experts. *Journal of Mental Health Counseling*, *29*, 81–92. Retrieved from http://connection.ebscohost.com/c/articles/23884033/sanctioned-supervision-voices-from-experts

Rapisarda, C. A., Desmond, K. J., & Nelson, J. R. (2011). Student reflections on the journey to being a supervisor. *The Clinical Supervisor*, *30*, 109–123. doi:10.1080/07325223.2011.564958

Rarick, S. L., & Ladany, N. (2012). The relationship of supervisor and trainee gender match and gender attitude match to supervisory style and the supervisory working alliance. *Counselling and Psychotherapy Research*, *13*, 138–144. doi:10.1080/14733145.2012.732592

Ratliff, D. A., Wampler, K. S., & Morris, G. H. (2000). Lack of consensus in supervision. *Journal of Marital and Family Therapy*, *26*, 373–384. doi:10.1111/j.17520606.2000.tb00306.x

Reese, R. J., Usher, E. L., Bowman, D. C., Nosworthy, L. A., Halstead, J. L., Rowlands, S. R., &Chisholm, R. (2009). Using client feedback in psychotherapy training: An analysis of its influence on supervision and counselor self-efficacy. *Training and Education in Professional Psychology*, *3*, 157–168. doi:10.1037/a0015673

Reichelt, S., & Skjerve, J. (2000). Supervision of inexperienced therapists: A qualitative analysis. *The Clinical Supervisor*, *19*, 25–43. doi:10.1300/J001v19n02_02

Reid, H. L. (2007). The shaping of discourse positions in the development of support and supervision for personal advisers in England. *British Journal of Guidance & Counselling*, *35*, 59–77. doi:10.1080/03069880601106807

Ronnestad, M. H., & Skovholt, T. M. (2003). The journey of the counsellor and therapist: Research findings and perspectives on professional development. *Journal of Career Development*, *30*, 5–44. doi: 10.1023/A:1025173508081

Roth, A.D., & Pilling, S. (2009). A competence framework for the supervision of psychological therapies. Retrieved from www.ucl.ac.uk/clinical-psychology/CORE/supervision_framework.htm

Rushton, A., & Nathan, J. (1996). The supervision of child protection work. *British Journal of Social Work*, *26*, 357–374. Retrieved from http://bjsw.oxfordjournals.org/content/26/3/357.short#cited-by

Saltzburg, S., Greene, G. J., & Drew, H. (2010). Using live supervision in field education: Preparing social work students for clinical practice. *Families in Society*, *91*, 293–299. doi:10.1606/1044 3894.4008

Sangganjanavanich, V., & Black, L. L. (2009). Clinical supervision for international counselors-in-training: Implications for supervisors. *Journal of Professional Counseling: Practice, Theory, and Research*, *37*(2), 52–65. Retrieved from http://connection.ebscohost.com/c/articles/48188420/clinical-supervision-international-counselors-in-training-implications-supervisors

Sangganjanavanich, V. F., & Black, L. L. (2011). The initial development of the multicultural supervision scale. *Journal of Professional Counseling: Practice, Theory, and Research*, *38*(2), 18–36. Retrieved from http://www.questia.com/library/p142246/journal-of-professional-counseling-practice-theory

Satterly, B. A., & Dyson, D. (2008). Sexual minority supervision. *The Clinical Supervisor*, *27*, 17–38. doi:10.1080/07325220802221462

Schoenwald, S. K., Sheidow, A. J., & Chapman, J. E. (2009). Clinical supervision in treatment transport: Effects on adherence and outcomes. *Journal of Consulting and Clinical Psychology*, *77*, 410–421. doi:10.1037/a0013788

Scott, K. J., Ingram, K. M., Vitanza, S. A., & Smith, N. G. (2000). Training in supervision: A survey of current practices. *The Counseling Psychologist*, *28*, 403–422. doi:10.1177/0011000000283007

Searles, H. F. (1955). The informational value of the supervisor's emotional experience. *Psychiatry*, *18*, 135–146.

Sells, J. N., Goodyear, R. K., Lichtenberg, J. W., & Polkinghorne, D. E. (1997). Relationship of supervisor and trainee gender to in-session verbal behavior and ratings of trainee skills. *Journal of Counseling Psychology*, *44*, 406–412. doi:10.1037//0022-0167.44.4.406

Sherr, L., Bergenstrom, A., & McCann, E. (1997). Running a counseling project in primary schools: The role of training and supervision. *Counselling Psychology Quarterly*, *10*, 261–270. doi:10.1080/09515079708254178

Slavin-Mulford, J. M., Hilsenroth, M. J., Blagys, M. D., & Blais, M. A. (2011). Experiences related to expert supervisors' views of ideal therapeutic practice. *Counselling and Psychotherapy Research*, *11*, 97–104. doi:10.1080/14733145.2010.485691

Sommer, C. A., & Cox, J. A. (2005). Elements of supervision in sexual violence counselors' narratives: A qualitative analysis. *Counselor Education and Supervision*, *45*, 119–134. doi:10.1002/j.1556-6978.2005.tb00135.x

Sommer, C. A., Ward, J. E., & Scofield, T. (2010). Metaphoric stories in supervision of internship: A qualitative atudy. *Journal of Counseling & Development*, *88*, 500–507. doi:10.1002/j.1556-6678.2010.tb00052.x

Szymanski, D. M. (2005). Feminist identity and theories as correlates of feminist supervision practices. *The Counseling Psychologist*, *33*, 729–747. doi:10.1177/0011000005278408

Talen, M. R., & Schindler, N. J. (1994). Goal-directed supervision plans: A model for trainee supervision and evaluation. *The Clinical Supervisor*, *11*, 77–88. doi:10.1300/J001v11n02_07

Taylor, B. A., Hernández, P., Deri, A., Rankin, I. R., & Siegel, A. (2006). Integrating diversity dimensions in supervision: Perspectives of ethnic minority AAMFT approved supervisors. *The Clinical Supervisor*, *25*, 3–21. doi:10.1300/J001v25n01_02

Toporek, R. L., Ortega-Villalobos, L., & Pope-Davis, D. B. (2004). Critical incidents in multicultural supervision: Exploring supervisees' and supervisors' experiences. *Journal of Multicultural Counseling and Development*, *32*, 66–83. doi:10.1002/j.2161 1912.2004.tb00362.x

Townend, M., Iannetta, L., & Freeston, M. H. (2002). Clinical supervision in practice: A survey of UK Cognitive Behavioural Psychotherapists accredited by the BABCP. *Behavioural and Cognitive Psychotherapy*, *30*, 485–500. doi:10.1017/S1352465802004095

Tracey, T. J. G., Bludworth, J., & Glidden-Tracey, C. E. (2012). Are there parallel processes in psychotherapy supervision? An empirical examination. *Psychotherapy*, *49*, 330–343. doi:10.1037/a0026246

Trepal, H. C., Bailie, J., & Leeth, C. (2010). Critical incidents in practicum supervision: Supervisees' perspectives. *Journal of Professional Counseling: Practice, Theory, and Research*, *38*, 28–38. Retrieved from http://web.ebscohost.com/abstract?direct=true&profile=ehost&scope=site&authtype=crawler&jrnl=15566382&AN=53279808&h=xFb4sBxPOjwt3Yc0aHcShKRwQ2kd4PRVPZ5SRMBgcI9zudO5UY265neISZca98KVcC2ELQiE49KxNb865Vc4NQ%3d%3d&crl=c

Tromski-Klingshirn, D. M., & Davis, T. E. (2007). Supervisees' perceptions of their clinical supervision: A study of the dual role of clinical and administrative supervisor. *Counselor Education and Supervision*, *46*, 294–304. doi:10.1002/j.1556-6978.2007.tb00033.x

Urdang, E. (1999). Becoming a field instructor: A key experience in professional development. *The Clinical Supervisor*, *18*, 85–103. doi:10.1300/J001v18n01_06

Vallance, K. (2004). Exploring counsellor perceptions of the impact of counselling supervision on clients. *British Journal of Guidance & Counselling*, *32*, 559–574. doi:10.1080/03069880412331303330

Vallance, K. (2005). Exploring counsellor perceptions of the impact of counselling supervision on clients. *Counselling and Psychotherapy Research*, *5*, 107–110. doi:10.1080/17441690500211106

VanderGast, T. S., Culbreth, J. R., & Flowers, C. (2010). An exploration of experiences and preferences in clinical supervision with play therapists. *International Journal of Play Therapy*, *19*, 174–185. doi:10.1037/a0018882

Verdinelli, S., & Biever, J. L. (2009). Experiences of Spanish/English bilingual supervisees. *Psychotherapy: Theory, Research, Practice, Training*, *46*, 158–170. doi:10.1037/a0016024

Vespia, K. M., Heckman-Stone, C., & Delworth, U. (2002). Describing and facilitating effective supervision behavior in counseling trainees. *Psychotherapy: Theory, Research, Practice, Training*, *39*, 56–65. doi:10.1037/0033-3204.39.1.56

Walker, J. A., Ladany, N., & Pate-Carolan, L. M. (2007). Gender-related events in psychotherapy supervision: Female trainee perspectives. *Counselling and Psychotherapy Research*, *7*, 12–18. doi:10.1080/14733140601140881

Wallace, M. J. D., Wilcoxon, S. A., & Satcher, J. (2010). Productive and nonproductive counselor supervision: Best and worst experiences of supervisees. *Alabama Counseling Association Journal*, *35*(2), 4–13. Retrieved from http://www.alabamacounseling.org

Wark, L. (1995a). Live supervision in family therapy: Qualitative interviews of supervision events as perceived by supervisors and supervisees. *The American Journal of Family Therapy*, *23*, 25–37. doi:10.1080/01926189508251333

Wark, L. (1995b). Defining the territory of live supervision in family therapy training. *The Clinical Supervisor*, *13*, 145–162. doi:10.1300/J001v13n01_11

Watkins, C. E. (1993). Development of the psychotherapy supervisor: Concepts, assumptions, and hypotheses of the supervisor complexity model. *American Journal of Psychotherapy*, *47*(1), 58–74.

Watkins, C. E., Jr. (Ed.). (1997). *Handbook of psychotherapy supervision*. New York, NY: Wiley.

Watkins, C. E., Jr. (2010). Psychoanalytic developmental psychology and the supervision of psychotherapy supervisor trainees. *Psychodynamic Practice*, *16*, 393–407. doi:10.1080/14753634.2010.510345

Watkins, C. E., Jr. (2011). Psychotherapy supervision since 1909: Some friendly observations about its first century. *Journal of Contemporary Psychotherapy*, *41*, 57–67. doi:10.1007/s10879-010-9152-2

Watkins, E. C. (2012). Development of the psychotherapy supervisor: Review of and reflections on 30 years of theory and research. *American Journal of Psychotherapy*, *66*, 45–83.

Watkins, C. E., & Milne, D. L. (Eds.). (2014). *The Wiley international handbook of clinical supervision*. Oxford, UK: John Wiley & Sons, Ltd.

Webb, A., & Wheeler, S. (1998). How honest do counsellors dare to be in the supervisory relationship? An exploratory study. *British Journal of Guidance & Counselling*, *26*, 509–524. doi:10.1080/03069889808253860

West, A. (2010). Supervising counselors and psychotherapists who work with trauma: A Delphi study. *British Journal of Guidance & Counselling*, *38*, 409–430. doi:10.1080/03069885.2010.503696

Wester, S. R., Vogel, D. L., & Archer, J., Jr. (2004). Male restricted emotionality and counseling supervision. *Journal of Counseling & Development*, *82*, 91–98. doi:10.1002/j.1556-6678.2004.tb00289.x

Wheeler, S., & King, D. (2000). Do counseling supervisors want or need to have their supervision supervised? An exploratory study. *British Journal of Guidance & Counselling*, *28*, 279–290.

White, M. B., & Russell, C. S. (1997). Examining the multifaceted notion of isomorphism in marriage and family therapy supervision: A quest for conceptual clarity. *Journal of Marital and Family Therapy*, *23*, 315–333. doi:10.1111/j.1752-0606.1997.tb01040.x

Wilcoxon, S. A., Norem, K., & Magnuson, S. (2005). Supervisees' contributions to lousy supervision outcomes. *Journal of Professional Counseling: Practice, Theory, and Research*, *33*(2), 31. Retrieved from http://web.ebscohost.com/abstract?direct=true&profile=ehost&scope=site&authtype=crawler&jrnl=15566382&AN=22969652&h=McAk%2b%2f7z7ySTjH9cVP9IUlJe95TASBM8N0jVVqPmA1eZqJI44PRse8qwMt71TE4B0rVfc7r0I9L4%2bNjMTK5LsQ%3d%3d&crl=c

Williams, E. N., Judge, A. B., Hill, C. E., & Hoffman, M. A. (1997). Experiences of novice therapists in prepracticum; Trainees', clients', and supervisors' perceptions of therapists' personal reactions and management strategies. *Journal of Counseling Psychology*, *44*, 390–399. doi:10.1037/0022-0167.44.4.390

Worthen, V., & McNeill, B. W. (1996). A phenomenological investigation of "good" supervision events. *Journal of Counseling Psychology*, *43*, 25–34. doi:10.1037/0022-0167.43.1.25

Worthington, R. L., Tan, J., & Poulin, K. (2002). Ethically questionable behaviors among supervisees: An exploratory investigation. *Ethics & Behavior, 12*, 323–351. doi:10.1207/S15327019EB1204_02

Wulf, J., & Nelson, M. L. (2001). Experienced psychologists' recollections of internship supervision and its contributions to their development. *The Clinical Supervisor, 19*, 123–145. doi:10.1300/J001v19n02_07

Ybrandt, H., & Armelius, K. (2009). Changes in self-image in psychotherapy supervisor training program. *The Clinical Supervisor, 28*, 113–123. doi:10.1080/07325220903343819

Young, J. S., & Borders, D. L. (1998). The impact of metaphor on clinical hypothesis formation and perceived supervisor characteristics. *Counselor Education and Supervision, 37*, 238–256. doi:10.1002/j.1556-6978.1998.tb00548.x

Young, J. S., & Borders, L. D. (1999). The intentional use of metaphor in counseling supervision. *The Clinical Supervisor, 18*, 137–149. doi:10.1300/J001v18n01_09

Yourman, D. B. (2003). Trainee disclosure in psychotherapy supervision: The impact of shame. *Journal of Clinical Psychology, 59*, 601–609. doi:10.1002/jclp.10162

Yourman, D. B., & Farber, B. A. (1996). Nondisclosure and distortion in psychotherapy supervision. *Psychotherapy, 33*, 567–575. doi:10.1037/0033-3204.33.4.567

Zarbrock, G., Drews, M., Bodansky, A., & Dahme, B. (2009). The evaluation of supervision: Construction of brief questionnaires for the supervisor and the supervisee. *Psychotherapy Research, 19*, 194–204. doi:10.1080/10503300802688478

5

Understanding How Supervision Works and What It Can Achieve

Tomaž Vec, Tanja Rupnik Vec, and Sonja Žorga

Introduction

The process of supervision presents one of the possible processes of life-long learning and development for adults. In this chapter, we introduce a few characteristics of the educational (or "formative") function of supervision as a specific method of professional reflection and counseling. The introduction is based on various concepts, seen as basics that explain learning and competence enhancement (i.e., generally valid, no matter what modalities, environments, or approaches they come from). These basics enable the integration of professional and personal development, as well as accepting and delimiting responsibilities for one's work. The aim of our contribution to this handbook is to demonstrate those basic properties and functions of the supervision process that reflect, for the most part, how this learning process works.

Supervision: A Field of Many Forms and Expressions

The area of supervision encompasses numerous approaches, models, and views, so that we cannot talk about supervision as something uniform. We agree with Carroll (2006, p. 8), who writes that supervision is a "combination of various elements – goals, functions, tasks, roles, strategies, focuses, process elements, personalities, beginnings, middles, endings, . . ." This variety is the consequence of a variety of meanings, hidden in the term supervision (the Latin expression means control, surveillance, as well as to see, to look over). Some so-called system-oriented authors (e.g., Brandau, 1991; Keeney, 1991) state, in their writing related to supervision, that it would have been better (due to the "power of language") to rename supervision into "super-audition" (super listening). That viewpoint is explained by the fact

The Wiley International Handbook of Clinical Supervision, First Edition. Edited by C. Edward Watkins, Jr. and Derek L. Milne.

that supervision, in its methods, is more related to the recount-listening than it is to presentation-seeing. The diversity of forms and functions of supervision practices has, of course, also evolved as a consequence of considering various needs of different environments, wherein it has been transferred by varied experts with different directions, preferences, knowledge, and so on.

We can conclude that, for supervision in general, the same holds true that has been said for clinical supervision by Ellis, Ladany, Krengal, and Schult (1996) and Milne, Aylott, Fitzpatrick, and Ellis (2008), which is, that it is poorly conceptualized with implicit theories, unrelated to empirical research, and inconsistent in the use of its own concepts.

In spite of these diverse models and definitions, we can nevertheless notice a fairly consensual acceptance of basic functions of (clinical) supervision, as defined by Kadushin (1985), for example, Bradley, Ladany, Hendricks, Whiting, and Rhode, (2011); Carroll (2006); Hawkins and Shohet (2002, 2006); Milne (2007); and Proctor and Inskipp (1988):

- Educative or formative: skills development, including the understanding and competence of the supervisee; carried out through explanations and study of the supervisee and their work with clients, thus directed toward lifelong professional development and increasing professional abilities and knowledge; some consider it one of the basic functions of supervision (e.g., Bradley et al., 2011; Falender et al., 2004).
- Supportive or restorative (renewing): oriented toward the emotional aspect of work with clients, which enables the supervisees to value their own cognitive and emotional response to professional issues. Through this, professional distance is established, set relationships analyzed, and a critical–analytical evaluation of their own action carried out.
- Managerial or normative (control, administrative): ensures the control over quality of work, in the sense of dealing away with "blind spots" – something that happens not only due to inadequate amounts of knowledge and experience, but also due to entirely human weaknesses, weak, or vulnerable areas, individual prejudice, and so on. In this function, the essence is control, direction, and evaluation of professional work, definition of roles, clarified responsibility, carrying out of agreements, and so on. It is also directed to the evaluation of efficiency of work carried out, as well as recognition and reduction of stress factors at work.

As described by Kadushin (1985), there is overlap among these functions, although every function differs from the others depending on the context within which the supervision is carried out, relative to the problems that are emphasized, and the supervision goals. The goal of supervision and its functions are co-dependent and represent a combination of the supervisor and the supervisee, who, with the help of a particular approach, work together on a particular sort of problems (O'Connor, 2008). Thus, it can be assumed that all three functions are interwoven and interdependent.

In this chapter, several concepts shall be presented to explain the processes of learning and development of professional competence in formative supervision. A special emphasis will be given to the explanation of the connection between personal and professional development through supervision and their integration into a so-called professional self. We intend to focus on supervision's educative functions (supervision is primarily an educational process, as pointed out by Carroll, 2006), which is also demonstrated by the developmental definition of supervision:

> Supervision is understood as a specific learning, developmental and supportive method of professional reflection and counselling, enabling professional workers (school counselors, teachers, child care workers, psychologists, social workers etc.), to acquire new professional and personal insights through their own experiences. It helps them to integrate practical experiences with theoretical knowledge and to reach their own solutions to the problems they meet at work, to face stress efficiently and to build up their professional identity. By this, supervision supports professional as well as personal learning and development of professional workers. (Žorga, 1995, 2002, p. 265)

The Necessity of Lifelong Learning and Development

Learning represents a central task for personal development and a successful professional career within our learning society, a task that is carried out throughout our entire life (Falender et al., 2004; Kolb, 1984; Kolb, Boyatzis, & Mainemelis, 1999). The environment that we work in does, in fact, change more rapidly than ever before. To use these changes to our advantage, we must become very skilled at learning, as this is the only way to respond suitably and quickly to these changes. Hay (1995) believes that future work organizations will need to become "learning communities" where people will be able to make use of all of their competencies, and where empowerment will become an indispensable strategy of every modern organization. Kolb (1984) believes that these organizations can draw on the necessary conceptual foundations and starting points, as well as the practical educational tools from experiential learning theory.

Everyday life situations offer many learning opportunities, mostly based on work and other life experiences, not only on formal education. Mezirow defines learning as the process of making a new or revised interpretation of the meaning of an experience, which guides subsequent understanding, assessment, and action (see Merriam & Clark, 1992). Like Piaget (1961), Mezirow (1990, see Merriam & Clark, 1992) also claims that several experiences from everyday life can easily be assimilated into our mental structure because they are congruent with earlier experiences. However, some life experiences are incongruent with past ones and cannot be properly interpreted with the existing mental structure. Examples of such experiences could be divorce, loss of job, a new position, the beginning of a new project, and many other unexpected situations one so frequently meets in work. Such experiences challenge our existing mental structure toward restructuring and lead to new recognitions (Piaget, 1961), or to perspective transformation (Mezirow, 1990, see Merriam & Clark, 1992). It is essential that professional workers are able to process their work experiences, learn from them, and reintegrate what has been learned.

However, experience alone does not suffice (Watkins, 1995, 2012; Worthington, 1987) and so supervision represents a vital process. But supervisors must also learn from experience, through education, seminars, constant involvement in their own supervision process, and so on. In particular, as Watkins (1995) said, the key characteristic distinguishing those who learn and grow is self-criticism. Self-criticism is to be understood as a constructive and evaluative stance of the individual, who regularly takes time to reflect on what he or she is doing and permanently educates himself or herself professionally. Self-criticism is not only a general reflective process that identify weaknesses, it also include other elements of learning: defining the criteria for self-evaluation, strengths awareness, goal-setting, planning strategies for learning, identification of resources in the environment, and so on. So we can consider it as contributing to a continuous process of learning. A supervisor should be committed to self-criticism, by actively and aggressively working on improving his or her professional skills and understanding. We believe that only experiences that are combined with such self-criticism can bring about development.

Learning from Experience in Supervision

In supervision, the learning process is of key importance, one of the main goals being to attract employees into the learning process. Within this they are helped to fuse what they do, think, and feel into a sensible whole. This involves mainly learning based on experience, which in supervision suits Kolb's (1984) model of learning as a cyclical process, where four activities are interwoven (Žorga, 2002):

1. Concrete experience: the supervisee's account of their actual work experience, where the event is carefully described (the supervision material).
2. Reflection on the experience: becoming aware, analyzing, and reflecting on the factors that influenced the experience and the supervisee's role in it.
3. Abstract conceptualization (or searching for the meaning of the experience): searching for and comparing possible connections between the reflections and other past experiences (one's own or the experiences of colleagues), linking this with theoretical knowledge, attitudes, and so on.
4. Practical experimentation (or doing things in a different manner): planning new behavioral patterns and strategies, and testing them out in practice.

The supervisor guides the supervisee in their learning process through the aforementioned four phases, including how the learning situations are shaped to encourage transition from one phase to the other. Here is an illustration from supervisee feedback (the final evaluation[1]): "The supervisor guided, connected and taught our group. In the supervision, he directed our conversations and discussions professionally. The red line of every supervision session followed, as well as keeping a positive atmosphere in our group. His knowledge was persistently and patiently transferred to us, and we were encouraged to think and participate intensively again and again. In this, none of his views were forced on us, but were given as free, while we were introduced into our own thought processes. He made sure that the meetings proceeded without complications. Every meeting was made pleasant and interesting. I

[1] From the written reflections of one of the supervisees.

accepted his warnings positively, as they helped me to learn some things and let go of some negative habits more easily."

Experiential learning is one of the key concepts of the developmental–educational model of supervision, as supervision may be understood as a dialectic learning process of the integration of working experience and theoretic concepts, the assimilation of these experiences into existing mental schemes and the adaptation of existing schemes, and thus a new perception of the situation. Kolb (1984; Kolb, Boyatzis, & Mainemelis, 1999), based his work on the concepts of Dewey, Lewin, and Piaget, which are treated as the most important predecessors of the experiential learning theory. Dewey (1955) and Lewin (1951) in their works emphasized learning as a dialectic process of integration of experience and concepts, while Piaget (1970, see Kolb, 1984) described the cognitive process as a dialectic process of assimilation of experiences. The most important dimensions of development of thinking in adulthood are, according to Piaget (1970; see Kolb, 1984), the dimensions of experience–learning and reflection–action. These dimensions also represent the basis of development in science. The learning process, being the foundation of development, thus takes place in constant interaction between an individual and the environment.

The process of learning and development in the supervision of professionals can be explained with the aid of Piaget's concepts of mental assimilation and mental accommodation. An individual in their everyday or professional experience tends toward the assimilation of their perceptions and emotions into the existing mental concepts or toward the understanding of concepts through the prism of existing schemas and concepts. But these very schemas and concepts can also prevent their perception of reality from different points of view. Through the process of critical reflection in supervision, their thoughts, perceptions, and emotions are questioned, doubted, confronted, and expanded with new alternatives. This leads to a process of reprogramming or "accommodation" of mental concepts or schemas. The constant tension between the processes of assimilation of experience into existing mental schemas and accommodation of these schemas under the influence of challenging or incongruent experience can trigger the resolution of this tension, resulting in mental adaptation or learning. This tension leads to a state of (temporary) destabilization ("dis-equilibration"; Piaget, 1961); however, the adaptation is always at a higher level. Levels follow one another in a way where the higher learning always includes the elements of the lower ones. In a general sense, an individual passes from the level of "concrete operations" to the level of "formal–logical" thinking. In the process of supervision, this passage is from the superficial understanding of individual events and experience, toward an ever more complex and wholesome insight into the situation and one's own role within it. If we are thus faced with behavior or emotional reactions that we cannot explain with existing knowledge and experience (be it our own behavior or knowledge, or that of a client, colleague, superior), we feel confusion, incompetence, and powerlessness. In Piaget's terminology, we experience a loss of balance (dis-equilibration). The conflict or loss of balance is experienced as incompatible with existing mental schemas. Reflecting on this behavior or emotional reaction enables adaptation of some elements of the experience into existing thinking schemas (assimilation). Sometimes this process triggers a transformation of existing views, implicit theories, and behavioral patterns (accommodation). The final result of both processes is the formulation of new knowledge, new skills, new experience, and new behavioral patterns and, as a consequence, preparedness for actions at a qualitatively different, higher level. The process of balancing existing views, knowledge, and behavioral patterns with a new experience (including new knowledge) is thus the process of equilibration.

Professionals constantly interact with their environment, and new experiences constantly trigger states of imbalance, encouraging the process of equilibration and thus professional development. The higher the levels of understanding of work situations of a professional, the more complex the thinking patterns and the more integrated the thought structures. The more intense the interaction of an individual with their environment, the more frequent and powerful are the impulses for the development of their thinking structures.

Kolb (1984) relates to Piaget's dimensions of development (concrete–abstract, active–reflecting) and points out that "(. . .) the poles of these dimensions are equipotent modes of knowing that through dialectic transformations result in learning. This learning proceeds along a third, developmental dimension that represents not the dominance of one learning mode over another but the integration of the four adaptive modes"(p. 40). Before Piaget, Dewey had already pointed out that the experiential learning cycle does not proceed in a circle, but in fact in a spiral, where every experience presents new potential for progress (Dewey, 1955). Thus, learning is a process that enables development.

Learning is also a social process, where the development of an individual is co-defined by the cultural system of social knowledge, as in supervision. The social dimension of learning and development has been conceptualized by Vygotsky (1977). According to this author, the development potentials of an individual are realized in the process of imitation and communication with others, through the interaction of an individual with the physical and social environment. These processes are practiced until they are not internalized as an independent developmental achievement. Vygotsky points out that development is optimal when carried out in the "zone of proximal development," which is defined as the difference between the individual's current and potential development. This development is evident in problems that an individual can solve through cooperation with a more experienced partner (the social other). In supervision, an individual similarly learns with the help of a more experienced colleague.

The way in which learning gives direction to development is described by Kolb (1984) with reference to four modalities of learning: affective, perceptive, symbolic, and behavioral. All are interwoven in the learning process and all transform in the direction of growing complexity. For example, affective complexity during concrete experience results in sentiments of a higher order (e.g., at the beginning when one enters the working process she or he experiences mainly black and white thinking regarding working relationships . Soon, she or he develops more complex relationships and becomes able to interact with a whole range of complex emotions, which are sometimes even contradictory, such as admiration, fear, embarrassment, jealousy, attraction); perceptive complexity in the phase of reflection results in more complex observations; symbolic complexity in the phase of abstract conceptualization results in more differentiated concepts; and behavioral complexity in the phase of active experimenting results in activities of a higher order, such as greater expertise. We next consider how supervision can build on these learning processes, drawing on more recent (post-Kolbian) thinking.

Learning in Supervision: Concepts from Cognitive Psychology

In addition to Kolb's (1984) summary, the process whereby individuals learn within supervision can also be understood through some cognitive psychology, concepts, and models. These include Argyris' model of double-loop learning (Argyris, 1976, 1995, 2002) and Senge's concept of the ladder of inference (Senge, 2001). We next outline this thinking, noting ways that supervisors can incorporate it within their practice. Argyris (1991) introduced the single-loop learning concept versus the double-loop learning concept. While the first type of learning is perceived very narrowly and is typical of experts and specialists (who focus on identification and correction of errors in the external environment when solving problems), double-loop learning (reflective learning) presents itself as a consequence of critical reflection of one's own actions, including the identification of potentially disturbing patterns or ways in which an individual contributes to the maintenance of the problems of the organization (or smaller systems). Double-loop learning also entails changing one's own thinking, experiencing, and acting. Learning within supervision fits with double-loop learning, as it is self- reflective, directed toward the exploration of the supervisee's planning (in relation to the client), the identification of potentially dysfunctional patterns of behavior, and planned self-change.

Argyris' concepts can help us to understand the events within the supervision process. In a discussion on the fundamental determinants of human behavior, Argyris (1976, 1995, 2002) defines a series of predispositions that control the actions of an individual, termed *theories of action*. These are used when deciding on the strategies to employ to achieve a goal. Theories of action are, in turn, controlled by a series of values, conditioning the use of particular strategies. The author defines two kinds of theories of action: *espoused theories* and *theories-in-use*. The most important finding of Argyris' research is that espoused theories differ significantly from the theories-in-use, but without individuals being aware of the fact. Another important finding is that the espoused theories are very different from one another, while the theories-in-use do not demonstrate a high variability.

The most common theory-in-use was named *Model I* by Argyris. It is typical in individuals of all races, both genders, all ages, education levels, and so on, and is very widespread. The Model I theory-in-use consists of four leading variables: (a) control events in one direction, (b) attempt to win, (c) suppress negative emotions, and (d) function rationally. Individuals with this theory-in-use chooses strategies that enable them to satisfy these values (i.e., to maintain their position, conclusions, and judgment). This prevents them from verifying their observations and conclusions, or from freely discussing them with others. The result of this kind of defensive behavior is a failure to understand, attempts to prove oneself, and shutting oneself away from others, so as to retain control.

Developmentally, the less common but more desired option is the *Model II theory-in-use*. Basic values of an individual with a Model II theory-in-use are (a) to exchange all valid information; (b) to decide freely, based on ample information on all points of view on the problem, to allow others to decide; and (c) to carefully follow and manage implementations. The most common illustrations are research and evaluation. An individual with this theory-in-use is aligned with learning and self-change.

Within supervision, there is a shift in an individual's thought, experience, and actions from Model I to Model II, meaning professional and personal development. It also means a move toward a more open and contemplative function within the world, and more tolerance toward initially foreign ideas, which in a process of deep thought may later be internalized. It is therefore important for a supervisor to work openly from the position of Model II. Thus, supervisees can be presented with the model, as the supervisor reflects the values and strategies that enable a more free and more understanding operation within the world: ideas are verified before they are implemented, constantly upgraded, and with that the needs and expectations of others are taken into consideration.

Close to Argyris' concept of theories-in-action is the concept of mental models, introduced by Senge (1993, 2001) as basic determinants of feeling and action. Senge (2001) defines the concept in the following way: "images, predispositions and stories that we carry within about ourselves, others, institutions and every aspect of the world. These images affect our knowledge and points of view. Usually, they are hidden and remain outside consciousness, thus they are often unverified and unexplored. Usually, they are 'invisible' until we direct attention to them" (p. 67).

Many beliefs are formed on the basis of conclusions that people make from their observation and in combination with previous experience. They are often hidden, subconscious, and thus unverified and unexplored. Schein (2004) calls them *basic predispositions* as they "are treated by members of the group as findings that cannot be negotiated . . . someone without these predispositions is perceived as a 'foreigner', as 'crazy' and automatically rejected" (p. 25). Brookfield (1995), too, emphasizes the implicit nature of predispositions and defines them "taken-for-granted beliefs about the world and our place in it which seem self-evident, so they do not need phrasing" (p. 2). The conscious acknowledgment of predispositions is one of the largest intellectual challenges for the individual, as it is accompanied by fearing the discovery that the key guidelines of thought and behavior up until then are senseless and unfounded. Supervision is a safe space within which an individual can acknowledge these beliefs, verify their suitability, and change them as required. This is because personal assumptions and experience are confronted with the assumptions and experience of colleagues, their importance is questioned, they are doubted, and they can change (Piaget's would say that under these conditions an individual "mentally adapts").

The process of belief-forming is represented by the *mental ladder of inference* (Schwarz, 2005; Senge, 2001). This recognizes that individuals perceive the environment selectively, only acknowledging and remembering that which supports their existing mental models or convictions. Based on this self-serving bias, individuals form unequivocal beliefs that predispose them to misguided action and further processes of misperception. Every level on the ladder of inference presents a higher level of abstraction, a further departure from the facts, more assigning of meanings, and thus often a greater distortion of reality. The process evolves quickly, but at the same time it seems that every step is a logical consequence of the previous one, and thus an individual is often unaware of the distorted reality. The supervisor can direct the supervisee toward more accurate beliefs by distinguishing facts from interpretations; by moving toward the exploration of different interpretations; and by encouraging their evaluation. This process can help supervisees toward acknowledging that their perception and judgment is significantly influenced by their expectations, prejudices, beliefs, and assumptions, which should be not be treated as indisputable. We are convinced that good supervision contributes to the correction of these biases and misperceptions, creating a deeper insight into clients and into professional situations and processes. This cognitive restructuring (mental adaptation) is accompanied by emotional relief, as well as a clearer understanding of the general laws of thinking, experiencing, and acting. In Kolb's diction, this would be called a formation of new concepts. As authors studying cognition and learning in educational context warn (Van Gelder, 2004), learning and practice are more efficient if they are accompanied by a certain level of theoretical insight.

Supervision and Change

Hopson (1981) finds that certain (un)expected events trigger predictable, general patterns of reactions and feelings, which the author named the "transition cycle." Within individuals, transition causes a change in perception of themselves and the world, consequentially demanding suitable changes in actions and relationships. Successfully facing important events in life through the search for new solutions enables an individual to grow and develop spiritually. These transitions are thus periods of risk and new opportunity, and supervision represents one of the methods that enables an individual to learn how to face stressful events in his or her professional life, including the periods of transition.

The transition cycle (Hopson, 1981) or the curve of competence (Hay, 1995) represents one of the possible frameworks through which we perceive the process of an individual's change more easily. Supervision enables an understanding of how efficiency, competence, or self-respect are transformed in relation to stressful events (Žorga, 1999, p. 62). Such an understanding of the process of change describes an initial immobilization, followed by a joyful reaction or one of denial (depending on the valuing and experiencing of the event itself), and, in accordance to it, the growth or fall of the feeling of competence, efficiency, or self-confidence. To illustrate, after one of the initial encounters, the supervisee reflected thus: "Supervision is something entirely new and unknown for me, thus I admit that I took part in the first meeting with mixed emotions and some fear of the unknown. However, the first impressions were pleasant, which helped me feel relaxed in all subsequent meetings, which was also aided by the fact that I received confirmation, that I work well." These feelings are usually followed by a phase of doubt or frustration and with it a drop in the sense of competence, which slowly resumes its rise only after an individual is faced with and accepts reality. The supervisee, in one of her reflections, wrote that she initially received some peace of mind (in the sense of feeling less responsibility), but later experienced some powerlessness, for her a source of frustration. The transition process continues through testing, giving sense, and integration (Hopson, 1981), referred to as development, application, and completion by Hay (1995). Both

Hopson and Hay view the process as leading to the establishment of enhanced competence.

Supervision and Personal Integration at Work

Supervision can be understood as one of those methods of self-development[2] that successfully contributes to constant learning and the integrated development of professionals across all of their functions. Work demands and expectations encourage especially the development of those characteristics and abilities that enable a more efficient functioning and adaptation to our profession. Such adaptation is often at the expense of our own needs for personal completion. Thus, we see the so-called specialization (Kolb, 1984), which simply means a one-sided development of our abilities. In this way, we accept the "win–lose" logic, instead of maintaining a personal change model, based on "learn–learn" (Hawkins & Smith, 2006). Exaggerated professional specialization can quickly lead to a narrowing of professional perspective, and to an ever larger rigidity and an increasingly routine existence (e.g., the special educator role, which over and over again deals only with dyscalculia, can begin to operate routinely in diagnosing). The consequence is that our professional knowledge gets pushed into the background in practice, with less thought directed at what we are actually doing. Thus, we even more frequently repeat the same mistakes and selectively overlook those facts that do not match our "knowledge in action," as Schön (1983) called it. So our work gets progressively more boring, and a "burnout" syndrome may appear. A part of this can be seen in the following reflection: "When I came into supervision, I thought that most client matters are solved along the way anyway, so there is no need to review something that's over for us. Then I realised that it's interesting to know how we felt when experiencing those matters, what kinds of dilemmas we faced when we solved them, and later what kind of things, which came out perfectly well, sometimes give me a bad feeling and I don't know why."

Reflection, provided by the supervision process, can help us prevent these negative consequences of specialization. The process of reflection makes us face our own understanding and subjective theories, which we have formed in relation to recurring but ignored experiences and lets us critically analyze them anew (e.g., "The meetings give me various new viewpoints for different situations in cases which I encounter and which are a real surprise for me, even in those situations which I thought I process easily."). This reflective process enables us to experience uncertainty and the unique nature of situations once again, thus giving us an opportunity to assign new meanings to them and to find a new challenge in our work, as well as opportunities for professional development.

Personal experience of a conflict between the demands of society and the need for personal accomplishment accelerates an individual's transition to the integrative stage of development. This can be helped by supervision, with its way of problem clarification and reflection on actions and decisions, combined with constant testing and exploration of situations, from various perspectives. In this way, supervision effectively

[2] This term, employed by Megginson and Whitaker (1996), emphasizes experiential learning as a cyclical process.

accelerates the development of the professional in the direction of recognizing and facing conflicts between their needs and the demands of the society, specifically the development of a more integrated personality. The higher the level of personal integration, the higher the level of work responsibility that a professional can assume. In research by the *Wall Street Journal* (Kolb, 1984), it was discovered that the leading professionals claimed integrity to be the characteristic that was the most important to their promotion. When professionals possess profession-related skills and knowledge that are suitably integrated into their personality traits, abilities, and sensitivities, this enables them to respond in tune when in professional situations, working in accordance with their thoughts, emotions, and wishes. It enables them to take heed of professional doctrines and demands, but also to recognize the actual possibilities offered by a particular, unique situation. This is illustrated by a conversation from a supervision meeting, when the supervisee said, "The answer why I come to supervision meetings is that supervision helps me raise my professional self confidence." Then her colleague added, "Yes, but I realised this when I found, in some of my actions, things I could be proud of, even though they may not be big things but simply matters I haven't been paying attention to up until now."

The Issue of Demands and Expectations When Working with People

Modern society demands efficiency and visible results from its professionals in the shortest time possible (i.e., achieving goals). The problem when this is applied to professional helping is that the visible results that are valued by others as a reflection of efficient work are not dependent exclusively on the experts themselves, but also on a wide range of other factors (e.g., situational and environmental factors; population characteristics; characteristics of individuals that the expert works with; social and systemic variables; personal history). Professionals are also subject to environmental factors, as when they are expected to achieve goals that are not their own. Thus, in working with clients, the supervisee internalizes socially designated goals (Bečaj, 1990; Gordon, 1980). Examples include a child successfully completing a grade; an adolescent beginning to act properly; a group establishing suitable relationships; or a family beginning to communicate (conflict levels being reduced, etc.). All too often it is overlooked that the professional's work is a minor influence on the achievement of such goals, being only one of the factors involved – and usually not the most important one. There are other considerations. It is a fact that no matter how well the professional work is carried out – sometimes we could claim that the harder the field of work, the more common this phenomenon – it does not always bring the desired results and achieve expected goals. The professional work input and the so-called efficiency (in the sense of attaining goals) are not always proportional, as there is no cause and effect relation between them. Thus, even the most expert professional with the most modern and efficient work methods cannot ensure that a below-average child could have the same efficiency in school as an average one. In the same way, no matter how competently an expert works with them, an adolescent with an already evolved antisocial personality will not begin to behave properly. The reverse can also be true, where the seeming success of an approach can lead to unethical practice. Thankfully, supervision allows professionals insight into such aspects of their work, providing more accurate feedback about its quality. Such insight also comes with professional studies, the reading of modern literature, conversations with co-workers, meetings with mentors, and so on, but these ways are less "convincing" for an individual than what can be achieved through supervision.

Modern society commonly places the expert in this goal-oriented situation, which is carried over from the business world, where "a professional's work must have visible effects." This occurs on a micro-social level as well, when one encounters the expectations of parents, leaders, or superiors, people in local communities, neighbors, and so on. Often, such expectations are not an issue, as long as the professional is aware of them and suitably corrects and reduces them; they become a real issue when they are internalized by the professional and accepted as their own. Such adaptation to the demands of the society (as in Žorga & Vec, 2004) does bring social recognition to an individual a sense of security, less conflict, and unification in thinking and acting with the majority, but it is often at the expense of neglecting their own needs and consequentially with unhappiness at work.

The consequence (as illustrated in Figure 5.1) is that professional knowledge is pushed into the background, as is self-critical reflection about what is done to respond to social pressures. This means that supervisees and others may repeat the same mistakes and selectively overlook any inconvenient facts. Thus, work begins to bore them, is carried out routinely, with feelings of depersonalization (cynicism) and inefficiency, forming the burnout syndrome (Maslach, 2003; Maslach, Schaufeli, & Leiter, 2001). The burnout syndrome has been discovered in 30–40% of teachers (Bauer et al., 2005; Vladut & Kállay, 2010), while it also has an above-average presence with school counselors (Wilkerson, 2009).

In addition to the advantages of individual supervision, there are particular advantages to group supervision, especially in relation to socially constructed goals. We

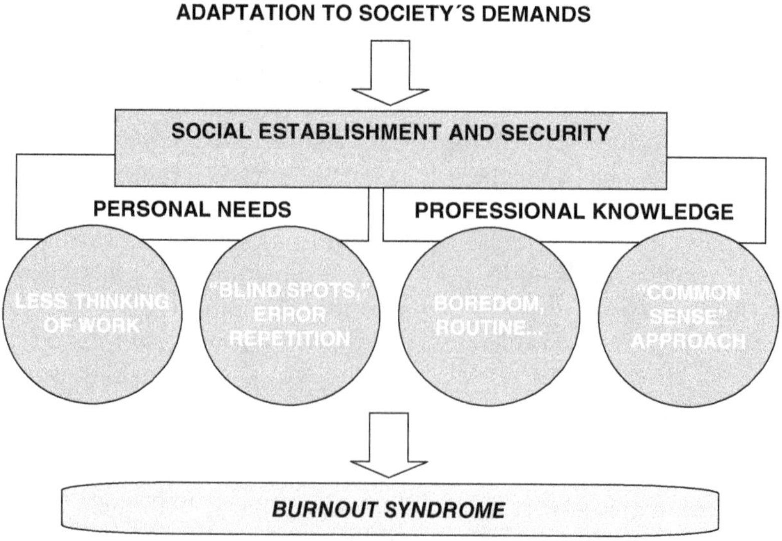

Figure 5.1 Burnout syndrome process.

could say that the supervision group is a separate field, one where we can form a group reality, along with the other participants.[3] As people, we truly believe and trust those points of view, thoughts, and suggestions that are exchanged and fortified with other people. Here, it is a matter of the group seeing participants co-create certain beliefs (the supervisor makes sure they truly follow professional principles), and due to the very reason that they co-create them, these beliefs become more "theirs," they believe in them, and also they function mostly in accordance with them.

The group also enables individuals to develop a critical view on their functioning, especially where there were desired outcomes. As one of the more problematic convictions of people involved in work with people, we have seen the belief that good results (i.e., kids being quiet in class, no conflicts expressed, no critical relation to adults expressed, etc.) mean good work by professionals. Thus, for example, an employee in an educational institution was perfectly convinced that the threat of slaps was in order (i.e., a good work method that others should copy) since the youths in his group were very obedient. In summary, supervision can help to challenge the assumed links between a supervisee's actions and goal-attainment, as there can be errors such as perfectly suitable processes bringing undesired results, and questionable practices providing good results.

Figure 5.2 indicates that outcomes from such situations can go in two directions:

1. The creation of faulty interpretations (false inferences), which can be:
   - false inference that good results always mean that good work has been done; and
   - false inference that bad results always mean poor, unprofessional work.
2. The establishment of general doubt about professional activities (e.g., whatever we do has no real effect or even a negative one, so in most cases it is best to do nothing, as things turn for the better eventually).

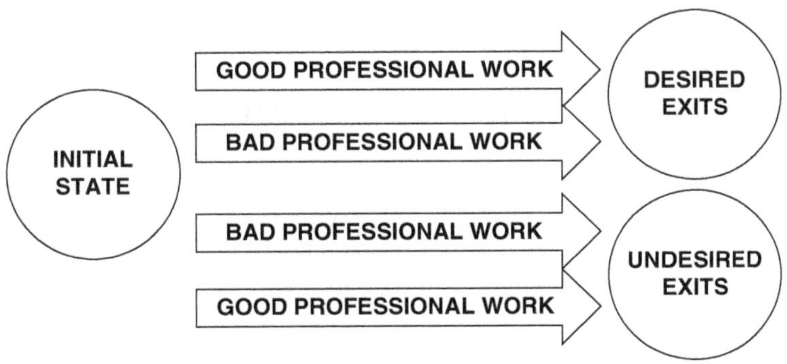

Figure 5.2 Effects of professional work on results/exits.

[3] Group reality is defined as Festinger's (1950) reflection that "an opinion, a belief and an attitude is perceived as 'correct,' 'valid' and 'proper' to the extent that is anchored in a group of people with similar beliefs, opinions, and attitudes" (pp. 272–273).

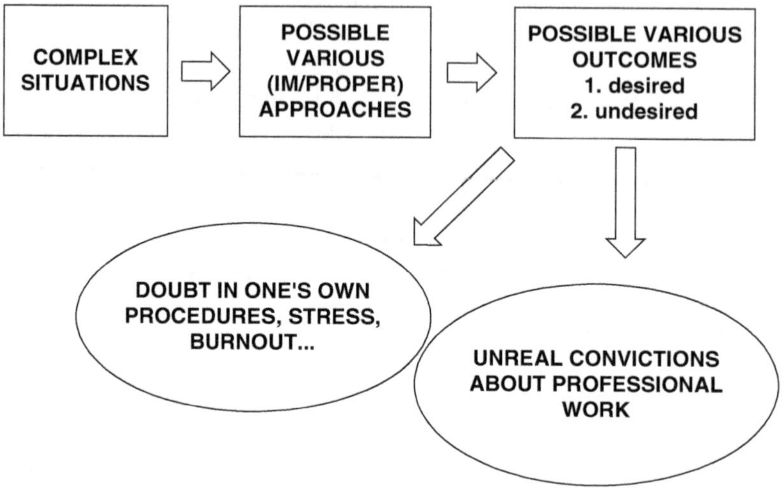

Figure 5.3 Consequence of complex situations when working with people.

We believe that the foundation of these faulty interpretations lies in the complexity of the therapeutic situations (e.g., various factors, interlaced, affect certain behaviors), which demand a variety of approaches, many of them combined or complex (no simple, one-size-fits-all recipes exist on how to solve problematic situations). That is, inferences are difficult when we cannot be sure precisely what has been done, or what has caused what, and when we do not have precise data from outcome measurement. As has been stated, because various therapeutic outcomes are possible (which are not only dependent on the supervisees' work, but also depend on other influences, such as clients' characteristics, organizational culture, and other systemic factors, etc.), mistaken beliefs about the work or self-doubt in supervisees about their competence, or a questioning of their therapeutic procedures can lead to occupational stress, burnout, and so on, as depicted in Figure 5.3.

Supervision Insight

Because of these difficulties in understanding therapy precisely, and the accompanying risks to the supervisees' own well-being, there is an additional role for the supervisor. This complements the formative function with some attention to the supportive and normative functions. Simplified, we could say that supervision, for example, with the help of a supervision group, enables supervisees to gain insight into professional work, and in a way that is independent of the so-called results of their therapeutic work, and regardless of whether the results were desired or not (Figure 5.4).

It is our opinion that the supervision process enables supervisees to gain insight into their own professional work in a way that is similar to that of a client in therapy (as described by Gee, 1996). Of course, this insight is not pleasant, as supervisees have to face their own imperfect understanding and subjective theories, formed from

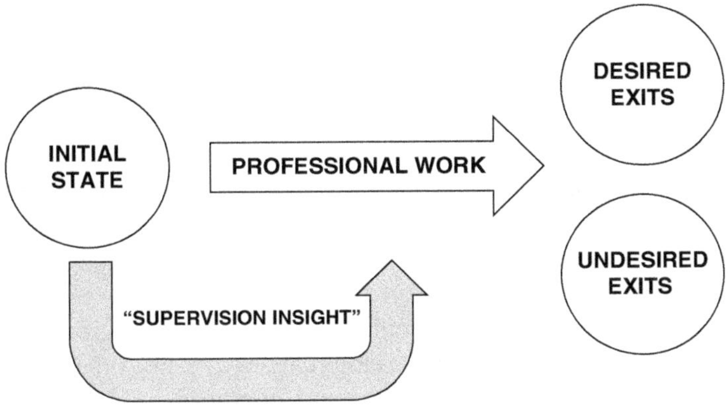

Figure 5.4 Supervision "insight."

limited and recurring experience. They are also faced with fresh information (e.g., supervisors' feedback on a session) about their own actions and feelings, areas about which they had not been thinking anymore. In this way, they are once more critically evaluated, which, for them, means (even assuming a safe and understanding environment) experiencing the insecurity and a greater awareness of the unique and challenging nature of their work. Only in this quasi-therapy way can they give new meanings to their growing experience and thus reinterpret the new challenges and possibilities for their professional development (Žorga & Vec, 2004). The supervision group helps with problem specification, by encouraging reflection on actions and decisions, and through constant questioning and shedding light on situations from various possible perspectives. In this way, the supervision process efficiently accelerates the development of a professional in the direction of recognizing and facing the aforementioned conflict between their needs and the demands of society.

In summary, we can say that "supervision insight" helps supervisees to

- specify problems, actions, and decisions;
- reflect on actions and decisions (including personal feelings of doubt or anxiety);
- develop constant questioning (and facilitates self-criticism); and
- shed light on situations, from various possible perspectives.

This also means that, overall, supervision enables the supervisees' development of a more integrated personality, where they can accept the higher the level of integration of a professional, together with the higher the level of professional responsibility. When supervisees possess profession-related skills and knowledge, ones that are suitably integrated into their personality traits, abilities, and sensitivities, this enables them to respond in tune when in professional situations. In turn, this helps them to work in accordance with their thoughts, emotions, and wishes, as well as taking heed of professional doctrines and demands, but also aware of the actual possibilities offered by a particular, unique situation.

Integration of Professional and Personal Development

Supervision thus enables insight and a higher quality of work, as theory supports the supervisees practice, and the practical experience of experts contributes to the research and development of new theories (Thompson & Thompson, 2008). However, when speaking about theory–practice integration, we do not believe that competence itself is enough, as there must also be a formation of professional identity, which we think of as a need for the integration of personal and professional development (Jarvis-Selinger, Pratt, & Regehr, 2012).

Personal and professional development should be fully connected (Bradley et al., 2011; Caspi & Reid, 2002), as the development of the personal characteristics of supervisees and their professional development condition one another. Again, we believe that supervision is no exception to the rule from personal psychotherapy, in the sense that both significantly influence the development of the professional self (Mackey & Mackey, 1994). We wish to emphasize that the process of supervision should be systematically directed toward this integration.

The fundamental precondition for the development of the integrated professional is an understanding of the need to change, to transform the inner world, and at the same time to always look for new opportunities for self-realization in professional life. An example lies in the improvement of professional self-awareness. Only in this kind of way can we avoid stagnation. Judging by the results of several research studies, mentioned by Mitina (1997), stagnation can appear with doctors and teachers after as little as 10 to 15 years, and even sooner with leading staff (i.e., after 5–7 years). Countering such stagnation, suitable supervision enables the professional to integrate what they do, feel, and think, and to integrate their practical experience with relevant theoretical knowledge, helping to transfer theory into practice and, over time, learning how to work independently. In this process, the supervisee grows professionally and personally, becoming better-equipped to deal with stagnation or burnout.

Kadushin (1985) points out a few fundamental conditions for more efficient personal development in supervision. He suggests that we learn better when

- we are highly motivated to do so (and since professionals are involved in the supervision process voluntarily, due to their own need, this should be true for them);
- in a learning situation, we dedicate most of our energy to learning (instead of expending our energy on defences for, anxiety, shame, guilt, fear in relation with failure, attack of our autonomy, unreal expectations, etc.);
- personal development is satisfactory (i.e., efficient and rewarded);
- we are actively involved in the learning process;
- content is provided sensibly; and
- the supervisor sees every individual in the process as unique.

In relation to this, Kadushin (1985) thought that the fundamental goal of supervision was actually the development of better self-awareness in the supervisee. This was because better self-awareness enabled independent, disciplined, and conscious professional functioning in the future. According to Kadushin, the development of higher levels of self awareness was also required since the problems faced by therapists soon affect them personally. Professional problems are thus tightly entwined with their own personal lives, and it may be extremely difficult to separate them. On top of this, awareness of similarities between one's own life experience as a therapist and the experience of the service user (client, student, youth, etc.) enables the professional to better understand the user's behavior.

While supervision can offer the supervisee an opportunity to review and recognize their personal strengths and weaknesses, which should improve their professional competence, we should also recognize that (as in therapy) such a review may also limit development. In theory, supervisees should reflect on their work experience in a safe environment with a group of colleagues, learning new patterns of professional activity. Van Kessel (1994) defines the final goal of such supervision as "two-dimensional integration," where supervisees are capable of efficiently synchronizing their functioning with their own personal characteristics (first dimension), and of synchronizing this with the properties of their professional work demands (second dimension), in a way that results in a professional self. However, it is important for supervision that work related to the personal dynamics of the supervisee is limited to the situations that stem from work experience, and that it is intended primarily for the supervisees' better professional functioning in the future. This is where supervision not only uses reflection as a learning tool, but also develops in the supervisee the ability to self-reflect, as a key goal of supervision. The more the supervisees can use this so-called internalized supervisor, the more capable they are of independent professional work. Figure 5.5 illustrates this integration.

The challenges of integrative development are enormous and not every supervisee is capable of facing them, regardless of how sophisticated his or her intelligence and professional training. We believe that, because of how it handles problems (e.g., by reflecting on the supervisee's actions and decisions, with the constant examination and elucidation of situations from various angles), supervision can effectively accelerate the development of a professional in the direction of facing conflicts (as between the demands of society and the needs of the individual for fulfillment) and consequently propel the supervisee toward the development of a more integrated personality.

This can be observed in an illustration from our own experience, concerning the evaluation reports written by school counselors, youth care workers, and teachers in higher education who had been involved in the supervision process for two or three years. The analysis (Žorga, 1997) showed that the experiences and knowledge gained in the course of the supervision process were reflected in their professional as well as private lives. Many professional workers claimed that the most important results of the supervision work pertained to the growth and development of their personality. They reported that the supervision meetings had helped them to reach deeper insights into their way of thinking, decision-making, and performance. They felt more self-confident, the level of their self-respect was raised, and they began to seek their own answers to questions, instead of looking for them from their superiors. Also, they became increasingly aware of their strengths and weaknesses, which they claimed enabled them to exploit and control them more consciously. Some of them reported how they had learned to better recognize and listen to their feelings. In turn, by being able to express their feelings and thoughts more clearly and adequately, they

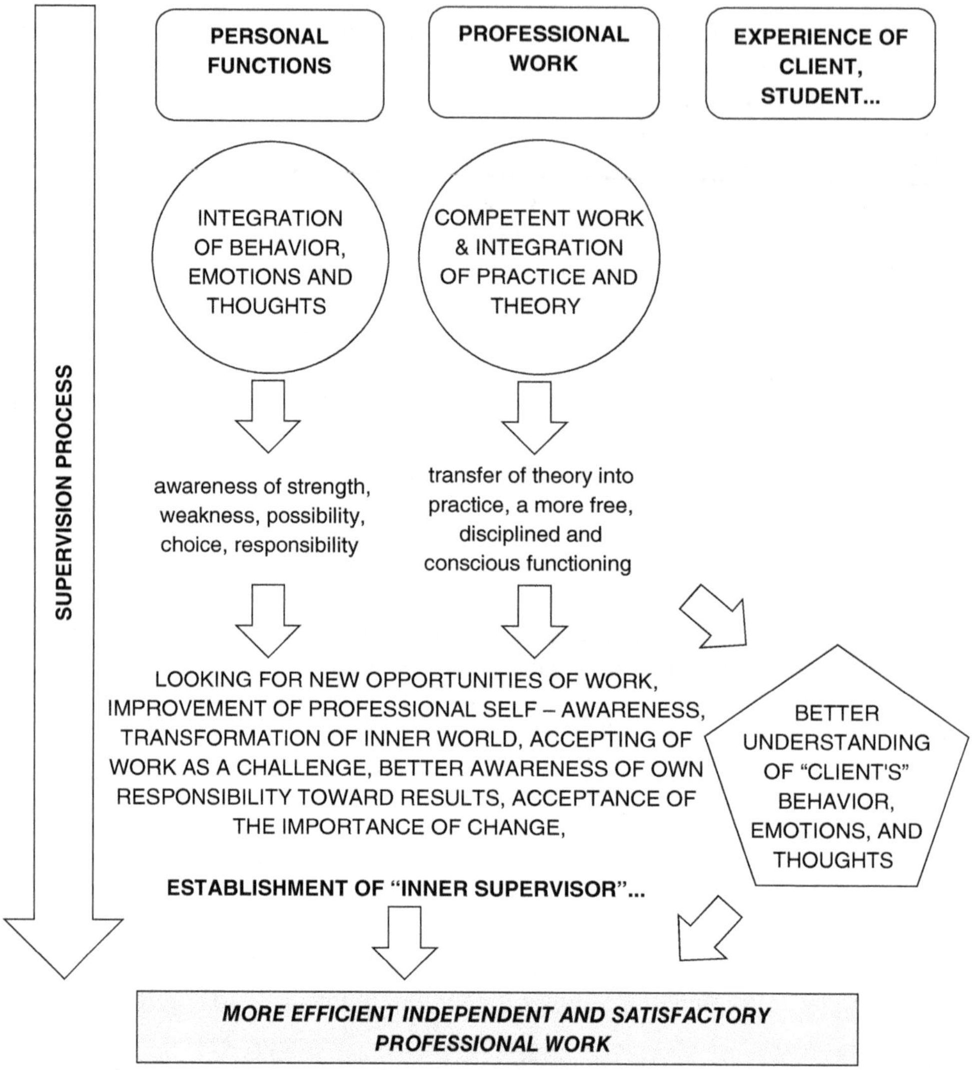

Figure 5.5 Two-dimensional integration and the "internal supervisor."

improved their communication. They also began to look after their health and well-being with greater care, and pay more attention to the balance between what they were allowed to do and what they desired. They had learned to more frequently take for themselves what they needed.

This new awareness that these participants reported allows a person to experience a change in his or her frame of reference, used to experience life, evaluate activities, and make decisions. In Kolb's (1984) opinion, the nature of this change depends on the peculiarities in the individual's dominant and nondominant (unexpressed) forms of adaptation. Thus, the awakening of an active form of adaptation empowers a reflective person with a new feeling for risk-taking. Rather than be influenced, the person wants to influence others. Instead of observing and accepting experiences as they happen, the challenge becomes forming one's own experiences. Development of our reflective side can also widen the possibility of choice and deepen the ability to feel the results of action. In Kolb's opinion, the pure effect of these changes lies in the increased feeling of oneself during the process. The learning process that was originally blocked by forms of nonspecialized adaptation is now experienced by the individual as the deep essence of oneself.

We should note that the role of reflection in developing the internal supervisor, and the formation of professional identity, does appear to be easier through social interactions (Jarvis-Selinger et al., 2012). Indeed, we think that social interactions, in the broadest sense of the word, are of key importance.

The Role of the Goals and Aims of Supervision in the Formation of a Supervision Group

A supervision group normally includes only a few individuals (recommended number is up to six). The reason for this is either financial or the management's decision about who within a workplace or service needs some supervision. As combination of both is normal, but due to financial reasons the number of participants in supervision groups is limited, so the principle of volunteering prevails. Sometimes a supervision group also forms as a consequence of some project in which a group of interested individuals has participated.

Supervision therefore stimulates participants to form a unique group culture, not only through specific knowledge, but primarily through (Vec, 2012)

- intensive participation in a small group (meetings are frequent; they last a few hours; participants during meetings share their reflections; everybody is active during each meeting; and everybody is obliged to prepare a case of their own);
- exchange of practical experiences, which are as a rule related to intensive emotional experiences (the majority of cases presented in the process of supervision are "problem-oriented," that is, people have not solved them the way that they wanted, which evokes feelings of powerlessness, fear, frustration, shame, etc.); and
- markedly personal participation since it is carried out in a small group, which provides intimacy, thus enabling insight into the mechanisms of personal backgrounds within professional work.

This supervision group culture, viewed from the perspective of social–psychological characteristics, is also established by forming distinctly specific group norms (for each group). In this way, certain knowledge and the manner or contents of communication become a habit and thus predictable. In this way, the clear structure of a group is formed, with its characteristic roles, stable interpersonal relationships, and defined expectations and goals. These norms are "internal pointers" (Bečaj, 2000) for behavior (there is a willingness to act according to a norm because one perceives it as sensible, proper, "normal," taken for granted). Members of a supervision group act in accordance with the norms both when alone (it is true, however, that some accept them more "intimately") and within a wider collective since the norms of a supervision group usually acquire the significance of reference groups' norms (Kelman, 2006; Turner, 1991).

The norms formed in a supervision group enhance reliability in deciding how to act in certain situations, especially in those that do not allow a uniform "recipe." In short, when the goal of supervision (harmonious regulation of one's thoughts, emotions, and wishes, taking into account the professional doctrines, demands, and factual possibilities in a concrete, unique situation) becomes normatively accepted by a group, individuals feel that their opinions and beliefs are appropriate. This feeling of appropriateness when conforming to a norm (Bečaj, 2000; Turner, 1991) will be internalized, remaining active in those participating in a supervision group when they are outside their supervision groups, so it will manifest in their actions in the wider clinical service.

In this sense, supervision therefore not only enables changes in the professional work of the individuals who participate in it, but can also affect change within an entire community (organization community) (through transferring the knowledge, beliefs, and the norms acquired in a supervision group). The relation of a supervision group toward those in a clinical service who are not included in a supervision group has, from the social–psychological point of view, all those group dynamics characteristic of minorities. By minority we mean a small number of people (or even one person) in relation to a group as a whole, whose behavior is perceived by a majority as antinormative (Vec, 2012). Until 1967, social psychology had primarily concerned itself with the ways others influence an individual (his or her behavior, thinking, perception, etc.). Then some of the experiments that were carried out (e.g., Moscovici & Faucheux, 1972; Moscovici, Lage, & Naffrechoux, 1969) suggested that the reverse might also take place: that a minority can influence a majority, at least when its work is consistent. Consistency is always a sign of conviction and confidence in being different. By responding differently, a minority becomes evidently different, exposed, and transparent, and it becomes the one bringing conflict and doubt. Through its consistency, a minority acts convincingly, thus introducing uncertainty concerning established norms. This consistency at the same time appears intransigent, which means that a majority can avoid unpleasant conflicts only by coming closer to a minority (Moscovici et al., 1969). The process in which a consistent minority can, under certain conditions, change a prevailing norm is called innovation.

The process of innovation is always initiated by an individual or a minority by being different. Historically, Moscovici and Faucheux (1972) spoke of three possible resolutions of the conflict (provoked by a minority being different): a majority coming closer to a minority; polarization; and avoidance of a minority (which is manifested by distrust). Polarization and avoidance were later sometimes referred to as the process of divergence, while approaching was termed validation (see, e.g., Mucchi-Faina & Cicoletti, 2006). These outcomes are captured in Figure 5.6.

Apart from the fact that being different (which supervisees gradually begin to present to others in a clinical service) itself brings potential for conflicts, a supervision group functions also according to other principles governing the work of a consistent minority (Turner, 1991). It thus follows:

1. A supervision group as a minority disturbs the established norms and causes doubt and insecurity in other members of a service.

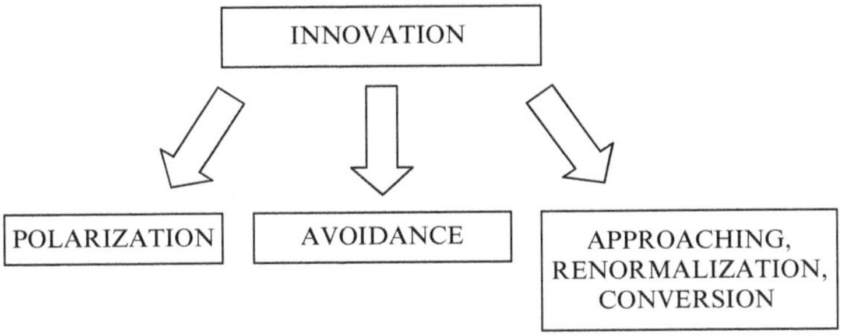

Figure 5.6 Possible implications of the process of innovation.

2. A supervision group is as a minority exposed, and it draws attention to itself.
3. It shows that there are also other, alternative and coherent aspects of working with people.
4. It expresses certainty, trust, and commitment to those different views.
5. It sends messages that it will not move or compromise.
6. This means that the only possible solution for resuming stability and the cognitive coherence of a service is that a majority comes closer to a minority.

According to the initial research carried out by Moscovici and his colleagues (Moscovici et al., 1969; Moscovici & Faucheux, 1972), we can conclude that a supervision group could bring changes to an entire service when they create a conflict (by being consistently different, in terms of conduct and forms of communication); when they are more original and flexible, like minorities that are willing to negotiate; when the starting points are closer to those of a majority (Mucchi-Faina, Maass, & Volpato, 1991; Nemeth, Swedlund, & Kanki, 1974); and when they are more active (Kerr, 2002). The objective consistency of supervision group as a minority is not as important as the fact that the rest of a service perceives its behavior as consistent, and that the message of such a minority (mediated by its behavior) is perceived by a majority as coherent, different, plausible, natural, in accordance with reality and objective (Turner, 1991), and that supervision group is in its entirety is perceived as convincing and trustworthy (Papastamou & Mugny, 1990). The resulting change of established norms is facilitated by the consistent behavior of supervision group members as a minority, but it should not be extreme in regard to its contents, lest it causes the so-called boomerang effect (Mugny, 1975). Martin and Hewstone (2003) concluded that the influence of a minority depends on the contents of a message, on whether a minority follows or disregards the behavior of a majority; and on whether it brings personally positive or negative outcomes. Mucchi-Faina and Cicoletti (2006) claimed that minorities assert their starting points more easily in less important circumstances, while in important situations they trigger disparities (polarization). One should bear in mind that consistency enables everybody in the role of a minority to influence others (i.e., members of a majority) even if they – which is often the case – do not publicly acknowledge, show, or admit this process. Of course, such a role can sometimes be harmful (in supervision, this can be avoided with good conditions for acquiring a license, as in the leader's own constant metasupervision, lifelong learning, etc.).

Conclusion

This chapter has focused on some universal processes of supervision (i.e., unrelated to the modality and theoretical foundations, the forms or fields where it is carried out, etc.). We suggest that supervision brings something that maybe the very profit orientation of work often takes away, that is, a humanistic orientation. By humanistic we mean seeing a human as an essentially social being who constantly learns and whose basic interaction tool is communication, with the help of which one creates reality. Through the supervision of therapy, the supervisee is encouraged to develop into a more efficient, independent, and professional worker. Full empowerment, a better awareness of one's strengths, a better awareness of one's possibilities, choices, and responsibilities, and a more autonomous style of work is encouraged by supervision, both in a professional and in a personal sense. Thus, the expectations of oneself and others, as well as professional actions (related to clients and also to other circumstances) are, through supervision, set into more personally meaningful frameworks. And if the supervisees as professional workers are more efficient and at the same time more satisfied with their work, the results achieved, as well as their personal functioning, we are led to the conclusion that a modern, outcome-oriented society should exhibit interest in supervision.

References

Argyris, C. (1976). Leadership, learning and changing the status quo. *Organisational Dynamics*, *4*(3), 29–43.

Argyris, C. (1991). Teaching smart people how to learn. *Harvard Business Review*, *4*(2), 4–15.

Argyris, C. (1995). Action science and organisational learning. *Journal of Managerial Psychology*, *10*(6), 20–26.

Argyris, C. (2002). Double loop learning, teaching and research. *Academy of Management Learning and Education*, *1*, 206–218.

Bauer, J., Stamm, A., Virnich, K., Wissing, K., Kriston, L., Muller, U., . . . Schaarschmidt, U. (2005). Correlation between burnout syndrome and psychological and psychosomatic symptoms among teachers. *International Archives of Occupational Health*, *79*, 199–204.

Bečaj, J. (1990). *Problem velikih pričakovanj in učiteljeve odgovornosti* [The problem of high expectations and teacher's responsibility]. Ljubljana, Slovenia: Svetovalni center za otroke, mladostnike in starše.

Bečaj, J. (2000). *Temelji socialnega vplivanja* [The basics of social influence]. Ljubljana, Slovenia: Filozofska fakulteta.

Bradley, L. J., Ladany, N., Hendricks, B., Whiting, P. P., & Rhode, K. M. (2011). Overview of counseling supervision. In N. Ladany & L. J. Bradley (Eds.), *Counselor supervision* (pp. 3–14). New York, NY: Routledge.

Brandau, H. (1991). NLP und systemische super–VISIONEN in trance [NLP and systemic super-VISIONS in trance]. In H. Brandau (Ed.), *Supervision aus systemischer Sicht* [Supervision from a systemic point of view] (pp. 176–193). Salzburg, Austria: Otto Müller Verlag.

Brookfield, S. (1995). *Becoming a criticaly reflective teacher.* San Francisco, CA: Jossey-Bass.

Carroll, M. (2006). *Counselling supervision: Theory, skills and practice.* London, UK: SAGE Publication Ltd.

Caspi, J., & Reid, W. J. (2002). *Educational supervision in social work: A task-centered model for field instruction and staff development.* New York, NY: Columbia University Press.

Dewey, J. (1955). *Experience and education.* New York, NY: Macmillan Company.

Ellis, M. V., Ladany, N., Krengal, M., & Schult, D. (1996). Clinical supervision research from 1981 to 1993: A methodological critique. *Journal of Counseling Psychology, 43*, 35–50.

Falender, C. A., Cornish, J. A. E., Goodyear, R., Hatcher, R., Kaslow, N. J., Leventhal, G., . . . Grus, C. (2004). Defining competencies in psychology supervision: A consensus statement. *Journal of Clinical Psychology, 60*, 771–785.

Festinger, L. (1950). Informal social communication. In D. Cartwright & A. Zander (1968) (Eds.), *Group dynamics* (pp. 57–63). New York, NY: A Harper International Edition.

Gee, H. (1996). Developing insight through supervision: Relating, then defining. *Journal of Analytical Psychology, 41*, 529–552.

Gordon, T. (1980). *Leader effectiveness training.* New York, NY: Bantam Books.

Hawkins, P., & Shohet, R. (2002). *Supervision in the helping professions: An individual, group and organizational approach.* Philadelphia, PA: Open University Press.

Hawkins, P., & Shohet, R. (2006). *Supervision in the helping professions: An individual, group and organizational approach.* Philadelphia, PA: Open University Press.

Hawkins, P., & Smith, N. (2006). *Coaching, mentoring and organizational consultancy: Supervision and development.* Maidenhead, UK: Open University Press.

Hay, J. (1995). *Transformational mentoring.* London, UK: McGraw-Hill Book Company.

Hopson, B. (1981). Response to papers by Schlossberg, Brammer and Abrego. *The Counseling Psychologist, 9*, 36–40.

Jarvis-Selinger, S., Pratt, D. D., & Regehr, G. (2012). Competency is not enough: Integrating identity formation into the medical education discourse. *Academic Medicine, 87*, 1185–1190.

Kadushin, A. (1985). *Supervision in social work.* London, UK: Columbia University Press.

Keeney, B. (1991). Hörst du die Melodie? Eine kurze Abhandlung des Wechsels von der "Super-vision" zur "Super-audition" [Do you hear the melody? A brief discussion of the change from the "super-vision" to the "super-audition." In H. Brandau (Ed.), *Supervision aus syste"mischer Sicht* [Supervision from a systemic point of view] (pp. 79–80). Salzburg, Austria: Otto Müller Verlag.

Kelman, H. C. (2006). Interests, relationships, identities: Three central issues for individuals and groups in negotiating their social environment. *Annual Reviews, 57*, 1–26.

Kerr, L. N. (2002). When is minority a minority? Active versus passive minority advocacy and social influence. *European Journal of Social Psychology, 32*, 471–483.

Kolb, D. A. (1984). *Experiential learning. Experience as the source of learning and development.* Engelwood Cliffs, NJ: Prentice Hall.

Kolb, D. A., Boyatzis, R. E., & Mainemelis, C. (1999). *Experiential learning theory: Previous research and new directions.* Retrieved from http://www.d.umn.edu/~kgilbert/educ5165-731/Readings/experiential-learning-theory.pdf

Lewin, K. (1951). *Field theory in social sciences.* New York, NY: Harper & Row.

Mackey, R. A., & Mackey, E. F. (1994). Personal psychotherapy and the development of a professional self. *Families in Society, 75*, 490–498.

Martin, R., & Hewstone, M. (2003). Majority versus minority influence: When, not whether, source status instigates heuristic or systematic processing. *European Journal of Social Psychology, 33*, 313–330.

Maslach, C. (2003). Job burnout: New directions in research and intervention. *Current Directions in Psychological Science, 12*, 189–192.

Maslach, C., Schaufeli, W. B., & Leiter, M. P. (2001). Job burnout. *Annual Review of Psychology, 52*, 397–422.

Megginson, D., & Whitaker, V. (1996). *Cultivating self-development.* London, UK: Institute for personnel and development.

Merriam, S. B., & Clark, M. C. (1992). Adult learning in good times and bad. *Studies in Continuing Education, 14*(1), 1–13.

Milne, D. (2007). An empirical definition of clinical supervision. *British Journal of Clinical Psychology, 46*, 437–447.

Milne, D., Aylott, H., Fitzpatrick, H., & Ellis, M. V. (2008). How does clinical supervision work? Using a "Best Evidence Synthesis" approach to construct a basic model of supervision. *The Clinical Supervisor, 27*, 170–190.

Mitina, L. (1997). Personal and professional development of the person in new socio economic conditions in Russia. In *33rd IAAP International Conference on Developing Human Relations and Ethnic Understanding* (pp. 80–85), Hardwar, India: Gurukul Kangri University.

Moscovici, S., & Faucheux, C. (1972). Social influence, conformity bias, and the study of active minorities. *Advances in experimental social psychology, 6*, 148–201.

Moscovici, S., Lage, E., & Naffrechoux, M. (1969). Influence of consistent minority on the responses of majority in a color perception task. *Sociometry, 32*, 365–380.

Mucchi-Faina, A., & Cicoletti, G. (2006). Divergence vs. ambivalence: Effects of personal relevance on minority influence. *European Journal of Social Psychology, 36*, 91–104.

Mucchi-Faina, A., Maass, A., & Volpato, C. (1991). Social influence: The role of originality. *European Journal of Social Psychology, 21*, 183–197.

Mugny, G. (1975). Negotiations, image of the other and the process of minority influence. *European Journal of Social Psychology, 5*, 209–228.

Nemeth, C., Swedlund, M., & Kanki, B. (1974). Patterning of the minority's responses and their influence on the majority. *European Journal of Social Psychology, 4*, 53–64.

O'Connor, L. C. (2008). A look at supervision in the 21st Century. *ASHA Leader, 13*(5), 14–18.

Papastamou, S., & Mugny, G. (1990). Synchronic consistency and psychologization in minority influence. *European Journal of Social Psychology, 20*, 85–98.

Piaget, J. (1961). *La psychologie de l'intelligence* [The psychology of intelligence]. Paris, France: Librairie Armand Colin.

Proctor, B., & Inskipp, F. (1988). *Skills for supervising and being supervised.* St Leonards on Sea, Sussex: Alexia Publications.

Schein, E. H. (2004). *Organisational culture and leadership* (3rd ed.). San Francisco, CA: Jossey-Bass.

Schön, D. A. (1983). *The reflective practitioner: How professionals think in action.* Boston, MA: Arena Publishing.

Schwarz, R. (2005). *The skilled facilitator fieldbook. Tips, tools and tested methods for consultants, facilitators, managers, trainers and coaches.* San Francisco, CA: Jossey-Bass.

Senge, P. M. (1993). *The fifth discipline. The art and practice of the learning organisation.* London, UK: Century Business.

Senge, P. M. (2001). *Schools that learn. A fifth discipline fieldbook for educators, parents and everyone who cares about education.* New York, NY, London, UK: Doubleday.

Thompson, S., & Thompson, N. (2008). *The critically reflective practitioner.* Basingstoke, UK: Palgrave. Macmillan.

Turner, J. C. (1991). *Social influence.* Buckingham, UK: Open University Press.

Van Gelder, T. (2004). Teaching critical thinking: Some lessons from cognitive science. *College Teaching, 45*, 41–46.

Van Kessel, L. (1994). The Duch concept of supervision as a teaching method for social work education. In *Social Work Education: State of the Art, Official congress publication*. Amsterdam: Hogeschool van Amsterdam.

Vec, T. (2012). Supervisor: Minority and minority facilitator. *IIASS – Innovative Issues and Approaches in Social Sciences*, *5*(2), 49–69.

Vladut, C. I., & Kállay, É. (2010). Work stress, personal life, and burnout. Causes, consequences, possible remedies: – A theoretical review. *Cognitie, Creier, Comportament/ Cognition, Brain, Behavior*, *14*, 261–280.

Vygotsky, L. S. (1977). *Mišljenje i govor* [Thought and speech]. Beograd, Serbia: Nolit.

Watkins, C. E. (2012). Development of the psychotherapy supervisor: Review of and reflections on 30 years of theory and research. *American Journal of Psychotherapy*, *66*, 45–83.

Watkins, C. E., Jr. (1995). Researching psychotherapy supervisor development: Four key considerations. *The Clinical Supervisor*, *13*, 111–119.

Wilkerson, K. (2009). An examination of burnout among school counselors guided by stress-strain-coping theory. *Journal of Counseling & Development*, *87*, 428–437.

Worthington, E. L., Jr. (1987). Changes in supervision as counselors and supervisors gain experience: A review. *Professional Psychology, Research and Practice*, *18*, 189–208.

Žorga, S. (1995). Supervizija v razvojnih projektih [Supervision in developmental projects]. In B. Dekleva (Ed.), *Supervizija za razvojne in preventive programe* [Supervision for developmental and preventive programme] (pp. 5–31). Ljubljana, Slovenia: Društvo za razvijanje preventivnega in prostovoljnega dela.

Žorga, S. (1997). Professionals as partners in their own professional development. In *33rd IAAP International Conference on Developing Human Relations and Ethnic Understanding* (pp. 134–143), Hardwar< India: Gurukul Kangri University.

Žorga, S. (1999). Razvoj in učenje v superviziji [Development and learning in supervision.] In A. Kobolt & S. Žorga (Eds.), *Supervizija – proces razvoja in učenja v poklicu [Supervision – The process of development and learning in profession]* (pp. 59–88). Ljubljana, Slovenia: Pedagoška fakulteta.

Žorga, S. (2002). Supervision: The process of life-long learning in social and educational professions. *Journal of Interprofessional Care*, *16*, 265–276.

Žorga, S., & Vec, T. (2004). Supervision: The process of professional reflection and development. In V. Švab (Ed.), *Education for change: Proceedings of the Conference Education for Change* (pp. 95–102). Ljubljana, Slovenia: ŠENT.

Part II

Practice Foundations
The Context for Clinical Supervision

6

International Ethics for Psychotherapy Supervisors

Principles, Practices, and Future Directions

Janet T. Thomas

Teaching the ethics of psychotherapy to developing professionals has been considered an essential function of supervisors over time and across continents. Early philosophers, on whose work the mental health professions are built, have described the ethical underpinnings of their methods for imparting knowledge and skills to novices and for overseeing their work as they learn. Understanding the ethics of such supervision and modeling ethical behavior are necessary prerequisites to effective performance of this critical function. Supervisors in every country and culture must be mindful of their ethical responsibilities for supervisees and their clients.

Mental health professionals in many countries have considered the ethical dimensions of supervision in different ways, and each contributes a valuable perspective. Sharing these perspectives will facilitate the further development of this important area of mental health practice. With this goal in mind, the following chapter will include

- a discussion of historical and contemporary conceptualizations of supervision;
- identification of commonalities in ethical principles guiding supervisors around the world;
- a sampling of ethical standards and professional guidelines and the context in which they have developed;
- an examination of specific ethical issues including boundaries and multiple relationships, informed consent, and competence; and
- future directions for ethical supervision in an international context.

Historical and Contemporary Conceptualizations of Supervision

Supervision has for centuries been addressed through teaching, mentoring, and professional oversight. The Buddha, Hippocrates, and Confucius all weighed in on the

The Wiley International Handbook of Clinical Supervision, First Edition. Edited by C. Edward Watkins, Jr. and Derek L. Milne.

subject. Bhikkhu Bodhi (2005) discussed the Buddha's reflections on the relationships of teachers and students, with direct implications for supervision. After listing the ways in which students should treat teachers, he reiterates the Buddha's perspective on how teachers should serve their students. In direct translation of the Digha Nikaya, the Buddhist scripture, he noted,

> There are five ways in which their teachers . . . reciprocate: they will give thorough instruction, make sure they [students] have grasped what they should have duly grasped, give them a thorough grounding in all skills, recommend them to their friends and colleagues, and provide them with security in all directions. (p. 117)

The Buddha's words suggest the critical functions of supervision: teaching, cultivating competence, evaluating, endorsing, and providing a safe environment in which supervisees can learn and grow.

From the fourth century BCE at least, teachers and helpers have understood that they hold influence over those they teach and serve. The Hippocratic oath, for physicians, is part of a comprehensive work, the Hippocratic Corpus. Unlike pledges for other guilds, the oath outlines the physician's responsibility to patients (Sinclair, 2012) and emphasizes the significance of teachers and mentors to subordinates:

> I will keep this Oath and this stipulation—to reckon him who taught me this Art equally dear to me as my parents, to share my substance with him, and relieve his necessities if required; to look upon his offspring in the same footing as my own brothers, and to teach them this art . . . without fee or stipulation; and that by precept, lecture, and every other mode of instruction. (Oath of Hippocrates, Greece, fourth century BCE)

This seminal "ethics code" conceptualizes the duties of the teacher or supervisor to include establishing rules, or precepts, and didactic instruction. Like the Digha Nikaya, the Hippocratic Oath suggests that the learner owes deference to the teacher.

The Chinese philosopher Confucius reportedly observed the process of learning a profession and wrote, "I hear, I know. I see, I remember. I do, I understand"(http://www.brainyquote.com/quotes/authors/c/confucius.html). Applied to supervision, this suggests that supervisors teach concepts, demonstrate related skills, and provide opportunities for supervisees to practice those concepts.

The concept of presiding over the work of a novice to teach the skills of a profession is not new, unique to psychotherapy, or originally a Western idea. But contemporary definitions of clinical supervision published in the United States, Canada, the United Kingdom, and New Zealand recognize its importance. Bernard and Goodyear (2014), for example, highlighted the supervisor's responsibility for supervisees and their clients and recognized them as the gatekeepers of the mental health professions. Falender and Shafranske (2004) emphasized supervisor competency and elucidated the skills required for effective supervision, suggesting it be provided in a manner "in which ethical standards, legal prescriptions, and professional practices are used to promote and protect the welfare of the client, the profession, and society" (p. 3).

The College of Psychologists of Ontario (2009) built on that definition, highlighting diversity in therapeutic and supervisory relationships, continuing evaluation, and the cultivation of ethical decision-making skills in supervisees. Hawkins and Shohet (2006) of the United Kingdom identified the three primary functions of supervision as managerial, educational, and supportive.

Mental health professionals in New Zealand have contributed significantly to state-of-the-art supervision. O'Donoghue and Tsui (2012) conceptualized social work supervision as having developed a "distinctive professional culture" (p. 5) with a strong emphasis on cultural competence. The New Zealand Psychologists Board (2010) detailed in *Guidelines on Supervision* a model contract for supervision and a form for creating a record of supervision. The document defines supervision as:

> a scheduled time to meet with a respected professional colleague for the purpose of conducting a self-reflective review of practice, to discuss professional issues, and to receive feedback on all elements of practice, with the objectives of ensuring quality of service, improving practice, and managing stress. (p. 2)

Also from New Zealand, an interdisciplinary group of Māori counselors, social workers, and psychologists defined supervision as "gathering the treasures of the past into the competencies of the present for the wellbeing of the future" (Carroll, 2006, p. 5). This definition reflects a seminal aspect of Māori culture and thinking: holistic consciousness. According to Syd Davies, "Māori culture takes into account past, present, and future, including those who have died and those who have yet to be born" (S. Davies, personal communication, October 17, 2012).

Implicit in these definitions is the influence of supervisors in supervisee understanding of professional ethics (Thomas, 2010). Graduate school coursework provides students with opportunities to learn the ethics codes of their professions and the rules applicable in their jurisdictions. They are exposed to the professional literature and may consider complex case vignettes or apply decision-making models. Yet only when they actually work with clients do they begin to appreciate the complexities of applying ethical principles to real-world mental healthcare. Handelsman, Gottlieb, and Knapp (2005) define such learning in their description of "ethical acculturation" (p. 59) as a developmental process through which students grow into their professional identities with the help of mentors and role models. Clearly, supervisors play a vital role in this process.

Commonalities in Ethical Principles Guiding Supervisors around the World

The *Universal Declaration of Ethical Principles for Psychologists* (International Union of Psychological Science, 2008) is one of the few documents identifying the human values that underlie professional ethics for psychologists in many countries. Janel Gauthier, one of its primary authors, described the objective of this publication in his 2008 address to the United Nations (http://www.apa.org/international/pi/2008/10/gauthier.aspx): "Psychologists are citizens of the world. Adherence to ethical principles in our work contributes to a stable society that enhances the quality of life – and respect for human rights – for all human beings" (Gauthier, 2008, p. 1). The *Universal Declaration of Ethical Principles for Psychologists*

> reaffirms the commitment of the psychology community to help build a better world where peace, freedom, responsibility, justice, humanity, and morality will prevail. Promoting the new universal declaration promises to be a contribution to the creation of a global society based on respect and caring for individuals and peoples. (Gauthier, 2008, p. 1)

Another effort to identify commonalities in ethical principles across countries is the *Code of Ethics* (n.d.) published by the International Academy of Behavioral Medicine, Counseling, and Psychotherapy, Inc. This code includes requirements that members maintain competence in all areas of practice, seek consultation when facing ethical dilemmas, and keep confidential information obtained in the course of professional consultations. Supervision is specifically referenced in a section prohibiting financial, emotional, and sexual exploitation of trainees and supervisees.

Like organizations representing psychologists and counselors, the International Federation of Social Workers, in cooperation with the International Association of Schools of Social Work, developed a document elucidating their shared values (2012). An earlier version of the *International Code of Ethics for the Professional Social Worker* clarifies that social work "originates variously from humanitarian, religious, and democratic ideals and philosophies and has universal application to meet human needs arising from personal-societal interactions and to develop human potential" (International Federation of Social Workers, 1978, p. 1).

The ethics codes of the profession of social work consistently reflect the commitment to social justice that permeates this international ethics code: "Social workers have a responsibility to promote social justice, in relation to society generally, and in relation to the people with whom they work" (International Federation of Social Workers, 2012). It specifically directs social workers to challenge discrimination and unjust policies, recognize diversity, work in solidarity, and to distribute resources equitably (International Federation of Social Workers, 2012). The International Federation of Social Workers Web site includes links to the social work ethics codes of 22 countries: http://ifsw.org/resources/publications/national-codes-of-ethics/.

These international ethics codes for mental health professions share a reverence for human rights. Further, they reflect a commitment to safeguarding the rights, welfare, and dignity of those who are served, and they lay the foundation for ethical principles informing all psychological and psychotherapeutic services, including the supervision that undergirds training and the maintenance of competence.

Contextual Factors in the Development of Ethics Codes and Supervision Guidelines

Ethical standards and guidelines differ in breadth, applicability, enforceability, and relation to legal requirements (Leach & Gauthier, 2011), often as related to the history of the profession in a specific country. The development of the mental health professions is relatively recent in many nations. As mental health services are increasingly recognized as valuable, the profession grows, associations are established, and ethics codes are created. Some of the newer professional associations do not yet have codes of their own. And, because the recognition of supervision as requiring a separate skill set is relatively new (Falender & Shafranske, 2004), supervision guidelines are even more uncommon.

Comprehension of the broader context of the development of the mental health professions is critical to understanding the current status of supervision ethics across nations. One important contextual factor is recognition that the profession of psychology predates that of counseling or *applied psychology* in most countries, and the development of counseling and other psychological services consistently predates the formalization of the supervision of those services.

One example of counseling following psychology comes from South Korea. American delegates introduced counseling to that country in the 1950s (Lee, Suh, Yang, & Jang, 2012), but the Korean Psychological Association (formerly Chosun Psychological Society) was founded in 1946 (Korean Psychological Association, n.d., http://www.koreanpsychology.or.kr/eng/). Malaysia's counseling profession began in the 1960s – as did that of many other countries – as school guidance, following the country's achievement of independence from England in 1957 (See & Ng, 2010). The increasing professionalization of the Malaysian Counseling Association, established in 1982, is evident. With the Malaysian Board of Counselors, it relies on an adaptation of the American Counseling Association's *Code of Ethics* (2005). Because this code was developed in the United States, it does not reflect Malaysian cultural sensibilities. See and Ng (2010) have recommended that its members work to develop a version of the code that is "contextualized and culturally relevant to Malaysia" (p. 21).

More recently, the Uganda Counselling Association, founded in 2002, published its first *Code of Ethics* in 2003 and revised it in 2009 (Senyonyi, Ochieng, & Sells, 2012), published its *Code of Ethics* (2003) and revised it in 2009. In Uganda, like other African countries in which corruption, poverty, disease, and war threaten stability, mental health services receive low priority (Okasha, 2002; Senyonyi et al., 2012). Botswana provides the exception in boasting one of the most stable governments on the continent (Stockton, Nitza, & Bhusumane, 2010). Nevertheless, the counseling profession is relatively young there: the Republic of Botswana Ministry of Education (2002), charged with the supervision of counseling in schools, first published a training curriculum in 2002, and the Botswana Counselling Association came into existence as late as 2004 (Stockton et al., 2010).

The mental health professions in other countries have longer, though interrupted, histories. One example is the Russian Federation. The Russian Psychological Society, first formed in 1885, continued to grow until the Russian Revolution in 1917, when its official activities were suspended until 1957 (Russian Psychological Society, 2012, http://www.psyrus.ru/en/about/). In Russia, a long history of mistrust, particularly of psychology and psychiatry, exists (Currie, Kuzmina, & Nadyuk, 2012). Despite the influence of Freud in the late 1800s and early 1900s (all of his works were translated into Russian), after the Revolution, the Russian government used psychological concepts to justify the psychiatric confinement of citizens whose ideas challenged those of Marx and Lenin (Sosland, 1997). "Psychology became a repressive power, a dangerous tool" (Currie et al., 2012, p. 489). As the government became more liberal, Mikhail Gorbachev, the last leader of the Soviet Union, introduced perestroika and glasnost in the mid-1980s, creating opportunity for the development of the mental health professions. More recently, the Ministry of Education and Science of the Russian Federation (2009) established the specialization *social psychological help*, under the umbrella of social work. These changes have opened the door to the growth of social work, psychology, addiction treatment, and pastoral counseling. The Russian Psychological Society published its most recent *Code of Ethics* in 2012 (Zinchenko & Petrenko, 2012), including specific standards for supervision.

Similarly, the study of psychology was introduced to Romania in the late 1890s (David, Moore, & Domuta, 2002; Foreman, 1996). Its government outlawed psychology as a separate discipline in the 1970s, but in 1990, after the collapse of the Ceausescu regime, psychology was reinstituted (Iliescu, Ispas, & Ilie, 2007). Applied psychology came into existence in the form of counseling in 1995 (Peteanu, 1997), and in 2009, a group of educators and practitioners established the Romanian Counseling Association under the supervision of the (American) National Board of Certified Counselors (Szilagyi & Paredes, 2010).

Only a few mental health professional associations have developed guidelines specifically for clinical supervisors. Examples include the American Association for Marriage and Family Therapy (2007), the Australian Psychological Society (2003), and the Canadian Psychological Association Committee on Ethics (2009). Similarly, only a few regulatory bodies have promulgated supervision guidelines: the American Board of Examiners in Clinical Social Work (2004), the College of Psychologists of Ontario (2009), and the New Zealand Psychologists Board (2010). The Association of State and Provincial Psychology Boards (2003), an international organization of regulatory bodies, also has developed supervision guidelines, and a revision is currently under way (J. Schaffer, personal communication, November 18, 2012).

Given the importance of ethical practice in supervision, the following section will highlight relevant ethics codes and guidelines from various countries, with particular emphasis on boundaries and multiple relationships, informed consent, competence, and multicultural competence in particular.

Boundaries and Multiple Relationships

Most codes recognize the power imbalance inherent in helping relationships. Whether explicitly stated or implied in particular ethics codes, supervisory relationships are characterized by this same dynamic. Professional literature, ethical standards, and supervision guidelines commonly alert supervisors to their need for vigilance and caution in relationships with supervisees.

Power imbalance in supervisory relationships

The intrinsic power imbalance of and commensurate professional responsibilities in therapeutic relationships are well documented (Gutheil & Simon, 2002; Haas & Malouf, 2005; Kaiser, 1997; Pope & Vasquez, 2007). Some authors have addressed the power inherent in the supervisory relationship (Gottlieb, Robinson, & Younggren, 2007; Peterson, 1992; Thomas, 2010). The principle underlying their work is the same: when one person is in a position to help another, the responsibility for the welfare of the recipient rests with the helper. For supervisors that responsibility is clinical, ethical, and legal, and it extends to the clients served by supervisees (Bernard & Goodyear, 2014; Saccuzzo, 2002).

French and Raven (1959) have explicated the nature and potential impact of power differentials in relationships. Special expertise imbues these helping relationships with additional power and responsibility (Peterson, 1992). Many authors have emphasized the responsibilities of professionals working with clients or patients. The seminal work of French and Raven elucidates the bases of social power and influence as reflected in supervisory relationships, defining the potency of power as the maximum potential ability of one social agent (O, a "person, role, norm group, or part of a group") to influence another person (P) (French & Raven, 1959, p. 151). They described five bases of social power:

1. reward power, based on P's perception that O has the ability to mediate rewards for him;
2. coercive power, based on P's perception that O has the ability to mediate punishments for him;
3. legitimate power, based on the perception by P that O has a legitimate right to prescribe behavior for him;
4. referent power, based on P's identification with O; and
5. expert power, based on the perception that O has some special knowledge or expertness (French & Raven, 1959, pp. 155–156).

Supervisory duties may include decisions that affect the careers of supervisees. Supervisors may be charged with hiring, firing, promoting, evaluating, and endorsing them for licensure or certification. These responsibilities give supervisors both *reward power* and *coercive power*. Supervisors are typically appointed to these roles by agencies or institutions, and their opinions receive the credence of licensing boards, academic programs, and professional associations. Recognizing such endorsement, supervisees afford their supervisors *legitimate power* as well as the *expert power* underscored by academic credentials and experience (French & Raven, 1959). The Hippocratic Oath reflects this power differential. The magnitude of debt owed to one's teacher imbues the teacher or supervisor with power over the learner and diminishes the learner's ability to challenge the teacher (Greece, fourth century BCE). The power differential enhances the difficulty faced by supervisees attempting to advocate for themselves with supervisors.

Direction from ethics codes and guidelines

Some national organizations, through ethics codes and guidelines, have addressed the issue of power inequity and the related potential for harm to supervisees. These include the American Association for Marriage and Family Therapy (2012), American Counseling Association (2005), American Psychological Association (2010), Australian Psychological Society (2007), Bulgarian Psychological Society (2005), Canadian Psychological Association (2000), Chinese Psychological Society (2007), Code of Ethics Review Group (New Zealand, 2002), German Psychological Society and Association of German Professional Psychologists (1999), and the Irish Association for Counselling and Psychotherapy (2005). Each of their documents recognizes that engaging in multiple roles with supervisees presents potential problems – conflicts of interest that may compromise the objectivity of the supervisor and exploit the supervisee.

The British Psychological Society's *Code of Ethics and Conduct* (2009) identifies eight areas of psychological practice creating ethical concerns. Multiple relationships and personal relationships are the first two: "Psychologists should . . . remain aware of the problems that may result from dual or multiple relationships, for example, supervising trainees to whom they are married, teaching students with whom they already have familial relationship" (p. 22).

The *Code of Ethics* of the American Association for Marriage and Family Therapy (2012) includes one of the most contemporary and perhaps clearest statements:

> 4.1 Exploitation. Marriage and family therapists who are in a supervisory role are aware of their influential positions with respect to students and supervisees, and they avoid exploiting the trust and dependency of such persons. Therapists, therefore, make every effort to avoid conditions and multiple relationships that could impair professional objectivity or increase the risk of exploitation. When the risk of impairment or exploitation exists due to conditions or multiple roles, therapists take appropriate precautions.

Another acknowledgment of the power differential appears in the Hong Kong Psychological Society's (1998)*Code of Professional Conduct*, addressing the protection of student privacy. The code states that association members

> who are providing supervision or training should not require or coerce supervisees or trainees to disclose personal information either directly or in the context of any training procedure. They should respect the right of a trainee to retain reasonable personal privacy. (p. 5)

Similarly, Germany's supervising psychologists are cautioned not to "either directly or indirectly require trainees to reveal personal information" (German Psychological Society and Association of German Professional Psychologists, 1999, p. 12).

The Code of Ethics for Psychologists Working in Aotearoa/New Zealand (2002) defines "work relationships" as including students and supervisees, and: "Psychologists do not exploit any work relationship to further their own personal or business interests" (p. 14). The Bulgarian Psychological Society *Ethical Code* (2005) states, "Inequity in regard of knowledge, influence, and power always affects the professional relationships of the psychologists with their clients and colleagues" (2005, p. 3).

The *Ethics Code of [the] Iranian Organization of Psychology and Counseling* (Iranian Psychological Association/Psychology and Counseling Organization of the Islamic Republic of Iran, n.d.) prohibits "making any kind of unprofessional relationship with . . . employees who work under their supervision" (p. 3). The section on education, training, and supervision elucidates the admonition, cautioning against taking advantage of professional relationships as well as against assuming a professional role "when there are conflicts between personal benefits and professional roles" (p. 3).

Other contemporary sources recognize the vulnerability of supervisees. The Colegio Oficial de Psicologos (Spain), the Australian Psychological Society (2007), and the German Psychological Society and Association of German Professional Psychologists (1999), for example, acknowledge the limited power of supervisees and elucidate commensurate responsibilities of supervisors and trainers. According to the

College of Psychologists of Ontario (2004): "The supervisory relationship is neither social nor egalitarian. Its evaluative and educative nature makes it hierarchical, thereby placing responsibility on supervisors to be cognizant of the inherent power differential that exists between them and their supervisees" (2009, p. 4). The Chinese Psychological Society (2007) prohibits counseling with supervisees, conducting sexual or romantic relationships, and supervising relatives or others with whom the supervisor has intimate relationships.

The British Psychological Society (Code of Ethics Review Group, 2009) goes a step further, recognizing that the power inherent in professional, including supervisory, relationships may persist beyond the conclusion of supervision and so instructs psychologists to recognize the continuing potential for abuse of this power. Accordingly, "Psychologists should (v) recognise that conflicts of interests and inequity of power may still reside after professional relationships are formally terminated, such that professional responsibilities may still apply" (p. 22).

International organizations have taken similar stands against the exploitation of supervisory relationships. The *Code of Ethics* of the International Academy of Behavioral Medicine, Counseling, and Psychotherapy, for example, states that academy diplomates "do not engage in any type of exploitation, either financially, emotionally, sexually or in any other way of clients, students, trainees, supervisees, colleagues, employees or any other individuals" (n.d., p. 3).

Obviously, supervisors must recognize their influence over supervisees and the trust placed in them by supervisees and the profession. Supervisees are not in a position to freely give or withhold consent to engage in behaviors with which they are uncomfortable. They may not realize what is and is not appropriate behavior for their supervisors. Challenging their supervisors may risk their careers. Therefore, supervisors must ensure that they consider carefully any request for a favor or for nonrequired participation in any professional activity (for example, co-presenting a workshop, co-authoring an article, or conducting a research project). In all of their interactions with supervisees, supervisors must be mindful of the power differential, the importance of establishing and maintaining professional boundaries, and their responsibility to serve as role models for ethical behavior.

That said, complete avoidance of all other connections with supervisees is not only difficult but also undesirable. F. Kaslow (2005) suggests that rather than establishing strict prohibition, ethics committees and professional associations "strongly recommend these (multiple relationships) be avoided where possible and handled cautiously and judiciously when inevitable" (p. 38). For example, supervisees sometimes are invited to work on research projects, co-present at professional conferences, or collaborate in writing articles with their supervisors. Such efforts provide valuable opportunities for mentoring.

After the supervisory relationship has ended, supervisees often become the colleagues of their former supervisors. Particularly in small communities, some supervisees may even work in the same settings (Schank & Skovholt, 2006). Although this is not necessarily problematic, supervisors must remember that supervisees may remain in positions of diminished consent.

Although the supervisory relationship is by nature one of unequal power, this power differential may be magnified – unfairly and unnecessarily – by the particular characteristics of supervisors and supervisees, and thus become a tool of exploitation, discrimination, or oppression. Any factor that affords one individual greater power, prestige, and privilege in a cultural context may exacerbate or diminish the power differential and decrease the relationship safety necessary for effective supervision (Hernãndez & McDowell, 2010). Race, ethnicity, gender, sexual orientation, social class, religion, age, relationship status, political affiliation, and physical ability/disability are examples.

The ways in which such factors can negatively impact supervision are illustrated by US researchers who have demonstrated that culturally diverse supervisees often enter into supervisory relationships feeling vulnerable relative to supervisors of the majority culture. Williams and Halgin (1995) reported that African-American supervisees commonly evade discussions of racial differences with Euro-American supervisors. Subjects reported insensitivity in supervisors as evidenced in their failure to recognize that their power relative to supervisees was enhanced by race. Allen, Szollos, and Williams (1986) and McRoy, Freeman, Logan, and Blackmon (1986) have reported similar findings.

Supervisees are encouraged to assume that their supervisors' decisions, requests, and recommendations are made in the supervisees' and clients' best interests and not motivated by their supervisors' personal or professional needs. The consensus for prevention of such exploitation is evident in the coverage of these issues.

In summary, regulatory bodies and professional associations in many countries have recognized the power differential inherent in supervisory relationships and addressed the maintenance of clear boundaries. Most caution supervisors against or specifically prohibit them from engaging in activities that may compromise their objectivity and effectiveness in the performance of supervisory duties. Further, supervisors are prohibited from exploiting supervisees – sexually, emotionally, or financially. Professional associations that directly address the issue of multiple relationships in supervision (for example, the American Psychological Association, 2010; British Psychological Society, 2009) typically prohibit sexual relationships with current students and supervisees. Further, these documents caution against the misuse of supervisory authority to further the supervisor's personal, political, financial, or social interests or advantage, and they discourage or prohibit providing mental health treatment to supervisees (e.g., the American Association for Marriage and Family Therapy, 2012; American Counseling Association, 2005; American Psychological Association, 2010; Association of State and Provincial Psychology Boards, 2005; German Psychological Society and Association of German Professional Psychologists, 1999).

The benefits of employing such caution extend not only to supervisees but also to their current and future clients. When supervisors model ethical behavior, they underscore the fundamental ethical principles on which the profession has been built (Handelsman, Gottlieb, & Knapp, 2005; Thomas, 2010).

Informed Consent to Supervision

Informed consent has been considered essential to establishing a foundation for a psychotherapeutic relationship (Haas & Malouf, 2005). Psychologists, counselors, and other mental health professionals attempt to identify and describe to prospective clients the potential benefits and risks of, and alternatives to, the proposed treatment, as well as inform them about their fees, qualifications, and the records that will be maintained. Further, they elucidate the limits to confidentiality, the procedures and methods, and other factors that bear on their decisions about engaging in treatment (Knapp & VandeCreek, 2006; Nagy, 2010).

The ethics codes of nearly every mental health profession address this issue. Examples include the ethics codes from the United Kingdom (Ethics Committee of the British Psychological Society, 2009), Hong Kong (Hong Kong Psychological Society, 1998), Canada (Canadian Psychological Association, 2000), China (Chinese Psychological Society, 2007), Bulgaria (Bulgarian Psychological Society, 2005), Aotearoa/New Zealand (Code of Ethics Review Group, 2002), Japan (International Mental Health Professionals Japan, 2008), Spain (Governing Committee of the Official College of Psychologists, 1993), and the United States (American Association for Marriage and Family Therapy, 2012; American Psychological Association, 2010; American Counseling Association, 2005). Further, informed consent is not a one-time event but a continuing strategy for keeping consumers apprised of their rights, the professional's responsibilities, and all the parameters that affect them through the process.

Obtaining informed consent in the context of clinical supervision is a more contemporary notion. Ethics codes are increasingly likely to include provisions to protect the rights and welfare of supervisees beyond their general emphasis on protections for clients. Providing supervisees with the information they need to make decisions about their participation in supervision conforms to many ethics codes and helps lay the foundation for positive supervisory relationships (American Counseling Association, 2005; Canadian Psychological Association Committee on Ethics, 2009; Cobia & Boes, 2000), mitigates the risk of misunderstanding and consequent substandard service to clients (Thomas, 2007, 2010), and offers an appropriate role model for supervisees (Cobia & Pipes, 2002). In addition, informed consent serves the interests of supervisees' clients in outlining a clear process for oversight of supervisee work. Informed consent may be conceptualized on two levels. First, supervisees must obtain the informed consent of their clients, and supervisors are responsible to ensure that this occurs. Second, supervisors must obtain the informed consent of their supervisees to participate in supervision.

Supervisees obtaining the informed consent of clients

Supervisors are ethically responsible for ensuring that supervisees are aware of and conform to professional ethical standards in working with clients (Thomas, 2010). Many ethics codes require supervisees to obtain the informed consent of their clients regarding the issues described above, and supervisors must train them in methods for doing so (American Association for Marriage and Family Therapy, 2012, American Psychological Association, 2010; Canadian Psychological Association, 2000; National Association of Social Workers, 2008). In addition to outlining parameters of treatment, they must inform clients about aspects of their psychotherapist's supervision that will directly affect them.

First, the video or audio recording of client sessions is a commonly used technique in training psychotherapists. Many ethics codes require the informed consent of clients for recording of sessions (American Counseling Association, 2005; American Psychological Association, 2010). Like other professional associations, the International Academy of Behavioral Medicine, Counseling and Psychotherapy, Inc (n.d.) in its *Code of Ethics* requires that "diplomates always obtain written informed consent from clients prior to video recording, audio taping or permitting third-party observation" (p. 4) of psychotherapy sessions.

The second issue involves the requirement that supervisees-in-training inform clients of their status as trainees. Some codes require that clients be provided with the name of the supervisor overseeing their treatment (American Psychological Association, 2010). Supervisors must ensure that supervisees obtain the informed consent of their clients.

Obtaining the informed consent of supervisees

Commitment to instituting clear expectations and clarifying the rights and responsibilities of supervisees and students is required in many ethics codes and reflected in the professional literature. The Hong Kong Psychological Society's *Code of Professional Conduct* (1998), for example, requires members to obtain the informed consent of students, including supervisees in training. Prospective students must be given accurate information about what will be expected of them and how they might benefit. Members of the Hong Kong Psychological Society must ensure that students' informed consent is obtained for participation in educational programs.

The Chinese Psychological Society offers one of the more comprehensive requirements regarding informed consent with supervisees in its *Code of Ethics for Counseling and Clinical Practice* (2007). This code requires supervisors to explain to supervisees the purpose and process of supervision, along with the methods and criteria that will be used to evaluate them. In addition to addressing evaluation methods and criteria, this association requires supervisors to advise supervisees about how to manage emergency situations and about how to proceed in case of interruption or termination of the supervisory relationship (Chinese Psychological Society, 2007).

The *Ethics Code of [the] Iranian Organization of Psychology and Counseling* (n.d.) requires teachers and supervisors to obtain the informed consent of the supervisees, specifically:"Psychologists and counselors should make students, trainees, and interns aware of the title, content, and process of the educational programs" (p. 5).

Supervisees benefit from receiving information about supervisory methods, their responsibilities relative to supervision, the supervisor's responsibilities, and about confidentiality policies pertaining to supervisees and clients (Thomas, 2007, 2010). Supervision must be documented (Falvey, 2002; Falvey, Caldwell, & Cohen, 2002; Luepker, 2012), and supervisees must be informed about the records that they are expected to maintain and about those that their supervisors will maintain. Evaluation criteria, interruption or termination of supervision, and ethical obligations are other elements to consider.

Each work setting reflects the culture in which it exists, so supervisors must modify the list of responsibilities to fit specific needs and ensure relevance. Whatever issues are deemed appropriate for inclusion should be addressed at least orally, if not in writing, to mitigate potential for misunderstanding (Thomas, 2010).

Competence in Supervisors and Supervisees

Establishing and maintaining competence is an essential element of ethical practice for all mental health professionals, and its import is reflected in the ethical principles, standards, and guidelines of virtually every country. Ethics codes around the world refer to supervision and consultation as critical components of establishing and maintaining professional competence and ethical practice (for example, American Psychological Association, 2010; Australian Psychological Society, 2007; Canadian Psychological Association, 2000; Chinese Psychological Society, 2007; Ethics Committee of the British Psychological Society, 2009; International Federation of Social Workers, 2012). The professional literature has increasingly focused on competency in providing counseling and psychological services (DeMers, Van Horne, & Rodolfa, 2008; Roberts, Borden, Christainsen, & Lopez, 2005). The American Psychological Association has published *Competency Benchmarks in Professional Psychology*, a document delineating essential components of competency at various levels of professional development (Fouad et al., 2009). More recently, N. J. Kaslow, Falender, and Grus (2012) have called for a "culture of competence" (p. 47) in the practice of psychology.

The need for competency-based supervision has been specifically recognized and addressed (Falender & Shafranske, 2004, 2007, 2008; N. J. Kaslow & Bell, 2008). In fact, in Ireland and the United Kingdom, "supervision is considered a career-long requirement for accredited counsellors and psychotherapists. It is recommended as best practice for clinical and counseling psychologists" (M. Creaner, personal communication, September 13, 2012). Competence in supervision is clearly valued.

Delegation of Responsibilities

Supervisors have an ethical and, in some cases, a legal responsibility to ensure that their supervisees are capable of providing the services assigned to them with the degree of supervision available (Bernard & Goodyear, 2014; Saccuzzo, 2002; Welfel, 2013). For example, the needs of a client with a serious mental illness who is suicidal and experiencing acute psychotic symptoms will strain, if not overwhelm, the skill set of a novice clinician, particularly when only minimal supervision is available. Conversely, the supervisor serving as the primary treating psychotherapist, with the supervisee playing a secondary role in managing such a case, may provide valuable learning without compromising client welfare. When case assignment reflects an appropriate match between the client's needs and the supervisee's skills, the best interests of both are served.

Ethical competency

Ensuring that supervisees understand their obligations and practice ethically is another responsibility of supervisors. Various professional associations and regulatory bodies have emphasized supervisor responsibility for inculcating supervisees with knowledge of professional ethics. The German Psychological Society and Association of German Professional Psychologists (1999) provide an example: "Psychologists who supervise the post graduate, practical activities of trainees or junior colleagues must ensure that such persons are familiar with, and monitor their compliance with, these ethical principles" (p. 8). The British *Code of Ethics and Conduct* states, "Psychologists should . . . seek to remain aware of the scientific and professional activities of others with whom they work, with particular attention to the ethical behavior of employees, assistants, supervisees, and students" (Ethics Committee of the British Psychological Society, 2009, p. 18). The *Code of Ethics for Psychologists Working in Aotearoa/New Zealand*states, "Psychologists should bring the Code to the attention of those they teach, supervise, and/or employ" (2002, p. 3).

Most novice supervisees begin clinical work having completed at least one graduate ethics course, but academic understanding of applicable codes, practice guidelines, and legal requirements is no substitute for experience as to how these directives apply in actual relationships with clients. This critical component of learning is actualized, in large measure, in the context of supervision. An important aspect of the supervisor's role then, is to observe supervisees' work, highlight ethical issues when they arise, and teach supervisees how to effect these principles and standards.

Supervisors' clinical competence

Supervisors must ensure that they themselves are competent in clinical supervision and in all of the areas of practice engaged in by their supervisees. To competently oversee the work of a subordinate, supervisors must have the training, education, and supervised experience necessary to establish competence in associated areas of practice.

Sometimes supervisees will want to develop skills in areas in which their supervisors are not adequately skilled. The Australian Psychological Society's *Guidelines on Supervision* (2003) offers guidance for supervisors who would like to accommodate the professional development needs of their supervisees but do not feel adequately prepared. If resources permit, a secondary supervisor may meet with the supervisee for the oversight of a specified portion of the individual's work. Administering and interpreting psychological tests, providing hypnosis, and working with a client with a particular cultural background are examples of the work that might be supervised by a second supervisor. The College of Psychologists of Ontario's *Supervision Resources Manual* (2009) highlights the advantages of a second supervisor and offers direction: "In most instances, primary and alternate supervisors will bring different skills, styles, and knowledge to the supervisor experience. In an effort to maximize the supervisees' learning, the focus of supervision in each of these two contexts should be coordinated" (p. 12).

Supervisor's multicultural competence

Supervisors must establish and maintain multicultural competence in their own clinical work, in their supervision of clinicians from various cultures, and in developing multicultural competence in their supervisees. This dimension of competence is reflected in most codes of ethics and supervision specialty guidelines, as it should be.

Yet the existence of such rules and recommendations is not enough to obviate problems resulting from culturally uninformed supervision. The professional literature, at least in the United States, is replete with studies revealing the negative experiences of ethnically and culturally diverse supervisees in their relationships with majority-culture supervisors (Hernãndez & McDowell, 2010; Lo, 2010; Murphy-Shigematsu, 2010). When supervisors are members of the majority culture, they may be oblivious to their unearned privilege and to their enhanced power relative to supervisees. When the implications of such privilege, along with those associated with other cultural variables, are acknowledged and effectively addressed throughout the course of supervision, multicultural competence will be enhanced, and supervisees will learn to address these issues in their clinical work (Constantine, 2001). Further, supervisors' attention to cultural variables results in greater supervisee satisfaction, better working alliances, and increased supervisor credibility (Ancis & Marshall, 2010; Inman, 2006; Toporek, Ortega-Villalobos, & Pope-Davis, 2004).

Another impediment to culturally competent supervision occurs when foreign models, often Western, are imported and implemented without consideration of their cross-cultural relevance or applicability (Ayyash-Abdo, Alamuddin, & Mukallid, 2010). Zebian, Alamuddin, Maalouf, and Chatila (2007) have observed the well-documented detrimental effects of reliance on Western assessment tools, professional training, and models in services provided by psychologists in Lebanon and other Arab countries (2007). Nelson et al. (2006) contend that the supervisory relationship is inherently Eurocentric and, therefore, fundamentally limited in regard to multicultural competence.

Supervisors must understand their own cultural backgrounds as well as the cultural contexts of their supervisees and supervisees' clients (Pack-Brown & Williams, 2003). Such understanding is reflected in most ethics codes and guidelines related to supervision. The American Counseling Association's *Code of Ethics* (2005) states, "Counseling supervisors are aware of and address the role of multiculturalism/diversity in the supervisory relationship" (p. 14). New Zealand's *Guidelines on Supervision* is among the most specific in articulating of this critical element of ethical supervision:

> Within the practice of psychology cultural safety demands of the psychologist a high degree of awareness of one's own culture, the cultural bias inherent in some psychological practice, as well as the cultural identity of the recipient of the psychological service offered. (New Zealand Psychologists Board, 2010, p. 2)

Hernãndez and McDowell (2010) have analyzed privilege and oppression in supervision and in the supervision of psychotherapy provided by tra inees. Using what they call a "critical postcolonial perspective" (p. 29), they examined intersectionality, power, and relationship safety in supervision, and illustrated how supervision has been used to "reproduce the status quo of inequities generated and maintained by the cultural and social capital of dominant groups" (p. 29). To guard against this risk, supervisors must recognize historical oppression and:

> be accountable for legacies of privilege within the local and global contexts. . . . Demonstrating critical social awareness and cultural humility allows supervisors and clinicians

> to build the trust and safety necessary to encourage growth across cultural and societal differences. (p. 29)

One strategy for increasing awareness of privilege is for supervisors or supervisees to consider and use any discrimination experienced by themselves to increase insight and openness to their own privilege (Hernāndez & Rankin, 2008). Cultivating a safe environment in which such factors may be acknowledged and addressed, as is culturally appropriate, may not only strengthen the supervisory relationship but also offer a model for supervisees to consider in their relationships with clients (Estrada, Frame, & Williams, 2004).

Although directly addressing such factors in supervision is commonly advocated, particularly in Western literature, *how* these factors are addressed varies with culture. In Chinese culture, for example, candid discussion of the dynamics of a supervisory relationship could cause one or both members of the supervisory dyad to "lose face," making such open communications impractical. Tsui, Ho, and Lam (2005) interviewed 40 Chinese social work supervisors and supervisees in Hong Kong, concluding that "supervisors . . . have the dominant power in decision-making" (p. 57). Supervisors preferred reaching consensus about decisions, yet the consensus did not always reflect agreement by the supervisees, who rarely objected to their supervisors' decisions directly. Rather, the authors report, "the supervisor passively acquires the consent of the staff" and will commonly "use consultation to incorporate the staff's ideas and to manipulate the decision-making process" (p. 58). According to Tsui et al., from the supervisee viewpoint " 'consensus' is only a political gesture on the part of the supervisor, so they dare not speak candidly in the consultation process" (p. 59). Consistent with Chinese culture, Tsui et al. indicated that such consensus "maintains the harmony between the supervisor and the supervisee in the power hierarchy" (p. 60). Despite the prevalence of these attitudes and practices, the authors recommended that supervisory competence rather than "culturally ascribed authority" (p. 62) be the foundation for power. Nevertheless, the Chinese supervisors wielded significant power over their supervisees.

Cultural self-awareness is important for every supervisor, regardless of race, ethnicity, sexual orientation, gender, social class, religion, physical condition, or other aspects of identity. No one is immune from bias that may compromise the safety of supervisees and the efficacy of supervision (Murphy-Shigematsu, 2010). Supervisees and even supervisors hold idealized notions of conflict-free, gratifying supervisory relationships when both members of the dyad share aspects of their identities. Yet the potential for relational challenges remains. Field, Chavez-Korell, and Domenech Rodríguez (2010) have described such challenges in Latina–Latina supervisory dyads, observing that the "desire for same-ethnic support that can lead to idealization and then unmet expectations, overidentification, difficulties negotiating boundaries, and cultural misunderstandings based on assumed similarities despite much within group variance" (p. 47). Such dynamics may characterize other supervisory dyads that include individuals of the same ethnicity, particularly when they are not members of the majority culture.

Self-awareness is particularly critical when the supervisor is a member of the majority culture. Such membership allows its beneficiaries to remain oblivious to their unearned privilege enjoyed at the expense of others. Inequities not recognized and addressed may be amplified in a supervisory context. Supervisory self-assessment is thus essential in developing the multicultural awareness necessary for competent, effective supervision and practice. Supervisors should model such assessment and teach it to supervisees (Pack-Brown & Williams, 2003). Helms and Cook (1999) have developed an instrument for assessing racial identity development, useful for self-assessment or as a vehicle for discussion with supervisees about multicultural issues in psychotherapy.

The New Zealand Psychologists Board promulgates the relatively comprehensive *Guidelines on Supervision* (2010). Its introduction emphasizes the importance of multicultural competence to effective, ethical supervision:

> Competence includes being culturally competent. Within the practice of psychology cultural safety demands of the psychologist a high degree of awareness of one's own culture, the cultural bias inherent in some psychological practice, as well as the cultural identity of the recipient of the psychological service offered. Although the Board is committed to ensuring that the training and practice of psychologists in New Zealand reflects paradigms and world views of both partners to the Treaty of Waitangi, the main body of knowledge within the psychology discipline is derived from Euro-American traditions. Furthermore the population of New Zealand is becoming increasingly multicultural. Attention to the cultural dimensions of professional practice is an important part of supervision. (p. 2)

Culturally competent supervision requires that supervisors consider the race, ethnicity, and cultural background of each party in the supervisory triad in case assignment. Exposure to members of other racial and ethnic groups during clinical supervision has been shown to have "a positive influence on the reduction of negative attitudes toward members of culturally different groups and thus . . . on the development of multicultural counseling competencies" (Diaz-Lazaro & Cohen, 2001, p. 44). Yet the identity and needs of the client are of primary importance (Bernard & Goodyear, 2014).

Supervisors must be cautious in their assumptions about supervisee competence based on ethnic identity. Assuming that a Spanish-speaking supervisee is clinically competent to work with any Spanish-speaking client, for example, is a generalization with potentially negative implications for supervisee and client. And identity-based supervisor bias is ethically problematic. The American Psychological Association prohibits psychologists from "unfair discrimination based on age, gender, gender identity, race, ethnicity, culture, national origin, religion, sexual orientation, disability, socioeconomic status, or any basis proscribed by law" (2010, p. 5).

Sue et al. (1998) described three components of cross-cultural competency skills: dynamic sizing (knowing when to attribute a particular behavior to culture and when to attribute it to individual or family differences within a culture); scientific mindedness (ability to form hypotheses and avoid drawing premature conclusions about a person based on culture), and culture-specific expertise (ability to obtain and appropriately use information about clients' cultures and subcultures). Such skills apply to working with clients from other countries who are dealing with the challenges of resettlement and adaptation to a new culture. Although the focus of this work was psychotherapy, the skills described are applicable to supervisors working cross-culturally with supervisees. Further, these skills are useful in training and evaluating supervisees' multicultural counseling skills (A. Northwood, personal communication, December 6, 2011).

The American Psychological Association's ethical standards have addressed "Boundaries of Competence" as related to diversity:

> Where scientific or professional knowledge in the discipline of psychology establishes that an understanding of age, gender, race, ethnicity, culture, national origin, religion, sexual orientation, disability, language, or socio-economic status is essential for effective implementation of services or research, psychologists have or obtain the training, experience, consultation, or supervision necessary to ensure the competence of their services, or they make appropriate referrals. (2010, p. 5)

Although many ethics codes stress the importance of multicultural competence in providing clinical and supervisory services, Aotearoa/New Zealand has addressed these issues in the context of nearly every section of its *Code of Ethics* (2002). In its section on "Vulnerability," the code recommends that psychologists understand the factors contributing to the vulnerability of certain individuals, groups, and communities. Further, "psychologists recognize that vulnerability is increased by unfamiliar cultural setting, unfamiliar clinical settings, unfamiliar language, overwhelming numbers of staff, and/or lack of advocate support" (p. 11). As discussed, there is a power imbalance in any supervisory relationship, and these additional factors only serve to enhance this vulnerability.

Native populations around the world

Indigenous peoples around the globe have long-standing traditions of helping one another and of training others to provide services. According to Senyonyi, Ochieng, and Sells, traditional cultures in Uganda

> upheld their legacies and passed on what was important through the nuclear family, extended families, and the community. These, in turn, were expected to meet the needs of guidance and support of members at fundamental life events, such as pregnancy, birth, adolescence, marriage, and death. The parents, aunts, uncles, grandparents, elders, and members of the community had clear roles and responsibilities for the wellbeing of the community. (Senyonyi et al., 2012, p. 500)

Although the international ethics codes do not specifically address the rights of indigenous peoples, the International Federation of Social Workers code (2004) includes a list of related documents on which the code is based. Among them is the *Indigenous and Tribal Peoples Convention, International Labour Organization 169*, ratified by 20 countries. *The United Nations Declaration on the Rights of Indigenous Peoples* might be used to develop ethical standards acknowledging the historical injustices of colonization and the legacy of intergenerational trauma. Particularly when supervisors are members of the dominant culture, the risk of perpetuating such historical inequities against indigenous supervisees and clients prevails (Hernāndez & McDowell, 2010). These include individuals who themselves or whose ancestors have survived cultural genocide, the Jewish Holocaust, slavery, or Apartheid, or who otherwise bring to psychotherapy and supervision what Duran (2006) has termed the *soul wound*. Duran and Duran (1995) have asserted:

> We should not be tolerant of the neocolonialism that runs unchecked through our knowledge-generating systems. We must ensure that the dissemination of thought through journals, media, and other avenues have "gatekeepers" who understand the effects of colonialism and are committed to fighting any perceived act of hegemony on our communities. Postcolonial thinkers should be placed in the positions that act as gatekeepers of knowledge in order to insure that western European thought be kept in its appropriate place. (p. 7)

Supervision might readily be conceptualized as one of those "knowledge-generating systems" (Duran & Duran, 1995, p. 7) responsible for perpetuating inequities. At its best, however, it functions as one of the "gatekeepers of knowledge" that may interrupt the long-standing practice of oppression in societies and in the mental health professions.

Future Directions

As globalization occurs, opportunities to share supervisory research and experience increase. The availability for cross-cultural supervision also increases, and thus the need for understanding other cultures is more important than ever. As those in the mental health professions learn from one another, they deepen their appreciation of ethical supervision.

Numerous ethical issues beyond the scope of this chapter will require attention. For example, supervisors must anticipate the ethical issues likely to arise as technology allows the practice of supervision and psychotherapy from remote locations. Theoretically, a supervisor in one country could provide supervision to a clinician in another country, who is providing psychotherapy to a client in a third country. The potential use of global technologies for cross-cultural supervision is exciting, as is the potential for mutual learning. But it also presents the possibility of harm, not the least of which might be the loss of unique healing traditions. Mental health professionals must be mindful of these risks and benefits as they continue to explore these new possibilities.

Another challenge involves the potential for conflict between national public policy and mental health ethics codes. Not all countries have protections for human rights embedded in their laws. In fact, some governments are systematically persecuting identified groups in their citizenry. There exists a potentially complicit role for mental health professionals in implementing discriminatory policies in the context of supervisory relationships. Conversely, there may be a risk to these individuals when they challenge such practices. Future ethics codes, guidelines, and regulations for supervisors should take into account these factors.

The ethical dimensions of supervision across nations and cultures are vast and multifaceted. This chapter is not intended to be a comprehensive treatment of the subject but rather, a beginning. The intersection of ethics with supervision represents a critical aspect of the foundation of clinical practice.

References

Allen, G. J., Szollos, S. J., & Williams, B. E. (1986). Doctoral students' comparative evaluations of best and worst psychotherapy supervision. *Professional Psychology, Research and Practice, 17*, 91–99.

American Association for Marriage and Family Therapy. (2007). *Approved supervisor designations standards and responsibilities handbook*. Alexandria, VA: Author.

American Association for Marriage and Family Therapy. (2012). *AAMFT code of ethics*. Alexandria, VA: Author.

American Board of Examiners in Clinical Social Work. (2004). *Clinical supervision: A practice specialty of clinical social work*. Salem, MA: Author.

American Counseling Association. (2005). *ACA code of ethics*. Alexandria, VA: Author.

American Psychological Association. (2010). *Ethical principles of psychologists and code of conduct*. Washington, DC: Author.

Ancis, J. R., & Marshall, D. S. (2010). Using a multicultural framework to assess supervisees' perceptions of culturally competent supervision. *Journal of Counseling & Development, 88*, 277–284.

Association of State and Provincial Psychology Boards. (2003). *Supervision guidelines*. Montgomery, AL: Author.

Association of State and Provincial Psychology Boards. (2005). *ASPPB code of conduct*. Peachtree City, GA: Author.

Australian Psychological Society. (2003). *Guidelines on supervision*. Victoria, Australia: Author.

Australian Psychological Society. (2007). *Code of ethics*. Victoria, Australia: Author.

Ayyash-Abdo, H., Alamuddin, R., & Mukallid, S. (2010). School counseling in Lebanon: Past, present, and future. *Journal of Counseling and Development, 88*, 13–17.

Bernard, J. M., & Goodyear, R. K. (2014). *Fundamentals of clinical supervision* (5th ed.). Boston, MA: Pearson.

Bodhi, B. (Ed.). (2005). *In the Buddha's words*. Boston, MA: Wisdom.

Bulgarian Psychological Society. (2005). *Ethical code*. Sofia, Bulgaria: Author.

Canadian Psychological Association. (2000). *Canadian code of ethics for psychologists* (3rd ed.). Ottawa, Canada: Author.

Canadian Psychological Association Committee on Ethics. (2009). *Ethical guidelines for supervision in psychology: Teaching, research, practice, and administration*. Ottawa, Canada: Author.

Carroll, M. (2006). Key issues in coaching psychology supervision. *The Coaching Psychologist*. The British Psychological Society, *2*, 4–8.

Chinese Psychological Society. (2007). *Code of ethics for counseling and clinical practice*. Beijing, China: Author.

Cobia, D. C., & Boes, S. R. (2000). Professional disclosure statements and formal plans for supervision: Two strategies for minimizing the risk of ethical conflicts in post master's supervision. *Journal of Counseling and Development, 78*, 293–296.

Cobia, D. C., & Pipes, R. (2002). Mandates supervision: An intervention for disciplines professionals. *Journal of Counseling and Development, 80*, 140–144.

Code of Ethics Review Group. (2002). *Code of ethics for psychologists working in Aotearoa/New Zealand*. Wellington, New Zealand: New Zealand Psychological Society, New Zealand College of Clinical Psychologists, New Zealand Psychologists Board.

College of Psychologists of Ontario. (2009). *Supervision resource manual for assistance to both supervisors and supervised members*. Toronto, Canada: Author.

Constantine, M. G. (2001). Multiculturally-focused counseling supervision: Its relativity to trainees' multicultural counseling self-efficacy. *The Clinical Supervisor, 20*, 87–96.

Currie, C. L., Kuzmina, M. V., & Nadyuk, R. I. (2012). The counseling profession in Russia: Historical roots, current trends, and future perspectives. *Journal of Counseling & Development, 90*, 488–493.

David, D., Moore, M., & Domuta, A. (2002). Romanian psychology on the international psychological scene: A preliminary critical and empirical appraisal. *European Psychologist, 7*, 153–160.

DeMers, S. T., Van Horne, B. A., & Rodolfa, E. R. (2008). Changes in training and practice of psychologists: Current challenges for licensing boards. *Professional Psychology, Research and Practice, 39*, 473–497.

Diaz-Lazaro, C. M., & Cohen, B. B. (2001). Cross-cultural contact in counselor training. *Journal of Multicultural Counseling and Development, 29*, 41–56.

Duran, E. (2006). *Healing the soul wound: Counseling with American Indians and other native peoples.* New York, NY: Teachers College Press.

Duran, E., & Duran, B. (1995). *Native American postcolonial psychology.* Albany, NY: University of New York Press.

Estrada, D., Frame, M. W., & Williams, C. B. (2004). Cross-cultural supervision: Guiding the conversation toward race and ethnicity. *Journal of Multicultural Counseling and Development, 32*, 307–319.

Ethics Committee of the British Psychological Society. (2009). *Code of ethics and conduct.* Leicester, England: British Psychological Society.

Falender, C. A., & Shafranske, E. P. (2004). *Clinical supervision: A competency-based approach.* Washington, DC: American Psychological Association.

Falender, C. A., & Shafranske, E. P. (2007). Competence in competency-based supervision practice: Construct and application. *Professional Psychology, Research and Practice, 38*, 232–240.

Falender, C. A., & Shafranske, E. P. (2008). *Casebook for clinical supervision: A competency-based approach.* Washington, DC: American Psychological Association.

Falvey, J. E. (2002). *Managing clinical supervision: Ethical practice and legal risk management.* Pacific Grove, CA: Brooks/Cole.

Falvey, J. E., Caldwell, C. F., & Cohen, C. R. (2002). *Documentation in supervision: The focused risk management supervision system.* Pacific Grove, CA: Brooks/Cole.

Field, L. D., Chavez-Korell, S., & Domenech Rodríguez, M. M. (2010). No hay rosas sin espinas: Conceptualizing Latina-Latina supervision from a multicultural developmental supervisory model. *Training and Education in Professional Psychology, 4*, 47–54.

Foreman, N. (1996). Psychology in Romania: Ilona Görög. *The Psychologist, 9*, 125–126.

Fouad, N. A., Grus, C. L., Hatcher, R. L., Kaslow, N. J., Hutchings, P. S., Madson, M., . . . Crossman, R. E. (2009). Competency benchmarks: A model for the understanding and measuring of competence in professional psychology across training levels. *Training and Education in Professional Psychology, 3*, S5–S26.

French, J. R. P., Jr., & Raven, B. (1959). Bases of social power. In D. Cartwright (Ed.), *Studies in social power* (pp. 17–43), Ann Arbor, MI: University of Michigan.

Gauthier, J. (2008, October). The universal declaration of ethical principles for psychologists presented at the United Nations DPI/NGO conference in Paris.*Psychology International Newsletter*, 1.

German Psychological Society and Association of German Professional Psychologists. (1999). *Ethical principles of the German Psychological Society and code of conduct of the German Professional Psychologists.* Berlin, Germany: Author.

Gottlieb, M. C., Robinson, K., & Younggren, J. N. (2007). Multiple relations in supervision: Guidance for administrators, supervisors, and students. *Professional Psychology, Research and Practice, 38*, 241–247.

Governing Committee of the Official College of Psychologists. (1993). *Code of ethics for the psychologist.* Madrid, Spain: Colegio Oficial de Psicologos.

Gutheil, T. G., & Simon, R. I. (2002). Non-sexual boundary crossings and boundary violations: The ethical dimension. *Psychiatric Clinics of North America, 25*, 585–592.

Haas, L. J., & Malouf, J. L. (2005). *Keeping up the good work: A practitioner's guide to mental health ethics* (4th ed.). Sarasota, FL: Professional Resource Exchange.

Handelsman, M. M., Gottlieb, M. C., & Knapp, S. C. (2005). Training ethical psychologists: An acculturation model. *Professional Psychology, Research and Practice, 36*, 59–65.

Hawkins, P., & Shohet, R. (2006). *Supervision in the helping professions* (3rd ed.). Berkshire, England: Open University Press.

Helms, J. E., & Cook, D. A. (1999). *Using race and culture in counseling and psychotherapy: Theory and process.* Needham Heights, MA: Allyn & Bacon.

Hernāndez, P., & McDowell, T. (2010). Intersectionality, power, and relational safety in context: Key concepts in clinical supervision. *Training and Education in Professional Psychology, 4*, 29–35.

Hernāndez, P., & Rankin, P. (2008). Relational safety in supervision. *Journal of Marital and Family Therapy, 34*, 58–74.

Hong Kong Psychological Society. (1998). *Code of professional conduct.* Hong Kong, China: Author.

Iliescu, D., Ispas, A., & Ilie, A. (2007). Psychology in Romania. *The Psychologist, 20*, 34–35.

Inman, A. (2006). Supervisor multicultural competence and its relation to supervisory process and outcome. *Journal of Marital and Family Therapy, 32*, 73–85.

International Academy of Behavioral Medicine, Counseling and Psychotherapy, Inc. (n.d.). *Code of ethics.* Dallas, TX: Author.

International Federation of Social Workers. (1978). *International code of ethics for the professional social worker.* Adopted in San Juan, Puerto Rico: Author.

International Federation of Social Workers. (2012). *Statement of ethical principles.* Berne, Switzerland: Author.

International Mental Health Professionals Japan. (2008). *Code of ethics of the international mental health professional Japan.* Tokyo, Japan: Author.

Iranian Organization of Psychology and Counseling. (n.d.). *Ethics code of Iranian organization of psychology and counseling.* Tehran, Iran: Author.

Irish Association for Counselling and Psychotherapy. (2005). *IACP code of ethics and practice for supervisors of counselors and psychotherapists.* Bray, County, Wicklow, Ireland: Author.

Kaiser, T. L. (1997). *Supervisory relationships: Exploring the human element.* Pacific Grove, CA: Brooks/Cole.

Kaslow, F. W. (2005, Summer). Ethical principles: Universal and absolute or county specific and relative? *The Family Psychologist, 21*, 37–44.

Kaslow, N. J., & Bell, K. D. (2008). A competency-based approach to supervision. In C. A. Falender & E. P. Shafranske (Eds.), *Casebook for clinical supervision: A competency-based approach* (pp. 17–38). Washington, DC: American Psychological Association.

Kaslow, N. J., Falender, C. A., & Grus, C. L. (2012). Valuing and practicing competency-based supervision: A transformational leadership perspective. *Training and Education in Professional Psychology, 6*, 47–54.

Knapp, S. J., & VandeCreek, L. (2006). *Practical ethics for psychologists: A positive approach.* Washington, DC: American Psychological Association.

Korean Psychological Association (n.d.). *About the KPA.* Seoul, Korea: Author. doi: http://www.koreanpsychology.or.kr/eng/About-the-KPA/sub_01.asp

Leach, M. M., & Gauthier, J. (2011). Internationalizing the professional ethics curriculum. In F. T. L. Leong, W. E. Pickren, M. M. Leach, & A. Marsella (Eds.), *Internationalizing the psychology curriculum: Meeting the challenges and opportunities of a global era* (pp. 29–50). New York, NY: Springer.

Lee, S. M., Suh, S., Yang, E., & Jang, Y. J. (2012). History, current status, and future prospects of counseling in South Korea. *Journal of Counseling & Development, 90*, 494–499.

Lo, H.-W. (2010). My racial identity development and supervision: A self reflection. *Training and Education in Professional Psychology, 4*, 26–28.

Luepker, E. T. (2012). *Record keeping in psychotherapy and counseling: Protecting confidentiality and the professional relationship* (2nd ed.). New York: Routledge.

McRoy, R. G., Freeman, E. M., Logan, S. L., & Blackmon, B. (1986). Cross-cultural field supervision: Implications for social work education. *Journal of Social Work Education, 22*, 50–56.

Ministry of Education and Science of the Russian Federation. (2009, December 8). *Federal educational standard for higher professional education* (in Russian). Retrieved from http://www.edu.ru/db/moData/d_09/prm709-1.pdf

Murphy-Shigematsu, S. (2010). Microaggressions by supervisors of color. *Training and Education in Professional Psychology, 4*, 16–18.

Nagy, T. F. (2010). *Essential ethics for psychologists: A primer for understanding and mastering core issues*. Washington, DC: American Psychological Association.

Nelson, M. L., Gizara, S., Hope, A. C., Phelps, R., Steward, R., & Weitzman, L. (2006). A feminist multicultural perspective on supervision. *Journal of Multicultural Counseling and Development, 34*, 105–115.

New Zealand Psychologists Board. (2010). *Guidelines on supervision*. Wellington, New Zealand: Author.

O'Donoghue, K., & Tsui, M. (2012). Towards a professional supervision culture: The development of social work supervision in Aotearoa New Zealand. *International Social Work, 55*, 5–28. doi: 10.1177/0020872810396109

Okasha, A. (2002). Mental health in Africa: The role of the WPA. *World Psychiatry, 1*, 32–35.

Pack-Brown, S. P., & Williams, C. B. (2003). *Ethics in a multicultural context*. Thousand Oaks, CA: Sage.

Peteanu, M. (1997). Educational and vocational guidance in Romania: Short history. *Revisita de Pedagogie, 1–12*, 314–324.

Peterson, M. R. (1992). *At personal risk: Boundary violations in professional-client relationships*. New York, NY: Norton.

Pope, K. S., & Vasquez, J. J. T. (2007). *Ethics in psychology and counseling: A practical guide* (3rd ed.). San Francisco, CA: Wiley.

Republic of Botswana Ministry of Education. (2002). *Primary curriculum guideline*. Garorone, Botswana: Botswana Government Printers.

Roberts, M. C., Borden, K. A., Christainsen, M. D., & Lopez, S. J. (2005). Fostering a culture shift: Assessment of competence in the education and careers of professional psychologists. *Professional Psychology, Research and Practice, 36*, 355–361.

Russian Psychological Society. (2012). *Code of ethics of the Russian Psychological Society*. Moscow, Russia: Author.

Saccuzzo, D. P. (2002). Liability for the failure to supervise adequately: Let the master beware (Part 1). *The Psychologist's Legal Update, 13*, 1–14. Washington, DC: Council for the National Register of Health Service Providers in Psychology.

Schank, J. A., & Skovholt, T. M. (2006). *Ethical practice in small communities: Challenges and rewards for psychologists*. Washington, DC: American Psychological Association.

See, C. M., & Ng, K.-M. (2010). Counseling in Malaysia: History, current status, and future trends. *Journal of Counseling & Development, 88*, 18–22.

Senyonyi, R. M., Ochieng, L. A., & Sells, J. (2012). The development of professional counseling in Uganda: Current status and future trends. *Journal of Counseling & Development, 90*, 500–504.

Sinclair, C. (2012). Ethical principles, values, and codes for psychologists: An historical journey. In M. M. Leach, M. J. Stevens, G. Lindsay, A. Ferrero, & Y. Korkut (Eds.), *Oxford handbook of international psychological ethics* (pp. 3–18). New York, NY: Oxford University Press.

Sosland, A. (1997). The state of psychotherapy in Moscow. *International Journal of Psychotherapy, 2*, 229–233.

Stockton, R., Nitza, A., & Bhusumane, D. B. (2010). The development of professional counseling in Botswana. *Journal of Counseling & Development, 88*, 9–12.

Sue, D. W., Carter, R. T., Casas, J. M., Fouad, N. A., Ivey, A., Jensen, M., Vazquez-Nuttall, E. (1998). *Multicultural counseling competencies: Individual and organizational development.* Thousand Oaks, CA: Sage.

Szilagyi, A., & Paredes, D. M. (2010). Professional counseling in Romania: An introduction. *Journal of Counseling & Development, 88*, 23–27.

Thomas, J. T. (2007). Informed consent through contracting for supervision: Minimizing risks, enhancing benefits. *Professional Psychology, Research and Practice, 38*, 221–231.

Thomas, J. T. (2010). *The ethics of supervision and consultation: Practical guidance for mental health professionals.* Washington, DC: American Psychological Association.

Toporek, R. L., Ortega-Villalobos, L., & Pope-Davis, D. B. (2004). Critical incidents in multicultural supervision: Exploring supervisees' and supervisors' experiences. *Journal of Multicultural Counseling and Development, 32*, 66–83.

Tsui, M., Ho, W., & Lam, C. (2005). The use of supervisor authority in Chinese cultural context. *Administration in Social Work, 29*, 51–68.

Uganda Counselling Association. (2009). *The counsellors' code of ethics.* Kampala, Uganda: Author.

International Union of Psychological Science. (2008). *Universal declaration of ethical principles for psychologists.* Retrieved from http://iupsys.net/index.php/policy/113-universal-declaration-of-ethical-principles-for-psychologists

Welfel, E. R. (2013). *Ethics in counseling and psychotherapy: Standards, research, and emerging issues* (5th ed.). Belmont, CA: Brooks/Cole.

Williams, S., & Halgin, R. P. (1995). Issues in psychotherapy supervision between the white supervisor and black supervisee. *The Clinical Supervisor, 13*, 39–61.

Zebian, S., Alamuddin, R. A., Maalouf, M., & Chatila, Y. (2007). Developing an appropriate psychology through culturally sensitive research practices in the Arabic speaking world: A content analysis of psychological research conducted between 1950 and 2004. *Journal of Cross-Cultural Psychology, 38*, 91–122.

Zinchenko, Y. P., & Petrenko, V. F. (2012). Introduction. *Psychology in Russia: State of the Art, Moscow, 5*, 7–10.

7

Organizational Change and Supervision

Mona Kihlgren and Görel Hansebo

Introduction

This chapter will focus on the concept of clinical supervision in the context of nursing care, discussing in particular the nursing care of the elderly. The health care system is characterized by many different specialties, each with its specific problems to solve. In the case of nursing, care is a 24-hr ongoing process, with complex caring situations, more or less urgent, which means that it is mostly unpredictable. The length of stay in different caring contexts for patients also varies and could differ between single days in emergency care, up to several years in a nursing home. This means that nurses play a central role and need to be prepared to deal with unexpected nursing care situations. There are also problems associated with predictable demands. Certain contexts, such as elderly care and mental health care, include staff who have limited education and who come from different cultural backgrounds, so sometimes there are communication problems and high staff turnover. The patients are often extremely dependent on these nurses, which puts special demands and responsibilities on them. Cooperation is important in order to reach the common goal that is best for addressing the patients' needs and wishes. Clinical supervision, with the possibility for reflection on such difficult caring situations, can therefore be important.

Defining clinical supervision in nursing health care

The use of clinical supervision in health care has, during recent years, become a rather common way to improve the quality of care in such challenging settings. The Department of Health in the United Kingdom defined 1993 clinical supervision as "a formal process of professional support and learning which enables individual practitioners to develop knowledge and competence, assume responsibility for their own practice and enhance consumer protection and safety of care in complex clinical situations."

The Wiley International Handbook of Clinical Supervision, First Edition. Edited by C. Edward Watkins, Jr. and Derek L. Milne.

In nursing care there are varied definitions, but the precision is poor (Butterworth & Faugier, 1992). Also, no consensus has been clarified on the concept of supervision in caring contexts, but there are some more or less common strategies. Clarifying the concept of clinical supervision within nursing care is not easy, as it is quite varied in its practice settings. Koivu, Hyrkäs, and Saarinen (2011) stated that there is still no common understanding of the nature or purpose of clinical supervision in nursing.

In order to define supervision, Butterworth and Faugier (1992) claimed that supervision was concerned with support and enabling, geared toward promoting growth and development of the supervisee. Butterworth et al. (1997) were among the first to argue the need for supervision for supporting nurses in their work. A concept analysis of clinical supervision was undertaken after conducting a literature review (Lyth, 2000). The proposed definition of clinical supervision that resulted was that it is a support mechanism for practicing professionals within which they can share clinical, organizational, developmental and emotional experiences with another professional in a secure, confidential environment, in order to enhance knowledge and skills. This process will lead to an increased awareness of other concepts, including accountability and reflective practice. In a systematic review, Milne (2007) noted that the functions of supervision within his sample of empirical studies were quality control, maintaining and facilitating the supervisees' competence and capability, and helping supervisees to work effectively. Similarly, Johansson, Holm, Lindqvist, and Severinsson (2006) argued that supervision is a supportive method for enabling reflection, with the potential to encourage and enhance the nurse's professional development and personal growth. In a later and more detailed analysis, Severinsson (1996) stated that clinical supervision was a pedagogical process of promoting human development, where both the supervisor and supervisee are raising questions, exploring, explaining, and systematizing experiences from a clinical care perspective. Still later, Severinsson (2001) described clinical supervision as a process whereby nurses discover facts and values with regard to a patient's recovery. Berggren (2005) viewed clinical supervision as valuable for nurses when reflecting on ethical dilemmas and when making decisions for the benefit of the individual patient. In almost every nursing care situation ethical dilemmas are present, and clinical supervision makes it possible for reflection on these ethical dilemmas (Berggren, Barbosa da Silva, & Severinsson, 2005). In summary, within the context of nursing health care, supervision has been viewed as a valuable means of supporting and developing professional practice. However, although many important processes and outcomes have been identified, there is as yet only an informal consensus on its definition within the nursing care profession.

Objectives of supervision

Although we have just touched on a few supervision objectives in summarizing the definitions within nursing, we next provide a more detailed synthesis. The objectives of clinical supervision are important, according to Hunter and Blair (1999), and are about creating a culture of change, based on the facilitating role of supervisor and the supervisory relationship. van Ooijen (2000) and Sloan, White, and Coit (2000) claimed that the focus should be on developing nurse–patient relationships, but it could also involve enhancing interactions between nurses and other members of the health care team. Winstanley and White (2002) concluded that the essence of supervision was a process that sought to create an environment in which participants have possibilities to evaluate, reflect on and develop their own clinical practice (e.g., therapeutic skills), providing empathic support for one another in facilitating reflective practice and the transmission of knowledge. There is reason to believe that supervision also achieves other objectives. In a study by Lindahl and Norberg (2002), the participants talked about their supervision as a space for relief, through sharing emotions and caring experiences. This helped these nurses to manage the demands of complex nursing care, a finding that was in accordance with a study by Hadfield (2000).

According to Severinsson (2001), some other general objectives of clinical supervision are to support the development of the supervisee's working identity, competence, skills and ethics; foster self-awareness and a self-critical perspective; and enable feelings to be clarified. Clinical supervision also challenges nurses to think differently about their professional work (Jones, 2006) and has also been highlighted as a possible strategy for recruitment and retention within nursing, including junior nurses (Cummins, 2009). Therefore, supervision can help nurses to achieve a number of valuable objectives. We next consider how supervision can best be understood and developed.

Models for clinical supervision in nursing care

A number of factors can support and enable supervision, including guiding theories. The three most frequently cited models were reported in a monograph by Winstanley and White (2002): the growth and support model; the integrative approach; and Proctor's interactive model, highlighting the normative (managerial), formative (educative), and restorative (supportive) functions of supervision. The use of caring and nursing theories in clinical supervision was emphasized as important by Bondas (2010).

In terms of developing supervision, several factors influence whether supervisors are likely to succeed or fail in their task (Winstanley & White, 2002). These include shared responsibility, the time available, and dedication to the organization. Supervisors have also claimed that it is important to have adequate training and to have their own supervision, to ensure quality for their supervisees (Butterworth, Bell, Jackson, & Pajnkihar, 2008; Hyrkäs, Appelqvist-Schmidlechner, & Kivimaki, 2005; Lyth, 2000; Winstanley & White, 2002). A review by Hyrkäs et al. (2005) underscored the importance of training and education in helping supervisors gain an unbiased perspective and distance, when discussing their supervisees' clinical practice. The authors also found in their review that it was important to enable supervisors to reflect on ethical decision-making. Berggren and Severinsson (2006) pointed out that an integral part of supervisors' ethical decision-making is to take responsibility for creating a good relationship with their supervisees.

Effects of supervision

There is a lack of empirical evidence to link the process of clinical supervision with real benefits to care quality, and so evaluating its effectiveness is therefore necessary

(Winstanley & White, 2002). Studies have reported that clinical supervision enhances the caring process, as well as the nurses' ability to provide care of the desired quality (Severinsson, 2001). In a literature review, Butterworth et al. (2008) found that most clinical supervision was seen as an educative and supportive process, but they also found in some studies that clinical supervision can be cost-effective and improve care.

The benefits of clinical supervision in psychiatric nursing were investigated in two further studies (Livni, Crowe, & Gonsalvez, 2012). The results indicated that participating in supervision was associated with more positive effectiveness, as measured with a quantitative instrument. This was contrary to the previous study by Buus, Angel, Traynor, and Gonge (2011), which found that participants thought that clinical supervision had made very little impact on clinical practice. Reasons for these discrepant findings could be that neither managers nor nurses prioritized clinical supervision. Using a quantitative design, Edwards et al. (2006) found a lower level of burnout among community mental health nurses when clinical supervision was effective. Similarly, Begat and Severinsson (2006) reported that clinical supervision had an influence on nurses' experiences of well-being. Based on a quantitative design, Choi and Johantgen (2012) showed that supportive supervision was important for job satisfaction among certified nursing assistants in nursing homes. This confirmed findings reported by Hyrkäs (2005) and Hyrkäs, Appelqvist-Schmidlechner, and Haatja (2006), who also found that levels of stress were decreased when supervision was available. Therefore, like the preceding sections, consideration of the effects of supervision again indicates that it is a multifaceted, complex intervention. We next consider the kinds of resources that are required to provide adequate supervision, then summarize the clinical benefits of supervision.

Time and organization

There is little evidence in the literature to suggest what might be a suitable standard for the amount of time or the frequency that is necessary for clinical supervision. However, a literature review by Butterworth et al. (2008) found that supervision was most effective when provided for around 45 min to 1 hr per month. Similarly, Hyrkäs (2005) also found support for a frequency of at least once a month, but it was noted that sessions that lasted for over 1 hr were positively evaluated. Organizational culture is consistently reported as another important determinant for the implementation of supervision (Butterworth et al., 2008; Jones, 2006). Brunero and Lamont (2012) made it clear that implementing clinical supervision with large numbers of nurses gave benefits, but logistical and resource challenges required attention.

Changes in Patients after Clinical Supervision

A reasonable assumption is that if the staff members have the proper knowledge and skills, the quality of the care for patients will improve. What follows is a discussion of some projects that tested this assumption by evaluating the effects of staff education and training on persons with a dementia diagnosis. A clinical supervision intervention study showed that the relational quality of patient–caregiver interaction improved after one year of clinical supervision (Edberg, Hallberg, & Gustafsson, 1996). Two wards at a psycho-geriatric clinic for patients with severe dementia were compared. Observation of nurse–patient cooperation was performed and sorted into predetermined categories. Statistically significant improvement was seen in the experimental ward, indicating a higher quality in nurse–patient cooperation. However, no statistically significant differences were found between a treatment and a control ward when Edberg, Norberg, and Hallberg (1999) evaluated the effects of one-year systematic clinical supervision. The effect of individually planned care on the mood and general behavior of patients with dementia was studied in relation to cognitive function and level of confusion.

The Prince Henry Hospital dementia caregivers' training program was studied by Brodaty and Gresham (1989), when comparing caregiver–patient dyads in a memory training group and a waiting list group. The program was broad, covering topics such as organizing the day and home; using community services; reducing caregiver distress, combating isolation, guilt and separation; finding new ways of thinking and new coping skills; fitness; diet; medical aspects of dementia; planning for the future; and coping with problem behaviors. The patient program included general ward activities and group discussions. Brodaty, Gresham, and Luscombe (1997) found that the program led to a statistically significant delay in the institutionalization of people with dementia, as well as reduced stress in the family caregivers. An eight-year survival analysis indicated that patients whose family caregivers received training stayed at home significantly longer ($p = .037$) and tended to live longer ($p = .08$). Patients as well as caregivers had received a 10-day program at the study start. The caregivers then received 12 months of support and follow-up interventions during the eight subsequent years, including telephone conferences, decreasing involvement by the coordinator, and visits to the hospital at 3, 6, and 12 months for assessment and reunion times with fellow caregivers. Wimo, Mattsson, Adolfsson, Eriksson, and Nelvig (1993) studied the effect of day care on patients with dementia who lived at home. By comparing those already in day care with those on a waiting list, changes in cognition, behavior, activities for daily living (ADL) function, and institutionalization after one year in day care was seen. The results showed that day care postponed institutionalization and gave spouses the relief they needed to recover their strength.

In addition to staff training and supervision, changes to the physical environment can enhance dementia care. We now summarize some relevant studies.

Organization of dementia care

The organization of care for the elderly has been studied by several authors (e.g., Bicket et al., 2010; Chalfont, 2011). Such authors claim that organizing the physical environment to promote greater resident dignity appears to be associated with better quality of life in residents. Studying the impact of the environment on resident outcomes in assisted living over time may also help us to better understand the relationship between the environment and the resident, especially regarding differences among patients with and without dementia (Bicket et al., 2010). Sandman, Norberg, and Adolfsson (1988) studied institutionalized patients' mealtime behavior and social interaction. A special dining room was organized, prepared with a set of china, cutlery, napkins, dishes, and bowls. The same staff members participated, and they received instructions to help the patients when needed. Patients ate alone during one of three observation periods, nurses wearing street (i.e., casual) clothes participated in a second period, and uniformed nurses participated in the final period. The results showed that two patients with milder dementia helped others when no nurse was available; one helped when nurses wore street clothes; and none helped when the nurses wore uniforms.

We next provide an outline of one of our own studies, which examined organizational factors in relation to supervision.

Illustration: a collective living unit versus a traditional nursing home Long-term influences on patients with dementia in different caring milieus were studied by Kihlgren et al. (1992). During a 22-month period, the environmental influences on demented patients in a collective living unit with special staff supervision were compared with those in a control group, living in a traditional nursing home. Five of six patients (one had aphasia but was not demented, so was excluded) from the collective living unit (CL group) were selected for the study, and five patients from the four nursing home wards (NH group) constituted the control group. They were matched for dementia, sex, age, and social background. The patients' medication was monitored during the study.

The collective living unit (CL unit) was specifically adapted for demented persons with regard to integrity, homeliness, and activities, according to the Bedömning av Fysisk Miljö för Äldre [Assessment of Physical Milieu for Elderly] scale (BFMÄ; Svensson, 1984), but less adapted for patients with physical disabilities. The assessment of the control wards at the nursing home (NH) showed low figures for orientation and high figures for activities. The CL group lived in a new home, but with their own private things.

Staff clinical supervision: Before the CL unit opened, all staff members went through a one-month training program about dementia diseases (DDs), home care, communication, and group relations. This training also included visits to other CL units. Supervision and support were offered to staff during the 22-month study period, from the research team as well as from the CL unit managers. The research team made observations of the work at least once a month and had regular discussions with the staff about their care practices. The staff also received feedback for the care delivered, including whether it was in line with the clinical supervision.

The results included intellectual functions, rated by the Gottfries–Bråne–Steen (GBS) scale (Gottfries, Bråne, Gullberg, & Steen, 1982), which indicated a significantly smaller deterioration in the CL group ($p < 0.05$). A quotient was also constructed of EEG alpha/delta activities, the ratio of which had increased in the CL group, indicating a reduction of dementia-induced changes, but which was reduced in the NH group ($p < .05$). The NH group showed signs of more passivity, sadness and depression, while the CL group showed greater activity, more individual initiatives, more signs of a will of their own, and also caused more "disturbances." But it seemed as if all activities were more accepted in the collective living, and so it was not necessary to follow the routines so rigorously.

Observations at the CL unit showed that physical aspects of the environment, daily activities, and the care were adapted to the patients, which made it easier for them to benefit. It was obvious that these patients were encouraged to participate in decisions, while the control patients at the NH wards were usually activated by means of suggestions, requests, and even orders.

The fundamental conclusion that we drew from our study was that the milieu of the CL unit could be assumed to give the patients an experience of wholeness and meaning. Probably several circumstances contributed to this effect. If the milieu was organized in small home-like units, it seemed to provide a humanizing element, permitting patients to live in a dignified way. The CL group showed more signs of integrity than the NH group. In this milieu, it indicated that staff, enabled by their clinical supervision and philosophy of care, could compensate for the patients' lack of resources and affect the patients' autonomy and well-being (Kihlgren et al., 1992).

Clinical supervision in relation to theoretical models of human functioning

Some psychosocial interventions that include staff training and supervision are based on theoretical models. Examples are the progressively lowered stress threshold model (Hall & Buckwalter, 1987).The theory of "eight stages of man" described by the Erikson couple together (E. H. Erikson, 1982; E. H. Erikson, J. M., Erikson, & H. Q. Kivnick, 1986; J. M. Erikson, 1988) and as used in elder care by Feil (1992), Ekman, Wahlin, Norberg, and Winblad (1993), Kihlgren (1992), Kihlgren, Hallgren, Norberg, Bråne, and Karlsson (1990), Kihlgren et al. (1993), Kihlgren, Hallgren, Norberg, and Karlsson (1994) and Kihlgren, Hallgren, Norberg, and Karlsson (1996), Hansebo (2000), Mamhidir, Karlsson, Norberg, and Kihlgren (2008); and the validation method (VM), introduced by Feil and used by Söderlund, Norberg, and Hansebo (2012). We will next outline and evaluate these models. We will say most about the eight stages model, as this features in the project illustration that follows.

The PLST model is based on the coping theories of Lazarus and Selye, focusing on the influence of the care environment (Hall & Buckwalter, 1987). The Hall et al. model, developed in mid-1980s, has been used by a great number of authors (Smith, Gerdner, Hall, & Buckwalter, 2004) and is designed to promote more adaptive and functional behavior in older adults with dementia. The model has been applied in a wide variety of settings to train caregivers in homes, adult day programs, nursing homes (NHs), and hospitals, serving as the conceptual basis for in-home and institutional studies. Extensive testing supports the use of the PLST model in decreasing depression, as well as diminishing the uncertainty and unpredictability associated with dementia caregiving, lessening caregiver appraisals of stress and burden. Less research-based information is available about the PLST model's effect on the behavioral symptoms experienced by the person with dementia.

In the Erikson theory of "eight stages of man" (1982, 1986, 1988) the experience of wholeness and meaning is described by the Erikson couple. The theory accounts for the process of psychosocial development in human beings, extending from infancy through adulthood and into old age. According to the theory, each stage is to be seen in relation to the previous and the future stages and is described as a crisis, leading to a synthesis, produced between two counteracting poles. This means that, at each age, one crisis is phase specific and the others are latent. In old age a person is normally in his or her last (eighth) stage of psychosocial development, and has to look back on life and forward toward death. As one alternative, a person can accept what has happened and anticipate what will happen; or as another alternative, one can be filled with grief and despair. The positive solution, leading to an experience of wholeness and meaning, is named *integrity*.

In a Swedish study, Ekman et al. (1993) applied the Erikson theory when analyzing communication, interaction, and relationship in the care of bilingual demented patients, who were Finnish immigrants. Caregivers who could/could not speak Finnish were included in the care organization. The conclusion was that an organization that makes it possible for patients with dementia to use their native language makes it easier for caregivers to promote the patients' integrity, which in turn enables patients to disclose more of their latent capacity.

Feil (1992) indicated that inner harmony (integrity) can only be reached if a person still has the cognitive ability to cope with problems. Therefore, she added a ninth stage to the Erikson developmental stage model. In this ninth stage, "resolution versus vegetation" is the central issue. Adding this stage makes it possible to give more specific attention to disoriented elderly people, who experience relief when validated on their feelings. This is a central aspect of the validation approach.

The VM, introduced by Feil (1992), focuses on the emotional content of what the people with a DD are expressing. The training in VM is provided to help nurses develop communication skills in their interactions with people with DD, by accepting these people's experiences of reality and by confirming their feelings, with the use of various verbal and nonverbal communication approaches. VM training is extensive and takes about one year (Feil, 1992).Several attempts have been made to evaluate the VM, primarily in quantitative studies. A Cochrane review reported insufficient scientific evidence for the efficacy of VM among people with DD (Neal & Briggs, 2003). Studies conducted later yielded no statistically significant results in favor of the VM regarding cognition, behavior, and emotional states (Deponte & Missan, 2007).

Illustration: the "integrity-promoting care" project A project was undertaken by Kihlgren et al. (1993, 1994, 1996) with the purpose of investigating if "integrity-promoting care" improves functioning in demented patients; and to describe changes over time in patients, the care delivered, the care routines and the environment. Two nursing home wards were selected, an intervention ward (I-ward) and a control ward (C-ward), each with similar staffing profiles and numbers of patients. The medical profiles of the two groups of patients were similar and drug regimes were unaltered during the study. The patients of both wards were severely demented and severely disabled in their ADL function. Data were collected before and after clinical supervision of the I-ward staff, including a three-month intervention period.

Clinical supervision in integrity-promoting care *Training course week* All staff members of the I-ward were given one week of training, aimed at promoting integrity in the patients with dementia according to an application of the Erikson theory to dementia care (Kihlgren, 1992). Different topics were covered, such as normal and pathological aging, confusion, and DDs, human relationship, communication, interaction, environment, human territory, and integrity. The staff were asked to discuss the theory, with the eight stages, in a concrete way: how trust, autonomy, initiative, industry, intimacy, generativity, and integrity could be best promoted during different care activities. The intention was that the patients should have a feeling of satisfaction and comfort in the caring activity (e.g., should be clean; should have had enough to eat), as well as have an experience of wholeness and meaning (integrity). The supervision also aimed at teaching the caregivers to increase the clarity of their communicative cues, to be attentive toward the patients, and to respond in a way that compensated for the patients' disabilities (see Barnard, 1981). The staff members were also instructed about the importance of a calm and homely environment to make it easier for the patients to interpret their surroundings. The staff made a group decision about how to change the care in accordance with the training.

A three-month intervention period followed, when the staff of the I-ward were encouraged to implement the changes in the daily nursing care. The researcher visited the ward three to four days a week, and a research assistant stayed at the ward throughout the intervention period. The staff members were asked questions about the patients' history during the course week. As this indicated a lack of historical knowledge, the staff were encouraged to interview the patients' relatives. This was done, and for each patient a summary was written which was accessible for all staff on the ward. Video recordings of patients and staff were taken from the daily work before the clinical supervision started. During the intervention period, these video recordings were used, with permission from the respective caregiver, in discussions with the ward staff of their delivery of care.

Findings *Neurochemical assessments* Cerebrospinal fluid (CSF) was obtained by means of a lumbar puncture. The CSF somatostatin (SRFI) concentrations increased significantly in all but one patient in the I-group after staff training. No increase was seen in the C-group (Bråne, Karlsson, Kihlgren, & Norberg, 1989). This may reflect an increased activity of neuromodulatory factors in the brain of the patients that are cared for in an integrity-promoting way.

Psychological ratings According to the GBS scale measurements (Gottfries et al., 1982), all observed differences provided evidence of improvement in the I-group patients. No significant changes were seen in the C group. Both intellectual improvement and increased motor performance were observed in the I-group, as well as a significant decrease in confusion, anxiety, and depressed mood. These improvements remained after a nine-month follow-up (Bråne et al., 1989).

Weight changes were followed to analyze how these related to biological and psychological parameters. The most prominent difference observed was weight increases in 13 of 18 patients of the I-ward, compared with only 2 of 15 patients in the control ward. The individual weight changes correlated significantly to changes in the intellectual functions (GBS). Relationships between weight change, increased motor function, and increased appetite were nonsignificant. There was also no significant relationship between weight changes and changes in biochemical parameters. According to the staff, increased contact with the patients and a more pleasant atmosphere resulted when the meal environment and routines were changed (Mamhidir et al., 2008).

Video recordings Recordings, including five patients/caregivers of each ward from before and after the supervision, were mixed randomly and nonrandomly, then an analysis was undertaken by one external researcher and one external co-assessor. During the nonrandomly selected video-recorded social activities, patients in the I-group were more active and sociable than the C group with their caregivers after training. They were also observed to be clearer in their cues and showed more sensitivity (see Barnard, 1981). It seems reasonable to believe that, as both patients and caregivers increased their clarity of cues and sensitivity, they also increased their capacity to interpret and their willingness to respond (Kihlgren et al., 1990). The analysis of morning care sessions ($n = 99$), using a coding scheme, showed, for example, more verbal contact initiated by the patients in the I-group after training, and slightly more participation and cooperation, compared with the C-group (Kihlgren et al., 1993). A phenomenological–hermeneutic analysis of the morning care sessions of the intervention ward (I-ward: $n = 49$) showed that, after training, 84% of the interactions were interpreted as positive, compared with 21% before. The care was supporting and permitting, and the activity was carried out in an intimate way, which led to the patients displaying more and more abilities (Kihlgren et al., 1994). An analysis of each of the I-group interactions showed patterns of action in the patients that seemed to reflect life-long characteristics. All the strengths/weaknesses described by the Erikson couple (1982, 1986, 1988) were seen in the patients after the training of staff, compared with before the training. More strengths were noted (e.g., hope, will, and purpose were observed in the patients) when the care was trustful and allowing. Patients showed a lot of competence in their conversations. Furthermore, the patients were seen praising the caregiver, expressing concern, facilitating the caregiver's work (interpreted as the strengths of love and care), and showing maturity (wisdom) when settling a problematic situation. The patients seemed to have the capacity to interpret the atmosphere properly, including the nonverbal communications from the caregiver, but were not able to respond and verbally express their own experience clearly (Kihlgren et al., 1996).

Oral reports More messages were given per report at the I-ward after the intervention compared with the C-ward, and the messages with psychosocial content had doubled. Thus, the oral reports between staff had undergone some changes, ones that could have contributed to the positive effects for the patients, as well as on the interactions between patients and staff (Kihlgren, Lindsten, Norberg, & Karlsson, 1992).

Conclusion From the findings that followed after clinical supervision was introduced into integrity-promoting care, as reported earlier, it was obvious that, together with an adapted physical environment, this kind of care improved functioning in patients with dementia over time (patients' medication was monitored during the study period and so could be excluded as an explanation). Clinical supervision followed the staff training and took place throughout the three-month intervention period, supplemented byintensive support from the research team and from management. This package of supervision and support seemed to be a necessary condition for staff accepting and implementing integrity-promoting care.

We next consider the influence of clinical supervision on family- and professional caregivers.

Changes in Formal and Informal Caregivers after Clinical Supervision

The number of older people over 80 years of age has increased in all parts of the Western world and has led to consequences in the care of older people (OECD, 2009). During the 1990s and the beginning of the twenty-first century, observations of the formal (professional) caregivers concerned with the care and nursing of the elderly have taken place. Little attention has been paid to the differences between formal (professional) and informal (family) caregivers when trying to compare studies concerning the benefits and effects of supervision-based interventions. We next contrast these caregivers' responses to supervision.

Informal caregivers

Most elderly people are women, and families (most often adult daughters) provide the majority of informal caregiving (Haberstroh, Hampel, & Pantel, 2010; OECD, 2009), though with a wide variation across countries in the number of hours of care provided per week. International intervention studies of informal caregivers, concerned with the care and nursing of people with a dementia diagnosis, with different supervision programs and support arrangements, were systematically evaluated and summarized by the Swedish Council on Technology Assessment in Health Care (SBU). SBU (2008) found four categories of international interventions:

1. psycho-educational and psychosocial interventions, with the purpose of maintaining and improving the emotional well-being of the caregivers;
2. skills training programs;
3. technological support programs; and
4. out-of-home activities and care placement.

In terms of the methodologies that were used in the studies already discussed, questions have arisen as to whether the commonly applied general indicators of a sense of burden (such as stress and dissatisfaction, as well as psychological and psychosomatic complaints) are the most relevant and discriminating outcome measures in researching support programs for informal caregivers (SBU, 2008). Perhaps more attention should be paid to the period during which caregivers are able to perform their tasks, variables that seem to be determined by situational and relation-specific factors, such as the feelings and experiences associated with caring for people with dementia. When interventions were multifaceted, it was difficult to identify which component was the most effective. The findings suggested that future interventions should assess the individual caregiver's specific training needs and tailor interventions to address those issues directly, in order to maximize the desired outcomes, such as reducing behavioral problems. For example, interventions based on the PLST model (Hall & Buckwalter, 1987) had a positive impact on both frequency and response to problem behavior among spousal caregivers (SBU, 2008).

Forty studies were included in the review by Cooke, McNally, Mulligan, Harrison, and Newman (2001). Approximately two-thirds of these interventions did not show improvements on any outcome measures. Among those studies that did demonstrate improvements, the inclusion of social components (e.g., social support) or a combination of social and cognitive components (e.g., problem-solving) seemed to be relatively effective. However, Cooke and co-workers claimed that the efficacy of psychosocial interventions for caregivers of people with dementia required a more systematic approach.

Haberstroh et al. (2010) claimed that there is a generally high consensus related to the effects of informal caregiver education and support, in order to enhance the quality of life of the informal caregiver. The authors see it as important to involve family caregivers in multimodal treatment settings, and to provide interventions that are both suitable and specifically tailored to their needs. Family caregivers have an important impact on clinical outcomes, such as quality of life. But as a consequence of this service, family caregivers may suffer high rates of psychological and physical illness, as well as social and financial burdens. In recent years, several clinical guidelines have been presented worldwide for evidence-based treatment of Alzheimer's disease (AD) and other forms of dementia. Most of these guidelines have considered family advice as integral to the optimal clinical management of AD. The article by Haberstroh et al. reviewed current and internationally relevant guidelines, with the emphasis on recommendations concerning family advice.

Having reviewed some research on informal caregivers, we next consider studies of formal caregivers. We again include a detailed account of our own research.

Formal caregivers

Structural and psychological empowerment topics have received increasing attention in nursing management, yet few theoretically informed intervention studies have been conducted in elderly care. In one rare example, a clinical supervision program aimed at strengthening caregivers' self-esteem and empowering them was evaluated. The program consisted of eight group sessions, each about 1.5-hr long, and took place over a nine-month period (a more detailed description is presented in Wadensten, Engström, & Häggström, 2009). Semi-structured interviews were conducted by Wadensten et al. (2009) to investigate how 14 of the female nurses experienced participating in the program. From the interviews it was obvious that the participants were generally satisfied with the clinical supervision. Their opinions about the benefits they received from the program can be described using three themes: "improved communication skills," "enhanced self esteem," and "sees work in a different way." Also, psychological empowerment and job satisfaction were studied and reported by Engström, Wadensten, and Häggström (2010). When compared over time there was significant improvement in the intervention group regarding the factor "criticism" (job satisfaction scale, Engström, Ljungren, & Lindqvist, 2006), in that the caregivers perceived less critique from their co-workers, supervisor, residents, and relatives. There were no statistically significant differences in the comparison group. The authors (Engström et al., 2010) concluded that caregivers' perception of criticism can improve through an intervention aimed at strengthening their self-esteem and by empowering them. Relationships between the variables were studied within the whole group; total empowerment and all empowerment factors (within the self-assessed empowerment scale (Spreitzer, 1995)) correlated positively with total job satisfaction. Six out of eight factors of job satisfaction correlated positively with total empowerment.

Illustration: supervision for individualized and documented nursing care Hansebo and Kihlgren (2004) illuminated changes in staff members' approach to nursing care after a one-year intervention based on clinical supervision. The intervention was introduced in three nursing home wards, in different parts of Sweden. Most patients had severe dementia. The intervention included supervision for individualized (and documented) nursing care, based on multidimensional assessments.

Intervention and staff training The intervention started with changing the ward organization in the three nursing home wards into caring teams, with a registered nurse as the leader and co-coordinator of a team of three to four staff. Each caring team was responsible for a group of seven to eight patients. All nurses were trained in implementation of an assessment instrument, the Resident Assessment Instrument/ Minimum Data Set (RAI/MDS; Morris et al., 1990), as a basis for individualized and documented nursing care, with practice sessions in working through the instrument. During the intervention year each caring team was supervised for 2 hr once a month in assessment, and in relation to their individualized and documented nursing care, with discussions as necessary for care planning about patients' needs, problems, and resources. The nursing process (Yura & Walsh, 1988) provided the model for the supervision. The focus was always on patients' remaining resources.

Findings from these different methods mirrored each other and added to the credibility of the intervention. In the review of nursing documentation, the main change after the intervention was that a nursing care plan was written for all patients, based on a complete assessment. Daily notes also increased, both in total and within parts of the nursing process used, but reflected mostly temporary situations. Medical treatment was still the most documented aspect (Hansebo, Kihlgren, & Ljunggren, 1999). Individually triggered Resident Assessment Protocols (RAPs) were used to compare items in the nursing care plans after the intervention. RAPs are included in the RAI-system and specify triggering items that identify potential problems (Morris et al., 1991). Fifty-two per cent of triggered RAPs were not documented. However, there were also items in the nursing care plans that were not triggered by the RAPs, such as communication for some patients, pressure ulcers, psychosocial well-being, and activities.

In the post-intervention comparison of caregivers' reports of patient life stories and current situation, the main finding was that caregivers gave fuller, more detailed accounts of their patients after the intervention (Hansebo & Kihlgren, 2000). This was more prominent if a caregiver spoke about the same patient before as well as after the intervention. Caregivers thought, however, that their knowledge was insufficient, even after the intervention. There were also caregivers who did not display any changes, and there were also differences between the wards. A changed perspective on patients became obvious, shifting from a focus on single facts to a greater emphasis on the unique person with resources and capabilities, despite the limitations resulting from old age and dementia.

In video-recorded interactions ($n = 24$) following the intervention, nurses used different methods and were differently skilled in managing the complexity of nursing situations involving patients suffering from severe dementia (Hansebo & Kihlgren,

2002). For example, nurses were balancing their interactions to promote a sense of mutual togetherness with the patient, through communication and actions, which promoted more competence. Nurses also showed more patience when they tried to get their patients more involved in activities, and took advantage of patients' initiatives and capabilities, trusting them. Furthermore, nurses tried to meet their patients in their world, and to convey feelings of security (e.g., they asked for the patient's permission before acting). Power dynamics were a further example of change, which could be seen as the nurses handing power over to the patient, seeking to avoid violating patients' autonomy and integrity. By contrast, interactions characterized by distance were seen in the nursing situations that were dominated by task- and action-centered care. Other signs of difficulty were silence, no concern for the patients' capabilities, and interactions that were characterized by stress (e.g., changing from one thing to another, without any connection).

Stimulated recall interviews (n = *12)* Four nurses were video-recorded before, during and after the one-year intervention. Interviews were conducted with each nurse after each recording. None of the nurses had any previous experience of watching themselves on video, as a way to reflect on their work. This gave them fresh possibilities to look critically at themselves, which was especially valuable, as they often worked in a nonreflective manner. This led to improvements in their ability to verbalize their reflections about their working. It also improved nurses' awareness and knowledge about their own influence on the quality of their care for the patients. Nurses expressed most of their negative self-criticism in the first and second interviews, together with reflections on their caring philosophy and thoughts about their duty (i.e., to do one's best for the patients). In the third interview other thoughts dominated, such as that they always tried to do the very best for the patients, but it was acknowledged that it was very difficult to interpret the world of the patient (Hansebo & Kihlgren, 2001).

Caregivers' views of using an assessment instrument, the RAI/MDS (Morris et al., 1991) As a basis for individualized and documented nursing care, a majority of caregivers answering the questionnaire agreed that the instrument could contribute to improving the quality of care (Hansebo, Kihlgren, Ljunggren, & Winblad, 1998). They thought that knowledge about the patient increased, as the instrument made them more aware of the importance of certain information. They thought that nursing care plans and documentation had improved through using the instrument, as had the responsibility for patient interventions, with more uniform care delivery and continuity for the patient. Furthermore, they claimed that another aspect of patients was seen, and a better understanding gained of different behaviors. Caregivers sought information that they had not paid attention to or bothered about before the intervention, and more of patients' capacity and interests were considered.

Despite shattered expectations, a willingness to care remained We next describe another of our studies, which drew on the points discussed earlier. A longitudinal multicenter study was performed, including three nursing homes in different parts of Sweden (Fläckman, 2008; Häggström, 2005). In two of the nursing homes, NH I and NH II, the whole staff group took part in a two-year intervention study, one that included education, clinical supervision, and support. The third home, NH III, served as a control nursing home (i.e., where no actions were taken by the research team during this period). NH I was newly opened and caregivers started planning how their work should be carried out. The management's role at the NH I was strictly administrative. Financial cutbacks at NH I became known shortly after its opening, in spite of promises of ample staffing. At NH II and NH III, rumors of cutbacks and some changes began around 12 months after the start of the project. Reduction in the number of employees and a simultaneous increase in number of residents took place at all three NHs.

The two-year support through education and clinical supervision started at NH I and NH II after collection of the initial baseline data. Caregivers were able to request the educational topics and could give their input regarding the approach taken to education and clinical supervision. A voluntary training program was offered about once a month and delivered by physicians and nurse specialists during the two years. Caregivers sought more knowledge about different diseases, as well as additional training in communication, through seeking literature, team cooperation, and conflict management. Lectures were also given on how to deliver integrity-promoting care (Kihlgren, 1992) and in using the RAI/MDS (Morris et al., 1990). Data from the RAI/MDS were used to establish individual resident care plans, which together with the formal education formed the basis for the clinical supervision.

NH I A first interview with caregivers of NH I were performed before the start of the intervention, which illuminated their perceptions of work satisfaction and dissatisfaction. Dissatisfaction dominated at NH I, being present in three of the four themes that emerged: experiences of betrayal, experiences of failing others, experiences of insufficiency in the workplace, and also experiences of work satisfaction (Häggström, Skovdahl, Fläckman, Kihlgren, & Kihlgren, 2004).

A second and a third interview, 12 and 24 months after the intervention at NH I, were reported by Häggström, Skovdahl, Fläckman, Kihlgren, and Kihlgren (2005). From the analysis, these themes emerged: "experiences of a changed perspective"; "experiences of open doors"; and "experiences of closed doors." Taken together, the caregivers had shifted to a position where work satisfaction dominated. No difference was seen in the content of the interviews after 12 and 24 months, which means that a change was seen after one year and remained after two years.

On both Creativity and Innovative Climate Questionnaire (CCQ; Ekvall, 1996) scores and Maslach Burnout Inventory (MBI; Maslach, Jackson, & Leiter, 1996) measurements, an improvement was seen over the two-year period. Significant improvements were found over time in the CCQ (for the dimensions of "idea support" and "idea time") and on the MBI (less burnout). At the 24-month assessment, the CCQ scores had passed the innovative level, in the positive direction. The scores for "conflict" and "trust" also improved, and a more playful and humorous atmosphere was reported (Fläckman, Hansebo, & Kihlgren, 2009).

NH II Interviews at the start showed that challenge, freedom, and playfulness were prevalent, with positive feelings in caregivers and positive expectations regarding their new work. The relationship with colleagues and residents showed emotional involvement, with security. Twelve months later, after being informed of the forthcoming changes, caregivers in the second interviews showed uncertainty, and their trust and openness with regard to the management had decreased. Furthermore, there were increasing conflicts in the work groups, and the freedom and independence in decision-making were no longer prominent. From having been focused on their work, staff members were now more focused on their own personal situation. After 24 months, the third interviews showed that the workplace was perceived as hectic and the caregivers were frustrated about conflicts that existed in the groups and the lack support for new ideas. Signs of fatigue and exhaustion now appeared. They realized that their expectations of giving good care would not be fulfilled, but they were not willing to give up. The CCQ scores progressed negatively from baseline to the 24 months follow-up. Some of the scores suggested stagnation in the organization. The scores for "conflict" and "trust" worsened over the study period. The MBI measurements showed low mean scores but worsened after 12 month, which corresponded to the time when staff received information about financial cutbacks, but still indicated a low degree of burnout. The more favorable scores were seen at 24 months (Fläckman et al., 2009). A second analysis of all NH II interviews was reported by Fläckman, Fagerberg, Häggström, Kihlgren, and Kihlgren (2007), with the conclusion that after two years the caregivers' willingness to care continued, despite their disappointment in the worsened working conditions. The main theme that resulted was that despite shattered expectations, a willingness to care for elders remained. The continued education and clinical supervision just described seems to be one factor behind this continued commitment. These findings demonstrate that support and caregiver involvement in educational programs are important during times of change and when disappointments arise in the workplace.

NH III Interviews at the start showed that trust, dynamism and playfulness predominated. However, after 12 months feelings of insecurity and increasing conflicts were expressed. Discussion about staff reductions and termination notes filled their days. After the 24-months follow-up, the caregivers talked about making the best of the situation. They were safeguarding of themselves and the residents, but their feelings of responsibility for the residents caused them to struggle. The CCQ scores were rather stable through the study. However, half of the dimensions demonstrated less favorable conditions at the 24-month follow-up. In the MBI measurements, the mean scores worsened at 12 months, but ultimately (i.e., after 24 months) improved from baseline (Fläckman et al., 2009).

Nursing managers Most studies that we found discussed clinical supervision for caregivers. Several organizational changes in the health care system have, however, also challenged nursing managers (Hyrkäs et al., 2005). One example is the two-year study reported earlier, which illuminated the managers' problem (Fläckman et al., 2007). First-line managers need support in their work, Hyrkäs et al. (2005) claimed, because of organizational changes and scarce economic resources. First-line managers believed that one of these supportive measures is clinical supervision. Dwyer (2011) conducted a systematic review about the experiences of registered nurses as managers and leaders in residential aged care facilities. This indicated that nurses show a strong motivation in the work and provide the best outcomes in nursing the elderly. They, however, experience a lack of professional support and collaboration from allied health and medical colleagues. In Sweden, there is a lack of specific education that is focused on clinical leadership and health team management, and no current structured pathway of learning and development for nursing careers. Nurses identify with their leadership role in residential aged care, and experience paradoxical feelings of being valued by the clients yet devalued by the system at the same time. Organizational barriers are strong in preventing continuing education and skills development for nurse leaders in aged care environments. Hyrkäs et al. followed up a group of first-line managers in a Finnish University hospital who had participated in a two-year clinical supervision intervention in 1999–2000. The managers' perceptions of the clinical supervision were assessed twice during the intervention and one year after (year 2001). The study aimed to describe how the first-line managers saw the future effects of the clinical supervision intervention, a year after its termination. Data were collected using empathy-based stories, which involved writing short essays. The managers indicated that clinical supervision had fostered, in the full three-year time frame, positive long-term effects on their leadership and communication skills, the desire for self-development, self-knowledge, and coping. Managers overall believed that, in the long run, clinical supervision would provide them with a broader perspective on work and would enhance the use of clinical supervision as a supportive measure among co-workers. First-line managers expected clinical supervision to have long-term positive effects on their work and coping. Empathy-based stories, as a method, were considered well suited to such studies, which aim to obtain future-oriented knowledge.

A second review, drawn from national and international databases (including doctoral dissertations, distinguished theses, and peer-reviewed articles), described administrative clinical supervision from the nursing leaders', directors', and administrators' perspectives (Sirola-Karvinen & Hyrkäs, 2006). The findings supported earlier perceptions concerning the importance and significance of administrative clinical supervision for nursing managers and administrators. Koivu et al. (2011) compared background characteristics and perceptions of work and health between medical and surgical nurses who had undertaken clinical supervision (n = 124) or who had decided not to undertake clinical supervision (n = 204). Differences in the perceptions of work and dimensions of burnout were found between the two groups. It appeared that nurses who were attracted to clinical supervision formed a distinctive group in the unit, standing out as self-confident, committed, and competent professionals who were supported by empowering and fair leadership.

Conclusions

Dementia care and treatment is not only a question of humanity, but also of economy (Butterworth et al., 2008; Jedenius, 2010). The rapid increase in the number of elderly and people with a DD (Jonsson & Wimo, 2009; OECD, 2009) makes it necessary to work with both topics. Biological and physiological changes in the elderly after clinical supervision are rarely reported in the international literature. In the work summarized here, we have indicated how efficient interventions can encourage those who care for elderly with cognitive impairment to accept and implement new knowledge about psychosocial methods, improving the quality of care. These interventions include ongoing supervision, training, and support, featuring feedback and concrete discussions around the daily work. We believe that such interventions, within a suitable milieu, contribute to a sense of well-being and an enhanced quality of life for both persons with cognitive impairment and their caregivers.

References

Barnard, K. E. (1981). Nursing child assessment satellite training. *Learner's manual.* Seattle, WA: University of Washington.

Begat, I., & Severinsson, E. (2006). Reflection on how clinical nursing supervision enhances nurses' experiences of wellbeing to their psychosocial work environment. *Journal of Nursing Management, 14*, 610–616.

Berggren, I. (2005). *Ethics in clinical nursing supervision – An analysis of fundamental ethical issues of the influence of clinical nursing supervision, with special reference to ethical decision making* (PhD Dissertation). Faculty of Medicine, Oslo university, Norway.

Berggren, I., Barbosa da Silva, A., & Severinsson, E. (2005). Core ethical issues of clinical nursing supervision. *Nursing and Health Services, 7*, 21–28.

Berggren, I., & Severinsson, E. (2006). The significance of nurse supervisors' different ethical decision-making styles. *Journal of Nursing Management, 14*, 637–643.

Bicket, M. C., Samus, Q. M., McNabney, M., Onyke, C. U., Mayer, L. S., Barndt, J., Rabins, P., . . . & Rosenblatt, A. (2010). The physical environment influences neuropsychiatric symptoms and other outcomes in assisted living residents. *International Journal of Geriatric Psychiatry, 25*, 1044–1054.

Bondas, T. (2010). Nursing leadership from the perspective of clinical group supervision: A paradoxical practice. *Journal of Nursing Management, 18*, 477–486.

Bråne, G., Karlsson, I., Kihlgren, M., & Norberg, A. (1989). Integrity promoting care of demented nursing home patients: Psychological and biochemical changes. *International Journal of Geriatric Psychiatry, 4*, 165–172.

Brodaty, H., & Gresham, M. (1989). Effect of a training program to reduce stress in carers of patients with dementia. *Brittish Medical Journal, 299*, 1375–1379.

Brodaty, H., Gresham, M., & Luscombe, G. (1997). The Prince Henry Hospital dementia caregivers' training program. *International Journal of Geriatric Psychiatry, 12*, 183–192.

Brunero, S., & Lamont, S. (2012). The process. Logistics and challenges of implementing clinical supervision in a generalist tertiary referral hospital. *Scandinavian Journal of Caring Sciences, 26*, 186–193.

Butterworth, T., Bell, L., Jackson, C., & Pajnkihar, M. (2008). Wicked spell or magic bullet?A review of the clinical supervision literature 2001–2007. *Nurse Education Today, 28*, 264–272.

Butterworth, T., Carson, J., White, K., Leacnck, J., Clcmenfi, A., & Bishop, V. (1997). *It is good to talk, clinical supervision and mentorship. An evaluation study in England and Scotland.* Manchester, UK: The University of Manchester.

Butterworth, T., & Faugier, J. (1992). *Clinical supervision and mentorship in nursing.* London, UK: Chapman and Hall.

Buus, N., Angel, S., Traynor, M., & Gonge, H. (2011). Psychiatric nursing staff members' reflections on participating in group-based clinical supervision: A semi structured interview study. *International Journal of Mental Health Nursing, 20*, 95–101.

Chalfont, G. (2011). Charnley Fold: A practice model of environmental design for enhanced dementia day care. *Social Care &Neurodisability, 2*(2), 71–79.

Choi, J., & Johantgen, M. (2012). The importance of supervision in retention of CNAs. *Research in Nursing & Health, 35*, 1–12.

Cooke, D. D., McNally, L., Mulligan, K. T., Harrison, M. J., & Newman, S. P. (2001). Psychosocial interventions for caregivers of people with dementia: A systematic review. *Aging and Mental Health, 5*, 120–135.

Cummins, A. (2009). Clinical supervision: The way forward? A review of the literature. *Nurse Education in Practice, 9*, 215–220.

Deponte, A., & Missan, R. (2007). Effectiveness of validation therapy (VT) in group: Preliminary results. *Archives of Gerontology and Geriatrics, 44*, 113–117.

Dwyer, D. (2011). Experiences of registered nurses as managers and leaders in residential aged care facilities: A systematic review. *International Journal of Evidence Based Health, 9*, 388–402.

Edberg, A. K., Hallberg, I. R., & Gustafsson, L. (1996). *Effects of clinical supervision on nurse patient cooperation quality: A controlled study of dementia care . . . including commentary by Iwasiw CL. and Bol N.* London, UK: Sage Publications.

Edberg, A. K., Norberg, A., & Hallberg, I. R. (1999). Mood and general behavior of patients with sevre dementia during one year of supervised, individualized planned care and systematic clinical supervision. Comparison with a similar control group. *Aging (Milan, Italy), 11*, 395–403.

Edwards, D., Burnard, P., Hanningan, B., Cooper, L., Adams, J., Juggessur, T., . . . Coyle, D. (2006). Clinical supervision and burnout: The influence of clinical supervision for community mental health nurses. *Journal of Clinical Nursing, 15*, 1007–1015.

Ekman, S.-L., Wahlin, T. B., Norberg, A., & Winblad, B. (1993). Relationship between bilingual dementedimmigrants and bilingual/monolingual caregivers. *International Journal of Aging and Human Development, 37*, 37–54.

Ekvall, G. (1996). Organizational climate for creativity and innovation. *European Journal of Work and Organizational Psychology, 5*, 105–123.

Engström, M., Ljungren, B., & Lindqvist, R. (2006). Staff satisfaction with work, perceived quality of care and stress in elderly care: Psychometric assessments and associations. *Journal of Nursing Management, 14*, 318–328.

Engström, M., Wadensten, B., & Häggström, E. (2010). Caregivers' job satisfaction and empowerment before and after an intervention focused on caregiver empowerment. *Journal of Nursing Management, 18*, 14–23.

Erikson, E. H. (1982). *The life cycle completed.* New York, NY: W.W. Norton & Company Inc.

Erikson, E. H., Erikson, J. M., & Kivnick, H. Q. (1986). *Vital involvement in old age.* New York, NY: W.W. Norton & Company Inc.

Erikson, J. M. (1988). *Wisdom and the senses. The way of creativity.* New York, NY: W.W. Norton & Company Inc.

Feil, N. (1992). Validation therapy with late-onset dementia populations. In G. M. M. Jones & B. M. L. Miesen (Eds.), *Care-giving in dementia, research and applications* (pp. 199–218). London, UK, New York, NY: Tavistock/Routledge.

Fläckman, B. (2008). *Work in eldercare – Staying or leaving. Caregivers' experiences of work and support during organizational changes* (PhD dissertation). Division of Geriatric Medicine, Karolinska Institutet, Sweden.

Fläckman, B., Fagerberg, I., Häggström, E., Kihlgren, A., & Kihlgren, M. (2007). Despite shattered expectations a willingness to care for elders remains with education and clinical supervision. *Scandinavian Journal of Caring Sciences, 21*, 379–389.

Fläckman, B., Hansebo, G., & Kihlgren, A. (2009). Struggling to adapt: Caring for older persons while under threat of organizational change and termination. *Nursing Inquiry, 16*, 82–91.

Gottfries, C. G., Bråne, G., Gullberg, B., & Steen, G. (1982). A new rating scale for dementia syndromes. *Archives of Gerontology and Geriatrics, 11*, 311–330.

Haberstroh, J., Hampel, H., & Pantel, J. (2010). Optimal management of Alzheimer's disease patients: Clinical guidelines and family advice. *Neuropsychiatric Disease and Treatment, 6*, 243–253.

Hadfield, D. (2000). Clinical supervision: Users' perspective. *Journal of Child Health Care, 4*, 30–34.

Häggström, E. (2005). *Municipal care for older people. Experiences narrated by caregivers and relatives* (PhD dissertation). Division of Geriatric Medicine, Karolinska Institutet, Sweden.

Häggström, E., Skovdahl, K., Fläckman, B., Kihlgren, A. L., & Kihlgren, M. (2004). To feel betrayed and to feel that you are betraying the old residents: Caregivers' experiences at a newly opened nursing home. *Journal of Clinical Nursing, 13*, 687–696.

Häggström, E., Skovdahl, K., Fläckman, B., Kihlgren, A. L., & Kihlgren, M. (2005). Work satisfaction and dissatisfaction – caregivers' experiences after a two-year intervention in a newly opened nursing home. *Journal of Clinical Nursing, 14*, 9–19.

Hall, G., & Buckwalter, K. (1987). Progressively lowered stress threshold: A conceptual model for care of adults with Alzheimer's disease. *Archives of Psychiatric Nursing, 1*, 399–406.

Hansebo, G. (2000). *Assessment of patients' needs and resources as a basis in supervision for individualized nursing care in nursing home wards. Evaluation of an intervention study* (PhD dissertation). Division of Geriatric Medicine, KarolinskaInstitutet, Sweden.

Hansebo, G., & Kihlgren, M. (2000). Patient life stories and current situation as told by carers in nursing home wards. *Clinical Nursing Research, 9*, 260–279.

Hansebo, G., & Kihlgren, M. (2001). Carers' reflections about their video recorded interactions with patients suffering from severe dementia. *Journal of Clinical Nursing, 10*, 737–747.

Hansebo, G., & Kihlgren, M. (2002). Carers' interactions with patients suffering from severe dementia – a difficult balance to facilitate mutual togetherness. *Journal of Clinical Nursing, 11*, 225–236.

Hansebo, G., & Kihlgren, M. (2004). Nursing home care: Changes after supervision. *Journal of Advanced Nursing, 45*, 269–279.

Hansebo, G., Kihlgren, M., & Ljunggren, G. (1999). Review of nursing documentation in nursing home wards – changes after intervention for individualised care. *Journal of Advanced Nursing, 29*, 1462–1473.

Hansebo, G., Kihlgren, M., Ljunggren, G., & Winblad, B. (1998). Staff views on the Resident Assessment Instrument, RAI/MDS in nursing homes, and the use of the Cognitive Performance Scale, CPS, in different levels of care in Stockholm, Sweden. *Journal of Advanced Nursing, 28*, 642–653.

Hunter, E. P., & Blair, S. E. E. (1999). Staff supervision for occupational therapists. *British Journal of Occupational Therapists, 62*, 344–350.

Hyrkäs, K. (2005). Clinical supervision, burnout, and jobsatisfaction among mental health and psychiatric nurses in Finland. *Issues in Mental Health Nursing, 26*, 531–556.

Hyrkäs, K., Appelqvist-Schmidlechner, K., & Haatja, R. (2006). Efficacy of clinical supervision: Influence on job satisfaction, burnout and quality of care. *Journal of Advanced Nursing, 55*, 521–535.

Hyrkäs, K., Appelqvist-Schmidlechner, K., & Kivimaki, K. (2005). First line managers' view of the long term effects of clinical supervision: How does clinical supervision support and develop leadership in health care? *Journal of Nursing Management, 13*, 209–220.

Jedenius, E. (2010). *Resource utilization in dementia – A question of collaboration* (PhD dissertation). Division of Geriatric Medicine, KarolinskaInstitutet, Sweden.

Johansson, I., Holm, A.-K., Lindqvist, I., & Severinsson, E. (2006). the value of caring in nursing supervision. *Journal of Nursing Management, 14*, 644–651.

Jones, A. (2006). Clinical supervision: What do we know and what do we need to know? A review and commentary. *Journal of Nursing Management, 14*, 577–585.

Jonsson, L., & Wimo, A. (2009). The cost of dementia in Europe: A review of the evidence, and methodological considerations. *Pharmaeconomics, 27*, 391–393.

Kihlgren, M. (1992). *Integrity promoting care of demented patients* (PhD dissertation). Umeå University, Umeå, Sweden.

Kihlgren, M., Bråne, G., Karlsson, I., Kuremyr, D., Leissner, P., & Norberg, A. (1992). Long-term influences on demented patients in different caring milieus, a collective living unit and a nursing home. A descriptive study. *Dementia (Basel, Switzerland)*, *3*, 342–349.

Kihlgren, M., Hallgren, A., Norberg, A., Bråne, G., & Karlsson, I. (1990). Effects of the training of integrity promoting care on the interaction at a long-term ward. Analysis of video-recorded social activities. *Scandinavian Journal of Caring Sciences*, *4*, 21–28.

Kihlgren, M., Hallgren, A., Norberg, A., & Karlsson, I. (1994). Integrity promoting care of demented patients. Patterns of interaction during morning care. *International Journal of Aging and Human Development*, *39*, 303–319.

Kihlgren, M., Hallgren, A., Norberg, A., & Karlsson, I. (1996). Disclosure of basic strengths and basic weaknesses in demented patients during morning care. Analysis of video-recordings by means of the Erikson theory of "eight stages of man". *International Journal of Aging and Human Development*, *43*, 219–233.

Kihlgren, M., Lindsten, I., Norberg, A., & Karlsson, I. (1992). The content of the oral daily reports at a long-term ward before and after staff training in integrity promoting care. *Scandinavian Journal of Caring Sciences*, *6*, 105–112.

Kihlgren, M., Kuremyr, D., Norberg, A., Bråne, G., Engström, B., Karlsson, I., & Melin, E. (1993). Nurse-patient interaction after training in integrity promoting care at a long-term ward. Analysis of video-recorded morning care sessions. *International Journal of Nursing Studies*, *30*, 1–13.

Koivu, A., Hyrkäs, K., & Saarinen, P. I. (2011). Who attends clinical supervision? The uptake of clinical supervision by hospital Nurses. *Journal of Nursing Management*, *19*, 69–79.

Lindahl, B., & Norberg, A. (2002). Clinical supervision in an intensive care unit: A space for relief, and for sharing emotions and experience of care. *Journal of Clinical Nursing*, *11*, 809–818.

Livni, D., Crowe, T. P., & Gonsalvez, C. J. (2012). Effects of supervision modality and intensity on alliance and outcomes for the supervisee. *Rehabilitation Psychology*, *5*, 178–186.

Lyth, G. M. (2000). Clinical supervision: A concept analysis. *Journal of Advanced Nursing*, *31*, 722–729.

Mamhidir, A.-G., Karlsson, I., Norberg, A., & Kihlgren, M. (2008). Weight increase in patients with dementia, and alteration in meal routines and meal environment after integrity promoting care. *Research and Practice in Alzheimer's Disease*, *13*, 1–4.

Maslach, C., Jackson, S. E., & Leiter, P. (1996). *Maslach burnout inventory manual*. Palo Alto, CA: Consulting Psychologists Press, Inc.

Milne, D. (2007). An empirical definition of clinical supervision. *British Journal of Clinical Psychology*, *46*, 437–447.

Morris, J. N., Hawes, C., Fries, B. E., Philips, C. D., Mor, V., et al. (1990). Designing the National Assessment Instrument for nursing homes. *The Gerontologist*, *30*, 293–03.

Morris, J. N., Hawes, C., Murphy, K., Nonemaker, S., Phillips, C., Fries, B. E., & Mor, V. (1991). *Resident Assessment Instrument training manual and resource guide*. Natick, MA: Elliot Press.

Neal, M., & Briggs, M. (2003). Validation therapy for dementia. *Cochrane Database of Systematic Reviews (Online)*, (3), CD001394.

OECD. Organisation for Economic Co-operation and Development. (2009). *Policies for healthy ageing: An overview*. OECD Health working papers no 42. Directorate for employment labour and social affairs health committee. Retrieved from http://www.oecd.org/LongAbstract/0,3425,en_2649_33929_42223436_119684_1_1_1,00.html

van Ooijen, E. (2000). *Clinical supervision: A practical guide*. Edinburgh, UK: Churchill Livingstone.

Sandman, P. O., Norberg, A., & Adolfsson, R. (1988). Verbal communication and behaviour during meals in five institutionalized patients with Alzheimer-type dementia. *Journal of Advanced Nursing*, *13*, 571–578.

SBU (The Swedish Council on Technology Assessment in Health Care). (2008). *Dementia – Caring, Ethics, Ethnical and Economical Aspects. A systematic review*. Volume 3.

Severinsson, E. (1996). Nurse supervisors' views of their supervisory styles in clinical supervision: A hermeneutic approach. *Journal of Nursing Management*, *4*, 191–199.

Severinsson, E. (2001). Confirmation, meaning and self-awareness as core concepts of the nursing supervision model. *Nursing Ethics*, *8*, 36–44.

Sirola-Karvinen, P., & Hyrkäs, K. (2006). Clinical supervision for nurses in administrative and leadership positions: A systematic literature review of the studies focusing on administrative clinical supervision. *Journal of Nursing Management*, *14*, 601–609.

Sloan, G., White, C., & Coit, F. (2000). Cognitive therapy supervision as a framework for clinical supervision in nursing: Using structure to guide. *Journal of Advanced Nursing*, *32*, 515–524.

Smith, M., Gerdner, L., Hall, G., & Buckwalter, K. C. (2004). History, development, and future of the progressively lowered stress threshold: A conceptual model for dementia care. *Journal of American Geriatric Society*, *52*, 1755–1760.

Söderlund, M., Norberg, A., & Hansebo, G. (2012). Implementation of the validation method: Nurses' descriptions of caring relationships with residents with dementia disease. *Dementia (Basel, Switzerland)*, *11*, 569–587.

Spreitzer, G. M. (1995). Psychological empowerment in the workplace: Dimensions, measurement, and validation. *Academy of Management Journal*, *38*, 1442–1465.

Svensson, T. (1984). *Aging and environment. Institutional aspects* (PhD dissertation). Department of Education and Psychology University of Linköping, Linköping, Sweden.

Wadensten, B., Engström, M., & Häggström, E. (2009). Public nursing home staff's experience of participating in an intervention aimed at enhancing their self-esteem. *Journal of Nursing Management*, *17*, 833–842.

Wimo, A., Mattsson, B., Adolfsson, R., Eriksson, T., & Nelvig, A. (1993). Dementia day care and its effects on symptoms and institutionalization – a controlled Swedish study. *Scandinavian Journal of Primary Health Care*, *11*, 117–123.

Winstanley, J., & White, E. (2002). Clinical supervision: Models, measures and best practice. *Nurse Researcher*, *10*, 7–38.

Yura, H., & Walsh, M. (1988). *The nursing process: Assessing, planning, implementing, evaluating* (5th ed.). New York, NY: Appelton & Lange.

8

On the Education of Clinical Supervisors

C. Edward Watkins, Jr. and Chiachih DC Wang

In accordance with Gordan (1997), we believe that "The training of psychotherapists [and counselors] can never be better than the competence of its supervisors" (p. 135). In this chapter, we would like to examine supervisor education as a vital means of enhancing supervisory competence.

Our Vision of Supervisor Education: Setting the Stage

The training and supervising of beginning *supervisors-in-learning* is very much a process of conviction and commitment, whereby supervisor educators have faith and belief in the power and preeminence of the supervisor education experience to best prepare and ready new supervisors for practice. As we envision it, supervisor education (training/supervision) is an *awe and wonder transmission process about an awe and wonder transmission process*: just as psychotherapy/counseling education is designed to transmit the awe and wonder of doing psychological treatment to therapy/counselor trainees, supervisor education is designed to transmit the awe and wonder of doing supervision to supervisor trainees. In doing that, we believe that supervisor educators – when they are at their best – generally hold to a collection of core, abiding convictions about clinical supervision that consistently informs and guides their conceptualization and conduct of the supervision education endeavor itself; in our view, the ever-expanding body of supervision literature explicitly or implicitly suggests that to be so as well. Some of what we see as being those most fundamental, foundational, supremely important supervision convictions are identified in Table 8.1. These 10 (nonexhaustive) convictions: (a) undergird good supervision practice; (b) are ideally held as sacrosanct by supervisors and supervisor educators;

The Wiley International Handbook of Clinical Supervision, First Edition. Edited by C. Edward Watkins, Jr. and Derek L. Milne.

Table 8.1 Fundamental guiding, abiding convictions that supervisors and supervisor educators ideally hold about clinical supervision.

1. Clinical supervision is a crucial means, if not *the crucial means*, by which the traditions, practice, and culture of psychotherapy/counseling are taught, transmitted, and perpetuated.
2. As a supremely important educational intervention, clinical supervision is a *unique, substantive area* of inquiry and practice, involving its own process, product, models, and methods, and deserves to be treated as such.
3. Clinical supervision is a process by which and through which supervisors eminently strive to *embrace, empower, and emancipate* the therapeutic potential of the supervisees with whom they have the privilege to work.
4. Clinical supervision is also a process whereby supervisors eminently strive to communicate and transmit the *awe and wonder* of doing psychological treatment and being a psychotherapist/counselor.
5. In psychotherapy/counseling education, clinical supervision is seemingly unmatched in being the *single most powerful learning experience* that most significantly contributes to the development and enhancement of the budding trainee's ability to (a) meaningfully apprehend, reflect on, and conceptualize the totality of the therapeutic process; and (b) appropriately intervene in, manage, and guide the treatment experience.
6. Clinical supervision is also seemingly unmatched in being the *single most powerful learning experience* that most significantly contributes to the development and enhancement of the budding trainee's sense of professional identity.
7. Clinical supervision practice forever deserves and is best when infused by the supervisor's *full investment* in, *complete commitment* to, and *incandescent passion* for the activity of supervision itself.
8. Competence in clinical supervision does not "fall from the sky" but, rather, results from the development and acquisition of a *special body of supervision knowledge, set of supervision skills, and corpus of supervision values* that serve to then informatively and consistently guide supervision conceptualization and conduct.
9. To be best learned, disseminated, and integrated, supervision knowledge, skills, and values *deserve substantial training attention* in graduate school, post graduation, or ideally during both periods of practice.
10. The process of being a competent, effective supervisor is embraced as an *ongoing, lifelong journey*, involving relatively continuous, if not continuous, efforts to remain current with developments in the field of supervision, challenge existing skills, and ensure that one's practice is forever grounded in, and guided by, a competency-based approach.

Source: Adapted from Watkins, C. E., Jr. (2013f). Reproduced with permission of the International Journal of Psychotherapy.

(c) are ideally lived and modeled throughout the supervision education process; and (d) form a substantive part of the message that we as supervisors wish to convey to our supervisor trainees. While not in and of themselves guaranteeing "good enough" supervision practice, these convictions do indeed appear present wherever such practice does occur and merit educational accentuation for that reason; they seemingly enliven, inspire, and impassion and, thereby, bring meaning and purpose to supervision. In proceeding, those 10 convictions will provide the substrate on which our subsequent supervisor education discussion is based.

Introduction

In contemporary therapist and counselor education, it is axiomatic, a foregone conclusion that to provide the most informed and competent clinical services, therapists and counselors need to be rigorously and vigorously trained in how to provide clinical services. It would accordingly stand to reason that if supervisors are to provide the most informed and competent supervision services, then they should be rigorously and vigorously trained themselves in how to provide supervision of such clinical work. But across the history of supervision, such rigorous, vigorous training has by no means been the norm: (a) training in how to supervise has generally been less recognized as *sine qua non* for supervisory practice; (b) being a supervisee oneself or gaining seniority have been seen as sufficiently qualifying supervision credentials; and (c) resistance to supervisor education has even been on display (e.g., Alonso, 2000; Fleming, 2012; Milne & James, 2002; Schlesinger, 1981; Whitman, Ryan, & Rubenstein, 2001). Approximately 25 years ago, Watkins (1992) referred to this lamentable absence of supervisor training for supervisors as the "persistent paradox without parallel" in psychotherapy education, and shortly thereafter summarized the then state of affairs as follows:

> . . . the facts here are staggering: (a) Psychotherapists-in-training typically are closely scrutinized and supervised because becoming a therapist is considered to be a labor-intensive endeavor for which much training and supervision are needed; (b) supervisors have the charge of facilitating the growth and development of their supervisees and, in turn, helping those supervisees facilitate the growth and development of their patients; and (c) though being the ultimately responsible party in the supervisor-supervisee-patient triad, supervisors typically receive little to no training in how to supervise and do supervision . . .. Something does not compute. We would never dream of turning untrained therapists loose on needy patients, so why would we turn those untrained supervisors loose on those untrained therapists who help those needy patients? (Watkins, 1997, p. 604).

While that educational paradox has not completely disappeared (cf. Watkins, 2013b), it appears to be much less prevalent today. A sea change has been evident in supervision's last generation, with far more attention being directed at supervisor training during that period than at any other time. Across the variety of mental health disciplines, the eminent value of competent supervision has been increasingly recognized, the value of supervisor training for supervisors has been increasingly acknowledged as potentially fostering competent supervision practice, and in some circles supervisor training programs have already been, or are, in the process of being implemented. As Borders (2010) has aptly stated, "Today, the need for supervisor training is widely accepted . . . although the practice of requiring, even offering, supervisor training in academic programs continues to vary rather substantially across disciplines . . ." (p. 130).

With regard to clinical supervisor training, what is its current status? In what directions does the area need to move to best advance and how do different countries address supervisor training now? In this chapter, we would like to examine those questions. For our purposes, "supervisor training" will be used to designate both supervisor instruction (e.g., through seminar or workshop participation) and supervisor supervision. The primary issues about supervisor training that we wish to consider are: (a) need and rationale for such training; (b) the best time to receive it; (c) critical areas of concern deemed most important to cover; (d) structure of training; (e) delivery; (f) educational methods, tools, and strategies deemed most useful; (g) the role of supervisor development; (h) the role of "competencies"; and (i) research.

What Do We Know or Believe about Supervisor Training?

Why is supervisor training needed?

Across supervision's history, psychotherapy educators have seemingly had a somewhat tortured relationship with the idea of supervision training for supervisors. We have moved from a period of neglect, where any need for supervisor training was not even considered at all, to ambivalence, where grudging recognition emerged that supervisor training could be important to consider, to embrace, where supervisor training is now generally recognized as needed or potentially beneficial. Disciplines still vary in the extent to which they provide or mandate actual supervisor training, but the seeming value of supervisor training appears to at least be on the collective educational radar screen now. But why is that? What has brought about such a change?

Perhaps the weight of logic itself would be a key factor in stimulating that change. As we stated at this chapter's outset, it would stand to reason that if supervisors are to provide the most informed and competent supervision services, then they should be rigorously and vigorously trained themselves in how to provide supervision of clinical work. While that logic currently seems incontrovertible and easy enough to readily acknowledge, it has been slow in becoming educational reality, having earlier gone wholly unrecognized as pivotal or even been resisted as important at various points along the way.

If we dial back the time clock on supervision, some of the thinking in decades past – unspoken though it may have been – seems to have clearly reflected the belief that "Anyone can supervise. No special skills required." While that belief appears to have lingered long in supervision and may not be completely extinguished even now, we are glad to say that it is largely either gone or on its way to fast becoming a relic of a bygone era.

The decades of supervision history and experience have taught us that (a) supervision and therapy, although similar in some respects, are different processes and should be treated as such; (b) supervision is a preeminently educational process that is designed to develop and enhance therapist competence, and supervisors would do well to foremost treat supervision as an educational enterprise and accordingly align their efforts with an educational role; (c) supervision is a unique, highly instrumental helping/learning experience in psychotherapy education that has its own special skill set, process, and product; (d) supervision, as a unique, instrumental helping/learning experience, needs to be studied in its own right; and (e) just as becoming a competent therapist greatly benefits from, even requires therapist training, becoming a competent supervisor greatly benefits from, even requires supervisor training. We have come to increasingly see that supervisor skills do not just fall from the sky, result from osmosis, or come fully formed from a "See one, do one, teach one" process (Gonsalvez, 2008; Whitman et al., 2001). Rather, if supervisor skills are to be had, they have to be earned through ongoing training, study, practice, and self-reflection.

Going along with this "weight of logic" factor, a number of other factors or reasons appear to have also played a prominent part in our coming to increasingly see the need for, or potential importance of, supervisor training. Gonsalvez and Milne (2010) have identified some of those factors as follows: (a) international expert consensus has supported the need for supervisor training; (b) clinical opinion and empirical data have converged to suggest that supervisor experience does not beget supervisor expertise; (c) indications point to unsound and inefficient supervision practices being widespread; (d) concerns have been raised that supervision practice without having had supervision training might be unethical; and (e) some research (limited though it may be) suggests that supervisor training can enhance supervisory functioning. Those identified factors are all matters of substantial import, and when considered collectively, have further added weight to the increasingly indisputable need for or potential significance of supervisor training. In our opinion, justifications for the need for, and value of, supervisor training are convincing, compelling, and eminently sound.

When is the best time to receive supervisor training?

From our observations and study, there appear to be two schools of thought on this issue. On the one hand, opinion has been expressed that learning supervision should only come after the student has learned about therapy and graduated to professional practice. The logic of this argument seems to be that therapy training is about learning therapy; students have enough to learn with therapy being their sole focus; students' attention should not be divided and diverted during therapy training; after having become fully equipped in therapy, the student cum professional should only then give attention to learning supervision. On the surface, there is a common sense, intuitive appeal to that logic. Yet we do admit to wondering if there has sometimes been an unspoken agenda also in operation here – where learning therapy reigns ascendant, learning supervision is viewed as an unnecessary distraction, and supervision in turn gets relegated to the professional "after-party." The hazard of that possibility is that if supervision is a "left-over" for after graduation, and if supervision training is not a required after-graduation requirement of professional associations, the learning of supervision becomes an entirely voluntary affair and all the easier to shuffle to lower priority status. Although that is a less likely scenario today, it still remains possible in some professional circles.

But if learning supervision is professional priority, then it should unequivocally be professionally prioritized. The second school of thought on this matter appears to readily reflect that emphasis: Affirming that supervisor training should begin during (not after) graduate training. For example, we now see such emphasis evident in psychology and counseling programs in Australia, the United Kingdom, and United States (Bernard & Goodyear, 2014; Fleming, 2012; Gonsalvez & Milne, 2010), and all indications suggest that incorporating supervisor training into the graduate curricula will remain or eventually be embraced as the recommended strategy (cf. Pegeron, 2008). Where that is the case, what are the real benefits of that inclusion?

Fleming (2012) provides a nice answer to that question: ". . .it is important to provide the skills to trainees to enable them to play an active part in their own supervision. In my experience this ability [supervisee's being able to make the most of supervision] is regularly discussed during supervisor training, and training in supervision skills and processes will inform and help trainees to enhance the effectiveness of the supervision they receive during training" (p. 87). With that perspective in mind, supervisor training, then, can be seen as being dual purposed: helping students learn about providing supervision while helping them to also be better supervision consumers themselves.

In our view, supervisor training during graduate school also affords students more opportunity to better process the training experience itself and contributes to their development of some beginning sense of supervisory identity. Just as students' learning of therapy is greatly benefited from their being ensconced in a rich educational, therapy-focused environment, where they are surrounded by like-minded and like-purposed confederates over time, the same applies for students who are learning supervision: they are most apt to be enriched by, and develop professionally when ensconced in a rich, supervision-focused environment, where they too are surrounded by like-minded and like-purposed confederates over time. Much as Ekstein and Wallerstein (1958) said almost 60 years ago, professional identity "originates . . . in the process of training" (p. 66). We believe that to be very much the case for clinical supervisors' professional identity and see that identity as being best developed first in a community training experience that ideally starts in graduate school. It may well be that some type of supervisor identity development occurs by means of far more abbreviated training (e.g., a one-day or two-day supervision workshop), but we see that as being much less likely.

What are the critical areas of concern deemed most important to cover in supervisor training?

In surveying various sources across various disciplines across various countries, there appears to be an international and interdisciplinary consensus about the crucial areas that seem most important to cover in supervisor training: supervisor/supervisee roles and responsibilities, ethical/legal issues in supervision, models of supervision, assessment/evaluation in supervision, models of therapist development, establishing and maintaining the supervision alliance, supervision interventions/strategies, diversity in supervision, and research about supervision (American Board of Examiners in Clinical Social Work, 2004; Bang & Park, 2009; Bernard & Goodyear, 2014; Borders, 2010, 2012; Borders et al., 1991; Dye & Borders, 1990; Falender et al., 2004; Fleming, 2012; Gonsalvez & Milne, 2010; Hoffman, 1990, 1994; Milne, Scaife, & Cliffe, 2009; Psychology Board of Australia, 2011; Riess & Fishel, 2000; Riess & Herman, 2008; Roth & Pilling, 2008; Turpin & Wheeler, 2011; Watkins, 2012b, 2013c; Westefeld, 2009). Each broad area of concern is composed of a number of key elements that require training attention. For example, under ethical and legal issues, some topics of interest would be privilege, confidentiality, informed consent, and dual relationships; under difference and diversity, some topics of interest would be individual differences, cultural and ethnic factors, and lifestyle considerations (Borders et al., 1991; Thomas, 2010).

In specifying the preeminent areas of concern in supervisor training and their constituent elements, a number of professional documents have been developed over the years to offer supervisor trainers with useful guidance and direction. Perhaps the Curriculum Guide for Training Counselor Supervisors (Borders et al., 1991) – supported by the Association for Counselor Education and Supervision (ACES) of the American Counseling Association – was the first, most ambitious, and most comprehensive example of such an effort: it specified seven primary areas of concern that needed supervisor training attention, identified three "threads" (knowledge, skills, self-awareness) that then needed attention within each area, and proposed learning objectives across those areas and threads. Although complex, that document still stands as a valuable resource for thinking about and structuring supervisor training and seems to have influenced or informed other supervisor training documents that have been subsequently produced (e.g., Falender et al., 2004). In one of its most recent initiatives, ACES has supported development of guidelines for Best Practices in Clinical Supervision (BPCS; Borders, 2012; in press). Like the Curriculum Guide, BPCS provides a comprehensive framework for development of supervisor training programs: it covers 12 broad areas of training concern and identifies a host of elements within each area that require attention. Although highly detailed, this guide also is an extremely valuable resource for stimulating thinking about training supervisors for best practices. While those two documents were developed within counselor education, they are highly relevant to, and potentially useful for, the training of clinical supervisors of any discipline.

How is supervisor training best structured?

In surveying various sources across various disciplines across various countries, there appears to be an international and interdisciplinary consensus that supervisor training should ideally involve both didactic and experiential components (e.g., American Board of Examiners in Clinical Social Work, 2004; Bernard & Goodyear, 2014; Borders, 2010; Borders et al., 1991; Dye & Borders, 1990; Falender et al., 2004; Fleming, 2012; Gonsalvez & Milne, 2010; Hoffman, 1990, 1994; Psychology Board of Australia, 2011; Roth & Pilling, 2008; Russell & Petrie, 1994; Sundin, Ogren, & Boethius, 2008; Turpin & Wheeler, 2011; Watkins, 1992, 2012a, 2012b; Westefeld, 2009; Whitman et al., 2001). The didactic component of training is designed to provide trainees with the needed conceptual/knowledge base about supervision and enhance their awareness about and understanding of substantive supervisory issues; it begins the process of learning to think like a supervisor (Borders, 1992). As Borders (2010) has indicated, some benefits of the didactic component include (a) "providing a framework for understanding supervisor's roles and the functions and goals of supervision" (p. 135); and (b) providing "a structure for conducting supervision sessions. . ." (p. 135). The experiential component of training – or supervision of supervision – is designed to provide trainees with opportunities to learn through doing. Just as therapy trainees benefit from having their treatment work supervised, supervisor trainees can also benefit from having their supervision sessions supervised. In current supervision thinking, the didactic and experiential are essential, complementary parts of an educational whole, where one without the other does not necessarily a supervisor make.

How is supervisor training best delivered?

Workshops, seminars, and class instruction are the primary means by which supervisor training occurs. Formal coursework in supervision can be offered as a part of the graduate curriculum. For practicing professionals, workshops that last anywhere from a few hours to a few days can be readily used to acquire such training (e.g., Milne, 2010; Psychology Board of Australia, 2011; Roth & Pilling, 2008). As indicated in the preceding paragraph, the didactic and experiential components would be ideally combined in any course or workshop format. Although that is not always the case, it has become increasingly common for coursework and workshops to include an experiential component, where trainees have opportunities to practice supervision skills and receive constructive feedback about their efforts. In the graduate curriculum, semester(s)-long supervision of supervision courses appear to have even become far more readily available at different universities around the world.

What are the educational methods and tools deemed most useful in supervisor training?

As part of any such formal coursework or workshops, a wide variety of methods and tools can potentially be employed to educate supervisor trainees. Some of these include: Group discussion, prescribed reading materials, Web-based instruction, e-learning materials, and training manuals (e.g., Frayn, 1991; Milne, 2010). Some face-to-face methods that tend to be frequently used in supervisor training include teaching, providing feedback, role-play, behavioral rehearsal, and modeling (cf. Milne, Aylott, Fitzpatrick, & Ellis, 2008; Milne, Sheikh, Pattison, & Wilkinson, 2011). In the experiential (or supervision of supervision) training component, supervisor trainees typically record tapes and/or process notes of their therapy supervision sessions, bring those to their own supervision for review and discussion, and their supervisor then helps them explore and consider their beginning efforts at doing supervision (e.g., Bernard, 2012; Haggerty & Hilsenroth, 2011). Furthermore, just as technological advances continue to affect and open up new vistas for enhancing therapist training and supervision (Barnett, 2011; Powell & Migdole, 2012), those advances will also continue to increasingly expand the digital arsenal of educational tools that supervisor trainers have at their disposal; such tools will continue to play an ever larger role in how supervisor training is conducted and become an ever more seamless, integrated part of how it is prosecuted (see Chapter 9 for elaboration).

What is the role of supervisor development in supervisor training?

To answer that question, let us first compare therapist versus supervisor development. We now have abundant data and professional opinion to support the widely accepted truth that "therapists develop": becoming a therapist or counselor is a growth process that involves steady accretions in therapist professional identity and skill development over time (Klein, Bernard, & Schermer, 2011; Orlinsky & Ronnestad, 2005; Ronnestad & Skovholt, 2003; Watkins, 2012c). Knowledge about the therapist development process can be highly useful to supervisors in facilitating understanding of supervisee struggles and needs and, thereby, allow for supervision to be tailored accordingly (Stoltenberg & McNeill, 2010; see Chapter 28). Those basic ideas about therapist development also apply when thinking about clinical supervisors: becoming a supervisor appears to involve a growth process that involves steady accretions in supervisor professional identity and skill development over time, and knowledge about the supervisor trainee development process can be highly useful in facilitating understanding of trainees' educational struggles and needs and, thereby, allow for the supervision of supervision experience to be better tailored accordingly (Watkins, 2012a, 2013a).

Models of supervisor development, products of the 1980s and 1990s, were proposed in an effort to capture the trajectory of that particular growth process and shine a light on the developmental nature of being and becoming a supervisor (see Alonso, 1983, 1985; Hess, 1986, 1987; Rodenhauser, 1994, 1997; Stoltenberg & Delworth, 1987; Watkins, 1990, 1993, 1994). Five of these models are summarized in Table 8.2. These models remain stage-oriented affairs, where changes that are speculated to occur over the course of supervisor development are charted; they (a) tend to be far more alike than different, being highly similar in their structure and content (Russell & Petrie, 1994; Watkins, 1995); and (b) can be helpful in providing "guidelines for supervisors to identify both the types of interventions and the kind of supervisory relationship that will promote . . . [supervisor trainees'] best growth and development. . ." (Chang & O'Hara, 2010, p. 149).

The core ideas that appear to underlie the supervisor development perspective include the following: (a) supervisor trainees can be expected to vary in their levels of conceptual understanding about and skillfulness in performing supervision; (b) supervisor trainees can be expected to vary in their readiness for, receptivity to, and ability to profit from supervisor training; (c) supervisor trainees appear to pass through a gradually unfolding developmental process, where over time they move from a beginning point where anxiety, discomfort, lack of confidence, and limited supervisory skill and identity preponderate to an endpoint where comfort, confidence, and heightened and solidified supervisory skill and identity preponderate; and (d) by taking their supervisor trainees' developmental variations in skillfulness, understanding, and readiness into account, supervisor educators are then better positioned to tailor training in ways that would be most meaningful to their respective trainees (Watkins, 2012a, 2012b). Becoming a supervisor, then, requires a host of shifts in perspective – developmental, perceptual, and conceptual – where the supervisor trainee establishes a supervisor identity, learns to think like a supervisor, and comes to conceive in terms of supervisor roles, functions, and tasks (Inman & Soheilian, 2010; Kemer, Borders, & Willse, in press; Watkins, 2013a). The supervisor development models reflect metatheoretical efforts, seemingly clinically valid (Russell & Petrie, 1994), to chart those shifts as they unfold over the course of supervisor trainees' process of learning and growth. In best stimulating those crucial shifts, supervisors ideally take into account their supervisor trainees' level of development, consider the according educational implications, and structure a training experience that is forever developmentally informed by that assessment.

Table 8.2 Stage summary for five supervisor development models.

Model	*Stage names and descriptions across models*			
	1	*2*	*3*	*4*
Alonso (1983, 1985)	Novice: Anxious, confused, conflicted; feels fraudulent; quest for identity; draws on experiences as supervisee to inform efforts	Midcareer: Internally settled; ideal mentor; generative, secure; stable sense of self; supervisory altruism in evidence	Late career: Adjusting to getting older personally/professionally. "The choice is between hope, wisdom, and integrity, and clinical despair and boredom" (Alonso, 1985, p. 75)	
Hess (1986, 1987)	Beginning: Often lack formal training; self-conscious, unaware, anxious; draws on experiences as supervisee for guidance	Exploration: Increasingly aware of importance of supervision and its impact on supervisees; needs of supervisees given priority; fluctuating though much improved performance; informal power base	Identity confirmation: Solidified supervisor identity; heightened sense of confidence and professionalism; high level of skillfulness	
Rodenhauser (1994, 1997)	Emulation: Draws on previous experiences as supervisee to provide direction; uses memories of past supervisor to guide work	Conceptualization: Conceptual foundation for supervision takes form; rough practice guidelines established; search for a "system" predominates	Incorporation: Increasingly aware of self as supervisor and impact on supervisees; increasingly sensitive to/respectful of differences and diversity; attention to parallel process phenomena emerges	Consolidation: Solidified identity; theoretically grounded; able to effectively address parallel process and supervisee counter-transference phenomena

Stoltenberg and McNeill (2010; cf. Stoltenberg & Delworth, 1987)	Level 1: Highly anxious, uncomfortable, confused; concerned about doing the "right thing"; can resort to "flight into structure"; draw on past supervisee experiences for direction	Level 2: Conflicted, confused, frustrated; fluctuating motivation and affectivity; assertion of autonomy mingled with lapses into dependency	Level 3: Consistent motivation; autonomous, comfortable, committed; able to engage in realistic self-appraisals; consults with colleagues on "as needed" basis	Level 3 integrated: "Master supervisor"; highly skilled and integrated; able to effectively work with wide variety of supervisees
Watkins (1990, 1993)	Role shock: Anxiety, confusion, turmoil; feels fraudulent (impostor phenomenon); limited to no supervisory confidence, identity, or self-awareness; great need for support from others	Role recovery/trransition: Some recognition of supervisory strengths and abilities; nascent identity core begins to take form; tension, anxiety, confusion, and turmoil abate; vacillating cognitive and affective experience	Role consolidation: Increasingly realistic sense of self and supervisory impact; general sense of confidence, solidified identity core; stable, consistent, secure; theoretically grounded; able to recognize and address supervisory transference, countertransference, and parallel process	Role mastery: "Master supervisor"; highest levels of awareness, skill, and identity achieved; consistency, stability, and consolidation predominate; highly committed to supervision as lifelong learning experience; highly adept at working with supervisory transference, countertransference, and parallel process

Source: Reprinted from Watkins (2012a, pp. 50–51) with permission of the Association for the Advancement of Psychotherapy.

What is the role of "competence" and "competencies" in supervisor training?

The enhancement of competence has always been a preeminent concern in clinical supervision, but since the dawn of the new millennium, focus on supervision competence and competencies has ratcheted up to a level of emphasis and scrutiny that lacks parallel across the entire 100-year-plus history of supervision (cf. Chapter 1 section on competency frameworks). Supervision competence, the more molar term, can be defined as the supervisor's "habitual and judicious use of communication, knowledge . . . technical [and supervision] skills, clinical [and educational] reasoning, emotions, values, and reflection in daily [supervision] practice for the benefit of . . . [supervisees, patients,] and the community being served" (adapted from Epstein & Hundert, 2002, p. 226). Supervisor competence, referring to the overall functioning of the supervisor, requires (a) possession of professional knowledge and skill, (b) professionally acting on that knowledge and skill, (c) public verification of what is achieved by such action, and (d) consistent demonstration over time (Rodolfa et al., 2005). Supervisor competency/competencies, the more molecular term, can be defined as the necessary combination of supervisor *skills/abilities, knowledge, and values* required to perform a specific supervisory task (e.g., form a relationship bond, provide effective feedback). Any supervisory competency, then, would be viewed as a *combination* or *bundling* of those three ingredients or components (Falender & Shafranske, 2004; Watkins, 2013b). In the competency movement today, skills/abilities (able performance), knowledge (know how), and values (e.g., respect for others) have come to be regarded across varied disciplines as essential ingredients for competency delineation.

If competence has always been of concern in supervision practice and training, what is really different now? How is the current competence push different from what we have been doing all along in supervision? As Falender and Shafranske (2012) have so nicely put it,

> What is new is the position that it is no longer acceptable to simply assume that competence has been attained. This critique challenges the implicit assumption that competence is necessarily or automatically achieved during the usual course of doctoral education and clinical training, and requires the explicit demonstration of competence. Such a shift involves an increased emphasis on evidence-based modes of assessment and places significant demands for accountability at all levels of training, i.e., on the institution, the supervisor and the supervisee, to ensure that professional capability has been attained and demonstrated. . .. efforts to address today's standards require steps to be taken to better identify the knowledge, skills and values that are assembled to form competencies as well as the means to reliably evaluate their development. (Falender & Shafranske, 2012, p. 129)

Their words have relevance for therapy/counseling supervision practice as well as the training of supervisors. The current competency movement, which is international in scope, is focused more so than ever before on the delineation and specification of training outcomes and demonstrating that those desired outcomes have been achieved (e.g., Fouad et al., 2009; Psychology Board of Australia, 2011, 2013; Rodolfa et al., 2005; Roth & Pilling, 2008; Turpin & Wheeler, 2011). Competence and competencies have well become "the zeitgeist of supervision discourse" (Holloway, 2012), and all indications suggest that that will remain the case for our near and distant future (Watkins, 2012d).

In surveying various sources across various disciplines across various countries, there does indeed appear to be an international and interdisciplinary consensus about the practice competencies that are deemed most important to acquire by means of supervisor training. Those core areas of competence include (a) knowledge about/understanding of supervision models, methods, and intervention; (b) knowledge about/skill in attending to matters of ethical, legal, and professional concern; (c) knowledge about/skill in managing supervision relationship processes; (d) knowledge about/skill in conducting supervisory assessment and evaluation; (e) knowledge about/skill in fostering attention to difference and diversity; and (f) openness to/utilization of a self-reflective, self-assessment stance in supervision (Watkins, 2012d, 2013c, 2013d, 2013e). Those six areas provide international guidance on what to address during the practice of therapy/counseling supervision *and* what to address during the training and supervision of supervisor trainees. For each core area of competence, a host of more specific defining competencies have been identified that would then require training attention. As of this writing, the most detailed competency-driven initiatives for supervision practice and education have emerged from Australia, the United Kingdom, and United States (e.g., Borders et al., 1991; Falender et al., 2004; Fouad et al., 2009; Psychology Board of Australia, 2013; Roth & Pilling, 2008; Turpin & Wheeler, 2011). Some examples of supervisor competencies by area, which seem to have cross-country applicability, are identified in Table 8.3.

A competence framework, so useful for thinking about the supervisor–therapist supervisee relationship, appears then to also have much to offer in thinking about the supervisor–supervisor trainee relationship and, thereby, help to enhance the training of clinical supervisors. Such a framework would seem of such value because it

> (1) consistently promotes educational clarity, specificity, and understanding for both supervisor and . . . [supervisor trainee]; (2) requires the identification of specific knowledge, skills, attitudes, and values that constitute specific competencies (thereby allowing training to be tailored accordingly); (3) facilitates, even requires, the articulation of specific training goals and learning objectives for . . . [supervisor trainees] (whereby supervision can be focused accordingly); (4) emphasizes collaborative identification and management of . . .[supervisor trainee] reactivity to particular supervision triggers (that elicit unusual affective response); (5) accents the importance of attending to supervisory relationship strains, ruptures, and their resolution; (6) supports the creation of conditions that make clear, targeted, and specific feedback increasingly possible (where areas of growth and areas in need of growth can be more concretely identified); (7) embraces competence, its maintenance, and its enhancement as an ongoing, continuous, lifelong educational process; and (8) provides means, motive, and opportunity for [therapist and] client welfare to be better guarded, protected, and enhanced. (Watkins, 2012d, p. 194)

With the potential weight and implications of those eight benefits considered, it becomes all the more clear why competency initiatives have had, and will most probably, continue to have such far-reaching educational ramifications in clinical supervision.

Table 8.3 Supervisor practice/training competencies of international import.

I. Knowledge about/understanding of supervision models, methods, and intervention
Supervisor demonstrates awareness/understanding of . . .
   1) . . . definition and purpose of supervisor role, its varied functions (e.g., to teach, to consult), and when implementation of those functions is most apropos;
   2) . . . supervision expectations and responsibilities for both supervisor and supervisee and the importance of consistently attending to those dimensions over the course of supervision; and
   3) . . . diverse supervision interventions and when to best implement them in practice.

II. Knowledge about/skill in attending to matters of ethical, legal, and professional concern
Supervisor demonstrates awareness/understanding of . . .
   1) . . . ethical principles as they relate to and guide supervisory action;
   2) . . . ethical decision-making skills and their appropriate application in supervision; and
   3) . . . ethical codes of conduct, laws, or statutes that impact the practice of supervision.

III. Knowledge about/skill in managing supervision relationship processes
Supervisor demonstrates knowledge about/skill in . . .
   1) . . . consistently creating a safe space for thinking and reflection characterized by empathy, respect, and trust;
   2) . . . modeling supervisory interventions that are informed by difference/diversity considerations; and
   3) . . . establishing a mutual supervision agreement that is guided by an ethos of openness and transparency.

IV. Knowledge about/skill in conducting supervisory assessment and evaluation
Supervisor demonstrates knowledge about/skill in . . .
   1) . . . conducting a learning-based supervisee assessment, where each supervisee's specific learning needs are determined;
   2) . . . developing fair and transparent evaluation procedures that are explicit in every respect; and
   3) . . . providing supervisees with constructive, focused feedback in a respectful fashion.

V. Knowledge about/skill in fostering attention to difference and diversity
Supervisor demonstrates awareness/understanding of . . .
   1) . . . one's own personal diversity and self as a cultural being;
   2) . . . the diversity of others and their lives as cultural beings; and
   3) . . . how to help supervisees formulate and apply a diversity-sensitive case conceptualization in psychotherapy/counseling practice.

VI. Openness to/utilization of a self-reflective, self-assessment stance in supervision
Supervisor demonstrates recognized need for/is committed to . . .
   1) . . . ongoing reflection about one's own supervision practice and personal impact on the supervision experience;
   2) . . . ongoing evaluation of one's own supervision practice; and
   3) . . . attending to matters of self-care and acting to insure that personal well-being is consistently fostered.

Adapted from Watkins, C. E., Jr. (2013f). Reproduced with permission of the International Journal of Psychotherapy.

What does the research say about supervisor training?

As supervisors and supervisor trainers, we believe in the power of supervision to mightily contribute to enhancing supervisor trainee and therapist/supervisee performance and even potentially improving patient treatment. But the research supporting supervision's "power" has yet to catch up to our firm conviction to that effect (Hill, 2012; Hill & Knox, 2013; Watkins, 2011). Supervision's clinical validity far outweighs its empirical validity, and nowhere is that more evident than when reviewing the supervisor training literature. For instance, consider these three quotes about supervisor training research that have consecutively appeared across the last approximate 15-year period:

> Thus, although there is some tentative evidence to suggest that training supervisors can produce change in supervisor practices and supervisee subjective ratings of the benefits of training, it remains to be demonstrated conclusively that such training achieves long-term impact on supervisee clinical practice and client outcomes. (Spence, Wilson, Kavanagh, Strong, & Worrall, 2001, p. 149)

> . . . perceptions beg the question of whether the training [of supervisors] does have effect. On this issue there is little literature to provide answer. . .. It is unclear why supervision training has not received more attention from researchers . . . (Kavanagh et al., 2008, pp. 96–97)

> Perhaps the strongest, safest conclusion that can be drawn from these [supervisor training] studies at this time is: There appears to be a tentative base of support for supervisor training (didactic/experiential mix) that suggests it can have value in stimulating the development of supervisor trainees and better preparing them for the supervisory role. Unfortunately, I am not sure that we are able to say more beyond that now. No, limited, or mixed results. . ., coupled with methodological compromises and weaknesses across studies. . ., temper what we can strongly and confidently conclude about any supervisor training benefits. Supervisor training may well have an impact, but that is by no means a solidly established empirical reality. (Watkins, 2012b)

While some more favorable conclusions about supervisor training have recently been drawn (based almost exclusively on nontherapy/counseling supervision studies; Milne et al., 2011), those quotes in our view still nicely capture the current state of research on therapist/counselor supervisor training and reflect our clear and pressing need for far more such study (cf. Bernard & Goodyear, 2014). (For more specifics on supervisor training research conducted thus far, see a review by Watkins (2012b) where 20 supervisor training studies were detailed regarding setting/sample characteristics, measures used, analyses/design, procedure, findings/conclusions, and limitations/strengths.)

But with the limitations of current studies recognized, what then can we say that we now know or need to know about supervisor training? From our reading and study, we believe that the following conclusions, which apply to both graduate students and postgraduate supervisor trainees, are justified.

1. Research suggests that supervisor training contributes to self-perceived increases in trainee confidence, knowledge, skills, self-image, and development.
2. Research suggests that supervisor training contributes to self-perceived decreases in trainee stress and anxiety.
3. Research has largely relied on self-report data.
4. In researching supervisor training, most study authors have either exclusively or in part used a self-created measure and/or interview guide for assessment purposes.
5. Studies in which any type of multimethod, multitrait approach has been used to investigate supervisor training impact are virtually nonexistent.
6. Studies that examine the impact of supervisor training on actual supervisor trainee in-session behavior (i.e., transfer of training) are virtually nonexistent.
7. Studies that examine the impact of supervisor training on the supervisor trainee's own supervisee are nonexistent.

Supervisor training perhaps is most useful because it provides trainees with an informed and informing mental map where one had not existed before. But does that training also lead to actual, desirable in-session supervisor behaviors that endure? If so, what are the mechanisms or variables that contribute to such changes? Furthermore, how much supervisor training is needed for optimal effect (e.g., can you really become equipped to supervise through taking a day-long workshop)? And how does supervisor training trickle down to affect the supervisor trainee's supervisees and their patients? Those are some of the burning questions that will require our empirical attention in the years ahead. To paraphrase Wheeler (2007), "future for research on . . . [supervisor training] is [very] wide open" (p. 1).

A Snapshot of Supervision Practice and Supervisor Training Requirements from an International Perspective

To round out our coverage about supervisor training, we thought it might be interesting to provide you with a snapshot of current supervision practice and supervisor training requirements across a diversity of countries and major international cities and states. In an effort to develop such a snapshot, we informally polled 20 highly knowledgeable, well-informed supervisors or supervisor educators from 15 different locales from around the world and invited them to complete a survey with the following questions: (a) What is the title of the mental health profession in your country with which you are most closely associated? (b) Is there a licensure/certificate system established for this profession? If so, who issues this license/certificate (e.g., government, professional association) and what are the required qualifications (e.g., degree, examination, clinical experience) to obtain it? Does the license/certificate allow the license holder to do private practice? (c) Is there a license, certificate, or required credential needed to become a clinical supervisor for this professional field? If so, what is the title, who issues this license/certificate, and what are the required qualifications (e.g., required courses, years of clinical experience)? (d) Where a license/certificate is not required, what are the typical qualifications possessed by those providing clinical supervision (e.g., academic degrees, continued education training, advanced clinical experiences)? (e) What are the typical topics/foci for supervisor training in your professional field and how are these supervisor training experiences delivered (e.g., graduate program curricula, intense weekend workshops as continued education, online training, one-on-one supervision)?

We received responses from 14 professionals, with 12 different countries or major cities/states being represented: Australia, China, Hong Kong, Italy, Japan, South Korea, Mexico, Singapore, Taiwan, United Kingdom, United States, and Venezuela. Table 8.4 presents a summary of the survey responses. Although by no means a formal, comprehensive poll, we believe the information offers a current picture of supervisor credentialing and training taken from myriad corners of the globe. In reviewing the survey responses, it appears that

1. In most locales, no designated license or required qualifications for clinical supervision practice have been established. It seems as if advanced clinical experience is the norm to become a clinical supervisor.
2. A few countries have a well-established credential system in place, which includes a specific training program to systematically train clinical supervisors.
3. Australia is the only country among those we surveyed that has in place a mandatory accreditation system to become a clinical supervisor, effective July 2013.
4. With some variation recognized, topics of supervisor training appear to focus on supervision models and skills, ethical issues, and the supervisory relationship.
5. Weekend workshops and seminars appear to be the most popular ways of delivering supervisor training.

The results of our admittedly informal poll suggest (a) that the importance of supervision has increasingly gained international traction and (b) that supervisor training is being increasingly recognized as important for the provision of competent supervision services. From our perspective, we expect those increases in the recognized importance of supervision and supervisor training to continue to further escalate internationally with time.

Conclusion

Calls for supervisor training began to first be made in the early to mid-1980s, those calls became even louder and more insistent in the 1990s and, today, the importance (or at least potential importance) of supervisor training is seemingly more widely recognized across more disciplines than at any other time in supervision's history. Supervisor training now appears to have come of age, and since the dawn of the new millennium, we have seen unprecedented attention given over to the education of clinical supervisors. In many respects, our work in supervisor training and research, largely a product of the last 25 years alone, is understandably still in its most formative stage. But a good beginning has indeed been made, needs and directions for future advancement have been identified, and the possibilities for the study and practice of supervisor training worldwide in the years ahead are vast.

Table 8.4 Licensure status and required qualifications of psychotherapists/counselors and clinical supervisors in 12 countries.

Country	*Titles of mental health professionals*	*License issuing body and if private practice allowed*	*Qualifications needed for mental health services*	*License/qualifications needed for supervisors*	*Typical topics of/means of delivery for supervisor training*
Australia	Psychologist Registered Psychologist	License issued by government Private practice allowed	Four years Psychology training (Bachelors and 1 year honors credit) with 2 years' supervised experience Or Six years of training (master's degree, two years of registrarship, or doctoral degree, and one year of registrarship)	Mandatory accreditation is required to be a clinical supervisor; fully effective as of July 2013; requires appropriate qualifications and passing a board-approved supervisor training program	Workshops that cover the Psychology Board of Australia's (PBA) requirements, supervision theories, supervision techniques, methods, and competencies PBA has developed guidelines for supervisor training course accreditation
China	Registered Psychologist Counselor Certificate	Registration status issued by the Division of Clinical and Counseling Psychology, Chinese Psychological Association No country-wide licensure law for private practice yet; currently reviewed by the Congress However, in some special economic zones, such as Shenzhen, regulatory legal codes have been passed by local governments in which the counselor certificate is issued by the city's Labor Department enabling professionals to provide counseling services legally	Registered psychologists require a master's or doctoral degree from a certificated counseling or clinical psychology program. The counselor certificate requires a bachelor's degree plus completion of an 18-day counseling training program	No designated license for clinical supervisor Senior clinicians with more clinical experiences are typically preferred Registered supervisor status is issued by the Division of Clinical and Counseling Psychology of the Chinese Psychological Association; applicants must be a registered clinical/counseling psychologist with a minimum of 800 direct clinical contact hours and 80 supervision practicum hours and recommended by two registered supervisors. Most of the current registered supervisors were trained in the German–Chinese training program in the 1990s, which includes three groups: psychoanalysis, cognitive-behavior, and family therapy.	Supervisor training courses are not regularly available in China

Hong Kong	Registered Psychologist	License issued by the Hong Kong Psychological Society (HKPS) Division of Clinical Psychology. Private practice allowed.	Master's or doctoral degree in Psychology with adequate course training in seven core areas (psychological assessment, theories of psychological problems, psychological therapy, professional and organizational issues, research methods, neuropsychology, and health and community psychology) and 220 days of postgraduation supervised clinical experience	No designated license for clinical supervisor. Advanced clinical experiences and invitations from universities to become supervisors.	Short courses, trainings, and sharing sessions are offered by the professional association (HKPS) or the two major universities (the University of Hong Kong and the Chinese University of Hong Kong) as Continuing Education (CE) credits for supervisors
Italy	Licensed Psychologist Licensed Psychotherapist	License issued by the government; also requires registration in the national professional register Private practice allowed	For psychologists, a graduate of Psychology and a period of apprenticeship For psychotherapists, a Psychology degree, a period of apprenticeship and five years of postgraduate training	Supervisor for a licensed psychologist requires being a university professor, member of the National Professional Register Supervisor for a licensed psychotherapist requires being a university professor or a psychotherapist member of the National Professional Register of Psychotherapists	No supervision training, advanced clinical experiences are preferred
Japan	Certified Clinical Psychologist	Certificate issued by the Foundation of the Japanese Certification Board for Clinical Psychologists. Private practice allowed.	Master's degree in clinical psychology from accredited graduate schools. Pass the post-master license exam.	No designated license for clinical supervisor. No requirements beyond having considerable clinical experience.	No graduate programs or course curricula, but workshops and one-on-one supervision options are offered Common topics for supervisor training workshops include enhancing therapists' self-awareness, clinical competences, and supervisory relationship

(*Continued*)

Table 8.4 (*Continued*)

Country	*Titles of mental health professionals*	*License issuing body and if private practice allowed*	*Qualifications needed for mental health services*	*License/qualifications needed for supervisors*	*Typical topics of/means of delivery for supervisor training*
(South) Korea	Counseling Psychologist	Certificates issued by the Korean Counseling Psychological Association. Private practice allowed	Two levels of certificates: Beginner level, a master's degree in counseling psychology or related fields plus 50 counseling sessions and 10 supervision sessions Advanced level, a master's degree in counseling psychology or related field plus 200 counseling sessions and 30 supervision sessions	Five years of practicing at the advanced level as counseling psychologist leads to a special status allowing supervisor positions and sponsorship of junior therapists	Experience gained through the advanced level of training and time requirement (five years) Common topics for supervisor training courses/workshops include case conceptualization and processing skills, exploration of supervisee personal issues, increasing level of competence by dealing with diverse clients
Mexico	Licensed Psychologist	License issued by government. Private practice allowed	Bachelor's in Psychology, which requires practicum hours and internship	No designated license for clinical supervisor Extensive clinical experience is needed and a master's or above is typically seen in supervisors but not a requirement	Extracurricular professional training in the form of courses or seminars, but it is not required or taken by most.
Singapore	Clinical Psychologist Counseling Psychologist Educational Psychologist Neuropsychologist Occupational Psychologist	Singapore Register of Psychologists (SPS) Affiliation is voluntary (not required) for there are no government offices or organizations regulating the practice of Psychology Able to practice privately even without SPS affiliation	First degree in psychology, then postgraduate training in a field of psychology that also includes practical training and not just academics, as determined by the SPS.	No designated license for clinical supervisor but the supervisor must have been a Registered Psychologist in Singapore for at least three years. The SPS Council then determines approved supervisor lists	Common topics for supervisor training workshops include ethical and professional standards of psychological practice, protecting clients/ patients, employers and supervisees, assisting supervisees in current work situations, enhancing the effectiveness of professional psychologists Supervision progress reports should be submitted to SPS Council every six months.

Taiwan	Licensed Counseling Psychologist	License issued by government Private practice allowed	Master's degree with one-year full-time internship Passing the national licensure exam	No designated license for clinical supervisor Senior clinicians with two to three years of clinical experience are typically preferred. Taiwan Counseling Psychology Association (TCPA) awards a certificate to those who complete 52-hr didactic courses and 32-hr supervised supervision sessions	Supervisor training workshops or seminars are offered frequently by universities or professional institutions with topics focusing on supervision models and supervisory relationship/interventions The didactic supervisor training courses offered by TCPA focus on the following seven areas: (1) supervision models, (2) ethics in supervision, (3) crisis intervention in supervision, (4) supervisory relationship, (5) evaluation in supervision, (6) supervision process, and (7) multicultural issues in supervision
United Kingdom	Practitioner Psychologist Counseling Psychologist Clinical Psychologist Registered Psychologist Sports and Exercise Psychologist	Registration with Health and Care Professions Council (HCPC), which is an independent government regulator to protect the public Private practice allowed	HCPC has detailed criteria as to what qualifications are needed to become registered	No designated license for clinical supervisor Registration to HCPC and appropriate clinical experiences The British Psychological Society provides a Register of Applied Psychology Practice Supervisors (RAPPS), which is designed to recognize psychologists with special expertise in supervision	The British Psychological Society provides a series of supervision skills training workshops; the training aims to facilitate supervisors' development and refine their own personal practice, and is tailored to the theoretical approaches, work settings, and clienteles of the supervisor-in-training

(*Continued*)

Table 8.4 (*Continued*)

Country	*Titles of mental health professionals*	*License issuing body and if private practice allowed*	*Qualifications needed for mental health services*	*License/qualifications needed for supervisors*	*Typical topics of/means of delivery for supervisor training*
United States	Licensed Professional Counselor (LPC) Licensed Marriage and Family Therapist (LMFT) Licensed Psychologist (LP)	All issued by State Government Private practice allowed	For LPC: master's or doctoral degree from counseling program or relevant field; passing the National Counselor Exam; and completion of a certain number of postgraduate clinical hours under supervision (exact hours vary from state to state) For LMFT: master's or doctoral degree from a marriage and family therapy program or relevant fields; passing the MFT National Exam; and completion of a certain number of postgraduate clinical hours under supervision. For LP: Doctoral degree in counseling/clinical/school Psychology; passing the Exam for the professional Practice of Psychology; and completion of a certain number of postdoctoral clinical hours under supervision	LPC-S: After two years of being fully licensed as an LPC, one may apply to become an LPC-Supervisor, issued by the state board. However, LPC-S is an add-on credential and it is not required for a supervisor to have the LPC-S to provide supervision Approved Supervisor issued by the American Association for Marriage and Family Therapy (AAMFT); must be an LMFT with at least 3,000 direct clinical hours, completion of approved supervision foundation courses and provide 180 hr of supervision to MFTs with at least 36 hr of supervision mentoring over a two-year period. No supervisor license or certificate is required to provide supervision for licensed psychologist; supervisors are usually those with more clinical experiences	Graduate-level classes, weekend workshops, one-on-one supervision are available for LPC and LPC-S on supervisory topics such as multiculturalism, legal, ethical issues in supervision. For AAMFT-approved supervisors, topics typically include sensitivity to multilevel implications of developmental, biological, sociocultural, gender and family-of-origin issues, ways in which personal values, beliefs, and experiences impact on the practice of supervision, theoretical consistency, and the rationale for choice of supervisory methods
Venezuela	Licensed Psychologist	License issued by the Venezuelan Federation of Psychology (FVA) in conjunction with the Ministry of Education. Private practice allowed	Bachelor with five years of undergraduate psychology work with 120 credits in Psychology-related fields Registration with the Ministry of Education Registration and enrollment with the Board of Licentiates in Psychology. Membership of the Institute of Protection of Psychologists (mandatory insurance)	No designated license for clinical supervisor Supervisors are typically those with 15 years or more of experience with clinical psychology, and there is no recognition as supervisor through the law or the field, unless it is psychoanalytic	Graduate program curricula, workshops, and one-on-one supervision are available to help supervisor gain additional experience

Note. During production of this book, some of the information in the table might have changed.

References

Alonso, A. (1983). A developmental theory of psychodynamic supervision. *The Clinical Supervisor, 1*(1), 23–36.

Alonso, A. (1985). *The quiet profession: Supervisors of psychotherapy.* New York, NY: Macmillan.

Alonso, A. (2000). On being skilled and deskilled as a psychotherapy supervisor. *Journal of Psychotherapy Practice and Research, 9*, 55–61.

American Board of Examiners in Clinical Social Work. (2004). *Clinical supervision: A practice specialty of clinical social work.* Retrieved from http://www.abecsw.org, July 17, 2013.

Bang, K., & Park, J. (2009). Korean supervisors' experiences in clinical supervision. *The Counseling Psychologist, 37*, 1042–1075.

Barnett, J. E. (Ed.). (2011). Special section: Internet and video technology in psychotherapy supervision and training. *Psychotherapy, 48*, 103–181.

Bernard, J. M. (2012). *An integrated approach to conceptualizing clinical supervision.* Presentation given at the Eighth International Interdisciplinary Conference on Clinical Supervision, Adelphi University, Garden City, NY.

Bernard, J. M., & Goodyear, R. (2014). *Fundamentals of clinical supervision* (5th ed.). Boston, MA: Allyn & Bacon.

Borders, L. D. (1992). Learning to think like a supervisor. *The Clinical Supervisor, 10*(2), 135–148.

Borders, L. D. (2010). Principles of best practices for clinical supervision training programs. In J. R. Culbreth & L. L. Brown (Eds.), *State of the art in clinical supervision* (pp. 127–150). New York, NY: Routledge.

Borders, L. D. (2012). *ACES best practices in clinical supervision.* Presentation given at the Eighth International Interdisciplinary Conference on Clinical Supervision, Adelphi University, Garden City, NY.

Borders, L. D. (in press). *Best Practices in Clinical Supervision*: Another step in delineating effective supervision practice. *American Journal of Psychotherapy.*

Borders, L. D., Bernard, J. M., Dye, H. A., Fong, M. L., Henderson, P., & Nance, D. W. (1991). Curriculum guide for training counseling supervisors: Rationale, development, and implementation. *Counselor Education and Supervision, 31*, 58–82.

Chang, C. Y., & O'Hara, C. (2010). Supervision-based integrative models of counselor supervision: Developmental models. In N. Ladany & L. Bradley (Eds.), *Counselor supervision* (4th ed., pp. 145–166). New York, NY: Routledge.

Dye, H. L., & Borders, L. D. (1990). Counseling supervisors: Standards for preparation and practice. *Journal of Counseling and Development, 69*, 27–29.

Ekstein, R., & Wallerstein, R. S. (1958). *The teaching and learning of psychotherapy.* New York, NY: Basic Books.

Epstein, R. M., & Hundert, E. M. (2002). Defining and assessing professional competence. *Journal of the American Medical Association, 287*, 226–235.

Falender, C. A., Cornish, J. A. E., Goodyear, R. K., Hatcher, R., Kaslow, N. J., Leventhal, G., . . . Grus, C. (2004). Defining competencies in psychology supervision: A consensus statement. *Journal of Clinical Psychology, 60*, 771–785.

Falender, C. A., & Shafranske, E. (2004). *Clinical supervision: A competency-based approach.* Washington, DC: American Psychological Association.

Falender, C. A., & Shafranske, E. P. (2012). The importance of competency-based clinical supervision and training in the 21st century: Why bother? *Journal of Contemporary Psychotherapy, 42*, 129–138.

Fleming, I. (2012). Developments in supervisor training. In I. Fleming & L. Steen (Eds.), *Supervision and clinical psychology: Theory, practice and perspectives* (2nd ed., pp. 77–95). London, UK: Routledge.

Fouad, N. A., Grus, C. L., Hatcher, R. L., Kaslow, N. J., Hutchings, P. S., Madson, M., . . . Crossman, R. E. (2009). Competency benchmarks: A model for the understanding and measuring of competence in professional psychology across training levels. *Training and Education in Professional Psychology*, *3*(4, Suppl), S5–S26.

Frayn, D. H. (1991). Supervising the supervisors: The evolution of a psychotherapy supervisors' group. *American Journal of Psychotherapy*, *45*, 31–42.

Gonsalvez, C. J. (2008). Introduction to the special section on clinical supervision. *Australian Psychologist*, *43*, 76–78.

Gonsalvez, C. J., & Milne, D. L. (2010). Clinical supervisor training in Australia: A review of current problems and possible solutions. *Australian Psychologist*, *45*, 233–242.

Gordan, K. (1997). An advanced training in the supervision and teaching of psychotherapy. In B. Martindale, M. Morner, M. E. C. Rodriguez, & J. Vidit (Eds.), *Supervision and its vicissitudes* (pp. 135–146). London, UK: Karnac.

Haggerty, G., & Hilsenroth, M. H. (2011). The use of video in psychotherapy supervision. *British Journal of Psychotherapy*, *27*, 193–210.

Hess, A. K. (1986). Growth in supervision: Stages of supervisee and supervisor development. *The Clinical Supervisor*, *4*, 51–67.

Hess, A. K. (1987). Psychotherapy supervision: Stages, Buber, and a theory of relationship. *Professional Psychology, Research and Practice*, *18*, 251–259.

Hill, C. E. (2012). *What we know empirically about the effects of training and supervision: Implications for practice.* Plenary address given at the Eighth International Interdisciplinary Conference on Clinical Supervision, Adelphi University, Garden City, NY.

Hill, C. E., & Knox, S. (2013). Training and supervision in psychotherapy. In M. J. Lambert (Ed.), *Garfield and Bergin's Handbook of psychotherapy and behavior change* (6th ed., pp. 775–812). Hoboken, NJ: Wiley.

Hoffman, L. W. (1990). *Old scapes, new maps: A training program for psychotherapy supervisors.* Cambridge, MA: Milusik Press.

Hoffman, L. W. (1994). The training of psychotherapy supervisors: A barren scape. *Psychotherapy in Private Practice*, *13*, 23–42.

Holloway, E. L. (2012). Professional competence in supervision. In J. N. Fuertes, A. Spokane, & E. L. Holloway (Eds.), *The professional competencies in counseling psychology* (pp. 165–181). New York, NY: Oxford University Press.

Inman, A. G., & Soheilian, S. S. (2010). Training supervisors: A core competency. In N. Ladany & L. Bradley (Eds.), *Counselor supervision* (4th ed., pp. 413–436). New York, NY: Routledge.

Kavanagh, D. J., Spence, S., Sturk, H., Strong, J., Wilson, J., Worrall, L., & Skerrett, R. (2008). Outcomes of training in supervision: Randomised controlled trial. *Australian Psychologist*, *43*, 96–104.

Kemer, G., Borders, L. D., & Willse, J. T. (in press). Cognitions of expert supervisors in academe: A concept mapping approach. *Counselor Education and Supervision.*

Klein, R. H., Bernard, H. S., & Schermer, V. L. (Eds.). (2011). *On becoming a psychotherapist: The personal and professional journey.* New York, NY: Oxford University Press.

Milne, D. L. (2010). Can we enhance the training of clinical supervisors? A national pilot study of an evidence-based approach. *Clinical Psychology and Psychotherapy*, *17*, 321–328.

Milne, D. L., Aylott, H., Fitzpatrick, H., & Ellis, M. V. (2008). How does clinical supervision work? Using a "best evidence synthesis" approach to construct a basic model of supervision. *The Clinical Supervisor*, *27*, 170–190.

Milne, D. L., & James, I. A. (2002). The observed impact of training on competence in clinical supervision. *British Journal of Clinical Psychology, 41*, 55–72.

Milne, D. L., Scaife, J., & Cliffe, T. (2009). How should we train effective supervisors? A British consensus on facilitating experiential learning. *Clinical Psychology Forum, 203*, 7–12.

Milne, D. L., Sheikh, A. I., Pattison, S., & Wilkinson, A. (2011). Evidence-based training for clinical supervisors: A systematic review of 11 controlled studies. *The Clinical Supervisor, 30*, 53–71.

Orlinsky, D. E., & Ronnestad, M. H. (2005). *How psychotherapists develop: A study of therapeutic work and professional growth.* Washington, DC: American Psychological Association.

Pegeron, J. (2008). A course on the supervisory process for candidates . . . and supervisors: An attempt to address inconsistencies in psychoanalytic education and fundamental paradox of psychoanalytic training. *Psychoanalytic Inquiry, 28*, 344–360.

Powell, D., & Migdole, S. (2012). *Can you hear me now? New frontiers of clinical supervision.* Plenary address given at the Eighth International Interdisciplinary Conference on Clinical Supervision, Adelphi University, Garden City, NY.

Psychology Board of Australia. (2011). *Exposure draft: Guideline for supervisors and supervisor training providers.* Retrieved from http://www.psychologyboard.gov.au/Registration/Supervision.aspx (see Past Consultations).

Psychology Board of Australia. (2013). *Guidelines for supervisors and supervisor training providers.* Retrieved from http://www.psychologyboard.gov.au/Registration/Supervision.aspx

Riess, H., & Fishel, A. K. (2000). The necessity of continuing education for psychotherapy supervisors. *Academic Psychiatry, 24*, 147–155.

Riess, H., & Herman, J. B. (2008). Teaching the teachers: A model course for psychodynamic psychotherapy supervisors. *Academic Psychiatry, 32*, 259–264.

Rodenhauser, P. (1994). Toward a multidimensional model for psychotherapy supervision based on developmental stages. *Journal of Psychotherapy Practice and Research, 3*, 1–15.

Rodenhauser, P. (1997). Psychotherapy supervision: Prerequisites and problems in the process. In C. E. Watkins, Jr. (Ed.), *Handbook of psychotherapy supervision* (pp. 527–548). New York, NY: Wiley.

Rodolfa, E., Bent, R., Eisman, E., Nelson, P., Rehm, L., & Ritchie, P. (2005). A cube model for competency development: Implications for psychology educators and regulators. *Professional Psychology, Research and Practice, 36*, 347–354.

Ronnestad, M. H., & Skovholt, T. M. (2003). The journey of the counselor and therapist: Research findings and perspectives on professional development. *Journal of Career Development, 30*, 5–44.

Roth, A., & Pilling, S. (2008). *A competence framework for the supervision of psychological therapies.* Retrieved from http://www.ucl.ac.uk/clinical-psychology/CORE/supervision_framework

Russell, R. K., & Petrie, T. (1994). Issues in training effective supervisors. *Applied and Preventive Psychology, 3*, 27–42.

Schlesinger, H. J. (1981). General principles of psychoanalytic supervision. In R. S. Wallerstein (Ed.), *Becoming a psychoanalyst: A study of psychoanalytic supervision* (pp. 29–38). New York, NY: International Universities Press.

Spence, S. H., Wilson, J., Kavanagh, D., Strong, J., & Worrall, L. (2001). Clinical supervision in four mental health professions: A review of the evidence. *Behaviour Change, 18*, 135–155.

Stoltenberg, C. D., & Delworth, U. (1987). *Supervising counselors and therapists.* San Francisco, CA: Jossey-Bass.

Stoltenberg, C. D., & McNeill, B. (2010). *The IDM: A developmental approach to supervising counselors and therapists.* San Francisco, CA: Jossey-Bass.

Sundin, E. C., Ogren, M., & Boethius, S. B. (2008). Supervisor trainees' and their supervisors' perceptions of attainment of knowledge and skills: An empirical evaluation of a psychotherapy supervisor training program. *British Journal of Clinical Psychology, 47,* 381–396.

Thomas, J. (2010). *Ethical and legal issues in supervision and consultation.* Washington, DC: American Psychological Association.

Turpin, G., & Wheeler, S. (2011). *IAPT supervision guidance.* Retrieved from http://www.iapt.nhs.uk/silo/files/iapt-supervision-guidance-revised-march-2011.pdf

Watkins, C. E., Jr. (1990). Development of the psychotherapy supervisor. *Psychotherapy, 27,* 553–560.

Watkins, C. E., Jr. (1992). Reflections on the preparation of psychotherapy supervisors. *Journal of Clinical Psychology, 47,* 145–147.

Watkins, C. E., Jr. (1993). Development of the psychotherapy supervisor: Concepts, assumptions, and hypotheses of the Supervisor Complexity Model. *American Journal of Psychotherapy, 47,* 58–74.

Watkins, C. E., Jr. (1994). The supervision of psychotherapy supervisor trainees. *American Journal of Psychotherapy, 48,* 417–431.

Watkins, C. E., Jr. (1995). Psychotherapy supervisor and supervisee: Developmental models and research nine years later. *Clinical Psychology Review, 15,* 647–680.

Watkins, C. E., Jr. (1997). Some concluding thoughts about psychotherapy supervision. In C. E. Watkins, Jr. (Ed.), *Handbook of psychotherapy supervision* (pp. 603–616). New York, NY: Wiley.

Watkins, C. E., Jr. (2011). Does psychotherapy supervision contribute to patient outcomes? Considering 30 years of research. *The Clinical Supervisor, 30,* 235–256.

Watkins, C. E., Jr. (2012a). Development of the psychotherapy supervisor: Review of and reflections on 30 years of theory and research. *American Journal of Psychotherapy, 66,* 45–83.

Watkins, C. E., Jr. (2012b). Educating psychotherapy supervisors. *American Journal of Psychotherapy, 66,* 279–307.

Watkins, C. E., Jr. (2012c). On demoralization, therapist identity development, and persuasion and healing in psychotherapy supervision. *Journal of Psychotherapy Integration, 22,* 187–205.

Watkins, C. E., Jr. (2012d). Psychotherapy supervision in the new millennium: Competency-based, evidence-based, particularized, and energized. *Journal of Contemporary Psychotherapy, 42,* 193–203.

Watkins, C. E., Jr. (2013a). Being and becoming a psychotherapy supervisor: The crucial triad of learning difficulties. *American Journal of Psychotherapy, 67,* 135–151.

Watkins, C. E., Jr. (2013b). On psychoanalytic supervisor competencies, the persistent paradox without parallel in psychoanalytic education, and dreaming of an evidence-based psychoanalytic supervision. *The Psychoanalytic Review, 100,* 609–646.

Watkins, C. E., Jr. (2013c). On psychotherapy supervision competencies in an international perspective: A short report. *International Journal of Psychotherapy, 17*(1), 78–83.

Watkins, C. E., Jr. (2013d). The competent psychoanalytic supervisor: Some thoughts about supervision competences for accountable practice and training. *International Forum of Psychoanalysis.* doi: 10.1080/0803706x.2012.712219.

Watkins, C. E., Jr. (2013e). The contemporary practice of effective psychoanalytic supervision. *Psychoanalytic Psychology, 30,* 300–328.

Watkins, C. E., Jr. (2013f). What matters in psychotherapy supervision? Some crucial features of international import. *International Journal of Psychotherapy, 17*(2), 63–73.

Westefeld, J. S. (2009). Supervision of psychotherapy: Models, issues, and recommendations. *The Counseling Psychologist*, *37*, 296–316.

Wheeler, S. (2007). Editorial. *Counselling and Psychotherapy Research*, *7*, 1–2.

Whitman, S. M., Ryan, B., & Rubenstein, D. F. (2001). Psychotherapy supervisor training: Differences between psychiatry and other mental health disciplines. *Academic Psychiatry*, *25*, 156–161.

9

Using Technology to Enhance Clinical Supervision and Training

Tony Rousmaniere

The past two decades has witnessed an explosion in the number of technologies being used to deliver and enhance supervision and training,[1] such as Web-based videoconference, the iPad, webcams, the Internet "cloud," clinical virtual reality software, Web-based software for tracking clinical outcomes, and software to code psychotherapy session videos. Around the world, supervisors have been rapidly moving their services online; clinical supervision and training is no longer restricted by geography. In June 2013, a Google search for "psychotherapy Skype supervision" resulted in over 300 listings for individual or group psychotherapy supervision by videoconference, provided by supervisors around the world, in a diverse range of modalities, including acceptance and commitment therapy (ACT), addictions treatment, cognitive-behavioral therapy (CBT), dialectical-behavioral therapy (DBT), emotion-focused therapy (EFT), eye-movement desensitization and reprocessing (EMDR), drama therapy, equine-assisted therapy, Gestalt, imago therapy, intensive short-term dynamic psychotherapy (ISTDP), music therapy, psychoanalysis, sandplay therapy, and sensory motor therapy. The Council for the Accreditation of Counseling and Related Educational Programs (CACREP) lists 12 Internet-based accredited masteral and doctoral programs (CACREP, 2012). Clinical research on technology-assisted supervision and training (TAST) has been conducted in Australia, Canada, England, Norway, and the United States (e.g., Rees, Krabbe, & Monaghan, 2009; Reese et al., 2009). TAST offers a promising range of potential benefits, including the following (Barnett, 2011; Berger, 2004; Jerome et al., 2000; Powell, 2011; Vaccaro & Lambie, 2007; Whipple et al., 2003):

[1] In this chapter, the term "supervision" refers to a training relationship in which the trainee is unlicensed and the supevisor has legal responsibility for clinical services. The term "consultation" refers to a training relationship where all parties are licensed and the trainer does not have such legal responsibility.

The Wiley International Handbook of Clinical Supervision, First Edition. Edited by C. Edward Watkins, Jr. and Derek L. Milne.

- increased accessibility of psychotherapy training, especially for clinicians in rural or remote areas;
- reduced cost for travel and improved flexibility of scheduling;
- increased access for peer consultation (in small groups via teleconference, or large groups via electronic mailing lists and Web forums);
- potentially enhanced diversity in trainees, due to improved accessibility of training;
- increased ease in recording and documenting supervision and training; and
- improved clinical services through continuous outcome assessment.

However, the rapid adoption of TAST also poses significant challenges for the field. For example, supervisors and trainers who did not grow up with Internet technology may find the ever-changing range of new technologies bewildering. A host of critical questions for supervisors and trainers remained unanswered, including the following:

- What are the legal risks that supervisors take by using these new technologies? For example, how can supervisors maintain confidentiality of client records if they are transmitted by, or stored on, mobile devices, or the cloud?
- What level of technological expertise are supervisors expected to have to use these technologies? For example, what are reasonable competency standards for use of software programs that are updated on a monthly, or even weekly basis?
- What are the effects of technology on the major domains of supervision? For example, how does cybersupervision affect the supervisory working alliance?
- What are the impact on patient care (e.g., clinical outcomes)?
- What are the implications for informed consent (by client and supervisee) if the client, supervisee, or supervisor do not fully understand the technologies being employed, or if those technologies change frequently?

The goal of this chapter is to provide clinical supervisors with a practical and accessible overview of current developments in supervision and training technology. The first section of this chapter reviews the technological developments of the past decade that apply to TAST, including two new directions of development that are likely to affect the next decade. The second section focuses on the ethical, legal, and regulatory issues raised by TAST. The third section presents a review of the published research and literature regarding TAST since 2000, and describes a case example of a TAST-integrated training program.

Terminology

A range of terminology has been used to describe various uses of technology in clinical supervision and training, including cybersupervision (Coker, Jones, Staples, & Harbach, 2002), Web-based training (Weingardt, Villafranca, & Levin, 2006), telemedicine and telehealth (Stamm & Perednia, 2000), computer-based learning and computer-assisted learning (Berger, 2004), technology-assisted distance supervision and consultation (Coker & Schooley, 2009; McAdams & Wyatt, 2010), E-learning

(Weingardt, Cucciare, Bellotti, & Lai, 2009), and computer-mediated training (Janoff & Schoenholtz-Read, 1999). In this chapter, the term technology-assisted supervision and training (TAST) will be used as an all-encompassing term to designate the use of technology to assist in clinical supervision or training. Previously, the term "face-to-face" has been used to designate when both the supervisor and trainee are in the same location (e.g., Chapman, Baker, Nassar-McMillian, & Gerler, 2011). However, this terminology is no longer accurate, due to the widespread adoption of videoconference (which is face-to-face but usually at a geographic distance), so the term "in-person" will be used instead.

The Past Decade of Technological Development

To many supervisors and trainers, the most noticeable change to technology over the past decade is that devices (e.g., video cameras and laptop computers) have become smaller, lighter, and more powerful. However, in addition to this clear change, a number of less obvious changes have occurred in the background, which may be more difficult for supervisors to detect, thus increasing the risks of inadvertent breaches of confidentiality.

The Evolution of Technology

Pre-2000	***Post-2000***
Devices are mechanical	Devices run on software
Devices stand alone	Devices connect via networks and the Internet
Devices are designed to save data	Devices are designed to share data
Devices turn on/off	Devices are designed to be always on
Devices are static	Devices constantly update themselves
Devices serve only the user	Devices can serve the user manufacturer, or others
Devices are single purpose	Devices are multifunctional
Data are stored locally	Data can be stored in multiple distant locations

Mechanical versus software-based devices

Except for computers, past technologies used in supervision (e.g., video cameras and tape recorders) were largely mechanical. It was clear when they were on, and what they were doing. Now, most technology runs on microprocessors and software. While this greatly increases the functionality of these devices, it can also make it challenging to know when the devices are on, and what they are doing. For example, most smart phones have dozens of "apps" running in the background at any given time, sharing a wide range of data with other devices, wirelessly via the Internet.

Technology that is connected

In the past, technological devices were mostly stand-alone, except for the phone, which was connected via a wire. Now, most devices are designed from the ground up to be connected to a network or the Internet, via cables or wirelessly. For example, most new smartphones and laptops come with wireless Bluetooth connections preinstalled. Additionally, an increasing amount of communication is being routed over the Internet. For example, all phone communications at the author's university is transmitted over the Internet, a system call voice over the Internet protocol (VOIP). As the ease of connectivity increases, so do the risks of privacy violations, via malicious intent or inadvertent accident.

Technology that wants to share

In the past, devices were designed with the sole purposes of capturing and saving data. Now, devices are also designed from the ground up to share data. All data are considered valuable to share, including photos, videos, e-mails, and even a person's physical location. Smart phones and some new cameras will automatically "share" their photos and videos through wireless connections, increasing the risk of confidentiality violations.

Technology that is always on

In the past, the default setting for devices was off, unless a user turned it on. Now, the default setting for many devices is on, unless a user turns it off. Having an "always on" standby mode is helpful because devices can run maintenance software while not in use, such as antivirus scanning software. However, it also increases the risk of unintentional use, or malicious use by others. For example, seven computer rental companies were recently caught secretly installing video-monitoring software that used webcams in rental computers to videotape customer without their knowledge (British Broadcasting Corporation, 2012).

Technology that is constantly updated

One advantage of new technology that runs on software and is connected to the Internet is that those devices can easily update themselves. Your computer or smartphone may frequently and automatically download new functionality, without any effort on your part. To some, this can feel like a never-ending learning curve that feels steeper by the day. Ensuring competence was much simpler when devices did not change themselves overnight. Staying current with software updates is important in order to avoid heightened risk of security threats (e.g., viruses). However, some programs and devices will reset their settings to "public sharing" every time they are updated, thereby raising the risk of privacy violations.

Technology that serves many masters

Previously, technological devices served only the person who used it. However, many new devices come with software preinstalled that is designed to benefit the manufacturer or advertisers. For example, most new computers and video cameras ship with software "suites" that are essentially paid product placements by other companies (i.e., "install monetization"). When you setup your new device, it may innocuously ask if you want to install a host of other programs as well. Many supervisors may not be technologically sophisticated enough to know what risks these programs may pose to privacy. Likewise, software preinstalled by the manufacturer may contain features that make your device more vulnerable to hackers.

Into the Social Cloud: A Look Forward to the Next Decade of Technological Development

Two major recent innovations have changed the direction of almost all new technological development: the Internet cloud and "social" technology. Both of these innovations greatly expand the power and efficiency of new technology, but in the context of clinical supervision and training, they also heighten the risk of privacy violations for both supervisees and clients. An increasing number of new technological devices have cloud and social features built into the operating system, so they function automatically in the background. For example, most new computers and smartphones come with cloud and social technologies preloaded, running in the background. As such, supervisors may not be aware when these features are operating. Understanding these two developments is key for supervisors to use new technologies safely.

Cloud computing

Think of the Internet cloud as thousands of computers in a warehouse, all connected to each other and the Internet. These computers are called servers and can be located anywhere in the world. Technology companies rent servers for a range of purposes, such as data storage or running complex software, because it is more efficient than buying their own computers. Many new devices and software programs (e.g., the iPhone and Google Docs) use these servers to store data (e.g., videos and documents). Server companies often contract with backup server companies, also located internationally, to keep copies of the data, in case of emergencies.

The clear advantage of cloud computing is efficiency: technology companies such as Apple, Amazon, or Google can provide high-quality services at very low prices. The disadvantage for clinical supervisors is the potential loss of control of confidential information because the data are stored in multiple locations. Although server and backup server companies may promise to keep data secure, it is impossible for supervisors to assess their compliance. Likewise, it is probable that the staff who operate those companies may not fully understand the scope and limits of clinical confidentiality. Furthermore, it can be challenging for supervisors unfamiliar with technology to ensure that the privacy settings on cloud computing software is set to "private." If privacy settings are set to "public" (which is sometimes the default setting), then any information uploaded to the cloud can be accessed by anyone on the Internet, or even found through Google searches. For this reason, the most conservative and safest option for the storage or transfer of confidential information (e.g., clinical notes or videotapes) is to not use cloud computing software (E. Rodolfa, personal communication, October 3, 2012). If cloud computing is used, it is recommended that confidential information be encrypted with strong passwords, a cloud computing service that permits compliance with the Health Insurance Portability and Accountability Act (HIPAA) is used, and the use of cloud services as part of the client consent process is disclosed. For additional information on cloud computing in a clinical context, see Devereaux and Gottlieb (2012).

HIPAA-Compatible Cloud-Based File Storage and Transfer Services

1. http://www.mydocsonline.com
2. http://www.foldergrid.com
3. http://www.braveriver.com
4. http://www.box.com
5. http://www.boxcryptor.com

Examples of Software That Use Cloud Computing

- Most backup software programs for computers and smartphones
- Internet-based photo and video organizing software (e.g., Apple iCloud)
- Internet-based file sharing programs (e.g., Dropbox)
- Internet-based e-mail programs (e.g., Gmail, Yahoo)
- Internet-based applications (e.g., Google Docs)

Social software

Another new major technological innovation is "social" technology. Software is considered social when it is designed to facilitate *connections* with other users and *sharing* of data. Some new software programs are entirely social, such as Facebook, which now connects almost one billion users. Most supervisors know to never post confidential information on social services like Facebook. However, an increasing number of new devices have built-in social features that users may not be aware of. Thus, supervisors run the risk of inadvertently "sharing" confidential information if they use a device with an active social feature. For example, some smartphones built on the Google Android operating system have a feature that will automatically upload data to the user's cloud-based Google+ account. Unless this account is set to private, the data will be available to anyone on the Internet. (If the data are labeled with a client's name, then they could be potentially be found whenever someone does a Google search for that name.) Furthermore, the companies that build these devices have a vested interest in promoting and facilitating open data sharing, so many of the social features in new devices have a default privacy setting of public. Thus, when using devices or software with social features, it is recommended that supervisors carefully check the privacy settings.

The "Supervision Technology Ecosystem"

In the past, the "toolbox" model for TAST was most appropriate. In this model, supervision technology consisted of a set of tools, such as video cameras for recording therapy sessions, or ear buds for one-way-mirror supervision. Supervisors could simply pick which tools they found helpful, and leave the others unused. In the toolbox model, devices were discrete, single-purpose, and only turned on when used. This model has become less applicable, however, as supervision increasingly takes place in an environment containing technologies that are interconnected, multifunctioning, and frequently never turned off. For example, many offices used for supervision have multiple "smart" devices running at any given time, including computers, cell phones, or tablets. Each of these devices has dozens of software programs running in the background, interacting with the Internet cloud, and frequently updating themselves with new functionality. As such, the toolbox model for TAST can dangerously mislead supervisors, increasing the risk of privacy violations. Therefore, it is proposed that the clinical supervision community move away from viewing technology as a set of tools to be used, and instead conceptualize technology as an environment in which we work, also called the "technology ecosystem" (Mantovani, 1996): a constantly evolving network of multifunctioning, interconnected software and hardware that is always on. Applied to the field of clinical supervision, this model can help supervisors become aware of the constantly evolving technological connections around them. For example, although supervisor may pay for a highly secure videoconference system that permits HIPAA compliance, that software will not ensure against confidentiality breaches due to other software programs or viruses on their computers. Likewise, locking a video camera in a filing cabinet will not provide security if that camera automatically shares videos wirelessly via the Internet.

Laws and Regulations Regarding Technology-Assisted Distance Supervision

While the development and experimentation in Internet-based TAST by clinicians has moved quickly, regulations regarding such practices are developing relatively slowly. The author was unable to find any regulations specific to Internet-based TAST at the national level in any country. However, many countries have regulations regarding the electronic transmission of confidential healthcare information, which applies to TAST. For example, in the United States, the HIPAA and Health Information Technology for Economic and Clinical Health Act (HITECH Act) set minimum standards requiring the protection of the confidentiality of all electronic health information.

In some countries, regulations specific to Internet-based supervision are being developed at the state level. For example, in their comprehensive survey of 46 state counseling regulatory boards in the United States, McAdams and Wyatt (2010) found regulations in six states, in development or discussion in 18 states, and prohibitions again Internet-based supervision in 19 states. Sixty percent of boards limited the hours that could be applied to licensure, with the limits ranging from 10% to

50% of total hours (McAdams & Wyatt, 2010). Similarly, in the United Kingdom, regulations are established by each different jurisdiction (S. Buller, personal communication, November 7, 2012). Supervisors who want to use Internet-based supervision should inquire with their local or national regulatory agencies regarding applicable laws and regulations. Supervisors and trainers should keep in mind that a lack of regulations specific to TAST does not mean that they are without risk of liability if a trainee or a client is harmed by the use of TAST (Kanz, 2001).The following is a list of issues commonly involved in the regulation of Internet-based TAST (Kanz, 2001; McAdams & Wyatt, 2010; Rousmaniere & Frederickson, 2013):

- Are there limits on the number of hours of TAST that can count toward licensure, continuing education credits, and so on?
- What jurisdiction has legal accountability when supervision or training is conducted across state lines or international borders?
- Is specialized training required for TAST?
- Are there informed-consent requirements specific to TAST?
- Are the standards of practice different for TAST?
- Are there regulations about reimbursement specific to TAST?
- Are there technological standards for the practice of TAST? For example, what level of data encryption in required?
- Should supervisors get informed consent from clients whose confidential information is shared via Internet supervision?
- Do professional liability insurance policies cover TAST, or supervision in multiple jurisdictions?

One complicating factor in international TAST is potential conflict between regulations in different countries. For example, in Canada, regulations prohibit clinicians from exchanging or storing confidential patient information in a manner that is not secure. However, in the United States, the Patriot Act permits a host of government agencies to gain access to confidential patient information, on the basis of suspicion of terrorist activity, without informing the patient. This means that Canadian supervisors may be deemed in violation of Canadian privacy regulations if they provide Internet-based videoconference supervision to a supervisee in the United States, or use any technology that transmits or stores confidential patient information on US servers, as the Patriot Act effectively prohibits the guarantee of confidentiality of patient information (R. Babins-Wagner, personal communication, October 23, 2012).

Professional association guidelines

A number of professional associations in the United States have developed guidelines for the practice of TAST. For example, in the United States the American Psychological Association has published a statement called the "Guidelines for the Practice of Telepsychology" (APA, 2013). In regard to supervision, the guidelines state that supervisors should be competent in technology, and balance online/in-person supervision:

> Psychologists using telepsychology to provide supervision or consultation remotely to individuals or organizations are encouraged to consult others who are knowledgeable about the unique issues telecommunication technologies pose for supervision or consultation. Psychologists providing telepsychology services strive to be familiar with professional literature regarding the delivery of services via telecommunication technologies, as well as competent with the use of the technological modality itself. In providing supervision and/or consultation via telepsychology, psychologists make reasonable efforts to be proficient in the professionalservices being offered, the telecommunication modality via which the services are being offered by the supervisee/consultee, and the technology medium being used to provide the supervision or consultation. In addition, since the development of basic professional competencies for supervisees is often conducted in-person, psychologists who use telepsychology for supervision are encouraged to consider and ensure that a sufficient amount of in-person supervision time is included so that the supervisees can attain the required competencies or supervised experiences. (APA, 2013)

Likewise, the National Association of Social Workers (NASW) published the "Standards for Technology and Social Work Practice," which require that supervisors "shall be competent in the technologies used" (National Association of Social Workers & Association of Social Work Boards, 2005).

Perhaps the most specific guidelines available regarding TAST are provided by the Association for Counselor Education and Supervision (ACES), which in their "Best Practices in Clinical Supervision" stipulate that TAST supervision must "clearly approximate face-to-face synchronous contact" and that TAST must be compliant with HIPAA guidelines regarding password protection and encryption (ACES, 2011). However, like the APA and NASW, ACES guidelines also stipulate that supervisors must be "competent in the use of the technology employed in supervision," without explicitly defining competence in regard to technology (ACES, 2011).

Ethical Issues Posed by TAST

TAST poses a host of ethical challenges for supervisors and trainers. For example, if TAST is conducted over the Internet, then all of the security and confidentiality challenges from e-therapy apply (e.g., when conducting supervision by videoconference, confidential client information may be transmitted via the Internet). This is especially true in supervision of pre-licensure trainees, where there is a greater burden of responsibility and, thus, competence, on the supervisor. For example, if the client or the trainee has an emergency, the supervisor will have to step in with knowledge of local resources and laws (e.g., Kanz, 2001). Or, if the trainee is found to be not competent, the supervisor might have to provide services from a distance, over the Internet. For this reason, it is recommended that supervisors using TAST for distance supervision of pre-licensure trainees become competent in telehealth best practices (e.g., Mallen, Vogel, & Rochlen, 2005).

A review of the literature (Barnett, 2011; Devereaux & Gottlieb, 2012; Kanz, 2001; McAdams & Wyatt, 2010; Panos, Panos, Cox, Roby, & Matheson, 2002; Powell & Migdole, 2012; Shaw & Shaw, 2006; Vaccaro & Lambie, 2007; Watson, 2003) revealed a range of ethical issues posed by TAST that can be grouped into three broad categories: supervision process, legal and regulatory, and technology.

Ethical Issues in TAST

- Supervision Process Issues
  - Methods of communication between supervisor and supervisee
  - Evaluation of trainee
  - Collaboration and the supervisory working alliance
  - Procedures for when trainee is judged not competent
  - Local backup supervisors (if using distance supervision)
  - Cultural competency for supervisor and supervisee
  - Procedures for termination of supervision
- Legal and Regulatory Issues
  - Locals laws and regulations applying to supervisor and supervisee's locations
    - Limitations of hours of TAST that can be applied to licensure
    - Issues that may apply if the supervisor's licensure is out of the supervisee's jurisdiction
  - Plans for client or supervisee emergencies
  - Informed-consent procedures for both client and supervisee
  - Liability insurance appropriate for TAST
- Technology Issues
  - Backup procedures for cases of technological failure
  - How and where data will be stored, backed up, and deleted
  - Rules for privacy, security, and confidentiality of both client and supervisee information
  - Software security standards for all computers (e.g., antivirus software)
  - Standards regarding use of mobile devices, social software, and cloud computing
  - Training and competency standards

Supervision process issues

It has been suggested that all supervisory relationships start with the collaborative review of a supervision agreement that clearly states the roles and responsibilities of the supervisor and the supervisee (Ellis, 2012). If TAST is utilized, the agreement should include a description of the technology that will be used for supervision. Supervisors can use the list of Ethical Issues in TAST (see sidebar) to aid in writing a supervision agreement.

In the case of distance supervision, it is particularly important for supervisors to have clearly defined procedures for situations where there are client emergencies, supervisees are judged to not be competent, or supervision must be terminated (e.g., Panos et al., 2002). Likewise, local backup supervisors should be identified (e.g., Abbass et al., 2011).

Supervisors are particularly recommended to explicitly state what technologies should be used to contact the supervisor in an emergency (e.g., phone, text, instant messaging, or e-mail), and how long supervisees should expect to wait for responses to nonemergency questions (Barnett, 2011; Kanz, 2001). This is especially pertinent when working with a younger generation of supervisees, who may be used to using text-messaging as a primary method of communication and expect to receive instant responses to text messages throughout the day.

One concern that has been raised repeatedly (e.g., Sørlie, Gammon, Bergvik, & Sexton, 1999; Vaccaro & Lambie, 2007) is the risk of TAST negatively impacting the supervisory working alliance due to the diminished capacity for subtle nonverbal communication when using videoconference, e-mail, and text chat. Although qualitative data have found that the range of communication in TAST may be limited when compared with in-person supervision (e.g., Sørlie et al., 1999), the published empirical studies and anecdotal reports to date have found no difference in the quality of the supervisory working alliance in TAST compared with in-person supervision (e.g., Reese et al., 2009; Rousmaniere & Frederickson, 2013; Sørlie et al., 1999). However, in light of data suggesting that the prevalence of collaboration in supervision may be quite low (at least from the supervisee's perspective; Rousmaniere & Ellis, 2013), it is recommended that supervisors utilizing TAST be especially alert for potential negative effects on the supervisory working alliance, and emphasize a collaborative approach to supervision.

Panos et al. (2002) discussed the cultural challenges that may be posed by TAST, when the supervisor may be geographically distant from the supervisee and client. David Powell, who provides TAST to supervisees in Turkey, Singapore, Vietnam, China, and throughout the United States, recommends supervisors to stay alert for cultural cues or miscommunications (Powell, 2011). Panos et al. proposed the "triad model", where supervisees have two supervisors: one on-site who is well versed in local culture, and one online.

Supervisors should also indicate to supervisees if and how TAST will be used in the evaluations. For example, many training programs now utilize software programs to assess clinical outcomes – will these be utilized to assess trainees' clinical competence?

Legal and regulatory issues

If Internet-based TAST is used, clients should sign an informed consent recognizing that their confidential information will be transmitted over the Internet (e.g., Kanz, 2001; Vaccaro & Lambie, 2007). The informed consent should state the technologies and security measures utilized, in as clear language as possible. For an example of a TAST-informed consent, see Abbass et al. (2011). Likewise, supervisors may consider having supervisees sign an informed consent for TAST since supervision can involve discussions of supervisees' confidential information (e.g., Kanz, 2001).

If distance-TAST is utilized for supervision of prelicensed trainees, supervisors should learn about local laws and/or regulations in the supervisee's location that are pertinent to client care (e.g., Panos et al., 2002). For example, in the United States, laws and regulations about child abuse reporting are determined at the state level. Likewise, supervisors should become competent in local laws and/or regulations relating to supervision, for example, the number of hours of supervision required per week, and the maximum amount of distance supervision that can be applied to licensure.

Supervisors are encouraged to consult with their liability insurance carrier to ensure that their use of TAST is covered. Supervisors providing distance-TAST may want to seek legal consultation about the possible liability implications of providing supervision services to a supervisee in a different jurisdiction.

Technology issues

When using TAST, supervisors should develop clear procedures for the use of technology, for example, how and where data will be stored, backed up, and deleted, and procedures for use in case of technological failure (e.g., Kanz, 2001). Security standards for technology should be specified (e.g., antivirus software.) In developing procedures, supervisors should be cognizant of all connections in the supervision ecosystem, including devices owned by supervisees that are only occasionally used for TAST. For example, if supervisees use their personal computers for TAST (e.g., to write clinical notes from home or use videoconference for supervision), then the supervisee's computer should be password-protected and have appropriate antivirus software installed. Supervisors are advised to pay particular attention to the use of mobile devices, social software, and cloud computing, as these technologies pose greater risk to violations of client confidentiality. Finally, both supervisors and supervisees should achieve competency in TAST, as will be discussed next.

Competency in technology

It has been proposed that supervisors and supervisees be assessed for achieving competence in fundamental clinical skills (e.g., Falender & Shafranske, 2004). Likewise, it can be argued that supervisors and supervisees should attain competency in whatever methods of TAST are utilized. However, defining and assessing competency in TAST is a thorny problem because the technologies used in TAST change frequently. Indeed, many software programs update themselves overnight, so a supervisor who is competent in a program one day may be mystified by it the next. Likewise, understanding how a particular technology works is only one piece of the technological competency puzzle: supervisors should ideally also understand the full network of connections underlying that technology (i.e., the supervision technology ecosystem). However, it is clearly not realistic for supervisors to be fully informed on this matter. For example, it is not feasible for supervisors who use videoconference for supervision to know the full network of connections used by software programs on the supervisees' computer. However, it is proposed that, at the least, supervisors attain knowledge of the basic functionality regarding how TAST devices/software work, and how to assess and adjust settings to provide maximum security.

Toward a Best-Practices Model of Technology-Assisted Distance Supervision

The current state of TAST is much like the old "Wild West": a vast, unregulated field, full of exciting potential to improve clinical supervision, being eagerly explored by early pioneers but also posing significant hazards. For the field of TAST to mature, it has been advised that the various stakeholders (e.g., supervisees, supervisors, clinical training programs, regulatory boards, professional associations) come together and collaboratively establish rules and regulations to guide supervisors toward safe and ethical practice (McAdams & Wyatt, 2010; Vaccaro & Lambie, 2007). The author proposes that a set of "best practices" for TAST be developed, covering competency in the three domains discussed earlier: supervision process, legal and regulatory issues, and technology. Specifically, three "pillars" are proposed to guide the development of a best-practices model for TAST, building off the guidance previously offered by the literature (e.g., Kanz, 2001; Powell, 2011; Stamm, 1998), and based on the best-practices models widely recognized in the supervision literature (e.g., Bernard & Goodyear, 2014):

Pillar 1: best interest

TAST should be used only when it is in the best interest of clients and supervisees, and never solely for the convenience of supervisors. A test of this is whether supervisees, and clients where appropriate, can explain why the technology being used represents their best interests and goals.

Pillar 2: transparency

Supervisors should make technological tools and procedures clear to supervisees, and clients where appropriate. A test of this is whether supervisees or clients can clearly describe those tools and procedures.

Pillar 3: collaboration

Supervisors should involve supervisees, and clients where appropriate, in determining when to use TAST. A test of this is whether supervisees or clients feel included and that their opinion is valued in this process.

Research on Internet-Based Supervision and Training

A growing body of published literature is forming a research basis to inform supervisors on how, when, and why to use Internet-based supervision and training. A literature review conducted in July 2013 revealed 49 publications that had a significant focus on Internet-based TAST published between 2000 and 2013. (See Table 9.2 (a) and (b); Note that this literature review focused only on Internet-based TAST.) Of these studies, 26 were original research, and 23 were discussion of new technologies, case examples, or reviews of current literature. Of the research studies, 18 used quantitative methods, seven used qualitative methods, and one used mixed methods. Twenty-two of the studies took place in the United States, three in Australia, and one in the United Kingdom. Treatment modalities studied included CBT, motivational interviewing, psychodynamic therapy, school counseling, and rehabilitation counseling. The number of participants in each study ranged from three to 166, and both licensed and prelicensure clinicians were included as participants. The quantitative studies assessed a wide range of outcomes, including supervision process (e.g., measures of the supervisory working alliance), skills acquisition (e.g., measures of adherence post-training), and supervisee satisfaction (e.g., questionnaires). At least six of the studies focused on the application of Internet-based supervision in rural areas.

Notably, most of the studies were conducted by researchers who are pioneers, or "early adopters," in the use of the technologies they studied (like the author of this chapter). Therefore, allegiance effects must be considered as a significant validity threat. It is important for future research on this subject to be conducted by investigators who are not personally biased pro-technology.

Summary of Research on TAST

Potential Benefits

- High levels of trainee satisfaction with TAST have been reported (e.g., Xavier, Shepherd, & Goldstein, 2007).
- TAST can be effective for increasing supervisee self-efficacy (e.g., Weingardt et al., 2009).
- TAST can be effective for transfer of knowledge (e.g., Rees et al., 2009).
- TAST can increase supervisee self-disclosure and reduce inhibition (e.g., Cummings, 2002).
- Internet-based training programs are highly efficient due to scalability (e.g., Weingardt et al., 2009).
- Videoconference supervision encouraged some supervisory dyads to prepare more thoroughly for supervision (e.g., Sørlie et al., 1999).
- TAST can be effective for international and cross-cultural supervision (e.g., Panos, 2005).
- The supervisory working alliance and collaboration can be maintained with TAST (e.g., Reese et al., 2009).
- TAST can be effective for distance-based live one-way-mirror supervision (e.g., Rousmaniere & Frederickson, 2013).

Potential Risks

- Challenges in understanding nonverbal communication could be heightened by electronic communication (e.g., Vaccaro & Lambie, 2007).
- Supervisors may be unable to provide help from a distance, or may be unfamiliar with local laws and regulations (e.g., Abbass et al., 2011).
- Risks of cultural misunderstandings may be increased by geographic distance between supervisors and supervisees (e.g., Powell & Migdole, 2012).
- Videoconference supervision may cause heightened anxiety in some supervisees (e.g., Sørlie et al., 1999).
- Training via videoconference may not be as effective as in-person training (e.g., Sholomskas et al., 2005) or mixed in-person and distance TAST ("blended learning," e.g., Weingardt et al., 2006).

Table 9.1 Videoconference software.

Software	*Price*	*Notes*
http://www.skype.com	Free for one-on-one, $10/month for group	Encrypted but not "secure"
http://www.vsee.com	Varies	HIPAA-compliant, PC only
http://www.ISupelive.com	$50+	For use with IPad
http://www.via3.com	$29/month	PC only
http://www.webex.com	Varies	PC and Apple
http://www.nefsis.com	Varies	PC only
Facetime	Free with iPad & iPhone	HIPAA compliant
Google video chat	Free	PC and Apple
Adobe Connect	$45+/month	PC and Apple
http://www.oovoo.com	Free	PC and Apple

Videoconference technology

The technological development with arguably the greatest impact on clinical supervision and training over the past decade is the rapidly increasing accessibility of videoconferencing (Table 9.1). Also termed "synchronous E-learning" (Weingardt et al., 2009), a videoconference permits two or more individuals to communicate simultaneously by audio and video via the Internet. Dedicated videoconference systems have been used for clinical purposes for over two decades (e.g., Stamm, 1998). However, the high cost of dedicated videoconferencing systems make them largely impracticable for use by individual clinicians. Over the past decade, however, the rapid rise in Internet connectivity speeds and decrease in computer cost has greatly increased the accessibility of videoconference technology. In the first quarter of 2012, the average global Internet speed was 2.6 Mbps (Akami, 2012; first-world countries had substantially higher average speeds), which is five times greater than the speed recommended for good quality videoconferencing. Readers can test their personal Internet connection speed at http://www.speedtest.net.

Multiple large technology companies provide free software for individual and group videoconferencing (e.g., Skype, Google). Most new personal computers, smart phones, and tablet computers come with videoconference software preinstalled. Although most videoconference programs use strong encryption protocols, they are not considered "secure" because employees of the videoconference company can listen in on calls. (However, it is worth noting that this risk is theoretically no greater than the risk of a telephone company employee "listening in" on a supervision or psychotherapy session done via telephone.) For this reason, it is important to fully inform supervisees about the limits of confidentiality, and patient consent should be obtained if Protected Health Information (PHI) is going to be transmitted over videoconference. Videoconferencing software that permits a level of security that is HIPAA compliant is now available at affordable pricing (e.g., http://www.vsee.com).

Reliability

The reliability of videoconference is mixed, so users should expect occasional problems with dropped calls or poor connectivity (e.g., Powell, 2011). For example, in the author's experience using a range of different videoconference software weekly for over three years at both a University Counseling Center and private practice, about 20% of calls had connectivity problems. Group videoconference requires more Internet bandwidth and thus may have worse reliability. The reliability issues with videoconference are often due to connectivity problems in the international Internet network, which is beyond the control of users. Network problems can affect all videoconference software companies, so no particular videoconference software has yet been demonstrated as more reliable than others. Thus, supervisory dyads should only use videoconference if they are comfortable with these reliability constraints, and backup plans should be designated (e.g., phone). To improve reliability, the following methods are recommended: (a) get the fastest Internet connection available in your area; (b) close Internet-intensive programs running in background while using videoconference (e.g., Internet-based file-sharing software); (c) limit the use of "screen sharing" features; and (d) turn off the video camera when Internet connectivity is poor.

Originally, videoconference was largely used to increase the accessibility of supervision in rural areas (e.g., Rees & Haythornthwaite, 2004; Stamm, 1998) However, it is increasingly being used by urban clinicians who seek supervision or training in particular specializations from geographically distant experts (e.g., Abbass et al., 2011; Rousmaniere & Frederickson, 2013). Videoconference is also being adopted for wide-scale use by large organizations. For example, the China American Psychoanalytic Alliance (CAPA) runs a program that uses videoconference to let a pool of 400 Western experts provide psychodynamic psychotherapy training via videoconference to 160 Chinese students across 18 cities in China (Fishkin, Fishkin, Leli, Katz, & Snyder, 2011).

The body of research on videoconference TAST is growing rapidly; highlights of this research are described here. In a study of six supervisory dyads using mixed videoconference and in-person supervision, Sørlie et al. (1999) found that the videoconference sessions were equivalently effective as the in-person sessions for communication and maintaining the supervisory working alliance, but included more disruptions than the in-person sessions. Although the videoconference supervision initially caused more anxiety in some supervisees, it also encouraged supervisees to prepare for supervision better and disclose more in supervision (Sørlie et al., 1999). Coker et al. (2002) reported the results of two studies that included 13 practicum students who had a combination of supervision by e-mail, text chat, videoconference, and in-person. Supervisees had mixed reports, with some reporting a preference for in-person supervision (Coker et al., 2002). In a study with 76 school counselor trainees, Conn, Roberts, and Powell (2009) found mixed in-person and videoconference training (also called "blended" training;Weingardt et al., 2006) to have better outcomes than solely in-person training. Rees and Gillam (2001) ran a pilot videoconference CBT training program for 12 therapists at remote clinics across Western Australia. In post-training assessments, most participants rated the training as effective, although three of the therapists reported that they would have preferred training in person (Rees & Gillam, 2001). In a follow-up assessment seven years later, data from 48 participants who had taken the CBT training program suggested both a significant increase in knowledge of CBT and positive satisfaction ratings about both content and delivery method (Rees et al., 2009). Xavier et al. (2007) studied the use of videoconference to provide group training and supervision to 20 mental health professionals working with oncology patients. Participants largely reported high levels of satisfaction with the course, with large gains in clinical knowledge and confidence (Xavier et al., 2007). In a study of nine counselor trainees, Reese et al. (2009) found that ratings of the supervisory working alliance, trainee satisfaction, and trainee self-efficacy were similar in both videoconference group supervision and in-person group supervision formats. Likewise, in a study on the use of videoconference-based supervision for international social work practicum students, trainees reported high levels of satisfaction with the technology (Panos, 2005). Weingardt et al. (2009) examined the combination of videoconference supervision and Web-based training software for cognitive-behavioral substance abuse training, and found positive effects on counselor knowledge and self-efficacy. Preliminary results from recent studies have found videoconference to be effective for training in behavioral activation (Puspitasari, Kanter, Murphy, Crowe, & Koerner, 2013), functional analytic psychotherapy (Kanter, Tsai, Holman, & Koerner, 2013), and school-based autism interventions (Ruble, McGrew, Toland, Dalrymple, & Jung, 2013).

Videoconference for live one-way-mirror supervision

A promising new use of videoconference technology is to provide live one-way-mirror supervision at any distance, from the next room to across the country, termed remote live supervision (RLS; Rousmaniere & Frederickson, 2013). In RLS a supervisor watches a live psychotherapy session via the Internet, and gives guidance to the therapist in real time. RLS removes the geographic restrictions of traditional in-person live supervision, allowing "live" training in any location with a good Internet connection. The use of videoconference for live supervision was possibly first proposed by Weingardt (2004). Rousmaniere and Frederickson (2013) found RLS to be effective for advanced, postgraduate training in Intensive Short-Term Dynamic Psychotherapy. Angelita Yu recently developed iSupe, an innovative new "app" that utilizes the iPad for live supervision, available at http://www.iSupeLive.com. Students using iSupe have reported increased perceived support and challenge in supervision, higher willingness to take risks in therapy sessions, additional client focus, and stronger supervisory bonds (Yu & Coiro, 2013).

E-mail and text chat supervision

Clingerman and Bernard (2004) studied the use of e-mail as a supervision tool supplemental to in-person supervision. Findings from a qualitative analysis of 137 e-mails sent by 19 students suggest that e-mail "should be considered a worthwhile supplement to traditional supervision modalities" (p. 93; Clingerman & Bernard, 2004). Likewise, qualitative analysis of supervision e-mails in three other studies (Graf & Stebnicki, 2002; Luke & Gordon, 2011; Stebnicki & Glover, 2001) suggest e-mail can be a positive addition to traditional in-person supervision. Three studies (Butler & Constantine, 2006; Cummings, 2002; Gainor & Constantine, 2002) have found e-mail and text chat to be effective for peer group counseling supervision. In a quantitative N of 1 study replicated five times, Chapman et al. (2011) found supervision via text chat and e-mail to be correlated with increased trainee self-efficacy.

Web-based training

Another growing Internet-based training method is putting training materials online (e.g., treatment manuals), termed "Web-based training" (WBT; Weingardt et al., 2006). In a controlled study comparing WBT, in-person training, and a control group with 166 substance abuse counselors, Weingardt et al. (2006) found the two training methods to be equivalent in knowledge transfer. In another study of 147 substance abuse counselors, Weingardt et al. (2009) found that two methods of WBT were both effective at increasing CBT knowledge and counselor self-efficacy.Weingardt et al. note that WBT can be highly cost-efficient for delivering training to large populations: after the initial costs of putting a training program online are paid, the costs of allowing access to extra clinicians is relatively minor. The authors propose that the "most effective clinical training applications may use a 'blended delivery' format that leverages the strengths of both WBT and face-to-face training" (p. 23; Weingardt et al., 2006). In a study with 78 substance abuse counselors, Sholomskas et al. (2005) found that adding a WBT component to traditional paper treatment manuals improved training outcomes, but not as much as in-person supervision.

Technology-based continuous assessment of clinical outcomes

Another new technological development becoming adopted in supervision and training is the use of computer software to facilitate session-by-session clinical outcome assessment, also called "continuous assessment" (CA; Sparks, Kisler, Adams, & Blumen, 2011) and "contextualized feedback systems" (CFS; Bickman, Kelley, & Athay, 2012). With CA software, clients can complete outcome measures on a desktop computer, laptop, tablet, or their smartphone, while still in the clinician's waiting room. The software can automatically graph the client's progress and highlight risk factors, such as projected clinical deterioration or suicidality. CA software greatly reduces the paperwork and time required by paper outcome measures, making it easier for supervisors to integrate continuous assessment into their supervision, and easier for licensed clinicians to add a quantitative tool to their self- and peer-supervision. Whipple et al. (2003) developed a package of "clinical support tools" (CSTs) that provides session-by-session feedback to clinicians on clients that are at risk for deterioration, via the Internet-based OQ Analyst software package (Lambert, Harmon, Slade, Whipple, & Hawkins, 2005). In a controlled study, therapists using the CSTs had reduced dropout rates, achieved better clinical outcomes, and had a reduced likelihood of client deterioration (Whipple et al., 2003).

Miller, Duncan, Sorrell, and Brown (2005) developed the Partners for Change Outcome Management System (PCOMS) that utilizes the Outcome Rating Scale (ORS) and Session Rating Scale (SRS), ultra-brief measures of clinical outcome and the therapeutic working alliance. In controlled studies (e.g., Anker, Duncan, &

Sparks, 2009), therapists using PCOMS achieved significantly better clinical outcomes. Two additional examples of CA technology are the Evidence-Based Assessment System for Clinicians, a collection of more than 30 Web-based assessment measures covering a wide range of issues, such as gambling, attention deficit hyperactivity disorder (ADHD), sports anxiety, and alcohol use, all of which can be completed by clients via the Internet or their smartphone (Smith et al., 2011), and the Contextualized Feedback System, a collection of Web-based measures designed for couples and family therapy (Bickman et al., 2012). While these tools were designed to aid in clinical treatment, they are also suitable for supervision of trainees or to aid licensed clinicians in self-supervision.

Software for Continuous Assessment (CA)

- OQ-Analyst (http://www.oqmeasures.com)
- CCAPS (http://ccmh.squarespace.com/ccaps/)
- Carepaths (http://www.carepaths.com.)
- ASIST (http://www.clientvoiceinnovations.com)
- Wellness Check (http://www.wellnesscheck.net)
- MyOutcomes (http://www.myoutcomes.com)
- FIT-Outcomes (http://www.FIT-Outcomes.com)
- CORE (http://www.coreims.co.uk)
- Celest Health (http://www.celesthealth.com)

Computer-based training software

Another recent line technological development are computer programs that facilitate training in specific psychotherapy skills. Two examples are Calipso, which aids in CBT training, and Coherence in Case Conceptualizations, which helps trainees learn to make individualized case conceptualizations (Berger, 2004). The Intensive Feedback Tool helps clinicians learn to identify clinically relevant information (Caspar, Berger, & Hautle, 2004). Beutler and Harwood (2004) developed the Systematic Treatment Selection, a virtual reality (VR) training program that helps trainees learn clinical assessment and treatment planning.

Video-coding software

One innovative new line of development is software that trains clinicians to code videotapes of therapy sessions. The Achievement of Therapeutic Objectives Scale (ATOS) is a Web-based program that trains clinicians to systematically review videos of psychotherapy sessions, starting with videos of established expert therapists (McCullough, Bhatia, Ulvenes, Berggraf, & Osborn, 2011). The System for Observing Family Therapy Alliances software package (e-SOFTA) focuses on training and supervision in family therapy (Escudero, Friedlander, & Heatherington, 2011). Notably, both ATOS and e-SOFTA are free for users, and are both being used for training in psychotherapy process research (Escudero et al., 2011; McCullough et al., 2011).

Electronic mailing lists and web forums as virtual consultation communities

Clinically focused electronic mailing lists serve effectively as Internet-based consultation communities, in which clinicians give and receive informal peer consultation via e-mail. Some mailing lists focus on a therapeutic modality, for example, the Experiential Dynamic Therapies (EDT) mailing list, where more than 400 clinicians ask consultation questions and have discussions concerning EDTs (A. Kalpin, personal communication, October 20, 2012). Other listservs have a diagnostic focus (e.g., the Dissociative Disorders listserv), a job sector focus (e.g., the American College Counseling Association electronic mailing list), or serve national or state-level professional organizations (e.g., the Alaska Psychological Association electronic mailing list). Although research on clinically focused listservs is not yet available, anecdotal evidence suggests they are widely used, and it is probable that most therapeutic modalities and diagnostic foci have a dedicated listserv. This is an important area for future research, as an increasing number of clinicians are using listservs for informal clinical consultations.

Another new development is clinically focused Web forums, in which clinicians give and receive peer consultation via message boards. For example, as of October 2012, the International Center for Clinical Excellence (ICCE) Web site had than 4,000 members who use forums to discuss topics such as "Using Outcome Measurements in Supervision "and develop standards for training, certification, and core competencies (S. D. Miller, personal communication, October 22, 2012).

Technology Integrated Into a Supervision and Training Program: A Case Example

The following is a case example of how technology can be fully integrated into a clinical training program, and utilized to enhance clinical supervision, from the practicum for clinical psychology doctoral students at the University of Alaska, Fairbanks, Student Health and Counseling Center.

Electronic medical records

All client charts at the clinic are 100% electronic, using the "Point and Click" secure e-chart software package. Paper documents, such as a release of information requests or consents for treatment, are scanned into the electronic charts and then shredded.

Outcome monitoring

Starting with their first session, all counseling intakes complete the Outcome Questionnaire (OQ-45), an overall assessment of mental health (Lambert et al., 2005), using an online program called OQAnalyst. This software allows both the trainee and

Table 9.2 (a) Literature review: Original research since 2000 that address internet-based technologyfor supervision and/or training.

Original research studies	*Type of study*	*Technologies studied*	*Tx modalities*	*No. of participants*	*Participant demographics*	*Outcomes assessed*	*Country*
Butler and Constantine, 2006	Controlled study	Web-based peer group supervision	School counseling	24	First year school counselor trainees	Collective self-esteem scale, case conceptualization skills	United States
Chapman et al., 2011	*N* of 1 A/B (replicated 5×)	E-mail, text chat	Counseling	5	Counselor self-efficacy scale, Evaluation of Counseling Behaviors scale, Computer Competency and Comfort Scale, Distance Education Course Satisfaction Rating Inventory Survey	Counselor self-efficacy, course satisfaction, competency	United States
Clingerman and Bernard, 2004	Mixed qualitative/quanitative study	E-mail supervision	Counseling	19	Counselor trainees	Content of e-mails, professionalism at practicum	United States
Coker and Schooley, 2009	Qualitative analysis	Web-based counselor education and supervision	Mental health counseling, marriage and family counseling, school counseling	77	Counselor trainees, 1st–3rd year	Supervisory working alliance	United States

Coker et al., 2002	Two small-*N* quantitative studies	Blended (text chat & video chat) supervision	Counseling	8.5	1st year counselor trainees	Supervisory working alliance	United States
Conn et al., 2009	Controlled study	E-mail and videoconference supervision	School counseling	76	1st year school counselor trainees	Supervisory working alliance, Supervision Questionnaire, Web-Based Distance Group Satisfaction Survey	United States
Cummings, 2002	Qualitative analysis	E-mail, text chat	Peer group supervision	3	Counselor trainees	Analysis of e-mail and chat content	United Kingdom
Gainor and Constantine, 2002	Controlled study	Web-based peer group supervision	School counseling	45	Novice school counselor trainees	Multicultural case conceptualization exercise, Supervisee Satisfaction Questionnaire	United States
Graf and Stebnicki, 2002	Qualitative analysis	Blended (e-mail) supervision	Rehabilitation counseling	3	Practicum trainees	Analysis of e-mail content	United States
Haythornthwaite, 2002	Controlled study	Videoconference training	Youth counseling	32	Licensed clinicians	Training questionnaire	Australia
Kanter et al., 2013	Controlled study	Blended (videoconference) supervision	Functional analytic psychotherapy	16	Mixed	Measures of skills acquisition and satisfaction with training	United States

(*Continued*)

Table 9.2 (a) (*Continued*)

Original research studies	*Type of study*	*Technologies studied*	*Tx modalities*	*No. of participants*	*Participant demographics*	*Outcomes assessed*	*Country*
Kobak, Craske, Rose, and Wolitsky-Taylor, 2013	Pre-/post-quantitative study	Web-based training and remote live supervision	CBT (anxiety disorders)	39	Mixed	Measures of skills acquisition and satisfaction with training	United States
Luke and Gordon, 2011	Qualitative analysis	Blended (e-mail) supervision	School counseling	6	School counselor interns	Analysis of e-mail content	United States
Luke and Gordon, 2012	Qualitative analysis	E-mail supervision	Mixed	38	Counselor trainees	Discourse analysis	United States
Panos, 2005	Qualitative analysis	E-mail and videoconference supervision	Social work	24	Social work practicum trainees	Interviews	United States
Puspitasari et al., 2013	Pre-/post-quantitative study	Videoconference training	Behavioral activation	9	Licensed clinicians	Measures of skills acquisition and satisfaction with training	United States
Rees and Gillam, 2001	Pre-/post-quantitative study	Videoconference training	Varried	11	Licensed clinicians	Satisfaction questionnaire, CBT Knowledge test	Australia
Reese et al., 2009	Pre-/post-quantitative study	Videoconference training	Varried	48	Licensed clinicians	Satisfaction questionnaire, CBT Knowledge test	Australia

Reese et al., 2009	A/B/A study	Blended (videoconference) supervision	Varried	9	Counselor trainees	Supervisory working alliance, Counselling Self-Estimate Inventory, Supervisory Satisfaction Questionnaire	United States
Renfro-Michel, O'Halloran, and Delaney, 2010	Controlled study	Blended (virtual reality, video podcast)	Counselor education	14	Counselor trainees	Academic grades	United States
Ruble et al., 2013	Controlled study	Web-based training	Autism interventions	49	Teachers	Treatment adherence measures	United States
Sholomskas et al., 2005	Controlled study	Web-based training	CBT (substance abuse)	78	Licensed clinicians	CBT adherence and skills	United States
Stebnicki and Glover, 2001	Qualitative analysis	Blended (e-mail) supervision	Rehabilitation counseling	5	Practicum trainees	Analysis of e-mail content	United States
Weingardt et al., 2009	Controlled study	Web-based training	CBT (substance abuse)	147	Licensed clinicians	Provider Efficacy Questionnaire, Maslach Burnout Inventory	United States
Weingardt et al., 2006	Controlled study	Web-based training	CBT (substance abuse)	166	Licensed clinicians	Multiple-choice knowledge test	United States
Xavier et al., 2007	Pre-/post-quantitative study	Videoconference training	Psycho-oncology	20	Licensed clinicians	Questionnaire re: satisfaction, comfort, knowledge gained	United States

Table 9.2 (b) Literature review: Other publications since 2000 that address internet-based technologyfor supervision and/or training.

Other publications	*Type of publication*	*Technologies discussed*	*Tx modalities*	*Country*
Abbass et al., 2011	Case example	Group videoconference supervision	Psychodynamic	Multinational
Barnett, 2011	Discussion of new technologies/approaches	Many	Unspecified	United States
Berger, 2004	Discussion of current literature	Many	Unspecified	Unspecified
Bickman et al., 2012	Discussion of new technologies/approaches	Contextualized feedback system	Couples and family therapy	United States
Bloom and Walz, 2004	Discussion of new technologies/approaches	Many	Counselor education and supervision	United States
Cucciare, Weingardt, and Villafranca, 2008	Discussion of new technologies/approaches	Blended learning, Web-based training	Empirically supported, manual-based therapies	United States
Devereaux and Gottlieb, 2012	Discussion of new technologies/approaches	Internet "cloud"-based record keeping	Unspecified	United States
Fishkin et al., 2011	Discussion of new technologies/approaches	Videoconference	Pschodynamic	China

Gilbert and Maxwell, 2011	Review of literature	Many	Unspecified	United States
Jerome et al., 2000	Discussion of current literature	Many	Unspecified	United States
Kanz, 2001	Discussion of current literature	Many	Unspecified	United States
Lessing and Blignault, 2001	Survey of extent of use of TAST	Videoconference	Unspecified	Australia
McAdams and Wyatt, 2010	Survey of state regulations re: cybersupervision	Many	Unspecified	United States
McIlwraith, Dyck, Holms, Carlson, and Prober, 2005	Discussion of new technologies/approaches	Blended (videoconference) supervision	Unspecified	Canada
Miller et al., 2003	Case example	Blended (videoconference, e-mail, bulletin boards, chat)	Child psychology	United States
Panos et al., 2002	Discussion of ethical issues	Videoconference	International social Work	Multinational

(*Continued*)

Table 9.2 (b) (*Continued*)

Other publications	*Type of publication*	*Technologies discussed*	*Tx modalities*	*Country*
Rees and Haythornthwaite, 2004	Discussion of new technologies/approaches	Many	Unspecified	Australia
Rousmaniere and Frederickson, 2013	Case example	Remote live supervision via videoconference	Psychodynamic	United States
Smith et al., 2011	Discussion of new technologies/approaches	Many	Many	United States
Vaccaro and Lambie, 2007	Discussion of ethical issues	Many	Unspecified	United States
Weingardt, 2004	Discussion of new technologies/approaches	Web-based training	Empirically supported, manual-based therapies	United States
Wolf, 2011	Discussion of new technologies/approaches	Many	Unspecified	Multinational
Wood, Miller, and Hargrove, 2005	Discussion of new technologies/approaches	Many	Unspecified	United States

Note. "Blended" = mix of in-person and technology-assisted supervision or training.

the supervisor to easily monitor client progress, and provides alerts for risk factors (e.g., suicidality, substance abuse, and clients at risk for clinical deterioration).

Videotaping counseling

Trainees videotape their counseling sessions using two webcams connected to a desktop computer. One webcam records the client and the other records the trainee. A program called Wirecast combines the two video streams into one side-by-side video (also called "picture-in-picture") that is automatically saved directly to a secure network drive, without the need for tapes, CDs, or DVDs. Videos can be viewed from any counseling office, making it easy to review the videos in individual or group supervision. After being used in supervision, videos are deleted from the network. As an additional layer of security, the network drive is encrypted using TrueCrypt software, protecting videos from unauthorized viewing, even by University Information Technology system administrators.

Training via videoconference

Expert psychotherapy trainers from around the country provide live trainings via videoconference software. Because the software's security features permits HIPAA compliance, the trainers can present demonstration videos of real psychotherapy sessions and trainees can present real cases for consultation. These trainings can be saved on a secure drive for future use.

Remote live one-way-mirror supervision

HIPAA-compliant Web-based videoconference software and webcams are used for live one-way-mirror supervision. This allows the supervisor to provide live one-way-mirror supervision between any two offices in the counseling center, without the need for expensive one-way-mirrors to be built into the walls. The software also permits trainees to get live one-way-mirror supervision from any psychotherapy expert in the world who has a good Internet connection. Recordings of these sessions can be saved and used for training purposes.

Post-treatment feedback

After terminating treatment (or dropping out), clients are offered the opportunity to take a secure online survey about their experiences in counseling. This feedback is used for training, quality assurance, and research purposes.

Concluding Thoughts and Future Directions: The Inventor/Experimenter Model of Supervision

Most of the research and theorizing on TAST has focused on evaluating whether TAST can approximate the experience of traditional in-person supervision and training. While this approach is valid, it implies an assumption of superiority in traditional supervision methods that may be limiting or even inaccurate. The traditional methods of supervision are in wide use not because they were determined by research to be the most effective (e.g., Ellis & Ladany, 1997), but rather because they were the only methods available. The assumption that the "old methods are best" may cause the field a disservice, by blinding us to new opportunities and alienating a younger generation of supervisees who feel more comfortable with new technologies. Rather than questioning whether TAST is "as good" as traditional supervision, supervisors and researchers are encouraged to instead ask, "What is now possible, and how can it serve my supervisees and their clients?" The roles of a supervisor are multifaceted: in addition to being gatekeepers, supervisors are also, by necessity, clinical explorers and inventors. The same skills that enable supervisors to be flexible and adaptable in an always-changing clinical environment can serve them well in the new technological frontier.

Recommendations for Internet Security

1. The single most helpful and easy security procedure supervisors can use is making their passwords "strong": do not use birthdays, names, or words in the dictionary; use at least eight characters; and use a combination of numbers, special characters (e.g., *&@), and upper/lower-case letters. Do not use the same passwords for multiple accounts, and change your passwords regularly.
2. Be extremely careful when downloading attachments in e-mails or clicking on links in e-mails. This is possibly the most common way to have your e-mail account hacked.
3. Find out if your TAST device or software uses the Internet cloud. If so, do not use it for confidential matters, or make sure it is securely encrypted.

References

Abbass, A., Arthey, S., Elliott, J., Fedak, T., Nowoweiski, D., Markovski, J., & Nowoweiski, S. (2011). Web conference supervision for advanced psychotherapy training: A practical guide. *Psychotherapy, 48*, 109–119. doi:10.1037/a0022427

Akami. (2012). *The state of the internet, first quarter 2012 report.* Retrieved from http://www.akamai.com/stateoftheinternet/

American Psychological Association. (2013). *Guidelines for the practice of telepsychology.* Retrieved from http://www.apapracticecentral.org/ce/guidelines/telepsychology-guidelines.pdf

Anker, M. G., Duncan, B. L., & Sparks, J. A. (2009). Using client feedback to improve couple therapy outcomes: A randomized clinical trial in a naturalistic setting. *Journal of Consulting and Clinical Psychology, 77*, 693–704. doi:10.1037/a0016062

Association for Counselor Education and Supervision. (2011). *Best practices in clinical supervision.* Retrieved from http://www.acesonline.net/wp-content/uploads/2011/10/ACES-Best-Practices-in-clinical-supervision-document-FINAL.pdf

Barnett, J. E. (2011). Utilizing technological innovations to enhance psychotherapy supervision, training, and outcomes. *Psychotherapy, 48*, 103–108. doi:10.1037/a0023381

Berger, T. (2004). Computer-based technological applications in psychotherapy training. *Journal of Clinical Psychology, 60*, 301–315. doi:10.1002/jclp.10265

Bernard, J. M., & Goodyear, R. K. (2014). *Fundamentals of clinical supervision* (5th ed.). Needham Heights, MA: Allyn & Bacon.

Beutler, L. E., & Harwood, T. M. (2004). Virtual reality in psychotherapy training. *Journal of Clinical Psychology, 60*, 317–330. doi:10.1002/jclp.10266

Bickman, L., Kelley, S. D., & Athay, M. (2012). The technology of measurement feedback systems. *Couple and Family Psychology: Research and Practice, 1*, 274–284. doi:10.1037/a0031022

Bloom, J. W., & Walz, J. R. (2004). *Cybercounseling and cyberlearning: An encore*. Greensboro, NC: CAPS Press.

British Broadcasting Corporation. (2012). *Rented computers secretly photographed users having sex*. Retrieved from http://www.bbc.co.uk/news/technology-19726954

Butler, S., & Constantine, M. G. (2006). Web-based peer supervision, collective self-esteem, and case conceptualization ability in school counselor trainees. *Professional School Counseling, 10*, 146–152. doi:10.1037/a0022427

Caspar, F., Berger, T., & Hautle, I. (2004). The right view of your patient: A computer-assisted, individualized module for psychotherapy training. *Psychotherapy: Theory, Research, Practice, Training, 41*, 125–135. doi:10.1037/0033-3204.41.2.125

Chapman, R., Baker, S. B., Nassar-McMillian, S. C., & Gerler, E. R. (2011). Cybersupervision: Further examination of synchronous and asynchronous modalities in counseling practicum supervision. *Counselor Education and Supervision, 50*, 298–313. doi:10.1002/j.1556-6978.2011.tb01917.x

Clingerman, T. L., & Bernard, J. M. (2004). An investigation of the use of e-mail as a supplemental modality for clinical supervision. *Counselor Education and Supervision, 44*, 82–95. doi:10.1002/j.1556-6978.2004.tb01862.x

Coker, J. K., Jones, W. P., Staples, P. A., & Harbach, R. L. (2002). Cybersupervision in the first practicum: Implications for research and practice. *Journal of Guidance and Counseling, 18*, 33–37.

Coker, J. K., & Schooley, A. L. (2009). *Investigating the effectiveness of clinical supervision in a CACREP accredited online counseling program*. Paper based on a program presented at the 2009 ACES Conference, San Diego, CA.

Conn, S. R., Roberts, R. L., & Powell, B. M. (2009). Attitudes and satisfaction with a hybrid model of counseling supervision. *Educational Technology & Society, 12*, 298–306.

Council for Accreditation of Counseling and Related Educational Programs. (2012). *CACREP list of accredited programs*. Retrieved from http://cacrep.org/directory/directory.cfm

Cucciare, M. A., Weingardt, K. R., & Villafranca, S. (2008). Using blended learning to implement evidence-based psychotherapies. *Clinical Psychology: Science & Practice, 15*, 299–307. doi:10.1111/j.1468-2850.2008.00141.x

Cummings, P. (2002). Cybervision: Virtual peer group counseling supervision – Hindrance or help? *Counseling & Psychotherapy Research, 2*, 223–229. doi:10.1080/14733140212331384705

Devereaux, R. L., & Gottlieb, M. C. (2012). Record keeping in the cloud: Ethical considerations. *Professional Psychology, Research and Practice, 43*, 627–632. doi:10.1037/a0028268

Ellis, M. V. (2012). *Inadequate clinical supervision: Am I among the 97% providing it?* Roundtable presented at the The Eighth International Interdisciplinary Conference on Clinical Supervision, Adelphi University, Garden City, NY.

Ellis, M. V., & Ladany, N. (1997). Inferences concerning supervisees and clients in clinical supervision: An integrative review. In C. E. Watkins (Ed.), *Handbook of psychotherapy supervision* (pp. 447–507). Hoboken, NJ: John Wiley & Sons, Inc.

Escudero, V., Friedlander, M. L., & Heatherington, L. (2011). Using the e-SOFTA for video training and research on alliance-related behavior. *Psychotherapy, 48*, 138–147. doi:10.1037/a0022188

Falender, C. A., & Shafranske, E. P. (2004). *Clinical supervision: A competency-based approach*. Washington, DC: American Psychological Association.

Fishkin, R., Fishkin, L., Leli, U., Katz, B., & Snyder, E. (2011). Psychodynamic treatment, training, and supervision using internet-based technologies. *Journal of the American Academy of Psychoanalysis & Dynamic Psychiatry, 39*, 155–168. doi:10.1521/jaap.2011.39.1.155

Gainor, K. A., & Constantine, M. G. (2002). Multicultural group supervision: A comparison of in-person versus web-based formats. *Professional School Counseling, 6*, 104–111.

Gilbert, C., & Maxwell, C. F. (2011). Clinical supervision in healthcare in the internet era. *Social Work Today, 11*, 24–26.

Graf, N. M., & Stebnicki, M. A. (2002). Using e-mail for clinical supervision in practicum: A qualitative analysis. *Journal of Rehabilitation, 68*, 41–49.

Haythornthwaite, S. (2002). Videoconferencing training for those working with at-risk young people in rural areas of Western Australia. *Journal of Telemedicine and Telecare, 8*(Suppl. 3S3), 29–33.

Janoff, D. S., & Schoenholtz-Read, J. (1999). Group supervision meets technology: A model for computer-mediated group training at a distance. *International Journal of Group Psychotherapy, 49*, 255–272.

Jerome, L. W., DeLeon, P. H., James, L. C., Folen, R., Earles, J., & Gedney, J. J. (2000). The coming age of telecommunications in psychological research and practice. *American Psychologist, 55*, 407–421. doi:10.1037//0003066X.55,4.407.407

Kanter, J. W., Tsai, M., Holman, G., & Koerner, K. (2013). Preliminary data from a randomized pilot study of web-based functional analytic psychotherapy therapist training. *Psychotherapy, 50*, 248–255. doi:10.1037/a0029814

Kanz, J. E. (2001). Clinical-supervision.com: Issues in the provision of online supervision. *Professional Psychology, Research and Practice, 32*, 415–420. doi:10.1037/0735-7028.32.4.415

Kobak, K. A., Craske, M. G., Rose, R. D., & Wolitsky-Taylor, K. (2013). Web-Based Therapist Training on Cognitive Behavior Therapy for Anxiety Disorders: A Pilot Study. *Psychotherapy, 50*, 235–247. doi:10.1037/a0030568

Lambert, M. J., Harmon, C., Slade, K., Whipple, J. L., & Hawkins, E. J. (2005). Providing feedback to psychotherapists on their patients' progress: Clinical results and practice suggestions. *Journal of Clinical Psychology, 61*, 165–174. doi:10.1002/jclp.20113

Lessing, K., & Blignault, I. (2001). Mental health telemedicine programmes in Australia. *Journal of Telemedicine and Telecare, 7*, 317–323.

Luke, M., & Gordon, C. (2011). A discourse analysis of school counseling supervisory e-mail. *Counselor Education & Supervision, 50*, 274–291. doi:10.1002/j.1556-6978.2011.tb00124.x

Luke, M., & Gordon, C. (2012). Supervisors' use of reinforcement, reframing, and advice to re-author the supervisory narrative through e-mail supervision. *Clinical Supervisor, 31*, 159–177. doi:10.1080/07325223.2013.730020

Mallen, M. J., Vogel, D. L., & Rochlen, A. B. (2005). The practical aspects of online counseling: Ethics, training, technology, and competency. *Counseling Psychologist, 33*, 776–818. doi:10.1177/0011000005278625.2005

Mantovani, G. (1996). *New communications environments: From everyday to virtual*. New York, NY: The CRC Press.

McAdams, C. R., & Wyatt, K. (2010). The regulation of technology-assisted distance counseling and supervision in the united states: An analysis of current extent, trends, and implications. *Counselor Education and Supervision, 49*, 179–192. doi:10.1002/j.1556-6978.2010.tb00097.x

McCullough, L., Bhatia, M., Ulvenes, P., Berggraf, L., & Osborn, K. (2011). Learning how to rate video-recorded therapy sessions: A practical guide for trainees and advanced clinicians. *Psychotherapy, 48*, 127–137. doi:10.1037/a0023131

McIlwraith, R. D., Dyck, K. G., Holms, V. L., Carlson, T. E., & Prober, N. G. (2005). Manitoba's rural and northern community-based training program for psychology interns and residents. *Professional Psychology, Research and Practice, 36*, 164–172. doi:10.1037/0735-7028.36.2.164

Miller, S. D., Duncan, B. L., Sorrell, R., & Brown, G. S. (2005). The partners for change outcome management system. *Journal of Clinical Psychology, 61*, 199–208.

Miller, T. W., Miller, J. M., Kraus, R. F., Kaak, O., Sprang, R., & Veltkamp, L. J. (2003). Telehealth: A clinical application model for rural consultation. *Consulting Psychology Journal: Practice And Research, 55*, 119–127. doi:10.1037/a0020051

National Association of Social Workers & Association of Social Work Boards. (2005). *NASW & ASWB standards for technology and social work practice.* Washington, DC: National Association of Social Workers.

Panos, P. T. (2005). A model for using videoconferencing technology to support international social work field practicum students. *International Social Work, 48*, 834–841.

Panos, P. T., Panos, A., Cox, S. E., Roby, J. L., & Matheson, K. W. (2002). Ethical issues concerning the use of videoconferencing to supervise international social work field practicum students. *Journal of Social Work Education, 38*, 421–437. doi:10.1177/0020872805057095

Powell, D. (2011). Cyber Supervision: Welcome to the 21st Century. *Counselor, 1*, 12–14.

Powell, D., & Migdole, S. (2012). *Can you hear me now? New frontiers of clinical supervision.* Plenary presented at the The Eighth International Interdisciplinary Conference on Clinical Supervision, Adelphi University, Garden City, NY.

Puspitasari, A., Kanter, J. W., Murphy, J., Crowe, A., & Koerner, K. (2013). Developing an online, modular, active learning training program for behavioral activation. *Psychotherapy, 50*, 256–265. doi:10.1037/a0030058

Rees, C., & Gillam, D. (2001). Training in cognitive-behavioural therapy for mental health professionals: A pilot study of videoconferencing. *Journal of Telemedicine and Telecare, 7*, 300–303.

Rees, C., & Haythornthwaite, S. (2004). Telepsychology and videoconferencing: Issues, opportunities and guidelines for psychologists. *Australian Psychologist, 39*, 212–219. doi:10.1080/00050060412331295108

Rees, C. S., Krabbe, M., & Monaghan, B. J. (2009). Education in cognitive-behavioural therapy for mental health professionals. *Journal Of Telemedicine & Telecare, 15*, 59–63. doi:10.1258/jtt.2008.008005

Reese, R. J., Aldarondo, F., Anderson, C. R., Seong-Jik, L., Miller, T. W., & Burton, D. (2009). Telehealth in clinical supervision: A comparison of supervision formats. *Journal of Telemedicine & Telecare, 15*, 356–361. doi:10.1258/jtt.2009.090401

Renfro-Michel, E. L., O'Halloran, K. C., & Delaney, M. E. (2010). Using technology to enhance adult learning in the counselor education classroom. *Adultspan Journal, 9*, 14–25. doi:10.1002/j.2161-0029.2010.tb00068.x

Rousmaniere, T., & Frederickson, J. (2013). Internet-based one-way-mirror supervision for advanced psychotherapy training. *The Clinical Supervisor, 32*, 40–55. doi:10.1080/07325223.2013.778683

Rousmaniere, T. G., & Ellis, M. V. (2013). Developing the construct and measure of collaborative clinical supervision: The supervisee's perspective. *Training and Education in Professional Psychology, 7*, 300–308. doi: 10.1037/a0033796.

Ruble, L. A., McGrew, J. H., Toland, M. D., Dalrymple, N. J., & Jung, L. A. (2013). A randomized controlled trial of COMPASS web-based and face-to-face teacher coaching in autism. *Journal of Consulting and Clinical Psychology, 81*, 566–572. doi:10.1037/a0032003

Shaw, H. E., & Shaw, S. F. (2006). Critical ethical issues in online counseling: Assessing current practices with an ethical intent checklist. *Journal Of Counseling & Development, 84*, 41–53. doi:10.1002/j.1556-6678.2006.tb00378.x

Sholomskas, D. E., Syracuse-Siewert, G., Rounsaville, B. J., Ball, S. A., Nuro, K. F., & Carroll, K. M. (2005). We don't train in vain: A dissemination trial of three strategies of training clinicians in cognitive-behavioral therapy. *Journal of Consulting and Clinical Psychology, 73*, 106–115. doi:10.1037/0022-006X.73.1.106

Smith, R. E., Fagan, C., Wilson, N. L., Chen, J., Corona, M., Nguyen, H., . . . Shoda, Y. (2011). Internet-based approaches to collaborative therapeutic assessment: New opportunities for professional psychologists. *Professional Psychology, Research and Practice, 42*, 494–504. doi:10.1037/a0025392

Sørlie, T., Gammon, D., Bergvik, S., & Sexton, H. (1999). Psychotherapy supervision face-to-face and by videoconferencing: A comparative study. *British Journal Of Psychotherapy, 15*, 452–462. doi:10.1111/j.1752-0118.1999.tb00475.x

Sparks, J. A., Kisler, T. S., Adams, J. F., & Blumen, D. G. (2011). Teaching accountability: Using client feedback to train effective family therapists. *Journal of Marital and Family Therapy, 37*, 452–467. doi:10.1111/j.1752-0606.2011.00224.x

Stamm, B. (1998). Clinical applications of telehealth in mental health care. *Professional Psychology, Research and Practice, 29*, 536–542.

Stamm, B. H., & Perednia, D. A. (2000). Evaluating psychosocial aspects of telemedicine and telehealth systems. *Professional Psychology, Research and Practice, 31*, 184–189. doi:10.1037//0735-7Q28.31.2.184.

Stebnicki, M. A., & Glover, N. M. (2001). E-supervision as a complementary approach to traditional face-to-face clinical supervision in rehabilitation counseling: Problems and solutions. *Rehabilitation Education, 15*, 283–293.

Vaccaro, N., & Lambie, G. W. (2007). Computer-based counselor-in-training supervision: Ethical and practical implications for counselor educators and supervisors. *Counselor Education & Supervision, 47*, 46–57. doi:10.1002/j.1556-6978.2007.tb00037.x

Watson, J. C. (2003). Computer-based supervision: Implementing computer technology into the delivery of counseling supervision. *Journal of Technology and Counseling, 3*, 23–29. Retrieved from http://jtc.columbusstate.edu/Vol4_1/Watson/Watson.htm

Weingardt, K. R. (2004). The role of instructional design and technology in the dissemination of empirically supported, manual-based therapies. *Clinical Psychology: Science & Practice, 11*, 313–331. doi:10.1093/clipsy.bph087

Weingardt, K. R., Villafranca, S. W., & Levin, C. (2006). Technology-based training in cognitive behavioral therapy for substance abuse counselors. *Substance Abuse, 27*, 19–26. doi:10.1300/J465v27n03

Weingardt, K. R., Cucciare, M. A., Bellotti, C., & Lai, W. (2009). A randomized trial comparing two models of web-based training in cognitive–behavioral therapy for substance abuse counselors. *Journal of Substance Abuse Treatment, 37*, 219–227. doi:10.1016/j.jsat.2009.01.002

Whipple, J. L., Lambert, M. J., Vermeersch, D. A., Smart, D. W., Nielsen, S. L., & Hawkins, E. J. (2003). Improving the effects of psychotherapy: The use of early identification of treatment and problem-solving strategies in routine practice. *Journal of Counseling Psychology, 50*, 59–68. doi:10.1037/0022-0167.50.1.59

Wolf, A. W. (2011). Internet and video technology in psychotherapy supervision and training. *Psychotherapy, 48*, 179–181. doi:10.1037/a0023532

Wood, J. V., Miller, T. W., & Hargrove, D. S. (2005). Clinical supervision in rural settings: A telehealth model. *Professional Psychology, Research and Practice, 36*, 173–179. doi:10.1037/0735-7028.36.2.173

Xavier, K., Shepherd, L., & Goldstein, D. (2007). Clinical supervision and education via videoconference: A feasibility project. *Journal of Telemedicine & Telecare, 13*, 206–209.

Yu, A., & Coiro, M. J. (2013, January). *The influence of live supervision on the supervisory relationship*. Poster presented at National Council of Schools and Programs of Professional Psychology (NCSPP) Midwinter Conference, Nassau, Bahamas.

10

Culturally Competent and Diversity-Sensitive Clinical Supervision

An International Perspective

Ming-sum Tsui, Kieran O'Donoghue, and Agnes K. T. Ng

Introduction

In this chapter, the authors will identify the essence and significance of cultural competence and sensitivity to diversity in the practice of clinical supervision. The chapter will also explore and examine how the following five perspectives influence the practice of clinical supervision:

1. Political context: This includes the structural differentiation, class differences, and political ideologies of the supervisee and the supervisor.
2. Cultural context: This is related to the values, norms, rituals, and customs of the social environment.
3. Organizational context: This refers to the occupational hierarchy, use of supervisory authority, and decision-making in the process of clinical supervision.
4. Professional practices: This involves the clinical expertise, professional roles, staff participation, learning process, and supervisory interaction.
5. Personal characteristics: This includes the personal background and uniqueness of individual supervisees and supervisors, for example, age, gender, race, religion, and physical characteristics.

After the discussion, the guiding principles for conducting cross-cultural supervision in clinical settings will be explored and discussed. In addition, the recommendations for the further development of culturally competent supervision will be made.

The Wiley International Handbook of Clinical Supervision, First Edition. Edited by C. Edward Watkins, Jr. and Derek L. Milne.

Importance of Culture to Clinical Supervision

Supervision is critical for ensuring service standards and qualities (Davys & Beddoe, 2010; Kadushin & Harkness, 2002; Munson, 2002; Tsui, 2005a). The goal of supervision is to enhance supervisees' professional knowledge, practice skills, and social functioning, and to enhance the quality of professional service that is provided to the clients. Supervision is also regarded as an ongoing process that allows the supervisees and supervisors to develop working relationships in which they can grow and develop (Bernard & Goodyear, 2004). To make our professional practice effective, clinicians (such as psychologists, therapists, nurses, counselors, and social workers) have been reminded to be culturally responsive to the needs and problems of their clients (Falender & Shafranske, 2004).

Culture as a term has been interpreted by scholars across different generations from different disciplines in a variety of different ways (Jahoda, 2012; Tsui, 2001). It is easy to differentiate but very difficult to define. It is a sum total of the learned behaviors of a group of people who shared patterns of values, beliefs, languages, ritual and customs, behaviors and interactions, cognitive constructs, and affective understanding through process of socialization in the community and society (Chamberlain, 99). These shared patterns identify the people of a culture group while also distinguishing those of another group. For example, Chinese culture is a relatively collectivist culture, which emphasizes the interdependence and long-term mutual obligations between individuals and organizations (Tsui & Chan, 1995). People are expected to respect and follow group norms and social values. Chinese people prefer small group-based operations with the emphasis on hierarchy and harmony, long-term relationships, interorganizational collaboration, and negotiation while avoiding public confrontation (Ho, 1976; Tsui, Ho, & Lam, 2005). We also note that within the helping professions the word "culture" is most often used interchangeably with the word "ethnicity" to describe the views, customs, and language of a social group (Laird, 1998).

One of the most effective ways for acquiring cultural competence is positive supervision experiences that uphold and cultivate cultural expertise (Pope-Davis & Coleman, 1997; Sue & Sue, 2008). According to Burkand et al.(2006), when supervisees discussed cultural issues with their supervisors, they felt more sensitized to the importance of cultural issues in the therapeutic process, which also positively affected the outcome of the therapeutic intervention. We all know that it is not easy to be a culturally competent helping professional because it involves individuals' understanding their cultural milieu, and having the ability to adjust to cultural differences and diversity within their working relationships without causing offense (O'Donoghue, 2010). However, in light of the growing diversity in the global world, it is essential for the helping professionals to enhance their awareness and knowledge of multicultural issues in supervision and become culturally competent supervisors.

In this chapter, we aim to bring culture to the forefront within clinical supervision. We shall also discuss the influence and prevalence of culture, and its relationship with notions of cultural competence within supervision. In addition, we aim to provide systemic and contextual frameworks for understanding, assessing, and addressing culturally competent and diversity-sensitive practice in clinical supervision in the hope of increasing professionals' self-awareness and self-evaluation in their own clinical practice.

Cultural Competence

Cultural competence in clinical supervision refers to the ability of supervisees and supervisors to relate to each other in order to achieve the objectives of clinical supervision, regardless of any diversity issues or contextual differences. According to Martin and Vaughn (2007), cultural competence consists of four elements: (1) awareness of one's own cultural background, (2) attitude toward differences, (3) knowledge of different cultural practices and worldviews, and (4) skills in interacting with peoples from different cultures.

First, both the supervisee and the supervisor become aware of their own reactions to the other who is from a different cultural background. Such awareness can be strength in becoming a culturally competent supervisee or supervisor, as in recognizing one's limitations. Second, in the supervisory process, both the supervisee and the supervisor are sensitive and inclusive in their close encounters with colleagues who have a different cultural worldview. Third, more knowledge about other cultures will be an advantage for the supervisee and the supervisor, enabling them to get along with each other in harmony and with respect. Such knowledge can be attained from traveling, friendship, readings, or training. Lastly, in supervision, cross-cultural skills are the practices that build on the first three elements: awareness, attitude, and knowledge. It involves subtle considerations in interpersonal communication and interaction. Of course, it includes gestures and other nonverbal communication, which have specific meanings from culture to culture. To summarize, cultural competence is a sincere and humble way of facing and welcoming the diversity of your colleague in the supervisory process. Diversity must be identified, addressed, valued, and respected before a professional practitioner becomes culturally competent. In this sense, the existence of diversity is a necessary condition for achieving cultural competence. When your worldview is relative and multiple, when you understand that how the world is perceived comes from different sources, and when you recognize that you are not the center of the world, you are becoming more culturally competent.

To further understand cultural competence, Cross (1988) provided a continuum that ranged from the most incompetent to the most competent: (1) cultural destructiveness, (2) cultural incapacity, (3) cultural blindness, (4) cultural pre-competence, and (5) advanced cultural competence. First, "cultural destructiveness" is the greatest form of incompetence, one which intentionally tries to undermine, or even destroy another's culture. Second, "cultural incapacity" would be indicated when the supervisor is not intentionally destructive, but rather he or she lacks the ability to be culturally competent and is extremely biased. Third, "cultural blindness" is the mid-point on the continuum. In this position, the supervisor tries to be fair to all and to treat everyone as the same. It is as if the inequalities and discrimination do not exist. However, it does not mean that the supervisor is culturally competent or culturally sensitive, because he or she just ignores the difference. By contrast, "cultural pre-competence" is characterized by acceptance and respect for difference. Although it is not fully accomplished, it is, at least, a good start toward cultural competence.

Lastly, "advanced cultural competence" is characterized by the supervisor's high respect for cultural differences and the pursuit of improved relationships between different peoples.

McPhatter (2004) also outlined a framework for culturally competent supervision that involved practical strategies supervisors can use to model culturally competent supervision within multicultural settings. These strategies included the development of a core knowledge base concerning cultural difference; an understanding of the context within which cultural challenges arise; effective cross-cultural communication and conflict management skills; and the ability to create an environment of safety within supervision. For McPhatter (2004), cultural competence is not just transactional, it is also contextual. In other words, it is necessary for professions and human service organizations to create a friendly environment within which supervisees and supervisors can exchange information and ideas, as well as understand the feelings of others, then they can practice in a culturally competent manner.

Hair and O'Donoghue (2009) explored notions of cultural competence and the cultural relevancy of supervision from a social constructionist framework. In doing so, they argued that the social constructionist lens enables

1. the recognition of plurality and diversity of knowledge;
2. an emphasis on collaboration;
3. the acknowledgment that supervisees have agency in a co-constructive process;
4. the engagement in various relational forms, such as dyadic, group, and in-session supervision;
5. an increased sensitivity to power and the politics of empowerment and disempowerment in supervision; and
6. the explicit recognition of the influence of the social and cultural context within which supervision is immersed (Hair & O'Donoghue, 2009, p. 77).

For Hair and O'Donoghue (2009), supervision is constructed through global, social, cultural, professional, organizational, and personal narratives. This means that there is a diversity of cultural discourses, with different positions for cultural insiders and outsiders, when interacting within these discourses. The complexity of this situation indicates that the dynamics of culture within supervisory relationships and the supervision of client practice are complex and context specific and that there are differences pertaining to the supervision of those who are cultural insiders (i.e., who have "emic" status) and those who are outsiders (i.e., have "etic" status; Kwong, 2009).

In summary, cultural competence is an interactive process in which supervisors "approach culturally different people with openness and respect [and] a willingness to learn" (O'Hagan, 2001, p. 235), and in doing so are critically conscious of their cultural and ethnic positioning in relation to the supervisee, as well as the influence of wider discourses on them both.

Cultural Competence within Clinical Supervision

Having established an understanding of cultural competence, in this next section we will explore and examine how the political context, organizational context, cultural context, professional practice, and personal characteristics influence the practice of clinical supervision. This exploration will draw from qualitative, mixed-method, and pilot studies undertaken in New Zealand and Hong Kong (Ng, 2011; O'Donoghue, 2010; Tsui, 2001, 2004).

Political Context

Politically, New Zealand is a liberal democracy based on the Westminster system, with two differences. The first is the use of a mixed-member, proportional electoral system, and the second is a specific allocation of Māori electoral seats, which is based on the percentage of Māori who choose to go on the Māori electorate roll (Mulgan & Aimer, 2004). The context from which twenty-first century New Zealand politics developed is derived from the bicultural relationship established between the Crown and Māori in the Treaty of Waitangi (1840; see Taylor, 1976). In the Treaty of Waitangi, Māori and the British Crown agreed to be partners in a process of nation-building and settlement, through the Crown being permitted to establish a government, with Māori retaining their rights of chieftainship, self-determination, and management of their resources and treasures, as well as gaining the rights and privileges of British subjects (Belich, 2001; Orange, 1987). The bicultural relationship between Māori and non-Māori is the background against which the politics of a New Zealand national identity and nationhood have emerged (Belich, 2001; Ruwhiu, 2001, 2009). From the 1850s to the 1980s, numerous breaches of the treaty resulted in oppression of the Māori people (Ministerial Advisory Committee on a Maori Perspective for the Department of Social Welfare, 1986). In the 1960s, the mono-ethnic dominance of New Zealanders of European descent also began to have prejudicial effects on the Pacific Island peoples who had migrated to New Zealand in response to a high demand for labor (Ministry of Pacific Island Affairs, 1999). Particularly through the 1970s, the Maori people began to collectively strengthen their resistance to the dominant narratives of racism, oppression, and marginalization. Subsequent proceedings helped to move the country toward biculturalism, such as settlements by the New Zealand government of land claims made by Māori tribes, the recognition of Māori as an official language, and the emergence of Iwi (tribal) social services (Bradley, 1996; Cheyne, O'Brien, & Belgrave, 2004). Despite these developments, Māori and Pacific Island peoples feature disproportionately across a wide range of social and health indicators, and are significant users of welfare, health, social service, and criminal justice services (Pega, Valentine, & Matheson, 2010).

The influence of this political context is such that it provides the background to the challenges inherent in New Zealand, arising from the discourses of indigenous Māori development, biculturalism, and multiculturalism. For those involved in the helping professions, these challenges are most keenly felt through high demands on Māori and Pasifika professionals to provide services to their own people and advice and support to their European colleagues. In addition, it contributes to the situation where two European New Zealanders are discussing Māori or Pasifika clients in supervision.

Since 1997, Hong Kong has been a Special Administrative Region of the People's Republic of China. Prior to this and from1842, Hong Kong was a British colony.

Chinese sovereignty of Hong Kong operates according to the "one country, two systems" principle. The Hong Kong Special Administrative Region's constitutional document, the Basic Law, ensures that the current political situation remains in effect until 2046. The rights and freedom of people in Hong Kong are derived from the impartial rule of law and an independent judiciary (People's Republic of China, 2012).

A residual welfare system was established in Hong Kong during the late colonial period. According to Lee (2005), the Hong Kong welfare system has been challenged by financial austerity resulting from the twin pressures of economic globalization and socioeconomic change to the extent that the Social Welfare Department and non-government organizations (NGOs) are able to provide a safety net of social and welfare services for the socially disadvantaged. Chua, Wong, and Shek (2009, pp. 537–538) identify the following four unequal societies within Hong Kong: (1) the well-off, who are immune from changes in the local economy; (2) the socially secure, who are able to protect themselves from all but the most extreme changes; (3) the socially insecure, who just get by with difficulty on a day-to-day basis; and (4) a growing underclass living in poverty with limited opportunity for social mobility. Chua et al. (2009) also noted that across these four societies, the most notable negative change in the social development index was to the family solidarity sub-index, which they identified as reflective of increasing rates of divorce, domestic violence, spouse abuse, elder abuse, and child abuse.

Cultural Context

From a population-based perspective, New Zealand is multicultural: 67.6% of the population are European;14.6% are Māori (the indigenous people); 11.1% are New Zealanders (previously this group was included under the European category); 9.2% are Asian; 6.9% are Pacific peoples; and 0.9% are Middle Eastern, Latin American, or African (Statistics New Zealand, 2007). Over the last two decades, the Asian and Pacific peoples' populations have had the highest rates of increase (Maidment, 2009). The multicultural reality of New Zealand occurs within the context of a bicultural polity between Māori and non-Māori, derived from the Treaty of Waitangi (1840; see Taylor, 1976). This is evident in New Zealand's two official languages, English and Māori, and the incorporation of Māori customs such as the *haka* (ceremonial dance) by national sporting teams and *powhiri* (a formal ceremonial welcome) to visiting dignitaries. In other words, present-day New Zealand culture is constituted by the historical relationships between Māori, the government, and migrant settler groups. According to O'Donoghue (2010), these three historical relationships manifest themselves in the practice of supervision through three specific cultural discourses, namely indigenous Māori development, biculturalism, and multiculturalism. These in turn have been influential in shaping the cultural framework for supervision, as presented in Table 10.1. This framework captures the challenges present within the New Zealand cultural context as they pertain to how

a. practitioners from indigenous and minority cultural groups develop professionally and are supervised from within their cultures and from their cultural worldview;

Table 10.1 Cultural framework for supervision in New Zealand.

Type of cultural engagement/ cultural positioning	*Cultural insider example*	*Cultural outsider example*
Indigenous	Kaupapa Māori supervision within an Iwi (tribal) social service where both the supervisee and the supervisor are from the same Iwi (tribe)	Māori supervision within a Kaupapa Māori setting where either the supervisee and/or supervisor are not from the local Iwi (tribe)
Bicultural	Cultural supervision for Māori staff in mainstream or bicultural settings provided by a Māori supervisor	Non-Māori engaging in cross-cultural supervision/ consultation with a Māori consultant supervisor/ supervisee. Non-Māori engaging in cross-cultural supervision/ consultation with a Māori consultant regarding the supervision of their work with Māori clients
Multicultural	Supervision within same culture group within a multicultural setting (e.g., Pasifika supervision, African, Chinese, European supervision)	Cross-cultural supervision relationships and the supervision of cross-cultural practice, involving supervisees and/or supervisors from different cultural backgrounds

Source: O'Donoghue(2010, p. 323).

b. cross-cultural supervision relationships and the supervision of cross-cultural practice; and
c. supervision where the supervisee and supervisor are from the same-cultural group, but the clients who are the subject of the supervision are from a different culture.

Unlike New Zealand, 95% of the population in Hong Kong is Chinese. The other 5% of population are Indonesian (133,377); Filipino (133,018); Indian (28,616); Pakistani (18,042); Nepalese (16,518); Japanese (12,580); Thai (11,213); Korean (5,209); and other Asian (7,037), totalling to 365,610 (Census and Statistics Department, 2011). Most, if not all, of social workers in Hong Kong are Chinese and have not received cultural competence training in working with the above listed minority groups. In addition, there have been complaints that some social workers handle problems of all groups in the same way and neglect cultural issues unique to each group. There are also complaints that some social workers lack the cultural sensitivity, basic knowledge, and skills necessary for serving ethnic minorities (Hong Kong Unison Limited, 2013).

The official languages of Hong Kong are Chinese and English. That said, 89.2% of the population speak Cantonese; 0.9% speak Putonghua; 5.5% speak other Chinese dialects; 3.2% speak English; and 1.2% speak other languages (Hong Kong Government, 2013). The linguistic diversity of these minority groups poses a challenge to the extent that social workers have to rely on translators. This reliance sometimes lowers the service users' motivation to come for help and their ability to secure adequate assistance. Thus, the demand of multicultural competence workers is deemed both necessary and significant.

Organizational Context

In New Zealand, the organizational context of supervision has developed in response to indigenous Māori developments (Māori services for Māori), biculturalism (Māori and non-Māori working in partnership), and multiculturalism (the population-based recognition of ethnic and cultural diversity; O'Donoghue, 2010). Indigenous Māori developments are apparent in the development of Iwi (tribal) social services, Māori-specific teams within mainstream social and health services (Bradley, 1996; Walsh-Tapiata, 2000; Walsh-Tapiata & Webster, 2004). These developments have contributed to the claiming of an indigenous position in relation to supervision through kaupapa Māori supervision, which Eruera (2005) defines as

> An agreed supervision relationship by Māori for Māori with the purpose of enabling the supervisee to achieve safe and accountable professional practice, cultural development and self-care according to the philosophy, principles, and practices derived from a Māori worldview. (p. 64)

Mainstream organizational responses to biculturalism and multiculturalism within New Zealand have also contributed to the development of specific forms of cultural supervision wherein some organizations have engaged cultural experts to work with staff in culturally specific supervision relationships (Masters, Trynes, Kaparu, Robertson, & Waitoki, 2003). These relationships are an adjunct to the clinical supervision relationship, as well as part of some organizations' supervision policies. The purpose of cultural supervision is to assist both cultural insiders and cultural outsiders to work through and practice safely and effectively, when cultural issues arise in practice (O'Donoghue, 2010). Su'a-Hawkins and Mafile'o (2004, p. 11) illustrate this when they describe cultural supervision (as it is related to Pacific peoples who are residents in New Zealand, known as Pasifika cultural supervision) as a "multifaceted yet ethnic-specific" process, one that may involve interactions between supervisors, practitioners, and clients from diverse backgrounds (e.g., a Tongan supervisor, a Cook Island practitioner, and a Samoan client); as well as interactions within the same cultural groups (e.g., a Tongan supervisor, a Tongan practitioner, and a Tongan client). For Su'a-Hawkins and Mafile'o, the focus of Pasifika cultural supervision concerns the "cultural development . . . of Pasifika practitioners through reflection, critique, and action" (p. 12) and by recognizing that, in New Zealand, they operate in primarily non-Pasifika contexts. These are contexts in which support is often needed to maintain a critical awareness of the dominant New Zealand culture, and to practice effectively from a Pasifika cultural base. Before moving on to the Hong Kong context it should be noted a few of the participants in O'Donoghue's (2010) study felt that some of their organization's effort toward biculturalism and multiculturalism were tokenistic, because of a lack or limited provision of cultural supervision, or that the rhetoric within the organization's policy did not align with their experience of organizational practice. This was particularly apparent among participants who worked in the health field. It also highlights the importance of what McPhatter (2004, p. 49) termed "culturally competent organizations," ones that actively pursue cultural competence through the employment of a culturally diverse and competent work force, and which deliberately include cultural competence within their policies, plans, and reporting.

In Hong Kong, social service organizations are increasingly controlled and structured in accordance with the "Lump Sum Grant Policy," which allows the agency heads of NGOs to have the autonomy to spend the government subvention (Social Welfare Department, 2013). The role that supervision plays within such organizations is as one of the institutional controls for both the availability and the standards of service. In this process, a common culture of doing more for less creates tensions between supervisees and supervisors because the staff are sometimes under great stress to meet some unrealistic demands. Munson (2002) mentioned that supervisors perceive themselves as caught between the organization and the clinicians. They are recognized as "managerial persons"; however, in reality, they are "marginal persons" (Tsui, 2005a). The supervisor has the administrative and educational functions to maintain the required service standards. Argument commonly occurs about the respective weight that should be given to each function (Tsui, 2005b). Conceptually, both functions are essential elements of supervisory practice as the organization is responsible for the results of its service: it must set up administrative controls as well as train up competent staff to carry out the tasks for service quality assurance. However, much has been reported in recent years about the inadequate supervision practice due to organizational restructuring, limited resources, and greater services demand. The frequency of supervision is not adequate for proper monitoring of job performance or the development of the professional competence of the supervisee (Tsui, 1998, 2001). For developing a competent team, the supervisors should have the responsibility to take a gatekeeping role in helping the top management to establish an effective organizational cultural for supervision practice.

According to Ng (2011), approximately 150 persons come to Hong Kong from the Chinese Mainland every day to reunite with other family members. These families, while also being ethnic Chinese, differ in their values, attitudes, language, living patterns, and practices from those imbued in Hong Kong culture. When these people seek help from social service organizations, it is expected that they will assimilate within the dominant culture rather than have the social service respond to them in a culturally responsive and friendly manner. Ng also measured the multicultural competence of supervisor–supervisee dyads. Her results indicated that most of the supervisors self-rated their multicultural supervision competencies as satisfactory. However, the supervisees' views on their supervisors' multicultural competence were that the supervisors' had very low and low levels of competence. This difference, while not statistically significant and derived from a small sample, still highlights the need for further study in order to have a clearer picture of this issue. Nonetheless, there is a need for organizations to educate supervisors to improve their attitude and beliefs toward the minority groups and the increasing number of clients from other diverse ethnic groups.

Professional Practices

At the professional practices level, O'Donoghue (2010) found that supervisors experienced clear differences between supervision that occurred within their own cultural groups by comparison with cross-cultural supervision. For example, Halle, a Māori supervisor, when commenting on the differences between supervising Māori and non-Māori, noted that Māori supervisees had "*an ability to relate to each other [within the context] of a Maori worldview and . . . [had] the humour, and . . . [were] able toengageinallthedifferentemotions . . . asMaoriinourunderstandingofthe situations.*" In other words, they "*have a sense of what it means and a commonality of understanding around being . . . Maori.*" But with non-Māori supervisees, "*quite extensive discussions [were needed] . . . at the beginning of [the] relationship around that cultural difference*" and from those discussions they "*wanted to . . . have another framework . . . to . . . explor[e] . . . their . . . worldview*" (O'Donoghue, 2010, p. 218). For Halle cross-cultural supervision relationships differed from those that occurred within her own culture because of the need to discuss the differences between her and the non-Māori supervisees, and the need to educate them with regard to Māori cultural perspectives. In contrast to Halle's experience was that of Elton, a European New Zealander, who had considerable experience supervising Māori practitioners. Elton stated that supervision with Māori supervisees differed from that with Europeans, because with Māori supervisees, he

> might go into a little more detail about how they awhi (support) a certain whanau (family) and it was quite detailed [whereas] . . . a European colleague wouldn't have spent so much time with the family and acknowledged the issues.

According to Elton his process with Māori supervisees involved more checking of their comfort and agreement with regard to his interventions by using questions such as, "*Are you happy with that? How would that sound to you?*"

Another area of cross-cultural supervision practice is the supervision of cultural matters presented in supervision, where the clients discussed in supervision differ culturally from the supervisee and the supervisor. For instance, O'Donoghue (2010) noted that New Zealand European supervisors and supervisees often discussed cultural matters concerning Māori within supervision. From these discussions, O'Donoghue identified a model of supervisory practice in regard to Māori content (when both parties were non-Māori and cultural outsiders). This model involved an exploration of cultural issues, and a discussion concerning the need for advice and support from Māori services.

Turning to supervisory practice in Hong Kong, Tsui (2004) found that the supervisee and the supervisee share the same professional goals in supervision. They also used it to address personal matters in the supervision process. Overall, the distinctive supervisor–supervisee relationship was mitigated by Chinese cultural values that stress reciprocity: *qing*, *yuan*, and *face*. As a result, the supervisory relationship is a consensual interaction that occurs without much friction.

Personal Characteristics

Supervisors and supervisees bring with them into the supervision relationship their cultural and ethnic identity, their past experiences, worldviews, and physical appearance and presence. Each of these features brings with it a set of assumptions from which the supervisee and supervisor will engage with each other. For example, in New Zealand, O'Donoghue (2010) found that supervision with Māori supervisees generally differed from supervision with non-Māori and that the nature of this difference concerned the use of a Māori worldview, Māori knowledge and Māori cultural practices (such as rituals of engagement, e.g., *hongi*, which is a traditional Māori form of greeting involving the pressing of noses, and/or the use of *karakia* [spiritual incantations] at the beginning and ending of sessions). At the individual level, the specific incorporation of cultural practices relies on the supervisee and the supervisor acknowledging their differences and exploring how they might work together. Central to this discussion is whether the supervisee wishes to have their cultural worldview and professional practice incorporated into the supervision. O'Donoghue emphasized the importance of enabling the supervisee to make this choice, as illustrated in the following examples. The first concerns Ted, a European supervisor who described how a Māori supervisee:

> Asked if she [could] occasionally . . . engage in karakia at the beginning, and she takes some leadership of that . . . A couple of times she's asked me if I would join her in a prayer . . . and . . . a couple of times I've participated in that . . . to the level . . . that I feel comfortable. (O'Donoghue, 2010, p. 266)

The second example was outlined by another European supervisor, Becky, who stated that one Māori supervisee that she worked with

> . . . was very very clear with me that she didn't want karakia with me, and she didn't want anything to do with her cultural identity in supervision with me . . . Very clear. (O'Donoghue, 2010, p. 264)

Both these examples were from supervisors who were sensitive to cultural differences and who were willing to engage cross-culturally and were open to challenge. In particular, Becky's example challenges supervisors not to presume that because their supervisee is of a particular ethnic and cultural background that supervision will necessarily incorporate cultural practices.

In Hong Kong, the form of supervisory practice is a combination of, and compromise between, the North American concept of supervision and the British system of government within the Chinese cultural context. Surprisingly, these contradictory components coexist without conflicts. This harmony can be explained by the five constants our Chinese core social values teach us to uphold namely, humaneness (*Ren*), righteousness or justice (*Yi*), propriety or etignettee (*Li*), knowledge (*Zhi*), and integrity (*Xin*), and four virtues covering loyalty (*Zhong*), filial piety (*Xiao*), continency (*Jie*), and righteousness (*Yi*) in dealing with human relationships. There are still many other elements, such as *Cheng* (honesty), *Shu* (kindness and forgiveness), *Lian* (honesty and cleanness), *Chi* (shame, judge and sense of right and wrong), *Yong* (bravery), *Wen* (kind andgentle), *Liang* (good, kindhearted), *Gong* (respectful, reverent), *Jian* (frugal), *Rang* (modestly, self-effacing). In Tsui's (2004) study, he found that supervisors are usually strongly motivated to be the leader, and their adoption of this role is more tolerable for their supervisees than it is for supervisees in North America. Although there is tension between the supervisor and the supervisee, the conflict is reduced to a minimum because supervisors take the role of a leader and the supervisees accept their position as followers. This intrapersonal compatibility of concepts of positional roles ensures stability and minimizes interpersonal conflicts. However, the attitudes of tolerance and deference among supervisees might not only contribute to the negative "conflict avoidance" reason. It may come from their upbringing by Chinese *Gong* (respectful, reverent) culture wherein they have been socialized to obey the "senior's position status and authority" in a natural manner. They accept their supervisor's authority and that the supervisor is responsible for how things work in a similar fashion to how young children accept the authority and guidance of their parents. In spite of this, some of these cultural values have been challenged by the new generation social work practitioners who see themselves as competent professionals and are not willing to become unconditional followers. Thus, the challenge for present-day supervisors is to be alert and attentive to their supervisees' expectations in order to achieve effective professional practice.

Although "cross-racial" supervisor–supervisee dyads are not common in Hong Kong, supervisors' sensitivity toward the "cross-racial" supervisee–client dynamic is important. In Hong Kong, the supervisory role carries a strong element of authority that includes making judgment about the promotion, reassignment, or dismissal of staff. This dynamic of power and control vested in the supervisor, coupled with the dependence and insecurity of the learner, and the closeness of the relationship can heighten anxiety reactions within the supervisor–supervisee dyads. It is notable that in this context the level of supervisor support experienced significantly influenced supervisees' evaluations of whether supervision was positive or not? Tsui (2001) reported that the supervisory relationship of social workers in Hong Kong is very distinctive. It is characterized by a dual perspective: personal and professional. The supervisor is a "senior," in both a personal and a professional sense. The tension arising from the dynamics of these two different types of relationships is lessened by the traditional Chinese cultural values of reciprocity: *qing*, *yuan*, and *face* can be maintained in a harmonious, stable, and sustainable manner.

Overall, the research we have reported from New Zealand and Hong Kong aligns and adds to the international research. For example, Pope-Davis, Reynolds, Dings, and Nielson (1995) and Pope-Davis, Reynolds, Dings, and Ottavi (1994) found that receiving multicultural supervision was significantly predictive of self-reported multicultural counseling competence. Constantine (1997) reported that some respondents in her study believed that their supervision relationship would have been more enhanced if they had spent more time addressing multicultural issues. Ladany, Inman, Constantine, and Hofheinz (1997) reported that supervisees who were "instructed" by their supervisors to focus on multicultural issues in their conceptualizations of a client's presenting concerns were better able to consider multicultural issues in these conceptualizations than supervisees who did not receive such instruction.

In summary, our exploration of how context, professional practices, and personal characteristics influence the practice of clinical supervision within New Zealand and Hong Kong shows that cultural competence within clinical supervision is complex, contextual, and contingent. It is influenced by relationships between cultural groups over time, the ongoing interplay within societies of political and cultural discourses, and the position of the supervisor, supervisee, and client as either cultural insiders or outsiders.

Guiding Principles for Conducting Intracultural and Cross-Cultural Supervision

The instruction and guidance in regard to cultural competence within the supervision practice literature for the most part encourages supervisors (1) to increase their understanding, awareness, and knowledge of their own cultural background; (2) to increase their knowledge and skills in regard to the different ethnic and cultural groups among their supervisee and client populations; (3) to engage in respectful dialogue within supervision, with an understanding of one's cultural positioning and power; and (4) to develop their supervisees' cultural competence, through modeling and instruction in supervision (Hawkins & Shohet, 2006; Haynes, Corey, & Moulton, 2003). These principles align with a recent study by Wong, Wong, and Ishiyama (2013) concerning the factors that help and hinder cross-cultural clinical supervision. The study found that (1) personal attributes of the supervisor, (2) supervision competence, (3) mentoring, (4) relationship, and (5) multicultural supervision competence were the most helpful factors. The most unhelpful were (1) personal difficulties as a visible minority, (2) negative personal attributes of the supervisor, (3) lack of a safe and trusting relationship, (4) lack of multicultural competence, and (5) lack of supervision competence.

Nonetheless, it is our view that these guidelines, while helpful, do not recognize the complex diversity of cultural engagements and discourses within clinical supervision. For example, they do not address the cultural development that occurs within cultural groups and the role that supervision can play. For instance, in New Zealand there are differences in regard to the level of cultural development within each cultural group. These differences can come to the forefront when the different groups engage in intracultural supervision (for example, one may be fluent in the language and the other may not; or one might be New Zealand born, and the other may be a migrant). The point here is that within cultural groups, as well as across cultural groups, there is a need for supervisees and supervisors to walk carefully as they enter other people's worlds, partly because within a cultural group people may be in different places in their cultural development. Regarding this observation, O'Donoghue (2010) argued that cultural competence within supervision concerned the contribution that supervision makes to the cultural development of practitioners and the cultural safety of clients from indigenous and minority cultural groups, as well as the cultural competence of practitioners from dominant cultural groups. Cultural competence needs to be conceived of both intraculturally and cross-culturally.

Clearly, in cross-cultural supervision, the enacting of the guidelines discussed earlier would appear to be helpful in relation to the supervisory process. Nevertheless, there remains a concern about the extent to which multicultural training is provided to supervisors. For example, Constantine (1997) reported that 70% of the supervisors she surveyed had never taken an academic course related to multicultural counseling issues, whereas 70% of the supervisees in her study had completed such a course. She concluded that supervisors, in general, might be less aware of multicultural counseling issues than their supervisees.

Conclusion and Recommendations

The aim of this chapter has been to bring culture to the forefront within clinical supervision. We have emphasized the influence and prevalence of culture and its relationship with notions of cultural competence within supervision. In addition, we have provided systemic and contextual frameworks for understanding, assessing, and addressing the culturally competent and diversity-sensitive practice in clinical supervision. We have done so in the hope of increasing professionals' self-awareness and self-evaluation in their clinical practice. In doing so, we have highlighted the influence of indigenous, bicultural, and multicultural discourses have on supervision. We have also encouraged you, the reader, to consider your cultural positioning as a cultural insider or outsider (or both), and to be aware that cultural competence is not just cross-cultural but also intracultural. We have also brought to your attention different models of supervision within New Zealand that are culturally competent forms of supervision and a culture-sensitive approach to supervision within Hong Kong.

Finally, there is a clear need internationally for a broader understanding of cultural competence within supervision, as well as a need for an interdisciplinary approach toward culturally competent professions and helping organizations. Alongside this, there is an obvious need for further model development. The New Zealand supervision model, with its culture-specific approaches to supervision, highlights the differences between supervision involving cultural insiders and supervision that is cross-cultural. This is perhaps one way for the international community to determine the role of supervision in the cultural development and well-being of practitioners from indigenous and minority groups, and in the development of the cultural competence of practitioners from majority and dominant cultural groups. Obviously, there are many challenges to multicultural supervision competence. To combat these challenges, continuous efforts need to be invested in improving supervision effectiveness for the benefit of practitioners' professional development and service users' well-being. Last of all, in culturally competent clinical supervision, both the supervisee and the supervisor have to try to be culturally sensitive, contextually specific, conceptually clear, consciously humanistic, and continuously humorous.

References

Belich, J. (2001). *Making peoples: A history of the New Zealanders from Polynesian settlement to the end of the nineteenth century.* Auckland, New Zealand: Penguin.

Bernard, J. M., & Goodyear, R. K. (2004). *Fundamentals of clinical supervision*. Boston, MA: Pearson.

Bradley, J. (1996). Iwi and cultural services policy: The state's best kept secret. *TeKomako II Social Work Review*, *8*(4), 3–5.

Burkand, A. W., Johnson, A. J., Madson, M. B., Pruitt, N. T., Contreras-Tadych, D. A., Kozlowski, J. M., . . . Knox, S. (2006). Supervisor cultural responsiveness and unresponsiveness in cross-cultural supervision. *Journal of Counseling Psychology*, *53*, 288–301.

Census and Statistics Department. (2011). *Hong Kong 2011 population census. Thematic report: Ethnic minorities*. Retrieved from http://www.statistics.gov.hk/pub/B11200622012XXXXB0100.pdf

Chamberlain, S. (2005). Recognizing and responding to cultural differences in the education of culturally and linguistically diverse learners. *Intervention in School and Clinic*, *40*, 195–211.

Cheyne, C., O'Brien, M., & Belgrave, M. (2004). *Social policy in Aotearoa New Zealand: A critical introduction* (3rd ed.), Auckland, New Zealand: Oxford University Press.

Chua, H. W., Wong, A. K., & Shek, D. T. (2009). Social development in Hong Kong: Development issues identified by Social Development Index (SDI). *Social Indicators Research*, *95*(3), 535–551.

Constantine, M. G. (1997). Facilitating multicultural competency in counseling supervision: Operationalizing a practical framework. In D. B. Pope-Davis & H. L. K. Coleman (Eds.), *Multicultural counseling competencies: Assessment, education and training, and supervision* (pp.310–324). Thousand Oaks, CA: Sage.

Cross, T. L. (1988). Cultural competence continuum. *Issue of "Focal Point" bulletin of the Research and Training Centre on Family Support and Children's Mental Health*, Portland State University, OR.

Davys, A., & Beddoe, L. (2010). *Best practice in professional supervision: A guide for the helping profession*. London, UK: Jessica Kingsley Publisher.

Eruera, M. (2005). *He korero korari. Supervision for Maori. Weaving the past, into the present for the future* (Unpublished MPhil Social Work thesis). Auckland, New Zealand: Massey University.

Falender, C. A., & Shafranske, E. P. (2004). *Clinical supervision: A competency-based approach*. Washington, DC: American Psychological Association.

Hair, H. J., & O'Donoghue, K. (2009). Culturally relevant, socially just social work supervision: Becoming visible through a social constructionist lens. *Journal of Ethnic and Cultural Diversity in Social Work*, *18*, 70–88.

Hawkins, P., & Shohet, R. (2006). *Supervision in the help professions*. Maidenhead, UK: Open University Press.

Haynes, R., Corey, G., & Moulton, P. (2003). *Clinical supervision in the helping professions: A practical guide*. Pacific Grove, CA: Thomson, Brooks/Cole.

Ho, D. Y. F. (1976). On the concept of face. *American Journal of Sociology*, *81*, 867–884.

Hong Kong Government. (2013). *Hong Kong – The facts*. Retrieved from http://www.gov.hk/en/about/abouthk/facts.htm

Hong Kong Unison Limited. (2013). *Hong Kong Unison's submissions on the second report of Hong Kong SAR on the international covenant on economic, social and cultural rights (part two) for the pre-sessional hearing in May 2013*. Retrieved from http://www2.ohchr.org/english/bodies/cescr/docs/ngos/HKUnison1_China51PSWG.pdf

Jahoda, G. (2012). Critical reflections on some recent definitions of culture. *Culture and Psychology*, *18*, 289–303.

Kadushin, A., & Harkness, D. (2002). *Supervision in social work* (4th ed.). New York, NY: Columbia University Press.

Kwong, M. (2009). Applying cultural competency in clinical practice: Findings from multicultural experts' experience. *Journal of Ethnic and Cultural Diversity in Social Work, 18*, 146–165.

Ladany, N., Inman, A. G., Constantine, M. G., & Hofheinz, E. W. (1997). Supervisee multicultural case conceptualization ability and self-reported multicultural competence as functions of supervisee racial identity and supervisor focus. *Journal of Counseling Psychology, 44*, 284–293.

Laird, J. (1998). Theorizing culture: Narrative ideas and practice principles. In M. McGoldrick (Ed.), *Re-visioning family therapy: Race, culture, and gender in clinical practice* (pp. 20–36). New York, NY: Guilford Press.

Lee, E. (2005). The renegotiation of the social pact in Hong Kong: Economic globalisation, socioeconomic change, and local politics. *Journal of Social Policy, 34*, 293–310.

Maidment, J. (2009). Cross-cultural practice. In M. Connolly & L. Harms (Eds.), *Social work: Contexts and practice* (2nd ed., pp.149–162). Melbourne, Australia: Oxford University Press.

Martin, M., & Vaughn, B. (2007). *Strategic diversity and inclusion management, Magazine* (pp. 31–36). San Francisco, CA: DTUI Publications Division.

Masters, B., Trynes, M., Kaparu, R., Robertson, N., & Waitoki, M. (2003). An evaluation of the cultural supervision prototype undertaken within the Department of Corrections, Hamilton. In L. W. Nikora, M. Levy, B. Masters, W. Waitoki, N. Te Awekotuku, & R. J. M. Etheredge (Eds.), *The Proceedings of the National Māori Graduates of Psychology Symposium 2002: Making a difference. Proceedings of a symposium hosted by the Māori & Psychology Research Unit at the University of Waikato, Hamilton, November 29–30, 2002* (pp. 49–55). Hamilton, New Zealand: Māori and Psychology Research Unit, University of Waikato.

McPhatter, A. (2004). Culturally competent practice. In M. Austin & K. Hopkins (Eds.), *Supervision as collaboration in the human services: Building a learning culture* (pp. 47–58). Thousand Oaks, CA: Sage.

Ministerial Advisory Committee on a Maori Perspective for the Department of Social Welfare. (1986). *Puao-te-ata-tu (Day break)*. Wellington, New Zealand: Department of Social Welfare.

Ministry of Pacific Island Affairs. (1999). *Pacific directions report: A report to government on a possible pathway for achieving Pacific people's aspirations*. Wellington, New Zealand: Ministry of Pacific Island Affairs.

Mulgan, R., & Aimer, P. (2004). *Politics in New Zealand* (3rd ed.). Auckland, New Zealand: Auckland University Press.

Munson, C. E. (2002). *Handbook of clinical social work supervision* (3rd ed.). New York, NY: The Haworth Press.

Ng, K. T. (2011). *A pilot study of clinical supervision practice in Hong Kong: Reality vs expected standards*. Unpublished manuscript.

O'Donoghue, K. (2010). *Towards the construction of social work supervision in AotearoaNew Zealand: A study of the perspectives of social work practitioners and supervisors* (PhD thesis). Massey University, Palmerston North.

O'Hagan, K. (2001). *Cultural competence in the caring professions*. London: Jessica Kingsley.

Orange, C. (1987). *The Treaty of Waitangi*. Wellington, New Zealand: Bridget Williams.

Pega, F., Valentine, N., & Matheson, D. (2010). *Social Determinants of Health Discussion Paper 3 (Case Studies)*. Geneva: World Health Organization. Monitoring Social Wellbeing to Support Policies on the Social Determinants of Health: the case of New Zealand's Social Reports/TePūrongoOrangaTangata.

People's Republic of China. (2012). *The Basic Law of the Hong Kong Special Administrative Region of the People's Republic of China*. Retrieved from http://www.basiclaw.gov.hk/en/index/index.html

Pope-Davis, D. B., & Coleman, H. L. (1997). *Multicultural counseling competencies: Assessment, education and training, and supervision*. CA: Sage.

Pope-Davis, D. B., Reynolds, A. L., Dings, J. G., & Ottavi, T. M. (1994). Multicultural competencies of doctoral interns at university counseling centers: An exploratory investigation. *Professional Psychology: Research and Practice*, *25*(4), 466–470. doi: 10.1037/0735-7028.25.4.466

Pope-Davis, D. B., Reynolds, A. L., Dings, J. G., & Nielson, D. (1995). Examining multicultural competencies of graduate students in psychology. *Professional Psychology, Research and Practice*, *26*, 322–329.

Ruwhiu, L. (2001). Bicultural issues in Aotearoa New Zealand. In M. Connolly (Ed.), *New Zealand social work: Contexts and fields of practice* (pp. 54–71), *Auckland*. New Zealand: Oxford University Press.

Ruwhiu, L. (2009). Indigenous issues in Aotearoa New Zealand. In M. Connolly & L. Harms (Eds.), *Social work: Contexts and practice* (2nd ed., pp.107–120). Melbourne, Victoria, Australia: Oxford University Press.

Social Welfare Department. (2013). *Lump sum grant mode*. Retrieved from http://www.swd.gov.hk/en/index/site_ngo/page_subventions/sub_modesofsub/id_lsgmanualc/

Statistics New Zealand. (2007). *QuickStats national highlights*. Retrieved from http://www.stats.govt.nz/~/media/Statistics/Census/2006-reports/quickstats-subject/Culture-Identity/qstats-about-culture-and-identity-2006-census.pdf

Su'a-Hawkins, A., & Mafile'o, T. (2004). What is cultural supervision? *Social Work Now*, *29*, 10–16.

Sue, D. W., & Sue, S. (2008). *Counseling the culturally diverse: Theory and practice*. Hoboken, NJ: Wiley.

Taylor, C. (1976). *Facsimilies of the Declaration of Independence and the Treaty of Waitangi*. Wellington, New Zealand: Government Printer.

Tsui, M. S. (1998). A job performance of professional social workers. *Asia Pacific Jorunal of Social Work*, *8*(2), 51–63.

Tsui, M. S. (2001). *Towards a culturally sensitive model of social work supervision in Hong Kong* (Unpublished PhD thesis). University of Toronto,Ann Arbor, MI: University Microfilms International.

Tsui, M. S. (2004). The supervisory relationship of Chinese social workers in Hong Kong. *The Clinical Supervisor*, *22*, 99–120.

Tsui, M. S. (2005a). *Social work supervision: Contexts and concepts*. Thousand Oaks, CA: Sage.

Tsui, M. S. (2005b). Functions of social work supervision in Hong Kong. *International Social Work*, *48*, 485–493.

Tsui, M. S., & Chan, R. K. H. (1995). East meets West: In search of a common base of the notion of the welfare state in China and in the West. New Global Development: *Journal of International & Comparative Social Welfare*, *XI*, 42–55.

Tsui, M. S., Ho, W. S., & Lam, C. M. (2005). The use of supervisory authority in chinese cultural context. *Administration in Social Work*, *29*, 51–68.

Walsh-Tapiata, W. (2000). Te tau ruamano. He aha ngaweroinaianei? The year 2000. What are the challenges for Maori social workers now? *Te Komako IV, Social Work Review*, *12*(4), 9–12.

Walsh-Tapiata, W., & Webster, J. (2004). Do you have a supervision plan? *Te Komako IV, Social Work Review*, *16*(2), 15–19.

Wong, L., Wong, P., & Ishiyama, I. (2013). What helps and what hinders in cross-cultural clinical supervision. *The Counseling Psychologist*, *41*, 66–85.

Part III

Core Skills in Clinical Supervision

11

Building and Sustaining the Supervisory Relationship

Helen Beinart

It is widely agreed that the development and maintenance of the supervisory relationship (SR) is critical to the delivery of effective supervision. This is supported by international competency frameworks (e.g., Roth & Fonagy, 2006 [United Kingdom]; Falender & Shafranske, 2004 [United States]; Psychology Board of Australia, 2011) and a growing body of research (e.g., Beinart & Clohessy, 2009; Ellis, 2010; Watkins, 2011). This chapter will explore definitions, theories, and research that inform our understanding of the SR. The qualities of the SR will be discussed, as well as its measurement and contribution to supervision outcomes. Many experienced clinicians and teachers believe that supervision is one of the most satisfying and enjoyable aspects of their professional roles and, when conducted well, it is one of the most influential. However, when SRs do not progress well they can be distressing and potentially destructive or harmful, for the supervisee and for the service user (Ellis, 2010; Falender & Shafranske, 2012). The chapter will therefore also explore, drawing on evidence from practice and research, in particular that of the Oxford Institute for Clinical Psychology Training Supervision Research Group, how to build and develop effective SRs, and how to sustain and develop these rewarding yet challenging professional relationships.

What Is the Supervisory Alliance/Supervisory Relationship? Definitions and Models

In the supervision literature the terms supervisory working alliance (SWA) and supervisory relationship (SR) tend to be used interchangeably. However, the SWA is a more theoretically driven construct defined by Bordin (1983) as a mutual agreement on the goals and tasks of supervision and the bond that develops between the

The Wiley International Handbook of Clinical Supervision, First Edition. Edited by C. Edward Watkins, Jr. and Derek L. Milne.

supervisor and supervisee. Bordin's definition stems from work on the therapeutic working alliance, which is supported by a strong body of research (e.g., Norcross, 2002). In particular, the rupture and repair of the therapeutic alliance is understood to be one of the key mutative factors in the psychological therapies (e.g., Safran, Muran, Stevens, & Rothman, 2007). However, it has been argued elsewhere (Beinart, 2012; Bernard & Goodyear, 2014; Ellis, D'Iuso, & Ladany, 2008) that to rely on translational models and research from psychotherapy to supervision can be restrictive because clinical supervision and therapy are fundamentally different. Clinical supervision is primarily educative and has a quality control function. During professional training, it is normally involuntary and involves formal evaluation (Bernard & Goodyear, 2014; Palomo, Beinart, & Cooper, 2010). Therefore, the SWA, defined as goals, tasks, and bond, is seen as only a partial explanation of the SR. The SR is understood here to include broader cultural, educational, and evaluative aspects. The chapter will use the more general term, SR, to describe the dyadic relationship between supervisee and supervisor unless referring to specific research on the SWA.

Although the SR is widely acknowledged in definitions and models of supervision, there are surprisingly few definitions and models of the SR itself, with the notable exception of Holloway (1995). She identified the balancing of power and involvement as central to the development of the SR over a period of time (including developmental phases of beginning, maturing, and terminating) which is supported by the supervision contract. "The relationship is the container of a dynamic process in which supervisor and supervisee negotiate a personal way of using a structure of power and involvement that accommodates the supervisee's progression of learning" (Holloway, 1995, pp. 41–42).

We know the SR is important. As stated by Ellis (2010)"good supervision is about the relationship, not the specific theory or techniques used (p. 106)." Additionally, Watkins (2014) emphasized that "the supervisor-supervisee alliance has increasingly emerged as a variable of preeminent importance in the conceptualisation and conduct of supervision . . . it is widely embraced as the very heart and soul of supervision". The SR has also been found to be central in supervision across cultures (Son, Ellis, & Yoo, 2007; Tsui, 2004). However, what we actually know about the SR is limited (Watkins, 2014). Research into the SR is complex and in its infancy. It is remarkably challenging to provide strong evidence on the specific effective ingredients of the SR and how it impacts on supervision outcomes. Currently, there is stronger evidence for SR outcomes related to supervisee learning and development than client outcomes. Positive client outcome is clearly an important goal of effective supervision and there is some promising early research in this area (Bambling, King, Raue, Schweitzer, & Lambert, 2006; Bradshaw, Butterworth, & Mairs, 2007; White & Winstanley, 2010). The learning and professional development of the supervisee is another important outcome, and there is a growing body of evidence to support the role of the SR in supervisee satisfaction (e.g., Ladany, Ellis, & Friedlander, 1999), perceived effectiveness (e.g., Palomo et al., 2010) and skills development (e.g., Ellis & Ladany, 1997).

There are numerous models of supervision (see Beinart, 2012; Hess, 2008); however, the majority pay minimal attention to the SR. This failure to clearly understand and define the specific and unique qualities of the SR is one of the factors that contribute to the slow development of a strong evidence base in this field (Ellis &

Ladany, 1997). Additionally, when discussing the conceptual basis to the SR it is important to consider the influences of relational models of supervision, such as parallel process and attachment theory. Early models of supervision (e.g., Ekstein & Wallerstein, 1972) used the term parallel process to describe the mirroring of conflicts and defenses in therapy within the SR (in systemic supervision models, patterns that develop in these relationships are termed isomorphism). Although it is important to notice, attend to, and reflect on similarities between the SR and the therapeutic relationship, the use of explanations that place the focus solely on the therapist and client could allow the avoidance of genuine issues of difference and difficulties within the SR, not least in the area of multiculturalism (Sue et al., 2007). Effective SRs are truly collaborative in that both parties mutually share their contribution and parallel process models may not fully support these discussions. Thus, although parallel process has historical and ongoing importance within certain psychotherapeutic traditions, it will not be further addressed in this chapter.

The application of attachment theory to our understanding of the SR has developed relatively more recently. There is some promising evidence to suggest that attachment theory may be helpful in conceptualizing the SR, particularly the influence of supervisor attachment pattern on SR quality (Dickson, Moberly, Marshall, & Reilly, 2011; Riggs & Bretz, 2006). It is also suggested that supervisees' with certain attachment patterns (avoidant, compulsive self-reliance), may be more vulnerable to developing weaker SRs (Bennett & Saks, 2006).This body of research is helpful to bear in mind when considering the importance of establishing a safe supervisory base, as discussed in the following section.

What Are the Unique Qualities of the SR? A Review of the Evidence

There has been considerable research in the United States exploring Bordin's model of the SWA using a questionnaire (Bahrick, 1990) adapted from a measure of the therapeutic alliance (Horvath & Greenberg, 1986). Findings suggest that the SWA is related to supervisee satisfaction (Inman, 2006; Ladany et al., 1999), supervisee role conflict (Ladany & Friedlander, 1995), supervisor evaluation and feedback practices (Lehrman-Waterman & Ladany, 2001), supervisor self-disclosure (Ladany & Lehrman-Waterman, 1999), supervisor interpersonal sensitivity (Ladany, Walker, & Melincoff, 2001), supervisors' ethical behavior (Ladany et al., 2001), and supervisor multicultural competence (Inman, 2006). Indeed, Watkins (2012) states, "while the relationship or alliance factor may be weighted and addressed differently across . . . supervision approaches . . . there seems to be no question that the factor is a (if not the) central pivotal component (p. 198)." This body of work has stimulated wider interest in other countries, including both the United Kingdom and Australia.

Research conducted by the Supervision Research Group in Oxford (United Kingdom) was initially prompted by the publication of the *Handbook of Psychotherapy Supervision* (Watkins, 1997), which outlined the poor quality of research in the field and drew attention to the significance of the SR. In particular, the comments from Ellis and Ladany (1997) "that until the unique qualities of the SR are both acknowledged and integrated into theorising . . . our understanding will continue to falter"

(p. 466) and that there is a "dearth of viable measures specific to clinical supervision" (p. 493) were stimuli to this research. In parallel, Milne and colleagues were developing standards for high-quality research into clinical supervision in the United Kingdom, and reached similar conclusions (Milne, 2009). Indeed, Milne states, "although the professional consensus is unanimous in affirming the importance of the supervisory alliance (e.g., Falender & Shafranske, 2004; Hatcher & Lassiter, 2007), evidence to support the assumption is surprisingly wanting" (Milne, 2009, p. 93). The body of research described in the next section aims to address a number of the issues already raised in this chapter. These specifically concern the employment of rigorous methods such as those suggested by Ellis and Ladany (1997) and Milne (2009), and avoidance of the use of translational models and measures from psychotherapy, based on the assumption that clinical supervision is primarily an educational activity (Holloway & Poulin, 1995; Milne & James, 2000), albeit often with the purpose of improving therapeutic outcomes. Additionally, it begins to address the recent recommendation for programmatic research into the SR including "investigation of the alliance in process, including attention to the alliance rupture and repair process" (Watkins, 2014).

Oxford supervision research

The research discussed here is based on clinical psychology training in the United Kingdom and aims to fill some of the gaps and address methodological flaws identified in the existing literature. Eight studies were conducted to specifically explore the SR from both supervisee and supervisor perspectives. The strategy was to start with robust qualitative research to answer some of the process questions concerning the particularity of SR qualities, experiences of difficulties, and attempts at resolution. Three empirically sound measures were developed from the qualitative research. All participants were working within the National Health Service in the United Kingdom, either in training or in qualified posts. The clinical areas are broad and include work with adults, children, people with intellectual disabilities, and the elderly, as well as more specialist areas such as neuropsychology and pediatrics. The competencies supervised are thus general psychological competencies and not specific to psychotherapy (although therapeutic competence is part of the broad portfolio of skills).

Five studies focused on supervisees, followed by a dyadic study on supervisees and supervisors, and two studies focused on supervisors.

Beinart (2002) used both quantitative and qualitative methodologies to test aspects of Bordin's model of the SWA (Bordin, 1983) and Holloway's model of the SR (Holloway, 1995), as described earlier. Clinical psychology supervisees (including trainees on doctoral programs and up to two years post qualification) participated in the study.

Supervisees were asked to complete a series of questionnaires and some open-ended questions on specific supervisors whom they believed had contributed most and least to their effectiveness; 49 supervisees responded and provided data on 98 SRs. The quantitative findings suggested that satisfaction with supervision, rapport (or bond) between supervisee and supervisor, and feeling supported by the supervisor were the main qualities of SRs that supervisees believed contributed to their effectiveness as practitioners.

A grounded theory analysis of the qualitative data, derived from written answers to open-ended questions, suggested that there were nine categories that described the quality of the SR (see Table 11.1 for details). These were a Boundaried, Supportive, Respectful, Open, and Committed relationship, where the supervisor remained Sensitive to the supervisees' needs, and acted in a Collaborative manner while performing Educative and Evaluative tasks.

A model (Figure 11.1) was developed that proposed that some of these categories represented a framework that needed to be in place for the supervision process to occur (i.e., the remaining categories). Central to the framework of the SR was the development of a boundaried relationship that included structural boundaries (such as regular, uninterrupted supervision) and personal/professional boundaries that enabled the supervisee to feel emotionally safe within the SR. The other aspects of the framework were the development of a mutually respectful, supportive, and open relationship, where the supervisee experienced the supervisor as committed to the supervision and the SR. The model proposed that in supervision certain optimal relationship conditions were necessary for the more formal processes of supervision (such as education and evaluation) to take place effectively.

The qualitative findings also suggested that more effective supervision practices were characterized by collaborative SRs, where both parties were involved in setting the agenda and the goals of supervision. The supervisory tasks of education and evaluation were facilitated by the supervisor responding sensitively to the supervisee's needs, taking into account previous experience, stage of learning, and the personal impact of the work. Supervisees valued formative feedback and challenge in boundaried, collaborative relationships. The formal elements of summative evaluation did not appear to impact when regular, mutual feedback was built into the SR. However, in less boundaried or effective SRs, the formal task of evaluation was often experienced as unsafe by supervisees (Beinart, 2002).

Palomo (2004) used the qualitative model described above to develop a psychometrically sound measure of the SR from the supervisees' perspective, the Supervisory Relationship Questionnaire (SRQ; Palomo et al., 2010). Exploratory factor analysis was used to analyze the responses from 284 trainee clinical psychologists to develop a valid and reliable measure of the SR, as well as to explore perceived impacts on client outcome and supervisee learning and development. The SRQ has 67 items and good psychometric properties. The analysis yielded six coherent factors: (1) Safe Base, (2) Structure, (3) Commitment, (4) Reflective Education, (5) Role Model, and (6) Formative Feedback. The components reflect the distinct nature of the SR, including its educative, involuntary, and evaluative nature, as well as its central core component, the "safe base," which reflects the more generic facilitative, relational characteristics (see discussion of SWA definition). As well as contributing to evidence and theory specific to the SR, this study provides a new measure in a field where empirical research is scarce, and provides a useful and practical tool for individual supervisors to invite feedback and to review their SRs. Milne (2009) has used the factors from the SRQ to develop implications for improving supervisory practice. These include establishing an emotional connection, sharing expectations, providing regular and structured supervision, being approachable and attentive, showing respect for clients and colleagues, encouraging reflection, and providing regular and balanced feedback (see Table 11.2 for details). The SRQ has also been widely incorporated

Table 11.1 Nine categories of the supervisory relationship and their defining features (Beinart, 2002).

Boundaried
- Organizational boundaries of supervision (regular/uninterrupted)
- Space and time
- Focus of session
- Professional boundaries
- Emotional boundaries (feeling contained)

Supportive
- Practical support
- Being valued
- Warm and encouraging
- Sense of humor

Open relationship
- Honesty and trust
- Open-minded (nonjudgmental)
- Approachable
- Discuss difficult issues

Respectful
- Respect for supervisor
- Being respected
- Mutual respect
- Respect for clients and colleagues

Committed
- Not a burden
- Enthusiastic
- Interested (in supervision and supervisee)
- Stimulating

Sensitive to needs
- Attentive to detail
- Attentive to process
- Meet at supervisees' level
- Professional and training needs

Collaborative
- Shared expectations and goals
- Shared agenda
- Flexibility
- Manages power differential
- Goodness of fit between supervisor and supervisee (for example, shared values, therapeutic model)

Educative
- Knowledge and experience
- Observational learning (role-model)
- Theory–practice links
- Flexibility (models, techniques, process)
- Challenge and reflection

Evaluative
- Regular, ongoing feedback
- Positive and negative feedback
- Reciprocal feedback
- Formal structures
- Fear of failure

Source: Reproduced with the permission of Beinart, H. (2002).

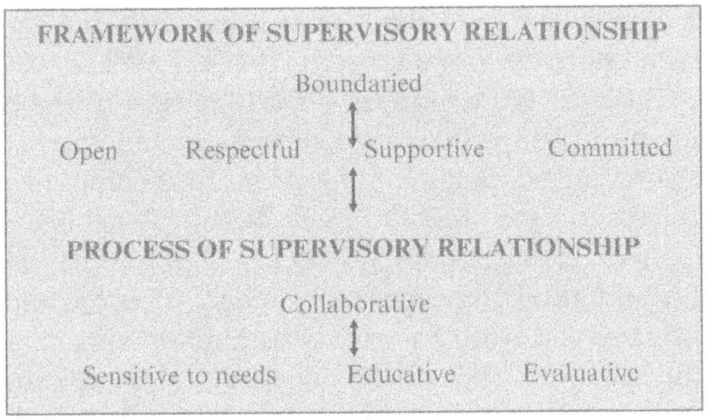

Figure 11.1 Model of the SR. Reproduced with the permission of Beinart, H. (2002).

Table 11.2 The six factors in the Supervisory Relationship Questionnaire (SRQ; Palomo, 2004), with actions (Milne 2009, p.80). Reproduced with permission of the authors.

Components	*Definitions and examples*	*Possible actions for supervisors*
1. Safe base	Supervisee feeling valued, respected and safe. Supervisor supportive, trustworthy, and responsive	Empathize and connect emotionally (e.g., through self-disclosure); seek understanding and consensus (e.g., shared expectations); offer warmth and respond to learner's needs; avoid hostility; criticism, and being judgmental
2. Structure	Maintaining practical boundaries, like time	Be clear about duration and purpose (including shared goals/joint agenda-setting); regular and structured supervision
3. Commitment	Supervisor interested in supervision and supervisee	Show interest and enthusiasm; be approachable and attentive; offer constructive feedback; address and repair alliance ruptures
4. Role model	Supervisor perceived as skilled, knowledgeable, and respectful	Draw on experience within system; provide practical support; demonstrate your approach and key skills, especially respect for patients and colleagues
5. Reflective education	Facilitating learning through supervisee's reflection; sensitive to supervisee's anxieties	Draw on multiple models flexibly; encourage reflection; foster theory–practice integration; promote interesting discussions of techniques; focus on the process of supervision (including acknowledging the power differential)
6. Formative feedback	Constructive and regular, including positive and negative feedback; tailored to stage of supervisee's development	Encourage interest in feedback from the supervisee, adapting it to fit his/her understanding and level of confidence; provide feedback regularly, including positive and negative comments, made in a balanced, constructive way

into supervisor training programs in the United Kingdom (Fleming & Steen, 2012). However, it has been criticized for its length (Wheeler, Aveline, & Barkham, 2011). In a recent study, Cliffe (2013) developed a short version of the SRQ, the S-SRQ. More than two hundred (203) UK trainee clinical psychologists completed a series of online questionnaires including the S-SRQ. A principal components analysis identified three components of the S-SRQ: "Safe Base,""Reflective Education," and "Structure." Analyses revealed that the S-SRQ has high internal reliability, adequate test–retest reliability and good convergent, divergent, criterion, and predictive validity. Participants also rated the S-SRQ as easy to use and potentially helpful for providing feedback on the SR within supervision. The S-SRQ (three subscales, total of 18 items) is a short, easy-to-use, valid, and reliable measure of the SR from the supervisee's perspective.

Two qualitative studies (Borsay, 2012 and Lemoir, 2013) examined why it can be so challenging for supervisees to raise difficult issues with their supervisors. Borsay (2012) recruited and interviewed 14 psychologists who had experienced difficult SRs during training, and explored the nature of these difficulties and how they were managed. Interview transcripts were analyzed using grounded theory. The findings suggested that difficulties arose in the context of the expectations and personal and professional circumstances that participants and supervisors brought to their SRs. Supervisees identified difficulties in three key areas (supervision structure and boundaries, interpersonal difficulties, external structure, and resource issues) and faced a number of dilemmas when deciding whether or not to approach their supervisor about these. It was challenging for supervisees to raise difficulties, and they experienced a variety of (more or less helpful) responses from their supervisors. The ending of a difficult SR was often a prompt for participants to begin the process of reflecting on, and learning from, their experiences.

In another grounded theory study, Lemoir (2013) explored disclosure and nondisclosure within supervision and found that a safe and trusting SR was pivotal to supervisees' ability to work effectively on placement. The content of nondisclosures included client work, personal issues, and SR issues. If disclosure was facilitated, positive impacts on the SR and supervisee learning were found. However, nondisclosure led to negative impacts on the SR, trainee learning and personal development, and, most importantly, clinical work.

Frost (2004) contributed one of the few dyadic, longitudinal studies to explore the development of the SR from both supervisee and supervisor perspectives over the course of a six-month training placement. Using qualitative methods (interpretative phenomenological analysis), Frost found that the early process of forming the SR was critical and, if "good beginnings" were established, the relationship continued to grow in warmth, collaboration, and openness. However, the converse was also suggested by this study, where unmet expectations led to difficulties that proved difficult to resolve. Additionally, themes generated for supervisees and supervisors at each phase (beginning, middle, and end) of the SR were different, suggesting that supervisees and supervisors may have somewhat different experiences of the SR over time. For example, at the beginning of relationships, supervisees described processes of adjustment and striving for acceptance, while supervisors described processes of nurture, influence, and commitment. At the midpoint, the supervisee focus was on learning and the supervisor focus was on settling into a sense of security and trust.

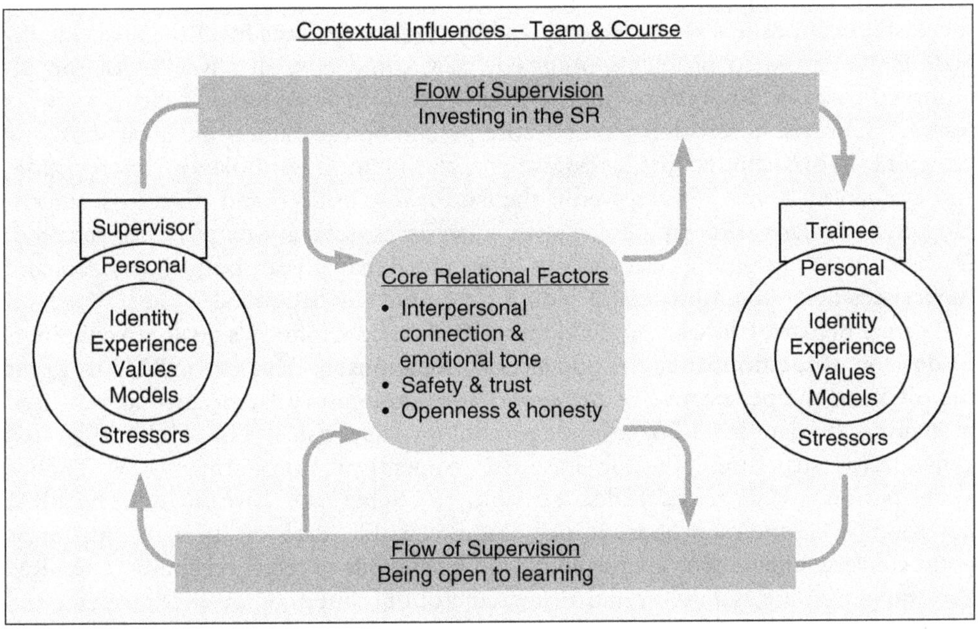

Figure 11.2 Quality of SR (Clohessy, 2008).

Toward the end of the SR, supervisees described the experience of resolution and empowerment while supervisors discussed collaboration and satisfaction. Further longitudinal dyadic research in this field is much needed.

Clohessy (2008) used a qualitative methodology (grounded theory) to explore supervisors' perspectives of their SRs with trainee clinical psychologists. The model developed from these supervisors' experiences suggested that three categories were important in the quality of the relationship (as illustrated in Figure 11.2): (a) contextual influences, (b) the flow of supervision, and (c) core relational factors. Contextual influences included the team/service in which the supervisee worked, the presence of the training course, and individual factors that the supervisor and supervisee brought to the relationship (for example, gender, cultural background, and prior experience). The flow of supervision reflected the supervisor's and supervisee's reciprocal contributions to the process of supervision. Supervisor contributions included "investing in the SR" by planning ahead for the trainee, spending time together (particularly in the early phase), establishing clear boundaries and expectations, encouraging learning, and responding to individual learning needs. Supervisee contributions included "being open to learning" by demonstrating enthusiasm and commitment, adopting a proactive stance, working hard, and making a productive contribution to the service. The more open to learning the trainee appeared to be, the more the supervisor invested in the relationship, creating a virtuous cycle that supported the development of positive core relational factors. The core relational factors described in this study were the interpersonal connection between the supervisor and supervisee; the emotional climate or atmosphere of the relationship; and the degree of safety, trust, openness, and honesty. The model suggests a reciprocal relationship between the core relational factors and the flow of supervision. The most successful relationships were characterized by positive features in all the areas identified. However, when problems occurred, they could arise in any facet of the SR (context, core, or flow), were often experienced as challenging, and did not always resolve. Supervisors resorted to their core psychological frameworks to resolve any difficulties. This included further assessment, consultation, formulation, intervention, and evaluation. Some SRs resolved if the issues were noticed and addressed quickly. However, similar to Borsay's study with supervisees, several SRs were not repaired. In the context of training relationships of no more than a year, both supervisors and supervisees described a process of biding time until the SR ended.

Pearce, Beinart, Clohessy, and Cooper (2013) used Clohessy's qualitative findings to develop a questionnaire, the Supervisory Relationship Measure (SRM) to assess the SR from the perspective of the supervisor. Exploratory factor analysis was used to analyze the data from 267 clinical psychology supervisors. The results suggested a five-factor structure: (1) Safe Base, (2) Supervisor Commitment, (3) Trainee Contribution, (4) External Influences, and (5) Supervisor Investment. The SRM has good psychometric properties including acceptable levels of internal consistency, good convergent and divergent validity, and high levels of retest reliability. The SRM also shows promise as a useful statistical predictor of trainee competence (as perceived by the supervisor) and supervisor satisfaction with supervision.

Aspects of Clohessy's model, such as the core relational factors, are reflected in the safe base and supervisor investment subscales. The concept of "flow" can be seen in the trainee contribution, supervisor commitment, and safe base subscales. The contextual factors are represented in the external influences subscale. Similar to its sister measure, the SRQ, "Safe Base" appeared to be the strongest predictor of supervision outcomes, including perceived effectiveness, lending strong support to the SWA being an important component of the SR. However, the SRM also suggests contextual factors and supervisee contribution are significant and confirms the hypothesis that although there are common elements, supervisors and supervisees have somewhat different views and experiences of their relationships. Table 11.3 outlines some of the action implications for supervisees, supervisors, and the supervisory dyad based on the SRM factors. These include being open and honest, demonstrating enthusiasm and commitment, and taking a personal interest in the unique characteristics of the supervisee.

The Oxford group's research makes a contribution to understanding the specific qualities of the relationship, and measuring the SR, and is supported by other research findings in the field (Inman & Ladany, 2008). Falender and Shafranske (2004, 2012), in their summary of the literature in this area, suggest that a good SR consists of facilitating attitudes, behaviors, and practices including, for example, a sense of teamwork (Henderson, Cawyer, Stringer, & Watkins, 1999), empathy (Worthen & McNeill, 1996), approachability and attentiveness (Henderson et al.,1999), encouragement of disclosures by supervisees (Ladany, Hill, Corbett, & Nutt, 1996), and supervisors' sensitivity to the developmental level of the supervisee (e.g., Magnuson, Wilcoxon, & Norem, 2000). Additionally, recent research (Ancis & Ladany, 2010; Constantine, 2001; Inman, 2006) suggests that the supervisor's multicultural competence is an important component of the SR, which supports the significance of contextual influences identified by the work of Clohessy (Beinart & Clohessy, 2009)

Table 11.3 The five factors in the Supervisory Relationship Measure (SRM; Pearce et al., 2013), with actions.

Components	*Definitions and examples*	*Possible actions for supervisors and supervisees*
1. Safe base	Core relationship and emotional bond between supervising dyad. Relationship feels safe, characterized by openness and honesty supervisee enthusiastic and responsive.	*For dyad:* Connect emotionally, be open, honest and willing to engage. Demonstrate enthusiasm and responsiveness. Reflect on learning and be open about any difficulties.
2. Supervisor commitment	Supervisor's professional commitment to supervision	*For supervisor:* Remain available and accessible, provide regular supervision, keep supervisees' needs in mind and pitch supervision accordingly, provide clear and honest feedback.
3. Trainee contribution	Supervisee investment, productivity, quality, professional values, integration	*For supervisee:* Take responsibility and work hard, make a useful contribution (e.g., manage a caseload) be organized and considerate of others
4. External influences	External stressors from personal/professional lives of supervisee and aupervisor including past supervisory relationships	*For dyad:* Remain mindful of external personal and professional stressors and how they impact current SR, avoid boundary violations between supervision and therapy, raise issues for discussion/negotiation
5. Supervisor investment	Supervisor's emotional investment in the relationship, getting to know the supervisee, emotionally open, for example, sharing strengths and weaknesses, self-disclosure	*For supervisor:* Take an interest in the supervisee, take time to get to know the supervisee's particular culture, interests, and learning needs, be open about your strengths and needs, approach/discuss difficult issues

and Pearce et al. (2013). In particular, the individual differences that supervisee and supervisor bring into their relationship appear to be significant. This has been discussed in some depth in relation to gender (Aitken & Dennis, 2012; Nillson, Barazanji, Schale, & Bahner, 2008), culture and racism (Constantine & Sue, 2007; Patel, 2012; Toldson & Utsey, 2008), and power (Tsui, 2004). These are important variables in the SR and support the proposal (Falender & Shafranske, 2012) that the SR is one of the three interrelated pillars in supervision competence (the other two being inquiry and educational praxis). These are in the context of super-ordinate values, which include "integrity in relationship, ethical values based practice, appreciation of all aspects of diversity, and science informed practice" (Falender & Shafranske, 2012, p. 8).

Norcross and Wampold (2011) conclude that the therapy relationship makes a substantive contribution to therapy outcome regardless of the therapeutic model used. A similar conclusion may be drawn for supervision, albeit the evidence base is still in development.

The qualities of the SR are similar to some of the alliance factors found in psychotherapy research. For example, the individuals within both the therapeutic and supervisory dyads bring their gender, culture, expectations, and personal preferences to the relationship, and it is helpful to tailor the relationship accordingly, gathering feedback regularly (Norcross & Wampold, 2011). The research described earlier points to some unique features of the SR, including the importance of establishing a safe base to support supervisee development and learning; providing a transparent structure for learning and quality monitoring; attending to supervisee developmental level; and the option for both parties to disclose, to attempt to address, and to resolve difficulties. In other words, the educational and evaluative/monitoring aspects of the SR require particular relational characteristics to thrive.

How Do We Measure the SR?

Having established the importance of the SR, we need to be able to measure it in order to further our understanding of supervision outcomes for both practice and research. Three measures, based on qualitative research on the SR, have been described in some detail in the previous section: the SRQ and the S-SRQ, for supervisees, and the SRM for supervisors. There are few measures of the SR and many have been criticized for being directly translated from psychotherapy instruments and for their poor construction (Ellis & Ladany, 1997). However, those recommended for use by previous reviews (Ellis & Ladany, 1997; Ellis et al., 2008; Wheeler et al., 2011) will be briefly described here. The Relationship Inventory (RI; Schacht, Howe, & Berman, 1988) is a measure of the SR based on facilitative conditions and is composed of five subscales measuring perceived supervisor regard, empathy, congruence, unconditionality, and willingness to be known. The inventory was originally developed to measure the therapeutic relationship (the Barrett–Lennard Relationship Inventory; Barrett-Lennard, 1962). Its use in supervision was validated using a sample of clinical and counseling psychologists in the United States. It is considered to have reasonable psychometric properties.

Bahrick (1990) developed the Working Alliance Inventory (WAI) to test Bordin's (1983) model of the SWA. The measure was adapted from a measure originally designed for the therapeutic alliance. It measures the three components of the SWA, that is, degree of agreement on the goals of supervision, tasks to be completed by each party, and the bond between supervisee and supervisor. The WAI has parallel trainee and supervisor versions and has good psychometric properties. Ellis et al. (2008) suggest that the three factors (goals, tasks, and bond) are highly correlated and hence suggest the WAI may only be measuring a single alliance factor.

Ellis and Ladany (1997) argue that the WAI is superior to another commonly used measure, the Supervisory Working Alliance Inventory (SWAI; Efstation, Patton, & Kardash, 1990). The SWAI is derived from both psychotherapy and supervision models and has nonparallel supervisor and supervisee versions. The supervisor version comprises three factors: client focus, rapport, and identification. The supervisee version comprises rapport and client focus. Low internal consistency has been reported. However, Wheeler et al. (2011), in their review of measures, recommend its use. Wheeler et al. also recommend an unpublished measure, the Brief Supervisory Alliance Scale – a trainee form (BSAS-TF) developed by Rønnestad and Lundquist (2009). This measure is considered to have acceptable psychometric properties and is recommended for its brevity (12 items). Another recommended measure is the Role Conflict and Role Ambiguity Scale (RCRA; Olk & Friedlander, 1992), which has been widely used and has good psychometric properties. Although this is not a measure of the SR per se, it is useful in identifying some of the issues that may arise. An interesting recent development is the Leeds Alliance in Supervision Scales (LASS), a three-item scale designed to provide session-by-session feedback on the supervisory alliance. It consists of three visual analog scales: approach to supervision, relationship, and the degree to which the supervisee found supervision helpful. It is based on measures of the SR and is reported to have acceptable levels of validity and reliability and, importantly, is sensitive to change (Wainwright, 2010). Apart from the LASS and the BSAS, all the SR measures mentioned earlier have normative data drawn from US populations (of counselors, psychotherapists, clinical, and counseling psychologists) and are adaptations of measures of the therapeutic relationship. The SRQ, S-SRQ, and SRM were developed with UK samples of psychologists working in the National Health Service. This makes them a strong alternative for use, particularly for non-US populations. These measures have the added advantage of being psychometrically sound and based explicitly on supervision theory and research.

How Do We Build an Effective SR?

The theory and research discussed earlier can guide us in building effective SRs as described in Table 11.2 and Table 11.3. The tasks are to establish safe, boundaried (emotionally containing and structured), and collaborative relationships where both supervisors and supervisees can be open and respectful, and learn from one another. Clarifying expectations and assumptions early on, including those that stem from ethnic, cultural, or gender differences, is one way of approaching the power differential inherent in these relationships, particularly during training. The danger for psychological therapists is that they (reasonably) assume that they are skilled in relationship formation and therefore positive relationships with their supervisees will develop naturally. This may be the case with some SRs but certainly not with all, and those that do not develop well can be damaging to both parties and impact relationships with clients (Ellis, 2010). It is therefore worthwhile to invest time and attention early on in these SRs to ensure "good beginnings." Research (Borsay, 2012; Clohessy, 2008; Frost, 2004) has shown that it is challenging to resolve difficulties once they have occurred and therefore essential to set solid foundations for success. The message is therefore preventative. How is this done? Clearly, many of the skills stem from general relationship-building skills. However, as discussed earlier in this chapter, the SR is a unique type of relationship with its primarily educative and monitoring/quality assurance (in training, evaluative) functions. The vehicle we have to discuss these issues is the supervision contract. Another chapter in this volume is focused on the general supervision contract. The discussion here will therefore be confined to contracting for the SR.

Contracting for the SR

Holloway (1995) describes the supervisory contract as a way of negotiating the goals, tasks, and parameters of the relationship. This is helpfully described as "a psychological contract" (Nelson, Barnes, Evans, & Triggiano, 2008), where mutual expectations are shared. One of the challenges in developing a psychological contract early on in SRs is that safety and trust are still in a fledgling state. The psychological contract therefore must be understood as a developing process rather than a static event and so subject to regular review. Scaife (2009) suggests the following reasons for establishing a supervision contract:

- to avoid misunderstandings;
- to begin to establish the SR;
- to clarify expectations, including those of the supervisor, supervisee, and training course/employing agency/professional body, and other third parties as appropriate;
- to encourage an atmosphere of collaboration and openness;
- to encourage supervisees to think about their developmental and learning needs;
- to encourage discussion about managing feedback (and the process of evaluation within a training contract); and
- to put the SR on the agenda as a subject for negotiation, discussion, and reflection.

It is also helpful to explore differences in assumptions and expectations that may arise from all aspects of diversity.

Over the years, the Oxford Supervision group have developed some processes that further support the development of effective SRs. These include arranging a preparatory meeting where information about organizational, ethical, and competency frameworks can be addressed. This allows both parties to raise any particular needs and constraints, and provides the opportunity to assess whether this is a contract in which both parties are able to invest. The initial meeting lays the foundations of the SR. The supervisor can prepare by being mindful of the contextual and personal issues that need to be considered in advance of the meeting. These may include, for example, finding out background information about the supervisee, preparing the team/service, and arranging practicalities such as office space. For the supervisee, preparation may include background reading, reflecting on their learning needs and competency development, and being aware of any personal or professional challenges that may arise. During the initial phases of the contracting process, it is helpful to establish the supervisee's learning needs and preferred learning style. For supervisees early in their career pathways, this may be a novel way of thinking, and making use of quick and easy questionnaires based, for example, on Kolb's (1984) experiential learning cycle, can provide a helpful starting point for these discussions. For those with previous experience of SRs, it is useful to discuss what has facilitated or hindered their learning and development in the past. It is also helpful for the supervisor to use judicious self-disclosure and be explicit about what they value in their SRs. For example, supervisors may explain that they value openness and honesty and find it challenging when they feel there are issues that the supervisees are not disclosing. These sorts of conversations begin to allow exploration of assumptions that are often not made explicit in other types of relationships. Similarly, exploration of assumptions based on culture, gender, or beliefs about psychological change, can begin to create an atmosphere of trust and give permission for later discussions in relation to clients or service issues. It is worthwhile, early on, to approach the issue of feedback (or evaluation). This can be discussed in terms of what has been helpful or challenging in the past, what sort of feedback may produce a defensive reaction, and how the supervisee may approach the supervisor if feedback is not meeting his or her needs. A typical example of this is a supervisee who feels that she/he is not getting sufficient feedback and a supervisor who believes everything is going well and therefore no specific feedback is needed. It may also be facilitative if the supervisor flags up any issues (personal or professional) that may impact the supervision from their perspective. Examples may include a supervisor who explains that she/he values uninterrupted supervision sessions but may have to answer a call due to a current crisis. By explaining this in advance, the supervisor gives a message of valuing and respecting protected supervision time and that an interruption is an unavoidable exception to the rule. Another supervisor may explain that she/he takes punctuality very seriously and that failure to attend sessions on time is likely to make her/him more alert to professional concerns.

It is helpful to clarify roles and responsibilities within the SR, for example, expectations regarding the supervision agenda, note-keeping, professional issues, issues regarding clinical and managerial supervision, or how confidentiality will be managed within the SR, particularly if ethical or fitness to practice issues arise.

It is worth remembering the strong evidence cited earlier about the importance of establishing a safe base for the SR, particularly the establishment of clear boundaries in which mutual trust, openness, and honesty can thrive.

The capacity to approach potentially challenging issues, and putting these on the agenda at the beginning as normative areas for discussion, is seen as key to building an effective SR.

How Do We Sustain an Effective SR?

There are two main ways of sustaining effective SRs. The first, discussed earlier, is to treat the contract as an ongoing process that is regularly reviewed and adjusted according to need. This keeps the discussion alive, tracks the developmental needs of the supervisee, and allows any potentially challenging issues to be addressed. The second method is to learn to give and receive feedback in a way that is sensitive and meaningful to each participant. Discussions about feedback preferences begin in the early phase of contracting. Different supervisor and supervisee dyads will have differences regarding how they prefer to review the contract and the SR. For example, some like to check in briefly during every supervision session and will have review and feedback as a standing item on the supervision agenda. Others prefer to set more time aside periodically to have a reflective review. Much of this will depend on personal style, preference, clinical and organizational contexts. However, the effectiveness of any feedback and review will depend to some extent on how honest the pair can be with one another.

Recent competency frameworks for supervision stress the importance of directly observing supervisee practice and giving specific feedback on observed performance, and this is considered good practice. However, it is probably the case that most supervision occurs by the supervisee reporting verbally to the supervisor. The process of supervision thus relies on supervisees being able to openly disclose all aspects of their work and its personal impact (Webb & Wheeler, 1998), including difficulties and clinical mistakes (Rønnestad & Skovholt, 1993). It is thus worthwhile to take a detour to the small but growing evidence on self-disclosure (both relating to clinical mistakes and personal responses) in supervision. In early work, Ladany et al. (1996) found that supervisee nondisclosure was related to poor SRs, supervisor incompetence, and fear of negative evaluation. More recently, Mehr, Ladany, and Caskie (2010) suggest that failure to disclose in supervision may have a direct impact on therapy outcomes including alliance ruptures and premature termination of therapy. However, the content of supervisee nondisclosure is most commonly related to difficulties in the SR, such as perceived incompetence of the supervisor (Lemoir, 2013; Reichelt, 2009), unclear expectations, and supervisor unprofessionalism (Inman et al., 2011). Where there are strong SRs, supervisee nondisclosures are more likely to be related to clinical issues, often related to performance anxiety or fear of criticism (Hess, Hess, & Hess, 2008). Inman et al. (2011) found that another reason for supervisee nondisclosure was fear of upsetting their supervisor or the SR. However, a strong SR was found to facilitate supervisee self-disclosure particularly in nontraining relationships (Webb & Wheeler, 1998) or those that have a strong sense of mutuality and greater balance of power (Walsh, Gillespie, Greer, & Eanes, 2003). Additionally, remaining sensitive to unspoken supervisee needs (Palomo et al., 2010) and attending to those needs, may facilitate disclosure on the part of the supervisee.

Falender and Shafranske (2012) list some of the actions that supervisees can take to enhance the SR. These include making supervision sessions a priority; avoiding being late or canceling; following through supervisory suggestions; taking responsibility for preparing for supervision; reporting back and following up suggestions from previous supervision sessions; identifying any specific supervision strategies that they find particularly helpful; being open and receptive to discussions of differences of assumptions and attitudes; respectfully raising any concerns; using outcome measures to add to the supervisory discussion; taking responsibility for professional development (e.g., reading); and discussing any innovative ideas in supervision before trying them out in practice. Above all, supervisees need to remain committed, open to learning and feedback, and show motivation and enthusiasm for the work (Clohessy, 2008).

Feedback in the SR

Feedback is clearly a significant aspect of supervision and features in many definitions; for example, Milne (2007) refers to “corrective feedback,” which implies a discrepancy between expected and actual performance in relation to agreed goals. Indeed, feedback (including praise and constructive criticism) is the most common supervision method (81%) cited in systematic reviews of effective supervision (Milne, 2009). Hoffman, Hill, Holmes, and Freitas (2005) define feedback as information that supervisors give supervisees about their skills, attitudes, and behavior that may influence their performance with clients or affect the SR. Feedback is generally understood to be most helpful in the context of a supportive and trusting relationship (Scaife, 2009). The limited research into supervisee preferences for feedback suggest that balanced, timely, objective, consistent, clear, and credible feedback in the context of a supportive relationship is experienced as most effective (Heckman-Stone, 2004). At its best, feedback is an integrated and mutual process within supervision (Hughes, 2012). Hawkins and Shohet (2012), in their much used mnemonic CORBS, stress that feedback should be given in a manner that is:

- Clear and unambiguous, so that the supervisee knows the issue to be addressed and how to go about this.
- Owned by the person giving feedback: that this is their opinion and not a universal truth (this is particularly important if the feedback is related to personal issues).
- Regular and an ongoing part of supervision (it is not helpful to save up feedback to the point that the issue becomes difficult to address or remedy).
- Balanced, including both positive and negative aspects, so that supervisees are aware of what they are doing well and what needs to be improved.
- Specific: this links to the concept of corrective feedback that relates to a specific achievable goal or learning need.

Hughes (2012) adds two other elements to this list: that feedback should be mutual and welcomed by the supervisor and that all feedback should be delivered in a respectful manner. Scaife (2009) draws the distinction between feedback and challenge, and encourages supervisees to self-evaluate alongside their supervisor and agree the next goals for their learning and development, thereby taking a more active role and embracing the opportunity to be challenged and stretched in their learning process. This has the added advantage of the feedback being invited, providing clear and realistic expectations of change, and being somewhat less judgmental. It is always worth clarifying with the supervisees how they prefer to receive feedback (perhaps referring back to the contract) and whether the feedback has been given and received in the preferred manner (and if not, how the supervisors could improve their performance). This provides an opportunity to reflect together on the process of giving and receiving feedback, and ensures that there are no misunderstandings and that the feedback given has been received as intended. It also creates an atmosphere of collaboration and models that feedback can be hard to give, that there are no perfect ways of providing it, and that what is important is giving feedback in a way that is mutually beneficial. Many supervisees find it challenging to give feedback to their supervisor and building in feedback about feedback is one way of facilitating this process.

Hoffman et al. (2005) in their research into supervisors' perspectives of giving feedback, suggest that supervisors find it easier to give feedback about clinical issues, such as clinical skills, and more challenging to provide feedback about supervisee personality, professional behavior (e.g., self-presentation), or the SR. Indeed, in

Hoffman et al., no feedback was given if costs were felt to outweigh benefits, or if there were concerns about the SR. The strength of SR played an important role in whether feedback was given and how it was received, integrated, and used. Ladany and Melincoff (1999) suggest that supervisors avoid giving feedback for a number of reasons, including avoiding confrontations or having a negative impact on the supervisee, a belief that supervisees will discover the issues themselves when they are developmentally ready, and fearing boundary violations between supervision and therapy.

Some guidelines to the supervisor for giving challenging feedback may include the following:

- clarifying your views and clearly naming the issue (it may be helpful to consult with a colleague or your own supervisor if needed);
- owning your concerns and inviting the supervisee to reflect/self-assess on the issue;
- if there are different views, providing the opportunity to explore the differences and possible reasons/influences;
- using models of supervision or the SR to make sense of the issues/differences;
- if the emotional climate is uncomfortable, drawing attention to the process and acknowledging the challenge of discussing difficult issues; and
- allowing time and space for further reflection and follow-up.

Another useful method for giving and receiving feedback is to apply measures of the SR described earlier. Used in a clinical setting, these can provide a starting point for discussions about the SR from both perspectives. For example, supervisors can use the SRQ (Palomo et al., 2010) or S-SRQ (Cliffe, 2013) to gather feedback from supervisees. The SRM (Pearce et al., 2013) provides the opportunity for the supervisor to provide feedback to supervisees and the session-by-session measure, the LASS (Wainwright, 2010), provides a quick measure for regular review. Other useful measures were discussed earlier in the chapter. Although many of these measures were developed for research purposes, they can also be helpful in clinical settings. Used in this way, there is a tendency to positively skew the results. However, any variation in the scores opens up opportunities for discussion and review. The measures developed in Oxford are available at http://www.oxicpt.co.uk.

This section has focused on review of the contract and the giving and receiving of feedback as key aspects of sustaining the SR. It has focused on formative rather than summative feedback (although it applies to both) and has not specifically addressed evaluation or unsatisfactory performance. Instead, the focus has been on preventing difficulties within the SR.

However, difficulties in the SR still do occur. Mueller and Kell (1972) argue that conflict in the SR is inevitable because of the power differential and the inherently complex nature of the SR, involving, as it does, conflicting demands of support, monitoring/evaluation, and learning.

Furthermore, the supervisee is expected to be receptive, to take risks, and to respond constructively to challenge in order to enable personal and professional development to occur. It is hypothesized that an effective SR may provide a safe base for conflict management, which can provide opportunities for growth and development but, if mishandled, may lead to difficulties and challenges. Difficulties can occur within the supervisory context and dyad, or be primarily related to what the supervisee or supervisor individually contributes to the relationship.

Contextual and dyadic challenges may include, for example, high rates of referrals and demands for service delivery, lack of clear expectations, having to manage dual relationships, ethical issues, conflictual teams, lack of time for processing conflicts or misunderstandings, not managing power differentials effectively (particularly if cultural/age/experience-related factors impinge), and a lack of an explicit psychological contract.

Supervisee challenges may include anxieties about evaluation, being over- or underconfident, being unable to hear or respond to feedback, displaying a lack of responsibility/engagement/investment, or experiencing a sense of being overwhelmed and feeling unable to manage demands. Additionally, supervisees may be unwilling to share or disclose their concerns because of performance or evaluation anxiety. In extreme cases, the supervisee may show inadequate competency development and/or violate ethical or professional standards.

Challenges related to the supervisor may include providing insufficient or substandard supervision. Supervisors may fail to clarify explicit expectations, or their expectations may be too high, unrealistic, or not matched to supervisee developmental needs. Additionally, supervisors may lack confidence and be anxious about the responsibilities of the role and thus not be able to provide realistic and appropriate feedback. Supervisors are also at risk from burnout and may not have the psychological resources to offer effective supervision. Also, they may be less than competent and not meet ethical or professional standards.

Nelson et al. (2008) in their study of experienced and "wise" supervisors, describe how the supervisors in their sample normalized conflict as part of learning and development. In this way learning is contextualized as a developmental need and supervisees are not humiliated or shamed by "not knowing" or needing to develop new competencies. Experienced supervisors were able to approach, rather than deny conflict, and were prepared and expected to give difficult feedback. They also used judicious amounts of humor, humility, and self-disclosure. On the whole, these supervisors accepted their own shortcomings and were comfortable in sharing these with their supervisees. Ladany, Friedlander, and Nelson (2005) suggest that there are typical conflict markers (for example, avoidance, nondisclosure) in all SRs and that experienced supervisors are alert to these.

Clohessy (2008), in her study of experienced supervisors' strategies for resolving difficulties, described a multifaceted process of noticing and tuning into the SR that included gathering information by checking with the supervisee and seeking advice from others, attempting to formulate the problem by exploring the issue with the supervisee, clarifying any misunderstandings, and reestablishing boundaries. This often required a commitment to spend more time together in order to build on the positives in the relationship, to maintain a positive and nonblaming stance, and to continue to work together collaboratively. Similarly, in a study of experienced Australian supervisors, Grant and Schofield (2012) found that supervisors used a range of strategies to manage difficulties. The majority employed reflective and confrontational strategies and some utilized avoidant strategies, particularly with regard to personal or sexual issues or if the SR was at risk.

Borsay (2012) found that supervisees struggled to raise difficult issues within a training SR and, if this did occur, it was usually toward the end of the relationship when any formal evaluation had been completed.

In summary, the strategies that experienced supervisors use to manage challenges in the SR are very similar to those already described in the development and maintenance of effective SRs. These include attending to the SR and developing a culture of trust and openness within the relationship, communicating clear expectations, providing regular feedback, identifying and addressing supervisee developmental needs, reframing difficulties as useful learning opportunities, maintaining clear boundaries, and reestablishing these as and when needed. It is generally helpful for supervisors to gain objective evidence through direct observation and detailed feedback. Supervisors who are able to monitor their own responses and use their own reflections and supervision to aid the process tend to be those that are more equipped to manage challenges in the SR. This often involves maintaining a sense of balance, humility, and humor.

Summary and Conclusions

This chapter has explored definitions, theories, evidence, and measurement of SRs. How to establish and maintain effective SRs in practice was discussed, with examples of good practice and relevant research highlighted. In particular, the fundamental methods of contracting and feedback were described. These are relatively simple and straightforward methods but, as with most simple things, hard to do well. The latter section has focused on preventing and managing difficulties within the SR. While again the methods appear simple (e.g., naming any concerns clearly, inviting feedback and self-assessment, using models and other resources to formulate, approaching rather than avoiding any difficulties, normalizing challenges as part of the process of development and learning, and maintaining a safe and accepting SR where it is possible to make mistakes and learn from them), their implementation requires both skill and sensitivity.

Part of the pleasure of supervision is creating unique SRs, which accept the individual and cultural differences that each supervisee and supervisor brings. All supervisory dyads will bring a set of different assumptions and attitudes into the SR, based on their personality, experience, socio-cultural backgrounds, and worldviews (as well as their hopes and fears of the supervisory process itself). While much of the research referred to here is based on studies from the United Kingdom and the United States, it is likely that the core principles will remain similar and the challenge for supervisors will be to genuinely listen, understand, and support the supervisee in assisting a process of learning and development that is specific to their needs and cultural context. Indeed, studies exploring effective multicultural supervision stress the importance of a safe, nonjudgmental, and supportive SR to explore cultural values and differences (Dressel, Consoli, Kim, & Atkinson, 2007).

The central significance of SRs to supervision experience is clearly established and research is emerging to also suggest their importance in supervision outcomes. Ongoing research is needed to further our understanding of the characteristics of SRs and how these specifically relate to clinical and learning outcomes. However, in the meantime, there are some helpful practical guidelines on how to develop and strengthen SRs and a promising early evidence base on which to build.

References

Aitken, G., & Dennis, M. (2012). Incorporating gender issues in clinical supervision. In I. Fleming & L. Steen (Eds.), *Supervision and clinical psychology: Theory, practice and perspectives* (pp. 118–141). Hove, UK: Routledge.

Ancis, J. R., & Ladany, N. (2010). A multicultural framework for counsellor supervision. In N. Ladany & L. J. Bradley (Eds.), *Counsellor supervision* (pp. 53–95). New York, NY: Routledge.

Bahrick, A. (1990). Role induction for counselor trainees: Effects on the supervisory working alliance. *Dissertation Abstracts International, 51*, 1484B.

Bambling, M., King, R., Raue, P., Schweitzer, R., & Lambert, W. (2006). Clinical supervision: Its influence on client-rated working alliance and client symptom reduction in the brief treatment of major depression. *Psychotherapy Research, 16*, 317–331.

Barrett-Lennard, G. T. (1962). Dimensions of therapist response as causal factors in therapeutic change. *Psychological Monographs, 76*(43), 1–36. (Whole No. 562).

Beinart, H. (2002). *An exploration of the factors which predict the quality of the relationship in clinical supervision* (Unpublished D.Clin. Psych. thesis). Open University/British Psychological Society.

Beinart, H. (2012). Models of supervision and the supervisory relationship. In I. Fleming & L. Steen (Eds.), *Supervision and clinical psychology: Theory, practice and perspectives* (pp. 47–62). Hove, UK: Routledge.

Beinart, H., & Clohessy, S. (2009). Supervision. In H. Beinart, P. Kennedy, & S. Llewelyn (Eds.), *Clinical psychology in practice* (pp. 319–335). Oxford, UK: British Psychological Society & Blackwell publishing.

Bennett, S., & Saks, L. (2006). A conceptual application of attachment theory and research to social work student-field instructor supervisory relationships. *Journal of Social Work Education, 42*, 669–682.

Bernard, J. M., & Goodyear, R. K. (2014). *Fundamentals of clinical supervision* (5th ed.). Upper Saddle River, NJ: Pearson.

Bordin, E. S. (1983). A working alliance model of supervision. *Counseling Psychologist, 11*, 35–42.

Borsay, C. (2012). *Understanding the supervisory relationship and what happens when difficulties occur* (Unpublished D.Clin. Psych. thesis). University of Oxford.

Bradshaw, T., Butterworth, A., & Mairs, H. (2007). Does structured clinical supervision during psychosocial intervention education enhance outcome for mental health nurses and the service users they work with *Journal of Psychiatric and Mental Health Nursing, 14*, 4–12.

Cliffe, T. (2013). *Development and validation of a short-version of the Supervisory Relationship Questionnaire (S-SRQ)* (Unpublished D.Clin.Psych. thesis). University of Oxford.

Clohessy, S. (2008).*Supervisors' perspectives on their supervisory relationships: A qualitative study* (Unpublished PsyD thesis). University of Hull.

Constantine, M. G., & Sue, D. W. (2007). Perceptions of racial microaggressions among black supervisees in cross-racial dyads. *Journal of Counselling Psychology, 54*, 142–153.

Constantine, M.G.. (2001). Perspectives on multicultural supervision. *Journal of Multicultural Counselling and Development, 29*, 98–101.

Dickson, J., Moberly, N., Marshall, Y., & Reilly, J. (2011). Attachment style and its relationship to working alliance in the supervision of British clinical psychology trainees. *Clinical Psychology and Psychotherapy, 18*, 322–330.

Dressel, J. L., Consoli, A. J., Kim, B. S., & Atkinson, D. R. (2007). Successful and unsuccessful multicultural supervisory behaviours: A Delphi poll. *Journal of Multicultural Counseling and Development, 35*, 51–64.

Efstation, J. F., Patton, M. J., & Kardash, C. M. (1990). Measuring the working alliance in counselor supervision. *Journal of Counseling Psychology, 37*, 322–329.

Ekstein, R., & Wallerstein, R. S. (1972). *The teaching and learning of psychotherapy* (2nd ed.). New York, NY: International Universities Press.

Ellis, M. (2010). Bridging the science and practice of clinical supervision: Some discoveries, some misconceptions. *The Clinical Supervisor, 29*, 95–116.

Ellis, M., D'Iuso, N., & Ladany, N. (2008). State of the art in the assessment, measurement, and evaluation of clinical supervision. In A. K. Hess, K. D. Hess, & T. H. Hess (Eds.), *Psychotherapy supervision: Theory, research and practice* (2nd ed., pp. 473–499). New York, NY: Wiley.

Ellis, M., & Ladany, N. (1997). Inferences concerning supervisees and clients in clinical supervision: An integrative review. In C. E. Watkins (Ed.), *Handbook of psychotherapy supervision* (pp. 447–507). New York, NY: Wiley.

Falender, C., & Shafranske, E. (2004). *Clinical supervision: A competency-based approach*. Washington, DC: American Psychological Association.

Falender, C., & Shafranske, E. (2012). *Getting the most out of clinical supervision: A guide for practicum students and interns*. Washington, DC: American Psychological Association.

Fleming, I., & Steen, L. (2012). *Supervision and clinical psychology: Theory, practice and perspectives*. Hove, UK: Routledge.

Frost, K. (2004). *A longitudinal exploration of the supervisory relationship: A qualitative study* (Unpublished D.Clin. Psych. thesis). University of Oxford.

Grant, J., & Schofield, M. J. (2012). Managing difficulties in supervision: Supervisors' perspectives. *Journal of Counseling Psychology, 59*, 528–541.

Hatcher, R., & Lassiter, K. (2007). Initial training in professional psychology: The practicum competencies outline. *Training in Education and Professional Psychology, 1*, 49–63.

Hawkins, P., & Shohet, R. (2012). *Supervision in the helping professions* (4th ed.). Buckingham, UK: Open University Press.

Heckman-Stone, C. (2004). Trainee preferences for feedback and evaluation in clinical supervision. *The Clinical Supervisor, 22*, 21–33.

Henderson, C. E., Cawyer, C., Stringer, C. E., & Watkins, C. E. (1999). A comparison of student and supervisor perceptions of effective practicum supervision. *Clinical Supervisor, 18*, 47–74.

Hess, A. K. (2008). Psychotherapy supervision: A conceptual review. In A. K. Hess, K. D. Hess, & T. H. Hess (Eds.), *Psychotherapy supervision: Theory, research and practice* (2nd ed., pp. 3–22). New York, NY: Wiley.

Hess, A. K., Hess, K. D., & Hess, T. H. (2008). *Psychotherapy supervision: Theory, research and practice*. New York, NY: Wiley.

Hoffman, M. A., Hill, C. E., Holmes, S. E., & Freitas, G. F. (2005). Supervisor perspective on the process and outcome of giving easy, difficult, or no feedback to supervisees. *Journal of Counseling Psychology, 52*, 3–13.

Holloway, E. L. (1995). *Clinical supervision: A systems approach*. Thousand Oaks, CA: Sage.

Holloway, E. L., & Poulin, K. (1995). Discourse in supervision. In J. Siegfried (Ed.), *Therapeutic and everyday discourse on behaviour change: Towards a microanalysis in psychotherapy process research* (pp. 245–273). New York, NY: Ablex.

Horvath, A. O., & Greenberg, L. S. (1986). The development of the Working Alliance Inventory. In L. S. Greenberg & W. M. Pinsof (Eds.), *The psychotherapeutic process: A research handbook* (pp. 529–556). New York, NY: Guilford.

Hughes, J. (2012). Practical aspects of supervision: All you ever wanted to know but were too afraid to ask. In I. Fleming & L. Steen (Eds.), *Supervision and clinical psychology: Theory, practice and perspectives* (pp. 184–206). Hove, UK: Routledge.

Inman, A. (2006). Supervisor multicultural competence and its relation to supervisory process and outcome. *Journal of Marital and Family Therapy, 32*, 73–85.

Inman, A., & Ladany, N. (2008). Research: The state of the field. In A. Hess, K. Hess, & T. Hess (Eds.), *Psychotherapy supervision: Theory, research and practice* (2nd ed., pp. 500–517). Hoboken, NJ: Wiley.

Inman, A. G., Schlosser, L. Z., Ladany, N., Howard, E. E., Boyd, D. L., Altman, A. N., & Stein, E. P. (2011). Advisee nondisclosures in doctoral-level advising relationships. *Training and Education in Professional Psychology, 5*, 149–159.

Kolb, D. (1984). Experiential learning: *Experience as the source of learning and development.* Englewood Cliffs, NJ: Prentice-Hall.

Ladany, N., Ellis, M., & Friedlander, M. (1999). The supervisory working alliance, trainee self-efficacy and satisfaction. *Journal of Counseling and Development, 77*, 447–455.

Ladany, N., & Friedlander, M. L. (1995). The relationship between the supervisory working alliance and trainees' experience of role conflict and role ambiguity. *Counselor Education and Supervision, 34*, 220–231.

Ladany, N., Friedlander, M. L., & Nelson, M. L. (2005). *Critical events in psychotherapy supervision. An interpersonal approach.* Washington, DC: American Psychological Association.

Ladany, N., Hill, C., Corbett, M., & Nutt, E. (1996). Nature, extent and importance of what psychotherapy trainees do not disclose to their supervisors. *Journal of Counseling Psychology, 43*, 10–24.

Ladany, N., & Lehrman-Waterman, D. (1999). The content and frequency of supervisor self disclosure and the relationship to supervisory working alliance and satisfaction with supervision. *Counselor Education and Supervision, 38*, 143–160.

Ladany, N., & Melincoff, D. (1999). The nature of counselor supervisor non-disclosure. *Counselor Education and Supervision, 38*, 161–176.

Ladany, N., Walker, J., & Melincoff, D.. (2001). Supervisee integrative complexity, experience and preference for supervisor style. *Counselor Education and Supervision, 40*, 203–219.

Lehrman-Waterman, D., & Ladany, N. (2001). Development and validation of the evaluation process within supervision inventory. *Journal of Counseling Psychology, 48*, 168–177.

Lemoir, V. (2013). *(Non) disclosure in the supervision of trainee clinical psychologists: A grounded theory analysis* (Unpublished D.Clin.Psych. thesis). University of Oxford.

Magnuson, S., Wilcoxon, S. E., & Norem, K. (2000). A profile of lousy supervision: Experienced counselors'perspectives. *Counselor Education and Supervision, 39*, 189–203.

Mehr, K., Ladany, N., & Caskie, G. I. L. (2010). Trainee nondisclosure in supervision: What are they not telling you?*Counselling and Psychotherapy Research, 10*, 103–113.

Milne, D. (2007). An empirical definition of clinical supervision. *British Journal of Clinical Psychology, 46*, 437–447.

Milne, D. (2009). *Evidence-based clinical supervision: Principles and practice.* Oxford, UK: British Psychological Society & Blackwell Publishing.

Milne, D. L., & James, I. (2000). A systematic review of effective cognitive-behavioural supervision. *British Journal of Clinical Psychology, 39*, 111–127.

Mueller, W. J., & Kell, B. L. (1972). *Coping with conflict: Supervising counselors and psychotherapists.* New York, NY: Appleton-Century-Crofts.

Nelson, M., Barnes, K., Evans, A., & Triggiano, P. (2008). Working with conflict in clinical supervision: Wise supervisors' perspectives. *Journal of Counseling Psychology, 55*, 172–184.

Nillson, J., Barazanji, D., Schale, C., & Bahner, A. (2008). Gender and sexual orientation in supervision. In A. Hess, K. Hess, & T. Hess (Eds.), *Psychotherapy supervision: Theory, research and practice* (2nd ed., pp. 560–575). Hoboken, NJ: Wiley.

Norcross, J. C. (Ed.). (2002). *Psychotherapy relationships that work. Therapist contributions and responsiveness to patients.* Oxford, UK: Oxford University Press.

Norcross, J. C., & Wampold, B. E. (2011). Evidence-based therapy relationships: Research conclusions and clinical practices. *Psychotherapy, 48*, 98–102.

Olk, M., & Friedlander, M. L. (1992). Trainees' experience of role conflict and role ambiguity in supervisory relationships. *Journal of Counseling Psychology, 39*, 389–397.

Palomo, M.(2004). *Development and validation of a questionnaire measure of the supervisory relationship (SRQ)* (Unpublished D.Clin. Psych.thesis). University of Oxford.

Palomo, M., Beinart, H., & Cooper, M. (2010). Development and validation of the supervisory relationship questionnaire (SRQ) in UK trainee clinical psychologists. *British Journal of Clinical Psychology, 49*, 131–149.

Patel, N. (2012). Difference and power in supervision: The case of culture and racism. In I. Fleming & L. Steen (Eds.), *Supervision and clinical psychology: Theory, practice and perspectives* (pp. 96–117). Hove, UK: Routledge.

Pearce, N., Beinart, H., Clohessy, S., & Cooper, M. (2013). Development and validation of the Supervisory Relationship Measure: A self report questionnaire for use with supervisors. *British Journal of Clinical Psychology, 52*, 249–268.

Psychology Board of Australia. (2011). *Supervised practice guidelines.* Victoria, Australia: Australian Psychological Society.

Reichelt, S., Gullestad, S. E., Hansen, B. R., Rønnestad, M. H., Torgersen, A. M., Jacobsen, C. H., . . . Skjerve, J. (2009). Nondisclosure in psychotherapy group supervision: The supervisee perspective. *Nordic Psychology, 61*, 5–27.

Riggs, S., & Bretz, K. (2006). Attachment processes in the supervisory relationship: An exploratory investigation. *Professional Psychology: Research & Practice, 37*, 558–566.

Roth, A., & Fonagy, P. (2006). *What works for whom: A critical review of psychotherapy research.* New York, NY: The Guilford Press.

Rønnestad, M. H., & Lundquist, K. (2009). *The Brief Supervisory Alliance Scale – Trainee Form.* Unpublished manuscript.

Rønnestad, M. H., & Skovholt, T. M. (1993). Supervision of beginning and advanced graduate students of counselling and psychotherapy. *Journal of Counseling & Development, 71*, 396–405.

Safran, J., Muran, C., Stevens, C., & Rothman, M. (2007). A relational approach to supervision: Addressing ruptures in the alliance. In C. Falender & E. Shafranske (Eds.), *Casebook for clinical supervision: A competency-based approach* (pp. 137–157). Washington, DC: American Psychological Association.

Scaife, J. (2009). *Supervision in clinical practice: A practitioner's guide.* Hove, UK: Routledge.

Schacht, A. J., Howe, H. E., & Berman, J. J. (1988). A short form of the Barrett-Lennard Inventory for supervisory relationships. *Psychological Reports, 63*, 699–703.

Son, E., Ellis, M., & Yoo, S. (2007). The relations among supervisory working alliance, role difficulties and supervision satisfaction: A cross-cultural comparison. *Korean Journal of Psychology, 26*, 161–182.

Sue, D., Capodilupo, C., Torino, G., Bucceri, J., Holder, A., Nadal, K., & Esquilin, M. (2007). Racial microaggressions in everyday life: Implications for clinical practice. *American Psychologist, 62*, 271–286.

Toldson, I., & Utsey, S. (2008). Racial and cultural aspects of psychotherapy supervision. In A. Hess, K. Hess, & T. Hess (Eds.), *Psychotherapy supervision: Theory, research and practice* (2nd ed., pp. 537–559). Hoboken, NJ: Wiley.

Tsui, M.-S. (2004). The supervisory relationship of Chinese social workers in Hong Kong. *The Clinical Supervisor*, *22*, 99–120.

Wainwright, N. A. (2010). *The development of the Leeds alliance in supervision scale (LASS): A brief sessional measure of the supervisory alliance* (unpublished D.Clin.Psych. thesis). University of Leeds.

Walsh, B. B., Gillespie, C. K., Greer, J. M., & Eanes, B. E. (2003). Influence of dyadic mutuality on counselor trainee willingness to self-disclose clinical mistakes to supervisors. *The Clinical Supervisor*, *21*, 83–98.

Watkins, C. E. (Ed.). (1997). *Handbook of psychotherapy supervision.* New York, NY: Wiley.

Watkins, C. E. (2011). Does psychotherapy supervision contribute to patient outcomes? Considering 30 years of research. *The Clinical Supervisor*, *30*, 235–236.

Watkins, C. E. (2012). Psychotherapy supervision in the new millennium: Competency-based, evidenced-based, particularized and energized. *Journal of Contemporary Psychotherapy*, *42*, 193–203.

Watkins, C. E. (2014). The supervisory alliance: A half century of theory, practice and research in critical perspective. *American Journal of Psychotherapy*, *68*, 1–37.

Webb, A., & Wheeler, S. (1998). How honest do counsellors dare to be in the supervisory relationship?: An exploratory study. *British Journal of Guidance & Counselling*, *26*, 509–524.

Wheeler, S., Aveline, M., & Barkham, M. (2011). Practice-based supervision research: A network of researchers using a common toolkit. *Counselling and Psychotherapy Research*, *11*, 88–96.

White, E., & Winstanley, J. (2010). A randomized control trial of clinical supervision: Selected findings from a novel Australian attempt to establish the evidence base for causal relationships with quality of care and patient outcomes, as an informed contribution to mental health nursing practice development. *Journal of Research in Nursing*, *15*, 151–167.

Worthen, V., & McNeill, B. W. (1996). A phenomenological investigation of "good" supervision events. *Journal of Counseling Psychology*, *43*, 25–34.

12

Establishing Supervision Goals and Formalizing a Supervision Agreement

A Competency-Based Approach

Craig J. Gonsalvez

Over the last decade, competency-based models have breathed new life into the education and training of professional psychologists, including their clinical supervision. The work of Falender and colleagues (Falender & Shafranske, 2004; Falender et al., 2004) and the objectives-based approach to supervision (Gonsalvez, Oades, & Freestone, 2002) are examples of such competency-based approaches. While the enhancement of competence has always been an important consideration within clinical supervision, "since the dawn of the new millennium, focus on supervision competence and [therapy] competencies has ratcheted up to a level of emphasis and scrutiny that lacks parallel across the entire 100 year plus history of supervision" (Watkins & Wang, 2014, p. 15). For the field-based clinical supervisor, the implications of these changes are not always apparent.

In this context, the present chapter serves the following functions: an information-disseminating function, by unpacking for supervisors how a competency-based paradigm might influence key aspects of supervision (namely, establishing supervision goals and formalizing a supervision contract); a reflective function, by inviting and challenging supervisors to carefully consider the merits and demerits of the paradigm (and its alignment to their own supervisory practices); and finally a supportive function, by providing guidelines, templates, and resources that may help supervisors adopt the paradigm.

Adopting a Competency Approach in Supervision

Although the notion of competence is old, the development of a taxonomy of competencies has only recently occurred (Fouad et al., 2009). Assessment require-

The Wiley International Handbook of Clinical Supervision, First Edition. Edited by
C. Edward Watkins, Jr. and Derek L. Milne.

ments within universities have long been weighted toward the traditional evaluation of knowledge, to the neglect of relevant skill, relationship and attitude-value competencies (Milne & James, 2002; Pachana, Sofronoff, Scott, & Helmes, 2011). Finally, contrary to the tenets of the competency paradigm, accreditation criteria for training programs have been weighted toward "inputs" such as the number of practicum, supervision, and coursework hours that a student should undertake; rather than "output" measures, such as whether students could demonstrate assessment and intervention skills at an acceptable level of proficiency (Pachana et al., 2011).

Competency-based models, appropriately tailored to the unique character and processes of clinical supervision, have the potential to improve the pedagogic standing, scientific status, and the overall effectiveness of supervisory practice. Significant initial progress has already been accomplished within psychology (Kaslow, 2004; Kaslow et al., 2007, 2009; Rubin et al., 2007). The discipline of clinical supervision has a rare opportunity to harness the momentum of a revolution to initiate systemic change and effect substantive progress.

The adoption of a competency approach to supervision plans involves at least three practical tasks: designing competency-based developmental plans (CDP) for supervisees within clinical placements;[1] high-fidelity implementation of such plans, and evaluation of all aspects of the supervision program against the principles of the competency approach. The focus of the current chapter is on the first aspect: designing a CDP for supervision. Designing a CDP has many similarities with goal-setting in supervision. However, in practice, goals in supervision plans rarely adhere to core principles of competency-based approaches. Therefore, the term, ***competency-based developmental plan*** will be used in the current chapter to identify a comprehensive supervision plan in which all components (learning activities, supervision methods, assessment, and evaluation) are guided by a competency-based pedagogy. A preliminary conceptualization of such a program has been outlined previously (Gonsalvez et al., 2002), and that earlier model will be revised and elaborated here. The stages may be schematically represented as per Figure 12.1.

The development of a CDP for supervision is an important and essential first step in the adoption of the competency paradigm. It forms the blueprint for all of the learning and teaching activities within the supervision program. It comprises three supervisory tasks, designated by the three rectangular boxes in Figure 12.1: (1) assisting supervisees to formulate their own competencies for the placement; (2) finalizing competencies for supervision through a process of information delivery, reflection, and consensus-building; and (3) designing an implementation plan. There are several overarching considerations and processes that have a bearing on each of the supervisory tasks (Figure 12.1, oval box). This chapter is structured into six sections. Overarching considerations are discussed first after which the three supervisory tasks are discussed. Establishing a supervision agreement or contract is discussed next, followed by a summary and concluding comments.

[1] The generic term *placement* will be used in this chapter to identify external field placements, clinical placements, external practicum, externships, clinical rotations, and internships.

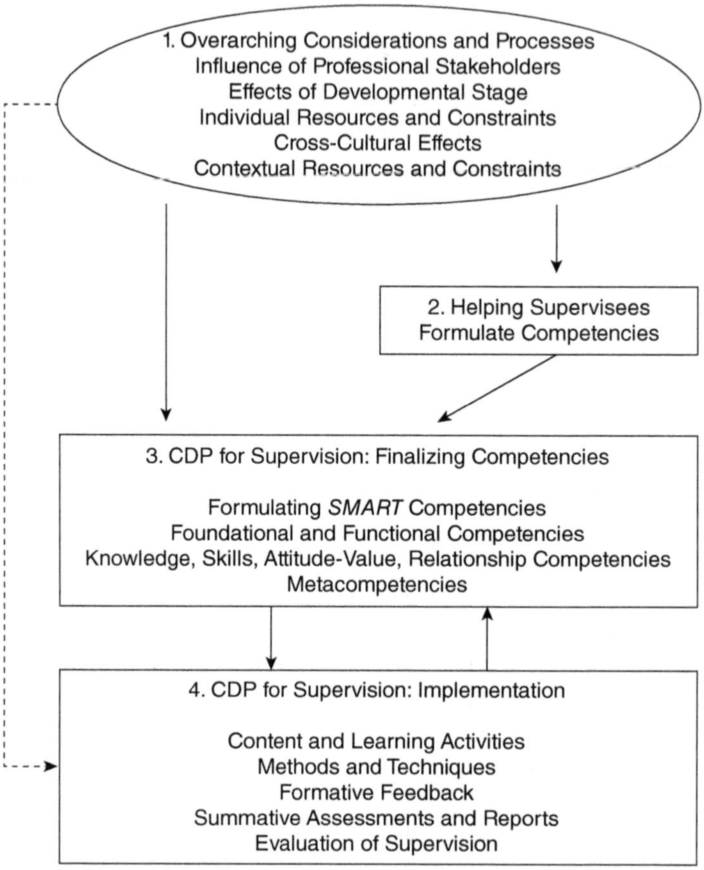

Figure 12.1 A competency-based developmental plan (CDP) for supervision: Supervisor tasks and processed. Adapted from Gonsalvez, Oades, and Freestone (2002). Reproduced with permission.

Overarching Considerations and Processes

Influence of professional stakeholders

In the past, the supervision space was, in a sense, hallowed turf, a private and confidential space shared between the supervisor and supervisee. An important change ushered in by competency-based approaches is the entry of a third entity into the supervision space: the professional stakeholder. While some supervisors have welcomed such enhanced professional interest in supervision, others have resented the intrusion or are ambivalent. Common concerns are that having "Big Brother" poring over the supervision process may change the delicate dynamic within the supervisor–supervisee relationship and undermine supervision effectiveness. Further, regulatory bodies appear keen to extend their audit from professions in training to fully qualified professionals, by attaching requirements to renewal of licensure or by introducing supervisor accreditation requirements (e.g.,Psychology Board of Australia, 2010).

Professional stakeholders include the regulatory bodies that can mandate teaching and training inputs, including coursework and practicum hours and the demonstration of key competencies (outputs) before a professional is registered or licensed. These regulatory bodies include the Health Professions Council (United Kingdom) and the Psychology Registration Board (Australia). In the United States, licensure is regulated on a state-by-state basis. A second group of stakeholders is constituted by professional societies, such as the American Psychological Association (APA, United States), or the British Psychological Society (BPS, United Kingdom). The third group comprises training institutes, such as universities. Service agencies in which placements are conducted form a fourth group. Until recently, competence statements from such regulatory and professional bodies were generic and couched in terms sufficiently amorphous to encompass most supervision conducted. The recent decade has witnessed significant progress in these statements, including a clearer specification and a more systematic organization of professional competencies (Fouad et al., 2009; Hatcher & Lassiter, 2007; Hunsley & Barker, 2011; Kaslow et al., 2007, 2009; Roth & Pilling, 2007, 2008).

An implication for training institutions (e.g., universities) is the requirement to design a curriculum of competencies that both aligns with the prescriptions of regulatory and professional bodies (Pachana et al., 2011), and captures their unique character (in terms of philosophy and pedagogic approaches to training).

For today's clinical supervisor, it is important to gain a good working knowledge of the competency frameworks of key stakeholders, and to understand their implications for supervision process and outcome *before* supervision commences. A key point of conflict is often the fact that the person designated the consumer varies between the stakeholders involved in clinical supervision. For example, the service agency's primary concern may be the benefits accrued by their clients (the client in the counseling room) and the welfare of and costs incurred by their staff (e.g., supervision time). For training institutions, the supervisee is the primary consumer, while regulatory authorities are primarily concerned with protecting the interests of the public. Such differences in perspective may create conflicting expectations for supervisees' caseloads, for the frequency of supervision, or for reporting requirements. It is important to recognize that multiple lists of essential and desirable learning outcomes from diverse stakeholders may compete for attention and crowd the supervision agenda. Valuable supervisor skills include the ability to differentiate among and prioritize competing demands, and to maintain good communication with competing stakeholders during the placement. It is also important for supervisors to become aware of their own reactions to the entry of professional stakeholders into the supervision space and ensure that negative reactions do not adversely impact the supervision process.

Effects of developmental stage

For decades, models of supervision have been dominated by developmental theories. However, these models have only offered broad brush stroke accounts of development. There has been lack of clarity with regard to detail, and poor specification of the nature and determinants of transitions between developmental stages (Watkins, 1995; Worthington, 1987). Supervision models that use a competency framework as their starting point and progress to applying this framework within professional education and training are more amenable to task analyses and specifications, leading to a taxonomy of competencies across domains and functions. It appears sensible to integrate these traditions, and initial attempts have been made (Falender et al., 2004; Fouad et al., 2009; Gonsalvez et al., 2002). When developmental stages are imposed on competency frameworks, a matrix emerges that includes two or more dimensions: domains of competence (e.g., counseling skills, ethical practice, professional skills) and stages of development (e.g., novice, advanced beginner, competent, proficient, expert; Blackburn et al., 2001). The competence domains may be further categorized into foundational and functional domains (Fouad et al., 2009; Rodolfa et al., 2005), or alternatively into competency types (knowledge, skills, attitude-value, and relationship; Gonsalvez et al., 2002), giving rise to two slightly different three dimensional matrices. In summary, developmental theory has the potential to inform and enrich competency-based models. The supervisee's developmental level in various domains should guide the choice of competency domains for the CDP and the levels of performance to be attained in each domain. Further, the supervisor's and supervisee's developmental stage will influence the way they respond to supervision activities, methods, and assessment.

For training institutions, the implication of an integration between developmental approaches and competency-based pedagogy is that the sequence of placements may influence training outcomes, with sequences that are developmentally appropriate, leading to better outcomes. The implication for research is that the model offers a theoretical framework that spawns a range of questions that have valuable training implications. For instance, what are the core competency domains? How independent or similar are the normative developmental trajectories across domains? Is progress among domains affected by similar or different supervision styles and methods? Does supervisory alliance affect all domains in a comparable manner?

Individual resources and constraints

Each supervisor brings to supervision a distinctive set of experiences, a range of expertise, and a unique profile of strengths that together have the potential to shape and alter supervision processes and outcomes. Psychologists work across diverse treatment settings, populations, client issues, and engage in a range of professional activities. Consequently, attempts to match competency lists prescribed by professional stakeholders with supervisor and supervisee preferences should occur early in supervision.

It is helpful to design CDPs that acknowledge and build on the professional and personal strengths of the supervisor and the supervisee. An implication for the supervisor is to become more aware of the range and limits of one's competence and expertise, and to plan professional development experiences for oneself, in a fashion that parallels the design of learning outcomes for the supervisee. Further, it is important to recognize that in the "new scheme of things" professionals are called on to demonstrate competencies (e.g., through completion of workshops and assignments, or through consultation and supervision), rather than to merely assume they have acquired competencies through experience (Gonsalvez & Milne, 2010). Becoming aware of the range and limits of one's competence and expertise, and planning professional development experiences for oneself, in a fashion that parallels the design of learning outcomes for the supervisee, is part of the fun and challenge of professional growth as a supervisor.

Effects of theoretical orientation Recent attempts to map out supervisor competencies have led to the description and detailing of general and specialist supervisor competencies (Roth & Pilling, 2008). The identification of generalist competencies is consistent with findings demonstrating that supervision across specializations in psychology (and indeed across disciplines;Kavanagh et al., 2003; Strong et al., 2004) share a large number of common elements. Specific competencies include competency sets associated with specific therapeutic orientations. This raises the question whether supervision outcomes are influenced by a supervisor–supervisee match for preferred therapeutic orientation. Unfortunately, the empirical research on orientation matching and supervision outcomes is paltry and preliminary, and the results have been inconsistent. Perceived theoretical similarity yielded higher perceived supervisor effectiveness for a group of counseling interns in one study (Putney, Worthington, & McCullough, 1992), but the superiority of such matching has not been demonstrated in relation to the supervisory working alliance or the supervisees' developmental progress (Blaisdell, 2000). Also, any observed advantages for matched orientation may be mediated by working alliance or by the way these differences are handled, rather than whether any such differences were present (Dodds, 1986). Nevertheless, it is reasonable to assume that the supervisor's perceived competence and confidence with regard to therapeutic orientation would influence their list of preferred competencies for the placement.

Supervision approaches, personal preferences, and relating styles In the face-to-face context of individual supervision, complementary interpersonal attitudes, approaches, and supervision styles have the potential to enhance the supervisory relationship and promote the acquisition of competencies. Significant differences among supervisors occur on a number of dimensions, including directiveness; structure and organization; support and caring; and ability to be challenging, to be consultative, and to be interpersonally sensitive. Further, supervisors differ in terms of their ability to vary their supervisory styles to meet situational demands. Despite wide differences among experts on several other matters concerning supervision, there is an expert consensus about the importance of the supervisor–supervisee relationship and its influence on supervision process and outcome (Beinart, 2014). This core determinant of supervision deserves special consideration in supervision planning. The current chapter is not focused on the effects of the supervisory relationship but on how this core determinant should be given appropriate consideration during supervision planning. Yet, despite the emphasis on the supervisory relationship within both the theoretical and empirical literature (Bernard & Goodyear, 2009; Milne, 2009), we know little about whether weak alliance early in supervision is predictive of future ruptures in the supervisory relationship. It is also unclear whether similar or complementary supervisor–supervisee styles or preferences strengthen working alliance and supervision effectiveness, and whether such effects are mediated by matching or complementary supervisor–supervisee developmental stages. Given the undeveloped state of knowledge in this area, the best approach in practice may be for supervisors to become aware of and avoid unhelpful supervisor styles and patterns (Liese & Beck, 1997), and to develop accurate awareness of their own supervision approach and style. Such heightened awareness may help the supervisors to be alert to the potential for mismatches between their supervision approaches and supervisees' expectations. The supervisory relationship is also likely to benefit if supervisors encourage supervisees to similarly engage in reflective practices (see, e.g., Bennett-Levy & Thwaites, 2007) aimed at enhancing awareness of professional and personal qualities, and their preferences in supervision. This will assist supervisors in adjusting their style to developmental level and learning style of the supervisee.

Cross-cultural effects

Factors such as ethnicity, gender, and religious identity of individuals in supervision, and cultural differences within the supervisor–supervisee dyad, have the potential to influence the supervision process. Effective supervisor strategies to engage supervisees in the formulation of a CDP may vary across countries and across culturally different supervisees within a country. For instance, Tsui and colleagues (Tsui, Ho, & Lam, 2005) have drawn attention to interesting differences between Chinese and Western perceptions of roles, boundaries, and "appropriate behaviors" within supervision. Specifically, strong Chinese conventions of "giving face" (protecting the supervisor from embarrassment or from "losing face" by superficial agreement with the supervisor's opinions and compliance with supervisory intentions) have the potential to affect the nature and meaning of a supervisee's interactions. If cultural differences are not appreciated, a Chinese supervisee's failure to articulate a different opinion may be misinterpreted as engagement and agreement, or as lack of independence. The concept of *qing* among the Chinese (Tsui, 2004) also has implications for the supervisory relationship. Maintaining an appropriate professional supervisory relationship (in Anglo-Saxon terms) may be construed as being overly formal, cold, aloof, and even as disapproval within Chinese and other south Asian cultures. Hence, while competency-based approaches are expected to be relevant across continents and countries, cultural factors are likely to influence the choice, form, and delivery of a supervisor's interventions. From the supervisor's perspective, it is important to be sensitive to cultural issues and their impact on supervision, to ensure that one acquires new cultural competencies or supervises within one's area of cultural competence (see Hernandez, 2008).

Contextual resources and constraints

Common contextual factors include the nature of the service provided (e.g., inpatient/outpatient) age, type, and severity of client/client problems (child/adult; anxiety/depression/relationship problems), and learning opportunities available during placement within psychology (e.g., case conferences, research seminars, group programs, and multidisciplinary activities, such as ward and grand rounds).Table 12.1 summarizes the main points about the foregoing procedures and processes.

Table 12.1 Overarching considerations for CDPs.

Best-practice guidelines
1. Acquire a good working knowledge of competency frameworks from key accreditation bodies and professional societies.
2. If the supervisee is a student, obtain competency lists from the supervisee's training institution along with "input" requirements concerning caseload, case type, and supervision.
3. If applicable, obtain competency lists and requirements/recommendations about the practicum from the service agency at which the placement will be conducted.
4. Obtain relevant information to help you assess the supervisee's developmental stage (e.g., previous supervisor's report; inventory to assess development). Have the supervisee submit representative samples of performance (e.g., recording of therapy session) if this is warranted.
5. Become aware, acknowledge, and build the program around your strengths and values.
6. Cultivate an awareness of how you are faring yourself, personally and professionally, on the burnout–thrive continuum and the effect of this on your supervision.
7. Become aware and acknowledge gaps within the supervision program and explore options to bridge these gaps.
8. Design a list of peer expertise and learning activities (e.g., ward and grand rounds) that will build on and enrich learning outcomes from the primary supervisor's input.
9. When supervising an individual from a different cultural background, gain an understanding of cultural factors affecting supervisory processes through education or supervision.

Helping Supervisees Formulate Their Competencies for Supervision

Goals and competencies in supervision

The task of formulating a program of competencies shares several characteristics with goal-setting, which has a long and valued tradition within clinical supervision. Within therapy, goal-setting skills are a key component of the therapeutic alliance (Horvath & Greenberg, 1989; Horvath & Symonds, 1991), which is recognized to be an important determinant of treatment outcome (Horvath & Symonds, 1991). There is expert consensus that the formulation of goals is also an important supervisor competency (Falender & Shafranske, 2004; Roth & Pilling, 2008) and this has empirical support (Milne, Sheikh, Pattison, & Wilkinson, 2011). Unfortunately, this supervisory task is often poorly prioritized or inadequately applied (Gonsalvez & Freestone, 2007). An examination of the reasons for this may help address the problem. First, there is often a lack of clarity with regard to goal definition, and a poor appreciation of characteristics contributing to effective goal formulation. It is worth remembering that clinical supervision has been primarily influenced by two traditions with their constituent paradigms and metaphors: teaching and therapy. Regrettably, the confluence of these two paradigms has also generated a host of terms with ambiguous and overlapping conceptual boundaries. To a large extent, goal-setting in supervision practice often mirrors procedures adopted in the counseling room. The term "goal," as in the negotiation of therapy goals, is often used in a fairly broad manner to designate both generic and specific goals. On the other hand, within the education parlance, a goal refers to a "broad and general statement of . . . intention" and not to be confused with a "learning objective or outcome" that refers to "a clear measurable outcome" that the learner can demonstrate (Newble & Canon, 1995).

Competence is defined as "the habitual and judicious use of communication, knowledge, technical skills, clinical reasoning, emotions, values, and reflection in daily practice for the benefit of the individual and community being served" (Epstein & Hundert, 2002, p. 227). Competencies are defined as "demonstrable elements or components of performance (knowledge, skills, and attitudes and their integration) that make up competence" (Kaslow et al., 2009, p. S34). In this context, competencies are more akin to specific learning outcomes that are executed at a high level of proficiency. In other words, a key characteristic of the competency paradigm is to start with the end in mind. This means that a key initial task for supervisors seeking to design a CDP is to invite supervisees to formulate a list of specific and personalized competencies that they plan to attain by the end of the placement.

Joint goal-setting with supervisees Supervisors often appreciate the advantages of engaging the supervisee in setting goals for supervision jointly. However, they observe that supervisees have problems formulating goals: supervisee goals are often overly general (*I want to become a good therapist/psychologist*), and/or are naive and ambitious (e.g., *I would like to become an expert in eating disorders*). Several factors contribute to poor goal-setting skills among supervisees. Peer conversations about "difficult and complex clients "sensitize novices to the difficulties rather than the rewards of being a counselor or psychologist, leaving them feeling uncertain, inadequate, and dependent. They often respond by being overly trusting and dependent, assuming that the supervisor knows best. Having no knowledge of the terrain, quite understandably, they have difficulty charting a path to progress. Under circumstances where several supervisees compete for an available placement, supervisees may consider it prudent to agree with whatever the supervisor suggests. The context makes it inviting for the supervisor to assume the mantle of the expert and prescribe a set of competencies for the placement.

There are several reasons why the supervisor should not be lured into taking sole charge of formulating the competencies for a placement. Thinking deeply about and articulating the competencies the supervisee desires to achieve is productive in its own right. It raises self-awareness, strengthens engagement in the supervision process, and is likely to enhance the supervisory alliance. Regardless of whether or not supervisees can explicitly articulate the competencies they would like to attain, it is likely that, at the conclusion of placements, supervisors will be evaluated against implicit expectations. Moreover, the opportunity to reflect on the set of competencies that one values is an excellent opportunity to foster reflective practice in an area central to professional identity. Finally, an important developmental transition is the progress from dependence to assuming responsibility over one's professional journey toward competence. There is no better place to start than with giving supervisees responsibility to jointly formulate their personal CDP. To this end, a more deliberate and systematic effort to help supervisees with this task is warranted. There are several strategies that are useful in assisting supervisees to identify, articulate, and compile a meaningful set of competencies for themselves. Information about how to formulate SMART competencies (covered in the next section) and the provision of templates with core domains (e.g., assessment, conceptualization, intervention skills), including examples of relevant competencies, may be a good initial step. Supervisees who require additional support may be offered, as examples, competency lists designed for peers at the same developmental stage. Almost invariably, supervisees have made considerable commitments of time, effort, and financial resources to their training. Above all, supervisees often have a large part of themselves invested in their careers and aspirations, which makes what transpires in supervision personally relevant and profoundly meaningful. Having supervisees' actively engage in setting their personalized set of competencies for placements provides the supervisors with an excellent opportunity to get to know and understand their individual supervisee.

Enhancing the supervisee's awareness of their own strengths and needs

Developing self-awareness through analysis and reflection is an important competency for all professionals, especially for psychologists and counselors. An awareness of one's personal and professional strengths and needs, and a nondefensive openness to both positive and corrective feedback, is probably the best predictor of a supervisee's response to supervision and potentially their rate of progress during a placement. Hence, having the supervisee participate in meaningful self-awareness exercises is a good way to commence supervision. Further, it is crucial that any blueprint for a supervision program attempts to build on the strengths of both supervisor and supervisee in addressing the supervisee's developmental needs.

Representative questions posed to the supervisee may include the following:

- What strengths and needs do you believe you bring to your role as a therapist/counselor?
- Do you have preferences in terms of a theoretical orientation? How strong are these preferences? What experiences have shaped your preference?
- How important to you is it for a supervisor to share/have a different therapeutic orientation than the one you have?
- What knowledge and skills do you believe you already possess as a family/cognitive-behavioural/psychodynamic therapist?
- What specific skills would you want to develop or enhance?
- How do you typically cope with the pressures of client work/academic load/combination of above? Are there self-care practices that work for you?

Novice supervisees may find this task more difficult and more anxiety provoking than their more experienced peers. Often, they are concerned about the possibility that their answers may be incorrect or are "not insightful enough." In fact, it is not expected that the task would reveal an accurate appraisal of a supervisee's capabilities and attitudes. Any focus on the valence or "correctness" of the answer is missing the point. The point is rather to emphasize the relevance of asking the question and to encourage supervisees to develop powerful self-awareness and reflective processing, skills that have largely been ignored in prior academic training.

Table 12.2 Assisting supervisees formulate a personalized list of competencies.

Best-practice guidelines
1. Ensure the supervisee understands the importance of formulating a personalized list of competencies that the supervisee would like to attain during the placement. Insist on a written draft.
2. Commence the process of goal setting and reflection several weeks before supervision commences. Assist them in this process by providing them with relevant resources (information about the placement, information about how to formulate *SMART* competencies, and guidelines you have drawn up, or examples of adequate and inadequately formulated competencies).
3. Offer additional support and scaffolding if initial effort by the supervisee is unsatisfactory. This can be achieved by providing supervisees with a template or matrix with common domains, offering examples of different types of competencies including knowledge, skills, attitude, and relationship, providing them with a program of competencies designed for a peer at the same developmental stage, or providing different sets of competencies that span developmental levels just below and just above the supervisee's current developmental stage.
4. Following submission of an initial draft of competencies, have supervisees identify the overlap and areas of mismatch between their personal list and the competencies recommended by relevant professional stakeholders. Supervisees may then progress to revise and prioritize their list of competencies.
5. Match the level of assistance you provide to the supervisee's developmental level.
6. Have the supervisee identify a profile of perceived strengths and needs that will help inform and customize planned learning outcomes.

A reflective focus on the supervisees' needs and strengths early in the supervision process has the potential to provoke self- doubt and anxiety. Supervisee anxiety is best evaluated and managed on a case-by-case basis. It is also important to bear in mind that designing supervision plans without a fair impression of how a supervisees view themselves, or what skills they believe they bring to their roles, is a good recipe for future ruptures in the supervisory relationship. Table 12.2 summarizes some of these points.

CDP for Supervision: Finalizing Competencies

Assisting the supervisee to formulate a personalized list of competencies for the placement experience is a useful first step, but a program of competencies formulated solely by a supervisee is rarely comprehensive or adequate simply because it requires expertise that professionals early in their career have not had the opportunity to develop. Therefore, the supervisor bears the ultimate responsibility to ensure that the supervision plan is comprehensive and meets best-practice guidelines. The supervisor's task is to facilitate informed discussion about and to align the supervisee's plan with the requirements and recommendations of relevant stakeholders, including the supervisor. Finalizing a list of competencies and designing an implementation strategy are arguably the most vital supervisor tasks, and so should be executed through active collaboration and consensus-building with the supervisee. It is hard to conceive of an effective supervision program without a carefully choreographed master plan that underpins its various activities and the active and open engagement of the supervisee in these activities. The ability to formulate *SMART* competencies and the ability to formulate a holistic program of competencies are two essential hallmarks of an adequate CDP for supervision. Each of these will be addressed later.

Formulating *SMART* competencies

There is evidence from a wide range of disciplines that attainment of optimal outcomes requires more than the activity of goal-setting; it requires that goals are operationalized and satisfy key criteria. For instance, Doran (1981) makes a compelling argument that planned outcomes must be SMART, a useful mnemonic that captures these criteria. In the current chapter, the mnemonic has been retained but the criteria have been modified to make them applicable to competencies for supervision (*S* = *specific; M* = *measureable; A* = *appropriate to developmental stage; R* = *relevant and recommended by relevant bodies; T* = *time-wise*). The first criterion for *SMART* competencies is that they be *specific*, rather than general. The most common problem with supervision goals is that they are overly generic. For instance, "improving a supervisee's diagnostic and therapeutic skills," are goals that could apply across a wide range of client populations, severity levels, and psychological disorders. More helpful, specific competencies for a placement in an anxiety clinic that offers services for adults would be "to make accurate diagnostic and differential diagnostic decisions for adult cases of anxiety disorders; to demonstrate competency in conducting exposure therapy across several phobic conditions; and to demonstrate Socratic dialogue skills that promote change of client belief structures."

The second criterion is that the competency is *measurable*. In the absence of tangible, quantifiable means by which to gauge progress (or lack thereof), there is a greater risk of deviating from the original objective or not meeting the desired outcome at all. For instance, exposure therapy competencies could be assessed by "standard or exemplar" cases, and "Socratic dialogue" could be assessed by validated scales (Blackburn et al., 2001; Milne & Reiser, 2013). Competency measurement will be discussed in greater detail later in the chapter.

The third criterion emphasizes that a goal is *appropriate from a developmental perspective*. This criterion helps differentiate competencies across training and professional levels. For instance, "fostering a therapeutic alliance with cooperative clients" may be an appropriate competency for a supervisee at the novice level, and "establishing and maintaining a therapeutic alliance with ambivalent or resistant clients" may constitute a more advanced competency. Similarly, "to be better able to manage transference and countertransference reactions in therapy" is inappropriately generic and could apply across developmental stages to both supervisee and supervisor.

The fourth criterion is *relevance*. That is, does the competency align with the "bigger picture" aims and competency frameworks recommended by accrediting bodies and professional stakeholders? For instance, "to become competent in hypnotherapy" may be a valuable optional competency under certain circumstances but may not be included among the list of essential competencies that the supervisor has to endorse at the end of placement.

Finally, a *SMART* competency is one that is *time-wise* and *time-bound.* In other words, attainment of the competency is realistic within the timeframe devoted for the placement and supervision. Hence, for a three-month placement, the ability "to conduct cognitive therapy at a competent level" may be unrealistic, whereas "the ability to conduct cognitive therapy at the advanced beginner level" may be *time-wise.*

Foundational and functional competencies

While we should be cognizant of the benefits of competency-based approaches, we should not lose sight of potential problems. One such potential problem is the proliferation of competency lists that become excessively detailed and tedious. The categorization of competencies into broad domains and the differentiation between foundational (e.g., relationships, ethical, and legal standards) and functional domains (e.g., assessment, intervention) appears meaningful (Rodolfa et al., 2005). There is evidence for at least four broad clusters of clinical psychology competencies (including assessment and intervention skills, psychometric skills, professional skills, and professional values and attributes), but these data are preliminary and warrant further research (Gonsalvez et al., 2013). The danger is that psychology's obsession to differentiate and divide, then differentiate and divide again, will lead to a maze of competency domains and matrices that will only serve to obscure rather than to accentuate the true character of the competent practitioner. To some extent, this trend may be apparent already, with competency taxonomies becoming more complex, and competency lists growing too bulky for implementation at the grassroots level (Fouad et al., 2009; Hatcher & Lassiter, 2007). Time will tell whether our passion for dissection will yield a clearer representation and a more accurate measure of the practitioner's core capabilities.

Knowledge, skills, attitude-value, relationship, and metacompetencies

In the past, pedagogic advances in curriculum development have had seemingly little appeal or impact on the way supervision was conducted. Supervisors have felt, with some justification, that the teaching–education paradigm was designed to focus on facts and concepts through the mechanics of cognitive processes. On the other hand, psychological therapies are concerned with subjective truth, and attend to feelings, attitudes, conflicts, and relationships through the mechanics of emotional processing. To have an impact on supervision, the competency-based paradigm has to go beyond knowledge and cognitions and embrace the data of emotions and relationship interactions. To the extent that these processes become legitimate competencies and are given pride of place within competency matrices, we will have taken the first steps toward ensuring we do not flush out the baby with the bath water.

In adapting the competency paradigm to supervision, it is therefore crucial for the supervisor to preserve a holistic approach to competence. One way of doing this is to discriminate among (and assign relevant priority to) the core and high-impact competencies. Gonsalvez et al. (2002) recommend that a holistic program will comprise a balanced commitment of supervision resources to the four competency types: knowledge (e.g., to demonstrate an awareness of the empirical literature governing cognitive therapy), skills (the ability to conduct with fluency a diagnostic assessment for eating disorders), attitude-value (to become aware of and my responses to clients, to be more open to negative feedback), and relationship competencies (e.g., to demonstrate the ability to form and maintain a working alliance with adult clients).

Within this context, it is of note that several competencies that are at the core of professional training are attitude-value competencies (for instance, unconditional positive regard, regard for scientific evidence, respect for ethics principles, commitment to a client's well-being, openness to corrective feedback). The problem at the root of unethical professional behavior is usually not a knowledge inadequacy or a skill deficiency, but a disregard for ethics principles and a lack of genuine commitment to client welfare, both attitude-value competencies. Devoid of the value aspects of the competency, an in-depth knowledge of the code of ethics will achieve little by way of fostering the development of a competent practitioner. Similarly, respect for empirical evidence and value attached to the scientific method are essential aspects of the scientist–practitioner competency, not knowledge of the empirical literature concerning treatment outcomes. Finally, because relationship competencies hold a preeminent position in professional psychology training, they are best regarded as an independent competency type in supervision (Gonsalvez et al., 2002).

Metacompetencies Recently, there has been a renewed focus on the notion of metacompetencies, such as reflective practice and the scientist-practitioner approach. The development of metacompetencies may be more important and more impactful on long-term outcomes for professional training than the focus on a large number of discrete and specific knowledge and skill competencies (Kagan & Kagan, 1997). Although there is little by way of empirical research to demonstrate the superiority of training programs that focus on metacompetencies early in training, there appears to be expert consensus that reflective practice is important (Bernard & Goodyear, 2009; Milne, 2009). Highlighting the importance of these competencies early in supervision, followed by systematic and ongoing attention during later stages of supervision, may be an effective supervisor strategy.

In summary, from the supervisor's perspective, it is important to ensure that the supervision plan represents a balanced program of competencies with appropriate relevance given to competency domains and competency types.

CDP for Supervision: Implementation

Once mutual agreement about a set of competencies has been achieved, the task for the supervisory dyad is to design an implementation plan that outlines how these competencies will be achieved. Such a plan will involve the planning of four aspects: placement and supervision activities; supervision methods and techniques; formative feedback and summative assessment tasks; and supervision evaluation. Each will be described briefly. A template that may be used to garner this information is provided in Appendix 12.A.

Content and learning activities

The content that may be covered in supervision is extensive and can span all foundational and functional domains (Fouad et al., 2009), client populations and client presentations. Practical considerations, such as the nature of the services provided at the placement site, may limit the nature of activities and caseload. Supervisees will benefit if supervisors are pro-active and provide them with information about the nature of client services provided at the placement, client-load, supervision frequency and modality (individual vs. group), and other essential practicalities. Additional information, including typical roles and responsibilities of supervisors within the agency, and generic information about the agency, agency staff and other resources (e.g., video recording facilities), will also enable supervisees to make better informed decisions. Where supervisees have an option of choosing between facilities, a visit to the agency site and discussions with staff may be of benefit. In the face of growing diversity of specializations in psychology, it is important for supervisors to openly discuss their area(s) of specialization and the limits of their expertise. It is a good strategy to recruit peer expertise, both within psychology and across disciplines to widen and enrich learning experiences. For instance, attending ward or grand rounds, and then reflecting on medical and nonmedical models, multidisciplinary interactions, and philosophies could be an insightful and stimulating experience for a supervisee. The activity could be used to foster knowledge (diagnostic decision-making trees), skills (case formulation and case presentation skills), attitude-value (the value self and others place on diagnostic labels; one's attitude towards nonpsychology disciplines), and relationship (the nature of one's relationship with peers and professionals from nonpsychology disciplines) competencies. The "reflective" component of the exercise could enhance self-awareness, professional identity formation, and reflective practice competencies. As may be apparent from the above example, the nature and type of competency targeted for growth will determine the range and nature of learning activities chosen for the placement.

Supervision methods and techniques

A range of supervision methods may be used to facilitate the attainment of supervision competencies, including case discussion, role-play, live observation and video review. Recent technological advances in computer technology have made possible the use of sophisticated live monitoring techniques such as bug-in-the-ear and bug-in-the-eye (Bernard & Goodyear, 2009). Real-time direct observation can now be conducted remotely, using video conferencing platforms. Despite current availability of these innovative methods of supervision, simple video recording and review remain practical, versatile and popular. From a competency-based perspective it is important that the supervision methods chosen match the competency-type targeted for change. The promotion of skills development requires opportunities for observation, review, behavior rehearsal and feedback. Hence, the selection of live (e.g., one-way mirror) or delayed monitoring (e.g., video review and feedback), together with the use of role-play would be consistent with skills-training pedagogies. Knowledge-application competencies can be promoted using case-presentations of actual cases and standardized case-scenarios. Participating in co-therapy and independent video review and feedback from supervisor or peers are recommended for enhancement of self-reflection and self-awareness, because they provide opportunities for self-observation against evaluation by others.

It is worth noting that each supervision method has its own characteristic strengths, rationale, and range of applications. For instance, real-time monitoring through a one-way mirror may be advantageous when direct and immediate intervention is warranted to ensure client care (e.g., during an assessment of suicide risk by a novice, or during a strategic intervention in family therapy; Bernard & Goodyear, 2009). Examples of competencies and examples of appropriate supervision methods for important competency domain are provided in Appendix 12.B and Appendix 12.C, respectively.

A cursory glance at Appendix 12.C highlights the value and versatility of observation methods. Specifically, while self-report may be justified for knowledge-competencies, observation methods are capable of addressing knowledge, skills, attitude-value, relationship, as well as the metacompetencies, such as reflective practice. Perhaps the most glaring example of supervision practice that is inconsistent with the foregoing expert consensus and empirical evidence is the widespread use of case presentation and subjective report in supervision, to the neglect of observation methods (Gonsalvez & McLeod, 2008; Kavanagh et al., 2003). It is illuminating that these practices persist despite recommendations to the contrary by experts (Liese & Beck, 1997; Milne, Leck, & Choudhrie, 2009; Padesky, 1996), despite supervisee preferences for skills training, and despite the acknowledgment by supervisors themselves that more extensive use of observation methods would be ideal (Gonsalvez et al., 2002). At the risk of being provocative, I would like to suggest that this unhealthy supervisory practice survives because of a possible collusion between supervisor and supervisee (see Milne et al., 2009 for more on collusion). From the supervisee's perspective, observation methods raise anxiety and exacerbate feelings of self-doubt and inadequacy in the short term, especially among novice supervisees. From the supervisor's perspective, observation often highlights a "stuck-point" in therapy, followed by a supervisee's request to the supervisor to demonstrate how the interaction could be handled differently. Impromptu role-plays place the supervisor's skills under scrutiny, which may provoke supervisor discomfort. Inadequate training in the effective use of observation methods might further accentuate ambivalence toward these methods (Kavanagh et al., 2003). Thus, avoidance of observation methods benefits both supervisor and supervisee in the short term but, unfortunately, yields less effective outcomes in the long term.

Formative feedback

A key characteristic of competency approaches is the systematic and ongoing monitoring of performance so that progress can be tracked across competency domains and over time. A comprehensive tool kit for the assessment of competencies has recently been published (Kaslow et al., 2009) and principles governing best-practice assessment and challenges in assessing competencies have been described (Leigh et al., 2007; Lichtenberg et al., 2007). Ongoing formative feedback, given in a constructive and interpersonally sensitive manner, has been the backbone of skills-shaping in supervision in the past. The supervision literature has a wealth of information on formative feedback (see Kluger & DeNisi, 1996), helpful discussions about approaches to feedback (Borders, 1993), and good-practice guidelines about providing balanced feedback (Hattie & Timperley, 2007; James, Milne, & Morse, 2008). From a competency-based perspective, feedback must be competency driven in that it should be sufficiently specific to shape and consolidate targeted competencies, or extend the application of such competencies to newer and more complex situations.

Summative assessments and reports

Summative assessments often provoke anxiety among supervisees. Assessments associated with live or delayed observation (e.g., videotapes of sessions) may accentuate these negative experiences. More recently, regulatory bodies have required training institutions and supervisors to certify that supervisees have demonstrated attainment of a checklist of competencies before declaring candidates ready for practice (e.g., Australian Psychology Accreditation Council, 2010). This gives supervisors less say in the matter. In any case, assessment tasks must be ecologically valid, capable of capturing essential elements of the competency, and be sensitive to changes in performance levels. In forthright terms, the excessive reliance on subjective report, a common practice in supervision, is inconsistent with the principles of valid assessment (Kaslow et al., 2007; Lichtenberg et al., 2007). Key competencies such as accurate diagnostic capabilities, case conceptualization, and counseling (and other intervention skills) require observation of therapist behaviors and performance. Further, the multiplicity of competencies that require monitoring and evaluation warrants a broad repertoire of assessment activities and tasks (Kaslow et al., 2009). Growing evidence suggests that supervisor judgments of supervisees may be vulnerable to rating biases, including halo and leniency effects (Gonsalvez & Freestone, 2007; Knight, 2013; Robiner, Saltzman, Hoberman, Semrud-Clikeman, & Schirvar, 1998). This has resulted in the recommendation for multimethod, multitrait, and multitask assessments (Leigh et al., 2007). The practice of scheduling some form of summative assessments at mid- and end-placement is common and often mandated by accreditation bodies and training institutions. However, a baseline assessment of key competencies, an essential task to track the progression of competency attainment during a placement, is rarely conducted (Gonsalvez & Freestone, 2007).

Several competencies central to professional training are attitude-value competencies that may not lend themselves to being captured by a brief inventory or rating scale (e.g., unconditional positive regard, regard for scientific evidence, respect for ethical principles, and commitment to client well-being). Therefore, supervision plans should identify behavioral anchors for these competencies, and recommend supervision methods (e.g., video review) that may capture these indices.

Evaluation of supervision

The current chapter is concerned with the formulation of CDPs for supervision, so a detailed coverage of evaluation falls outside its scope. However, it is worthwhile mentioning that key aspects of evaluation must be given due consideration during the planning stage. Ideally, evaluation should include an evaluation of supervisor competencies during implementation of the CDP and assess whether the CDP blueprint for the supervision program satisfies best-practice guidelines. To be credible, evaluation data obtained from supervisees are best complemented by expert/peer observation and critique.

Resolving differences

It is of paramount importance that the final CDP for supervision is arrived at through consensus and that it reflects a genuine attempt to meet supervisee needs. However, the supervisor also holds responsibilities to protect client welfare and to ensure that professional standards are not compromised. Supervisee anxiety toward observation methods may be effectively managed in a variety of ways, including graduated exposure to the task or, where appropriate, through the use of alternative observational methods (e.g., the use of videotapes in lieu of the one-way mirror). In my opinion, the supervisory practice of certifying the attainment of skills and relationship competencies on the basis of supervisee self-report is indefensible. Should observational methods not be feasible for one reason or another, the set of competencies targeted for development in supervision will require revision or confirmation at a later date.

Establishing the nature of summative assessment tasks and finalizing the schedule for lodgment of supervisor reports (if applicable) are challenging tasks for most supervisors. This is reflective of conflicting roles (supportive and facilitative vs. objective assessor) that the supervisor is called on to assume during supervision. In my opinion, where possible, the summative assessor function should be delegated to an independent professional. Evidence that supervisor judgments of supervisees may be systematically biased is an additional reason to support such a change. (Gonsalvez & Freestone, 2007; Robiner et al., 1998). Table 12.3 summarizes the preceding points.

Table 12.3 CDP Implementation.

Best-practice guidelines
1. Ensure that the CDP is the outcome of active collaboration between the supervisor and supervisee.
2. Formulate competencies that satisfy *SMART* criteria.
3. Ensure balanced coverage of competency domains and competency types.
4. Match type and nature of competencies to supervision methods
5. Match type and nature of competencies to assessment tasks.
6. Manage supervisee anxiety with tact and understanding without compromising competency standards.
7. Ensure the CDP capitalizes on supervisor and supervisee strengths and addresses important supervisee needs.
8. Recruit the expertise of colleagues and access learning opportunities within the placement context to extend and enrich the supervisee's learning experience.
9. Design strategies to resolve potential problems/barriers affecting implementation.
10. Incorporate ongoing and systematic evaluation of all program components.

Establishing a Supervision Agreement or Contract

Establishing a supervision plan that includes an agreement about the competencies to be attained during placement, and a blueprint to achieve this may form the basis of a more formal supervision agreement or contract. A legally binding supervision contract may be applicable when the supervisee is paying for the supervision provided. Regulatory, legal, and ethical guidelines differ across countries, states, or provinces within a country, and situations. Hence, offering a general template for a supervision contract will be of limited value. Sample supervision contract outlines are available in several textbooks (see Bernard & Goodyear, 2009; Falender & Shafranske, 2004).

Many supervisors across disciplines and countries provide supervision to trainees or junior professionals as part of their commitment to the profession, or as their roles as senior professionals within an organization. A signed supervision agreement between the supervisor and supervisee(s) will be more appropriate in these circumstances. Key issues that are likely to be of relevance to supervision agreements and contracts are as follows:

- Professional qualifications and expertise of supervisor: Include name, qualifications, current registration/licensure status, areas of specializations if appropriate, training in specialized interventions if relevant (e.g., hypnotherapy), training in supervision, and membership in professional societies.
- Professional details of supervisee(s): Include name, qualifications, current registration/licensure status, areas of specializations if appropriate, and years of experience if applicable.
- Financial terms and other practicalities: List fees, cancellations, and payment for resources if applicable.
- Supervision details: Include frequency, times, and modality of supervision, periods of leave if applicable, and provisions for backup supervision.
- Supervision goals, activities, and methods: Include copies of competency lists and copies of supervision plans for implementation.
- Assessment: Provide details of assessment tasks, schedule of assessments, and assessment reports.
- Roles and responsibilities: Include descriptions of supervisor and supervisee roles and responsibilities. In circumstances where several different persons hold supervisory or management roles (e.g., online managers), identify lines of accountability for what and to whom.
- Case work: Identify document that summarizes (or include details regarding) policies and procedures governing key aspects of case work including caseload and case documentation.
- Adherence to professional code of ethics: Mention the professional code of ethics to which supervisor and supervisee will adhere.
    - Mention issues of specific relevance to supervision and how they will be managed (e.g., including extent of vicarious liability, confidentiality, assessment materials).
- Insurance: Mention indemnity/malpractice insurance requirements, if relevant.

Summary and Concluding Comments

Competency-based models have breathed new life into the theoretical conceptualization and practical delivery of supervision. An essential supervisor competency is the ability to formulate an effective, competency-based developmental plan for supervision (CDP). The chapter outlines for the supervisor a stepwise approach to designing a CDP and provides best-practice guidelines for key components of the task. First, an effective CDP comprises the formulation of *SMART* competencies to be achieved during a placement. To ensure a holistic program, supervisors must then ensure coverage of (and appropriate prioritizing among) foundational and functional competency domains, and across competency types (including knowledge, skills, attitude-value, relationship, and metacompetencies). Further, a well-designed CDP includes a carefully considered schedule of supervision activities, methods, assessment, feedback, and evaluation, activities that are each informed by and aligned with the competencies to be demonstrated. The active engagement of and close collaboration with the supervisee are essential during all stages of the CDP.

Faithful adherence to the principles of competency approaches has the potential to generate major and enduring changes to supervision effectiveness and efficiency. A key challenge is the competency paradigm's ability to effectively capture and accurately measure the less tangible attitude-value and relationship competencies that constitute the essence of psychotherapy training. It is hard to conduct a clinical supervision workshop without an animated discussion about the unhelpful attitudes of "resistant" and "difficult" supervisees: their reluctance to be scrutinized through observational strategies, their hypersensitivity to critical feedback, and their penchant to be less than diligent in their responsibilities to clients and organizations. While these supervisor observations are accurate, progress within the discipline of supervision will depend also on the readiness for change among "resistant" and "difficult" supervisors and supervisor trainers; our reluctance to submit our supervision to peer observation and expert critique, and our hypersensitivity to challenges that our judgments may be biased. Above all, as supervisors, we could be more diligent in our pursuit of opportunities for growth: to learn from and inspire our supervisees and peers, and to develop competencies that will enhance the "awe and wonder" (Watkins & Wang, 2014) experience in supervision.

References

Australian Psychology Accreditation Council. (2010). *Rules for accreditation and accreditation standards for psychology courses.* Melbourne, Australia: Author.

Beinart, H. (2014). Building and sustaining the supervision alliance. In C. E. Watkins, Jr. & D. L. Milne (Eds.), *The Wiley international handbook of clinical supervision*, (pp. 257–281). Oxford, UK: John Wiley & Sons, Ltd.

Bennett-Levy, J., & Thwaites, R. (2007). Self and self-reflection in the therapeutic relationship: A conceptual map and practical strategies for the training, supervision and self-supervision of interpersonal skills. In P. Gilbert & R. L. Leahy (Eds.), *The therapeutic relationship in the cognitive behavioral psychotherapies* (pp. 255–281). New York, NY: Routledge/Taylor & Francis Group.

Bernard, J. M., & Goodyear, R. K. (2009). *Fundamentals of clinical supervision* (4th ed.). Upper Saddle River, NJ: Pearson Education.

Blackburn, I.-M., James, I. A., Milne, D. L., Baker, C., Standart, S., Garland, A., & Reichelt, F. K. (2001). The revised cognitive therapy scale (CTS-R): Psychometric properties. *Behavioural & Cognitive Psychotherapy, 29*, 431–446.

Blaisdell, K. D. (2000). *An investigation of the effects of theoretical orientation, supervisory style, and supervisee preferred supervisory style on supervisee development* (PhD thesis). Louisville: Spalding University.

Borders, L. (1993). Learning to think like a supervisor. *The Clinical Supervisor, 10*, 135–148.

Dodds, J. B. (1986). Supervision of psychology trainees in field placements. *Professional Psychology: Research & Practice, 17*, 296–300.

Doran, G. T. (1981). There's a S.M.A.R.T. way to write managements' goals and objectives. *Management Review, 70*(11), 35.

Epstein, R. M., & Hundert, E. M. (2002). Defining and assessing professional competence. *Journal of the American Medical Association, 287*, 226–235.

Falender, C. A., Cornish, J. A. E., Goodyear, R., Hatcher, R., Kaslow, N. J., Leventhal, G., & Grus, C. (2004). Defining competencies in psychology supervision: A consensus statement. *Journal of Clinical Psychology, 60*, 771–785.

Falender, C. A., & Shafranske, E. P. (2004). *Clinical supervision: A competency-based approach.* Washington, DC: American Psychological Association.

Fouad, N. A., Grus, C. L., Hatcher, R. L., Kaslow, N. J., Hutchings, P. S., Madson, M. B., & Crossman, R. E. (2009). Competency benchmarks: A model for understanding and measuring competence in professional psychology across training levels. *Training and Education in Professional Psychology, 3*(4 Suppl. 1), S5–S26.

Gonsalvez, C. J., Bushnell, J., Blackman, R., Deane, F., Bliokas, V., Nicholson-Perry, K., Shires, A., Nasstasia, Y., Allan, C., & Knight, R. (2013). Assessment of psychology competencies in field placements: Standardized vignettes reduce rater bias. *Training and Education in Professional Psychology, 7*, 99–111.

Gonsalvez, C. J., & Freestone, J. (2007). Field supervisors' assessments of trainee performance: Are they reliable and valid?*Australian Psychologist, 42*(1), 23–32.

Gonsalvez, C. J., & McLeod, H. J. (2008). Toward the science-informed practice of clinical supervision: The Australian context. *Australian Psychologist, 43*, 79–87.

Gonsalvez, C. J., & Milne, D. L. (2010). Clinical supervisor training in Australia: A review of current problems and possible solutions. *Australian Psychologist, 45*, 233–242.

Gonsalvez, C. J., Oades, L. G., & Freestone, J. (2002). The objectives approach to clinical supervision: Towards integration and empirical evaluation. *Australian Psychologist, 37*, 68–77.

Hatcher, R. L., & Lassiter, K. D. (2007). Initial training in professional psychology: The practicum competencies outline. *Training and Education in Professional Psychology, 1*, 49–63.

Hattie, J., & Timperley, H. (2007). The power of feedback. *Review of Educational Research, 77*, 81–112.

Hernandez, P. (2008). The cultural context model in clinical supervision. *Training and Education in Professional Psychology, 2*, 10–17.

Horvath, A. O., & Greenberg, L. S. (1989). Development and validation of the Working Alliance Inventory. *Journal of Counseling Psychology, 36*, 223–233.

Horvath, A. O., & Symonds, D. (1991). Relation between working alliance and outcome in psychotherapy: A meta-analysis. *Journal of Counseling Psychology, 38*, 139–149.

Hunsley, J., & Barker, K. (2011). Training for competency in professional psychology: A Canadian perspective. *Australian Psychologist, 46*, 142–145.

James, I. A., Milne, D., & Morse, R. (2008). Microskills of clinical supervision: Scaffolding skills. *Journal of Cognitive Psychotherapy: An International Quarterly*, *22*, 29–36.

Kagan, H., & Kagan, N. (1997). Interpersonal Process Recall: Influencing human interaction. In C. E. Watkins, Jr. (Ed.), *Handbook of psychotherapy supervision* (pp. 421–446). New York, NY: Wiley.

Kaslow, N. J. (2004). Competencies in professional psychology. *American Psychologist*, *59*, 774–781.

Kaslow, N. J., Grus, C. L., Campbell, L. F., Fouad, N. A., Hatcher, R. L., & Rodolfa, E. R. (2009). Competency assessment toolkit for professional psychology. *Training and Education in Professional Psychology*, *3*(4 Suppl. 1), S27–S45.

Kaslow, N. J., Rubin, N., Bebeau, M., Leigh, I., Lichtenberg, J., Nelson, P., & Smith, L. (2007). Guiding principles and recommendations for the assessment of competence. *Professional Psychology: Research & Practice*, *38*, 441–451.

Kavanagh, D. J., Spence, S. H., Strong, J., Wilson, J., Sturk, H., & Crow, N. (2003). Supervision practices in allied mental health: Relationships of supervision characteristics to perceived impact and job satisfaction. *Mental Health Services Research*, *5*, 187–195.

Kluger, A. N., & DeNisi, A. (1996). The effects of feedback interventions on performance: A historical review, a meta-analysis, and a preliminary feedback intervention theory. *Psychological Bulletin*, *119*, 254–284.

Leigh, I., Smith, L., Bebeau, M., Lichtenberg, J., Nelson, P., Portnoy, S., & Kaslow, N. J. (2007). Competency assessment models. *Professional Psychology: Research & Practice*, *38*, 463–473.

Lichtenberg, J., Portnoy, S., Bebeau, M., Leigh, I., Nelson, P., Rubin, N., & Kaslow, N. J. (2007). Challenges to the assessment of competence and competencies. *Professional Psychology: Research & Practice*, *38*, 474–478.

Liese, B. S., & Beck, J. S. (1997). Cognitive therapy supervision. In C. E. Watkins, Jr. (Ed.), *Handbook of psychotherapy supervision* (pp.114–133). New York, NY: Wiley.

Milne, D. L. (2009). *Evidence-based clinical supervision: Principles and practice.* Oxford, UK: Wiley-Blackwell.

Milne, D. L., & James, I. A. (2002). The observed impact of training on competence in clinical supervision. *British Journal of Clinical Psychology*, *41*, 55–72.

Milne, D. L., Leck, C., & Choudhrie, N. Z. (2009). Collusion in clinical supervision: Literature review and case study in self-reflection. *The Cognitive Behaviour Therapist*, *2*, 106–114.

Milne, D. L., & Reiser, R. (2014). SAGE: A scale for rating competence in CBT supervision. In C. E. Watkins, Jr. & D. L. Milne (Eds.), *The Wiley international handbook of clinical supervision*, (pp. 402–415). Oxford, UK: John Wiley & Sons, Ltd.

Milne, D. L., Sheikh, A. I., Pattison, S., & Wilkinson, A. (2011). Evidence-based training for clinical supervisors: A systematic review of 11 controlled studies. *The Clinical Supervisor*, *30*, 53–71.

Newble, D., & Canon, R. (1995). *A handbook for teachers in universities and colleges* (3rd ed.). London, UK: Kogan Page.

Pachana, N. A., Sofronoff, K., Scott, T., & Helmes, E. (2011). Attainment of competencies in clinical psychology training: Ways forward in the Australian context. *Australian Psychologist*, *46*(2), 67–76.

Padesky, C. A. (1996). Developing cognitive therapist competency: Teaching and supervision models. In P. M. Salkovskis (Ed.), *Frontiers of cognitive therapy* (pp. 266–292). New York, NY: Guilford Press.

Psychology Board of Australia. (2010). *Continuing professional development registration standards.* Retrieved from http://www.psychologyboard.gov.au/Standards-and-Guidelines/Registration-Standards.aspx

Putney, M., Worthington, E., & McCullough, M. (1992). Effects of supervisor and supervisee theoretical orientation and supervisor-supervisee matching on interns' perceptions of supervision. *Journal of Counseling Psychology*, *39*, 258–265.

Robiner, W. N., Saltzman, S. R., Hoberman, H. M., Semrud-Clikeman, M., & Schirvar, J. A. (1998). Psychology supervisors' bias in evaluations and letters of recommendation. *Clinical Supervisor*, *16*(2), 49–72.

Rodolfa, E., Bent, R., Eisman, E., Nelson, P., Rehm, L., & Ritchie, P. (2005). A Cube Model for competency development: Implications for psychology educators and regulators. *Professional Psychology, Research and Practice*, *36*, 347–354.

Roth, A. D., & Pilling, S. (2007). *The competencies required to deliver effective cognitive and behavioural therapy for people with depression and with anxiety disorders.* Retrieved from http://www.ucl.ac.uk/clinical-psychology/CORE/CBT_Competences/CBT_Competence_List.pdf

Roth, A. D., & Pilling, S. (2008). *A competence framework for the supervision of psychological therapies.* Retrieved from http://www.ucl.ac.uk/clinical-psychology/CORE/supervision_framework.htm

Rubin, N. J., Bebeau, M., Leigh, I. W., Lichtenberg, J. W., Nelson, P. D., Portnoy, S., & Kaslow, N. J. (2007). The competency movement within psychology: An historical perspective. *Professional Psychology, Research and Practice*, *38*, 452–462.

Strong, J., Kavanagh, D., Wilson, J., Spence, S., Worrall, L., & Crow, N. (2004). Supervision practice for allied health professionals within a large mental health service: Exploring the phenomenon. *The Clinical Supervisor*, *22*, 191–210.

Tsui, M.-S. (2004). The supervisory relationship of chinese social workers in Hong Kong. *The Clinical Supervisor*, *22*, 99–120.

Tsui, M.-S., Ho, W.-S., & Lam, C.-M. (2005). The use of supervisory authority in chinese cultural context. *Administration in Social Work*, *29*(4), 51–68.

Watkins, C. E., Jr. (1995). Psychotherapy supervisor and supervisee: Developmental models and research nine years later. *Clinical Psychology Review*, *15*, 647–680.

Watkins, C. E., Jr. & Wang, C. C. D. C. (2014). On the education of clinical supervisors. In C. E. Watkins, Jr., & D. L. Milne (Eds.), *The Wiley international handbook of clinical supervision*, (pp. 177–203). Oxford, UK: John Wiley & Sons, Ltd.

Worthington, E. L. (1987). Changes in supervision as counselors and supervisors gain experience: A review. *Professional Psychology – Research & Practice*, *18*, 189–208.

Appendix 12.A Trainee A. Agency: Adult anxiety unit, Northfields Clinic. Placement hours: 300 hr.

Domain and competency type	*Competency*	*Content, casework, time, resources*	*Methods and procedures*	*Formative feedback (ff) and summative assessment tasks (S) measures (M)*
I. Clinical assessment (knowledge application)	To make accurate diagnoses and differential diagnoses for adult presentations of anxiety	Real cases from clinic (Tue) Standardized cases from case book Feedback: Weekly individual supervision sessions	Case presentation and feedback Use standardized cases scenarios to make diagnoses, followed by discussion in weekly supervision	Feedback following weekly case presentations S: Week 10 (mid-placement) Week 20 (end-placement); M: Therapist performance rating scale: Assessment
II. Intervention (skills)	(a) Conduct a cognitive-behavioral assessment at advanced beginner level (b) Demonstrate Socratic dialogue skills with clients with anxiety disorders kill in structuring therapy sessions without jeopardizing progress through therapy	Real clients from clinic (Tue)	Supervisor demonstration, DVD record of client sessions, role-play	ff: Feedback on DVD, feedback following role-plays S: Week 10 (mid placement); Week 20 (end-placement); M: Cognitive therapy rating scale: self and supervisor
III. Professional multidisciplinary(attitude-value)	(a) Self-awareness: Gain insights into attitudes toward discipline of psychiatry, and medical model, an understanding of cognitive-behavioral interventions for anxiety disorders and to demonstrate level of competence in their application	Grand rounds (Wed) Discussions with registrar and social worker	Complete self-reflective exercise Discuss during supervision	NA
IV. Intervention, multicultural(relationship)	(b) Demonstrate empathy and rapport building with client (a) Demonstrate empathy and rapport building with a client from a different cultural background	Real clients from clinic Client from Aboriginal center	DVD record of client sessions, video review, and feedback	ff: feedback on DVD from supervisor; M = client ratings ff: feedback on DVD from supervisor and Aboriginal psychologist; M = client ratings

Appendix 12.B Competency grid showing sample competencies.

Competency domains		*Competency types*			
		Knowledge and knowledge application (WHAT)	*Skills (HOW)*	*Relationship*	*Attitude-value*
Assessment	Disorders: e.g., anxiety Population: e.g., adult Psychological tests Reporting Documentation	Diagnostic issues Accurate diagnoses Case conceptualization	Ability to conduct assessments in a competent fashion (includes elements of fluency, time efficiency, pace, and communication style)	Therapist–client relationship while conducting assessments. Ability to engage difficult clients, enhance alliance while doing assessments	Attitudes toward profession and key professional roles including assessment, intervention, professional development Self: self-doubt, anxiety/ confidence
Intervention	Disorders: e.g., anxiety Population: e.g., adult Psychological tests Reporting Documentation	Knowledge about indications/ contraindications for interventions Procedural knowledge Rationale for choice of interventions Models of psychopathology	Ability to conduct interventions in a competent fashion (includes elements of fluency, time efficiency, pace, and communication style)	Therapist–client relationship and interactions while conducting interventions CBT: Key cognitions about client and self during interventions Psychodynamic: Transference and countertransference	Clients: positive regard/, caring, cynical, pessimistic Work: e.g., conscientious, overly responsible, tardy Others including supervisors: e.g., open and responsive vs. defensive
Professional	Ethical–legal: Communication skills Intra- and inter disciplinary aspects: Sociocultural aspects: Professional identity:	Knowledge about ethical issues. Competencies to make ethical judgments when given case scenarios	Oral and written communication skills with other professionals	Supervisor–therapist relationship Relationship with other psychologists and health professionals	Ability to think and act ethically demonstrated in ethical conduct Burn out vs. thriving Professional development
Metacompetencies		Scientist-practitioner mindset (respect for empirical evidence, scientific method, objectivity) Reflective practice capabilities Unconditional positive regard			

Appendix 12.C Competency grid showing appropriate supervision methods.

		Competency types			
		Knowledge and knowledge application (WHAT)	*Skills (HOW)*	*Relationship*	*Attitude-value*
Competency domains	Assessment: Disorders: e.g., anxiety Population: e.g., adult Psychological tests Reporting Documentation Intervention: Disorders: e.g., anxiety Population: e.g., adult Psychological tests Reporting Documentation Professional: Ethical–legal Intra and inter disciplinary Identity Metacompetencies	Case presentation and discussion Case scenarios Venn Diagrams Conceptualization charts Test or "standardized" cases Prescribe readings Trainee presentations and seminars Lectures Essays, short answers Multiple choice questions, quizzes Literature searches	Live demonstration by supervisor Expert videos Monitoring techniques (e.g., one-way mirror) Video tape review (e.g., interpersonal process recall) Role-play activities Assessment by structured, validated scales (if available)	Videotape review methods (e.g., interpersonal process review) Concordance between self- and supervisor report following video review Self-reflection and discussion exercises following role plays Positive feedback on/ discussion of observed behavior and conduct Modeling and mentoring Encounter group strategies Assessment by structured, validated scales or inventories (if available) Live supervision methods (if available)	Videotape review methods (e.g., interpersonal process review) Concordance between self and supervisor report following video review Self-reflection and discussion exercises following actual or e-role play activities Positive feedback on/discussion of observed behavior and conduct Modeling and mentoring Encounter group strategies Experiential work including mindfulness Maintaining personal journals Self-care exercises Assessment by structured, validated scales or inventories (if available)

13

Using the Major Formats of Clinical Supervision

Mary Lee Nelson

When you think about the process of conducting clinical supervision, what comes to your mind? Do you imagine sitting in a room with a professional-in-training, one-on-one, discussing cases? Do you imagine sitting behind a one-way mirror observing a supervisee working with a family, occasionally contacting the supervisee by telephone or earpiece to provide options and support? Do you imagine doing co-therapy with your supervisee, modeling useful techniques and collaborating with the supervisee? Do you imagine sitting in a room with a group of trainees, making case presentations and discussing challenges? Do you imagine logging on to your computer to have a conversation with your supervisee or a group of supervisees in voice chat over an Internet connection? Or do you imagine sitting down with a group of professional peers to support each other and share ideas on case assessment and treatment problems?

How we define supervision format depends on a variety of factors including geographical location, clinical subspecialty, theoretical orientation, supervisee developmental level, and training setting. In the past decade, worldwide efforts have been made to identify best supervision modalities and practices. In this chapter I will work to include multiple efforts of supervision scholars across the globe. Although the most commonly used format for supervision is the individual face-to-face model (Goodyear & Nelson, 1997; McKenzie, Atkinson, Quinn, & Heath, 1986; Wetchler, Piercy, & Sprenkle, 1989), many other modalities are practiced. In addition, within the aforementioned formats we also find a variety of within-session structures and practices. The purpose of this chapter will be to illustrate the major supervision formats and the contexts in which they occur. Additionally, I will address within-session supervision practices, their purposes, and their perceived value. To avoid redundancy and repetition, the terms "format," "modality," and "model" will be used interchangeably to define both the structure and in-session practice of supervision. The primary supervision formats I will examine in the chapter are verbal reports,

The Wiley International Handbook of Clinical Supervision, First Edition. Edited by C. Edward Watkins, Jr. and Derek L. Milne.

audiotape review, videotape review, direct observation, live supervision, distance supervision using technology, and group supervision.

There have been curiously few investigations into the prevalence of use of different supervision modalities across disciplines. In the 1980s, family therapy researchers attempted to document the types of family therapy supervision used by the American Association for Marriage and Family Therapy (AAMFT) approved supervisors in multiple settings, along with supervisor perceptions of the effectiveness of each format (see Goodyear & Nelson, 1997, Table 19.1 which summarizes some of the data from these studies). McKenzie et al. (1986) obtained data from 550 supervisors who were AAMFT approved at the time, and Wetchler et al. (1989) compiled data from 318 AAMFT supervisors and 299 of their supervisees. Whereas the McKenzie et al. study documented simply the types and frequency of supervision used, the Wetchler et al. study documented supervisor and supervisee effectiveness ratings (1–5 format) for each of the formats used.

Relation of Setting to Delivery Format

The choice of supervision delivery format is often influenced by the type of setting in which the supervision takes place. For instance, in academic training institutions and training agency settings, clinical training laboratories may house counseling and therapy rooms equipped with sophisticated cameras and microphones that allow for recording of sessions or closed circuit live viewing of sessions or both. In some settings, training rooms also contain one-way mirrors that allow for live observation of sessions through the glass. In settings like this, it is common for supervisors to watch their supervisees' work before a supervision session and/or for the supervision session to involve viewing and discussion of recorded segments of the therapy session.

If the training program involves couples and family therapy, training rooms may also allow for a variety of supervision practices including phone-in, bug-in-the ear, or computer monitor supervisor assistance, as well as reflecting-team supervision (Anderson, 1987; Barnett, 2011; Carlson & Lambie, 2012; Champe & Kleist, 2003; Goldberg, 1985; Haggerty & Hilsenroth, 2011; Mauzy & Erdman, 2008; Scherl & Haley, 2000; Wetchler et al., 1989; Wright & Griffiths, 2010). In reflecting-team supervision, a team of supervisors observes a family therapy session and at some point allows the therapist and family to look back through a two-way mirror to observe the supervisory team discussing and thinking about the family's situation. These later approaches will be discussed further in a section of this chapter dedicated to family therapy supervision. It is clear, however, that in institutional settings that benefit from large, on-site training clinics equipped with technological observation tools, supervision involves some form of visual observation of therapy sessions and that various approaches to observation may be employed.

In agency or private practice settings, on the other hand, supervisors may not have access to the same types of technology. It is more common for supervision in these settings to rely on supervisee report and/or audio recordings of therapy sessions. In addition, in some training settings, the use of technology in supervision may be avoided because it is thought to interfere with the supervisory relationship (Kernberg, 2010).

In settings where individual face-to-face supervision may not be feasible, group supervision may be the practice of choice. Supervision by telephone, over an Internet connection such as Skype, or within a virtual world such as Second Life (Barnett, 2011; Cummings, 2002; Manring, Greenberg, Gregory, & Gallinger, 2011; Stebnicki & Glover, 2001; Wright & Griffiths, 2010), may be practiced when physical distance between supervisor and supervisee is impractical or impossible. In the case of distance supervision utilizing technology, ethical challenges arise. This topic will be addressed further in a subsequent chapter on distance supervision.

It appears that the practice of supervision will find a way, regardless of setting, theoretical orientation, training philosophy differences, or technical challenges. The following sections will address each of the aforementioned supervision formats, with research on, and critiques of, each of them.

Basic Supervision Formats

Supervisee report

The most commonly used supervision format appears to be the supervisee providing verbal reports to the supervisor about client issues, diagnosis or assessment, interventions used, and treatment plans (McCarthy, Kulakowski, & Kenfield, 1994; McKenzie et al., 1986; Wetchler et al., 1989). Often this verbal report includes the presentation of clinical case notes, which, in many settings, must be signed by the supervisor.

It is possible that the frequency with which this format is used may derive more from its convenience and ease of implementation than from its effectiveness. In fact, whereas Wetchler et al. (1989) found that their sample of supervisors used it most often, supervisee report was rated lower on effectiveness than 13 other formats cited. Many writers, however, maintain that self-report is highly useful and informative.

Some psychodynamically oriented supervisors believe that supervisee reports reveal as much about the supervisee and the therapeutic relationship as they do about the client and that these observations are important for identifying and working with client–therapist and therapist–supervisor relational patterns. From this viewpoint, the isomorphism between psychotherapy and supervision relationships is important in that it allows the supervisor to analyze his or her experiences with the supervisee (Aveline, 1992; Kernberg, 2010; Sarnat, 2012). Moreover, the more interaction the supervisor and supervisee have in session, the more amenable the session is to analysis of parallel processes (Kernberg, 2010; Ladany, Friedlander, & Nelson, 2005; McNeill & Worthen, 1989; Watkins, 2010).

The concept of parallel process holds that interpersonal dynamics that occur in the therapeutic relationship may transfer into the supervisory relationship and vice versa. For example, a supervisee may feel challenged by a client who presents with a consistent complaint of not being able to understand what why she persists in a particular behavior. Likewise, the supervisee may consistently complain to the supervisor that she cannot understand the client. The supervisor may in turn develop the feeling that she cannot understand the supervisee. Thus, the dynamic between the supervisee and the client has presented itself to the supervisor in such a way that the supervisor experiences it directly. The supervisor then has the opportunity to take steps to better understand the supervisee, thus modeling for the supervisee what it is like to have someone work to understand her. The supervisee, having been able to directly experience the act of being understood, may then take steps to understand the client better, an outcome that will hopefully lead to the client's improved self-understanding. This kind of "working through" of a parallel process is possible only when the supervisory dyad has sufficient time to do it. Kernberg (2010) states that too much emphasis on other supervision formats such as video or audio recordings or examination of detailed case notes may be detrimental to working with parallel process in this fashion. He cautions, however, that other types of supervision formats have their legitimate place in supervision, even psychoanalytic supervision.

Audio and video recordings in supervision

Rogers (1942) and Covner (1942) reported the first use of electronically recorded interviews for supervision purposes. Their articles described recording the therapy interview directly onto phonograph records. Those interviews were then transcribed, and both the recordings and transcripts were used in supervision. Rogers identified three primary advantages to using recordings of therapy sessions for supervision. First, he observed that clinical trainees tended to be much more directive in their interviews than they had supposed. Rogers' early experiences with recording therapy interviews revealed that mere didactic training in nondirective methods was insufficient for training many students and that only when the students had direct access to the content of their interviews could they identify their natural tendencies to provide advice and otherwise control their sessions. He provided a quotation from margin notes that a student had made on one of his training transcripts:

> Not until the counselor read these interviews did he realize the deep dark depths to which his counseling had fallen. He could hardly believe that he actually had said such things. The assumption is made that he knew better. He thinks that he can recognize many of his errors, even though he evidently didn't, during the interview. (Rogers, 1942, p. 432)

Such an observation directly illustrates the type of advance in clinical training that was to develop as a result of the capacity to observe oneself in action in the therapy session. Nondirective listening is difficult to master, as most of us want to direct, control, and advise. Through the use of audio recordings, Rogers was able to do better training in the techniques that he valued so highly through helping supervisees identify and modify their tendency to be directive.

The act of actually listening to one's work with clients provided an avenue for supervisees to test their guesses about what they had said in session against the reality of what they actually said and to reflect on discrepancies between the two. Rogers suggested that a second advantage to session recordings was their capacity to reveal resistances, conflicts, and blocks that occur in session. He referred to the common experience of being aware of something happening in session but being unable to pinpoint what it was. Electronic recordings provided the means by which trainee and supervisor could return to a specific moment in the session and examine particular processes and dynamics. They enabled the supervisory pair to evaluate specific supervisee interventions and to develop intervention changes for use in future sessions.

Rogers saw additional advantages to observing supervisees' work using technology. Recordings also allowed supervisees and supervisors to specify what interventions and techniques led to insight or change on the part of the client. Moreover, for the first time they allowed supervisees to directly observe their strengths and talents as psychotherapists.

Although we no longer produce phonograph recordings to preserve therapy sessions for supervision, audio recording is still one of the most widely used forms of technology in psychotherapy training settings (Bernard & Goodyear, 2009; Wetchler et al., 1989). One of the reasons for its popularity is the degree of mobility provided by the size and portability of audio recorders. Offices of therapists-in-training are often not equipped with special observation equipment such as one-way mirrors and video recorders.

Supervising clinicians assume various approaches to using recorded therapy sessions. Of the 21 training sites that Goodyear and Nelson (1997) surveyed, 18 reported that supervisors listened to audiotapes of their supervisee's sessions before meeting with the supervisees. The frequency of this practice ranged from once in a while to always. Whether one uses audio or video recordings, the advantage of this approach is that the supervisor gets a picture of how the therapist in training manages a session from orienting to concluding material. The supervisor can make notes while going through the tape and can share the notes either before or during the supervision session.

As documented by Goodyear and Nelson (1997), McKenzie et al. (1986), and Wetchler et al. (1989), videotaping is used in many settings as an integral part of individual, as well as family therapy supervision. The use of videotape was first suggested by Norman Kagan (1976) for the conduct of interpersonal process recall (IPR), a nondirective, supervisee-centered method for helping supervisees identify and discuss their reactions to events in their therapy sessions. Videotaping held a distinct advantage over audiotaping in that it provided access to nonverbal cues and nonverbal interpersonal exchanges that would not be observable on audiotape.

Videotaping, however, is more difficult to undertake because of its cost, size, and complexity. Many modern training clinics have video cameras installed in counseling rooms or behind one-way mirrors behind observation and counseling rooms. Some clinics still use videotape as a medium for recording, whereas more modernized clinics simply allow for saving a recorded session to a hard drive. The recording can then be transferred to a DVD, jump drive, cell phone, tablet, or other device for portability. Innovations have permitted compact video cameras to be installed in very small offices and still provide accurate images of the activity in the room while remaining unobtrusive. Still, the cost of installing such systems is prohibitive in many settings.

More recently the advent of small hand-held video recorders is permitting videotaping where it might not have been possible a decade ago, for example, taping a counseling session in an office housed in an academic department. Although the cost of purchasing small video recorders is coming down, it has not yet reached the affordability of audio recording devices; hence, the practice of audio recording may continue in settings where affordability of technology is an issue. Video recording as part of a training program, however, seems to be more widely adopted now than ever before, as equipment becomes easier to purchase and implement (Manring et al., 2011).

The recorded session as an adjunct to reflective processing

The reflective process (Neufeldt, Karno, & Nelson, 1996; Schon, 1983) involves assuming an observational stance toward the work that one is undertaking for the purpose of developing self-awareness, relational awareness, and intentionality in one's work. Reflectivity also provides information about what works and what does not. Schon distinguished between "reflection-in-action" and "reflection-on-action." Reflection-in-action involves observing one's process while it is taking place, or deliberately noticing ones feeling states, actions, and reactions to others while involved in the undertaking. Reflection-on-action involves looking back on a process that is finished to reflect on how one engaged in the process. Videotaping of therapy sessions provides an opportunity to examine past behaviors in light of present reflections. In supervision, videotaping allows for the supervisor to facilitate the reflective process so that the supervisee can closely examine the dynamics of the therapy situation. IPR (Kagan, 1976), described in another chapter of this book, details a method of inviting supervisees to engage in reflective processing through the use of videotape in the supervision sessions.

Supervisee resistance in audio and videotaping

Goldberg (1983) discussed two potential hazards inherent to video recording of counseling sessions for use in supervision: (a) the resistance of the client and (b) the resistance of the therapist-in-training. Indeed, Pharis (1986) described in detail a case example of how the audiotaping of therapy sessions produced profound resistance in a client. In the example the therapist was able to uncover the meaning of the resistance to the client and use it to help the client understand the underlying dynamics in the client's relationships. It takes a sophisticated therapist, however, to skillfully use resistance in the therapeutic work, and novice and early-career therapists may not have the necessary degree of skill. In most training settings, clients are informed that recording is a requirement of the therapist in training and referred to a different therapist if they refuse to be recorded.

The psychiatric training literature has documented that both clients and therapists in training tend to be anxious about taping early on but adapt over time (Barnes & Pilowsky, 1969; Suess, 1970). Moreover, Ellis, Krengel, and Beck (2002) found little evidence for pronounced supervisee anxiety about being taped, even in their initial sessions with clients.

Influence of Theoretical Orientation on Supervision Delivery Format

Theoretical orientation has been viewed as a major influence in supervision practice, influencing not only how psychotherapy is defined but also how it is taught

(Goodyear & Bradley, 1983; Watkins, 1997). Supervision formats, in particular, seem to vary in relation to the guiding philosophy of the training setting and supervisor. Even so, practitioners within theoretical orientations also seem to differ on appropriate formats for conducting supervision. In this section, I will examine supervision formats as they have been described for several theoretical orientations: psychodynamic therapy, cognitive-behavioral therapy (CBT) solution-focused therapy, and family therapy. These orientations were chosen because they have received a great deal of attention in the literature for their strong discourses with regard to appropriate choice of supervision formats. I will address the structure of in-session work, as well as the types of technology used in the various forms of supervision.

Formats in psychodynamic supervision

Psychodynamic supervision formats are as varied as are psychodynamic theoretical perspectives. According to Ogden (2005) and Zachrisson (2011), the essence of supervisory work is to provide a space for supervisee reverie wherein the supervisee can "dream up" the patient, or create a "fiction" of the patient that accords with the supervisee's emotional experience of him or her. The supervisor thus invites the supervisee to present the patient's story as the supervisee sees and experiences it. On this view, the supervisee's presentation of the patient is never completely factual; rather it contains the supervisee's transference and counter-transference material, which is rich with information and educational potential. This process enables both supervisee and patient material and the dynamics between them to be considered in the supervisory hour. For many psychoanalytic trainers, the supervision hour is a clinical experience in itself, representing a partial reflection of the analytic hour. Thus, the time in supervision may be quite unstructured, leaving open space for the supervisee to provide associations, which constitute material for reflection and analysis.

As mentioned in the previous paragraph, because supervision is viewed as a place of safety and reverie where an analyst in training can understand and learn from his or her associations, it can be difficult to introduce audio or video recording into the process. Viewing a videotaped session can be experienced as jarring or intrusive, and many analytic trainers advise against it. Zachrisson (2011), however, proposes that if videotaping is regular and expected, rather than occasional, it may come to be experienced as part of the process and not constitute the invasive influence about which some trainers are concerned.

Not all psychodynamic supervision is the same, however, and approaches vary by context and training philosophy. One novel approach to psychodynamic supervision was proposed by Alpher and Kobos (1988), proponents of supervisor–supervisee co-therapy in psychodynamic therapy groups. The goals of co-therapy with supervisor and supervisee are to mutually manage transferences and counter-transferences as they arise throughout predictable stages of group development (Bion, 1959) and provide an opportunity for the supervisor to model psychodynamic group leadership for the supervisee. In the co-therapy model, the supervisor serves as a live observer of all of the supervisee's interventions in the group, as well as a trainer who helps the supervisee resolve tensions with group members, within himself or herself, and with the supervisor.

Formats in CBT

CBT therapy supervision is often viewed as more structured and goal oriented than supervision from other theoretical perspectives in that it emphasizes teaching, as well as cognitive restructuring of supervisees' faulty assumptions (Liese & Beck, 1997; Pretorius, 2006; Ronen & Rosenbaum, 1998; Rosenbaum & Ronen, 1998). And whereas numerous CBT supervision experts recommend somewhat structured supervision (e.g., Liese & Beck, 1997), in fact it is not clear how much structure is actually used by CBT supervisors in everyday practice (Townend, Iannetta, & Freeston, 2002). UK scholars Reiser and Milne (2012) recommend not only that the field of CBT supervision operationalize clearer goals and objectives for supervision, but also create structures that will more clearly delineate what is to take place in the supervision hour (see also Milne & Reiser, 2012). They suggest that evaluations reflect these goals and objectives so that supervision outcomes can be more directly assessed. Thus, it seems that the identification of clearer goals and processes for supervision is a priority for some CBT experts.

It is clear that the use of audio and videotaped recordings is valued in the literature on CBT supervision. Dryden (1983) endorsed the use of audiotapes in an early call for the use of technology in distance supervision. Moreover, although in many settings video or audio recording may not be feasible or deemed essential (Townend et al., 2002), most experts in CBT supervision speak freely about the use of recording review in sessions and see it as complementary, if not essential, to the teaching of CBT (James, Milne, Marie-Blackburn, & Armstrong, 2007; Liese & Beck, 1997; Pretorius, 2006). Recordings document the use of skills and techniques and thus allow for assessment of clinician development, effectiveness, and adherence to CBT protocols.

Formats in solution-focused therapy supervision

The thrust of a solution focused supervisor's work in session is to model the therapeutic strategy through the use of the same tools that are used in solution-focused therapy. It is no surprise then that Marek, Sandifer, Beach, Coward, and Protinsky (1994) suggest that solution focused supervision be used primarily when the supervisee is in training to do solution-focused therapy. Whereas the supervision of cognitive-behavioral therapists is often quite didactic, solution-focused supervisors try to avoid direct teaching (Knight, 2004). The relationship between supervisor and supervisee is intended to be collegial and empowering, and the supervisor works to use supervisee language and assumptions, positive reframing, and support in session (Selekman & Todd, 1995). The supervisor engages the supervisee in a process of identifying and emphasizing the supervisee's own goals and strengths (Knight, 2004; Selekman & Todd, 1995). As problem talk is avoided, when a supervisee's interventions do not lead to observable change, he or she is invited to explore what might be done differently. Thus, the supervisor tries to focus the session on positive goals and outcomes. So-called miracle questions such as "When this family is doing well, what will that look like?" are common in solution-focused supervision. Scaling questions are used, such as "On a scale of one to five, how improved would you say your client is this week?" Thus, the solution-focused supervisor models confidence in the intervention model by using its very techniques with the supervisee while demonstrating firsthand how those strategies are intended to work.

Selekman and Todd (1995) raise the very real concern that to attempt to remain positive in the presence of inappropriate supervisee interpersonal behaviors and goals for therapy would be irresponsible. Thus, the authors recommend taking supervisees' normal developmental learning needs into account, acknowledging that teaching and some direction may be necessary. Ideally, however, the needs should be identified by the supervisees.

Formats in family therapy supervision

Although family therapy supervision is informed by multiple theories, it is often considered to be a specific form of psychotherapy. I include it in this section because family therapy trainers have developed multiple and sophisticated technologies for conducting supervision and in some respects lead the supervision field in innovative supervision formats.

Family therapists have been the primary, though not the exclusive, proponents of live supervision (cf. Beddoe, Ackroyd, Chinnery, & Appleton, 2011). Direct observation, or live viewing of therapy sessions, is a key component of family therapy supervision, although it is not sufficient in the family therapy model because the supervisor must also actively intervene in some way. Live supervision, or direct observation combined with real-time intervention, is a highly developed modality in family therapy supervision. Direct observation may take place through the use of a one-way mirror installed in the wall of a consulting room with an observation space behind the mirror, or through the use of closed circuit video cameras where supervisors can view live sessions in a room with video monitors. Some training clinics maintain both technologies. This section will address four commonly used live supervision formats: phone-ins, consultation breaks, bug-in-the-ear, and reflecting team supervision.

Phone-ins and consultation breaks In these versions of live supervision, the supervisor interrupts the therapy session to intervene in some manner with the supervisee. For phone-in supervision, both live observation viewing spaces and therapy rooms are equipped with telephones so that the supervisor can call the supervisee to provide guidance during the therapy session. When telephones are not available, supervisors may simply tap on the door of the therapy room and invite the supervisee for a brief consultation.

Some novel twists on the live supervision format include having the supervisor phone in to the client about how to help the therapist help the client (Keeney, 1990), and sending in a note to the client to give support and encouragement or having the supervisee and client compose a note to the supervisor in which the client disagrees with the supervisor (Goodman, 1985).

Of course, all of these techniques can be experienced as highly invasive to the supervisee and to the client. In their report on a study of the effects of supervisor interruptions of counseling sessions Hendrickson, McCarthy Veach, and LeRoy (2002) suggested that clients may experience supervisor oversight and guidance as productive but that they can also experience confusion about it if not appropriately educated about the role of the supervisor in their treatment. Bartle-Haring, Silverthorn, Meyer, and Toviessi (2009) found that whereas family therapy trainees perceived their progress in therapy to be superior when they received live supervision, their clients did not. Role induction for clients regarding the purpose and potential benefits of live supervision may enhance their appreciation for, and benefit from, greater supervisor participation in their therapy.

Liddle and Schwartz (1983) suggested questions supervisors should entertain as they consider making a live intervention. For example, what are the consequences if the suggested intervention is not delivered? If the supervisor waits, what is the likelihood that the supervisee will make the desired interventions on his or her own? Is the supervisee capable of actually making the desired intervention if the supervisor suggests it? Will the intervention foster unnecessary dependency on the supervisor? Liddle and Schwartz also suggest factors to consider in evaluating the intervention. For example, if the supervisor's suggestion was not followed, to what extent does this represent one or more of the following: (a) a relationship problem between supervisor and supervisee, (b) lack of clarity on the supervisor's part in suggesting the intervention, (c) the supervisee's inability to carry out the intervention, or (d) the supervisee's decision not to follow the directive?

Based on her review of more than 150 phone-ins, Wright (1986) suggested that the supervisor should

- Practice phone-ins with the supervisee (e.g., via role plays) prior to actually using it to supervise a therapy session
- Use phone-ins sparingly (e.g., not using phone-ins during the first 20 min of the therapy session)
- Limit the phone-in to 25 s or less and generally save process discussions for after the session
- Give no more than two instructions per phone-in
- Provide positive comments to the supervisee in at least the first one or two phone-ins of a session
- Use more specific and concrete directives with beginning supervisees, and more global and abstract comments with more advanced supervisees
- Be the only team member to conduct the phone-ins (at least with beginning supervisees)

These suggestions are useful in that they provide strategies for maximizing the effectiveness of the supervisory alliance in live supervision. Studies of supervisee anxiety in live supervision have indicated that when supervisees perceived their relationships with their supervisors to be supportive, they experience decreased anxiety in session, as well as enhanced levels of skill and professional development (Hendrickson et al., 2002; Wark, 1995).

The number of supervisor interruptions per counseling session undoubtedly varies according to characteristics of the supervisee, the client, and both the counseling and supervision relationships. However, it is possible that not enough supervisor interventions may be as detrimental as too many. Moorhouse and Carr (1991) found that when supervisors intervened infrequently, their conversations with supervisees were more collaborative; however, the supervisees were then less likely to collaborate with their clients. This finding indicates a need for more research on session interruptions and their outcomes.

Reflective teams in live supervision Reflecting team supervision is a highly innovative and not uncontroversial method for conducting live supervision in a format that involves the client intimately with a supervisory team (Anderson, 1987). This model involves a "reflecting team" that views the live counseling session and at some point trades places with the client and the therapist so that they can view the team discussing and conceptualizing the content of the case and the therapy process. The intent of reflecting team therapy and supervision is to empower clients by offering multiple perspectives on the problem and allowing clients to select the viewpoint that makes the most sense to them. Thus, reflecting team supervision is not simply a structure that allows clients to watch a live discussion of their case; its intent is to inform and edify clients, allowing them to feel like collaborators in their own therapy (Chang, 2010).

Technology-Based Distance Supervision

The advent of multiple, sophisticated technologies that can allow individuals to communicate electronically and across major distances has made supervision more feasible for practitioners and supervisors who for one reason or another must work together without meeting in person. Rural settings sometimes experience a paucity of health practitioners, who choose to locate in urban areas, where there is greater access to practice communities, as well as services and cultural amenities. This concentration of health practitioners in urban settings sometimes renders it difficult for rural practitioners and trainees to obtain the supervision they need to meet clinical needs and training requirements. Thus, distance or "telehealth" (Reese et al., 2009; Wood, Miller, & Hargrove, 2005) technologies have become more widely used in supervision.

Distance technologies are widespread in the fields of education, medicine, and psychotherapy, and are becoming part of the landscape for supervision as well (Cummings, 2002; Emmelkamp, 2006; Harwood et al., 2011; Wood et al., 2005; Wright & Griffiths, 2010). These technologies may involve asynchronous (record and forward) formats such as e-mail, exchanges of video or audio recordings, and facsimile transmissions, or synchronous (real time) formats such as telephone, instant messaging, and video conferencing (Chapman, Baker, Nassar-McMillan, & Gerler, 2011; Wood et al., 2005).

Distance technologies have been used to conduct supervision for at least two decades. In the early 1990s, Wetchler, Trepper, McCollum, and Nelson (1993) described a procedure of doing supervision by telephone to facilitate the learning of marriage and family therapists in training who were at a nondrivable distance from their supervisors. In their model, the entire supervision relationship took place by telephone, beginning with a relationship-building telephone supervision session. Because family therapy training relies heavily on what the authors termed "raw data," in their model a supervisee would video record a family therapy session, which the supervisee then viewed and critiqued in writing. The supervisee then sent the videotape, along with the written critique and case notes, to the supervisor. After the supervisor had an opportunity to review the written documents and view the videotaped session, both parties would take part in a telephone supervision session that would consist of discussing the supervisee's work, addressing concerns and questions, and planning subsequent treatment.

Clearly, long-distance supervision by telephone is not an optimal approach, particularly because the entire process may prevent feedback from reaching the supervisee in a timely fashion. This method also poses ethical challenges in that immediate crises may not receive adequate real-time attention. In addition, supervision by telephone does not allow for the supervisor to observe nonverbal markers (Ladany et al., 2005) that might signal a need for here and now intervention. Luckily, we now have technological products that permit real-time distance supervision. Supervision sessions can be recorded and sent over the Internet, and supervisors and supervisees can talk in real time over technologies such as Skype, which make conversational partners visible to each other through cameras attached to computer monitors or installed on laptop computers.

Supervision by e-mail has been gaining popularity in recent years because of e-mail's capacity to deliver messages of any length between parties on their own time, rather than at appointed times. In a recent investigation of school counseling supervision by e-mail, Gordon and Luke (2012) examined how supervisees developed a sense of "face" or professional self by responding to e-mails, rather than nonverbal cues. Wright and Griffiths (2010) described their process of using telephone and e-mail when distance was prohibitive of face-to-face supervision in rural New Zealand. They noted how supervision by e-mail permitted the supervisee, who benefits greatly from writing, to engage in reflective journaling. This journaling, perhaps not surprisingly, had a powerful impact on the supervisee in that it permitted her to convey to the supervisor a depth of reflectivity that she might have overlooked in conversation. She noted, however, that when she and the supervisor did converse over the telephone, she felt less inclined to convey strong emotional reactions, which she preferred to reserve for face-to-face sessions when they were possible.

A similar approach was suggested by Cummings (2002), who examined the experiences of peer supervision groups who read each other's e-mailed case presentations and provided group supervision through the use of what the author termed "cybervision," or supervision via online chat room texting. Cummings' analysis of participant responses to this process revealed that although they did not convene in person, participants had been able to establish a surprising degree of trust and openness. They experienced the supervision as engaging and stimulating and appreciated the degree of professional development gained from the group process. Some participants speculated that the degree of distance offered by the chat room format allowed them to feel safer, hence more open, than they might have felt in a face-to-face supervision setting.

Often telehealth supervision will be used in combination with face-to-face supervision, providing for valued in-person communication while allowing supervisors and supervisees to commute long distances less frequently. Distance technologies such as videoconferencing require supervisee efforts to familiarize themselves with and become comfortable using programs such as Skype or Wimba; thus they have the potential to cause supervisee anxiety or frustration (Sorlie, Gammon, Bergvik, & Sexton, 1999). However, research on supervisee satisfaction with this hybrid supervision format has been largely encouraging. Supervisees typically report that they are able to achieve the same goals through the use of distance technology than they are through face-to-face supervision (Abbass et al., 2011; Reese et al., 2009; Sorlie et al., 1999; Wright & Griffiths, 2010). In a comparison of Web-based peer supervision and conventional group supervision of school counseling trainees, Butler and Constantine (2006) found that students in the Web-based supervision groups reported heightened levels of collective self-esteem and case conceptualization skill than did their counterparts. Thus, strong support is beginning to accrue for the utility of Internet technologies in supervision.

The delivery of supervision via Internet has several ethical implications (Shaw & Shaw, 2006; Vaccaro & Lambie, 2007). Because multiple networks have varying degrees of confidentiality, several authors have recommended including a statement in client informed-consent forms that notifies them of Internet use for supervision of their case (Shaw & Shaw, 2006; Welfel, 2006). In the consent form, clients should be educated about the highly unlikely but possible breach of confidentiality that could occur should Internet security be violated. Crisis management is another concern when supervisors are not available for professional consultation on site. Distance supervisors and their supervisees should have clear plans in place to collaborate on managing emergencies should they arise (Shaw & Shaw, 2006). Another major ethical issue that affects distance psychotherapy and supervision is the concern about jurisdiction. The locality where the supervisor is licensed may not be the same locality where the therapist-in-training is practicing; thus, supervisor and therapist might be bound by conflicting laws and ethical constraints. Moreover, the vicarious liability of supervisors (Falvey, 2002) complicates legal risk management of cases across jurisdictions. Barnett and Scheetz (2003) recommend that telehealth practitioners know all laws regarding practice in jurisdictions where they are not themselves licensed and that they clarify whether their liability insurance covers cases in other jurisdictions. Because various states and countries have differing laws and ethical guidelines and the field has not yet developed a consolidated set of mandates regarding ethical and legal telehealth practice, a good rule of thumb at this point in time may be to not practice outside one's legal jurisdiction.

Group Supervision Formats

In the mid-1980s, the status of group supervision was succinctly summarized in the title of Holloway and Johnston's (1985) article on the dynamics of group supervision. The title of the article stated that group supervision was "widely practiced but poorly understood." Group supervision in one form or another is ubiquitous in the training not only of mental health professionals but also of other health professionals (e.g., Balint groups; Balint, 1985; Brock & Stock, 1990). There is no doubt that group supervision has its benefits and drawbacks. As compared with individual supervision, the use of groups involves economy of time and energy. Because supervisees in groups can learn vicariously from each other, working with a group of trainees means that each can be learning even while someone else is the focus of attention.

As Hillerbrand (1989) has pointed out, group members are often able to give each other feedback that is more understandable than what the supervisor offers. Thus, it has been important to supervision researchers to further clarify the uses and efficacy of group supervision as a supervision format.

Altthough peer feedback can be perceived as central to supervisee learning experiences, supervisee anxiety about being judged by their peers may be particularly present in the early stages of group development (Mastoras & Andrews, 2011). In a cluster analysis of supervisee experiences in group supervision, Carter, Enyedy, Goodyear, Arcinue, and Puri (2009) found that supervisees feel the impact of both supervisor and peer influences and that experiences of support or lack of support are impactful on supervisees. Supervisors' open and validating style, willingness to didactically contribute to supervisees' knowledge, and use of in vivo techniques were important aspects of supervisees' experiences of helpful group supervision. Supervisees also indicated that one outcome of group supervision was greater self-awareness. On the other hand, Enyedy et al. (2003) identified hindering events as perceived by trainees in supervision groups. These hindering events included competition among supervisees in the groups, less-than expert feedback, supervisors' lack of skill with conducting groups, different theoretical orientations between group co-supervisors, and lack of adequate group time management. These findings caution the field that training in group supervision, as well as individual supervision, might be advisable for developing supervisors.

Efforts to uncover the utility and learning needs in the field of group supervision are well under way in Sweden, where basic psychotherapy trainees are required to take part in 120 hr of group supervision over an 18-month period, and advanced trainees are required to participate in 150 sessions of group supervision over a period of 30 months. In addition, the two-year, part-time supervisor training program requires 150 hr of group supervision of supervisors (Ögren & Sundin, 2009).

Ögren and Sundin (2009) collected both qualitative and quantitative data on supervision groups as they developed over a period of four years. They found that regardless of theoretical orientation of supervision groups (e.g., psychodynamic vs. CBT) both supervisors and supervisees characterized their group experiences as individual supervision delivered in a group format. Proctor and Inskipp (2001) described this type of authority-driven supervision as "supervision in the group," compared with what they called "supervision with the group," wherein the supervisor focuses on an individual but invites all members to participate, or "supervision by the group," a collaborative form of supervision in which power is more equalized. In discussing group supervision from a Gestalt perspective, Melnick and Fall (2008) remind us that a group is greater than the sum of its parts and that it is highly challenging to supervisors to manage the complexity of group dynamics. Thus, it may be simpler for a group supervisor to focus on individuals at the expense of the group and its dynamics, but group supervision can, and some argue must be, taken to a deeper level.

Ögren and Sundin found significant differences between levels of perceived group processing in supervision groups and the desire for group processing. This difference was partially accounted for by theoretical orientation, with psychodynamic participants expressing a greater desire than CBT therapists for group processing. The authors indicate that training of supervisors in Sweden has recently begun to involve working with group processing in supervision groups. Other supervision experts are also calling for a greater emphasis on group processing in group supervision, particularly at advanced levels such as supervision of supervision groups (DiMino & Risler, 2012).

Research on supervision groups that do focus on group processes seems to indicate that supervision groups pass through a series of stages similar to the stages of group psychotherapy (Boalt Boëthius & Ögren, 2000; Ögren, Apelman, & Klawitter, 2001). Boalt Boëthius and Ögren (2000) also found that supervision groups of fewer than four supervisees tended to be less beneficial than groups of four or more; moreover, they also noted that groups seemed to function better when there was a gender balance of members. Further research on the outcomes, thus utility, of this type of group format will no doubt provide useful guidance for the field of group supervision as it develops.

Peer group supervision: a special case of group supervision

Peer group supervision has been defined differently by numerous authors (Bernard & Goodyear, 2009; Christensen & Kline, 2001; Wilkerson, 2006). Wilkerson (2006) makes an important distinction between peer groups that are facilitated by more experienced supervisors and groups that are self-guided, without the hierarchical presence of a more expert facilitator. Wilkerson offers the following definition of peer group supervision:

> Peer supervision is a structured, supportive process in which counselor colleagues (or trainees), in pairs or in groups, use their professional knowledge and relationship expertise to monitor practice and effectiveness on a regular basis for the purpose of improving specific counseling, conceptualization, and theoretical skills. (p. 62)

It is the later definition I will address in this section, as groups that are facilitated by professional supervisors seem to fall more logically into the general group supervision category.

Peer supervision is particularly valuable to professional school counselors in the United States, who technically receive no professional supervision after completing the master's degree (Borders & Usher, 1992; Page, Pietrzak, & Sutton, 2001). This lack of assistance with professional development renders school counselors particularly at risk of committing gross clinical errors or ethical violations. Moreover, it leaves many school counselors feeling a lack of professional support because they do not have regular contact with professionals other than teachers and principals, who can express support but are not trained in the delivery of mental health interventions. When school counselors have access to professional peer support, they experience less anxiety and burnout (Culbreth, Scarborough, Banks-Johnson, & Solomon, 2005). Numerous authors have called for practicing school counselors to recognize their responsibility for pursuing ongoing input and oversight in the form of individual or group peer supervision (Fischetti & Lines, 2003; Gruman & Nelson, 2008; Wilkerson, 2006). They urge the field to develop an ongoing network of peer supervision opportunities for school counselors.

Other professionals have touted the value of peer supervision groups for practicing professionals (Counselman & Weber, 2004; Goldsmith, Honeywell, & Mettler, 2011; Granello, Kindsvatter, Granello, Underfer-Babalis, & Hartwig Moorhead, 2008). In a novel approach to ongoing professional peer supervision, a group of Canadian genetic counselors developed a system of obtaining peer perspectives by having teams conduct live observations of a therapist's work and providing feedback later in a group format (Goldsmith et al., 2011).

Research on the outcomes of peer group supervision is scant. However, the few efforts to study its benefits have indicated that participants experience a heightened sense of responsibility for one's professionalism (Wagner & Smith, 1979) and increased opportunities to engage in professional development (Runkel & Hackney, 1982). It is likely that professionals from all counseling and psychotherapy fields would benefit from ongoing peer supervision.

Conclusions

Although most psychotherapy practitioners have undoubtedly experienced supervision as an individual face-to-face weekly encounter, it is clear that a wide variety of formats are available to accommodate different settings, theoretical orientations, and resource provisions. Recent developments in technology are broadening the range of options for supervision delivery format and increasing opportunities for creativity in designing situation-specific supervision modalities. These new technologies also present both clinical and ethical questions that will challenge the field to question what practices actually enhance the effectiveness of supervision and resulting psychotherapy. It is my hope that this chapter will be informative to educators and practitioners of all types of supervision and that it may inspire some to expand their views about how supervision can be approached. I encourage supervision researchers to continue to carefully examine both the conduct and the content of supervision practice in an ongoing effort to evaluate and define our very best practices.

References

Abbass, A., Arthey, S., Elliott, J., Fedak, T., Nowoweiski, D., Markovski, J., & Nowoweiski, S. (2011). Web-conference supervision for advanced psychotherapy training: A practical guide. *Psychotherapy, 48*, 109–118.

Alpher, V. S., & Kobos, J. C. (1988). Cotherapy in psychodynamic group psychotherapy: An approach to training. *Group, 12*, 135–144.

Anderson, T. (1987). The reflecting team: Dialog and meta-dialog in clinical work. *Family Process, 25*, 415–428.

Aveline, M. (1992). The use of audio and videotape recordings of therapy sessions in the supervision and practice of dynamic psychotherapy. *British Journal of Psychotherapy, 8*, 347–358.

Balint, E. (1985). The history of training and research in Balint groups. *Psychoanalytic Psychotherapy, 1*, 1–9.

Barnes, L. H., & Pilowsky, I. (1969). Psychiatric patients and closed-circuit television teaching: A study of their reactions. *British Journal of Medical Education, 40*, 1159–1161.

Barnett, J. E. (2011). Utilizing technological innovations to enhance psychotherapy supervision, training, and outcomes. *Psychotherapy, 48*, 103.

Barnett, J. E., & Scheetz, K. (2003). Technological advances and telehealth: Ethics, law, and the practice of psychotherapy. *Psychotherapy: Theory, Research, Practice, Training, 40*(1–2), 86.

Bartle-Haring, S., Silverthorn, B. C., Meyer, K., & Toviessi, P. (2009). Does live supervision make a difference? A multilevel analysis. *Journal of Marital and Family Therapy, 35*, 406–414.

Beddoe, L., Ackroyd, J., Chinnery, S. A., & Appleton, C. (2011). Live supervision of students in field placement: More than just watching. *Social Work Education, 30*, 512–528.

Bernard, J. M., & Goodyear, R. K. (2009). *Fundamentals of clinical supervision* (4th ed.). Upper Saddle River, NJ: Pearson Education.

Bion, W. (1959). *Experiences in groups.* New York, NY: Basic Books.

Boalt Boëthius, S., & Ögren, M.-L. (2000). Role patterns in group supervision. *The Clinical Supervisor, 19*, 45–69.

Borders, L. D., & Usher, C. H. (1992). Post-degree supervision: Existing and preferred practices. *Journal of Counseling and Development, 74*, 314–318.

Brock, C. D., & Stock, R. D. (1990). A survey of Balint group activities in U.S. family practice residency programs. *Family Medicine, 22*, 33–37.

Butler, S. K., & Constantine, M. G. (2006). Web-based peer supervision, collective self-esteem, and case conceptualization ability in school counselor trainees. *Professional School Counseling, 10*, 146–152.

Carlson, R. G., & Lambie, G. W. (2012). Systemic-developmental supervision: Clinical supervisory approach for family counseling student interns. *The Family Journal, 20*, 29–36.

Carter, J. W., Enyedy, K. C., Goodyear, R. K., Arcinue, F., & Puri, N. N. (2009). Concept mapping of the events supervisees find helpful in group supervision. *Training and Education in Professional Psychology, 3*, 1.

Champe, J., & Kleist, D. M. (2003). Live supervision: A review of the research. *The Family Journal, 11*, 268–275.

Chang, J. (2010). The reflecting team: A training method for family counselors. *The Family Journal, 18*, 36–44.

Chapman, R. A., Baker, S. B., Nassar-McMillan, S. C., & Gerler, E. R., Jr. (2011). Cybersupervision: Further examination of synchronous and asynchronous modalities in counseling practicum supervision. *Counselor Education and Supervision, 50*, 298–313.

Christensen, T. M., & Kline, W. B. (2001). The qualitative exploration of process-sensitive peer group supervision. *Journal for Specialists in Group Work, 26*, 81–99.

Counselman, E. F., & Weber, R. L. (2004). Organizing and maintaining peer supervision groups. *International Journal of Group Psychotherapy, 54*, 125–143.

Covner, B. J. (1942). Studies in phonographic recordings of verbal material: I. The use of phonographic recordings in counseling practice and research. *Journal of Consulting Psychology, 6*, 105–113.

Culbreth, J. R., Scarborough, J. L., Banks-Johnson, A., & Solomon, S. (2005). Role stress among practicing school counselors. *Counselor Education and Supervision, 45*, 58–71.

Cummings, P. (2002). Cybervision: Virtual peer group counselling supervision – Hindrance or help? *Counselling and Psychotherapy Research, 2*, 223–229.

Dimino, J. L. & Risler, R. (2012). Group supervision of supervision: A relational approach for training supervisors. *Journal of College Student Psychotherapy, 26*, 61–72.

Dryden, W. (1983). Audiotape supervision by mail: A rational-emotive perspective. *British Journal of Cognitive Psychotherapy, 1*, 57–64.

Ellis, M. V., Krengel, M., & Beck, M. (2002). Testing self-focused attention theory in clinical supervision: Effects of supervisee anxiety and performance. *Journal of Counseling Psychology, 49*, 101.

Emmelkamp, P. M. G. (2006). Technological innovations in clinical assessment and psychotherapy. *Psychotherapy and Psychosomatics, 34*, 336–343.

Enyedy, K. C., Arcinue, F., Puri, N. N., Carter, J. W., Goodyear, R. K., & Getzelman, M. A. (2003). Hindering phenomena in group supervision: Implications for practice. *Professional Psychology, Research and Practice, 34*, 312.

Falvey, J. E. (2002). *Managing clinical supervision: Ethical practice and legal risk management.* Pacific Grove, CA: Brooks/Cole.

Fischetti, B. A., & Lines, C. L. (2003). Views from the field: Models for school-based clinical supervision. *The Clinical Supervisor, 22*, 75–86.

Goldberg, D. A. (1983). Resistance to the use of video in individual psychotherapy training. *American Journal of Psychiatry, 140*, 1172–1176.

Goldberg, D. A. (1985). Process notes, audio, and videotape. *The Clinical Supervisor, 3*, 3–14.

Goldsmith, C., Honeywell, C., & Mettler, G. (2011). Peer-observed interaction and structured evaluation (POISE): A Canadian experience with peer supervision for genetic counselors. *Journal of Genetic Counseling, 20*, 204–214.

Goodman, R. W. (1985). The live supervision model in clinical training. *The Clinical Supervisor, 2*, 43–49.

Goodyear, R. K., & Bradley, F. O. (1983). Supervision in counseling: II. Integration and evaluation: Theories of counselor supervision: Points of convergence and divergence. *The Counseling Psychologist, 11*, 59–67.

Goodyear, R. K., & Nelson, M. L. (1997). The major formats of psychotherapy supervision. In C. E. Watkins, Jr. (Ed.), *Handbook of psychotherapy supervision* (pp. 328–344). New York, NY: John Wiley and Sons.

Gordon, C., & Luke, M. (2012). Discursive negotiation of face via email: Professional identity development in school counseling supervision. *Linguistics and Education, 23*, 112–122.

Granello, D. H., Kindsvatter, A., Granello, P. F., Underfer-Babalis, J., & Hartwig Moorhead, H. J. (2008). Multiple perspectives in supervision: Using a peer consultation model to enhance supervisor development. *Counselor Education and Supervision, 48*, 32–47.

Gruman, D., & Nelson, M. L. (2008). Supervision of professional school counselors. In H. L. K. Coleman & C. Yeh (Eds.), *Handbook of school counseling* (pp. 309–319). New York, NY: Erlbaum.

Haggerty, G., & Hilsenroth, M. J. (2011). The use of video in psychotherapy supervision. *British Journal of Psychotherapy, 27*, 193–210.

Harwood, T. M., Pratt, D., Beutler, L. E., Bongar, B. M., Lenore, S., & Forrester, B. T. (2011). Technology, telehealth, treatment enhancement, and selection. *Professional Psychology, Research and Practice, 42*, 448.

Hendrickson, S. M., McCarthy Veach, P., & LeRoy, B. S. (2002). A qualitative investigation of student and supervisor perceptions of live supervision in genetic counseling. *Journal of Genetic Counseling, 11*, 25–49.

Hillerbrand, E. T. (1989). Cognitive differences between experts and novices: Implications for group supervision. *Journal of Counseling and Development, 67*, 293–296.

Holloway, E., & Johnston, R. (1985). Group supervision: Widely practiced, but poorly understood. *Counselor Education and Supervision, 24*, 332–340.

James, I. A., Milne, D., Marie-Blackburn, I., & Armstrong, P. (2007). Conducting successful supervision: Novel elements towards an integrative approach. *Behavioural and Cognitive Psychotherapy, 35*, 191.

Kagan, N. (1976). *Influencing human interaction*. Mason, MI: Mason Media; Washington, DC: American Counseling Association.

Keeney, B. P. (1990). Supervising client conversation: A note on a conceptual structure for evoking therapeutic creativity. *Journal of Family Psychotherapy*, *1*, 51–56.

Kernberg, O. F. (2010). Psychoanalytic supervision: The supervisor's tasks. *Psychoanalytic Quarterly*, *79*, 603–627.

Knight, C. (2004). Integrating solution-focused principles and techniques into clinical practice and supervision. *The Clinical Supervisor*, *23*, 153–173.

Ladany, N., Friedlander, M., & Nelson, M. L. (2005). *Critical events in psychotherapy supervision: An interpersonal approach*. Washington, DC: American Psychological Association.

Liddle, H. A., & Schwartz, R. C. (1983). Live supervision/consultation: Conceptual and pragmatic guidelines for family therapy trainers. *Family Process*, *22*, 477–490.

Liese, B. S., & Beck, J. S. (1997). Cognitive therapy supervision. In C. E. Watkins (Ed.), *Handbook of psychotherapy supervision* (pp. 114–133). Hoboken, NJ: John Wiley & Sons.

Manring, J., Greenberg, R. P., Gregory, R., & Gallinger, L. (2011). Learning psychotherapy in the digital age. *Psychotherapy*, *48*, 119.

Marek, L. I., Sandifer, D. M., Beach, A., Coward, R. L., & Protinsky, H. O. (1994). Supervision without the problem. *Journal of Family Psychotherapy*, *5*, 57–64.

Mastoras, S. M., & Andrews, J. J. W. (2011). The supervisee experience of group supervision: Implications for research and practice. *Training and Education in Professional Psychology*, *5*, 102–111.

Mauzy, E., & Erdman, P. (2008). Trainee perceptions of live supervision phone-ins: A phenomenological inquiry. *The Clinical Supervisor*, *15*, 115–128.

McCarthy, P., Kulakowski, D., & Kenfield, J. A. (1994). Clinical supervision practices of licensed psychologists. *Professional Psychology, Research and Practice*, *25*, 177.

McKenzie, P. N., Atkinson, B. J., Quinn, W. H., & Heath, A. W. (1986). Training and supervision in marriage and family therapy: A national survey. *American Journal of Family Therapy*, *10*, 21–25.

McNeill, B. W., & Worthen, V. (1989). The parallel process in psychotherapy supervision. *Professional Psychology, Research and Practice*, *20*, 329.

Melnick, J., & Fall, M. (2008). A gestalt approach to group supervision. *Counselor Education and Supervision*, *48*, 48–60. ACA.

Milne, D., & Reiser, R. P. (2012). A rationale for evidenced-based clinical supervision. *Journal of Contemporary Psychotherapy*, *42*, 139–149.

Moorhouse, A., & Carr, A. (1991). The correlates of phone-in frequency, duration and the number of suggestions made in live supervision. *Journal of Family Therapy*, *21*, 407–418.

Neufeldt, S. A., Karno, M. P., &Nelson, M. L. (1996). A qualitative analysis of experts' conceptualization of supervisee reflectivity. *Journal of Counseling Psychology*, *43*, 3–9.

Ogden, T. (2005). On psychoanalytic supervision. *The International Journal of Psycho-Analysis*, *86*, 1265–1280.

Ögren, M.-L., Apelman, A., & Klawitter, M. (2001). The group in psychotherapy supervision. *The Clinical Supervisor*, *20*, 147–176.

Ögren, M.-L., & Sundin, E. C. (2009). Group supervision in psychotherapy. Main findings from a Swedish research project on psychotherapy supervision in a group format. *British Journal of Guidance & Counselling*, *37*, 129–139.

Page, B. J., Pietrzak, D. R., & Sutton, J. M., Jr. (2001). National survey of school counseling supervision. *Counselor Education and Supervision*, *41*, 142–150.

Pharis, M. E. (1986). The object relations implications of taping individual therapy sessions. *Clinical Social Work Journal*, *14*, 361–374.

Pretorius, W. M. (2006). Cognitive behavioural therapy supervision: Recommended practice. *Behavioural and Cognitive Psychotherapy, 34*, 413–420.

Proctor, B., & Inskipp, F. (2001). Group supervision. In J. Scaife (Ed.), *Supervision in mental health settings: A practitioner' guide* (pp. 99–121). London, UK: Bruner-Routledge.

Reese, R. J., Aldarondo, F., Anderson, C. R., Lee, S. J., Miller, T. W., & Burton, D. (2009). Telehealth in clinical supervision: A comparison of supervision formats. *Journal of Telemedicine and Telecare, 15*, 356–361.

Reiser, R. P., & Milne, D. (2012). Supervising cognitive-behavioral psychotherapy: Pressing needs, impressing possibilities. *Journal of Contemporary Psychotherapy, 42*, 161–171.

Rogers, C. R. (1942). The use of electrically recorded interviews in improving psychotherapeutic techniques. *American Journal of Orthopsychiatry, 12*, 429–434.

Ronen, T., & Rosenbaum, M. (1998). Beyond direct verbal instructions in cognitive behavioral supervision. *Cognitive and Behavioral Practice, 5*, 7–23. Elsevier.

Rosenbaum, M., & Ronen, T. (1998). Clinical supervision from the standpoint of cognitive-behavior therapy. *Psychotherapy: Theory, Research, Practice, Training, 35*, 220.

Runkel, T., & Hackney, H. (1982). Counselor peer supervision: A model and challenge. *The Personnel and Guidance Journal, 61*, 113–115.

Sarnat, J. E. (2012). Supervising psychoanalytic psychotherapy: Present knowledge, pressing needs, future possibilities. *Journal of Contemporary Psychotherapy, 42*, 151–160.

Schon, D. (1983). *The reflective practitioner: How professionals think in action.* New York, NY: Basic Books.

Scherl, C. R., & Haley, J. (2000). Computer monitor supervision: A clinical note. *American Journal of Family Therapy, 28*, 275–282.

Selekman, M. D., & Todd, T. (1995). Co-creating a context for change in the supervisory system: The solution-focused supervision model. *Journal of Systemic Therapies, 14*, 21–33.

Shaw, H. E., & Shaw, S. F. (2006). Critical ethical issues in online counseling: Assessing current practices with an ethical intent checklist. *Journal of Counseling and Development, 85*, 41–53.

Sorlie, T., Gammon, D., Bergvik, S., & Sexton, H. (1999). Psychotherapy supervision face-to face and by video conferencing: A comparative study. *British Journal of Psychotherapy, 15*, 452–462.

Stebnicki, M., & Glover, N. (2001). E-supervision as a complementary approach to traditional face-to-face clinical supervision in rehabilitation counseling: Problems and solutions. *Rehabilitation Education, 15*, 283–294.

Suess, J. (1970). Self-confrontation of videotaped psychotherapy as a teaching device for psychiatric residents. *Journal of Medical Education, 45*, 271–282.

Townend, M., Iannetta, L., & Freeston, M. H. (2002). Clinical supervision in practice: A survey of UK cognitive behavioural psychotherapists accredited by the BABCP. *Behavioural and Cognitive Psychotherapy, 30*, 485–500.

Vaccaro, N., & Lambie, G. W. (2007). Computer-based counselor-in-training supervision: Ethical and practical implications for counselor educators and supervisors. *Counselor Education and Supervision, 47*, 46–57.

Wagner, C. A., & Smith, J. P., Jr. (1979). Peer supervision: Toward more effective training. *Counselor Education and Supervision, 18*, 288–293.

Wark, L. (1995). Live supervision in family therapy: Qualitative interviews of supervision events as perceived by supervisors and supervisees. *American Journal of Family Therapy, 23*, 25–37.

Watkins, C. E. (2010). Psychoanalytic constructs in psychotherapy supervision. *American Journal of Psychotherapy, 64*, 393–416.

Watkins, E. C., Jr. (1997). Defining psychotherapy supervision and understanding supervisor functioning. In E. C. Watkins, Jr. (Ed.), *Handbook of psychotherapy supervision* (pp. 3–10). New York, NY: John Wiley and Sons.

Welfel, E. R. (2006). *Ethics in counseling and psychotherapy: Standards, research, and emerging issues* (3rd ed.). Pacific Grove, CA: Brooks/Cole.

Wetchler, J. L., Piercy, F. P., & Sprenkle, D. H. (1989). Supervisors' and supervisees' perceptions of the effectiveness of family therapy supervisory techniques. *American Journal of Family Therapy, 17*, 35–47.

Wetchler, J. L., Trepper, T. S., McCollum, E. E., & Nelson, T. S. (1993). Videotape supervision via long-distance telephone. *American Journal of Family Therapy, 21*, 242–247.

Wilkerson, K. (2006). Peer supervision for the professional development of school counselors: Toward an understanding of terms and findings. *Counselor Education and Supervision, 46*, 59–67.

Wood, J. A. V., Miller, T. W., & Hargrove, D. S. (2005). Clinical supervision in rural settings: A telehealth model. *Professional Psychology, Research and Practice, 36*, 173.

Wright, J., & Griffiths, F. (2010). Reflective practice at a distance: Using technology in counselling supervision. *Reflective Practice, 11*, 693–703.

Wright, L. M. (1986). An analysis of live supervision "phone-ins" in family therapy. *Journal of Marital and Family Therapy, 12*, 187–191.

Zachrisson, A. (2011). Dynamics of psychoanalytic supervision: A heuristic model. *The International Journal of Psycho-Analysis, 92*, 943–961.

14

Helping Skills Training
Implications for Supervision

Clara E. Hill

Helping skills training involves a structured group approach to teaching novice trainees about counseling and psychotherapy. Trainees are typically taught to use less of some behaviors (e.g., advice, self-disclosure, interruptions) that they might use frequently with friends, and instead use behaviors that are thought to be more therapeutic (e.g., attending, listening, reflections of feelings, open questions). Teaching typically incorporates a didactic component (reading and lecture), modeling, practice with classmates and volunteer clients, and positive and constructive feedback for each individual skill. The assumption is that these helping skills can best be taught in a group format, with trainees benefiting from considerable practice with easy clients.

Helping skills training is typically the first formal training for novice therapists, who typically spend one to two semesters learning and practicing these skills before they go on to more individualized practica and supervision. Thus, helping skills training provides a foundation on which supervision can build. There is of course an element of supervision in the helping skills training in that instructors provide trainees with individualized feedback (e.g., give more eye contact, keep your interventions shorter). Similarly, there is often an element of skills training in supervision in that supervisors might individually work with trainees to practice a particular skill (e.g., using role-play to help trainees use reflection of feelings more empathically). If therapists lack adequate helping skills or are unable to use the skills appropriately in a particular situation (e.g., because of major counter-transference), supervisors may need to focus on the skills, particularly through helping the supervisees understand the blocks and role-playing. Supervisors often especially need to work individually with novice therapists to enable them to implement insight skills (e.g., challenge, interpretation, immediacy) given that these skills are difficult to use, require sensitivity, and vary in implementation based on the dynamics of working with specific clients.

The Wiley International Handbook of Clinical Supervision, First Edition. Edited by C. Edward Watkins, Jr. and Derek L. Milne.

The purpose of the present chapter is to present a brief background of the various approaches to helping skills training, focus more in depth on the model that I have developed over the years (Hill, 2004, 2009; Hill & O'Brien, 1999), and review the research related to helping skills training, drawing heavily on previous reviews (Hill & Knox, 2013; Hill & Lent, 2006). I hope to convince readers of the benefits of providing helping skills training prior to supervision. And, finally, I hope to stimulate research on the differential effects of helping skills training and supervision.

The Origins of Helping Skills Training

Imagine the excitement when Carl Rogers leaped onto the stage of American psychology in the 1940s and presented a major alternative to psychoanalysis and behaviorism. His fundamentally positive approach (Rogers, 1942, 1951, 1957) reflected the American idealism and belief in the possibilities of growth and self-actualization.

Not only did Rogers have a major impact on psychotherapy, but he also had a major impact on the field of training psychotherapists. Given that his initial theory (Rogers, 1942) emphasized that therapists should be sounding boards or mirrors who reflect back to clients, the resulting training approach emphasized teaching therapists to restate and mirror clients, to not go beyond what clients said but to allow clients to hear what they were thinking and feeling and elaborate on that. By having such a mirror held up, clients could learn to listen to themselves and self-correct and trust themselves. A large number of programs were developed in the 1960s and 1970s that proposed methods for teaching helping skills to professionals, paraprofessionals, teachers, and parents.

Three programs were quite popular and received a lot of empirical attention. These programs were developed by Carkhuff (1969; human relations training [HRT]), Ivey (1971; microcounseling [MC]), and Kagan (1984; interpersonal process recall [IPR]). In HRT and MC, trainees are taught specific skills (e.g., reflection of feeling). IPR, in contrast, helps trainees articulate their thoughts and feelings about their interventions; Kagan's assumption was that students are blocked from effectively using native skills because of performance anxiety.

As Rogers evolved (e.g., Rogers, 1957), he shifted away from thinking that therapists served merely as mirrors of what clients were saying. Rather, he came to think that therapists at the core must communicate the facilitative attitudes of empathy, warmth, and genuineness to their clients. When therapists can accept clients fully and nonjudgmentally, Rogers believed that clients come to accept and heal themselves. He indeed began to question whether these attitudes could be taught. If the attitudes are inherent to the individual, he reasoned that we need to shift from an emphasis on teaching specific skills to focusing on the facilitative conditions. In fact, Rogers seemed quite disturbed by the way that training programs developed because they often were simplistic and almost seemed like cookbooks rather than having a lot of clinical sensitivity (see Rogers, 1986). At any rate, people who developed the helping skills training programs continued with the original proposition that skills could be taught.

To diverge for a moment, let me disclose how my personal experiences fit into this history. I was lucky enough to be taught helping skills in my first semester of graduate school in 1970 by Bill Anthony, who had studied with Robert Carkhuff, who had worked with Charles Truax, who had worked with Carl Rogers. I so clearly remember going into the class totally unsure of myself and my ability to help anyone. I was empathic but was not skilled at all other than in listening (usually so that I did not have to talk). At the end of the semester, I felt far more confidence because I had some specific skills on which I could rely: I knew how to use nonverbal behaviors and to do a level 3 reflection of feelings. And even more exciting was having the opportunity the next semester to lead my own lab in helping skills, an experience that allowed me to continue to work on my skills. I have been teaching helping skills ever since and feel like I continue to evolve and change in my thinking about how the skills can be taught. At this point, I believe that a combination of helping skills and a facilitative attitude is crucial, a point I will elaborate in this chapter.

Early Research on Helping Skills Training Programs

Most of the research on helping skills training was conducted in the 1960s and 1970s. Compared with today's standards, this research is methodologically flawed and of questionable validity in terms of providing evidence for the efficacy of helping skills training. To provide a historical context, however, I briefly review older literature on the effects of training, the maintenance of skills, predictors of the outcome of training, and the components of training.

The effectiveness of helping skills training

Narrative reviews of helping skills training Narrative reviews refer to authors examining a body of studies and intuitively rather than statistically summarizing the results. Several such reviews about helping skills training (Ford, 1979; Kasdorf & Gustafson, 1978; Lambert, DeJulio, & Stein, 1978; Matarazzo, 1971, 1978; Matarazzo & Patterson, 1986; Russell, Crimmings, & Lent, 1984) have generally concluded that helping skills training is effective. Matarazzo's reviews in the three early editions of the *Handbook of Psychotherapy and Behavior Change* were the most comprehensive and credible. She concluded that warmth and empathy could be taught and that there was sufficient evidence for the effectiveness of teaching Ivey's MC program to appropriately selected students. She dismissed, however, the studies of Carkhuff's HRT because of numerous methodological problems (e.g., skills were not well defined, assessment of skills was crude and subjective; the training itself was not well specified; controls were not adequate; the same rating scales were used to assess training and outcome introducing bias; outcome was assessed through analog methods rather than through behavior in an interview setting; judges were not adequately trained to code outcome measures; and the sequencing of training methods was not assessed). Thus, the early reviews of helping skills training were relatively positive, with some cautions based on the methods used in studies.

Meta-analytic reviews of helping skills training More recently, meta-analytic methods have been developed that have enabled reviewers to quantitatively summarize findings across studies. In the Baker and Daniels (1989) review, for example, the authors reported evidence that Ivey's MC was effective. More specifically, they reported a large effect size for undergraduate trainees (1.18) and a moderate effect size for graduate trainees (.66). Goodyear and Guzzardo (2000) suggested that graduate trainees probably had more clinical experience at the start of training than did undergraduates and thus may not have had as much room for growth.

Baker, Daniels, and Greeley (1990) conducted a meta-analysis comparing MC, HRT, and IPR for graduate trainees. Although there were only eight HRT studies, 23 MC studies, and 10 IPR studies, they found a large effect (1.07) for Carkhuff's HRT, a medium effect (.63) for Ivey's MC, and a small (.20) effect for Kagan's IPR. Type and amount of training may have been confounded, however, given that HRT averaged 37 hr of training whereas MC and IPR averaged 19 and 9.5 hr, respectively. And it should be noted, that these programs were generally shorter than what we would now recommend (a minimum of 1–2 semesters).

As noted previously, however, the results of these studies need to be considered with caution. In addition to the methodological problems that Matarazzo (1971, 1978; Matarazzo & Patterson, 1986) noted, Hill and Lent (2006) added a few concerns. They noted that the content of the training programs was seldom specified so we do not know much about the content of training. Furthermore, most studies only used one trainer, so that we do not know anything about trainer effects. In addition, random assignment was almost never used, so trainees were not randomly assigned to training versus control conditions, which could lead to bias. Finally, to assess outcome, trainees were typically asked to respond in writing or via tape recordings to written or taped analog stimuli, rather than through assessing therapist behavior or client outcomes in more naturalistic clinical settings. Responding to a written client statement is much different from responding within context to a client presenting an actual problem. Hence, although the meta-analyses provide more precision in the summaries of findings than were possible in the narrative reviews, we must still be cautious about interpreting studies that are seriously flawed in terms of methodology.

Maintenance of skills post-training

If training is effective, we would expect that trainees would retain the skills over time. In the three studies that addressed this issue, undergraduate trainees decreased in rated facilitativeness (Collingwood, 1971; Gormally, Hill, Gulanick, & McGovern, 1975), and beginning graduate trainees either maintained or increased in rated facilitativeness (Butler & Hansen, 1973; Gormally et al., 1975). It may be, as Gormally et al. suggested, that undergraduates did not maintain the skills because they did not continue to use them in a professional setting, whereas graduate students maintained their skills because they continued to use them in professional settings.

Predictors of outcome of helping skills training

Only five studies have been conducted predicting outcome from trainee characteristics (see review in Hill & Lent, 2006). None of these studies used the same variables or measures, however, so it is not possible to draw any conclusions about whether some types of trainees benefit more than others from helping skills training.

Effectiveness of components of helping skills training

In their review, Hill and Lent (2006) noted that several components have been suggested as important components of helping skills training: modeling, rehearsal/practice, instruction, feedback/supervision, self-observation/confrontation, co-counseling, and de-conditioning of anxiety. The theoretical foundation for these components is Bandura's (1969, 1997) social cognitive theory, in which Bandura proposed that instruction, modeling, practice, and feedback are essential for learning to occur. The application of this theory to helping skills training suggests that the importance of providing a rationale, giving examples of how to use the skills, structuring opportunities to practice the skills, and offering positive and constructive feedback about the performance of the skills.

In the research on components, instruction was typically operationalized as 5–10 min of written or taped didactic information about how the skill was defined and giving a rationale for using the skill. Modeling was typically operationalized through brief (less than 30 min) videos of expert therapists using the skill. Practice involved an opportunity to use the skill in some way. Feedback involved visual reinforcement with lights, verbal reinforcement through earphones or speakers, or a 20- to 30-min feedback session with a supervisor.

Hill and Lent conducted two meta-analyses of the research involving components. The first meta-analysis compared components across studies; participants thus came from different studies for each component and were not randomly assigned. When effects were combined across components, a large effect (.79) was found, indicating that using any component was better than no component. When components were examined individually compared with no training, however, medium to large effects for modeling (.90), feedback (.89), and instruction (.63) were reported. Unfortunately, practice was not included in the meta-analysis because there were not enough studies. An examination of outcome measure (averaged across components) revealed medium effects for judges' ratings of trainee empathy during short practice interviews (.75), and for judges' ratings of trainee empathy in written/taped responses to written/taped analog stimuli (.62). Finally, Hill and Lent found that both graduate (.88) and undergraduate (.77) trainees had large effects. This analysis thus revealed that modeling, feedback, and instruction had effects on rated empathy for both graduate and undergraduate trainees.

Hill and Lent then conducted a second meta-analysis on within-studies data (e.g., comparisons of components were made within the same study). They noted that within-studies estimates provide better estimates of the effects of components because researchers randomly assign participants to condition (either to receive one component or another), thus controlling for variations across trainees and methods. In this within-studies meta-analysis, Hill and Lent found a medium effect (.67) that modeling was better than instruction or feedback. Furthermore, using multiple components was better than using any single component (effect size = .51). Thus, modeling seemed to be more effective than instruction or feedback, and more impact was obtained by combining components.

Hill and Lent noted that these results should be considered with caution because of numerous methodological problems. Of particular relevance to this chapter, skills were not taught within the context of an ongoing training program. Rather they were taught in isolation, often to introductory psychology students within the space of five minutes to an hour. Thus, trainees were not given the opportunity to learn the complexity of the skill and how to use the skill clinically and how to judge the client's response, but rather were taught just to formulate a simple grammatical statement. Relatedly, the only skill that was typically taught was usually some variation of reflection of feeling, which is relatively easy to teach in a simplistic way (although not easy to apply in an actual clinical situation). Notably, other skills that are more complex and difficult to teach (e.g., interpretation, challenge, immediacy) were not investigated. Furthermore, the definition and implementation of training was vague. Also, as with the research on training programs, assessments of outcomes typically involved written/oral responses to written/oral analog vignettes, which probably do not generalize to behavior in an actual clinical setting. Finally, although these components were tested as separate entities, it is hard to imagine how one could model a skill without defining what it is being modeled and how one could give realistic feedback without basing it on practice.

Recent Research on Helping Skills Training

The Hill model of helping skills training

Current research has focused mostly on the helping skills model that I developed (Hill, 2004, 2009; Hill & O'Brien, 1999). This approach grew out of my own training in Carkhuff's (1969) HRT, which I have modified extensively based on teaching the approach to both upper-level undergraduates and beginning graduate students. In addition, I have also integrated findings from more than 40 years of research that I have conducted on therapist techniques and therapy process. I use the term "helper" rather than "therapist" because this model is taught to a wide range of students, not all of whom go on to be therapists in professional mental health settings.

The Hill model comprises three stages, with goals and skills for each stage. In the exploration stage, the goals are to help clients tell their stories and explore their thoughts (through using the skills of open questions and restatements) and feelings (through using the skills of open questions, reflections of feelings, and disclosures of feelings). In the insight stage, the goals are to facilitate awareness (through using the skill of challenge), promote insight (through using the skills of open questions, interpretation, and disclosure of insight), and work with the therapeutic relationship (through using the skill of immediacy). In the action stage, the goal is to help the client change, which the helper accomplishes through combining the skills of open questions, information, and direct guidance combined into four different modules (relaxation, behavior change, behavior rehearsal, and decision-making). In the training, the skills within the three stages are presented sequentially. Instructors provide and discuss the theoretical rationale and empirical findings for each stage. Within each stage, instructors focus on providing a rationale for each skill (through reading and lecture), they then provide examples in a variety formats (videos, demonstrations), and finally they provide many opportunities to practice in small groups and dyads with supportive coaching and feedback. Students also have the opportunity to participate as volunteer clients to practice the skills and to see how it feels experientially to be the recipient of the skills and be vulnerable as a client. In addition, students do self-reflection papers so that they can learn more about themselves, and they conduct and transcribe sessions so that they can have the experience of coding the skills and slowing the process down to hear the client's reactions.

Importantly, we do not teach the skills in a cookbook approach suggesting that certain skills must always be used. Rather, we try to teach students that a variety of skills can be useful and that the manner in which they implement the skills is important. We also try to teach flexibility and empathy, noting that not all clients respond in the same way and that clients have different needs (e.g., some like to focus on feelings, others do not). In addition, we try to teach students to be aware of their own needs and reactions so that they can be aware of what is coming from the client and what is coming from them. Finally, we teach professionalism, encouraging students to have a professional demeanor, maintain confidentiality, and follow ethical guidelines.

Finally, I should note that we teach the course slightly differently at the undergraduate and graduate levels. At the undergraduate level, students have a 4-credit semester-long class that meets 4 hr a week. They focus on helping skills for the whole class (2 hr lecture/discussion and 2 hr lab per week, for a total of 60 hr) and practice extensively with classmates. In the graduate class, we spend 20 hr in the first month of the semester going over the exploration stage with extensive practice in class. We then start trainees seeing a volunteer client from an undergraduate class. They are supervised by a more advanced graduate student (who has gone through this experience) who observes every session live and also meets with the trainee individually during the week. In addition, trainees meet in group supervision immediately after seeing their clients. Later in the semester, students receive more training in the insight and action stages, each for about 6 hr. In addition to reading the text as do the undergraduates, the graduate students also read a number of other primary texts on various theories of psychotherapy.

Effectiveness of the Hill model of helping skills training

A few studies have now been conducted on the outcomes of this training model. In the first study, Hill and Kellems (2002) developed the Helping Skills Measure, the Relationship Scale, and the Session Evaluation Scale so that there would be measures available to assess the effects of training in brief sessions with volunteer clients (recall that a major criticism of the previous research was the use of analog methods for assessing outcomes). By completing these measures after helping sessions, clients and therapists indicate how much they thought that the exploration, insight, and action skills were used; they also evaluate the quality of the therapeutic relationship; and finally they evaluate the quality of the overall session. Using these measures, Hill and Kellems found that undergraduate students in helping skills classes were perceived by clients as using more exploration, insight, and action skills at the end of the semester than they had at the beginning of the semester. In addition, trainees received higher ratings from clients in terms of being able to establish a therapeutic relationship and also higher ratings in terms of session evaluation. Thus, trainees changed over the course of a semester of training in interactions with volunteer clients (different ones at each time period).

One could argue, however, that Hill and Kellems did not assess actual behavior but rather that they investigated perceptions of behavior. Hence, we set out to design a more ambitious study, where we investigated the effects of helping skills training from the perspectives not only of helpers and clients, but also of judgments of behavior in sessions. For this study (Hill et al., 2008), we were able to study training across the course of a semester for different helping skills classes with different instructors (responding to criticisms of earlier research that used only one instructor/trainer). We found that in a helping session with a classmate conducted mid-semester after training in the exploration stage as compared with a helping session conducted with a different classmate at the beginning of the semester, undergraduate students were more able to use exploration skills, were judged more empathic, talked less, and were evaluated as more effective in using the exploration stage skills. In addition, trainees were asked to complete self-evaluations at the end of the 15-week semester. In this post-semester self-evaluation, trainees reported having higher self-efficacy for using helping skills than they had at the beginning of the semester. Trainees also completed weekly estimates during the semester of their confidence in being able to use the helping skills. Their confidence ratings increased steadily while they were learning exploration skills, but decreased as they learned insight skills, and then again increased as they learned action skills. We speculated that exploration and action skills are easier to learn because they are closer to skills used in everyday life. Insight skills, in contrast, are more difficult to learn because they are different from typical communication with friends. Interestingly, we were not able to predict who profited most from training using initial grade-point average, self-rated empathy, and self-rated perfectionism.

We also conducted two qualitative studies of the experiences of beginning master's level students learning helping skills and implementing these skills with volunteer clients under supervision. Williams, Judge, Hill, and Hoffman (1997) found that students had substantial decreases in anxiety across the course of a semester, and had positive reactions to the training. Hill, Sullivan, Knox, and Schlosser (2007) found that as a result of training, trainees were more able to use exploration and insight skills, felt better about themselves as therapists, were less anxious, had more self-efficacy, were more comfortable in the role of therapist, were less self-critical, and felt themselves more able to connect with clients.

Thus, the results from two quantitative and two qualitative studies indicate that training in the Hill helping skills model was effective. We caution, however, that these studies were all conducted by our group at the University of Maryland and need to be replicated by other investigators at other universities.

Effectiveness of the components of training using the Hill model

In addition to studying the overall effects of training in helping skills, we have been investigating the effects of the components. Our starting point in these studies was the previous literature (reviewed above) that focused on instruction, modeling, practice, and feedback based on Bandura's (1969, 1997) social cognitive theory. In the three studies that I review next, we focused on insight skills that are typically more difficult to teach (immediacy, challenge, and interpretation, respectively). These studies were all conducted within the context of semester-long helping skills classes, so that the skills were taught within the context of training as it usually occurs. In the first half of the semester, students learned and practiced the exploration skills. In the second half of the semester, the specific skill was introduced. Typically, students were asked to read about the skill, then they heard a lecture, next they observed a modeling of the skill, and finally they practiced the skill in a variety of exercises. After each component (e.g., reading, lecture, modeling, large group practice, dyadic practice), they completed a measure of self-efficacy for using the skill. After the entire 4 hr of training, students wrote a narrative describing what was effective and not effective about the training; this narrative was examined qualitatively. Note that although we recognize the importance of feedback, it was difficult within the context of large classes to provide much individual feedback, and so this component was not intentionally manipulated.

Although somewhat different results emerged from each of the three studies, the general conclusions were that instruction, modeling, practice, and feedback were all effective components of training. The most effective, however, from the perspective of the student narrative reports was practice. Students emphatically stated that in retrospect, although the other components were helpful, what really made the difference was having the opportunity to practice. In fact, many students said that the skills sounded easy when they read about them, heard about them in lecture, and observed them being used, but they really realized how difficult they were to implement when they tried them. They found that hands-on experience invaluable in terms of learning how to use the skills. These findings for the importance of practice support the literature that students learn a lot from their clients (Stahl et al., 2009).

In summary, we found evidence for the effectiveness of instruction, modeling, practice, and feedback in teaching insight skills in the Hill model. We know less, however, about other possible components of training, such as self-observation/confrontation, co-counseling, anxiety-reduction techniques, support, and transcribing and coding interventions used in sessions. In addition, we do not know the best sequence for the components of training. Although it makes sense that trainees need to read first, then hear about a skill through lecture, then see models of the skill, then practice, and then receive feedback, other sequences might be as useful, and sequences might vary for different skills.

Implications for Training Students

Helping skills training is strongly embedded in many programs as the initial training experience that students receive. This focus on helping skills training as the first exposure seems prudent because trainees are learning to shift from communication that is appropriate in friendship to communication that is appropriate for therapy. Hence, they must learn to move from evenly shared conversations to listening more, giving less self-disclosure and less opinion, and interrupting less. In addition, they learn to become self-aware, and to think about their intentions. They get an opportunity to practice the skills, in increasingly more challenging situations. They learn how to observe clients and be responsive to their needs in the moment. Moreover, they are involved in a professionalization process, whereby they begin to see themselves in the role of therapist (including taking an ethical stance toward working with another person). Thus, helping skills training involves much more than just learning specific grammatical ways of phrasing statements. It makes sense, then, to provide this type of structured experience early in their careers so that trainees can begin to self-reflect and observe their behaviors in a supportive environment. The group setting also helps because students learn from each other and have the opportunity to practice with each other.

I thus recommend that trainees be exposed to helping skills training prior to the experience of seeing their first clients and engaging in individual supervision. Helping skills training allows trainees to focus on themselves before they are placed in a setting where they have to diagnose and treat clients. It is hard to do both at once, so it makes sense to focus first on the person of the therapist.

It is important that the helping skills training be implemented with flexibility so that trainees learn that they need to use their own style rather than follow a cookbook approach. Thus, rather than, for example, learning that reflection of feelings is the only skill to use, trainees can be taught to practice the various skills, think about their intentions in the moment, and observe client responses to see what the most effective skills are to use in various situations. In effect, trainees are being taught to be good personal scientists and to develop their own styles.

The goal of helping skills training is thus to teach students to think broadly about the skills, to practice them in a variety of situations, to learn when and why to use skills, and to observe client reactions and adjust their approach to be responsive to client's needs. Given that every client is different, and thus that therapists must respond to each client's needs, it is not only unfeasible, but also perhaps dangerous, to dictate what skills "should" be used in a given situation. Thus, the goal of training is to provide trainees with a broad set of skills on which they can rely, and which they can astutely use in various clinical situations depending on the client's needs.

After helping skills training, students are more likely to be ready to profit from individual supervision. They typically have some confidence, they have some skills, and they are eager to try out their skills with clients. At this point, they are ready for the individual attention that comes from working with an individual supervisor. And rather than having to teach the individual skills, the supervisor can spend his or her time coaching the trainee in using the skills with specific clients and helping the trainee examine the barriers that arise in trying to use the skills with specific clients.

International Implications

The helping skills are by no means unique to the United States. Rather, these are skills that are used throughout the world. Just as the skills are used differently by therapists of differing orientations (e.g., Hill, Thames, & Rardin, 1979), however, they are undoubtedly used to different extents and perhaps in different ways by therapists in different countries (although this requires empirical validation).

Helping skills workshops that I have conducted in Taiwan, China, and Korea have been well received. In general, participants had no problems with the exploration skills. Empathy works well universally, although some therapists and clients have trouble identifying and especially deepening feelings. Asian therapists were generally most comfortable with questions (as are novice therapist trainees in the United States). With the insight skills, they were quite intrigued but also had many concerns. They talked at length about how challenges would have to be used in a very gentle and indirect way, rather than being too aggressive or direct. They were also concerned about interpreting too quickly, and suggested that perhaps it might be better for therapists to use open questions to invite clients to interpret for themselves. Immediacy is the skill that was most difficult for Asian therapists. Thus, immediacy may need to be modified to be more of an invitation to talk about the relationship rather than the therapist stating his or her reactions too directly. In terms of the action stage, many Asian therapists focus more heavily on action than we do in the United States. Interestingly, Asian clients seem to expect directives from people in authority, although they may not necessarily follow the directives completely (see also Duan et al., 2012).

As I have modified the model over the years based on my experiences both in the United States and abroad, I have increasingly asked trainees to think about how and when to use the skills. Rather than having a prescribed way to use the skills, I ask trainees to think about their intentions, to try out the skills, and to watch the clients' reactions. Thus, for some clients, reflections of feelings are very appropriate, but others explore more readily with open questions. Thus, therapists need to be responsive to clients' needs, whatever the culture, rather than slavishly following any model.

Conclusions

In closing, I would like to encourage people not only to teach helping skills but also to do research on the effectiveness of helping skills training and on the effective components of helping skills training. It would be particularly useful to have evidence about whether supervision is enhanced if students have first gone through helping skills training.

References

Baker, S. B., & Daniels, T. G. (1989). Integrating research on the microcounseling program: A meta-analysis. *Journal of Counseling Psychology, 36*, 213–222. doi:10.1037/0022-0167.36.2.213

Baker, S. B., Daniels, T. G., & Greeley, A. T. (1990). Systematic training of graduate-level therapists: Narrative and meta-analytic reviews of three major programs. *The Counseling Psychologist, 18*, 355–421. doi:10.1177/0011000090183001

Bandura, A. (1969). *Principles of behavior modification.* New York, NY: Holt, Rinehart, & Winston.

Bandura, A. (1997). *Self-efficacy: The exercise of control.* New York, NY: W. H. Freeman.

Butler, E. R., & Hansen, J. C. (1973). Facilitative training: Acquisition, retention, and modes of assessment. *Journal of Counseling Psychology, 20*, 60–65. doi:10.1037/h0033989

Carkhuff, R. R. (1969). *Human and helping relations* (Vols. 1 & 2). New York: Holt, Rinehart, & Winston.

Collingwood, T. R. (1971). Retention and retraining of interpersonal communication skills. *Journal of Clinical Psychology, 27*, 294–296.

Duan, C., Hill, C. E., Jiang, G., Hu, B., Chui, H., Hui, K., Yu, L. (2012). Therapist directives: Use and outcomes in China. *Psychotherapy Research. 22*, 442–457.

Ford, J. D. (1979). Research on training therapists and clinicians. *Review of Educational Research, 49*, 87–130.

Goodyear, R. K., & Guzzardo, C. R. (2000). Psychotherapy supervision and training. In S. Brown & R. W. Lent (Eds.), *Handbook of counseling psychology* (3rd ed., pp. 83–108). New York, NY: Wiley.

Gormally, J., Hill, C. E., Gulanick, N., & McGovern, T. (1975). The persistence of communication skills for undergraduate trainees. *Journal of Clinical Psychology, 31*, 369–372.

Hill, C. E. (2004). *Helping skills: Facilitating exploration, insight, and action* (2nd ed.). Washington, DC: American Psychological Association.

Hill, C. E. (2009). *Helping skills: Facilitating exploration, insight, and action* (3rd ed.). Washington, DC: American Psychological Association.

Hill, C. E., & Kellems, I. S. (2002). Development and use of the Helping Skills Measure to assess client perceptions of the effects of training and of helping skills in sessions. *Journal of Counseling Psychology, 49*, 264–272. doi:10.1037/0022-0167.49.2.264

Hill, C. E., & Knox, S. (2013). Training and supervision in psychotherapy: Evidence for effective practice. In M. J. Lambert (Ed.), *Handbook of psychotherapy and behavior change* (6th ed., pp. 775–811). New York, NY: Wiley.

Hill, C. E., & Lent, R. W. (2006). A narrative and meta-analytic review of helping skills training: Time to revive a dormant area of inquiry. *Psychotherapy: Theory, Research, Practice, Training, 43*, 154–172. doi:10.1037/0033-3204.43.2.154

Hill, C. E., & O'Brien, K. (1999). *Helping skills: Facilitating exploration, insight, and action.* Washington, DC: American Psychological Association.

Hill, C. E., Roffman, M., Stahl, J., Friedman, S., Hummel, A., & Wallace, C. (2008). Helping skills training for undergraduates: Outcomes and predictors of outcomes. *Journal of Counseling Psychology, 55*, 359–370. doi:10.1037/0022-0167.55.3.359

Hill, C. E., Sullivan, C., Knox, S., & Schlosser, L. (2007). Becoming psychotherapists: The experiences of novice therapists in a beginning graduate class. *Psychotherapy: Theory, Research, Practice, Training, 44*, 434–449. doi:10.1037/0033-3204.44.4.434

Hill, C. E., Thames, T. B., & Rardin, D. (1979). A comparison of Rogers, Perls, and Ellis on the Hill Counselor Verbal Response Category System. *Journal of Counseling Psychology, 26*, 198–203.

Ivey, A. E. (1971). *Microcounseling: Innovations in interviewing training.* Springfield, IL: Charles C. Thomas.

Kagan, N. (1984). Interpersonal process recall: Basic methods and recent research. In D. Larson (Ed.), *Teaching psychological skills: Models for giving psychology away* (pp. 229–244). Monterey, CA: Brooks/Cole.

Kasdorf, J., & Gustafson, L. (1978). Research related to microtraining. In A. E. Ivey & J. Authier (Eds.), *Microcounseling: Innovations in interviewing, counseling, psychotherapy, and psychoeducation* (pp. 323–376). Springfield, IL: Thomas.

Lambert, M. J., DeJulio, S. S., & Stein, D. M. (1978). Therapist interpersonal skills: Process, outcome, methodological considerations, and recommendations for future research. *Psychological Bulletin, 85*, 467–489.

Matarazzo, R. G. (1971). The systematic study of learning psychotherapy skills. In A. E. Bergin & S. L. Garfield (Eds.), *Handbook of psychotherapy and behavior change* (pp. 895–924). New York, NY: Wiley.

Matarazzo, R. G. (1978). Research on the teaching and learning of psychotherapeutic skills. In S. L. Garfield & A. E. Bergin (Eds.), *Handbook of psychotherapy and behavior change* (2nd ed., pp. 941–966). New York, NY: Wiley.

Matarazzo, R. G., & Patterson, D. (1986). Research on the teaching and learning of therapeutic skills. In S. L. Garfield & A. E. Bergin (Eds.), *Handbook of psychotherapy and behavior change* (3rd ed., pp. 821–843). New York, NY: Wiley.

Rogers, C. R. (1942). *Counseling and psychotherapy*. Boston, MA: Houghton Mifflin.

Rogers, C. R. (1951). *Client-centered therapy: Its current practice, implications, and theory*. Boston, MA: Houghton Mifflin.

Rogers, C. R. (1957). The necessary and sufficient conditions of therapeutic personality change. *Journal of Consulting Psychology, 21*, 95–103. doi:10.1037/h0045357

Rogers, C. R. (1986). Carl Rogers's column: Reflection of feelings. *Person-Centered Review, 1*, 375–377.

Russell, R. R., Crimmings, A. M., & Lent, R. W. (1984). Therapist training and supervision. In S. Brown & R. W. Lent (Eds.), *Handbook of counseling psychology* (pp. 625–681). New York, NY: Wiley.

Stahl, J. V., Hill, C. E., Jacobs, T., Kleinman, S., Isenberg, D., & Stern, A. (2009). When the shoe is on the other foot: A qualitative study of intern-level trainees' perceived learning from clients. *Psychotherapy: Theory, Research, Practice, Training, 46*, 376–389. doi:10.1037/a0017000

Williams, E., Judge, A., Hill, C. E., & Hoffman, M. A. (1997). Experiences of novice therapists in prepracticum: Trainees', clients', and supervisors' perceptions of personal reactions and management strategies. *Journal of Counseling Psychology, 44*, 390–399. doi:10.1037/0022-0167.44.4.390

15

Developing Understanding in Clinical Supervision

Marie-Louise Ögren and Siv Boalt Boëthius

Introduction

Learning in psychotherapy supervision is complex right from the start, in the encounter between the supervisor and the supervisee, with their different personalities, attitudes, life experiences, professional experiences, and capacities, in a specific work environment and with various clients. Psychotherapy supervision aims to fulfill a number of tasks, such as enhancing the supervisee's understanding of the client's problems and of how psychotherapy works. Moreover, it is of importance to help supervisees to improve diagnostic and therapeutic skills. To develop and consolidate a therapeutic attitude and to integrate theory with practice, as well as to enhance the capacity for reflection and awareness of the professional work, are fundamental goals. In addition to helping supervisees maintain their professional competence, supervision is also considered to give the supervisees a certain buffer against burn-out or stagnation. Another aspect of the learning situation is that the supervisees also need to understand how the host organization works and how it can support the learning situation in supervision (Orlinsky & Rønnestad, 2005; Skovholt & Rønnestad, 1992; Watkins, 1997, 1998). Psychotherapy supervision also functions as a quality assurance of the supervisees' psychotherapy work (Milne & James, 2002).

Psychotherapy training has a long tradition. Individual supervision was, for many years, the predominant form. From the start, supervision constituted, alongside personal psychoanalysis or psychotherapy, the chief element in training for psychoanalysts and psychotherapists (Flemming & Benedek, 1966). Internationally, since the Second World War, psychotherapy courses have become formalized and have increased in number and scope. Psychotherapy training programs appear to have a similar structure and design, namely didactic theory seminars, supervision, clinical work with patients or clients, and sometimes personal psychotherapy. Supervisor training courses

The Wiley International Handbook of Clinical Supervision, First Edition. Edited by C. Edward Watkins, Jr. and Derek L. Milne.

have also appeared during the past decades and have adopted a formalized structure in the United States and Europe as well as Australia (Barnett, 1998; Carroll, 2001; Gonsalvez & Milne, 2010; Ögren, Boalt Boëthius, & Sundin, 2008; Pearson, 2004; Sundin, Ögren, & Boalt Boëthius, 2008; Whitman, Ryan, & Rubenstein, 2001).

The goals and frames of psychotherapy supervision are of decisive importance for the design of the supervision. Goals, frames, and content are influenced in turn by whether the supervision is conducted within a formal academic program or as part of a competence-raising program for a working team, such as a mental health care unit. In a review, Watkins (1997) described the following aspects of supervision: the reciprocity of the supervision's relations, the importance of the assessment component, the focus on enhancing professional competence in the form of quality assurance of patient work, and therewith the supervisor's responsibility as "gatekeeper." The goals of supervision vary according to the stage of training. At the basic training level, the purpose of supervision is to provide a basic professional standard, while at the advanced training level it is to contribute to the maintenance and deepening of competence (Orlinsky, Botermans, & Rønnestad, 2001). Psychotherapy supervision offers a learning situation that combines theoretical, practical, and personal aspects. This learning is unique and can be most stimulating and positive. However, to achieve a constructive working climate, some challenges have to be faced.

The Learning Situation in Supervision

To acquire new knowledge and to integrate theoretical aspects with clinical practice is, in general, very much appreciated by the supervisees. However, to be confronted with a new clinical and supervision situation may evoke anxiety, at least for the novice supervisee (Bernard & Goodyear, 2009; Gray, Ladany, Walker, & Ancis, 2001; Hansen, Svendsen, & Hagen, 2010; Hawkins & Shohet, 1989, 2012; Jacobsson, Lindgren, & Hau, 2012; Nielsen, Haugaard Jacobsen, & Bork Mathiesen, 2012; Skovholt & Rønnestad, 1992, 2003; Stoltenberg, McNeill, & Delworth, 1998; Strømme, 2012; Watkins, 2012; Yourman, 2003). All learning situations contain both cognitive and emotional elements, which need to be balanced in order to promote a constructive climate. Decisive for the effective acquisition of knowledge is ultimately the supervisor's/teacher's ability to adjust the teaching to the specific conditions of the learning situation (Boalt Boëthius & Ögren, 2000; Glickauf-Hughes, 1994). Greenhalgh (2000) draws attention to both the student's emotional need for meaningfulness and security in the learning situation, and the obstacles to, and defense against, learning and therewith related emotional development. The individual supervisee's learning is affected by earlier favorable or unfavorable experiences of being able to feel trust, and of daring to be dependent on authorities.

Psychotherapy supervision, compared with traditional academic theory courses, is based on a somewhat different form of tuition, which, among other things, has evolved from various forms of self-exploration. The supervisees are not only to incorporate cognitive material, which in itself may be emotionally absorbing, but also to expose parts of their private, emotional sphere to the supervisor. Therapy presupposes that the therapists' inner emotional consistency makes it possible to meet the clients and receive their problems, transference reactions, and projections. At the same time, from an emotional self-awareness, the therapists have to be able to maintain integrity and not be enticed into over-identifying with the clients. In other words, the supervisees are to absorb an "outer" body of knowledge and in addition be encouraged to pay attention to and expose their inner thoughts, feelings, and reactions as they are actualized in the encounter with the clients' emotional problems. Furthermore, they are to make these the objects of scrutiny and reflection with the supervisors. As a next stage in the learning process, supervisees need to be able to process, digest, and integrate the newly-won experiences about themselves and their professional attitude in relation to the clinical situation.

The supervisees are also expected to be able to integrate theoretical knowledge with the clinical work. Paradoxically, a part of the learning situation is also the matter of learning to endure not being able to understand the clients' and one's own reactions, and in this connection to refrain from all too rapidly seeking theoretical explanatory models, which would "save" the supervised therapist from a painful feeling of not mastering or having control over the situation. Psychotherapy supervision is thus a special form of learning, in which the experience-based and emotional components have an important and prominent place beside the cognitive components. In psychotherapy supervision, the therapist is exposed to situations in which old ways of feeling and thinking must be reconsidered, and in which a new state of equilibrium between knowledge and emotion must be attained.

Deepened learning

In-depth learning, that is to say learning which presupposes that learners must reconsider certain parts of themselves – that they have to "reshuffle" their knowledge – is significantly more demanding than learning that merely calls for placing new knowledge into already existing structures. Piaget suggested that it is possible to discern two types of learning, namely assimilative and accommodative learning. Assimilative learning is a matter of arranging new knowledge within existing structures. When the assimilative no longer functions in the encounter with new knowledge, an imbalance arises in which the equilibrium regarding perception, thinking, and action is upset. There then arises a demand to find accommodation for the new knowledge, which means that one must find a new way of interpreting and absorbing that with which one has come into contact (Flavell, 1963). Every attempt to learn something new entails a change, which, despite being desired, also awakens anxiety and insecurity and sometimes a feeling of shame (Salzberger-Wittenberg, Williams, & Osborne, 1999; Shane, 1980, 2010; Festinger, 1957).

A starting point for this dimension of learning is that when we are placed in new situations, earlier experiences are aroused with roots in our earlier life, which sometimes may be associated with insecurity, fear, and anxiety. Supervisees, like all students, harbor, in general, both hope and fear regarding their supervisor and other authority figures involved in a training course. These feelings may also apply in relation to other group members in a supervision group. Helplessness, confusion, and fear of the unknown are the price we have to pay for daring to think and react in new ways and acquire new insights. It is suggested by Salzberger-Wittenberg et al. (1999) that genuine learning must start out from a condition of nonawareness, which on many levels can be felt as painful and sometimes even shameful. This implies the need for balancing the supervisees' positive expectations and joy of learning with the challenges in acquiring new knowledge.

Interactive learning

The dialectic process encompassing both the learners' experiences and their attempts to take in new material through, for example, observations and action, is a starting point for interactive learning. Dewey (1938) does not rule out the teacher's having information to impart to the student but is of the opinion that the information can become lifeless and mechanical if the student does not have to struggle with a problem on a personal level.

One of the first to take advantage of the possibilities to systematically stimulate an interactive learning process based on the individual's own needs and interests was Lewin (1948). The main thrust of his theory is that concrete experience forms the basis for both new learning and re-evaluating earlier knowledge. Direct personal experience gives life and meaning to abstract concepts and makes it possible to test the new situation or these concepts in a tangible reality. Lewin's general principle states that concrete experience is followed by observations, which provide more thorough information on whatever has been experienced. At the same time, the learner reflects over what he or she sees and feels. Thanks to these observations and reflections, it is possible to make generalizations and form concepts. In other words, the principal idea in the interactive and experienced-based learning tradition is that learning, in order to be efficient, must be anchored in a real situation, in which the learner is given the opportunity for input and points of view from different personal levels.

Vygotsky, another pioneer within the field of learning theory, contributed theories that are still of great contemporary relevance (Gindis, 1999). He argued that development in the learning process proceeds from an interpsychological to an intrapsychological stage. Social activity forms the basis for all higher psychological processes. According to Vygotsky, the relational aspect of learning is even a prerequisite for the individual's ability to acquire knowledge on an inner, personal, and higher level. Psychotherapy supervision corresponds in many respects to the aforementioned situations. Linked to aspects of supervision as a social situation are the different roles of supervisee and supervisor and the interdependency between these roles.

Roles, Power, and Dependency

The interplay between supervisor and supervisee is impacted by the basic fact that the two are unequal: they have an asymmetrical role division. The supervisee is dependent on the supervisor, who is the one holding the power. The supervisee's dependency revolves around his or her need to develop into a good therapist, in part with the help of the supervisor's greater experience and expertise. The power that supervisors have is partly based on their experience and theoretical knowledge, and partly on their responsibility for assessing the supervisees' capacities as therapists. In practice, however, the balance between power and dependency can vary and the supervisees can relate to their position of dependency in many ways, as can the supervisors, in relation to their position of power. In her study, Holloway (1984) showed that trainees experienced a substantial shift in power and responsibility as they moved across trainee and counselor roles (Boalt Boëthius & Ögren, 2000; Holloway, 1984; Salzberger-Wittenberg et al., 1999).

The supervisee has a subordinate position in relation to the supervisor but an authoritative one in relation to the client. The formal aspect of the role remains for all parties during the whole process, while the informal dimension must be able to evolve over time. A client becomes less and less dependent on the therapist over time as the therapeutic work progresses. Correspondingly, it is reasonable to expect the supervisee's dependency on the supervisor to decrease over time as well. Openness toward the informal power shift that occurs over time is vital for effective supervision. As pointed out by Salzberger-Wittenberg et al. (1999), a part of this shift in roles can be perceived as embedded in the learning situation of supervision.

The formal role and the experienced role in supervision

While clarity is an important aspect of any role, a certain role ambiguity arises even in the most distinct situations (Oyster, 2000). In a learning situation, this tension is constantly present in the student role – on the one hand, as a wish to be confirmed for already existing knowledge, and on the other hand, as a wish for learning and development, which presupposes that one must expose what one cannot do, or does not know or does not understand. In psychotherapy supervision, these elements become reinforced inasmuch as the individual, in the role of supervisee, is meant to "lift out," examine, and sometimes reconsider parts of his or her own personality.

Psychotherapy supervision aims to lay the foundations for a professional role and a professional identity and thereby purports to provide supervisees with a basic confidence in their future ability to carry out their professional role. The supervisee situation means having to enter the role of supervised psychotherapist. The meaning of the role of supervisee is, in other words, central, but has not, in the context of psychotherapy supervision, been the object of systematic studies. In an early Tavistock publication, Banton (1965) gives, as a starting point for his line of argument about roles, examples of simple and complex role systems. The simple role system could be described as easy to define from its social context, whereas the more complex role systems are constructed from expectations, earlier experiences, and situations that elicit the adoption of certain roles and role identifications. In a similar way, Brown (2000) discusses the concept of role in terms of the formally prescribed and the informally experienced role. In psychotherapy supervision, the discrepancy between the formal, "simple," and the experienced, "complex" role becomes evident and interesting. The role of supervisee implies a learning situation in which parts of one's own personality are exposed, which adds to the complexity.

The supervisee role On a formal level, the role of supervisee in a training situation may appear as well defined and distinct. The pre-knowledge requirements, the goal of the training, content and design, as well as the standards for receiving a passing or better mark, are generally, on an overarching level, well defined and made clear from the beginning. However, the supervision component, because of its complexity, has a tendency to be more diffusely described than the theoretical elements (Boalt

Boëthius & Ögren, 2000). Prospective students probably form an idea of the student role from the formal training plan, but at the same time it is difficult to put themselves into the informal, experience-based role of supervisee.

However, supervisees need to handle many different roles. They are supposed to be both a treating psychotherapist and a student/supervisee (Holloway, 1984; Olk & Friedlander, 1992; Skovholt & Rønnestad, 2003). It is supposed that supervisees are gaining experience of the patient role through their work as psychotherapists and are thus increasing their professional awareness. These different roles may sometimes lead to certain role conflicts and uncertainty (Nelson & Friedlander, 2001; Olk & Friedlander, 1992). A stable working alliance is held to be crucial if the role division is to stand out as clearly and self-evidently as it should for the supervisees. An important precondition for this clarity is that the supervisees have been informed from the start about the assessment procedures being used, as well as the ethical grounds on which their patient work and supervision participation rest (Ladany, 2004).

To change one's role is only in one respect a matter of a process on an uncomplicated cognitive and conscious level. Development, change, and learning always mean a challenge to self-esteem, on both a personal and a professional level. This is because, at a beginner's stage, during a basic training or advanced training course (either of which aims to create a new professional identity), the ability to acquire a new professional skill is challenged. However, at the advanced training level, the previously attained professional identity may also feel threatened (Skovholt & Rønnestad, 1992). Moreover, the experience aspect of the role of supervisee is impacted by the previously discussed exposure in the learning situation, an exposure with regard to knowledge, emotional maturity, and personality (Salzberger-Wittenberg et al., 1999; Szecsödy, 1990).

The supervisor role The supervisor has a responsibility for facilitating learning and for contributing to an enhanced understanding of the clinical work carried out by the supervisees (Aasheim, 2012; Holloway, 1984). The supervisor also has a function as a role model in order to contribute to the development of the supervisee's professional identity (Gordan, 1996; Watkins, 1997). In his or her role, the supervisor must take responsibility for ensuring satisfactory quality in the clinical work of the students, and in connection with this he or she also has the role of gatekeeper (Watkins, 1997). A fundamental aspect of the role as supervisor is that the focus should be placed on how genuine learning can be stimulated in the supervisee. Accordingly, the supervisor should not fall for the temptation of taking over the patient work in critical circumstances but should keep the focus on the supervisee's learning. A prerequisite for this is a supervisory alliance built on trust and confidence and in which the supervisee feels seen and understood.

An important aspect of the role as supervisor is to be attentive to the problems with which the supervisees are wrestling. We have found repeatedly in our studies of group supervision (see Chapter 31) that the supervisor generally underestimates the difficulties and the insecurities that the supervisees feel, in terms of climate and freedom of expression in the supervision (Ögren & Sundin, 2009). Similar findings are seen in other studies (Carlsson, 2012; Strømme, 2012). Supervisors thus have cause to heighten their attention and empathy toward the developmental process in which the supervisees have been placed. The primary task of a supervisor is unquestionably to support and facilitate each and every supervisee's learning process. It is appropriate for supervisors in their roles as supervisors to make a self-disclosure, if it is deemed helpful, thereby deepening the supervisee's understanding of a specific situation. This means that supervisors can give examples of situations similar to those that the supervisee is talking about, as long as they refrain from sharing personal information about themselves and from furthering a personal agenda of no benefit to the supervisees' learning (Aasheim, 2012; Ögren, Boalt Boëthius, & Sundin, 2008).

Power and dependency

An important part of the supervisor's role is to create a climate that is accepting enough for the supervisee to feel free to describe, in the most open and honest way possible, both what the patient and the therapist have said and done (Arlow, 1963). Several studies have shown, though, that this often is not the case. Greben (1991) asserts that if a supervisee does not give an accurate account of what has happened in therapy, the supervision has failed in a crucial way. Through interviews with four psychotherapy trainees, Hantoot (2000) examined what supervisees purposely left out or changed in the account of the therapy session that they gave in supervision. The examples Hantoot described point to how the supervisees were afraid of their supervisors' criticism and therefore held back much of their own interventions and emotional reactions. One supervisee also talked about how she had deliberately held back information about part of what had happened during her sessions because she did not want the supervisor to have full insight into her work. In this way, she could, as a supervisee, retain control over her work. Another example was of a supervisee who did not mention the advice she had given her patient because she thought her supervisor would disapprove. The examples also showed that when the supervisees were more secure in their roles it was easier to recount what had occurred in the therapy session and not worry about the supervisor's judgment. In general, these studies underscore the importance of developing a good learning environment. To do so, supervisors must be aware of supervisees' vulnerability and possible tendencies toward overadaption and dependency or, at the opposite pole, resistance toward dependency and fear of losing their integrity (Carlsson, 2012; Strømme, 2012).

A supervision process goes through various phases. As the supervisee increases in knowledge and maturity, it is natural that the tone becomes more collegial and that the supervision begins to have more and more symmetrical qualities. As the supervisee's knowledge and ability to take responsibility for the professional work increase, the supervisor can loosen the strings on control and oversight and instead affirm the supervisee's increased ability to manage the work situation by himself or herself. There are reasons to compare the supervisor role with the parenting role in some respects. First, it is a matter of supporting, helping, and teaching, and then of being present in the training phase. The supervisor, like the parent, must be on hand when the liberation takes place: "I want to use what I've learned and to try doing it my way." Curiosity, tolerance, and a safety net need to be offered at this point. A supervision situation is always embedded in an organizational context and framework, which has different psychological implications for the learning situation. This will be elaborated in the following section.

The Organizational Framework and Learning

Organizational frames of relevance for the learning process in psychotherapy supervision are for example the contract between the supervisee and the supervisor as well as between the host organization and the supervisee and the supervisor, respectively. Moreover, it includes time frames, routines for evaluations and examination requirements. When it comes to group supervision, the organizational framework also includes the group's composition, size, and inter-group relationships. Supervision that takes place in a training context requires regular staff meetings with the supervisors and the course tutors.

The importance of the organizational frames with regard to clarity and explicitness in the learning situation, is emphasized by several authors (Boalt Boëthius & Ögren, 2000; Greenhalgh, 2000; Ögren, Boalt Boëthius, & Olsson, 2008; Proctor, 2008). Proctor proposes that explicitness regarding the organizational framework, including the contract between the supervisor and the responsible institution (as well as the one between the supervisor and the supervisee or the supervision group), constitutes the essential basis on which supervision works. Proctor maintains that a mutual responsibility exists between the supervisor and the supervisee, in which both parties must be informed of their respective undertakings. Greenhalgh (2000) points out that a prerequisite for the emotional containing of difficult feelings in the supervisee or supervisees is that the organization serves and strengthens the teachers and supervisors in their containing functions. Within the organizational frame, the training institution should assist with a clear, "load-bearing" structure, as in being able to offer the supervisor an opportunity for support and scope for reflection about the supervision process.

Supervisors should receive the kind of support from their organization that makes it possible to help supervisees tolerate a certain amount of uncertainty and noncontrol, so-called negative capability (French, 2001). The learning in supervision is not only about taking on a specific technique, but just as much about being able to deal with complex situations, which can make the supervisee feel lost and powerless. In one of our studies, the results indicated that the supervisor's and the supervision group's ability to harbor the group's process and internal dialogue affected how the supervised therapists could strengthen their ability to harbor emotionally charged patient material in a therapy situation (Ögren, Jonsson, & Sundin, 2005).

Ekstein and Wallerstein (1958, 1977) developed the concept of the "clinical rhombus" to describe the complexity of intrapsychological and interpersonal problems in the supervision situation. The model refers to the interaction between the patient's problems, the supervisee's training institution, and the clinical institution. Szecsödy (1990) extended this model and suggested that the interaction between patient, therapist, and supervisor is mutually influenced by each party and, moreover, influenced by other interdependent relationships. Based on models for individual supervision as well as on studies of small work groups, a framework for supervision has been described by Boalt Boëthius (1993). The basic idea is to call attention to the degree to which the supervision is supported by an adequate organizational framework and how this concordance (or lack of concordance) between frame conditions and core content affects the supervisor–supervisee relationship (see Chapter 31).

Contract for learning and supervision

A clear contract between the different parties in psychotherapy supervision, regardless of area of specialty, is not infrequently a determining factor for the supervisory work. The significance of clear agreements in the form of a contract has been emphasized by several authors and researchers (Holloway, 1995; Norcross & Halgin, 1997; Osborn & Davis, 1996). Stiwne (1993) pointed out that the contract, among other things, should clarify supervision's primary task, purpose, and limits, as well as the participants' various roles, responsibilities, and tasks in relation to the goal. The agreement reached should function as a protection for the weaker party, in relationship to the supervisor's power and influence. It should also have a stabilizing effect on the learning process. The contract should be the backdrop against which the parties can lean, and against which various problems that come up can be examined and understood.

To facilitate supervision and to secure the best relationship between the supervisor and the supervisee, Stiwne underlines the need to develop a contractual relationship, as it is described by Szasz (1965). This is characterized by solidarity with the task, mutual demands, a respect for boundaries, and an acceptance of differences, among other things. Szasz described two kinds of status relationships that should be avoided. One is characterized by seeing the supervisor as an expert who dominates and the supervisee as a subordinate who idealizes the supervisor. The other is characterized by a supervisee who is the dominant one while the supervisor idealizes the supervisee.

Various pitfalls can exist in which supervisors allow themselves to be enticed onto paths where they risk losing the grounding that should come with their designated role. Theoretically sophisticated supervisees can sometimes challenge the supervisor to discuss theory in order to avoid confrontation with their uncertainty about how to manage their role as a professional helper, which is the goal of supervision work, strictly speaking. If supervisors let themselves get pulled into such avoidance strategies, the balance is upset in the supervision work. A supervisor must never veer from the boundaries that have to be respected, based on the contract that stipulates each and every party's role and responsibilities.

Routines for evaluations How evaluations of the ongoing supervision are to be made can be seen as a part of the initial contract settlement. Reaching clear agreements about how evaluation of supervision will take place and how often it will be done creates stability as part of the framework (Boalt Boëthius & Ögren, 2009; Falender & Shafranske, 2004; Ögren, Boalt Boëthius, & Olsson, 2008). According to one study (Hoffman, Hill, Holmes, & Freitas, 2005), supervisors were more likely to give positive feedback than to bring up things up that were disturbing and troublesome. They felt it was difficult to give feedback on the supervisees' problems in handling their clinical situations, as well as their personal and professional issues. As a result, this type of difficult feedback was often given more or less indirectly and thereby had a varying degree of effectiveness. Supervisors may also find it tempting to give evaluations that were far too positive in order to avoid difficult confrontations and to put themselves in a good light as supervisors. Needless to say, it is of great value for supervisors to be brave, honest, and conscientious when giving feedback.

If supervisees are coddled into thinking there are no problems, they can miss out on an essential part of a necessary learning process. Here again a clear organizational framework is needed in order for the supervisor to know which evaluation criteria must be used.

Examination demands What is expected of the supervisee in the learning situation is an important point of departure for both the supervisor and the supervisee. This is an essential aspect of the contract and organizational frame. Samec (1995), in his study of failure in psychotherapy training, illuminates the trauma, for both supervisees and supervisors, of failing a student. An individual supervisee's dissatisfaction with the supervision and complaints about the examination requirements are not infrequently expressions of resistance toward seeing his or her own difficulties. Stumbling blocks and conflicts may also have their origins in the supervisor's personality and blind spots (Szecsödy, 1990).

Supervisors have a delicate task. They are authority figures but they also need to be welcoming and understanding. They should be ready and able to suggest ways of learning from mistakes while they refrain from taking a condemning role. As if this balancing act were not difficult enough, they must also handle the role of gatekeeper and make sure the supervisees stand up for good quality in their patient work. Based on our experience, we see it as absolutely crucial for this work to have stable organizational support. Administrators or course tutors should provide clear information and supportive educational input and serve the interests of all parties: the patient, the supervisees, and the supervisor (Skovholt & Rønnestad, 1992). A lack of stable support at any level of the system could pose the same problem at some other level, as there needs to be consistency in the system as a whole.

The assessment situation in supervision is in many regards paradoxical, a matter that both the supervisor and the organization must be able to handle with foresight (Falender & Shafranske, 2004; Watkins, 1997). Right from the start, the organization should provide clear information to both the supervisees and the supervisor about the goals of the supervision in order for the learning process not to suffer (and again to show clear support). Supervision taking place as part of an education program differs from supervision in other contexts by having specific frame conditions that define goals and content, examination criteria and criteria for passing, as well as time frames for the supervisees' treatment work. Supervision that is part of an education program has an inherent dilemma that must be addressed and managed correctly, namely that the supervisees are being asked to expose their difficulties to the supervisor at the same time as they are being assessed and working to convince the supervisor that they are competent to pass.

It is highly likely that the assessment aspect of the supervision affects the power relationship between the supervisor and the supervisee. A "fail" result is difficult not only for the supervisee but also for supervisors. The supervisor obviously has the responsibility for assuring that future professionals from various education levels are "up to snuff" and will be able do a satisfactory job. It also happens that students, as is their full right, react negatively if someone whom they feel is doing poor work "slips through." They begin to question the value of their own knowledge and hard work.

Setting a fail mark is also sometimes necessary if established professionals are to be able to take responsibility for the next generation's professional competence.

Clarity in norms and demands from the course tutors must form the basis for protecting each individual's interests. Signs of problems should be shared and discussed with the course tutors at an early stage so that possible assistance (such as increased supervision) can be put into place. To receive a fail mark can be devastating. The only workable way we can see of confronting this matter is to be as clear as possible when informing presumptive supervisees and their supervisors about the requirements for a passing mark and about the routines of the course tutors. Such a pool of information can then form the basis for measures to be taken when a student is deemed to be in the risk zone for a failing mark.

Fail marks can usually be attributed to a high rate of absence, where the supervisee has missed too much of the supervision and needs to make a fresh start; or to an unsatisfactory level of participation, where the supervisee has attended but has not wanted to speak openly about his or her patient work or other difficulties. However, the student might also have too many personal problems or be unsuited for the profession. In this context, it is important to remember that all parties involved have a responsibility to make sure that a good supervision climate is maintained. Everyone must keep it from getting to the point where supervisees only pick what they want to share in supervision, while they hide or distort mistakes and difficulties (Ruskin & Greben, 1994; Samec, 1995; Strømme, 2012).

Learning in an organizational context

To examine how psychotherapy supervision can be seen in terms of the learning situation within the organization as a whole, we can draw parallels to the concepts organizational learning (Levitt & March, 1998) and learning organizations (Senge, 1990). A basic premise of this thinking is that the desire to learn is a natural trait in all individuals. When we run a psychotherapeutic service and cooperate in teams, learning is going to take place. Organizations in and of themselves are obviously not capable of learning in a literal sense, but individuals within an organization can do so and thereby contribute to organizational learning and development. However, supervision within one part of an organization will be of benefit to the entire organization only if the culture of the organization is characterized by openness and interest in stimulating learning. Organizations that do not have learning as one of their guidelines in their personnel advancement policies risk losing people who have ambitions to develop further, which then also undermines the organizations' ability to learn and grow.

Learning Climate in Supervision

It is of utmost importance to create a favorable climate that stimulates learning and equally so to have participants in supervision who have a personal motivation to learn (Ögren & Jonsson, 2003; Wheeler & Richards, 2007). To capture the favorable factors for a creative learning climate is not an easy task. The supervisee's personal qualities and earlier relationship to learning situations and authorities carry weight. Likewise, the supervisor's ability to find an appropriate way to understand and to relate to the supervisee is significant.

We cannot simply state that a friendly and conflict-avoiding climate is the same as an optimal learning climate. If participants want to learn something about themselves and to be able to evolve in their professional roles, it is necessary for them to bear hearing different views about their work. They are thereby confronted with new angles and different ways of looking at things. At certain stages they are forced to face the fact that the old equilibrium is being shaken and that cognitive dissonance is arising in its aftermath.

It seems that most participants experience the climate for cooperation as somewhat awkward in the beginning but that they often gradually become more comfortable. Also, it seems that supervisors do not always realize how unsure a supervisee can feel (Boalt Boëthius, Ögren, Sjøvold, & Sundin, 2005; Carlsson, 2012; Hill, Sullivan, Knox, & Scholsser, 2007; Ögren, Apelman, & Klawitter, 2001; Strømme, 2012). A reaffirming intervention from the supervisor often suffices. It is probably just as important for a supervisee as for a patient to feel intuitively that the person in whom he or she is putting trust during a perhaps painful developmental process has a "good handle on the situation."

Learning resistance

As a supervisor and teacher it is important to recognize that an individual's desire to learn in most cases goes hand-in-hand with a discomfort and shame about discovering and exposing what he or she does not know. Feelings of shame are often at the root of a resistance to learning and a fear of exposing a need for help (Ladany, Klinger, & Kulp, 2011). When supervisees withhold or distort material it often stems from discomfort about exposing their shortcomings and insecurities (Talbot, 1995; Yourman, 2003; Yourman & Farber, 1996). Other forms of resistance described in the literature are submission, self-depreciation, helplessness, and projection (Bauman, 1972) as well as flattery, redefining the supervisor's power, concealing problems, and distorting what actually happens in the therapy session (Kadushin, 1976).

Another way of thinking about resistance in supervision has been described by Liddle (1986), who defined supervision resistance as a defensive response to a perceived threat. According to Liddle, some possible sources of threat in supervision include evaluation anxiety, performance anxiety, deficits in the supervisory relationship, and personal issues of the supervisee. This last aspect has been taken further by Glickauf-Hughes (1994), who, by means of a developmental model, has explored some underlying issues that may cause resistance to learning. These issues are primarily related to the task of forming a professional identity and include autonomy and control, insufficiently developed sense of self or identity, lack of basic trust, shame, and narcissism (see also Carlsson, 2012; Strømme, 2012).

We might suppose that therapists with more experience in the profession or on a higher level of education would find it less threatening to open up about their working methods and degree of knowledge. However, based on our research, the opposite appears to be the case. The more knowledge and experience therapists have, the more they tend to be tied to a professional self-esteem that can be threatened, thus giving them for a period of time a new kind of vulnerability (Boalt Boëthius & Ögren, 2000). Our conclusion is that despite age and level of education, and no matter how great their motivation is to learn something new, they can be stricken with feelings of discomfort when they are forced to question old ideas that they have taken for granted and forced to discover new dimensions. Therefore, just as we may well underestimate the supervisees anxiety, it is possible that supervisors also engage in avoidance behaviors so as to minimize various threats (e.g., by declining to let the supervisee observe their therapy).

Another element of the picture is that professionals in their roles as supervisors can also feel exposed in different ways, which can lead them to falter in their interplay with the supervisees. One such situation takes place when a supervisor forms an alliance with a supervisee and becomes more of a friend than a supervisor. Another instance can be found when the supervisor feels threatened by a supervisee and puts up a defense by, for example, trying to trump the supervisee through excessive theorizing or distancing (Ögren et al., 2005). In this way, supervisors can contribute to the buildup of various forms of resistance, as has been discussed in relation to countertransference aspects, matching between supervisor and supervisee, and the personal characteristics of the supervisor. Such a course of events can lead to power struggles or to a complete standstill, so that the supervision must be terminated (Glickauf-Hughes, 1994; Ruskin & Greben, 1994).

Watkins (2010) pinpointed three types of supervisor resistance, based on personal shortcomings in the supervisor that make him or her unable to engage in an authentic relatedness with psychotherapy supervisees. These are autonomy-based resistance, shame-based resistance, and narcissism-based resistance. Watkins puts these resistances within a developmental context and sees them as particularly problematic for supervisors new to the role of supervising. "While these resistances can subside over time, they still have a decidedly negative impact on the supervision experience and can restrain supervisee learning and growth as a therapist. Self-analysis, psychotherapy, psychotherapy supervision coursework, and the supervision-of-supervision are presented as methods by which supervisors' characterological resistances can be attacked" (Watkins, 2010, p. 239).

Supervisor style

A decisive factor for learning and development in supervision is the supervisor's skill as a teacher and supervisor. As mentioned earlier, there are different ways to view the function that the supervisor can and should have (Scaife & Inskipp, 2001). Supervisors are governed in their ways of shaping the supervision by the nature of the work situation in which the supervisees are involved, as well as by the expectations tied to the assignment. Supervisors' own professional and personal life experiences have an impact on the supervision, as does their theoretical orientation (Ögren, Boalt Boëthius, & Olsson, 2008).

Several of our studies have shown that supervisors with relatively inexperienced supervisees should use a more supportive teaching style in the beginning. Beginners need more concrete help and support in order to understand what they do or do not know, and how they can expand their skill. When they have built up a foundation of knowledge, the supervisor can be more process oriented and stimulate the students to put forth their own points of view about the case being discussed. Our findings showed that the most appreciated supervisors were those who were straightforward, expressed empathy, and held an autonomous position that conveyed their care about how things turned out for the students and their clients (Ögren, Boalt Boëthius, & Olsson, 2008). The supervisor's ability to be a containing authority, as opposed to being too nice and accepting, was of significance. We have also found that the supervision turned problematic if the supervisors became entirely too authoritarian and rigid and only promoted a line they believed to be "the absolute truth." For example, the supervisees' demands on themselves to perform increased if the supervisor's style was authoritarian, which led to a stifling of their creativity.

Containing environment for the supervisors

In the context of these various dynamics, a functioning forum that provides opportunities for mirroring of the respective supervisor's current supervision situation has proven to be of great significance. In the context of education, the course tutors can create a collegial meeting place for supervisors where they have a sufficient sense of security and sufficient freedom from defending their prestige to allow them to discuss the problems they encounter in their respective supervision groups. Just as supervisees are assumed to be understood by their supervisors, the supervisors also need a forum where they can take up their concerns and shortcomings in their work and where they can be open for new angles, ideas, and support from colleagues. The point is that the supervisees must feel confidence in their supervisors and the supervisors in their course tutors (Ögren, Boalt Boëthius, & Olsson, 2008).

The course tutors should be in regular contact with the supervisors to ensure that they will be notified should a problematic situation arise. In a similar manner, the course tutors should be careful to maintain the trust of the supervisors. This is a daunting balancing act that once again rests on the organizational framework and policy. The middle position of the course tutors requires them to show respect for the trust that they receive from the different parties and not take sides directly and make judgment, but instead encourage communication between the parties in a conflict. As the ones responsible, they should take care to retain the trust of both parties to be able to function as a moderator and to help in clearing up problematic situations.

Supervisors' needs for mirroring and reflecting around their own roles and work in supervision exist outside educational institutions as well, but it is most likely easier to create this type of forum within the framework of an education program. At the same time, we would like to emphasize the importance of the recommendations put forth by several authors. They point out that supervisors should be provided with this type of forum together with their supervisor colleagues to ensure that the dilemmas and difficulties they can encounter can be elucidated in a collegial context (Baruch, 2004; Guy, 2000).

Supervision and Learning in Different Treatment Traditions

In earlier sections of this chapter, the focus was placed primarily on general aspects, when it comes to the learning process in psychotherapy supervision. However, it is obvious that every treatment tradition calls for a specific focus and content in order to increase the therapists' knowledge and to enhance their professionalism within the area in question (Henderson, 2009; Watkins, 1997).

Both *the cognitive and the behavioral therapeutic (CBT) perspectives* permeate CBT supervision (Lewis, 2005; Liese & Beck, 1997). Teaching in supervision focuses here, among other things, on problematizing cognitive patterns and modifying the non-functional attitudes and notions that have negative consequences for the individual. Many representatives of CBT have asserted that the supervision should be set up in parallel to the treatment to the greatest extent possible. They thus suggest approximately the same structure for a supervision session as for a treatment session. According to this approach, the supervisors and supervisees are expected to set up a problem list and agenda for the supervision, formulate goals, and enter into a Socratic dialogue and behavioral experiment using several approaches in parallel with the principles for treatment within CBT (Liese & Beck, 1997).

Teaching in supervision and teaching in general overlap with each other and the supervisor can in many respects be seen as a teacher. What seems to prevail today as a recommendation for effective learning in supervision within the CBT area (Bennett-Levy, 2006; James, Milne, Blackburn, & Armstrong, 2006; Milne & James, 2005) can be described as follows: supervision should be built up on the basis on a number of steps, namely (1) definition of the supervisee's learning needs, (2) the developmental potential of the supervisee, and (3) assessment of the supervisee's learning needs. Furthermore, it is deemed essential for the supervisor to be able to listen, observe, give feedback, support, challenge, counter-argue, confront, evaluate, and, finally, provide training opportunities, for example in the form of educational role-play.

The *systemic treatment model* is represented among other contexts within the areas of couples and family therapy (Burnham, 1993). The basic view behind the treatment is that all individuals are part of interplay and systems. The understanding that we as individuals can gain about a situation is created based on a system of relating to the people around us, primarily to those closest to us. Accordingly, systemic psychotherapy directs its focus toward existing mutual relationships, in terms of understanding and action. The understanding of social interplay and communicative processes is accentuated. The teaching goals within this area focus in part on the development of an interview technique, in order to help the therapists in question to give their clients an opportunity to enter into and to experience different positions in an interplay and to witness the consequences thereof. The purpose of both the treatment and the supervision is to bring to the fore a glimpse of a new interplay scenario. Therapists are expected to focus on their own reflections about their ability to think, feel, and act in a systemic respect during supervision. Similarities and differences in relationship to other dimensions of systems are taken into account.

Psychodynamic-oriented supervision focuses on both manifested and latent content and process. The therapist's alliance with the client is put into focus, and likewise how different stages of the treatment process take shape in terms of factual material, as well as changes in the client's life situation. An important premise is that psychic symptoms are seen as meaning-bearing and understandable. They arise as a result of the individual's striving to deal with and resolve contradictory and problematic relationships and inner conflicts, often on an unconscious level. The goal in psychodynamic psychotherapy is therefore not primarily to arrive at a relief of the symptoms

– even if this is also important – but rather to help the client to understand and to work through the inner conflicts that form the basis for the various symptoms. Last but not least, the supervisee's emotional reactions are to be taken into consideration as a source of information for a deeper understanding of the client material at hand as well as for the developmental process that the supervisee is going through.

In psychodynamic supervision, the participants also work with different kinds of parallel phenomena or mirroring (Searles, 1955; Sumerel, 1994). These phenomena are also common for work in the psychiatric ward with patients who have severe personality disorders. According to this approach, many conflicts, for example, between different members of a therapy team or between a therapy unit and the units around it, can be understood from a psychodynamic perspective. Patients can unconsciously expose different sides of their split personalities to different actors in the therapeutic system, which can lead to notions of omnipotence or other extremes in the personnel. This course of events can be highly destructive if the personnel are not aware of their function as helpbearers of the patients' inner lives. Such developments can create serious problems on many levels, not only for supervision.

Reporting in supervision

The interplay between a client and a therapist can be recorded in various ways with different dimensions of cooperation and technical aids. Without a doubt, the video- and audio-recorded conversation captures an important dimension, whereas video recordings also capture nonverbal material (Haggerty & Hilsenroth, 2011; Sorli et al., 1999). Within cognitive-behavioral psychotherapy, excerpts from video-recorded sessions are the most common form of documentation used in supervision. In psychodynamic psychotherapy supervision, the use of video-recorded sessions in combination with verbal reports, has increased substantially. A verbal or written account of a meeting with a client captures yet other aspects of the supervisee's experience of the session as a complement to video-recorded sessions. Documenting what happens in a supervised psychotherapy is important not only with respect to learning but also with respect to risk management and possible legal processes (Recupero & Samara, 2007). However, there are not many studies that have examined which type of supervision reports contribute best to a favorable learning situation on different education levels.

Supervisor and Teacher Competence

Supervisor competence

It is neither realistic nor fair for supervisors to assume that they are good supervisors based solely on their long experiences as psychotherapists(Bernard & Goodyear, 2009). The shift in focus from the role as therapist to the role as supervisor can be difficult to handle, especially for new supervisors (Holloway, 1992; Sundin et al., 2008). The supervisor must be able to stay focused on making it easier for the supervisees to conduct their work. In certain supervision assignments, the task can be to function as moderator, helping the supervisees put their thoughts into words. In other supervision assignments, the task can be to relate to an entire treatment organization. The supervisor's role is tied to challenges on different levels and must be founded on competence.

Awareness of the necessity for specific education courses on the pedagogical aspects of supervision has become more and more prevalent. A precondition for a satisfactory supervision effort is that the supervisor has solid pedagogical knowledge with respect to how to help the supervisees to develop their professional competence so that their knowledge of and their confidence in their own ability are enhanced. To supervise is not primarily a matter of telling supervisees what to do, but rather of guiding them so that they can find their own style in their professional role. "Super"-"vision" can therefore mean to give supervisees a vision from a standpoint above them, but then they have to see what part of the vision is useful to them. The supervisor's experience and competence with regard to the organizational culture and the treatment orientation in question are important foundational factors.

Currently, it is seen as unquestionable that high-quality supervision calls for supervisors who have completed an education program with a focus on the specific pedagogical methods needed for supervision. In the Nordic countries, education programs for supervisors who are preparing for supervision of psychotherapists have been in operation for several decades (Ögren, Boalt Boëthius, & Sundin, 2008; Sundin et al., 2008),and such programs have become mandatory in order to practice as a psychotherapy supervisor. The pedagogical challenge the supervisors faces is in knowing how to help younger colleagues find their identity and role, and be aware of the difference between role as a psychotherapist and role as a supervisor.

Teacher competence

We do not automatically become a supervisor or a teacher, and certainly not a good teacher, based on our having solid knowledge and experience within a certain domain. At the university level in Sweden, it was previously not unusual for researchers to be forced to teach a certain number of classes, even though they had no pedagogical background. Granted, it was of great value for university students to learn about ongoing research and the most up-to-date research findings. However, the problem was that the researchers were frequently without interest or knowledge about teaching and had no idea of how to prepare a lecture so that it would stimulate students' interest.

As teachers and supervisors we sometimes have the privilege of meeting highly gifted students, who with all probability are going to be better clinicians, supervisors, and researchers than we ourselves have ever been. A part of the task of a supervisor and an educator is to be able to help these supervisees to find their own style and to believe in it (Watkins, 1992). Just as is the case for a good psychotherapist or a good parent, part of our task as experienced and well-educated professionals is to be capable of feeling joy about the next generation, who, perhaps partly thanks to our efforts, will be profoundly successful within our "preciously guarded area."

Conclusions

Some main prerequisites for a solid learning environment and optimal learning climate are, according to our experiences and research, a competent and supporting organizational context and framework. Moreover, the supervisors' pedagogic skills and style, as well as awareness of the role balance between the supervisor and the supervisee, are of vital importance.

An increased awareness regarding the pedagogical competence of university clinical teachers and supervisors has emerged over time. Lately, supervisor training courses have gained recognition on an international level. In some countries (e.g., Sweden), the completion of a basic pedagogical training program is required for those who seek to qualify for a position as associate professor or university lecturer in the field (Biggs & Tang, 2007). The main factors we want to pinpoint are thus supervisors' pedagogical competence and psychotherapeutic knowledge. Both course administrators and supervisors are helped by an awareness of how to cultivate appropriate organizational support.

References

Aasheim, L. (2012). *Practical clinical supervision for counselors: An experiential guide.* New York, NY: Springer Publishing Company, LLC.

Arlow, J. A. (1963). The supervisory situation. *Journal of American Psychoanalytic Association, 11*, 576–594.

Banton, M. (1965). *Roles. An introduction to the study of social relations.* London, UK: Tavistock Publications.

Barnett, M. (1998). *Roles: An introduction to the study of social relations.* London, UK: Tavistock Publications.

Baruch, V. (2004). Self-care for therapists: Prevention of compassion fatigue and burnout. *Psychotherapy in Australia, 10*(4), 64–68.

Bauman, W. F. (1972). Games counselor trainees play: Dealing with trainee resistance. *Counselor Education and Supervision, 11*, 251–256.

Bennett-Levy, J. (2006). Therapist skills: A cognitive model of their acquisitions and refinement. *Behavioural and Cognitive Psychotherapy, 34*, 57–58.

Bernard, J., & Goodyear, R. (2009). *Fundamentals of clinical supervision.* Boston, MA: Pearson.

Biggs, J. B., & Tang, C. (2007). *Teaching for quality learning at university.* London, UK: Open University Press.

Boalt Boëthius, S. (1993). Grupphandledning och samspelsprocesser [Group supervision and interaction processes]. In D. Stiwne (Ed.), *Perspektiv på handledning [Perspectives on supervision]* (pp. 160–188). Stockholm, Sweden: Natur & Kultur.

Boalt Boëthius, S., & Ögren, M.-L. (2000). Role patterns in group supervision. *The Clinical Supervisor, 19*, 45–69.

Boalt Boëthius, S., Ögren, M.-L., Sjøvold, E., & Sundin, E. (2005). Experiences of group culture and patterns of interaction in psychotherapy supervision groups. *The Clinical Supervisor, 23*, 101–121.

Boalt Boëthius, S. & Ögren, M-L. (2009). Organizational framework and psychotherapy supervision. Dynamics within and outside the lab. *Proceedings from the 6th GRASP conference, Lund University. May, pp.* 53–66.

Brown, R. (2000). *Group processes. Dynamics within and between groups.* Oxford, UK: Blackwell Publisher.

Burnham, J. (1993). Systemic supervision. The evolution of reflexivity in the context of the supervisory relationship. *Human Systems, 4*, 349–381.

Carlsson, J. (2012). Research on psychotherapists' professional development during and after training. *Nordic Psychology, 64*, 150–167.

Carroll, M. (2001). *Counselling supervision: Theory, skills and practice.* London, UK: Continuum.

Dewey, J. (1938, 1997). *Experience and education.* New York, NY: Simon and Schuster.

Ekstein, R., & Wallerstein, R. S. (1958, 1977). *The teaching and learning of psychotherapy* (2nd ed.). New York, NY: International Universities Press.

Falender, C. A., & Shafranske, E. P. (2004). *Clinical supervision. A competency-based approach.* Washington, DC: APA.

Festinger, W. (1957). *A theory of cognitive dissonance.* Stanford, CA: Stanford University Press.

Flavell, J. H. (1963). *The developmental psychology of Jean Piaget.* Princeton, NJ: van Nostrand Company Inc.

Flemming, J., & Benedek, T. (1966). *A method of clinical teaching.* New York, NY: Grune & Stratton.

French, R. (2001). Negative capability. Managing the confusion uncertainty of change. *Journal of Organizational Change Management, 13*, 480–492.

Gindis, B. (1999). Vygotsky's vision: Reshaping the practice of special education for the 21st century. *Remedial and Special Education, 20*(6), 32–64.

Glickauf-Hughes, C. (1994). Characterological resistances in psychotherapy supervision. *Psychotherapy, 31*, 58–66.

Gonsalvez, C., & Milne, D. (2010). Clinical supervisor training in Australia: A review of current problems and possible solutions. *Australian Psychologist, 45*, 233–242.

Gordan, K. (1996). *Psychotherapy supervision in education, clinical practice, and institutions.* New York, NY: Jason Aronson.

Gray, L. A., Ladany, N., Walker, J. A., & Ancis, J. R. (2001). Psychotherapy trainees' experience of counterproductive events in supervision. *Journal of Counseling Psychology, 48*, 371–383.

Greben, S. F. (1991). Interpersonal aspects of the supervision of individual psychotherapy. *American Journal of Psychotherapy, 45*, 306–316.

Greenhalgh, P. (2000). *Emotional growth and learning.* New York, NY: Routledge.

Guy, J. D. (2000). Holding the holding environment together: Self-psychology and psychotherapist care. *Professional Psychology, Research and Practice, 31*(3), 351–352.

Haggerty, G., & Hilsenroth, M. H. (2011). The use of video in psychotherapy supervision. *British Journal of Psychotherapy, 27*, 193–210.

Hansen, T. I., Svendsen, B., & Hagen, R. (2010). Worry related to clinical training of Norwegian psychology students. *Journal of the Norwegian Psychological Association, 47*, 505–510.

Hantoot, M. S. (2000). Lying in psychotherapy supervision: Why residents say one thing and do another. *Academic Psychiatry, 24*, 179–187.

Hawkins, P., & Shohet, R. (1989, 2012). *Supervision in the helping professions.* Philadelphia, PA: Open University Press.

Henderson, P. (2009). *Supervision training. Issues and approaches.* London, UK: Karnac Books.

Hill, C. E., Sullivan, C., Knox, S., & Scholsser, L. Z. (2007). Becoming psychotherapists: Experiences of novice trainees in a beginning graduate class. *Psychotherapy: Theory, Research, Practice, Training, 44*, 434–439.

Hoffman, M. A., Hill, C. E., Holmes, S. E., & Freitas, G. F. (2005). Supervisor perspective on the process and outcome of giving easy, difficult, and no feedback to supervisees. *Journal of Counseling Psychology, 52*, 3–13.

Holloway, E. (1984). Outcome evaluation in supervision research. *The Counseling Psychologist, 12*, 166–174.

Holloway, E. (1992). Supervision: A way of teaching and learning. In S. Brown & R. Lent (Eds.), *Handbook of counseling psychology* (2nd ed., pp. 177–214). New York, NY: Wiley.

Holloway, E. (1995). *Clinical supervision: A systems approach.* London, UK: Sage.

Jacobsson, G., Lindgren, T., & Hau, S. (2012). Rites of passages – Novice students experiences of becoming psychotherapists. *Nordic Psychology, 64*, 192–202.

James, I. A., Milne, D. L., Blackburn, I.-M., & Armstrong, P. (2006). Conduction successful supervision: Novel elements towards an integrative approach. *Behavioural and Cognitive Psychotherapy, 35*, 191–200.

Kadushin, A. (1976). *Supervision in social work.* New York, NY: Columbia University Press.

Ladany, N. (2004). Psychotherapy supervision: What lies beneath. *Psychotherapy Research, 14*, 1–19.

Ladany, N., Klinger, R., & Kulp, K. (2011). Therapist shame: Implications for therapy and supervision. In R. L. Dearing & J. P. Tagney (Eds.), *Shame in the therapy hour* (pp. 307–323). Washington, DC: APA.

Levitt, B., & March, J. (1998). Organizational learning. *Annual Review of Sociology, 14*, 319–338.

Lewin, K. (1948). *Resolving social conflict: Selected papers on group dynamics.* New York, NY: Harper & Row.

Lewis, I. (2005). The supervision of cognitive and behavioural psychotherapist. *BABCP Magazine: Supervision Supplement, 33*(2), 1–4.

Liddle, B. (1986). Resistance in supervision: A response to perceived threat. *Counselor Education and Supervision, 26*, 117–127.

Liese, B. S., & Beck, J. S. (1997). Cognitive therapy supervision. In C. E. Watkins (Ed.), *Handbook of psychotherapy supervision*(pp. 114–133). New York, NY: Wiley.

Milne, D., & James, I. (2002). The observed impact of training on competence in clinical supervision. *British Journal of Clinical Psychology, 41*, 55–72.

Milne, D., & James, I. (2005). A systemic review of effective cognitive-behavioural supervision. *British Journal of Clinical Psychology, 39*, 111–129.

Nelson, M. L., & Friedlander, M. L. (2001). A close look at conflictual supervisory relationships: The trainee's perspective. *Journal of Counseling Psychology, 48*, 384–395.

Nielsen, J., Haugaard Jacobsen, C., & Bork Mathiesen, B. (2012). Novice supervisors' task and training – A descriptive study. *Nordic Psychology, 64*, 182–191.

Norcross, J. C., & Halgin, R. P. (1997). Integrative approaches to psychotherapy supervision. In C. E. Watkins (Ed.), *Handbook of psychotherapy supervision* (pp. 203–223). New York, NY: John Wiley & Sons.

Ögren, M.-L., Apelman, A., & Klawitter, M. (2001). The group in psychotherapy supervision. *The Clinical Supervisor, 20*, 147–176.

Ögren, M.-L., Boalt Boëthius, S., & Olsson, U. (2008). Organizational structure and framework. A case study of Swedish training programs in psychotherapy. *Organisational and Social Dynamics, 8*(22), 256–278.

Ögren, M.-L., Boalt Boëthius, S., & Sundin, E. (2008). From psychotherapist to supervisor. The significance of group format and supervisors' function as role models in psychotherapy supervision. *Nordic Psychology, 60*, 3–23.

Ögren, M.-L., & Jonsson, C.-O. (2003). Psychotherapy skill following group supervision according to supervisees and supervisors. *The Clinical Supervisor, 22*, 35–59.

Ögren, M.-L., Jonsson, C.-O., & Sundin, E. (2005). Group supervision in psychotherapy. The relationship between focus, group climate and perceived attained skill. *Journal of Clinical Psychology, 61*, 373–389.

Ögren, M.-L., & Sundin, E. (2009). Group supervision in psychotherapy. Main results from a Swedish project on psychotherapy supervision in a group format. *British Journal of Guidance and Counselling, 37*, 129–139.

Olk, M., & Friedlander, M. (1992). Trainees' experiences of role conflict and role ambiguity in supervisory relationships. *Journal of Counseling Psychology, 39*, 389–397.

Orlinsky, D. E., Botermans, J. F., & Rønnestad, M. H. (2001). Towards an empirically grounded model of psychotherapy training: Four thousand therapists rate influences on their development. *Australian Psychologist, 36*, 1–10.

Orlinsky, D. E., & Rønnestad, M. H. (2005). Aspects of professional development. In D. E. Orlinsky & M. H. Rønnestad (Eds.), *How psychotherapists develop: A study of therapeutic work and professional growth* (pp. 103–116). Washington, DC: American Psychological Association.

Osborn, C. J., & Davis, T. D. (1996). The supervision contract: Making it perfectly clear. *The Clinical Supervisor, 14*, 121–134.

Oyster, C. K. (2000). *Groups. A users's guide.* New York, NY: MacGrawhill.

Pearson, Q. (2004). Getting the most out of clinical supervision: Strategies for mental health. *Journal of Mental Health Counseling, 26*, 361–373.

Proctor, B. (2008). *Group supervision. A guide to creative practice.* London, UK: Sage.

Recupero, P. R., & Samara, E. R. (2007). Liability and risk management in outpatient psychotherapy supervision. *Journal of the American Academy of Psychiatry and the Law, 35*, 188–195.

Ruskin, R., & Greben, S. (1994). When supervision may fail: Difficulties and impasses. In S. E. Greben & R. Ruskin (Eds.), *Clinical perspectives on psychotherapy supervision* (pp. 213–261). Washington, DC: American Psychiatric Press.

Salzberger-Wittenberg, I., Williams, G., & Osborne, E. (1999). *The emotional experience of learning and teaching.* London, UK: Karnac.

Samec, J. (1995). Shame, guilt and trauma. Failing the psychotherapy candidate's clinical work. *The Clinical Supervisor, 13*, 1–18.

Scaife, J., & Inskipp, F. (2001). *Supervision in mental professions: A practitioner's guide.* London, UK: Psychology Press.

Searles, H. F. (1955). The informational value of the supervisor's emotional experience. *Psychiatry, 18*, 135–146.

Senge, P. (1990). *The Fifth Discipline. The art and practice of the learning organization.* London, UK: Random House.

Shane, P. (1980, 2010). Shame and learning. *American Journal of Orthopsychiatry, 50*, 348–355.

Skovholt, T. M., & Rønnestad, H. M. (1992). *The evolving professional self. Stages and themes in therapist and counselor development.* New York, NY: Wiley & Sons.

Skovholt, T. M., & Rønnestad, M. H. (2003). Struggles of the novice counselor and therapist. *Journal of Career Development, 30*, 45–58.

Sorli, T., Gammon, D., Bergvik, S., & Sexton, H. (1999). Psychotherapy supervision faceto face and by video conferencing: A comparative study. *British Journal of Psychotherapy, 15*, 452–462.

Stiwne, D. (1993). Om psykoterapihandledningens vanskligheter (On the hazard of supervision and adjacent areas) (pp. 23–47). In D. Stiwne (Ed.), *Om psykoterapihandledningens vanskligheter (On the hazard of supervision and adjacent areas).* Stockholm, Sweden: Natur & Kultur.

Stoltenberg, C. D., McNeill, B., & Delworth, U. (1998). *IDM supervision: An integrated developmental model for supervising counselors and therapists.* San Francisco, CA: Jossey-Bass Publishers.

Strømme, H. (2012). Confronting helplessness. A study of psychology students' acquisition of dynamic psychotherapeutic competence. *Nordic Psychology, 64*, 203–217.

Sumerel, M. B. (1994). *Parallel process in supervision.*Washington, DC:ERIC Clearinghouse.

Sundin, E., Ögren, M.-L., & Boalt Boëthius, S. (2008). Supervisor trainees' and their supervisors' perceptions of attainment of knowledge and skills: An empirical evaluation of a psychotherapy supervisor training programme. *British Journal of Clinical Psychology*, *47*, 381–496.

Szasz, T. (1965). *The ethics of psychoanalysis. The theory and method of autonomous psychotherapy.* New York, NY: Basic Books.

Szecsödy, I. (1990). The learning process in psychotherapy supervision. Stockholm, Sweden: The Karolinska Institute.

Talbot, N. L. (1995). Unerthing shame in the supervisory experience. *American Journal of Psychotherapy*, *49*, 338–349.

Watkins, C. E., Jr. (1992). Psychotherapy supervision and the separation-individuation process: Autonomy versus dependency issues. *The Clinical Supervisor*, *10*, 111–120.

Watkins, C. E., Jr. (1997). Defining psychotherapy supervision and understanding supervisor functioning. In C. E. Watkins, Jr. (Ed.), *Handbook of psychotherapy supervision* (pp. 3–10). New York, NY: John Wiley & Sons.

Watkins, C. E., Jr. (1998). Psychotherapy supervision in the 21st century: Some pressing needs and impressing possibilities. *Journal of Psychotherapy Practice and Research*, *7*, 93–101.

Watkins, C. E., Jr. (2010). Considering characterological resistances in the psychotherapy supervisor. *American Journal of Psychotherapy*, *64*, 239–256.

Watkins, C. E., Jr. (2012). On demoralization, therapist identity development, and persuasion and healing in psychotherapy supervision. *Journal of Psychotherapy Integration*, *22*, 187–205.

Wheeler, S., & Richards, K. (2007). The impact of clinical supervision on counsellors and therapists, their practice and their clients. A systematic review of the literature. *Counselling and Psychotherapy Research*, *7*, 54–65.

Whitman, S., Ryan, B., & Rubenstein, D. F. (2001). Psychotherapy supervisor training: Differences between psychiatry and other mental health disciplines. *Academic Psychiatry*, *25*, 156–161.

Yourman, D. B. (2003). Trainee disclosure in psychotherapy supervision: The impact of shame. *Journal of Clinical Psychology*, *59*, 601–609.

Yourman, D. B., & Farber, B. A. (1996). Nondisclosure and distortion in psychotherapy supervision. *Psychotherapy*, *33*, 567–575.

Part IV

Measuring Competence
In Supervisees and Supervisors

16

A Core Evaluation Battery for Supervision

Sue Wheeler and Michael Barkham

Research on clinical supervision has been prolific over the past few decades, but there are still few headlines that can really claim that supervision is essential to good practice or that it makes a difference to the outcomes of clients. And yet, many practitioners believe that supervision is essential to good practice and much time and resources are invested in the provision of supervision as an important part of safe and competent practice. In this chapter, we set out a summary of the evidence and its shortcomings and, in response, consider the utility of building a cumulative body of evidence on supervision via the adoption of a core supervision battery in routine practice.

The State of the Evidence Base

There have been a number of systematic reviews of supervision research in the past two decades (see Ellis & Ladany, 1997; Ellis, Ladany, Krengel, & Schult, 1996; Freitas, 2002; Milne & James, 2000; Wheeler, 2003). Wheeler and Richards (2007) conducted a systematic review of supervision literature specifically to evaluate the impact of clinical supervision on counselors and therapists, their practice, and their clients. A total of 25 studies met the inclusion criteria for the review. Between them 32 different instruments were used, only one of which was used in more than one study. Accordingly, it was not possible to conduct a meta-analysis. The authors considered there to be a lack of logical progression between the studies and minimal evidence that researchers were trying to build on the experience of previous research. Each study, and supervision instrument, stood in isolation from the existing body of literature and there appeared no strategy for building on previous work in order to yield a cumulative and coherent evidence base for the field. In addition, there is little replication of supervision studies, even though there are many cultural differences in supervision across the globe and across modality.

The Wiley International Handbook of Clinical Supervision, First Edition. Edited by C. Edward Watkins, Jr. and Derek L. Milne.

The Wheeler and Richards (2007) systematic review of the supervision literature revealed an array of weaknesses in supervision research to date. The research questions were often convoluted and difficult to relate to routine practice. The majority of studies were on trainees, making it difficult to evaluate the impact of supervision as opposed to other elements of training, and there was a reliance on self-report instruments. Very little information was presented on the supervisees (theoretical orientation, length of experience, number of clients seen, etc.), the supervisors (training in supervision, length of time supervising the individual, relationship with the organization, etc.), and almost no information was provided about clients being seen by the supervisees. Supervision was often not clearly defined. Many studies were cross-sectional (i.e., with measures only taken at one time point) and the same measures were rarely used in more than one study. Many analog studies were identified (i.e., laboratory-based simulations of supervision), but these studies were excluded from the review. As a result, there is little information about supervision with experienced practitioners and equally limited information about the effect of supervision over time. In particular, little is known about supervision as routinely practiced by counselors and psychotherapists across theoretical orientation, organization, practice duration, and client groups. In an age where evidence-based practice is espoused throughout healthcare systems, evidence on the effectiveness of supervision is sorely lacking.

The methodological weakness of supervision research was also an overarching concern of a subsequent critical review of 30 years of supervision research carried out by Watkins (2011). The review considered a total of 18 studies focusing on supervision and client outcomes as identified from a search of earlier reviews and recent studies via searches of electronic databases. Watkins determined that only three studies met reasonable standards of methodological rigor, two of which were randomized controlled trials (RCT; Bambling, King, Raue, Schweitzer, & Lambert, 2006; White & Winstanley, 2010) while the third study used a quasi-experimental controlled design (Bradshaw, Butterworth, & Mairs, 2007). Although Watkins saw promise and potential arising from these three studies (i.e., showing that good quality research *can* be carried out), overall he concluded, "In surveying the last 30 years of supervision outcome research (actual and purported), the drawing of any conclusions about supervision's effects on patient outcome seems premature" (p. 252).

Practice-Based Supervision Research

While the RCT might be viewed by some as the gold standard for research, there is, of course, a healthy debate concerning the degree to which tightly controlled efficacy trials provide the most robust evidence for routine care (see Barkham, Stiles, Lambert, & Mellor-Clark, 2010). However, in the field of supervision, with few exceptions, evidence from trials is virtually nonexistent and small-scale research is unlikely to convince paymasters. By contrast, there is the potential for large amounts of routine practice-based data to be collected that can complement or even supersede the limited evidence from RCTs. In recognition of this potential, there has been increasing interest in the development of practice research networkss (PRNs) whereby practitioners in different settings adopt a similar methodology in order to collect and combine data (e.g., British Association for Counselling & Psychotherapy, 2013; Castonguay et al., 2010). Some practitioner networks are well established and producing impressive results (Levant, 2005; Margison et al., 2000; Parry, Castonguay, Borkovec, & Wolf, 2010). If practice-based research networks can be established to work together, collaboratively pooling data from many sources, the products of such systems can make a substantial contribution to the evidence base for supervision.

As a result of an initiative of the British Association for Counselling and Psychotherapy (BACP) to promote research into supervision, the authors secured funding to develop a network of supervision researchers. The project, named SuPReNet (Supervision Practice Research Network), had three specific aims: (1) to develop and sustain a network of people interested and engaged in supervision research, (2) to promote the network through a series of supervision research seminars and a conference, and (3) to explore instruments used in supervision research, in order to find a set of tools that could be promoted to the network for adoption in practitioner research. A plan was drawn up for the infrastructure needed to encourage a sustainable network of researchers, each collecting data and answering research questions related to supervision. The aim was to develop a research paradigm that would be sustainable, given a diverse group of counselors and psychotherapists with little research training or knowledge, but with the enthusiasm to contribute to an evidence base for supervision. The infrastructure needed some pragmatic research project designs, an agreed set of instruments, an agreed method of data collection, and a means to store and access the data to be used in agreed projects.

In order to support the fledgling network, the authors and colleagues undertook to identify a battery of instruments that could be recommended to the network in order to encourage replication, collaboration, and pooling of data collected in different settings. The first step was to identify as many measures as possible that had been used in published research, and the second (even more demanding) task was to locate and collate the instruments.

The Purpose of a Core Battery of Research Instruments Related to Supervision

If there is to be a practitioner research network collecting supervision data (as well as routine outcome data on their clients), the whole network needs to be using the same instruments so that data can be pooled and securely managed in a central location. Most counselors and psychotherapists have not been trained as scientist practitioners (Lane & Corrie, 2006).While the imperative of evidence-based practice has galvanized many therapists into research action, there is often resistance to any form of data collection related to clinical practice. In the search for instruments that can be used routinely in clinical and supervision practice, they need to be acceptable to the supervisors, therapists, and clients.

The use of the Clinical Outcomes in Routine Evaluation-Outcome Measure (CORE-OM; Barkham, Mellor-Clark,et al., 2010) in counseling and psychotherapy services throughout the United Kingdom has demonstrated how institutions can work with their staff to familiarize them with outcome measures that can be routinely used in therapy. Within the United Kingdom, there is now a vast national database of questionnaires completed in hundreds of services. The measure is well constructed, easy to use, and easy to understand. Furthermore, it has the potential to be used as part of the process of therapy in order to increase understanding and hence the effectiveness of the work. It can also be a valuable tool to use in supervision so that supervisors can gain some insight into the progress that clients are making.

The Process of Identifying the Proposed Core Battery

Many counseling and psychotherapy services use the CORE-OM and as a result a plethora of publications reporting on the outcome of therapy have appeared (e.g., Barkham et al., 2006; Stiles, Barkham, Connell, & Mellor-Clark, 2008). The model of the success of the CORE-OM inspired the search for measures that could routinely be used in supervision. It was quickly decided that the development of new instruments would be a long-term project and that time should be used to identify those already in existence that would be fit for purpose.

We sourced and obtained instruments that had been used in supervision research since 1980 based on cited work in Wheeler and Richards (2007) as well as recent texts (Bernard & Goodyear, 2009; Falender & Shafranske, 2004; Gould & Bradley, 2001; Ladany & Muse-Burke, 2001). In addition, we searched more recent articles as well as relevant Web sites. Electronic databases searched were Psych Lit, Psych Art, Medline, and Scopus. Terms included a combination of Counsel*, supervis*, psychothera*, evaluat*, assess*, instrument*, measure*, questionnaire*, scale*, inventor*, reliability*, valid*, therap*, develop*. Some databases had restricted access (i.e., Infotrac, Swetswise, and APA). Our search yielded 150 instruments of which hard copy was obtained for 67 measures. A total of eight instruments were rejected on the following grounds: they tapped mental state ($n = 3$); therapy process as opposed to supervision process ($n = 3$); and alliance in education, a focus that appeared to be qualitatively different from ours ($n = 2$). Of the resulting 59 instruments, 10 were variants of the Supervisory Working Alliance (SWA). We therefore excluded these 10 variants but retained the original version, yielding a total of 49 instruments (see Table 16.1). The paucity of instruments reflects two related factors: an under-researched field and an overrepresentation of one-off degree projects, often from long ago and rarely revisited. Many of the other instruments were used in supervision projects but were actually evaluating counseling process and outcome.

The Process of Evaluating Existing Instruments

Our analytic strategy adopted pragmatic and functional criteria to evaluate the features of instruments that could be used in routine practice. We adopted seven criteria (see the following list) that we applied with a degree of tolerance (e.g., any criterion relating to psychometrics would not be applicable to an instrument capturing qualitative material).

- First, we deemed it important that instruments were pan-theoretical (i.e., universally applicable to supervision of therapists working with any theoretical orientation).

Table 16.1 Measures related to supervision that were considered by the research team.

	Scale title	*For supervisee*	*For supervisor*	*Author(s)*[a]
1.	Anticipatory Supervisee Anxiety Scale (ASAS)			Ellis, Singh, Dennin, and Tosado, 2014
2.	Change Interview Record – supervisees, supervisors			Elliott, 1999
3.	Competencies of Supervisors			Borders and Leddick, 1987
4.	Counselor Supervisor Self-efficacy Scale			Barnes, 2002
5.	Critical Incidents in Supervision			Ellis, 1991
6.	Cross-Cultural Counseling Inventory – revised – CCI-R-Supervisor/counselor			LaFromboise, Coleman, and Hernandez, 1991 – modified (Hird, Tao, & Gloria, 2005)
7.	Development of Psychotherapists Common Core Questionnaire – supervisor/trainer			Orlinsky et al., 1999
8.	EKARGS – Evaluation of Knowledge and Relations in Group Supervision – student; supervisor			Sundin, Ögren, and Boalt Boëthius, 2008
9.	Evaluation Process within Supervision Inventory	•		Lehrman-Waterman and Ladany, 2001
10.	Feminist Supervision Scale – FSS			Szymanski, 2003
11.	Supervision Outcomes Survey	•		Worthen and Isakson, 2000
12.	Form for Evaluation of Supervisor-in-training		•	Bradley and Whiting, 2001
13.	Group Climate in Group Supervision – supervisor, supervisee	•	•	Ögren and Sundin, 2009
14.	Group Supervision Scale	•		Arcinue, 2002
15.	Helpful Aspects of Supervision – supervisors, supervisees			Llewelyn, 1988
16.	Internal Consistency of the Supervision Attitude Scale – 2003			Kavanagh et al., 2003
17.	Manchester Clinical Supervision Scale	•		Winstanley, 2000
18.	Multicultural Supervision Competencies Questionnaire	•		Wong and Wong, 2014

(*Continued*)

Table 16.1 (*Continued*)

	Scale title	For supervisee	For supervisor	Author(s)[a]
19.	Brief Supervisory Alliance Scale (BSAS); supervisor form (BSAS-SF); trainee form (BSAS-TF)	•	•	Rønnestad and Lundquist, 2009
20.	Supervisor and Supervisee Rating Form 1976	•	•	Doehrman, 1976
21.	Role Conflict and Role Ambiguity Inventory	•		Olk andFriedlander, 1992
22.	Structured Interview, Inner Emotional Process	•	•	Rožič and Mandelj, 2008 (unpublished)
23.	Supervisee Levels Questionnaire – revised	•		McNeill, Stoltenberg, and Pierce, 1985
24.	Supervisee Satisfaction Questionnaire – SSQ	•		Larsen, Attkisson, Hargreaves, and Nguyen, 1979
25.	Supervision Emphasis Rating Form – revised		•	Lanning and Freeman, 1994
26.	Supervisor Focus and Style Measure		•	Yager, Wilson, Brewer, and Kinnetz, 1989
27.	Supervisor Style; Work Climate Questionnaire – student/supervisor	•	•	Ögren, Jonsson, and Sundin, 2005
28.	Supervision Estimate Questionnaire		•	Haley, 2002
29.	Supervision Questionnaire – 1983	•		Zucker, 1984 Worthington and Roehlke, 1979
30.	Supervision Questionnaire	•		Protivnak, 2003 Protivnak and Davis, 2008
31.	Supervision Questionnaire	•		After Ladany, Hill, and Nutt, 1996
32.	Supervision Self-efficacy Questionnaire		•	Haley, 2002
33.	Supervisory Working Alliance (SWA) supervisor/ supervisee version 2)	•	•	Efstation, Patton, and Kardash, 1990
34.	Supervisor/Peer Rating Form		•	Hill, 2009
35.	Supervisor Feedback	•		Hall-Marley, 2001
36.	Supervisor perception form		•	Heppner and Handley, 1982
37.	Supervisor Personal Reaction Scale	•	•	Holloway and Wampold, 1984
38.	Supervisor Self-disclosure Index	•		Ladany and Walker, 2003
39.	Supervisor Style Questionnaire – student and supervisor versions			Ögren, Boalt Boëthius, and Sundin, 2008

Table 16.1 (*Continued*)

	Scale title	*For supervisee*	*For supervisor*	*Author(s)*[a]
40.	Supervisory Embodiment Scale	•		Geller, Farber, and Schaffer, 2010 Geller, Lehman, and Farber, 2002 Geller, Smith-Behrends, and Hartley, 1981
41.	Supervisory Relationship Questionnaire	•		Farber, 2003
42.	Supervisory Styles Inventory – SSI	•		Friedlander and Ward, 1984
43.	Therapist Evaluation Checklist		•	Hall-Marley, 2001
44.	Trainee Anxiety Scale	•		Ladany, Walker, Pate-Carolan, and Gray, 2007
45.	Trainee–Client Sexual Misconduct	•	•	Hamilton and Spruill, 1999
46.	Trainee Disclosure Scale	•		Walker, Ladany, and Pate-Carolan, 2007
47.	Workforce Survey	•		Grant and Schofield, 2007
48.	(Supervision)Working Alliance Inventory – WAI	•	•	Horvath and Greenberg, 1989 Also attributed to Bahrick, 1989
49.	Working Alliance Inventory/ supervision – short form (supervisor and trainee forms)	•	•	Ladany, Mori, and Mehr, 2007

[a]Further reference information is available on request from the first author (sw103@le.ac.uk).

- Second, instruments needed to be relatively short so that they could be completed repeatedly without causing irritation (and hence being ignored and not completed).
- Third, instruments needed to have face validity and address issues that would be immediately recognizable to practitioners as relevant to their supervisory practice.
- Fourth, ideally, instruments should be able to capture both the supervisor and the supervisee perspectives.
- Fifth, wherever possible, instruments should have been tested and have psychometric support for reliability, validity, sensitivity, and internal consistency.
- Sixth, instruments should be suitable for repeated use over a long-term period in order to be consistent with the paradigm of practice-based research on the process and outcome of supervision over a period of time. Clinical utility was

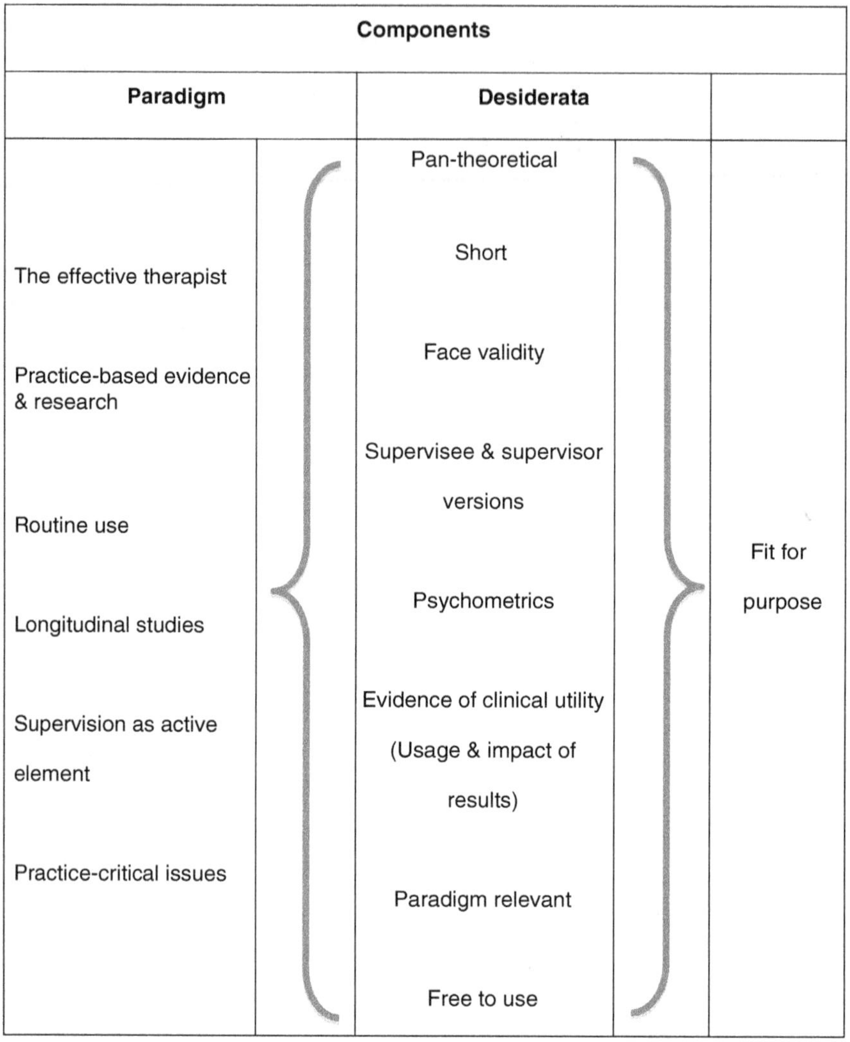

Figure 16.1 Desiderata.

assessed by addressing the way in which instruments had been used in relevant research studies and the yield achieved through these studies.

- Finally, an overarching consideration was whether the measures were free to use. As it was the intention that many practitioners would use the chosen instruments routinely in their practice, they needed to be easily and freely accessible (see Figure 16.1).

A rating system was devised for scoring the identified measures on all the above criteria, a procedure carried out by the authors and their colleagues.[1] Some criteria

[1] The four reviewers were Mark Aveline, Michael Barkham, Delia Cushway, and Sue Wheeler.

suggested a binary response (Yes/No), for example, whether the instrument was free to use. Other criteria warranted a more graduated scoring system, for example, the extent of clinical utility and available psychometrics. The four reviewers independently assessed all sourced instruments, together with relevant articles and other available information, and graded them against each of the criteria. Disagreements were resolved through a consensus-meeting. In many cases, information about instruments was sparse and it was difficult to make a complete assessment. The instruments were then ranked on the basis of their scores on each criterion, with those scoring the highest being considered for a core battery that would be fit for purpose (Wheeler, Aveline, & Barkham, 2011).

We blended the scores from this review process with consideration as to whether the instruments would be user-friendly and acceptable to practitioners in the British context. Hence, we combined science and pragmatism in the assessment of the instruments collected. While the summing of the scores gave an indication of which instruments it might be worth giving closer consideration to, in practice the procedure shifted from criteria to desiderata. A single fit for purpose rating emerged and was used for decision-making using a 0–3 scale as follows: 3 = *use in routine practice*; ≥2 *special purpose/occasional use*; and >1 *development potential.* The instruments selected as a result of this process reflected five different domains of supervision: (1) supervisor and trainee characteristics (SC); (2) supervision process (SP); (3) supervision outcome (SO); (4) counseling process (CP); and (5) counseling outcome (CO).

The Toolkit

The mean ratings for all the instruments using the agreed criteria were calculated. One measure received a maximum mean score of 3 points and five measures received a mean score >2. A total of 23 measures received mean scores between 1 and 2, and the remaining 20 scored <1. We set a mean score of >2 as being the threshold for possible inclusion in the core battery. Setting this criterion yielded a total of six instruments that could be recommended for both routine and occasional use (although the cost of the Manchester Clinical Supervision Scale makes it less accessible). The intention was not to convey anything about whether some instruments were better than others, but to choose those that would fit best with practitioner research. This meant that the chosen instruments would need to be acceptable to practitioners that would, in turn, promote collaboration and cooperation in data collection and synergy of effort. A wide range of instruments might be suitable for specific projects and the assembly of the bank of instruments may, in itself, prove to be useful to researchers at some point. We therefore conceptualized this battery of instruments as a *toolkit*, which was subsequently road tested at various meetings and conferences.[2]

[2] These included the 2009 BACP Research Conference workshop on supervision measures and the 2010 ESRC Seminar Series on supervision research. The toolkit was also reviewed by an International Advisory Board of supervision research experts who were recruited to support the SuPReNet project.

Permission to use the instruments in the toolkit was sought from all the authors and copyright holders. Permissions were granted to use them, provided that they were accessed through membership of the SuPReNet network and that the authors of the measures were appropriately acknowledged and referenced in any publication.

Details of Instruments in the Toolkit

Several of the instruments in the evaluation toolkit were recognized to be questionnaires that had been adapted from earlier versions designed to measure aspects of the counseling process or therapeutic alliance, rather than specifically intended for supervision. On close inspection, it was clear that the subtleties of the supervisory relationship and the supervision process were not being accurately captured. Some instruments had a range of questions that seemed to be tapping the same concept, while others employed scales with excessive points on the scale in order to achieve reliable differentiation (e.g., 10). Instruments that were not judged favorably were those where an inferred perspective was taken. For example, asking the supervisor to estimate trainee thought processes, when the trainee would have been in a better position to answer such questions for themselves. Also, some instruments used language that might not be universally understood, pertaining strongly to a particular culture or client group.

In total, five measures were selected for routine use in supervision practitioner research. Their details are summarized in Table 16.2. The five selected measures serve different purposes and will be relevant to projects addressing diverse research questions.

Routine measurement of supervision

Given that a primary aim is to develop practitioner research and to encourage the routine collection of data related to supervision, only one instrument was deemed appropriate for routine data collection at every supervision session.

- The Brief Supervisory Alliance Scale (BSAS-T&S; Rønnestad & Lundquist, 2009).It comprises 12 items and has a trainee/supervisee and supervisor version, good face validity, valid psychometric properties, and is free to use. Two factor-analytic derived scales – Bond and Co-action – were constructed from an original set of 23 questions.

A broader core battery for supervision

The other four chosen instruments serve different and specific purposes.

- The Development of Psychotherapist Common Core Questionnaire (Supervisor and Trainee versions) is derived from the longer and more comprehensive Development of Psychotherapist Questionnaire (Orlinsky & Rønnestad, 2005). It is valuable in that it collects information on a range of therapist/trainee/supervisee and supervisor characteristics. This questionnaire would be good to use at the

Table 16.2 Summary of core battery measures for clinical supervision research.

Form	*Characteristics*	*Comments*	*Domain(s) and use*	*Example questions*
Routine use				
Brief Supervisory Alliance Scale (BSAS-T&S Forms) Rønnestad and Lundquist (University of Oslo)	Supervisee and supervisor mirror versions. 12 items 6-point scales	Short, repeatable, relevant, and free. Being used in the Leicester CORE-Net trial. Rating: 3	SO/SC/SP Routine	1. My supervisor treats me with respect 2. My supervisor helps me to talk openly in supervision 3. My supervisor and I trust each other 4. In supervision, I feel free to address the negative feelings I may have toward my supervisor
Measures for special purposes				
1. Delineating therapist experience, focus, and ability				
Psychotherapists' Professional Development Scales Orlinsky and Rønnestad (2005)	21 Qs, 6-point scales. Overall career development, currently experienced growth and depletion scales	Opportunity to contribute to and be informed by large international dataset collected by SPR Collaborative Research Network Rating: 2	TC Baseline	1. How well do you understand what happens moment-by-moment during therapy sessions? 2. How well are you able to detect and deal with your patients' emotional reactions to you? 3. How good are you at making constructive use of your personal reactions to patients?
2. Identifying supervisory issues				
Role Conflict and Role Ambiguity Inventory (Olk & Friedlander, 1992)	29 Qs, 5-point scales, supervisee. Role conflict and ambiguity scales	Good for identifying issues. Our rating: 2.5	SO/SP Occasional	Rating: *almost never. . . .almost always* 1. My supervisor treats me like a colleague in our supervisory sessions 2. My supervisor helps me talk freely in our sessions 3. In supervision, my supervisor places a high priority on our understanding the client's perspective

(*Continued*)

Table 16.2 (*Continued*)

Form	*Characteristics*	*Comments*	*Domain(s) and use*	*Example questions*
3. Process				
Helpful Aspects of Supervision – Supervisors, Supervisees (adapted from Llewelyn, 1988)	7 and 3 Qs, free text answers	Variant of a classic. Useful in identifying events for further inquiry, complements Ambiguity Inventory. Our rating: 2.5	SP Occasional and routine	Complete no more than 24 hr after supervision 1. Of all the events which occurred in this session, which do you feel was the most helpful to yourself and/or work with your client(s)? 2. Please describe what made this event helpful/important and what you got out of it 3. How helpful was this particular event?
4. Classic alliance measure				
Supervisory Working Alliance (SWA; Efstation et al., 1990)	23 Qs, 8-point scales, supervisor/ supervisee versions	The original, widely used, factor analyzed. Use if direct comparability with pioneering studies is vital	SP Baseline and occasional	Rating: *almost never. . . . almost always* 1. My supervisor treats me like a colleague in our supervisory sessions 2. My supervisor helps me talk freely in our sessions 3. In supervision, my supervisor places a high priority on our understanding the client's perspective

Note. Measures are free to use by SuPReNet members but must be used in original form.

Q , Questionnaire; SC, Supervisor Characteristics; SP, Supervision Process; SO, Supervision Outcome; TC, Therapist Characteristics.

Table 16.3 Measures sourced or developed after the initial evaluation.

	Scale title	*For supervisee*	*For supervisor*	*Author(s)*
1.	The Supervisory Relationship Questionnaire	•		Palomo, Beinart, and Cooper, 2010
2.	Leeds Alliance in Supervision Scale	•		Wainwright, 2010 (unpublished DClinPsy thesis)

beginning and end of any project involving supervision, in order to capture biographical information (so often absent in supervision research) and change over time.

- The Helpful Aspects of Supervision Questionnaire (HASQ; adapted from Llewelyn, 1988) is derived from her Helpful Aspects of Therapy form. It has a short series of open-ended questions that have the potential to generate rich qualitative data. Although a variant of an earlier form, this instrument was considered to capture material that other instruments did not.
- The Role Conflict and Role Ambiguity Inventory (Olk & Friedlander, 1992) is a questionnaire to be completed by supervisees that captures some of the nuances of the experience of supervision that could be useful in some projects.
- The SWA (Efstation, Patton, & Kardash, 1990) is a questionnaire of which there are various versions that have been developed over time. The version referenced has 23 items that would not be unduly burdensome for selected use in research projects. It may be useful in longitudinal projects, measuring change over time.

Recent developments of measures

Subsequent to the BSAS being chosen as the primary relationship measure, two other measures have become available (see Table 16.3). Palomo, Beinart, and Cooper (2010) have published their Supervisor Relationship Questionnaire. This is a questionnaire that addresses the supervisory relationship from the supervisee perspective, although a supervisor version is in the process of development. It has 67 items, which makes it long for routine use, but it would certainly have been included as a recommended measure had it been available at the time of the selection. The other measure is the three-item Leeds Alliance in Supervision Measure (LASS; Wainwright, 2010). Again this measure could be useful for routine use given its brevity, but it captures the relationship only from the supervisee perspective. The team liked the Manchester Clinical Supervision Scale (Osman Consulting, 2013), but its major disadvantage is that it is not free to use or easy to access, as well as being too long (34 items plus biographical details page) to be used routinely.

The Toolkit in Practice

The toolkit was launched at a workshop at the BACP Research Conference in May 2009 and was also distributed at three Economic and Social Research Council

(ESRC)-funded supervision research seminars (2010/2011). In addition, members of the SuPReNet network have requested copies. There is limited information about how and where the measures are being used, but two projects are known to have incorporated them into research protocols.

The first is the University of Leicester Research Clinic established in 2010. A core battery of questionnaires was included in the protocol for the clinic that included the BSAS to be used by supervisor and supervisee at every session. It also included the Development of Psychotherapist Common Core Questionnaire (Orlinsky & Rønnestad, 2005). This was completed by all therapists and supervisors involved in the clinic.Wheeler (2010) reported on the relationship between therapist and supervisor, noting that supervisors tended to score the relationships lower than supervisees. The second project used the HASQ (supervisor and supervisee versions) and the BSAS in research on supervision for safeguarding (child protection) social workers (Wheeler & Cushway, 2013). The BSAS proved to be very useful in confirming that the four supervisors engaged in the project had similar levels of (good) relationship with their supervisees and in tracking the way that relationships developed over time. The HASQ produced the most valuable results of the whole project. While it was difficult to measure change over time in the social workers' level of stress or their sickness absence rates while they were receiving consultative supervision support, the data from the questionnaire produced a rich picture of their experiences of supervision and the way in which it was used.

Summary and Recommendations for the Future

In summary, the core battery – toolkit – for supervision was developed in response to a context in which there is a lack of a clear, coherent, collective, and cumulative research agenda for supervision that is built on the use of a common measurement approach. Our aspiration is that practitioners will use the toolkit to aid their selection of instruments and thereby provide greater opportunity for building a cumulative evidence base for supervision. However, we are mindful that focusing on a single instrument that then becomes dominant runs the risk of freezing the field in that there may be a disincentive for researchers to develop better measures. As is always the case in most research, decisions inevitably involve trade-offs. In our view, there is more to be gained for the foreseeable future by reigning in the number of measures used by supervision researchers. Focusing on building a cumulative and coherent knowledge base will not only lead to the provision of supervision universally but will also deliver more robust evidence of its contribution to the processes and outcomes of the psychological therapies.

References

Arcinue, F. (2002). *The development and validation of the Group Supervision Scale* (Unpublished doctoral dissertation). University Southern California.

Bahrick, A. S. (1989). Role induction for counselor trainees: Effects on the supervisory alliance. *Dissertation Abstracts International, 51*(03), 1484. (UMI No. 9014392).

Bambling, M., King, R., Raue, P., Schweitzer, R., & Lambert, W. (2006). Clinical supervision: Its influence on client-rated working alliance and client symptom reduction in the brief treatment of major depression. *Psychotherapy Research, 16*, 317–331.

Barkham, M., Connell, J., Stiles, W. B., Miles, J. N. V., Margison, F., Evans, C., & Mellor-Clark, J. (2006). Dose-effect relations and responsive regulation of treatment duration: The good enough level. *Journal of Consulting and Clinical Psychology, 74*, 160–167.

Barkham, M., Mellor-Clark, J., Connell, J., Evans, R., Evans, C., & Margison, F. (2010). The CORE measures & CORE system: Measuring, monitoring, and managing quality evaluation in the psychological therapies. In M. Barkham, G. E. Hardy, & J. Mellor-Clark (Eds.), *Developing and delivering practice-based evidence: A guide for the psychological therapies* (pp. 175–219). Chichester, UK: Wiley.

Barkham, M., Stiles, W. B., Lambert, M. J., & Mellor-Clark, J. (2010). Building a rigorous and relevant knowledge-base for the psychological therapies. In M. Barkham, G. E. Hardy, & J. Mellor-Clark (Eds.), *Developing and delivering practice-based evidence: A guide for the psychological therapies* (pp. 21–61). Chichester, UK: Wiley.

Barnes, K. L. (2002). Development and initial validation of a measure of counselor supervisor self-efficacy. *Counseling and Human Services – Dissertations*. Paper 16. Retrieved from http://surface.syr.edu/chs_etd/16

Bernard, J. M., & Goodyear, R. K. (2009). *Fundamentals of clinical supervision* (4th ed.). Upper Saddle River, NJ: Pearson Education Inc.

Borders, L. D., & Leddick, G. R. (1987). *Handbook of counseling supervision*. Alexandria, VA: Association for Counselor Education and Supervision.

Bradley, L. J., & Whiting, P. P. (2001). Supervision training: A model. In L. J. Bradley & N. Ladany (Eds.), *Counselor supervision: Principles, process, and practice* (3rd ed., pp. 63–90). New York, NY: Brunner-Routledge.

Bradshaw, T., Butterworth, A., & Mairs, H. (2007). Does structured clinical supervision during psychosocial intervention education enhance outcome for mental health nurses and the service users they work with? *Journal of Psychiatric and Mental Health Nursing, 14*, 4–12.

British Association for Counselling & Psychotherapy. (2013). *Children and Young People Practice Research Network, formerly SCoPReNet*. Retrieved from http://www.bacp.co.uk/schools/

Castonguay, L. G., Boswell, J. F., Zack, S., Baker, S., Boutselis, M., Chiswick, N., . . . Grosse Holtforth, M. (2010). Helpful and hindering events in psychotherapy: A practice research network study. *Psychotherapy: Theory, Research, Practice, Training, 47*, 327–344.

Doehrman, M. J. (1976). Parallel processes in supervision and psychotherapy. *Bulletin of the Menninger Clinic, 40*, 1–104.

Efstation, J. F., Patton, M. J., & Kardash, C. M. (1990). Measuring the working alliance in counselor supervision. *Journal of Counseling Psychology, 37*, 322–329.

Elliott, R. (1999). Client Change Interview protocol. Network for Research on Experiential Psychotherapies website. Retrieved from http://experiential-researchers.org/instruments/elliott/changei.html

Ellis, K. L. (1991). Critical incidents in clinical supervision and in supervisor supervision: Assessing supervisory issues. *Journal of Counseling Psychology, 38*, 342–349.

Ellis, M., Singh, N. N., Dennin, M. K., & Tosado, M. (2014). Anticipatory supervisee anxiety scale. Unpublished instrument. In J. M. Bernard & R. K. Goodyear (Eds.), *Fundamentals of clinical supervisioned.*, pp. 330–331). Boston, MA: Pearsson.

Ellis, M. V., & Ladany, N. (1997). Inferences concerning supervisees and clients in clinical supervision. In C. E. Watkins (Ed.), *Handbook of psychotherapy supervision* (pp. 447–507). New York, NY: Wiley.

Ellis, M. V., Ladany, N., Krengel, M., & Schult, D. (1996). Clinical supervision research from 1981 to 1993: A methodological critique. *Journal of Counseling Psychology, 43*, 35–50.

Falender, C. A., & Shafranske, P. A. (2004). *Clinical supervision: A competency based approach.* Washington, DC: American Psychological Association.

Farber, B. A. (2003). Self-Disclosure in psychotherapy practice and supervision: An introduction. *Journal of Clinical Psychology, 59*, 525–528.

Freitas, G. J. (2002). The impact of psychotherapy supervision on client outcome: A critical examination of 2 decades of research. *Psychotherapy, 39*, 354–367.

Friedlander, M. L., & Ward, L. G. (1984). Development and validation of the supervisory styles inventory. *Journal of Counseling Psychology, 31*, 541–557.

Geller, J., Farber, B. A., & Schaffer, C. E. (2010). Representations of the supervisory dialogue and the development of psychotherapists. *Psychotherapy: Theory, Research, Practice, Training, 47*, 211–220.

Geller, J. D., Lehman, A. K., & Farber, B. A. (2002). Psychotherapists' representations of their patients. *Journal of Clinical Psychology, 58*, 733–745.

Geller, J. D., Smith-Behrends, R., & Hartley, D. (1981). Images of the psychotherapist: A theoretical and methodological perspective. *Imagination, Cognition, and Personality, 1*, 123–146.

Gould, L. J., & Bradley, L. J. (2001). Evaluation in supervision. In L. J. Bradley & N. Ladany (Eds.), *Counselor supervision: Principles, process and practice* (3rd ed.). Philadelphia, PA: Brunner-Routledge.

Grant, J., & Schofield, M. J. (2007). Career-long supervision: Patterns and perspectives. *Counselling and Psychotherapy Research, 7*, 3–11.

Haley, S. J. (2002). The influence of supervision training on supervisor self-efficacy among doctoral interns at university counseling centers. *Dissertation Abstracts International: Section B. Sciences and Engineering, 62*(7-B), 3378. (UMI No. AAI3022046).

Hall-Marley, S. (2001). Unpublished instrument. In C. Falender & E. Shafranske (2004). *Clinical supervision: A competency-based approach.* Washington, DC: American Psychiatric Association.

Hamilton, J. C., & Spruill, J. (1999). Identifying and reducing risk factors related to trainee-client sexual misconduct. *Professional Psychology, Research and Practice, 30*, 318–327.

Heppner, P. P., & Handley, P. (1982). The relationship between supervisory behaviors and perceived supervisor expertness, attractiveness, or trustworthiness. *Counselor Education and Supervision, 22*, 37–46.

Hill, C. E. (2009). *Helping skills: Facilitating exploration, insight, and action* (3rd ed.). Washington, DC: American Psychological Association.

Hird, J. S., Tao, K. W., & Gloria, A. M. (2005). Examining multicultural supervision competence in racially similar and different supervision dyads. *The Clinical Supervisor, 23*, 107–122.

Holloway, E. L., & Wampold, B. E. (1984). *Dimensions of satisfaction in the supervision interview.* Paper presented at the Proceedings of the American Psychological Association Convention, Toronto, Canada.

Horvath, A. O., & Greenberg, L. S. (1989). Development and validation of the Working Alliance Inventory. *Journal of Counseling Psychology, 36*, 223–233.

Kavanagh, D. J., Spence, S. H., Strong, J., Wilson, J., Sturk, H., & Crow, N. (2003). Supervision practices in allied mental health: Relationships of supervision characteristics to perceived impact and job satisfaction. *Mental Health Services Research, 5*, 187–195.

Ladany, N., Hill, C. E., & Nutt, E. A. (1996). Unpublished instrument. In J. M. Bernard & R. K. Goodyear (2009). *Fundamentals of clinical supervision.* Columbus, OH: Merrill.

Ladany, N., Mori, Y., & Mehr, K. E. (2007). Trainee perceptions of effective and ineffective supervision interventions. Unpublished manuscript, Lehigh University, Bethlehem, PA.

Ladany, N., & Muse-Burke, J. L. (2001). Understanding and conducting supervision research. In L. J. Bradley & N. Ladany (Eds.), *Counselor supervision: Principles, process and practice* (3rd ed., pp. 304–320). Philadelphia, PA: Brunner-Routledge.

Ladany, N., & Walker, J. A. (2003). Supervisor self-disclosure. *In Session/Journal of Clinical Psychology*, *59*, 611–621.

Ladany, N., Walker, J. A., Pate-Carolan, L., & Gray, L. (2007). *Experiencing counseling and psychotherapy: Insights from psychotherapy trainees, their clients, and their supervisors.* London, England: Routledge.

LaFromboise, T. D., Coleman, H. L., & Hernandez, A. (1991). Development and factor analysis of the Cross-cultural Counseling Inventory – Revised. *Professional Psychology, Research and Practice*, *22*, 380–388.

Lane, D. A., & Corrie, S. (2006). *The modern scientist practitioner: A guide to practice in psychology.* London, UK: Routledge.

Lanning, W., & Freeman, B. (1994). The Supervisor Emphasis Rating Form-Revised. *Counselor Education and Supervision*, *33*, 294–304.

Larsen, D. L., Attkisson, C. C., Hargreaves, W. A., & Nguyen, T. D. (1979). Assessment of client/patient satisfaction: Development of a general scale. *Evaluation and Program Planning*, *2*, 197–207.

Lehrman-Waterman, D., & Ladany, N. (2001). Development and validation of the evaluation process within supervision inventory. *Journal of Counseling Psychology*, *48*, 168–177.

Levant, R. (2005). Evidence based practice in psychology: President's column. *Monitor on Psychology*, *36*(2), 5.

Llewelyn, S. P. (1988). Psychological therapy as viewed by clients and therapists. *British Journal of Clinical Psychology*, *27*, 223–237.

Margison, F., Barkham, M., Evans, C., McGrath, G., Mellor-Clark, J., Audin, K., & Connell, J. (2000). Evidence-based practice and practice-based evidence. *British Journal of Psychiatry*, *177*, 123–130.

McNeill, B. W., Stoltenberg, C. D., & Pierce, R. A. (1985). Supervisees' perceptions of their development: A test of the counselor complexity model. *Journal of Counseling Psychology*, *32*, 630–633.

Milne, D., & James, I. (2000). A systematic review of effective cognitive-behavioural supervision. *British Journal of Clinical Psychology*, *39*, 111–127.

Ögren, M.-L., Boalt Boëthius, S., & Sundin, E. (2008). From Psychotherapist to Supervisor: The significance of group format and supervisors' function as role models in psychotherapy supervision. *Nordic Psychology*, *60*, 3–23.

Ögren, M.-L., Jonsson, C.-O., & Sundin, E. (2005). Group supervision in psychotherapy. The relationship between focus, group climate and perceived attained skill. *Journal of Clinical Psychology*, *61*, 373–389.

Ögren, M.-L., & Sundin, E. (2009). Group supervision in psychotherapy. Main results from a Swedish project on psychotherapy supervision in a group format. *British Journal of Guidance and Counselling*, *37*, 129–139.

Olk, M., & Friedlander, M. L. (1992). Trainees' experience of role conflict and role ambiguity in supervisory relationships. *Journal of Counseling Psychology*, *39*, 389–397.

Orlinsky, D. E., Ambuhl, H., Ronnestad, M. H., Davis, J. D., Gerin, P., Davis, M., . . . & the SPR Collaborative Research Network (1999). The development of psychotherapists: Concepts questions, and methods of a collaborative international study. *Psychotherapy Research*, *9*, 127–153.

Orlinsky, D. E., & Rønnestad, M. H. (2005). *How psychotherapists develop: A study of therapeutic work and professional growth.* Washington, DC: APA.

Osman Consulting. (2013). *The Manchester clinical supervision scale.* Retrieved from http://www.osmanconsulting.com.au/

Palomo, M., Beinart, H., & Cooper, M. J. (2010). Development and validation of the Supervisory Relationship Questionnaire (SRQ) in UK trainee clinical psychologists. *British Journal of Clinical Psychology, 49*, 131–149.

Parry, G. D., Castonguay, L., Borkovec, T. D., & Wolf, A. B. (2010). Practice research networks and psychological services research in the UK and US. In M. Barkham, G. E. Hardy, & J. Mellor-Clark (Eds.), *Developing and delivering practice-based evidence: A guide for the psychological therapies* (pp. 311–325). Chichester, UK: Wiley.

Protivnak, J. J. (2003). *Developmentally appropriate school counselor supervision modalities.* (ERIC Document Reproduction Service No. ED475587).

Protivnak, J. J., & Davis, T. E. (2008). The impact of the supervision relationship on the behaviors of school counseling interns. *Journal of School Counseling*, Retrieved from http://www.jsc.montana.edu/articles/v6n19.pdf

Rønnestad, H., & Lundquist, K. (2009). *Brief supervisory alliance questionnaire*: Oslo, Norway: Department of Psychology, University of Oslo.

Rožič, T., & Mandelj, T. R. (2008). Relational family supervision in the therapeutic practice. Unpublished.

Stiles, W. B., Barkham, M., Connell, J., & Mellor-Clark, J. (2008). Responsive regulation of treatment duration in routine practice in United Kingdom primary care settings: Replication in a larger sample. *Journal of Consulting and Clinical Psychology, 76*, 298–305.

Sundin, E., Ögren, M.-L., & Boalt Boëthius, S. (2008). Supervisors trainees' and their supervisors' perceptions of attainment of knowledge and skills: An empirical evaluation of a psychotherapy supervisor training programme. *British Journal of Clinical Psychology, 47*, 381–496.

Szymanski, D. M. (2003). The Feminist Supervision Scale (FSS): A rational/theoretical approach. *Psychology of Women Quarterly, 27*, 221–232.

Wainwright, N. A. (2010). *The development of the Leeds alliance in supervision scale (LASS): A brief sessional measure of the supervisory alliance* (D.Clin.Psychol thesis). University of Leeds.

Walker, J., Ladany, N., & Pate-Carolan, L. (2007). Gender-related events in psychotherapy supervision: Female trainee perspectives. *Counselling and Psychotherapy Research, 7*, 12–18.

Watkins, C. E., Jr. (2011). Does psychotherapy supervision contribute to patient outcomes? Considering thirty years of research. *The Clinical Supervisor, 30*, 235–256.

Wheeler, S. (2003). *Research on supervision of counsellors and psychotherapists: A systematic scoping search.* Rugby: BACP.

Wheeler, S. (2010). The therapeutic relationship and the supervisory relationship: An exploratory Study. *BACP Supervision Research Conference*, London.

Wheeler, S., Aveline, M., & Barkham, M. (2011). Practice-based supervision research: A network of researchers using a common toolkit. *Counselling and Psychotherapy Research, 11*, 88–96.

Wheeler, S., & Cushway, D. (2013). How effective is clinical supervision in alleviating the stress of social workers involved with the safeguarding of children and young people? *BACP Research Conference*, Warwick, UK, May.

Wheeler, S., & Richards, K. (2007). *The impact of clinical supervision on counsellors and therapists, their practice and their clients: A systematic review of the literature.* Lutterworth, BACP.

White, E., & Winstanley, J. (2010). A randomised controlled trial of clinical supervision: Selected findings from a novel Australian attempt to establish the evidence base for causal relationships with quality of care and patient outcomes, as an informed contribution to mental health nursing practice development. *Journal of Research in Nursing*, *15*, 151–167.

Winstanley, J. (2000). Manchester Clinical Supervision Scale. *Nursing Standard*, *14*(19), 31–32.

Wong, P. T. P., & Wong, L. C. J. (2014). Multicultural Supervision Competencies Questionnaire. In J. M. Bernard & R. K. Goodyear (Eds.), *Fundamentals of clinical supervision* (5th ed., pp. 334–337). Boston, MA: Pearson.

Worthen, V. E., & Isakson, R. L. (2000). Appendix J Supervision outcomes survey. Unpublished scale pp. 271–272. In C. A. Falender & E. P. Shafranske (2004). *Clinical supervision: A competency-based approach*. pp. 271–272 Washington, DC: American Psychological Association.

Worthington, E. L., Jr., & Roehlke, H. J. (1979). Effective supervision as perceived by beginning counselors-in-training. *Journal of Counseling Psychology*, *26*, 64–73.

Yager, G. G., Wilson, F. R., Brewer, D., & Kinnetz, P. (1989). *The development and validation of an instrument to measure counseling supervisor focus and style*. Paper presented at the American Educational Research Association, San Francisco, CA.

Zucker, P. J. (1984). An examination of advanced counseling and psychotherapy supervision, (Doctoral dissertation, Virginia Commonwealth University, 1983). *Dissertation Abstracts International*, *45*, 1035B. (University Microfilms No. DA8413071).

17

The Manchester Clinical Supervision Scale© *MCSS-26*©

Julie Winstanley and Edward White

Historical Context

Contemporary clinical supervision (CS) practice owes provenance to a number of key figures associated with East Coast American charitable organizations (Richmond, 1899; Yale University, 2012) and, in their turn, to a European heritage (Crooker, 1917). These early developments were subsequently engaged by the groundbreaking scholarship of academics and practitioners (Bernard & Goodyear, 1998; Butterworth et al., 1997; Ellis & Ladany, 1997; Milne, Aylott, Fitzpatrick, & Ellis, 2008; Proctor, 1986; Shulman, 1981; Watkins, 1997) and two human service agencies were at the vanguard: social work (Kadushin, 1976; Munson, 1993) and counseling (Leddick & Bernard, 1980).

Shortly before the Great Depression in the United States, Dawson (1926, p. 293) published a generic list of duties for supervisors of case workers in the New Haven Community Chest, Connecticut. The list included making available the results of casework experience necessary for the formulation of policies and methods and the educational development of each individual worker on the staff in a manner calculated to enable her to fully realize her possibilities of usefulness in her chosen field of work. Half a century later, Kadushin (1976) acknowledged Dawson's list and conceded that his earlier training as a social worker had not prepared him for the job. As a distinguished academic, he decided to devote himself to what he called "the professionalization of helping" and to the "probabilities of increasing the effectiveness of what is taught for professional social work" (Morgenbesser, 2011). Brown (1994) observed that, until the early 1970s, British social work academics and practitioners relied heavily on this North American social work literature. It seemed to him that, with the exception of the published work of Shulman (1993), "the pendulum then swung the other way, with a tendency to underuse transatlantic texts, perhaps due

The Wiley International Handbook of Clinical Supervision, First Edition. Edited by C. Edward Watkins, Jr. and Derek L. Milne.

to the substantial British literature, difficulties in obtaining books, and price" (Brown, 1994, p. 118). Brown later made his own contribution to the literature (Brown & Bourne, 1995), believed to be the first comprehensive British text on the supervision of staff in social work, community care, and social welfare settings.

In contemporaneous developments in the United Kingdom, the establishment of the Standing Conference for the Advancement of Counselling (SCAC) in 1970 was the landmark in recent European CS history. Thirty years later, it changed to the British Association for Counselling (BAC) and, having recognized that it no longer represented counseling alone, but also psychotherapy, changed again to the British Association for Counselling and Psychotherapy (BACP). It remains the largest and broadest body within this sector, with a principal remit to ensure public protection (BACP, 2012). Brigid Proctor was associated with the early development of the SCAC and, while training as a probation officer, had been a recipient of supervision. Later, as tutor at the South West London College, she supervised students enrolled on a Diploma course in Counseling and Interpersonal Skills. From this collective experience, she "wanted to use and promote supervision as a cooperative, facilitating process with a two-fold aim. The first is to enable the student or worker 'being supervised' to develop as an effective working person. The second related aim is to offer a forum in which the worker renders account of herself in order to assure herself, and anyone who may be requiring her to be accountable, that she is practicing responsibly" (Proctor, 1986, p. 23). She developed one of the most influential models of CS in contemporary health care practice, particularly among nurses and allied health staff (Proctor, 1986). With echoes of Kadushin's professional background and with similarities to his three-function model, Proctor's organizing framework also nominated three functional domains: normative, restorative, and formative.

In the wake of the Allitt Inquiry (1991) in England and subsequent Clothier Report (Department of Health, 1994a), Faugier and Butterworth (1994) explicitly referred to the Proctor Model and argued that CS should be considered a necessary part of the clinical governance agenda for safer nursing care in Britain. This position was later publicly endorsed by the United Kingdom Central Council for Nursing, Midwifery and Health Visiting (UKCC, 1996) and by the Department of Health (1994b), London. By 1999, Butterworth and Woods (1999) were sufficiently confident to describe CS and clinical governance as "an obvious relationship" (p. 1).

Measurement of CS

Not only were elements of these pioneering models of CS sympathetic to each other in terms of their guidance for practice, but they also contained the essential framework for evaluating the outcomes of CS. Donabedian (1966) had already described three similarly related domains for measuring quality in health care and his structure, process, and outcome trilogy has since become the best known framework in health services research (see Figure 17.1). Of these, Donabedian regarded outcomes as the ultimate validation of the effectiveness and quality of health care, a sentiment later shared by Ellis and Ladany (1997), who also regarded long-term improvements in clinical practice and better client outcomes as "the acid test of good supervision" (p. 485).

Donabedian (1966)*	Kadushin (1976)**	Proctor (1986)***
Structure	Administrative	Normative
Process	Supportive	Restorative
Outcome	Educational	Formative

Figure 17.1 The sympathetic features of the Donabedian, Kadushin, and Proctor models. *Donabedian defined *structural* measures of quality as the professional and organizational resources associated with the provision of care, such as staff credentials and facility operating capacities. *Process* measures of quality refer to the things done to and for patients by practitioners in the course of treatment. *Outcome* measures are the desired states resulting from care processes, which may include reduction in morbidity and mortality, and improvement in the quality of life. **Kadushin defined *administrative* as the correct, effective, and appropriate implementation of policies and procedures; *supportive* as the improvement of staff morale and job satisfaction; and *educational* as reflection on and exploration of work. ***Proctor defined the *normative* domain as being concerned with maintaining and monitoring the effectiveness of the practitioner's everyday practice; the *restorative* domain with how the practitioner responds emotionally to the stresses and demands of practice; and the *formative* domain with the development of knowledge, skills, and attitudes through regular reflection on practice in health care.

Kadushin (1974) made a precocious attempt to describe significant aspects of social work supervisory practice across the United States. His 20-page questionnaire analyzed data from 469 supervisors and 384 supervisees to provide a national overview in this respect. Later, again in social work, Shulman (1981) reported an example of how to identify the skills required for effective practice, to develop instruments to measure them, and to design an approach to teach them effectively. His embryonic Social Worker Behavior Questionnaire (SWBQ), a client-perception instrument, was an early attempt to move into the empirical examination of practice which, "would become increasingly sophisticated as we strengthen our spirit of investigation in this area and our tools of examination" (Shulman, 1981, p. vi). Within three years, Friedlander and Ward (1984) had designed a CS-specific measurement instrument, arising from a series of studies conducted to develop and validate the Supervisory Styles Inventory (SSI), a 33-item 7-point self-report measure that assessed trainees' perceptions of their supervisor's style. Later, a novel general purpose scale, the Client Satisfaction Questionnaire (CSQ), was developed as a response to several problems and issues that "clouded the measurement of consumer satisfaction in health and human systems" (Larsen, Attkisson, Hargreaves, & Nguyen, 1979, p. 197). The CSQ provided Ladany, Hill, Corbett, and Nutt (1996) with an opportunity to replace the terms *counseling* and *services*, with the term *supervision*. Although the resultant eight-item 4-point Supervisory Satisfaction Questionnaire (SSQ) has never been published on its own, it has been used in studies that ask participants to rate their satisfaction with various aspects of their supervision (e.g., Reese et al., 2009). Since these pioneering attempts, *supervision checklists* also began to emerge (Bernard & Goodyear, 1998; Gawande, 2009; Management Sciences for Health, 1998; Shulman, 1993), on both seaboards of the United States. These "home grown scales" were essentially used to evaluate student performance in educational settings. By way of example, the Supervision Checklist has been used in mock supervision exercises to "quickly point out areas that supervisors failed to address, or addressed well" (D. Schoech, personal communication, 2012). Similarly, ratable scales have also been developed recently (Palomo, Beinart, & Cooper, 2010), although many others remain unpublished (e.g., Arcinue, 2002), or are yet to be fully validated and/or reported (e.g., Horton, de Lourdes Drachler, Fuller, & de Carvalho Leite, 2008; Saarikoski, Isoaho, Warne, & Leino-Kilpi, 2008) or, thereafter, little used (Milne & Reiser, 2011).

Thus, while it has always been difficult to link therapeutic intervention to client outcomes (Wampold & Brown, 2005), attempts to link *supervision* to client outcomes, particularly through efficacy studies, have been even more problematic. With notable exceptions (Bambling, King, Patrick, Schweitzer, & Lambert, 2006; Bradshaw, Butterworth, & Mairs, 2007; White & Winstanley, 2010), few studies have yet been concerned with causally linked clinical outcomes. In part, this has been because robust large-scale CS research studies remain difficult to design, conduct, interpret, and fund (White & Winstanley, 2011), and may also help to explain why much of the international CS literature thus far has been contained to reports of small-scale qualitative studies (Cross, Moore, Sampson, Kitch, & Ockerby, 2012), or undemanding quantitative studies (Hancox, Lynch, Happell, & Biondo, 2004), and/or those judged methodologically weak (Cape & Barkham, 2002).

The Manchester Clinical Supervision Scale© (MCSS© 36-Item Version)

The continuous measurement of CS to assure quality, therefore, became one of the most important contemporary challenges on the international clinical governance agenda. This was formally acknowledged in March 1995, when the Department of Health, England, funded a national workshop to consider the use of selected tools in the assessment of CS. The National Health Service (NHS) Nursing Directorate subsequently funded a CS evaluation in 23 sites across England and Scotland (Butterworth et al., 1997). Data collection for the Clinical Supervision Evaluation Project (CSEP) began in June 1995 and was to be regarded as "possibly the most useful large-scale evaluation of the effectiveness of clinical supervision in the United Kingdom" (Williamson & Dodds, 1999, p. 341). One of the aims of the CSEP was to provide an informed view on assessment tools that could be used to report on the impact of CS. Findings revealed that not all research instruments were helpful in this respect, save two that were found to be especially sensitive to change: the Maslach Burnout Inventory (Maslach & Jackson, 1986) and the Minnesota Job Satisfaction Scale (Weiss, 1967). The CSEP demonstrated scope, therefore, to design and conduct a parallel study to develop a new CS-specific research instrument, eventually code-named the Manchester Clinical Supervision Scale© (MCSS©), in deference to The

University of Manchester, England, which was the lead host institution of the CSEP (and the alma mater of both present authors).

The first version of the MCSS© had 45 items. A full replication study was then performed on another large sample of 467 nurses from five centers in the United Kingdom (Winstanley, 2000). The final factor analysis established a scale that contained 36 items, a seven-factor solution, which accounted for 64.6% of the variance. Moreover, subsequent analyses also found that these seven subscales tapped into the three domains of the Proctor Model of Clinical Supervision (Figure 17.2). Thus, in recent years, a sympathetic relationship has been established between an important issue in professional practice (CS), an operational definition (Open University, 1998),

MCSS-26© subscales and Proctor domains	Number of items	Interpretation
Importance/ Value of CS	5	A measure of the importance of receiving CS and whether the CS process is valued or necessary to improve quality of care
Finding Time	4	A measure of the time available for the Supervisee to attend CS sessions
NORMATIVE domain Summary Score	**9**	
Trust/ Rapport	5	Level of the trust/rapport with the Supervisor during the CS sessions/ability to discuss sensitive/confidential issues
Supervisor Advice/ Support	5	Extent to which the Supervisee feels supported by the Supervisor and a measure of the level of advice and guidance received
RESTORATIVE domain Summary Score	**10**	
Improved Care/Skills	4	Extent to which the Supervisee feels that CS has affected their delivery of care and improvement in skills
Reflection	3	A measure of how supported the Supervisee feels with reflecting on complex clinical experiences
FORMATIVE domain Summary Score	**7**	

Figure 17.2 Relationship between the six subscales of the MCSS-26© and the three domains of the Proctor Model of Clinical Supervision.

a conceptual model (Proctor, 1986), and a dedicated research instrument (MCSS©). The MCSS© has since been used as a quantitative outcome measure in upwards of 100 licensed studies, in 13 countries worldwide, and translated into seven languages other than English.

Revision of the Manchester Clinical Supervision Scale to the MCSS-26©

Rasch Analysis was developed to test scales against a mathematical model (Rasch, 1960) and rigorously assess how well each question behaved in accordance with the rest of the questions in that scale and provide a range of fit statistics to check whether adding together the scores of a research instrument was justified or not. For ordinal scales, this may not be true and means and standard deviations may not have validity (Stevens, 1946). The essential rule in successful (interval) measurement, which is ubiquitously used for money, length, area, weight, and temperature, is that "one more unit means the same amount extra, no matter how much there already is. This is exactly what Rasch measurement operationalizes for social science" (Linacre, 2007, p. ix). For that reason, the original factor structure and response format of the MCSS© were tested for goodness of fit to the Rasch Model (Winstanley & White, 2011) using RUMM 2030 software (RUMM Laboratory Pty Ltd, 2011), according to guidelines developed by Pallant and Tennant (2007). Real data (n = 385; 225 nursing staff and 160 allied health staff) were amalgamated from several international CS evaluations that had been previously commissioned from Osman Consulting Pty Ltd., Sydney (http://www.osmanconsulting.com). The findings reconfirmed the validity of the 5-point response format of the original MCSS©, from *Strongly Disagree* to *Strongly Agree* (see Figure 17.3).

The MCSS-26©					
Drawing on your **current experience of receiving Clinical Supervision**, indicate your level of agreement with the following 26 statements by ticking the box which best represents your answer. 0 means you strongly disagree, 1 means you disagree, 2 means you have no opinion, 3 means you agree, 4 means you strongly agree	Strongly disagree	Disagree	No opinion	Agree	Strongly agree
1. My CS sessions are an important part of my work routine	0☐	1☐	2☐	3☐	4☐
2. I learn from my supervisor's experiences	0☐	1☐	2☐	3☐	4☐
3. It is important to make time for CS sessions	0☐	1☐	2☐	3☐	4☐
4. My supervisor provides me with valuable advice	0☐	1☐	2☐	3☐	4☐

Figure 17.3 An example of the MCSS-26© response format.

Moreover, they justified a remodeled version, the MCSS-26© (Winstanley & White, 2011), in which the 36-item version could be reduced to 26 items, with increased structural integrity, and result in improved fit statistics for six subscales, rather than the original seven. By way of independent vindication, the 10 items omitted to create the MCSS-26© included those that were later identified as challenging, when translated by local researchers into Swedish/Norwegian and Danish (Winstanley & White, 2012). The MCSS-26©therefore retained the design capability to suit all grades of personnel in human service agencies, working in a variety of settings, to accommodate the myriad of evaluation conditions and disparate CS delivery methods.

Conditions for Optimal CS

The original version of the MCSS© rated 36 individual items between 1 and 5; the total score therefore ranged from 36 to 180. On the basis of median scores returned on several international CS evaluations, White and Winstanley (2010) have hypothesized that an overall score of 136 might be the indicative threshold for efficacious CS provision. This was broadly equivalent to a score of about 70% of the possible maximum. Figure 17.4 shows the strong correlation ($R_s = 0.975$) between the total

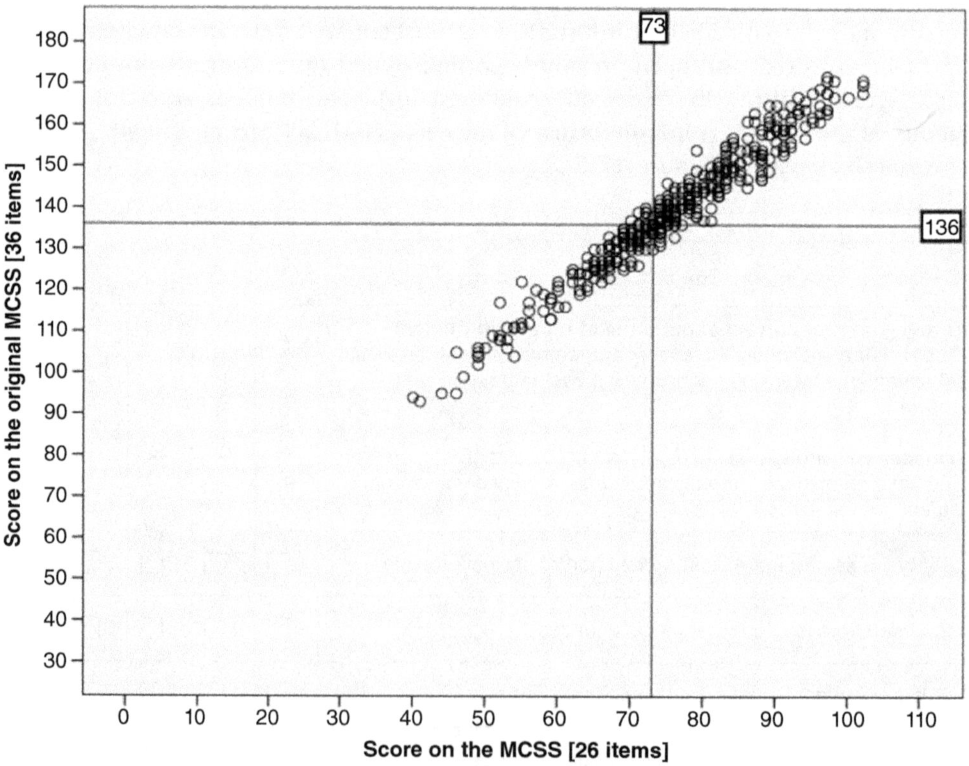

Figure 17.4 A scatter diagram of the correlation between the total score on MCSS-26© with the original MCSS© ($R_s = 0.975$).

scores on the original MCSS© and the MCSS-26©. The MCSS-26© scores 26 individual items between 0 and 4; the total score therefore ranges from 0 to104. It can be posited that a threshold score of 73 is broadly equivalent to the previous score of 136 at which CS efficacy might be apparent.

For the first time, these data have now been subjected to multivariate analysis in an attempt to identify the important factors that predict a high score. Classification and Regression Tree (CART) analysis (Breiman, Friedman, Olshen, & Stone, 1984), or *Decision Trees* as they are known, are useful because they are easy to interpret unbecoming familiar with the concept. CART analysis is a nonparametric recursive-partitioning algorithm that yields a tree-structured rule for prediction. No assumptions are made regarding the underlying distribution of values of the predictor variables. Thus, CART analysis can handle numerical data that are highly skewed or multimodal, as well as categorical predictors with either ordinal or non-ordinal structure, and the model can be validated using statistical tests.

In this example, the "predictor" variables were factors associated with CS received and characteristics of the Supervisee. The predicted outcome was the total score on the MCSS©. CART analysis begins with the complete supervisee group and proceeds to split the group into descendent subsets. The aim is to select optimal discriminator values for splits yielding descending subsets "purer" with respect to the original classification problem. For this analysis, the MCSS© score was introduced as a continuous variable. The analysis was repeated with staff base (hospital or community) forced in as the first variable, to discover if the predicted model fitted both major staff groups. This procedure was conducted because it has long been acknowledged that CS is delivered in different ways in these two environments. The CART method, which dichotomizes the tree at each point and calculates the model that shows the greatest separation in the two nodes, was used. The tree was pruned back to omit any nodes that showed a separation of less than .5 standard error.

Characteristics of the Amalgamated Dataset

For this analysis, 1,272 supervisees with complete data for the 36 items that comprise the MCSS© were available for analysis. These included international studies that were conducted using the MCSS© as an outcome measure in palliative care, forensic mental health, and hospital and community health settings, and involved both nursing (general and mental health) and allied health staff groups. The following variables were introduced to the model:

1. Sex of supervisee
2. Age of supervisee
3. Length of time in post (<1 year, 1–2 years, 3–5 years, >5years)
4. Place of CS sessions (within, away from the workplace, both)
5. Type of CS (one to one/other, group)
6. Length of sessions (<15 min, 15–30 min, 31–45 min, 46–60, >60 min)
7. Frequency of sessions (every week, every 2 weeks, monthly, 2–3 monthly, more than 3 months apart)
8. Supervisor (allocated, chosen)

Table 17.1 Mean, standard deviation (*SD*), and median MCSS© total score for the predictor variables.

Predictor variables	*Mean*	*SD*	*Median*	*n*	%	*Significance*[a]
Sex						
Male	131.1	18.8	134	152	12	Not significant
Female	132.2	19.9	134	1114	88	
Supervisee's usual work base						
Hospital	129.9	21.3	133	604	48	$\chi^2 = 9.69$, $df = 2$,
Community	133.6	18.3	135	583	46	$p = .008$
Both	135.8	16.8	134	69	5	
Length of time in post						
<1 year	136.6	17.8	138	239	19	$\chi^2 = 33.7$, $df = 3$,
1–2 years	135.1	19.5	136	235	19	$p < .0005$
3–5 years	131.9	19.2	134	239	19	
>5 years	128.6	20.6	131	549	44	
Supervisor chosen or allocated						
Allocated	132.1	19.2	134	663	53	Not significant
Chosen by yourself	131.3	20.9	133	535	43	
Other	137.2	15.9	139	46	4	
Frequency of CS sessions						
Every week	139.2	16.4	142	40	3	$\chi^2 = 120.2$,
Every 2 weeks	141.6	14.9	142	88	7	$df = 4$,
Monthly	136.6	18.3	137	513	41	$p < .0005$
2–3 months	128.8	18.2	131	281	23	
Over 3 months apart	123.5	21.2	127	320	26	
Where CS sessions took place						
Within the workplace	130.5	20.1	133	912	72	$\chi^2 = 16.2$, $df = 2$,
Away from the workplace	135.4	18.7	136	278	22	$p < .0005$
Both	136.8	17.7	138	71	6	
Type of CS						
One to one basis	130.0	20.2	132	859	6	$\chi^2 = 26.3$, $df = 2$,
Group sessions	136.9	17.8	137	314	25	$p < .0005$
Other/Combination	133.0	19.5	136	98	8	
Length of CS sessions						
<15 min	121.8	25.3	133	12	1	$\chi^2 = 75.2$, $df = 4$,
15–30 min	123.1	19.6	125	218	17	$p < .0005$
31–45 min	130.3	20.7	133	236	19	
46–60 min	133.9	18.7	135	510	41	
>60 min	136.9	18.5	138	282	22	

[a]Univariate analyses, Kruskal–Wallis analysis of variance.

Group differences were analyzed using nonparametric tests and the results of preliminary univariate analyses showed (Table 17.1) that all predictor variables, except sex of the supervisee and whether the supervisor was chosen or allocated, had the potential to influence the MCSS© total score.

At the commencement of the CART analysis (Node 0), the mean MCSS© total score for the whole group of supervisees was 132.0 ($SD = 19.8$) and the median was

134 (see Figure 17.5). Node 1 represents supervisees having CS sessions more than one month apart recorded a mean MCSS© total score of 126.0. In contrast, Node 2 shows that supervisees having CS sessions at least monthly are predicted to achieve a mean MCSS© total score of 137.5. This difference (~11 points) in the MCSS© total score represents a significant improvement in the effectiveness of the CS being delivered at least monthly (equivalent of .5 of a standard deviation, moderate effect size). The scenario that predicted the highest mean MCSS© total score can be seen at Node 10. Thus, when a supervisee has CS sessions at least monthly, is a younger staff member (<35 years old), and has supervision away from the workplace, his or her predicted MCSS© total score would be 147.4. The arrangement that predicted the lowest score (116.4; see Node 11) would be when the CS sessions were less than 30 min and more than 3 three months apart.

This analysis was repeated for hospital- and community-based staff separately (by forcing this predictor variable into the model first) and the model was found to be very similar (Figure 17.6). However, for hospital-based staff, the most significant threshold for how often the sessions are held was 3 months or more. The optimum scenario for the hospital-based group (Node 10) was for CS to be delivered more frequently than every 3 months and for greater than 30 min. The predicted score would be 139.3, which was effective (according to the proposed threshold of 136). The worst case scenario would be for staff who had been in post for more than 3 years and to receive CS sessions more than 3 months apart.

For community-based staff, the most significant threshold for how often the CS sessions are held was monthly or more. The optimum scenario for the community-based group (Node 14) was for CS to be received at least monthly and away from the workplace. The predicted score would be 141.4, which was effective (according to the proposed threshold of 136). The worst case scenario would be for community-based staff to receive CS sessions more than 1 month apart, for less than 45 min. The choice of supervisor and length of time in post influenced the model only slightly, and sex of supervisee and type of CS had no effect. Thus, if the CS sessions were short (up to 30 min), the frequency of the sessions was also of crucial importance. The MCSS© total score varied from a minimum of 117 when sessions were more than 3 months apart, to a maximum of 140 when they were held every fortnight. When the sessions were of 60 min or more duration, however, the influence of frequency was less remarkable. The mean MCSS© total score varied only between 135 and140.

Summary

The international development of contemporary clinical supervision (CS) has been tracked back to innovations within human service agencies, prompted by charitable organizations in Europe and the United States (White & Winstanley, in press). Key individuals have been identified for their pioneering scholarship in the construction and refinement of appropriate ways in which CS can be measured and early examples of research instruments have been acknowledged. The Manchester Clinical Supervision Scale© (MCSS©) has since established a leading position in this lineage. The worldwide use of the MCSS© has permitted a large normative dataset to be accumulated, which has been systematically interrogated over more than a decade, not only

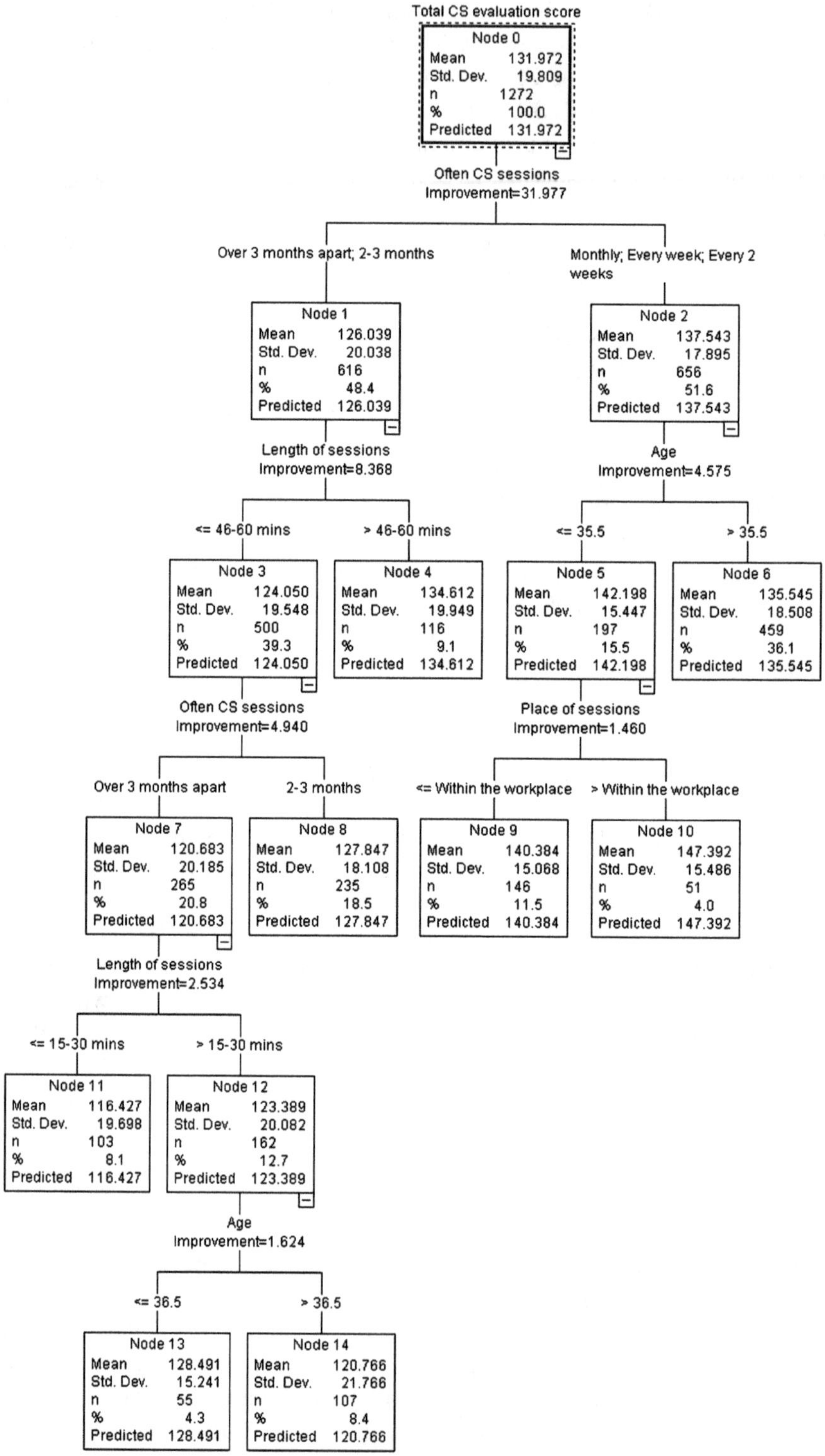

Figure 17.5 CART analysis of the whole group of supervisees (n = 1,272).

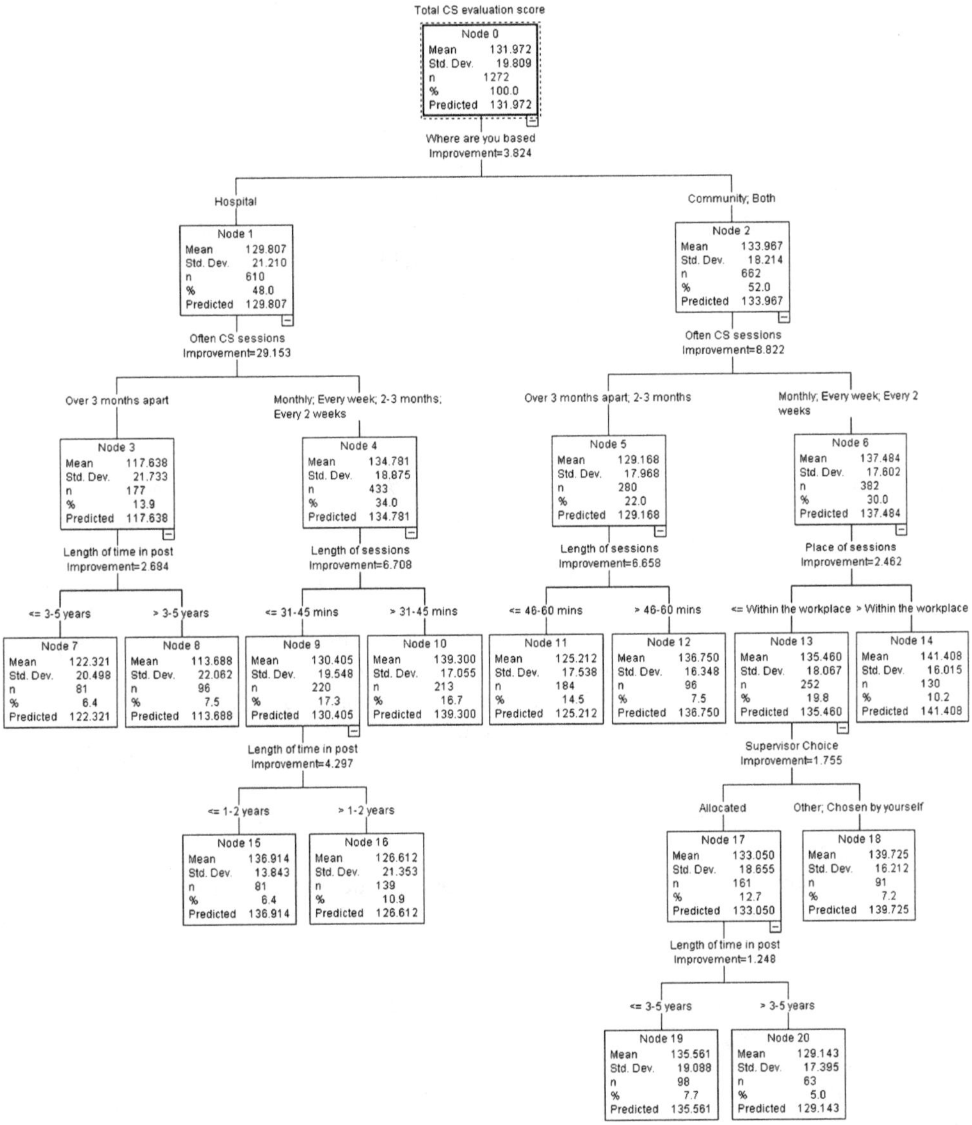

Figure 17.6 CART analysis of the whole group of supervisees (n = 1,272); staff group forced in as first variable.

to refine and strengthen the psychometric properties, but also to make a modest contribution to the development of testable theoretical insights and suggestions of practical CS guidelines.

The research and development of the MCSS© and its derivatives continue, and, in common with other approaches to practice-based evidence (Barkham, Mellor-Clark, Connell, & Carhill, 2006), this includes making best use of reliable information technology and the Internet, to develop even more robust ways to collect data, and to establish a feedback loop with services and individual practitioners. In the present example, a novel secondary analysis of real MCSS© data, using mathematical models and sophisticated software, revealed empirical evidence in support of two important factors which, in combination, result in the optimization of the MCSS© total score. These factors are the frequency and the length of CS sessions.

Given the infinite range of international practice environments, human service agencies now have the opportunity to harvest measurement data using the Manchester Clinical Supervision Scale© (MCSS-26©) and other complementary measures, and conduct CART analyses that take account of particular circumstances and resources. With prudent parsimony, the resultant findings will reveal a number of delivery permutations, which can be considered within the context of local service characteristics, to predict the likelihood of the most effective model of CS.

References

Allitt Inquiry. (1991). *Independent inquiry relating to the deaths and injuries on the children's ward at Grantham and Kesteven General Hospital during the period February to April 1991.* London, UK: HMSO.

Arcinue, F. (2002). *The development and validation of the Group Supervision Scale* (Unpublished doctoral dissertation). University of Southern California, USA.

Bambling, M., King, R., Patrick, R., Schweitzer, R., & Lambert, W. (2006). Clinical supervision: Its influence on client-rated working alliance and client symptom reduction in the brief treatment of major depression. *Psychotherapy Research, 16*, 317–331.

Barkham, M., Mellor-Clark, J., Connell, J., & Carhill, J. (2006). A core approach to practice-based evidence: A brief history of the origins and applications of the CORE-OM and CORE System. *Counselling and Psychotherapy Research, 6*, 3–15.

Bernard, J., & Goodyear, R. (1998). *Fundamentals of clinical supervision* (2nd ed.). Needham Heights, MA: Allyn and Bacon.

Bradshaw, T., Butterworth, A., & Mairs, H. (2007). Does structured clinical supervision during psychosocial intervention education enhance outcome for mental health nurses and the service users they work with? *Journal of Psychiatric and Mental Health Nursing, 14*, 4–12.

Breiman, L., Friedman, J., Olshen, R., & Stone, C. (1984). *Classification and regression trees.* Belmont, CA: Wadsworth.

British Association for Counselling and Psychotherapy. (2012). *About BACP. British Association for Counselling and Psychotherapy Web site.* Retrieved from http://www.bacp.co.uk

Brown, A. (1994). Interactional Supervision (Review of the book by L. Shulman, 1993, National Association of Social Workers Press, Washington DC). *British Journal of Social Work, 24*, 118–119.

Brown, A., & Bourne, I. (1995). *The social work supervisor.* Buckingham, UK: Open University Press.

Butterworth, T., Carson, J., White, E., Jeacock, J., Clements, A., & Bishop, V. (1997). *It is good to talk. Clinical supervision and mentorship: An evaluation in England and Scotland.* The University of Manchester, England.

Butterworth, T., & Woods, D. (1999). *Clinical Governance and Clinical Supervision; working together to ensure safe and accountable practice.* Briefing Paper. School of Nursing, Midwifery and Health Visiting, The University of Manchester, England.

Cape, J., & Barkham, M. (2002). Practice improvement methods: Conceptual base, evidence-based research, and practice-based recommendations. *The British Journal of Clinical Psychology, 41*, 285–307.

Crooker, J. (1917). *The true origin of modern methods of scientific charity.* Volume BSAC 074:297. April. Bibliotheca Sacra, Dallas.

Cross, W., Moore, A., Sampson, T., Kitch, C., & Ockerby, C. (2012). Implementing clinical supervision for ICU Outreach Nurses: A case study of their journey. *Australian Critical Care, 25*, 263–270. doi: 10.1016/j.aucc.2012.01.004.

Dawson, J. (1926). The case supervisor in a family agency without district offices. *The Family, 6*, 293–295.

Department of Health. (1994a). *Independent inquiry relating to deaths and injuries on the children's ward at Grantham and Kesteven General Hospital.* Clothier Report. HMSO, London.

Department of Health. (1994b). *Clinical supervision for the nursing and health visiting professions.* CNO letter 94(5). Department of Health, London.

Donabedian, A. (1966). Evaluating the quality of medical care. *Millbank Memorial Fund Quarterly, 44*, 166–203.

Ellis, M., & Ladany, N. (1997). Inferences concerning supervisees and clients in clinical supervision: An integrative review. In C. Watkins (Ed.), *Handbook of psychotherapy supervision* (pp. 447–507). New York, NY: Wiley.

Faugier, J., & Butterworth, T. (1994). *Clinical Supervision: A position paper.* School of Nursing Studies, University of Manchester, England.

Friedlander, M., & Ward, L. (1984). Development and validation of the supervisory styles inventory. *Journal of Counseling Psychology, 31*, 541–657.

Gawande, A. (2009). *The Checklist Manifesto: How to get things right.* New York, NY: Metropolitan Books.

Hancox, K., Lynch, L., Happell, B., & Biondo, S. (2004). An evaluation of an educational program for clinical supervision. *International Journal of Mental Health Nursing, 13*, 198–203.

Horton, S., deLourdes Drachler, M., Fuller, A., & deCarvalho Leite, J. (2008). Development and preliminary validation of a measure for assessing staff perspectives on the quality of clinical group supervision. *International Journal of Language and Communication Disorders, 43*, 126–134.

Kadushin, A. (1974). Supervisor-Supervisee: A survey. *Social Work, 19*, 288–297.

Kadushin, A. (1976). *Supervision in social work* (4th ed., 2002, with D. Harkness). New York, NY: Columbia University Press.

Ladany, N., Hill, C., Corbett, M., & Nutt, E. (1996). Nature, extent and importance of what psychotherapy trainees do not disclose to their supervisors. *Journal of Counseling Psychology, 43*, 10–24.

Larsen, D., Attkisson, C., Hargreaves, W., & Nguyen, T. (1979). Assessment of client/patient satisfaction: Development of a general scale. *Evaluation and Program Planning, 2*, 197–207.

Leddick, G., & Bernard, J. (1980). The history of supervision: A critical review. *Counselor Education and Supervision, 19*, 186–196.

Linacre, J. (2007). Foreword. In T. Bond & C. Fox (Eds.), *Applying the Rasch model: Fundamental measurement in the human sciences* (2nd ed.). Mahwah, NJ: Lawrence Erlbaum Associates.

Management Sciences for Health. (1998). *Supervisor Competency Self-Assessment Inventory.* October. Management Sciences for Health. Cambridge, Massachusetts.

Maslach, C., & Jackson, S. (1986). *Maslach burnout inventory.* Palo Alto, CA: Consulting Psychologists Press.

Milne, D., Aylott, H., Fitzpatrick, H., & Ellis, M. (2008). How does clinical supervision work? Using a "best evidence synthesis" approach to construct a basic model of supervision. *The Clinical Supervisor, 27*, 170–190.

Milne, D., & Reiser, R. (2011). Observing competence in CBT supervision: A systematic review of the available instruments. *The Cognitive Behaviour Therapist, 4*, 89–100.

Morgenbesser, M. (2011). *Complete Professor Alfred Kadushin interview. Part 1–5*. An interview University of Wisconsin-Madison Professor Emeritus Mel Morgenbesser. Retrieved from http://www.youtube.com/watch?v=_EVhcgedW-E

Munson, C. (1993). *Handbook of clinical social work supervision* (3rd ed., 2012). New York, NY: Taylor and Francis.

Open University. (1998). *K509: Clinical Supervision: A development pack for nurses*. Milton Keynes, UK: Oxford University Press.

Pallant, J., & Tennant, A. (2007). An introduction to the Rasch measurement model: An example using the Hospital Anxiety and Depression Scale HADS. *British Journal of Clinical Psychology, 46*, 1–18.

Palomo, M., Beinart, H., & Cooper, M. (2010). Development and validation of the Supervisory Relationship Questionnaire (SRQ) in UK trainee clinical psychologists. *British Journal of Clinical Psychology, 49*, 131–149.

Proctor, B. (1986). Supervision: A cooperative exercise in accountability. In M. Marken & M. Payne (Eds.), *Enabling and ensuring: Supervision in practice* (pp. 21–34). (Original printing). Leicester, UK: National Youth Bureau and Council for Education and Training in Youth and Community Work. (NB: Reprinted in May 1988. Inside page shows first publication date as April 1987. ISBN reveals June 1987).

Rasch, G. (1960). *Probabilistic models for some intelligence and attainment tests*. Danish Institute for Educational Research, Copenhagen. Expanded edition 1980, foreword and afterword by B. Wright. Chicago, IL: The University of Chicago Press.

Reese, R., Aldarondo, F., Anderson, C., Lee, S., Miller, T., & Burton, D. (2009). Telehealth in clinical supervision: A comparison of supervision formats. *Journal of Telemedicine and Telecare, 15*, 356–361.

Richmond, M. (1899). *Friendly visiting among the poor: A handbook for charity workers*. New York, NY: Macmillan.

RUMM Laboratory Pty Ltd. (2011). *RUMM2030 software*. Retrieved from http://www.rummlab.com.au

Saarikoski, M., Isoaho, H., Warne, T., & Leino-Kilpi, H. (2008). The nurse teacher in clinical practice: Developing the new sub-dimension to the clinical learning environment and supervision (CLES) scale. *International Journal of Nursing Studies, 45*, 1233–1237.

Shulman, L. (1981). *Identifying, measuring, and teaching helping skills*. Council on Social Work Education, New York and the Canadian Association of Schools of Social Work, Ottawa.

Shulman, L. (1993). *Interactional supervision*. Washington, DC: NASW Press.

Stevens, S. (1946). On the theory of scales of measurement. *Science, 103*(2684), 677–680.

United Kingdom Central Council for Nursing, Midwifery and Health Visiting. (1996). *Position statement on clinical supervision for nursing and health visiting*. London, UK: UKCC.

Wampold, B., & Brown, G. (2005). Estimating variability in outcomes attributable to therapists: A naturalistic study of outcomes in managed care. *Journal of Consulting and Clinical Psychology, 73*, 914–923.

Watkins, C. E. (1997). *Handbook of psychotherapy supervision*. New York, NY: Wiley.

Weiss, M. (1967). *Manual for the Minnesota Satisfaction Questionnaire*. University of Minnesota, Minneapolis.

White, E., & Winstanley, J. (2010). A randomised controlled trial of Clinical Supervision: Selected findings from a novel Australian attempt to establish the evidence base for causal relationships with quality of care and patient outcomes, as an informed contribution to mental health nursing practice development. *Journal of Research in Nursing, 15*, 151–167.

White, E., & Winstanley, J. (2011). Clinical Supervision for mental health professionals: The evidence base. *Social Work and Social Sciences Review*, *14*(3), 77–94.

White, E., & Winstanley, J. (in press). Clinical Supervision and the helping professions: An interpretation of history. *The Clinical Supervisor*.

Williamson, G., & Dodds, S. (1999). The effectiveness of a group approach to clinical supervision in reducing stress: A review of the literature. *Journal of Clinical Nursing*, *8*, 338–344.

Winstanley, J. (2000). Manchester Clinical Supervision Scale©. *Nursing Standard*, *14*(19), 31–32.

Winstanley, J., & White, E. (2011). The MCSS-26©: Revision of The Manchester Clinical Supervision Scale© using the Rasch Measurement Model. *Journal of Nursing Measurement*, *19*, 160–178.

Winstanley, J., & White, E. (2012). Nordic translations of the Manchester Clinical Supervision Scale: A rejoinder. *Journal of Nursing Management*, *20*, 948–950.

Yale University. (2012). *Family Counselling of Greater New Haven, Inc.* Records (MS 1808). Manuscripts and Archives, Yale University Library. Retrieved from http://hdl.handle.net/10079/fa/mssa.ms.1808

18

SAGE
A Scale for Rating Competence in CBT Supervision

Derek L. Milne and Robert P. Reiser

Introduction

In Chapter 1 of this handbook it was noted how the context could influence supervision. In the present chapter we will outline how the British National Health Service (NHS) created a favorable cultural context for the development of an instrument for directly observing competence in supervision, SAGE (Supervision: Adherence and Guidance Evaluation). We will outline this NHS context before providing details on this instrument. To add qualitative color to this description, we will then present cross-cultural material from a longitudinal $n = 1$ study that used evidence-based clinical supervision (EBCS; Milne, 2009) in conjunction with SAGE. We end by noting that there exist cross-cultural and professional barriers to this form of supervision, as well as to the direct observation of supervisory competence, but conclude that such barriers can and should be overcome if supervision is to benefit.

The British Context

"Modernization" of the British NHS became a pressing priority with the election of the Labour government in 1997 (Department of Health, 1998). Supervision was increasingly specified, latterly gaining the status of an essential element within high-quality patient care: "regular clinical supervision will encourage reflective practice and needs to be available to all staff . . . the importance of staff training and support cannot be underestimated" (Department of Health, 2004, p. 35). The status of supervision was further strengthened within the recent Improving Access to Psychological Treatment initiative (IAPT; Layard, 2005), a major fresh investment of government money in psychological therapies. Turpin (2012) noted the "central role" that high-quality supervision was to play within IAPT (p. 39).

The Wiley International Handbook of Clinical Supervision, First Edition. Edited by C. Edward Watkins, Jr. and Derek L. Milne.

High-quality supervision necessitates sound measurement and corrective feedback, yet these have been hampered by the lack of suitable instruments: "one of the most pernicious problems confronting supervision researchers is the dearth of psychometrically sound measures specific to a clinical supervision context" (Ellis & Ladany, 1997, p. 488). Ellis and Ladany concluded that there were no suitable instruments designed to measure competence in clinical supervision. In the United Kingdom, the supervision competence framework (Roth & Pilling, 2008) advocated direct observation of supervisors, possibly using tapes and by reference to specific criteria or competences. In summary, the British NHS reforms introduced a culture within which supervision came of age, creating a favorable context for developing a suitable instrument.

Systematic Review of Observational Tools

In three relevant papers we reported a review of the existing instruments for observing supervisory competence (Milne & Reiser, 2011), described the preliminary evaluation of a new instrument for measuring competence in supervision (SAGE; Milne, Reiser, Cliffe, & Raine, 2011), and applied SAGE within an 11-month study of supervision (Milne, Reiser, & Cliffe, 2013). We summarize this psychometric evaluation work here, then present for the first time some of the raw qualitative data from SAGE, as used within this longitudinal study, to offer a cross-cultural perspective on some of the barriers to direct observation.

Development of a New Supervision Instrument: SAGE

Because of our research program and the emphasis on evidence-based practices (EBP) in the United Kingdom and the United States, we developed a tool to observe the competence of supervision in relation to cognitive-behavioral therapy (CBT) and the closely related approach of evidence-based clinical supervision (EBCS; Milne, 2009, see p. 71). In essence, EBCS is an enhancement of CBT supervision, strengthening the emphasis on experiential learning (e.g., more emotional experiencing). EBCS also differs by drawing systematically on applied psychology and adult learning (e.g., educational needs assessment; developmental model), reflected in nonequivalent qualitative and quantitative outcomes (Milne, Reiser, Cliffe, Breese, et al., 2011; Milne et al., 2013). The resulting instrument, SAGE, was initially a 23-item instrument, as summarized in Table 18.1 (in later versions we dropped item 9).

Three factors were assumed in constructing SAGE, reflecting the EBCS model (Milne, 2009). Items 1–4 were termed "The common factors," designed to assess the supervisory relationship or alliance. Items 5–18 were termed "The supervision cycle," designed to assess supervision competencies. This allowed for an assessment of the fidelity of supervision to the CBT or EBCS models (i.e., whether there was *adherence* to one of these models). Items 19–23 were termed "The supervisee's learning cycle," designed to assess the initial signs of experiential learning (so providing the *evaluation* part of the acronym). Each of these 23 SAGE items was defined within a coding manual (available on request). Competence is rated after observing

Table 18.1 A summary of the instrument SAGE, intended to rate supervisory competence based on direct observation.

SAGE items	*Brief definition*
Common factors	
1. Relating	Core conditions; "restorative"
2. Collaborating	Alliance
3. Managing	Scaffolded; optimal challenge; "normative"
4. Facilitating	Improving grasp (including perplexity)
Supervision cycle	
5. Agenda-setting	Needs-led/developmental objectives
6. Demonstrating	Modeling
7. Discussing	Review; disagree; problem-solving
8. Evaluating	Closely monitor (e.g., clinical data)
9. Experiencing	Expressing and processing affective aspects
10. Feeding back (giving)	Offer praise; strengths/weaknesses
11. Feeding back (receiving)	Elicit (e.g., helpful events/transfer)
12. Formulating	Analysis, synthesis, explanation
13. Listening	Attending and summarizing
14. Observing	Live/tape material
15. Prompting	Reminders and cues
16. Questioning	Gather information; raise awareness
17. Teaching	Informing/educating (symbolic)
18. Training	Experiential learning (e.g., role-play)
Supervisees cycle	
19. Experiencing	Awareness, identification, and processing of affect
20. Reflecting	Summarizing and integrating subjective material
21. Conceptualizing	Integrating objective material (e.g., theories/ findings)
22. Planning	Decision-making about actions
23. Experimenting	Enacting plans (in and out of supervision, e.g., trial and error learning through role-play/ reality-checking)

a supervision session, typically from an audiotape recording, using a scale from *incompetent* to *expert*. Table 18.2 outlines the rating scale. Qualitatively, the observer also adds any notes, such as explaining high or low ratings, and suggests ways to improve the observed sample of supervision (see Table 18.3 for an example). We will draw on examples of this qualitative material to note some cultural differences, to illustrate an international dimension. Our EBCS model assumes that a competent supervisor would utilize a range of skills to enable the supervisee to commence experiential learning (i.e., a combination of action, reflection, conceptualization, and experiencing; Kolb, 1984), within an effective supervisory relationship.

The preliminary psychometric work on SAGE is detailed in Milne, Reiser, Cliffe, and Raine (2011). To summarize, we started with content validity, drawing exten-

Table 18.2 The scoring key for SAGE, drawn from the rating manual.

Competence level		*Examples*
Incompetent	0	Absence of feature, or highly inappropriate performance
Novice	1	Inappropriate performance, with major problems evident
Advanced beginner	2	Evidence of competence, but numerous problems
Competent	3	Competent, but some problems and/or inconsistencies
Proficient	4	Good features, but minor problems and/or inconsistencies
Expert	5	Very good features, minimal problems, and/or inconsistencies
Expert+	6	Excellent performance, or very good even in the face of difficulties

sively on "Teachers' PETS" (Process Evaluation of Training and Supervision; Milne, James, Keegan, & Dudley, 2002) and "CBT STARS" (James, Blackburn, Milne, Freeston, & Armstrong, 2005). The items for Teachers' PETS were derived from the applied psychology literature, particularly from instruments designed to assess different forms of leadership (e.g., teachers, coaches, and supervisors). The items for CBT STARS were based on an expert consensus by a group of experienced CBT supervisors.

Second, construct validity was assessed by factor analysis, based on data from $n = 176$ mental health professionals. This indicated a single factor, Supervisory Competence, accounting for 77% of the variance. Internal consistency was .98. In contrast to the aforementioned rationale for SAGE, this analysis suggested that the three intuited factors could be collapsed into one, at least for this sample. A second preliminary and as yet unpublished principal components factor analysis on the original 23-item version of SAGE has recently been completed. It was based on a survey of $n = 114$ supervisor and supervisee pairs and suggested a three-factor solution akin to the original conception of SAGE: Structured Learning Environment, Supervisory Alliance, and Experiential Learning. Full-scale and respective subscale internal consistencies (based on Cronbach's coefficient alpha) of .92, .91, .91, and .80 were obtained. While a more definitive analysis will require a larger n, this finding is intriguing in that these factors reflect well-supported elements in the literature on effective supervision practices.

Third, we looked at the predictive (criterion) validity, reasoning that EBCS should have a significantly greater effect on experiential learning (i.e., SAGE items 19–23) than CBT supervision, due to drawing on supervision methods with evidence to support their effectiveness (Milne, 2009). We utilized a longitudinal study for this assessment (Milne et al., 2013) with an $n = 1$ multiple phase (ABAB) design. The phases within the design were alternating baseline phases (Phase A: CBT supervision as usual), and intervention phases (Phase B: EBCS). Both forms of intervention involved supervision-of-supervision, to promote adherence to these different approaches to supervision. The SAGE data indicated that EBCS did result in greater learning by the supervisee with a mean 32% improvement. Statistical analysis of covariation across the overall ABAB sequence supported this interpretation: the

Table 18.3 A sample SAGE record sheet, from the Milne et al. (2013) study.

Record sheet completed by (rater/observer): Derek
Date of rating: January 29

Supervisor: RR; *Supervisee:* B.
Date of Supervision Session: January 28

Items	*Circle your rating*						
The common factors	*Incompetent*			*Competent*			*Expert*
1. Relating (Interpersonally effective)	0	1	2	3	4	5√	6
2. Collaborating	0	1	2	3	4	5√	6
3. Managing	0	1	2	3	4√	5	6
4. Facilitating	0	1	2	3	4	5√	6
The supervision cycle							
5. Agenda-setting (and adherence)	0	1	2	3	4	5√	6
6. Demonstrating	0	1	2	3	4√	5	6
7. Discussing	0	1	2	3	4√	5	6
8. Evaluating	0	1	2	3	4	5√	6
9. Experiencing	0	1	2	3	4√	5	6
10. Feedback (giving)	0	1	2	3√	4	5	6
11. Feedback (eliciting)	0	1√	2	3	4	5	6
12. Formulating	0	1	2	3	4	5√	6
13. Listening	0	1	2	3	4	5√	6
14. Observing	0	1	2	3	4	5√	6
15. Prompting	0	1	2	3	4√	5	6
16. Questioning	0	1	2	3	4√	5	6
17. Teaching	0	1	2	3√	4	5	6
18. Training	0	1	2	3	4√	5	6
The supervisee's learning							
19. Experiencing	0	1	2	3	4√	5	6
20. Reflecting	0	1	2	3	4	5√	6
21. Conceptualizing	0	1	2	3	4√	5	6
22. Planning	0	1	2	3	4√	5	6
23. Experimenting	0	1	2	3	4	5√	6

NOTES: Good example of EBCS, with exceptionally thorough attention to agenda-setting, drawing on the "Learning Outcomes list" effectively (including training B in its use). I've said this before, but it struck me again today, faced with a supervisee who's sweet but actually rather unhelpful in supervision (e.g., not planned; rather unforthcoming when questioned) you were consistently poised and patient, with that high degree of concern/caring. Also (as noted before, but still striking and commendable) skillfully and persistently taking B with you; ensuring that she is signed up to the challenging action plan.

SUGGESTIONS: I realize that you got through a lot, and that doing that thorough job of goal-setting initially took ages, but we need to ensure that all the main bases are covered, so please try to always end by seeking her feedback (item 11), which might also strengthen her "experiencing," as in asking her how she felt about the supervision session.

supervisee's learning significantly covaried with EBCS. By contrast, nonsignificant findings were obtained for all CBT sequences.

Fourth, to assess the discriminant validity of SAGE, we compared naturalistic recordings of three supervision sessions believed to represent three distinct approaches: CBT, psychodynamic, and systemic supervision. Modifying the recording to that of frequencies (as per Teachers' PETS), we found that the CBT supervision session contained all but one of the SAGE items (i.e., item 18, "experiencing," was not observed). SAGE ratings indicated that this CBT session mostly contained teaching (13% of observed behaviors) and supervisee reflecting (12%), followed by questioning the supervisee (10%), the supervisor observing (10%), and the supervisor listening to the supervisee (7%). The psychodynamic supervision session mostly contained supervisee reflecting (32%), related to the supervisor's extensive listening (19%), questioning (9%), and teaching (11%).This psychodynamic session did not include any agenda-setting, demonstrating, receiving feedback, observing, training, or experimenting. By contrast, within the systemic supervision session again only one SAGE item was not observed: demonstrating. Similar to the psychodynamic session, the systemic session was predominantly a combination of reflecting (33%), listening (25%), questioning (12%), and discussing (5%).

Lastly, we assessed inter-rater reliability in the use of SAGE between two novice (undergraduate) raters. Their independent ratings of a representative supervision session indicated an exact percent agreement of 73%, with a Pearson's correlation of $r = .815$ ($p = .001$). The more robust reliability measure, Cohen's Kappa coefficient, was K = .54, which equates to moderate agreement. In summary, SAGE shows promise in terms of a sorely neglected sphere: measuring competence in supervision through direct observation. In the future, we plan to undertake a generalizability study of SAGE to better examine its characteristics.

Next we outline how SAGE served as the main measure within our longitudinal study (Milne et al., 2013). This was a rare comparative evaluation of two methods of supervision, CBT and EBCS. The only prior examples to our knowledge are the randomized controlled trials by Bambling, King, Raue, Schweitzer, and Lambert (2006), and by Uys, Minnaar, and Simpson (2005). Bambling et al. compared CBT and psychodynamic supervision, finding no significant difference in patients' depression scores at the end of an eight-session treatment period. However, both forms of supervision improved patient outcome. Uyset al. found that the two supervision approaches that they compared (i.e., a developmental model and Holloway's 1995 matrix model) both produced significantly improved supervisee ratings of supervision but that neither approach was superior.

These studies followed the dominant methodology of large-group designs. A complementary strategy is to use small-sample designs, such as the $n = 1$ method, which affords benefits in terms of exceptionally high internal validity, partly as a result of the precise control that is possible over the supervision intervention. We have been utilizing this methodology throughout our analyses of supervision, finding it manageable and illuminating. Our reasoning is that it is a preferable "upstream" method to use in the early development of an intervention like supervision, as it allows one to better specify, test, and refine the key variables (including a dependent variable like SAGE). The first such study was Milne and Westerman (2001), in which we studied the effects of fortnightly consultation (supervision-of-supervision) on the clinical supervision of three supervisees over an eight-month period, using a multiple baseline design. As anticipated, we found an increased use of the key EBCS activity "guided experiential learning" (i.e., item 18, "training," in Table 18.1). Encouraged, we next compared routine CBT supervision and EBCS with the help of one supervisor and six supervisees (Milne & James, 2002). The results indicated that the supervisors could develop their CBT approach with the aid of consultancy, again when judged in terms of the supervisees' initial experiential learning. Other related $n = 1$ studies, all conducted within the NHS under naturalistic conditions, have yielded consistently similar results (i.e., Milne, Lombardo, Kennedy, Freeston, & Day, 2008; Milne, Pilkington, Gracie, & James, 2003). This has been corroborated and elaborated by qualitative analyses of the $n = 1$ material, such as studies of the content of supervision "episodes" (e.g., Breese, Boon, & Milne, 2012; Milne, Reiser, Cliffe, Breese, et al., 2011).

The present study built on this $n = 1$ work by looking more closely at adherence to the CBT and EBCS approaches and by using SAGE as the measure of adherence. Like the studies cited earlier, we alternated these two approaches across patients, adopting ABA and ABAB phases across three clients (A = CBT; B = EBCS). We included all 37 consecutive, audiotaped sessions of supervision that took place over 11 months and included discussion of at least one of the patients. Each of these sessions was rated with SAGE and then aggregated into an overall supervisor competence score (i.e., SAGE items 1–18). The final five SAGE items (19–23) were also aggregated to give a "supervisee learning" score for each supervision session. The study was based on a community psychology training clinic in the United States serving adults presenting with complex mental health problems. The participants were one male consultant (i.e., the first author, based in the United Kingdom and serving as the supervisor of the supervisor), one male supervisor (the second author), one female therapist (i.e., supervisee), and three clients (two males and one female) presenting with anxiety and depression. During the study, consultancy involved fortnightly phone calls for hour-long reviews of the preceding week's tape-recorded supervision (i.e., supervision-of-supervision). Corrective feedback was provided to the supervisor based on the consultant's ratings of the prior session using SAGE. Consultancy included offering support and guidance to the supervisor in the form of discussion, advice, teaching, supervision guidelines, experiential exercises (e.g., role-plays), DVD illustrations, and other supportive materials.

In terms of analyzing these SAGE ratings, we used a combination of visual inspection of the descriptive (longitudinal) data and inferential statistics. As indicated in Figure 18.1, visual inspection suggested to us that the EBCS phases yielded the highest SAGE scores for all three clients, although there is considerable variability. The mean values for clients in each of the phases (CBT or EBCS) are indicated by the broken horizontal lines and supports this interpretation (i.e., all the EBCS phases have higher mean SAGE scores than the CBT phases). This suggested that there was good adherence to the two approaches, as SAGE was designed to be most sensitive to EBCS. Specifically, when we compared the SAGE items considered to best distinguish EBCS, we found support for this interpretation, with ratings .63 points higher during EBCS phases for "emotional engagement,""challenging,""training," and "experiencing." Conversely, CBT supervision had higher ratings for "conceptualiz-

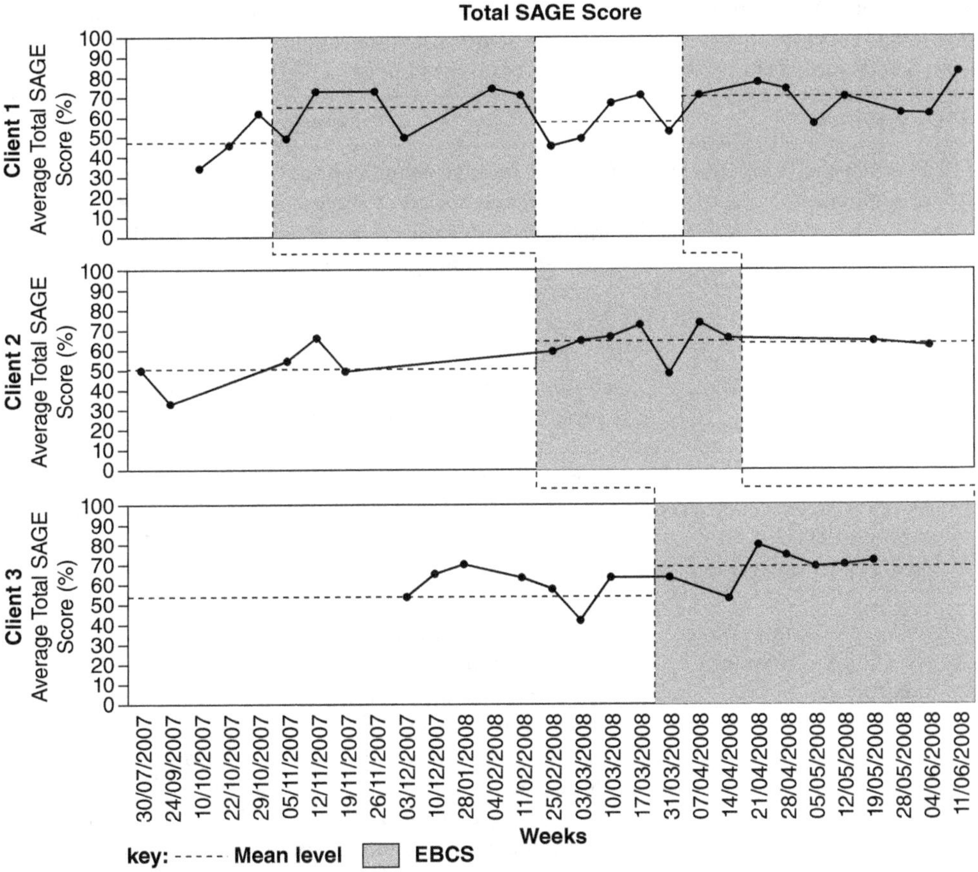

Figure 18.1 A diagrammatic summary of the authors' longitudinal, $n = 1$ study design (from Milne et al., 2013, together with the total SAGE scores in relation to CBT supervision and EBCS [shaded phases]).

ing" (mean: .2), reflecting the relative emphasis on case discussion and reformulation within this approach.

When we analyzed these SAGE ratings statistically, we obtained trends for each successive client's supervision. This indicated in each case that EBCS resulted in greater engagement in experiential learning by the supervisee (i.e., the mean values within the EBCS phases all exceeded those within the CBT phases). The two phases, CBT supervision and EBCS, were then compared across all three clients combined, in order to increase statistical power, in terms of the supervisee's learning data (i.e., the relevant SAGE items, 19–23: see Table 18.1). Statistically significant differences between the supervisee's learning in the CBT and EBCS phases were obtained ($p < .05$). Expressed in terms of the differences in the SAGE learning scores between phases for all three clients, EBCS was associated with enhanced engagement in experiential learning on four of the five SAGE learning items, amounting to a mean improvement of 32%.

Table 18.4 An illustration of how written qualitative feedback from the consultant (i.e., providing "supervision-of-supervision") can achieve the four functions of SAGE (quotes drawn from SAGE record sheets within the $n = 1$ study: Milne et al., 2013).

SAGE Functions	*Examples*
1. Evaluate the competence of supervisors	"This was an engrossing session, rich in content, appropriately varied in the use of methods, great intensity, and featuring an exceptionally good alliance (esp. mutual engagement, partly through superb 'titration' of the challenge/threat to the supervisee) . . . Congratulations!"
2. Audit adherence to supervision standards	"Another 'straight-down-the-middle', traditional, didactic session, spiced up with some persistent, helpful questioning/guided discovery, and by the welcome use of a tape of recent therapy" (i.e., adherence to CBT "supervision-as-usual" during a baseline phase).
3. Develop practice, through detailed feedback to supervisors (e.g., on the supervisee's reaction/learning; or on the clinical outcomes/ transfer)	"Agenda-setting: you did OK to begin with, but then during the feedback at the close (which was otherwise improved on last time) I wasn't struck by any explicit reference back (e.g., you might say: 'OK, we set out to do A, B & C: to what extent do you think . . .?'). If you wish, let's rehearse this in consultancy. . . ." "Supervisee was highly engaged and collaborative. She appeared to emerge more confident." "Great management . . . particularly in ensuring that the three patients got roughly equal attention." "Supervisee becoming more directive, so complementing her strengths in the more supportive and exploratory therapeutic modes."
4. Profile different styles of supervision (e.g., contrast two approaches)	"I thought that these were two contrasting but equally excellent examples of supervision: with patient X the emphasis was on the supervisee's long-term development, including your parallel process interpretation . . . Then, with patient Y you were more experiential, sticking squarely and expertly to the EBCS model."

Not reported in the Milne et al. (2013), or elsewhere, was the material within the notes and suggestions parts of the SAGE instrument. Examples of these qualitative remarks are therefore combined within Table 18.4 in relation to the four main functions that can be served by SAGE. According to the SAGE manual, the instrument can be used to evaluate the competence of supervisors; to audit adherence to standards for supervision (especially CBT supervision); to develop practice, by enabling detailed feedback to be provided to supervisors; and to profile different styles of supervision. Of course, we have already seen how SAGE can be used for such purposes by means of the quantitative ratings (as in Table 18.3). Here we hope to show how the qualitative material can complement these ratings, enhancing the potential value of SAGE. Table 18.4 illustrates how these four functions were addressed within our longitudinal study.

Cultural Considerations

We next reflect briefly on the international dimension underlying our longitudinal study (i.e., Milne et al., 2013). We draw on the fact that the British consultant (the first author) was speaking by telephone with his American colleague (the second author) every fortnight throughout the study during the period from 2007 to 2008. As we will illustrate, although both had English as a first language, there were some noteworthy cross-cultural differences. From the consultant's British perspective, the supervisor appeared extremely positive in the way he spoke, almost a caricature of the American upbeat, "can-do" attitude. Nothing was a problem, and the sky was the limit. Perhaps such an attitude was necessary for us to embark on such a challenging project. And this style was certainly a refreshing contrast with the British bent for caution, understatement, and dour self-deprecation. But the positive style of speech, with its affirmative, emotionally charged tone also felt effusive and uncomfortable to the consultant, as he was working in the emotionally restricted world of northern England and had been brought up in post-Second World War Scotland (for a sense of that critical, evaluative environment, see Duncan, 2004). In short, the supervisor's positive emotional tone was not consistent with the consultant's upbringing, or the way that the consultant would normally speak professionally in the United Kingdom. Within British professional circles, such an uncritical style might even be regarded with suspicion, as a form of politeness that was suggestive of an unspoken, substantive problem (e.g., that the consultancy was so downright poor that the supervisor felt that all he could do was to emphasize the few available positives). In practice, this was sometimes so marked a difference that one of us would feel obliged to begin by stating, perhaps in a jocular way, that the other person should please bear this stylistic difference in mind. Also, the consultant learned to try and be a notch or two more positive during these international calls or when completing the qualitative part of the fortnightly SAGE record sheet (see Table 18.4).

From the perspective of the supervisor, there were several other potential barriers to international collaboration. First of all, EBCS itself is a relatively challenging and emotionally arousing method. As a result, this style of supervision often creates a significant level of discomfort in the supervisory relationship, particularly during affectively charged learning episodes, both for the supervisor himself and for his or her trainee. This tension may have been accentuated by cross-cultural differences, as EBCS had been developed in the context of the evidence-based practice and the British NHS. The EBCS platform may not be consistent with certain styles of supervision or for supervisors who rely primarily on a supportive stance and are uncomfortable in providing specific and concrete and challenging feedback directly to supervisees. We have emphasized in a prior article (Reiser & Milne, 2013) that optimal levels of anxiety play a vital role in learning, as also noted specifically in the IAPT supervision competencies (Roth & Pilling, 2008). The supervisor who is unwilling to tolerate supervisee discomfort is likely to convey to the supervisee that "being comfortable" is an acceptable goal for supervision and psychotherapy. A parallel process may also emerge, one in which both the supervisor and the supervisee prefers a supportive and "soft" style of supervision, a comfortable collusion (for a case study, see Milne, Leck, & Choudhri, 2009). This kind of avoidance can deeply undermine therapeutic progress for clients who need to face their discomfort and discontinue escape/avoidance strategies, as well as providing very poor modeling for supervisee learning and training experiences. In one of the critical incidents identified in our research program (Breese et al., 2012), providing the supervisee with direct and challenging feedback about her avoidance of difficult issues and low expectations of her client resulted in dramatic positive changes, in both the supervisee and her client's subsequent behavior. Arguably, managing this tension between support and challenge is at the core of effective supervision.

A second major barrier was the use of direct observation with SAGE, as it is potentially threatening for supervisors, who may fear that close observation will result in negative evaluation of their supervision. Indeed, this was the experience of the second author, who, despite 20 years of supervising and five years directing a doctoral-level training clinic, felt profoundly intimidated by having to send off tapes of his own supervision for external review. It was humbling that several initial tapes fell below the cutoff for competence on SAGE, leading to some very challenging feedback and one or two quite significant course corrections to the supervision. In one notable moment of the consultancy, the supervisor had veered off course and received both very low scores (50% average rating on Supervision Cycle Rating Items of SAGE) and very pointed feedback on the qualitative section on SAGE: "I then listened to the last available session with S002, who is supposed to be receiving EBCS, but I didn't hear anything different from the CBT session. For example, in both sessions the agenda-setting episodes were effectively abandoned . . ." (SAGE Record Sheet, December 3, 2007). As this example illustrates, the evaluation of competence and adherence to this direct observation method required hardiness and a willingness to persevere, despite setbacks or frustrating moments. This higher level of challenge and directive feedback was particularly challenging for the supervisor to accept, perhaps as it was emanating from a different context and culture.

The cultural context is noteworthy in that few supervisors in doctoral training programs in the United States have ever had their supervision directly observed. Specifically, when pre-doctoral training program directors were asked to endorse supervision training competencies, there was only weak agreement with the item concerned with whether the supervisor had received supervision of his or her supervision, including some form of observation (audio or video; Rings, Genuchi, Hall, Angelo, & Erickson Cornich, 2009). It appears that there may be slightly more endorsement in Britain in that direct observation has been recommended as part of core competency training in recent IAPT supervisor training guidelines. Nonetheless, it is apparent that the underlying technology (in terms of pairing a direct observational method with the use of a standardized instrument to rate competency in supervisors) is still early in its acceptance and development, even within the modernizing ethos of the NHS (". . . reliable scales of supervision competence have yet to be developed and agreed.": IAPT Education and Training Group, 2011, p. 3). We have noted elsewhere that this difficulty in implementing direct observation of supervision appears to be international (Reiser & Milne, 2012). Based in part on our $n = 1$ study experience (Milne et al., 2013), we speculate that this difficulty represents an understandable avoidance behavior. This avoidance may be especially pronounced in cultures that (unlike the United Kingdom and the United States) view direct feedback as potentially rude or offensive.

In summary, even these relatively minor cultural differences regarding the emotional challenge within supervision and participants' willingness to tolerate the discomfort of direct observation (and directive feedback) probably affected how supervision-of-supervision took place, influencing in turn the general way that we used SAGE.

Conclusion

We have summarized our initial work on SAGE, a promising observational instrument for rating supervisory competence, placing it in the context of the British NHS. Despite clear support for measurement within the NHS, and an American culture where ". . . accountability rules the day . . ." (Watkins, 2012, p. 201), there has been a lack of sound instruments for evaluating supervision. In particular, the absence of a tool for assessing competence in supervision is a serious omission. Competence now lies at the heart of professional training and licensing (Falender & Shafranske, 2012), so instruments are required to help us to develop proficient, accountable, evidence-based clinical services. Such tools should define the technical, cognitive, and emotional competencies of supervision that promote safe and effective mental health practice (Roth & Pilling, 2008). We believe that SAGE meets these criteria and has shown promise in evaluating and fostering supervisory competence, although further psychometric work is planned. Additionally, as the above section illustrates, we acknowledge that supervisors and students face cross-cultural and professional barriers to this more direct and emotionally arousing form of supervision and observation. However, it is our belief that these barriers need to be overcome if we are to reap the benefits of more vigorous supervision and its more rigorous evaluation.

References

Bambling, M., King, R., Raue, P., Schweitzer, R., & Lambert, W. (2006). Clinical supervision: Its influence on client-rated working alliance and client symptom reduction in the brief treatment of major depression. *Psychotherapy Research*, *16*, 317–331.

Breese, L., Boon, A., & Milne, D. L. (2012). Detecting excellent episodes in clinical supervision: A case study, comparing two approaches. *The Clinical Supervisor*, *31*, 121–137. doi: 10.1080/07325223.2013.730012.

Department of Health. (1998). *A first class service: Quality in the new NHS.* London, UK: Department of Health.

Department of Health. (2004). *Organising and delivering psychological therapies.* London, UK: Department of Health.

Duncan, B. (2004). *The wee book of Calvin.* London, UK: Penguin.

Ellis, M. V., & Ladany, N. (1997). Inferences concerning supervisees and clients in clinical supervision: An integrative review. In C. E. Watkins (Ed.), *Handbook of psychotherapy supervision* (pp. 447–507). New York, NY: Wiley.

Falender, C. A., & Shafranske, E. P. (2012). The importance of competency-based clinical supervision and training in the twenty-first century: Why bother? *Journal of Contemporary Psychotherapy*, *42*, 129–137.

IAPT Education and Training Group. (2011). *Guidance for commissioning IAPT supervisor training (revised 2011)*. Retrieved from http://www.iapt.nhs.uk/silo/files/guidance-for-commissioning-iapt-supervisor-training-revised-2011.pdf

James, I. A., Blackburn, I.-M., Milne, D. L., Freeston, M., & Armstrong, P. (2005). *Supervision training and assessment rating scale for gognitive therapy (STARS – CT)*. Unpublished instrument, available from Ian James (ianjamesncht@yahoo.com); the centre for the health of the elderly, Newcastle General Hospital, England, NE4 6BE.

Kolb, D. A. (1984). *Experiential learning: Experience as the source of learning and development*. Englewood Cliffs, NJ: Prentice-Hall.

Layard, R. (2005). *Therapy for all on the NHS*. Sainsbury Centre Lecture, September 6, 2005. London, UK: Sainsbury Centre.

Milne, D. L. (2009). *Evidence-based clinical supervision: Principles and practice*. Malden, MA: BPS/Blackwell.

Milne, D. L., & James, I. A. (2002). The observed impact of training on competence in clinical supervision. *British Journal of Clinical Psychology*, *41*, 55–72.

Milne, D. L., James, I. A., Keegan, D., & Dudley, M. (2002). Teachers' PETS: A new observational measure of experiential training interactions. *Clinical Psychology and Psychotherapy*, *9*, 187–199.

Milne, D. L., Leck, C., & Choudhri, N. Z. (2009). Collusion in clinical supervision: Literature review and case study in self-reflection. *The Cognitive Behaviour Therapist*, *2*, 106–114.

Milne, D. L., Lombardo, C., Kennedy, E., Freeston, M., & Day, A. (2008). Zooming in on clinical supervision. *Behavioural and Cognitive Psychotherapy*, *3*, 619–624.

Milne, D. L., Pilkington, J., Gracie, J., & James, I. A. (2003). Transferring skills from supervision to therapy: A qualitative and quantitative N=1 analysis. *Behavioural and Cognitive Psychotherapy*, *31*, 193–202.

Milne, D. L., & Reiser, R. P. (2011). Observing competence in CBT supervision: A systematic review of the available instruments. *The Cognitive Behaviour Therapist*, *4*, 89–100.

Milne, D. L., Reiser, R. P., & Cliffe, T. (2013). An N=1 evaluation of enhanced CBT supervision. *Behavioural and Cognitive Psychotherapy*, *41*, 210–220.

Milne, D. L., Reiser, R. P., Cliffe, T., Breese, L., Boon, A., Raine, R., & Scarratt, P. (2011). A qualitative comparison of cognitive-behavioural and evidence-based clinical supervision. *The Cognitive Behaviour Therapist*, *4*, 152–166.

Milne, D. L., Reiser, R. P., Cliffe, T., & Raine, R. (2011). SAGE: Preliminary evaluation of an instrument for observing competence in CBT supervision. *The Cognitive Behaviour Therapist*, *4*, 123–138.

Milne, D. L., & Westerman, C. (2001). Evidence-based clinical supervision: Rationale and illustration. *Clinical Psychology and Psychotherapy*, *8*, 444–445.

Reiser, R., & Milne, D. L. (2012). Supervising cognitive-behavioral psychotherapy: Pressing needs, impressing possibilities. *Journal of Contemporary Psychotherapy*, *42*, 161–171. doi: 10.1007/s10879-011-9200-6

Reiser, R., & Milne, D. L. (2013). CBT supervision in a university-based training clinic: A case study in bridging the gap between rigor and relevance. *Journal of Cognitive Psychotherapy*, *27*, 30–41.

Rings, J. A., Genuchi, M. C., Hall, M. D., Angelo, M., & Erickson Cornich, J. A. (2009). Is there consensus among predoctoral internship training directors regarding clinical supervision competencies? A descriptive analysis. *Training and Education in Professional Psychology*, *3*, 140–147.

Roth, A., & Pilling, S. (2008). *The competence framework for supervision*. Retrieved from http://www.ucl.ac.uk/clinical-psychology/CORE/supervision_framework.htm

Turpin, G. (2012). The impact of recent NHS policy on supervision in clinical psychology. In I. Fleming & L. Steen (Eds.), *Supervision and clinical psychology* (2nd ed., pp. 23–46). London, UK: Routledge.

Uys, L. R., Minnaar, S., & Simpson, B. (2005). The effect of two models of supervision on selected outcomes. *Journal of Nursing Scholarship*, *37*, 282–288.

Watkins, C. E. (2012). Psychotherapy supervision in the new millennium: Competency-based, evidence-based, particularized and energised. *Journal of Contemporary Psychotherapy*, *42*, 193–203.

19

The Supervision Scale *Measurement of the Clinical Learning Environment Components in a Nursing Context*

Mikko Saarikoski

Introduction

Being a researcher with a nursing background, I will offer in this chapter a snapshot of nursing as science and professional practice by considering the link between clinical supervision (CS) and students' training for clinical practice. As a field of science, nursing is young. The first Masters Programs for nurse teachers started in the 1920s in the United States at the University of Columbia. Research-oriented professorial posts in nursing were established in the 1950s in the United States, and approximately two decades later in Europe. Nursing care as a modern profession can be seen as "a right hand of medical treatment" and as an interaction where a nurse shares in their patient's life situation, assisting the patient to cope with her or his illness. According to Florence Nightingale, who laid the foundation of professional nursing in the nineteenth century, both perspectives were seen as an essential part of nursing. Nowadays these approaches can still be seen in the research topics of nursing science. As a person of her own century, Nightingale (1859) highlighted "hard" scientific methods. For example, she made systematic observations about her patients and kept careful documentation as an essential part of nursing practice, and her orientation as a researcher gave direction for survey-type research in nursing science (White, 2003). Similarly, her opinions about the nurse–patient relationship were also quite modern and so can still act as a basis for qualitative research.

These approaches are valid in modern nursing practice: contemporary thinking within the profession considers nursing to entail a clinical role (mainly as a part of the medical treatment program) and an interaction process, where the nurse faces the patient as *a person*. In both of these roles, nurses' contacts with patients are often characterized by high levels of emotion, which can be experienced by nurse practi-

The Wiley International Handbook of Clinical Supervision, First Edition. Edited by C. Edward Watkins, Jr. and Derek L. Milne.

tioners and students alike. Warne and McAndrew (2009) have argued that the ability of nurses to manage their own emotional life, while attending to the emotions of other people, is a prerequisite skill for any caring profession. Nurses act within all fields of health care, including services where the orientation of health care processes can vary strongly. For example, quite different elements of care are present in the operating room, or in elderly psychiatric care. One factor that introduces differences in the approaches taken across such settings is the nurse–patient relationship, especially its interactional nature. Of course, some forms of communication are present also in medical treatment and even in the operating room, but their nature is different from a patient relationship (e.g., in mental health nursing). A key point is how well a nurse can consciously understand and use this interaction. In this communication role, *reflection* is a notable element. It is a self-awareness process, where a nurse monitors consciously her or his own feeling and emotional reactions, as they arise from the nurse–patient relationship. In this kind of professional activity, elements of CS are regarded as a crucial vehicle to help nurses to face professional challenges, as they are in all fields of social and health care. I will shortly outline an instrument that has been developed to measure supervision, alongside other aspects of the learning environment for nurses in Finland. But first I wish to note some important background considerations.

Background

Nursing is a practice-oriented profession and approximately half of the training program is carried out in health care organizations. Nursing students are naturally interested in the quality of their clinical learning and supervisory experiences. It is also important to their training programs to estimate the quality of the practice placement experiences because these are a crucial part of students' professional development. The role of the student's personal supervisor is especially important because this mentor (the term used in some parts of Europe) acts as professional role model for the nursing student.

The Clinical Learning Environment and Supervision (CLES) scales described in this section are based on the assumption that students are key evaluators of the quality of supervision within a clinical placement. A review of approximately 100 publications within the nursing science literature supports this view: in 61% of the surveyed empirical studies, the only informants were the students, and in a further 30% of these studies, students, teachers, and supervisors were involved in the quality evaluation of the learning environment and supervisory activities. Only the relatively small number of remaining studies (9%) did not involve students' perceptions at all (Saarikoski, 2002). Quantitative measurement is not the first idea one might have when considering CS as a research topic. At the first glance, its nature as a place to consider socioemotional experiences suggests a qualitative approach. This chapter is too brief for considerations about *positivism in human sciences*, but we have clear evidence within psychology and the social sciences that a quantitative research methodology can give reliable and valid information about individuals' attitudes, experiences, and emotions. Also, all research approaches contain error, and in qualitative analyses we can make faulty interpretations; in quantitative studies, error can come from respondents' inaccurate understanding of questions, or from coding mistakes, inappropriate statistical analyses, or erroneous interpretations. Similarly, these research approaches both have ways to minimize error. A notable example for a quantitative researcher is power analysis, a technique that guides sampling (i.e., the sample size needed to detect a likely effect, considering the research design and the instrument's item number). Bigger samples will tend to have smaller measurement errors. The sample sizes used in the CLES and CLES+T scale validation studies have varied between 400 and nearly 2,000 individual respondents.

These considerations were in focus when the work began on developing the CLES scale (Saarikoski, 1998; Saarikoski & Leino-Kilpi, 2002), started in University of Turku at the end of the 1990s. The scale's first internationally tested version (Saarikoski, 2002) was published within the author's Ph.D. The second version (Saarikoski, Isoaho, Warne, & Leino-Kilpi, 2008) included an additional dimension, adding the nurse teacher's role in the students' CS. This new questionnaire is called the Clinical Learning Environment, Supervision, and Nurse Teacher (CLES+T) scale, which has been tested in many empirical studies (e.g.,Bergjan & Hertel, 2013; Bos, Alinaghizadeh-Mollasaraie, Saarikoski, & Kaila, 2012; Johansson et al., 2010; Saarikoski, Warne, Kaila, & Leino-Kilpi, 2009; Skaalvik, Normann, & Henriksen, 2011; Tichelaar, Harps-Timmerman, Docter, & Janmaat, 2012; Tomietto et al., 2012; Warne et al., 2010; Watson et al., 2014). At present, there are 26 language versions of the CLES or CLES+T scales, and more than 60 researcher links in 45 countries.

Clinical Learning Environment, Supervision and Nurse Teacher (CLES+T) Evaluation Scale

Theoretical basis

The theoretical framework of the scale draws on a number of empirical studies into the clinical learning environment, supervision, and the clinical role of nurse teachers undertaken since the 1980s. The initial literature review utilized Cinahl, Medline, and indexes of all Finnish universities. These searches identified 87 empirical studies, eight literature reviews, and four audit instruments (and related discussion papers). The empirical studies and theoretical articles were used in the development of the theoretical structure and to produce the items for testing in the pilot study. These items were first carefully evaluated, using an expert panel. The first version was then tested, using test–retest reliability estimates and explorative factor analysis (Saarikoski, 2002). A concurrent validity instrument (Dunn & Burnett, 1995) was also used in empirical testing. In the second development phase of the CLES+T scale (Saarikoski et al., 2008), the final form of the scale was achieved (Figure 19.1).

As indicated in column three of Figure 19.1, the CLES+T scale's 33 items are divided into five subdimensions: (a) Pedagogical atmosphere in the unit – 8 items; (b) Leadership style of the unit manager – 4 items; (c) Quality of (nursing) care on the unit – 4 items; (d) Supervisory relationship – 8 items; and (e) Role of the nurse teacher – 9 items. The contextual nature of these subdimensions will be detailed later. The underpinning idea behind the selection of these items was that they reflect elements of a learning environment's optimal state. The scale items of the CLES+T

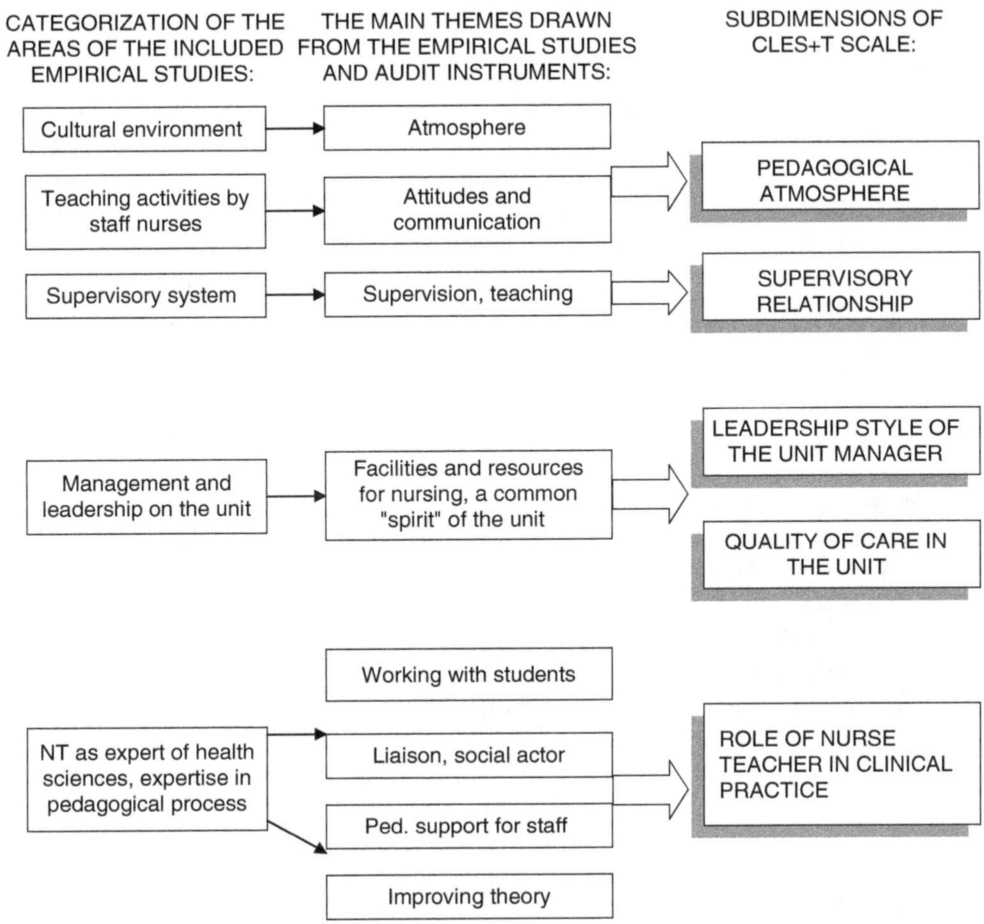

Figure 19.1 Theoretical framework of the CLES+T scale (Saarikoski et al., 2008). Reproduced with permission of Elsevier. NT = Nurse Teacher; Ped. Support = Pedagogical support.

scale and the structural items of Supervisory relationship are presented in Appendix 19.A (the instrument version used in the European validation study 2007–2009).

In terms of the procedure for completing the CLES, the students evaluate their experiences at the end of every clinical placement with the questionnaire, which includes a number of background variables and 34 items from the validated CLES+T scale. The absence of negative or mirrored statements diminishes the errors in completing and coding the CLES items. The response format utilizes a 5-point Likert scale: (a) *fully disagree*, (b) *disagree to some extent*, (c) *neither agree nor disagree*, (d) *agree to some extent*, and (e) *fully agree* (Saarikoski et al., 2008).

Scale dimensions

Pedagogical atmosphere in the unit One of the most important features of a good clinical learning environment is psychological security. This is achieved in an environment in which the atmosphere is fair and where students can solve problems concerning their learning. Also, a "good" clinical learning environment has a culture that tolerates faults and mistakes (as part of the learning process), is characterized by a nonhierarchical structure, and can be identified as displaying teamwork and good communication. Ideally, students are placed in such a learning environment, and their workload is also optimal.

Several studies support this logic. Smith (1987) noted similarities between the relationships between students and qualified staff, and the relationships between patients and qualified staff. It is possible to argue that, where nursing practice effectively reflects a shared sense of *caring* in the relationships between staff and patients and staff and students, such relationships result in mutual respect (and a greater sense of trust also in student–nursing staff relationships). Similarly, a few studies have demonstrated what a "poor" or suboptimal learning environment is like. If the spirit of the unit is poor, students feel that they "are not present," the staff do not get to know students by their personal names, and the students' learning needs are not adequately met (Hosoda, 2006; Ramage, 2004). This appears to be the case even when formally everything appears okay (e.g., they do not experience any clear discrimination or visible abuses: Ogden et al., 2005).

Studies evaluating the learning environments in terms of the ward type are few in number. From these limited studies, students have generally experienced the less technically oriented departments, in which the patients' stay is long, as the worst learning environments (e.g., geriatric wards). By contrast, surgical wards are more often perceived as "good" learning environments by students. However, it appears that clinical learning environments in the health and social care service systems are a complex entity, where many subsystems interact.

Supervisory relationship From the perspective of CS, supervisory relationship is the most important element of the CLES+T scale, whether supervision takes place in a group or individually. More traditional models for student supervision were earlier group supervisory approaches, but contemporary models emphasize individual supervision. In practice, clinical nurses' act as students' personal supervisors (called *mentors* in Finland). The aim of the supervisory system in nurse education is to enable a close relationship to develop between mentor and student, providing individual support and guidance through the students' clinical placements. Supervision tends to be "more than teaching," which focuses mainly on practical nursing skills.

There is considerable evidence that such a *one-to-one* relationship is one of the most important contributors to students' learning and professional development in clinical practice. The mentorship relationship has largely been studied from the perspective of professional socialization. The key question has been *how to support a new nurse in the transition when he or she is leaving the studying phase and starting working life*. A mentor or preceptor relationship is a crucial factor in this transition process. Individuals perceive their professional identity as this is experienced in relation to those with whom they associate, those who have related roles, and those who affect or are affected by an individual's identity. In professional socialization, the goal is the integration of the personal and professional *self* (Warne et al., 2010).

Additionally, the mentorship relationship is important from the viewpoint of "emotional work." Students do not yet have an emotional readiness to meet difficult situations in a way that is similar to experienced staff nurses. To succeed in this important work, the mentorship relationship must be based on official agreement between the education and service organizations. It is also suggested that mentor and student make an appointment for weekly meetings. These kind of private meetings enable a working culture that approaches models of CS. Confidential supervision sessions are a part of the mentorship relationship, enabling the student to talk about not only clinical situations but also personal experiences and feelings. Reflecting on one's own emotions is possible only if the supervisory relationship is based on equality and mutual respect. According to relevant studies (Saarikoski, 2002; Warne et al., 2010), this mentoring relationship is the most important element in support of clinical experience for the nursing student. Clinical experience is often overwhelming, but if a student has a "good" mentorship experience, he or she tends to evaluate other elements of the learning experience as positive.

Leadership style of the unit manager Another crucial factor influencing the clinical environment is the leadership style of the unit manager. The subdimension "Leadership style of unit manager" is a key factor for the ward culture, affecting how nurses work and study. This style can create or inhibit a positive environment. The ward atmosphere is a measurable concept, which reflects the ward culture at the level of human experience. This was pioneered with the "Social Climate" scales (see Moos, 2008). In all the scale validation processes of CLES and CLES+T, the ward atmosphere has had the strongest correlation with the subdimension "Supervisory relationship," which reveals the integrated and holistic experiences of student nurses in clinical practice.

The unit manager's role is hidden in relation to the supervision of student nurses, but is still a basic condition for the good team spirit which contributes to positive relationships between students and clinical staff. This role is both organizationally and professionally challenging when she or he is trying to put together the elements of management and leadership.

Quality of (nursing) care in the unit As illustrated in Figure 19.1, the quality of care is also influenced primarily by the unit's leadership. The content of care is an important issue in students' clinical experiences, as it provides the context within which clinical learning occurs. Some care settings are more stimulating for students than others; working with childhood cancer patients is more touching than working, for example, in occupational health services for young, healthy adults. The quality of patient care is also a crucial factor in achieving meaningful learning experiences. High-quality nursing care has been defined as care that is holistic and individual, provided by a nursing team with a defined nursing philosophy. Clinical learning and nursing care should always be considered together because they are both necessary and interrelated (Suikkala, 2007). For example, the student nurse who sees the whole individual nursing process has a much clearer picture than one who has only participated in series of disconnected tasks.

Contacts with patients are important elements in learning a caring attitude in clinical practice. Students are exposed to authentic life stories, for example people with serious illness, and these experiences can arouse strong emotions while also offering meaningful learning experiences. These kinds of clinical situations are important impulses and challenges to professional development, but without a CS-oriented working culture, they can even act as stressful factors and impulses to leave the profession.

Workload on the unit is best viewed as having two dimensions: the amount and the nature of work. It can be argued that a heavy physical workload and the pace of work will result in a decrease in the levels of work satisfaction of both nursing staff and students. However, in many research studies (e.g., Egan & Jaye, 2009; Leveck & Jones, 1996), the evidence is contradictory; for example, nurses experiencing a heavy workload in the intensive care units suffer lower occupational stress than do nurses working on conventional medical and surgical wards with minimal patient contacts and nursing interventions. This kind of light workload experience actually leads to idleness and stressful emotions. It seems that good leadership balances these two factors, creating an optimal amount of work that tends to be associated with less work-related distress and better satisfaction with the working environment.

Role of the nurse teacher This is the fifth and final subdimension of the CLES+T scale, as shown in Figure 19.1. In this chapter, the general concept of nurse teacher (NT) describes an educationally certified lecturer who is employed by a university or polytechnic to supervise and train nurses. The concept covers all variations of the roles and functions a teacher has in nursing education. The CLES+T's subdimension "Role of NT" is more complicated than other subdimensions because there are notable differences between the countries that have participated in the questionnaire's development. In some, the NT's role is based on clinical practice, alongside the nursing students. In other countries the role has changed from the *clinical skilled practitioner* to a *liaison* person, working between the education and health care provider organizations. These two working models indicate the development phase of the nurse education system within a country. Where there has been a transfer to a more academically oriented system (e.g., Finland and the United Kingdom), the NT's role in clinical practice has increasingly separated from everyday clinical practices (Saarikoski et al., 2013; Warne et al., 2010).

Psychometric properties of the CLES+T scale

In the international nursing literature there are only a limited numbers of tools available for measuring the quality of a clinical learning environment (including supervision), and none of them have been validated internationally. International and cross-cultural studies are considered important for the advancement of nursing knowledge. In the statistical testing and in factor analyses of the CLES+T scale (Johansson et al., 2010; Saarikoski et al., 2008; Tomietto et al., 2012; Watson et al., 2014), different models with 4–8 factors have been proposed. Methodologically, the most remarkable validation study was carried out in nine European countries during 2007–2009 (Warne et al., 2010; Saarikoski et al., 2013). The purposive sample ($N = 1{,}903$) for the study was collected from 17 nursing schools located across the northern, middle, and southern parts of Western Europe. The countries were Cyprus, Belgium, England, Finland, Ireland, Italy, the Netherlands, Spain, and Sweden. Schools from Eastern European countries were not included because of cultural differences in the education systems within old and new European Union countries. For example, in old Eastern Europe, nursing was not an independent academic discipline and the nurse training programs were strongly influenced by the medical profession (Kalnins, Barkauskas, & Seskevicius, 2001; Richards, 2005). First, to enable international participation, a contact person from every cooperating country translated the CLES+T items of the scale to his or her own language. Second, an English lecturer translated this new language version back to English as a check on accuracy. Finally, in the consensus phase, a native English-speaking nurse teacher reviewed the original items and the double-translated items to ensure that the basic idea of the item had not been changed.

In the initial factor analyses of the CLES+T scale, the five subdimensions model, as summarized in Figure 19.1, was the best fitting model (Saarikoski et al., 2008). In the subsequent European study, this five-factor model was not confirmed completely, but the factors' eigenvalues and explanation percentages remained high (Saarikoski et al., 2013; Warne et al., 2010). In this pan-European analysis, the subdimensions "Pedagogical atmosphere in the unit" and "Quality of care" overlapped, and the subdimension "Role of nurse teacher" split into two different factors. As per the initial factor analysis, the chosen six-factor model still explained 73% of the variance.

The reliability of the instrument was estimated in both of these factor analytic studies, using Cronbach's alpha coefficients. This analysis measures how consistent items are within each factor (subdimension). The reliability of the CLES+T scale was moderately high in both analyses. In the European sample ($N = 1{,}903$), the alpha values varied between .83 and .96. These values were higher than in the earlier analysis, where they varied between .77 and .96. As an interpretation, we can say the values are very high and give clear evidence for instrument's trustworthiness. The mean values of the subdimensions varied to a remarkable extent. The subdimension reflecting the Supervisory relationship got the highest mean (3.91), while another "Nurse teacher" subdimension (nurse teacher improving theoretical understanding) received the lowest mean value.

A test–retest reliability assessment was also conducted in order to evaluate the instrument's stability (Saarikoski, 2002). The test–retest group ($n = 38$) was formed from two student groups that had just ended their clinical placement. They were asked to evaluate the learning environment and supervision of their last clinical placement with the CLES+T over a five-week interval. The correlation of single items ranged from .52 to .89 ($p < .001$), and the coefficients for the subdimensions ranged from .71 to.91. The higher correlation of subdimensions is explained by the high internal consistency of items inside each subdimension. The total instrument test–retest reliability was good, at .81.

Conclusion and Implications for Practice

The CLES+T scale has been developed successfully and can help to measure CS in relation to other important educational and health service factors. Following this development, the CLES+T scale has become part of a quality assurance system within Finnish health care (i.e., the education in clinical practice aspect), covering approximately 80% of health care service organizations in the country, and is used via electronic survey portals (Meretoja & Saarikoski, 2012).

A key question that arises with the CLES+T scale is how we understand nursing as a practical field of health care. If we consider nursing only as a "helping hand of medical treatment," then CS has little value for nursing. In general, a biomedical approach emphasizes task-oriented practices, and the demands for efficiency tend to restrict and hinder communication between patients and nurses, obstructing the development of the nurse–patient relationship. For nurses, there may be many associated feelings, but instead of being discussed they stay "inside" and so can become a reason for professional stress. Might this be a reason for the high turnover among new nurses working in such traditional environments?

If inadequate discussion contributes to turnover, it demands closer consideration: we know that critical personal feelings and contextual factors exist (e.g., perceptions of self in relation to others and the emotions arising from nursing acts). If we understand nursing also as therapeutic interaction, we can identify many psycho-emotional aspects that are also essential parts of the nursing process. A few classical nursing theorists (e.g.,Leininger, 1981; Watson, 1988) have described professional nursing using the concept of *caring*. They highlighted a nurse–patient relationship as reflective, sensitive, and interpretative, which carries many deeper meanings than a "biomedical" professional relationship. Caring means a holistic approach, a concept which may constitute part of nursing, and also part of a person's private life. Ontologically, the caring perspective means a relationship of *being-with*. This kind of approach to nursing practice parallels the therapeutic approach defined in chapter 1 of this book. If nursing practice means a therapeutic relationship – *being with* – then CS should be included to guide and support nurses working in any field of health care.

A related question is whether CS and the rest of the nurse education system "feeds" a biomedical orientation rather than a holistic approach to caring? Unfortunately, my own answer is, yes. My experience as a lecturer and researcher in the Finnish nurse education system strengthens that interpretation. In her classical studies, the British author Pam Smith (1987, 1991) noticed that students described nursing in terms of caring at the start of their education program, but during their final year their language was transformed into more of a biomedical rhetoric, and they were most interested in different techniques and medical investigations.

One development that has occurred in many European countries during the past 10–20 years has been the transition of nurse education from vocational colleges or hospital-based nursing schools to higher education institutions (HEI). Of course, this transition has strengthened the theoretical structure of the curriculum, but maybe its disadvantage has been that many practical aspects of training programs have been neglected (e.g., clinical placements in health care services). This has consequences for caring and for nursing relationships. Instead, the theoretically rich academic topics have determined the content of the curriculum, decreasing the value of clinical learning experiences. For instance, in order to gain experience of the different types of treatment, the clinical placements have been shortened (sometimes to only 1–2 weeks), which means that many of the students' contacts with patients occur only once. By contrast, longer placements enable more intensive patient relationships to develop, ones in which students can learn to recognize crucial elements of caring. The student can also become aware of their own emotional reactions in patient relationships, and understand that this element is as important as the different techniques and investigations. The importance of the length of clinical placements was indicated in the European study (the validation of the CLES+T scale, as summarized earlier): the students with longer placements and with active mentorship relationships were more satisfied with their learning experience than those students who had had a short placements and only 2–3 meetings with their mentors. Educators need to consider carefully the balance of providing many short (e.g., 1–2 weeks) clinical experiences of different specialties against the holistic experience of nursing care that might be achieved during longer placements (Warne et al., 2010).

References

Bergjan, M., & Hertel, F. (2013). Evaluating students' perception of their clinical placements – Testing the clinical learning and supervision and nurse teacher scale (CLES+T scale) in Germany. *Nurse Education Today*, *33*, 1393–1398.

Bos, E., Alinaghizadeh-Mollasaraie, F., Saarikoski, M., & Kaila, P. (2012). Validation the clinical learning environment, supervision and nurse teacher CLES+T instrument in primary health care settings using confirmatory factor analysis. *Journal of Clinical Nursing*, *21*, 1785–1788.

Dunn, S. V., & Burnett, P. (1995). The development of a clinical learning environment scale. *Journal of Advanced Nursing*, *22*, 1166–1173.

Egan, T., & Jaye, C. (2009). Communities of clinical practice: The social organization of clinical learning. *Health: An Interdisciplinary Journal for the Social and Health, Illness and Medicine*, *16*, 107–125.

Hosoda, Y. (2006). Development and testing of a clinical learning environment diagnostic inventory for baccalaureate nursing students. *Journal of Advanced Nursing*, *56*, 480–490.

Johansson, U.-B., Kaila, P., Ahlner-Elmqvist, M., Leksell, J., Isoaho, H., & Saarikoski, M. (2010). Psychometric evaluation of the Swedish version of Clinical Learning Environment, Supervision and Nurse Teacher evaluation scale. *Journal of Advanced Nursing*, *66*(9), 2085–2093.

Kalnins, I., Barkauskas, V. H., & Seskevicius, A. (2001). Baccalaureate nursing education development in 2 Baltic countries: Outcomes 10 years after initation. *Nursing Outlook*, *49*, 142–147.

Leininger, M. M. (1981). The phenomenon of caring: Importance, research questions and theoretical considerations. In M. M.Leininger (Ed.), *Caring: An essential human need* (pp. 2–15), Thorofare, NJ: Slack.

Leveck, M. L., & Jones, C. B. (1996). The nursing practice environment, staff retention, and quality of care. *Research in Nursing & Health*, *19*, 331–343.

Meretoja, R., & Saarikoski, M. (2012). Evidence based development of clinical learning environment in Finnish health care services. Improvement by Evaluation/ Eval2012 Conference (proceedings article), University of Tampere, 150–156.

Moos, R. (2008). Context and mechanism of reactivity to assessment and treatment. *Addiction (Abingdon, England)*, *103*(2), 249–250.

Nightingale, F. (1859). *Notes on nursing: What it is and what it is not.* London, England: Harrison & Sons.

Ogden, P. E., Wu, E. H., Elnicki, M. D., Battistone, M. J., Cleary, L. M., Fagan, M. J., . . . Wong, R. Y. (2005). Do attending physicians, nurses, residents, and medical students agree on what constitutes medical student abuse?*Academic Medicine*, *80*, S80–S83.

Ramage, C. (2004). Negotiating multiple roles: Link teachers in clinical practice. *Journal of Advanced Nursing*, *45*, 287–296.

Richards, R. (2005). Development in Eastern Europe. *Mental Health Nursing*, *25*, 10–12.

Saarikoski, M. (1998). Clinical learning environment and supervision by staff nurses – Development of the instrument and the main results. Licentiate study (in Finnish, English abstract), University of Turku, Department of Nursing Science. Unpublished.

Saarikoski, M. (2002). *Clinical learning environment and supervision. Development and validation of the CLES evaluation scale* (Doctoral dissertation). University of Turku, Annales Universitatis Turkuensis, Ser. D 525. ISBN951-29-2157-X. Turku: Kirjapaino Pika Oy.

Saarikoski, M., Isoaho, H., Warne, T., & Leino-Kilpi, H. (2008). The nurse teacher in clinical practice: Developing the new sub-dimension to Clinical Learning Environment and Supervision (CLES) scale. *International Journal of Nursing Studies*, *45*, 1233–1237.

Saarikoski, M., Kaila, P., Lambrinou, E., Pérez Cañaveras, R. M., Tichelaar, E., Tomietto, M., & Warne, T. (2013). Students' experiences of cooperation with nurse teacher during their clinical placements: An empirical study in a Western European context. *Nurse Education in Practice*, *13*, 78–82.

Saarikoski, M., & Leino-Kilpi, H. (2002). The clinical learning environment and supervision by *staff nurses: Developing the instrument. International Journal of Nursing Studies*, *39*, 259–267.

Saarikoski, M., Warne, T., Kaila, P., & Leino-Kilpi, H. (2009). The role of nurse teacher in clinical practice; an empirical study of Finnish student nurse experiences. *Nurse Education Today*, *29*, 595–600.

Skaalvik, M. W., Normann, H. K., & Henriksen, N. (2011). Clinical learning environment and supervision: Experiences of Norwegian nursing students – a questionnaire survey. *Journal of Clinical Nursing*, *20*, 2294–2304.

Smith, P. (1987). The relationship between quality of nursing care and the ward as a learning environment: Developing a methodology. *Journal of Advanced Nursing*, *12*, 413–420.

Smith, P. (1991). The nursing process: Raising the profile of emotional care in nurse training. *Journal of Advanced Nursing*, *16*, 74–81.

Suikkala, A. (2007). *Nursing student-patient relationship and associated factors* (Doctoral dissertation). University of Turku, Annales Universitatis Turkuensis, Ser. D 788. ISBN978-951-29-3462-1. Turku: Painosalama Oy.

Tichelaar, E., Harps-Timmerman, A., Docter, M., & Janmaat, N. (2012). Dutch student nurses' experience with clinical learning environment: A challenge for the changing role of the nurse teacher. *Nursing Education, Research and Practice*, *2*, 55–61.

Tomietto, M., Saiani, L., Palese, A., Cunico, L., Cicolini, G., Watson, P., & Saarikoski, M. (2012). Clinical Learning Environment and Supervision plus Nurse Teacher (CLES+T) scale: Testing the psychometric characteristics of the Italian version. *Giornale Italiano Di Medicina Del Lavoro Ed Ergonomia*, *34*(N2), B72–B80.

Warne, T., Johansson, U.-B., Papastavrou, E., Tichelaar, E., Tomietto, M., Van den Bossche, K., . . . Saarikoski, M. (2010). An exploration of the clinical learning experience of nursing students in nine European countries. *Nurse Education Today*, *30*, 809–815.

Warne, T., & McAndrew, S. (2009). *Creative approaches to health and social care – knowing me, understanding you.* Basingstoke, England: Palgrave Publishers.

Watson, J. (1988). *Nursing: Human science and human care.* New York, NY: National League for Nursing.

Watson, P. B., Seaton, P., Sims, D., Jamieson, I., Mountier, J., Whittle, R., & Saarikoski, M. (2014). Exploratory factor analysis of the Clinical Learning Environment, Supervision and Nurse Teacher Scale (CLES+T). *Journal of Nursing Measurement*, *22*, 163–179.

White, E. (2003). The struggle for methodological orthodoxy in nursing research: The case of mental health. *International Journal of Mental Health Nursing*, *12*, 88–95.

Appendix 19.A
Clinical Learning Environment, Supervision, and NurseTeacher (CLES+T) Evaluation Scale (Saarikoski et al., 2008)

The following statements concerning the learning environment, supervision, and the role of nurse teacher are grounded into main areas, each with their own title.

For each statement, please choose the option that best describes your own opinion.

Evaluation scale:
1 = fully disagree
2 = disagree to some extent
3 = neither agree nor disagree
4 = agree to some extent
5 = fully agree

The learning environment

Pedagogical atmosphere:					
The staff were easy to approach	1	2	3	4	5
I felt comfortable going to the ward at the start of my shift	1	2	3	4	5
During staff meetings (e.g., before shifts) I felt comfortable taking part in the discussions	1	2	3	4	5
There was a positive atmosphere on the ward	1	2	3	4	5
The staff were generally interested in student supervision	1	2	3	4	5
The staff learned to know the student by their personal names	1	2	3	4	5
There were sufficient meaningful learning situations on the ward	1	2	3	4	5
The learning situations were multidimensional in terms of content	1	2	3	4	5
The ward can be regarded as a good learning environment	1	2	3	4	5

Leadership style of the unit/ward manager (WM):					
The WM regarded the staff on her/his ward as a key resource	1	2	3	4	5
The WM was a team member	1	2	3	4	5
Feedback from the WM could easily be considered as a learning situation	1	2	3	4	5
The effort of individual employees was appreciated	1	2	3	4	5

Nursing care on the ward:					
The wards nursing philosophy was clearly defined	1	2	3	4	5
Patients received individual nursing care	1	2	3	4	5
There were no problems in the information flow related to patients' care	1	2	3	4	5
Documentation of nursing (e.g., nursing plans, daily recording of nursing procedures etc.) was clear	1	2	3	4	5

The supervisory relationship

In this form, the concept of supervision refers guiding, supporting, and assessing of student nurses made by clinical staff nurses. Supervision can occur as individual supervision, or as group (or team) supervision.

The concept of mentor means a named personal supervisor.

Occupational title of supervisor:	nurse	1
	nurse specialist	2
	assistant ward manager	3
	sister/ ward manager	4
	other, what?	______________

Occurrence of supervision: (circle one alternative only)

I did not have a supervisor at all	1
A personal supervisor was named, but the relationship with this person did not work during the placement	2
The named supervisor changed during the placement, even though no change had been planned	3
The supervisor varied according to shift or place of work	4
Same supervisor had several students and was a group supervisor rather than an individual supervisor	5
A personal supervisor was named and our relationship worked during this placement	6
Other method of supervision, please specify?	. . . .

How often did you have separate private unscheduled supervision with the supervisor (without nurse teacher):	not at all	1
	once or twice during the course	2
	less than once a week	3
	about once a week	4
	more often	5

The content of supervisory relationship:

The following statements concerning the supervisory relationship.

For each statement, please choose the option that best describes your own opinion.

Evaluation scale:
1 = fully disagree
2 = disagree to some extent
3 = neither agree nor disagree
4 = agree to some extent
5 = fully agree

My supervisor showed a positive attitude toward supervision	1	2	3	4	5
I felt that I received individual supervision	1	2	3	4	5
I continuously received feedback from my supervisor	1	2	3	4	5
Overall I am satisfied with the supervision I received	1	2	3	4	5
The supervision was based on a relationship of equality and promoted my learning	1	2	3	4	5
There was a mutual interaction in the supervisory relationship	1	2	3	4	5
Mutual respect prevailed in the supervisory relationship	1	2	3	4	5
The supervisory relationship was characterized by a sense of trust	1	2	3	4	5

Role of the nurse teacher

Nurse teacher is a lecturer (employed by a university or polytechnic) who is responding to the clinical placement.

The following statements concerning the linking nurse teacher are grounded into main areas, each with their own title.

For each statement, please choose the option that best describes your own opinion.

Evaluation scale:
1 = fully disagree
2 = disagree to some extent
3 = neither agree nor disagree
4 = agree to some extent
5 = fully agree

Nurse teacher as enabling the integration of theory and practice:

In my opinion, the nurse teacher was capable to integrate theoretical knowledge and everyday practice of nursing	1	2	3	4	5

The teacher was capable of operationalizing the learning goals of this clinical placement	1	2	3	4	5
The nurse teacher helped me to reduce the theory–practice gap	1	2	3	4	5
Cooperation between placement staff and nurse teacher:					
The nurse teacher was like a member of the nursing team	1	2	3	4	5
The nurse teacher was capable to give his or her pedagogical expertise to the clinical team	1	2	3	4	5
The nurse teacher and the clinical team worked together in supporting my learning	1	2	3	4	5
Relationship among student, mentor, and nurse teacher:					
The common meetings between myself, mentor, and nurse teacher were comfortable experience	1	2	3	4	5
In our common meetings I felt that we are colleagues	1	2	3	4	5
Focus on the meetings was in my learning needs	1	2	3	4	5

Thank you for your time and help!

20

A Qualitative Approach for Measuring Competence in Clinical Supervision

Gellisse Bagnall and Graham Sloan

Introduction

Despite its history, breadth of implementation, and extent of engagement among a broad range of professions, it is surprising that consistent formalized supervision training, competences appropriate to clinical supervision, and accreditation processes for clinical supervisors are lacking (Reiser & Milne, 2012). In the majority of health care organizations throughout the United Kingdom, for example, although clinical supervision is integral to many staff positions, no formal qualifications or supervision training are necessarily expected of clinical supervisors (Sloan & Fleming, 2011). Often, clinical supervisors' previous experience of being supervised was expected to provide them with the knowledge, skills, and attitudes necessary for their provision of competent and effective supervision for their own supervisees (Milne, 2009). It is only in the relatively recent past that generic and modality-specific competency frameworks for supervision of psychological therapies have been developed (Falender & Shafranske, 2004; Roth & Pilling, 2008).

The measurement of supervisory competence poses many challenges in terms of both robust methodologies and related resources. In other chapters, the development of measurement tools and questionnaires of supervision competence are described. This chapter describes an alternative, qualitative approach to addressing some of these challenges, drawing on an educational intervention for clinical psychology supervisors.

This project will be described, with particular emphasis on the use of portfolios of evidence for supervisory competence, and the process developed for assessing/evaluating these. The main message from this will be that, while portfolios were a useful source of evidence for competence in clinical supervision, there is a need to enhance such measurements by triangulating portfolio outcomes with other relevant

The Wiley International Handbook of Clinical Supervision, First Edition. Edited by C. Edward Watkins, Jr. and Derek L. Milne.

information. This is in line with the findings of a recent systematic review of the effectiveness of portfolios for postgraduate assessment and education, which included 56 articles from 10 countries covering seven health care professions (Tochel et al., 2009). Despite the extensive evidence base, this review concluded that there were few high-quality studies with generalizable messages. The authors noted that reports of inter-rater reliability for summative assessment of portfolio data are varied, and they recommend triangulation with other assessment methods.

Clinical Supervision Training and Portfolios as Evidence of Supervisory Competence

In the United Kingdom's National Health Service (NHS), postgraduate clinical psychology trainees gain a doctoral qualification by combining academic study and clinical placements. Clinical supervision throughout these placements is regarded as essential to facilitating trainee development, as well as protecting patient safety. To prepare clinical supervisors for this crucial role, NHS Education for Scotland (NES)[1] developed a new educational intervention that aimed to quality assure and standardize such clinical supervision throughout Scotland.

The project described here was operational between 2001 and 2009, specifically targeting the development of supervisory competence for recently qualified clinical psychologists about to supervise their first trainee (Bagnall, 2010). The project began with a training needs analysis (Allan, Bagnall, & Campbell, 2003) that identified the priority target group, and made key recommendations for the content of the educational intervention. This scoping exercise combined qualitative and quantitative methods, comprising a questionnaire survey of all clinical psychologists in Scotland, interviews with preregistration trainees, a focus group with key clinical psychology staff, and a Delphi consensus-building process with expert groups. The training needs for clinical supervisors that emerged from the study fell into four distinct categories, which offered an evidence-based framework for developing a syllabus for relevant training. These four categories were

- delivery of supervision – theories of learning, models and methods of supervision, management of trainee with difficulties;
- evaluation of process and outcome of supervision;
- legal, ethical, and professional standards; and
- integration of trainees' needs with professional requirements and service need.

In addition, both trainees and clinical supervisors acknowledged the importance of formal support for the supervision process in terms of time and resources, with some suggestion that formal accreditation for supervisors could enhance the perceived value of the process for all stakeholders. There was also considerable support for online delivery of supervisor training.

[1] NES is a special health board set up as part of NHS Scotland to support the education and lifelong learning need of all NHS Scotland staff. The overall aim of this education and training body is to ensure that patients and their families get the best health care possible from well-trained and educated staff.

Taking these recommendations on board, and following recommended guidelines for curriculum development in clinical professions (Grant, 2006), the next stage was to clarify and agree the intended learning outcomes (ILOs) for a new educational resource/module aiming to "prepare new supervisors for their role with trainees by developing understanding of best supervisory practice." Preliminary ILOs for the module were developed by an advisory group of experienced clinical psychology supervisors. These were subsequently reinforced by a parallel development in a UK-wide group of clinical psychologists working together to promote the development and recognition of supervisory skills (DROSS).

These ILOs were mapped onto 12 statements of supervisory competence, so providing an explicit framework for the module and for evaluating/assessing the development of individual supervisory competence.[2] These statements are listed in Box 20.1.

The *educational rationale* underpinning the module was based on Kolb's (1984) learning cycle, emphasizing the principles of adult learning and constructivism, reflective learning, and theory–practice links. The experiential element integral to Kolb's cycle was reinforced by the requirement that all participants would actively supervise a clinical psychology trainee during the period of module study, using that experience to reflect on and develop their supervisory practice.

Module delivery was designed to offer flexible learning at a distance, with a blended learning approach combining "face-to-face" (F2F) workshops and a virtual learning environment (VLE) that was supported by facilitated online discussion and collaborative learning. The VLE was developed and managed using the open-source software Moodle, which is a widely recognized tool to support online course development and administration (Figure 20.1).

The module *content* was subdivided into four "study blocks" addressing, respectively,

Block 1: Course Introduction and Overview,
Block 2: Educational Principles and Good Supervision,
Block 3: Supervision in Practice – Power and Difference,
Block 4: Professional and Ethical issues in Supervision.

The combination of didactic and experiential learning and the broad areas of concern addressed in this NES module closely parallel those identified in the relevant literature – see, for example, Chapter 8 by Watkins and Wang. Throughout all content areas, the three threads of knowledge, skills, and self-awareness are addressed, reflecting the recommendations in the Curriculum Guide for Training Counselor Supervisors, also cited in Chapter 8. This approach to supervisor training was developed as a Scotland-wide initiative by NES as a consolidation of what was already taking place in an ad hoc manner, pulling it together in a comprehensive and innovative format, and grounded in educational theory emphasizing experiential learning and reflective practice.

[2] This work preceded the publication of Roth and Pilling's (2008) framework of generic supervisory competences in psychological therapies. See http://www.iapt.nhs.uk/2008/02supervision-competence-framework/

Box 20.1

Scottish statements of supervisory competence

1. Organise a placement prior to the trainee starting, covering induction, resources, and clinical workload/experience. This will include instructing the trainee about relevant departmental and operational issues.
2. Organise the ongoing supervision of the placement, including negotiating supervision agenda, regular monitoring and review of trainee progress and developmental needs.
3. Set and negotiate appropriate learning objectives with the trainee, taking account of formal professional requirements and the trainee's previous experience and preferences.
4. Discuss, set, and review appropriate boundaries for supervision.
5. Maintain a balance in supervision between supporting and leading the trainee as appropriate.
6. Monitor the well-being of the trainee and raise concerns with the trainee as appropriate.
7. Monitor trainee placement experience, including use of supporting paperwork, to ensure that placement objectives are met and that a judgment of clinical competence can be made at the end of the placement.
8. Negotiate the style and content of supervision, taking account of trainee and supervisor preferences and identified needs.
9. Maintain a balance in supervision between positive feedback and constructive criticism.
10. Take timely remedial action should unpredictable problems, outwith supervisor control, develop around the provision of placement experience during the course of the placement.
11. Take appropriate action when the supervisor perceives that the trainee's competencies on the placement are not developing satisfactorily or may lead to a recommendation of placement failure.
12. Identify and appropriately manage potential disagreements and differences between the trainee and the client/other professional colleagues/supervisor.

Total anticipated *study time* was 50 hr, spread over four months. This began with two F2F days, which enabled each cohort of participants to meet their study peers (important for subsequent online discussion forum). The content of these two days promoted discussion around clinical supervision, introducing some of the key issues of the module, such as models of supervision and giving constructive feedback to facilitate trainee learning. A "hands-on" introduction to using the online components of the course was included, along with a practical example and a discussion about what a portfolio of evidence might look like. This initial F2F component thus comprised approximately 14 hr.

The recommended time for online study was 28–30 hr with an average of 7 hr suggested for each of the four online study blocks, which combined set readings and

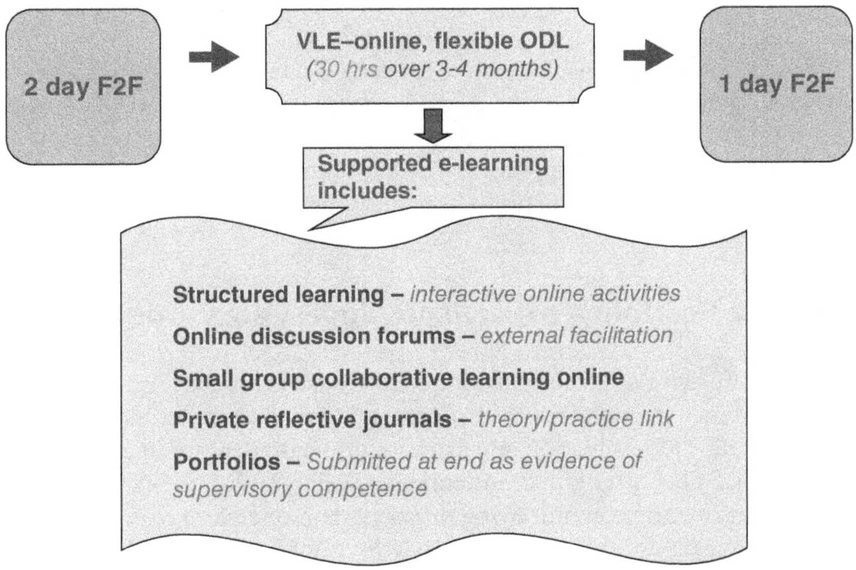

Figure 20.1 Overview of NES induction to supervision module structure. Key: F2F = face-to-face (workshop); VLE = virtual learning environment; ODL = open and distance learning. Reproduced with permission from Bagnall (2010).

their critical review with interactive activities including a self-assessed "quiz" and critical debate via the online discussion forum. As noted, the participants were encouraged to maintain a private reflective log throughout their study, focusing on module content and relating that to ongoing supervisory experience. Questions were built into the online text to facilitate this. As well as promoting reflective learning, individual reflective logs would be an important source of evidence for inclusion in the portfolio of evidence for supervisory competence. It was recommended that portfolio evidence was compiled as an ongoing activity, and it was anticipated that 8 hr would be required to prepare the portfolio for submission.

Protected study time was secured for each participant by a formal contract between NES and the head of psychological services in the participant's health board (i.e., the employing organization).

Agreement was also secured from each participant's line manager to ensure that module study was formally recognized.

Evaluation/assessment of portfolios

A robust process was developed for reviewing individual portfolios of evidence for supervisory competence. This was similar to the internal and external examiner process commonly used in higher education, where preliminary assessments are made internally (often by two independent assessors) and consensus about final outcomes is ratified at formal examination boards, involving relevant external examiners.

Portfolio evaluation was primarily summative but included extensive formative individual feedback on developing supervisory competence. Successful submission was required to obtain a formal Certificate of Completion but was never in practice an explicit requirement for supervisors. Despite the absence of any true sanction for inadequate portfolios or nonsubmission, it was expected that line managers would follow this up at the local level. As discussed later, successful portfolios conferred eligibility for formal (but voluntary) recognition as a clinical supervisor by the British Psychological Society, and completion rates were high.

Further description of the portfolio evaluation process follows later.

Why Use Portfolios to Evaluate Supervisory Competence?

As already noted, successful module completion was contingent on submission of a portfolio of evidence for supervisory competence. There is a developing literature on the use of portfolios for evaluation and assessment of competence in a clinical setting. This suggests that a key strength is authenticity (Miller, 1990), for example, by charting development over time and drawing on more than one piece of evidence (Chang, 2001; Driessen, van der Vleuten, Schurwirth, van Tartwijk, & Vermunt, 2005; Duque, 2003). However, portfolios also raise questions about reliability and feasibility (Driessen, 2008). In the case study described here, for example, portfolio evidence was selected by the individual supervisors themselves and based on self-report, with no corroborating evidence from alternative sources.

The module portfolios aimed to provide evidence of developing supervisory competence for evaluation purposes. Using the 12 items defining supervisory competence (which reflected the module ILOs, as summarized in Box 20.1), the participants monitored their own progress against each of these statements and gathered supporting evidence from their current experience as a supervisor. The content of submitted portfolios thus included relevant extracts from the participants'

- reflective learning journals (private, online);
- personal supervision notes; and
- communications with trainees (e.g., e-mail).

To facilitate portfolio compilation, and in line with the various recommendations from the literature (see, e.g., Abrami & Barrett, 2005, Klenowski, Askew, & Carnell, 2006), the participants were asked to structure their evidence for each statement of competence under three headings:

- experiential evidence of supervisory competence,
- rationale for selecting that particular piece of evidence, and
- what the portfolio creator learned.

It should be noted that the last two statements of supervisory competence (relating to underperforming or difficult trainees) were not likely to be experienced by all module participants. A scenario was thus provided for those two situations, providing an opportunity for participants to offer hypothetical evidence of how they *would* have dealt with such problems in supervision.

How were the portfolios reviewed and evaluated?

On module completion, each participant submitted his or her portfolio for formal review. An increasingly robust review process was established over time, including explicit criteria against which portfolios would be evaluated. These criteria were made explicit to participants and reviewers to help them judge whether the evidence submitted

- adequately illustrated each specific statement of supervisory competence,
- explicitly linked supervisory theory and practice, and
- adequately illustrated reflective learning.

For example, to provide evidence of linking supervisory theory to practice for statement 8 (*negotiating style and content of supervision . . .*) a participant might include an extract from his/her own supervision notes:

> we agreed today that we would use role play next week to help (trainee) address the difficulty they are having in dealing with the client's distress at parental divorce (this stems from recent divorce of trainee's own parents)

After the role play has been tried out, the new supervisor could provide an illustration of reflective learning for this competence statement by including a relevant extract from their private "reflective log," reflecting on how they felt the role play had gone and whether it appeared to have helped the trainee. This could have been further enhanced by including a subsequent extract from supervision notes (or e-mail communication with the trainee), discussing if the role play had helped the trainee to make progress with this aspect of his/her clinical work.

Successful portfolios had to include a minimum of three examples of theory–practice links and six of reflective learning. The review procedure is described as follows:

1. Each portfolio was evaluated (blind) independently by two reviewers, reviewing the evidence for each statement of supervisory competence under the three headings provided. An evaluation template was used for each portfolio, recording the initial evaluation for each statement, along with any comments to be noted/feedback for portfolio author. Finally, an overall, global grade of "very good," "good," or "needs revision/resubmit" was awarded, along with qualitative feedback for each participant.
2. Review pairs then compared their assessments, with any disagreements resolved by a third party.
3. The internal review panel met to validate grades, discuss anomalies, and agree on individual feedback for each participant.
4. Portfolios (or a representative subset) were submitted to external reviewers.
5. Internal and external panels met to ratify "grades" and feedback and to review the process.

This process reflects Driessen, van Tartwijk, van der Vleuten, and Wass (2007), Jasper and Fulton (2005), and Rees and Sheard (2004, p. 142), who argued:

discussion and negotiation between independent assessors can enhance the reliability of assessment criteria for portfolios.

How Effective Has the NES Supervision Module Been?

The first module ran in 2005. The portfolio evaluation process became increasingly robust as criteria and standards became more explicit. An audit of portfolio outcomes suggested that the supervisory competencies were achieved by the majority of participants. Table 20.1 highlights a summary of the audit findings, which show the high completion rate for portfolios, the great majority of which were judged "good."

Table 20.1 Portfolio outcomes: audit summary.

Study year	*Total n*	*Portfolios submitted*	*Portfolio grade*		
			Very good	*Good*	*Resubmit*
2005 (Pilot 1)	12	12	n/a (developmental)		
2006 (Pilot 2)	10	10	n/a (submitted for individual feedback – not graded)		
2007	33	31	4	23	4[a]
2008	25	23	9	7	7[b]
	33	30[c]	10	16	4[d]
2009	10	9	3	4	2[e]

[a]After resubmission, three participants obtained a "good" grade and one did not resubmit.
[b]After resubmission, six "good" grades and 1 "resubmit again" (subsequently "good").
[c]One participant dropped out; two portfolios were deferred, one of which was evaluated as "good" with 2009 cohort review panel, and the other was not completed.
[d]After resubmission, all graded as "good."
[e]Delayed resubmissions, plus one maternity leave, all subsequently "good."
Source: Reproduced with permission from Bagnall (2010).

Impact Evaluation

In order to triangulate the portfolio outcome data, an additional measure of supervisory competence was used, enabling us to conduct a simple impact evaluation at the end of each module for each cohort. Drawing on the work of Hall-Marley (2001), a pre/postmodule questionnaire was devised with questions divided into four domains:

1. atmosphere for learning (9 items),
2. supervision style (9 items),
3. supervision conduct (13 items), and
4. supervision impact (5 items).

For each question, the participants were asked to self-rate their confidence to supervise using a 3-point self-rating scale where

- 1: "no confidence, significant development required,"
- 2: "some confidence but need to develop further," and
- 3: "confident."

The perceived development of supervisory competence was measured by the individual "shift" in self-rating before and after module completion and portfolio submission.

Impact evaluation outcomes

Full evaluation outcomes were reported internally, and increased confidence was consistently evident across all four domains. This suggests generally that the ILOs of the module were achieved and reinforced the high proportion of "good" portfolios. However, it should be noted that these questionnaires were anonymous, relying on respondents using an allocated code to self-report. Identifiable pre and postreturns were typically well below 50%, meaning this triangulation was not representative.

Formative feedback from module participants

Structured questionnaire feedback suggests that participants underestimated the time required to complete their portfolios, leaving too much until the end. Some were concerned that the portfolio format reduced supervisory competence to a "tick-box" exercise. However, participant feedback also reinforced the module aim: for example,

> portfolio is good idea and links well to process of learning to supervise.

What Can We Conclude from This Approach to Measuring Supervisory Competence?

The outcomes from this case study are summarized as follows in terms of the various key stakeholders.

External/professional recognition of supervisor training

One of the key successes was that the British Psychological Society formally recognized successful module completion as conferring eligibility for their professional register of supervisors. This professional recognition goes some way to addressing the need for formal accreditation of supervisor training (albeit still not compulsory) identified in the original needs analysis. It also reinforced the value of the portfolio process for participants, tutors, and reviewers.

Participants

Although the portfolio assessment was the most innovative aspect of the supervisor training, it was clear that some participants found portfolio completion stressful and time-consuming. However, it should also be noted that the anxiety and fear commonly aroused by any formal assessment or evaluation can result in negatively biased feedback on the process.

Course administration

The portfolio submission process was time-consuming to administer, requiring support for participants; the setting up of blind, paired portfolio reviews; internal and external examiner meetings; and collating reviewer feedback to individual participants. Although this may have been no more demanding than the administration required for a typical postgraduate course, it could be perceived as disproportionate to the module study time and greatly exceeded the time accorded to the evaluation of more traditional supervision workshops.

Portfolio reviewers

These were fundamentally "volunteer" senior clinical psychologists who added this task to an already full work schedule and who additionally found the process time-consuming. They also had some concerns about the reliability and validity of their judgments for qualitative "grading" and feedback, and thus strongly supported the double-blind aspect of reviewing, and the ratification by external examiners.

External examiners

They were very supportive of the portfolio review process, regarding it as a "definite" strength of the module. For them "the fact that all candidates expected to revise or resubmit their portfolios actually did so demonstrated the development of a robust learning culture . . . and a serious commitment to CPD."

In response to the expansion of psychological therapies under the government agenda for Improving Access to Psychological Therapies (IAPT; Department of Health, 2007) in England and guidance within the matrix for psychological services in Scotland (NHS Education for Scotland and The Scottish Government, 2011), the provision of supervisor training by NES has been expanded to cover all psychological therapists practicing in NHS Scotland (Bagnall, Sloan, Platz, & Murphy, 2011). While the experience of the module for clinical psychology supervisors described earlier made a major contribution to these new developments, the increased breadth (and thus numbers) of target group participants meant that it would not be feasible, in terms of assessing the portfolios, to include portfolios to measure competence in clinical supervision.

Lessons Learned

The portfolio format provides a qualitative method for the assessment of clinical supervisor competence. As suggested earlier, this strategy has the potential of being enhanced with the addition of corroborative evidence. It is understood that the incorporation of a range of data-gathering options during research is thought to facilitate the emergence of a more comprehensive picture on the problem being studied. Campbell and Fiske (1959) were the first to use the navigational term, triangulation, in a research context, which appears appropriate since the phenomenon being investigated during qualitative research is much like a ship at sea. At the outset of a qualitative study, the phenomenon is unclear. In order to establish a clearer perspective, researchers study the issue from a specific reference point. Importantly, knowledge and understanding at this point is imprecise and potentially lacking in crucial detail or description. Consequently, researchers investigate the phenomenon further, but from an alternative perspective. Ultimately, incorporating a range of perspectives contributes toward creating a fuller, more comprehensive understanding of the phenomenon.

Initially, researchers described the process of triangulation as though it were a means of reaching confirmation (Denzin, 1970). However, the purpose of triangulation is now also extended to achieving completeness (Jick, 1979). Multiple triangulation exists when "a combination of multiple observers, theoretical perspectives, sources of data and methodologies are used" (Denzin, 1989, p. 310). In this regard, multiple triangulation is thought to capture a more complete, holistic and contextual appreciation of that being investigated and can include data (source, space, and time), methods (qualitative interviews, questionnaires, tests), and analysis strategies (two or more approaches to analyze the same data set) (Merriam, 2009; Thurmond, 2001).

To illustrate, in an investigation of clinical supervision in mental health nursing (Sloan, 2004, 2006), multiple triangulation was used, incorporating data triangulation (source, space, and time), methodological triangulation (qualitative interviews, clinical supervision session documents, critical incident journals, audio recordings of clinical supervision), and analytic triangulation (thematic analysis and six category intervention analysis as an analytic framework). This generated a more complete data set and confirmation of the conclusions, ultimately enhancing both the rigor and trustworthiness of its findings.

Might this approach have relevance to the assessment and evaluation of the competence of clinical supervisors? Perhaps in addition to the portfolios that were completed by the clinical supervisors, confirmation and completeness could be achieved by incorporating (at least as a minimum) data and methodological triangulation strategies. For instance, the supervisees, who are after all an important source given the essential requirement of a good supervisory relationship in the provision of effective clinical supervision, could be requested to provide evaluation of their clinical supervisors' performance during clinical supervision. Though potentially time-consuming, supervisees could also be asked to maintain a reflective journal of key learning points during supervision, and be invited to tease out the supervisors' contribution/competence to these points. Another option might be to observe clinical supervisors' provision of supervision and to rate their competence quantitatively using an appropriate competence measure, for example, the Supervision Adherence and Guidance Evaluation (Milne & Reiser, 2008), thus combining self-report by way of portfolios with objective observer evaluation.

Conclusion

This chapter has described an approach to measure supervisory competence, which was an integral part of an innovative supervision training module for clinical psychologists in Scotland, United Kingdom. Through an extension of existing qualitative methods, module participants were required to compile a personal portfolio of evidence for supervisory competence, drawing on their ongoing experience in supervising a clinical psychology trainee. The portfolio evidence was gathered from several different sources and mapped onto 12 specially developed statements of supervisory competence, which in turn reflected the intended learning outcomes of the module content. Portfolios were submitted for formal review and evaluation, with internal and external examiners using agreed criteria to make judgments about evidence for linking supervision theory to practice and for reflective learning about clinical supervision.

While the case study described here was innovative and developed rigorously and collaboratively over several years, there were perhaps inevitably some emergent weaknesses. These have been noted in this chapter, with some reference to the time-consuming nature of portfolio compilation and review, and thus its feasibility in practical terms. Reference was also made to the need for more robust triangulation to validate the self-reported supervisory competence, for example, by combining essentially qualitative evaluation of personal portfolios with objective observer evaluation.

Overall however, we believe that the approach described in this chapter, based on sound educational principles, could offer a way forward, ideally in a context of compulsory accreditation for clinical supervisors. One of the key strengths of this approach was the authenticity offered by portfolio evidence drawn from a range of supervisory experiences over a period of time. Furthermore, the pilot phase, which included pre and postmeasures, suggested that the training was successful, and indeed completion of the module was formally recognized by the relevant professional body in the United Kingdom. The authors are unaware of other training programs for clinical supervision which have adopted a similarly educationally sound and robust process for evaluating the development of supervisory competence. Given the increased recognition of the importance of formal supervisor training, as identified in Chapter 8, the portfolio process described here offers a possible future approach by combining an educational tool to promote reflective learning with a robust process for evaluating individual supervisory competence.

References

Abrami, P. C., & Barrett, H. (2005). Directions for research and development on electronic portfolios. *Canadian Journal of Learning and Technology*, *31*(3), 1–15. Online version.

Allan, C., Bagnall, G., & Campbell, E. (2003) *Analysis of education and training needs for supervisors in clinical psychology across Scotland: Final Report to NHS Education for Scotland.*

Bagnall, G. (2010). Preparing for clinical supervision in psychology: What can we learn from the Scottish experience? *Clinical Psychology Forum*, *216*, 15–20.

Bagnall, G., Sloan, G., Platz, S., & Murphy, S. (2011). Generic supervision competencies for psychological therapies. *Mental Health Practice*, *14*(6), 18–23.

Campbell, D. T., & Fiske, D. W. (1959). Convergent and discriminant validity by the multitrait, multi-method matrix. *Psychological Bulletin*, *56*(1), 81–105.

Chang, C. (2001). Construction and evaluation of a web-based learning portfolio system: An electronic assessment tool. *Innovations in Education and Teaching International*, *38*(2), 144–155.

Denzin, N. K. (1970). *The research act in society: A theoretical introduction to sociological methods*. London, England: Butterworth.

Denzin, N. K. (1989). *The research act: A theoretical introduction to sociological methods* (3rd ed.). Englewood Cliffs, NJ: Prentice Hall.

Department of Health (2007) Johnson Announces £170 Million Boost to Mental Health Therapies. Department of Health, London.

Driessen, E., van der Vleuten, C., Schurwirth, L., van Tartwijk, J., & Vermunt, J. (2005). The use of qualitative research criteria for portfolio assessment as an alternative to reliability evaluation: A case study. *Medical Education*, *39*(2), 214–220.

Driessen, E. (2008). Are learning portfolios worth the effort? Yes. *BMJ (Clinical Research Ed.)*, 337:39540 415822.AD. Online version. Retrieved from http://www.bmj.com/cgi/content/full/337/jul11_1/a513.

Driessen, E., van Tartwijk, J., van der Vleuten, C., & Wass, V. (2007). Portfolios in medical education: Why do they meet with mixed success? A systematic review. *Medical Education*, *41*, 1224–1233.

Duque, G. (2003). Web-based evaluation of medical clerkships: A new approach to immediacy and efficacy of feedback and assessment. *Medical Teacher*, *25*(5), 510–514.

Falender, C. A., & Shafranske, E. P. (2004). *Clinical supervision: A competency-based approach*. Washington, DC: American Psychological Association.

Grant, J. (2006). *Principles of curriculum design*. Understanding medical education monograph series. Oxford: Association for the Study of Medical Education (ASME), Blackwell Press.

Hall-Marley, S. (2001). *Supervisor Feedback Form*. Retrieved from www.cfalendEr.com

Jasper, M. A., & Fulton, J. (2005). Marking criteria for assessing practice-based portfolios at masters' level. *Nurse Education Today*, *25*, 377–389.

Jick, T. D. (1979). Mixing qualitative and quantitative methods: Triangulation in action. *Administrative Science Quarterly*, *24*, 602–611.

Klenowski, V., Askew, S., & Carnell, E. (2006). Portfolios for learning, assessment and professional development in higher education. *Assessment and Evaluation in Higher Education*, *31*(3), 267–286.

Kolb, D. A. (1984). *Experiential learning, Englewood Cliffs, New Jersey: Prentice Hall. Cited in Fry et al. (1999) A handbook for teaching and learning in higher education*. London, England: Kogan Page.

Merriam, S. B. (2009). *Qualitative research: A guide to design and implementation*. San Francisco, CA: John Wiley & Sons.

Miller, G. (1990). Assessment of clinical skills/competence/performance. *Academic Medicine*, *65*(Suppl.), S63–S67.

Milne, D. (2009). *Evidence-based clinical supervision: Principles and practice*. West Sussex, UK: BPS Wiley-Blackwell.

Milne, D. L., & Reiser, R. (2008). *SAGE: Manual for the supervision adherence and guidance evaluation instrument*. Newcastle: Newcastle University.

NHS Education for Scotland and The Scottish Government. (2011). Mental Health in Scotland: A Guide to Delivering Evidence-Based Psychological Therapies in Scotland The Matrix 2011. Edinburgh.

Rees, C., & Sheard, C. (2004). The reliability of assessment criteria for undergraduate medical students' communication skills portfolios: The Nottingham experience. *Medical Education*, *38*(2), 138–144.

Reiser, R. P., & Milne, D. (2012). Supervising cognitive-behavioural psychotherapy: Pressing needs, impressing possibilities. *Journal of Contemporary Psychotherapy*, *42*, 161–171.

Roth, A., & Pilling, S. (2008) *A Competence Framework for the Supervision of Psychological Therapies*. Retrieved from www.ucl.ac.uk/CORE/

Sloan, G. (2004) *An Illuminative Evaluation of Clinical Supervision in Mental Health Nursing*. (Unpublished PhD thesis). Department of Nursing and Community Health, Glasgow Caledonian University.

Sloan, G. (2006). *Clinical supervision in mental health nursing*. London, England: John Wiley & Sons.

Sloan, G., & Fleming, M. (2011). Training requirement for clinical supervision in the UK. In J. R. Cutcliffe, K. Hyrkas, & J. Fowler (Eds.), *Routledge handbook of clinical supervision: Global perspectives on fundamental themes – 2nd edition of fundamental themes of clinical supervision* (pp. 79–92), London: Routledge.

Thurmond, V. A. (2001). The point of triangulation. *Journal of Nursing Scholarship*, *33*(3), 253–258.

Tochel, C., Haig, A., Hesketh, A., Cadzow, A., Beggs, K., Colthart, I., & Peacock, H. (2009). Effectiveness of portfolios for postgraduate assessment and education. BEME Guide No 12. *Medical Teacher*, *31*(4), 299–318. Retrieved from http://www.beme.org

21

Creating Positive Outcomes in Clinical Supervision

Matthew Bambling

The research into supervision outcome has been criticized for methodological reasons, as well as a general view that it is disproportionately drawn from training settings, is out dated, and the arguments presented in previous reviews are tired, being based on reworking the same literature (Watkins, 2011). While acknowledging these limitations, this chapter includes some more recent research regarding the kinds of supervision outcomes that are thought important for both competence development for practitioners and clinical outcomes for clients (Bambling, 2009).

What Is Supervision and Who Thinks It Matters?

Supervision is considered an important professional practice that develops the ongoing competency of practitioners (O'Donovan, Halford, & Walters, 2011). Proctor (1986) provided a core definition of the outcomes of supervision, viewing it as providing restorative, normative, and formative functions. Supervision is restorative (supportive and stress management): therapists like participating in supervision; they evaluate supervision as an important part of their professional development and ongoing practice (Steven, Goodyear, & Robertson, 1998; Tromski-Klingshirn & Davis, 2007). Supervision may improve role performance and reduce burnout in stressful mental health settings (Bégat, Ellefsen, & Severinsson, 2005; White & Winstanley, 2010a). Supervision is formative (skill and knowledge development): Bernard and Goodyear (2004) conclude that supervisees assessed supervision as increasing the development of self-awareness and therapeutic awareness and professional practice skills and issues. Supervision also appears to develop greater self-efficacy in supervisees (Cashwell & Dooley, 2001). Supervision is regarded as a method of teaching and evaluating practice competencies (Falender & Shafranske, 2004). Supervision is normative (professional accountability): Bradley and Olson (1980) found that higher hours of

The Wiley International Handbook of Clinical Supervision, First Edition. Edited by C. Edward Watkins, Jr. and Derek L. Milne.

supervision and greater numbers of supervisors predicted positive assessments of clinical students' developing competence (Holloway & Neufeldt, 1995). In graduate settings, supervision provides a method of monitoring practice and practitioner standards (Australian Health Practitioner Regulation Agency [AHPRA], 2012). For example, in Australia, supervision is mandatory in clinical psychology training programs, and for graduate practitioners, it is part of the conditions of maintaining licensure.

Given the importance of supervision, what is the evidence base for effectiveness across the process and technical dimensions defined by Proctor? There are five broad research themes worthy of consideration (Bambling & King, 2000):

1. the supervisory relationship and clinical competencies,
2. individual supervisee and supervisor characteristics,
3. structure of supervision and learning environment,
4. supervision as a means of providing training in counseling skills, and
5. outcomes for clients.

Working Alliance, Supervisee Confidence, Feedback, and Evaluation

The supervisory relationship and clinical competencies

The supervisory relationship is thought to underpin effective supervision and has been conceptualized from different theoretical perspectives. Early investigation into the supervisory relationship was informed by the client-centered framework (Rogers, 1957). The assumption was made that the therapeutic relationship facilitated client change; therefore, the same process would occur in supervision for supervisees (Holloway & Wampold, 1986).

The facilitative conditions

The early supervision literature examining the quality of the relationship between the supervisor and supervisee focused primarily on the provision of facilitative conditions (Barrett-Lennard, 1985). When supervisors provided high levels of facilitative conditions, supervisees demonstrated growth in the use of these skills in therapy, which were retained in practice over a 12-month period (Holloway & Wampold, 1986). In comparison, supervisees whose supervisors provided low levels of facilitative conditions experienced a small decline in the provision of these skills when compared with baseline (Pierce & Schauble, 1971).

Facilitative conditions in supervision are subjectively important to supervisees and affect self-assessment of skill acquisition (Kennard, Stewart, & Gluck, 1987). Low facilitative conditions within the supervisory relationship increase supervisee experience of dissatisfaction and anxiety, negatively impacting on self-efficacy (Friedlander, Siegel, & Brenack, 1989). Schacht, Howe, and Berman (1989) found that in postgraduate training, a positive supervisee rating of supervisors' contribution to skill development directly related to supervisor provision of facilitative conditions. Supervisees also assessed supervisors more highly on facilitative conditions than on technical ability and experience (Schacht et al., 1989). The use of facilitative conditions may enhance supervisee capacity to learn core therapeutic interpersonal skills and to demonstrate these in therapy practice (Kostick, Whitley, & Bush, 2010; Pierce & Schauble, 1971).

The supervisory alliance

The supervisory relationship has been examined through the more contemporary construct of supervisory working alliance (Bambling & King, 2000). High ratings of supervisory alliance reduce conflict and ambiguity with supervisees perceiving the supervision as accommodating their expectations and preferences (Landany & Friedlander, 1995). It is also likely that supervisors who achieve high ratings of supervisory alliance intentionally focus on developing rapport, encourage supervisee identification, as well as maintain a strong focus on the therapeutic casework (Bambling & King, 2013). In a recent study (Bambling & King, 2013), supervisee-rated alliance predicted learning evaluation for both technical and interpersonal skill development. The supervisory alliance might be considered a fundamental requirement to achieve positive outcomes (Lampropoulos, 2003).

The supervisory working alliance, strains, ruptures, and management

The supervisory alliance may be subject to strains and ruptures much in the same way as the working alliance in therapy (Safran, Muran, Stevens, & Rothman, 2007). Supervisees may experience strains in the supervisory relationship due to the demands created by supervision, for example, formal responsibilities and attribution and role demands (Friedlander et al., 1989; Landany & Friedlander, 1995). The failure of a supervisor to adequately attend to supervisory alliance strains and ruptures may lead to unmet supervisee expectations and learning needs, anxiety, or conflict (Gray, Ladany, Walker, & Ancis, 2001; Kulp, 2012). Likewise, supervisee struggles in client work may create strains and ruptures in the supervisory relationship (Nelson & Friedlander, 2001). Overt or underlying conflict is thought to harm the quality of supervisory alliance and outcome. Conflict results in a negative assessment of the supervisory relationship, self-efficacy, and satisfaction with supervision (Friedlander et al., 1989; Nelson & Friedlander, 2001). A lack of clear supervisory roles results in more supervisee anxiety and less self-efficacy and predicts conflict with the supervisor. Conflict affects supervisor evaluation of supervisee practice. Supervisees who reported low conflict tended to be evaluated more highly by supervisors than those who reported high levels of conflict (Kulp, 2012).

A positive experience of supervision, assessed along indices of support, instructional and interpretative competence produces less role conflict and anxiety and more role satisfaction than negative ratings (Kulp, 2012). A good match between the theoretical orientation of the supervisor and supervisee predicts low role conflict and positive evaluation of supervisory relationship and outcome (Friedlander et al., 1989; Kennard et al., 1987). Supervisors who communicate trustworthiness, expertness, and attractiveness positively influence supervisee judgment of supervisory alliance. Trustworthiness accounted for more variance in judgments than expertness and attractiveness. Trustworthiness is required for supervisees to disclose struggles with practice and to accept corrective feedback, and is related to supervisor and supervisee assessment of skill development. While the relationship between supervisor trustworthiness, expertness and attractiveness, and skill development is unclear, it supports the importance of positive interpersonal supervisor behavior underpinning supervisory alliance and learning outcomes (Bambling & King, 2013).

Supervisors are often concerned about providing critical feedback to supervisees to preserve the supervisory alliance (Friedlander et al., 1989; Hoffman, Hill, Holmes, & Freitas, 2005). This concern may be unfounded as Reese et al. (2009) found that using client feedback measures to inform supervision encouraged higher levels of corrective feedback to trainees, which did not negatively impact the supervisory alliance and enhanced the development of supervisee self-efficacy (Falender & Shafranske, 2004). Supervisors can do much to enhance the supervisees' perception of supervision by ensuring there is little overt confusion and conflict around roles and learning environment, and by negotiating these directly. In addition, supervisors can provide role induction and corrective feedback, and manage the supervisory alliance. When alliance strains and ruptures occur, they can be corrected through addressing issues of concern, to reduce negative supervisee experience (Landany & Friedlander, 1995; Safran et al., 2007).

Flexibility and Practice Demands

Supervisor characteristics

Supervisors have characteristics that may predict supervision outcome. For example, higher stability in supervisor attachment style may predict the development of supervisory alliance (Riggs & Bretz, 2006; White & Queener, 2003). In a recent study, the level of supervisor verbal and nonverbal interpersonal skills as measured by the Social Skills Inventory (SSI) (Riggio, 1986) predicted supervisee ratings of supervisory alliance and supervision evaluation (Bambling & King, 2013). However, only three subscales of the SSI predicted supervisory working alliance. These were supervisor emotional sensitivity (ES), social expressivity (SE), and social control (SC). The ES subscale measures sensitivity to the emotional state of others and awareness of underlying feelings, motivations in communication and receiving and decoding the nonverbal communications of others (Riggio, 1986). Supervisors high in ES are concerned with and vigilant in observing the nonverbal emotional cues of their supervisee. Because they are able to decode emotional communication rapidly and efficiently, they could identify supervisee feelings and concerns and address these as part of the supervision process. The negative is that they may be more susceptible to becoming emotionally aroused by their supervisees and sympathetically experiencing their emotional states. SE refers to a general verbal speaking skill and an ability to engage others in social interaction. Supervisors high in SE are experienced by their supervisees as outgoing because of their ability to initiate conversations and to speak spontaneously with them (Riggio, 1986). In the supervision context, this ability would allow supervisors to utilize interpersonal engagement as the main method to relate to, and to conduct supervisory discussions with their supervisee. SC control refers to a general skill in social self-presentation. Supervisors high in SC are tactful, socially adept, and self-confident and can play various social roles and easily take a particular stance or orientation in a discussion. Consequently, they are able to adjust personal behavior to be appropriate to any given supervisory situation. SC would provide an important skill to balance SE in supervision. Supervisors could match their interpersonal style to suit the individual needs of the supervisee as well as provide feedback, thereby directing the process of supervision without being unduly influenced by competing issues or demands. Supervisors high in SC are likely to be experienced as sophisticated and wise by their supervisees (Riggio, 1986). The other subscales, emotional control (EC), emotional expresivity (EE), and social sensitivity (SS), did not relate to supervisory working alliance. The evidence suggests that effective supervisors use interpersonal skills that actively facilitate supervisee perception of supervisory alliance and managing the learning environment (Bambling & King, 2013).

Supervisee characteristics

Supervisees have individual characteristics that influence supervision learning outcome such as stability of attachments, attitudes, ego strength, and learning and cognitive style (Bernstein & Lecomte, 1979; White & Queener, 2003). Higher supervisee interpersonal and therapeutic skill and stability in interpersonal relationships predict flexibility in learning style and therapeutic attitudes. Likewise, stable attachment and relationships are related to greater ego strength and the demonstration of empathy and application of facilitative skills (White & Queener, 2003). Supervisees who are more internally oriented regarding learning style and decision-making evaluate supervisor feedback more positively than supervisees who are externally oriented.

Holloway and Wampold (1986) examined the ability to acquire counseling skills between cognitively concrete and cognitively complex trainees in supervision. Cognitively complex individuals were better able to perform complex and ambiguous therapy tasks than concrete supervisees. In a similar study, Winter and Holloway (1992) examined the relation of supervisee cognitive complexity with choice of audiotaped content for discussion. Cognitively complex supervisees demonstrated a more critical evaluation of their work and requested more feedback on demonstrated skills. Supervisee characteristics such as orientation to learning style and decision-making, cognitive style, and ego strength may mediate skill acquisition and are important considerations for structuring the supervisory learning environment (Holloway & Wampold, 1986).

There is little doubt that supervisors and supervisees bring individual characteristics to supervision that influences process and outcome. The effects of individual characteristics are not well understood and more research is needed. While supervision theory does not recognize these effects as being important for conducting supervision, it is prudent for the supervisor to understand and account for these characteristics in practice.

Supervisor Style and Learning Environment

Supervisor approach to the practice of supervision may impact on supervisee expectancies and the learning environment of supervision (Landany, Walker, & Melincoff, 2000). Supervisees have a preference for supervision style that includes a high level of supervisor interest in them, equitable distribution of power, being a teacher and consultant, acknowledging concerns, providing a theory-based framework for practice, modeling approach and skills, practical skills training, clear communication, and provision of evaluative feedback (Kulp, 2012). For example, Schoenwald, Sheidow, and Chapman (2009) found that when supervisors focused on adhering to treatment principles using a supportive style, supervisees were more likely to adhere to the treatment approach in youth treatment programs. It appears supervisors in part meet these supervisee expectations, providing more technical and theory-based responses; however, significantly fewer responses related to emotional development and well-being (Holloway & Neufeldt, 1995; Holloway & Wampold, 1986).

These studies demonstrate that there may not be a great variation regarding how supervisors conduct supervision: they tend to be more educative, focusing less on supervisees' emotional life. While supervisors should aim to meet supervisee expectancies, there is insufficient evidence to conclude that meeting all supervisee expectancies is required for supervisee outcomes. At best, it can be concluded that a primary educative and learning focus and a secondary focus on affective issues in supervision are sufficient.

Intervention Skills and Evaluation

Supervision as a means of providing training in counseling skills

Supervision is often used to both teach and evaluate counselor skill acquisition and other practice competencies. O'Donovan et al. (2011) conclude supervision is well suited to provide these formative functions. Norcross and Stevenson (1984) and Norcross, Stevenson, and Nash (1986) were unable to identify any reliable competency data from graduate psychology programs and concluded the evaluation processes used were informal and not empirically validated. Stevenson, Norcross, King, and Tobin (1984) found that personal impressions and qualitative evaluation were most commonly used to evaluate supervisee skill acquisition. Little has changed as supervisee evaluation methods in clinical psychology training programs are still subject to these criticisms. In a large Australian study, supervised practicum evaluations were found to involve subjective supervisor assessment of supervisee performance for counseling and other competency dimensions. Supervisor assessments were found to be inaccurate, typically inflated, and evaluations did not relate to later practicum performance (Gonsalvez & Freestone, 2007). However, this does not mean that supervised training programs have no impact on supervisee skill development. Reese et al. (2009) found that by the end of a 12-month supervised practicum, interns had significantly improved, achieving better outcomes in their client work than at baseline on all competencies measured. At least for graduate psychology training, the evaluation of multiple domains of skill acquisition in supervision is not reliable and the assessment of learning outcomes is inaccurate. Simple strategies such as including client outcome data and standardized measures of competence and skill achievement would make the evaluation process stronger.

Supervision has a positive impact on the development of specific counseling-related skills. Heaven, Clegg, and Maguire (2005) found that training in therapeutic communication skills improves competency but is not generalized to clinical practice without supervision. Henry, Schacht, Strupp, Butler, and Binder (1993) concluded that basic cognitive-behavioral therapy (CBT) counseling skill can be learned rapidly through supervisory training, but higher-order skills such as timing, judgment, and insight take longer to learn. Lambert and Ogles (1997) concluded that CBT supervision can teach basic behavioral counseling skills through instruction without supervisor modeling. With regard to more complex therapy skills, Williams, Judge, Hill, and Hoffman (1997) found that trainees are better able to manage countertransference in client work as a result of supervision. Complex interpersonal skills such as establishing a positive early alliance and alliance rupture management can be taught through supervision (Bambling, King, Raue, Schweitzer, & Lambert, 2006). Treatment plans devised in supervision might be consistently delivered in therapy (Schoenwald et al., 2009). Falender and Shafranske (2007) concluded that practice competencies can be taught through supervision. While the evidence is encouraging regarding skill outcome for supervisees, the role of supervision in teaching advanced skills such as theoretical treatment model, case conceptualization, and treatment planning require more investigation.

Supervision Approaches and Supervisee Learning Outcome

Which approaches to supervision are best to achieve supervisee competence?

Supervision can be divided into two broad categories, those that are related to a therapy approach (such as *CBT* or psychodynamic supervision) or are distinct, such as the developmental approach. Milne and James (2000, 2002) and Milne and Dunkerley (2010) conclude there is evidence that supervision, especially CBT supervision, has a positive impact on supervisee clinical development. There is also reason to believe that it impacts positively on client work (Ng & Cheung, 2007). Bambling et al. (2006) evaluated two different approaches to supervision (CBT vs. psychodynamic therapy) in relation to quality of client work and found both were equally effective with no difference in outcome. However, this study was not measuring approach-specific outcomes but rather evaluating if there was a differential impact for supervision techniques on client outcome. The *developmental approach* is a non-therapy supervision model. All developmental supervision models share key assumptions regarding the structuring of learning environment, based on supervisee experience level (Bambling, 2004). Essentially, developmental theory describes a process where the supervisor modifies the structure of supervisory activity through a series of prescribed stages to match the growing clinical experience of the supervisee. The importance of altering supervisory structure to match growing supervisee competency cannot be overemphasized, as it provides the method by which more advanced skills are developed (Bambling, 2004; Biggs, Bambling, & Pearce, 2009; Stoltenberg, 1997).

Research into developmental processes and the learning environment has been criticized (Holloway, 1987). However, some important conclusions can be drawn (Bambling, 2004; Biggs et al., 2009). Supervisors are well able to use the development model, assessing the different needs of beginning and advanced level supervisees and structuring the learning environment accordingly. Beginning level supervisees preferred structure and direction by their supervisor, and experienced supervisees preferred less structure and direction. Experienced supervisees focused on advanced skills such transference and countertransference, and self-efficacy and self-awareness when conceptualizing cases. Newer supervisees focused on basic technical skills necessary to conceptualize and work with cases. No effects have yet been found for intermediate or transitional levels of skill development (Biggs et al., 2009). However, the effect of developmental level are lost when situational factors occurred, such as engaging a new supervisor or dealing with a crisis situation. In these instances, the need for structure and support was present in supervision regardless of experience level (Bambling, 2004; Biggs et al., 2009). In summary, while there is evidence that supervision approaches may be effective, there is much that needs to be done to define approach-specific outcomes and learning processes (Milne & James, 2002; O'Donovan et al., 2011).

The Effect of Supervision on Client Outcome

An important test of supervision is the impact on client outcome. Evaluating supervision in relation to client outcomes is a complex task, due to the multitude of variables operative between supervisor, supervisee, and client. Examining either an aspect or aspects of this supervisory triad, rather than evaluating a system of supervision, has been the dominant approach to date (Bambling & King, 2000).

To illustrate, Stein and Lambert (1995) reviewed graduate training and client outcome through internships at mental health clinics and found modest positive results. Reese et al. (2009) found a positive effect on client outcome for supervised internships. Supervision may also promote supervisees' ability to work with client transference, helping them to become aware of parallel processes and influencing therapist behavior with clients (Friedlander et al., 1989). White and Winstanley (2010a) demonstrated that supervision reduces burnout, increases staff retention in health agencies, and improves practice outcomes in some health settings. Supervisor and supervisee adherence to supervision structure and focus on supervisee development was found to relate to better client outcomes (Schoenwald et al., 2009). Bradshaw, Butterworth, and Mairs (2007) demonstrated that workplace supervision of mental health nurses after training in psychosocial rehabilitation methods created a reduction in positive symptoms and improved function for patients with schizophrenia. The supervision focused on the application of the psychosocial model learned in training. In another study, White and Winstanley (2010b) found that in public mental health agencies, there may be significant impediments to effective supervision and it only improves outcomes where there is dedicated commitment to supervision among unit staff and managers.

Bambling et al. (2006), in a three-group clinical trial using a standardized therapy approach, found that supervised graduate therapists achieved superior outcomes to unsupervised therapists. The supervision approaches included a strong focus on the interpersonal process of therapy following either a CBT or a psychodynamic therapy framework. Compared with the unsupervised therapist group, both supervision approaches achieved equivalent and positive results for symptom outcome, client-rated working alliance, treatment retention, and client evaluation of therapy. The supervision conditions significantly outperformed the control group, which also achieved acceptable results. There was a significantly higher dropout rate in the control group than the supervised groups. While this study provides evidence that supervision may directly enhance client outcomes, the mechanisms of action do not appear to be related to the theoretical approach within supervision but rather to the focus on therapeutic processes. Hill and Knox (2013) suggest that supervision achieves outcomes based on common mechanisms rather than theoretically embedded procedures.

A major advancement in enhancing psychotherapy outcomes has been the development of outcome informed practice through client session-by-session feedback (Lambert, 2001). Feedback provides immediate information to therapists about client progress and identifies cases that are not progressing as expected, allowing remedial action to be taken (Ackerman et al., 2001). The use of feedback may also reduce treatment noncompletion and improve outcomes for clients considered to be treatment resistant (Brown & Jones, 2005; Whipple et al., 2003).

Supervision typically relies on supervisee reports of client work and less frequently recordings of sessions for review. Therapists and perhaps supervisors (regardless of experience) tend to misjudge "at-risk" cases and deterioration (Grove, Zald, Lebow, Snitz, & Nelson, 2000). Reese et al. (2009) examined the impact of trainee therapists using client feedback in supervision over a one-year practicum. Both feedback and nonfeedback supervision conditions demonstrated significantly better client outcomes at the end of practicum. However, clients in the feedback supervision condition improved significantly more than the nonfeedback condition. Supervisees in both conditions rated the supervisory relationship and satisfaction with supervision equally, although the relationship between supervisee self-efficacy and client outcome was strongest in the supervision feedback condition. The impact of supervision on client outcome may be improved by supervisees taking feedback reports to supervision, at least for training therapists.

Conclusion

There is sufficient evidence to conclude supervision creates a variety of positive outcomes for both therapists and clients. Supervision may enhance supervisee self-efficacy, knowledge, and skills, at least in the training setting. Most encouragingly, there is evidence that supervision might also improve the quality of client work and enhance treatment outcomes for clients. Process factors, such as supervisory alliance, are important to ensure the quality of supervision and the achievement of learning goals and clinical outcomes. There is insufficient data as yet to explain the mechanisms by which supervision achieves these outcomes. A systematic approach to evaluating supervision outcome based on the practice competencies has utility to both the practice and training settings (Milne & Dunkerley, 2010; Watkins, 2011). This would represent a constructive and systematic way forward to better evaluate the mechanisms and processes by which supervision may achieve the outcomes required for mental health practice.

References

Ackerman, S. J., Benjamin, L. S., Beutler, L. E., Gelso, C. J., Goldfried, M. R., Hill, C., Rainer, J. (2001). Empirically supported therapy relationships: Conclusions and recommendations of the Division 29 Task Force. *Psychotherapy: Theory, Research, Practice, Training, 38*, 495–497. doi:10.1037/0033-3204.38.4.495

Australian Health Practitioner Regulation Agency (AHPRA). (2012). *Psychology Board of Australia*. Retrieved from http://www.psychologyboard.gov.au/

Bambling, M. (2004). The developmental model of supervision and contemporary practice. *Psychotherapy in Australia, 11*(1), 30–35. Retrieved from http://search.informit.com.au

Bambling, M. (2009). Working alliance Supervision. In N. Pelling, J. Barletta, & P. Armstrong (Eds.), *The practice of clinical supervision* (pp. 121–137), Brisbane, Australia: Australian Academic Press.

Bambling, M., & King, R. (2000). The effect of clinical supervision on the development of counsellor competency. *Psychotherapy in Australia, 6*(4), 58–63. Retrieved from http://search.informit.com.au

Bambling, M., & King, R. (2013). Supervisor social skill and supervision outcome. *Counselling and Psychotherapy Research*, 121–138, 1–7. doi:10.1080/14733145.2013.835849

Bambling, M., King, R., Raue, P., Schweitzer, R., & Lambert, W. (2006). Clinical supervision: Its impact on working alliance and outcome in the treatment of major depression. *Psychotherapy Research, 16*, 317–331. doi:10.1080/10503300500268524

Barrett-Lennard, G. (1985). The helping relationship: Crisis and advance in theory and research. *The Counseling Psychologist, 13*, 278–294. doi:10.1177/0011000085132006

Bégat, I., Ellefsen, B., & Severinsson, E. (2005). Nurses satisfaction with their work environment and the outcomes of clinical nursing supervision on nurses experiences of well-being – A Norwegian study. *Journal of Nursing Management, 13*, 221–230. doi:10.1111/j.1365-2834.2004.00527.x

Bernard, J., & Goodyear, R. (2004). *Fundamentals of clinical supervision* (3rd ed.). Columbus, OH: Pearson Education.

Bernstein, B., & Lecomte, C. (1979). Supervisory type feedback effects: Feedback discrepancy level, trainee psychological differentiation, and immediate responses. *Journal of Counselling Psychology, 26*, 295–303. doi:10.1037/0022-0167.26.4.295

Biggs, H., Bambling, M., & Pearce, Z. (2009). Approaches to supervision. In N. Pelling, J. Barletta, & P. Armstrong (Eds.), *The practice of clinical supervision* (pp. 94–120), Brisbane, Australia: Australian Academic Press.

Bradley, J., & Olson, J. (1980). Training factors influencing felt psychotherapeutic competence of psychology trainees. *Professional Psychology, 11*, 930–934. doi:10.1037/0735-7028.11.6.930

Bradshaw, T., Butterworth, A., & Mairs, H. (2007). Does structured clinical supervision during psychosocial intervention education enhance outcome for mental health nurses and the service users they work with? *Journal of Psychiatric and Mental Health Nursing, 14*(1), 4–12. Retrieved from http://www.ncbi.nlm.nih.gov

Brown, G. S., & Jones, D. R. (2005). Implementation of a feedback system in a managed care environment: What are patients teaching us? *Journal of Clinical Psychology, 61*, 187–198. doi:10.1002/jclp.20110

Cashwell, T. H., & Dooley, K. (2001). The impact of supervision on counselor self-efficacy. *The Clinical Supervisor, 20*, 39–47. doi:10.1300/J001v20n01_03

Falender, C., & Shafranske, E. (2004). *Clinical supervision: A competence-based approach.* Washington, DC: American Psychological Association.

Falender, C., & Shafranske, E. (2007). Competence in competency-based supervision practice: Construct and application. *Professional Psychology: Research and Practice, 38*, 232–240.

Friedlander, M. L., Siegel, S. M., & Brenack, K. (1989). Parallel processing in counseling and supervision: A case study. *Journal of Counseling Psychology, 36*, 149–157. doi:10.1037/0022-0167.36.2.149

Gonsalvez, C., & Freestone, J. (2007). Field supervisors' assessments of trainee performance: Are they reliable and valid? *Australian Psychologist, 42*, 23–32. doi:10.1080/00050060600827615

Gray, L. A., Ladany, N., Walker, J. A., & Ancis, J. R. (2001). Psychotherapy trainees' experience of counterproductive events in supervision. *Journal of Counseling Psychology, 48*, 371–383. doi:10.1037/0022-0167.48.4.371

Grove, W. M., Zald, D. H., Lebow, B. S., Snitz, B. E., & Nelson, C. (2000). Clinical versus mechanical prediction: A meta-analysis. *Psychological Assessment, 12*, 19–30. doi:10.1037//1040-3590.12.1.19

Heaven, C., Clegg, J., & Maguire, P. (2005). Transfer of communication skills training from workshop to workplace: The impact of clinical supervision. *Patient Education and Counselling, 60*, 313–325. doi:10.1016/j.pec.2005.08.008

Henry, W., Schacht, T., Strupp, H., Butler, S., & Binder, J. (1993). Effects of training in time-limited dynamic psychotherapy: Mediators of therapists' responses to training. *Journal of Consulting and Clinical Psychology, 61*(3), 441–447. Retrieved from http://psycnet.apa.org

Hill, C. E., & Knox, S. (2013). Training and supervision in psychotherapy. In M. J. Lambert (Ed.), *Bergin and Garfield's handbook of psychotherapy and behavior change* (6th ed., pp. 775–811), Hoboken, NJ: Wiley.

Hoffman, M. A., Hill, C. E., Holmes, S. E., & Freitas, G. F. (2005). Supervisor perspective on the process and outcome of giving easy, difficult, or no feedback to supervisees. *Journal of Counseling Psychology, 52*, 3–13. doi:10.1037/0022-0167.52.1.3

Holloway, E. (1987). Developmental models of supervision: Is it development? *Professional Psychology: Research and Practice, 18*, 209–216.

Holloway, E., & Neufeldt, S. (1995). Supervision: Its contribution to treatment efficacy. *Journal of Consulting and Clinical Psychology, 63*, 207–213.

Holloway, E., & Wampold, B. (1986). Relation between conceptual level and counselling related tasks, a meta-analysis. *Journal of Counselling Psychology, 33*, 310–319. doi:10.1037/0022-0167.33.3.310

Kennard, B., Stewart, S., & Gluck, M. (1987). The supervision relationship: Variables contributing to positive versus negative experiences. *Professional Psychology, Research and Practice, 18*, 172–175. doi:10.1037/0735-7028.18.2.172

Kostick, K., Whitley, R., & Bush, P. (2010). Client-centeredness in supported employment: Specialist and supervisor perspectives. *Journal of Mental Health, 19*, 523–531. doi:10.3109/09638237.2010.520364

Kulp, L. (2012). *Supervision factors that predict trainee role conflict and role ambiguity* (Unpublished doctoral thesis). Lehigh University, Bethlehem, PA.

Lambert, M., & Ogles, B. (1997). The effectiveness of psychotherapy supervision. In C. Watkins, Jr. (Ed.), *Handbook of psychotherapy supervision* (pp. 421–446), New York: John Wiley & Sons. Ch 24.

Lambert, M. J. (2001). Psychotherapy outcome and quality improvement: Introduction to the special section on patient-focused research. *Journal of Consulting and Clinical Psychology, 69*, 147–149. doi:10.1037//0022-006X.69.2.147

Lampropoulos, G. K. (2003). A common factors view of counseling supervision process. *The Clinical Supervisor, 21*, 77–95. doi:10.1300/J001v21n01_06

Landany, N., & Friedlander, M. (1995). The relationship between the supervisory working alliance and trainees' experience of role conflict and role ambiguity. *Counselor Education and Supervision*, *34*, 220–231. doi:10.1002/j.1556-6978.1995.tb00244.x

Landany, N., Walker, J., & Melincoff, D. (2000). Supervisory style: Its relation to the supervisory working alliance and supervisor self-disclosure. *Counselor Education and Supervision*, *38*, 215–225. doi:10.1002/j.1556-6978.2001.tb01259.x

Milne, D., & Dunkerley, C. (2010). Towards evidence-based clinical supervision: The development and evaluation of four CBT guidelines. *The Cognitive Behaviour Therapist*, *3*, 43–57. doi:10.1017/S1754470X10000048

Milne, D., & James, I. (2000). A systematic review of effective cognitive-behavioural supervision. *The British Journal of Clinical Psychology*, *39*, 111–127. doi:10.1348/014466500163149

Milne, D., & James, I. (2002). The observed impact of training on competence in clinical supervision. *The British Journal of Clinical Psychology*, *41*, 55–72. doi:10.1348/014466502163796

Nelson, M. L., & Friedlander, M. L. (2001). A close look at conflictual supervisory relationships: The trainee's perspective. *Journal of Counseling Psychology*, *48*, 384–395. doi:10.1037/0022-0167.48.4.384

Ng, R., & Cheung, M. (2007). Supervision of cognitive behavioural therapy for psychosis: A Hong Kong experience. *Hong Kong Journal of Psychiatry*, *17*(4), 124–130. Retrieved from http://www.questia.com/library/p136885/hong-kong-journal-of-psychiatry

Norcross, J., & Stevenson, J. (1984). How shall we judge ourselves? Training evaluation in clinical psychology programs. *Professional Psychology, Research and Practice*, *15*, 497–508. doi:10.1037/0735-7028.15.4.497

Norcross, J., Stevenson, J., & Nash, J. (1986). Evaluation of internship training: Practices, problems and prospects. *Professional Psychology, Research and Practice*, *17*, 280–282. doi:10.1037/0735-7028.17.3.280

O'Donovan, A., Halford, K., & Walters, B. (2011). Towards best practice supervision of clinical psychology trainees. *Australian Psychologist*, *46*, 101–112. doi:10.1111/j.1742-9544.2011.00033.x

Pierce, M., & Schauble, G. (1971). Graduate training of facilitative counsellors: The effects of individual supervision. *Journal of Counselling Psychology*, *17*, 210–215. doi:10.1037/h0029221

Proctor, B. (1986). Supervision: A cooperative exercise in accountability. In M. Marken & M. Payne (Eds.), *Enabling and ensuring: Supervision in practice* (pp. 21–34), Leicester, England: National Youth Bureau and Council for Education and Training in Youth and Community Work.

Reese, R., Usher, E., Bowman, D., Norsworthy, L., Halstead, J., Rowlands, S., & Chisholm, R. (2009). Using client feedback in psychotherapy training: An analysis of its influence on supervision and counselor self-efficacy. *Training and Education in Professional Psychology*, *3*, 157–168. doi:10.1037/a0015673

Riggio, R. (1986). Assessment of basic social skills. *Journal of Personality and Social Psychology*, *51*, 649–660. doi:10.1037/0022-3514.51.3.649

Riggs, S. A., & Bretz, K. M. (2006). Attachment processes in the supervisory relationship: An exploratory investigation. *Professional Psychology, Research and Practice*, *37*, 558–566. doi:10.1037/0735-7028.37.5.558

Rogers, C. (1957). Training individuals to engage in the therapeutic process. In C. Strother (Ed.), *Psychology and mental health* (pp. 95–103), Washington, DC: American Psychological Association.

Safran, J. D., Muran, J. C., Stevens, C., & Rothman, M. (2007). A relational approach to supervision. In C. A. Falender & E. P. Shafranske (Eds.), *Casebook for clinical supervision:*

A competency-based approach (pp. 137–157), Washington, DC: American Psychological Association.

Schacht, J., Howe, E., Jr., & Berman, J. (1989). Supervisor facilitative conditions and effectiveness as perceived by thinking – and feeling – type supervisees. *Psychotherapy, 26*, 475–483. doi:10.1037/h0085466

Schoenwald, S., Sheidow, A., & Chapman, J. (2009). Clinical supervision in treatment transport: Effects on adherence and outcomes. *Journal of Consulting and Clinical Psychology, 77*, 410–421. doi:10.1037/a0013788

Stein, D., & Lambert, M. (1995). Graduate training in psychotherapy: Are therapy outcomes enhanced? *Journal of Consulting and Clinical Psychology, 63*, 182–196. doi:10.1037/0022-006X.63.5.717

Steven, D., Goodyear, R., & Robertson, P. (1998). Supervisor development: An exploratory study in changes in stance and emphasis. *The Clinical Supervisor, 16*, 73–88. doi:10.1300/J001v16n02_05

Stevenson, J., Norcross, J., King, J., & Tobin, K. (1984). Evaluating clinical training programs: A formative effort. *Professional Psychology, Research and Practice, 15*, 218–229.

Stoltenberg, C. (1997). The integrated developmental model of supervision: Supervision across levels. *Psychotherapy in Private Practice, 16*, 59–69. doi:10.1300/J294v16n02_07

Tromski-Klingshirn, D. M., & Davis, T. E. (2007). Supervisees perceptions of their clinical supervision: A study of the dual role of clinical and administrative supervisor. *Counselor Education and Supervision, 46*, 294–304. doi:10.1002/j.1556-6978.2007.tb00033.x

Watkins, C. E. (2011). Does psychotherapy supervision contribute to patient outcomes? Considering thirty years of research. *The Clinical Supervisor, 30*, 235–256. doi:10.1080/07325223.2011.619417

Whipple, J. L., Lambert, M. J., Vermeersch, D. A., Smart, D. W., Hawkins, E. J., & Nielsen, S. L. (2003). Improving the effects of psychotherapy: The use of early identification of treatment failure and problem solving strategies in outcome. *Journal of Counseling Psychology, 50*, 59–68. doi:10.1037/0022-0167.50.1.59

White, E., & Winstanley, J. (2010a). Does clinical supervision lead to better patient outcomes in mental health nursing? *Nursing Times, 106*(16), 16–18. Retrieved from http://www.nursingtimes.net

White, E., & Winstanley, J. (2010b). A randomised controlled trial of clinical supervision: Selected findings from a novel Australian attempt to establish the evidence base for causal relationships with quality of care and patient outcomes as an informed contribution to mental health nursing practice development. *Journal of Research in Nursing, 15*, 151–167. doi:10.1177/1744987109357816

White, V., & Queener, J. (2003). Supervisor and supervisee attachments and social provisions related to the supervisory working alliance. *Counselor Education and Supervision, 42*, 203–218. doi:10.1002/j.1556-6978.2003.tb01812.x

Williams, E., Judge, A., Hill, C., & Hoffman, M. (1997). Experiences of novice therapists in prepracticum: Trainees', clients', and supervisors' perceptions of therapists' personal reactions and management strategies. *Journal of Counseling Psychology, 44*, 390–399.

Winter, M., & Holloway, E. (1992). Relation of trainee experience, conceptual level and supervisor approach to selection of audiotaped counseling passages. *The Clinical Supervisor, 9*(2), 87–103.

22

Measuring Competence in Supervisees and Supervisors *Satisfaction and Related Reactions in Supervision*

Analise O'Donovan and David J. Kavanagh

Supervision is a highly valued component of practitioner training. A recent survey of Australian postgraduate clinical students found that individual clinical supervision was viewed as the most effective teaching method in their program (Scott, Pachana, & Sofranoff, 2011). There is also an international consensus by educationalists about its central position in training practitioners (Lambert & Ogles, 1997; Roth & Pilling, 2007; Watkins, 1997). As discussed elsewhere in this handbook, supervision potentially translates concepts, principles, and therapy descriptions into specific practices, shaping practitioners' skill acquisition (Holloway & Neufeldt, 1995). Supervision can have effects that extend well beyond effective practice: for example, a stronger supervisory working alliance has been found to predict higher work satisfaction and decreased work-related stress (Sterner, 2009).

The high expectations of supervision by all parties throw a spotlight on indicators of its quality. A summary measure of this is satisfaction – implicitly, a measure of the extent that the reality of a particular supervision experience matches those expectations. In fact, supervisees' satisfaction tends to be the most common way that supervision is evaluated, particularly in routine or repeated measurement (Milne, 2009). Simple summary measures of satisfaction with supervision can be highly predictive. For example, a large study of mental health practitioners found that a single-item measure of supervisees' satisfaction with supervision correlated .71, $p < .001$, with the ratings of its perceived impact on their clinical practice (Kavanagh et al., 2003).

In this chapter, we discuss the following: factors influencing perceived satisfaction and alliance; how satisfaction, alliance, and supervision relationships are currently measured; and review issues with the concept and its assessment.

The Wiley International Handbook of Clinical Supervision, First Edition. Edited by C. Edward Watkins, Jr. and Derek L. Milne.

Characteristics of Supervision That Promote Satisfaction and Alliance

The literature is replete with examples of supervisees thriving in a collaborative and effective supervision relationship, or drowning in ineffective, harmful supervision situations. Supervision comprises the best and worst of times for its recipients. Many supervisees continue to report a significant impact from their early supervisory experience years after its completion (Guest & Beutler, 1988).

Effective supervision can enhance supervisee reactions and experiences positively. For example, supportive supervision can enhance supervisee confidence and reduce supervisee anxiety (Bambling, King, Raue, Schweitzer, & Lambert, 2006; Kennard, Stewart, & Gluck, 1987), and the breadth and depth of supervision are significant predictors of a therapist's sense of competence (Bradley & Olsen, 1980). In particular, a focus on detecting and rewarding successive approximations to effective practice (instead of focusing primarily on ways the trainee falls short) builds self-efficacy, as does communicating a belief in their potential for achievement (Bandura, 1982). This assists in maintaining motivation and effort, reduces anxiety about performance, and increases the pace of skill acquisition (Bandura, 1982). Conversely, a detrimental supervisory experience can impair the supervisee's self-efficacy (Bambling, 2000; Gray, Ladany, Walker, & Ancis, 2001).

Supervision achieves its ends within a relationship, which (as in therapy) has a strong influence on its effectiveness (Ellis & Ladany, 1997). An essential characteristic of an effective supervisory relationship is its provision of a safe context for disclosure of problems and suboptimal practice, and for progressive skill acquisition. Anxiety about the supervisor's reactions can impair learning during sessions, both by inducing distracting cognitions and by inhibiting disclosure. An anxious supervisee may choose to only discuss those cases that they feel confident with, reducing learning opportunities within supervision and potentially persisting with ineffective or even harmful practice. So, positive supervisory characteristics such as empathy enhance supervisee disclosure (O'Donovan, Halford, & Walters, 2011), and if supervisees anticipate negative reactions by their supervisor, they limit disclosure (Ladany, Hill, Corbett, & Nutt, 1996). Nondisclosure is remarkably common: Mehr, Ladany, and Caskie (2010) found an average of 2.8 instances of nondisclosure in each supervision session and demonstrated that the supervisory working alliance and trainee anxiety were both significantly associated with willingness to disclose.

Low supervisee satisfaction can be a proxy measure of negative supervisory experiences and therefore is also associated with supervisee nondisclosure (Ladany et al., 1996). Greater supervisory alliance is predictive of the overall progress of a supervisee (e.g., Bradley & Ladany, 2001; Holloway, 1995). Specifically, Ladany, Lehrman-Waterman, Molinaro, and Wolgast (1999) found that the emotional bond aspect of alliance is more closely associated with supervisees being more satisfied than is an agreement on supervision goals and tasks.

There has been considerable research attention on features of supervisors that enhance or detract from relationship quality, alliance, and satisfaction. Supervisees report that "good" supervisors are trustworthy, supportive, and create a safe atmosphere. They also provide clear and direct feedback, allocate sufficient time to the supervisee, and are expert (e.g., Bernard & Goodyear, 2009; Campbell, 2000). In contrast, "poor" supervisors are overly critical, uninterested, authoritarian, rigid, inept, and vague (Shanfield, Matthews, & Hetherley, 1993). Similarly, O'Donovan, Dyck, and Bain (2001) found that supervisees indicated that effective supervisors were supportive, caring, and available; skillfully provided feedback; and elicited mutual trust and respect. Ineffective supervisors were disinterested, discouraging, nonrespectful, negative, uncaring, hostile, egocentric, and out-of-date.

Negative supervisory behaviors have potential not only to be ineffective but also to be harmful. Such behaviors may include abusing power at the supervisee's expense, being demeaning, overly critical, and vindictive, violating boundaries, and even subjecting the supervisee to public humiliation and derision (Gray et al., 2001; Nelson & Friedlander, 2001).

Given the importance of the supervisory relationship and of the supervisory alliance for the effectiveness of supervision and for the welfare of supervisees, the routine, repeated measurement of both these concepts, together with supervisee satisfaction, also assumes considerable utility. This assessment gives trainees a voice, moderating the power imbalance in the supervisory relationship; when results are given to supervisors, it provides feedback that can build their confidence as supervisors or offer suggestions for improvement; when used by training programs, it enables them to monitor and maintain the quality of their supervision. Reliable and valid measurement therefore assumes some importance. The next section describes a selection of some commonly used measures.

Measurement of Satisfaction, Relationship Quality, and Alliance

Supervisee Satisfaction Questionnaire (SSQ)

The SSQ is an eight-item self-report measure that is based on the Client Satisfaction Questionnaire (Ladany et al., 1996). Respondents rate their satisfaction with aspects of supervision on a Likert scale from 1 (low) to 4 (high). Examples include "How would you rate the quality of the supervision you have received?" and "If a friend were in need of supervision, would you recommend this supervisor to him or her?" Four items are reversed scored. Items are summed to form a satisfaction score, with higher scores reflecting greater satisfaction. The SSQ has high internal consistency, with coefficient alphas of .96–.97 (Ladany et al., 1996, 1999).

Supervisory Relationship Questionnaire (SRQ)

The 67-item SRQ was developed to measure the quality of the supervisory relationship from the perspective of the supervisee (Palomo, Beinart, & Cooper, 2010). This measure has six subscales: safe base (15 items), structure (8 items), commitment (10 items), reflective education (11 items), role model (12 items), and formative feedback (11 items). The safe base subscale accounts for 52% of the variance in SRQ total scores. Internal consistency for the total questionnaire is high ($\alpha = .98$), test–retest reliability is excellent (.97 over an average of 30 days), and all six subscales are significantly but moderately correlated with each other. Importantly, the SRQ was found to be able to predict supervisees' satisfaction with supervision, its contribution to personal and professional development, impact on behaviors in therapy, and perceived impact on clients' progress.

Supervisory Relationship Measure (SRM)

The SRM is a 51-item scale that is completed by the supervisor, and is intended to provide a companion measure to the SRQ (Pearce, Beinart, Clohessy, & Cooper, 2013). Like the SRQ, it has subscales of "safe base" (15 items – 21% of the variance) and "supervisor commitment" (9 items), but the other subscales identified by principal component analysis were "trainee contribution" (13 items), "external influences" (8 items), and "supervisor investment" (6 items), and the SRM was derived separately, from statements by supervisors in qualitative research. Like the SRQ, the total scale has high internal consistency ($\alpha = .90$) and test–retest reliability (.94 over an average of 17 days), and subscales have moderate intercorrelations.

Supervision Attitude Scale (SAS)

The 16-item SAS was adapted from the Family Attitude Scale (FAS) (Kavanagh et al., 1997; Kavanagh et al., 2003), which has very high internal consistency and satisfactory validity as a measure of criticism and burden within a family (Kavanagh et al., 1997), and is predictive of relapse of psychosis (Kavanagh et al., 2008). To construct the SAS, the FAS items with the highest item–total correlations were selected and their content altered to suit supervision (e.g., "I enjoy working with them" rather than "living with them"). Items are rated from 0 (never) to 4 (all the time), giving a total score from 0 to 64, with higher scores denoting greater positivity. Both supervisor (SAS-OR) and supervisee (SAS-EE) versions were constructed. In large multidisciplinary studies of practitioners in government mental health services, both versions had high internal consistency (OR: .90–.95, EE: .91–.94) and high stability over 3 months (EE: $r = .70$, OR: $r = .74$; with no significant change in mean scores). Despite the fact that SAS scores were confidential (i.e., not disclosed to the supervisory partner), median total scores were positive (e.g., EE = 56.5), with only 9% of supervisees giving scores below the midpoint. The SAS-EE was highly predictive of perceived impact of supervision ($r = .63$, $p < .001$) and was moderately correlated ($r = .30$, $p < .001$) with scores on the Hoppock Job Satisfaction Measure (Hoppock, 1935; McNichols, Stahl, & Manley, 1978) – a scale testing whether a person wanted to remain in his or her job.

Supervisory Working Alliance Inventory (SWAI)

Bordin (1983) drew an analogy between the supervisory and therapeutic alliances, arguing that alliance was important for collaboration, goal-setting, and a strong emotional bond. The SWAI is a general measure of supervisee and supervisor perceptions of the quality of the supervisory relationship in terms of bond, goals, and tasks (Efstation, Patton, & Kardash, 1990). Along with the supervisory version of the Working Alliance Inventory developed by Bahrick (1989), it remains a commonly utilized measure of supervisory working alliance.

The supervisor version of the SWAI includes subscales on client focus, rapport, and identification (the supervisor's perception of the trainee's identification with them). The trainee version only includes client focus and rapport. Cronbach's alphas for both versions range from .71 to .90, and the measures show adequate convergent and divergent validities. However, correlations within supervisor/supervisee dyads ranged from .03 to .36, suggesting that supervisors and supervisees may have very different perceptions of the relationship.

Supervisory Styles Inventory (SSI)

While supervisees value a supportive and practice-focused approach in supervision, regardless of their experience, a more directive, skills-oriented supervision tends to be preferred when facing a new, challenging situation, whereas more confident practitioners tend to want supervision that is more like peer support (Heppner & Roehlke, 1984; Tracey, Ellickson, & Sherry, 1989). It is therefore important that supervisors are able to match their styles to their trainee's level of experience (Miars et al., 1983).

The SSI is a 25-item measure that can be administered to both the trainee (SSI-T) and supervisor (SSI-S), allowing an assessment of the degree of perceived matching (Friedlander & Ward, 1984). Repeated measurement can allow adjustment of style over time as the trainee gains skills and confidence (Stoltenberg, McNeill, & Crethar, 1994). The SSI provides scores on three subscales: attractiveness (e.g., warm, supportive, friendly, flexible), interpersonal sensitivity (e.g., invested, committed, perceptive), and task orientation (content-focused – e.g., thorough, focused, practical, structured). The SSI has sound psychometric properties, with alphas of .76–.93 and a test–retest reliability of .92. Trainees who rate their supervisors as highly interpersonally sensitive also tend to report positive effects of supervision on their professional development and clients' progress ($R_c = .76$, $p < .0001$).

Role Conflict and Ambiguity Inventory (RCAIC)

Supervisory working alliance is impaired if role conflict and ambiguity are present (Ladany & Friedlander, 1995; Olk & Friedlander, 1992). When asked about their most detrimental supervision experiences, supervisees who report feeling deeply hurt and confused typically attribute these feelings to power struggles or opposing expectations about how supervision should occur (Nelson & Friedlander, 2001). These supervisees felt unsupported and became guarded with their supervisors instead relying on peers or other practitioners for support.

The 16-item Role Ambiguity (RA) scale of the RCAIC measures uncertainty about supervisory expectations and how the trainee will be evaluated, while its 13-item Role Conflict (RC) scale focuses on experiences where role expectations of the trainee and supervisor differ. For example, as students, trainees are expected to follow their supervisor's suggestions, while as therapists, they are expected to show autonomous decision-making. The RA and RC scales should not be combined for a total score, as they relate to different constructs. Each has excellent internal consistency (.89–.91) and high construct validity. Up to now, the RCAIC has been primarily tested and applied with psychologist trainees rather than with other professions or later supervisory relationships.

Evaluation process within supervision inventory (EPSI)

This 21-item measure has two scales: goal-setting and feedback, and is intended to measure trainees' satisfaction with evaluative processes in supervision (Lehrman-Waterman & Ladany, 2001). Trainees indicate the extent that they agree or disagree with items such as "My supervisor and I created goals that were realistic" and "My supervisor balanced his or her feedback between positive and negative statements." Its psychometric properties were investigated in postgraduate clinical and counseling psychology trainees and can only be tentatively applied in other contexts (Ellis, D'Iuso, & Ladany, 2008). In the developmental study, the alpha coefficient of goal-setting was .89, while feedback gave .69. The EPSI is significantly related to a measure of working alliance and can be distinguished from trainee self-efficacy and satisfaction with supervision (Lehrman-Waterman & Ladany, 2001). Importantly, EPSI scores do not vary according to training level, and it therefore can be used at any stage of training.

Limitations of Satisfaction as an Index of Supervision Quality

Despite the ubiquitous use of supervisee satisfaction to assess supervision (Milne, 2009), there is long-standing concern about over-reliance on it (e.g., Borders, 1989; Holloway & Neufeldt, 1995). Goodyear and Bernard (1998) used the analogy that liking doughnuts does not necessarily mean they are nutritious. Effective supervisory relationships sometimes need to accommodate corrective feedback and elicit progressively more demanding goals and achievements: a comfortable, undemanding relationship may be pleasant but not encouraging of growth. As noted at the start of this chapter, satisfaction with supervision implies a match to the supervisee's expectations: the extent that satisfaction provides an accurate index of supervision quality relies on the supervisee having an accurate understanding of effective supervision characteristics and being able to distinguish those from their emotional responses to sessions. These insights may not always be present.

As important as safety and empathy in supervision are for its clinical impact (Kavanagh et al., 2003), so is a focus on skill acquisition and confidence-building. In Kavanagh et al. (2003), each was strongly related to clinical impact (r = .66) and each offered unique predictive variance in a multivariate regression. However, observation of clinical practice and rehearsal of skills is rare (Kavanagh et al., 2003; Scott et al., 2011). Instead, sessions rely heavily on self-reported practice, which is subject to the supervisee's self-perception and editing. Observation is time-consuming for supervisors and potentially confronting for supervisees: when modeling is included, supervisors are also open to scrutiny. While an accepting and rewarding supervision relationship minimizes anxiety, it may not eliminate it, and the most effective relationships may retain some discomfort over exposing suboptimal practice – our incompetence may finally be found out! As with therapy and with parenting, an effective supervisor cannot please his or her supervisees at all times and at any cost, nor will such an indiscriminate approach be valued by discerning supervisees.

Satisfaction with supervision may also be impaired by external factors. As with a therapeutic relationship, the supervisory relationship can meet resistance – to the supervisor's role and influence, the supervisory experience, session tasks, or practice-related plans (Bernard & Goodyear, 2009). Like client resistance, this can occur for many reasons. While it may reflect a lack of trust, overly directive supervision, or disagreements about supervision tasks and goals, it may also involve a difficulty accepting alternative ideas, transference of responses to a previous relationship (or to other aspects of their work or training), or an uncritical acceptance of the client's perception of their problems. Expert supervisors may often be able to address such resistance, but in some cases, this may not be readily achievable. A satisfaction rating in such a context may well mean that the supervision is not effective, but it may not mean that it lacks quality.

Despite these limitations, we argue that supervisees' satisfaction should continue to be assessed, as it emphasizes the importance of their views, their right to receive high-quality supervision, and the idea that supervision is best when it is collaborative. Suboptimal satisfaction requires investigation to see if it does reflect suboptimal supervision practice or to trigger discussion of mutual expectations.

Optimising the Accuracy of Assessment

Supervisee reports of satisfaction, alliance, and relationship characteristics are often made in a context of significant power differentials: the supervisor often has an evaluative or gate-keeping role and, in clinical services, may also be the practitioner's manager. In these contexts, open communication of dissatisfaction may have the potential for negative consequences.

To test the accuracy of supervisees' feedback to supervisors, responses on the SSQ were compared for 83 supervisees in two contexts: where they provided the feedback to a supervisor and where they were asked the same questions in confidence (O'Donovan, Riley, & Kavanagh, in preparation). The confidential feedback condition resulted in significantly lower scores (M = 80.50, SD = 16.92) than where supervisors received their feedback (M = 86.81, SD = 15.95; $t(82) = 4.17$, $p < .001$, $\eta = .15$). These results indicate that supervisors and agencies, using supervisee satisfaction ratings to judge how well supervision is progressing, should keep in mind that the results may be positively skewed, unless ratings are provided anonymously.

To increase the accuracy of supervisee feedback, the importance of open feedback could be discussed before a measure is completed, and measures could be used repeatedly, to demonstrate that it is safe to provide honest feedback (O'Donovan et al., 2011). A similar process is increasingly being used in obtaining client measures of therapy (Overington & Ionita, 2012). To further reduce the perceived risk in training contexts, supervisee measures might be shared only after evaluations are submitted.

Conclusion

Satisfaction with supervision may be a subjective impression of its quality – with all the limitations that it has – but it offers a summary that can trigger further assessment and discussion. Similarly, measures of alliance and relationship quality may not capture all of the elements necessary for effective supervision, but they do offer assessments of necessary features. Being aware of the possible reactions to supervision that supervisees may experience brings a responsibility to ensure that supervision is helpful and not harmful. Supervisees will not necessarily disclose counterproductive events to their supervisor unless specifically encouraged to do so, and undisclosed issues will generally remain unresolved (Gray et al., 2001). It is important, therefore, to foster conditions that encourage disclosure. Repeated use of measures such as those in this chapter will assist with this process.

References

Bahrick, A. S. (1989). Role induction for counselor trainees: Effects on the supervisory working alliance. *Dissertation Abstracts International*, *51*, 1484B.

Bambling, M. (2000). The effect of clinical supervision on the development of counsellor competency. *Psychotherapy in Australia*, *6*, 58–63.

Bambling, M., King, R., Raue, P., Schweitzer, R., & Lambert, W. (2006). Clinical supervision: Its influence on client-rated working alliance and client symptom reduction in the brief treatment of major depression. *Psychotherapy Research*, *16*(3), 317–331.

Bandura, A. (1982). Self-efficacy mechanism in human agency. *American Psychologist*, *37*, 122–147.

Bernard, J. M., & Goodyear, R. K. (2009). *Fundamentals of clinical supervision* (4th ed.). Upper Saddle River, NJ: Merrill/Pearson.

Borders, L. D. (1989). A pragmatic agenda for developmental supervision research. *Counselor Education and Supervision*, *29*, 16–24.

Bordin, E. S. (1983). A working alliance model of supervision. *The Counseling Psychologist*, *11*, 35–42.

Bradley, J., & Olsen, J. (1980). Training factors influencing felt psychotherapeutic competence of psychology trainees. *Professional Psychology*, *11*, 930–934.

Bradley, L. J., & Ladany, N. (2001). *Counselor supervision: Principles, process, and practice.* Ann Arbor, MI: Brunner-Routledge.

Campbell, J. M. (2000). *Becoming an effective supervisor. A workbook for counselors and psychotherapists.* Ann Arbor, MI: Sheridan Books.

Efstation, J. F., Patton, M. J., & Kardash, C. M. (1990). Measuring the working alliance in counselor supervision. *Journal of Counseling Psychology*, *37*, 322–329.

Ellis, M. V., D'Iuso, N., & Ladany, N. (2008). State of the art in the assessment, measurement and evaluation of clinical supervision. In A. K. Hess, K. D. Hess, & T. H. Hess (Eds.), *Psychotherapy supervision: Theory, research, and practice* (2nd ed., pp. 473–499), Hoboken, NJ: John Wiley & Sons.

Ellis, M. V., & Ladany, N. (1997). Inferences concerning supervisees and clients in clinical supervision: An integrative review. In C. E. Watkins, Jr. (Ed.), *Handbook of psychotherapy supervision* (pp. 567–607), New York, NY: Wiley.

Friedlander, M. L., & Ward, C. (1984). Development and validation of the Supervisory Styles Inventory. *Journal of Counseling Psychology*, *31*, 541–557.

Goodyear, R. K., & Bernard, J. M. (1998). Clinical supervision: Lessons from the literature. *Counselor Education and Supervision*, *38*(1), 6–17.

Gray, L. A., Ladany, N., Walker, J. A., & Ancis, J. R. (2001). Psychotherapy trainees' experience of counterproductive events in supervision. *Journal of Counseling Psychology*, *48*(4), 371–383.

Guest, P. D., & Beutler, L. E. (1988). Impact of psychotherapy supervision on therapist orientation and values. *Journal of Consulting and Clinical Psychology*, *56*, 653–658.

Heppner, P. P., & Roehlke, H. J. (1984). Differences among supervisees at different levels of training: Implications for a developmental model of supervision. *Journal of Counseling Psychology*, *31*, 76–90.

Holloway, E. L. (1995). *Clinical supervision: A systems approach*. Thousand Oaks, CA: Sage Publications.

Holloway, E. L., & Neufeldt, S. A. (1995). Supervision: Its contributions to treatment efficacy. *Journal of Consulting and Clinical Psychology*, *63*, 207–213.

Hoppock, R. (1935). *Job satisfaction*. New York, NY: Harper & Row.

Kavanagh, D. J., O'Halloran, P., Manicavasagar, V., Clark, D., Piatkowska, O., Tennant, C., & Rosen, A. (1997). The Family Attitude Scale: Reliability and validity of a new scale for measuring the emotional climate of families. *Psychiatry Research*, *70*, 185–195.

Kavanagh, D. J., Spence, S. H., Strong, J., Wilson, J., Sturk, H., & Crow, N. (2003). Supervision practices in allied mental health: Relationships of supervision characteristics to perceived impact and job satisfaction. *Mental Health Services Research*, *5*(4), 187–195.

Kavanagh, D. J., Pourmand, D., White, A., Robertson, D., Halford, K., & Vaughan, K. (2008). Predictive validity of the Family Attitude Scale in people with psychosis. *Psychiatry Research*, *160*, 356–363.

Kennard, B. D., Stewart, S. M., & Gluck, M. R. (1987). The supervision relationship: Variables contributing to positive versus negative experiences. *Professional Psychology, Research and Practice*, *18*, 172–175.

Ladany, N., & Friedlander, M. L. (1995). The relationship between the supervisory working alliance and trainees' experience of role conflict and role ambiguity. *Counselor Education and Supervision*, *34*, 220–231.

Ladany, N., Hill, C. E., Corbett, M. M., & Nutt, E. A. (1996). Nature, extent, and importance of what psychotherapy trainees do not disclose to their supervisors. *Journal of Counseling Psychology*, *43*, 10–24.

Ladany, N., Lehrman-Waterman, D., Molinaro, M., & Wolgast, B. (1999). Psychotherapy supervisor ethical practice: Adherence to guidelines, the supervisory working alliance, and supervisee satisfaction. *The Counseling Psychologist*, *27*, 443–475.

Lambert, M. J., & Ogles, B. M. (1997). The effectiveness of psychotherapy supervision. In C. E. Watkins (Ed.), *Handbook of psychotherapy supervision* (pp. 421–446), New York, NY: Wiley.

Lehrman-Waterman, D., & Ladany, N. (2001). Development and validation of the evaluation process within supervision inventory. *Journal of Counseling Psychology*, *48*, 168–177.

McNichols, C. W., Stahl, M. J., & Manley, T. R. (1978). A validation of Hoppock's job satisfaction measure. *Academy of Management Journal*, *21*, 737–742.

Mehr, K. E., Ladany, N., & Caskie, G. I. L. (2010). Trainee nondisclosure in supervision: What are they not telling you? *Counselling and Psychotherapy Research: Linking Research with Practice*, *10*, 103–113.

Miars, R. D., Tracey, T. J., Ray, P. B., Cornfield, L., O'Farrell, M., & Gelso, C. J. (1983). Variation in supervision process across trainee experience levels. *Journal of Counseling Psychology*, *30*, 403–412.

Milne, D. (2009). *Evidence-based clinical supervision: Principles and practice*. Chichester, England: BPS Blackwell.

Nelson, M. L., & Friedlander, M. L. (2001). A close look at conflictual supervisor relationships: The trainee's perspective. *Journal of Counseling Psychology*, *48*, 384–395.

O'Donovan, A., Dyck, M., & Bain, J. D. (2001). Trainees' experience of postgraduate clinical training. *Australian Psychologist*, *36*, 149–156.

O'Donovan, A., Halford, W. K., & Walters, B. (2011). Toward best practice supervision of clinical psychology trainees. *Australian Psychologist*, *46*, 101–112.

O'Donovan, A., Riley, M., & Kavanagh, D. (in preparation). How accurate is the evaluative feedback supervisors are provided by supervisees?

Olk, M., & Friedlander, M. L. (1992). Trainees' experiences of role conflict and role ambiguity in supervisory relationships. *Journal of Counseling Psychology, 39*, 389–397.

Overington, L., & Ionita, G. (2012). Progress monitoring measures: A brief guide. *Canadian Psychology, 53*(2), 82–92.

Palomo, M., Beinart, H., & Cooper, M. J. (2010). Development and validation of the Supervisory Relationship Questionnaire (SRQ) in UK trainee clinical psychologists. *The British Journal of Clinical Psychology, 49*, 131–149.

Pearce, N., Beinart, H., Clohessy, S., & Cooper, M. (2013). Development and validation of the Supervisory Relationship Measure: A self-report questionnaire for use with supervisors. *The British Journal of Clinical Psychology, 52*(3), 249–268. doi:10.1111/bjc.12012

Roth, A. D., & Pilling, S. (2007). *The competences required to deliver effective cognitive and behavioural therapy for people with depression and anxiety disorders.* London, UK: Department of Health.

Scott, T. L., Pachana, N. A., & Sofranoff, K. (2011). Survey of current curriculum practices within Australian postgraduate clinical training programmes: Students' and program directors' perspectives. *Australian Psychologist, 46*, 77–89.

Shanfield, S. B., Matthews, K. L., & Hetherley, V. V. (1993). What do excellent psychotherapy supervisors do? *The American Journal of Psychiatry, 150*, 1081–1084.

Sterner, W. R. (2009). Influence of the supervisory working alliance on supervisee work satisfaction and work-related stress. *Journal of Mental Health Counseling, 31*, 249–263.

Stoltenberg, C. D., McNeill, B. W., & Crethar, H. C. (1994). Changes in supervision as counsellors and therapists gain experience: A review. *Professional Psychology: Research & Practice, 25*, 416–449.

Tracey, T. J., Ellickson, J. L., & Sherry, P. (1989). Reactance in relation to different supervisory environments and counsellor development. *Journal of Counseling Psychology, 36*, 336–344.

Watkins, C. E., Jr. (Ed.). (1997). *Handbook of psychotherapy supervision.* New York, NY: John Wiley & Sons.

Part V

Supervising Psychotherapies – Theory-Specific, Developmental, and Social Role Perspectives

23

Supervision of Psychoanalytic/ Psychodynamic Psychotherapy

Gillian Eagle and Carol Long

Introduction

It has been argued that "no approach to psychotherapy supervision exists today that has not in some way been touched and influenced by the insights developed in psychoanalytic supervision over the last century" (Watkins, 2011a, p. 402). Psychoanalytic supervision has also enjoyed a pivotal position in the training and ongoing development of psychoanalysts and psychotherapists. Furthermore, as the original model for supervision, many of its principles and practices have influenced the development of supervision approaches in other theoretical orientations and professions. Over the last century, however, approaches to psychotherapy have proliferated, with interest turning to shorter-term interventions tailored to specific forms of presenting problems. In the current zeitgeist, the tendency is for different orientations to compete with rather than inform one another, often in the face of increasingly limited resources, creating specific languages and ways of thinking that can be alienating to those of different theoretical persuasions. Psychoanalysis is no exception in this regard. Writing about psychoanalytic supervision in the context of an inclusive handbook about psychotherapy supervision, therefore, offers the challenge of being true to the language of psychoanalysis while being aware of the sometimes specialized nature of psychoanalytic concepts. Our hope in writing this chapter is that psychotherapists and supervisors from various therapeutic and professional persuasions may once again find resonance and inspiration from psychoanalytic approaches to supervision, and debates about supervision, that will enrich their own practices. To this end, we aim to offer a general, inclusive, and accessible overview of the development of psychoanalytic supervision, the characteristics and aims of supervision, and the important debates that have emerged over time, drawing from the large body of writing on supervision within the psychoanalytic literature and our own practice experience.

The Wiley International Handbook of Clinical Supervision, First Edition. Edited by C. Edward Watkins, Jr. and Derek L. Milne.

By far the majority of work on psychoanalytic supervision has taken place within the context of institutes of psychoanalysis, largely located in first world countries. In contrast, our experiences of supervision are rooted in the South African context in which we live. South Africa has had a very different history of engagement with psychoanalytic ideas and practices. Until very recently, it has not been possible to train as a psychoanalyst in South Africa. The majority of supervision work we conduct takes place in the context of training psychoanalytically oriented clinical psychology students at the University of the Witwatersrand, Johannesburg. Within this context, we supervise both long-term psychoanalytic psychotherapy (18–24 months) and shorter-term interventions (1–4 months). Furthermore, because the apartheid history of the country continues to mark everyday reality, it is often counterproductive to focus supervision on intrapsychic dynamics alone since therapy material is so often imbued with the interpersonal and the sociopolitical context (Eagle, Haynes, & Long, 2007). Therefore, while the overall aim of this chapter is to offer an overview of international approaches to psychoanalytic supervision, we have endeavored to include examples from the South African situation.

Historical Developments in Psychoanalytic Supervision

Psychotherapy can be a lonely and messy undertaking that involves an intimate and intense relationship between therapist and patient. A psychoanalytic approach presupposes that the therapist engage with the unconscious of the patient. From the beginnings of psychoanalysis, there has been a recognition that colleagues are essential in helping the therapist to think about what is happening in the therapeutic process and relationship. From 1902, Freud held regular meetings in his home where clinical cases were discussed (Watkins, 2011a, 2011b). Although Freud wrote almost nothing on supervision, the value of theoretical and clinical discussion was clearly entrenched from early on. Interestingly, one of the few references Freud did make to supervision included a comment, when Freud was in conflict with Jung, that Jung was "immature himself and in need of supervision" (Freud, 1912a, p. 434). In another comment on the dispensability of universities for the development of psychoanalysis, Freud (1919) noted that the psychoanalyst could do well without universities, provided the analyst gained theoretical knowledge from psychoanalytic institutes, was in his own personal analysis, gained practical experience from his own patients, and, in addition, "provided that he can get supervision and guidance from recognized psycho-analysts" (Freud, 1919, p. 171). "Recognized analysts" was later refined to "older and more experienced analysts" (Freud, 1926, p. 228).

In these very brief reflections can be found the kernels of the model that remains dominant today: that training should consist of an apprenticeship wherein a clinician treats patients under the supervision of a more experienced colleague while also receiving theoretical input and experiencing his or her own psychotherapy. This model was formalized by Eitingon (in Watkins, 2011a), in what is known as the Eitingon model, which remains largely followed today (although not without critique; see, e.g., Hanoch, 2006; Kernberg, 2006). These brief reflections also, perhaps, hint at some of the debates that fueled further developments in psychoanalytic approaches to supervision, for example, that supervision is particularly needed for the "immature," that it involves a hierarchical relationship, and that it is properly found in institutes of psychoanalysis.

In the Eitingon model, the supervisor and the supervisee's personal analysis therapist are necessarily different people. This is based on the assumption that the therapist should focus on personal issues, while the supervisor should focus only on the patient. In the initial formulation, supervision was understood as a didactic enterprise. In practice, however, it is very difficult for the supervisor to separate the supervisee's personal issues, including countertransference, from the supervisee's therapeutic work being conducted with the patient. As Brown and Miller (2002) point out, this difficulty in supervision is reflected in psychotherapy and even Freud struggled to decide on the function of a therapist's countertransference and how to engage with this. On the one hand, as they argue, he felt that the therapist should turn his/her unconscious "like a receptive organ towards the transmitting unconscious of the patient" (Freud, 1912b, p. 115), implying that the therapist's unconscious is always part of the therapeutic process. On the other hand, Freud advocated the metaphor of analysis as surgery, where the therapist/surgeon dispassionately performs an operation on the patient with a certain "emotional coldness" (p. 115). There has been much debate about the meaning of countertransference in psychotherapy supervision: how can one teach in a dispassionate and authoritative manner and focus on the unconscious of the patient without also focusing on the receptive unconscious of the supervisee-therapist? If the therapist's personality is the primary "tool" of psychotherapy, how can supervision focus only on the patient (Berman, 2000a; Brown & Miller, 2002; Frawley-O'Dea, 2003)? Conversely, how can one do supervision that maintains focus on the patient if focus on the therapist risks turning the supervision into psychotherapy (Levy & Parnell, 2001; Sedlak, 2003)?

Amidst all these questions about how best to undertake supervision, a number of theoretical developments in psychoanalysis have taken place over the years, and it has been observed that the supervisor's theoretical orientation influences supervisory style and input (Frawley-O'Dea, 2003; Hanoch, 2006). It is not possible to trace all these developments here, but it is helpful to focus on two developments that directly influenced evolving models of supervision. The first concerns the shift from drive theory to theories that focused on the intrapsychic and the interpersonal. This shift, particularly in recent years, has offered new models of supervision that are less didactic and theoretically led and that understand the undertaking of supervision not as authoritative correction but as a creative endeavor in which the supervisor and the therapist can productively "waste time" (Ogden, 2005) by dreaming up the patient together, can understand supervision as a containment of the patient *and* the therapist's raw experiences (Ungar & De Ahumada, 2001), and can introduce Winnicott's (1971) concept of play so as to "explore and enjoy the 'bloody serious play' of supervision" (Szecsödy, 2008, p. 383). This shift has encouraged both supervisors and supervisees to approach supervision in a more creative manner.

The second, and related, shift was inspired by psychoanalytic theories of intersubjectivity, which understood the therapeutic endeavor not only as interpersonal and relational but also as deeply shaped by the therapist's contribution (both conscious and unconscious) (Mitchell, 1998). This theory challenged the notion of therapeutic objectivity and stressed the mutual interchange between therapist and patient. This theoretical development opened new approaches to supervision (Brown & Miller,

2002; Frawley-O'Dea, 2003), including an emphasis on the relational interchange in supervision (Berman, 2004; Frawley-O'Dea & Sarnat, 2001), recognition of the supervisor's countertransference (Marshall, 1997), and an appreciation that supervisor and supervisee in some ways create a "fiction" together of the therapeutic interchange and should acknowledge this in order to productively use supervision (Ogden, 2005). It has been noted, however, that the relational turn influenced psychotherapy long before it began to influence supervision (Frawley-O'Dea, 2003) and that the mutuality of the supervisory relationship continues to be an area of debate.

One area where less debate has taken place, at least in psychoanalytic journals, concerns the implications of supervising psychoanalytic psychotherapy as opposed to psychoanalysis proper. Psychoanalytic psychotherapy usually takes place once weekly, as opposed to three, four, or five times weekly psychoanalysis, and is also sometimes of shorter duration. It is less intense than psychoanalysis and is therefore less amenable to work with the deep unconscious, although it may be more applicable to work with more disturbed patients who do not have the ego strength to tolerate psychoanalysis (Binder, Strupp, & Schacht, 1983; Joannidis, 2006). As mentioned earlier, the dominant practice in South Africa is of psychoanalytic psychotherapy. Models of supervision in South Africa have been less plagued by debates about the influence of institutes on supervision, simply because there has not been a psychoanalytic institute and most practitioners are trained in a university environment. Practitioners tend to be psychologists but also include other professionals, such as social workers and expressive therapists. Interdisciplinary supervision is thus regularly undertaken. Trainees are offered obligatory supervision, but many psychotherapists continue supervision as part of their professional development. There is a relatively large and vibrant community of psychoanalytically oriented psychotherapists to whom many continuing professional development activities, including clinical discussion groups, are offered. South Africa has enjoyed visits from international (largely British) psychoanalysts for a number of decades and this provides a context for specialist supervision. More recently, a small number of psychoanalysts have relocated to South Africa and training as a psychoanalyst has commenced. These general conditions may have offered a less restrictive supervisory environment, although it has also been noted that South African practitioners can sometimes worry about their legitimacy and can feel "inferior" to "proper" psychoanalysts (Swartz, 2007), perhaps overemphasizing the orthodoxy of theory and practice. This no doubt plays itself out in the supervisory context.

Aims and Characteristics of Psychoanalytically Oriented Supervision

Given the diverse history of psychoanalytic supervision, it is unsurprising that there are also diverse approaches to supervision, particularly regarding whether supervision should be primarily didactic or primarily experiential (Szecsödy, 2008). Werbart (2007) traces the etymology of the word supervision to two very different meanings: "the profane meaning of 'control and inspection', and the sacral meaning of 'divine guidance', are sometimes difficult to separate" (p. 1397). Supervision simultaneously aims to teach, to inspect, and to guide the therapist on his or her own unique developmental pathway. Somewhat more cryptically, Pedder (1986) describes supervision as "more than education and less than psychotherapy" (p. 1). While the components of supervision may include teaching, monitoring, and guiding, it seems to us that capturing the spirit of supervision seems more helpful than trying, in the midst of debate, to break it too rigidly into its component features. It is helpful to understand supervision as a process through which the supervisor provides "optimal conditions for the candidate to integrate his experiences, his theoretical knowledge, and his personality for a competent participation in and handling of the psychoanalytic situation and process" (Szecsödy, 2008, p. 373). Such a definition foregrounds the primary aim of supervision as facilitative of the therapist's growth. Within this process, it is also helpful to understand supervision as a reflective space that "furthers the reconsideration of the therapist's clinical task, promoting the examination of the evidence, the sharing of doubts and the harbouring of evolving ideas" (Ungar & De Ahumada, 2001, p. 80).

These statements of the aims of supervision are far from exhaustive and offer only broad parameters in which to approach supervision; they favor a facilitative approach to supervision which we have found to be particularly productive. Pedder (1986), reflecting on Fleming's (1967) taxonomy of supervision, encompassing Jug, Potter, and Gardener models, stresses that "we have to take [therapists] from where they are . . . They are not empty vessels into whom we pour from a jug; nor inert lumps of clay to be fashioned after our own image. We are facilitators; gardeners, accepting the plants that spring up in our gardens and doing what we can by pruning" (p. 2). Following this metaphor, we have foregrounded the facilitative characteristics of supervision as follows.

The supervisory setting

Basescu (2006) notes that psychotherapeutic work itself can be a "breeding ground for anxiety" (p. 169). The regularity and predictability of supervision goes some way toward providing a consistent setting in which to hold the reflective work of supervision. We try as far as possible to meet at the same time in the same place every week and to protect supervision from any interruptions or deviations. There has been some debate regarding the relative merits of group versus individual supervision (Yerushalmi, 1999). We find that group supervision is particularly useful in the beginning stages of training as the group feels less exposing and therapists have the opportunity to learn both about each other's patients and also about different styles of engagement and transference and countertransference dynamics. Groups of three trainees are assigned to a supervisor and work together in the same cohort over the duration of the academic year. The consistency of the group allows for the deepening of trust over time. Therapists are often active in engaging in the supervision of their colleagues' work, thereby learning not only passively but also actively about the therapeutic process. As trainee therapists become more experienced, it can be helpful to alternate between group and individual supervision. This is particularly effective as therapists become more aware of their own contributions to the therapeutic process. Supervision focuses primarily on a conversation concerning session content. Supervisees present a particular session and we then engage in reflection about that session. Although we recognize that "dutiful presentation of clinical material may serve as a defense against a more freely associative form of thinking" (Ogden, 2005, pp. 1272–1273), we generally encourage therapists to produce session notes, as well as questions for supervision, in advance. These serve to guide the supervision hour. We have also found, particularly toward the beginning of training, that supervisees' memories of the session are not always the best reflections of what happened in the session. In our supervision of long-term therapy, we ask therapists to videorecord their sessions and to produce a verbatim transcription (from the recording) of every third session. Therapists often initially experience this as anxiety-provoking but generally find that both video recordings and transcripts offer an invaluable learning experience. It appears that recording and transcription have not conventionally been widely utilized as supervision aids within the analytic context (Fink, 2007; Pedder, 1986); however, we find that the recordings help therapists to become more aware not only of their nonverbal communication but also that of their patients' and to see the session from a distance. Transcripts are particularly useful in helping to track process and to help therapists refine their interventions.

Facilitation of the supervisory process

Despite differences between theoretical orientations, psychoanalytic psychotherapy is commonly characterized by a focus on the therapeutic process, including the seemingly irrelevant, unimportant, nonsensical, or disagreeable (Freud, 1924). Psychoanalytically oriented supervision similarly differs depending on theoretical preferences but generally remains true to the nondirective and exploratory goal of psychotherapy. Although the didactic aim – to teach the therapist how to intervene and think about the patient and to ensure that the therapist can integrate theory into practice – remains important to many supervisors (Szecsödy, 2008), it is also often understood that supervision itself is a process (Vaslamatzis, 2008). A primary aim of supervision should therefore be to facilitate the unfolding of this process (Ogden, 2005); in other words, the process of supervision should mirror the exploratory and nondirective style of psychotherapy.

Since supervision, like psychotherapy, is not always a comfortable process, it is important that the supervisor and supervisee establish a good learning alliance (Watkins, 2011a, 2011b). "Just as the analyst's empathic perceptiveness and responsiveness are instrumental in establishing a therapeutic alliance with the patient, so the supervisor's empathic perceptiveness and responsiveness are instrumental in establishing and maintaining a *learning alliance*" (Fleming & Benedek, 1966, in Watkins, 2011b, pp. 561–562). A learning alliance implies that both supervisor and supervisee are allied together in their common goal. Watkins (2011b) also notes that the importance of the real relationship in supervision has been largely overlooked, despite the clear importance of genuineness and authenticity to the supervisory endeavor. Indeed, various studies have suggested that the supervisory alliance is "at the heart of effective supervision" (Inman & Ladany, 2008, in Watkins, 2011a, p. 411).

Together with the real relationship, the availability of the supervisor as a model is also important. Supervisees often model themselves on their supervisors, and the manner in which this process takes place can have very different consequences for the supervision process. At one extreme, the supervisor can be imitated rather than internalized (Debell, 1963; Szecsödy, 2008). This may come about not only because of the supervisee's dynamics but also as a result of the supervisor's need to be admired (Debell, 1963; Yerushalmi, 1999) as well as institutional authoritarian dynamics (Berman, 2000b; Kernberg, 2006). A false analytic self is developed that prevents the therapist from discovering his or her own way of being (Berman, 2000b). Rather than the supervisor becoming a source of guidance and inspiration, the therapist can mimic the supervisor in what has been described as supervision by ventriloquism (Fiscalini, 1985) or supervision by remote control (Frawley-O'Dea & Sarnat, 2001). We have often observed that supervisees cannot find their own words in therapy because their minds are too crowded by the words of their supervisors. This is perhaps an inevitable process but should give way to the more important supervisory goal of facilitating the therapist's own unique development. At the other extreme, then, one strives toward not an imitation but an introjection of the supervisor into the therapist's internal world. Casement's (1991) well-known concept of the "internal supervisor," through which the therapist, over time, becomes more able to engage in an internal dialogue in order to test out how a particular intervention may be received by the patient, is often particularly helpful to our supervisees and gives them permission to introject their supervisor in a fluid rather than prescriptive manner. We also find it helpful for therapists to be exposed to different supervisors in different contexts. Since each supervisor inevitably has his or her own style and personality, this offers therapists different models upon which to draw in their work. The supervisory process, therefore, needs to be able to accommodate ambiguity and to foreground a tolerance for the process of psychotherapy in all its complexities (Werbart, 2007).

Facilitation of the developmental process

The process of supervision is fluid and should also be responsive to changing needs over time. Supervising a therapist just beginning to undertake therapy is very different from supervising a qualified and experienced practitioner. An appreciation of how the supervisory process unfolds over time holds crucial implications for facilitation. Although supervision should be understood from the outset as a shared responsibility between therapist and supervisor (Frawley-O'Dea & Sarnat, 2001), the supervisor's role should ideally become increasingly collaborative over time. At first, the therapist is likely to require more direction and help mastering the basics of therapy. To expect the therapist to begin to develop his or her own style at this stage of the process can be experienced as overwhelming and counterproductive. As the therapist develops and becomes more sophisticated, it is equally counterproductive to adhere to an authoritarian position in which the supervisor always knows best. Levy and Parnell (2001) helpfully suggest that the supervisor should allow movement from being seen as an experienced guide toward being understood as a trusted mediator.

Skills and knowledge generally also develop as the therapist becomes more experienced. Therapists initially find it easier to develop basic listening and reflective skills. More interpretive skills require a more careful reading of the process and awareness of the transference. It generally takes time for these skills to develop, and it is very difficult to explain how to read the process or to understand the transference without some exposure to these phenomena as initially identified by the supervisor. Supervision can offer modeling in this regard, and the reflective process of supervision generally deepens supervisees' capacity to listen for the unconscious and for the latent meanings of a therapeutic session. It is the development of both the therapist's theoretical and self-knowledge that allows for greater awareness of what is happening in a therapy. Supervision has an important role to play in aiding such knowledge development, but the therapist's own therapy and growing experience are formative (Berman, 2000a). It is also helpful to distinguish between the development of an ability to formulate – a more patient-focused activity centered on the therapist's ability to think about the patient – and the development of technique – a more therapist-focused activity that requires the ability to operate in the room.

Inexperienced therapists understandably need more guidance. They often come to supervision with fundamental questions, such as "What do I do?" or "How can I understand this?" Although it is sometimes important to try to directly answer these questions, a general ethos of reflection, even at the beginning stages of supervision, can be very helpful. Instead of answering questions, Kaufman (2006) suggests redirecting therapists "toward reflecting on their own feelings, articulating the interaction between themselves and their patients, finding their own knowledge and their own voice" (p. 152). Ungar and De Ahumada (2001) similarly suggest that when a supervisee asks, "Did I do it right?" an invitation to explore the anxieties this question suggests can be more productive than focusing on what is "correct" or "incorrect." As therapists become more experienced, the process of reflection rather than direction should be deepened.

For this developmental process to optimally unfold, supervisees need to feel that they can bring their authentic experience, and not what they think they are "supposed" to be doing, to supervision. This is easier said than done: it is normative that this kind of learning evokes in supervisees feelings of inadequacy, shame, competitiveness, and both envy and fear of envy (Berman, 2004). Supervisees often feel great pressure to conform to the "rules" of psychoanalysis and are often ashamed to admit to interventions (such as giving advice or answering questions) that they know are unapproved of (Schaffer, 2006). It is often the "mistakes" of psychotherapy that offer the greatest learning opportunities, however, and sometimes these mistakes can offer productive opportunities for the therapeutic process. We encourage our supervisees to bring mistakes, suggesting to them that a therapist who makes mistakes is a better therapist than one who does not allow mistakes to be made. It is recognized that some mistakes, particularly toward the beginning of training, do need correcting rather than reflecting upon. However, encouraging the supervisee to increasingly self-supervise in the presence of the supervisor (Aronson, 2000; Schaffer, 2006) and to engage with the supervisor in reflecting on their own development facilitates recognition of their progress.

Key Issues and Debates

Having covered the history of supervision within the psychodynamic tradition and issues related to the characteristics and aims of such supervision, this third section of the chapter introduces discussion of a number of core areas of debate and contestation. This discussion introduces some new topics but also revisits some already signposted issues, aiming to offer a deepening of reflection on these issues. The debates reflect tensions in both the conceptualization and practice of supervision. The following three topics are identified as particularly salient in thinking about the delivery of psychodynamic/psychoanalytic psychotherapy supervision: (1) the evaluative component of supervision and the supervisee's vulnerability to narcissistic injury, (2) the supervisor's role in engaging with trainee countertransference and differentiation of training and treatment roles, and (3) the triadic nature of the supervisory relationship and understanding of parallel process dynamics.

Supervision as both facilitative and evaluative

The inherent tension in almost all psychotherapy supervisory relationships is that in the process of providing the kind of scaffolding and support required for a trainee to become competent, there is an ongoing evaluation that takes place. The very person to whom the supervisee is expected to reveal insecurities, "mistakes," gaps in knowledge, and anxieties about mastery of technique is the person who, in most instances, will assess his or her ability to meet the "qualifying" criteria for entry into the profession or practice. Given the levels of self-disclosure and engagement characteristic of psychodynamic supervision, this issue becomes particularly delicate to manage. As Debell (1963) argues, there are two "quite separate purposes of the supervisory process . . . sometimes working at cross purposes" (p. 546), these being "the function of teaching and the function of testing" (p. 546). Referring to the supervisor, Szecsödy (1989) suggests that there is a "crowd" present in the analytic supervisory situation that includes "a mentor, teacher, evaluator, judge, supervisor, future colleague" (p. 245) among others. While the bulk of supervision literature tends to be concerned with the facilitative or training function and how best to optimize this, the hard fact of the evaluative or gate-keeping function of supervision remains. This is one of the reasons why within the psychoanalytic community only analysts with sufficient experience and credibility are viewed as competent to take on a supervisory role. It is not only that such status is necessary to provide the kind of mentorship that trainees require from someone who has accumulated wisdom of a range of kinds, but also that such people are adjudged to have the necessary acumen to determine whether the trainee is ready to become an independent practitioner.

Within analytic institutes, graduation into full status as an analyst requires the scrutiny of several parties, including the supervisor of the candidate's patient analyses. (The "candidate" is a telling term capturing the idea that the supervisee is aware of being in a kind of trial position in which he or she is dependent upon the supervisor's approval in order to achieve the status they desire.) The supervisor thus becomes the custodian of certain standards and has a dual responsibility to the analytic institute and the analytic trainee. Such arrangements are also true of less elite or analytically purist training bodies, including university-based training programs and psychotherapy training institutes. This gate-keeping function has bearing not only for the profession but also, of course, for patient or client welfare, as is emphasized in the ethical codes for all psychotherapeutic practitioners. The supervisor is the representative of their institutional base with regard to assessing whether the trainee has met the necessary criteria to "pass" as a competent enough psychotherapist, demonstrating the required knowledge base, practice skills, self-awareness, and ethical capability in this regard. This is a complex set of attributes to evaluate and clearly requires more than assessment based on the writing of some form of theoretical examination (although this may be a legitimate component of evaluation). This is part of what makes the roles of trainer and evaluator impossible to separate. The management of likely tensions between these aspects of supervision is something of which supervisors need to remain constantly aware, particularly psychodynamic supervisors who recognize that the supervisory context is one in which a range of transference and countertransference dynamics may be at play. It is easy to see how, for example, projections related to the sense of a judging, superior parent/supervisor might interfere with those aspects of supervision that require trust and self-disclosure. Given the uneasy alignment of assessor and facilitator functions, theorists have attempted to address this point of tension by considering whether it is possible to assign evaluative functions to individuals who have not been engaged in supervision of trainees, that is, to separate out the personages of those who "train" from those who "evaluate" (Hanoch, 2006; Werbart, 2007). One of the considerations in attempting to separate the two roles, however, is that any attempt to give priority to an external evaluator is likely to mean that summative evaluation takes precedence over formative evaluation. While it is debatable whether a purely summative evaluation is ever desirable in assessing the competence of psychotherapists, it is clearly more feasible in therapeutic approaches that are more technique or protocol driven. As indicated previously, in psychodynamic psychotherapy, in addition to the micro-skills that are the basis for all interventions, there is enormous weight placed upon the person of the therapist, their capacity for self-insight, their attunement to each specific patient, their awareness of dynamic and relational elements, and their ability to be cognizant of unconscious and preconscious forms of communication. Such capacities are not easily observed in summative-type evaluations. Thus, it appears not only untenable, but also perhaps undesirable, for supervisors not to be involved in trainee evaluation. In order to acknowledge the kind of personal and professional journey that a psychodynamic psychotherapist needs to undertake to begin to be able to practice independently, it is necessary to have accompanied the trainee on this journey, the place conventionally taken by a supervisor. Ultimately then, in large measure to serve the interests of the trainee as importantly as those of the profession or the public, the supervisor is obligated to take on and manage the role of evaluator. Debell (1963) makes the point that the supervisee's anxiety at being scrutinized in this way may be inhibiting at times but that it may "also frequently . . . spur to greater achievement" (p. 546). It appears important for supervisors to be comfortable with and transparent about assuming this evaluative part of the supervisory role. Their necessary "ambiguity tolerance" (Szecsödy, 1989, p. 245) should assist supervisors to take on this mantle in addition to their mentoring, supporting, stretching, didactic, and containing functions.

In the context within which we work, in South Africa it is understood that the supervisor should play an assessor and evaluator role, in part because of resource constraints but primarily because this person is viewed as having the most comprehensive knowledge of the student's performance in this area. Thus, students are awarded a percentage mark based on their presentation in, and employment of, supervision across the year. Supervisees are also given supervisory feedback based on a set of criteria made available to them at the outset of their training, which includes, for example, the ability to apply appropriate theory, awareness of countertransference elements in their work, and the ability to make use of supervisory input. However, supervisor evaluations are complemented both by team (of at least three staff) evaluation of a case conference presentation, as well as by "external examination" (by a senior clinician) of a supervisee-selected, audiotaped, psychotherapy session accompanied by a dynamic formulation of the patient, written transcript, and commentary on the session. In this way, we seek to combine both summative and formative forms of evaluation. We also hope to strike a balance in giving due weight to the supervisor's assessment without giving him or her sole responsibility or absolute power to make the determination about a candidate's competence. Using a range of assessment practices and outcomes and involving a further assessor beyond the primary supervisor may offer a practical means of reducing some of the tensions inherent in straddling the trainer–evaluator divide, complementing the more complex management of interpersonal dynamics in this regard.

Having looked at this dilemma primarily through the lens of the supervisor, it is also important to look at this aspect of the supervisory relationship from the perspective of the trainee. Beyond the fear of formal evaluation and the possibility that one might ultimately fail in one's goal of becoming a recognized psychodynamic psychotherapist, supervision requires that candidates subject themselves to critical scrutiny on an ongoing basis. Such necessary scrutiny tends to evoke anxiety about performance, and in the case of psychodynamic psychotherapy, almost inevitably about the self. "The boundaries between exposure of the candidate's weaknesses as a professional and exposure of her flaws as a person are blurred, and professional criticism might easily feel like attacks on the self" (Hanoch, 2006, p. 133). Several authors writing about psychodynamic supervision have made reference to the risk of narcissistic wounding that trainees face in such territory. "One of the important functions of supervision is helping supervisees cope with the great narcissistic vulnerability (Brightman, 1984) occasioned by the position of being beginning psychotherapists" (Yerushalmi, 1999, p. 432). By virtue of their having applied for and committed into training, it is apparent that supervisees value the identity they seek to acquire and are willing to make sacrifices to achieve this. Such sacrifices include giving up a degree of autonomy and personal comfort to become aware not only of mistakes in the application of theory and technique but also of personal limitations, defensive patterns, and unconscious enactments. It has been recognized that supervisees may be challenged by both "dumb spots" and "blind spots" (cited in Szecsödy, 1989), the former referring primarily to gaps in knowledge and the latter to repressed, avoided, and/or unconscious material. A significant role of the supervisor is to identify and explore with the supervisee precisely these "blind spots." It is evident that learning psychodynamic psychotherapy requires willingness to be exposed and challenged in the context of supervision. Given such expectations, it is not unexpected that many trainees experience psychodynamic psychotherapy supervision as taxing of the self and become vulnerable to shame and narcissistic injury. "Training is a regressive experience, and supervision can produce self-fragmentation anxiety (Fuqua, 1994; Wolf, 1995), difficulties maintaining self-cohesion, destructuring, and restructuring and the like" (Kaufman, 2006, p. 148). Supervisors need to manage this kind of risk with sensitivity without becoming overprotective.

It has been suggested that providing psychodynamic psychotherapy supervision within a group may be one means of reducing the likelihood of narcissistic injury. Although this may seem somewhat paradoxical, in that a group suggests a larger audience to perceive one's shortcomings, it has been observed that group supervision reduces some of the discomfort associated with being the sole object of scrutiny. Wolstein, cited in Yerushalmi (1999), suggests that " a group of equals generally dispels tensions, dissipates resistance to the supervisor, and minimizes supervisees' anxieties about being manipulated and invaded while still allowing for the requisite and reasonable exposure of their countertransference reactions" (p. 429). Within a supervisory group, there is shared inexperience and the reassurance that others too have dumb and blind spots.

As discussed previously, group supervision is predominant in our setting, but there is also the opportunity for individual supervision when supervisees so request or when supervisors may wish to address a particular issue in greater depth than might be possible in the group setting, such as particularly sensitive countertransference dynamics. This last mentioned point offers a useful link into the next area of focus.

To teach and/or treat: concerns about the boundary between supervision and psychotherapy

A further issue that has engendered considerable debate within the literature on psychoanalytic and psychodynamics supervision is what is generally referred to as the "teach or treat" dilemma (Kaufman, 2006). Put simply, this dilemma relates to the question of whether supervision is viewed as primarily didactic or whether it involves some sort of exploratory or even interpretive function in relation to the supervisee that verges on being a form of "treatment." With the recognition that transference and countertransference are core dimensions of psychodynamic psychotherapy, it becomes incumbent on supervisors to assist trainees to become aware of, to be able to identify, to be able to reflect upon, and to be able to work with transference dynamics.

Revised views on countertransference have meant that this dimension of the therapist's experience is no longer understood as largely problematic and as reflecting unresolved issues in his/her psyche, but has rather come to be understood as an important source of information about the patient and the course of therapy. Levy and Parnell (2001) observe that since 1980, there has been a "growing trend toward publishing elaborate and detailed data on the working through of analyst's countertransference based interventions" (p. 93). Racker's (1968) work on concordant and complementary countertransferences, for example, suggests that responses evoked in the therapist may provide important information not only about the patient's internal world but also about the patient's characteristic object-relational (or interpersonal/interactional) patterns. The concept of "projective identification" (Klein, 1946/1975) has extended the notion of countertransference even further. It is suggested that when projective identification is operating, therapists may find themselves experiencing alien or ego-dystonic kinds of feelings or states that are understood to be unconsciously evacuated and projected by the patient into the therapist. This kind of communication is perceived to take place at a very primitive level that bypasses verbal exchange. It is thus apparent that it is impossible for supervision not to involve some examination of countertransference and that this element of supervision may be revealing of the supervisee at a number of levels. For example, supervision may require teasing out with the supervisee what elements of their response appear to stem from their own "transference" or unresolved issues, as opposed to those that are primarily evoked by the patient. Kaufman (2006) asserts "we cannot teach psychoanalysis without the supervisee's disclosure of countertransference as well as some disclosure of their own lives and history" (p. 147).

It is difficult to think of any other form of therapy that might require this level of personal awareness and personal disclosure in supervision. The protocol-based treatments and cognitive-behavioral therapy (CBT) approaches that are becoming increasingly popular rely almost entirely upon the teaching element of supervision. Although aspects of the therapist's personality, such as those that might affect the development of rapport and style of delivery of treatment, may be highlighted, this is a very different level of engagement than that required to work with countertransference dynamics. More recent cognitive-behavioral approaches have, however, begun to stress the importance of fostering self-reflection (e.g., Bennett-Levy, Lee, Travers, Pohlman, & Hamernik, 2003) and empathy (e.g., Thwaites & Bennett-Levy, 2007) in therapists. Such work may reflect a growing convergence of recognition of the importance of personal awareness in conducting psychotherapy. While psychodynamic theorists would suggest that almost all supervisory relationships will carry some transference elements between supervisor and supervisee, given the hierarchical nature of such exchanges, it is evident that psychodynamic supervision is that much more likely to evoke such dynamics because of the level of sharing that is assumed or required. Thus, not only are the supervisor and supervisee expected to think about countertransference in respect of the patient but they are also expected to pay attention to the dynamics of their supervisory relationship, as will be discussed more fully in the next subsection.

While there is no debate that attention to countertransference is an integral component of psychodynamic supervision, where there is some difference of opinion is in the degree to which it is appropriate for the supervisor to open up, explore, and attempt to work through these issues with the trainee. When does the overlap between supervision and personal psychotherapy become inappropriate? When might the supervisor usurp or possibly rival the place of the trainee's psychotherapist and when might they work in a way that perhaps complements or enables work in this domain? "The ever-present hazards of working through the candidate's countertransference in supervision are related to various sources. Exploring the candidate's experiences may reach a point where it intrudes into the domain of personal analysis tacitly encourages split transferences (e.g., supportive growth-promoting supervisor versus restricting, frustrating, distant training analyst). We understand the concern of training analysts who tend to view this approach to supervision as turning it into pseudotreatment" (Levy & Parnell, 2001, p. 113). Although this quotation refers to analytic training rather than psychodynamic psychotherapy supervision, it is possible to see that the same tensions apply to the latter, although perhaps with somewhat less intensity. Sedlak (2003) is concerned that the intersubjective paradigm, particularly, is likely to promote the blurring of boundaries between supervision and personal psychotherapy, as exemplified in an article by Berman (2000a). Sedlak (2003) is of the opinion that supervisory work with countertransference dynamics can be largely restricted to that which is generated from close attention to the patient's material and the responses this evokes in the therapist. Where the main point of contention seems to lie is in how appropriate it is to explore aspects of the supervisee's personal history, defensive structure, core conflicts, and relational patterns when these appear to be counterproductive in the work with the patient. What many supervisors appear to do is not to ignore these elements altogether but rather to attempt to reflect upon such dynamics in a collaborative way, inviting the supervisee to identify possible links, and then to suggest that full exploration of these issues be taken to personal psychotherapy. The trick is to retain a supervision boundary while at the same time not feeling overly restricted to raise what might be important countertransferences features.

The following is a fairly straightforward illustration of this kind of aspect of supervision. A clinical psychology master's student had been seeing a tertiary level student for several months and had identified that her patient had introjected a rather harsh, demanding superego based on her relationship with an idealized, disciplinarian maternal aunt who had been her primary caretaker in the face of parents who were constructed as highly irresponsible. Following some important therapeutic work, the patient became disinvested in her academic work, feeling that her expectations of herself in this regard related to her need to dis-identify from her parents and to live up to the expectations of her powerfully influential (introjected) aunt. At the same time, her depression lifted and her interpersonal relationships improved. At this point, the trainee therapist became highly anxious about his role in possibly having facilitated a change that might lead the patient to underperform or even fail her academic courses. Although this was an important therapeutic issue to explore for the sake of the patient, what became apparent through some exploration of the intensity of his anxiety and sense of responsibility in supervision was that the trainee's countertransference was playing a role in his response to the patient. His investment in his own studies and his sense of how important it was to be diligent and to live up to both his own expectations as well as his parents' was clouding his ability to examine what this change in attitude might mean for the patient. Once this dynamic had been identified, in part with some prompting from the supervisor who was sensitive to the trainee's own high performance demands, it was possible to suggest that this issue should continue to be examined within the trainee's personal psychotherapy. Interestingly, following identification of this countertransference dynamic in supervision, some two or three sessions later, the patient reflected that she had reengaged with her studies and wished to allow herself freedom to choose future options by making sure she passed her current courses. It is evident from this example that some aspects of countertransference may be more easily accessible and more easily dealt with than others. The more unconscious and the more challenging or shameful countertransferential material is (such as, e.g., the identification of erotic, competitive, disgusted, dismissive, envious, or punitive feelings), the more difficult for the supervisor to take up and the more likely that supervisees may feel that boundaries have been transgressed. While it is evident that it is not easy to determine exactly where the defining line lies between supervision and the exploration of personal material, it is important for both parties to hold in mind that the main aim of working with countertransference is to enable a better understanding of, and to work with, the patient, that is, to locate such work within the supervisory alliance. In addition, it has been suggested that there should be some negotiation of this element of supervision at the outset and some guarantee around confidentiality with respect to any highly exposing material that might be revealed. The supervisor may also need to protect the supervisee against over-disclosure every bit as much as under-disclosure, in part by giving respectful feedback at points at which particularly personal material or associations are proffered.

One further element that complicates the negotiation of the teach–treat balance is the fact that the supervisory relationship creates a further context within which transference dynamics emerge in response to aspects of both personal and structural or group identity characteristics such as gender and racial differences (Eagle, 2005). Both supervisee and supervisor are likely to be aware of such dynamics at points and also have to negotiate how best to engage with them. Again this requires sensitivity, especially in light of the evaluative element discussed previously. What recognition of the relational elements of the supervision dyad suggests is the now well-established idea that psychodynamic supervision is triadic, involving sets of relationships between three different parties: the patient, the supervisee, and the supervisor.

Supervision as triadic and the entertainment of parallel process

Building on some of the previous discussion about countertransference and its importance, one of the constructs that has taken central place in writing about psychodynamic supervision is that of the "triadic relationship" (Brown & Miller, 2002; Marshall, 1997; Werbart, 2007). Relatively early in the study of psychodynamic supervision, it became recognized that supervision was not a dyadic or two-person relationship between trainee and supervisor. The person of the patient was understood to occupy an important relational place within supervision. Not only was the therapist's relationship with the patient considered important, but also that between the supervisor and the patient, even if this relationship was mediated by the supervisee's particular presentation of the patient. Thus, it is always borne in mind that supervision needs to encompass understanding of at least three sets of relational dynamics – those between patient and supervisee, supervisee and supervisor, and supervisor and patient. "Gediman and Wolkenfeld conceptualized the supervisory relationship as a 'triadic system' in which influence does not run in a one-dimensional path, originating in either the patient or the supervisor, but as a 'complex multidirectional network' (1980, p. 236)" (cited in Brown & Miller, 2002, p. 812).

Although different vertices of this triadic constellation may be foregrounded at different moments in supervision (most often that between the patient and the therapist), it is understood that they are interrelated and are reciprocally influential. For example, a supervisee's awareness of an erotic transference from a patient may be brought into supervision with some embarrassment, the supervisee fearing that the supervisor may think that they have been responsible for the evocation of such transference. The supervisor, in turn, may feel some sense of protectiveness toward the supervisee who is being thrown off balance by a highly seductive patient, or alternatively may feel some sympathy for the patient who has landed up with an inexperienced therapist who is unable to manage this kind of transference. The patient may be behaving flirtatiously toward the therapist in order to seduce the therapist into a more intimate relationship that excludes the supervisor and the training institution. What is evident in this kind of scenario is that the dynamics between all three sets of parties are complex and require careful disentangling. The supervisor is obligated to be aware of and to examine his/her countertransference responses to both supervisee and patient, in the same way that the supervisee is expected to be. Yet again, it is evident that the requirements of psychodynamic supervisors are rather different from those of supervisors in many other therapeutic modalities. Not only are supervisees expected to be mindful of their particular contributions to their work but so too are supervisors. This has led some authors to suggest that supervisors need supervisory support as discussed later.

In addition, it has been proposed that it may be important to acknowledge the quadratic nature of supervision in some instances, the fourth element in the mix being the training institution within which the supervisor and the supervisee are both located and to which they might both have transference feelings (Szecsödy, 1989; Watkins, 2011a). For example, supervisors may also have narcissistic investments in being viewed as "good" with regard to this aspect of their work. Even outside of analytic institutes, it is often the case that the taking on of a supervisory role is understood as reflecting a kind of coming of age and is desired and aspired to. While such quadratic dynamics may be less evident in supervision of psychodynamic psychotherapy that takes place post qualification and outside of formal training settings, supervisors are still mindful of their professional reputations and the manner in which their supervisees may reflect upon experiences of supervision with colleagues. It is thus evident that supervisors need to manage a range of conscious and unconscious features that may impede (or possibly enhance) their supervisory capacity.

With the intersubjective and relational developments in psychodynamic practice, a more egalitarian understanding of the contributions of both supervisor and supervisee (in parallel with more egalitarian understandings of the therapeutic relationship) has gained considerable purchase (Berman, 2000a; Frawley-O'Dea, 2003). The supervisory relationship is understood to be co-constructed rather than as the product of an objective, wise supervisor engaged with a dependent, unformed learner. While this more postmodern understanding of supervisory exchanges is compelling, even within this new framework of understanding, it is still important for certain boundaries to be observed, such as those that have previously been outlined. In addition, it is apparent that not every nuance of the triadic matrix can be addressed and that again it requires sound judgment and flexibility on the part of the supervisor to choose how far to take any one issue. One of the constructs that may offer guidance in determining when supervision dynamics should be directly tackled is the idea of "parallel process."

First identified as a "reflective process" by Searles (1955) and later captured terminologically by Doehrman (1976), the idea of *parallel process* refers to the observation that in certain instances there is an unconsciously produced "correspondence between the supervisory and treatment relationships" (Brown & Miller, 2002, p. 812). Patterns and conflicts within the therapeutic dyad become in some way repeated, *paralleled*, in the supervision dyad (and vice versa as has been more recently recognized). Doehrman emphasized that parallel processes "were not symptomatic of difficulties in either the analytic or supervisory relationships, but were rather an expectable part of every supervised treatment" (cited in Brown & Miller, 2002, p. 812). Having gained considerable credibility as a framework for thinking about the dynamic interplay between therapy and supervision processes, many pieces of writing about psychodynamic supervision make reference to parallel process dynamics. The examination of these dynamics is often understood to offer a tool toward thinking about more irrational and "stuck" aspects of supervision.

While there are numerous case-based illustrations of parallel processes in the psychodynamic literature, a brief example from our training context is offered in order to highlight how this way of understanding supervisory material may be helpful. Some years previously, one of the authors found that she became unusually irritated and dismayed in reading the transcription of a session by a trainee. She found it hard to restrain herself from writing overly harsh and highly critical comments on the transcript and, in fact, did give some strongly worded feedback. Later, she regretted her actions and wondered whether some kind of enactment had taken place. While the trainee had made some evident errors, these did not appear to warrant quite the level of criticism provoked. She invited the supervisee to a meeting at which she apologized for the manner in which the feedback had been delivered and invited the trainee to explore the issue a bit further. What emerged from the discussion was the supervisee's considerable frustration and irritation with his patient, who he felt was not "pulling her weight" in contributing to the therapy. He doubted his own capacity to think interpretively about his patient and expected her to demonstrate greater insight and to provide him with more to work with. When this was not forthcoming, he responded rather punitively toward her, which was one of the features of the session that the supervisor had picked up on in the transcript. In addition, the supervisor became more aware that she had felt some frustration and disquiet at the apparent lack of skill demonstrated by the trainee, despite exposure to training input. What became apparent was that the supervisor's disappointed, critical, punitive response and underlying anxiety about the efficacy of training input in relation to the supervisee were reflective of the supervisee's similar struggle with his patient. Although not all of this was laid bare in the supervisory exchange, the discussion allowed the supervisee to engage with the patient in a more gentle and helpful way and assisted the supervisor to tone down the intensity of her negative evaluation. While such dynamics can be much less accessible to conscious exploration, it is helpful to entertain the possibility of parallel process dynamics even in the supervision of once weekly psychodynamic psychotherapy. There has been some concern about the possibly defensive overemployment of parallel process as a framework for understanding supervisory dynamics, with the suggestion that supervisors may sometimes hide behind this kind of formulation rather than acknowledging what may be personally driven transference and countertransference dynamics. This is perhaps an important caution, as like projective identification, the notion of parallel process is very captivating, tending to locate supervision difficulties largely outside of the supervisor, and offering intellectual appeal. Despite this caution, it is evident that an understanding of parallel process dynamics is an important part of the armamentarium of the psychodynamic supervisor.

The discussion of these selected core elements of psychodynamic supervision is clearly not exhaustive; however, the aim has been to introduce and signal some key aspects of supervision that appear to be largely unique to psychodynamic ways of working.

Support for Supervisors

There has been increasing recognition that supervisors do not necessarily have "super vision" (Teitelbaum, 1990) and are not neutral, objective parties in the supervisory interchange. On the contrary, supervisors themselves may have narcissistic vulnerabilities and may be prone toward feelings of rivalry, which may play out in the supervisory setting (Debell, 1963). Given the typical structures of training, where supervisors are expected to evaluate supervisees, the temptation to break confidentiality or to gossip is also present (Yerushalmi, 1999). As suggested previously, supervisors may bring their own feelings, including their own unconscious conflicts and internal worlds (Werbart, 2007), into the supervisory setting in what Teitelbaum (1990) has termed "supertransference." Berman (2000a) terms the avoidance or denial of the supervisor's subjective role the "myth of the supervisory situation" (p. 277).

As a result of increasing acknowledgment of the subjectivity of the supervisor, attention has turned to the importance of training and support for supervisors. Some institutes, for example, the Swedish Psychoanalytic Institute, have set up training programs for supervisors, where elements of supervision and the supervisory process are discussed and the competencies of supervisors explored (Szecsödy, 2008). Suggestions have also been made that supervisors themselves need supervision (e.g., Fink, 2007; Vaslamatzis, 2008; Yerushalmi, 1999). Yerushamli (1999) makes an interesting case for the advantages of group supervision of supervision. The domination of writing about supervision by supervisors has also been challenged as more supervisees have started to contribute to this literature (e.g., Basescu, 2006; Hanoch, 2006; Pedder, 1986; Secrest, 2006) and joint papers incorporating the perspectives of supervisors and supervisees have been produced (e.g., Brown & Miller, 2002; Levy & Parnell, 2001; Ungar & De Ahumada, 2001). There has also been increasing recognition that psychodynamic supervision requires more rigorous research (Watkins, 2011b), definition, and role delineation (Szecsödy, 2008).

These shifts have encouraged recognition that supervisors themselves need support. It is more comfortable being in the supervisor's seat than in the therapist's seat, but, of course, the work evokes feelings in the supervisor as well as the supervisee. Offering support for the supervisor has the potential of opening the reflective space and enriching supervision for all parties, including to the benefit of the patient.

Conclusion

We hope in this chapter to have presented psychoanalytic approaches to supervision that are of relevance to supervisors of psychoanalysis and psychoanalytic psychotherapy, and to have offered readers working in other modalities with tools that can be incorporated into their work. In contrast to concerns that psychoanalytic psychotherapy offers only "an expensive treatment for the worried well" (Lemma & Patrick, 2010, p. 6), there is a great deal of contemporary interest in the application of psychoanalysis in a variety of settings. Psychoanalytic thinking is "on a remarkable accelerating upward spiral" (Wallerstein, 1991, in Patterson & Watkins, 1997, p. 32) in many parts of the globe, including Central and Eastern Europe, South America, and Asia. As a model of supervision, a psychoanalytic approach holds global relevance.

Since this handbook is explicitly invested in exploring international aspects of supervisory models, work, and experiences, this final section of the chapter briefly explores some of the particular contextual demands involved in offering psychodynamic psychotherapy supervision in South Africa. As indicated earlier, although there has previously been no formal psychoanalytic training institute in the country, many universities and organizations offering psychotherapy training have been influenced by psychodynamic ways of thinking, and psychodynamic psychotherapy is practiced fairly widely in all the major cities in the country. Despite historically embedded reservations about this approach linked to notions of psychodynamic practice as elitist and necessarily long term, practitioners have taken psychodynamic understandings into a range of different contexts and, in fact, we would argue that within the psychotherapeutic community, it is psychodynamically oriented theorists who have engaged most substantively with sociopolitical issues, such as racial discrimination and youth violence.

In thinking about psychodynamic supervision, two particularly salient contextual issues are identified. First, the history of race and class discrimination in the country, which continues to affect the population today, means that race and class differences become highly salient in any therapeutic and supervisory encounter and need to be carefully attended to and engaged (Eagle, 2005; Swartz, 2007). Racial oppression in South Africa was marked by particularly discriminatory, demeaning, exploitative, and brutal interactions, and the legacy of White dominance and Black invalidation continues to shape people's consciousness and everyday experiences. Although the emergence of a new postapartheid generation of young South Africans and shifts in political and economic power (in part the product of Black Economic Empowerment policies) are bringing about rapid transformations in society, there is still considerable sensitivity in race relations. Because of discriminatory educational practices and economic hardship, very few Black South Africans were previously able to train as psychologists and professional psychotherapy is still heavily dominated by White practitioners, despite the fact that over 80% of the population is Black. This means that it is still largely the case that Black trainees (who are slowly increasing in number) are supervised by White staff. As with therapeutic exchanges, supervisory exchanges are also rendered more complex by such dynamics: "at worst it is a relationship overloaded, burdened and profoundly affected by the past, generally speaking, and by the past lives of the two people engaging in the counseling relationship specifically" (Lago & Thompson, 1996, p. 27, cited in Eagle, 2005, p. 201). Not only do supervisors need to assist supervisees to deal with difference in the therapeutic encounter, dealing with their own and others group identities and stereotypes, but, in line with parallel process and triadic ways of understanding what takes place in supervision, supervisors also need to be willing to engage with their own relational dynamics in this regard. While such "multicultural awareness" is becoming mainstreamed with increasing gobalization, in contexts in which relations of oppression and intergroup conflict have been particularly salient, this is a delicate area to negotiate in supervision. Once again, it is perhaps important to signal that engaging in exploration of the meanings of such differences may be enormously productive rather than inevitably difficult (Eagle et al., 2007; Swartz, 2007).

A second important contextual issue concerns the kinds of patients and problems that present in our training context and what this requires of trainees and, in turn, of supervisors. We strive to encourage our students to be aware of the sociopolitical context within which they live and to gain experience in working with marginalized populations that would not necessarily have access to psychotherapy under normal circumstances. Their clinic-based work involves seeing a range of patients for shorter-term interventions, many of these patients managing social deprivation and poverty in addition to psychological distress. Exposure to extreme and complex traumatic stressors (such as rape, violent assault, and murder) is also common, given very high crime levels in South Africa. The stressfulness of the work thus goes beyond that of mastering psychotherapeutic theory and skills, but extends to countertransference effects that are situation and context driven. Supervision thus often requires debriefing and containment beyond that which might normally be expected (Eagle, 2005; Eagle et al., 2007). Supervisors themselves are not unaffected by hearing about the deprived and dangerous circumstances within which patients live. They need to be mindful of their own value systems and the kind of vicarious traumatization that can be evoked by such material if they are to assist supervisees to digest what are often very toxic and taxing experiences. In this respect, we believe that it may be important for supervisors to seek peer support, of the kind discussed earlier. We would contend that psychodynamic ways of thinking and working can provide psychotherapists and supervisors with important tools for understanding the impact of work with minority or oppressed groups in countries in which mental health care is severely under-resourced. In these kinds of contexts, we would suggest that the supervisory armamentarium previously referred to needs to be expanded to incorporate a sociopolitical consciousness that remains a consistent backdrop against which much of what is managed in supervision takes place. In order to supervise ethically and meaningfully in these kinds of contexts, supervisors need to expand their understanding of their role to encompass contextually sensitive forms of understanding, interpersonal engagement, and support.

References

Aronson, S. (2000). Analytic supervision: All work and no play? *Contemporary Psychoanalysis, 36*, 121–132.

Basescu, S. (2006). Discussion of "candidates' anxiety in supervision." *Psychoanalytic Perspectives, 3*, 167–170.

Bennett-Levy, J., Lee, N., Travers, K., Pohlman, S., & Hamernik, E. (2003). Cognitive therapy from the inside: Enhancing therapists skills through practicing what we preach. *Behavioural and Cognitive Psychotherapy, 31*, 143–158.

Berman, E. (2000a). Psychoanalytic supervision: The intersubjective development. *International Journal of Psychoanalysis, 81*, 273–290.

Berman, E. (2000b). The utopian fantasy of a new person and the danger of a false analytic self. *Psychoanalytic Psychology, 17*, 38–60.

Berman, E. (2004). *Impossible training: A relational view of psychoanalytic education.* Hillsdale, NJ: The Analytic Press.

Binder, J., Strupp, H., & Schacht, T. (1983). Countertransference in time-limited dynamic psychotherapy – Further extending the range of treatable patients. *Contemporary Psychoanalysis, 19*, 605–622.

Brown, L., & Miller, M. (2002). The triadic intersubjective matrix in supervision: The use of disclosure to work through painful affects. *International Journal of Psychoanalysis, 83*, 811–823.

Casement, P. (1991). *Learning from the patient.* New York, NY: The Guildford Press.

Debell, D. (1963). A critical digest of the literature on psychoanalytic supervision. *Journal of the American Psychoanalytic Association, 11*, 546–575.

Doehrman, M. (1976). Parallel processes in supervision and psychotherapy. *Bulletin of the Menninger Clinic, 40*(1), 3–104.

Eagle, G. (2005). Grasping the thorn: The impact and supervision of traumatic stress therapy in the South African context. *Journal of Psychology in Africa, 15*(2), 197–208.

Eagle, G., Haynes, H., & Long, C. (2007). Eyes wide open: Facilitating student therapists' experiences with the unfamiliar. *European Journal of Psychotherapy and Counselling, 9*(2), 133–146.

Fink, K. (2007). Supervision, transference and countertransference. *International Journal of Psychoanalysis, 88*, 1263–1273.

Fiscalini, J. (1985). On supervisory parataxis and dialogue. *Contemporary Psychoanalysis, 21*, 591–608.

Frawley-O'Dea, M. (2003). Supervision is a relationship too: A contemporary approach to psychoanalytic supervision. *Psychoanalytic Dialogues, 13*, 355–366.

Frawley-O'Dea, M., & Sarnat, J. (2001). *The supervisory relationship: A contemporary psychodynamic approach.* New York, NY: Guildford Press.

Freud, S. (1912a). Letter from Sigmund Freud to Sandor Ferenczi, November 26, 1912. In E. Brabant & E. Falzeder (Eds.), *The correspondence of Sigmund Freud and Sandor Ferenczi* (Vol. 1, pp. 433–435), Cambridge, MA: Harvard University Press, 1993.

Freud, S. (1912b). Recommendations to physicians practising psycho-analysis. In J. Strachey (Ed. and Trans.), *The standard edition of the complete psychological works of Sigmund Freud* (Vol. 12, pp. 109–120), London, England: Hogarth Press.

Freud, S. (1919). On the teaching of psycho-analysis in universities. In J. Strachey (Ed. and Trans.), *The standard edition of the complete psychological works of Sigmund Freud* (Vol. 17, pp. 169–174), London, England: Hogarth Press.

Freud, S. (1924). A short account of psycho-analysis. In J. Strachey (Ed. and Trans.), *The standard edition of the complete psychological works of Sigmund Freud* (Vol. 19, pp. 189–210), London, England: Hogarth Press.

Freud, S. (1926). The question of lay analysis. In J. Strachey (Ed.), *The standard edition of the complete psychological works of Sigmund Freud* (Vol. 20, pp. 177–258), London, England: Hogarth Press.

Hanoch, E. (2006). The loudness of the unspoken: Candidates' anxiety in supervision. *Psychoanalytic Perspectives, 3*, 127–146.

Joannidis, C. (2006). Psychoanalysis and psychoanalytic psychotherapy. *Psychoanalytic Psychotherapy, 20*, 30–39.

Kaufman, J. (2006). Candidates' anxiety in supervision: A discussion. *Psychoanalytic Perspectives, 3*, 147–157.

Kernberg, O. (2006). The coming changes in psychoanalytic education: Part I. *International Journal of Psychoanalysis, 87*, 1649–1673.

Klein, M. (1946/1975). *Envy and Gratitude.* New York, NY: Delacorte Press.

Lemma, A., & Patrick, M. (2010). *Off the Couch: Contemporary psychoanalytic applications.* East Sussex, England: Routledge.

Levy, J., & Parnell, Y. (2001). The benefits and hazards of working through the supervisee's countertransference in psychoanalytic supervision. *Journal of Clinical Psychoanalysis, 10*, 91–116.

Marshall, R. (1997). A dynamic and structural model of the triad in supervision. *Modern Psychoanalysis, 22*, 41–57.

Mitchell, S. A. (1998). *Relational concepts in psychoanalysis: An integration.* Cambridge, MA: Harvard University Press.

Ogden, T. (2005). On psychoanalytic supervision. *International Journal of Psychoanalysis, 86*, 1265–1280.

Patterson, C. H., & Watkins, C. E. (1997). *Theories of psychotherapy.* New York, NY: Pearson.

Pedder, J. (1986). Reflections on the theory and practice of supervision. *Psychoanalytic Psychotherapy, 2*, 1–12.

Racker, H. (1968). *Transference and countertransference.* New York, NY: Int. Univ. Press.

Schaffer, A. (2006). The analyst's curative fantasies: Implications for supervision and self-supervision. *Contemporary Psychoanalysis, 42*, 349–366.

Searles, H. (1955). The informational value of the supervisor's emotional experiences. Psychiatry: *Journal for the study of interpersonal processes, 18*, 135–146.

Secrest, M. (2006). Aspects of angst in analytic supervision: A candidate weighs in. *Psychoanalytic Perspectives, 3*, 159–165.

Sedlak, V. (2003). The patient's material as an aid to the disciplined working through of the countertransference and supervision. *International Journal of Psychoanalysis, 84*, 1487–1500.

Swartz, S. (2007). The power to name: South African intersubjective psychoanalytic psychotherapy and the negotiation of racialized histories. *European Journal of Psychotherapy and Counselling, 9*(2), 177–190.

Szecsödy, I. (1989). Supervision: A didactic or mutative situation. *Psychoanalytic Psychotherapy, 4*, 245–261.

Szecsödy, I. (2008). Does anything go in psychoanalytic supervision? *Psychoanalytic Inquiry, 28*, 373–386.

Teitelbaum, S. (1990). Supertransference: The role of the supervisor's blind spots. *Psychoanalytic Psychology, 7*, 243–258.

Thwaites, R., & Bennett-Levy, J. (2007). Conceptualizing empathy on cognitive behavior therapy: Making the implicit explicit. *Behavioural and Cognitive Psychotherapy, 35*, 591–612.

Ungar, V., & De Ahumada, L. (2001). Supervision: A container-contained approach. *International Journal of Psychoanalysis, 82*, 71–81.

Vaslamatzis, G. (2008). On: Supervision, transference and countertransference. *International Journal of Psychoanalysis, 89*, 655–656.

Watkins, C. (2011a). Celebrating psychoanalytic supervision: Considering a century of seminal contribution. *Psychoanalytic Review, 98*(3), 401–418.

Watkins, C. (2011b). Toward a tripartite vision of supervision for psychoanalysis and psychoanalytic psychotherapies: Alliance, transference-countertransference configuration, and real relationship. *Psychoanalytic Review, 98*(4), 557–590.

Werbart, A. (2007). Utopic ideas of cure and joint exploration in psychoanalytic supervision. *International Journal of Psychoanalysis, 88*, 1391–1408.

Winnicott, D. (1971). *Playing and reality.* London, England: Tavistock.

Yerushalmi, H. (1999). The roles of group supervision of supervision. *Psychoanalytic Psychology, 16*, 426–447.

24

Supervising Cognitive and Behavioral Therapies

Robert P. Reiser

Introduction

This chapter provides a comprehensive review of the current status of supervision in the cognitive and behavioral therapies (CBT). Since the publication of the *Handbook of Psychotherapy Supervision* (Watkins, 1997), there have been a number of very significant developments in the field that should inform and enrich the current practice of clinical supervision. Some of these important international developments have already been outlined in the introductory chapter of this handbook, namely defining a core set of fundamental competencies and identifying empirically supported elements of effective supervisory practice (Falender et al., 2004; Falender & Shafranske, 2004; Falender & Shafranske, 2012; O'Donovan, Slattery, Kavanagh, & Dooley, 2008; Psychology Board of Australia, 2011; Roth & Pilling, 2008a; Turpin & Wheeler, 2011). In this chapter, I highlight some of the current challenges and opportunities associated with these trends as they apply to the supervision of CBT. I start with a review of the foundational texts in CBT supervision that provide the core elements of a platform for practice. Next, I identify significant updates integrating a competency-based framework, and provide illustrative vignettes highlighting empirically supported practices in CBT supervision. Finally, I address the need for an enhanced methodology and technology for further development of competent CBT supervisory practices.

Foundations of cognitive therapy supervision

As a starting point it would be helpful to review the status of CBT supervision as illustrated in Liese and Beck's original chapter in the *Handbook of Psychotherapy Supervision* (Liese & Beck, 1997). Their discussion of supervision, along with Padesky (1996), can be seen as providing an early framework for the development of clinical

The Wiley International Handbook of Clinical Supervision, First Edition. Edited by C. Edward Watkins, Jr. and Derek L. Milne.

Table 24.1 Specifying key elements in CBT supervision (Liese & Beck, 1997; Padesky, 1996).

Session structure
Check-in
Prioritization and discussion of supervision agenda
Bridge from previous session: inquiry about last supervision session and previously supervised cases
Review of assigned homework
Supervisor provides capsule summaries throughout session
Supervisor assigns new homework
Supervisor elicits feedback from therapist
Session content
Discuss cognitive therapy individual case formulation
Focus on structuring of therapy sessions
Teach specific cognitive and behavioral techniques
Make primary use of audio- or videotapes for supervision
Use standardized supervision instruments (e.g., CTS; Young & Beck, 1980)
Session process
Take an empirical stance with therapist (finding out what works)
Utilize guided discovery and Socratic questioning
Utilize experiential exercises and learning experiments
Take a collaborative approach
Address the therapist's interpersonal issues in supervision and personal issues that interfere with therapy
Identify therapist's maladaptive beliefs about therapy

supervision. Indeed, these key texts were cited most frequently in a survey of practicing CBT supervisors (Townend, Iannetta, & Freeston, 2002) and can be seen as templates for best practices in CBT supervision, setting forth the unique and fundamental characteristics of CBT supervision. In particular, they emphasized the strong parallels between the overall structure of a CBT session and the closely related framework for supervision, thereby providing scaffolding for the structural elements of a supervision session that can be clearly delineated (see Table 24.1).

Liese and Beck (1997) identify key shared elements between psychotherapy and supervision sessions including a check-in, a bridge to the last session, setting the current session agenda, prioritizing and working on problems presented by the supervisee, using capsule summaries throughout the session, assigning homework, and providing specific detailed feedback. Other critical features identified include consistent adherence to setting session structure; the use of fundamental CBT tools such as Socratic questioning and guided empiricism; using homework assignments; the emphasis on collaboration; routine use of recorded sessions of therapy; use of standardized instruments to ascertain supervisee competence; and an underpinning cognitive conceptualization model that drives interventions in both supervision and psychotherapy. Finally, Liese and Beck challenge some common misconceptions of cognitive therapy, perhaps reflecting the still dominant cultural zeitgeist of dynamic therapies at the time of their review. They emphasized the following corrective

Table 24.2 Definition of CBT supervision.

CBT supervision can be defined as clinical supervision which meets the general definition (Milne, 2007), and which has the following distinctive emphases:

1. Has a structured agenda, as per cognitive therapy
2. Takes an active, pragmatic, and problem-oriented approach to enhance the learning process
3. Makes primary use of cognitive case conceptualization, through case discussion (i.e., symbolic learning) and diagrammatic CBT formulations (i.e., iconic learning)
4. Uses cognitive therapy techniques to teach wherever appropriate, especially Socratic questioning, guided discovery, educational role-play, and behavioral rehearsal with corrective feedback (i.e., enactive learning)
5. Is collaborative
6. Attends to personal and interpersonal dynamics affecting therapy and supervision (e.g., discuss supervisee's automatic thoughts), insofar as these affect therapy (i.e., not for the therapist's personal growth/development: for therapy fidelity)
7. Teaches evidence-based procedures
8. Makes use of therapy tapes to assesses and enhance competence, ideally using psychometric tools (e.g., the CTS)
9. Utilizes empirically supported methods, and makes use of psychometric tools to monitor the supervisee's clinical effectiveness, using patient's responses for corrective feedback, and so on (e.g., the Beck Depression Inventory).

Note. Developed in collaboration with Derek L. Milne.

themes: eschewing a simplified, mechanistic view; the importance of a developmental historical understanding of the client's problems; the value of the therapeutic alliance; and the vital role of interpersonal factors and emotions in psychotherapy.

In summary, these original accounts of CBT supervision provided a roadmap picturing session structure and key elements of supervision, thereby offering practitioners an explicit framework for supervision. CBT supervision is clearly differentiated from other psychotherapy-based supervision models. For example, the emphasis on direct observation and routine review of complete recorded sessions as well as utilizing standardized rating scales of competence is entirely distinctive to CBT supervision. CBT supervision as a highly structured, agenda-driven procedure poses a sharp contrast to psychodynamic, humanistic–existential, and integrative accounts of supervision, which focus almost exclusively on process-oriented and interpersonal elements of supervision (Boswell, Nelson, Nordberg, McAleavey, & Castonguay, 2010; Farber, 2010; Sarnat, 2010). (See Table 24.2 for a definition of CBT supervision.) This clear delineation of the CBT supervision model promotes adherence in dissemination and implementation efforts: in order to improve adherence, supervisors must attend to the prescribed elements of CBT supervision and omit or minimize the proscribed elements.

The integration of competencies within CBT supervision

Taken together, key elements of CBT supervision identified above – a well-defined structure and attention to directly observing the trainee using standardized rating scales to assess supervisee competence – set the stage for the evolution of CBT supervision toward a competency-based model. Direct observation and objective assessment of outcomes is consistent with a competency-based model that assumes a "criterion-based conceptualization and assessment" where objective standards can be applied (Falender et al., 2004, p. 77). This approach can be distinguished from a purely normative ranking system in which trainees are simply compared with each other without regard to any objective standard. This reconceptualization of supervision demands clear specification of the elements of supervision, a set of well-defined and replicable standards, and objective measurement of outcomes.

The next step in the maturational process of CBT supervision was aided by parallel developments in the broader evolution of supervision that established a competency-based framework setting forth specific supervision competencies and recognizing supervision itself as a core professional competency (Falender et al., 2004). Competency-based supervision has been defined as "an approach that explicitly identifies the knowledge, skills, and values that are assembled to form a clinical competency and develops learning strategies and evaluation procedures to meet criterion referenced competence standards in keeping with evidence-based practices and requirements of the local clinical setting" (Falender & Shafranske, 2007, p. 233). This new approach to supervision presented important challenges to a field that had taken a rather lackadaisical approach to training supervisors. Falender et al. (2004) note that "the majority of clinicians have not received formal training and supervision in this area of competence" (p. 774). This reframing of clinical supervision as a complex, competency-based task provided a corrective measure aimed at increasing attention paid to supervision as a key component of effective training (Watkins, 1997). Falender et al. set the research, assessment, and clinical training agenda for supervision by noting that "direct observation of supervision (e.g., videotape, audiotape) was deemed another excellent way to assess competence" (p. 780). I will return later to the important question of how well this agenda has been addressed in the intervening decade.

While providing an explicit, well-differentiated model for supervision, one of the inherent weaknesses in the first stage of dissemination of CBT supervision was over-reliance on a psychotherapy-based, reflexive model. This fashioning of supervision utilizing a model based on cognitive therapy served to obscure or minimize the unique features and tasks of supervision: developmentally focused training, ethical and gatekeeping dimensions, summative feedback, and attention to the organizational context. Newman (2010) addressed some of these problems by repositioning CBT supervision within a competency-based framework, drawing on Rodolfa et al.'s (2005) cube model, addressing foundational, functional, and developmental dimensions of supervision. Kaslow et al. (2009) had earlier identified foundational competencies, cross-cutting professional practice in all functional areas including supervision: "professionalism, reflective practice, scientific knowledge and methods, relationships, individual and cultural diversity, ethical and legal standards and policy, and interdisciplinary systems" (p. S28). Newman (2010) emphasized the relational and ethical aspects of supervision, balancing the difficult tasks of creating a safe environment for optimal learning and serving as professional gatekeepers with an ethical obligation to protect the client and the public. He also broadened the base of earlier reviews by including a much stronger emphasis on the importance of diversity and cultural factors as a key foundational competency in supervisory practice. Importantly, he also reiterated the vital role of direct observation and systematic ratings using the Cognitive Therapy Scale (CTS; Young & Beck, 1980).

By repositioning CBT supervision squarely in a competency-based model, Newman (2010) made way for a critical third stage of development where purely narrative accounts of CBT supervision could be informed by empirically derived supervision and training methods. Initial efforts at defining the competencies of CBT supervision lacked an explicit set of procedures that could be specified and replicated and a clear scientific foundation based on empirical research identifying the underlying competencies associated with effective training and supervision. While addressing competencies in CBT supervision, Newman's review can be seen as transitional in that it provides more of an outline for conducting cognitive therapy supervision than a blueprint or an operationalizable checklist. In order to clear the way for further development of supervisory practice in CBT, there was a need to define the underlying competencies specific to CBT supervision in a manner that could lead to objective and reliable measurement. I have noted elsewhere (Reiser & Milne, 2012) the tendency toward addressing key elements of CBT supervision in a broadly descriptive, discursive manner that falls short of identifying explicit and clear procedures that can be measured and replicated. If we compare these accounts of CBT supervision with the same scientific standard that has been applied in clinical trials of CBT, the following elements are absent: clearly and explicitly defined procedures in a manualized format so that fidelity to the model can be established; a reliable method of characterizing supervisory; and demonstrations of the effectiveness of supervision on trainee learning and client outcomes.

The Current Picture

Redefining the competencies of CBT supervision

The international trend toward a competency-based conceptualization of clinical supervision over the past 10 years has been a fundamental driver in the continuing evolution of clinical supervision. Competency-based statements and models for supervisory practice have become increasingly refined with the potential to define and operationalize components of supervision in a very specific and explicit manner (Falender & Shafranske, 2004; Fouad et al., 2009; IAPT Education and Training Group, 2011; Gonsalvez & Milne, 2010; Kaslow et al., 2004). This development has enormous implications for constructing empirically supported supervision training models; establishing standards for entry level and advanced supervisors; establishing effective methods of evaluating supervisors' competence and appropriate continuing professional development requirements; and, finally, for improving overall supervision, training, and dissemination efforts.

In a final critical stage of development in the competency-based model, Roth and Pilling (2007, 2008b) created an empirically derived competency-based framework for supervision. This approach was founded on an initial report commissioned by the Improving Access to Psychological Therapies (IAPT) program (Roth & Pilling, 2007). The authors collated the underlying competencies associated with CBT through a review of effective treatments delivered in clinical trials. This approach, extending the earlier Falender et al. (2004) consensus statement on competency-based supervision, takes forward a "criterion-based conceptualization and assessment" (p. 771) founded on objective external standards (versus a normative approach that looks at what therapists/supervisors are doing in practice) and sets the stage for a new empirically supported competency-based model of supervision.

Roth and Pilling (2008a) specified several levels of supervisory competence including generic supervision competencies, specific supervision competencies, applications of supervision to specific theoretical models, and metacompetencies. Generic competencies are cross-cutting features common to all types of supervision regardless of the theory specific model. Specific supervision competencies identify supervisory tasks common to all theoretical domains. Model specific supervision competencies differentiate the unique characteristics of supervision within different theoretical models. Metacompetencies include higher order decision-making and clinical reasoning skills, nonspecific superordinate capabilities that are the hallmark of highly competent supervisors of all orientations.

The IAPT competency model, although intended to be generically applicable to multiple theoretical orientations, also incorporates the standard elements of CBT supervision defined in earlier works (Liese & Beck, 1997; Padesky, 1996). Some of the methods espoused in earlier CBT supervision and training models, especially the use of direct observation in assessing supervisee competence and the focus on the assessment of therapy process and outcome through standardized rating scales, are well adapted to this new framework. The IAPT framework also provides additional important emphasis on several areas absent from earlier discussions of CBT-specific supervisory competence (Liese & Beck, 1997; Newman, 2010; Padesky, 1996). In particular, there is a clearer and more explicit emphasis on underlying adult learning theories and educational principles. The development of new knowledge occurs within an experiential learning framework where iterative cycles of new ideas, opportunities to practice, reflecting on experience in applying this new learning to future work proceed toward a deepening of the trainee's knowledge base. There is also a more direct emphasis on methods of facilitating learning that have strong empirical support, specifically the use of role-play, rehearsal, modeling, and feedback. These additional empirically supported features are summarized in Table 24.3.

Challenges in the implementation of CBT supervision and training

These trends toward specifying the competencies of CBT supervision have served to highlight ongoing weaknesses and deficiencies in the actual practice of CBT supervision. Now, there is a pressing need to further operationalize CBT supervision competencies in a concrete and specific fashion to construct an empirically supported set of training guidelines. In some ways, supervision has languished as a "blackbox" condition in professional clinical training and clinical trials that has remained poorly defined. In their review of therapist training and supervision in 27 randomized clinical trials, Roth, Pilling, and Turner (2010) noted that training and supervision conditions have not been systematically reported in a consistent manner. The authors suggest a minimum set of standards for reporting on training and supervision in clinical trials (p. 297). They conclude their review: "What emerges from this review

Table 24.3 Development of CBT supervision framework: Moving towards a clearer empirical basis.

Element of supervision	*Liese and Beck (1997)*	*Roth and Pilling (2008a)*
Structure for CBT supervision prioritizing agenda-setting	x	x
Use of direct observation, review of tapes	x	x
Use of standardized rating scales	x	x
Assigns and reviews homework	x	x
Teaches individual case conceptualization	x	x
Collaborative and addresses supervisory relationship and related interpersonal issues	x	x
Takes an empirical stance in determining "what works" (Use of Socratic questioning, "collaborative empiricism," guided discovery)	x	x
Competency-based framework empirically derived from clinical trials		x
Explicit use of underlying adult learning theories and educational principles – experiential learning framework		x
Emphasis on close monitoring and provision of specific, corrective, and detailed feedback		x
Facilitating learning using a range of empirically supported methods (including observation, role-play, rehearsal, and modeling)		x
Use of session-by-session client outcome measures		x
Importance of culture and working with differences		x

is a picture of the major investment in training and supervision made by researchers in high-quality trials. Therapists are. . . . supervised intensively, and monitored closely, usually on the basis of tape-recordings" (p. 296). They conclude: "but if it is the case that client outcomes are enhanced by matching levels of supervision and training to those available in clinical trials then this needs to be recognized in the commissioning of routine clinical services" (p. 298).

In theory, practicing CBT supervisors now have a clear set of guidelines and a framework for improving the clinical practice of supervision by incorporating empirically supported practices. In actual practice, it appears that supervisors in the real world do not routinely or consistently use a number of empirically supported methods. For example, in a survey of CBT supervisors in the United Kingdom, a majority of very experienced CBT practitioners were not routinely using practices such as video or audiotaping, direct observation, and use of role-play and enactive methods (Townend et al., 2002; Townend, Iannetta, Freeston, & Hayes, 2007). Surprisingly, only 60% of practitioners surveyed indicated that they used agenda-setting in supervision. Agenda-setting linked to goal-setting in supervision has been a distinguishing, critical, and well-supported element of CBT supervisory practice established in the original account of Liese and Beck (1997) almost 15 years ago. Milne (2008) has

Table 24.4 Signs of supervisor drift (derived in part from Townend et al., 2007).

Poorly structured or unstructured supervision sessions
Limited use of a supervision contract with explicit learning goals
No well-defined learning agenda within sessions
Excessive reliance on symbolic methods, case conceptualization, and case discussion
Low levels of active experiential learning, over-reliance on teaching, directing
Limited use of homework
Lack of direct observation utilizing audio- or videotapes
Poverty of enactive learning methods utilized in the session (role-play, rehearsal, and feedback)
None or limited use of routine clinical outcomes monitoring
None or limited use of objective evaluation methods – use of adherence competence rating instruments (CTS)
Failure to use a range of methods to provide accurate and constructive feedback
Not explicitly addressing culture and issues of difference in the supervisory relationship

also documented continuing poor fidelity between empirical accounts of CBT supervision and actual practice, noting several critical areas (agenda-setting, structuring, review of therapy tapes, use of role-plays, eliciting feedback, and using standardized assessments of competence) where adherence appears to be especially weak.

Therapist drift linked presumably to poor quality or ineffective supervision has been noted as a significant problem even among experienced practitioners who espouse adherence to an empirically supported CBT model of treatment (Brosan, Reynolds, & Moore, 2006; Reiser & Milne, 2012; Townend et al., 2007; Waller, Stringer, & Meyer, 2012). Table 24.4 summarizes some of the main problems that have been identified in terms of poor fidelity to the model. As noted by Roth et al. (2010) in their review of effective clinical trials, routine psychotherapy services, if they are to be effective, require similarly intensive levels of training and supervision often absent in the design, implementation, and planning of services. Therefore, proper ongoing supervision with high fidelity to the model is inextricably linked to providing effective services and improving client outcomes.

In an effort to address standardizing supervisory training, Milne and Dunkerley (2009) developed a set of manualized guidelines with graded recommendations as to the level of empirical support modeled along the lines of the National Institute for Clinical Excellence (NICE).

Milne and Dunkerley (2010) described the development and evaluation of these guidelines, which included a systematic review of the evidence, a theoretical model for clinical supervision, and the use of an expert reference group of key stakeholders to provide ongoing evaluation and consensus on the scope, content, and utility of the guidelines. In a second study, Culloty, Milne, and Sheikh (2010) then evaluated the use of these standardized training guidelines in a training workshop of supervisors in terms of the Borelli et al. (2005) fidelity model. They examined the design of the supervision program (model), training of supervisors (adherence to the model), delivery of supervisor training, receipt of training, and enactment (transfer, generalization, learning impact).

Best Practices in CBT Supervision

Overall, since the publication of the *Handbook of Psychotherapy Supervision* (Watkins, 1997), CBT has advanced and broadened its position considerably as a well-recognized and empirically supported treatment for a wide range of problems and disorders (Butler, Chapman, Forman, & Beck, 2006). A number of large-scope, high-visibility national programs are currently under way involving training, dissemination, and implementation of cognitive behavioral treatment methods on an unprecedented scale (Clark et al., 2009; Karlin, Brown, Trockel, Cunning, & Zeiss, 2012). These projects seek to expand the dissemination and implementation of evidence-based treatments and have received significant governmental support and funding (McHugh & Barlow, 2010). It appears that a new era has dawned for CBT, in terms of increased demand and broad acceptance by governmental agencies and insurance companies. Underlying this support is a compelling rationale as to the cost-effectiveness of properly conducted psychotherapy accompanied by appropriate levels of ongoing supervision. Given this plethora of exciting developments in the evolution, acceptance, and dissemination of CBT, CBT supervision now occupies an even more central position in assuring that effective, high-quality treatments are delivered on an ever broader scale. This new scaling up of training and supervision programs itself presents substantial and complex problems in terms of future large-scale and cross-cultural dissemination efforts.

How can CBT supervision best adapt itself to some of the challenges noted earlier, especially in the context of the need for rapid development of new training programs? What are the optimal problem-solving strategies to address future development? Having formulated some of the weaknesses and deficiencies in the evolving model of CBT supervision, in the following section I attempt to summarize what can be learned from empirical reviews of supervision and training in order to enhance the actual practice of CBT supervision. There are risks to taking guidance based solely on an empirical review of what is known about effective supervision practices. Roth and Pilling (2008a) clearly note the need for "integrating empirical findings with professional consensus" (p. 6). Published studies must still be considered preliminary, incomplete, and subject to consistent reevaluation. However, ignoring the available empirical data risks falling into a kind of nihilistic antiscientific view where all practice is based on oral traditions and we continue to supervise as we were supervised without regard to any objective data or science.

A review of the evidence on effective supervision and training practices

While Ellis and Ladany (1997) criticized research on supervision due to limitations in terms of design and methodology, there have been a number of studies that can provide guidance about effective supervisory and training practices. Milne and James (2000) systematically reviewed 28 methodologically sound studies where supervision was manipulated as a variable. They noted that a range of training techniques were utilized but that there was a consistent focus on goal-setting, close observation of the trainee using audiotapes, and the use of enactive methods including modeling, behavioral rehearsal, and corrective feedback. Milne and James' review has been critiqued as having limited validity and generalizability problems because of the preponderance of studies involving individuals with learning disabilities (Roth & Pilling, 2008a). A follow-up review comparing CBT supervisory practices culled from empirical studies (Milne et al., 2010) with theoretically derived accounts of CBT supervision (Liese & Beck, 1997; Padesky, 1996) identified several opportunities for improvements in practice, including "setting an agenda for supervision, using audio–video tapes, utilizing multimodal methods of teaching including experiential exercises and learning experiments, and giving feedback to the therapist" (p. 287). This review noted significant heterogeneity in supervisory and training methods and surprising deficits in terms of competencies that were identified infrequently ("clinical reasoning, reflective practice, appropriately collaborative and supportive affective stance toward supervisee" [p. 297]).

These findings are consistent with other reviews of supervision and training practices (Roth et al., 2010; Watkins, 2012) that have noted that effective training involves a rich experiential mix of teaching, modeling, demonstrating, working from treatment manuals and role-play; and, includes a demonstration of competence. Roth and Pilling (2010) concluded that more than 90% of the 27 clinical trials reviewed specifically included recording and monitoring of therapist adherence as well as using standardized measures of competence. A second review of the role of therapist training (Herschell, Kolko, Baumann, & Davis, 2010) concluded that "some methods appear to be more effective in changing knowledge and skill (e.g. multi-component training packages, feedback, consultation, supervision) than others (e.g. reading a treatment manual and attending workshops" (p. 18).

This finding is echoed in a recent review that examined training methods in clinical trials of CBT associated with improved client outcomes (Rakovshik & McManus, 2010). The researchers concluded that better clinical outcomes were associated with higher doses of experiential and interactive training methods involving close adherence monitoring of performance and feedback in addition to didactic and theoretical instruction (not in itself sufficient). Rakovshik and McManus (2010) also addressed the underlying learning model that appeared to best explain the training infrastructure in studies that demonstrated improved clinical outcomes in terms of dosage, order, timing, and sequencing of training. They point to two compelling models of how learning takes place: the use of "scaffolding" to foster the acquisition and development of new skills (consistent with the use of guided discovery and Socratic questioning) and Kolb's (1984) experiential learning theory where learning occurs within iterative cycles of experiencing, reflecting, conceptualizing, and experimenting. Milne, Reiser, and Cliffe (2013) have recently provided data from an $n = 1$ longitudinal study that supports these review findings by demonstrating enhanced learning when utilizing an experiential learning model in supervision (also see Chapter 18, SAGE).

Conclusion

Guidance on CBT supervision has evolved from a collection of narrative reviews to a set of well-defined empirically supported competency statements. Methods of effective training have been formulated based on data from clinical trials where treatment has been shown to improve clinical outcomes. There is now a series of compelling and empirically supported recommendations as to best practices in CBT supervision that can be gleaned from competency sets, systematic reviews of supervision, and reviews of training and supervision in clinical trials that have demonstrated effectiveness. These additional elements of training and supervision have been summarized in Table 24.3. However, the field still lacks a consistent consensus as to the value of fully implementing empirical procedures in the training of supervisors so that adherence and competence can be reliably assessed through direct observation and standardized measures of competence. There is a continuing research–practice gap such that many supervisors provide poorly structured supervision without an explicit learning agenda; fail to utilize effective methods including role-play, behavioral rehearsal, modeling, and feedback; and, finally, of greatest concern, have no reliable method for rating the competence of their supervisees in terms of using either audio- or videotaping, direct observation, or a standardized competence rating scale. In order to address this gap, in the next section, I provide some illustrations of supervision closely linked to empirically supported models of practice.

Supervision vignettes incorporating principles of evidence-based CBT supervision

The following vignettes (the first set directly transcribed from tapes of the author's supervision with a post-doctoral-level psychology student) illustrate key competencies including goal-setting, maintaining the learning agenda in supervision, using experiential learning principles, and addressing culture and issues of difference.

The setting was a university-based doctoral-level training clinic in the United States treating a wide range of complex mental health problems in the community. These supervision sessions were conducted as part of an Institutional Review Board-approved research program examining the impact of telephone-based consultation with a goal of enhancing supervision by using a manualized, evidence-based approach. Consultant feedback was derived from a standardized rating scale of supervisory behaviors (SAGE) in order to enhance standard CBT supervision (Milne, Reiser, & Cliffe, 2013). Feedback to the supervisor was based on review of audiotaped sessions, completion of a competence rating scale (SAGE; Milne & Reiser, 2011), and session-by-session feedback from the supervisee. This approach to supervisory training emphasizes audiotape review, session-based competence rating, and feedback using an experiential learning model (modeling, role-play and rehearsal, and feedback). The underlying model of evidence-based clinical supervision as developed by Derek Milne is described elsewhere (Breese, Boon, & Milne, 2012; Milne, 2009; Milne & Reiser, 2011; Milne, Reiser, Cliffe, Breese, et al., 2011; Milne, Reiser, Cliffe, & Raine, 2011; Milne et al., 2013).

Setting and maintaining the learning agenda in supervision

SUPERVISOR: (After a brief check-in) Let's look at your learning agenda for today's supervision session.

SUPERVISEE: (Referring to a list of written learning outcomes: Milne, 2009, pp. 151–152) So for clients A and B it would be updating you, telling their story, summarizing. . . .

SUPERVISOR: And then after the update what were you hoping to carry away from the session? What are you hoping to learn? [Supervisor emphasizes an explicit leaning agenda, not just general case discussion or case conceptualization – this is more consistent with a well-structured supervision session and the IAPT generic competency "Ability to structure supervision sessions" (Roth & Pilling, 2008a)].

SUPERVISEE: Umm, good question, I guess in terms of your feedback, do you think I should "stay the course," or do you see something else I should be doing?

SUPERVISOR: And by "staying the course," you mean? [Prompts for further clarification, reflection]

SUPERVISEE: I mean just proceeding as I have been going along. . . .

This comment is clarified as referencing the supervisees' work over the past several weeks on becoming more appropriately directive, assertive, and active as a therapist. His counseling skills in the area of listening, attending, emotional attunement to his clients, and empathic responding are excellent, but he has difficulty when more active interventions are required. This discussion is followed by a summary and discussion of two cases and watching a video of a role-play with a client is put on the agenda with the supervisee feeling unsure of how it went and suggesting a role-play with the supervisor to help him technically. (Use of modeling, rehearsal, and enactive techniques; IAPT generic competency: "Ability to incorporate direct observation into supervision"; CBT specific competency area: "An ability to use a range of observational and participative methods [listening to and reviewing audio and video recordings of clinical sessions, role-play, modelling etc.] to develop specific skills in the application of CBT techniques" [Roth & Pilling, 2008a]).

SUPERVISOR: (Reviewing feedback form for past session) You gave me generally high marks except in the "experiencing of feelings" area; and your main feedback was that it was helpful talking about your confidence level on the tape in the session. [Use of observation, reflection, feedback IAPT generic competency: "Ability to use a range of methods to give accurate and constructive feedback" (Roth & Pilling, 2008a, p. 10)] So, if we bridge back to that confidence issue [Bridging back to past session, clarifying the learning agenda], how did that seem to affect your confidence over the past week?

SUPERVISEE: It did seem to carry over.

SUPERVISOR: It did?

SUPERVISEE: Yes, like I felt more confident in the sessions, especially with Client A when we were planning homework for next week. I felt like I was "in the driver's seat," more grounded and like, "OK," more confident.

SUPERVISOR: How do you understand that? [Prompting for more reflection: IAPT generic competency: "Ability to help supervisee's ability to reflect on their work and on the usefulness of supervision: (Roth & Pilling, 2008. p. 10)].

SUPERVISEE: If I hadn't gotten that feedback, it's almost like that "fake it until you make it" thing. OK, I see myself as being confident, like "I can do this, I know that I can do this."

SUPERVISOR: So somehow my validating that you looked confident, like a professional therapist on the tape, helped you get an internal sense of feeling confident and you felt more "I can do this." Is that right? [Note the use of scaffolding and experiential learning principles here.]

SUPERVISEE: Yeah.

SUPERVISOR: (Then moves on to discuss more challenging interventions that the supervisee has been experimenting with that require more confidence and assertiveness) Yes, it's risky to do these experimenting enactments in session as you don't know how they are going to turn out . . .

you have to have more confidence. (IAPT generic competency "Ability to structure supervision sessions" [Roth & Pilling, 2008a]).

Utilizing the experiential learning cycle (Kolb, 1984)

SUPERVISOR: [Starts with a check-in and then reviews supervisee's written feedback from past session, and summarizes] You appreciated the reflection (in last session) of your growing confidence and ability to direct sessions and you felt that this type of discussion was helpful . . . explain more about that to me . . . [Prompts for formulating/reflecting].

SUPERVISEE: So over the past weeks, I've been behaving more directively in sessions and have been able to kind of "take the helm" and I like the fact that we reflected on that . . . actually talking about it makes the learning stick better. . . . I'm doing it and then we are talking about it. [Note elements of conceptualizing, reflecting, planning and practicing learning cycle; IAPT generic competency "Ability to employ educational principles which enhance learning" (Roth & Pilling, 2008a)].

SUPERVISOR: I think that's so true . . . It makes it "sticky" . . . maybe increases self-monitoring in some ways . . .

SUPERVISOR: [Sets learning agenda for session collaboratively] So, where would you like to start, here? What's your clinical agenda today?

SUPERVISEE: I would like to touch base with what we talked about – how I have been more directive and we've been moving things along more, experimenting more so I want to let you know about what's happened with Client A over the past week. It's probably pretty clear from the outcomes questionnaire that he filled out (Outcomes Questionnaire-45: Lambert et al. (1996) that there has been a huge change [Use of clinical outcome measures in each session to track client progress in supervision: IAPT CBT specific competency area: "Monitoring supervisee's work: An ability to use session by session outcome measures to guide the supervision agenda" (Roth & Pilling, 2008a)].

SUPERVISOR: [Reviewing client session outcome measure] Well, there was a huge decrease in his overall distress level! (sounding quite animated)

SUPERVISEE: Exactly!

SUPERVISEE: Well, we have been talking about whether this is due to his antidepressant medication or therapy and I think that this has a lot to do with the therapy – this big drop . . . How our supervision has fed directly into this.

SUPERVISOR: Wow! (sounding very excited and animated) . . . So, just to summarize, Client A had a big drop in his total OQ-45 scores, in his Symptom Distress subscale score (measures distress, anxiety and depressive symptoms) and I think also a big drop on his Interpersonal Relations subscale score (measures interpersonal problems, difficulties and satisfaction with quality of intimate relationships) right? Well, we'll want to talk about that and understand in the context of changes in your behaviour and approach particularly being more directive . . .

SUPERVISEE: Yeah . . .

SUPERVISOR: And presumably more exposing in many ways.

SUPERVISEE: Right, yeah, totally. What he was talking about applied directly to what we have been doing . . .

(Supervisor then returns to agenda setting, making sure that other clients are prioritized appropriately in terms of risk factors and training opportunities before continuing. Three additional clients are briefly discussed focusing on the same theme of the supervisee's level of directiveness in setting up session structure and assigning homework. There is an agreement to use modeling, role-play, feedback, and rehearsal of a specific issue that came up in therapy. Supervisor then summarizes the agenda for the balance of the supervision session prioritizing the theme of being more appropriately directive as a key learning agenda for the session.) [Use of session structuring – modeling appropriate structure and directiveness in supervision; Use of enactive methods to facilitate learning: IAPT CBT specific competency: "An ability to use a range of observational and participative methods (listening to and reviewing audio and video recordings of clinical sessions, role-play, modeling etc.) to develop specific skills in the application of CBT techniques" (Roth & Pilling, 2008)].

SUPERVISOR: So, where should we start here?

SUPERVISEE: With Client A, because it's really exciting! (sounding very animated)

SUPERVISOR: (Summarizes clinically significant changes in client's assessment) You're smiling. [Integrating affective elements to enhance learning]

SUPERVISEE: (Summarizes several of client's improvements in social functioning and reduced avoidance behaviors related to following through on a behavioral activation homework assignment) . . . to be honest it (homework assignment) had a much bigger effect than I anticipated.

SUPERVISOR: You were really surprised.

SUPERVISEE: Exactly (laughing excitedly).

SUPERVISOR: This was an unexpected outcome for him. Tell me a little bit more about how you reviewed the outcome of this behavioral experiment with him . . . I think there's a great opportunity to address some changes in cognitions, core beliefs. Sometime you can do some very nice schema work by asking how the outcome fit with their usual thinking . . . especially if there was a surprise here . . . how does this change your theory? . . . [Prompts for reconceptualizing based on new experiences/experimenting].

SUPERVISEE: (Summarizes discussion with the client)

SUPERVISOR: (Asks supervisee for a summary of supervision discussion up to this point on Client A, use of behavioral activation, supervisee's increased directiveness, and cognitive change) [Structuring, facilitating reflection]. The point we haven't discussed so directly is that you took a more directive approach here . . . you modeled being more directive, more explicit, maybe you were even a little bit pushy in assigning the homework [behavioral activation, behavioral experiments to help client test out predictions related to their social anxiety] . . . so that seemed to be the antecedent for him (the client) pushing the envelope a little bit.

SUPERVISEE: Yeah . . . that's true. I really didn't think of it exactly as modeling.

SUPERVISOR: So, what's your metacognitive conclusion about you and (doing) therapy? How do you think that this might change your beliefs about being a therapist? [Encouraging reflection and reconceptualizing, use of experiential learning model]

SUPERVISEE: (Laughs excitedly) [Note strong affective element associated with new learning] This is a good discussion to have because I really do need to make this stick. I see myself going back to my old ways. This is good . . . in terms of my own learning, the emotions I have when I am faced with a situation of being more directive, I feel like this is going to hurt the client. Oh, I'm going to hurt the client by stepping in and giving them suggestions or homework.

SUPERVISOR: And what's the theory behind that idea – that you're going to hurt the client?

SUPERVISEE: It's more on an emotional level, in terms of my own experience, that I am "stepping on their feet," they're going to be intruded on . . . I want the session to be the clients and the feeling is that they are going to feel invalidated.

SUPERVISOR: They're going to feel intruded on, invalidated . . . it's going to disrupt their sense of autonomy. [Emphasizing underlying affects supporting this belief]

SUPERVISEE: Right, right. Exactly! But then . . . the new learning (laughs very excitedly) [Note powerful affective elements here]

SUPERVISOR: So the old (maladaptive) cognitions are: "It's going to hurt the client, they're going to feel intruded upon, they're going to experience a loss of autonomy" . . . And what feels the worst about this? What's the most powerful part of this (for you)?

SUPERVISEE: Like what's interfering?

SUPERVISOR: As you look at the thoughts, which thought has a big pull – that "I have to be careful and minimize my directiveness."

SUPERVISEE: I think it's the first one – that it will hurt the client. Like it's just this gut feeling that "God, I'm going to hurt them, hurt their feelings, . . ." [Note high levels of affect].

SUPERVISOR: It's just this automatic assumption that whenever you step in it's going to be harmful, hurtful . . . [Summarizing]. If we had to make the new adaptive therapist assumption, what would that be? I can see you have already got it by the look on your face. [Supervisor notes a surprised, amused expression].

SUPERVISEE: Yeah. Like when I'm appropriately directive it helps the client . . . it helps them a lot! (laughs) [Reformulating old belief with high levels of affect]

SUPERVISOR: Isn't that nice! [Emphasizing underlying affects]

SUPERVISEE: (Laughs)Yeah.

SUPERVISOR: [Summarizes, structuring] So, "when I'm appropriately assertive it helps the client a lot."

SUPERVISEE: Yeah, I am just going to have to keep pulling out this (coping) card again and again [Planning, experimenting; Use of coping card with written feedback to enhance learning] just to remind myself that here's this experience . . . this really happened, it happened. Look how his score went way down.

SUPERVISOR: Yeah, so it's really important to have this flexible rule: sometimes it's okay to be assertive, sometimes it's in the client's best interest. [Structuring, summarizing]

SUPERVISEE: Right!

SUPERVISOR: And it certainly may hurt the client if I'm too nondirective.

(The remainder of the session is spent reviewing videotapes related to the client issues discussed earlier.)

The supervisee's written feedback about this session was collected on a structured feedback form (REACTS: Rating of Experiential Learning And Components of Teaching & Supervision; Milne et al., 2012; Wilson, 2007). REACTS is an 11-item paper-and-pencil rating of supervision designed to emphasize the formative aspects of supervision by addressing Kolb's (1984) experiential learning cycle modes of experiencing, reflecting, conceptualizing, experimenting, and planning. This feedback also seemed to confirm the receipt of new knowledge in terms of experiential learning around the theme of appropriate directiveness and assertiveness: "This session definitely covered all the bases. Good balance between planning/trying things out and reflecting. It really feels like things are coming together." The supervisee rated the session highly (5 out of a possible score of 5) in the following areas: "I was able to recognize relevant feelings becoming more self-aware"; "I was able to reflect on events and perceive things more clearly"; and "The supervisor helped me to try things out and to try and solve problems/practice skills."

Cultural competence in CBT supervision

The following vignette illustrates the IAPT competency area: "Ability to help supervisees consider the relevance of issues of difference: to ensure that issues of difference that are relevant to the supervisor and supervisee themselves are included in supervision discussions" (Roth & Pilling, 2008a). The ability to work with differences as a supervisor has been recognized as an important key competency area both in earlier (Falender et al., 2004) and in more recent (Roth & Pilling, 2008a) competency frameworks.

> The main aim of considering issues of difference is to maximise the efficacy of clinical practice for all clients. This is done by helping supervisees to see the potential relevance of difference and to integrate this thinking into their work. This includes – indeed often

> starts from – reflection on the assumptions introduced by the supervisor and supervisee's own experience of difference, whether this be from a "majority" or a "minority" cultural perspective. (Roth & Pilling, 2008)

Iwamasa, Pai, and Sorrocco (2006) note a dearth of CBT specific treatments of multicultural issues in CBT supervision and they affirm that "it is the supervisor's responsibility to address and invite discussion of diversity issues in supervision, much as it is the supervisor's responsibility to train the student in the CBT model" (p. 274).

However, despite agreement on the growing importance of culture and recognizing cultural differences, there is little concrete guidance as to how supervisors might accomplish this goal. Ancis and Ladany (2001, 2010) have proposed a framework for multicultural supervision involving the following domains: personal development, conceptualization, interventions, process, and evaluation. The personal development domain entails both supervisor- and supervisee-focused personal development in the area of openly exploring values, biases, and knowledge about cultural differences as part of the supervision process. Logically, if we are asking our supervisees to be knowledgeable and transparent about the impact of culture on the psychotherapy process, this discussion should also be reflected in a parallel process within supervision itself. Ideally, the supervisor should directly address cultural differences as an integral part of setting up the framework for supervision in the needs assessment and establishment of the learning contract phase (both strongly empirically supported practices; Milne & Dunkerley, 2009). The following questions are useful prompts: How might our cultural differences affect your learning in supervision? What barriers might there be and what opportunities could we find to surmount these barriers? This type of focused questioning offers a sense of open recognition of cultural differences and a model for transparent and open discussion and resolution of problems or issues that might arise.

The following vignette addresses the IAPT competency element: "Ability to foster competence in working with difference" (Roth & Pilling, 2008a) by demonstrating how culture can be woven into the initial framework of supervision as a matter of course.

Vignette: addressing cultural differences in supervision

A 25-year-old female Asian American doctoral psychology student in the third quarter of a first year practicum is being supervised by a European Caucasian American male supervisor in his late 50s.This trainee was transferred from another European Caucasian American male supervisor and had been put on probation with a written warning: she often appeared unprepared, only superficially engaged, and failed to respond to questions in depth. Prior to the first supervision session, all students are asked to review a supervision contract and to reflect on culture, roles, expectations, and preferred learning styles. This student "forgot" her assignment, resulting in a direct and rather challenging discussion of being unprepared – exactly the problem specified in her written performance improvement plan.

In a follow-up session, cultural differences were addressed by initiating a discussion about the supervisor's European American background, the impact of having had immigrant parents in shaping his beliefs, and expectations about the importance of education and learning. As this discussion continued, it became clear that the student, although considering herself (and appearing) highly acculturated in terms of her style and tastes, also retained some important values of her own parents' culture, including deference to authority, a tendency to avoid responding directly to "respected elders," and a proclivity to avoid interpersonal conflict. These cultural values were discussed directly identifying potential strengths and possible obstacles to the student's full participation in CBT supervision.

This open discussion of culture helped the supervisor reconceptualize the student's problems and reframe her tendency toward passivity and deference to authority within a cultural context instead of viewing her as aloof, disinterested, or uninvested in supervision. Supervision was then structured collaboratively to help her become progressively more comfortable with participating, being open, and taking a more assertive stance. In the following three months, the trainee became progressively more outspoken and actively participatory with the result that she was able to advance to her next practicum year on schedule with no further problems.

Improving Cognitive Therapy Supervision: The Way Forward

Standardizing the training of supervisors

Surprisingly, there is no clear agreement on what constitutes an appropriate course of training in terms of content, frequency, or duration in order to establish a minimum level of competence for supervisors (Watkins, 2012). Indeed, recent surveys of graduate psychology programs in the United States have indicated significant disagreement as to key elements of training for supervisors, including only weak endorsement of requiring direct observation with specific feedback (Rings, Genuchi, Hall, Angelo, & Cornish, 2009, p. 143). Overall, there is a dearth of underlying empirical data as to what level, method, and type of training might be required to ensure supervisor competence. Roth et al. (2010) have argued that if treatments in community settings are to be equivalently effective as clinical trials, then comparable training and supervision methods must be considered to establish possible standards for competence.

In fact, this relative neglect for establishing standards for supervisory training within current regulatory and government frameworks is reflected in an extremely wide variance in state, national, and governmental standards. In California, for example, the minimum standard set for psychologists who wish to supervise is a 6-hr workshop repeated every two years. The content, delivery, and quality of these trainings vary wildly. There is no consistent requirement in terms of content (e.g., focus on established competencies, training methods with empirical support). By contrast, the Psychology Board of Australia (2011) is now promulgating a rigorous approved training program for clinical supervisors which identifies a specific set of competencies and includes 7 hours of preparatory self-study, 14 hours of face-to-face instruction, and a series of systematic assessments of supervisory competence over time, including direct observation, review of a tape of supervision, and a short test. In the United Kingdom, the IAPT initiative requires 5–7 days of coursework with didactic training over 6–9 months (Guidance for Commissioning IAPT Supervisor Training, 2011, pp. 2–3). But IAPT guidance falls disappointingly short of requiring direct observation and feedback as a required component of training.

Standardizing assessments of supervisory competence

The underlying empirical research on clinical supervision presents only a modestly supportive picture in demonstrating substantial training effects closely tied to client outcomes (Ellis, Ladany, Krengel, & Schult, 1996; Milne & James, 2000; Milne et al., 2010; Roth & Pilling, 2008a; Watkins, 2012). Reviews of controlled studies have indicated that the provision of supervision provides some positive benefits for trainees in terms of achieving higher levels of competence, skills, self-awareness, and self-efficacy (Mannix et al., 2006; Wheeler & Richards, 2007). Few studies have been designed to link supervision directly to client outcomes (Watkins, 2011). An exception would be Bambling, King, Raue, Schweitzer, and Lambert (2006), which compared clinical outcomes associated with two forms of supervision (problem-solving and alliance focused) and determined that both types of supervision were effective versus no supervision, in terms of reducing symptoms of depression and in improving the therapeutic alliance.

Dual problems that have hampered the development of supervision as an empirical science are the limited degree to which competency sets actually provide operationalizable details and the slow implementation of adequate technologies to observe and measure the provision of supervision. Nearly 15years ago, Watkins (1998) called for the urgent development of supervision manuals comparable to the development of psychotherapy treatment manuals in order to specify training content and standardize the training of supervisors. While the IAPT supervisory competence framework is explicitly based on competencies extracted from clinical trials where CBT has demonstrated effectiveness, data from the results of this model, confirming that training in supervision competencies is indeed effective, is still preliminary (Clark et al., 2009).

Closing this gap in determining fidelity in supervisory practices is an important continuing problem because, as noted previously, surveys of real-world practice continue to demonstrate relatively poor adherence to best practices as defined in recent competency sets (Milne, 2008; Townend et al., 2007). In their 2007 survey of supervision techniques in a UK study of accredited CBT therapists with a 47% response rate, Townend et al. (2007) determined that only a minority of practitioners were utilizing role-play (32%), video review (28%), or direct observation (11%). Only 60% of practitioners reported using agenda-setting, a foundational element of both CBT therapy and supervision identified in the earliest texts on CBT supervision.

While there has been a trend toward increasing specification of the elements of supervisory competence, measurement of these specific competencies has lagged behind. Lichtenberg et al. (2007) noted early on in the development of competencies in professional psychology that there are significant challenges in the assessment of competencies due to the very complex nature of the construct of competency itself. By definition, competency entails a sophisticated integration of knowledge skills and attitudes in the performance of a complex professional task. Our abilities to assess knowledge tend to be more refined than our ability to assess skills and attitudes (Lichtenberg et al., 2007):

> More importantly, psychology does not currently have methods to readily or reliably assess the integration of knowledge, skills, and attitudes in the performance of professional functions that comprise competence (e.g., professional judgment, scientific mindedness, relationship skills, team work, internalized ethical orientation, reflective practice/self-awareness, openness to learning, and commitment to professional growth).Yet it is this integration that reflects the construct of competence. (Lichtenberg et al., 2007, p. 476)

Furthermore, many commonly used assessment measures (such as multiple choice tests and paper-and-pencil assessments, and course work) lack fidelity and are not relevant to assessing the complex skills required for competent practice: "Assessment techniques typically used do not involve the observation of the persons being evaluated in simulated or actual situations, do not include feedback from patients/clients or peers, and are not indicative of clinical outcomes" (Lichtenberg et al., 2007).

While the IAPT program has addressed some of these specification and assessment issues, procedures for implementing sound measurements of supervisory competence to evaluate training are still in an early stage of development. More than 15 years ago, Watkins (1998) observed: ". . . one of the most pressing needs for psychotherapy supervision in the next century remains the development and establishment of reliable, valid criterion measures to guide supervision research" (p. 94). In a more recent review, Milne and Reiser (2011) surveyed the limited domain of instruments available that have significant utility in terms of reliably observing and recording supervisory competence. However, there are promising developments under way in this area in terms of approaches to measuring supervisory competence (Milne, Reiser, Cliffe, Breese, et al., 2011; Milne, Reiser, Cliffe, & Raine, 2011; Milne et al., 2013; also see Chapter 18).

Future Directions for CBT Supervision

In this review of the current status of supervision in cognitive and behavioral therapies, several important challenges have been identified in terms of the ongoing evolution of CBT supervision. I began by noting the distinctive grounding of CBT supervision on the firm foundation of the methods of cognitive therapy (Liese & Beck, 1997; Padesky, 1996). In the intervening period, significant developments have occurred in several areas including: more fully operationalizing broad competency statements to make them more CBT-specific and user-friendly; providing a comprehensive underlying theory of adult learning to complement the application of therapy principles to better underpin supervision; incorporating empirically supported teaching methods to make supervision more effective; creating a CBT-relevant developmental framework that addresses the staging of supervision, based on the developmental level of the trainee; and increasing attention to the role of culture in supervisory practice.

Finally, there are significant challenges to dissemination efforts in terms of the need to expand training and consultation more broadly and to look to new training models and technologies to assist in this effort. Several national and regional programs have utilized innovative methods for training at a distance (Karlin et al., 2012;

McHugh & Barlow, 2010), but there is no doubt that training remains a hands-on, labor-intensive process and that alternative strategies and innovation via the internet are still in the early stages of development. The IAPT model has provided a blueprint for training and dissemination efforts aimed at qualifying trainers and supervisors that addresses the scope, costs, and resource requirements of a national-level training program. Bennett-Levy, Richards, and Farrand (2010) have developed an innovative training model for "low-intensity" practitioners (or non-mental health specialists) to provide greater access to evidence-based services. With the expansion of effective treatments to new populations, the scope of further training efforts that will be required to assure adequate numbers of fully qualified supervisors in order to support these evidence-based treatments is rather daunting. However, the developments in CBT supervision noted earlier indicate that we may now be positioned for a next stage of dissemination utilizing competency-based supervisory training that makes use of methods that are empirically supported, that offers a standardized curriculum, and that is subject to ongoing evaluation.

References

Ancis, J. R., & Ladany, N. (2001). A multicultural framework for counseling supervision. In L. J. Bradley & N. Ladany (Eds.), *Counselor supervision: Principles, process, and practice* (3rd ed., pp. 63–90), Philadelphia, PA: Brunner-Routledge.

Ancis, J. R., & Ladany, N. (2010). A multicultural framework for counselor supervision. In N. Ladany& L. J. Bradley (Eds.), *Counselor supervision* (4th ed., pp. 53–94), New York, NY: Routledge.

Bambling, M., King, R., Raue, P., Schweitzer, R., & Lambert, W. (2006). Clinical supervision: Its influence on client rated working alliance and client symptom reduction in the brief treatment of major depression. *Psychotherapy Research*, *16*(3), 317–331. doi:10.1080/10503300500268524

Bennett-Levy, J., Richards, D. A., & Farrand, P. (2010). Low intensity CBT interventions: A revolution in mental health care. In J. Bennett-Levy, D.V Richards, P. Farrand, H. Christensen, & K. Griffiths (Eds.), *Oxford guide to low intensity CBT interventions* (pp. 3–18), Oxford, UK: Oxford University Press.

Borelli, B., Sepinwall, D., Ernst, D., Bellg, A.J., Czajkowski, S., Breger, R., . . . Orwig, D. (2005). A new tool to assess treatment fidelity and evaluation of treatment fidelity across 10 years of health behavior research. *Journal of Consulting and Clinical Psychology*, *73*, 852–860. doi:10.1037/0022-006X.73.5.852

Boswell, J. F., Nelson, D. L., Nordberg, S. S., McAleavey, A. A., & Castonguay, L. G. (2010). Competency in integrative psychotherapy: Perspectives on training and supervision. *Psychotherapy: Theory, Research, Practice, Training*, *47*(1), 3–11. doi:10.1037/a0018848

Breese, L., Boon, A., & Milne, D. (2012). Detecting excellent episodes in clinical supervision: A case-study, comparing two approaches. *The Clinical Supervisor*, *31*(2), 121–137. doi :10.1080/07325223.2013.730012

Brosan, L., Reynolds, S., & Moore, R. G. (2006). Factors associated with competence in cognitive therapists. *Behavioural and Cognitive Psychotherapy*, *35*, 179–190. doi:10.1017/S1352465806003304

Butler, A. C., Chapman, J. E., Forman, E. M., & Beck, A. T. (2006). The empirical status of cognitive-behavioral therapy: A review of meta-analyses. *Clinical Psychology Review*, *26*, 17–31. doi:10.1016/j.cpr.2005.07.003

Clark, D. M., Layard, R., Smithies, R., Richards, D. A., Suckling, R., & Wright, B. (2009). Improving access to psychological therapy: Initial evaluation of two UK demonstration sites. *Behaviour Research and Therapy, 47*, 910–920. doi:10.1016/j.brat.2009.07.010

Culloty, T., Milne, D. H., & Sheikh, A. I. (2010). Evaluating the training of clinical supervisors: A pilot study using the fidelity framework. *The Cognitive Behaviour Therapist, 3*, 132–144. doi:10.1017/S1754470X10000139

Ellis, M. V., Ladany, N., Krengel, M., & Schult, D. (1996). Clinical supervision research from 1981 to 1993: A methodological critique. *Journal of Counseling Psychology, 43*(1), 35.

Ellis, M. V., & Ladany, N. (1997). Inferences concerning supervisees and clients in clinical supervision: An integrative review. In C. E. Watkins, Jr. (Ed.), *Handbook of psychotherapy supervision* (pp. 447–507), New York, NY: Wiley.

Falender, C., Cornish, J. A. E., Goodyear, R., Hatcher, R., Kaslow, N. J., Leventhal, G., . . . Grus, C. (2004). Defining competencies in psychology supervision: A consensus statement. *Journal of Clinical Psychology, 60*, 771–785. doi:10.1002/jclp.20013

Falender, C. A., & Shafranske, E. P. (2004). *Clinical supervision: A competency-based approach* (pp. 37–58). Washington, DC: American Psychological Association.

Falender, C. A., & Shafranske, E. P. (2007). Competence in competency-based supervision practice: Construct and application. *Professional Psychology, Research and Practice, 36*(3), 232–240. doi:10.1037/0735-7028.38.3.232

Falender, C. A., & Shafranske, E. P. (2012). The importance of competency-based clinical supervision and training in the 21st century: Why bother? *Journal of Contemporary Psychotherapy, 42*, 5–13. doi:10.1037/0735-7028.38.3.232

Farber, E. W. (2010). Humanistic–existential psychotherapy competencies and the supervisory process. *Psychotherapy: Theory, Research, Practice, Training, 47*(1), 28–34. doi:10.1037/a0018847

Fouad, N. A., Grus, C. L., Hatcher, R. L., Kaslow, N. J., Hutchings, P. S., Madson, M., . . . Crossman, R. E. (2009). Competency benchmarks: A model for the understanding and measuring of competence in professional psychology across training levels. *Training and Education in Professional Psychology, 3*(4 Suppl.), S5. doi:10.1037/a0015832

Gonsalvez, C. J., & Milne, D. L. (2010). Clinical supervisor training in Australia: A review of current problems and possible solutions. *Australian Psychologist, 45*, 233–242. doi:10.1080/00050067.2010.512612

Herschell, A. D., Kolko, D. J., Baumann, B. L., & Davis, A. C. (2010). The role of therapist training in the implementation of psychosocial treatments: A review and critique with recommendations. *Clinical Psychology Review, 30*(4), 448–466. doi:10.1016/j.cpr.2010.02.005

IAPT Education and Training Group (2011). *Guidance for Commissioning IAPT Supervisor Training* (Revised 2011). Retrieved from http://www.iapt.nhs.uk/silo/files/guidancefor-commissioning-iapt-supervisor-training-revised-2011.pdf

Iwamasa, G. Y., Pai, S. M., & Sorrocco, K. H. (2006). Multicultural cognitive-behavioral supervision. In P. A. Hays & G. Y. Iwamasa (Eds.), *Culturally responsive cognitive-behavioral therapy* (pp. 267–281), Washington, DC: American Psychological Association.

Karlin, B. E., Brown, G. K., Trockel, M., Cunning, D., & Zeiss, A. M. (2012). National dissemination of cognitive behavioural therapy for depression in the Department of Veterans Affairs health care system: Therapist and patient level outcomes. *Journal of Consulting and Clinical Psychology, 80*(5), 707–718. doi:10.1037/a0029328

Kaslow, N. J., Borden, K. A., Collins, F. L., Jr., Forrest, L., Illfelder-Kaye, J., & Nelson, P. D. (2004). Competencies conference: Future directions in education and credentialing in professional psychology. *Journal of Clinical Psychology, Special Issue, 60*, 699–712. doi:10.1002/jclp.20016

Kaslow, N. J., Grus, C. L., Campbell, L. F., Fouad, N. A., Hatcher, R. L., & Rodolfa, E. R. (2009). Competency assessment toolkit for professional psychology. *Training and Education in Professional Psychology*, *3*(4 Suppl.), S27–S45. doi:10.1037/a0015833

Kolb, D. A. (1984). *Experiential learning: Experience as the source of learning and development* (Vol. 1). Englewood Cliffs, NJ: Prentice-Hall.

Lambert, M. J., Hansen, N.B., Umphress, V., Lunnen, K., Okiishi, J., Burlingame, G.M., & Reisenger, C.W (1996). Administration and Scoring Manual for the OQ-45.2.

Lichtenberg, J. W., Portnoy, S. M., Bebeau, M. J., Leigh, I. W., Nelson, P. D., Rubin, N. J., . . . Kaslow, N. J. (2007). Challenges to the assessment of competence and competencies. *Professional Psychology, Research and Practice*, *38*(5), 474–478. doi: 10.1037/0735-7028.38.5.474

Liese, B. S., & Beck, J. S. (1997). Cognitive therapy supervision. In C. E. Watkins (Ed.), *Handbook of psychotherapy supervision* (pp. 114–133).New York, NY: Wiley.

Mannix, K. A., Blackburn, I. V., Garland, A., Gracie, J., Moorey, S., Reid, B., . . . Scott, J. (2006). Effectiveness of brief training in cognitive behaviour therapy techniques for palliative care practitioners. *Palliative Medicine*, *20*, 579–584. doi:10.1177/0269216306071058

McHugh, R. K., & Barlow, D. H. (2010). The dissemination and implementation of evidence-based psychological treatments: A review of current efforts. *The American Psychologist*, *65*, 73–84. doi:10.1037/a0018121

Milne, D. L. (2008). CBT supervision: From reflexivity to specialisation. *Behavioural and Cognitive Psychotherapy*, *36*, 779–786. doi:10.1017/S1352465808004773

Milne, D. L. (2009). *Evidence-based clinical supervision: Principles and practice*. Chichester, UK: BPS/Blackwell.

Milne, D. L., & Dunkerley, C. (2009). *Evidence-based clinical supervision guidelines*. Unpublished manuscript.

Milne, D. L., & Dunkerley, C. (2010). Towards evidence-based clinical supervision: The development and evaluation of four CBT guidelines. *The Cognitive Behaviour Therapist*, *3*, 43–57. doi:10.1017/S1754470X10000048

Milne, D. L., & James, I. A. (2000). A systematic review of effective cognitive-behavioural supervision. *The British Journal of Clinical Psychology*, *39*(2), 111–127. doi:10.1348/014466500163149

Milne, D. L., Leck, C., James, I., Wilson, M., Procter, R., & Ramm, L. (2012). High fidelity in clinical supervision research. In I. Fleming & L.Steen (Eds.), *Supervision and Clinical Psychology* (pp. 142–158), London, UK: Routledge.

Milne, D. L., & Reiser, R. (2011). Observing competence in CBT supervision: A systematic review of the available instruments. *The Cognitive Behaviour Therapist*, *4*, 89–100. doi:10.1017/S1754470X11000067

Milne, D. L., Reiser, R., Aylott, H., Dunkerley, C., Fitzpatrick, H., & Wharton, S. (2010). The systematic review as an empirical approach to improving CBT supervision. *International Journal of Cognitive Therapy*, *3*, 278–294. doi:10.1521/ijct.2010.3.3.278

Milne, D. L., Reiser, R. P., & Cliffe, T. (2013). An N = 1 evaluation of enhanced CBT supervision. *Behavioural and Cognitive Psychotherapy*, *41*(2), 210–220. doi:10.1017/S1352465812000434

Milne, D. L., Reiser, R. P., Cliffe, T., Breese, L., Boon, A., Raine, R., & Scarratt, P. (2011). A qualitative comparison of cognitive-behavioural and evidence-based clinical supervision.*The Cognitive Behaviour Therapist*, *4*(4), 152–166. doi:10.1017/S1754470X1100009

Milne, D. L., Reiser, R., Cliffe, T., & Raine, R. (2011). SAGE: Preliminary evaluation of an instrument for observing competence in CBT supervision. *The Cognitive Behaviour Therapist*, *4*, 123–138. doi:10.1017/S1754470X11000079

Newman, C. F. (2010). Competency in conducting cognitive–behavioral therapy: Foundational, functional, and supervisory aspects. *Professional Psychology, Research and Practice, 47*(1), 12–19. doi:10.1037/a0018849

O'Donovan, A., Slattery, L., Kavanagh, D., & Dooley, R. (2008). Opinions of Australian Psychological Society College Chairs about process and content in supervision training: Preliminary investigation in Queensland. *Australian Psychologist, 43*, 114–120. doi:10.1080/00050060801978654

Padesky, C. A. (1996). Developing cognitive therapist competency: Teaching and supervision models. In P. M. Salkovskis (Ed.), *Frontiers of cognitive therapy* (pp. 266–292), London, UK: Guilford Press.

Psychology Board of Australia (2011). *Exposure draft: Guideline for supervisors and supervisor training providers.* Retrieved from http://www.psychologyboard.gov.au/news/current-consultations.aspx

Rakovshik, S. G., & McManus, F. (2010). Establishing evidence-based training in cognitive behavioral therapy: A review of current empirical findings and theoretical guidance. *Clinical Psychology Review, 30*(5), 496–516. doi:10.1016/j.cpr.2010.03.004

Reiser, R., & Milne, D. L. (2012). Supervising cognitive-behavioral psychotherapy: Pressing needs, impressing possibilities. *Journal of Contemporary Psychotherapy, 42*, 161–171. doi:10.1007/s10879-011-9200-6

Rings, J. A., Genuchi, M. C., Hall, M. D., Angelo, M. A., & Cornish, J. A. E. (2009). Is there consensus among predoctoral internship training directors regarding clinical supervision competencies? A descriptive analysis. *Training and Education in Professional Psychology, 3*(3), 140. doi:10.1037/a0015054

Rodolfa, E., Bent, R., Eisman, E., Nelson, P., Rehm, L., & Ritchie, P. (2005). A cube model for competency development: Implications for psychology educators and regulators. *Professional Psychology, Research and Practice, 36*(4), 347–354. doi:10.1037/0735-7028.36.4.347

Roth, A., & Pilling, S. (2007). *The competences required to deliver effective cognitive and behavioural therapy for people with depression and with anxiety disorders.* London, UK: Department of Health.

Roth, A., & Pilling, S. (2008a). *A competence framework for the supervision of psychological therapies.*Retrieved from http://www.ucl.ac.uk/clinical-psychology/CORE/supervision_framework.htm

Roth, A., & Pilling, S. (2008b). Using an evidence-based methodology to identify the competencies required to deliver effective cognitive and behavioural therapy for depression and anxiety disorders. *Behavioural and Cognitive Psychotherapy, 36*, 129–147. doi:10.1017/S1352465808004141

Roth, A., Pilling, S., & Turner, J. (2010). Therapist training and supervision in clinical trials: Implications for clinical practice. *Behavioural and Cognitive Psychotherapy, 38*, 291–302. doi:10.1017/S1352465810000068

Sarnat, J. (2010). Key competencies of the psychodynamic psychotherapist and how to teach them in supervision. *Psychotherapy: Theory, Research, Practice, Training, 47*(1), 20–27. doi:10.1037/a0018846

Townend, M., Iannetta, L., & Freeston, M. H. (2002). Clinical supervision in practice: A survey of UK cognitive-behavioural psychotherapists accredited by the BABCP. *Behavioural and Cognitive Psychotherapy, 30*, 485–500.

Townend, M., Iannetta, L., Freeston, M., & Hayes, J.(July, 2007). Supervision practices of UK cognitive-behavioural psychotherapists, 2001 and 2006. Paper presented at the 5th World Congress of Behavioural and Cognitive Therapies, Barcelona.

Turpin, G., &Wheeler, S. (2011). *IAPT supervision guidance.*Retrieved from http://www.iapt.nhs.uk/silo/files/iapt-supervision-guidance-revised-march-2011.pdf

Waller, G., Stringer, H., & Meyer, C. (2012). What cognitive behavioral techniques do therapists report using when delivering cognitive behavioral therapy for the eating disorders? *Journal of Consulting and Clinical Psychology*, *80*(1), 171–175. doi:10.1037/a0026559

Watkins, C. E. (1997). *Handbook of psychotherapy supervision*. New York, NY: Wiley.

Watkins, C. E. (1998). Psychotherapy supervision in the 21st century: Some pressing needs and impressing possibilities. *The Journal of Psychotherapy Practice and Research*, *7*, 93–101.

Watkins, C. E. (2011). Does psychotherapy supervision contribute to patient outcomes? Considering thirty years of research. *The Clinical Supervisor*, *30*, 235–256. doi: 10.1080/07325223.2011.619417

Watkins, C. E. (2012). Educating psychotherapy supervisors. *American Journal of Psychotherapy*, *66*(3), 279–307.

Wheeler, S., & Richards, K. (2007). The impact of clinical supervision on counsellors and therapists, their practice and their clients: A systematic review of the literature. *Counselling & Psychotherapy Research*, *7*(1), 54–65. doi:10.1080/14733140601185274

Wilson, M. (2007) *Can experiences of supervision be quantified? REACTS: A new tool for measuring supervisee's perceived satisfaction with clinical supervision* (Unpublished thesis). Psychology Department, Newcastle University.

Young, J., & Beck, A. T. (1980). *The cognitive therapy rating scale manual (revised)*. Philadelphia, PA: Center for Cognitive Therapy, University of Pennsylvania.

25

Clinical Case Management Supervision

Using Clinical Outcome Monitoring and Therapy Progress Feedback to Drive Supervision

David A. Richards

Introduction

This chapter will describe a model of supervision that has been developed for high-volume psychological therapy environments. These environments often employ a nontraditional workforce with highly specific clinical competences to deliver "low-intensity" psychological treatments. Clinical case management supervision (CCMS) is driven by patient-determined factors and is often automated through computer-based patient management systems. Algorithm-led patient selection and the use of routine, sessional outcome measures are key defining features of CCMS. The chapter will describe the history of CCMS, its core features, information, and training support needs followed by a brief discussion on how CCMS addresses different aspects of core supervision models. The chapter is written from the perspective of the author's expertise as the principal developer of the low-intensity psychological therapy clinical method employed throughout England within the Improving Access to Psychological Therapies (IAPT) initiative.

Background

In the latter part of the twentieth century, a team of US clinicians and researchers recognized that the routine treatment of patients with depression was suboptimal (Katon et al., 1995). In particular, the outcomes achieved through antidepressant regimes in primary care were not at the levels expected from clinical trial data. Given

The Wiley International Handbook of Clinical Supervision, First Edition. Edited by C. Edward Watkins, Jr. and Derek L. Milne.

that most people with depression were treated in primary care, this team and others began to believe that there was a need for specialists in mental health care to advise primary care physicians on their treatment practices in order to improve clinical outcomes.

Initially, this led to the development and testing of "consultation liaison" services, whereby psychiatrists would give direct advice to responsible primary care doctors on the care of individual patients (reviewed by Gask, Sibbald, & Creed, 1997). However, it quickly became apparent that this system was highly inefficient. Given the prevalence of depression in primary care, it was simply not possible to use scarce and very expensive specialist liaison resources to discuss individual cases. These considerations led to the development of an enhanced version of consultation liaison – collaborative care (Miller, Kessler, Peek, & Kallenberg, 2011).

Collaborative care involves the insertion of a third mental health care worker into the liaison system. These "case managers" were designed to act as a conduit for specialist mental health advice to generalist clinicians. Case managers were less expert (Simon, VonKorff, Rutter, & Wagner, 2000) than specialist mental health professionals (and therefore less expensive to employ), but those specialists could supervise their practice. Case managers then liaised with the primary care medical team on behalf of the specialist (Gunn, Diggens, Hegarty, & Blashki, 2006).

Over a number of clinical trials and other studies, the model of collaborative care was refined to include both liaison and direct patient care (Gilbody, Bower, Fletcher, Richards, & Sutton, 2006). Case managers now met regularly with patients and helped them make best use of their medication regimes as well as advising primary care physicians on the most effective regime to prescribe. Given the danger of patients with depression losing touch with health care services, contacts between case managers and patients were conducted in an assertive manner, case managers always trying to ensure that patients in need did not drop out of treatment.

Although medication management was the focus of early trials (Katon et al., 1995), psychological interventions quickly became part of advanced collaborative care protocols (Katon et al., 1996). Researchers, specialists, and case managers recognized that many patients wanted more from their contacts with case managers and began to include brief psychological advice into their clinical practice. Some trials formalized this by training case managers to use interventions such as "problem-solving," "brief cognitive-behavioral therapy (CBT)," or "low-intensity behavioral activation" (e.g., Richards et al., 2008).

During the course of these developments, specialist clinical and research teams began to recognize a problem. From a research perspective, clinical research teams needed to ensure fidelity with the collaborative care model being tested. This required them to supervise the work of case managers in both their medication advice work and their psychological treatment delivery. Many case managers came from counseling or nursing backgrounds and had no previous experience of either medication adherence or structured psychological treatments (Hunkeler et al., 2000). Clinically, teams were equally concerned that inexperienced workers should operate safely and should not put patients at any risk. The solution adopted was clinical supervision.

However, one could argue that standard supervision models in use in traditional psychological therapy environments are ill-fitted to the case managers' working practices and the collaborative care model. Case managers hold high caseloads, treatment contacts are short, and patients may not remain in long-term contact with workers (Gunn et al., 2006). A supervision model that focused on in-depth discussion of a small number of cases did not satisfy the research and clinical teams who were concerned primarily about patient safety, model fidelity, and clinical decision-making at an individual – and numerically high – patient level.

A model of supervision that requires a supervisee to identify, select, and "bring cases" to supervision may leave many patients out of discussions in supervision encounters. High-volume caseloads and short-duration clinical practices mean that these patients will be very numerous. Furthermore, case managers may not have the experience or skills to deal with cases that challenge their standard clinical protocols. Such workers can develop repetitive and undesirable patterns of clinical decision-making that are unlikely to be identified, recognized, and remedied in supervision unless all cases are discussed at some point (Richards, 2010).

A final reservation about the suitability of traditional supervision models is that these rarely address the patient who has failed to attend therapy – the "do not attends," "defaulters," or "dropouts." In a collaborative care model, it is precisely these patients who are of most interest, since collaborative care is designed to enable depressed patients to stick with effective therapeutic regimes when the anhedonic and motivational phenomenology of their disorder often mitigates against this.

These are significant challenges: high-volume caseloads, short-duration treatment programs, a potentially de-motivated patient group, inexperienced workers and finally, traditionally trained supervisors unequipped with competences to address these requirements. In England, the issue became acute during the mid years of the first decade of the twenty-first century as the IAPT program began to invest over £700 million (US$1140 million) in clinical services (Layard, 2006). These services use the case management model as one of six core elements of a stepped care system to deliver short or "low-intensity" psychological treatments to hundreds of thousands of patients (Richards, 2012).

The solution adopted, CCMS, was both ingenious and in itself challenging (Richards, Chellingsworth, Hope, Turpin, & Whyte, 2010).

In CCMS, the focus is (at least apparently – more on this later in the chapter) exclusively on the patient, not the mental health worker. Algorithm-led patient selection and the use of routine, sessional outcome measures are key defining features of CCMS. Supervision is focused toward the needs of all patients rather than on a few selected by the supervisee or supervisor. The key features are as follows.

Case Selection

Box 25.1 summarizes the categories of patients to be discussed using patient-defined and therapy progress algorithms driving case selection. In CCMS, the supervision encounter starts with a review of the supervisee's total caseload. This includes the number of active patients, the number of new referrals, and numbers of patients discharged since the last supervision session. This helps the supervisor put the supervisee's workload into context, alongside that expected for a worker of comparable experience and available workload hours. Supervisors are able to identify if a worker's caseload numbers are silting up or if their ability to discharge patients is being blocked

Box 25.1

Categories of patients to be discussed using patient-defined and therapy progress algorithms driving case selection

Supervision should usually start with an overall discussion of a worker's full caseload numbers, to enable the supervisor to assess the worker's ability to manage his or her caseload. Following this first stage, the following principles should guide the selection of cases for discussion:

- Any new patients.
- All patients on the worker's caseload should be discussed regularly, and certainly no less frequently than at four-weekly intervals.
- Any patients with risk levels above a predetermined threshold.
- All patients whose scores on clinical measures are above a predetermined threshold.
- All patients whose appointments are overdue or who have not been contacted recently by the case manager.
- Any patient for whom the worker requires further support.

by potential case mix issues or competency problems, such as a reluctance to finish treatment programs. Any early warning signs can be investigated further as the supervision session progresses.

Next, the supervisee summarizes all cases to be discussed during the supervision session itself. The critical focus here is that cases are selected based on *predetermined* patient-defined and therapy progress characteristics. Initially, a supervisor in CCMS would expect all new cases to be presented. Next, she/he would want the supervisee to present all other cases that have reached a series of specific milestones in therapy. These are usually determined by the number of sessions that have been delivered by the mental health worker in therapy, say, every 4, 8, 12 sessions. At this stage in the supervision session, the supervisee presents a count of these different categories.

Next, the supervisee outlines the number of patients whose clinical presentations remain at a level that might cause concern. Although the mental health worker can determine this subjectively, the more usual practice is for these people to be identified by their scores on standardized clinical outcome scales. So, for example, in the English IAPT system, it is recommended that any patients whose PHQ9 (Kroenke, Spitzer, & Williams, 2001) score at the last appointment remains at a moderately severe level, generally considered to be a score of 15 or higher out of a possible total of 27, requires supervision. It will be apparent that in order to reliably detect patients with specific severity scores on clinical outcome scales, mental health workers must collect these measures from patients at each clinical session. This is one of the defining features of the English IAPT system (Richards & Borglin, 2011) and of other case management systems in general. Psychological therapists undertake routine clinical monitoring using such scales with patients at *each appointment*.

Next, supervisees will indicate to their supervisor how many other patients they wish to discuss. Again, for most cases, this will be driven by other predetermined patient factors. Supervisees will highlight patients who present with a risk to self, to, or from others. In addition, case managers will list patients that have defaulted from planned appointments without prior discussion with the mental health worker (so called "DNAs" or "did not attends"). Once again, this is a defining feature of CCMS, initially developed as it was to manage collaborative care systems, one of the main objectives of which is to minimize patients loosing touch with therapeutic services.

Finally, CCMS allows space for supervisees to raise additional clinical cases with their supervisor. These will be patients for whom the case manager thinks they need to receive supervision, but have not been identified in any of the preceding categories. They usually involve patients who seem to fall outside the case manager's usual clinical "comfort zone" or competences. For example, in a stepped care system (Bower & Gilbody, 2005; Davison, 2000), case managers might identify patients whom they think might require a higher intensity of psychological treatment than the briefer versions provided in collaborative care.

Presenting and Reviewing Information

There are three phases to each patient CCMS discussion (Richards et al., 2010):

1. information giving,
2. case discussion, and
3. shared decision-making.

Information Giving

It has already been noted that case managers carry higher caseloads than many other types of psychological therapists. With the focus in CCMS so clearly on patient-defined case review factors, the numbers of cases that need to be discussed can be quite large. It will be apparent that individual patient discussions will need to be carefully organized and efficient. Indeed, CCMS can be as high-volume as the actual clinical work of case managers themselves. Case managers present case review information in a succinct yet comprehensive manner. Box 25.2 summarizes the information required for each case discussion.

As can be seen from Box 25.2, at the first presentation, information includes basic demographic data (age, gender etc.), a summary of the person's main clinical problem, a risk profile, problem history including treatment and previous episodes, physical and psychological comorbidities, social and cultural factors, and finally a summary of the treatment plan. Case managers will also report scores derived from patient outcome questionnaires measuring salient difficulties such as depression, anxiety, and work and social adjustment. When case managers present patients who are at predetermined supervision points or have been identified for supervision for any other

Box 25.2

Information required for each case discussion in clinical case management supervision

For all cases:

- Gender, age, main problem statement, level of risk, onset and duration of current problem, previous episodes, past treatment, current scores on clinical measures, any comorbidity issues, any cultural, language or disability considerations, employment status, current treatment from general practitioner (GP) or other workers, low-intensity treatment plan, low-intensity action already initiated

Where supervision is concerned with patients being reviewed at predetermined intervals (e.g., every four weeks), where risk level causes concern or where outcome measures remain high:

- An episode treatment summary that includes intervention summary; number of contacts; duration of contacts; patient progress report including patients' engagement with and response to low-intensity treatment; risk management plan, scores on sessional clinical outcome measures; alternative low-intensity treatments available and suggestions for alternative treatments where necessary, for example, stepping up to high-intensity treatment

Where patients' appointments are overdue, if patients have not attended scheduled contacts (including telephone appointments) or have "dropped out" of treatment:

- Number of attempts made to contact the patient including telephone calls, time of calls, letters, and other contact attempts

reason, they will also summarize the number and duration of their clinical contacts, their treatment interventions, patients' response to this and their progress, and the sessional scores derived from repeated clinical outcome scales. Where the discussion concerns a patient who has dropped out or who has not attended planned sessions, case managers will also report the number of attempts they have made to contact the person.

The information giving section may seem somewhat daunting. However, experience tells us that with practice, case managers are able to cover this basic information in a matter of a minute or two. In CCMS, supervisors and supervisees quickly become adept at reporting and listening to informational patterns, highlighting where elements are missing, and these patterns are disturbed. Furthermore, no patient is ever discussed less than four weekly after the initial new presentation session, so some accounts become quite familiar to both parties in the supervision, particularly those with high levels of symptoms.

Case Discussion

In this stage of the process, the focus moves from presentation of information to a more discursive approach. Supervisees and supervisors jointly problem-solve any issues that have been brought up. This requires the supervisee to both listen to and reflect on suggestions given by the supervisor. Equally, supervisors will facilitate supervisees offering their own suggestions as to next steps. CCMS is by no means the one-way transfer of advice from an experienced supervisor to a junior supervisee. Supervisors in CCMS work hard to develop the clinical decision-making skills of case managers by seeking supervisee suggestions, mirroring the process of therapy between a patient and a psychological therapist. As discussions proceed, supervisees reflect on and clarify the emerging clinical plan.

Shared Decision-Making

For each patient discussed, the supervision discussion comes to an end with an agreement on what the supervisee will do next in terms of his or her clinical plan. This requires the supervisees to do three things. First, they summarize the discussions accurately, highlighting the main points covered. Second, they formulate a clear plan that contains the action to be undertaken by the case manager for the care of that patient. Actions agreed are generally specific, achievable, and have a clear time frame. Finally, supervisees will move on to the next case in an unambiguous manner, following the case selection process highlighted earlier.

Evidence for CCMS

As noted previously, CCMS was developed by the Center for Health Studies, a joint endeavor between the University of Washington and Group Health Cooperative, a Seattle-based health care provider (see Katon et al., 2004). Its usefulness was highlighted empirically in a systematic review, meta-analysis, and meta-regression of collaborative care studies (Bower, Gilbody, Richards, Fletcher, & Sutton, 2006). This review showed that the presence of planned and organized supervision, as opposed to non-programmatic, ad hoc "take it or leave it" process, predicted better patient outcomes in collaborative care studies. Consequently, CCMS was included in the first modern clinical trial of collaborative care in the United Kingdom (Richards et al., 2008). This trial showed that collaborative care, using this supervision model as one of its core components, was significantly more effective than usual treatment for patients with depression in primary care. At around the same time CCMS was used in the first IAPT prototype "demonstration site," in Doncaster, United Kingdom (Richards & Borglin, 2011; Richards & Suckling, 2008, 2009). In these uncontrolled studies, CCMS contributed to the achievement of clinical outcomes from low-intensity psychological therapies that were equivalent to those achieved in clinical trials of CBT.

That CCMS could be predictive of better patient outcomes is a startling effect. Patient health is a more distal outcome for supervision than proximal measures of supervisee clinical competence, for example. There are few, if any, examples of such evidence where a process once-removed from direct clinical contact can actually lead to better outcomes. Currently, no studies have unpicked this relationship for CCMS. If the proposed mechanism of effect is that CCMS leads to better clinical decision-making and case manager competence, studies are required to demonstrate this mediating effect directly.

Supporting CCMS

In high-volume clinical environments where CCMS is as high-volume as the clinical activity itself, it would be easy for both case managers and supervisees to lose track of their caseloads in treatment, and for presentation in supervision. The selection of cases for supervision could be time-consuming and subject to errors, negating the whole rationale behind the CCMS model. Consequently, an electronic patient management system is almost certainly essential to manage this process.

This system should do two things. First, it must provide a place where routine clinical outcome measures and risk profiles can be entered on a patient record immediately once they have been collected. Given these are gathered at every clinical encounter, the system should be quick and efficient to ease administrative burden. The system should also automatically record every completed patient therapy session *and* those that patients have missed. These elements of clinical practice – clinical outcomes and session records – are the key drivers of CCMS so IT systems must be able to collect them reliably with minimum operator burden.

Second, these data should be linked to an alert system that is able to identify patients who need discussion in CCMS. Electronic patient management systems that automatically select patients for discussion according to the criteria discussed earlier ensure that no patient can "slip through the net." Case managers also do not have to spend precious administrative time selecting patients for discussion from their sizeable caseloads. If this alert system is linked to electronic supervisor records, then both supervisee and supervisor can access supervision lists and the case records of patients who have been automatically selected for supervision based on the predetermined selection algorithms referred to earlier in this chapter. Using such systems, it is not even necessary to be in the same room. Supervision can occur remotely via the telephone or video conferencing, providing both parties have access to the clinical records and lists of patients for supervision.

Such systems do exist in other areas of health care where patients with long-term conditions such as diabetes are called for routine screening or enhanced care using risk algorithms built into clinical records. The first such system for CCMS was developed for a trial run by the Seattle group (Katon et al., 2004) and then developed at the University of York, United Kingdom, to help manage England's first IAPT service in Doncaster: PC-MIS (http://www.pc-mis.co.uk). PC-MIS is Web-based, facilitating remote access, and provides workers and supervisors with a weekly list of all patients for discussion in supervision. This saves considerable administration time and ensures that the system is clinically safe. Once an individual patient has been discussed, supervisors make notes on their supervision and "close" the case record. This automatically logs that supervision has taken place and removes the patient from the list of current supervision alerts. This provides a unique way of ensuring a high standard of clinical governance that can be audited at any time.

Another area of support is in both supervisee and supervisor competence. In England, IAPT case managers (called psychological well-being practitioners [PWPs]) are trained at postgraduate level (Department of Health Mental Health Programme, 2008) to deliver low-intensity psychological therapy and to help patients manage their medication regimes. Their year-long postgraduate certificate course requires them to pass a summative competency assessment that judges their ability to use CCMS. As noted earlier, these competences include the ability to select appropriate cases for discussion, to produce a summary overview of these cases, to present patient-centered information accurately and succinctly, to engage in case discussion, and to come to a shared decision on future patient care (Richards et al., 2010). Equally, CCM supervisors are also trained to manage the process of CCMS via elements of a standard five- to seven-day continuing professional development course (IAPT Education and Training Group, 2011). In some respects, this can be more of a challenge for supervisors than case managers. Supervisors are often drawn from professional groups who are used to supervision models in which individual patients are selected for supervisee learning purposes and discussed in depth. Supervisors can feel very exposed and worried about CCMS discussions implying a lack of detail and rigor. Ironically, it is often only by experiencing case managers presenting highly organized information and details of clinical decision-making that supervisors become more comfortable and competent in the model.

Placing CCMS in Context

This book has brought together many aspects of supervision and discussed them in great depth. How does CCMS fit into these discussions? At first glance, one might presume that CCMS is narrowly focused on the "normative" function of supervision (see Chapter 1), directing its attention solely to case management and quality control. Using the model described by Turpin and Wheeler (2011, revised), CCMS seems to best serve the fidelity, case management, and clinical governance functions of supervision. Certainly, removing almost all elements of supervisee and supervisor choices in selecting patients for discussion might lead one to presume that the focus on patients might be at the expense of restorative and formative functions (see Chapter 1) designed to enhance worker skill development and to provide support (Turpin & Wheeler, 2011).

However, on closer inspection and reflection, one might come to a different conclusion. The very organized and systematic methods at the core of CCMS could be seen to provide a secure structure for supervisees. The initial review of caseload numbers and status of patients will alert supervisors to workload management problems before they get out of hand. Automated systems, in particular, do not allow inexperienced therapists to hide emerging problems though fear being judged negatively by supervisors. CCMS is a very open system and such transparency can provide safety and security for junior clinicians. Supervisors can then engage in the restorative agenda with supervisees, either directly or through recommendations to use other opportunities available to workers in the service.

In a similar way, skills development is also not ignored, since CCSM is driven by two main factors, clinical outcomes and patient engagement. In supervision, supervisees are discussing patient progress via clinical feedback for every patient on a regular basis. Pattern recognition and subsequent learning opportunities abound. Supervisors will draw supervisees' attention to successful and less successful clinical strategies, providing multiple opportunities for reflection and skills development and shaping supervisees' behaviours. Not unlike Mike Lambert's pioneering work on recording and feeding back collated clinical outcome scores to therapists in order to improve practice (e.g., Brown, Lambert, Jones, & Minami, 2005), CCMS provides immediate and regular patient-facing feedback to practitioners and their supervisors. So although CCMS is apparently more focused on control than development, skilled supervisors can and do use it as a vehicle for support and learning. Anecdotal comments from PWPs in the United Kingdom do indeed support this view.

Nonetheless, it is probably more accurate to refer to these learning opportunities as reactive rather than prioritized. Time in CCMS is limited – in high-volume clinical environments such as the stepped care English IAPT services, CCMS is usually undertaken for 1 hr on an individual basis weekly. So, although supervisors may recommend additional skills practice, they may not know whether these learning opportunities are being taken up and may not attend to them formally in CCMS sessions. As a consequence, many services take clinical issues raised during CCMS into more traditional supervision sessions held less frequently and often in groups of supervisees. This permits a greater degree of in-depth discussion around specific clinical techniques, similar to a more traditional group supervision session and very like that offered to high-intensity CBT therapists in the English IAPT system. However, one should note that even here, the issues for discussion are raised from patterns of uncertainty identified during CCMS. In this care, therefore, CCMS enhances the more traditional supervision practice.

Summary

CCMS is a novel package of supervisory procedures that was developed to meet a highly specific need, implemented with considerable sophistication and for which there is evidence of a positive effect on patient outcomes. Modern mental health care practices, where brief psychological therapies are combined with medication management and delivered to high volumes of patients challenge received wisdom and traditional "professional" supervision practices. The distinguishing features of CCMS are that automated algorithms select cases for discussion on the basis of predefined patient characteristics and therapy progress data. The collection, collation, and feedback of routine clinical outcome measures play a significant part in driving the CCMS system. Where CCMS is supported by sophisticated patient information systems including automated supervision alerts, and both supervisees and supervisors are appropriately trained to attain the relevant competences, CCMS not only can address the normative functions of supervision but can also deliver restorative and formative objectives.

References

Bower, P., & Gilbody, S. (2005). Stepped care in psychological therapies: Access, effectiveness and efficiency: Narrative literature review. *The British Journal of Psychiatry*, *186*(1), 11–17.

Bower, P., Gilbody, S., Richards, D. A., Fletcher, J., & Sutton, A. (2006). Collaborative care for depression in primary care. Making sense of a complex intervention: Systematic review and meta regression. *The British Journal of Psychiatry*, *189*, 484–493.

Brown, G. S., Lambert, M. J., Jones, E. R., & Minami, T. (2005). Identifying highly effective psychotherapists in a managed care environment. *American Journal of Managed Care*, *11*(8), 513–520.

Davison, G. (2000). Stepped care: Doing more with less? *Journal of Consulting and Clinical Psychology*, *68*(4), 580–585.

Department of Health Mental Health Programme. (2008). *Improving Access to Psychological Therapies implementation plan: Curriculum for low intensity therapies workers.* London: Department of Health.

Gask, L., Sibbald, B., & Creed, F. (1997). Evaluating models of working at the interface between mental health services and primary care. *The British Journal of Psychiatry*, *170*, 6–11.

Gilbody, S., Bower, P., Fletcher, J., Richards, D., & Sutton, A. J. (2006). Collaborative care for depression: A cumulative meta-analysis and review of longer-term outcomes. *Archives of Internal Medicine*, *166*, 2314–2321.

Gunn, J., Diggens, J., Hegarty, K., & Blashki, G. (2006). A systematic review of complex system interventions designed to increase recovery from depression in primary care. *BMC Health Services Research*, *6*, 88.

Hunkeler, E., Meresman, J., Hargreaves, W., Fireman, B., Berman, W. H., Kirsch, A. J., . . . Salzer, M. (2000). Efficacy of nurse telehealth care and peer support in augmenting treatment of depression in primary care. *Archives of Family Medicine*, *9*, 700–708.

IAPT Education and Training Group. (2011). *Guidance for Commissioning IAPT Supervisor Training (Revised 2011).* Retrieved from http://www.iapt.nhs.uk/silo/files/guidance-for-commissioning-iapt-supervisor-training-revised-2011.pdf

Katon, W., Robinson, P., Von Korff, M., Lin, E., Bush, T., Ludman, E., . . . Walker, E. (1996). A multifaceted intervention to improve treatment of depression in primary care. *Archives of General Psychiatry*, *53*, 924–932.

Katon, W., Von Korff, M., Lin, E., Walker, E., Simon, G. E., Bush, T., . . . Russo, J. (1995). Collaborative management to achieve treatment guidelines: Impact on depression in primary care. *Journal of the American Medical Association*, *273*, 1026–1031.

Katon, W. J., Von Korff, M., Lin, E. H. B., Simon, G., Ludman, E., Russo, J., . . . Bush, T. (2004). The Pathways Study: A: Randomized trial of collaborative care in patients with diabetes and depression. *Archives of General Psychiatry*, *61*(10), 1042–1049.

Kroenke, K., Spitzer, R. L., & Williams, J. B. (2001). The PHQ-9: Validity of a brief depression severity measure. *Journal of General Internal Medicine*, *16*(9), 606–613.

Layard, R. (2006). The case for psychological treatment centres. *British Medical Journal, 332*, 1030–1032.

Miller, B. F., Kessler, R., Peek, C. J., & Kallenberg, G. A. (2011). *A National Agenda for Research in Collaborative Care: Papers from the Collaborative Care Research Network Research Development Conference. AHRQ Publication No. 11-0067*. Rockville, MD: Agency for Healthcare Research and Quality.

Richards, D. A. (2010). Chapter 11, Supervising low-intensity workers in high volume clinical environments. In J. Bennett-Levy, D. A. Richards, P. Farrand, H. Christensen, K. Griffiths, D. Kavanagh, . . . C. Williams (Eds.), *The Oxford guide to low intensity CBT interventions* (pp. 129–136), Oxford, UK: Oxford University Press.

Richards, D. A. (2012). Stepped care: A method to deliver increased access to psychological therapies. *Canadian Journal of Psychiatry. Revue Canadienne de Psychiatrie, 57*(4), 210–215.

Richards, D. A., & Borglin, G. (2011). Implementation of psychological therapies for anxiety and depression in routine practice: Two year prospective cohort study. *Journal of Affective Disorders, 133*, 51–60.

Richards, D. A., Chellingsworth, M., Hope, R., Turpin, G., & Whyte, M. (2010). *Reach Out: National programme supervisor materials to support the delivery of training for psychological well-being practitioners delivering low intensity interventions*. London: Rethink.

Richards, D. A., Lovell, K., Gilbody, S., Gask, L., Torgerson, D., Barkham, M., . . . Richardson, R. (2008). Collaborative care for depression in UK primary care: A randomised controlled trial. *Psychological Medicine, 38*, 279–288.

Richards, D. A., & Suckling, R. (2008). Improving access to psychological therapy: The Doncaster demonstration site organisational model. *Clinical Psychology Forum, 181*, 9–16.

Richards, D. A., & Suckling, R. (2009). Improving Access to Psychological Therapies (IAPT): Phase IV prospective cohort study. *The British Journal of Clinical Psychology, 48*, 377–396.

Simon, G., VonKorff, M., Rutter, C., & Wagner, E. (2000). A randomized trial of monitoring, feedback, and management of care by telephone to improve depression treatment in primary care. *British Medical Journal, 320*, 550–554.

Turpin, G., & Wheeler, S. (2011). *IAPT supervision guidance*. Retrieved from http://www.iapt.nhs.uk/silo/files/iapt-supervision-guidance-revised-march-2011.pdf

26

Supervising Humanistic and Existential Psychotherapies

Eugene W. Farber

Having come of age as the "signature pedagogy" for psychotherapy education and training, supervision is experiencing a dynamic process of growth and evolution that corresponds to the changing landscape of the psychotherapy field as a whole (Bernard & Goodyear, 2009; Watkins, 2011, 2012). The intent of this chapter is to describe a general framework for clinical supervision of humanistic and existential psychotherapies as conceived and practiced in the United States, explore applications in the context of emerging developments in twenty-first century psychotherapy supervision, and consider the approach from an international perspective.

An array of psychotherapies falls under the broad rubric of humanistic and existential psychotherapy approaches. Major examples, each of which has enjoyed international reach and influence, include person-centered psychotherapy (Cooper, O'Hara, Schmid, & Wyatt, 2007; Rogers, 1961), Gestalt therapy (Brownell, 2008; Perls, 1969), existential psychotherapy (van Deurzen, 2010; Yalom, 1980), existential–humanistic psychotherapy (Bugental, 1978; Schneider & Krug, 2010), and experiential psychotherapy (Elliott, Watson, Goldman, & Greenberg, 2004; Gendlin, 1996). Given the sheer breadth of these psychotherapies, attempting a serial description of specific supervision requirements and activities that correspond to each of them is beyond the scope of this chapter. Rather, the primary aim is to articulate broad humanistic and existential psychotherapy supervision principles and processes. An additional aim is to explore the status of humanistic and existential psychotherapy supervision relative to contemporary trends in the field.

To accomplish these tasks, a set of key overarching questions will guide the discussion. These questions include the following: (1) What are the theoretically grounded core principles and processes that comprise a general framework for humanistic and existential psychotherapy supervision? (2) How might these supervision principles and processes contribute to evolving competency-based approaches to psychotherapy

The Wiley International Handbook of Clinical Supervision, First Edition. Edited by C. Edward Watkins, Jr. and Derek L. Milne.

education and training? (3) How might humanistic and existential ideas inform the dialogue on the role of supervision in preparing psychotherapists to (a) work in diverse health care settings, and (b) utilize integrative frameworks for psychotherapy practice? (4) Apropos of the subject matter of this handbook, how might an international perspective of humanistic–existential supervision be envisioned, particularly as this relates to its cultural applicability? All theoretically based clinical training frameworks, including approaches to psychotherapy supervision, are anchored by a core set of guiding conceptual assumptions (for review, see Farber, in press). As such, in order to provide a context for the discussion that follows, the chapter begins with a brief overview of the theoretical origins of the humanistic and existential psychotherapies and the conceptual foundations of the supervision approach.

Theoretical Origins and Foundations

Origins of existential and humanistic psychotherapies

The rich conceptual traditions that undergird existential and humanistic psychotherapy frameworks are international in scope and can be traced to two theoretical lineages, the earlier of which began in 1920s and 1930s Europe with critiques by some psychiatrists of the orthodoxy of the psychoanalytic approach as it was conceptualized and practiced in that era. These psychiatrists, among the first of whom were Karl Jaspers of Germany and Ludwig Binswanger of Switzerland, drew inspiration from European existential philosophy to pioneer theories and psychotherapies concerned with the fundamental dimensions of existence that characterize the human condition (Burston, 2003).

Meanwhile, in 1940s and 1950s North America, psychologists in the United States were, like the European existential psychotherapists, articulating both theoretical and psychotherapeutic alternatives to the prevailing psychoanalytic and behavioral frameworks of the time under the umbrella of what came to be known as the "third force" of humanistic psychology (Burston, 2003; Cain, 2002). Pivotal contributions from this period include Abraham Maslow's (1954, 1968) formulation of a growth-oriented motivational theory, and work by Carl Rogers (1957) to articulate key facilitating processes in his person-centered psychotherapy approach, including congruence, empathy, and unconditional positive regard.

Although European existential psychotherapy and North American humanistic psychology developed separately at first, certain parallel ideas were apparent across the two approaches, such as the respective phenomenological concepts associated with the existential and person-centered psychotherapies (Cooper, 2007a). It was the introduction of European existential concepts to North America by May, Angel, and Ellenberger (1958), however, that marked the beginning of active efforts to blend existential and humanistic ideas. Reflecting this conceptual cross-fertilization, the term humanistic–existential is used widely in the United States to refer to the spectrum of humanistic and existential psychotherapies, while some in Europe and elsewhere classify the humanistic and existential psychotherapies as distinct orientations (Burston, 2003). Although both mindful and respectful of these differing viewpoints regarding the proper classification of the humanistic and existential frameworks, the term humanistic–existential will be employed throughout the discussion as a kind of shorthand that refers to the array of approaches that fall within the humanistic and existential psychotherapy spectrum. This use of terminology is consistent with a key purpose of this chapter, which is to illuminate a general characterization of the principles and processes of supervision across the range of the humanistic and existential psychotherapies.

Central theoretical concepts

The legacy of European existential psychotherapy has been to provide a foundational set of philosophically based theoretical positions, beginning with a contextual view of existence as fundamentally in relation to a world that encompasses physical, social, psychological, and spiritual realms of being (Binswanger, 1946/1958; van Deurzen, 2009). Existential psychotherapy also is framed by a phenomenological epistemology centered on conscious experiencing, and a conceptualization of human personality functioning as continually unfolding and becoming rather than fixed or static (Cooper, 2008). Additionally, existential theory posits that human beings are possessed of a freedom to choose and are in many respects defined by their choices and in this sense responsible for how their lives unfold. Human freedom is viewed as limited, however, such that not all possibilities can be fulfilled, a premise that points to inherent existential tensions that characterize the tragic aspects of the human condition (Burston, 2003; Cooper, 2008; van Deurzen, 2009).

Relative to this European existentialist framework, the North American humanistic psychotherapy movement has tended to convey a more expansive and optimistic view of human psychological life (Burston, 2003). The concept of the actualizing tendency, a cornerstone of humanistic theory, reflects this position in that it refers to a presumed biologically based organismic striving toward increasing levels of organization in the service of growth, optimal coping, and use of potentiality (Bohart, 2007; Cain, 2002). This difference in tone relative to human potentiality notwithstanding, humanistic psychotherapy shares many points of convergence with the existential framework. Specifically, both emphasize the primacy of experiencing as a source of knowing self and world, highlight free choice, personal agency, and authenticity in living, and take a contextual whole person perspective on psychological functioning (Burston, 2003; Cain, 2002; Cooper, 2007a; Pos, Greenberg, & Elliott, 2008).

A theoretically grounded humanistic–existential supervision framework

Having briefly encapsulated the theoretical origins and foundations of the existential and humanistic psychotherapies, attention now turns to the first major task of the chapter, which is to characterize a general humanistic–existential supervision approach. Although no unitary supervision framework exists that encompasses all of the specific training requirements and activities associated with the diverse psychotherapies that have been developed under the mantle of the humanistic and existential traditions, general principles for conducting supervision can be discerned from shared points of theoretical convergence that span the varieties of humanistic–existential psychotherapies. These include suppositions that (1) thoughts, feelings, and behavior are best understood in relation to the overall context and functioning of the whole person as a biopsychosocial unity; (2) relationships characterized by genuineness, authenticity, empathy, basic regard, and presence are facilitative of growth; (3) experiencing represents a primary avenue for self-knowledge and change; (4) human freedom, while not unconstrained by limits, constitutes a basis for personal agency along with an associated responsibility for the impact of choices made; and (5) psychological symptoms represent more than mere problems to be removed but serve an orienting function that encourages meaningful self-reflection and self-evaluation of one's life circumstances and life path (Farber, 2012). As will be illustrated presently, these theoretical premises inform the humanistic–existential supervision context, the supervisory relationship, and the process and content of supervision.

The context of supervision

As has been described, humanistic–existential theory posits that psychological life must be understood in a contextual way. This idea is expressed in the existential notion of being-in-the-world as living in connection to one's environment and relationships (e.g., Cooper, 2008), as well as in the gestalt therapy field–theoretical conceptualization of psychological life as influenced by interrelationships among experiential and environmental phenomena (e.g., Brownell, 2010; Crocker, 2008). Anchored by this theoretical framework, supervision is viewed as a contextual enterprise that is centered on the relationship between the supervisor and supervisee, but also is influenced to varying degrees by additional contextual layers. These include the exigencies of the psychotherapy client, the client–supervisee relationship, the clinical setting, the training environment, the training philosophy and priorities, and the prevailing *zeitgeist* that frames the overarching ethics, values, norms, practices, and expectations of the profession. Illustrative of this contextual perspective, Pack (2009) suggests that supervision within a gestalt psychotherapy framework must facilitate the supervisee's awareness of self in relation to the supervisor, the client, the clinical team, professional colleagues, the clinical setting, and broader social systems. Each of these factors has a bearing on the supervisory relationship, the process of supervision, and the contents that comprise the supervisory focus.

Even given this contextual emphasis, humanistic–existential supervision as depicted in this chapter historically has tended to center itself on the individual development of the supervisee as an autonomous professional, which is consistent with the largely individualist Western cultural milieu within which it has evolved. As will be demonstrated later, however, recent work that more fully applies the contextual theoretical underpinnings of humanistic–existential supervision yields a ready pathway for accommodating a more collectivist or interdependent perspective, thereby enhancing the potential international applicability of the supervision approach.

The supervisory relationship

Clinical supervision generally is defined as a relationship-based activity (Bernard & Goodyear, 2009; Milne, 2007). Within the humanistic–existential tradition, just as the quality of the psychotherapy relationship is viewed as facilitative of client healing, the quality of the supervisory relationship is regarded as facilitative of supervisee learning (Barnett, 2009; Bryant-Jefferies, 2005; Farber, 2010; Lambers, 2007;

Nassif, Schulenberg, Hutzell, & Rogina, 2010; Pack, 2009). In accordance with theoretical assumptions regarding the role of the psychotherapy relationship in the change process, the humanistic–existential psychotherapy supervisor cultivates a relationship with the supervisee that is respectful, collaborative, empathic, and genuine while also retaining the necessary posture required to evaluate the work of the supervisee and ensure the quality of the services provided (Farber, 2012). This overarching relational supervisory stance is consistent with how the supervisory relationship is characterized in current definitions of supervision (e.g., Milne, 2007).

This basic conceptualization of the supervisory relationship is evident across the spectrum of humanistic-existential psychotherapy training frameworks. For instance, working within a person-centered perspective, Lambers (2007) characterizes the facilitative supervisory relationship as one in which the supervisor evidences high degrees of presence, empathy, congruence, and regard for the supervisee. These qualities of the supervisory relationship engender a relational context that is authentic, encouraging of mutual dialogue, collaborative, and supportive of the supervisee's development as a psychotherapist. The supervisory relationship offers the opportunity for the supervisor and supervisee to collaborate in an effort to grasp the psychological world of the client, the psychotherapy process, and the client–supervisee relationship (Bryant-Jefferies, 2005). Drawing upon an existential view, Barnett (2009) points to the value of a trusting supervisory relationship in providing a context for honest self-reflection and self-evaluation that supports supervisee learning. Within a gestalt framework, Pack (2009) describes the need for the supervisor to provide a combination of support, encouragement, and challenge in the supervisory relationship, a stance that parallels that of the psychotherapy relationship in the gestalt approach. The supervisor balances logistical and goal directed aspects of supervision that ensures safe practice with what is referred to as a dialogic relationship in which the supervisor seeks to grasp the supervisee's experience of psychotherapy, is present and authentic, and is willing to engage with the supervisee in ". . . a mutual journey of discovery" (Pack, 2009, p. 75).

Within a humanistic–existential supervision framework, the supervisor's basic respect for the supervisee and commitment to the supervisee's learning process provides a relational context that is not only fundamentally supportive but also allows for appropriate challenge and evaluative reflection on the supervisee's work. At its heart, an effective supervision relationship incorporates relational depth, where both the supervisor and supervisee fully and willingly immerse themselves in an authentic and open dialogue regarding the supervisee's experience in working with the client and their shared experience of the supervisory relationship in the service of the supervisee's development as a psychotherapist (Lambers, 2007).

The process and content of supervision

The process of humanistic–existential supervision involves discussion and review of the supervisee's psychotherapy sessions with the client, including key psychological themes and concerns that are present, patterns of interaction between supervisee and client, and the supervisee's psychotherapeutic actions and responses to the client. Dialogue on theoretical and technical aspects of psychotherapy, discussion centered on professional values and ethics, review of session audiotapes or videotapes, and role-play all may be a part of this supervisory process. In keeping with the theoretical centrality within the humanistic–existential framework of experiencing as a source of self-knowledge, the supervision process emphasizes experiential learning as a vehicle for advancing the supervisee's development as a psychotherapist (Farber, 2010). For example, the supervisor frequently invites the supervisee to reflect on the experience of being with the client and to articulate impressions of the affective tone of the psychotherapeutic encounter. The intent of this approach is to cultivate supervisee skills in using experiential knowledge both to illuminate predominant clinical themes and to direct clinical intervention. In parallel fashion, the supervisor and supervisee also attend to their experiencing of the supervisory encounter as a means of grasping specific training needs of the supervisee as they arise and direct the training process accordingly.

Consistent with humanistic–existential conceptualizations of the importance of personal agency in psychological life, the experiential process in supervision facilitates the emergence of the supervisee's unique experience and personal ownership of self as a psychotherapist. For example, the experiential process serves as a vehicle to illuminate supervisee choice points for psychotherapeutic action with clients, articulate or clarify supervisee beliefs, values, and attitudes as a psychotherapist, and facilitate supervisee authorship and responsibility for psychotherapeutic action. The degree of emphasis on these aspects of training in the supervisory process varies in accordance with the supervisee's level of clinical experience and development as a clinician and corresponding readiness to explore increasing degrees of independent thought and action as a psychotherapist (Farber, 2010).

Theoretical assumptions regarding the primary facilitators of psychotherapy change suggest a general roadmap for guiding the content focus of humanistic-existential supervision; namely, deepening experiential self-awareness and using the psychotherapy relationship as an instrument of change (Farber, 2010). As such, supervision cultivates supervisee knowledge of experiential and phenomenological theory, skill in the application of psychotherapy methods that deepen self-awareness and experiential self-reflection, and an attitude of openness and receptivity to the client's experiential world. Additionally, supervision attends to the development of supervisee knowledge regarding the facilitative dimensions of the psychotherapy relationship, along with corresponding interpersonal capacities, skills, and attitudes required to create a relational context that promotes growth and change in the client. Because the conduct of humanistic–existential psychotherapy relies heavily on use of the relationship and experiential learning, clinical supervision also places a premium on developing the person of the psychotherapist and psychotherapist use of self as an instrument of change (Farber, 2010, 2012).

The process and content elements of humanistic–existential supervision reveal the theoretically guided training priorities of the approach. Put differently, they point to domains of knowledge, attitudes, and skills that humanistic–existential supervisors regard as important competency domains to cultivate in the work of their supervisees. Since a key function of supervision is to develop competent psychotherapists, it is important to reflect on how this occurs in the context of humanistic–existential supervision. Accordingly, attention now is directed to considering humanistic–existential psychotherapy competency concepts and contributions to emerging approaches to competency-based professional education and training.

Humanistic–Existential Supervision and Competency-Based Clinical Training

A competency-based framework for professional psychology education and training has been gaining increasing international attention. This is exemplified by efforts to articulate key competencies for professional practice in Australia (e.g., Pachana, Sofronoff, Scott, & Helmes, 2011), the United Kingdom (e.g., Roth & Pilling, 2008), and the United States (e.g., Rodolfa et al., 2005; Falender & Shafranske, 2012). From the standpoint of clinical supervision, the focus of these efforts is on identifying competency domains that supervision as a pedagogy aims to cultivate in supervisees (e.g., Farber & Kaslow, 2010) as well as on articulating competency in conducting clinical supervision (e.g., Falender & Shafranske, 2004, 2012). Both are considered presently as they pertain to humanistic–existential supervision.

Supervisee competencies

As with any supervision approach, the conceptual underpinnings of humanistic–existential supervision inform its particular pedagogical goals (i.e., learning objectives for the supervisee). That is, supervision aims to support the development of specific competencies relevant to the conduct of psychotherapy. In the United States, the emerging competency-based model defines competencies as domains of professional knowledge, skills, attitudes, and values, and includes efforts to articulate competency benchmarks and tools for assessing competency in the context of professional education and training (Fouad et al., 2009; Kaslow et al., 2009; Rodolfa et al., 2005). This model specifies foundational competencies that presumably are applicable across all domains of professional functioning (i.e., professionalism, reflective practice, relationships, ethical and legal standards and policy, individual and cultural diversity, interdisciplinary systems, scientific knowledge and methods). The model also specifies functional competencies, two of which, assessment and intervention, are directly relevant to supervisee development in the context of psychotherapy supervision.

Foundational competencies A competency-based framework for humanistic–existential supervision is just beginning to be explored (for review, see Farber, 2010, 2012). Figure 26.1 provides a schematic snapshot of how the focus of humanistic–existential supervision might be conceptualized in the context of the evolving competency model as articulated in the United States. As depicted, specific activities that characterize the supervision focus are presumed to correspond to the cultivation of particular foundational competencies.

For example, the experiential focus in supervision taps the self-reflective processes that are part and parcel of reflective practice. To the extent that this focus involves facilitating the development of supervisee expertise relative to experiential understanding of relational processes, it also has pertinence for the development of relationships competency in the supervisee.

The person of the psychotherapist emphasis in supervision concerns itself with articulating the supervisee's unique qualities and capacities as an emotional healer and facilitating supervisee skill in the use of self-knowledge to advance the well-being

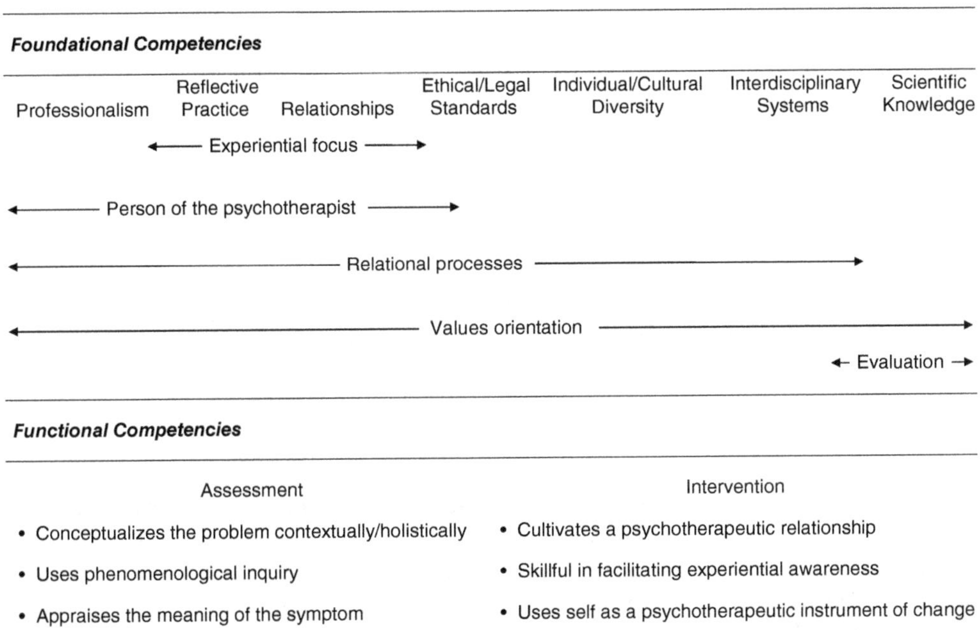

Figure 26.1 Humanistic–existential psychotherapy supervision and competency-based training.

of psychotherapy clients. These activities require cultivation of self-reflection, self-monitoring, and self-evaluation abilities as these pertain to psychotherapy skill sets, psychotherapist roles and responsibilities, clinical blind spots and susceptibilities that affect clinical performance, the interface of personal and professional functioning, self-care, professional development, and the emergence of a professional identity. As such, the person of the psychotherapist focus in humanistic–existential supervision is pertinent to supervisee development in the competency domains of reflective practice, professionalism, and relationships.

The supervisory focus of humanistic–existential supervision on the relational conditions of psychotherapy that are facilitative of change (e.g., genuineness, positive regard, relational presence) along with supervisor modeling of the corresponding relational conditions that promote the growth and professional development of the supervisee is relevant to a broad range of foundational competency domains. Aside from the more obvious significance of this focus to relationships, reflective practice, and professionalism competencies, it also has a bearing on cultivating ethical standards (e.g., conducting oneself appropriately and professionally relative to relational boundaries), diversity (e.g., capacity to relate effectively with persons from diverse backgrounds), and interdisciplinary systems (e.g., professional communication and collaboration skills) competencies as well.

The humanistic–existential tradition is anchored by an explicitly values-based frame of reference that highlights the importance of valuing the humanity of each individual, a commitment to facilitating self-determination, and basic regard for differing world views, personal narratives, ways of living, and lifestyles. (Cain, 2002;

Cooper, 2007b). This frame, when applied to the supervisory situation, encourages consciousness of an ethical perspective that has implications for training across the spectrum of the foundational competency domains. Examples of this broad influence include the nurturing of integrity and accountability as a part of professionalism, a commitment to awareness of how personal values influence clinical assumptions, priorities, and actions as a component of reflective practice, and an ethical approach to scientific methods and applying scientific knowledge in clinical work.

Functional competencies Figure 26.1 shows the functional assessment and intervention competencies that humanistic–existential supervision highlights. Relative to psychotherapy assessment, the supervisor works collaboratively with the supervisee to understand the client's problems and concerns in the context of the client's biopsychosocial situation and attend to how clinical symptoms are expressed in interrelated emotional, cognitive, behavioral, and somatic spheres (e.g., affective expression, predominant narratives of the problem, gestures, bodily tension; Farber, 2010, 2012). The supervisor encourages the supervisee to adopt a similarly collaborative and holistic frame with the client in assessing the problem. The supervisor also works to cultivate the supervisee's skill in conducting phenomenological inquiry, which involves a process of setting aside preconceptions and assumptions as much as possible and understanding descriptively the client's experiential expressions (Adams, 2009; Cain, 2002; Cooper, 2007b; Etzi, 2008). The supervisor models the phenomenological approach in the supervisory process and guides the supervisee in applying principles of phenomenology in the psychotherapeutic encounter with the client. Overlapping with a focus on phenomenological assessment is a supervisory emphasis on illuminating the meaning of the symptom or problem. Accordingly, in addition to formulating a traditional categorical diagnosis, supervision aims to cultivate the supervisee's competency in collaborating with the client to shed light on themes that the symptom may be expressing relative to the client's life circumstances and life path. For instance, the supervisee learns to engage the anxious client in a mutual process of reflecting upon what the anxiety might be calling attention to that needs addressing in the client's life rather than focusing exclusively on removing anxiety symptoms.

Figure 26.1 also shows the priorities of humanistic–existential supervision as pertaining to the functional competency domain of intervention. As has been described previously, supervision focuses on developing supervisee capacities to create the relational conditions within which the work of psychotherapy can unfold. Just as the supervisor cultivates relational depth in the service of the development of the supervisee (Lambers, 2007), the supervisee learns to engage with the client in an authentic and substantive way that encompasses ". . . a realness *in the service of* the client" (Cooper, 2007b, p. 14). To engage clients in this way requires the supervision also to focus on facilitating the supervisee's capacity to be self-aware relative to the experience of being with the client in psychotherapy (Cooper, 2007b). This supervisory focus on cultivating the psychotherapeutic relationship intersects with efforts to advance supervisee competency in facilitating experiential exploration of the client's psychological life, including use of active listening and empathic reflection; psychotherapeutic strategies that direct awareness to key concerns, themes, and moments of experiential avoidance; and techniques that illuminate experiential conflicts. A thread that runs through the supervision focus on intervention competency is development of the supervisee's ability to make use of self in the service of client change. Accordingly, the supervisor and supervisee work together to help the supervisee become proficient in using internal responses both to grasp the experiential process in the psychotherapy encounter and to engage relationally with the client in ways that facilitate the change process.

Supervisor competencies

The development of a competency-based framework for conducting clinical supervision is well under way and its reach is international in scope (Falender & Shafranske, 2004, 2012; Milne & Watkins, 2014; Watkins, 2012). Milne and Watkins (2014), in the introductory chapter to this volume, outline six supervision competency domains that reflect points of convergence across competency-based frameworks for clinical supervision developed in several different countries, including Australia, the United Kingdom, and the United States. Although an explicitly competency-based framework for conducting humanistic–existential supervision has yet to be outlined, a close reading of the humanistic–existential supervision literature reveals efforts to elucidate supervisor qualities and skills that are thought to be essential for conducting supervision within the model (e.g., Bryant-Jefferies, 2005; Lambers, 2007; Pack, 2009; van Deurzen, 2009). How might the six supervisor competency domains outlined by Milne and Watkins (2014) help organize these supervisor qualities and skills into a competency-based vision of humanistic–existential supervision? This question is addressed presently.

Knowledge of supervision models, methods, and intervention Within a humanistic–existential framework, this competency domain refers to the supervisor's mastery of the theoretical principles that underlie the approach and how they inform supervision practices and procedures, including use of experiential learning and the supervisory relationship to support the professional growth of the supervisee. Ideally, the supervisor also should have general expertise of supervision models and methods beyond those specified within the humanistic–existential approach.

Knowledge and skill in addressing ethical, legal, and professional matters Given the values-based orientation of the humanistic–existential tradition, it is not surprising that discussions of humanistic–existential supervision commonly highlight the supervisor's ethical sense and responsibility, along with the obligation of the supervisor to ensure the safety of both the client and the supervisee (Bryant-Jefferies, 2005; Lambers, 2007; Pack, 2009; van Deurzen, 2009). A distinctive contribution of a humanistic–existential frame in this regard is the supervisor's use of the experiential process in the supervision relationship to raise ethical challenges or clarifications of responsibility with a supervisee where needed (Lambers, 2007; Mitchell, 2009). For example, the supervisor might share a sense of visceral discomfort that directs the supervisee's attention to ethical concerns that they can then openly discuss. Guiding supervisee reflection on the ethics and values inherent in psychotherapeutic engagement in the context of cultivating professional development via a person of the psychotherapist focus also constitutes a key humanistic–existential supervisor competency.

Knowledge and skill in managing supervision relationship processes As has been described, the supervisor's relational capacities in many respects represent the *sine qua non* of the effectiveness of humanistic–existential supervision (Barnett, 2009; Bryant-Jefferies, 2005; Farber, 2010; Pack, 2009). Specifically, the quality of the relationship sets the conditions that make possible the supervisee's willingness to engage the process of experiential learning and to accept challenge and evaluative feedback from the supervisor. Anchored by an existential point of view, Barnett (2009) observes that a well-functioning supervisory relationship ". . . offers us a place to think out loud, to question our assumptions, values, and the projects we have and the past we carry" (p. 65). Similarly, drawing upon a gestalt framework, Pack (2009) notes that genuineness and presence on the part of the supervisor contributes to creating a relationship that ". . . supports the safe exploration of existential themes, uncertainty and complexity" (p. 72). While reflecting in this way can powerfully advance the development of the supervisee as a psychotherapist, it is critical that the supervisor ensure that the boundaries and purposes of the supervisory relationship to support the training of the supervisee remain clear (Farber, 2010; Lambers, 2007).

Knowledge and skill in assessing and evaluating the work of the supervisee As with all supervision models, the humanistic–existential approach recognizes the responsibility of the supervisor to ensure the safety and welfare of clients as well as the vital need for the supervisor to be skilled in providing evaluative feedback to the supervisee (e.g., Pack, 2009). The supervisor commonly offers feedback in the context of a collaborative dialogue through which the supervisor shares experiential observations of the work of the supervisee and invites the supervisee to respond to this input. Challenges or concerns about the work of the supervisee also are shared as experiential impressions that emerge in the context of the ongoing supervisory dialogue. In this process, the supervisor also invites the supervisee to engage in a process of reflective self-evaluation.

Knowledge and skill in cultivating attention to difference and diversity The contextual and highly idiographic foundations of the humanistic–existential approach make a focus on capturing the uniqueness of each individual a key element of the supervisor's approach in training supervisees. This basic framework is complemented by the supervisory emphasis on striving to understand the client's world with as much clarity as is feasible by setting aside preconceptions, biases, and expectations (Cain, 2007). Among the hallmarks of a humanistic–existential stance is ". . . a commitment to conceptualizing, and engaging with people in a deeply valuing and respectful way" Cooper, 2007b, p. 11). Collectively, these aspects of the approach converge such that the competent humanistic–existential supervisor organically engages with the supervisee in ways that highlight awareness of, and basic regard for, difference and diversity.

Use of self-reflection and self-assessment in supervision The experiential focus of the approach, including the premium placed on attending to the subtleties of both the client–supervisee and the supervisor–supervisee process, makes self-reflective skills and openness to self-evaluation essential for effective humanistic–existential supervisory work. Additionally, the humanistic–existential supervision process presents learning opportunities not just for the supervisee but for the supervisor as well, as both are conceptualized as engaged in a mutual process in the service of the professional development of the supervisee (Lambers, 2007; Pack, 2009). Supervisor self-reflection and self-assessment are essential to this process.

Humanistic–existential supervision and contemporary trends in psychotherapy training

The competency-based movement is illustrative of the dynamic and evolving professional landscape. In order to ensure that supervisees develop the competencies necessary for contemporary clinical practice, supervisors must remain cognizant of unfolding trends in the field and adapt their supervisory practices accordingly. With this in mind, ways in which humanistic–existential supervision may inform emerging training needs for supervisees are considered presently relative to two contemporary trends in the field: (1) the growing embeddedness of psychotherapy practice within health care settings; and (2) the increasing emphasis on integrative frameworks for psychotherapy.

Supervision of psychotherapy practice in medical care settings

In the United States, recent years have witnessed increased movement toward the integration of psychological services into medical care settings (e.g., Auxier, Farley, & Seifert, 2011; Vogel, Kirkpatrick, Collings, Cederna-Meko, & Grey, 2012), a trend that is consistent both with strategic initiatives within the American Psychological Association and with national health policy and reform activities (Runyon, 2011; Vogel et al., 2012). A key emerging model of integrative care is the patient-centered medical home, which is grounded in a holistic framework for conceptualizing health and illness (Runyon, 2011). The growing interest in patient-centered care in medicine is by no means limited to the United States, but rather is international in its reach and scope. This is evidenced by the convening of the Geneva Conferences on Person-Centered Medicine beginning in 2008 (Mezzich, 2011) and the launch in 2011 of an international journal focusing on person-centered approaches to medicine (Miles & Mezzich, 2011).

Person-centered medicine is conceptualized as a framework ". . . dedicated to the promotion of health as a state of physical, mental, social, and spiritual well-being as well as to the reduction of disease" (Mezzich, 2011, p. 335). As it turns out, this essentially biopsychosocial/spiritual view parallels closely the holistic and contextual framework of the humanistic–existential psychotherapy tradition, as exemplified by existential conceptualizations of physical, social, psychological, and spiritual dimensions of being (van Deurzen, 2009). Similarly, the patient-centered concept of a "humanistic aspect" (Schattner, 2009, p. 1095) of the relationship between health provider and patient is virtually identical to the humanistic–existential view of the psychotherapist's relational stance with clients. Specifically, the patient-centered relationship in medicine is conceptualized in terms of basic respect, empathy, compassion, sensitivity to patient concerns, and collaboration on behalf of the patient's health and well-being (Epstein & Street, 2011; Schattner, 2009). As the movement toward integration of mental health services into medical settings unfolds, the need to develop training frameworks that prepare clinicians for such work is gaining increased attention (McDaniel, Belar, Schroeder, Hargrove, & Freeman, 2002; Runyon, 2011). The obvious conceptual and practical overlap between patient-centered care models in medicine and humanistic–existential psychotherapy underscores the potential for the humanistic–existential supervision approach to add significant value to emerging models for training psychotherapists to work in medical settings.

For example, the relational focus of humanistic–existential supervision organically cultivates the supervisee's capacity to engender a collaborative healing relationship with the client that is wholly consistent with the medical concept of a patient-centered relationship. By extension, this supervisory focus also can help support the supervisee in learning to assume a consultative role with interdisciplinary colleagues on behalf of clients, such as in instances where medical colleagues might look to the supervisee for guidance on how to maximize their relational effectiveness in their medical encounters with clients. As such, supervision provides an opportunity for the supervisee to gain confidence in working within interdisciplinary contexts. Specifically, the supervisee learns to understand the value of interdisciplinary roles and care philosophies of differing health disciplines, and gain facility with interdisciplinary communication, collaboration, and working as part of a clinical team. Collectively, these activities serve to cultivate the supervisee's overarching foundational competency in working within interdisciplinary systems (Fouad et al., 2009; Rodolfa et al., 2005), which is critical to professional functioning in health care settings.

Several content elements of humanistic–existential supervision also can be adapted to guide the specific training of supervisees for work in medical settings. For instance, given the differences between humanistic–existential clinical formulation frameworks and the categorical diagnostic formulation systems that typically are required in medical settings, it is important that the supervisor explore with the supervisee ways of integrating traditional diagnosis with phenomenological and adaptation-focused formulations that are individualized and contextualized in accordance with the biopsychosocial situation of a given client. As a part of this focus, the supervisee has an opportunity to educate interdisciplinary colleagues about the value added by including a whole-person clinical formulation that is consistent with an overarching patient-centered care framework. Given that a meaning-focused perspective is a salient characteristic of humanistic–existential psychotherapy (e.g., Wong, 2010), humanistic–existential supervision also is well positioned to guide the clinical work of the supervisee as it pertains to client themes regarding the meaning of illness and health-related concerns. Assisting the supervisee in promoting the client's experience of personal agency and efficacy relative to health-related adaptation is a key supervisory priority, as is cultivating the supervisee's skill in facilitating client awareness of personal choice and responsibility relative to health behaviors, self-care, relationships with health providers, and navigation of health care systems. Finally, because psychological services conducted in health care settings frequently are intermittent or occur in conjunction with medical visits or procedures, supervisees must gain skill and comfort in working in a time-sensitive manner while remaining within a humanistic–existential frame. Principles from brief humanistic–existential psychotherapy models are quite useful in guiding this supervisory focus (e.g., Elliot, 2001; Tudor, 2008; Williams, 2001).

Psychology, like medicine, has placed increasing emphasis on preparing trainees to utilize an evidence-based practice framework for clinical work, with the evidence-based model gaining strength as psychological services increasingly are integrated within medical care settings. As such, it is vital that scientific knowledge and methods as a foundational competency domain (Fouad et al., 2009; Rodolfa et al., 2005) be incorporated as a routine focus of humanistic–existential psychotherapy supervision (Farber, 2012). Yet systematic consideration of the scientific literature in the context of humanistic–existential supervision historically has been de-emphasized by many supervisors based on the rationale that the nomothetic and quantitative bases of evidence-based practice are out of step with the highly idiographic and phenomenological bases of humanistic–existential psychotherapy. In medicine, the patient-centered model is recognized as complementary to evidence-based medical practice (Epstein & Street, 2011; Schattner, 2009), as it ". . . seeks to articulate science and humanism in a balanced manner, engaging them at the service of the whole person" (Mezzich, 2011, p. 335). The pluralism inherent in this vision of the complementarity of a patient-centered approach and evidence-based medicine suggests a compelling way forward for incorporating a science-oriented focus into humanistic–existential psychotherapy supervision.

Important models already exist for the integration of a scientific orientation within the humanistic–existential perspective. For example, Carl Rogers was a pioneer of psychotherapy research (Rogers & Dymond, 1954), and some contemporary experiential psychotherapy approaches, notably emotion-focused psychotherapy, are well-researched using traditional quantitative methods (Pos et al., 2008; Pos, Greenberg, & Warwar, 2009). Furthermore, rich qualitative human science research frameworks have been elaborated from within a humanistic–existential perspective (Giorgi, 2009). It would be of great value for supervisors to encourage their supervisees to learn about these scientific developments within the humanistic–existential tradition, and to engage actively with their supervisees in a dialogue regarding the uses, applications, and challenges of science and research in the context of humanistic–existential psychotherapy (Cooper, 2010). Specifically, supervisors might explore with their supervisees the place of pluralism in scientific inquiry, as well as examine the strengths and limitations of quantitative and qualitative psychotherapy research for informing clinical practice. Additionally, supervisors might invite their supervisees to pursue knowledge of the extant psychotherapy research literature and consider its practical applications for psychotherapy, as well as reflect on the relative contributions of scientific and experiential knowledge in guiding the psychotherapy process (Farber, 2012).

Humanistic–existential supervision and psychotherapy integration

A ". . . *zeitgeist* of informed pluralism" (Norcross, 2005, p. 4) regarding psychotherapy has gained ascendency in recent years as psychotherapy theorists, clinicians, and researchers increasingly appreciate that no one theoretical orientation sufficiently captures the complexity of human psychological life. This pursuit of pathways to psychotherapy integration extends to the psychotherapy education and training arena, including psychotherapy supervision (Norcross & Halgin, 2005; Scaturo, 2012).

In reflecting on potential contributions of humanistic–existential supervision to an integrative approach to psychotherapy training, perhaps a logical starting point is to consider the broad contributions of the psychotherapy approach itself. Along these lines, Cain (2007) has characterized several overarching themes from humanistic–existential psychotherapy that are broadly applicable to the field of psychotherapy as a whole, highlighting the humanistic–existential relational framework as a hallmark contribution in this regard. This includes the familiar humanistic–existential emphasis on basic regard, listening, responding empathically, being present, and suspending preconceptions to the degree possible while immersing oneself in the client's experiential world. It also refers to the psychotherapist's use of self, including genuineness, spontaneity, openness to the experiential impact of working with the client, and willingness to share experiences of being with the client in the service of psychotherapeutic healing. Discussions of integrative psychotherapy training have highlighted the importance of learning the core interpersonal skill fundamentals early on in the training process (e.g., Norcross & Halgin, 2005). Given its emphasis on the therapeutic relationship in the psychotherapy process, humanistic–existential supervision is ideally situated to contribute to the development of these supervisee relational skills that are presumably foundational to good psychotherapy practice in general. Consistent with this view, Scaturo (2012) highlights the usefulness of humanistic–existential principles for an integrative psychotherapy supervision framework, particularly as applied to skills that pertain to clinical interviewing and the psychotherapy alliance. Further underscoring the key role of humanism in an integrative supervision framework, Scaturo (2012) notes that ". . . the fields associated with the practice of psychotherapy should be at the vanguard of recognizing the healing power of genuine human contact" (p. 186).

Returning to the musings of Cain (2007) on the contributions of a humanistic–existential perspective to psychotherapy as a whole, the emphasis on experiential attunement in the psychotherapy process is also highlighted. Specifically, humanistic–existential psychotherapy has a lot to say about discerning and tracking key psychotherapeutic issues by attending to repeating themes expressed by the client, emotional cues, nonverbal communication, the client's use of language, and client references to self as clues to guide the psychotherapeutic focus and intervention. A focus on illuminating personal choice and responsibility also is a key element of the approach. To the extent that humanistic–existential supervision promotes development of these skills in supervisees, it has the potential to contribute to an integrative supervision approach in that it focuses on assisting supervisees in knowing how, when, and where to focus psychotherapeutic efforts most productively along with empowering clients to make the changes they seek. Collectively, these capacities comprise a key skill set for general psychotherapy practice across theoretical orientations.

Reflections on the international applicability of humanistic–existential supervision

Having described a general humanistic–existential framework for psychotherapy supervision, considered its applicability in the context of a competency-based training perspective, and explored the supervision approach relative to emerging trends in the field, attention now is turned to examining the international applicability of humanistic–existential supervision. Specifically, what can be said about its international resonance across the rich diversity of cultures that comprise the global community of psychotherapists and psychotherapy supervisors? This sense of resonance refers not only to the potential for the humanistic–existential perspective to contribute meaningfully to international frameworks for clinical supervision, but also to the potential for existing humanistic–existential supervision models to themselves experience meaningful growth and evolution based on insights gleaned from the vibrant exchange of cultural viewpoints as the international dialogue on supervision unfolds.

When reflecting on the prospects for the international applicability of any theoretically grounded system of psychotherapy supervision, the diversity of cultural frameworks represented across global regions springs to the forefront as a central matter requiring consideration. The concepts of individualism and collectivism have been widely utilized as categories for understanding basic differences in cultural organization, with individualism emphasizing autonomy, independence, and personal fulfillment, and collectivism prioritizing interdependence, belonging, and acting in the service of group-oriented goals (Triandis, 2001). Conceived from theories and methods of psychotherapy developed and elaborated in Europe and North America, the humanistic–existential supervision framework represented in this chapter is rooted in a decidedly Western individualist worldview. Specifically, the model shines a light on supervisory principles and processes that promote an individualist self-oriented focus relative to both the supervisee and the work of psychotherapy. For instance, as has been described, significant attention is given in supervision to developing the person of the psychotherapist based on an individualist conceptualization of professional identity. In parallel fashion, supervision orients the supervisee clinically toward development of the client's self through a focus on illuminating the client's internal experiential world. At the same time, relatively little attention is given in supervision to social and cultural influences on the supervisee's professional development. Similarly, supervision typically focuses only minimally on how social and cultural context influence a client's presenting problems and concerns, experience of self, and the psychotherapy relationship.

As currently articulated, therefore, the international applicability and reach of the humanistic–existential supervision approach is apt to be greatest in global regions where an individualist value is predominant. Yet the contextual foundations of humanistic–existential psychotherapy provide a basis for envisioning new adaptations of humanistic–existential psychotherapy supervision with international applicability of increased breadth. This is reflected in emerging humanistic–existential psychotherapy models that more fully incorporate the cultural dimensions of human life into the scope and focus of the approach than previously has been the case (e.g., Fernbacher & Plummer, 2005; Hoffman & Cleare-Hoffman, 2011; Hoffman, Yang, Kaklauskas, & Chan, 2009: Jenkins, 2001; Lago, 2007, Vontress & Epp, 2001).

For example, in describing a cultural–existential psychotherapy approach, Felder and Robbins (2011) suggest that psychotherapy must proceed at both depth and breadth, meaning that illuminating the inner life of the individual requires articulation of that person's cultural milieu. According to this view, psychotherapy should not be ". . . limited to placing the patient in dialogue with various aspects of his or her interiority. The patient should instead be encouraged to catch sight of the web of cultural discourses coiling over and through his or her being" (Felder & Robbins, 2011, p. 369). Drawing on a person-centered framework, Tudor (2010) similarly highlights the inseparability of the person and environmental context, and proposes that the individual strives simultaneously both toward increasing autonomy and belonging. As such, Tudor (2010) frames person-centered psychotherapy as a relational approach ". . . which acknowledges the impact of the environment/biosphere on the individual person/organism; of the person on her or his environment; of the individual/environmental biospheric occurance [*sic*] itself; and of the therapist's response to this integral reality" (p. 61). Accordingly, while the autonomy dimensions have tended to be emphasized in Western person-centered practice, a truly contextual framework requires also that attention be directed to the dimensions of interdependence and belonging.

What then do these ideas about extending the cultural reach of humanistic–existential psychotherapy suggest about how the corresponding supervision framework might broaden its international applicability? One clear point is that the contents and processes of supervision need to transcend the traditional emphasis on interiority such that guiding the supervisee in the process of illuminating the self of the client is expanded to incorporate reflection on the broader social and cultural context. Relative to the professional development of the supervisee, when the scope of supervision broadens to fully incorporate contextual breadth, the supervisory process of cultivating the supervisee's professional growth is recast to incorporate not only the unfolding of an individuated sense of personal identity as a psychotherapist, but also of professional interdependence. This includes facilitating the supervisee's appreciation for belonging within the professional community with its collective sense of professional history, values, ethics, traditions, and priorities, along with peer support for the process of lifelong professional engagement and growth.

Although the organization of a given culture can be characterized as more or less individualist or collectivist, there is tremendous diversity in the degree to which a particular individual within that culture subscribes to its predominant worldview (Triandis, 2001). Within a humanistic–existential framework, diversity is inherent in the processes of growth and development of the human organism (Tudor, 2010). Each person is wholly unique, making it imperative that psychotherapists and supervisors alike adopt an idiographic frame of reference grounded in the recognition of ". . . the vast diversity and unknowability of human being" (Cooper & McLeod, 2011, p. 221). A key focus, therefore, involves the illumination of the ways in which culture is expressed uniquely in the life world of a given individual.

In reflecting on the implications of this point for humanistic–existential supervision from the perspective of expanding its international applicability, it is clear that the contextual and idiographic underpinnings of the model must be applied such that the supervisory encounter is one that takes stock of the converging multiplicity of sociocultural dimensions that comprise the cultural backgrounds of the supervisor, the supervisee, and the psychotherapy client. A way forward in this regard is suggested by the concept of intersectionality, which Brown (2009) characterizes as an integrative culturally competent way to frame the psychotherapy enterprise. Intersectionality refers to the idea ". . . that each of us is more than the most obvious component of our identity and that these mixtures of aspects of self occur in a myriad of ways" (p. 344). Accordingly, clinical understanding in psychotherapy requires consideration of the unique intersection of such social and cultural characteristics as age, gender, race, ethnicity, sexual orientation, national/regional origin, spiritual/religious background, and socioeconomic status in the client's life. Incorporating the intersectionality construct as a focus of humanistic–existential supervision encourages a process inquiry aimed at honing the supervisee's capacity to conceptualize the ways in which multiple diversity characteristics converge uniquely to inform a given client's social and personal identities and experiences. Specifically, the supervisee learns to synthesize a contextual and idiographic understanding of the interplay of social/cultural background, social roles, and identities in the client's life and consider implications for the client's experience of clinical problems, aspirations and expectations for psychotherapy, and the psychotherapy relationship (Farber, 2012). The supervisory relationship and process also can be examined within an intersectionality framework, encouraging the supervisor and supervisee alike to reflect on ways in which the intersection of characteristics that comprise their respective social/cultural backgrounds influence their understanding of the focus and process of supervision, the supervisor–supervisee relationship, and the goals of supervision.

Conclusions

Among the signature themes of the current era in psychotherapy education and training with significant implications for the conceptualization, practice, and research of clinical supervision is that of convergence. This is exemplified by trends toward gaining consensus regarding competency-based training frameworks, articulating integrative ways to conceptualize psychotherapy and psychotherapy training, understanding the training implications of integrating psychological and medical services based on whole-person models of transdisciplinary care (e.g., patient-centered medical home), and exploring the international state of the art in psychotherapy supervision. Humanistic–existential psychotherapy supervision is rooted in a rich tradition with significant contributions to make to the unfolding dialogue on the status and evolution of clinical supervision in relation to these trends. A particular strength of the approach is its well-articulated supervisory methods for guiding training activities that focus on experiential learning and the psychotherapy relationship. Additionally, the value placed on pluralism and complementarity within the humanistic–existential approach make it especially well positioned to add to ongoing reflections on converging themes in clinical supervision. Of equal significance, the humanistic–existential psychotherapy supervision approach also is itself poised for significant enrichment and growth as the discourse on clinical supervision expands in scope to encompass a truly international conversation.

References

Adams, M. (2009). Phenomenology and supervision. In E. van Deurzen & S. Young (Eds.), *Existential perspectives on supervision: Widening the horizon of psychotherapy and counselling* (pp. 43–55). Houndmills, Basingstoke, Hampshire, UK: Palgrave Macmillan.

Auxier, A., Farley, T., & Seifert, K. (2011). Establishing an integrated care practice in a community health center. *Professional Psychology, Research and Practice*, *42*, 391–397.

Barnett, L. (2009). The supervisory relationship. In E. van Deurzen & S. Young (Eds.), *Existential perspectives on supervision: Widening the horizon of psychotherapy and counselling* (pp. 56–67), Houndmills, Basingstoke, Hampshire, UK: Palgrave Macmillan.

Bernard, J. M., & Goodyear, R. K. (2009). *Fundamentals of clinical supervision* (4th ed.). Upper Saddle River, NJ: Pearson.

Binswanger, L. (1946/1958). The existential analysis school of thought. In R. May, E. Angel, & H. Ellenberger (Eds.), *Existence: A new dimension in psychiatry and psychology* (pp. 191–213). New York, NY: Basic Books.

Bohart, A. C. (2007). The actualizing person. In M. Cooper, M. O'Hara, P. F. Schmid, & G. Wyatt (Eds.), *The handbook of person-centred psychotherapy and counselling* (pp. 47–63). New York, NY: Palgrave Macmillan.

Brown, L. S. (2009). Cultural competence: A new way of thinking about integration in therapy. *Journal of Psychotherapy Integration, 19*, 340–353.

Brownell, P. (Ed.). (2008). *Handbook for theory, research, and practice in gestalt therapy.* Newcastle, UK: Cambridge Scholars Publishing.

Brownell, P. (2010). *Gestalt therapy: A guide to contemporary practice.* New York, NY: Springer.

Bryant-Jefferies, R. (2005). *Person-centred counselling supervision: Personal and professional.* Oxford, UK: Radcliffe.

Bugental, J. F. T. (1978). *Psychotherapy and process: The fundamentals of an existential-humanistic approach.* Reading, MA: Addison-Wesley.

Burston, D. (2003). Existentialism, humanism, and psychotherapy. *Existential Analysis, 14*, 309–319.

Cain, D. J. (2002). Defining characteristics, history, and evolution of humanistic psychotherapies. In D. J. Cain & J. Seeman (Eds.), *Humanistic psychotherapies: Handbook of research and practice* (pp. 3–54). Washington, DC: American Psychological Association.

Cain, D. J. (2007). What every therapist should know, be, and do: Contributions from humanistic psychotherapies. *Journal of Contemporary Psychotherapy, 37*, 3–10.

Cooper, M. (2007a). Experiential and phenomenological foundations. In M. Cooper, M. O'Hara, P. F. Schmid, & G. Wyatt (Eds.), *The handbook of person-centred psychotherapy and counselling* (pp. 64–76). New York, NY: Palgrave Macmillan.

Cooper, M. (2007b). Humanizing psychotherapy. *Journal of Contemporary Psychotherapy, 37*, 11–16.

Cooper, M. (2008). Existential psychotherapy. In J. L. Lebow (Ed.), *Twenty-first century psychotherapies: Contemporary approaches to theory and practice* (pp. 237–276). Hoboken, NJ: John Wiley & Sons.

Cooper, M. (2010). The challenge of counselling and psychotherapy research. *Counselling and Psychotherapy Research, 10*, 183–191.

Cooper, M., & McLeod, J. (2011). Person-centered therapy: A pluralistic perspective. *Person-Centered & Experiential Psychotherapies, 10*, 210–223.

Cooper, M., O'Hara, M., Schmid, P. F., & Wyatt, G. (Eds.). (2007). *The handbook of person-centred psychotherapy and counselling* (pp. 64–76). New York, NY: Palgrave Macmillan.

Crocker, S. F. (2008). A unified theory. In P. Brownell (Ed.), *Handbook for theory, research, and practice in gestalt therapy* (pp. 124–150). Newcastle, UK: Cambridge Scholars Publishing.

Elliot, R. (2001). Contemporary brief experiential psychotherapy. *Clinical Psychology: Science and Practice, 8*, 38–50.

Elliott, R., Watson, J. C., Goldman, R. N., & Greenberg, L. S. (2004). *Learning emotion-focused therapy: The process-experiential approach to change.* Washington, DC: American Psychological Association.

Epstein, R. M., & Street, R. L. (2011). The values and value of patient-centered care. *Annals of Family Medicine, 9*, 100–103.

Etzi, J. L. (2008). Psychotherapy clients as human phenomena. *American Journal of Psychotherapy, 62*, 83–96.

Falender, C. A., & Shafranske, E. P. (2004). *Clinical supervision: A competency-based approach.* Washington, DC: American Psychological Association.

Falender, C. A., & Shafranske, E. P. (2012). The importance of competency-based clinical supervision and training in the 21st century: Why bother? *Journal of Contemporary Psychotherapy*, *42*, 129–137.

Farber, E. W. (2010). Humanistic-existential psychotherapy competencies and the supervisory process. *Psychotherapy Theory, Research, Practice, Training*, *47*, 28–34.

Farber, E. W. (2012). Supervising humanistic-existential psychotherapy: Needs, possibilities. *Journal of Contemporary Psychotherapy*, *42*, 173–182.

Farber, E. W. (in press). Theoretical orientation in the education and training of psychologists. In W. B. Johnson & N. J. Kaslow (Eds.), *Oxford handbook of education and training in professional psychology*. New York, NY: Oxford University Press.

Farber, E. W., & Kaslow, N. J. (2010). Introduction to the special section: The role of supervision in ensuring the development of psychotherapy competencies across diverse theoretical perspectives. *Psychotherapy Theory, Research, Practice, Training*, *47*, 1–2.

Felder, A. J., & Robbins, B. D. (2011). A cultural-existential approach to therapy: Merleau-Ponty's phenomenology of embodiment and its implications for practice. *Theory & Psychology*, *21*, 355–376.

Fernbacher, S., & Plummer, D. (2005). Cultural influences and considerations in gestalt therapy. In A. L. Woldt & S. M. Toman (Eds.), *Gestalt therapy: History, theory, and practice* (pp. 117–132). Thousand Oaks, CA: Sage.

Fouad, N. A., Grus, C. L., Hatcher, R. L., Kaslow, N. J., Hutchings, P. S., Madson, M. B., & Crossman, R. E. (2009). Competency benchmarks: A model for understanding and measuring competence in professional psychology across training levels. *Training and Education in Professional Psychology*, *3*(4 Suppl.), S5–S26.

Gendlin, E. T. (1996). *Focusing-oriented psychotherapy*. New York, NY: Guilford Press.

Giorgi, A. (2009). *The descriptive phenomenological method in psychology: A modified husserlian approach*. Pittsburgh, PA: Duquesne University Press.

Hoffman, L., & Cleare-Hoffman, H. (2011). Existential therapy and emotions: Lessons from cross-cultural exchange. *The Humanistic Psychologist*, *39*, 261–267.

Hoffman, L., Yang, M., Kaklauskas, F. J., & Chan, A. (Eds.). (2009). *Existential psychology east-west*. Colorado Springs, CO: University of the Rockies Press.

Jenkins, A. H. (2001). Humanistic psychology and multiculturalism. In K. J. Schneider, J. F. T. Bugental, & J. F. Pierson (Eds.), *The handbook of humanistic psychology: Leading edges in theory, practice, and research* (pp. 37–45). Thousand Oaks, CA: Sage.

Kaslow, N. J., Grus, C. L., Campbell, L. F., Fouad, N. A., Hatcher, R. L., & Rodolfa, E. R. (2009). Competency assessment toolkit for professional psychology. *Training and Education in Professional Psychology*, *3*(4 Suppl.), S27–S45.

Lago, C. (2007). Counselling across difference and diversity. In M. Cooper, M. O'Hara, P. F. Schmid, & G. Wyatt (Eds.), *The handbook of person-centred psychotherapy and counselling* (pp. 251–265). New York, NY: Palgrave Macmillan.

Lambers, E. (2007). A person-centred perspective on supervision. In M. Cooper, M. O'Hara, P. F. Schmid, & G. Wyatt (Eds.), *The handbook of person-centred psychotherapy and counselling* (pp. 366–378). New York, NY: Palgrave Macmillan.

Maslow, A. H. (1954). *Motivation and personality*. New York, NY: Harper.

Maslow, A. H. (1968). *Toward a psychology of being* (2nd ed.). New York, NY: D. Van Nostrand Company.

May, R., Angel, E., & Ellenberger, H. F. (Eds.). (1958). *Existence: A new dimension in psychiatry and psychology*. New York, NY: Simon & Schuster.

McDaniel, S. H., Belar, C. D., Schroeder, C., Hargrove, D. S., & Freeman, E. L. (2002). A training curriculum for professional psychologists in primary care. *Professional Psychology, Research and Practice*, *33*, 65–72.

Mezzich, J. E. (2011). The Geneva conferences and the emergence of the international network for person-centered medicine. *Journal of Evaluation in Clinical Practice, 17*, 333–336.

Milne, D. (2007). An empirical definition of clinical supervision. *British Journal of Clinical Psychology, 46*, 437–447.

Miles, A., & Mezzich, J. E. (2011). Advancing the global communication of scholarship and research for personalized healthcare. *International Journal of Person Centered Medicine, 1*, 1–5.

Milne, D. L., & Watkins, C. E., Jr. (2014). Defining and understanding clinical supervision: A functional approach. In C. E. Watkins Jr. & D. L. Milne (Eds.), *The Wiley international handbook of clinical supervision*, (pp. 3–19). Oxford, UK: John Wiley & Sons, Ltd.

Mitchell, D. (2009). Responsibility in existential supervision. In E. van Deurzen & S. Young (Eds.), *Existential perspectives on supervision: Widening the horizon of psychotherapy and counselling* (pp. 160–171). Houndmills, Basingstoke, Hampshire, UK: Palgrave Macmillan.

Nassif, C., Schulenberg, S. E., Hutzell, R. R., & Rogina, J. M. (2010). Clinical supervision and logotherapy: Discovering meaning in the supervisory relationship. *Journal of Contemporary Psychotherapy, 40*, 21–29.

Norcross, J. C. (2005). A primer on psychotherapy integration. In J. C. Norcross & M. R. Goldfried (Eds.), *Handbook of psychotherapy integration* (2nd ed., pp. 3–23). New York, NY: Oxford University Press.

Norcross, J. C., & Halgin, R. P. (2005). Training in psychotherapy integration. In J. C. Norcross & M. R. Goldfried (Eds.), *Handbook of Psychotherapy Integration* (2nd ed., pp. 439–458). New York, NY: Oxford University Press.

Pachana, N. A., Sofronoff, K., Scott, T., & Helmes, E. (2011). Attainment of competencies in clinical psychology training: Ways forward in the Australian context. *Australian Psychologist, 46*, 67–76.

Pack, M. (2009). Supervision as a liminal space: Towards a dialogic relationship. *Gestalt Journal of Australia and New Zealand, 5*, 60–78.

Perls, F. S. (1969). *Gestalt therapy verbatim*. Lafayette, CA: Real People Press.

Pos, A. E., Greenberg, L. S., & Elliott, R. (2008). Experiential therapy. In J. L. Lebow (Ed.), *Twenty-first century psychotherapies: Contemporary approaches to theory and practice* (pp. 80–122). Hoboken, NJ: John Wiley & Sons.

Pos, A. E., Greenberg, L. S., & Warwar, S. H. (2009). Testing a model of change in the experiential treatment of depression. *Journal of Consulting and Clinical Psychology, 77*, 1055–1066.

Rodolfa, E., Bent, R., Eisman, E., Nelson, P., Rehm, L., & Ritchie, P. (2005). A cube model for competency development: Implications for psychology educators and regulators. *Professional Psychology, Research and Practice, 36*, 347–354.

Rogers, C. R. (1957). The necessary and sufficient conditions of therapeutic personality change. *Journal of Consulting Psychology, 21*, 95–103.

Rogers, C. R. (1961). *On becoming a person*. Boston, MA: Houghton-Mifflin.

Rogers, C. R., & Dymond, R. F. (Eds.). (1954). *Psychotherapy and personality change*. Chicago, IL: University of Chicago Press.

Roth, A. D., & Pilling, S. (2008). Using an evidence-based methodology to identify the competences required to deliver effective cognitive and behavioural therapy for depression and anxiety disorders. *Behavioural and Cognitive Psychotherapy, 36*, 129–147.

Runyon, C. N. (2011). Psychology can be indispensable to health care reform and the patient-centered medical home. *Psychological Services, 8*, 53–68.

Scaturo, D. J. (2012). Supervising integrative psychotherapy in the 21st century: Pressing needs, impressing possibilities. *Journal of Contemporary Psychotherapy, 42*, 183–192.

Schattner, A. (2009). The silent dimension: Expressing humanism in each medical encounter. *Archives of Internal Medicine, 169*, 1095–1099.

Schneider, K. J., & Krug, O. T. (2010). *Existential-humanistic therapy.* Washington, DC: American Psychological Association.

Triandis, H. C. (2001). Individualism-collectivism and personality. *Journal of Personality, 69*, 907–924.

Tudor, K. (Ed.). (2008). *Brief person-centred therapies.* London, UK: Sage.

Tudor, K. (2010). Person-centered relational therapy: An organismic perspective. *Person-Centered and Experiential Psychotherapies, 9*, 52–68.

van Deurzen, E. (2009). Aims of existential supervision: Truth as a guiding light. In E. van Deurzen & S. Young (Eds.), *Existential perspectives on supervision: Widening the horizon of psychotherapy and counselling* (pp. 83–95). Houndmills, Basingstoke, Hampshire, UK: Palgrave Macmillan.

van Deurzen, E. (2010). *Everyday mysteries: A handbook of existential psychotherapy* (2nd ed.). New York, NY: Routledge.

Vogel, M. E., Kirkpatrick, H. A., Collings, A. S., Cederna-Meko, C. L., & Grey, M. J. (2012). Integrated care: Maturing the relationship between psychology and primary care. *Professional Psychology, Research and Practice, 43*, 271–280.

Vontress, C. E., & Epp, L. R. (2001). Existential cross-cultural counseling: When hearts and cultures share. In K. J. Schneider, J. F. T. Bugental, & J. F. Pierson (Eds.), *The handbook of humanistic psychology: Leading edges in theory, practice, and research* (pp. 371–387). Thousand Oaks, CA: Sage.

Watkins, C. E. (2011). Psychotherapy supervision since 1909: Some friendly observations about its first century. *Journal of Contemporary Psychotherapy, 41*, 57–67.

Watkins, C. E. (2012). Psychotherapy supervision in the new millennium: Competency-based, evidence-based, particularized, and energized. *Journal of Contemporary Psychotherapy, 42*, 193–203.

Williams, B. (2001). The practice of gestalt therapy within a brief therapy context. *Gestalt Journal, 24*, 7–62.

Wong, P. T. P. (2010). Meaning therapy: An integrative and positive existential psychotherapy. *Journal of Contemporary Psychotherapy, 40*, 85–93.

Yalom, I. (1980). *Existential psychotherapy.* New York, NY: Basic Books.

27

Supervising Integrative and Eclectic Psychotherapies[1]

Douglas J. Scaturo and C. Edward Watkins, Jr.

Introduction

The following chapter is divided into two parts. In Part I, we focus on helping trainees and supervisees learn "how to think about doing psychotherapy" from an integrative and eclectic perspective. We propose four *bona fide* schools of psychotherapy with relatively nonoverlapping foci that are most useful in training and supervision that would contribute to either case conceptualization and the process of clinical interviewing: psychodynamic psychotherapy, cognitive-behavioral psychotherapy, family systems therapy, and humanistic/client-centered therapy. The goal for such broadly based clinical instruction is for students, trainees, and interns to have an ability to provide a multilevel case conceptualization for any of the psychotherapy cases for which they are providing treatment. In Part II, we focus on providing clinical supervisors with an integrative, transtheoretical structure for "how to think about doing supervision." To this end, we propose a common-language, learning-based, integrative model for guiding the practice of psychotherapy supervision, identifying three supervisory processes: alliance building and maintenance, educational interventions, and learning/relearning (see Watkins & Scaturo, 2013). These processes comprise both new learning and relearning, providing corrective experiences for supervisees within the cognitive, affective, and behavioral domains.

[1] This chapter is an adaptation of "Supervising integrative psychotherapy in the 21st century: pressing needs, impressing possibilities," by D. J. Scaturo, 2012a, *Journal of Contemporary Psychotherapy*, *42*, 183–192, copyright 2012 by Springer Science+Business Media, LLC, and "Toward an integrative, learning-based model of psychotherapy supervision: supervisory alliance, educational interventions, and supervisee learning/relearning" by C. E. Watkins, Jr., & D. J. Scaturo, 2013, *Journal of Psychotherapy Integration*, *23*, 75–95, copyright 2013 by the American Psychological Association. Adapted with permission.

The Wiley International Handbook of Clinical Supervision, First Edition. Edited by C. Edward Watkins, Jr. and Derek L. Milne.

Part I. The Breadth and Range of Integrative and Eclectic Psychotherapies

Clinical supervision in integrative and eclectic psychotherapy occupies a somewhat unique place in the field of supervision in much the same way that it does in the field of psychotherapy overall. While it becomes the task of practitioners and teachers of any given form of psychotherapy to keep current on the developments within that particular school of treatment (e.g., cognitive-behavioral, psychodynamic), supervisors and instructors in the areas of integrative and eclectic psychotherapies have had the dual task of initially *surveying* the considerable range of approaches that have developed and subsequently *distilling* these approaches down to a manageable number of influences that have been found to have the greatest impact on clinical practice over time. For example, Garfield (1995) reviewed the burgeoning array of psychotherapeutic approaches that has emerged over the history of the field. In the mid-1960s, he identified over 60 different approaches to psychotherapy. By the mid-1970s, the National Institute of Mental Health reported that over 130 approaches could be documented (Report of the Research Task Force of the National Institute of Mental Health, 1975). After only five more years had passed, Herink (1980) cited 250 forms of psychotherapy being performed in practice. And, by the mid-1980s, Kazdin (1986) found over 400 psychotherapeutic techniques in existence.

To contend with this proliferation of diverse approaches and techniques, some practitioners have attempted to find a common theoretical language that can help us grapple with this conceptual Tower of Babel (e.g., Goldfried, 1995; Marks et al., 2005; Messer, 1987; Miller, Duncan, & Hubble, 1997; Scaturo, 2005, 2010a, 2012b). At present, an international task force has been assembled for a Common Language for Psychotherapy (CLP) Project sponsored by 12 psychological, psychiatric, and psychotherapeutic organizations worldwide. This ambitious undertaking, designed to create an ecumenical lexicon of psychotherapy procedures, is being spearheaded by Isaac Marks at the Institute of Psychiatry at King's College in London, England (Marks et al., 2011). Presently, the cataloging effort has thus far accepted 94 procedures into its registry authored by 107 mental health professionals. The intent of the CLP is to arrive at a consensus of *bona fide* psychotherapy procedures in use by practitioners across the globe.

Whether or not a single unifying language for psychotherapy can ultimately emerge, it remains the job of those interested in psychotherapy integration to distill the diversity of approaches down to a set of major theoretical paradigms that serve to explain the preponderance of clinical data in any given psychotherapy case. One of the primary functions of theory in psychotherapy is to organize seemingly varied approaches under a rubric that shares common assumptions about psychopathology and its treatment (Scaturo, 2010b). The American Psychological Association (APA) has recently published an excellent series of books intended to distill the diversity of psychotherapy approaches down to what it regards as the major theoretical models currently practiced by psychotherapists (http://www.apa.org/pubs/books/theories-series-and-dvds.aspx). Of the 19 volumes in this series, 16 of these might be regarded as emanating from single-theory methods of treatment: psychoanalysis and psychoanalytic therapies, brief dynamic therapy, behavior therapy, cognitive therapy, cognitive-behavioral therapy, rational emotive behavior therapy, acceptance and commitment therapy (ACT), reality therapy, family therapy, existential-humanistic therapy, person-centered psychotherapies, interpersonal psychotherapy (IPT), emotion-focused therapy, narrative therapy, feminist therapy, and relational-cultural therapy.

Another approach to distillation is to subsume related methods of treatment into what form broader "schools of thought." Scaturo (2001, 2005) has proposed a distillation of schools of psychotherapy that has focused on three *bona fide* schools of treatment as the foundation of theoretical pluralism for psychotherapeutic treatment and supervision that have "withstood the test of time" for case conceptualization: (a) *psychoanalytic and psychodynamic psychotherapy*, (b) *behavioral and cognitive-behavioral therapy*, and (c) *family systems therapy*. In addition, *humanistic and client-centered therapy* constitutes a major theoretical force in understanding the process of psychotherapy (Scaturo, 2002, 2005, 2010b), although its primary contribution to training may be more relevant to teaching effective clinical interviewing skills (Truax & Carkhuff, 1967) and negotiating a sound therapeutic alliance (Safran & Muran, 2003) rather than as a diagnostic system that contributes substantively to case formulation (Ells, 2010). Thus, we believe that the literature suggests that four major schools of thought in psychotherapy are likely to provide most comprehensive, nonoverlapping perspectives for training and supervision of integrative psychotherapy.

Designing integrative graduate curricula and education

While the primary focus of this chapter is targeted toward the supervision of psychotherapy, it is difficult to talk about supervision in *integrative* psychotherapy without making some mention of graduate school curricula. In part, this is because pluralism precedes integration. Integrative clinicians in our field require, first of all, a pluralistic exposure to a variety of forms of treatment and case conceptualization. Some of the earliest writings on the supervision of integrative psychotherapy have recognized that training in multiple systems of psychotherapy poses an inherent difficulty in training (Norcross, 1988a). As Castonguay (2000) pointed out, "Integrative and eclectic therapists are confronted with unique and complex questions (e.g., How and when should different methods be combined? How can one determine which approach to use for a particular client faced with a specific problem?) . . ." (p. 230). Such questions underscore the importance of systematic training models for teaching eclectic approaches to treatment. According to Norcross and Halgin (2005, p. 451), "A systematic model determines in large part whether integrative supervision is experienced as intelligible or bewildering" to the supervisee.

By contrast, it has been our general impression that most traditional PhD programs in clinical and counseling psychology tend to provide an introductory course in the methods of psychotherapy (e.g., Bloch, 2006), and then relegate the more in-depth understanding of those methods to the trainees' clinical supervisors at their pre-internship practicum and field placements, thereby exposing them, perhaps somewhat unsystematically, to whatever orientation the particular supervisor might hold. Furthermore, if more in-depth coverage of psychotherapy is provided in graduate school, the focus of that instruction tends to be skewed predominately in the direction of cognitive-behavioral treatments, in part, because cognitive-behavioral therapies have, in the past, tended to dominate the lists of treatments that have been empirically validated (DeRubeis & Crits-Christoph, 1998). Only more recently have the psychodynamically oriented therapies provided a substantial body of evidence of their efficacy (Levy & Ablon, 2010; Shedler, 2010). Graduate programs in clinical social work have likely taken a similar approach in familiarizing students with psychological interventions. Training programs in marriage and family therapy may be even more focused in their approach by providing an introduction to treatment that tends to be limited to only family systems conceptualizations of case material (e.g., Goldenberg & Goldenberg, 2007).

Three primary approaches to case conceptualization In our supervisory experience, a truly pluralistic approach to training would supplement an introductory course in psychotherapy with coursework that covers what we consider to be the "three primary approaches to case conceptualization": psychodynamic and insight-oriented psychotherapy, cognitive-behavioral therapy, and family systems therapy. First, coursework in *psychodynamic and insight-oriented therapies* (Scaturo, 2002, 2010b) should include a review of long-term psychodynamic therapy (Gabbard, 2010), brief psychodynamic psychotherapy (Levenson, 2010), IPT (e.g., Klerman, Weissman, Rounsaville, & Chervon, 1984; Markowitz, 1998; Stuart & Robertson, 2003), and the principles of supportive psychotherapy (Winston, Pinsker, & Rosenthal, 2004). Second, coursework in *cognitive-behavioral therapy* should include an understanding of the origins of clinical behavior therapy (Goldfried & Davison, 1994), the cognitive revolution in the 1970s (Mahoney, 1974; Meichenbaum, 1977) that led to the cognitive therapy of today (Beck, 1995), as well as the so-called third wave of behavioral and cognitive therapies (Cloud, 2006; Hayes, 2004) that includes ACT (Hayes, Strosahl, & Wilson, 1999) and schema therapy (Young, Klosko, & Weishaar, 2003). And third, an in-depth course on *family systems therapy* should provide a detailed look at couples therapy (Gurman & Fraenkel, 2002), family structure (Minuchin, 1974) and family therapy (Nichols, 2009), as well as an integrated understanding of family dynamics and periodic family consultations with patients in individual psychotherapy (Wachtel & Wachtel, 1991).

Additional critical elements of instruction In addition to these three approaches to case conceptualization, a background in *humanistic psychology and psychotherapy* (Bugental, Pierson, & Schneider, 2002) that serves as the theoretical underpinnings for the facilitative factors of genuineness, empathy, and positive regard in client-centered therapy (Rogers, 1951), which enables the building and maintenance of a constructive therapeutic alliance (Safran & Muran, 2003) through both nondirective (Carkhuff & Berenson, 1967; Truax & Carkhuff, 1967) and more directive motivational interviewing techniques (Miller, Rollnick, & Conforti, 2002) should be thoroughly comprehended by students in the clinical and counseling fields. Finally, an overview of *psychotherapy integration* should serve as a capstone of the doctoral psychotherapy curriculum and include exposure to the four major approaches to integrative treatment (Norcross & Halgin, 2005): (a) "technical eclecticism," which attempts to select the best method of treatment for the person and problem presented; (b) "theoretical integration" that attempts to blend two or more therapeutic approaches with the goal of arriving at an improved form of treatment; (c) "assimilative integration" that likewise attempts to arrive at a synthesis with firm grounding in a single method of treatment with a willingness to selectively include other therapeutic perspectives; and, finally, (d) a "common factors" approach to integration that emphasizes the core ingredients that different forms of therapy have in common with one another (e.g., the therapeutic alliance).

Toward multilevel case conceptualization The desired result of such broadly based instruction would be the ability for students to provide a multilevel case conceptualization for any of their psychotherapy cases. When the first author has taught Advanced Clinical Practicum in Integrative Psychotherapy at Syracuse University, he has typically required that graduate students learn to conceptualize case material from these three different sets of "theoretical lenses": psychodynamic, cognitive-behavioral, and family systems formulations. Specifically, students are asked to select a case from their practicum caseload and write three different formulations from the same clinical data and case material. We want our students to understand the case from a symptomatic/behavioral, an intrapsychic, and an interpersonal level of theoretical analysis. While such a three-part exercise is, admittedly, impractical for every case in a full clinical caseload, the broadly based comprehensive understanding of case material which it provides in selected cases proves to be invaluable for conceptualizing subsequent cases and clinical material.

Clinical interviewing and the therapeutic alliance: a place for humanism

In the midst of such multilevel conceptualization, both the patient and therapist live and struggle within the human domain of their respective lives. While humanism has a *bona fide* place in all of the health care professions, the fields associated with the practice of psychotherapy should be at the vanguard of recognizing and understanding the healing power of genuine human contact (Scaturo & Huszonek, 2009). An illustrative example can be given from the integrative psychotherapy practicum at Syracuse University taught by the first author as noted earlier. A part of this seminar consisted of instruction that took place in the context of observed psychotherapy sessions. At any given point in the seminar, one of the psychology trainees in this practicum would carry a psychotherapy case where the supervisor and the other practicum students observed the session behind a one-way mirror, providing more "microscopic supervision" of therapeutic interactions. Prior to one such observed interview, the trainee who was to conduct the session came to the pre-session briefing appearing troubled and expressing concern.

The trainee, who was a particularly bright, capable, and adept young clinician, came to the pre-session briefing obviously distressed by an event that had just occurred in her personal life as every clinician ultimately is likely to have happen at some point in his or her professional career. She posed a somewhat atypical but instructive question for the supervisor about what to do when something takes place in the therapist's personal life that may affect their ability to conduct a given session with a patient. As her supervisor, the first author suggested to her that she first evaluate for herself whether or not she feels that she can give adequate attention to the session. The supervisor noted that, although less desirable, she may need to cancel the session, which may be the best alternative under certain conditions. After affirming her belief that she felt now sufficiently centered to conduct the session, the supervisor then suggested to her that not every session in an entire course of psychotherapy needs to have an elegant multilevel intervention associated with it in order to be of help to the patient. The supervisor reminded her of the facilitative factors in psychotherapy originally noted by Carl Rogers (1951). The supervisor suggested to her that, in her upcoming session, if she simply *listens attentively* to her patient and *responds empathically* that she will already be providing a "corrective emotional experience" (Alexander & French, 1946) for someone who has suffered a lifetime of emotional neglect from significant others whom never fully weighed their words (Scaturo & McPeak, 1998). While most present-day authors have doubts about whether Roger's facilitative conditions can be regarded as *both* "necessary and sufficient" (Rogers, 1957) to accomplish what one hopes to achieve in a completed course of psychotherapy, they are often more than adequate to facilitate a genuine human connection and therapeutic alliance. This continuity is frequently the heart of what we provide as clinicians in our profession much of the time. Further, it is doubtful that any of the other therapeutic tasks can be met by most psychotherapy patients without these initial conditions for treatment being achieved.

Integrative and eclectic supervision in practicum and internship settings

Historically, the field of psychotherapy has been characterized by, what Norcross (1988b) has called, a "dogma eat dogma" competitiveness among its architects, each of whom has been primarily invested in demonstrating the superiority of their own particular methodology. As Goldfried (2001) once observed, academic careers are "made by making history, not knowing it." And, while considerable progress has been made in recent years in dispelling the "exclusivity myth" in psychotherapy (Norcross, 1988b, 1995), one continues to find repetitive studies using "horse race" outcome research designs, attempting to demonstrate the empirical support of a given treatment program over another. In an age when psychoanalysis was the dominant theoretical paradigm, Harry Stack Sullivan once noted astonishment at how difficult it was for most clinicians of that day to seriously entertain even one rival hypothesis to explain a given case history (Strupp, 1981). Isaac Disraeli, the nineteenth-century literary scholar and father of one of Great Britain's most eminent prime ministers, Benjamin Disraeli, was fond of quoting an old Latin proverb, "*Cave ab homine unius libri*" or "Be cautious of the man of one book" (Disraeli, 1861). In the new millennium, the mental health consumer would be wise to, "Be cautious of the psychotherapist with one manual" (Scaturo, 2005). Regrettably, there remains considerable disincentive among academicians to advance plurality, eclecticism, and common factors in the understanding of this profession; incentivizing training in eclectic and integrative approaches remains a challenge for the field.

The challenge for integrative and eclectic supervisors in the age of empirically supported single-theory single-method treatments

Even in accredited internship settings, where there is considerably less academic pressure to advance a given "brand name" of therapy, there is often the problem that "birds of a theoretical feather flock together" in a common work setting. Like-minded psychotherapists are often most comfortable in conducting their teaching and practice among similarly minded practitioners. This form of theoretical homogeneity in the profession poses a problem for the trainee who requires a broadly based education and sampling of ways to interact with a range of psychotherapy patients. One cannot fault therapists for being comfortable with a specific approach or orientation. Even therapists who regard themselves as integrationists are likely to have a "primary theoretical orientation" or a theoretical language in which they tend to "think" or conceptualize their clinical work. As Wachtel (1991, p. 53) noted, "most efforts at integration have a 'flavor' that derives from the therapist's original orientation." But, the ideal setting for *training* is one in which the staff has made an effort to select therapists whose primary orientation provides a somewhat nonoverlapping theoretical perspective, each of whom models for their trainees and interns a *genuine respect* for what each other offers that they themselves may not. Sadly, the latter condition may frequently be as difficult to achieve as the former, given the rivalries among staff that often occur.

Eclectic practice, integrative aspirations

The eclectic practice of psychotherapy largely hinges on having a *clinical rationale*, a critical concept for utilizing a given intervention or paradigm at a given phase of treatment (Scaturo, 1994, 2005). Without a carefully deliberated rationale, attempts at eclecticism and integration can become haphazard at best and may often be based on methods and techniques that are considered "fashionable" among clinicians at that time (Dryden, 1984) rather than those that are employed in the patient's clinical best interest. Teaching our students and trainees the importance of deriving a sound clinical rationale for treatment may be among the most important activities that we can impart to them in the course of their training. Once again, this is a concept that presently tends to be delegated to their clinical supervisors in practicum and internship settings. While it is true that the concept of a treatment rationale is best understood within the context of a given case, learning "clinical reasoning" and acquiring "clinical decision-making skills" through instruction and discussion in graduate seminars before internship is a task that would provide trainees with worthwhile preparation for more sophisticated clinical work later on in their training and their careers (Scaturo, 2005). Beyond eclecticism, it is important for clinical supervisors in the twenty first century to help their trainees to think *synergistically* about how interventions that are predicated upon differing theoretical paradigms can serve to enhance one another to provide a stronger form of intervention together than each approach may be able to accomplish on its own (e.g., Wachtel & McKinney, 1992).

Regardless of the manner in which a student or trainee attempts integration in psychotherapy, as supervisors we must have a deep and abiding respect for the fact that there is always a "theoretical language," in which one thinks and provides a base for a given practitioner's clinical work. This is even more applicable to younger clinicians and novice learners (Norcross & Halgin, 2005). Clinical supervisors must realize that, whatever their integrative goals are for their students, the trainee's original orientation and framework for understanding of a case is like a "theoretical life preserver" in a vast sea of clinical information. Developing an integrative process from multiple perspectives takes time. The notion that a given approach to psychotherapy integration may combine interventions that are drawn from a variety of treatment approaches, but remain guided by a unitary theoretical framework has been nicely captured by the term *assimilative integration* (Messer, 1992; Stricker, 2010).

As Wachtel (1991, p. 44) has wisely observed, "for most of us integration remains more a goal than a constant daily reality. Eclecticism in practice and integration in aspiration is an accurate description of what most of us in the integrative movement do much of the time." As supervisors, we can more quickly approximate those aspirations by providing our trainees with formative experiences in multiple perspectives and treatments earlier on in their training and urging them to think creatively and eclectically about their patients, psychotherapy, and behavior change. To this end, we propose in the second part of this chapter the following three-phase model of psychotherapy supervision, the concepts of which are predicated upon learning theory, but have broad applicability for the clinical supervision of psychotherapy conducted from an extensive range of theoretical paradigms.

International perspectives: East and West

Internationally, the supervision and training in integrative and eclectic psychotherapy understandably mirror the trends toward such attitudes about practice of integration in current treatments. Knobloch (2003) has noted that there have been early influences in Europe toward the notion of psychotherapy integration. He points out that the heuristic path that integrative psychotherapy had taken within this context involved an extension of Freud's individual psychology toward a more interpersonal and social psychological perspective. More recently, in a series of papers on the topic of humanism in psychotherapy (*Psychotherapy*, 2012, Vol. 49, No. 4), Kriz and Langle (2012, p. 477) discussed the European perspective on this aspect of psychotherapy that serves as an integrative concept in treatment and has significant implications for supervision and training: "An important focus of our discussion concerns training because this is where the fundamentals of HP [humanistic psychology] are clearly visible." These authors feel that, while the technical aspects of training are important, the central focus of humanistic psychology in terms of training should be on the development of the aspiring clinician's personality. As a result, they conclude that, "one's own personal growth stands at the forefront of training, whereas teaching technique is of secondary importance" (p. 477).

Eastern concepts of mental health and mindfulness began to appear prominently nearly two decades ago as Linehan and her colleagues proposed dialectical behavior therapy (DBT) as an integrative approach to the treatment of borderline personality disorder (Heard & Linehan, 1994). With this approach, these authors describe how dialectical philosophy and Eastern concepts of Zen practice are integrated into Western notions of behavior therapy. Andersen (2005) conceptualized Zen meditation as a Buddhist contribution to the common factors perspective that can be integrated across various forms of psychotherapy and clinical practice. Finally, Iwakabe (2008) reported that psychotherapy integration in Japan has necessitated adjusting and modifying the technical procedures of Western psychotherapeutic practice to better suit the Japanese population and culture, emphasizing the importance of a "nontalking cure," "silent processes," and nonverbal therapeutic tasks (e.g., drawing, sandtray work). As a result, supervision and training in these approaches, like the process of therapy itself, are likely to take on a broader philosophical approach to treatment and human functioning, as well as a mentoring and apprenticeship approach to modeling these facets of therapeutic style and interaction.

The cause of psychotherapy integration – its theory, research, practice, and education – is championed nationally and internationally by several vital professional associations. For example, the Society of Psychotherapy Integration (SEPI) is an international, interdisciplinary organization with the aim of promoting "the exploration and development of approaches to psychotherapy that integrate across theoretical orientations, clinical practices, and diverse methods of inquiry"; its members can be found in such countries as Argentina, Australia, Brazil, Canada, Chile, Cyprus, Czech Republic, Denmark, Finland, France, Germany, Greece, China, India, Iran, Ireland, Israel, Italy, Japan, Mexico, Norway, Poland, Portugal, Republic of Singapore, Slovakia, Spain, Sweden, Switzerland, The Netherlands, Turkey, the United Kingdom, the United States of America (from SEPI website, http://www.sepiweb.com). Other such associations, with a mission identical to SEPI, include the European Association for Integrative Psychotherapy (http://www.europeanintegrativepsychotherapy.com), United Kingdom Association for Psychotherapy Integration (http://www.ukapi.com), and International Integrative Psychotherapy Association (IIPA; http://www.integrativeassociation.com). Particularly germane to our chapter's topic, the IIPA has developed downloadable documents that address (a) requirements for conducting integrative psychotherapy supervision and (b) requirements for becoming an integrative psychotherapy supervisor (http://www.integrativeassociation.com/Training_ENGLISH.html).

Part II. Toward an Integrative Learning-Based Model of Psychotherapy Supervision: Supervisory Alliance, Educational Interventions, and Supervisee Learning/Relearning

We have considered whether some useful unifying metric could be identified by which we as supervisors across orientations (a) could profitably consider and conceptualize our supervisory efforts, (b) meaningfully discuss case dynamics and action within the context of a common, integrative language, and (c) perhaps even speed supervision's evolution as a science. We subsequently would like to outline a tripartite, learning-based model of psychotherapy supervision (previously proposed in greater detail elsewhere, Watkins & Scaturo, 2013b; cf. Watkins & Scaturo, in press) that (a) has both integrative, common-language properties, (b) is grounded in the foundational building blocks of learning theory/educational psychology, (c) is transtheoretical in structure, and (d) is informed by and seemingly compatible with existing psychotherapy-focused supervision approaches (e.g., Beck, Sarnat, & Barenstein, 2008). Psychotherapy-focused approaches to supervision have generally not been based in or linked to learning theory and educational process in any way. We feature such an educational model, striving to ground our triphasic view within a learning framework.

To consider commonalities across psychotherapy-focused supervision approaches, we first need a common language in place in order to do that. To look more specifically at psychotherapy supervision as a supremely educational process, then we need a vision of supervision that is informed foremost by an educational perspective. Our educationally grounded framework is an attempt to capture some of the most salient facets of supervision that are shared across diverse psychotherapy-focused supervision approaches.

Psychotherapy supervision, learning domains, and educational processes

Learning domains In educational psychology, it has long been recognized that there is more than one type of learning (Scaturo, 2010a, 2012b). Bloom and his colleagues (Bloom, Englehart, Furst, Hill, & Krathwohl, 1956; Krathwohl, Bloom, & Masia, 1964; Simpson, 1972) identified three domains of learning: cognitive (intellectual), affective (emotional), and psychomotor (behavioral). *Cognitive learning* involves the acquisition of factual knowledge and the development of intellectual skills, abilities, and thought processes. *Affective learning* involves the ways in which people process information and stimuli emotionally. Emotional learning and development are essential to the construction of the learner's feelings, values, and motives and are at the foundation of one's receptivity to information. Finally, *psychomotor learning* involves behavior and activity connected with one's perceptual responses to inputs, to the activity of imitation (modeling), and to the manipulation of one's environment (instrumental learning).

Tripartite learning model of psychotherapy Our supervision model is built upon, informed by, and extrapolated from recent efforts to apply a learning-based approach to psychotherapy (Scaturo, 2005, 2010a, 2012b). The tripartite learning model of psychotherapy incorporates the contributions of the (a) *emotional learning* that takes place in establishing a working *therapeutic alliance* with the psychotherapist, (b) *cognitive aspects* of the therapist's *technical interventions* in treatment that are intended to accelerate change, and (c) the *behavioral elements* of *relearning* more adaptive coping responses that take place in the patient's life outside of the consulting room.

Psychotherapy supervision is similarly considered to be an educational process in which various types of personal and professional learning occur. Drawing upon the seminal works of Bloom and his colleagues and students (Anderson & Krathwohl, 2001; Bloom et al., 1956; Krathwohl et al., 1964), the cognitive, affective, and psychomotor domains of learning can be (a) posited to occur in psychotherapy supervision; (b) viewed as being primarily knowledge based (think), attitudinal based (feel), and skills based (do); and (c) considered to capture the primary ways in which varied supervisee learning occurs. Within the *cognitive domain*, identification, comprehension, analysis, synthesis, and evaluation are viewed as highly important components of cognitive function. Some supervision-relevant examples are recall of pertinent patient data, identifying and evaluating interpersonal patterns, and formulating case conceptualizations. Within the *affective domain*, feelings, values, motives, and attitudes emerge as most important here. Some supervision-relevant examples are being able to actively and attentively listen, being able to identify and empathize with the patient's plight and the supervisee's struggle to learn, actively participating and meaningfully engaging in treatment/supervision, and coming to prize and value one's patients. Within the *psychomotor/behavioral domain*, practice, imitation, and repetition emerge as highly important to successful learning. Some supervision-relevant examples are practicing specific techniques by means of role play in

Table 27.1 Tripartite, learning-based conceptualization of psychotherapy supervision.

Alliance building and maintenance	*Educational interventions*	*Learning/relearning*
Secure base/facilitating environment	Case conceptualization	Behavioral practice
Empathy, genuineness, positive regard	Stimulus questions	Mental practice
Remoralization	Feedback	Corrective behavioral experiences
Alliance rupture/repair processes	Modeling	
Supervisee readiness/preparation	Stimulus control	
Corrective affective experiences	Corrective cognitive experiences	

Source: Copyright © by the American Psychological Association. Adapted with permission.

supervision, repeating empty chair with a client over sessions, and deliberately focusing on and reflecting cognitive or affective content in one's responses.

An integrative three-part model of psychotherapy supervision Our three-stage supervision structure corresponds to the three types of learning: (a) supervision alliance building and maintenance (affective learning), (b) educational interventions (cognitive learning), and (c) learning/relearning (psychomotor learning or "putting it into practice"). Both new learning and relearning (i.e., replacing dysfunctional responses or mindsets) occur over the course of supervision. Relearning can be thought of as largely "corrective" behaviors; supervision entails supervisee corrective cognitive experiences, corrective affective experiences, and corrective behavioral experiences. Table 27.1 provides some of the specifics of our learning model.

Alliance building and maintenance in psychotherapy supervision: the affective domain

In this section, we examine the contribution of six factors to building and maintaining the supervision alliance: (a) secure base/facilitating environment; (b) empathy, genuineness, and positive regard; (c) remoralization; (d) alliance rupture/repair processes; (e) supervisee readiness and preparation; and (f) corrective affective experiences. Each of those factors has increasingly gained currency in how supervision is conceptualized and practiced and can be seen as instrumental in fostering supervision of any ideological stripe. Across the affective domain, the primary components of supervisee learning are (Krathwohl et al., 1964) receiving (supervision receptivity), responding (supervision responsiveness), valuing (developing conviction about therapy's meaningfulness), organizing (forming a wholistic psychotherapy conceptualization), and internalizing (developing an internal supervisor).

Secure base/facilitating environment A safe, secure supervisory space has long been recognized as pivotal in fostering supervisee receptivity toward, openness in, and active engagement in the supervisory process. Borrowing from Bowlby (1988), Winnicott (1965), and Bion (1962), the supervision environment and atmosphere have been likened to a holding environment, safe haven, and secure base where trust, emotional containment, and safety predominate (Mollon, 1989; Pistole & Watkins,

1995; Watkins, 2011b, 2012a), where constructive attachments are formed (Fitch, Pistole, & Gunn, 2010; Neswald-McCalip, 2001; Watkins & Riggs, 2012), and where a relationally rich, accepting context is developed within which affectively laden learnings can be acquired (Sarnat, 2012). A secure hold ultimately contributes to the "freeing" of supervisees and stimulating their growth possibilities. The supervisor also frequently assumes the broader role function of a *mentor* for the trainee; a capable mentor in young adulthood is analogous to Winnicott's (1965) "good enough" parent in childhood (Levinson, Darrow, Klein, Levinson, & McKee, 1978). The mentor also nurtures the novice's emotional development by providing advice, mature judgment, moral support, and encouragement in critical moments of occupational socialization (Keith, Scaturo, Marron, & Baird, 1993).

Empathy, genuineness, and positive regard Empathy, genuineness, and positive regard can be conceived of as central to the development of a secure base or holding environment in supervision; those conditions play a crucial role in fostering supervisee receptivity, trust, and building of the supervisory alliance (Farber, 2012). The desired effect is to create a climate in supervision in which fear and anxiety are minimized, and an optimal learning situation is created (cf. Watkins, 2013). That type of accepting, facilitative atmosphere contributes substantially to making successful educational experiences increasingly possible. Over the decades, supervisor empathy, warmth, genuineness, understanding, acceptance, respect, and a nonjudgmental attitude have rather consistently been cited by supervisees as favorably contributing to their supervision experiences (see Carifio & Hess, 1987; Falender & Shafranske, 2004; Henderson, Cawyer, & Watkins, 1999; Shanfield, Hetherly, & Matthews, 2001; Watkins, 2011a). As Keith et al. (1993) have aptly noted: "As professionals, we learn to empathize best by experiencing empathy from our role models. We learn caring by being cared for. We learn to tolerate uncertainty by being supported in our uncertainty" (p. 380).

Supervisory alliance ruptures/repairs Rupture in the therapeutic alliance has been identified as a highly significant transtheoretical phenomenon (Safran, 1993). Rupture in the supervision alliance can also be considered a transtheoretical phenomenon of considerable significance. Bordin (1983) first proposed a vision of the supervisory alliance centered around *bond*, *goals*, and *tasks*; he further viewed the supervisory endeavor as being characterized by a series of relationship rupture and repair events. A supervision alliance rupture could be defined as a strain, breakdown, or deterioration in relatedness and communication in the interaction or the failure to develop a collaboration at the outset of the supervisory relationship. Some possible examples of rupture events or triggers would include the following: Supervisees having feelings of being controlled by their supervisor's suggestions or interventions and responding in a psychologically reactant manner; supervisors becoming overly defensive at having their case comments questioned by supervisees; supervisees becoming overly defensive in having their own behaviors examined in relation to treatment process; and supervisors inducing supervisee negativity through acting in dictatorial fashion.

Remoralization Because supervision calls upon students to expose their nascent, raw, and undeveloped therapist selves, it has the potential to be a far more personally threatening and deeply disturbing experience than didactic coursework and seminars (Eckler-Hart, 1987; Watkins, 2012b). For example, patients who seek psychotherapy have often undergone some profoundly disturbing life experience or trauma that has encumbered them with a profound sense of human suffering, and learning to bear that suffering with patients can be therapeutically taxing for supervisees. Patients who suffer from post-traumatic stress disorder symptoms can often evoke substantial, disorienting countertransferential feelings in clinicians, particularly young clinicians. Discussion with a sage and trusted supervisor may provide the primary emotional compass to help supervisees get back on track and find an appropriate and balanced empathic response. Thus, this transition from classroom to clinic can indeed be punctuated by episodes of doubt, anxiety, and confusion. Furthermore, beginning supervisees – due to being increasingly mired in the ambiguities and struggle of the therapist identity development process – can become despondent, deflated, and demoralized and, in turn, come to increasingly question their ability to truly be a therapist; where that is the case, supervisee "remoralization" has been identified as a critical transtheoretical task that may well require supervisory attention and action (Lampropoulos, 2002; Watkins, 1996, 2012a, 2012b).

Supervisee readiness and preparation Since supervision is an educative, learning process at its core, the crucial question for supervisors at the outset of supervision becomes: What are the particular learning needs of this particular supervisee that most require attention at this particular point in time? Thus, assessment of supervisee readiness for and learning needs in supervision are considered to be preeminent concerns that merit addressing early on in supervision. The need for that assessment appears to be guided by what has come to be a widely embraced tenet across most, if not all, supervision approaches: supervisees vary in their therapeutic knowledge, skills, and readiness for practice, and to best facilitate supervisee development, supervisors need to gain an informed understanding of their supervisees' current practice knowledge and skill strengths and deficits. Just as psychotherapy needs to be tailored to the patient, a similar realization appears to have increasingly become a crucial part of the supervision landscape: to be most effective, supervision should be individualized – tailored to fit the needs of each supervisee – rather than being prosecuted to "fit the tailor" (Alonso, 2000; Aten, Strain, & Gillespie, 2008; Beck et al., 2008; Bernard & Goodyear, 2014; Carroll, 2009, 2010; Falender & Shafranske, 2004; Farber, 2012; Reiser & Milne, 2012; Sarnat, 2012; Stoltenberg & McNeill, 2010; Watkins, 2012a, 2012c). That fundamental tenet now seems to generally hold across all models of psychotherapy supervision. It is incumbent upon supervisors to accommodate and adapt their supervisory interventions and teaching methods to meet the learning styles of their supervisees, not vice versa (Carroll, 2010).

Corrective affective experiencing We propose that, to some degree, supervision is itself a type of corrective affective experience: in learning to be a therapist, supervisees oftentimes have to let go of interfering (although sometimes natural) affect and adopt a way of being that is emotionally foreign to them at the outset of training. For example, the ability to tolerate ambiguity and appreciate that facet of treatment is not typically a part of the beginning supervisee's repertoire (Pica, 1998; Skovholt & Ronnestad, 2003); neither is the ability to tolerate nor appreciate the need for "optimally frustrating" patients. In learning to be therapists, supervisees must be able to eventually contain and meaningfully transform the affectively charged components of those experiences (e.g., where therapist anxiety and tension give way to "settling down" and "settling in") for therapy to be successful. To a great degree, the supervision alliance provides the laboratory and container within which that transformative learning can begin to occur across approaches (cf. Beck et al., 2008; Sarnat, 2012).

Educational interventions: the cognitive domain

In this section, we wish to examine the contribution of the following factors to the educational intervention process in psychotherapy supervision: (a) case conceptualization, (b) stimulus questions, (c) feedback, (d) modeling, (e) stimulus control, and (f) corrective cognitive experiences. Those six possibilities, while by no means an exhaustive list, seemingly capture some of the more commonly used interventions that are employed by supervisors across most, if not all, supervision approaches. The primary cognitive components of supervisee learning are knowledge (acquisition/ remembering), understanding, application, analysis, synthesis, and evaluation (Anderson & Krathwohl, 2001; Bloom et al., 1956). As supervisors, we hope to ultimately facilitate supervisee movement toward a higher-order cognitive organization of therapeutic process (e.g., identifying recurring interpersonal patterns or dysfunctional thoughts, meaningfully synthesizing disparate elements of patient treatment presentation). The educational interventions identified here contribute to the stimulation of learning process across the cognitive domain.

Case conceptualization Case conceptualization has always been and will always remain a core, decisive educational element of the psychotherapy supervision situation. In large part, supervision is about striving to meaningfully apprehend the specifics, uniqueness, and dynamics of each therapy case as well as the specifics, uniqueness, and dynamics of each therapist–patient relationship. Without a sound case conceptual framework, supervision can become rather haphazard (Neufeldt, 2007). Across supervision approaches, case conceptualization allows for a theory-informed lens to be brought to bear on the individual psychotherapy case – thereby providing understanding, organization, direction, and guidance for the treatment process and nuclear focus for the supervision process: it is a crucial, pivotal transtheoretical educational intervention in psychotherapy supervision. Abundant testament to that fact can be found throughout the supervision literature (e.g., Beck et al., 2008; Norcross & Halgin, 1997; Rubinstein, 2007; Stoltenberg & McNeill, 2010).

Stimulus questions Reflective questioning appears to be a commonly used intervention that is employed to stimulate and expand supervisees' critical thought processes. Since the development of supervisee reflectivity tends to be regarded transtheoretically as a crucial supervision goal (e.g., Neufeldt, Karno, & Nelson, 1996), such questioning or "active inquiry" (Neufeldt, 1999) holds a special place in encouraging supervisee understanding, application, analysis, synthesis, and evaluation. The process of reflection during supervision is a search to understand the psychotherapy session, with attention being given to the therapist's own thoughts, feelings, and actions (Neufeldt et al., 1996). The initial task of the supervisor may well be to create a context within which reflection becomes possible (Bernard & Goodyear, 2014). Helping supervisees to engage in reflective clinical practice is best developed by example. The reflective supervisor demonstrates a natural curiosity and interest in patient behavior, motivations, and concerns, remains ever eager to entertain rival hypotheses in initial case conceptualizations, and welcomes new information and clinical data.

Feedback Over 30 years ago, Goldfried (1980) identified the therapist's giving of feedback to patients as a crucial element of treatment process across all psychotherapies; it is no different for supervision process: the *supervisor's giving of feedback* to supervisees is a crucial component of the supervision process across all supervision approaches (Bernard & Goodyear, 2014; Falender & Shafranske, 2004; Watkins, 1997). Supervision feedback refers to the information that supervisors provide, which demonstrates whether or not supervisees are approaching clinical competence (Green, 2011; Phelps, 2011). Positive feedback has been described as "those instances when supervisors affirm that supervisees are on the right track . . ., while negative [or corrective] feedback is described as communication in which a supervisor notes that a supervisee is off track and should consider making a change" (Phelps, 2011, p. 14). The nature of that feedback can be expected to vary according to the theoretical lens or focus that informs supervision (e.g., Beck et al., 2008), but such a constructive, educative giving–receiving feedback process is to a great extent the transtheoretical spine that supports and guides supervisee growth and development.

Modeling Across the decades, research has tended to support the value of modeling in the learning of psychotherapy skills (Hill & Lent, 2006). Modeling – "to show to do" – is equally valuable in the process of psychotherapy supervision (Hess, 2011; Jacobs, David, & Meyer, 1995): supervisors serve as models of professional behavior and practice (Holloway, 1997). It is perhaps no wonder that so many psychology trainees and interns comment on how they value the "apprenticeship model" of learning in which they have the opportunity to co-conduct initial assessment interviews and the even rarer opportunity to conduct co-therapy with a respected supervisor. While modeling (like feedback) can be expected to vary according to the theoretical lens or focus that informs supervision, it appears to be a vital, readily used intervention across supervision approaches.

Stimulus control "The process of stimulus control involves avoiding or mitigating stimuli believed to impede growth or elicit problem behaviors resulting from supervisees' ongoing adaptation to supervision and the supervisory relationship" (Aten et al., 2008, p. 4). Stimulus control, or what we see as *the judicious exercise of environmental manipulation*, entails: The supervisor's close, careful monitoring of supervisory process, evaluating when problematic supervisee issues or concerns arise or could arise, and intervening to produce the most favorable learning outcome for the supervisee. Aten et al. (2008) presented the potentially crippling effects of supervisee shame as one example where supervisor intervention could be required to help mitigate such an experience. Case review and selection would be yet another way in which supervisors generally intervene to best arrange the supervisory experience and environment for supervisees, at least early on. We want to be sure that, in beginning their work as therapists, our supervisees are not thrown into the deep end of the treatment pool without a life preserver (e.g., being assigned a borderline case as one's first client). We hope to select cases and clinical experiences that will serve to develop a foundation of basic clinical skills first, then to be followed with greater sophistication and complexity as readiness is demonstrated by the supervisee. We maintain that, across all supervision approaches to varying degrees, judicious use of environmental manipulation is used as an intervention to enhance supervisory experience. In doing so, the supervisor should be cognizant that ongoing modification of the supervisory context is needed to meet the evolving needs of supervisees (Aten et al., 2008).

Corrective cognitive experiences We propose that, to some extent, supervision is also a type of corrective cognitive experience: in learning to be a therapist, supervisees oftentimes have to let go of interfering, inappropriate, and dysfunctional treatment mind sets or beliefs about the therapy role itself. For example, beginning supervisees can sometimes view their treatment function as more akin to advice giver, motivational coach, or savior than otherwise. Therapists can also hold different perceptual biases about what may or may not be helpful to patients based on their own defensive styles and theoretical biases (Scaturo, 2005). Such problematic perspectives need to be addressed over the course of supervision (and perhaps in personal therapy as well) and ultimately replaced if the supervisee is to be able to most successfully provide therapeutic services. We maintain, then, that the provision of "cognitive correction," while taking varied forms, appears to generally be a part of the supervision process across approaches.

Learning/relearning: the behavioral domain

In this section, we wish to examine the contribution of the following factors to the learning/relearning process in psychotherapy supervision: (a) behavioral practice, (b) mental practice, and (c) corrective behavioral experiences. Those three possibilities, while by no means an exhaustive list, seemingly capture some of the more commonly used interventions that are employed by supervisors across most, if not all, supervision approaches. The primary behavioral components of supervisee learning are (extrapolating from Dave, 1970; cf. Harrow, 1972; Simpson, 1972) imitation, manipulation, precision, articulation, and naturalization. Within this domain, movement (or actual observable performance) progressively winds its way from less refined to increasing refinement through to expertise (or naturalization). As supervisors, we hope to ultimately facilitate supervisee movement toward a more seamless, polished behavioral organization and presentation of therapeutic process (e.g., where practice proceeds comfortably and therapeutic interventions are offered with greater craft and precision). The learning/relearning factors identified here are considered to substantially contribute to the stimulation of learning process across the psychomotor domain.

Behavioral practice Experiential learning is the foundation of good supervision (Carroll, 2009). Regardless of supervisory approach, consensus has long been, continues to be, and will no doubt remain that actual prolonged therapeutic practice is indeed *sine qua non* if supervisees are to best learn how to do psychotherapy. Through supervised practice, the goal of meaningfully integrating declarative and procedural knowledge seemingly has a far greater chance of becoming reality. With behavioral practice, the experiential learning cycle is initiated (Kolb, 1984): doing, reflecting, learning, and application. That learning cycle – practicing to learn – has been demonstrated to be a very prominent part of the supervisory process (Milne, 2009). Behavioral practice should consist of an experiential process that encompasses graded efforts to address matters of therapist imitation, manipulation, precision, articulation, and naturalization through training and supervision.

Mental practice Reflection is best accomplished before and after therapy sessions rather than in the midst of them (Carroll, 2010). We define mental practice as mindful processing of, preparing for, and repeating in vitro actions or possibilities of action that can or will occur in psychotherapy. As supervisors, we encourage our supervisees to "think about" various therapeutic situations and eventualities before and after therapy and before, during, and after supervision. Some common examples would include thinking out how one wishes to introduce and provide patient orientation for psychotherapy, considering how you wish to (ideally) respond when a patient asks a particular question, practicing how you want to introduce and provide patient orientation for specific interventions, and practicing actual interventions imaginally (e.g., one's relaxation pattern, delivering constructive feedback, formulating and delivering mutative interpretations). In some way or other, mental practice appears to have a role across the variety of supervision approaches and is very much a part or extension of the reflective process itself.

Corrective behavioral experiences Just as supervision can be cognitively and affectively corrective, we further propose that, to some extent, supervision can also be a type of corrective behavioral experience: in learning to be a therapist, supervisees oftentimes have to let go of inappropriate or dysfunctional verbal or physical behaviors that can interfere with their implementation of the therapy role itself. Some such examples would be constantly interrupting patients, fidgetiness, slouching posture, being overly intrusive and controlling, or asking nothing but questions ad infinitum. Such troubling, even potentially derailing, therapist behaviors will require redress in supervision and, ultimately, supervisee correction and replacement if treatment is to most viably proceed.

The supervision experience can also be considered a type of counterconditioning process, whereby supervisees (a) are exposed to a new and anxiety-provoking situation in which their therapy behavior is scrutinized, (b) receive constructive supervisory feedback over time about that behavior, and (c) learn to adapt to and derive benefit from the supervisory situation. The review of recorded therapy sessions is one such counterconditioning intervention: it offers supervisees the opportunity to observe their clinical work, receive direct feedback about how they are doing, and discuss session content (Aten et al., 2008). Thus, to be successful, supervision to some degree must become a successful educational "exposure" experience.

Research on supervision: alliance building/maintenance, educational interventions, and learning/relearning

A number of research studies have relevance for and offer support for some facet of this three-stage model. While it is beyond the scope of this chapter or space available to review this literature here, the interested reader is referred to Watkins and Scaturo (2013) for a summary of the existing research.

Concluding Remarks

In this chapter, we have provided a perspective for trainees and supervisees of how to conceptualize psychotherapy from an integrative and eclectic approach, and have then provided for clinical supervisors an integrative framework for conceptualizing the process of psychotherapy supervision. In so doing, we have presented a tripartite, integrative, learning-based model of clinical supervision – alliance building and maintenance, educational interventions, and learning/relearning – that seemingly has transtheoretical applicability. The field has lacked for an educationally grounded, common-language model of psychotherapy supervision. Our model is offered as a way to consider how those missing elements might begin to be addressed. Psychotherapy supervision has long been and remains a critical means by which the culture of psychotherapy is taught and perpetuated. Supervision is now readily recognized as a core competency in psychological practice; its eminence in psychotherapy education seems well established and well assured. As we work to provide competent, effective supervision services, our current conceptual supervisory Tower of Babel does us no favors. Much as considered efforts are now being made to derive a common language for psychotherapy, considered efforts to derive a common language for psychotherapy supervision also seem needed.

References

Alexander, F., & French, T. M. (1946). *Psychoanalytic therapy: Principles and applications.* New York: Ronald Press.

Alonso, A. (2000). On being skilled and deskilled as a psychotherapy supervisor. *Journal of Psychotherapy Practice and Research*, *9*, 55–61.

Andersen, D. T. (2005). Empathy, psychotherapy integration, and meditation: A Buddhist contribution to the common factors movement. *Journal of Humanistic Psychology*, *45*(4), 483–502.

Anderson, L. W., & Krathwohl, D. R. (Eds.). (2001). *A taxonomy for learning, teaching, and assessing: A revision of Bloom's taxonomy for educational objectives.* New York: Longman.

Aten, J. D., Strain, J. D., & Gillespie, R. E. (2008). A transtheoretical model of clinical supervision. *Training and Education in Professional Psychology*, *2*, 1–9.

Beck, J., Sarnat, J. E., & Barenstein, V. (2008). Psychotherapy-based approaches to supervision. In C. Falender & E. Shafranske (Eds.), *Casebook for clinical supervision: A competency-based approach* (pp. 57–96). Washington, DC: American Psychological Association.

Beck, J. S. (1995). *Cognitive therapy: Basics and beyond.* New York: Guilford Press.

Bernard, J. M., & Goodyear, R. K. (2014). *Fundamentals of clinical supervision* (5th ed.). Upper Saddle River, NJ: Merrill.

Bion, W. R. (1962). The psycho-analytic study of thinking: A theory of thinking. *International Journal of Psychoanalysis, 43*, 306–310.

Bloch, S. (Ed.). (2006). *An introduction to the psychotherapies* (4th ed.). New York: Oxford University Press.

Bloom, B. S., Englehart, M. D., Furst, E. J., Hill, W. H., & Krathwohl, D. R. (Eds.). (1956). *Taxonomy of educational objectives: The classification of goals. Handbook I: cognitive domain.* New York: David McKay Co.

Bordin, E. S. (1983). A working alliance model of supervision. *The Counseling Psychologist, 11*, 35–42.

Bowlby, J. (1988). *A secure base.* New York: Basic Books.

Bugental, J. F., Pierson, J. F., & Schneider, K. J. (Eds.). (2002). *The handbook of humanistic psychology: Leading edges in theory, research, and practice.* Thousand Oaks, CA: Sage Publications.

Carifio, M. S., & Hess, A. K. (1987). Who is the ideal supervisor? *Professional Psychology, Research and Practice, 18*, 244–250.

Carkhuff, R. R., & Berenson, B. G. (1967). *Beyond counseling and therapy.* New York: Holt, Rinehart, & Winston.

Carroll, M. (2009). Supervision: Critical reflection for transformational learning (Part 1). *The Clinical Supervisor, 28*, 210–220.

Carroll, M. (2010). Supervision: Critical reflection for transformational learning (Part 2). *The Clinical Supervisor, 29*, 1–19.

Castonguay, L. G. (2000). Training in psychotherapy integration: Introduction to current efforts and future visions. *Journal of Psychotherapy Integration, 10*(3), 229–231.

Cloud, J. (2006). The third wave of therapy. *Time Magazine*, February 13. Retrieved from http://www.time.com/time/magazine/article/0,9171,1156613,00.html. Retrieved May 12, 2011.

Dave, R. H. (1970). Psychomotor levels. In R. J. Armstrong (Ed.), *Developing and writing educational objectives* (pp. 33–34). Tucson, AZ: Educational Innovators Press.

DeRubeis, R. J., & Crits-Christoph, P. (1998). Empirically supported individual and group psychological treatments for adult mental disorders. *Journal of Consulting and Clinical Psychology, 66*, 37–52.

Disraeli, I. (1861). *Curiosities of literature* (Vol. IV). Boston, MA: Crosby, Nichols, Lee.

Dryden, W. (1984). Issues in the eclectic practice of individual psychotherapy. In W. Dryden (Ed.), *Individual therapy in Britain* (pp. 341–363). London: Harper & Row.

Eckler-Hart, A. H. (1987). True and false self in the development of the psychotherapist. *Psychotherapy, 24*, 683–692.

Ells, T. D. (Ed.). (2010). *Handbook of psychotherapy case formulation* (2nd ed.). New York: Guilford Publications, Inc.

Falender, C. A., & Shafranske, E. P. (2004). *Clinical supervision: A competency-based approach.* Washington, DC: American Psychological Association.

Farber, E. W. (2012). Supervising humanistic-existential psychotherapy in the 21st century: Needs, possibilities. *Journal of Contemporary Psychotherapy, 42*, 173–182.

Fitch, J. C., Pistole, C., & Gunn, J. E. (2010). The bonds of development: An attachment-caregiving model of supervision. *The Clinical Supervisor, 29*, 20–34.

Gabbard, G. O. (2010). *Long-term psychodynamic psychotherapy: A basic text* (2nd ed.). Washington, DC: American Psychiatric Publishing, Inc.

Garfield, S. L. (1995). *Psychotherapy: An eclectic-integrative approach.* New York: John Wiley & Sons, Inc.

Goldenberg, H., & Goldenberg, I. (2007). *Family therapy: An overview* (7th ed.). Belmont, CA: Brooks/Cole.

Goldfried, M. R. (1980). Toward the delineation of therapeutic change principles. *American Psychologist, 25*, 991–999.

Goldfried, M. R. (1995). Toward a common language for case formulation. *Journal of Psychotherapy Integration, 5*(3), 221–244.

Goldfried, M. R. (Ed.). (2001). *How therapists change: Personal and professional reflections.* Washington, DC: American Psychological Association.

Goldfried, M. R., & Davison, G. C. (1994). *Clinical behavior therapy* (2nd ed.). New York: John Wiley & Sons.

Green, H. J. (2011). Skills training and self-esteem: Educational and clinical perspectives on giving feedback to clinical trainees. *Behaviour Change, 28*, 87–96.

Gurman, A. S., & Fraenkel, P. (2002). The history of couple therapy: A millennial review. *Family Process, 41*, 199–260.

Harrow, A. J. (1972). *A taxonomy of the psychomotor domain.* New York: David McKay Co.

Hayes, S. C. (2004). Acceptance and commitment therapy: Relational frame theory, and the third wave of behavioral and cognitive therapies. *Behavior Therapy, 35*, 639–665.

Hayes, S. C., Strosahl, K. D., & Wilson, K. G. (1999). *Acceptance and commitment therapy: An experiential approach to behavior change.* New York: Guilford Press.

Heard, H. L., & Linehan, M. M. (1994). Dialectical behavior therapy: An integrative approach to the treatment of borderline personality disorder. *Journal of Psychotherapy Integration, 4*(1), 55–82.

Henderson, C. E., Cawyer, C. S., & Watkins, C. E., Jr. (1999). A comparison of student and supervisor perceptions of effective practicum supervision. *The Clinical Supervisor, 18*, 47–74.

Herink, R. (Ed.). (1980). *The psychotherapy handbook: The A to Z guide to more than 250 different therapies in use today.* New York: A Meridian Book, New American Library.

Hess, A. K. (2011). Psychotherapy supervision. In J. C. Norcross, G. R. Vandenbos, & D. K. Freedheim (Eds.), *History of psychotherapy* (2nd ed., pp. 703–722). Washington, D. C.: American Psychological Association.

Hill, C. E., & Lent, R. W. (2006). A narrative and meta-analytic review of helping skills training: Time to revive a dormant area of inquiry. *Psychotherapy, 43*, 154–172.

Holloway, E. L. (1997). Structures for the analysis and teaching of supervision. In C. E. Watkins Jr. (Ed.), *Handbook of psychotherapy supervision* (pp. 249–276). New York: Wiley.

Iwakabe, S. (2008). Psychotherapy integration in Japan. *Journal of Psychotherapy Integration, 18*(1), 103–125.

Jacobs, D., David, P., & Meyer, D. J. (1995). *The supervisory encounter: A guide for teachers of psychodynamic psychotherapy and analysis.* New Haven, CT: Yale University Press.

Kazdin, A. E. (1986). Comparative outcome studies of psychotherapy: Methodological issues and strategies. *Journal of Consulting and Clinical Psychology, 54*, 95–105.

Keith, D. V., Scaturo, D. J., Marron, J. T., & Baird, M. A. (1993). A Balint-oriented case consultation group with residents in family practice: Considerations for training, mentoring, and the doctor-patient relationship. *Family Systems Medicine, 11*(4), 375–383.

Klerman, G. L., Weissman, M. M., Rounsaville, B. J., & Chervon, E. S. (1984). *Interpersonal psychotherapy of depression.* New York: Basic Books.

Knobloch, F. (2003). A heuristic path to psychotherapy integration: One early European development. *Journal of Psychotherapy Integration, 13*(2), 107–129.

Kolb, D. A. (1984). *Experiential learning: Experience as a source of learning and development.* Englewood Cliffs, NJ: Prentice-Hall.

Krathwohl, D. R., Bloom, B. S., & Masia, B. B. (1964). *Taxonomy of educational objectives: the classification of goals. Handbook II: Affective domain.* New York: David McKay Co.

Kriz, J., & Langle, A. (2012). A European perspective on the position papers. *Psychotherapy, 49*(4), 475–479.

Lampropoulos, G. K. (2002). A common factors view of counseling supervision process. *The Clinical Supervisor, 21*, 77–94.

Levenson, H. (2010). *Brief dynamic therapy.* Washington, DC: American Psychological Association.

Levinson, D. J., Darrow, C. N., Klein, E. B., Levinson, M. H., & McKee, B. (1978). *The seasons of a man's life.* New York: Alfred A. Knopf.

Levy, R. A., & Ablon, S. (Eds.). (2010). *Handbook of evidence-based psychodynamic psychotherapy.* New York: Springer-Verlag.

Mahoney, M. J. (1974). *Cognition and behavior modification.* Cambridge, MA: Ballinger.

Markowitz, J. C. (Ed.). (1998). *Interpersonal psychotherapy.* Washington, DC: American Psychiatric Press, Inc.

Marks, I. M., Goldfried, M., Sungur, M., Newman, M. G., Moore, K., & Stricker, G. (November 18, 2005). *Towards a common language in psychotherapy.* Panel discussion at the Association of Behavioral and Cognitive Therapies, Washington, DC.

Marks, I. M., Tortella-Feliu, M., Fernández de la Cruz, L., Fullana, M. A., Newman, M. G., & Sungur, M. (2011). Classifying what psychotherapists do: A first step. Paper for the Common Language for Psychotherapy Task Force. Retrieved June 4, 2011, from http://www.commonlanguagepsychotherapy.org

Meichenbaum, D. (1977). *Cognitive-behavior modification: An integrative approach.* New York: Plenum Press.

Messer, S. B. (1987). Can the Tower of Babel be completed? A critique of the common language proposal. *Journal of Integrative and Eclectic Psychotherapy, 6*, 195–199.

Messer, S. B. (1992). A critical examination of belief structures in interpretive and eclectic psychotherapy. In J. C. Norcross & M. R. Goldfried (Eds.), *Handbook of psychotherapy integration* (pp. 130–165). New York: Basic Books.

Miller, S. D., Duncan, B. L., & Hubble, M. A. (1997). *Escape from Babel: Toward a unifying language for psychotherapy practice.* New York: W. W. Norton & Company.

Miller, W. R., Rollnick, S., & Conforti, K. (2002). *Motivational interviewing: Preparing people for change.* New York: Guilford Press.

Milne, D. (2009). *Evidence-based clinical supervision: Principles and practice.* Hoboken, NJ: Wiley.

Minuchin, S. (1974). *Families and family therapy.* Cambridge, MA: Harvard University Press.

Mollon, P. (1989). Anxiety, supervision and a space for thinking: Some narcissistic perils for clinical psychologists in learning psychotherapy. *British Journal of Medical Psychology, 62*, 113–122.

Neswald-McCalip, R. (2001). Development of the secure counselor: Case examples supporting Pistole and Watkins' (1995) discussion of attachment theory in counseling supervision. *Counselor Education and Supervision, 41*, 18–27.

Neufeldt, S. A. (1999). Training in reflective processes in supervision. In M. Carroll & E. L. Holloway (Eds.), *Education of clinical supervisors* (pp. 92–105). London: Sage.

Neufeldt, S. A. (2007). *Supervision strategies for the first practicum* (3rd ed.). Falls Church, VA: American Counseling Association.

Neufeldt, S. A., Karno, M. P., & Nelson, M. L. (1996). A qualitative analysis of experts' conceptualization of supervisee reflectivity. *Journal of Counseling Psychology, 43*, 3–9.

Nichols, M. P. (2009). *Family therapy: Concepts and methods.* Boston, MA: Allyn & Bacon.

Norcross, J. C. (1988a). Supervision of integrative psychotherapy. *Journal of Integrative and Eclectic Psychotherapy, 7*(2), 157–166.

Norcross, J. C. (1988b). The exclusivity myth and the equifinality principle in psychotherapy. *Journal of Integrative and Eclectic Psychotherapy, 7*(4), 415–421.

Norcross, J. C. (1995). Dispelling the Dodo Bird Verdict and the exclusivity myth in psychotherapy. *Psychotherapy, 32*(3), 500–504.

Norcross, J. C., & Halgin, R. P. (1997). Integrative approaches to psychotherapy supervision. In C. E. Watkins Jr. (Ed.), *Handbook of psychotherapy supervision* (pp. 203–222). New York: Wiley.

Norcross, J. C., & Halgin, R. P. (2005). Training in psychotherapy integration. In J. C. Norcross & M. R. Golfried (Eds.), *Handbook of psychotherapy integration* (2nd ed., pp. 439–458). New York: Oxford University Press.

Phelps, D. L. (2011). Supervisee experiences of corrective feedback in clinical supervision. *The Psychotherapy Bulletin*, *46*(3), 14–18.

Pica, M. (1998). The ambiguous nature of clinical training and its impact on the development of student clinicians. *Psychotherapy*, *35*, 361–365.

Pistole, C., & Watkins, C. E., Jr. (1995). Attachment theory, counseling process, and supervision. *The Counseling Psychologist*, *23*, 457–478.

Reiser, R., & Milne, D. (2012). Supervising cognitive-behavioral psychotherapy in the 21st century: Pressing needs, impressing possibilities. *Journal of Contemporary Psychotherapy*, *42*, 161–171.

Report of the Research Task Force of the National Institute of Mental Health (NIMH). (1975). *Research in the service of mental health*. Rockville, MD: DHEW Publication No. (ADM) 75-236.

Rogers, C. R. (1951). *Client-centered therapy: Its current practice, implications, and theory*. Boston, MA: Houghton Mifflin.

Rogers, C. R. (1957). The necessary and sufficient conditions of therapeutic personality change. *Journal of Consulting Psychology*, *21*, 95–103.

Rubinstein, L. E. (Ed.). (2007). *Talking about supervision: 10 questions, 10 analysts = 100 answers*. London: Karnac.

Safran, J. D. (1993). The therapeutic alliance rupture as a transtheoretical phenomenon: Definitional and conceptual issues. *Journal of Psychotherapy Integration*, *3*, 33–39.

Safran, J. D., & Muran, J. C. (2003). *Negotiating the therapeutic alliance: A relational treatment guide*. New York: Guilford Publications, Inc.

Sarnat, J. (2012). Supervising psychoanalytic psychotherapy: Present knowledge, pressing needs, future possibilities. *Journal of Contemporary Psychotherapy*, *42*, 151–160.

Scaturo, D. J. (1994). Integrative psychotherapy for panic disorder an agoraphobia in clinical practice. *Journal of Psychotherapy Integration*, *4*, 253–272.

Scaturo, D. J. (2001). The evolution of psychotherapy and the concept of manualization: An integrative perspective. *Professional Psychology: Research and Practice*, *32*, 522–530.

Scaturo, D. J. (2002). Fundamental dilemmas in contemporary psychodynamic and insight-oriented psychotherapy. *Journal of Contemporary Psychotherapy*, *32*, 143–163.

Scaturo, D. J. (2005). *Clinical dilemmas in psychotherapy: A transtheoretical approach to psychotherapy integration*. Washington, DC: American Psychological Association.

Scaturo, D. J. (2010a). A tripartite learning conceptualization of psychotherapy: The therapeutic alliance, technical interventions, and relearning. *American Journal of Psychotherapy*, *64*(1), 1–27.

Scaturo, D. J. (2010b). Insight-oriented psychotherapy. In I. Weiner & E. Craighead (Eds.), *Corsini's Encyclopedia of Psychology* (Vol. 2, 4th ed., pp. 823–826). New York: John Wiley and Sons.

Scaturo, D. J. (2012a). Supervising integrative psychotherapy in the 21st century: Pressing needs, impressing possibilities. *Journal of Contemporary Psychotherapy*, *42*, 183–192.

Scaturo, D. J. (2012b). A tripartite learning conceptualization of psychotherapy. In N. Seele (Ed.), *Encyclopedia of the Sciences of Learning* (pp. 7–10). Heidelberg, Germany: Springer. DOI 10.1007/978-1-4419-1428-6_1759

Scaturo, D. J., & Huszonek, J. J. (2009). Collaborative academic training of psychiatrists and psychologists in VA and medical school settings. *Academic Psychiatry*, *33*(1), 4–12.

Scaturo, D. J., & McPeak, W. R. (1998). Clinical dilemmas in contemporary psychotherapy: The search for clinical wisdom. *Psychotherapy, 35*(1), 1–12.

Shanfield, S. B., Hetherly, V. V., & Matthews, K. L. (2001). Excellent supervision: The residents' perspective. *Journal of Psychotherapy Practice and Research, 10*, 23–27.

Shedler, J. (2010). The efficacy of psychodynamic psychotherapy. *American Psychologist, 65*(2), 98–109.

Simpson, E. J. (1972). *The classification of educational objectives in the psychomotor domain.* Washington, DC: Gryphon House.

Skovholt, T. M., & Ronnestad, M. H. (2003). Struggles of the novice counselor and therapist. *Journal of Career Development, 30*, 45–58.

Stoltenberg, C. D., & McNeill, B. W. (2010). *IDM supervision: An integrated developmental model for supervising counselors and therapists* (3rd ed.). San Francisco, CA: Jossey-Bass.

Stricker, G. (2010). *Psychotherapy integration.* Washington, DC: American Psychological Association.

Strupp, H. H. (1981). Clinical research, practice and the crisis of confidence. *Journal of Consulting and Clinical Psychology, 49*, 216–219.

Stuart, S., & Robertson, M. (2003). *Interpersonal psychotherapy: A clinician's guide.* London: Arnold Publishers.

Truax, C. B., & Carkhuff, R. R. (1967). *Toward effective counseling and psychotherapy: Training and practice.* Chicago, IL: Aldine.

Wachtel, E. F., & Wachtel, P. L. (1991). *Family dynamics in individual psychotherapy: A guide to clinical strategies.* New York: Guilford Press.

Wachtel, P. L. (1991). From eclecticism to synthesis: Toward a more seamless psychotherapy integration. *Journal of Psychotherapy Integration, 1*, 43–54.

Wachtel, P. L., & McKinney, M. K. (1992). Cyclical psychodynamics and integrative psychodynamic psychotherapy. In J. C. Norcross & M. R. Goldfried (Eds.), *Handbook of psychotherapy integration* (pp. 335–370). New York: Basic Books.

Watkins, C. E., Jr. (1996). On demoralization and awe in psychotherapy supervision. *The Clinical Supervisor, 14*, 139–148.

Watkins, C. E., Jr. (Ed.). (1997). *Handbook of psychotherapy supervision.* New York: Wiley.

Watkins, C. E., Jr. (2011a). Psychotherapy supervision since 1909: Some friendly observations about its first century. *Journal of Contemporary Psychotherapy, 41*, 57–67.

Watkins, C. E., Jr. (2011b). Toward a tripartite vision of supervision for psychoanalysis and psychoanalytic psychotherapies: Alliance, transference-countertransference configuration, and real relationship. *The Psychoanalytic Review, 98*, 557–590.

Watkins, C. E., Jr. (2012a). Fortification strategies for supervisory relationship enhancement. *The Psychotherapy Bulletin, 47*, 46–50, 70–73.

Watkins, C. E., Jr. (2012b). On demoralization, therapist identity development, and persuasion and healing in psychotherapy supervision. *Journal of Psychotherapy Integration, 22*, 187–205.

Watkins, C. E., Jr. (2012c). Psychotherapy supervision in the new millennium: Competency-based, evidence-based, particularized, and energized. *Journal of Contemporary Psychotherapy, 42*, 193–203.

Watkins, C. E., Jr. (2013). Why subject-centered listening is so crucial in the supervision of beginning psychoanalytic supervisees. *International Journal of Psychoanalytic Self Psychology, 8*, 525–527.

Watkins, C. E., Jr., & Riggs, S. A. (2012). Psychotherapy supervision and attachment theory: Review, reflections, and recommendations. *The Clinical Supervisor, 31*, 256–289.

Watkins, C. E., Jr., & Scaturo, D. J. (in press). Proposal for a common language, educationally-informed model of psychoanalytic supervision. *Psychoanalytic Inquiry.*

Watkins, C. E., Jr., & Scaturo, D. J. (2013). Toward an integrative, learning-based model of psychotherapy supervision: Supervisory alliance, educational interventions, and supervisee learning/relearning. *Journal of Psychotherapy Integration*, *23*, 75–95.

Winnicott, D. W. (1965). *The maturational processes and the facilitating environment.* New York: International Universities Press.

Winston, A., Pinsker, H., & Rosenthal, R. N. (2004). *Introduction to supportive psychotherapy.* Washington, DC: American Psychiatric Publishing, Inc.

Young, J. E., Klosko, J. S., & Weishaar, M. E. (2003). *Schema therapy: A practitioner's guide.* New York: Guilford Press.

28

The Integrative Developmental Model of Supervision

Cal D. Stoltenberg, Kenneth C. Bailey, Craigery B. Cruzan, Jonathan T. Hart, and Uchechi Ukuku

The integrative developmental model of supervision (IDM) has been in development for over 30 years (Loganbill, Hardy, & Delworth, 1982; Stoltenberg, 1981; Stoltenberg & Delworth, 1987; Stoltenberg & McNeill, 2010; Stoltenberg, McNeill, & Delworth, 1998), integrating work in supervision with relevant perspectives from cognitive and emotion processing, schema theory, development of expertise, social psychology, and motivation. The IDM describes counselor development as movement over time, experience, and training through three levels (levels 1–3) with a final integrated level (3*i*). This conceptualization describes a domain-specific form of professional development and learning which, over time and growth in various domains, can be descriptive of a more general level of integrative professional development across relevant domains. Key processes include attending to the change over time in three overarching structures (motivation, autonomy, self-, and other awareness) as well as competency across domains of professional practice. This change or growth can be facilitated by the provision of level appropriate supervision (and related training) environments. Consistent with our "integrative" frame of reference, we will begin our discussion with a broad review of work in other relevant areas of theory and research, including international studies, before moving on to a more detailed discussion incorporating this material into an understanding of the supervision process according to the IDM.

Cognitive Processing, Skill, and Schema Development

Stoltenberg and McNeill (2010) have discussed how the metaphor of development has been useful in describing and enabling the effective implementation of clinical supervision. The stages of skill acquisition and the development of expertise by Anderson (2005) is relevant (see Stoltenberg & McNeill, 2010). In the first, or

The Wiley International Handbook of Clinical Supervision, First Edition. Edited by C. Edward Watkins, Jr. and Derek L. Milne.

cognitive, stage, a rudimentary understanding of the task is enabled through the declarative verbal or image representation of a skill or procedure that is learned. Facts relevant to the skill are committed to memory, which requires retrieval and interpretation to perform the skill (brought into working memory). This suggests that access to cogent and useful information (theory, intent, skill utility, evidence) is necessary. In the second, or associative, stage, errors are identified and altered. allowing for a more effective application of the skill. Connections among the necessary elements are strengthened and procedures are refined and streamlined over time through careful self-examination and corrective feedback from others. For the supervision process, encouraging self-reflection (Schön's, 1987 reflection-in-action [R-I-A], reflection-on-action [R-O-A], and knowledge-in-action [K-I-A]) along with clear and specific feedback provided by supervisors and peers will enhance this process. Thus, procedural knowledge develops and the skill can be implemented quickly (recognition of condition–action pairs and patterns) without the requirement of mental rehearsal or recall of specific components of the skill (K-I-A). To avoid the risk of limited schemas reflecting restrictive or inaccurate stereotypes, the supervisee should be provided with varied experiences during skill development. In the third, autonomous, stage of developing expertise, the practice and feedback processes enable the implementation of the procedure to become more automatic, requiring less processing (greater K-I-A) and less additional practice. Over time, experts develop the ability to use forward-inference procedures (rather than reasoning backward from a problem statement), which enable them to come up with creative applications for various contexts, going beyond the initial learning experiences. As noted by Stoltenberg and McNeill (2010), "Sets, or patterns, of characteristics, including personality style, the therapist's reactions to the client, and environmental circumstances, will be recognized by expert therapists and lead to forward thinking about paths to solutions or problems not even mentioned by the client . . ." (p. 6).

An area of concern is the possible danger associated with automaticity in counseling or supervision if empathy or perspective taking of the client or supervisee is lacking. Automaticity suggests that as tasks become practiced, they become more automatic and require less central cognition (thinking) to execute (Anderson, 2010). Some automaticity (K-I-A) is needed and efficient for clinicians to be able to manage all of the concurrent activities being conducted (e.g., diagnosing, assessing of risk, building rapport, gathering relevant history, nonverbal attending). However, clinicians and supervisors must guard against acting through habit (mindlessness, social automaticity; Mather & Romo, 2007) and remain focused and intentional, concerning the context and process of therapy and supervision (mindfulness, R-I-A, R-O-A).

Social Psychology and Supervision

An integral part of a supervisee's training lies in developing accurate attributional skills when conceptualizing their clients. Jones and Nisbett (1971) described a process, now known as the fundamental attribution error, in which supervisees may err: the "pervasive tendency for actors to attribute their actions to situational requirements, whereas observers tend to attribute the same actions to stable personal dispositions" (p. 2). This phenomenon has been studied in the counseling realm, where counselors tend to take on an "observer" role and attribute client problems to personality (Batson, O'Quin, & Pych, 1982). A consideration of these processes might suggest that high levels of identification can move a counselor more toward an "actor" role with the client's experience than merely an observer role, leading to counselors erringly attributing their clients' problems more consistently to situational circumstances and ignoring personal contributions. This would require the supervisor to challenge and model: demonstrating empathy and situational causation when supervisees are too "observer minded," and demonstrating objectivity and dispositional causation when supervisees are too "actor minded."

Another potentially significant contribution are the concepts of goal-directed attention and category accessibility (Bruner, 1957). Goal-directed attention describes the process by which one's currently active goals drive what one attends to in the surrounding environment. Category accessibility is a theoretical process that describes how readily available prior knowledge is when relevant stimuli are in the environment (similar to schema activation). As applied to supervision, these concepts would suggest that a supervisee's current goals for therapy likely serve to both focus and limit what behavioral cues are noticed from the client. For example, if a supervisee's goals for therapy are more focused on improving and practicing specific techniques than on the problems expressed by the client (IDM level 1), the supervisee is more likely to pick up on cues from the client that indicate personal success or failure on the supervisee's part rather than stimuli relevant to the client's position. Similarly, if a supervisee is actively seeking to explore or treat a client's reported anxiety, cues and stimuli that point toward anxiety-related issues should be more readily salient in therapy and lead to a greater sense of direction (versus lack of direction; see Strozier, Barnett-Queen, & Bennett, 2000).

Priming research has long examined the mechanisms by which certain stimuli become salient to a person's perception, thoughts, and behaviors (Bargh, 2006). In a study by Fluckiger and Holtforth (2008), therapists were primed to focus on their clients' strengths immediately prior to a session with the client, subsequently resulting in greater attention to client strengths as opposed to client weaknesses during therapy as well as improved therapy outcome. These concepts underlie the importance of collaboratively developing a relevant treatment plan for a client with a supervisee and assisting the supervisee in being mindful of the stated goals, and reviewing the goals and strengths of the client prior to each session.

Supervisors may also be susceptible to allowing automatic social cognitions to interfere with the supervisory process. The halo effect (Thorndike, 1920) is the tendency for a person to judge another's general characteristics based on one especially salient characteristic. Supervisees learn and develop along different domains of counseling, and their ability in one area of supervision may not reflect equivalent ability in another area as expertise tends to remain domain-specific (Anderson, 2010; Stoltenberg & McNeill, 2010). Stoltenberg (2008) discussed this process for supervisees who functioned at two appreciably different levels in their counseling ability with individuals and with couples. Supervisors may err by focusing on one domain too heavily and working under the assumption that the supervisee's skills will naturally transfer across domains. The more similar the domains are to each other, the greater the likelihood of skills transferring or generalizing across domains, the less generalization is likely with dissimilar domains. Experience does not necessarily lead to expertise on its own (e.g., Ward, Hodges, Starkes, & Williams, 2007); rather, the evidence suggests that expertise relies more on careful practice aimed at improvement and attending to both differences and similarities across domains and contexts (see also Anderson, 2010). If supervisees are not given adequate opportunity to explore and deepen their expertise in a given domain, they are less likely to develop in that domain. Recent research in the training of medical residents (Thomas, Beckman, Mauck, Cha, & Thomas, 2011) has shown that group assessment of trainees may work to counteract the halo effects of supervision, potentially due to the varying foci of multiple supervisors across multiple domains. Also, the impact of deliberate practice with focused concentration in sports psychology encourages the development of expertise (Ericsson, 2006).

Emerging areas of social neuroscience (Cacioppo, 2002; Cacioppo & Berntson, 1992) and social cognitive neuroscience (Ochsner & Lieberman, 2001) provide additional perspectives combining social influences, cognitive processes (including emotion processing), and neuroscience. Goleman (2006) provided a summary of some of this work which helps connect cognition and emotion, which Greenberg (2002) had argued are somewhat arbitrarily separated. Greenberg (2002; Greenberg & Goldman, 2008) explicated the roles of primary and secondary emotions in interpersonal relationships, and the importance of experiencing and labeling them to allow for adequate processing of experience and exerting emotion regulation. Space does not allow for a full treatment of these processes and their effects on supervision (and therapy; see Stoltenberg & McNeill, 2010 for a more detailed discussion), but it is important to acknowledge that how we process our experiences, not simply the experiences themselves, plays a crucial role in schema development, and our ability to understand our world and interact in facilitative ways with others which is, in part, a goal of supervision and training.

The elaboration likelihood model (ELM) of persuasion has its roots in the social psychology of attitude formation and change, and adds important information processing constructs that impact one's motivation and ability to process information in developing and changing attitudes. Our discussion will rely heavily on discussion by Stoltenberg and McNeill (2010) in considering the utility of the ELM for clinical supervision. The ELM describes information processing along a continuum of approaches with "peripheral route" processing on one end and "central route processing" anchoring the other pole.

When an issue is viewed by an individual as being of limited importance or personal relevance to them, or if they have limited knowledge or experience with the issue, the likelihood increases that they will conserve cognitive energy and rely primarily on contextual cues to develop attitudes and make decisions. In the supervision context, one source of contextual cues is the perceived credibility of the supervisor and/or others in the environment, eliciting peripheral route processing by the supervisee that can result in an uncritical acceptance of supervisor input or recommendations without careful and effortful processing. Opinions and decisions formed through peripheral route processing appear to be less stable across contexts and less predictive of future behavior than those derived through more central route processing, which is more likely when the individual is sufficiently motivated (sees the issue as personally relevant) and knowledgeable to elaborate upon the information relevant to the context. Central route processing allows the supervisee to fully engage his or her attention to issue-relevant information provided in the situation, access and process relevant schemas and other sources of information to consider the pros and cons of various options, and finally derive an overall attitude toward the issue.

Biased processing (selectively focusing on information consistent with one's pre-existing attitudes or schemas) is also a concern within the ELM when strongly personally relevant attitudes and beliefs are threatened by new information and perspectives. This can short circuit the positive aspects of central route processing in favor of protecting existing beliefs. Cacioppo, Petty, and Sidera (1982) framed persuasive messages according to participant's preferred self-schema (in this case, religious or legalistic frameworks) and found that the messages were perceived more positively and stimulated more favorable elaboration than persuasive messages framed from the nondominant perspective. Other ways to effectively deal with this process are addressed by another theory of motivation: self-determination theory (Ryan & Deci, 2000).

Self-determination theory (SDT) is a macrotheory that conceptualizes growth, integration, and well-being as being driven by competence (Harter, 1978; White, 1963), relatedness (Baumeister & Leary, 1995), and autonomy (deCharms, 1968; Deci, 1975; Ryan & Deci, 2000). SDT coincides with how the IDM emphasizes integration while viewing learning and growth in context-specific ways (La Guardia & Patrick, 2008; Vansteenkiste, Simons, Lens, Sheldon, & Deci, 2004). Of particular relevance here is the documented generalizability of SDT across both collectivistic and individualistic cultures (Jang, Reeve, Ryan, & Kim, 2009; Jiang, Yau, Bonner, & Chiang, 2011). For our purposes, the construct of motivational styles and locus of causality are understood to be universal drives in SDT research, and we see this as useful to inform our understanding of the supervision process (see also Stoltenberg & McNeill, 2010).

Ryan, Lynch, Vansteenkiste, and Deci (2011) have conceptualized motivation into seven motivational styles, five existing along a continuum from external regulation, introjected regulation, identified regulation, integrated regulation, to intrinsic motivation (moving from external to internal, respectively). Two styles considered to be outside of this continuum include amotivation I (low value) and amotivation II (low efficacy). For the SDT, "motivation implies both the energy and direction of action" (p. 198). Amotivation is considered nonregulation and a perceived lack of control from either perceptions of low value for the action or a low sense of efficacy. Intrinsic motivation is characterized as being driven by interest, enjoyment, and inherent satisfaction. Of particular relevance for supervision and training is the understanding that motivation can vary by action, issue, context, and so on. For example, a supervisee may have a motivational style toward the intrinsic end of the continuum for becoming a counselor (or getting a degree), but may have amotivation or more external motivation for learning specific skills, interventions, theories, and so on. Supervisors need to be cognizant of how they attend to their supervisees in order to avoid unintentionally reinforcing an external locus of causality for supervisees and frustrating growth toward intrinsic motivation. This influence is more likely with early trainees due to the more extrinsic locus of control and higher levels of anxiety often present in the supervisee in the many counseling contexts (this is similar to peripheral route processing in the ELM).

A successful supervisor would be one who attends to how the content of the supervision sessions impacts the supervisee's perception of his or her own autonomy, competence, and relatedness in relation to the supervision relationship. Providing autonomy support in supervision would include perspective taking of the supervisee and client by the supervisor, supporting supervisee intervention choices and conceptualizations when they are viewed as appropriate for the particular client and context, prescribing interventions only when necessary or helpful (providing options from which to choose from when possible), and minimizing pressure and control by the supervisor on the supervisee's behavior in therapy (and supervision) within the constraints of client welfare.

The supervisory relationship can be impacted by a variety of factors. For example, a supervisee could have had a very positive and growth inducing supervisory relationship prior to engaging in a new one. If the supervisee experiences the new relationship as not supportive of his or her needs, one's autonomous self-regulation (gained from the past relationship) can help mediate the perceived poor relationship with the current supervisor. This is consistent with the observation of Stoltenberg and McNeill (2010) that more advanced supervisees, when paired with less developed supervisors, will often seek supervisory input elsewhere or "lay low" until the unsatisfactory supervision relationship ends. Another study (Norem, Magnuson, Wilcoxon, & Arbel, 2006) found that autonomous supervisees move "developmentally quicker" and are accepting of feedback. Motivation was described as willingness to "take risks in academic settings" and "commitment to learning and being a really good counselor," as well as "proactive" (p. 42). Other results demonstrate that supervisees who are intrinsically motivated find the act of counseling and learning about counseling inherently rewarding.

Ryan et al. (2011) noted, "There is simply no change without movement and no movement without motivation" (p. 199). For the supervision process, the goals that are set must be appropriate for the energy and the direction of movement desired. Due to variations among supervisees at different levels of development in self-perceptions of competence and motivation (and possibly relatedness), the goals of the supervisor from an SDT (and by extension, an IDM) framework would benefit from focusing on where the supervisee is oriented, through empathy and perspective taking, in motivation and regulatory styles for various aspects of the supervision and therapy processes, and encourage movement from helplessness through volition. Although client welfare in supervision remains an ultimate concern, supporting appropriate levels of supervisee autonomy in conceptualizing and intervening with clients while encouraging continued exploration of alternative views and interventions should lead to a more intrinsic motivation and more internal locus of causality for the trainee, and enhance development. By exerting the least necessary pressure and control on the supervisees, the supervisor can support trainees in assuming responsibility for their learning and behavior and positively influence their sense of well-being as well as their level of professional competency.

International and Cultural Considerations

The globalization movement requires the theory and practice of clinical supervision to become more internationalized and culturally adaptable, much as has the field of counseling psychology (Leong & Ponterotto, 2003). Important considerations for translating or transporting the IDM for applications in non-Western cultures include the focus or goals of supervision in terms of expected or desired competencies (see Chapter 1), the nature of hierarchical relationships relevant to supervision and counseling, typical goals of the counseling (and supervision process), types of counseling or therapy approaches should be taught and supervised based on applicability to the given cultural context, and how the model of supervision should be adapted or implemented based on other important cultural mores and traditions. Within the IDM, an important domain of professional development is individual differences, in which we have argued supervisees develop in similar ways as they do in other domains (Stoltenberg & McNeill, 2010). The supervision context, particularly in countries with representation of a number of diverse cultural influences, can be more complex in terms of a multiplicity of cultural influences across multiple types of relationships (e.g., supervisor–supervisee, therapist–client, supervisor–client).

An extensive review of these issues as related to the IDM is beyond the scope of this chapter, but examining some issues and contexts may shed some light on the process of adapting this model of supervision to new environments. Of course, as Pedersen (2003) has noted, testing and cross-validation processes are necessary, which have only begun and in only some countries. Lynch, Vansteenkiste, Deci, and Ryan (2011) have noted, for example, that personal volition regarding behavior that is consistent with collectivist societies is not inconsistent with a collectivist orientation. They describe the continuum of motivation as "content-free," "situation specific," and "dynamic." In other words, one can choose to be "autonomously dependent on others" or "heteronomously independent." Thus, considering separately how one learns and develops from the culturally specific goals or applications of learning and development is an important process in the cultural adaptation of the IDM, or any other supervision model.

Bang (2006) applied the IDM to Korean supervisees and found that age, education, and counseling experience had positive effects on self- and other awareness, motivation, and autonomy of participants. The significance of age for the counselor's development implies that within the Korean context, special attention should be paid to the ages of the supervisee and supervisor. Due to the social norm regarding age and expectations within supervisory roles, problems may arise when the supervisor is younger than the supervisee (Bang, 2006). Thus, the concept of age may well have implications for the relational and hierarchical dimensions of supervision that may then influence learning and development. This study provides support for aspects of the IDM and highlights how cultural differences must be examined when trying to adapt a supervision model to other societies. Supervision aids in the process of professional change for counselors and individual change processes are influenced by cultural background (Berry & Kim, 1988) and environment.

In another Eastern culture, Taiwan, counseling is seen as a Western import that has been adapted to the Taiwanese indigenous culture. An example of an integrated model is Jin's (1997) (as cited in Gerstein, Heppner, Aegisdottir, Leung, & Norsworthy, 2009) approach to career counseling that blends the Buddhist four Noble truths (nature of suffering, origin of suffering, cessation, way leading to cessation) with the Western theory of career counseling to create a Taiwanese career counseling model.

In Turkey, the term "mentor" has been used as an alternative to "supervisor" (Buyukgoze-Kavas, Taylor, Neimeyer, & Guneri, 2010) and, as relationships are defined more on a hierarchical basis than they are in the United States, the mentor is expected to give advice and provide direction (Buyukgoze-Kavas et al., 2010). A study of Turkish and American students (Bakioğlu & Gürdal, 2001) examined the components, expectations, and level of satisfaction of the mentoring relationship. Higher levels of perceived socioemotional support were positively related to a satisfactory mentor relationship for both Turkish and American students. However, Turkish students reported significantly lower levels of socioemotional support when compared to American counterparts. The author noted that this may be due to Turkish students looking to friends for socioemotional support rather than teachers or mentors.

Counselor supervision should not be taken out of the cultural context in which it was developed and simply implemented in another context (Richards, 2000). For example, in Zimbabwe, a historical contextual lens is required to understand and adapt counselor supervision for implementation. Todisco and Salomone (1991) argued that Eurocentric approaches to counselor supervision may have some legitimacy in Zimbabwe, but the Afrocentric world view is so oppositional to the Eurocentric world view that there may be more value in developing theory and practice that is more relevant specifically for the Zimbabwean context. This may be especially true in regard to the collectivist nature of the society, although the same arguments made by Lynch et al. (2011) for the SDT discussed earlier may be applicable here. Supervisors must be willing to incorporate aspects of the cultural context within supervision. "One way of demonstrating cultural respect is to recognize the value of the traditional network of helpers in the supervision/counseling process. The supervisee should be trained so that he/she is able to empower the client to integrate as many helpers, and types of helpers that the client feels necessary to solve his/her problem" (Mpofu, 1998, as cited in Richards, 2000).

It is essential for supervisors to encourage development in a way that will be effective in the cultural contexts in which the supervisee is being trained to function. Another area where culture matters is religion and spirituality. In a quantitative and qualitative study of supervisors in Jamaica, it was noted that spirituality is a large part of the cultural context and, indeed, most of the supervisors in this study worked in graduate seminaries (Stupart, Rehfuss, & Parks-Savage, 2010). This highlights the fact that spirituality and religion are important factors to consider in the supervision process, and the implications of cultural considerations based on these should be a part of how training is conducted as well as in what approaches, what competencies, and for what goals, for which supervisees are trained in Jaimaca and elsewhere.

Within a given country, there can be considerable cultural variation. For example, the Maori people of New Zealand have been a historically oppressed group who underwent colonization. Recently, as counseling has become more widespread, a movement to include Maori people and integrate their practices within counseling and counselor training has occurred. Within the counseling context, there has been the inclusion of faith healers/helpers called Maori Kalawhina to help facilitate counseling (Lang, 2005).

There are no simple ways to adapt any given model of supervision to all cultures as the variations of the cultures themselves will dictate how a model should be adapted. The more deeply we understand a particular culture, and the more extensive our understanding of a particular model of supervision (e.g., IDM), the more relevant and useful the modified model should be for implementation within a particular cultural context.

Integrative Developmental Model of Supervision

We see the IDM as a pantheoretical model that may be applied, to varying degrees, to the training of supervisees in diverse therapy orientations. The following discussion of the IDM draws from recent and more expansive treatments of the model including Stoltenberg and McNeill (2010) as well as related research (Stoltenberg & McNeill, 2012) and viewing the model as a form of evidence-based practice (Stoltenberg & Pace, 2008).

Overarching structures

The decision to include three overarching structures as an important part of the foundation of the IDM was based on the assumption (and observations) that once one has developed in a given area, it is possible to regress in response to stress or significant environmental changes, but development in the same domain should not recur with regularity, although it will be expressed differently across contexts and will be impacted by additional life experiences (see Stoltenberg & Delworth, 1987 for a discussion). Thus, although learning continues throughout life, the notion of recycling through the same developmental processes time and again (as posited by Loganbill et al., 1982) appeared to be inconsistent with models of development; however, cycling through similar developmental processes for various domains of clinical practice would be consistent with models of development and learning. This growth is not always characterized as a steady progression, however, and trainees may, at times, appear to regress. Tracking development becomes very important and three "overarching" structures were offered as constructs or markers with which to monitor trainee development over time. Changes in these structures help us assess what developmental level is most characteristic of a supervisee at any specific time in their professional growth for a given domain or activity. This is an aspect of the IDM that appears to be often misinterpreted or overlooked. A given supervisee may be functioning, in general, at a particular level of professional development, but as training and experience progress, the likelihood is that for particular domains of clinical practice, the supervisee may actually be functioning at various developmental levels. Thus, when one refers to a level 1 or level 2 therapist, one should specify level 1 or level 2 for which specific domains of professional practice, understanding that the therapist may be functioning at level 3 in other domains of practice. Development is domain specific (see Table 28.1 for an overview of developmental levels and structures). This view is consistent with present approaches to training in professional competencies, although the specific domains traditionally included in the IDM (intervention skills competence, assessment techniques, interpersonal assessment, case conceptualization, individual differences, theoretical orientation, treatment plans and goals, and professional ethics) differ somewhat from the foundational and functional competency benchmarks (see Crossman, 2009; Kaslow et al., 2009). The three overarching

Table 28.1 Developmental levels.

Level	*Motivation*	*Autonomy*	*Self-other awareness*
I	Focus on acquisition of skills Intrinsic motivation for learning or getting degree Range from amotivation, external, through introjected regulation for efficacy	Dependent on supervisor Need for structure, positive feedback, minimal direct confrontation Impersonal for amotivation Varied external locus of causality Susceptible to peripheral route processing	Limited self-awareness Focus on self Evaluation apprehension Relatively high performance anxiety Difficulty seeing strengths, weaknesses Limited K-I-A, limited R-I-A, reliance on R-O-A
Transition issues	Motivation for learning new approaches and techniques may be limited (amotivation-external: low value, low efficacy)	May desire more independence than is warranted Internality is increasing	Focus changes more to the client and away from own thoughts and performance
II	Motivation fluctuates from confident to lacking confidence Increased efficacy, movement toward identified regulation but still questions efficacy, still considerable external regulation	Dependency–autonomy conflict Locus of causality can vary, external to internal depending on perceptions of value and efficacy More central, less peripheral route processing depending on context	Can focus more on client with increasing K-I-A, greater empathy or potential for perspective taking Potential for enmeshment (overidentification) with client Developing appropriate balance/boundaries Better R-I-A, R-O-A still very important
Transition issues	Increased desire to personalize orientation, movement toward integrated regulation	Becoming more conditionally independent; better understanding of parameters of competence Movement toward more internal locus of causality	Can begin to alternate focus on client and more self-aware focus on own reactions More sensitive to and aware of contexts
III	Motivation is more stable, more integrated to intrinsic Doubts remain regarding competence, but less troubling, domain specific Concerned with broad professional identity and how therapist role fits in	Firm belief in own autonomy, not easily shaken, highly internal locus of causality, more aware of what cannot be controlled Reflective practice Better understanding of personal/professional competence Knows when to seek consultation Largely central route processing	Accepts own strengths, weaknesses, optimizes use of personal characteristics in therapy High empathy, perspective taking, pattern matching, high K-I-A Good R-I-A and R-O-A process skills Good cognitive and affective reflecting abilities Good intersubjective and more objective processing skills, aware of time and context
Transition to 3*i*	Aware of and reflects upon domains in which motivation is stable versus those where it isn't (extrinsic – intrinsic)	Better able to move conceptually and behaviorally from one domain to another Professional identity is solid across most relevant domains Largely internal locus of causality, high awareness of what is uncontrollable	Personalized/integrative understanding crosses domains Monitors impact of work on personal life, changes in professional identity/performance Good K-I-A, R-I-A, R-O-A

Source: Adapted from Stoltenberg & McNeill, 2010, and Ryan & Deci, 2000.

structures by which we mark development in the IDM are motivation, autonomy, and self- and other awareness.

Structures across levels of professional development

The overarching structures help us track development across levels for various domains of training and practice. As noted earlier, the IDM views development as progressing through levels 1–3 with a culminating level 3*i* that reflects a focus on integration across domains with functioning at level 3. Thus, any given trainee (or practicing professional) may be functioning at different developmental levels for different domains of practice at any given point in time. Characteristics for levels 1–3 supervisees are summarized in Table 28.1.

Level 1 There appear to be some common characteristics of many beginning trainees who would be expected to be functioning at level 1. In the most prototypical case, the trainee would enter a training program with little or no direct experience in counseling or psychotherapy, assessment, and so on, but would, of course, have had considerable experience interacting with others in various other social, school, and work contexts. As trainees approach the direct clinical training experience, which varies by types of training programs for various mental health professions, they often have been exposed (in the United States) at least at an introductory level to theories of counseling and psychotherapy, perhaps initial training in core counseling techniques, issues of psychological measurement, and so on, and they have often had a broad exposure to psychology or related fields through prior undergraduate educational experiences. Level 1 trainees will have limited knowledge, skills, and exposure to the specific domain of focus in the supervisory context. Of course, even experienced professionals who desire to build competence in new domains (perhaps new modalities of therapy, populations, or theoretical approaches) are often likely to be functioning at level 1 if the new domain of focus significantly differs from prior training and experience. This lack of experience and background knowledge has implications for learning from cognitive, skill, and schema development models (e.g., Anderson, 2010; Schön, 1987; Stoltenberg & Pace, 2008), other information processing models (Petty & Cacioppo, 1986; Petty & Wegener, 1999), and theories of motivation (e.g., SDT; Ryan & Deci, 2000).

Motivation This structure reflects the level of interest, personal investment, and effort the supervisee is willing to invest in clinical training and practice. As with theories of motivation, including SDT (Ryan & Deci, 2000), motivation can be seen as having multiple targets depending on the context. Aspects of the SDT can be useful in considering how motivational style is affected for various levels of trainees with different targets of motivation. We have regularly referred to level 1 (beginning) trainees as demonstrating high levels of motivation. With reference to SDT, this motivation might be viewed as largely intrinsic for learning to become a counselor or therapist, or perhaps, simply intrinsic for wanting to obtain a degree, license, or certification to practice with other levels of motivation related to other targets. In terms of the beginner's sense of self-efficacy as it relates to being a good therapist (competence) and the associated focus on the acquisition of skills (often dictated by the training environment), the motivational style may range from amotivation (believing he or she cannot learn or sees little value in the particular skills being taught) to external motivational styles, where external reward or punishment and approval are more relevant, through the more intrinsic end of the continuum where value of the activity fits more with personal values and goals. From an ELM (Petty & Cacioppo, 1986) perspective, the supervisor, and other authorities, would typically be viewed as credible sources, so with activities viewed as being low in personal relevance or with one's perception of low ability to effectively engage in the activity, the supervisor's input may be accepted at face value with little active information processing occurring. If personal value and related abilities are viewed as adequate (often not the case for abilities), the supervisee will be more motivated to engage in effortful central route processing. The desire to move from novice to expert as quickly as possible is often quite strong, but the ability to do so will come more slowly. As will be noted later, some early success in skills and initial knowledge acquisition can lead to less motivation (in terms of value) to learn new more complicated skills and more complex conceptualizations and theories (reticence to reexperience reduced self-efficacy).

Autonomy Novice trainees typically (and appropriately) show considerable dependence on their supervisors and others in authority with reference to their training programs (see Stoltenberg & McNeill, 2012 for review of relevant research). The IDM views this as an appropriate response to the level 1 trainee's low degree of experience and knowledge as well as a limited understanding of the processes involved in effective counseling or therapy. Supervisees often indicate a need for externally provided structure for the supervision context as well as for counseling situations, and it is expected that this structure and guidance will be provided by the supervisor. Their relevant schemas for supervision and counseling (and other related activities; K-I-A) tend to be limited, and they expect useful information, good examples, and skills training to occur in supervision and other training contexts. This would reflect a largely external locus of causality from an SDT framework and, possibly, more peripheral route processing in terms of the ELM. Early perceptions of success, often based on positive feedback or praise from the supervisor, and sometimes from clients, tend to encourage a more internal sense of causality and decreasing dependency on the supervisor. This increases one's sense of personal control and the desire for greater independence, often reflected in less compliance to directives from supervisors or others. A rather limited or simplistic understanding of the supervision and counseling processes can lead to a greater desire for independence than is warranted by levels of competence (as viewed by the supervisor and/or client). As noted earlier, this early sense of mastery of somewhat limited skills and knowledge can reduce the perceived value of learning more complex theories, conceptualization processes, and so on.

Self- and other awareness The new declarative knowledge acquired by level 1 trainees is necessary, but not sufficient for adequate practice or implementation of skills. With retrieval of information from memory in the counseling situation, level 1 trainees may develop the ability to adequately perform a particular skill or follow a simple strategy in counseling, but sufficient procedural knowledge is lacking. In other words, knowing how and when to effectively implement skills and apply knowledge has not yet developed as the schemas are insufficiently refined. The amount of cognitive effort and working memory used to retrieve and implement what has been learned leaves little attentional capacity for empathic attunement or perspective taking regarding the client. This cognitive self-focus tends to yield limited self-awareness (more self-consciousness) with accompanying performance anxiety, evaluation apprehension, difficulty assessing one's own strengths and weaknesses, as well as little K-I-A and R-I-A capacity. At this point, there is considerable reliance on R-O-A, particularly in the supervision context, to make sense of sessions and consolidate learning into efficient procedures and more developed schemas.

In the cognitive realm, lack of self-efficacy or understanding regarding what to do (whether one believes him or herself capable of doing it) characterizes the insufficient knowledge as well as interference with trainee cognitive processes at this level. The regular need to retrieve information (rules and procedures, weak schema activation links) from memory during sessions tends to interfere with the trainee's ability to attend to and understand the client's experience. In sports terms, this has been called "analysis paralysis." Relevant experience, review (video) and reflection on the experience (R-O-A), relevant additional practice, and accurate feedback provided by the supervisor are necessary to facilitate trainee development.

Affective self-awareness is also important for the trainee. From a developmental perspective, the disequilibrium elicited by one's perception of insufficient understanding (inability to assimilate new experiences) can result in internal conflict or discomfort for the trainee. The fear and anxiety associated with perceived negative evaluation by the supervisor and others for inadequate skills (external regulation) as well as one's own evaluation of inadequate competence set the stage for considerable uncertainty and discomfort on the part of the novice therapist. The self-focus, or even self-preoccupation, is understandable as skills and knowledge are being developed and one is attuned to one's own performance. In addition, the lack of understanding of and experience with the counseling process can elicit "low-road" social processing of effect with regard to the client with little conscious awareness of the origins of the experienced emotions (lack of high-road conscious processing). As familiarity with skills and counseling processes improve with feedback and practice, trainees have greater K-I-A with less distracting R-I-A focused on their own behavior, thoughts, and feelings of self-efficacy and a more internal locus of causality starts to increase. This frees up more attentional capacity and trainees can begin to focus more on the client's experience and the impact of their interventions on the client. The appropriate supervision environment for level 1 supervisees is summarized on Table 28.2.

Level 2 As supervisees resolve level 1 challenges and move into level 2 for at least some domains, we see some implications of the increased availability of attentional capacity. By moving away from the largely necessary self-focus of level 1, the supervisee has an opportunity to use this new capacity for attending more carefully to the client's experience both within and outside of session.

Motivation Prior to movement to level 2, we will often see increased self-efficacy in supervisees and higher self-perceptions of their abilities and understanding of counseling and related processes. Thus, less self-conscious attention to their own behavior, thoughts, and feelings allow them to focus more intently on the client,

Table 28.2 Level 1 supervision environment.

General considerations	Focus on basic information, skills, and attitudes Initial focus on breadth of theories Initial focus on client perspective taking, empathy Initial focus on awareness of culturally/environmentally influenced attitudes/values of self and others Provide structure and keep anxiety at manageable levels Provide specific resources, opportunities to practice Provide specific behavioral positive and corrective feedback Provide autonomy support (perspective taking of trainee and client, support supervisee intervention choices when appropriate, prescribe when not, minimize pressure and control within constraints of client welfare)
Client assignment	Mild presenting problems or maintenance cases, few in number Some culturally diverse clients
Interventions	Facilitative (supportive, encouraging) Prescriptive (suggest approaches, modeling interventions, etc.) Conceptual (somewhat limited, tie theory-Dx-Tx) Catalytic (late level 1; see level 2)
Mechanisms	Observation (video or live) Beginning skills training (microskills, empathy, perspective taking) Role playing Detailed case conceptualizations with supporting evidence Interpret dynamics (limited, client or trainee) Readings, literature searches Group supervision Appropriate balance of ambiguity/conflict Address strengths, then weaknesses, then strengths (feedback sandwich) Closely monitor clients Multicultural experiences Exploration of personal life experiences

Source: Adapted from Stoltenberg & McNeill, 2010, and Ryan & Deci, 2000.

which can bring more complexity to the process by adding additional dimensions to consider and evaluate. Emerging patterns of understanding may be challenged as insufficient when trainees are more aware of the client's reactions and not so focused on their own specific performance. In addition, the progression of other training experiences tends to add to the complexity of the learning process. One of us recalls coaching kids' league basketball and working with a young person who had developed considerable skills in dribbling a basketball by practicing alone at home. These skills proved inadequate when other players, and offensive and defensive schemes, were added to the context. This increased degree of complexity can challenge prior perceptions of self-efficacy and, at times, return the trainee to more extrinsic motivation for certain activities as well as a more external locus of causality accompanied by reduced competency (fluctuating motivation, competence; see Stoltenberg & McNeill, 2010 for detailed discussion). This process has also been referred to as deskilling (see

Lombardo, Milne, & Proctor, 2009 for discussion). For some, the intrinsic motivation to learn remains, while for others, there can be low or amotivation to learn certain procedures due to the view of limited value or limited efficacy. The realization that "one size does not fit all" in terms of effective therapy can result in disequilibrium and discomfort with regards to one's suitability for the profession. One may either retreat to earlier cognitive structures or push through (with support from the supervisor) for greater schema refinement and improved procedures via useful feedback and additional deliberate practice. Issues of relevance to this level of trainee include a broader and deeper understanding of the therapeutic process, incorporating better empathy and perspective taking, better self-understanding concerning the impact of one's experience and culture on values and perceptions, and (consistent with Wampold, 2010, therapist effects) developing a better understanding of one's personal strengths and weaknesses, and behavior and their impact on clients and professional competencies.

Autonomy The dependency that we noted as characteristic of level 1 has given way to a greater desire for independence, at least when perceptions of one's professional performance are positive. When, as noted earlier, increased attention to client reactions and experiences, and increased awareness of the bewildering amount of research and literature relevant to professional practice come to the awareness of the trainee; she or he may retreat to more dependency, at times, on the supervisor or, if fear of negative evaluation is high (external regulation or reality-based assessment of power), fail to disclose these insecurities and retreat to simple solutions or inadequate, but comfortable, schemas (e.g., the client's inability to form relationships, the client is not ready to change, measuring outcomes is not important). Essentially, we find that a trainee's K-I-A and R-I-A will be viewed by the trainee as adequate at times while inadequate at other times, with a greater need for supervisor assisted R-O-A and the provision of additional perspectives (including feedback), resources, and deliberate practice. This can lead to decreased competence in certain areas as the additional perceived complexity, emotional reactions, and challenges of therapy confuses and shakes the confidence of the trainee, resulting in a negative impact on performance. This dependency–autonomy conflict constitutes the adolescence (a metaphor, of course) of professional development as striving for autonomy and competence is met with successes and failures.

Self- and other awareness The IDM posits that the trainee's growing ability to engage in counseling processes without the need to regularly retrieve information from memory leaves more working memory (and attentional capacity) available to intensively focus on the client (if encouraged to do so), which allows him or her to more deeply and completely understand the client's perspective, the client's environment and reactions to it, and the client's emotional experience. Although this can be, at times, nearly overwhelming, this allows for a more complex understanding of counseling, provides additional crucial perspectives on the process and outcomes of counseling, and pushes the trainee to accommodate to this more complex picture, enabling better schema refinement, the development of more effective procedural knowledge, and greater more refined pattern recognition as growth toward expertise continues. This has implications for cognitive awareness (understanding, perceptual perspective taking) as well as awareness of the client's emotional experience. The possibility of greater awareness of the emotional climate of the counseling session, and the trainee's increased self-awareness regarding his or her own emotional processes, sets the stage for more complex processing as well as confusion. For example, less self-preoccupation on the part of the trainee expands the perceived emotional experience beyond performance anxiety and evaluation apprehension to the potential to respond emotionally to the client. Sorting out these emotional reactions, according to the IDM, is an important process for the level 2 trainee. Briefly, the trainee, in response to interacting with the client, may have an emotional reaction that is (a) similar to emotional reactions that many others in the client's life may have to the client (generalizable reaction), (b) may be an idiosyncratic emotional reaction to the client based on the trainee's particular life experiences and reactions to them (idiosyncratic countertransference), or (c) be a function of the trainee's emotional resonance with the client's emotional experience (true empathy). All of these are important sources of information, but misattributing the source of the trainee's emotion can negatively impact the counseling process. If, as Goleman (2006) suggested, the trainee's emotional reactions remain "low road," understanding is limited and behavior is automatic. If the trainee is able to symbolize his or her emotional experience and use "high road" processing (effective R-I-A), better social facilitation (in this case, better therapy) is enabled. See Table 28.3 for a summary of characteristics of the supervision environment appropriate for level 2 supervisees.

Level 3 Successful resolution of level 2 issues enables movement to level 3 which is characterized by a more stable intrinsic motivation toward most activities within given domains of professional practice, which leads to higher reality-based perceptions of self-efficacy and competence including a more internal locus of causality for professional behavior, with greater ability to engage in reflective practice. More effective (accurate) declarative and production schemas have been developed that more adequately incorporate a more complex therapeutic perspective in addition to higher skill levels. Effectively processed and integrated continued experience (through reflection, feedback, deliberate practice, self- and other initiated seeking of resources, and continued autonomy support) has "enabled the therapist to move toward greater expertise with more functional awareness of patterns and the ability to match patterns perceived in current practice with others encountered in prior experiences" (Stoltenberg & McNeill, 2010, p. 37). Unique or unexpected events unfolding in practice, which would have required extensive supervisor directed R-O-A in the past, can now more easily be handled by the therapist by R-I-A as the events occur. A greater awareness of the impact of one's personal characteristics on professional competence, through greater self-awareness and self-understanding, in addition to the processing of considerable professional experiences and greater awareness and command of theory and research, allows one to more accurately place reactions to clients within subjective, empathic, and more objective (e.g., nomothetic research or theory based) perspectives.

Motivation The vacillation between poles of external to intrinsic motivation for learning and specific activities has stabilized toward the intrinsic end of the continuum with greater internal locus of causality (SDT; more self-determined). Effortful

Table 28.3 Level 2 supervision environment.

General considerations	Advanced skill development More focus on advanced critical thinking/theory, pattern matching More focus on empathy, emotional competence Less structure provided by supervisor More supervisee provided structure encouraged Support self-directed literature searches Support utilizing increasing breadth of resources/perspectives Continue to provide specific behavioral feedback (positive, corrective) Continue to provide opportunities to practice, broaden range Continue to provide autonomy support (perspective taking of trainee and client, support supervisee intervention choices (now more broad and appropriate), suggest alternatives when choices not appropriate, minimize pressure, and control within constraints of client welfare)
Client assignment	More difficult clients with more severe presenting problems (for example, axis II disorders), greater number of active clients More breadth of diversity of clients
Interventions	Facilitative (supportive, encouraging) Prescriptive: used only occasionally compared with level I Confrontive: now able to handle confrontation through supportive corrective feedback, highlighting discrepancies Conceptual: introduce more alternative views (can be mild confrontation, pointing out discrepancies), advanced theory/ empirical literature reviews/integration, encourage pattern matching, integrate empathy/perspective taking of client with personal self-awareness (during and outside of sessions) and awareness of the influence of context/culture across time and place Catalytic: process comments, highlight countertransference, cognitive and affective reactions to client and/or supervisor, parallel process, encourage intersubjectivity and objectivity in R-I-A and R-O-A
Mechanisms	Observation (video or live) Role playing (although less important than at level 1) Advanced skills training Interpret dynamics (see catalytic earlier), parallel process Group supervision More complex or focused resources to address more diverse clients Monitor client welfare, but less close monitoring necessary Multicultural experiences Continued focus on own interpretation of personal life experiences to build self-awareness

Source: Adapted from Stoltenberg & McNeill, 2010, and Ryan & Deci, 2000.

self-monitoring and self-evaluation by the trainee enhanced with effective and accurate feedback by the supervisor across a range of experiences (educational as well as professional) enables more complex and comprehensive schema development and refinement as well as effective procedural knowledge and pattern matching (K-I-A, R-I-A). One's professional identity and how various professional roles fit into that identity become an increasing focus.

Table 28.4 Level 3 supervision environment.

General considerations	Most structure provided by trainee, more focus on personal and professional integration and career decisions Continue to provide autonomy support (perspective taking of trainee and client, support supervisee intervention choices [now much more broad and appropriate], suggest alternatives to consider, minimize pressure and control) Orient toward development of integration across domains
Client assignment	Complex range of clients with diverse presenting problems, broad cultural diversity Fully functioning professional across relevant domains able to handle range of clients
Interventions	Facilitative (support, encouragement) Confrontive: highlighting discrepancies occasionally necessary, including contrasting cultural perspectives Conceptual: from personal integrative orientation, continue to introduce alternative views and evidence Catalytic: in response to blocks or stagnation Train/encourage reflective practice
Mechanisms	Group supervision Strive for integration across domains Reflective practice Monitor and reflect on changing life experiences

Source: Adapted from Stoltenberg & McNeill, 2010, and Ryan & Deci, 2000.

Autonomy The dependency–autonomy conflict yields to greater independence and internal locus of causality. The level 3 therapist, while seeking consultation when necessary, retains personal responsibility for her or his clinical work. Thus, with greater ability, the level 3 therapist is less influenced by peripheral route processing (less susceptible to "expert" directives) and more likely to engage in central route processing when issues arise and feedback or suggestions differ from one's own perspective. In contrast to what can occur with level 2 trainees, this central route processing appears less reactant, and characteristic of effortful and informed information processing. Independent reflective practice now becomes more of a reality, and less aspirational. Supervision, if available, is still useful in providing additional breadth of perspective, but has become increasingly collegial and less hierarchical (see Table 28.4 for level 3 supervision environments).

Self- and other awareness The focus on the self that was characteristic of level 1 (self-preoccupation, self-consciousness) has developed into more insightful self-awareness for the level 3 professional. In the cognitive realm, the therapist can alternate among an informed awareness of one's own life experiences and perspectives (self-focus), an awareness and understanding of the client's perceptual and experiential world (other focus), and a more integrated awareness of what theory and research (and prior learning experiences) can contribute to the ongoing counseling process (cultural context, useful and predictable patterns, and relevant processes). The therapist's emotional awareness has also expanded with greater self-understanding, client empathy, and a broad and deep understanding of the role of emotion in profession practice. The therapist's "K-I-A is more adequate to handle a broader array of practice events, and the therapist's abilities in R-I-A allow for more effective changes in strategies to occur on the fly in the therapeutic context" (Stoltenberg & McNeill, 2010, p. 37). R-O-A through reflective practice, as well as appropriate supervision (if this is still available) can continue to aid in the therapist's effectiveness and development with a greater focus on integration of development across relevant domains (level 3*i*).

Conclusion

In this chapter we have attempted to present brief synopses of relevant models and theories from diverse perspectives that we believe add breadth and depth to the discussion of the supervision process and the implementation of the IDM. Given space limitations, it is not possible to completely develop how these constructs and processes can be fully integrated into the IDM, but we believe that awareness of how we learn and process information and experience, how we move from novice to expert, the role of emotion and emotion processing, the role of motivation and locus of causality, as well as the influence of frames of reference, priming, biased processing, and other social psychological factors provide valuable perspective on mediating and moderating factors that can influence the supervision process (as well as counseling and other professional processes). Our commitment to the scientist–practitioner framework has influenced our choice of theories, models, and constructs to those that have considerable empirical support as well as relevance to learning and development in professional domains of practice. Supervision, and other domains of professional practice, will benefit from considering and integrating theory and research from broad areas of human learning and interaction rather than restricting our focus to only a narrow range of content or processes and research we call clinical supervision or psychotherapy.

There is considerable evidence that developmental models of supervision are useful and largely consistent with research on the supervision process (Johnston & Milne, 2012; Ladany & Inman, 2008; Stoltenberg, 2005; Stoltenberg & McNeill, 2010, 2012; Stoltenberg & Pace, 2008). How relevant the IDM or other developmental models of supervision prove to be for non-Western cultures that focus on different professional roles and competencies remains a practical and empirical question. Nonetheless, as the focus on the IDM is primarily on how trainees learn and develop, with less specific focus on particular culture-based competencies, we would hope that the basic constructs prove to be useful and their application evaluated for any given cultural context.

References

Anderson, J. R. (2005). *Cognitive psychology and its implications* (6th ed.). New York: Worth Publishers.

Anderson, J. R. (2010). *Cognitive psychology and its implications* (Seventh ed.). New York: Worth Publishing.

Bakioğlu, A., & Gürdal, A. (2001). Lisansüstü tezlerde danışman ve öğrencilerin rol algıları:Yönetim için göstergeler [The role perceptions of advisees and supervisors 396 A. Buyukgoze-Kavas et al. regarding dissertations: Implications for administrators]. *Hacettepe Üniversitesi Eğitim Fakültesi Dergisi, 21*, 9–18.

Bang, K. (2006). Applying the integrated development model to Korean supervisees. *Asia Pacific Education Review, 7*(1), 11–18. Retrieved from http://www.eric.ed.gov/PDFS/EJ752323.pdf

Bargh, J. (2006). Agenda 2006: What have we been priming all these years? On the development, mechanisms, and ecology of nonconscious social behavior. *European Journal of Social Psychology, 36*(2), 147–168.

Batson, C. D., O'Quin, K., & Pych, V. (1982). An attribution theory analysis of trained helpers' inferences about clients' needs. In T. A. Wills (Ed.), *Basic processes in helping relationships* (pp. 59–80). New York: Academic Press.

Baumeister, R., & Leary, M. R. (1995). The need to belong: Desire for interpersonal attachments as a fundamental human motivation. *Psychological Bulletin, 117*, 497–529.

Berry, J. W., & Kim, U. (1988). Acculturation and mental health. In P. R. Dasen, J. W. Berry, & N. Sartorius (Eds.), *Health and cross-cultural psychology: Toward applications* (pp. 207–236). Thousand Oaks, CA: Sage Publications, Inc.

Bruner, J. S. (1957). On perceptual readiness. *Psychological Review, 64*, 123–152.

Buyukgoze-Kavas, A., Taylor, J. M., Neimeyer, G. J., & Guneri, O. (2010). The mentoring relationship: A comparison of counselling students in the United States of America and Turkey. *Counselling Psychology Quarterly, 23*(4), 387–398. doi:10.1080/09515070.2010.529677.

Cacioppo, J. T. (2002). Social neuroscience: Understanding the pieces fosters understanding the whole and vice versa. *American Psychologist, 57*, 819–827.

Cacioppo, J. T., & Berntson, G. G. (1992). Social psychological contributions to the decade of the brain: Doctrine of multilevel analysis. *American Psychologist, 47*, 1019–1028.

Cacioppo, J. T., Petty, R. E., & Sidera, J. A. (1982). The effects of a salient self-schema on the evaluation of proattitudinal editorials: Top-down versus bottom-up message processing. *Journal of Experimental Social Psychology, 18*, 324–338.

Crossman, R. E. (2009). Competency benchmarks: A model for understanding and measuring competence in professional psychology across training levels. *Training and Education in Professional Psychology, 3*, S5–S26.

deCharms, R. (1968). *Personal causation*. New York: Academic Press.

Deci, E. L. (1975). *Intrinsic motivation*. New York: Plenum.

Ericsson, K. A. (2006). The influence of expertise and deliberate practice on the development of superior expert performance. In K. A. Ericsson, N. Charness, P. Feltovich, & R. R. Hoffman (Eds.), *Cambridge handbook of expertise and expert performance* (pp. 685–706). Cambridge: Cambridge University Press.

Fluckiger, C., & Holtforth, M. G. (2008). Focusing the therapist's attention on the patient's strengths: A preliminary study to foster a mechanism of change in outpatient psychotherapy. *Journal of Clinical Psychology, 64*(7), 876–890.

Gerstein, L., Heppner, P., Aegisdottir, S., Leung, A., & Norsworthy, K. (2009). *International handbook of cross-cultural counseling: Cultural assumptions and practices worldwide* (p. 200). Thousand Oaks, CA: Sage Publications.

Goleman, D. (2006). *Social intelligence: The new science of human relationships*. New York: Bantam.

Greenberg, L. S. (2002). Integrating an emotion-focused approach to treatment into psychotherapy integration. *Journal of Psychotherapy Integration, 12*, 154–189.

Greenberg, L. S., & Goldman, R. N. (2008). *Emotion-focused couples therapy: The dynamics of emotion, love and power*. Washington, D.C.: American Psychological Association.

Harter, S. (1978). Effectance motivation reconsidered: Towards a developmental model. *Human Development*, *1*, 661–669.

Jang, H., Reeve, J., Ryan, R. M., & Kim, A. (2009). Can self-determination theory explain what underlies the productive, satisfying learning experiences of collectivistically oriented Korean students? *Journal of Educational Psychology*, *101*(3), 644–661.

Jiang, Y., Yau, J., Bonner, P., & Chiang, L. (2011). The role of perceived parental autonomy support in academic achievement of Asian and Latin American adolescents. *Electronic Journal Of Research In Educational Psychology*, *9*(2), 497–522.

Johnston, L. H., & Milne, D. L. (2012). How do supervisees learn during supervision? A grounded theory study of the perceived developmental process. *The Cognitive Behaviour Therapist*, *5*, 1–23.

Jones, E. E., & Nisbett, R. E. (1971). *The actor and the observer: Divergent perceptions of the causes of behaviors*. New York: General Learning Press.

Kaslow, N. J., Grus, C. L., Campbell, L. F., Fouad, N. A., Hatcher, R. L., & Rodolfa, E. R. (2009). Competency assessment toolkit for professional psychology. *Training and Education in Professional Psychology*, *3*, S27–S45.

La Guardia, J. G., & Patrick, H. (2008). Self-determination theory as a fundamental theory of close relationship. *Canadian Psychology*, *49*(3), 201–209.

Ladany, N., & Inman, A. G. (2008). Developments in counseling skills training and supervision. In S. D. Brown & R. W. Lent (Eds.), *Handbook of counseling psychology* (4th ed., pp. 338–354). Hoboken, NJ: Wiley.

Lang, S. W. (2005). 'Decolonialism' and the counselling profession: The aotearoa/New Zealand experience. *International Journal For The Advancement of Counselling*, *27*(4), 557–572.

Leong, F. L., & Ponterotto, J. G. (2003). A proposal for internationalizing counseling psychology in the United States: Rationale, recommendations, and challenges. *Counseling Psychologist*, *31*(4), 381–395.

Loganbill, C., Hardy, E., & Delworth, U. (1982). Supervision: A conceptual model. *The Counseling Psychologist*, *10*(1), 3–42.

Lombardo, C., Milne, D., & Proctor, R. (2009). Getting to the heart of clinical supervision: A theoretical review of the role of emotions in professional development. *Behavioural and Cognitive Psychotherapy*, *37*, 207–219.

Lynch, M. F., Vansteenkiste, M., Deci, E. L., & Ryan, R. M. (2011). Autonomy as process and outcome: Revisiting cultural and practical issues in motivation for counseling. *The Counseling Psychologist*, *39*, 286–302.

Mather, R., & Romo, A. (2007). *Automaticity and cognitive control in social behavior*. Southlake, TX: Fountainhead Press.

Norem, K., Magnuson, S., Wilcoxon, S. A., & Arbel, O. (2006). Supervisees' contributions to stellar supervision outcomes. *Journal of Professional Counseling Practice, Theory, and Research*, *34*(1&2), 33–48.

Ochsner, K., & Lieberman, M. (2001). The emergence of social cognitive neuroscience. *American Psychologist*, *56*, 717–734.

Pedersen, P. B. (2003). Culturally biased assumptions in counseling psychology. *The Counseling Psychologist*, *31*, 396–403.

Petty, R. E., & Cacioppo, J. T. (1986). *Communication and persuasion: Central and peripheral routes to attitude change*. New York: Springer-Verlag.

Petty, R. E., & Wegener, D. T. (1999). The Elaboration Likelihood Model: Current status and controversies. In S. Chaiken & T. Trope (Eds.), *Dual process theories in social psychology* (pp. 41–72). New York: Guilford Press.

Richards, K. (2000). Counsellor supervision in Zimbabwe: A new direction. *International Journal for the Advancement of Counselling, 22*(2), 143–155.
Ryan, R. M., & Deci, E. L. (2000). Self-determination theory and the facilitation of intrinsic motivation, social development, and well-being. *American Psychologist, 55*, 68–78.
Ryan, R. M., Lynch, M. F., Vansteenkiste, M., & Deci, E. L. (2011). Motivation and autonomy in counseling, psychotherapy, and behavior change: A look at theory and practice. *The Counseling Psychologist, 39*, 193–260.
Schön, D. A. (1987). *Educating the reflective practitioner.* San Francisco, CA: Jossey-Bass.
Stoltenberg, C. D. (1981). Approaching supervision from a developmental perspective: The counselor complexity model. *Journal of Counseling Psychology, 28*, 59–65.
Stoltenberg, C. D. (2005). Enhancing professional competence through developmental approaches to supervision. *American Psychologist, 6*, 855–864.
Stoltenberg, C. D. (2008). Developmental approaches to supervision: A case example. In C. A. Felander & E. P. Shafranske (Eds.), *Casebook for clinical supervision: A competency-based approach* (pp. 39–56). New York: American Psychological Association.
Stoltenberg, C. D., & Delworth, U. (1987). *Supervising counselors and therapists.* San Francisco, CA: Jossey-Bass.
Stoltenberg, C. D., & McNeill, B. W. (2010). *IDM supervision: An integrative developmental model for supervising counselors and therapists* (3rd ed.). New York: Routledge.
Stoltenberg, C. D., & McNeill, B. W. (2012). Supervision: Research, models, competence. In N. A. Fouad (Ed.), *APA handbook of counseling psychology* (pp. 295–327). Washington, DC: American Psychological Association.
Stoltenberg, C. D., & Pace, T. M. (2008). Science and practice in supervision: An evidence-based practice in psychology approach. In B. W. Walsh (Ed.), *Biennial review of counseling psychology* (pp. 71–95). New York: Routledge.
Stoltenberg, C. D., McNeill, B. W., & Delworth, U. (1998). *IDM Supervision: An integrated developmental model for supervising counselors and therapists.* San Francisco, CA: Jossey-Bass.
Strozier, A. L., Barnett-Queen, T., & Bennett, C. K. (2000). Supervision: Critical process and outcome variables. *The Clinical Supervisor, 19*(1), 21–39.
Stupart, Y., Rehfuss, M., & Parks-Savage, A. (2010). Counselor supervision in Jamaica: An initial exploration. *Journal for International Counselor Education, 2*, 74–95.
Thomas, M. R., Beckman, T. J., Mauck, K. F., Cha, S. S., & Thomas, K. G. (2011). Group assessments of resident physicians improve reliability and decrease halo error. *Journal of General Internal Medicine, 26*(7), 759–764.
Thorndike, E. L. (1920). A constant error in psychological ratings. *Journal of Applied Psychology, 4*(1), 25–29.
Todisco, M., & Salomone, P. R. (1991). Facilitating effective cross-cultural relationships: The White counselor and the Black client. *Journal of Multicultural Counselling and Development, 19*, 146–157.
Vansteenkiste, M., Simons, J., Lens, W., Sheldon, K. M., & Deci, E. L. (2004). Motivated learning, performance, and persistence: The synergistic effects of intrinsic goal contents and autonomy-supportive contexts. *Journal of Personality and Social Psychology, 87*(2), 246–260.
Wampold, B. E. (2010). The research evidence for common factors models: A historically situated perspective. In B. L. Duncan, S. D. Miller, B. E. Wampold, & M. A. Hubble (Eds.), *The heart & soul of change* (*2nd ed.*, pp. 49–81). Washington, D.C.: American Psychological Association.
Ward, P., Hodges, N. J., Starkes, J. L., & Williams, A. M. (2007). The road to excellence: Deliberate practice and the development of expertise. *High Ability Studies, 18*(2), 119–153.
White, R. W. (1963). *Ego and reality in psychoanalytic theory.* International Universities Press.

29

Supervisory Roles within Systems of Practice

Elizabeth L. Holloway

Theoretical models of supervisory practice in professional psychology have proliferated over the last 70 years, beginning with long-term psychoanalysis of the budding psychoanalytic therapist as the best method of learning practice. Early models of supervision were also aligned with a theoretical approach to counseling; however, supervision was viewed as a teaching activity distinct from counseling. Thus, supervision models were named after their counseling counterparts—rational emotive supervision, client-centered supervision, social learning, and working alliance (Goodyear, Bradley, & Bartlett, 1983). These models were built on the assumption that the method of teaching a specific approach to practice must mirror the counseling approach being taught. In spite of the prominence of these counseling-based approaches, there were murmurings from a minority of scholars in counseling psychology that the practice of supervision must be considered as a *praxis* that involved competencies and skills distinct from counseling (Holloway, 1984; Kagan & Kagan, 1990; Loganbill, Hardy, & Delworth, 1982; Stoltenberg & Delworth, 1987). Holloway and her colleagues (Holloway, 1992; Holloway & Poulin, 1995; Holloway & Wolleat, 1981; Holloway, Freund, Gardner, Nelson, & Walker, 1989), Stoltenberg and associates (Stoltenberg, McNeill, & Crethar, 1994; Stoltenberg, McNeill, & Delworth, 1998), and Ladany and associates (Ladany & Friedlander, 1995; Ladany & Lehrman-Waterman, 1999; Ladany, Inman, Constantine, & Hofheinz, 1997) published a persuasive body of research in the 1980s and 1990s that corroborated this contention. It is from this second generation of counseling models that *social role models of supervision* emerged.

The models that adhered to the theoretical premise that supervision embodied the awareness and skills of multiple teaching-like roles are numerous and began with Ekstein and Wallerstein's work of the 1950s. During the next 30 years, several models that might be classified as social role models were proposed in the United Kingdom and the United States. These models are charted by Bernard and Goodyear (2009),

---

The Wiley International Handbook of Clinical Supervision, First Edition. Edited by C. Edward Watkins, Jr. and Derek L. Milne.

who identified the work of Ekstein (1964; Ekstein & Wallerstein, 1958), Bernard (1979), Hess (1980), Hawkins and Shohet (1991), Holloway (1995), and Carroll (1996a; 1996b). Four well-known models were described in greater detail: the discrimination model by Janine Bernard (1979) and the systems approach to supervision (SAS) by Elizabeth Holloway (1995) both originating in the United States, and the seven-eyed model of supervision by Peter Hawkins and Robin Shohet (1991) and the seven tasks of supervision by Michael Carroll (1996a) of the United Kingdom.

Although programs of counseling psychology in the United States dominated the research and training of supervision in the latter part of the twentieth century, theory and research in supervision has proliferated over the last 15 years in England, Australia, New Zealand, and the European Union. The first conference in counseling devoted specifically to supervisory issues was in 1991 in London and named the British Association of Supervision Practice and Research. It was followed in 1992 by the International Conference of Supervision held in Hannover, Germany at the INITA Institute of Training. In England and Europe, supervision became a field of study taught not only in clinical areas but also across many other professions. For example, supervision certification is available through freestanding training institutes of study that align curriculum with government requirements. Professionals from different areas of practice including social work, psychology, education, medicine, business to name a few may participate in a one- to two-year course to gain supervision certification. The Association of National Organisations for Supervision in Europe was formed in 1997 in an effort to provide an exchange of views on training initiatives, and research and theories related to supervision as a practice of process-oriented consulting. Many European countries, such as the United Kingdom, require career-long supervision of clinical practice; thus, the models of supervision have an emphasis on the supporting (restorative), coaching, and consulting roles of supervision. In contrast, the United States supervisory models are designed for therapists in training from practicum through post-residency clinical placements and thus must include a gate-keeping, evaluative function. The development of the SAS model was greatly influenced by English and European scholars, in particular, Michael Carroll, Maria Gilbert, Brigid Protor, and Julie Hewson of England, Willem Lammers of Switzerland, Mathias Sells of Germany, and Karin Van Beekum of the Netherlands, during the many workshops that this author was privileged to offer at their training institutes and universities from 1988 to 2006. With this international influence, the SAS model has been adapted to both a training and consulting context of supervision, and it is hoped that supervisors will choose the emphasis on role that is most suited to the situation and supervisee with whom they work.

Social role theories are based on the supervisor taking on several potential roles. The most frequently recognized roles are teacher, counselor, and consultant; however, the roles of evaluator, lecturer, and role model of professional practice have also been used to describe supervisor behaviors and attitudes. Role theories of supervision outline the expectancies and behaviors that are considered part of the supervisory relationship and, specifically, part of the supervisor role. Studies have investigated roles typical of the supervisor (Bernard, 1979; Byrne & Sias, 2010; Ellis & Dell, 1986; Ellis, Dell, & Good, 1988; Gysbers & Johnston, 1965; Hart & Nance, 2003; Luke, Ellis, & Bernard, 2011; Stenack & Dye, 1982). Since Gysbers and Johnston's early study in 1965 that asked supervisors and supervisees to respond to the Supervisor Role Analysis Form (SRAF) to more recent studies of supervisory style by Byrne and Sias (2010), the concept of naming supervisors' actions as being aligned with role types has been confirmed.

The Advent of Competency Models

By 2004, the zeitgeist of supervision discourse was *competency-based training* for supervisors. The profession as a whole has promoted the competency movement through professional conferences that have resulted in a series of papers that identify supervision competencies and methods for the education and training of these competencies as well as their assessment (e.g., Falender et al., 2004). In this movement, such prominent scholars as Falender and Shrafranske (2004, 2008) and Pilling and Roth (see Chapter 2) have contributed in the development of models for competency-based supervision.

Supervision as a primary teaching method in practice is implicated in the competency movement, not only as a functional competency itself but also as a primary or secondary method of teaching the foundational competencies. For example, in the United States, six essential practice elements have been identified within the functional competency in supervision: expectations and roles, processes and procedures, skills development, awareness of the factors affecting quality, participation process, and ethical and legal issues. Thus, the articulation of best practices for assessment of each of the benchmarks becomes a critical component of the supervisor's education (Kaslow et al., 2009). In the twenty-first century, it seems warranted to revisit the social role supervisory models in light of the current thinking on supervision. The purpose of this chapter will be to update the model SAS, created by this author, in light of recent empirical studies on supervision and the competency-based movement in professional psychology.

The Systems Approach to Supervision: Theoretical Foundations

Although the SAS model is distinguished as a *social role* approach to supervision, first and foremost, it honors a relational approach to teaching the highly complex skills of therapeutic practice. Supervision is an intense and demanding relationship that requires both participants to be fully engaged while traversing the boundaries of their respective roles. SAS relationship is theoretically grounded in concepts of symbolic interactionism (Blumer, 1969), social role theory (Blumer & Morrione, 2004), and relational cultural theory (RCT) (Jordan & Walker, 2004). As such, it honors the principles of these theories while integrating them into a pragmatic heuristic with the intent of guiding practice.

Symbolic interactionism is made up of three interdependent constructs: the self, the world (as represented by others), and the social action. The self creates meaning through social interaction with the world as represented by other humans and events. Critical to creating a "sense of self" is the dynamic interplay between the "I" as reflector of action and the "me" as the object of self-reflection (Mead, 1934). Bowers

(1988), in describing the fundamental principles of symbolic interactionism in contrast to other ontological positions, stated,

> The I is the active, interactive, dynamic, interpreting component of the self . . . Rather than simply taking on a role by internalizing external expectations, the self is the accumulation of all previously experienced social interaction as interpreted and synthesized by the I. (p. 38)

The elevation of a reflective, dynamic, and interactive self with others and through social engagement is the essence of the learning alliance in supervision. As the supervisor engages in the teaching of therapeutic skills, the supervisee is further empowered by gaining knowledge through experiencing, reflecting, and articulating social processes that emerge in the counseling and supervisory relationship. The relationship becomes the central vehicle to understand social processes within the complex systems of organizational work, client needs, and supervisory actions.

The nature of the supervisory relationship is guided also by relational cultural theory or RCT. RCT emerged from the works of Gilligan (1993) and Belenky (1997) on women's development. They posited the importance of connection rather than separation in human learning and that educators as partners in learning can "encourage students to evolve their own patterns of work based on the problems they are pursuing" (Belenky, 1997, p. 229). This approach to collaborative problem-solving is foundational to the case method teaching promoted by the SAS model. Miller and Stiver (1997) claimed that when people collaborate through their interaction and relation with another, there are five essential qualities that enhance learning: zest, action, knowledge, worth, and desire for more connection. The generation of these qualities in relationship creates a learning alliance that can hold emotional intensity, conflict, and differences in cultural understandings. These qualities are precisely those needed in maintaining therapeutic bonds of trust and interpersonal sensitivity. The origin of RCT thinking came from the psychotherapeutic approach of Judith Jordan and her colleagues at the Stone Center (Jordan & Walker, 2004).

Supervision is also an intellectually challenging experience for both participants, and one might ask how these relational qualities contribute to heightened learning. Fredrickson and Losada (2005) devoted their research to the creation of intellectual communities of human relationships. Particularly relevant to supervisory practice are the relationships among good feelings (i.e., positive emotions, moods, and sentiments) and widened scope of attention, broadened behavioral repertoires, increased intuition, and creativity. These are all critical attributes in creating, engaging, and understanding the complex emotional fabric of therapeutic relationships. In the teaching of psychotherapeutic practice, of specific import is Fredrickson's suggestion that a positive feeling state will promote increased intellectual functioning. However, positive emotional states are not the only possible avenue for learning and connection, for issues of disagreement and conflict emerge in any healthy relationship (Schwartz, 2009). In order for the creation and facilitation of the supervisory relationship to be in accord with the theoretical principles of RCT, the supervisor must consider the client and the counseling relationship as well as the emotional conditions of the supervisor and the supervisory relationship (Jordan, 2004). In SAS, supervision a strong base of mutual connection in relationship, honoring the principles of RCT, provides an opportunity for positive professional growth, reflection, knowledge, skills, and resiliency through the judicious use of relational roles.

Elements of the SAS Model

The SAS model can be used as a frame of reference for an individual practitioner to problem solve a case dilemma, to strategize a supervisory approach, or to design a supervisory training. It provides a strategy for systematically using a "case method" approach that encompasses the presentation of client or supervisee histories, accompanied at times with examples of the on-going interaction, followed by a conceptualization of the clinical situation and suggestions for interventions. It is an effort to understand supervision by offering a common language that is relevant to supervisors and educators across different theoretical points of view. In testament to its visual accessibility and heuristic appeal, the SAS model has been translated into four languages (Chinese, German, Hebrew, and Portuguese) as well as having been taught to trainers on four continents. The model is meant to raise questions about what each of us does as a supervisor rather than to tell a supervisor what to think and what to do.

The SAS framework provides four components of support for educators and practitioners to uncover their own thinking, attitudes, decision-making, and behaviors: (a) a descriptive base, (b) guidelines stating common goals and objectives, (c) a way to discover meaning as it relates to participants and the profession, and (d) a systematic mode of inquiry to determine objectives and strategies for interaction during supervision. The confines of this chapter prevent the detailed discussion of the SAS structure, but, nonetheless, the heuristics of the model will be presented. The reader is referred to Holloway (1995) for a complete presentation of the theoretical and empirical underpinnings of the components of SAS.

The SAS model was designed to provide a visual roadmap for supervisors to intentionally and strategically consider the numerous factors that could impinge on their teaching and learning. Figure 29.1 presents the full model and the properties that describe each of the seven dimensions encompassed by the model.

Although the supervisory relationship is the core factor in the SAS model, there are a total of seven dimensions in the SAS model, each gleaned from the empirical, conceptual, and practice bases of knowledge in the field. In Figure 29.1, Six factors are represented around the periphery of the circle; they point to the core dimension, the supervisory relationship. Supervisor and supervisee engage to create the inner circle of the relationship. At the bottom of the figure are the learning tasks of the supervisee and the supervisor's strategies for teaching. At the top of the figure are the two contextual factors—client and institution—that influence the relationship as well as the process that unfolds in implementing strategies and tasks for teaching and learning. The components of the model are part of a dynamic process in which they interrelate and mutually influence one another. Whether trainer, consultant, or supervisor, reflection on these categories can guide questions that will lead to an integrated understanding of the relationship's potential to promote individual relational learning and professional expertise. Although the SAS model is classified as a social role model, it is evident from the figure that the importance of understanding the role of supervision in the context of the system in which it takes shape is critical to the model. Thus,

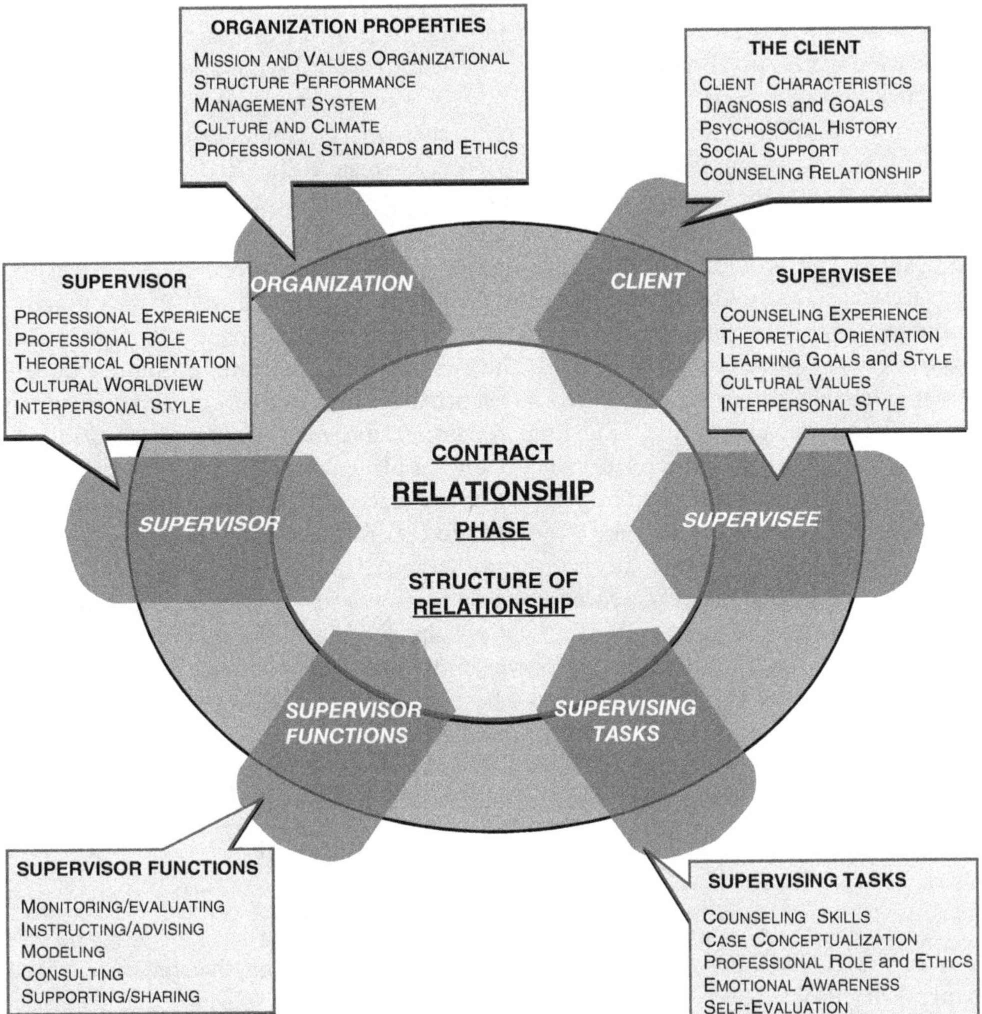

Figure 29.1 The systems approach to supervision (SAS) model includes the core factor of supervision – relationship; four contextual factors – supervisor, supervisee, client, and organization; and two process factors – task and function. (Graphic by T. Ullrich, 2009.)

the supervisor's decision-making and actions are always consciously or tacitly related to the system in which they are embedded. Systems models of supervision are most prominent in the supervision of family therapists (e.g., Burck, 2010; Burnham, 2010) and in European models, such as Schilling (2005). In the remainder of this chapter, I will describe the seven dimensions of SAS and make reference to the research that substantiates their inclusion in the model.

The relationship

The relationship of supervision is central to the learning alliance of supervision and creates the holding environment for the supervisee's reflection on and growth as a developing professional. The process of interaction between supervisor and trainee ideally creates a growth enhancing relationship as discussed earlier in the work of positive psychology and RCT. Learning to be a therapist requires self- and other awareness as well as responsibility for one's interpersonal behaviors and actions. Forrest has written extensively on interpersonal competence in the profession (Elman, Forrest, Vacha-Haase, & Gizara, 1999; Forrest, 2008, 2010; Forrest, Miller, & Elman, 2008; Johnson, Barnett, Elman, Forrest, & Kaslow, 2012) and supports the significance of emotional reflection within the context of relationship. Interpersonal awareness and skill are now included in the new competency benchmarks for psychologists (Kaslow et al., 2009). Supervision plays a critical role in recognizing and developing this competency area that has the potential to expand a person's *whole understanding* of self as engaged with the various social contexts presented by the client. This self-learning is embedded in relational structures that demand a knowing awareness of the processing, adjusting, repairing, and maintaining of relationship. The interstitial space of the relationship itself is a place where self- and other knowledge is mutually imparted and negotiated; it is a place of risk and opportunity. Relationships with these characteristics can greatly contribute to a student's embracing the role complexity and skills of the psychotherapist.

In the SAS model, there are three essential elements that guide the understanding of the formation and quality of the relationship: (a) the interpersonal structure of the relationship as described by the power and engagement across the five subroles of supervision, (b) the developmental phase of relationship, and (c) the learning contract of supervision. These are conceptual constructs that have been defined from empirical findings in supervision (Inman & Ladany, 2008). The use of these larger organizing constructs in the SAS model makes them more accessible to the practitioner.

Interpersonal structure of relationship

Power and involvement are helpful constructs in understanding the structure of the supervisory relationship. These two constructs have been used in social and personality psychology to understand the transactions and implicit rules that govern formal and informal relationships. Follett (1941) introduced *power with*, a concept that was pluralistic and dynamic, representing an ever-evolving process of human interaction. Follett's alternative conception of power is based on the relationship of involvement and mutual influence similar to the more current constructs of mutuality found in RCT research. Involvement might also be referred to as intimacy that includes *attachments*, the degree to which each person uses the other as a source of self-confirmation (Miller, 1976). This basis of power is consistent with the ideals of psychotherapy and supervision where the intent is not to control, but rather to empower individuals to exercise choice and self-determination.

Clinical supervision of therapists in training requires a formal relationship in which the supervisor has responsibility for imparting expert knowledge, making judgments of trainees' performance, and acting as a gatekeeper to the profession. These aspects of the role create a hierarchical relational structure that depends on *power over*. Yet the creation of a learning alliance that encourages transparency, vulnerability, and trust requires a *power with* orientation in the relationship. The existence of both power over and power with has caused considerable consternation for clinical supervisors because of the tension created by having to monitor the trainee's competency to ensure client safety and, at the same time, support the trainee's growing autonomy. The shifts of power and engagement in the relationship are described in the social role models through a number of supervisor *subroles* that are activated dependent on the immediate supervisory process, the trainee's learning needs, and the client's welfare. As supervisors, we hold the relational tension among the often conflicting roles of monitor, advisor, role model, consultant, and mentor, requiring us to use a delicate and firm hand in guiding the supervisee through the intellectual and emotional demands of therapeutic work. The seemingly conflicting responsibility for evaluation and a development focus has been discussed in the literature (Benson & Holloway, 2005).

The impact of power and involvement on the process of supervision has been studied by researchers using different models of power. Three preferred methods have been used in supervision research to describe the power of the supervisor: sociological typology of French and Raven (1960) (see also Raven and French, 1958; Robyak, Goodyear, & Prange, 1987), circumplex model of Strong, Hills, and Nelson (1988), and Penman's communication matrix (1980) (see also Holloway et al., 1989). Studies, in general, have confirmed the shifting use of power dependent on the supervisor's exercise of different functional roles in the relationship. For example, the supervisor is responsible for evaluation of the trainee and gatekeeping to the profession. In this role, the supervisor's power over is perceived by the trainee, whereas, when collaborating and consulting with the trainee, power with is more influential in the engagement. The shifts of power across roles are further discussed by considering supervisor functions.

Phase of relationship

The conceptualization of the developing, maturing, and terminating phases of the supervisory relationship (see Table 29.1) by Mueller and Kell (1972) is a useful,

Table 29.1 Phases of the supervisory relationship.

Developing phase	*Mature phase*	*Terminating phase*
• Clarifying relationship with supervisor • Establishment of supervision contract • Supporting teaching interventions • Developing competencies • Developing treatment plans	• Increasing individual nature of relationship, becoming less role bound • Increasing social bonding and influence potential • Developing skills of case conceptualization • Increasing self-confidence and self-efficacy in counseling • Confronting personal issues as they relate to professional performance	• Understanding connections between theory and practice in relation to particular clients • Decreasing need for direction from supervisor

heuristic to the evolving phases. As the supervisory relationship develops, the participants, using more personally relevant, interpersonal, psychological, and differentiated information in an effort to reduce interpersonal uncertainty, will attempt to predict each other's behavior. Relationship crises might entail periods of a lack of mutuality as new information is incorporated and the relationship is redefined. If mutuality, or a shared definition of the relationship, cannot be attained, then the relationship is usually terminated (Morton, Alexander, & Altman, 1976, p. 105). In one grounded dimensional analysis study, professional counselors with 5–20 years of experience identified mutuality as a core dimension when asked what made for good supervision (Holloway, 1998). Other studies have examined the changing patterns of communication across time in the supervision relationship (Holloway & Poulin, 1995). Wedeking and Scott (1976) found that supervisor messages changed from the beginning to the final stages of the relationship. Additionally, the association of relationship phase with supervisory behaviors has been investigated in case study designs that used microanalytic techniques (Garb, 1989; Martin, Goodyear, & Newton, 1987; Strozier, Kivlighan, & Thoreson, 1993) to point out that supervisees decreased the proportional use of deferential messages across the span of the supervisory relationship.

The facilitative conditions of genuineness, empathy, and unconditional positive regard, so important in building the therapeutic relationship, are equally important in building the supervisory relationship, particularly at the beginning. Therapists in training, like clients, need to feel safe, supported, and trusting of their environment before they can feel comfortable enough to take risks and engage in self-reflexivity, practice new behaviors, and actively seek feedback. Advanced supervisees, having a blueprint for the relationship of supervision from previous experiences, are able to truncate the discomfort of uncertainty and the need for reassurance by relying on known general expectancies for supervisory roles. Thus, they can move more quickly to establish specific expectancies for an interpersonal relationship. In contrast, beginning-level trainees are, perhaps, still learning their own role expectations and those of their supervisor, and, thus, are not as quick to enter into the interpersonal supervisory relationship. It is important to note that no matter what level of experience a trainee might have, it seems that there is a natural relationship stage in which participants need to become familiar with the role expectations set up by the supervisor and the supervisory context (Rabinowitz, Heppner, & Roehlke, 1986). This initial stage of building familiarity serves to reduce ambiguity and uncertainty in the relationship overall.

The contract of supervision

Each supervisor and supervisee will have idiosyncratic expectations of roles and function in supervision. As in any working relationship, the clarity of these expectations directly affects the relationship and the establishment of specific learning goals. The supervisor has a responsibility to ensure that the supervisee is clearly informed of the evaluative structure of the relationship, the expectancies and goals for supervision, the criteria for evaluation, and the limits of confidentiality in supervision.

Inskipp and Proctor (1989), among others (Hewson, 1999; Schilling, Haargaad Jacobsen, & Nielsen, 2010), have identified the supervisory contract as critical to establishing a way of being together in the supervisory relationship. Not only do the supervisor and supervisee need to negotiate specific tasks but they also need to define the process parameters of the relationship. By acting openly and purposefully, the supervisor increases the probability that both participants will behave congruently with established expectations. The negotiation of norms, rules, and commitments at the beginning of any relationship can reduce anxiety and move the involvement to a level of trust that will promote the degree of vulnerability needed for the task to be accomplished.

Additionally, the supervisor must be alerted to the changing character of the relationship and thereafter initiate discussion on renewed goals and relational expectations. Not only will the trainee's learning needs change as experience increases or clients develop but also his or her increasing skill and interpersonal confidence will influence issues of relational control. Research studies have corroborated that trainees, particularly beginning trainees, can greatly benefit from making role expectations clear and detailing competency-based expectations at various intermediary stages of evaluation (Friedlander, Keller, Peca-Baker, & Olk, 1986; Holloway, 1998; Ladany & Friedlander, 1995; Ladany, Brittan-Powell, & Pannu, 1997; Muse-Burke, Ladany, & Deck, 2001; Olk & Friedlander, 1992).

The process of supervision

The teaching tasks of supervision are comprised of those competencies defined in the benchmarks and toolkits of competency-based learning: expectations and roles, processes and procedures, skills development, awareness of the factors affecting quality, participation process, and ethical and legal issues (Falender et al., 2004). For the SAS model, these competencies have been grouped into five broad learning objectives based on the empirical literature: counseling skills, case conceptualization, professional role, including ethical practice, intra- and interpersonal awarenesses, and self-evaluation (Carroll, 1996; Holloway, 1992; Inman & Ladany, 2008). It is from this larger pool of knowledge that the supervisor and student will choose those specific learning goals that match the individual needs of the supervisee.

Supervisor functions are "the kind of action or activity proper to a person, thing or institution" (Webster's Encyclopedic Unabridged Dictionary, 1989, p. 574). Role labels have been useful in providing a common language for describing the specialized actions of the supervisor (Bernard & Goodyear, 2009; Carroll, 1996; Ellis & Dell, 1986; Ellis et al., 1988; Hess, 1980). In the SAS model, there are five subroles of supervision that have been named with active verbs to emphasize the dynamic, interweaving shifts inherent in these activities. Thus, the supervisor might use the functions of monitoring/evaluating, instructing/advising, modeling, consulting, and supporting/sharing. Each of these functions can be characterized by behaviors typical of its respective social role and by the form of relational power governing the role as discussed earlier in the interpersonal structure of the relationship. In Figure 29.1, the functions are listed from top to bottom: "power over" being dominant to "power with" being more dominant. The strategies aligned with these roles have been studied by researchers using discourse analysis and classification of supervisor verbal behaviors. A summary of these findings can be found in Holloway and Poulin (1995).

Supervisor tasks and functions are the combination of the supervisor and supervisee working together on a particular learning task which, in turn, creates a process

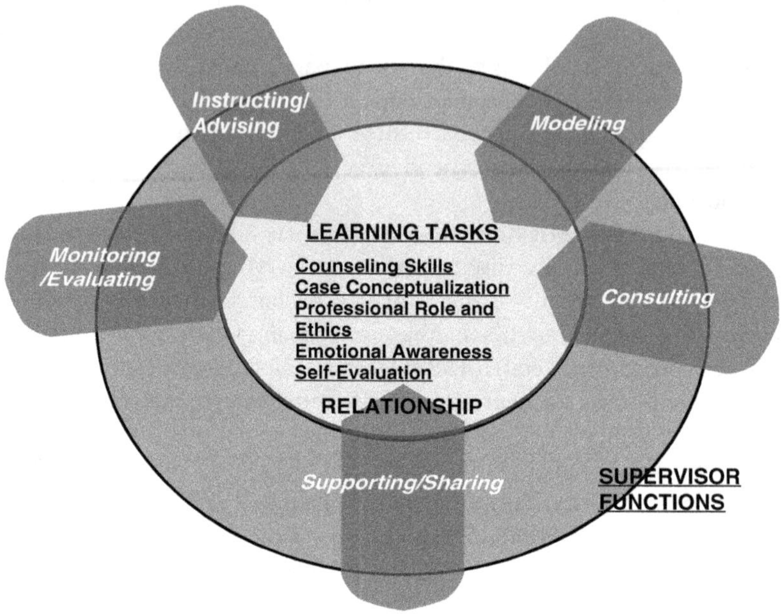

Figure 29.2 The SAS wheel of supervisory process–learning tasks and supervisory subroles. Graphic by T. Ullrich (2009).

of interaction. In SAS, the process can be illustrated by imaging the wheel of supervisory functions on the outside circle turning to choose a specific teaching task at a particular point in time (see Figure 29.2). The supervisor's use of different subroles may be influenced not only by the trainee's learning needs at the moment, but also by the other contextual factors described in the model. For example, if a neophyte trainee is just beginning with a new client, the supervisor may choose to use an advising function around case conceptualization. On the other hand, an experienced counselor experiencing resistance from a client may warrant a consulting approach by the supervisor. The use of the task-function matching to describe supervisory process has been explored by DeCato (2002) in the supervision of psychological testing, by Arnon and Hellman (2004) with school counseling supervisors, and by Xi-Qing (2004) in the observation of clinical supervision in China.

Contextual Factors of Supervision

The contextual factors in the SAS model are the supervisor, the trainee, the client, and the institution or organization in which the trainee is delivering service (see Figure 29.1). Contextual factors of supervision are conditions that are related empirically and practically to the supervisor and supervisee's choice of task and function and the formation of the relationship. Whereas task and function can be inferred from the process of communication, contextual factors are sometimes not obvious to the observer and sometimes not apparent to the participants. Based on their tacit knowledge and experience, supervisor and trainee make decisions about their engagement and topic of conversation. In teaching supervision, the properties of the contextual factors are guideposts for supervisors to consider in a reflective process that uncovers the motivations and intent of their actions in supervision. Factors that might influence information processing and decision-making have been studied by asking supervisors or trainees to reflect on their own or the other's actions (Holloway, 2000; Neufeldt, Karno, & Nelson, 1996; Skovholt & Ronnestad, 1992).

Supervisor factors The supervisor brings to the supervisory relationship an independent way of viewing human behavior, interpersonal relations, and social institutions, all of which are largely influenced by cultural socialization. Supervisors' views and experiences are described by five factors – professional experience, professional role, theoretical orientation to therapy, cultural worldview, interpersonal style – have been included, based on the empirical literature. Because cultural perspectives are relevant to the conceptualization of professionalism and mental health, the SAS model considers cultural values to be embedded in the supervisor's attitudes and actions. Cultural characteristics, which include gender, ethnicity, race, sexual orientation, religious beliefs, and personal values, strongly influence an individual's social and moral judgments. Such nuances of the supervisory relationship are sometimes subtle, but they are always critical aspects of the supervisory work. The potential for mutuality and emotional awareness in the supervisory relationship provides a unique opportunity to teach and learn the salience of culturally congruent treatment (Bernard & Goodyear, 2009; Burkard, Knox, Hess, & Schultz, 2009; Constantine, Warren, & Miville, 2005; Ladany, Friedlander, & Nelson, 2005). The SAS model is meant to encourage supervisors to recognize the importance of cultural factors in supervision and to pay attention to how these issues interact with each of the other contextual factors; for example, are cultural differences acknowledged as salient in client treatment? Does the organization includes cultural sensitivity as a part of professional development?

Other supervisor factors in the model – experience level, theoretical orientation, and interpersonal style – have been related to trainee satisfaction with supervision (Bernard & Goodyear, 2009; Holloway, 1992; Inman & Ladany, 2008). Empirically, it has been shown that the amount of experience a supervisor has in counseling and supervision seems related to the judgments the supervisor will make regarding self-disclosure, trainee performance, and choice of instructional approach to supervision (Stoltenberg et al., 1994). Additionally, supervisor experience has been examined in relation to supervisor use of facilitative behaviors, preplanning of supervisory sessions, and judgments of trainee performance (Marikis, Russell, & Dell, 1985; Stone, 1980; Sundland & Feinberg, 1972; Worthington, 1984a, 1984b). These studies suggest that experience in supervision frees supervisors from making global personality judgments of the trainee, allowing them to focus on the situational characteristics that might be influencing the trainee's performance.

The influence of the supervisor's theoretical orientation on supervisory behavior has been the subject of several studies (Beutler & McNabb, 1981; Goodyear & Robyak, 1982; Goodyear, Abadie, & Efros, 1984; Guest & Beutler, 1988; Sundland, 1977). Holloway et al. (1989) studied the Goodyear (1982) videotape series and concluded that theoretical orientation of the supervisor was related to perceived differences in supervisory behavior and actual differences in supervisory discourse.

Goldberg (1985) maintained the supervisor's personality or character style and theoretical orientation is the single most influential factor in the supervisor's behavior. Studies relating supervisor theoretical orientation and supervisor methods strongly support Goldberg's claim (Putney, Worthington, & McCullough, 1992).

Interpersonal style as perceived by the trainee has been operationalized in the research literature by several instruments, such as the supervisory working alliance (SWAI) (Patton & Kivlighan, 1997), the supervisory relationship questionnaire (SRQ) (Palomo, Beinart, & Cooper, 2010), the supervision questionnaire (SQ-R) (Worthington & Roehlke, 1979), and the supervisory styles inventory (SSI) (Friedlander & Ward, 1984). These instruments have been used extensively to understand the connection in quality of relationship, such as supervisor communication, task orientation, trust, interpersonal sensitivity, facilitative conditions, evaluative process, perceptions of conflict resolution, self-reflection, skills attainment, and personal growth (see reviews) (Ellis, Ladany, Krengel, & Schult, 1996; Ladany, Ellis, & Friedlander, 1999; Muse-Burke et al., 2001).

Trainee factors In SAS, characteristics of the supervisee, identified in the empirical literature, have been grouped into five supervisee factors: experience in counseling, theoretical orientation in counseling, learning goals and style, cultural worldview, and interpersonal style.

Trainee experience level has been a frequently studied factor in supervision research. Experience level of the trainee has been related to perceived supervisory needs and satisfaction with supervision (Stoltenberg et al., 1994). The predominant finding that distinguishes the expressed needs of very beginning-level trainees from those of intern-level trainees centers on different relationship characteristics (Heppner & Roehlke, 1984; Miars et al., 1983; Wiley & Ray, 1986; Worthington, 1984a, 1984b). For example, initial-level trainees appear to require more support, encouragement, and structure in supervision, whereas interns demonstrate increasing independence from the supervisor (Hill, Charles, & Reed, 1981; McNeil, Stoltenberg, & Pierce, 1985; Reising & Daniels, 1983; Wiley & Ray, 1986; Worthington, 1984a; Worthington & Stern, 1985) and more interest in exploring higher-level skills and personal issues affecting counseling (Heppner & Roehlke, 1984; Hill et al., 1981; McNeil et al., 1985; Stoltenberg et al., 1994; Worthington & Stern, 1985). Tracey, Ellickson, and Sherry (1989) designed an analog study to examine the relationship between supervisory structure and trainee learning. Their findings partially support some of the previous work that has indicated that, as they progress through levels of experience, trainees' need for supervisory structure diminishes (McNeil et al., 1985; Reising & Daniels, 1983; Stoltenberg et al., 1994; Wiley & Ray, 1986). However, the structure–experience relation is moderated by personality variables of the trainees (such as reactance potential) and the situational determinants of the supervisory focus (crisis versus noncrisis client).

Ward, Friedlander, Schoen, and Klein (1985) examined the influence of different self-presentational styles (in the SAS model referred to as interpersonal style) on supervisors' judgments of counselor competence. This was an analog study in which the investigators created stimulus conditions where trainees took a defensive or counterdefensive interpersonal style. Supervisors evaluated the defensive trainee as more self-confident, whereas the counterdefensive trainee was evaluated as more socially skilled. Interestingly, when the client was reported to have improved, trainees were judged to be altogether more competent, self-confident, expert, and attractive than when the client worsened, regardless of trainee style. Importantly, it appeared from this study that supervisors were influenced more by client progress in judging trainee professional skills than trainees' presentation style.

Competency models in counseling psychology, including supervision, have delineated the importance of multicultural sensitivity and skill in therapeutic contexts. In the SAS model, cultural values, such as ethnicity, race, sexual orientation, and religious beliefs, are seen as salient to trainees' attitudes and actions toward their clients and supervisors. Research in this supervision area is relatively limited (Constantine, Fuertes, Roysircar, & Kindaichi, 2008) although there has been significantly more research on the relation of cultural variables to counseling relationship and counselor effectiveness (Fuertes, Spokane, & Holloway, 2012).

Client factors

The characteristics of clients and the issues that they bring to the therapeutic context are central to the teaching and learning of supervision. The dynamics that unfold in the therapeutic relationship often are reenacted in the supervisory relationship. Thus, the importance of employing the client material as a springboard to designing appropriate teaching objectives and strategies cannot be underestimated. In SAS, there are five client factors: client characteristics (social, psychological, and biological), client identified problem and diagnosis, client history, client social and familial context, and counseling relationship.

Supervisors routinely screen clients for beginning-level trainees to ensure that they are only assigned cases that are appropriate to their level of competence and supervisors' areas of expertise. Competency guidelines created in the last decade delineate the progression of skills acquisition for psychologists from practicum to internship. Thus, supervisors need to align the matching of client needs to the training level of the trainee. Research on client attributes, as related to the process and outcome of psychotherapy, are relevant to supervisor decision-making. For example, the literature on matching client gender or ethnic identity with that of therapists suggests that, although there appears to be a preference for ethnically similar counselors, this is not consistently evident in the empirical literature (Coleman, Wampold, & Casali, 1994; Miville et al., 2009; Ober, Granello, & Henfield, 2009). It behooves the supervisor to recognize that variables, such as social desirability, socioeconomic status, attitudes, or values, may play an important role in the counselor's potential effectiveness. Therapeutic ineffectiveness may be falsely attributed to the lack of similarity between client and therapist on general qualities when a more in-depth analysis might reveal more implicit characteristics of the client or counselor to be inhibiting progress.

The evaluation of therapist effectiveness ultimately rests with the client's progress, symptom reduction, and relational bonding. Supervisors have frequently relied on trainees' reports of client change and audio- or videotaped recordings of trainees' counseling sessions. The advent of evidence-based therapy (EBT) has raised once again the question – What supervisory strategies and process impact therapist effectiveness and client change?

There has been considerable debate over the years on the efficacy of supervision on client outcomes (Bambling & King, 2000; Ellis & Ladany, 1997; Holloway &

Neufeldt, 1995; Stein & Lambert, 1995; Wampold & Holloway, 1997; Watkins, 2011). Research on the efficacy of supervision in relation to client change has begun in earnest in the last decade with the rise of EBT in psychotherapy. However, linking the impact of supervision to client outcomes has been challenging, given the considerable volume of findings that have revealed that therapists and supervisors are more generous in their assessment of client improvement and underestimate clients' deterioration when compared to client reports (Worthen & Lambert, 2007). In an effort to provide clients' perception of improvement, Lambert and associates have developed a client feedback approach that systematically sends client feedback to the therapist after each therapeutic session (Hawkins, Lambert, Vemeersch, Slade, & Tuttle, 2004; Lambert, Harmon, Slade, Whipple, & Hawkins, 2005; Lambert & Hawkins, 2001; Lambert et al., 2002; Whipple et al., 2003). When a client was not making progress, training therapists were at a loss as to how to rectify the course of therapy; this led to the investigation of supervisors' receptivity to using client data in supervision. Supervisors were not overly positive about the use of client outcome data in the early stages of this program of research (not surprising, given the history and studies that demonstrate clinicians prefer to rely on their intuitive clinical knowledge). However, as the utility of the client progress data became more persuasive, clinicians used this information to focus supervisory discussions. The evidence that client progress and outcome trajectory data can significantly affect client improvement by influencing the therapist's intervention strategies is a strong argument in favor of supervisors utilizing such client outcome information to guide their supervisory strategies. As Worthen and Lambert concluded, "We believe the use of (client-monitoring) feedback (system) will significantly assist our mandate as supervisors to monitor client welfare and through supervision, enhance client outcomes. Thus, outcome-oriented supervision can help facilitate the two primary aims of supervision, enhanced practice and improved client outcomes" (2007, p. 53).

Organizational factors

Supervision, whether a part of a training program or continuing professional development, takes place in the context of institutional organizations, such as in-house departmental clinics, university counseling centers, hospitals, or community mental health or other service settings. The role of supervision with respect to the service demands of the organization is an important consideration in establishing goals and functions of supervision (Carroll & Holloway, 1999; Proctor, 1997). Yet the influence of organizational variables on supervision has rarely been investigated or discussed in the professional literature (Holloway & Roehlke, 1987).

Institutional characteristics were first defined in SAS as organizational clientele, organizational structure and climate, and professional ethics and standards. However, the SAS model has been adapted to multidisciplinary, organizational systems. In these environments, the supervisor needs to attend to a more detailed knowledge of the organization's characteristics, such as mission, staffing practices, decision-making (formal and informal), and the history of the organization, among others unique to the supervisor's contract with the organization.

All of these factors might potentially have influence on the supervisory contract with the trainee. In the past 10 years, training programs in psychology have become more focused on competency-based criteria in evaluating trainees' preparation for the counselor role. For their part, researchers have been studying the conditions that are thought to influence the acquisition of counselor behaviors deemed necessary for effective counseling. In particular, the uses of empirically supported intervention programs are having a considerable influence on the training of therapists (Holloway & Gonzalez-Doupe, 1999), and standards of competence are being linked to manual adherence. If this training trend continues, supervisors will need to include such criteria in training contracts with their supervisees (Calhoun, Moras, Pilkonis, & Rehm, 1998).

Implications for Practice

It has been my intention in this chapter to describe the SAS model as a comprehensive model of supervision that emphasizes the importance of social roles, relational practice, and contextual factors that influence the supervisory process. In this description, I have emphasized the empirical literature that substantiates the significance of the seven factors of the SAS model and their respective properties. The model's value must be determined by the utility of its application to real-world supervisory practice and the challenges that emerge therein.

Supervisors carry an important responsibility of providing the appropriate degree of support, structure, and technical guidance most suitable to their supervisees' learning. Beginning supervisees with little to no previous supervisory training are not only being taught what supervision expects of them but also what to expect from a supervisor. The importance of a clear contract which is both procedural and psychological is central to the establishment of boundaries and expectations in the SAS model. Both supervisor and supervisee bring to the relationship expectations of how the learning process will unfold based on past experiences of supervision, formal and informal relational experiences; still others will develop from knowledge of supervision gained through anecdotal materials and empirical literature. These past experiences will shape the process or the relationship structure that will, in turn, influence the participants' engagement in the process (Holloway & Gonzalez-Doupe, 2002).

Once the initial contract is forged, the development of the relationship will result through the tacit creation of shared idiosyncratic rules governing the exercise of power and involvement between supervisor and supervisee. Supervision initially provides a general expectancy base for certain interactive behaviors; however, as the working relationship develops, it is individualized around the learning needs of the trainee and the teaching approaches of the supervisor. From the very first meeting, it is important for the supervisor to provide the supervisee with a road map of what to expect from supervision as well as the necessary information or tools to be an informed consumer of supervision. Thus, the supervisor can make explicit (a) the philosophical and theoretical orientation to supervision and psychotherapy, (b) work expectations, and (c) the conditions and timing of evaluation. Research indicates that supervisees benefit from being educated in how to *be* a supervisee because it is a distinct role from that of counselor, client, or student; and each supervisory encounter is unique (Ladany & Friedlander, 1995). If the role and work expectations are not made clear, trainees can begin to feel role ambiguity or role conflict (Friedlander et al., 1986; Ladany & Friedlander, 1995; Ladany et al., 1999; Nelson & Friedlander, 2001).

Counselors are in a vulnerable position for role conflict because they are the linchpin, or the common factor, in the therapeutic and the supervisory relationships. The trainee has to become versatile at alternating power roles between a superordinate power position (counselor) and the subordinate power position (student/trainee). Supervisors can encourage supervisees to discuss their experiences of power and influence in their roles as trainee, student, counselor, and supervisee. Using the SAS model as a starting point for explanation of relational power and moving the trainee to reflect on both the therapy and supervision relationship can serve as a model for importance of emotional awareness and self-evaluation.

Regardless of the trainees' level of experience, they will feel initial uncertainty about the role expectations and the conditions for evaluation; therefore, trainees require specific information, particularly at the beginning of the supervision relationship, about the criteria on which they will be evaluated, when they will be evaluated, and what options will be available to them when their clinical work does not meet expectations (Benson & Holloway, 2005). Formative evaluation, or evaluation conducted at critical points during the course of supervision, has several objectives: (1) it reassures trainees that they are developing clinical skills as expected; (2) it refocuses trainees on necessary skills that are underdeveloped; and (3) it points out progress and indicates new directions for skill development. Summative evaluation occurs at the termination of the training relationship, and it usually carries the gatekeeping responsibility of asserting who passes and who does not. This final evaluation, however, should include comments that the trainee has already heard throughout supervision because the trainee should have been given ample opportunity to address and correct any pertinent clinical skill. Trainees will have different comfort levels with supervisory feedback; however, research seems to indicate that as trainees gain confidence in their clinical skill and trust the supervisory relationship, they tend to actively seek out feedback on their clinical work and on personal issues that might be impacting their clinical work.

The advent of competency guidelines for supervisors and EBT mandates have added significant guidance and responsibility to the supervision training and implementation. To guide the assignment of clients to their trainees as well as teach the most efficacious therapeutic strategies for that client, supervisors need to recognize the limits of their own therapeutic competencies in evidence-based practice. Further, the importance of educating supervisors in the ethics, process, and multiple roles and responsibilities of supervision as outlined in the competency guidelines for supervisors has become even more critical. It is intended that the SAS model plays a role in guiding the supervisor and supervisor educator to ask critical questions of self, trainee, relationship, and context and in the interweaving of these in the dynamic, relational process of supervision.

Author Notes

Portions of this chapter have appeared in Holloway, E. L. & Gonzalez-Doupe, P. (2001). The Learning Alliance of Supervision: Research to Practice. In *Counseling Based on Process Research* by G. S. Tyron (Ed.), Allyn & Bacon: Needham Heights, MA.

References

Arnon, C., & Hellman, S. (2004). On supervision and professional development of school counselors. In R. Erhardt & A. Klingman (Eds.), *School counseling in a changing world* (pp. 443–464). Tel Aviv: Ramot.

Bambling, M., & King, R. (2000). Supervision and the development of counselor competency. *Psychotherapy in Australia*, *6*, 4.

Belenky, M. F. (1997). *Women's ways of knowing: The development of self, voice, and mind* (10th anniversary). New York: BasicBooks.

Benson, K., & Holloway, E. L. (2005). Achieving influence: A grounded theory of how clinical supervisors evaluate trainees. *Qualitative Research in Psychology*, *2*, 117–140.

Bernard, J. M. (1979). Supervisor training: A discrimination model. *Counselor Education and Supervision*, *19*, 60–68.

Bernard, J. M., & Goodyear, R. K. (2009). *Fundamentals of critical supervision*. Boston: Allyn & Bacon.

Beutler, L. E., & McNabb, C. E. (1981). Self-evaluation for the psychotherapist. In C. E. Walker (Ed.), *Clinical practice of psychology* (pp. 397–439). New York: Pergamon Press.

Blumer, H. (1969). *Symbolic interactionism: Perspective and method*. Englewood Cliffs, NJ: Prentice-Hall.

Blumer, H., & Morrione, T. J. (Eds.). (2004). *George Herbert Mead and human conduct*. Lanham, MD: Rowman & Littlefield.

Bowers, B. (1988). Grounded theory. In B. J. Sarter (Ed.), *Paths to knowledge: Innovative research methods for nursing* (pp. 33–59). New York: National League for Nursing.

Burck, C. (2010). From hazardous to collaborative learning: Thinking systemically about live supervision group processes. In C. Burck & G. Daniel (Eds.), *Mirrors and reflections: Processes of systemic supervision*. London: Karnac Books.

Burkard, A. W., Knox, S., Hess, S. A., & Schultz, J. (2009). Lesbian, gay, and bisexual supervisees' experiences of LGB-affirmative and nonaffirmative supervision. *Journal of Counseling Psychology*, *56*, 176–188.

Burnham, J. (2010). Creating reflexive relationships between practices of systemic supervision and theories of learning and education. In C. Burck & G. Daniel (Eds.), *Mirrors and reflections: Processes of systemic supervision* (pp. 49–77). London: Karnac Books.

Byrne, A. M., & Sias, S. M. (2010). Conceptual application of the discrimination model of clinical supervision for direct care workers in adolescent residential treatment settings. *Child & Youth Care Forum*, *39*(3), 201–209. doi: 10.1007/s10566-010-9100-z

Calhoun, K. S., Moras, K., Pilkonis, P. A., & Rehm, L. P. (1998). Empirically supported treatments: Implications for training. *Journal of Consulting and Clinical Psychology*, *66*, 151–162.

Carroll, M. (1996a). *Counselling in supervision: Theory, skills and practice*. London: Cassell.

Carroll, M. (1996b). *Workplace counseling*. London: Sage.

Carroll, M., & Holloway, E. L. (Eds.). (1999). *Counseling supervision in context*. London: Sage.

Coleman, H. L. K., Wampold, B. E., & Casali, S. L. (1994). Ethnic minorities' ratings of ethnically similar and European American counselors: A meta-analysis. *Journal of Counseling Psychology*, *42*, 247–294.

Constantine, M. G., Warren, A. K., & Miville, M. L. (2005). White racial identity dyadic interactions in supervision: Implications for supervisees' multicultural counseling competence. *Journal of Counseling Psychology*, *52*(4), 490–496.

Constantine, M. G., Fuertes, J. N., Roysircar, G., & Kindaichi, M. M. (2008). Multicultural competence: Clinical practice, training and supervision, and research. In W. B. Walsh

(Ed.), *Biennial review of counseling psychology* (pp. 97–127). New York: Routledge/Taylor & Francis.

DeCato, C. (2002). A quantitative method for studying the testing supervision process. *Psychological Reports, 90*(1), 137–138. doi: 10.2466/PR0.90.1.137-138

Ekstein, R. (1964). Supervision of psychotherapy: Is it teaching? Is it administration? Or is it therapy?. *Psychotherapy: Theory, Research, and Practice, 1*, 137–138.

Ekstein, R., & Wallerstein, R. S. (1958). *The teaching and learning of psychotherapy*. New York: Basic Books.

Ellis, M. V., & Dell, D. M. (1986). Dimensionality of supervisor roles: Supervisors' perceptions of supervision. *Journal of Counseling Psychology, 3*, 282–291.

Ellis, M. V., & Ladany, N. (1997). Inferences concerning supervisees and clients in clinical supervision: An integrative review. In C. E. Watkins Jr. (Ed.), *Handbook of psychotherapy supervision* (pp. 447–507). New York: John Wiley & Sons.

Ellis, M. V., Dell, D. M., & Good, G. E. (1988). Counselor trainees' perceptions of supervisor roles: Two studies testing the dimensionality of supervision. *Journal of Counseling Psychology, 35*, 315–324.

Ellis, M. V., Ladany, N., Krengel, M., & Schult, D. (1996). Clinical supervision research from 1981 to 1993: A methodological critique. *Journal of Counseling Psychology, 43*(1), 35–50.

Elman, N., Forrest, L., Vacha-Haase, T., & Gizara, S. (1999). A systems perspective on trainee impairment: Continuing the dialogue. *The Counseling Psychologist, 27*(5), 712–721. doi: 10.1177/0011000099275005

Falender, C., Cornish, J., Goodyear, R., Hatcher, R., Kaslow, N., Leventhal, G., & Grus, C. (2004). Defining competencies in psychology supervision: A consensus statement. *Journal of Clinical Psychology, 60*(7), 771–785. doi: 10.1002/jclp.20013

Falender, C. A., & Shrafranske, E. P. (2004). *Clinical supervision: A competency-based approach*. Washington, DC: American Psychological Association.

Falender, C. A., & Shrafranske, E. P. (2008). *A casebook for clinical supervision: A competency-based approach*. Washington, DC: American Psychological Association.

Follett, M. P. (1941). The meaning of responsibility in business management. In H. C. Metcalf & L. Urwick (Eds.), *Dynamic administration: The collected papers of Mary Parker Follett* (pp. 141–166). London: Sir Issac Pitman and Sons.

Forrest, L. M. (2008). The ever evolving identity of counseling psychologists: Musings of the society of counseling psychology president. *The Counseling Psychologist, 36*(2), 281–289. doi: 10.1177/0011000007313552

Forrest, L. M. (2010). Linking international psychology, professional competence, and leadership: Counseling psychologists as learning partners. *The Counseling Psychologist, 38*(1), 96–120. doi: 10.1177/0011000009350585

Forrest, L. M., Miller, D. S., & Elman, L. S. (2008). Psychology trainees with competence problems: From individual to ecological conceptualizations. *Training and Education in Professional Psychology, 2*, 183–192. doi: 10,1037/1931-3918.2.4.183

Fredrickson, B. L., & Losada, M. F. (2005). Positive affect and the complex dynamics of human flourishing. *American Psychologist, 60*(7), 678–686.

French, J. R. P., Jr., & Raven, B. M. (1960). The bases of social power. In D. Cartwright & A. Zander (Eds.), *Group dynamics: Research and theory* (2nd ed., pp. 607–623). New York: Peterson.

Friedlander, M. L., & Ward, L. G. (1984). Development and validation of the Supervisory Styles Inventory. *Journal of Counseling Psychology, 4*, 541–557.

Friedlander, M. L., Keller, K. E., Peca-Baker, T. A., & Olk, M. E. (1986). Effects of role conflict on counselor trainees' self-statements, anxiety level, and performance. *Journal of Counseling Psychology, 33*, 1–5.

Fuertes, J. N., Spokane, A., & Holloway, E. L. (2012). *The professional competencies in counseling psychology.* London: Oxford University Press.

Garb, H. N. (1989). Clinical judgment, clinical training, and professional experience. *Psychological Bulletin, 105,* 387–396.

Gilligan, C. (1993). *In a different voice: Psychological theory and women's development.* Cambridge, MA: Harvard University Press.

Goldberg, D. A. (1985). Process, notes, audio and videotape: Modes of presentation in psychotherapy. *The Clinical Supervisor, 3*(3), 3–13.

Goodyear, R. K. (1982). *Psychotherapy supervision by major theorists.* Manhattan, KS: Instructional Media Center, Kansas State University.

Goodyear, R. K., & Robyak, J. E. (1982). Supervisors' theory and experience in supervisory focus. *Psychological Reports, 51,* 978.

Goodyear, R. K., Bradley, F. O., & Bartlett, W. E. (1983). An introduction to theories of counselor supervision. *The Counseling Psychologist, 11*(1), 19–20. doi: 10.1177/0011000083111004

Goodyear, R. K., Abadie, P. D., & Efros, F. (1984). Supervisory theory into practice: Differential perception of supervision by Ekstein, Ellis, Polster, and Rogers. *Journal of Counseling Psychology, 31,* 228–237.

Guest, P. D., & Beutler, L. E. (1988). Impact of psychotherapy supervision on therapist orientation and values. *Journal of Consulting and Clinical Psychology, 56,* 653–658.

Gysbers, N. C., & Johnston, J. A. (1965). Expectations of a practicum supervisor's role. *Counselor Education and Supervision, 2,* 68–75.

Hart, G. M., & Nance, D. (2003). Styles of counselor supervision as perceived by supervisors and supervisees. *Counselor Education and Supervision, 43,* 146–159.

Hawkins, E. J., Lambert, M. J., Vemeersch, D., Slade, K., & Tuttle, K. (2004). The effects of providing patient progress information to therapists and patients. *Psychotherapy Research, 31,* 308–327.

Hawkins, P., & Shohet, R. (1989). *Supervision in the helping professions.* Bristol, PA: Open University Press.

Hawkins, P., & Shohet, R. (1991). Approaches to the supervision of counselors. In W. Dryden & B. Thorne (Eds.), *Positive affect and the complex dynamics of human flourishing* (pp. 99–115). Thousand Oaks, CA: Sage.

Heppner, P. P., & Roehlke, H. J. (1984). Differences among supervisees at different levels of training: Implications for a developmental model of supervision. *Journal of Counseling Psychology, 31,* 76–90.

Hess, A. K. (Ed.). (1980). *Psychotherapy supervision: Theory, research and practice.* New York: Wiley.

Hewson, J. (1999). Training supervisors to contract in supervision. In E. Holloway & M. Carroll (Eds.), *Training counseling supervisors* (pp. 67–91). London: Sage.

Hill, C. E., Charles, D., & Reed, K. G. (1981). A longitudinal analysis of changes in counseling skills during doctoral training in counseling psychology. *Journal of Counseling Psychology, 28,* 428–436.

Holloway, E. L. (1984). Outcome evaluation in supervision research. *The Counseling Psychologist, 12*(4), 167–174.

Holloway, E. L. (1992). Supervision: A way of teaching and learning. In S. D. Brown & R. W. Lent (Eds.), *Handbook of counseling psychology* (pp. 177–214). New York: Wiley.

Holloway, E. L. (1995). *Clinical supervision: A systems approach.* Thousand Oaks, CA: Sage.

Holloway, E. L. (1998, October 29). *The supervisee's view: An international sample.* Paper presented at the meeting of the Department of Educational Counseling Psychology, University of Illinois, Urbana-Champaign.

Holloway, E. L. (2000, July 1). *Through the eyes of the supervisee.* Paper presented to the Queensland Guidance and Counseling Association, Brisbane, Queensland, Australia.

Holloway, E. L., & Gonzalez-Doupe, P. (1999, August). *Empirically supported intervention programs: implications for supervision as a training modality.* Paper presented at The American Psychology Convention, Boston, MA.

Holloway, E. L., & Gonzalez-Doupe, P. (2002). The learning alliance of supervision: Research to practice. In G. S. Tyron (Ed.), *Counseling based on process research.* Needham Heights, MA: Allyn & Bacon.

Holloway, E. L., & Neufeldt, S. N. (1995). Supervision: Contributions to treatment efficacy. *Journal of Consulting and Clinical Psychology, 63,* 207–213.

Holloway, E. L., & Poulin, K. (1995). Discourse in supervision. In J. Siegfried (Ed.), *Therapeutic and everyday discourse as behavior change: Towards a micro-analysis in psychotherapy process research* (pp. 245–276). New York: Ablex.

Holloway, E. L., & Roehlke, H. J. (1987). Internship: The applied training of a counseling psychologist. *The Counseling Psychologist, 2,* 205–260.

Holloway, E. L., & Wolleat, P. L. (1981). Style differences of beginning supervisors: An interactional analysis. *Journal of Counseling Psychology, 28,* 373–376.

Holloway, E. L., Freund, R. D., Gardner, S. L., Nelson, M. L., & Walker, B. E. (1989). The relation of power and involvement to theoretical orientation supervision: An analysis of discourse. *Journal of Counseling Psychology, 36,* 88–102.

Inman, A. G., & Ladany, N. (2008). Research: The state of the field. In T. H. Hess (Ed.), *Psychotherapy supervision: theory, research, and practice* (2nd ed., pp. 500–517). Hoboken, NJ: John Wiley & Sons.

Inskipp, F., & Proctor, B. (1989). *Skills for supervising and being supervised [Principle of counseling audiotape series].* East Sussex: Alexia.

Johnson, W. B., Barnett, J. E., Elman, N., Forrest, L., & Kaslow, N. J. (2012). The competent community. *American Psychologist, 67,* 557–569.

Jordan, J. V. (2004). Relational learning in psychotherapy consultation and supervision. In M. Walker & W. B. Rosen (Eds), *How connections heal: Stories from relational-cultural therapy* (pp. 22–30). New York: The Guilford Press.

Jordan, J. V., & Walker, M. (2004). Introduction. In J. V. Jordan, M. Walker, & M. Hartling (Eds.), *The complexity of connection: Writings from the Stone Center's Jean Baker Miller Training Institute* (pp. 1–8). New York: The Guilford Press.

Kagan, N. I., & Kagan, H. (1990). IPR: A validated model for the 1990s and beyond. *The Counseling Psychologist, 18*(3), 436–440.

Kaslow, M. J., Grus, C. L., Campbell, L. F., Fouad, N. A., Hatcher, R. L., & Rodolfa, E. R. (2009). Competency assessment toolkit for professional psychology. *Training and Education in Professional Psychology, 3,* S27–S45.

Ladany, N., & Friedlander, M. L. (1995). The relationship between the supervisory working alliance and trainees' experience of role conflict and role ambiguity. *Counselor Education and Supervision, 34,* 220–231.

Ladany, N., & Lehrman-Waterman, D. E. (1999). The content and frequency of supervisor self-disclosures and their relationship to supervisor style and the supervisory working alliance. *Counselor Education and Supervision, 38,* 143–160.

Ladany, N., Brittan-Powell, C. S., & Pannu, R. K. (1997). The influence of supervisory racial identity interaction and racial matching on the supervisory working alliance and supervisee multicultural competence. *Counselor Education and Supervision, 36,* 284–304.

Ladany, N., Inman, A. G., Constantine, M. G., & Hofheinz, E. W. (1997). Supervisee multicultural case conceptualization ability and self-reported multicultural competence as functions of supervisee racial identity and supervisor focus. *Journal of Counseling Psychology, 44,* 284–293.

Ladany, N., Ellis, M. V., & Friedlander, M. L. (1999). The supervisory working alliance, trainee self-efficacy, and satisfaction. *Journal of Counseling & Development, 77*(4), 447–455.

Ladany, N., Friedlander, M. L., & Nelson, M. L. (2005). Heightening multicultural awareness: It's never been about political correctness. In N. Ladany (Ed.), *Critical events in psychotherapy supervision: An interpersonal approach* (pp. 53–77). Washington, DC: American Psychological Association.

Lambert, M. J., & Hawkins, E. J. (2001). Using information about patient progress in supervision: Are outcomes enhanced? *Australian Psychologist, 36*, 131–138.

Lambert, M. J., Whipple, J. L., Vermeersch, D., Smart, D. W., Hawkins, E. J., & Nielsen, S. L. (2002). Enhancing psychotherapy outcomes via providing feedback on client progress: A replication. *Clinical Psychology and Psychotherapy, 9*, 91–103.

Lambert, M. J., Harmon, C., Slade, K., Whipple, J. L., & Hawkins, E. J. (2005). Providing feedback to psychotherapists on their patients' progress: Clinical results and practice suggestions. *Journal of Clinical Psychology, 61*(2), 165–174. doi: 10.1002/jclp.20113

Loganbill, C., Hardy, E., & Delworth, U. (1982). Supervision: A conceptual model. *The Counseling Psychologist, 10*(1), 3–42.

Luke, M., Ellis, M. V., & Bernard, J. M. (2011). School counselor supervisors' perceptions of the discrimination model of supervision. *Counselor Education and Supervision, 50*, 328–343.

Marikis, D. A., Russell, R. K., & Dell, D. M. (1985). Effects of supervisor experience level on planning and in-session supervisor verbal behavior. *Journal of Counseling Psychology, 32*, 410–416.

Martin, J. S., Goodyear, R. K., & Newton, F. B. (1987). Clinical supervision: An intensive case study. *Professional Psychology, Research and Practice, 18*, 225–235.

McNeil, B. W., Stoltenberg, C. D., & Pierce, R. A. (1985). Supervisees' perceptions of their development: A test of the counselor complexity model. *Journal of Counseling Psychology, 32*, 630–633.

Mead, G. H. (1934). *Mind, self, and society: From the standpoint of a social behaviorist.* Chicago, IL: University of Chicago Press.

Miars, R. D., Tracey, T. J., Ray, P. B., Cornfeld, J. L., Q'Farrel, M., & Gelson, C. J. (1983). Variation in supervision process across trainee experience levels. *Journal of Counseling Psychology, 30*, 403–412.

Miller, G. R. (1976). *Explorations in interpersonal communication.* Newbury Park, CA: Sage.

Miller, J. B., & Stiver, I. P. (1997). *The healing connection: How women form relationships in therapy and in life.* Boston: Beacon Press.

Miville, M. L., Duan, C., Nutt, R. L., Waehler, C. A., Suzuki, L., Pistole, M. C., & Corpus, M. (2009). Integrating practice guidelines into professional training implications for diversity competence. *Counseling Psychologist, 37*(4), 519–563. doi: 10.1177/0011000008323651

Morton, T., Alexander, C., & Altman, I. (1976). Communication and relationship definition. In G. Miller (Ed.), *Explorations in interpersonal communication* (pp. 105–125). Beverly Hills, CA: Sage.

Mueller, W. J., & Kell, B. L. (1972). *Coping with conflict: Supervising counselors and psychotherapists.* Englewood Cliffs, NJ: Prentice-Hall.

Muse-Burke, J., Ladany, N., & Deck, M. D. (2001). The supervisory relationship. In L. J. Bradley & N. Ladany (Eds.), *Counselor supervision: Principles, process, and practice* (3rd ed., pp. 28–62). New York: Brunner-Routledge.

Nelson, M., & Friedlander, M. (2001). A close look at conflictual supervisory relationships: The trainee's perspective. *Journal of Counseling Psychology, 48*(4), 384–395. doi: 10.1037//0022-0167.48.4.384

Neufeldt, I. S. A., Karno, M. P., & Nelson, M. L. (1996). A qualitative study of experts' conceptualization of supervisee reflectivity. *Journal of Counseling Psychology, 43*, 3–9.

Ober, A. M., Granello, D. H., & Henfield, M. S. (2009). A synergistic model to enhance multicultural competence in supervision. *Counselor Education & Supervision, 48*(3), 204–221.

Olk, M., & Friedlander, M. L. (1992). Trainees' experiences of role conflict and role ambiguity in supervisory relationships. *Journal of Counseling Psychology, 39*, 389–397.

Palomo, M., Beinart, H., & Cooper, M. J. (2010). Development and validation of the supervisory relationship questionnaire (SRQ) in UK trainee clinical psychologists RID F-7769-2010. *British Journal of Clinical Psychology, 49*, 131–149. doi: 10.1348/014466509X441033

Patton, M. J., & Kivlighan, D. M., Jr. (1997). Relevance of the supervisory alliance to the counseling alliance and to treatment adherence in counselor training. *Journal of Counseling Psychology, 44*, 108–115.

Penman, R. (1980). *Communication processes and relationship.* London: Academic Press.

Proctor, T. I. (1997). Contracting in supervision. In C. Sills (Ed.), *Contracts in counseling* (pp. 161–175). London: Sage.

Putney, M. W., Worthington, E. L., Jr., & McCullough, M. E. (1992). Effects of supervisor and supervisee, theoretical orientation and supervisor-supervisee matching on interns' perceptions of supervision. *Journal of Counseling Psychology, 39*, 258–265.

Rabinowitz, F. E., Heppner, P. P., & Roehlke, H. J. (1986). Descriptive study of process and outcome variables of supervision over time. *Journal of Counseling Psychology, 33*, 292–300.

Raven, B. H. & French, J. R. P., Jr. (1958). Legitimate power, coercive power, and observability in social influence. *Sociometry, 21*(2), 83–97.

Reising, G. N., & Daniels, M. H. (1983). A study of Bogan's model of counselor development and supervision. *Journal of Counseling Psychology, 30*, 235–244.

Robyak, J. E., Goodyear, R. K., & Prange, M. (1987). Effects of supervisors' sex, focus, and experience on preferences for interpersonal power bases. *Counselor Education and Supervision, 26*, 299–309.

Schilling, B. (2005). *Systemisk supervisionsmetodik: Et sprogspil for professionelle, der anvender supervision.* Virum: Dansk Psykologisk Forlag.

Schilling, B., Haugaard Jacobsen, C., & Nielsen, J. (2010 March). Supervision og de 3 K'er (Supervision and the 3 C's: Context, contract and control). *Dansk Psykolog Nyt, 5*, 1–22.

Schwartz, H. (2009). *Thankful learning: A grounded theory study of relational practice between master's students and professors* (Doctoral dissertation). Retrieved from https://etd.ohiolink.edu/

Skovholt, T. M., & Ronnestad, M. H. (1992). *The evolving professional self: Stages and themes in therapist and counselor development.* Chichester: Wiley.

Stein, D. M., & Lambert, M. J. (1995). Graduate training in psychotherapy: Are therapy outcomes enhanced? *Journal of Consulting and Clinical Psychology, 63*, 182–196.

Stenack, R. J., & Dye, H. A. (1982). Behavioral description of counseling supervision roles. *Counselor Education and Supervision, 21*, 295–304.

Stoltenberg, C. D., & Delworth, U. (1987). *Supervising counselors and therapists.* San Francisco, CA: Jossey-Bass.

Stoltenberg, C. D., McNeill, B., & Crethar, H. C. (1994). Changes in supervision as counselors and therapists gain experience: A review. *Professional Psychology, Research and Practice, 25*, 416–449.

Stoltenberg, C. D., McNeill, B. W., & Delworth, U. (1998). *IDM supervision: An integrated developmental model for supervising counselors and therapists.* San Francisco, CA: Jossey-Bass.

Stone, G. L. (1980). Effects of experience on supervisor planning. *Journal of Counseling Psychology*, *27*, 84–88.

Strong, S. R., Hills, H. I., & Nelson, B. N. (1988). *Interpersonal communication rating scale* (Rev. ed). Richmond: Department of Psychology, Virginia Commonwealth University.

Strozier, A. L., Kivlighan, D. M., & Thoreson, R. W. (1993). Supervisor intentions, supervisee reactions, and helpfulness: A case study of the process of supervision. *Psychotherapy: Theory, Research and Practice*, *24*, 13–19.

Sundland, D. M. (1977). The relationship of interpersonal attraction, experience, and supervisors' level of functioning in dyadic counseling supervision. *Counselor Education and supervision*, *12*, 187–193.

Sundland, L. M., & Feinberg, L. B. (1972). The relationship of interpersonal attraction, experience, and supervisors' level of functioning in dyadic counseling supervision. *Counselor Education and Supervision*, *12*, 187–193.

Tracey, T. J., Ellickson, J. L., & Sherry, P. (1989). Reactance in relation to different supervisory environments and counselor development. *Journal of Counseling Psychology*, *36*, 336–344.

Wampold, B. E., & Holloway, E. L. (1997). Methodology, design, and evaluation in psychotherapy supervision research. In J. C. E. Watkins (Ed.), *Methodology, design, and evaluation in psychotherapy supervision research* (pp. 11–27). New York: Wiley.

Ward, L. G., Friedlander, M. L., Schoen, L. G., & Klein, J. C. (1985). Strategic self-presentation. *Journal of Counseling Psychology*, *32*, 111–118.

Watkins, C. E., Jr. (2011). Does psychotherapy supervision contribute to patient outcomes? Considering thirty years of research. *The Clinical Supervisor*, *30*, 235–256.

Webster's Encyclopedic Unabridged Dictionary. (1989). *Webster's encyclopedic unabridged dictionary of the English language*. New York: Dilithium Press.

Wedeking, D. F., & Scott, T. B. (1976). A study of the relationship between supervisor and trainee behaviors in counseling practicum. *Counselor Education and Supervision*, *15*, 259–266.

Whipple, J. L., Lambert, M. J., Vemeesch, D., Smart, D. W., Nielsen, S. L., & Hawkins, E. J. (2003). Improving the effects of psychotherapy: The use of early identification of treatment failure and problem solving strategies in routine practice. *Journal of Counseling Psychology*, *50*, 59–68.

Wiley, M. O., & Ray, P. B. (1986). Counseling supervision by developmental level. *Journal of Counseling Psychology*, *33*, 439–445.

Worthen, V. E., & Lambert, M. J. (2007). Outcome oriented supervision: Advantages of adding systematic client tracking to supportive consultations. *Counseling & Psychotherapy Research*, *7*(1), 48–53.

Worthington, E. L., Jr. (1984a). Empirical investigation of supervision of counselors as they gain experience. *Journal of Counseling Psychology*, *31*, 63–75.

Worthington, E. L., Jr. (1984b). Use of trait labels in counseling supervision by experienced and inexperienced supervisors. *Professional Psychology, Research and Practice*, *15*, 457–461.

Worthington, E. L., Jr., & Roehlke, H. J. (1979). Effective supervision as perceived by beginning counselors-in-training. *Journal of Counseling Psychology*, *26*, 64–73.

Worthington, E. L., Jr., & Stern, A. (1985). The effects of supervisor and supervisee degree level and gender on the supervisory relationship. *Journal of Counseling Psychology*, *32*, 252–262.

Xi-Qing, S. (2004). The implication of the Holloway's SAS model for the clinical supervision in China. *Chinese Journal of Clinical Psychology*, *12*(1), 92–95.

30

Supervising Couple and Family Therapy Practitioners

Sandra A. Rigazio-DiGilio

Supervising therapists working with client systems beyond individuals requires a systemic framework that promotes therapists' understanding of the multiple perspectives operating in a client system's life space and in the therapeutic alliance (Burck & Daniel, 2010; Todd & Storm, 2014). Helping practitioners understand and apply the deeper meanings of therapeutic constructs, derived from the mathematical and physical science theories of complexity theory, quantum physics, and chaos theory, is the primary work of the marriage and family therapy (MFT) supervisor. These supervisors work from a systemic worldview, which provides a lens for organizing various systems theories and for integrating the constructs and techniques associated with these theories to best serve the needs of the wide range of clients whom supervisees serve. Building on the Boulder scientist–practitioner model (Hodgson, Johnson, Ketring, Wampler, & Lamson, 2005; Karam & Sprenkle, 2010), this chapter posits that it is the integration of research and practice that provides the cornerstone for ensuring that optimal services are provided to couples, families, and wider systems through the decrease or elimination of inhibiting forces that impact development and functioning (Donnelly & Gosbee, 2009).

Mental Health Professions Supervising MFT Practitioners

At the heart of MFT supervision is a focus on the systemic dimensions and characteristics of the couple, the family, and the larger organizational systems that might be working with the clinician (Stokes & Molarte, 2011; Storm, 2011; Styczynski & Greenberg, 2008). Descriptions and constellations of these dimensions and characteristics vary across MFT models and mental health disciplines. Systemic supervision is available across a wide range of mental health disciplines (e.g., counseling, MFT, psychiatry, psychology, social work), but it is rare that MFT supervision models are

The Wiley International Handbook of Clinical Supervision, First Edition. Edited by C. Edward Watkins, Jr. and Derek L. Milne.

shared beyond the discipline, even though most disciplines rely on similar theoretical and practical approaches to MFT therapy (DeRoma, Hickey, & Stanek, 2007).

The discipline through which supervision is delivered affects the content and the process of the encounter (Moore, Hamilton, Crane, & Fawcett, 2011). MFT supervision provided within psychiatry will be considerably different from community-based supervision for MFT interns. While the focus of both is on the client system and supervisee development, the professional socialization associated with each discipline is distinct (Miller, Todahl, & Platt, 2010). Sometimes, professionals from several disciplines may come together for supervision in specific marriage and family models but rarely are collaborations sustained (Saayman, Saayman, & Wiens, 2006).

Supervising couple and family therapists requires a multidimensional view of the work. The therapeutic alliance, supervisory alliance, and contextual and cultural environments surrounding these relationships are all important considerations in delivering systemic supervision (Aponte, 2009). As with all mental health supervision, there are five domains that systemic supervisors must attend to: reflective teachers, gatekeepers, mentors, colleagues, and evaluators who are charged with the responsibility of ensuring ethical service for the public (Russell, DuPree, Beggs, Peterson, & Anderson, 2007).

Therapeutic and Supervisory Contexts: From Local to Community to Global Networks

In our ever-shrinking, digital world, couples, families, and wider systems increasingly work and live in different cities, countries, and hemispheres. It is not unusual for some members of a family to move for economic, educational, and/or human rights and safety reasons and to become separated from their families of origin or procreation. While such separations have occurred throughout history, our current social communication technology makes it possible to conduct synchronous and asynchronous treatment with family members even when they are miles apart. While not the norm, there is a growing need to provide treatment when a family member, who may be on military duty, is geographically far from home but able to participate through digital technology.

MFT supervisors adopt a multicultural perspective which holds that individuals are embedded within a family culture, which, in turn, is embedded in a community culture, that is itself positioned within a geopolitical culture (region of a state, providence, or country), and an even larger ideological culture (e.g., religion, political preferences, occupational status, educational level). Regardless of where MFT services are delivered, the MFT supervisor monitors the influence of supervision for the therapist, the client system, and the relevant wider networks that contribute to defining and managing distress and/or disorder (Aponte & Johnson, 2000; McDonald, Billingham, Conrad, Morgan, & Payton, 1997; Rigazio-DiGilio, 2000).

Figure 30.1 is a graphic representation of the multiple contexts in which systemic supervision takes place. The *Participants' Worldviews* represent the personal and professional assumptions all members of the supervisory alliance bring to the encounter – factors that significantly determine our conceptualizations of distress and disorder and the ways in which these are managed, as well as our conceptualizations of

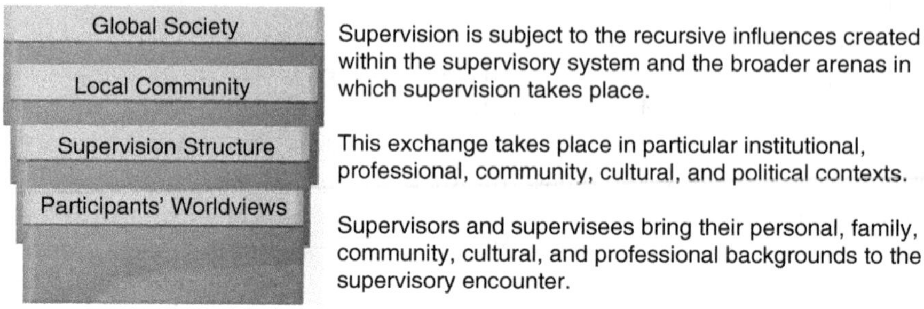

Figure 30.1 The multiple contexts of systemic supervision. Source: Rigazio-DiGilio and LaPlante (2009).

supervisee development and the ways in which it is enhanced. The *Supervision Structure* includes factors such as positions of power, authority, accountability, and responsibility. These factors directly influence what issues are brought to the foreground, relegated to the background, or not addressed at all.

The *Local Community* represents the particular institutional, professional, community, and political systems and cultural mores that contribute to long-held beliefs about the work of mental health professionals and those we serve. By recognizing this wider, local domain, supervisors are able to broaden the scope of inquiry beyond the supervisory and therapeutic systems to include the voices of the local community and create an open context promoting social justice by facilitating equality, social acceptance, and the credibility of multiple views. Finally, the *Global Society* refers to the shifting social and professional issues that frame the work of mental health professionals in a diverse and increasingly pluralistic and technological world. Increasingly, complex issues arise within this domain including the need to review the degree to which our work addresses sociocultural and sociopolitical forces that promote oppression, mental distress, and disease (Rigazio-DiGilio, Ivey, & Locke, 1997; U.S. Department of Health and Human Services, 2001).

This multicultural perspective provides opportunities to (a) activate resources within and beyond the therapy room (Green & Dekkers, 2010; Storm, Todd, Sprenkle, & Morgan, 2001) and (b) systematically access venues to provide effective and relevant services to all those in need, including underrepresented and underserved populations and under-resourced communities (Leong & Kalibatseva, 2013).

Essential Attributes of Couple and Family Therapy Supervision

The cybernetics revolution in science, prominent in the first half of the twentieth century, culminated in the writings of Wiener (1948) and set the stage to extend the systems theories of von Bertalanffy (1950) and the communication theories of Bateson (1951), which in turn helped to reliably identify the interactional relationships that compose couple and family life (Lee, Nichols, Nichols, & Odom, 2004). Within this philosophical environment, Bateson postulated the family dynamics implicated in the transmission of schizophrenia through generations. Searching for a behavioral explanation, Bateson (1951) concluded that it was contradictory communication that seemed to be at work within the family. The role of language in forming and sustaining relationships has always been essential to the work of the MFT ever since then (e.g., Wittgenstein, 1966).

Systemic worldview

The systems approach to understanding human interactions entered the professional lexicon in the 1950s and the popular culture in the 1960s. The theories outlined at that time provided a framework based on a set of foundational assumptions that guided practitioners' work with couples, families, and wider relational networks. Systemic supervisors assist supervisees to develop deeper, more integrated understandings of the following principles drawn from the fields of biology and social psychology (von Bertalanffy, 1950).

1. The whole is greater than the sum of its parts.
2. Individuals within a family relate to one another in some consistent fashion.
3. The family system is structured by these relationships.
4. Relationships can be complementary, where their differences fit together, or symmetrical, where their similarities overshadow differences.
5. Sometimes, third parties are brought in to diffuse high emotionality and anxiety within dyads.
6. Boundaries among family members and between the family and the external environment regulate degrees of influence.
7. Systems tend to be self-regulating and attempt to maintain homeostasis or equilibrium.
8. Feedback loops help maintain the structure of the family. Negative feedback limits change or deviation and helps maintain the equilibrium of the family. Positive feedback amplifies change.
9. Feedback systems and patterns can be rigid or flexible.
10. Changes in one part of a social system influence all other parts of that same system.
11. The solutions families employ to restore equilibrium may become causes of stress for some or all of its members.
12. The concept of equifinality is used to explain that there are multiple causes and effects associated with any thought, action, or situation and that the final state of the system can be achieved via numerous routes.
13. Linear cause and effect reasoning is not as powerful as circular or recursive reasoning to understand systems.

A systemic view of the therapeutic exchange Today, systems therapists are socialized to think about and act upon the interactive processes occurring within and among individuals, families, and wider social systems (e.g., Wynne, Shields, & Sirkin, 1992). To accomplish this, most MFT models offer guidelines for weighing the importance of individual, family, and wider contextual variables when working with clients or client systems. Additionally, the models provide intervention strategies that can be used within and across a client system's multiple life spaces so that balanced attention can be given to internalized cognition and emotion, individual and collective identities, wider sociocultural and sociopolitical realities, and individual and collective action.

This broader territory of investigation and intervention relies on a systemic view of the therapeutic alliance. That is, therapists are generally called upon to establish relationships of trust, credibility, unconditional regard, and authenticity with individuals, couples, families, local community members, and institutions with the intention of providing interactive exchanges capable of generating multiple perspectives and options toward resolving psychological distress and disorder. To accomplish this, MFT therapists must possess a wide array of therapeutic knowledge and skills, competencies generally advanced and refined in supervision.

MFT supervision models and approaches generally drawn from MFT therapeutic frameworks to train professionals. Table 30.1 provides an overview of MFT supervisory models and their relationship to MFT treatment approaches. Regardless of model or approach, supervision should assist supervisees to (a) access some clinical models with fidelity (Todd & Storm, 2014), (b) develop personal approaches to treatment, and (c) tailor various models and approaches to meet the unique needs of those seeking treatment within the communities in which they work (Rigazio-DiGilio, 2014).

Table 30.1 Model-specific MFT supervision approaches.

Supervision approaches	*MFT models*
Transgenerational approaches (Gilberto-Rorman, 2014; Roberto, 1997)	• Bowen family systems therapy • Symbolic-experiential family therapy • Contextual family therapy
Psychoanalytic approaches (Reiner, 2014)	• Psychoanalytic family therapy • Psychodynamic family therapy • Object relations family therapy
Purposive-systemic approaches (Todd, 2014; 1997)	• Structural family therapy • Strategic family therapy • MRI (Mental Research Institute) • Milan family therapy • Solution-focused family therapy
Emotionally focused approaches (Palmer-Olsen, Gold, & Woolley, 2011).	• Emotionally focused family therapy
Post-modern approaches (Bobele & Biever, 2014; Ungar, 2006)	• Constructivism • Social constructionism • Coconstructivism • Narrative family therapy
Feminist approaches (Lyness & Helmeke, 2008; Prouty, 2001)	• Feminist family therapy
Evidenced-based supervision approaches (Lebow, 2014)	• Evidenced-based family therapy
Integrative approaches (Breunlin et al., 2011; Rigazio-DiGilio, 2014)	• Integrative-problem-centered family therapy • Systemic cognitive-developmental therapy • Metaframeworks

A systemic view of the supervisory exchange A systems perspective of supervision extends the ideas that language is essential to understanding the work and needs of the therapist and that holding multiple perspectives simultaneously is important (Rigazio-DiGilio, 2014; Smith, 2011). Supervision with MFTs requires that the same systemic concepts be applied to the supervisory relationship (Nichols, Nichols, & Hardy, 1990).

Supervision always takes place in a specific context: a clinic, a university, a place of worship, a hospital (Woolley, 2010). Supervisors must simultaneously attend to variables in the following three categories: the supervisor–supervisee relationship, the therapist–client relationship, and the context where supervision takes place. According to Harper-Jaques and Limacher (2009), the influence of the clinical setting can affect the process in four ways. It defines the role of supervision within the setting, the quality and quantity of multiple problem definitions, the organizational structure, and the influence of power.

A systemic view of supervisory, therapeutic, client, and wider networks Practitioners using a systemic mind set always see the relationship between the objects in the foreground and the forces in the background influencing those objects. The ecosystemic nature of this work is captured in Figure 30.2. Couples and families are viewed

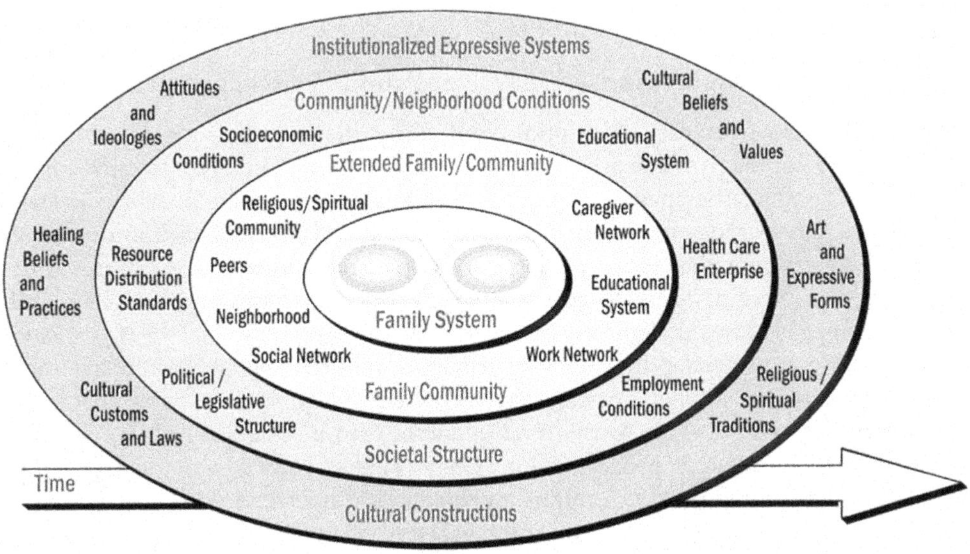

Figure 30.2 Conceptualizing the family's mediating role across time and contexts. Families provide the primal socialization unit matrix for individuals to develop. Over the course of development, families' boundaries extend to include wider contexts that influence various aspects of individual members', relationships', and families' development and functioning as a whole. Families also are subsystems of wider social units and, as such, rely on their developmental and contextual histories to give meaning to and participate in larger social entities. This figure demonstrates one ecosystemic model for conceptualizing this multilayered life-span interactive process. The dynamics within each of the life spaces is conceptualized as four concentric circles, specifying that cultural societal, community, and family dynamics are constantly operating within and across these four domains. Source: Rigazio-DiGilio et al. (2005).

as subsystems of larger social units. The dynamics within and among the levels are conceptualized as four concentric circles, specifying that cultural, societal, community, and family dynamics are operating within the relationship development of family members (Rigazio-DiGilio, Ivey, Kunkler-Peck, & Grady, 2005). Beginning with the interaction that happens within the family boundary, the systemic professional understands that those interactions are forged within the family and the extended family/community milieu. By understanding the ways the extended family/community influences the interactions of the family, the therapist and supervisor are able to assess the constraints and resources the family has available to affect change. The extended family/community also is influenced by the wider community and its sociopolitical culture. Finally, the wider community also is a conduit for the institutionalized expressive aspects of the greater society. This ecosystemic interaction happens over time and contributes directly to the development of family members.

Using this type of analysis, the extended network beyond the therapist/supervisor relationship can be identified. Questions about the setting of the supervision, about significant others who may not be present in the family, and about what cultural issues are affecting the client system can be explored. The systemic supervisor continually strives to account for both visible and invisible dynamics that may be operating on the supervisory encounter. Evidence to support the development of a systemic perspective in supervision is found in Lee and Vennum (2010) and Lee et al. (2004).

Therapy and supervision as clinical and cultural exchange processes

Contextual issues operating in multiple and sometimes overlapping environments influence the interactive discourse of MFT supervision. The interactions among individuals, families, therapeutic alliances, and wider environments provide the stage upon which supervisee competence can be developed. It is the dialectic and recursive nature of supervision that is the dynamic force of development. The nature of the person–environment dialectic co-constructed in MFT supervision is viewed as a cultural exchange process, as depicted in Figure 30.3.

A supervisee's understanding of and participation in the therapeutic environment is co-constructed in a constant person–environment dialectic transaction enacted in the supervisory relationship. At the level of the human interaction in MFT supervision, the cultural exchange process includes issues such as professional identify factors of gender, race, ethnic, and community background; physical and psychological variations; and socioeconomic and educational levels of both the supervisor and the supervisee. As these personal qualities interact to form the supervisory alliance, the supervisee and supervisor together examine issues of clinical practice pertinent to the needs of the client system. The family identity factors directly affect the worldviews the therapist and the supervisor holds about family health and dysfunction which stem from their experience as family members. Cultural factors directly enter the supervisory exchange and must be identified as they may interfere with both treatment and supervision progress. The degree to which each member of the supervisory encounter holds onto their tactic and explicit assumptions is identified as the two-way arrows. The systemic supervisor is aware that when power differentials exist, the nature of the interaction is altered (Murphy & Wright, 2005). Using this concept

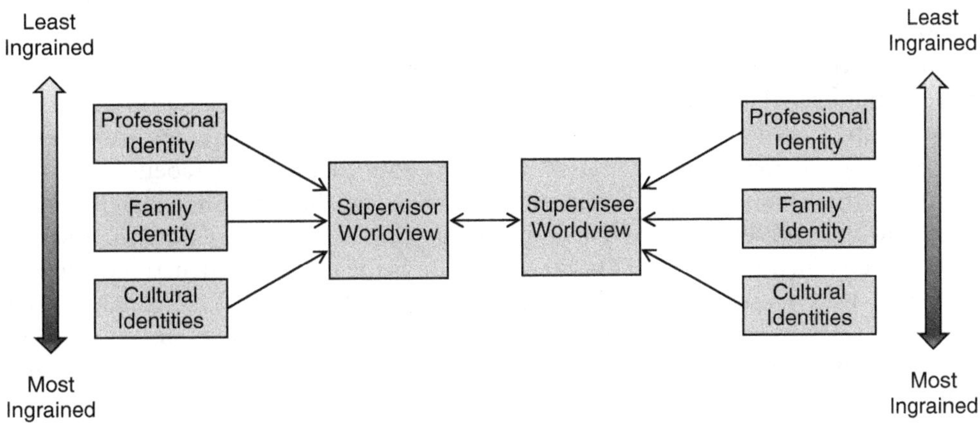

Figure 30.3 Systemic supervision as a cultural exchange process.
Professional worldviews/formal theory guide. Personal worldviews add texture to these guides in the way of our idiosyncratic/personal definitions about (a) our roles and the supervisory and therapeutic processes; (b) our intentions; (c) our assumptions about health, disorder, and its management; and (d) our assumptions about therapist growth and development. The more ingrained the roles or learning that have come to shape our personal worldviews, the more likely such factors contribute to our later learned roles. Thus, family and cultural identities are more ingrained and tend to be more influential (and outside of our awareness) than other learned professional roles. Concomitantly, professional roles and worldviews (learned later) are more within our awareness and available for intentional use in conceptualizing and working with supervisees and families. Source: Rigazio-DiGilio (2007).

of dialectic exchange, the systemic supervisor can monitor the use of power in both the supervisory and the therapeutic alliances.

Understanding multiple voices and perspectives When two or more persons are together, there are many levels of meaning making at play. At the supervisory level, the many levels involve the technical, conceptual, executive knowledge, skills, and attitudes the therapist brings to the session. Similarly, the levels of supervisory skills, professional confidence, and the perceived primary functions a supervisor must fulfill are some of the multiple perspectives supervisors carry into the relationship. The work of Aponte (1992) on the self of the therapist provides strategies that supervisors can use to surface the multiple voices that therapists bring to the encounter (García & Guevara, 2007).

At the level of treatment, this multiplicity is contained within the interpretations the client makes of the therapist's words and deeds, and the interpretations the therapist makes of the client's words and deeds. Understanding the predominant narratives at the level of client involves identifying the way individuals and subgroups engage in, and maintain or transform, or reject such narratives in the fluid interaction of the family. This clinical information informs the system practitioner about the resources being used by the client and the resources that could be tapped in the future. Each member of the client system sitting in the session has a worldview about the way the presenting issues entwine themselves and other family members. It is important to activate the individual voice throughout therapy.

At the wider systems level, the supervisor applies the systemic, contextual, and cultural theoretical assumptions to understand the dynamics infringing on the therapeutic system. What external agencies or individuals and groups are influencing the patterns of interaction evident at the client level or in the therapeutic alliance? What external resources may be activated to assist the client in resolving the issues related to their presenting problem and to enhancing their adaptive potential? Miller (2011) recommended that MFT supervision adopts the Objective Structured Clinical Exercises, widely used in the medical profession to assess clinical competence, as a formative assessment tool to work with supervisees in a competency-based learning environment to monitor their growth and development. Attneave (1982) and Boyd (2010) have spoken about the benefits and strategies for bringing voices from the wider community into the treatment and supervisory process.

Understanding alliances within supervisory, therapeutic, client, and wider networks Applying the systemic assumption that all larger systems have smaller subsystems in operation, Murray Bowen (1978) identified the concept of alliances in family clients. Watching the flow of communication among members, he and his associates were able to reliably identify, use, and intervene in subgroups of family members that formed alliances to support or defeat one of the family narratives being spoken about or played out in the here and now of the session. Alliances are dynamic and as such may shift, gain prominence, recede in prominence, or emerge over time. Some alliances are stable and the involved individuals hold together and maintain their roles within the relationship for long periods of time. Some well-established alliances experience changes to their composition, roles, and purposes for existence and communication styles as they evolve through time. These are fluid alliances and maintain some characteristics of the past but are morphing as the time and circumstances move on. Finally, emergent alliances are the spontaneous relationships that form in the heat of a stressful or growthful situation. Sometimes, members of alliances that hold exactly opposite worldviews about a given issue may find themselves aligned in relation to a new issue. These emergent alliances may end up being the new fluid and stable alliances of the future or they may only exist for a short period of time. The systemic practitioner is aware that alliances are dynamic and uses this energy to forge new alliances and modify the impact of existing alliances when necessary.

At the supervisory level, members of the wider therapeutic system can be engaged in alliances within the worldviews of either or both the supervisor and the therapist. For example, the family client, the therapist, and the referring agency may all be in an alliance to help the adolescent daughter to stop abusing drugs. On the other hand, the supervisor and insurance company may be more interested in reducing the level of psychological violence displayed by members of the spousal unit. Competing alliances are not unusual at the level of supervision and the systemic supervisor will monitor them closely to be sure mixed messages are not sent in either direction.

External forces in the wider community often are experienced in the therapy room. Deciphering where and why those forces emerge are helpful in understanding the full cultural context of the family system. The daughter who is abusing drugs may have stronger ties to her peers outside the therapy room and this alliance needs to be accounted for in the therapy. Similarly, the religious or cultural expectations of peers who influence the parents of the client system also need to be attended in the goals, content, and process of treatment. These external alliances from the wider community often enter the therapeutic and supervisory exchange and, unless acknowledged in MFT supervision, may derail the treatment or supervisory outcomes.

Understanding and accessing effective and relevant resources The ecological thinking inherent in systemic practice makes visible many individual, biologic, sociopolitical networks, and wider-community variables that may be activated or constrained by the client to resolve its presenting and emergent issues. As always, the needs of the client seeking treatment should be paramount in the supervisor's mind. How effective is the supervisee in assisting the client to open new channels of internal communication and problem-solving styles? Helping systemic therapists understand and integrate the individual dynamics and needs operating in the treatment process is just as important as understanding the alliances active in the family structure. Alliances may or may not involve significant others outside the client. These outside members of key family alliances offer extended possibilities to access resources for the family beyond the family itself. These external connections to the wider community reveal opportunities for the systemic therapists to consider in the conceptualization of the family and the goals of treatment.

The final domain supervisors need to help supervisees consider is the resources contained in the extended supervisory relationship. Many therapists, especially beginning therapists, may be so overwhelmed with emotional interactions between individuals and primary alliances that they do not consider the wider contextual and cultural dynamics at play in the client interactions. Systemic supervision attends to the cognitive, affective, and behavioral resources that can be found throughout the human network the client and the therapist bring into treatment.

Couple and Family Therapy Supervision Skills Promoting and Monitoring Clinical, Cultural, and Contextual Competence

The American Association for Marriage and Family Therapy (AAMFT) has issued the competencies MFTs are expected to demonstrate upon licensing (Nelson & Graves, 2011). This list identifies the clinical, cultural, and contextual skills MFTs are expected to possess and perfect over their careers. Supervisors and supervisees use the list to identify the skills, competences, and dispositions that will become the focus of supervision. Lee and Vennum (2010) described the powerful use of journals in helping supervisees monitor and analyze critical incidents in their practice. By demonstrating the scientist–practitioner perspective, supervisees applied the qualitative analysis method of open coding to review critical incidents reported in their journals. The authors note that the new knowledge directly led to action plans for growth that were used in supervision to achieve the AAMFT competencies.

Developing supervisees' systemic perspective and approach

At the philosophical level, supervision helps the therapist maintain and enhance his or her application of a systemic perspective. Helping therapists adopt and refine their systemic perspective is some of the most intellectually challenging work systemic supervisors face. Initially, therapists, novice or veterans, fail to see a systemic force operating in the client system that neutralizes treatment interventions and maintains a status quo posture by the client. Systemic supervision provides an environment for therapists to expand their systemic analysis of the client within a particular context and cultural milieu and to adapt a more robust systemic perspective.

Systemic supervisory conversations focus on making the invisible dynamic forces and alliances operating in and on the family visible. Three theoretical orientations to supervision have been described in the literature: (a) the common factor models (Gardner & Butler, 2009; Morgan & Sprenkle, 2007), (b) the integrated models of supervisee development (Breunlin, Pinsof, Russell, & Lebow, 2011; Rigazio-DiGilio, 2014), and (c) the practice-oriented model of Todd and Storm (2014). All provide structures for MFT supervisors to guide their work with supervisees. Bitar, Bean, and Bermúdez (2007) provided a comprehensive inventory that can be used in supervision to access and examine a supervisee's preferred theoretical orientations and to consider the systemic nature of their conceptualization of therapy and the role of the therapist.

Technically, systemic supervision also focuses on the conceptual, executive, and operational skills of the therapist to apply a systemic perspective. The general theory of change and approach to therapy each school of MFT espouses is unique and requires sustained practice to master these approaches. The systemic supervisor is constantly assessing the therapist's level of application of a systems approach to treatment. Today, some supervision is school specific and some supervision is integrative. Training in structural, psychodynamic, experiential-symbolic, narrative, cognitive-behavioral, emotionally focused, and problem-focused approaches are all examples of school-specific systemic supervision. Alternatively, systemic cognitive developmental supervision (Rigazio-DiGilio, 2014), the integrative problem-centered metaframework supervision (Breunlin et al., 2011), the consultation model (Green, Shilts, & Bacigalupe, 2001), and the family systems approach (Gingrich, 2001) are examples of integrative systemic supervision that help therapists make connections across schools of couple and family therapies. Monitoring the development and maintenance of a systems perspective by the therapist is foundational to systemic supervision regardless of the school-specific or integrative approach adopted.

Developing supervisees' cultural and contextual competencies

Numerous models of MFT supervision for contextual and cultural competency are available for use in today's supervisory encounter (Guanipa, 2002; Lawless, Gale, & Bacigalupe, 2001; Tyson, Pérusse, & Stone, 2008). Hernández (2003) has demonstrated the importance of supervisors bringing up issues on how to integrate diversity into the supervision process. Green and Dekkers (2010) found that when supervision attends to power and diversity, it provides a supportive environment that influence (a) positive clinical outcomes for clients because of isomorphism, (b) satisfaction with supervision, and (c) enhanced learning outcomes for supervisees. Culture and context involve all aspects of life, and Long and Serovich (2003) provided MFT supervisors with tools to integrate issues of sexual orientation into the supervision process. Inman (2006) has demonstrated that the level of multicultural competence of the supervisor is directly related to the process and outcome of the supervisory experience.

Developing supervisees' ability to provide effective and relevant services

All supervision is aimed at enhancing the technical skills of the supervisee. Whether that person is a first year graduate student or a seasoned professional, the goals of supervision always focus on expanding the clinical repertoire of the supervisee (Celano, Smith, & Kaslow, 2010).

The ability to apply a systemic perspective while foundational is a never-ending process. Following the basic framework of therapy, the family therapy supervisor monitors and directs the supervisee's ability to engage the family client through all stages of the supervisory encounter.

Facilitating Supervisee's Engagement in the Supervisory Process

The need to participate fully in the supervision process is an expectation of all supervisees. Briggs, Fournier, and Hendrix (1999) identified that MFT supervisees must come prepared for individual and group supervision, set appropriate supervision goals, accurately assess their part in the therapeutic system, and incorporate input from supervision during session. Maintaining a focus on clinical, cultural, and contextual competencies is demanding and the particular skill sets the supervisee is working on should be explicitly stated in the supervisory contract. As part of the work of supervision, the supervisor has the responsibility to monitor the personal efforts supervisees put forward in examining and improving their practice (Ali & Bachicha, 2012). When issues of biases and privileges do surface, the response of the supervisee is critical. The attitudes supervisees rely on in working through these issues reflect their ability to engage deeply in supervision that does examine the social justice issues in any case and the natural and logical biases and privileges they bring to the work (Schindler Zimmerman & Haddock, 2001). Occasionally, the issues of disproportionality of power and its excesses are evident in the supervisory alliance (Ren, 2008). At times like this, the systemic supervisor could consider engaging in peer supervision or contracting for his/her own supervision of supervision.

In MFT supervision, therapists must master cognitive, emotional, behavioral, and relational understanding of effective systemic treatment, whether using school-specific or integrative theories and approaches. The professional competence and confidence of the supervisee to provide what Bernal and Zera (2012) have labeled universal design for learning (UDL) principles are important aspects to monitor. That is, how is the supervisee growing in their ability to provide universal access to quality care for all clients? Having the supervisee identify professional goals in the clinical, cultural, and contextual areas of technical competence is the starting point. Using self-of-the-therapist activities (Aponte, 1992) to reflect clinically and professionally on client-system progress and the competence of therapists to conceptualize, execute, and assess the impact of their work, systemic supervisors lead supervisees to connect this learning to their professional worldview (Johnson & Caldwell, 2011).

Ensuring Supervisors' Ability to Create Effective and Relevant Environments

Systemic cognitive-developmental supervision (SCDS) (Rigazio-DiGilio, 2014) provides one example of how to create supervisory environments that are personalized for MFT supervisees. Table 30.2 provides an overview of the four supervisory environments that systemic supervisors can use to scaffold the technical, conceptual, and executive development of supervisees. There are five foundational assumptions to the SCDS process:

1. The information processing style of the MFT supervisee can be reliably identified.
2. Supervisory environments can be matched to the supervisee's information processing style and the clinical demands of the client system.
3. Supervisors can design activities that match the current information processing style of the supervisee and can introduce activities that promote movement to other supervisory environments.
4. Supervisors can monitor both supervisee competence and client system progress.
5. Supervisors can monitor supervisee confidence from a dependent, to an independent, to an interdependent stance in supervision.

Table 30.2 presents a description of the four different supervisory environments, the objectives associated with each environment, and an example of the types of techniques that can be used to match (horizontal development) or move the supervisee's information processing style to another environment (vertical development). These environments can be used to differentiate supervision to the unique worldview of each supervisee. The descriptions in Table 30.2 can be used by supervisors to monitor their own ability to tailor supervision to the developmental needs of their supervisees.

Supervisory Formats in Couple and Family Therapy

MFT supervisors have a wide array of supervisory formats to choose from when working with therapists. Live, video, and digital formats provide different windows into the work of the therapist. The setting under which the family and couple therapy is delivered also influences the goals, focus, and processes of supervision.

Individual supervision: case conceptualization and electronic recordings

Verbal presentation of case material is widely used in MFT supervision and can be personally communicated or audio or video recorded. Regardless of the mode of presentation, the content needs to be structured to maintain a systemic focus. To help therapists focus on important elements of their cases, numerous case presentation guidelines have been developed. Maione (2011) provided case guidelines to open and focus the supervisory dialogue. These guidelines maximize the time supervisees and supervisors spend engaged in clinical conversations. Smith, Finn, Swain, and Handler (2010) described that a therapeutic assessment protocol supervisees can use to conceptualize cases that focus on the needs of a child receiving medical care. Brenner (2010) offered guidelines to consider cases that are struggling with

Table 30.2 The four SCDS environments associated with each cognitive-developmental information processing style.

SCDS constructs environments that assist supervisees to access the broad range of perceptual, conceptual, and executive resources available within each of four cognitive-developmental information processing styles. Over the course of supervision, supervisors and supervisees co-construct these environments to facilitate both horizontal (skill mastery) and vertical (skill extension) development.

Sensorimotor/elemental information processing style structured supervision environment		
Supervision environment	*Supervision objective*	*Illustrative modalities/techniques*
Supervisors introduce a directive style to encourage supervisees to safely explore immediate sensory-based experiences and integrate salient aspects of these experiences into a coherent framework.	• Develop case conceptualization skills • Clarify and directly experience client and supervisee feelings • Reduce anxiety • Identify transference/countertransference issues	• Live supervision, bug-in-ear, phone-in • Co-therapy • Digital supervision focused on case conceptualization • Team supervision focused on case conceptualization • Instruction, independent readings • Role plays, sculpting, experiential activities
Concrete/situational information processing style coaching supervision environment		
Supervision environment	*Supervision objective*	*Illustrative modalities/techniques*
Supervisors introduce a semi-directive coaching style to assist supervisees to frame thoughts, feelings, and behaviors from an if/then linear perspective and to assist them to act more predictably/intentionally during the therapeutic encounter.	• Learn/practice strategies and techniques • Become proficient at if/then reasoning • Enhance tracking skills • Increase predictability/intentionality • Understand decision-making processes across therapy and supervision	• Live supervision with pre/mid/post-session coaching • Digital supervision focused on conceptual and executive mastery • Practice exercises focused on conceptual and executive skills • Case presentation focused on accurate description

(*Continued*)

Table 30.2 (*Continued*)

Formal/reflective information processing style consulting supervision environment		
Supervision environment	*Supervision objective*	*Illustrative modalities/techniques*
Supervisor takes on a consultation role, working with supervisee to better understand the constancy of patterns within self, client, therapeutic theories and therapies, and therapeutic and supervisory relationships. This environment stresses work on reflective and abstract analytical skills.	• Reflect/analyze self and clinical information • Generalize assessment and intervention skills • Identify themes and patterns in self, client, therapy, and supervision • Co-construct parallel analogs to help clients expand perspectives and actions	• Edited digital segments focused on identifying similar patterns and themes across cases and therapeutic encounters • Assistance in constructing and using integrative metaframeworks • Independent, self-appraisal exercises
Dialectic/systemic collaborating environment		
Supervision environment	*Supervision objective*	*Illustrative modalities/techniques*
Supervisor and supervisee engage in a collegial, collaborative venture focused on core cognitive and meta-cognitive processes such as the person–environment dialectic and personal constructs.	• Recognize/challenge assumptions and rules • Recognize/challenge developmental and contextual influences on worldview constructions and behaviors • Evaluate parameters of one's beliefs and constructions	• Supervision focused on epistemological and ontological issues • Co-therapy • Peer consultation • Co-constructing hypotheses and plans • Analyze self and therapeutic framework for generalizability and unrecognized bias

Source: Table 30.2 is reproduced here with permission from Sandra A. Rigazio-DiGilio, copyright 2007.

items the family-system consider taboo, such as homosexuality and alternative gender identity.

Live supervision: co-therapy and observation

Marriage and family therapy supervisors have long used a variety of in-session supervisory techniques (Birchler, 1975). Live supervision behind a one-way mirror allows supervisors to make immediate interventions in the here and now of the session. Sometimes, therapists wear an earpiece that permits them to receive messages from the supervisor (Moorhouse & Carr, 2001). Co-therapy, where the supervisor and supervisee serve the client, also has been effective in modeling the skills and strategies for the therapist with real clients (Hendrix, Fournier, & Briggs, 2001). This permits supervisors to use their clinical acumen to simultaneously help the family client and to demonstrate clinical-problem solving for their co-therapists (Charlés, Ticheli-Kallikas, Tyner, & Barber-Stephens, 2005). Hendrix et al. (2001) found that co-therapy benefitted both clients and supervisees to a greater degree than traditional sole therapist approaches to treatment.

Team supervision

Team supervision is common and serves as a consulting group to the therapist. A chorus of therapists behind the mirror offer commentary and recommendations directly to the family-client and therapist. In some MFT approaches, the team has been used to develop paradoxical prescriptions for the family (Lowe, Hunt, & Simmons, 2008). In general, the team serves as a collective supervisory environment where therapists have an opportunity to be observed by the team and to receive feedback on both their performance and the reaction of the family client.

Group supervision

Another common mode of supervision involves a group of individual MFT's who convene on a regular basis to process their cases. Video tapes, audio tapes, case notes, and live observations are all means of displaying client material for the group members to analyze, and generate multiple perspectives about diagnoses and treatment of the client system under examination (Boston, 2010). Some groups may focus on issues of generic systemic treatment and other groups might have a particular focus that is MFT theory specific or are related to diagnostic and treatment categories, such as families with substance abusers, families with schizophrenic members, or couple treatment (Burck, 2010). Edwards and Heshmati (2003) provided detailed information for supervisors wishing to begin a group supervision process. They articulate a seven stage model that includes (a) checking, (b) case presentation, (c) questions from the audience (d) video review, (e) commentator reflections, (f) audience reflections, and (g) post-supervision supervisor reflections.

Outcomes of Effective and Relevant Couple and Family Therapy Supervision

MFT supervision research primarily consists of studies that investigate small samples of MFT graduate students as they progress through an academic program (e.g., Mcneil, Pavkov, Hecker, & Killmer, 2012; Samara, 2006). Numerous studies report the impact or effect of some supervisory innovation. Sometimes, these innovations are in the content or the focus of supervision as in the learning of a MFT school-specific approach; other times, the innovations are in the supervisory format as in live, digital, individual, or group settings (Bradley et al., 2010; Silverthorn, Bartle-Haring, Meyer, & Toviessi, 2009). The content of these studies has small historical trajectories, and often the studies do not build on prior research findings, or explicitly connect to the longitudinal body of knowledge that does exist in MFT supervision. The majority of MFT supervision research articles rely on convenient samples of graduate students either participating as supervisees or supervisors. In 2001, Storm et al. identified that the field of MFT supervision is based on spurious and capricious assumptions. Citing that the AAMFT supervision practice standards were not grounded in empirical findings and were generated from a committee process, they challenged the field to institute a research-based approach to the identification of supervisory competences. To date, the field has not responded to this challenge and continues to promulgate the eight standards originally identified.

Recently, Karam and Sprenkle (2010) raised the question about how far the scientist–practitioner model can be realized in master's level students training for clinical careers. They argued that the researched-informed perspective should be adopted as one of the goals of effective systemic supervision. Similarly, Hodgson et al. (2005) reported on how socialization into the scientist–practitioner model was differentiated at four MFT training programs serving master's and doctoral students. They found that helping students question the therapy process and integrate research through the supervisory process was helpful in having students work with the scientist–practitioner model.

Therapist growth as a practitioner and supervisee

The vast majority of published articles in MFT supervision focus on the growth of the therapist as a practitioner or supervisee. Supervision tailored to school-specific training, integrative models, evidence-based models, and common core models are available and all report positive findings. This illustrates the fundamental issue in MFT supervision; with a lack of a unifying conceptual theory of supervisee development, all theories and constructs are valid areas for investigation, thus research on MFT supervision on therapist growth is fragmented and disconnected.

Treatment outcome clinical and supervisory

Nelson and Smock (2005) traced the history of MFT education and, by extension, supervision. Their research indicates that the field has undergone many changes and that core training experiences vary widely across training programs and supervisory expectations today. They note that the current movement toward outcome-based education has strong potential to improve the consistency and diversity of MFT professionals. Research is underway to identify to what degree outcome-based practices, such as rubric-anchored competences aligned to learning and supervisory experiences, attention of interdisciplinary issues, and personalization of the expected program outcomes, are in use in the field (Baker, 2013).

MFT supervision, like its wider field of MFT education, is in transition in terms of research methodology. An investigation on outcomes by Sexton, Kinser, and Hanes (2008) indicates that randomized clinical trials have come to dominate the research landscape for both treatment and supervision. However, they state that

> Despite becoming the "gold standard" for evaluating clinical research and clinical practices, there is a growing debate regarding the reliance on randomized clinical trials as

> the primary basis for evaluating clinical intervention in MFT. Given the natural diversity of clients, settings, and clinical problems faced by practitioners and the relational and recursive interactional process of MFT, one of the major challenges for the field of MFT will be to come to grips with the research–practice gap by moving beyond a single methodological standard through adopting a "levels of evidence" approach as a framework that promotes diverse research methods, different methodological criteria (depending on the method), and evaluation based on the accumulated type of evidence needed to answer a specific policy, clinical practice choice, or within a model clinical decision. (p. 392)

Research on MFT supervision is in the same transition and will benefit from a systematic approach to supervision.

Institutional capacity

The role of the institutional context in which MFT supervision is provided has been studied. Context does matter (Harper-Jaques & Limacher, 2009). Every setting from institutions of higher educational to hospitals and community mental health settings, to private and for-profit clinics have all been evaluated for their effect on the development of the MFT professional. Knowledge about the unique influences that can be accessed to improve either clinical practice or supervision is important for the systemic supervisor to consider when co-constructing supervisory goals with a therapist providing service at a particular facility (London & Tarragona, 2007). Because the MFT supervisee provides service in the facility, effective supervision must include professional orientation and oversight of the trainee's compliance with best practices and institutional reporting protocols.

Helping MFT therapists to consider the implications of their context in the development of case conceptualizations and treatment plans helps them tailor treatment to the full client system. Even in institutional settings where the MFT trainee is only one of many professionals serving the community, the development of the therapist's competence is essential to the integrity and continuous growth of that organization. It is therefore critical that systemic supervision focuses on the delivery of quality service to widening groups of family clients. In this fashion, supervision is building institutional capacity to meet its goals and mission statement. As supervisees become junior and then senior staff members in those institutions, they pass on organizational cultural mores that enhance, diminish, or transform the institution.

Community resilience

As MFTs have opened new venues to provide systemic therapy, coupled with an ecosystemic philosophy that emphasizes the reciprocal nature of context and client system, it is not surprising that an emerging focus of systemic supervision is on community development as an outcome of MFT treatment. Today, several states have recognized the importance of providing MFT services in public schools (Vennum & Vennum, 2013). These states have established licensing provisions that include school-centered MFT supervision. McDonald et al. (1997) provided guidelines for systemic supervisors to integrate how to use school-based services to promote community development through clinical strategies. Ganong and Coleman (2002) demonstrated how developing family resilience needs to be conceived within a community resilience model. They focus on how MFT services can enhance community resilience when working with clients suffering from chronic illness, living in poverty, or are members of the gay, bisexual, lesbian, and transgendered community (Green, Murphy, Blumer, & Palmanteer, 2009) to name a few of the wider social networks that directly or indirectly benefit from effective MFT treatment.

Systemic supervisors must account for the potential impact their extended work may have on wide communities of citizens. This theme was reinforced by Koepke (2007) in her presidential address to the Groves Conference on Marriage and Family, where she emphasized all work needs to attend to issues affecting all families and professionals advocate for policies supportive of family well-being. Explicit in her presentation was information about how the roles and responsibilities of the systemic supervisor are shifting to attend to the development of long-term community solutions as well as the amelioration of presenting problems by the client system.

Emerging Issues for the Twenty First Century

Internet and wider system involvement

As the social bonds shift from physical to digital, the definition and makeup of the family morph into the future. Therapy in the future will be more about opening digital means to participate than it will be about getting the family in one office (Chapman, Baker, Nassar-McMillan, & Gerler, 2011). Systemic supervisors know how to use basic social communication technology such as the use of phones, videos, Skype, and e-mail to create meaningful therapeutic and supervisory environments. Innovative ways of using educational platforms, such as blackboard, and social media such as Facebook, Twitter, and Diigo, also are capturing the attention of training programs around the world (Pimmer, Linxen, & Gröhbiel, 2012).

Understanding and applying supervision in international contexts

MFT supervision co-mingles with the migration of MFT delivery systems. The systems in North America are well documented and researched. European models of training for systemic family therapy are similar to the models used in the North America. Welter-Enderlin (2005) provided an overview of the training and supervision MFT students in Zurich, Switzerland receive in the multidimensional treatment and training model. Significantly, the Zurich model is inspired by the tradition of enlightenment in European philosophy. Supervision must be isomorphic with these cultural and contextual influences if it is to remain viable. The concept of tailoring supervision to the unique cultural and social beliefs of a country (and even continent) is evident in the reports of international supervisory practices. For examples, MFT supervisors had better understand the role of the national ideology of socialism in many communist countries, such as Hungary (Cseh-Szombathy & Somlai, 1996) and the Czech Republic (Chvala, Trapkova, Novak, & Lattova, 2012).

In Australia, Darracott (2007) noted that if the MFT field is to become stronger, then it must consider "systemic influences upon indigenous Australians . . . unless the danger for family therapy is becoming stuck in a closed system that ignores the wider system" (p. 6). Lamer (2011) argued that Australian and New Zealand MFT supervision needs to focus on relational ethics and systemic treatment methods.

Reports about MFT services that have found their root in a culture have done so by adapting both Western views of family well-being and treatment, and indigenous cultural mores about family life. Bebtschuk, Smirnova, and Khayretdinov (2012) emphasized that recent changes in Russian society that directly influence family life must be accounted for by the MFT profession in that country. In China, Miller and Fang (2012) stated that by integrating the rich cultural traditions of valuing and activating multigenerational family connections, the field has emerged as a popular modality of mental health service. The same pathway to acceptance of MFT treatment by the Singapore public was reported by Sim (2012).

In India, Rastogi, Natrajan, and Thomas (2005) reflected on the long history of MFT service and indicate that as MFT adapted to the cultural context of India and its unique communities, the field gained more public and governmental approval. They suggested that for MFT to continue to gain stature, MFT providers will need supervisors who are skillful in the areas of system-based therapy training and the practice of MFT in India.

The portrait of MFT services in Africa as presented by Nwoye (2004) clearly defines the boundaries of professional practice. The systemic MFT supervisor must be aware of

> In a manner similar to its indigenous paradigm, modern African therapy incorporates sociological dimensions that are either ignored or quite unrecognized by Western therapists. The indigenous paradigm in personal agency terms emphasizes the idea of both spouses as centers of initiative, and blames marriage failures and conflicts on the inability of the spouses to live up to their respective traditional marriage role expectations (2000, p. 353).

Recently, Charlés (2010) detailed the support that family therapists who are acting as front line mental health providers in war-affected regions of Africa need as they deliver MFT services.

Conclusion

MFT systemic supervision is a complex and evolving undertaking. Not only do supervisors need to attend to the professional development and evaluation of therapists who can conceptualize and execute treatment practices in a systemic and culturally sensitive fashion but they also must consider the multidimensional needs of the client system and its wider community. The interaction between and among all elements of the systemic supervisory relationship follows a cultural exchange process where language, thoughts, and emotions co-mingle to form shared understandings of treatment goals and methods in therapy and supervision. Effective systemic supervisors understand how to use the natural context in the co-construction of learning environments that promote therapist growth and client success.

References

Ali, R., & Bachicha, D. (2012). Systemic supervision practices compared: A closer look at "reflection" and "self" in multisystemic therapy and family therapy supervision. *Clinical Child Psychology & Psychiatry, 17*(2), 192–207.

Aponte, H. (1992). Training the person of the therapist in structural family therapy. *Journal of Marital & Family Therapy, 18*(3), 269–281.

Aponte, H. (2009). Introduction for special section on training and supervision. *Journal of Marital & Family Therapy, 35*(4), 369–369.

Aponte, J., & Johnson, L. (2000). Ethnicity and supervision: Models, methods, processes, and issues. In J. F. Aponte & J. Wohl (Eds.), In *Psychological intervention and cultural diversity* (pp. 268–285). Needham Heights, MA: Allyn & Bacon.

Attneave, C. (1982). The role of support systems in building family strengths. *Family Strengths, 4*, 309–314.

Baker, L. K. (2013). *Perceptions and practices in MFT educational reform* (unpublished doctoral dissertation). University of Connecticut, Storrs, CT.

Bateson, G. (1951). Information and codification: A philosophical approach. In J. Ruesch & G. Bateson (Eds.), *Communication: The social matrix of psychiatry* (pp. 168–211). New York: Norton.

Bebtschuk, M., Smirnova, D., & Khayretdinov, O. (2012). Family and family therapy in Russia. *International Review of Psychiatry, 24*(2), 121–127.

Bernal, A., & Zera, D. (2012). Increasing accessibility in couple and family therapy training: Incorporating universal design for instruction. *Contemporary Family Therapy: An International Journal, 34*(1), 112–123.

Birchler, G. R. (1975). Live supervision and instant feedback in marriage and family therapy. *Journal of Marriage and Family Counseling, 1*(4), 331–342.

Bitar, G., Bean, R., & Bermúdez, J. (2007). Influences and processes in theoretical orientation development: A grounded theory pilot study. *American Journal of Family Therapy, 35*(2), 109–121.

Bobele, M. & Biever, J. (2014). Postmodern models of systemic therapy supervision. In T. Todd and C. Storm (Eds.), *The complete systemic supervisor: Context, philosophy, and methods* (2nd ed.). Oxford England: John Wiley.

Boston, P. (2010). The three faces of supervision: Individual learning, group learning, and supervisor accountability. In C. Burck & G. Daniel (Eds.), In *Mirrors and reflections: Processes of systemic supervision* (pp. 27–48). London: Karnac Books.

Bowen, M. (1978). *Family therapy in clinical practice.* New York: Jason Aronson.

Boyd, E. (2010). "Voice entitlement" narratives in supervision: Cultural and gendered influences on speaking and dilemmas in practice. In C. Burck & G. Daniel (Eds.), *Mirrors and reflections: Processes of systemic supervision* (pp. 203–223). London: Karnac Books.

Bradley, P. D., Bergen, L. P., Ginter, E. J., Williams, L. M., & Scalise, J. J. (2010). A survey of North American marriage and family therapy practitioners: A role delineation study. *American Journal of Family Therapy, 38*(4), 281–291. doi: 10.1080/01926187.2010.493119

Brenner, G. (2010). To speak or not to speak-the taboo of communication. *Journal of Gay & Lesbian Mental Health, 14*(3), 230–239.

Breunlin, D., Pinsof, W., Russell, W., & Lebow, J. (2011). Integrative problem-centered metaframeworks therapy I: Core concepts and hypothesizing. *Family Process, 50*(3), 293–313.

Briggs, K., Fournier, D., & Hendrix, C. (1999). Evaluating trainees' skill development: The family therapy skills checklist. *Contemporary Family Therapy: An International Journal, 21*(3), 353–371.

Burck, C. (2010). From hazardous to collaborative learning: Thinking systemically about live supervision group processes. In C. Burck & G. Daniel (Eds.), *Mirrors and reflections: Processes of systemic supervision* (pp. 141–162). London: Karnac Books.

Burck, C., & Daniel, G. (2010). Feminism and strategic therapy: Contradiction or complementarity?. In C. Burck & G. Daniel (Eds.), *Mirrors and reflections: Processes of systemic supervision.* London: Karnac Books.

Celano, M., Smith, C., & Kaslow, N. (2010). A competency-based approach to couple and family therapy supervision. *Psychotherapy: Theory, Research, Practice, and Training, 47*(1), 35–44.

Chapman, R., Baker, S., Nassar-McMillan, S., & Gerler, E., Jr. (2011). Cybersupervision: Further examination of synchronous and asynchronous modalities in counseling practicum supervision. *Counselor Education & Supervision, 50*(5), 298–313.

Charlés, L. (2010). Family therapists as front line mental health providers in war-affected regions: Using reflecting teams, scaling questions, and family members in a hospital in Central Africa. *Journal of Family Therapy, 32*(1), 27–42.

Charlés, L., Ticheli-Kallikas, M., Tyner, K., & Barber-Stephens, B. (2005). Crisis management during "live" supervision: Clinical and instructional matters. *Journal of Marital & Family Therapy, 31*(3), 207–219.

Chvala, V., Trapkova, L., Novak, T., & Lattova, Z. (2012). Family therapy in the Czech Republic. *International Review of Psychiatry, 24*(2), 157–161.

Cseh-Szombathy, L., & Somlai, P. (1996). Family theory and research in Hungary. *Marriage & Family Review, 22*(3–4), 181–201.

Darracott, R. (2007). Australian family therapy: Have we lived up to our mission statement? *Australian & New Zealand Journal of Family Therapy, 28*(1), 1–10.

DeRoma, V., Hickey, D., & Stanek, K. (2007). Methods of supervision in marriage and family therapist training: A brief report. *North American Journal of Psychology, 9*(3), 415–422.

Donnelly, H., & Gosbee, M. (2009). Family of origin supervision in the workplace: Impacts on therapist and team functioning. *Australian & New Zealand Journal of Family Therapy, 30*(4), 300–314.

Edwards, T., & Heshmati, A. (2003). A guide for beginning family therapy group supervisors. *American Journal of Family Therapy, 31*(4), 295–304.

Ganong, L., & Coleman, M. (2002). Family resilience in multiple contexts. *Journal of Marriage & the Family, 64*(2), 346–348.

García, A., & Guevara, L. (2007). Voicing voices. In H. Anderson & P. Jensen (Eds.), *Innovations in the reflecting process* (pp. 58–73). London: Karnac Books.

Gardner, B., & Butler, M. (2009). Enacting relationships in MFT: The empirical, theoretical, and clinical case for incorporating enactments as common factors in the best practice model. *Journal of Couple & Relationship Therapy, 8*(4), 306–324.

Gilberto-Rorman, L. (2014). The transgenerational models. In T. Todd and C. Storm (Eds.), *The complete systemic supervisor: Context, philosophy, and methods* (2nd ed.). Oxford England: John Wiley.

Gingrich, F. (2001). A family systems model of marriage and family therapy supervision. *Marriage & Family: A Christian Journal, 4*(4), 343–365.

Green, M., & Dekkers, T. (2010). Attending to power and diversity in supervision: An exploration of supervisee learning outcomes and satisfaction with supervision. *Journal of ist Family Therapy, 22*(4), 293–312.

Green, M., Murphy, M., Blumer, M., & Palmanteer, D. (2009). Marriage and family therapists' comfort level working with gay and lesbian individuals, couples, and families. *American Journal of Family Therapy, 37*(2), 159–168.

Green, S., Shilts, L., & Bacigalupe, G. (2001). When approved is not enough: Development of a supervision consultation model. *Journal of Marital & Family Therapy, 27*(4), 515–525.

Guanipa, C. (2002). A preliminary instrument to evaluate multicultural issues in marriage and family therapy supervision. *Clinical Supervisor, 21*(1), 59–75.

Harper-Jaques, S., & Limacher, L. (2009). Providing marriage and family therapy supervision in a multidisciplinary psychiatric setting: Contextual sensitivity as a cornerstone of supervision. *Journal of Systemic Therapies, 28*(3), 49–58.

Hendrix, C., Fournier, D., & Briggs, K. (2001). Impact of co-therapy teams on client outcomes and therapist training in marriage and family therapy. *Contemporary Family Therapy, 23*(1), 63–82.

Hernández, P. (2003). The cultural context model in supervision: An illustration. *Journal of Feminist Family Therapy: An International Forum, 15*(4), 1–18.

Hodgson, J., Johnson, L., Ketring, S., Wampler, R., & Lamson, A. (2005). Integrating research and clinical training in marriage and family therapy training programs. *Journal of Marital & Family Therapy, 31*(1), 75–88.

Inman, A. (2006). Supervisor multicultural competence and its relation to supervisory process and outcome. *Journal of Marital & Family Therapy, 32*(1), 73–85.

Johnson, L., & Caldwell, B. (2011). Race, gender, and therapist confidence: Effects on satisfaction with the therapeutic relationship in MFT. *American Journal of Family Therapy, 39*(4), 307–324.

Karam, E., & Sprenkle, D. (2010). The research-informed clinician: A guide to training the next-generation MFT. *Journal of Marital & Family Therapy, 36*(3), 307–319.

Koepke, L. (2007). A call to action: Five policy proposals on behalf of all families – President's address to the 2007 groves conference on marriage and family. *Journal of Feminist Family Therapy, 19*(3), 1–12.

Lamer, G. (2011). Relational ethics and systemic therapy. *Australian & New Zealand Journal of Family Therapy, 32*(1), 1–1.

Lawless, J., Gale, J., & Bacigalupe, G. (2001). The discourse of race and culture in family therapy supervision: A conversation analysis. *Contemporary Family Therapy: An International Journal, 23*(2), 181–197.

Lebow, J. (2014). Research, evidence-based models, and supervision. In T. Todd and C. Storm (Eds.), *The complete systemic supervisor: Context, philosophy, and methods* (2nd ed.). Oxford England: John Wiley.

Lee, M., & Vennum, A. (2010). Using critical incident journaling to encourage cultural awareness in doctoral marriage and family therapy students. *Journal of Family Psychotherapy, 21*(4), 238–252.

Lee, R., Nichols, D., Nichols, W., & Odom, T. (2004). Trends in family therapy supervision: The past 25 years and into the future. *Journal of Marital & Family Therapy, 30*(1), 61–69.

Leong, F., & Kalibatseva, Z. (2013). *The Oxford handbook of research strategies for clinical psychology* (pp. 413–433). Comer, J. S., & Kendall, P. C. (Ed.). New York: Oxford University Press.

London, S., & Tarragona, M. (2007). Collaborative therapy and supervision in a psychiatric hospital. In H. Anderson & D. Gehart (Eds.), *Collaborative therapy: Relationships and conversations that make a difference* (pp. 251–267). New York: Routledge/Taylor & Francis Group.

Long, J., & Serovich, J. (2003). Incorporating sexual orientation into MFT training programs: Infusion and inclusion. *Journal of Marital & Family Therapy, 29*(1), 59–67.

Lowe, R., Hunt, C., & Simmons, P. (2008). Towards multi-positioned live supervision in family therapy: Combining treatment and observation teams with first- and second-order perspectives. *Contemporary Family Therapy: An International Journal, 30*(1), 3–14.

Lyness, A., & Helmeke, K. (2008). Clinical mentorship: One more aspect of feminist supervision. *Journal of Feminist Family Therapy: An International Forum, 20*(2), 166–199.

Maione, P. (2011). Help me help you: Suggested guidelines for case presentation. *Contemporary Family Therapy: An International Journal, 33*(1), 17–24.

McDonald, L., Billingham, S., Conrad, T., Morgan, A., & Payton, E. (1997). Families and schools together (FAST): Integrating community development with clinical strategies. *Families in Society: The Journal of Contemporary Social Services, 78*(2), 140–155.

Mcneil, S., Pavkov, T., Hecker, L., & Killmer, J. (2012). Marriage and family therapy graduate students' satisfaction with training regarding religion and spirituality. *Contemporary Family Therapy: An International Journal, 34*(4), 468–480.

Miller, J. (2011). Special section: International issues in clinical practice and training. *Journal of Systemic Therapies, 30*(2), 41–42.

Miller, J., & Fang, X. (2012). Marriage and family therapy in the people's republic of China: Current issues and challenges. *Journal of Family Psychotherapy, 23*(3), 173–183.

Miller, J., Todahl, J., & Platt, J. (2010). The core competency movement in marriage and family therapy: Key considerations from other disciplines. *Journal of Marital & Family Therapy, 36*(1), 59–70.

Moore, A., Hamilton, S., Crane, D., & Fawcett, D. (2011). The influence of professional license type on the outcome of family therapy. *American Journal of Family Therapy, 39*(2), 149–161.

Moorhouse, A., & Carr, A. (2001). A study of live supervisory phone-ins in collaborative family therapy: Correlates of client cooperation. *Journal of Marital and Family Therapy, 27*(2), 241–249.

Morgan, M., & Sprenkle, D. (2007). Toward a common-factors approach to supervision. *Journal of Marital & Family Therapy, 33*(1), 1–17.

Murphy, M., & Wright, D. (2005). Supervisees' perspectives of power use in supervision. *Journal of Marital & Family Therapy, 31*(3), 283–295.

Nelson, T., & Graves, T. (2011). Core competencies in advanced training: What supervisors say about graduate training. *Journal of Marital & Family Therapy, 37*(4), 429–451.

Nelson, T., & Smock, S. (2005). Challenges of an outcome-based perspective for marriage and family therapy education. *Family Process, 44*(3), 355–362.

Nichols, W., Nichols, D., & Hardy, K. (1990). Supervision in family therapy: A decade restudy. *Journal of Marital & Family Therapy, 16*(3), 275–285.

Nwoye, A. (2004). The shattered microcosm: Imperatives for improved family therapy in Africa in the 21st century. *Contemporary Family Therapy: An International Journal, 26*(2), 143–164.

Palmer-Olsen, L., Gold, L., & Woolley, S. (2011). Supervising emotionally focused therapists: A systematic research-based model. *Journal of Marital & Family Therapy, 37*(4), 411–426.

Pimmer, C., Linxen, S., & Gröhbiel, U. (2012). Facebook as a learning tool? A case study on the appropriation of social network sites from mobile phones in developing countries. *British Journal of Educational Technology, 43*(5), 726–738.

Rastogi, M., Natrajan, R., & Thomas, V. (2005). On becoming a profession: The growth of marriage and family therapy in India. *Contemporary Family Therapy: An International Journal, 27*(4), 453–471.

Reiner, P. (2014). Psychoanalytic approaches to systemic therapy supervision. In T. Todd and C. Storm (Eds.), *The complete systemic supervisor: Context, philosophy, and methods* (2nd ed.). Oxford England: John Wiley.

Ren, R. (2008). Quality of supervisor-subordinate relationship, cultural values, and organizational justice. Doctoral dissertation, Texas A&M University. Available electronically from http://hdl.handle.net/1969.1/ETD-TAMU-2554

Rigazio-DiGilio, S. A. (2014). Expanding the focus of supervision: Common themes across integrative models. In T. Todd & C. Storm (Eds.), *The complete systemic supervisor: Context, philosophy, and methods* (2nd ed.,). Oxford England: John Wiley.

Rigazio-DiGilio, S., Ivey, A., Kunkler-Peck, K., & Grady, L. (2005). *Community genograms: Using individual, family, and cultural narratives with clients.* New York: Teachers College Press.

Rigazio-DiGilio, S. A. (2000). Reconstructing psychological distress and disorder from a relational perspective: A systemic, coconstructive-developmental framework. In R. Neimeyer & J. Raskin (Eds.), *Constructions of disorder* (pp. 309–332). Washington, DC: American Psychological Association.

Rigazio-DiGilio, S. A. (2007). Systemic cognitive-developmental supervision: Accessing and extending meaning and options within the supervisory exchange. Invited workshop for the Third International Interdisciplinary Conference on Clinical Supervision. Sponsored by the National Institute of Drug Abuse and the University of Buffalo. Amherst, New York.

Rigazio-DiGilio, S. A., & LaPlante, D. (2009) Supervision refresher course. Invited Pre-Conference Institute for the Annual AAMFT Conference: Sacramento, CA.

Rigazio-DiGilio, S. A., Ivey, A. E., & Locke, D. C. (1997). Continuing the post-modern dialogue: Enhancing and contextualizing multiple voices. *Journal of Mental Health Counseling, 19*, 233–255.

Roberto, L. (1997). Supervision: The transgenerational models. In T. Todd and C. Storm (Eds.), *The complete systemic supervisor: Context, philosophy, and methods* (pp. 135–155). Needham Heights, MA: Allyn and Bacon.

Russell, C., DuPree, W., Beggs, M., Peterson, C., & Anderson, M. (2007). Responding to remediation and gatekeeping challenges in supervision. *Journal of Marital & Family Therapy, 33*(2), 227–244.

Saayman, R., Saayman, G., & Wiens, S. (2006). Training staff in multiple family therapy in a children's psychiatric hospital: From theory to practice. *Journal of Family Therapy, 28*(4), 404–419.

Samara, A. (2006). Group supervision in graduate education: A process of supervision skill development and text improvement. *Higher Education Research and Development, 25*(2), 115–129.

Schindler Zimmerman, T., & Haddock, S. (2001). The weave of gender and culture in the tapestry of a family therapy training program: Promoting social justice in the practice of family therapy. *Journal of Feminist Family Therapy: An International Forum, 12*(2–3), 1–31.

Sexton, T., Kinser, J., & Hanes, C. (2008). Beyond a single standard: Levels of evidence approach for evaluating marriage and family therapy research and practice. *Journal of Family Therapy, 30*(4), 386–398.

Silverthorn, B., Bartle-Haring, S., Meyer, K., & Toviessi, P. (2009). Does live supervision make a difference? A multilevel analysis. *Journal of Marital & Family Therapy, 35*(4), 406–414.

Sim, T. (2012). The growing pains of family therapy in Singapore. *Journal of Family Therapy, 34*(2), 204–224.

Smith, G. (2011). Cut the crap: Language – Risks and relationships in systemic therapy and supervision. *Australian & New Zealand Journal of Family Therapy*, *32*(1), 58–69.

Smith, J., Finn, S., Swain, N., & Handler, L. (2010). Therapeutic assessment of families in healthcare settings: A case presentation of the model's application. *Families, Systems, & Health*, *28*(4), 369–386.

Stokes, S., & Molarte, B. (2011). Supervision in marriage and family therapy. In L. Metcalf (Ed.), *Marriage and family therapy: A practice-oriented approach* (pp. 411–442). New York: Springer Publishing Co.

Storm, C. (2011). What is unique about supervising couple therapists? One supervisor's beginning answer. In J. L. Wetchler (Ed.), *Handbook of clinical issues in couple therapy* (2nd ed.) (pp. 329–343). New York: Routledge/Taylor & Francis Group.

Storm, C., Todd, T., Sprenkle, D., & Morgan, M. (2001). Gaps between MFT supervision assumptions and common practice: Suggested best practices. *Journal of Marital & Family Therapy*, *27*(2), 227–239.

Styczynski, L., & Greenberg, L. (2008). Supervision of couples and family therapy. In A. K. Hess, K. D. Hess, & T. H. Hess (Eds.), *Psychotherapy supervision: Theory, research, and practice* (2nd ed.) (pp. 179–199). Hoboken, NJ: John Wiley & Sons Inc.

Todd, T. (1997). Purposive systemic supervision models. In T. Todd and C. Storm (Eds.), *The complete systemic supervisor: Context, philosophy, and methods* (pp. 173–194). Needham Heights, MA: Allyn and Bacon.

Todd, T. (2014). Classic systemic supervision models and beyond. In T. Todd and C. Storm (Eds.), *The complete systemic supervisor: Context, philosophy, and methods* (2nd ed.). Oxford England: John Wiley.

Todd, T., & Storm, C. (2014). *The complete systemic supervisor: Context, philosophy, and methods* (2nd ed.). Oxford: John Wiley.

Tyson, L., Pérusse, R., & Stone, C. (2008). Providing culturally responsive supervision. In L. E. Tyson, J. R. Culbreth, & J. A. Harrington (Eds.), *Critical incidents in clinical supervision: Addictions, community, and school counselling* (pp. 191–197). Alexandria, VA: American Counseling Association.

Ungar, M. (2006). Practicing as a postmodern supervisor. *Journal of Marital and Family Therapy*, *32*(1), 59–71.

U.S. Department of Health and Human Services. (2001). Mental health: culture, race, and ethnicity – A supplement to mental health: A report of the Surgeon General. Rockville, MD: U.S. Public Health Service.

von Bertalanffy, L. (1950). An outline of general system theory. *British Journal of the Philosophy of Science*, *1*, 134–165.

Vennum, A., & Vennum, D. (2013). Expanding our reach: Marriage and family therapists in the public school system. *Contemporary Family Therapy: An International Journal*, *35*, 41.

Welter-Enderlin, R. (2005). The state of the art of training in systemic family therapy in Switzerland. *Family Process*, *44*(3), 303–320.

Wiener, N. (1948). *Cybernetics; or control and communication in the animal and the machine.* Oxford: John Wiley.

Wittgenstein, L. (1966). *Philosophical investigations.* Oxford: Macmillian.

Woolley, S. (2010). Purposes, diversities, and futures in MFT doctoral education. *Journal of Marital & Family Therapy*, *36*(3), 282–290.

Wynne, L., Shields, C., & Sirkin, M. (1992). Illness, family theory, and family therapy: Part I. Conceptual issues. *Family Process*, *31*, 3–18.

31

Challenges and Possibilities in Group Supervision

Marie-Louise Ögren, Siv Boalt Boëthius, and Eva Sundin

Introduction

Supervision is mandatory in most psychotherapy training programmes today. In 1978, the Swedish National Board of Health and Welfare required a license for psychotherapists. Criteria were stipulated for psychotherapy education which gave supervision an important role. A minimum level for quantity and quality of supervision was established. A 5-year university education leading to a psychology degree was established in 1982. The Swedish education is a two-step process, where the second step after basic course work is a 3-year continuing education in psychotherapy at undergraduate level. After completing basic course work, it is possible to work with psychotherapy under supervision. When the higher education level has been completed, it is possible to apply for licensing as a psychotherapist with the National Board of Health and Welfare. The education programmes mentioned were for many years based on individual supervision, but the trend is that courses on both levels are trading individual supervision for group supervision. As far as education programmes for supervisors are concerned, the tradition of group supervision was established right from the start, with the first programme in 1974.

Group supervision can be described as ". . . the regular meeting of a group of supervisees (a) with a designated supervisor or supervisors, (b) to monitor the quality of their work, and (c) to further their understanding of themselves as clinicians, of the clients with whom they work, and of service delivery in general. These supervisees are aided in achieving these goals by their supervisor(s) and by their feedback from and interactions with each other" (Bernard & Goodyear, 2009, p. 244). Holloway and Johnston (1985) summarized the situation of group supervision as "widely practiced, but little understood," which at that point in time was most relevant. Ten years later, Wampold and Holloway (1997) emphasized the need for more research on psychotherapy supervision. As a step in approaching and gradually encompassing

The Wiley International Handbook of Clinical Supervision, First Edition. Edited by C. Edward Watkins, Jr. and Derek L. Milne.

the complexity of the field, it is suggested that the various components involved in supervision should be examined systematically and related to one another (Rønnestad & Ladany, 2006). Our studies of psychotherapy supervision in a group setting have investigated some components of this complex training field; for example, the trainee's attainment of knowledge and skills, relationships among trainees in the supervisory group and between trainee and supervisor, as well as supervisory style and the importance of the organizational frameworks.

Group supervision has a lot to offer, provided that the supervisor has the competence to handle the dynamics in a small group and to understand the impact of organizational structures. Supervision in a group can never be seen as an isolated phenomenon. It is always part of a context defined by the surrounding organizational structure. Group supervision is also the type of supervision that is most often possible from the standpoint of an organization's economic framework and conditions. Marked advantages with group supervision are the broader frame of reference that the group members' combined experience and competence can offer, together with the exposure to a greater number of clients (Andersson, 2008; Baruch, 2009; Bernard & Goodyear, 2009; Hayes, Blackman, & Brennan, 2001; Jacobsson, Lindgren, & Hau, 2012; Mastoras & Andrews, 2011; Ögren & Sundin, 2009; Ögren, Boalt Boëthius, & Sundin, 2008b; Riva & Cornish, 1995). Group supervision also seems to diminish hierarchical issues between supervisor and supervisee, increase the variety of behavioral and experiential supervision strategies, and help alleviate novices' perceptions of intellectual and emotional isolation (Goodyear & Nelson, 1997; Watkins, 1997).

From Individual to Group Supervision

The supervision situation involves, among other things, an encounter between the supervisor and the supervisee, with their different personalities, attitudes, life experiences, professional experiences, and capacities, in a specific work environment and with various clients. Unique constellations are therefore formed in the encounter. It is natural that the situation becomes unique and extremely complex. Group supervision contributes, to a still higher degree than individual supervision, to the complexity of the supervision situation. The group can convey a multitude of views regarding the work of the individual and, furthermore, in favorable cases, contribute to a feeling in the individual group member of being less exposed since the uncertainty of the other group members is made apparent. However, the group also stimulates transferences and projections, both toward the supervisor and between the group members. Exposing one's difficulties and shortcomings, not only to the supervisor but also to the others in the group, may be accompanied by feelings of shame, just as success in the therapy may result in collegial competition and rivalry (Gautier, 2009). The evaluation of the supervisees' work also takes place within the frame of the group, contributing further to the complexity of the situation.

Individual supervision, compared with group supervision, can offer more depth and more chances to highlight the individual therapist's assets and shortcomings. This is possibly one reason for the individual format of supervision's having been the main type of training for so long, as has been confirmed by a number of reviews (e.g., Holloway, 1984; Lambert & Arnold, 1987; Stoltenberg, McNeill, & Crethar, 1994; Worthington, 1987). However, as was pointed out by Milne and James (2002), the research literature includes only a small number of systematic evaluations of supervision programmes. Whitman and colleagues (Whitman, Ryan, & Rubenstein, 2001) suggested that the lack of comparative analysis of different supervision formats is probably at least partly due to the fact that the courses vary widely in terms of length, format, content, who teaches the course, and for whom the course is designed. A small number of studies have been published which compare individual and group supervision in psychotherapy (Grigg, 2006; Hawkins & Shohet, 1989; Nguyen, 2003). In an early study, Lanning (1971) reported no significant difference between individual and group supervision based on measuring the client's perceptions of the trainee's capacity to engage in the therapeutic relationship, the trainee's perception of his/her own therapeutic relationship, and the trainee's perception of the supervisory relationship. Similar results, that is, no substantial differences between training formats, were found in a study that compared small-group supervision, large group supervision, and combined group and individual supervision (Ray & Altekruse, 2000).

Research on group supervision started in Sweden in the beginning of the 1990s. It used as its vantage point the challenge of showing benefits rather than downsides to group supervision. Generally, experienced supervisors were, at this point in time, educated in the dyadic perspective and had limited knowledge about a group's interaction and dynamics. Often, supervisors were skeptical about the potential success of conducting supervisory work in a group setting. Nor was it unusual that supervisors with experience of individual supervision concluded after having conducted group supervision "never again group supervision."

Group supervision places demands on the supervisor's knowledge of the dynamics of the small group. To favor constructive and prevent destructive group processes, the supervisors must be well acquainted with the dynamics that characterize small work group and, at the same time, be able to handle his or her role as a supervisor and leader. These necessary qualities in supervisors make it possible for them to educate the supervisees in how best to take advantage of the group's potential for an optimal exchange of experiences (Goodyear & Nelson, 1997; Ögren & Jonsson, 2003; Ögren, Boalt Boëthius, & Olsson, 2008a; Proctor & Inskipp, 2001; Sundin, Ögren, & Boalt Boëthius, 2008). As a whole, it has been found that therapists who have participated in the exchange of experiences made possible in group supervision feel a greater confidence in their ability to deal with a diversity of clinical scenarios (Goodyear & Nelson, 1997; Jacobsson et al., 2012; Wheeler & Richards, 2007). It seems as though supervisees, regardless of the context, see a value in the extended frame of reference and appreciate the chance to get insight into the clinical experiences of the other group members.

Different Formats in Group Supervision

Group supervision as a concept appears to have been used broadly for support efforts within education and health-care often without its being clear what is actually intended in terms of purpose, goals, and methods. Goals and framework within a programme of education are usually clear and definite. When it comes to supervision within a treatment context, goals and frame structures can show significant variations. It is of great importance in such cases for the supervisor to obtain solid information about the expectations of management as well as of the supervision group. A prerequisite for achieving a satisfying supervisory performance is for the supervisor to anchor his or her assignment with both management and the supervision group and – in other words – to have an organizational mind set as well.

Group supervision can be described from various perspectives, one of which is the group's approach to its work. Proctor and Inskipp (2001) asserted – from a clinical perspective – that there are four different ways of using the group in psychotherapy supervision: *authoritative*, *participative*, *cooperative*, and *peer-group supervision*. The main difference among these four types of supervision is the extent to which group interactions are taken into account in the learning process. The two first categories appear to describe the format most often seen within various types of educational and organizational programmes, which is why the focus is on these two formats in this chapter.

Studies on group supervision concerning the usage of a group format have indicated that in the initial phase of group supervision, there is a need to receive supervision *in* a group. One supervisee presents a clinical situation, after which the presenter and then the other supervisees, in turn, explore this situation with the supervisor. In the next phase, it appears that the unique exchange of experiences that the group can offer is most valued. In other words, supervision gradually moves toward involving the group members in listening to each others' opinions and perspectives (Baruch, 2009; Goodyear & Nelson, 1997).

It is important to note that the various treatment traditions are necessarily connected to specific supervision concepts. Within the cognitive-behavioral therapy (CBT) tradition, the conviction is often expressed that supervision should be primarily individually focused – that is, supervision in a group. At the same time, the supervision in this case does take place in a group setting, meaning that the supervisor even here needs to have solid knowledge of small-group interaction processes. In one of our studies, we examined differences between supervisors' and novice supervisees' experiences of actual and desired usage of the group format in psychotherapy supervision (Ögren & Sundin, 2006). We also examined differences between supervisors and supervisees who worked with psychodynamic versus cognitive-behavioral group supervision. The results showed significant differences between actual and ideal usage of the group format examined. The differences pointed in the same direction; the group format should be used to a larger degree as a teaching tool. Psychodynamic supervisors and supervisees presented, to some extent, higher wish ratings compared with those of cognitive-behavioral supervisors and supervisees. However, from a supervisor and supervisee perspective, a higher awareness and a greater focus on group processes in the supervision group were desired. A reasonable way to interpret these results is to discern a wish for increased competence at handling the group format in order to make the supervision meaningful.

The conclusion we have drawn is that a deepened understanding about the group's dynamic is significant no matter which treatment tradition is being followed. To handle various group situations requires experience and knowledge on the part of the supervisor. Supervisees feel intuitively whether supervisors in their leadership roles understand the group's ongoing interaction or not. Obviously, the group supervision must never be allowed to break down so that the supervision is primarily about the group members' internal relationships. The focus must be kept on the task – namely, to supervise the handling of current cases. At the same time, the dynamic that inevitably arises in a group can, in some cases, cause blockages that in turn create obstacles to learning and creativity. Here supervisors must put their experience to use. They need to be able to identify what is happening as well as to find appropriate solutions and interventions to resolve the blockages. The best case scenario in such situations is found when the supervisees gain valuable insights about the group's interaction and about aspects of the client case.

Organizational Frames, Core Contents, Interaction: A Model

In order to give an overview of the phenomena that can be observed in various types of supervision groups, we have used a model based on analyses of small groups in the workplace (Boalt Boëthius, 1993). This framework enables the process in group supervision to be described and analyzed with regard to three perspectives. These are (a) the organizational framework of the supervision group, (b) the core content, the object of supervision, and (c) the interaction among the group members and their relationships with the supervisor as an authority. The basic purpose of our model is to find out to what degree the work done by a group is supported by an adequate organizational framework and how this concordance or lack of concordance between framework conditions and core content reverberates in the relationships among the group members and in relation to management authorities. The model can be seen as a further development of models with a focus on supervision and as a complement to existing models (Ekstein & Wallerstein, 1958, 1977; Hawkins & Shohet, 1989; Szecsödy, 1990).

Organizational frameworks refer to the relationships that can be defined as basic conditions for supervision. The fact that these basic conditions are clear does not necessarily mean that the group members perceive them in the same way as do the supervisor or those in charge of the work. The individual group members' experience of different framework conditions is at least as important to understand as the actual external conditions for the work in question. The organizational framework that is built up around a supervision group automatically gives rise to different processes. The structure, that is, the combination of framework factors and the interaction among these, has a deciding significance for how, for example, communication, information, decision-making, and role-assuming play out.

The object of supervision or the core content in psychotherapy training is the psychotherapeutic process between therapist and patient. It includes the therapist's attitude to the clinical material and the way regression and other defense mechanisms are dealt with as well as transference and countertransference. Variations in clients' problems and motivation level may naturally also have an effect on an inexperienced supervisee's experience of the therapist role and the supervision process. The third perspective, which refers to *interactional relationships*, holds true primarily for the internal relationships among the supervisees (horizontal relationships) and between the supervisees and the supervisor. It concerns how these interactional processes change over time and it also concerns relationships to authorities such as course tutors and managers and to various theory constellations that have controlling effects (vertical relationships). This third perspective – interactional relationships – can be seen as an effect of the two formerly discussed perspectives. The perspectives can be well cut off from each other at times; at other times, they overlap. One way to use the model is to view it as a spotlight that can be pointed in one way or the other, creating a grid through which we can interpret a certain pattern of behavior.

Using this model, we believe it is possible to arrive at a comprehensible description of even relatively complex phenomena in various types of work groups, including group supervision. To keep the three perspectives in mind demands that we include – in addition to the client's, the therapist's, and the group's perspective (core content and interaction) – a clear picture of the organizational conditions. The model allows us to alternate the focus from core content to organizational framework conditions including the surrounding society, herewith facilitating the understanding of interactions that arise among group members and of interactions connected to how the group works as a unit. The following section presents an application of the model that purports to give a deeper understanding of phenomena in group supervision.

Application of the Model

As a basis for any operation to function optimally, be it an activity, an organization, or a group, there must be clear but flexible organizational frameworks in place that can both bind together and integrate the various functions that bear up the operation. At the same time, the frameworks need to be formed so that they can harbor feelings and experiences associated with the current task. For example, they should be strong enough to withstand various strains and testing of limits. To be concrete, let us say that a health-care operation begins to draw its patients from a different patient group than earlier. Accordingly, the entire organizational framework must be reevaluated. The framework is supposed to constitute the foundation thanks to which the operation can harbor and withstand challenges and criticism internally and externally. It is not enough to make small adjustments, for example, adding a new activity or changing the conference system. It is necessary to look over the core operation in its entirety and to examine to what degree the framework can provide the supports that are needed. If there are clear shortcomings, it is important to figure out how the frameworks actually look in relation to the core operation and how they are perceived by the parties involved.

To be part of a supervision group can be rewarding and enlightening, but it is also possible to feel excluded and inhibited. Whether a supervisor or supervisee, it is necessary for every member of a small group to understand what is happening when the situation suddenly changes from feeling right to feeling boring or unpleasant. A member might suddenly go from feeling energetic and productive to feeling that he or she has nothing to contribute and that participating is meaningless. Many people often blame themselves when they have not achieved what was expected or when they feel that the supervisor or someone else in the group has not understood or supported them adequately. It should be remembered that a bad feeling in a group does not always have to be about ourselves or another individual member. There are many reasons why a group underperforms, loses its creativity, or comes to a standstill. It might stem from the interaction in the group, the work content, or the external framework conditions such as the group's composition and size or the leadership. Weak leadership, for example, can leave room for strong informal leaders to take over. Further, the group might end up in a situation dominated by destructive competition and envy. The composition of the group might mean that some members take or are given room at the expense of others. Finally, the setup of the operation might make it more or less impossible for the group members to do a good job (Gautier, 2009; Plant & Smith, 2009).

When conflicts arise in a work group or between groups in an organization, the first reaction is often to look for causes in the interaction within the group, between individuals, or in relation to the leadership. It is easy to perceive an individual group member's difficulties in therapy supervision as an expression of his or her personal problems. This might, in fact, be true, but it might just as well be a case of the member's receiving a patient with complications that he or she does not understand and that the supervision group cannot handle within the existing framework (core content). It might also be so that the group's composition is so unfortunate that an individual group member cannot find his or her place within it. Perhaps the dynamics in the relationship between supervisor and supervisee do not work equally well for everyone (the organizational framework). A benefit of our model is that it can increase the awareness of the fact that many conflicts and difficulties do not primarily have to do with the individual group members, but can instead have arisen or have been reinforced by deficiencies in concordance between core content and framework conditions. Certain educational backgrounds lead people to be extra alert to relationships and patterns of interaction, making it easy to get caught up in personal relationships. In such cases, there is a risk that the significance of the content of the work will be overlooked or that the needed support by an adequate organization with a well-thought-out framework will not be taken into account. In the following, previous and current research is described using the model as a point of departure.

Group Supervision and the Organizational Framework

Core content and interactional processes at the group and organizational levels can have deficiencies such that decision-making is undermined and well-prepared plans are thwarted. An adequate quality control can be rendered difficult or impossible. Boundary functions that concern responsibility and delegation are put out of play and agreement about time and place is neglected. When it comes to group supervision, there is a reason, especially in the beginning, to reflect on how different dimensions of dependency are generated and handled. On the part of the supervisees, a wish to be seen and confirmed sparks early emotional needs and can easily create a strong dependency or its opposite in the form of an active distance-taking stance as a shield against closeness and dependency. Supervisors should be aware of their corresponding needs to be confirmed not only by their supervision group but also by the course tutors, needs that sometimes can contradict each other. The most significant organizational frameworks appear to be the group's goal, organizational context, earlier history and culture, leadership style, and financial frameworks. Frameworks of special importance for the functioning of group supervision are the group's composition, size, time frame, and inter-group relationships. In addition, there are other special conditions to bear in mind, such as contract and examination requirements as well as the need for regular staff meetings with the supervisors and the course tutors.

The organizational frameworks that have been built around an operation give rise to different group processes, such as communication, information, decision-making, norm-building, and role-taking. In the beginning, the structure (i.e., the combination of frameworks and the interplay among them) has a great significance for how the different processes that follow in their wake are evolved. But with time, the predominance of structure changes and various group processes tend to take over the main significance. As a consequence, it fairly soon becomes difficult to distinguish between structure and process. They tend to be woven together into an intricate pattern and they take on a character of their own. By thinking through the framework conditions for the operation before it starts, it is possible to create reasonable chances for a group to function in a satisfactory manner. In a corresponding way, it is easy, despite the best intentions of the group members, supervisor, and course tutor, to end up in frustrating and uncomfortable group situations. When this happens, it often stems from a deficient understanding of the initial framework conditions.

The Goal and Purpose of the Supervision

In a study of how organizational framework conditions within Swedish education programmes for psychotherapy are perceived by course tutors and supervisors, respectively (Ögren et al., 2008a), the results showed a very good agreement when it came to the goal of the supervision and the over-arching frameworks. It was clear that course tutors and supervisors had similar perceptions about the significance of clear goals and a clearly defined aim for the group supervision. At the same time, matters took a more varied shape in reality. The supervisors emphasized primarily the importance of a clear framework, clear information, and fixed routines for evaluation, assessment, and conflict resolution. The accessibility and general competence of the course tutors were also considered to be important.

However, formalized training situations have drawbacks as well as advantages. It might be worthwhile mentioning that apart from increased knowledge and work satisfaction, there is also a risk for a normative culture that promotes too much conformity. An expression of such a process is that supervisees who are enrolled in an education programme tend to adapt to what they perceive that the supervisor wants rather than what they actually believe in. In a longitudinal study of a continuing education course in psychotherapy, Carlsson (2012) found that many students, a few years after having finished their education, had changed their focus compared with what they had described during their education. Not until then had they felt free to find their own model. Their compliance in relation to their supervisors during their education was interpreted to stem from a need to receive confirmation and to adapt to an expected role as a professional therapist.

The Supervisor's Leadership Style

Common to all group supervision is that supervisors must find a way to relate and a leadership style that matches the group's format. Earlier studies suggest that the supervisor's teaching style and function as a role model influence the development of the learning process as well as group processes and the group climate (Ögren, Apelman, & Klawitter, 2001; Proctor, 2008; Proctor & Inskipp, 2001). Ögren, Jonsson, and Sundin (2005) reported evidence that the supervisor's style affected the focus of the supervision, the experience of the group climate, and the perception of how much one learned as a supervisee.

In a qualitative interview study of 18 supervision pairs (supervisor–supervisee), Reichelt and Skjerve (2002) found that supervisors with a nonauthoritarian style, who were accepting and affirming, were perceived as facilitating positive development. In the same way, supervisors who both brought forth and reinforced the group's competence and were prepared to share their own experiences with the supervisees were perceived as contributing to the supervisees' development. On the other hand, supervisors who were perceived as directive and authoritarian, and who intervened too quickly with their own interpretations and instructions, contributed to the supervisees' feeling uncertain and inhibited.

The research of Rutter (2007) on effective group supervision indicates that experienced counselors considered the main factors for creating a good working climate to be the installment of trust and a sense of security, the relationships among group members, and the opportunities to learn from the supervisor and from one another. Most studies on the role of the supervisor in group supervision show that the balance between the different needs of the members, the requirements of the education programme, and not least the supervisors own ambition can be considerably taxing.

Group Composition

In general, heterogeneous groups tend to function better than homogeneous groups, and this applies to supervision groups as well. However, many studies indicate that too great a degree of heterogeneity with regard to personal and professional background, education, and nationality, as well as previous contact with other group members, may be a negative contributory factor. Individual differences in motivation, suitability for the professional task, maturity, and, in serious cases, individual supervisee dysfunction may contribute to difficulties in establishing good supervision. Moreover, group dynamics also tend to work toward a "least common denominator" when it is a matter of exploiting intellectual and emotional resources, in that the members unconsciously tend to calibrate themselves toward the member with the lowest level of anxiety tolerance or even the lowest level of professional competence (Boalt Boëthius, 1983).

In a study of supervisors' perception of group supervision, Sussman, Bogo, and Globerman (2007) found that supervisors distinguished between external and internal barriers to establishing trust and a sense of security in the group members.

External barriers included the members' prior histories with each other and internal barriers including difficult group members such as the nonreflective ones and the ones who cannot take risks. However, if group members can ultimately manage to create a climate for good supervision, variations in style, beliefs, emotionality, competence, experience, gender, class, ethnicity, and age may be useful (Proctor, 2008). Even if we prepare for such factors as age, sex, nationality, and personality in advance, it is almost impossible to predict what mixture will lead to good participation. Individual students will contribute differently according to the composition of the group. Nonetheless, the results from various studies point to the importance of thinking through the member composition in group supervision so that relevant dimensions can be balanced. Where relevant, the relationships among various supervision groups within the framework for an education programme must also be kept in mind. An interesting finding in our study of organizational framework relationships (Ögren et al., 2008b) was that the composition initially agreed upon rarely changed. When changes were made, they could be attributed to a group member's long-term illness or decision to drop out or to irresolvable conflicts and thus a break up of the group.

Although age and gender of individual group members may be viewed as fairly obvious determinants of behavior in adult groups, few studies have supported this proposition, partly because studies of age as a determinant more frequently involve children and adolescents than adults. With regard to gender differences among adults, a number of studies indicate that men and women display different types of behavior (Brown, 2000). However, Wheelan (1996) argued that differences in status might be even more important than gender differences. Another factor of importance for the composition of groups found in our studies (Ögren et al., 2005) was the varied ability of individual group members, which determined how effectively they could perform as they wished in the group. This, in turn, influenced how others reacted to them as group members. In this study, each supervision group contained two to four members of similar age while the groups' gender composition varied.

The Size of the Group and Intergroup Relationships

In a training context, the supervision group usually comprises a supervisor and three to four participants. In one of our studies, the results indicated that groups with four supervisees provided a more beneficial learning climate than groups with fewer supervisees (Boalt Boëthius, Sundin, & Ögren, 2006). It is possible that the three-member group constellation activates a certain type of competitiveness to a greater extent than if the group comprises four members and a supervisor. In the four-member group constellation, the members also have a greater opportunity to relate to one another in dyadic relations (Boalt Boëthius & Ögren, 2000).

When the supervision group is large, the pool of talent and experience available for solving problems or sharing the effort is evident. However, as the size increases, some members may begin to dominate and reticent members will fail to contribute, although they may well enjoy the relative anonymity a large group affords them. The smaller the group, the greater is the likelihood of close relationships, full participation, and consonance of aims, but this closeness might also be an obstacle.

In group supervision, it is important to be on the look out not only for parallel processes between the client material and the course of events in the small group but also for *intergroup processes*. Different regressive processes may occur, such as tendencies toward projections or displacements of responsibility. Intergroup processes can be hard to discern in a single specific supervision group since the supervisor is working with only a part of a larger social system. The important thing is to be aware that a part of what comes to the fore in an individual group can be rooted primarily in the training group as a whole rather than in the small group.

Contract and Examination Requirements

When a supervision group starts out, it is important that all of the members are given an opportunity to talk about expectations and reality in the face of their imminent cooperation. The importance of encasing the supervision within a well-thought-out organizational framework has been emphasized earlier. A clear-cut contractual agreement between all parties involved carries utmost significance. A spoken contract is essential in which everyone goes through together what is expected of each individual group member; for example, in terms of being willing and able to come forward with one's own material as well as viewpoints on the other participants' case presentations (Osborn & Davis, 1996; Proctor, 2008). Each and every individual is responsible for making room for his or her own training needs and at the same time allowing room and showing involvement in the others' needs. A key aspect of the actual agreement is the discussion of how each member wants to relate to the supervision group. There are different traditions in this respect.

The most basic aspect, as we see it, is that everyone, the course tutor, the supervisor, and the supervisees, must be ready to relate to the fact that the supervision is going to take place in a group form. Likewise, the level and the degree of ambition must govern the manner in which the members wish to relate to the group context in which the supervision takes place. A further aspect of the organizational frame consists of the examination requirements. On the organizational and administrative levels, there is a great responsibility to make it clear right from the start for both the supervisor and supervisees what criteria are going to be used for determining a passing mark for the clinical work within the framework of a group supervision. Samec (1995), in his study of failure in psychotherapy training, illuminated the trauma, for both supervisees and supervisors, of failing a student.

It is reasonable to assume that the group's composition and size, as well as the contract and the relation to the examination requirements, affect the interaction in the group and the perception of the group climate. An individual supervisee's dissatisfaction with the supervision and objections to the examination requirements are not infrequently expressions of resistance toward seeing his or her own difficulties. Stumbling blocks and conflicts may also have their origins in the supervisor's personality and blind spots (Szecsödy, 1990). However, the supervisor's transferences, influence, and power over the individual group members tend to be reduced in group supervision, as a consequence of the reactions of the other group members (Gerrard, 1998).

Core Content of Supervision

The supervision situation is affected by the nature of the case in focus. Moreover, it plays a role which set of problems the client in question is dealing with as well as which experiences the supervisees bring with them. All these things considered, it is also a question of how well the supervisor and the supervision group are able to take care of these factors and respond to them. Processes that come to the fore in therapy work with a client will inevitably involve aspects of the therapist's own life situation and activate earlier experiences and patterns (Gerson, 1996; Jacobsson et al., 2012).

The therapist and the supervision will be impacted if the client has a set of problems that are similar to a high degree to the difficulties with which the therapist himself or herself is grappling. To recognize oneself in one's client can enhance feelings of involvement and empathy, but at the same time it can also give the supervisee, the additional task of differentiating between his or her experiences and those of the client. The more inexperienced the supervisees are, the more help they need in keeping their experiences and reactions separate from those of their clients. In such cases, supervision fills an important function. In recent studies of novice supervisees and their supervisors, it was found that the clients' defenses on the one hand, and the therapists' helplessness and lack of therapeutic skills on the other, could affect the psychotherapies negatively (Strømme, 2012). The author suggests an extended focus on how therapeutic practical skills and personal traits develop in the supervision situation under psychotherapy training programmes.

It can take time for a specific client's set of problems and, by extension, the interaction between client and therapist to become discernible in a supervision group. When a therapist gets a client whom he or she understands and with whom a good therapeutic alliance can be established, it is easy to feel self-satisfaction. The supervisee can describe the patient in such a way as to give the supervisor and the other group members a clear picture of the therapeutic process. It can be tempting to equate a "functioning treatment" with a "good therapist" and the two may well be synonymous, but not necessarily. It can be just as likely for an inexperienced therapist to meet a client with a set of problems that are difficult to handle. Perhaps the client gives vague and incomplete material or gives voice to his or her difficulties by means of a constant contentiousness toward the therapist. Perhaps the client is only superficially motivated toward the treatment. It is easy in such cases, especially for novices, to feel inadequate and to lose self-esteem. It is then common to equate a "dubious treatment" with a "dubious helper." In the context of training, it is not uncommon for an initially unsure therapist to become even more unsure if he or she gets a client with whom it is difficult to develop a good working alliance or, alternatively, a client who for one reason or another quits therapy prematurely. This clinical observation has been corroborated by several researchers, as reviewed by Ellis, Krengel, and Beck (2002), who also reported findings from two studies on a group of counseling trainees ($n = 71$) on doctoral level (70%), master's level (25%), and undergraduate level (3%). The trainees perceived significantly higher anxiety when they had a session with a "difficult client," that is, a client with severe problems or with a strong negative mood.

It matters considerably for a supervisor in a group supervision to emphasize that everyone in the group has a valuable treatment scenario to contribute. The therapists with the hard-to-handle cases can have especially valuable experiences to contribute to the shared knowledge bank of the supervision group. The stance of the supervisor has significance for how the group's dynamic develops in terms of a sense of security, role division, opportunities for exchange of experiences, and learning. A sense of self-doubt is almost always activated in supervisees. Against this background, there can be a risk for the group situation to enhance the role division among the group members in an undesirable way. It is unfortunate for the entire group if the one who has a client with severe problems and who feels less confirmed in his or her clinical work is made to bear the role of the unsure and failed group member.

Group phenomena that emanate from the supervisees' client material are often not taken up in a conscious and systematic manner until these phenomena have been expressed in the interaction among the group participants or in relation to the supervisor. In order to avoid blockages of various kinds in the group, it is essential to try to identify the effect of patient problem sets (core content) on the group's interaction (Andersson, 2008). The client material's influence upon the therapist and the group is considerable. The supervisor's stance is decisive for how interaction and learning will develop in the long run.

Interaction Processes in Group Supervision

The interaction that arises in a supervision group, among the group members and in relation to the supervisor, is affected by many different factors. We have earlier discussed the organizational framework's significance for the supervision group's interaction as well as how the core content in the supervision can give rise to different interaction patterns. In order to be able to fully understand the different aspects of a supervision group's dynamics, we must be on the look out for the specific patterns that small work groups generally tend to generate. Important factors may be influences from earlier group experiences and competition among group members. The foremost factor is the group climate, how a good group climate is created and how it influences learning. There is also reason to reflect on roles, role balance, power, and dependency, as well as on the starting and the terminating of a supervision group. We have carried out a research project in which self-evaluation has been shown to increase the understanding of different phenomena in a supervision group. Accordingly, we introduce a strategy for reflecting on different dynamics in supervision groups (Boalt Boëthius & Ögren, 2000).

Everybody has experiences of belonging to a small group, for example, school experiences, friendship experiences, and different work groups. Memories from earlier group contexts can be tinted with a wide range of emotions. In a similar manner, we have experiences from our earlier years of relating to authorities such as parents and teachers and other adults. These experiences have their special implications for every individual and can be more or less conscious and worked through. No matter what experiences we have with us, they seem to be awakened to life when we become a part of a new group constellation. It is a well-known phenomenon that when we join groups, we assign ourselves and others different roles in a more or less conscious and predetermined way.

Competition in Group Supervision

How we as group members and supervisors can take a position in competition situations often comes to a head in a group supervision situation. Competition in a group can originate in the interaction between the different group members but can also be related to competitive aspects of the client material. Competition in education and work contexts can be a driving and stimulating force, but it can also have a destructive effect. In supervision groups, the hidden, non-acknowledged and unspoken competition often tends to be the greatest threat (Sussman et al., 2007). In a study of group supervision (Ögren et al., 2001) in which the supervisees described the climate as characterized by friendly interaction and mutual understanding, it could be suspected that matters that were sensitive and that had to do with conflict or competition had been eliminated. This would be a dubious strategy, considering that the life situations that our clients confront often involve problems connected to competition and conflict. The supervisor, therefore, has an important task in this regard as well, which is to put the competition that he or she sees into words and talk about it as an issue in terms of the various force fields that are activated in psychotherapy treatment.

Group Climate

The group members' feelings about the group climate, likewise the climate's influence on learning, are important aspects of group supervision. Research has been conducted, particularly within work-life, to identify what characterizes a good group climate. The group climate can be regarded as the product of the characteristics of the individual members multiplied by the role of the individual members in the group plus the relationship of this product to the organizational climate. Organizational climate is often defined as the recurring patterns of behavior, attitudes, and feelings that characterize life in the organization (Burningham & West, 1995).

However, a limited amount of research has been conducted on group climate with specific focus on psychotherapy supervision groups. The group provides opportunities for its members to explore personal meanings and experiences by identification with, and provocation by, others. The model of Bion's (1989) for how groups function suggests that "provocations and projections enable others in the group to feel things which they have not felt before, and rediscover aspects of themselves which have been projected or denied" (Greenhalgh, 2000, p. 192).

Group supervision may be an opportunity for the supervisee to make use of the reflective space offered in the group. Supervisees are confronted with attitudes and evaluations both from the supervisor and the other supervisees. Such confrontations may lead to positive developments, but they can also be risky for the inexperienced supervisee, who is often extra sensitive and fluctuating in his/her self-esteem (Higgs, Richardson, & Abrandt, 2004; Skovholt & Rønnestad, 1992; Strømme, 2012). Against the background of the aspects of the group's activity and task mentioned earlier, it is reasonable to conclude that the concept of climate in group supervision is very complex. The supervisees' experience of the climate will probably be imbued by the dynamics emerging from their personal experiences, the encounter with a client material, and the relationship with their peers and the supervisor.

Professional development presumes a sufficiently safe and challenging supervision experience. In the initial phase of group supervision, supervisees need to be informed about facts concerning organizational frames and learning goals. Moreover, supervisees may need to be reminded about "group life," about the way that people normally bring hopes, fears, and expectations to the group, which will affect the group experiences. It is most important that the organizational frames – the conditions for the supervision in an educational setting, the group supervision contract, the learning goals, and examination demands – are clearly outlined for the supervisees. Proctor (2008) opined that when a group gets into difficulties and is not carrying out good enough supervision because of extreme individual emotional vulnerability or withdrawal, the supervisor has a responsibility to both the group and the clients to take reparative measures. Group members may choose to leave or be asked to leave if they cannot share in the commitment to the ground rules. Reviewing the contract and working agreement is of primary importance in this context. The author is also of the opinion that preventive measures rely on the supervisor's development of clear, unambiguous communication, emanating from an organizational structure of the type mentioned earlier.

The concept of group climate in psychotherapy supervision groups is multifaceted due to the group's and the supervisor's tasks in the form of both supporting and confronting the group members in the supervision process and ensuring good quality in the client work. The psychotherapy supervision group is the forum that is to bear the vulnerable process of the supervisees' development. The groups encompass the supervision and the client work with arising transference and countertransference problems (Andersson, 2008). Moreover, it is also reasonable to suppose that important parts of the total training situation are captured and condensed in the supervision group. In other words, the group has to be strong enough to endure a number of strains, during certain periods, which contribute to the psychotherapy supervision group's complexity. Thoroughly permissive climates are probably not compatible with the task of the supervision to both support and confront in order to promote development and learning. The supervisor has to be clear about intentions and priorities concerning the supervision task, learning goals, and the life of the group (Proctor, 2008). Explicit organizational frames should constitute the fundamental security for the group's work so that the group is able to bear the dynamic insecurity that is necessarily actualized in the learning process.

However, in spite of the paradoxical components of the learning situation discussed earlier (i.e., with conflicting goals of sense of security, challenge, and uncertainty), there are remarkably few empirical and systematic evaluations of attained skill following supervision and a complete lack of systematic evaluations of attained skill after group supervision (Boalt Boëthius et al., 2006).

Creating a Good Learning Climate

A trusting climate in supervision must be built up by the group members and the supervisor together based on support and a basic structure from the course designers. All members in the supervision group are important contributors. It is usually beneficial to discuss this at an early stage. It can be good to point out that it is natural for people to feel a certain discomfort toward speaking about their dissatisfaction with their own work efforts. It should also be strongly stated that overcoming this discomfort and being open constitute the best way of getting the maximum exchange from supervision. Since all members per definition will have difficult matters to talk about, the supervisor can encourage them to "open" with their own examples so that others can follow their lead. The supervisor can also emphasize how important it is for the group members to show engagement in each others' work. They need to be as generous as possible in giving their views on each others' cases in order to learn as much as possible. It can be good to remind them that the scenario that another group member is now confronting can confront them as well at some later point in time.

One way to promote the potential of the group is to have a case presented first and then to encourage each and every participant to voice comments and associations. The member who has presented his or her case can then concentrate fully on listening, after which he or she can reflect over the viewpoints that seem fruitful. This is a variation on the model of working with a so-called reflecting team (Willott, Hatton, & Oyebode, 2012). Such a procedure seems to reduce the risk of the presenter's feeling bombarded with suggestions from the others, which can lead to reduced self-esteem.

The group context offers a unique opportunity to gain access to a "space for reflection" together with others. Viewpoints from the supervisor as well as from the other group members can introduce valuable new angles of approach. This situation can be experienced as both stimulating and provocative, especially for novice supervisees when it is their turn to take the role of presenter. Their self-esteem can be strengthened or it can begin to waver (Altfeld, 1999; Counselman & Gumpert, 1993; Enyedy et al., 2003; Ögren et al., 2005; Skovholt & Rønnestad, 1992). The presenter can feel strengthened by the group, leading to a feeling of confidence that he or she is "okay." But it is just as likely that the group members will respond in such a way as to cause each other to hold back and to bring up only matters that feel opportune or "right."

The difficulties that come up during group supervision can lead to exhaustion and strain for individual group members, but, at the same time, they can also serve as starting points and preconditions for meaningful and genuine insights. Important knowledge about one's own "professional persona" can be necessary to "bring to life painfully" with the help of the group. This knowledge is thereafter beneficial for the individual group member in the continuation of his or her work. The perception of a "bad group climate," given a holding frame and a good basis in terms of group composition, can actually enhance the possibility of processing central questions and promote a unique development for the group's members. In contrast, a "genuinely bad climate," based on other factors, can be devastating for a group. Distinguishing between the "fruitfully bad climate" and the "genuinely bad climate" in a group is difficult, as, for example, knowing when it is, in fact, best to break up a group and find other ways, such as individual supervision.

Some of the studies of group supervision that we have carried out indicate that the group climate in the beginning of a supervision situation can feel awkward and uncertain, but that it gradually seems to improve in line with an increasing sense of security in the group. If the supervisor shows tolerance for divergent ways of thinking about various issues in the initial phase of a group supervision, it has a significant effect on what happens subsequently (Boalt Boëthius, Ögren, Sjøvold, & Sundin, 2005). A good group climate most importantly should favor the learning process that is going to take place. Supervisors have the task of promoting the development of a sufficient sense of security in the supervisees in their group as a precondition for each and every one of them to have the strength to explore dilemmas, difficulties, and their own shortcomings in their clinical work. At the same time, the supervisor must make sure that the climate does not become so "nice" that the group members can be assumed to have made a silent pact to avoid bringing up client- and interaction-related material concerning, for example, competitiveness, negative feelings, and countertransference (Ögren et al., 2001). A good balance is essential between facilitating alliance-making as a basis for a sense of security within the group and allowing necessary frustration and confrontation to further the professional psychotherapeutic development of the supervisees.

In this context, it is important to point out that when participants have been asked to evaluate the climate in a supervision group, the supervisors' evaluations have generally been more favorable and positive than those of the supervisees. There is thus reason for supervisors to sharpen their attention concerning the group climate and to be on the lookout for how each individual supervisee can perceive the situation. Studies show that supervisors tend to underestimate how unsure the supervisees, especially novice psychotherapy candidates, can be (Carlsson, 2012; Strømme, 2012). Another point of concern is that the supervisor might not understand to what extent the internal dynamics in a supervision group can inhibit certain individual group participants (Sussman et al., 2007). In this context, the supervisor's knowledge and experience when it comes to interpreting a group situation play a crucial role.

Roles, Role Balance, Power, and Dependency

The roles of the supervisees should be clearly demarcated and clarified in accordance with what has been previously been pointed out with regard to the contract for group supervision between the supervisor and the supervisees. The supervisees should be prepared to take responsibility for their own learning as well as to give the other supervisees' work an active and engaged response. The information from the course designers to the parties involved should form the basis of the contract, stipulating the forms of cooperation that the supervisor expects of the supervisees in the group. Everyone's joint responsibility for creating a group climate that is conducive to learning and development should be made clear. It is essential to impress upon the supervisees at an early stage that each and every one of them has a great influence upon how the learning climate is going to develop. It is more often than not a matter of daring to "break the ice."

Supervisees need to talk about issues that are difficult and in such situations be met with appreciation for raising the stakes for what is allowed to be talked about and "exposed." The other group members should be encouraged to accept this type of material as a natural opening for them to speak of their own mistakes and feelings of insecurity. This generally leads to the group's taking on a containing function that is desirable. The important function of the supervisor in such cases is to show backing for the one who begins exposing his or her shortcomings. It should be pointed out that this person is opening up opportunities for the group instead of letting him or her be given the role of "the therapist who is unsure and who is making a fool of him/herself." The relationship between the supervisor and the supervisees is asymmetrical. If a person is being supervised within the framework of an education programme, the situation becomes even more apparent since the supervisor is carrying out regular assessments of the work of the supervisees.

According to Carlsson's study (2012) based on interviews with supervisees in an advanced training programme, the supervisees seemed to be motivated by a desire to achieve acknowledgment of their preformed professional self from their supervisors. This led to conflicts in supervision. The author recommends that training institutes, teachers, and supervisors should learn how to handle students' preformed professional selves in order to avoid compliance and conflicts during training. The balance of power between supervisor and their supervisees was stressed.

Self-Evaluations as a Way of Describing Interaction and Climate

One of our first research efforts in the area of group supervision, which indirectly opened up the dialogue between supervisors within a collegial body of supervisors, was to collect data from supervisees and supervisors at different levels of education using Symlog self-ratings (Bales & Cohen, 1979; Boalt Boëthius & Ögren, 2000; Boalt Boëthius et al., 2005). These self-ratings build upon individual group members' responses to 26 items about how they perceive that they function in the group at the time of the ratings and how they wish they could function.

Supervisors and supervisees in different supervision groups evaluated both the "actual" and the "wish" situations with regard to their roles in the supervision group. The field diagrams generated from the ratings were used as bases both for research and for discussion in the collegial body of supervisors and in the respective supervision groups. The diagrams for the different groups were presented for the supervisors at recurring supervisor meetings, after which the supervisors took the diagrams of "their own groups" back to their respective supervision groups for continued discussion. This procedure was considered to be of good help in enabling the group members to discuss their group's interaction. It also brought about an opening in the dialogue among the supervisors, who could begin to share experiences with other supervisor colleagues and reflect together over how they could understand the "pictures of the group" that took form. The discussion progressed to concern the different groups' interaction and dynamics. Our studies have shown that well-prepared regular supervision meetings were considered to be of great significance by supervisors (Ögren et al., 2008b). The supervisors valued the support they could receive from colleagues when dealing with a problematic situation.

Conclusion

Group supervision is, under favorable circumstances, a powerful educational instrument that seems able to condense and harbor the clinical material and create a stable foundation for learning. The supervisees' clinical experience is expanded through the insight they receive into the work of their co-supervisees. It should be remembered that it seems to be an equally great challenge and balancing act to find one's role whether as a supervisor or a supervisee and regardless of level of education. Group supervision places high demands on the supervisors' knowledge and understanding with regard to both organizational issues and group dynamics.

References

Altfeld, D. (1999). An experiential group model for psychotherapy supervision. *International Journal of Group Psychotherapy, 49*, 237–254.

Andersson, L. (2008). Psychodynamic supervision in a group setting: Benefits and limitations. *Psychotherapy in Australia, 14*, 36–41.

Bales, R. F., & Cohen, S. (1979). SYMLOG. *A system for the multiple level observations of groups.* New York: The Free Press.

Baruch, V. (2009). Supervision groups in private practice: An integrative approach. *Psychotherapy in Australia, 15*(3), 72–76.

Bernard, J., & Goodyear, R. (2009). *Fundamentals of clinical supervision.* Boston: Pearson.

Bion, W. R. (1989). *Experiences in groups and other papers.* London: Routledge.

Boalt Boëthius, S. (1983). *Autonomy, coping and defence in small work groups.* Stockholm: Almqvist & Wiksell International.

Boalt Boëthius, S. (1993). Grupphandledning och samspelsprocesser. [Group supervision and interaction processes.]. In D. Stiwne (Ed.), *Perspektiv på handledning i psykoterapi och angränsande områden [Perspectives in psychotherapy supervision]* (pp. 160–187). Stockholm: Natur och Kultur.

Boalt Boëthius, S., & Ögren, M.-L. (2000). Role patterns in group supervision. *The Clinical Supervisor, 19*, 45–69.

Boalt Boëthius, S., Ögren, M.-L., Sjøvold, E., & Sundin, E. (2005). Experiences of group culture and patterns of interaction in psychotherapy supervision groups. *e Clinical Supervisor, 23*, 101–121.

Boalt Boëthius, S., Sundin, E., & Ögren, M.-L. (2006). Group supervision from a small group perspective. *Nordic Psychology, 58*, 22–42.

Brown, R. (2000). *Group processes.* Oxford: Blackwell Publisher.

Burningham, C., & West, M. (1995). Individual, climate, and group interaction processes as predictors of work team. *Small Group Research, 26*(1), 106–117.

Carlsson, J. (2012). Research on psychotherapists' professional development during and after training. *J. Nordic Psychology, 3*, 150–167.

Counselman, E., & Gumpert, P. (1993). Psychotherapy supervision in small leader-led groups. *Group, 17*, 25–32.

Ekstein, R., & Wallerstein, R. S. (1958, 1977). *The teaching and learning of psychotherapy* (2nd ed.). New York: International Universities Press.

Ellis, M., Krengel, M., & Beck, M. (2002). Testing self focused attention theory in clinical supervision: Effects on supervisee anxiety and performance. *Journal of Counseling Psychology, 49*, 102–116.

Enyedy, K. C., Arcinue, F., Puri, N. N., Carter, M. C., Goodyear, R. K., & Getzelman, M. A. (2003). Hindering phenomena in group supervision: Implications for practice. *Professional Psychology, Research and Practice, 34*, 312–317.

Gautier, D. (2009). The impact of sibling rivalry in group supervision. *The Journal of the British Association for Psychoanalytic & Psychodynamic Supervision, 1*, 6–8.

Gerrard, J. (1998). Supervision, its vicissitudes and issues of frequency. In P. Clarkson (Ed.), *Supervision. Psychoanalytic and Jungian perspectives* (pp. 34–53). London: Whurr Publishers Ltd.

Gerson, B. (1996). *The therapist as a person: Life crises, life choices, life experiences, and their effects on treatment.* Hillsdale, NJ: The Analytic Press.

Goodyear, R. K., & Nelson, M. L. (1997). The major formats of psychotherapy supervision. In E. Watkins (Ed.), *Handbook of psychotherapy supervision* (pp. 11–27). New York: John Wiley & Sons, Inc.

Greenhalgh, P. (2000). *Emotional growth and learning.* London and New York: Routledge.

Grigg, G. (2006). Designs and discriminations for clinical group supervision in Counselling Psychology: An analysis. *Canadian Journal of Counselling, 40*(2), 110–122.

Hawkins, P., & Shohet, R. (1989). *Supervision in the helping professions.* Philadelphia: Open University Press.

Hayes, R. L., Blackman, L. S., & Brennan, C. (2001). Group supervision. In L. J. Bradley & N. Ladany (Eds.), *Counselor supervision* (3rd ed., pp. 183–206). Philadelphia: Brunner-Routledge.

Higgs, J., Richardson, B., & Abrandt, M. (Eds.). (2004). *Developing practice knowledge for health professionals.* London: Butterworth-Heinemann.

Holloway, E. (1984). Outcome evaluation in supervision research. *Counseling Psychologist, 12*, 167–174.

Holloway, E., & Johnston, R. (1985). Group supervision: Widely used but poorly understood. *Counselor Education and Supervision, 12*(24), 332–340.

Jacobsson, G., Lindgren, T., & Hau, S. (2012). Rites of passages – Novice students experiences of becoming psychotherapists. *Nordic Psychology, 64*(3), 192–202.

Lambert, M., & Arnold, R. (1987). Research and the supervisory process. *Professional Psychology, Research and Practice, 18*, 217–224.

Lanning, W. (1971). A study of the relation between group and individual counseling supervision and three relationship measures. *Journal of Counseling Psychology, 18*, 401–406.

Mastoras, S. M., & Andrews, J. J. (2011). The supervisee experience of group supervision: Implications for research and practice. *Training and Education in Professional Psychology, 5*, 102–111.

Milne, D., & James, I. (2002). The observed impact of training on competence in clinical supervision. *British Journal of Clinical Psychology, 41*, 55–72.

Nguyen, T. V. (2003). A comparison of individual and triadic supervision. doctoral dissertation, University of North Texas.

Ögren, M.-L., & Jonsson, C.-O. (2003). Psychotherapy skill following group supervision according to supervisees and supervisors. *The Clinical Supervisor, 22*(1), 35–59.

Ögren, M.-L., & Sundin, E. (2006). Experiences of the group format in psychotherapy supervision. *The Clinical Supervisor, 25*(1/2), 69–82.

Ögren, M.-L., & Sundin, E. (2009). Group supervision in psychotherapy. Main results from a Swedish project on psychotherapy supervision in a group format. *British Journal of Guidance and Counselling, 37*(2), 129–139.

Ögren, M.-L., Apelman, A., & Klawitter, M. (2001). The group in psychotherapy supervision. *The Clinical Supervisor, 20*(2), 147–176.

Ögren, M.-L., Jonsson, C.-O., & Sundin, E. (2005). Group supervision in psychotherapy. The relationship between focus, group climate and perceived attained skill. *Journal of Clinical Psychology, 61*(4), 373–389.

Ögren, M.-L., Boalt Boëthius, S., & Olsson, U. (2008a). Organizational structure and framework. A case study of Swedish training programs in psychotherapy. *Organisational and Social Dynamics, 8*(22), 256–278.

Ögren, M.-L., Boalt Boëthius, S., & Sundin, E. (2008b). From psychotherapist to supervisor. The significance of group format and supervisors' function as role models in psychotherapy supervision. *Nordic Psychology, 60*(1), 3–23.

Osborn, C. J., & Davis, T. D. (1996). The supervision contract: Making it perfectly clear. *The Clinical Supervisor, 14*, 121–134.

Plant, R., & Smith, M. (2009). Counter transference and parallel process in supervision groups. Supervision Review. *The Journal of the British Association for Psychoanalytic & Psychodynamic Supervision*, 15–18. Available at http://www.supervision.org.uk/BAPPS_SReview/SR09_spring.pdf

Proctor, B. (2008). *Group supervision. A guide to creative practice*. London: Sage Publications.

Proctor, B., & Inskipp, F. (2001). Group supervision. In J. Scaife (Ed.), *Supervision in mental health professions. A practitioner's guide* (pp. 99–121). London: Brunner-Routledge.

Ray, D. C., & Altekruse, M. (2000). Effectiveness of group supervision versus combined group and individual supervision. *Counselor Education and Supervision, 40*(1), 119–130.

Reichelt, S., & Skjerve, J. (2002). Correspondence between supervisors and trainees in their perception of supervision events. *Journal of Clinical Psychology, 58*, 759–772.

Riva, M. T., & Cornish, J. A. E. (1995). Group supervision practices at psychology predoctoral internship programs: A national survey. *Professional Psychology, Research and Practice, 26*, 523–525.

Rønnestad, M., & Ladany, N. (2006). The impact of psychotherapy training: Introduction to the special section. *Psychotherapy Research, 16*(3), 261–267.

Rutter, M. E. (2007). Group supervision with practicing school counsellors. *Guidance & Counseling, 21*(3), 160–167.

Samec, J. (1995). Shame, guilt and trauma: Failing the psychotherapy candidate's clinical work. *The Clinical Supervisor, 13*, 1–18.

Skovholt, T. M., & Rønnestad, H. M. (1992). *The evolving professional self. Stages and themes in therapist and counselor development*. New York: Wiley & Sons.

Stoltenberg, C., McNeill, B., & Crethar, H. (1994). Changes in supervision as counselors and therapists gain experience: A review. *Professional Psychology, Research and Practice, 25*, 416–449.

Strømme, H. (2012). Confronting helplessness. A study of psychology students' acquisition of dynamic psychotherapeutic competence by psychology students. *Nordic Psychology, 64*, 203–217.

Sundin, E., Ögren, M.-L., & Boalt Boëthius, S. (2008). Supervisors trainees' and their supervisors' perceptions of attainment of knowledge and skills: An empirical evaluation of a psychotherapy supervisor training programme. *British Journal of Clinical Psychology, 47*, 381–496.

Sussman, T., Bogo, M., & Globerman, J. (2007). Field instructor competence in group supervision. Establishing trust through managing group dynamics. *The Clinical Supervisor, 26*(1/2), 61–80.

Szecsödy, I. (1990). *The learning process in psychotherapy supervision.* Doctoral thesis, Stockholm: Karolinska Institutet.

Wampold, B. E., & Holloway, E. (1997). Methodology, design and evaluation in psychotherapy supervision research. In E. Watkins (Ed.), *Handbook of psychotherapy supervision* (pp. 11–27). New York: John Wiley & Sons, Inc.

Watkins, C. E. (1997). Defining psychotherapy supervision and understanding supervisor functioning. In C. E. Watkins Jr. (Ed.), *Handbook of psychotherapy supervision* (pp. 3–10). New York: John Wiley & Sons.

Wheelan, S. (1996). Effects of gender composition and group status differences on member's perceptions of group developmental patterns, effectiveness, and productivity. *Sex Roles, 34*, 665–686.

Wheeler, S., & Richards, K. (2007). The impact of clinical supervision on counsellors and therapists, their practice and their clients. A systematic review of the literature. *Counseling and Psychotherapeutic Research, 7*(1), 54–65.

Whitman, S. M., Ryan, B., & Rubenstein, D. F. (2001). Psychotherapy training: Differences between psychiatry and other mental health disciplines. *Academic Psychiatry, 25*, 156–161.

Willott, S., Hatton, T., & Oyebode, J. (2012). Reflecting team processes in family therapy: A search for research. *Journal of Family Therapy, 34*(2), 180–203.

Worthington, E. L. (1987). Changes in supervision as counselors and supervisors gain experience: A review. *Professional Psychology, Research and Practice, 18*, 189–208.

Part VI
Endnotes

32

Clinical Supervision at the International Crossroads
Current Status and Future Directions

C. Edward Watkins, Jr., and Derek L. Milne

Perhaps if there is one safe, robust conclusion that could be made about the rich and enriching material found throughout this book, it would be this: in best training psychotherapists and counselors for competent practice across the professional life span, clinical supervision has increasingly become a far more readily recognized, widely accepted, and integrally vital part of the international educational landscape down through the decades. Based on our reading of the preceding 31 chapters, more of the same can certainly be expected. The reach and reward of clinical supervision will continue to be on prominent international display in the decades ahead, and its professional contribution to the teaching and career-long learning of psychotherapy/counseling will accordingly gain in refinement, power, and impact.

The substantive supervision efforts that have shaped this international educational landscape have been noted here by contributors from Australia, Finland, Hong Kong, New Zealand, Slovenia, South Africa, Sweden, the United Kingdom, and the United States. As a vital educational practice, supervision's presence is also beginning to be felt in many other corners of our globe. For example, at a recent meeting of the International Interdisciplinary Conference on Clinical Supervision, supervision practice and training now occurring in Bulgaria, Cyprus, Germany, Greece, Macedonia, Portugal, Romania, Korea, Botswana, and Venezuela were considered (Lim & Hong, 2013; Msimanga, 2013; Szilagyi, 2013; Vera & Barreto, 2013). We are fast becoming a world committed to supervision and its enhancement. In our view, all indications point to further embrace and strengthening of supervision's stature as educational *sine qua non* across countries and continents, and these varied and valuable chapters provide particularly compelling testament to that effect.

In this concluding chapter, we would like to use these preceding 31 chapters as a fulcrum to look back and look forward: in considering clinical supervision's 100 year plus history and evolution, what can we say about its current status? And as we

The Wiley International Handbook of Clinical Supervision, First Edition. Edited by C. Edward Watkins, Jr. and Derek L. Milne.

gaze into the future, what can be said about supervision from this point forward? In what follows, we would like to examine those two questions by giving focus to 10 fundamental themes: (a) competencies and competency frameworks; (b) theoretical models; (c) the supervisory relationship; (d) assessment, measurement, and evaluation; (e) research; (f) difference and diversity; (g) ethical and legal concerns; (h) organizational matters; (i) technology; and (j) training and education. We will identify by area what, in our view, are some of the most robust, durable, and enduring features or themes that now define clinical supervision around the world; and then we will identify some of the needs that now seem most pressing if supervision is to maintain its vital advance in the years ahead. We believe that these 10 themes, while by no means exhaustive, provide a representative international picture of what clinical supervision has become, helping us to anticipate where it appears to be moving and to suggest what needs to happen for the most profitable progress.

Looking Back and Looking Forward in Clinical Supervision

Competencies and competency frameworks

Competencies and competency frameworks, emerging in full over the past approximate 15 year period, have become all the rage in supervision and fittingly so. Holloway (2012) has even referred to this competency thrust as the very Zeitgeist of contemporary supervision practice. Indeed, there has perhaps never been a more sweeping and all-pervasive singular change to so rapidly impact the entirety of the supervision enterprise than the advent of the competency movement itself. While competence has always been a focus of much concern in supervision, current competency frameworks have ratcheted up that focus as never before. This development is surely proof of the way that supervision has latterly gained in international recognition and importance. These frameworks have also provided an abundance of benefits for all parties across the supervision triad. Some of those benefits include promoting supervisor/supervisee educational clarity, specificity, and understanding; requiring identification of specific knowledge, skills, attitudes, and values that define specific competencies; facilitating articulation of supervisee training goals and learning objectives; emphasizing collaborative identification and management of supervisee reactivity; accenting attention to supervisory relationship strains, ruptures, and their resolution; supporting creation of conditions that increase clear, targeted, and specific feedback; embracing competence and its enhancement as ongoing, continuous, lifelong educational process; and providing means, motive, and opportunity for better safeguarding client welfare (Falender & Shafranske, 2012; Watkins, 2012b). Competency initiatives are grounded in and guided by an ethos of transparency, measurability, concreteness, and specificity. With that being the case, supervision is thereby positioned to have a far better chance of becoming much more accountable practice and a demonstrably explicit educational reality (cf. Falender & Shafranske, 2012). Such is the desideratum that underlies all competency endeavors.

As emphasized by Milne and Watkins, and detailed by Pilling and Roth (in Chapters 1 and 2), comprehensive supervision competency frameworks have been developed for use in Australia, the United Kingdom, and the United States, but those are neither lone nor necessarily finished products. For example, the European Association for Psychotherapy is currently in the middle of a 10-year project to designate competencies for psychotherapy practice throughout Europe (Young, Schulthess, Szyszkowitx, Oudijks, & Stabingis, 2013), and supervision competencies are very much a part of that framework (see domain 9, http://www.psychotherapy-competency.eu). A host of other international efforts to better address, consider, or reevaluate matters of supervision competencies can also be readily identified (e.g., Bang & Park, 2009; Hunsley & Barker, 2011; Owens-Pugh & Symons, 2013; Rodolfa et al., 2013). Based on work done over the past 15 years, we have not lacked, nor are we apt to lack, for continued emphasis on and vigorous scrutiny of competencies, their significance for supervision practice and training, and attempts to build an ever more effective and eminently user friendly competency framework. While all this ongoing emphasis and scrutiny may reflect an endeavor that in some respects is still a "work in progress" (cf. Owens-Pugh & Symons, 2013; Roth, 2013), we appear well on our way to realizing a far more solid, anchored educational vision about how best to make supervision practice and training more accountable and optimally effective. Current competency frameworks provide viable means of translating that ideal into reality and have led us to a place of far greater international consensus than ever before about the critical components of clinical supervision and their implementation (Milne, Gonsalvez, & Watkins, 2013). We expect that such consensus will only broaden and strengthen internationally in the years ahead.

However, we perceive a significant threat: as competency considerations move forward, *practical economy* perhaps has been and will continue to be the most crucial and bedeviling framework issue to bear in mind. Much like a good personality or psychotherapy theory should be comprehensive, parsimonius, and practical, a good competency framework should ideally be sufficiently comprehensive, efficiently parsimonious, and preeminently practical itself. While long and detailed lists of competencies can readily be developed, the danger is that – as such lists lengthen and their detail increases – the weight and ponderousness of any proposed framework will cause it to implode due to sheer lack of practicality. Achieving proper balance between comprehensiveness, parsimony, and practicality is by no means an easy feat, but it is the superordinate challenge with which competency frameworks must forever contend. Finding that proper balance can ultimately mean the difference between embrace and dismissal. For that very reason, we now see more substantive professional effort being given to streamlining competency frameworks for more user friendly implementation (Foo Kune & Rodolfa, 2013; Hatcher et al., 2013; Rodolfa et al., 2013; Schaffer, Rodolfa, Hatcher, & Fouad, 2013). In our view, such work is most welcome and much needed in further enhancing, disseminating, and rendering most central the role of competencies for supervision practice and training.

Theoretical models and their advancement

As indicated in this *handbook's* Part V, three different types of models have thus far been identified in the supervision literature: theory-specific (or psychotherapy focused), developmental, and social role perspectives. Theory-specific approaches originally developed from psychotherapy theories and remain so aligned (see Chapters 23–27); developmental and social role approaches have been created specifically to explain supervision and are not linked to any psychotherapy theory (see Chapters 28–29) (Beinart, 2012). In surveying the chapters in Part V and considering other recent discussions about model needs and possibilities (e.g., Farber, 2010, 2012; Reiser & Milne, 2012; Sarnat, 2010, 2012; Scaturo, 2012; Watkins, 2012b), what could be identified as the salient developmental themes across the varied theoretical models at this time? From our reading, supervision models appear to have evolved in such direction that they all now share one highly robust and indisputable cardinal feature that merits mention here. Furthermore, all models appear to now be increasingly confronted by at least two fundamental questions of eminent concern that merit mention here as well. Let us review each of those considerations in turn.

First, if there is one feature that now seems to characterize the tenor of all supervision models, it might best be stated as follows: across the decades, supervision conceptualization and conduct have come to increasingly reflect a more egalitarian, collaborative, co-participative, and co-constructed vision of process and outcome, where supervisor and supervisee actively and fully work together to create a supervision experience that is jointly optimal and productive. At its core, that evolving shift is ultimately about power, influence, and agency – the move toward recognizing that (a) both supervisor *and* supervisee have power and influence in the supervisory endeavor and (b) supervision works best when that power and influence are mutually used and shared for its enhancement. With some of the perspectives that are covered in Part V, matters of power and influence seem to have been built in and addressed from the very outset (e.g., Holloway's systems approach to supervision; see Chapter 29). In other cases, those matters seem to have emerged only after decades of perspective development (e.g., as is so for psychoanalytic supervision; Watkins, 2013b, 2013c; Eagle & Long, Chapter 23). Such convergence toward an empowering stance seems much in line with contemporary adult learning theory and the core principles by which adults most effectively learn (see Knowles, Swanson, & Holton, 2011). This kind of internal consistency or reflexivity (between how supervision is conducted and how it works) is surely a valuable strength. In our view, this evolved and ever evolving egalitarian stance across models – eminently filtered through the practical prism of culture – has much to commend it and should continue to serve supervision well in its decades of practice ahead.

Next, let us turn attention to our other topic of consideration: what are some of the most pressing questions that confront all theoretical models at this time? We specifically would like to focus on two issues that we regard as most problematic. First, how will each model better address and incorporate the matter of competencies into its particular theoretical fabric? That is a pivotal question that will continue to command answer. It requires that the specifics of each model – constructs, techniques, and skills – be defined from competency vantage point. Theory-specific competency frameworks that have been developed in the United Kingdom already provide some fruitful direction for any such considerations (see Chapter 2; Roth & Pilling, 2008); they provide blueprints for action that could potentially prove internationally informative and merit close examination for that very reason. With that being the case, however, such frameworks or consensus statements can still lack the high degree of specificity and procedural detail that are needed for effective implementation, and further modifications may indeed be required to make that possible (Reiser & Milne, 2012). Falender and Shafranske (2010) have gone so far as to state that the advancement of supervision actually requires re-envisioning and reaffirming – via competency-based perspective – the unique role of psychotherapy-focused supervision in professional training. To some extent, the same could perhaps be said with regard to the developmental and social role visions as well.

For our second question, it seems most important to ask: how can a base of supervision research be more effectively established or reignited across the psychotherapy-focused, developmental, and social role models? That question also speaks to need to render each perspective more evidence based and accountable (see Milne's account in Chapter 3; also Milne, 2009; Milne & Reiser, 2012). Research foundation across models is notably lacking in some cases and calls to remedy that reality have been repeatedly made (e.g., Ladany & Inman, 2012; Reiser & Milne, 2012; Sarnat, 2012; Watkins, in press, 2014a). In other cases, model-specific supervision research (e.g., developmental: see Stoltenberg et al., Chapter 28) appears to have significantly diminished over time and may well be in need of a jump start (Goodyear & Guzzardo, 2000; Inman & Ladany, 2008; Ladany & Inman, 2012). But others feel that a significant start has already been made. For one, Reiser (Chapter 24) took an upbeat stance, noting a "plethora of exciting developments" in relation to the cognitive behavior therapy (CBT) model. Similarly, Farber (Chapter 26) referred to "an exciting, dynamic process of growth and development" in relation to the humanistic and existential models. As has often been lamented in the supervision literature, a virtual absence of adequate supervision measures has long been identified as being the culprit in generally frustrating the development of a more substantive body of supervision research (Ellis, 2010; Ellis & Ladany, 1997; Ellis, D'Iuso, & Ladany, 2008; Milne et al., 2012). That absence of measures has certainly affected advance in studying particular supervision models as well. Any research is only as good as the measures upon which it is based. While some highly positive developments in supervision measurement have occurred more recently (see Part IV chapters), model-specific supervision still has much ground to cover to compensate for its slow empirical beginnings. Answering the research call in more compelling and convincing fashion will perhaps remain the greatest challenge for models of supervision in the decades that lie ahead.

The supervisory relationship

Extrapolating from the work of Gelso and Carter (1985), Bernard and Goodyear (2014) have defined the supervisory relationship as "The supervision participants' attitudes and feelings toward each other and the way in which those attitudes and feelings are expressed. The supervision relationship, an eminently triadic affair, encompasses such variables as the supervision alliance, attachment style, supervisory style, parallel process, and personality factors." Beinart's Chapter 11 provides a particularly useful and informed perspective on the current status of the supervisory relationship. To varying degrees, other chapters throughout the book also touch on the crucial importance of the supervisory relationship for effectiveness of supervision process and outcome. In a fascinating account of some particularly challenging, rarely mentioned aspects of the alliance within group supervision, Ogren, Boethius, and Sundin (Chapter 31) noted how "the supervisor must make sure that the climate does not become so 'nice' that the group members can be assumed to have made a silent pact to avoid . . . competitiveness, negative feelings and counter-transference (Ogren et al., 2001). A good balance is essential between facilitating alliance-making as a basis for a sense of security within the group and allowing necessary frustration and confrontation to further the professional psychotherapeutic development of the supervisees."

In considering this various material about the supervision relationship, the most robust point that has emerged from our reading would be this: more so than at any other time in supervision's 100-year plus history, the supervisory relationship has evolved in such a way that (a) far more equal weight is now assigned to each party's particular importance in the supervision triad, (b) far more deliberate and studious attention is now given to how each party specifically affects the supervision triad (client, supervisee, *and* supervisor), and (c) far more emphasis is now placed on the ways in which participants' respective psychologies intersect and how that intersection impacts supervision process and outcome. We have progressed from a monolithic, top–down arrangement to the valuing of dynamic collaboration and the recognition of recursive processes and co-construction (see Rigazio-DiGilio, Chapter 30). The supervisory relationship has perhaps come to truly be viewed and more fully appreciated as triadic, systemic phenomenon as never before. When organized supervision efforts began nearly a century ago at the Berlin Poliklinik (Watkins, 2013a), focus seemed to be solely on the psychology of the patient receiving treatment and what to do about it therapeutically. The impact of the interpersonal, relational aspects of treatment and supervision had yet to be recognized and was decades away from receiving its due. The psychology of the supervisee and its potential effects on the supervisory encounter did not begin to substantively enter the picture until the 1950s; the psychology of the supervisor and its potential effects on the supervisory encounter did not begin to substantively enter the picture until decades later. Today, it is axiomatic to think of and refer to supervision as triadic event. But in the grand scope of its history, this deeper and more complete appreciation of supervision's triadic nature is only about a generation old.

In our reading and study of these chapters, a second point of consensus shines through and perhaps could best be stated as follows: across any and all perspectives on the supervisory relationship, supervisors appear to readily recognize that (a) supervisees differ in their skills, abilities, potentials, and learning needs; (b) to provide supervision with most solid foundation, those variables need to routinely be considered for planning purposes from the outset; and (c) based on that consideration, a more effective tailoring of supervision to best match particular supervisee needs can thereby be achieved. This point, as with the preceding one, can also be thought of as axiomatic, but that seemingly has not always been standard fare. Over the course of supervision's history, we get the sense that in times past a "one size fits all" mentality may have been far more the guiding ethos for supervisory practice than otherwise – where supervisee learning needs were not adequately taken into account, any tailoring of supervision to accommodate those supervisee needs was left undone and, instead, supervision was prosecuted to "fit the tailor." But over the last generation, if there is a mantra that has come to increasingly define supervision practice, then "one size does not fit all" would be it (cf. Bernard & Goodyear, 2014; Borders, 2014; Borders & Brown, 2005; Farber, 2012; Ladany & Bradley, 2010; Milne, 2009; Reiser & Milne, 2012; Sarnat, 2012; Scaturo, 2012; Stoltenberg & McNeill, 2010;

Watkins, 2012a; Watkins & Scaturo, 2013). What we have consequently seen are more widely pervasive and substantive supervision efforts to live out the spirit of that mantra in every respect, and the chapters in this book bear powerful testament to that reality.

Of all the varied components and facets that comprise the supervisory relationship, none has received more consistent and thorough going attention than the alliance between supervisor and supervisee. Now half a century old (Fleming & Benedek, 1964, 1966), the supervisory alliance – defined by means of supervisor–supervisee rapport or bond, mutual understandings and agreements about supervision goals, and mutual understandings and agreements about tasks to be executed in the service of goal attainment – has, in our view, emerged as the preeminent organizing construct of the supervision encounter. Referred to as "quintessential integrative variable" and the very "heart and soul of supervision" (Watkins, 2014b, 2014c), the alliance also seems to provide a point of unequivocal convergence across supervision perspectives and practitioners: (a) it appears to be uniformly regarded as a necessary, although not sufficient, component of the supervisory relationship; (b) it appears to be viewed as a relational facilitator, not only making the action of supervision possible but also having the potential to increase the power of its action; and (c) it is typically considered to substantially contribute to the nature of both supervision process and its eventual outcome, with favorably perceived alliances being far more apt to have highly favorable impact and unfavorably perceived alliances being far more apt to have highly unfavorable impact. Based on current perspective (see Beinart, Chapter 11), some of the chief features of such favorably perceived alliances – from the supervisees' perspective – would include the supervisor's being empathic, collaborative, engaged, flexible, adaptive, creative, respectful, genuine, encouraging, affirming, calming, guiding, teaching, structuring, and challenging. Where such features have been on display, more positive supervisee perceptions about supervision have, in turn, been reported (e.g., more satisfaction with supervision, greater perceived effectiveness of supervision). Where such features have been absent or their converse has been on display, negative supervisee perceptions about supervision have routinely been reported (e.g., higher degree of perceived stress, more exhaustion and burnout, greater amount of role conflict and role ambiguity). The power and promise of the alliance for making or breaking supervision experience seem now to be a well-acknowledged reality in contemporary supervision, and from our reading, much in this book gives loud and irrepressible voice to that being so. For example, in Chapter 27, Scaturo and Watkins integrated the alliance within a transtheoretical framework, helping supervisors to think about the rationale for their approach.

But as Milne (2009) has so aptly indicated, ". . . although the professional consensus is unanimous in affirming the importance of the supervisory alliance . . ., evidence to support the assumption is surprisingly wanting" (p. 93). While an important empirical building block, the available evidence thus far has virtually all been correlational, cross sectional, and ex post facto in nature. What more appears to be needed to provide complementary empirical traction and profitably advance alliance studies? Because the alliance is indeed so unanimously affirmed and continues to be granted such hallowed supervision status, that question seems highly pertinent to consider. Based on recent review, Watkins (2013d, in press 2014c) has identified three particular directions that, if pursued, hold much promise for substantively advancing supervision alliance understanding: (a) investigation of the supervisory alliance in process, including attention to the alliance rupture and repair experience; (b) tapping multiple perspectives when measuring alliance; and (c) taking a methodologically diverse and diversified approach to alliance research. As yet, none of those directions have been much on research display and, instead, the most typical supervision alliance study has been a one-shot, self-report examination of supervisee perspective only. If supervision alliance knowledge, understanding, and practice are to be more empirically informed and empirically grounded, then building a base of future research studies that incorporate those three recommended directions will be required.

The "real" or personal relationship between supervisor and supervisee, not specifically addressed throughout these chapters, is a last area that we would like to mention here as matter for future consideration. Over the last near 20-year period, the personal relationship between therapist and patient (occurring as a part of their professional interaction) has received an increasing amount of conceptual, practical, and empirical attention in the psychotherapy literature; data now strongly suggest that the real or personal relationship matters and can indeed matter greatly for the entirety of the psychotherapy relationship (Gelso, 2009, 2011, 2014). But how might the real or personal relationship matter in clinical supervision? We believe that to be an empirical question that also needs study. The real or personal relationship in supervision refers to those supervisor–supervisee interactions or experiences that fall outside of their proper working relationship or alliance. Examples of real relationship experiences in supervision (similar for psychotherapy as well) could include the following: greetings and salutations, parting comments, shaking hands, tact, courtesy, friendly interest, self-expression, warmth, liking, "clicking," trust, expressing feelings about events that impact the supervisee's or supervisor's life (e.g., birth of a child, death of a parent), and the genuine and appropriate feelings the supervisor and supervisee experience toward one another as a part of the supervisory process (e.g., sadness over supervision's termination, happiness over supervisee successes). While there is no denying the reality of such supervisor–supervisee interactions or experiences, they have not been the focus of substantive attention in supervision thus far. Yet the real or personal relationship has been identified as being a crucial component of the supervision relationship, perhaps on par with the significance of the alliance itself, and suggestion for empirical test to that effect (based on the work of Gelso) has been made (Watkins, 2011a, 2011b, 2013b). If the totality of the supervision relationship is to be most fully taken into account, then we believe that future attention to the real or personal relationship will be integral to any such consideration. It appears to very much be a component of the supervision relationship, although almost completely neglected as of this writing.

Difference and diversity (or multicultural considerations)

To some extent, every interpersonal encounter can be considered an experience in difference and diversity (Bernard & Goodyear, 2014). No two individuals are ever exactly alike, differences are to be expected, and those differences can widely vary across individuals. As our knowledge of psychotherapy/counseling and supervision has evolved, increasing attention – conceptual, practical, and empirical – has been given to trying to better understand the ways in which difference and diversity (or multicultural) variables impact those respective helping processes and their constituents. As currently defined, difference and diversity variables include "gender, race, ethnicity, sexual orientation, disability, socioeconomic status, age, and religion, as well as their intersections" (Ancis & Ladany, 2010, p. 54). While Chapter 10 by Tsui, O'Donoghue, and Ng gives primary focus to culture alone, it also provides an instructive overview about issues of crucial importance to consider across any and all difference and diversity encounters. As Tsui et al. accentuate, diversity-sensitive and diversity-informed awareness, knowledge, attitudes, and skills are requisite for competent supervision practice and ideally should serve as the nucleus for the development of supervisor training programs as well.

Across the last generation of scholarship and practice, matters of difference and diversity have increasingly moved out of the supervision shadows to currently being viewed as a guiding ethos: They are rightly considered to be inextricably intertwined in every facet of the supervisory endeavour. Difference and diversity are now routinely included in existing supervision competency frameworks; supervision training experiences and professional development opportunities, be they graduate or post-graduate in nature; and any and all instructive text materials that elucidate the essentials of clinical supervision practice (e,g., Bernard & Goodyear, 2014; Falender, 2004; Fleming & Steen, 2012; Hawkins & Shohet, 2012; Pelling, Barletta, & Armstrong, 2009; Psychology Board of Australia, 2013; Roth & Pilling, 2008). Furthermore, a slowly growing body of multicultural supervision research has also become evident (e.g., Son & Ellis, 2013). But if there is one unanimous opinion about the current status of this area that seems to be shared across the supervision community now, it would be this: while this increasing attention to difference and diversity in supervision is most welcome and informative, such effort has only just begun in so many respects, and if a substantive advance is to occur in our multicultural supervision understanding, then far more intensive and extensive consideration will need to be given to the many facets of this area. From our perspective, that deliberate and studious consideration is vital for supervision's future. As we see it, important advances in supervision will largely be predicated upon the very advancement of our multicultural supervision knowledge and understanding. Significant supervision progress will not happen in the absence of multicultural supervision progress.

In reflecting upon the future of the supervision-multicultural area, what particular needs seem most pressing to address now? What are the concerns of most critical import for supervision-difference/diversity advancement? In answer to those questions, two crucial issues bear emphasis: (a) working to best place supervision within a competency-based multicultural context and (b) striving to build a broader, more informed multicultural supervision research base. As Arthur and Collins (2009) have indicated, attention to multicultural competence is generally a rather recent phenomenon, and in thinking about supervision, such attention is even more recent still. In a 2013 issue of *The Counseling Psychologist*, which included an excellent set of papers on multicultural supervision, Falender, Burnes, and Ellis (2013) accentuated that very point: "there exists a critical need . . . to understand and promote supervision using a competency-based multicultural framework" (p. 19). While some effort has indeed been made to address that need (Inman & Kreider, 2013; Inman & Ladany, 2014), it still remains uncharted territory in many respects and will require serious, continuing attention in the years ahead if multicultural supervision competence is to ever become a more highly substantive practical and educational reality. As a complement to that desideratum, serious, continuing attention will also be sorely needed from an empirical perspective. Ancis and Ladany (2010) have actually referred to such need as "imperative," indicating that multicultural research is necessary for enhancing understanding and best serving all parties developmentally across the totality of the supervisory triad. Their opinion is well in accordance with and generally reflective of what appears to now be consensus about the vital importance of and supreme necessity for more and better multicultural supervision research. In looking ahead, we believe that need will remain relentless in its press and ideally will command much empirical redress in supervision's future.

Measurement and evaluation

In drawing conclusions about the state of play nearly 20 years ago, Watkins (1997) urged researchers to develop better measures, ones that were specific to supervision. In the same overview, Watkins also extended the concept of a core outcome battery to supervision, first suggested in relation to psychotherapy outcome evaluation nearly 40 years ago (Waskow & Parloff, 1975). Watkins (1997, p. 609) predicted that such a battery was "a good way off." Yet here we are a few short years later with a rich seam of psychometrically robust, supervision-specific instruments, together with the initial version of a core outcome battery (Wheeler and Barkham, Chapter 16). This is heartening progress, complemented most helpfully by a suitably diverse range of measures. O'Donovan and Kavanagh have helpfully reviewed the most popular measure, supervisee satisfaction (Chapter 22). We particularly applaud the grounding of such instruments in relevant theory, as this enhances hypothesis validity and enables the interpretation of data. For example, The Manchester Clinical Supervision Scale (Winstanley and White, Chapter 17) operationalizes the normative–formative–restorative model of supervision (Kadushin, 1976), while Milne and Reiser's SAGE instrument (Chapter 18) draws on experiential learning theory.

Another major development within supervision that builds directly on psychotherapy is clinical outcome monitoring. This links measurement, evaluation, and supervision in a systematic fashion, as illustrated impressively in Chapter 25 by Richards. Based on work in the United States on collaborative care, Richards introduced "clinical case management supervision" as one part of the united Kingdom's innovative Improving Access to Psychological Therapies (IAPT) program, a stepped care system designed to deliver "low-intensity" psychological treatments to thousands of patients. Supervision pivots on sessional clinical outcome data, which is automated through computer-based patient management systems and presented to the supervisor as the basis for routine supervision. Cases discussed within clinical case management supervision are based on the emergent clinical outcome data. This approach to supervision contrasts markedly with traditional professional supervision, with this form of IAPT supervision being concerned primarily with the patient, fidelity to the (CBT) model, and clinical decision-making affecting all patients on the supervisee's caseload. Chapters 9 (Rousmaniere) and 21 (Bambling) provide more ideas on outcome monitoring.

How might this uplifting progress unfold over the next decade? Surely one major challenge is dissemination: the business of generalizing developments of these kinds to the majority of supervisors. In this sense, the maintenance of IAPT (and clinical case management supervision) appears vulnerable to the transitory nature of governmental priorities, whereas the core outcome battery logic integrates dissemination through research networks. Again, this builds on success in the field of therapy, where Barkham and colleagues have developed and disseminated clinical outcome instruments that have been administered to thousands of patients in England. There are important lessons to be learned from the innovation literature (Rotheram-Borus, Swendeman, & Chorpita, 2012), so we believe that the biggest step forward would be for the good technical progress in measurement to be matched by large-scale technological dissemination. Competence-based evaluation and socially valid measurement are likely to be features of any such dissemination, as illustrated by Bagnall and Sloan (Chapter 20).

In complete contrast, another development that we would wish to encourage is the measurement of small-scale supervision processes. These would enable us to "zoom in" on the mechanisms or processes that govern effectiveness, the variables which encourage "sudden gains" or which repair alliance ruptures, and so on (Milne et al., 2008). We take up this theme next.

Research

A striking feature of supervision research, in general, is the scarcity of process–outcome evaluations. This is a glaring omission for a field with such a strong foundation in therapy research, as there is so much to be learned from a careful scrutiny of the relationship between what was done and its effect. As noted in our introductory chapter, definitions of supervision are decidedly diverse, something that is especially problematic because supervision is a complex intervention that is not easily conceptualized (Wampold & Holloway, 1997). Furthermore, some forms of supervision take complexity to very challenging levels, using concepts such as co-construction and recursive processes, making it hardly surprising that limited research has taken place (see Rigazio-DiGilio, Chapter 30). With such complexity, one of the associated difficulties has been a lack of transparency regarding what was actually done in the name of supervision: process evaluations of supervision fidelity are rare, at least when linked to an operational definition or supervision manual. Within therapy research, there is some broad agreement on the kinds of variables that constitute an outcome (i.e., symptomatic relief, improved quality of life and functional impairment: Comer & Kendall, 2013). Reviews of supervision outcomes again indicate relatively diverse definitions in terms of the focus (supervisees or their patients?) and selected outcome. While client outcomes are broadly thought to refer to positive changes in the patient as a result of therapy (Wampold & Holloway, 1997), this subsumes various indices: several studies have treated client satisfaction or contentment as an outcome, while others selected social functioning, symptom relief, risk reduction, or quality of life (Milne, 2009).

We think that part of a working solution is the already-noted progress on measurement (e.g., a core outcome battery), but the lesson from therapy research is also surely complementary progress on process evaluation. We agree with Bambling (Chapter 21, and the other contributors to this handbook) that supervision is a complex, multilayered, interactive process. We need evaluations to illuminate such processes as experiential learning (see Milne and Reiser, Chapter 18). Process evaluations should be matched in scale to the study hypotheses, as in considering how microelements of supervisor training (e.g., corrective feedback) impact on supervisors' reflections, as recorded by such means as portfolios (Bagnall and Sloan, Chapter 20), or in considering how larger-scale interventions, such as the IAPT initiative (Richards, Chapter 25), impact on the clinical outcomes of thousands of patients.

In gazing into our crystal ball, we glimpse signs that therapy research will continue to exert a powerful influence on supervision research. To illustrate, we translate some current, relevant therapy research (as per the cited references further on), predicting the following themes within supervision research.

- "Signature supervision": the methods used within supervision are personalized by taking into account supervisee characteristics (see Carpenter et al., 2012).
- "Sudden gains": penetrating analyses of the moderators, mediators, and mechanisms that combine to produce dramatic progress (see Aderka, Nickerson, Boe, & Hofman, 2012).
- "Super supervision": component analyses which compare standard supervision with supervision which has components added or dismantled (Bell, Marcus, & Goodlad, 2012).
- "Remote possibilities": supplementing supervisor training workshops with teleconferencing, designed to provide live supervision of supervision and to better disseminate evidence-based practice (EBP) (Smith et al., 2012).
- "Sticking at it": manipulations of the supervision dose (i.e., total supervision received) and supervisee engagement (i.e., extent of active participation) influence therapist adherence and client outcomes (Glenn et al., 2012).
- "Accurate observation": more objective forms of evaluation will be developed, including training raters to observe accurately the critical aspects of supervision (Chapman, McCart, Letourneau, & Sheidow, 2012).

These examples were sampled from one year of one journal's contents (i.e., Journal of Consulting & Clinical Psychology, 2012), so many other ideas could be gleaned from a larger sample. We enthusiastically anticipate suitable variants within the supervision literature.

Ethical and legal aspects

Like one's theoretical orientation, an ethical dimension runs through the very heart of supervision, encouraging us to do what is right. Observing ethical principles is like observing the rules of a game: although rarely discussed, they bear on everything we do in our professional life, helping to regulate, educate, and guide us (e.g., with respect to doing no harm, doing what is beneficial, and doing justice). Supervisors should heighten awareness of ethical matters in a positive, prospective vein (e.g., recognizing how a supervisee has respected a client's autonomy).

For the novice supervisee, this "heartbeat" may be only dimly apprehended, but with experience, it becomes a significant point of reference, a "moral compass" (Hess, 2008). And when there are ethical transgressions, it is usually the supervisee who suffers most (e.g., through the supervisors' abuse of power, as in blurring relationship boundaries for their personal gain). For supervisors, there are usually quite prominent challenges, such as attending properly to one's duties, managing complex confidentiality issues, and ensuring that the appropriate accountability arrangements are in place. One source of complexity is that the guiding principles may seem to contradict one another. For instance, we naturally wish to respect the supervisee's autonomy (the right to act freely and to exercise choice), but situations may arise where this forms a tension with the supervisor's accountability (e.g., exercising authority over the supervisee when a situation is judged to require intervention). As noted by Thomas (Chapter 6) in her wonderfully international review, such ethical dimensions are complex and multifaceted, representing an aspect of supervision that is critical to a stable, trusting, and productive relationship. It is partly critical as supervisors must behave ethically when dealing with such tensions, seeking to follow due process in identifying and addressing any concerns (e.g., referring to established procedures or consulting with appropriate colleagues). This includes an appropriate problem-solving approach (Knapp & VandeCreek, 2006). Dealing skillfully with such complexities is illustrated in Chapter 10 (Tsui, O'Donoghue and Ng), in the context of cross-cultural supervision, where rather different concepts of ethical practice may exist. Thus, in the context of authority versus autonomy in New Zealand, one experienced European New Zealander supervisor followed a process with his Maori supervisees that involved more checking of their comfort and agreement with regard to his interventions, relative to non-Maori supervisees.

Legal issues are much less prominent within the present handbook and within international supervision. However, the few legal cases to date (and the threats of legal action) relate directly to ethical principles. For example, in the United States, a supervisor lost her licence to practice because she allowed her supervisee to counsel a friend, blurring relationship boundaries. In our own experience, the most common legal risk that supervisors take is to treat supervisees as equals, effectively denying their supervisory accountability and authority. Whether due to some misplaced "cult of the positive" or excessive "niceness" (Fleming, Gone, Diver, & Fowler, 2007), this can result in a reluctance to conduct observations or take other measures to orient themselves to what the supervisee is actually doing, or to be unwilling to take steps to enhance the supervisee's ethical practice. Another possible explanation is that rarely do supervisors obtain a thorough training in supervision, even though their code of ethics may well require them to operate within the boundaries of their competence (Knapp & VandeCreek, 1997). Whatever the reason, this avoidance or denial is a risky stance, avoiding the exercise of legitimate and expert power: as Thomas makes clear, there is an international consensus that supervisors carry the ultimate clinical, ethical, and legal responsibility for their supervisees. In the British National Health Service, some supervisees have a similarly suspect arrangement, called "peer supervision," in which they take turns to "supervise" one another, often within a small group. But peer supervision is an informal, leaderless arrangement where no one has authority, making the term an oxymoron, a dangerous nonsense because it negates these responsibilities and flattens the necessarily hierarchical relationship. This is not to devalue the benefits of discussing work with peers, but that should properly be called something like "peer consultation" (Counselman & Weber, 2004), and it should be clearly understood that no group member has authority or responsibility in relation to the other members (to minimize legal liability). It should also be supplemented by clinical supervision, whether in a group or otherwise.

We hope that the practice of supervision will be increasingly recognized as a bonafide subspecialty within the mental health professions. The hallmarks of such recognition will include the explicit teaching of ethics within supervisor training programs by trainers, negotiating supervision contracts that reflect educational and organizational needs, the direct observation of supervisees' therapy, and training programs developing in supervisees the requisite competencies for recognizing and addressing ethical issues. Over the next decades, we hope that the growing status of supervision will witness a more thorough and sophisticated embrace of its ethical heart, with the current instances of avoidance and denial replaced by positive ethical practices.

Technology

What are some of the new or emerging educational tools that could be of most potential benefit to the supervisory experience now? As we work to keep our models and methods fresh and most educationally vital, continued consideration of that question seems supremely important to bear in mind. Striving to forever enhance educational experience within and across supervision models is eminent, enduring objective that can never be allowed to lapse. In contemporary practice, one such enhancement possibility can certainly be found in ongoing technological advances and their implications for supervision practice and training. Whereas solely talking with supervisees about their treatment sessions or reviewing process notes may have once been standard fare for the supervisory hour, neither appears to be used as much so in exclusion today. First used in psychotherapy training and supervision in the 1960s (Abbass, 2004), videorecording appears to now be used with far greater frequency to good effect and with good reason: it has the potential to make the work of supervision come alive via viewing the treatment hour in moment by moment real time. Such perspective, in our view, is invaluable and irreplaceable for optimal supervision practice. Absent videorecord, memory problems can surface via transience, absent mindedness, misattribution, and bias; videorecording can serve as a counter to such possibilities and increase the chances of a much more accurate treatment picture being displayed in supervision (Haggerty & Hilsenroth, 2011). As Haggerty and Hilsenroth (2011) have rightly opined, "With the cost of videotape equipment dropping and technological advances [rising] there is little reason why almost all training programmes could not include videotaping sessions as at least some part of their training programme" (p. 205). Where cost is not a prohibitive issue, we could not agree more about the power and possibility of videorecording to enhance the supervisory experience.

But as we also see from Chapters 9 (by Rousmaniere) and 13 (by Nelson) and other recent like publications (Barnett, 2011; Rousmaniere & Frederickson, 2013), the march of technological innovation does not stop with supervisor and supervisee in-house review of videorecord. Individual and group supervision by means of videoconference and remote live supervision – with potential to stretch across cities, states, countries, and continents – are readily available and already being put to excellent programmatic use (e.g., the China American Psychoanalytic Alliance, where American psychoanalysts are involved in providing psychodynamic psychotherapy training to a large number of students across 18 Chinese cities; Fishkin, Fishkin, Leli, Katz, & Snyder, 2011; Varvin & Gerlach, 2011). In conjunction with Web-conferencing, interactive computer programs, virtual human technology, and psychotherapy-specific Web sites (e.g., http://www.ATOStrainer.com for watching/rating treatment sessions) have become reality for training and supervision purposes (Abbass et al., 2011; Manring, Greenberg, Gregory, & Gallinger, 2011; McCullough, Bhatia, Ulvenes, Berggraf, & Osborn, 2011). The possibilities for technological advancement in psychotherapy education show no signs of diminishing. As Watkins (2012b) recently stated, such developments "have impacted how many of us already think about and conduct psychotherapy [or counseling] supervision and . . . will continue to do so in the years and decades ahead. These ongoing advances will open up new, exciting, and instructive possibilities that have the potential to further enhance the supervision learning experience for both supervisee and supervisor" (p. 201). Yet with that immense enhancement potential recognized, the real challenge for supervisors perhaps will forever be remaining sufficiently abreast of technological advances and, in effort to best develop supervisee learning, working to routinely and most meaningfully incorporate such advances into supervision. Based on Rousmaniere's superb treatment of this topic in Chapter 9, we believe that to be a manageable challenge whose benefits will far outweigh any costs that might be incurred in the process.

Training and education

What might be said now about the international status of supervisor education – preparing supervisors for supervising and subsequently enhancing their continuing professional supervisory development? When the *Handbook of Psychotherapy Supervision* first appeared in 1997, the general absence of supervision training for supervisors was loudly lamented and the need for a course correction in that regard was vigorously voiced: "something does not compute" (Watkins, 1997, p. 604). Over the past approximate 20-year period, evidence of such course correction seemingly has been widely building to varying degrees around our globe. Because supervision's importance in enhancing therapeutic competence appears to be an international given at this point (cf. Bang & Park, 2009; Bomba, 2011; Lim & Hong, 2013; Msimanga, 2013; Stupart, Rehfuss, & Parks-Savage, 2010; Szilagyi, 2013; Vera & Barreto, 2013), we, perhaps, are at a place where the following statements about supervisor education seem accordingly safe to make: (a) across mental health disciplines, the potential importance of supervision training – for developing and enhancing competent supervisory practice – also appears to now be increasingly recognized and appreciated internationally as never before; (b) over time, that growing recognition and appreciation have led to and, we believe, will continue to lead to the proliferation of supervision training opportunities – voluntary and required – for supervision practitioners, whatever might be their country or continent, mental health discipline, or theoretical perspective; and (c) more so now than at any previous time, the crucial competencies that are so essential to good supervision practice have been consensually identified internationally, have been recommended for program use as systematic blueprint for the training of new supervisors, and, in turn, have served to organize and systematize the implementation of supervisor training efforts on an increasingly worldwide scale. In our view, these are all most welcome developments, giving greater recognition and exciting momentum to the overdue transformation of supervisory practice and education.

As these positive changes continue to be built upon, what might also be some of the more consequential challenges that still require redress if supervisor education is to most viably advance? Fleming (2012) has identified several such highly important issues as being the development of advanced training for supervisors, giving focus to transfer of training (i.e., examining if supervisory training actually translates into supervisory practice), and striving to establish a more solid base of evaluation and research for supervisor training (evaluations of helping skills training may help guide this work: see Hill, Chapter 14). Fleming (2012) also rightly indicated that little is still known about supervision of supervision, and a remedy for that lack is sorely needed on both practical and research fronts. We heartily agree with Fleming's assessment and see each of those concerns as continuing to be pressing matters in the education of clinical supervisors. Furthermore, if – as Falender and Shafranske (2004) asserted a decade ago – an empirical, evidence-based theoretical foundation is requisite for the practice of clinical supervision, then supervisor training ideally should also be grounded in such foundation as well. While substantive work that provides some foundation in that very direction has been programmatically developed by Milne and his colleagues (e.g., see Chapters 3 and 18; Milne, 2008, 2009, 2010; Milne & Reiser, 2012; Milne, Sheikh, Pattison, & Wilkinson, 2011; Milne & Westerman, 2001), more consistent, sustained, and systematic attention across researchers and educators will be needed if the evidence-based challenge of supervisor training is to be most fully realized as practical reality. As psychotherapy/counseling supervision has increasingly moved onto the fast track to becoming "competency-based, evidence-based, particularized, and energized" (Watkins, 2012b), then the necessity for supervisor training to follow suit would seem a foregone conclusion.

Organizational matters

Several contributors have emphasized how contextual factors influence supervision, interacting with supervisor training. For example, Saarikoski's Chapter 19 describes an instrument for measuring the training context, including the supervisory relationship, the managers' leadership styles, and the staffing "spirit" on the ward. Kihlgren and Hansebo (Chapter 7) note how organizational culture determines the implementation of supervision, as in logistical and resource challenges requiring attention. They also noted that the staff group may require consideration, particularly if coming from different cultural backgrounds, as this can contribute to communication problems and high staff turnover. Additionally, their older adult client group was often extremely dependent (being dementia sufferers). These various organizational considerations meant that supervision was a vital opportunity for the nurses to reflect on their mental health work, seeking enhanced cooperation. But to improve their care, nurses also needed training, ongoing and intensive support (e.g., practical discussions), feedback, and changes to the physical environment. Kihlgren and Hansebo concluded that "This package of supervision and support seemed to be a necessary condition for staff accepting and implementing integrity-promoting care." A second necessary condition was a suitable milieu. Once implemented, this care contributed to an enhanced quality of life for the clients and their caregivers. In Chapter 15, their Swedish compatriots Ögren and Boëthius made similar observations, namely, that the organization should facilitate supervision with a "load-bearing" structure, giving the supervisors a forum for support and reflection about the supervision process. In turn, this enables them to help supervisees deal with complex situations and tolerate uncertainty and powerlessness, strengthening their ability to contain emotionally charged material in therapy.

Both of these accounts exemplify the development of the "right" kind of system to embed and nourish supervision, a system where important contextual factors are identified and managed. Within this context, having the right kind of staff is also important, matched to the client group, consistent with findings from the staff development literature (e.g., Colquitt, LePine, & Noe, 2000). This kind of approach, designed to foster the transfer of training by creating the right milieu or culture for the right people who have received the right training, is also recommended in relation to staff development (e.g., Beidas & Kendall, 2010) and is consistent with the model embedded within Chapter 8 (Watkins and Wang) and Chapter 12 (Gonsalvez).

But reflecting on this approach now, helped by these Swedish chapters (and other models within this handbook), we might note that this "transfer model" is rather passive and simplistic, in that supervisors and supervisees are credited with little power to control their workplace or their own behavior. In this sense, Ögren and Boëthius also helped supervisors to be aware of how they could cultivate appropriate organizational support, an element within a more suitably interactive, self-regulation model. Vec, Vec, and Žorga (Chapter 5) provided another example in recounting their supervision groups, partly created to reduce burnout. They suggested that the clear structure of the group, including "characteristic roles, stable interpersonal relationships, and defined expectations and goals," also created a consistent minority within their organizations. They believed that this helped the supervisees to be more independent, more efficient, more satisfied with their work, and more effective clinically. As a group, it also fostered innovation within the host organizations.

What does this foretell of future developments? Continued reference to the inspiring staff development literature would suggest that suitably cunning approaches to supervisor development would start to take a whole-system approach, empowering supervisors to effect holistic changes in their organizations, and that these would lead to helpful changes in themselves: a general transactional model, referred to in this literature as the "systems-contextual approach" (Sanders & Turner, 2005). Illustrations in the staff development literature include extending therapeutic concepts to staff, such as relapse prevention. For example, Tziner, Haccoun, and Kadish (1991) described how they "immunized" staff against the challenges of transferring their training by such means as heightened awareness, group problem-solving, realistic goal-setting, and encouraging the appropriate personal coping skills. Clear illustrations are hard to find within the supervision literature, but within the neighboring parent development literature, there is some guidance from an impressive project that incorporated supervision. In reflecting on the success of their Positive Parenting Program, Sanders and Turner (2005) described how they had taken an ecological approach, one that assumed that changing professionals' practices entailed a complex interaction among the quality of the therapy, the training, and the practitioner's post-training environment. Like Vec et al., they recognized that they were engaged in innovation, and so were guided by the innovation literature (e.g., Rogers, 1995). Reflexively, they based their innovation strategy on the same self-regulatory approach that was used in their parent education programs. This facilitated professional behavior change through self-directed learning and personal responsibility for skill development, linked to appropriate training (including how to self-monitor, set personal goals, and self-evaluate). As a result, practitioners (therapists) become activc, confident, and self-sufficient problem-solvers. This developmental process was supported by supervision, which also drew on the same approach. Specific features were supervision networks to encourage peer support, the provision of supervision guidelines, and support to overcome administrative barriers.

Conclusions

When we tried to crystallize the progress reflected within this handbook for a brief conference presentation (Milne et al., 2013), we identified three major themes, contrasting them with the status of supervision as captured within the main prior handbook (Watkins, 1997).

- Conceptualization has progressed from chaos to consensus: In 1997, Watkins noted that "(supervision is). . .driven by the theory of therapy that one is trying to teach . . ." (p. 605). At that stage, models of supervision were a "methodological morass" (Falender & Shafranske, 2004, p. 15). The present handbook indicates progress in developing an empirical definition of supervision and in building expert consensus, resulting in a much clearer conceptualization of clinical supervision.
- Operationalization has progressed from soft to solid: In 1997, Watkins recommended that ". . . we need to work toward . . . measures that are supervision-specific . . . not take-offs on a psychotherapy measure." (p. 606). There are now a number of sound and useful instruments that are specific to clinical supervision, alongside suggestions for a core outcome battery.
- Evaluation has advanced from nuisance to necessity: In 1997, Watkins noted that ". . . certain aspects of the evaluative component of supervision have been little addressed . . ." (p. 611). Within the present handbook, we can see evidence that evaluation is now being implemented within clinical supervision, across individuals (supervisors and supervisees), and within systems (hospital and training contexts).

These advances in conceptualization, operationalization, and evaluation set the scene for significant developments, consistent with the growing recognition of supervision as a specialized professional role, an essential part of high-quality mental health services. We can now note these important developments: competency-based supervisor training, instruments to monitor alliances/learning/effectiveness/and so on, more sophisticated ways of understanding how supervision works, systemic analysis of supervision-support arrangements, enhanced clinical outcome monitoring as feedback to supervisors, supervision-specific measurement to improve research, technology-assisted techniques ("remote" supervision, etc.), and a growing recognition of difference and diversity.

In 1997, Watkins declared that "We have a way to go, but we are getting there" (p. 613). Subsequent international advances indicate that we have now reached another important milestone, as reviewed masterfully by Inman and colleagues in Chapter 4. But there remains much to do, and much that has been done will benefit from refinement. This is a vibrant time for developments in supervision. We feel privileged to have helped to summarize this vital international field of professional activity.

References

Abbass, A. (2004). Small-group videotape training for psychotherapy skills development. *Academic Psychiatry, 28*, 151–155.

Abbass, A., Arthey, S., Elliott, J., Fedak, T., Nowoweiski, D., Markovski, J., & Nowoweiski, S. (2011). Utilizing technological innovations to enhance psychotherapy supervision, training, and outcomes. *Psychotherapy, 48*, 109–118.

Aderka, I. M., Nickerson, A., Boe, H. J., & Hofman, S. G. (2012). Sudden gains during psychological treatments of anxiety and depression: A meta-analysis. *Journal of Consulting & Clinical Psychology, 80*, 93–101.

Ancis, J. R., & Ladany, N. (2010). A multicultural framework for counseling supervision. In N. Ladany & L. J. Bradley (Eds.), *Counselor supervision: Principles, process, and practice* (4th ed., pp. 53–95). Philadelphia: Brunner-Routledge.

Arthur, N., & Collins, S. (2009). Culture-infused counselling supervision. In N. Pelling, J. Barletta, & P. Armstrong (Eds.), *The practice of clinical supervision* (pp. 267–295). Bowen Hills: Australia Academic Press.

Bang, K., & Park, J. (2009). Korean supervisors' experiences in clinical supervision. *The Counseling Psychologist, 37*, 1042–1075.

Barnett, J. E. (2011). Special section: Internet and video technology in psychotherapy supervision and training. *Psychotherapy, 48*, 103–181.

Beidas, R. S., & Kendall, P. C. (2010). Training therapists in evidence-based practice: A critical review of studies from a systems-contextual perspective. *Clinical Psychology: Science & Practice, 17*, 1–30.

Beinart, H. (2012). Models of supervision and the supervisory relationship. In I. Fleming & L. Steen (Eds.), *Supervision and clinical psychology: Theory, practice and perspectives* (2nd ed., pp. 47–61). London: Routledge.

Bell, E. C., Marcus, D. K., & Goodlad, J. K. (2012). Are the parts as good as the whole? A meta-analysis of component treatment studies. *Journal of Consulting & Clinical Psychology, 81*, 722–736.

Bernard, J. M., & Goodyear, R. K. (2014). *Fundamentals of clinical supervision* (5th ed.). Upper Saddle River, NJ: Merrill.

Bomba, J. (2011). Psychotherapy supervision as viewed from psychodynamic standpoint. *Archives of Psychiatry and Psychotherapy, 4*, 45–49.

Borders, L. D. (2014). Best Practices in Clinical Supervision: Another step in delineating effective supervision practice. *American Journal of Psychotherapy.*

Borders, L. D., & Brown, L. L. (2005). *The new handbook of counseling supervision* (2nd ed.). New York: Taylor & Francis.

Carpenter, K. M., Cheng, W. Y., Smith, J. L., Brooks, A. C., Amrhein, P. C., Wain, R. M., & Nunes, E. V. (2012). Old dogs and new skills: How clinician characteristics relate to motivational interviewing skills before, during and after training. *Journal of Consulting & Clinical Psychology, 80*, 560–573.

Chapman, J. E., McCart, M. R., Letourneau, E. J., & Sheidow, A. J. (2012). Comparison of youth, caregiver, therapist, trained and treatment expert raters of therapist adherence to a substance abuse treatment protocol. *Journal of Consulting & Clinical Psychology, 81*, 674–680.

Colquitt, J. A., LePine, J. A., & Noe, R. A. (2000). Toward an integrative theory of training motivation: A meta-analytic path analysis of twenty years of research. *Journal of Applied Psychology, 85*, 678–707.

Comer, J. S., & Kendall, P. C. (2013). Methodology, design and evaluation inpsychotherapy research. In M. J. Lambert (Ed.), *Bergin and Garfield's handbook of psychotherapy and behavior change* (6th ed., pp. 21–48). Hoboken, NJ: Wiley.

Counselman, E. F., & Weber, R. L. (2004). Organizing and maintaining peer supervision groups. *International Journal of Group Psychotherapy, 54*, 125–143.

Ellis, M. V. (2010). Bridging the science and practice of clinical supervision: Some discoveries, some misconceptions. *The Clinical Supervisor, 29*, 95–116.

Ellis, M. V., & Ladany, N. (1997). Inferences concerning supervisees and clients in clinical supervision: An integrative review. In C. E. Watkins Jr. (Ed.), *Handbook of psychotherapy supervision* (pp. 447–507). New York: Wiley.

Ellis, M. V., D'Iuso, N., & Ladany, N. (2008). State of the art in assessment, measurement, and evaluation of clinical supervision. In A. K. Hess, et al. (Eds.), *Psychotherapy supervision: Theory, research, and practice* (2nd ed., pp. 473–499). Hoboken, NJ: Wiley.

Falender, C. A., Cornish, J. A. E., Goodyear, R., Hatcher, R., Kaslow, N. J., Leventhal, G., et al. (2004). Defining competencies in psychology supervision: A consensus statement. *Journal of Clinical Psychology, 60*, 771–785.

Falender, C. A., & Shafranske, E. P. (2004). *Clinical supervision: A competency-based approach.* Washington, DC: American Psychological Association.

Falender, C. A., & Shafranske, E. P. (2010). Psychotherapy-based supervision models in an emerging competency-based era: A commentary. *Psychotherapy, 47*, 45–50.

Falender, C. A., & Shafranske, E. P. (2012). The importance of competency-based clinical supervision and training in the 21st century: Why bother? *Journal of Contemporary Psychotherapy, 42*, 5–13.

Falender, C. A., Burnes, T. R., & Ellis, M. V. (2013). Multicultural clinical supervision and benchmarks: Empirical support informing practice and supervisor training. *The Counseling Psychologist, 41*, 8–27.

Farber, E. W. (2010). Humanistic-existential psychotherapy competencies and the supervisory process. *Psychotherapy, 47*, 28–34.

Farber, E. W. (2012). Supervising humanistic-existential psychotherapy in the 21st century: Pressing needs, impressing possibilities. *Journal of Contemporary Psychotherapy, 42*, 173–182.

Fishkin, R., Fishkin, L., Leli, U., Katz, B., & Snyder, E. (2011). Psychodynamic treatment, training, and supervision using internet-based technologies. *Journal of the American Academy of Psychoanalysis and Dynamic Psychiatry, 39*, 155–168.

Fleming, I. (2012). Developments in supervisor training. In I. Fleming & L. Steen (Eds.), *Supervision and clinical psychology: Theory, practice and perspectives* (2nd ed., pp. 77–95). London: Routledge.

Fleming, I., & Steen, L. (Eds.). (2012). *Supervision and clinical psychology: Theory, practice and perspectives* (2nd ed.). London: Routledge.

Fleming, I., Gone, R., Diver, A., & Fowler, B. (2007). Risk supervision in Rochdale. *Clinical Psychology Forum, 176*, 22–25.

Fleming, J., & Benedek, T. F. (1964). Supervision. A method of teaching psychoanalysis. *The Psychoanalytic Quarterly, 33*, 71–96.

Fleming, J., & Benedek, T. F. (1966). *Psychoanalytic supervision: A method of clinical teaching*. New York: Grune & Stratton.

Foo Kune, N. M. R., & Rodolfa, E. R. (2013). Putting the benchmarks into practice: Multiculturally competent supervisors–effective supervision. *The Counseling Psychologist, 41*, 121–130.

Gelso, C. J. (2009). The real relationship in a postmodern world: Theoretical and empirical explorations. *Psychotherapy Research, 19*, 253–264.

Gelso, C. J. (2011). *The real relationship in psychotherapy: The hidden foundation of change*. Washington, D.C.: American Psychological Association.

Gelso, C. J. (2014). A tripartite model of the therapeutic relationship: Theory, research, and practice. *Psychotherapy Research, 24*, 117–131.

Gelso, C. J., & Carter, J. A. (1985). The relationship in counseling and psychotherapy: Components, consequences, and theoretical antecedents. *The Counseling Psychologist, 13*, 155–244.

Glenn, D., Golinelli, D., Rose, R. D., Roy-Byrne, P., Stein, M. B., Sullivan, G., . . . Craske, M. G. (2012). Who gets the most out of cognitive-behavioral therapy for anxiety disorders? The role of treatment dose and patient engagement. *Journal of Consulting & Clinical Psychology, 81*, 639–649.

Goodyear, R. K., & Guzzardo, C. R. (2000). Psychotherapy supervision and training. In S. D. Brown & R. W. Lent (Eds.), *Handbook of counseling psychology* (3rd ed., pp. 83–108). New York: Wiley.

Haggerty, G., & Hilsenroth, M. H. (2011). The use of video in psychotherapy supervision. *British Journal of Psychotherapy, 27*, 193–210.

Hatcher, R., Fouad, N., Grus, C., McCutcheon, S., Campbell, L., & Leahy, K. (2013). Competency benchmarks: Practical steps toward a culture of competence. *Training and Education in Professional Psychology, 7*, 84–91.

Hawkins, P., & Shohet, R. (2012). *Supervision in the helping professions: An individual, group and organizational approach* (4th ed.). Berkshire: Open University Press.

Hess, A. K. (2008). Ethical and legal considerations in psychotherapy supervision. In A. K. Hess, K. D. Hess, & T. H. Hess (Eds.), *Psychotherapy supervision: Theory, research & practice* (2nd ed., pp. 521–534). New York: Wiley.

Holloway, E. L. (2012). Professional competence in supervision. In J. N. Fuertes, A. Spokane, & E. L. Holloway (Eds.), *Specialty competencies in counseling psychology* (pp. 165–181). New York: Oxford University Press.

Hunsley, J., & Barker, K. K. (2011). Training for competency in professional psychology: A Canadian perspective. *Australian Psychologist, 46*, 142–145.

Inman, A. G., & Kreider, E. D. (2013). Multicultural competence: Psychotherapy practice and supervision. *Psychotherapy, 50*, 346–350.

Inman, A. G., & Ladany, N. (2008). Research: The state of the field. In A. K. Hess, K. D. Hess, & T. H. Hess (Eds.), *Psychotherapy supervision: Theory, research, and practice* (2nd ed., pp. 500–517). Hoboken, NJ: Wiley.

Inman, A. G., & Ladany, N. (2014). Multicultural competencies in psychotherapy supervision. In F. T. L. Leong (Ed.), *APA handbook of multicultural psychology: Applications and training* (pp. 643–658). Washington, DC: American Psychological Association.

Kadushin, A. (1976). *Supervision in social work*. New York: Columbia University Press.

Knapp, S., & VandeCreek, L. (1997). Ethical and legal aspects of clinical supervision. In C. E. Watkins (Ed.), *Handbook of psychotherapy supervision* (pp. 589–602). New York: Wiley.

Knapp, S. J., & VandeCreek, L. D. (2006). *Practical ethics for psychologists: A positive approach*. Washington, DC: APA.

Knowles, M. S., Swanson, R. A., & Holton, E. F. (2011). *The adult learner: The definitive classic in adult education and human resource development* (7th ed.). Saint Louis, MO: Routledge.

Ladany, N., & Bradley, L. J. (Eds.). (2010). *Counselor supervision: Principles, process, and practice* (4th ed.). Philadelphia: Brunner-Routledge.

Ladany, N., & Inman, A. G. (2012). Training and supervision. In E. Altmaier & J. C. Hansen (Eds.), *Oxford handbook of counseling psychology* (pp. 179–207). New York: Oxford University Press.

Lim, J., & Hong, S. Y. (2013). *Improving standardized classification tool of the Korean long-term care program: From the perspectives of clinical supervisors and directors.* Presentation given at the International Interdisciplinary Conference on Clinical Supervision, Adelphi University, Garden City, New York (June 14).

Manring, J., Greenberg, R. P., Gregory, R., & Gallinger, L. (2011). Learning psychotherapy in the digital age. *Psychotherapy, 48*, 119–126.

McCullough, L., Bhatia, M., Ulvenes, P., Berggraf, L., & Osborn, K. (2011). Learning how to rate video-recorded therapy sessions: A practical guide for trainees and advanced clinicians. *Psychotherapy, 48*, 127–137.

Milne, D. (2008). Evaluating and enhancing supervision: An experiential model. In C. Falender & E. Shafranske (Eds.), *Casebook for clinical supervision: A competency-based approach* (pp. 211–245). Washington, DC: American Psychological Association.

Milne, D. (2009). *Evidence-based clinical supervision: Principles and practice.* Hoboken, NJ: Wiley.

Milne, D. (2010). Can we enhance the training of clinical supervisors? A national pilot study of an evidence-based approach. *Clinical Psychology and Psychotherapy, 17*, 321–328.

Milne, D., & Reiser, R. P. (2012). A rationale for evidence-based clinical supervision. *Journal of Contemporary Psychotherapy, 42*, 139–150.

Milne, D., Leck, C., James, I., Wilson, M., Procter, R., Ramm, L., & Weetman, J. (2012). High fidelity in clinical supervision research. In I. Fleming & L. Steen (Eds.), *Supervision and clinical psychology: Theory, practice and perspectives* (2nd ed., pp. 142–158). London: Routledge.

Milne, D., Gonsalvez, C., & Watkins, C. E., Jr. (2013). *International advances in clinical supervision.* Presentation given at the Advances in Clinical Supervision Conference, Sydney, Australia (June 5th).

Milne, D. L., & Westerman, C. (2001). Evidence-based clinical supervision: Rationale and illustration. *Clinical Psychology and Psychotherapy, 8*, 444–457.

Milne, D. L., Kennedy, E., Todd, H., Lombardo, C., Freeston, M., & Day, A. (2008). Zooming in on CBT supervision: A comparison of two levels of effectiveness evaluation. *Behavioural & Cognitive Psychotherapy, 36*, 619–624.

Milne, D. L., Sheikh, A. I., Pattison, S., & Wilkinson, A. (2011). Evidence-based training for clinical supervisors: A systematic review of 11 controlled studies. *The Clinical Supervisor, 30*, 53–71.

Msimanga, S. (2013). *Hurdles of clinical supervision in Botswana.* Roundtable discussion conducted at the International Interdisciplinary Conference on Clinical Supervision, Adelphi University, Garden City, New York (June 14).

Owens-Pugh, V., & Symons, C. (2013). Roth and Pilling's competence framework for clinical supervision: How generalizable is it? *Counselling and Psychotherapy Research, 13*, 126–135.

Pelling, N., Barletta, J., & Armstrong, P. (Eds.). (2009). *The practice of clinical supervision.* Bowen Hills: Australia Academic Press.

Psychology Board of Australia (2013). *Guidelines for supervisors and supervisor training providers.* Retrieved 10/1/2013 from http://www.psychologyboard.gov.au/Registration/Supervision.aspx

Reiser, R., & Milne, D. (2012). Supervising cognitive-behavioral psychotherapy in the 21st century: Pressing needs, impressing possibilities. *Journal of Contemporary Psychotherapy, 42*, 161–171.

Rodolfa, E., Greenberg, S., Hunsley, J., Smith-Zoeller, M., Cox, D., Sammons, M., & Spivak, H. (2013). A competency model for the practice of psychology. *Training and Education in Professional Psychology, 7*, 71–83.

Rogers, E. M. (1995). *Diffusion of innovations* (4th ed.). New York: Free Press.

Roth, A. (2013). Commentary on Owens-Pugh and Symons. *Counselling and Psychotherapy Research, 13*, 136–137.

Roth, A., & Pilling, S. (2008). *A competence framework for the supervision of psychological therapies.* Retrieved 10/1/2013 from http://www.ucl.ac.uk/clinical-psychology/CORE/supervision_framework

Rotheram-Borus, M. J., Swendeman, D., & Chorpita, B. F. (2012). Disruptive innovations for designing and diffusing evidence-based interventions. *American Psychologist, 67*, 463–476.

Rousmaniere, T. G., & Frederickson, J. (2013). Internet-based one-way-mirror supervision for advanced psychotherapy training. *The Clinical Supervisor, 32*, 40–55.

Sanders, M. R., & Turner, M. T. (2005). Reflections on the challenges of effective dissemination of behavioral family intervention: Our experience with the Triple P- positive parenting program. *Child & Adolescent Mental Health, 10*, 158–169.

Sarnat, J. (2010). Key competencies of the psychodynamic psychotherapist and how to teach them in supervision. *Psychotherapy, 47*, 20–27.

Sarnat, J. (2012). Supervising psychoanalytic psychotherapy in the 21st century: Pressing needs, impressing possibilities. *Journal of Contemporary Psychotherapy, 42*, 151–160.

Scaturo, D. J. (2012). Supervising integrative psychotherapy in the 21st century: Pressing needs, impressing possibilities. *Journal of Contemporary Psychotherapy, 42*, 183–192.

Schaffer, J. B., Rodolfa, E. R., Hatcher, R. L., & Fouad, N. A. (2013). Professional psychology competency initiatives: Reflections, contrasts, and recommendations for next steps. *Training and Education in Professional Psychology, 7*, 92–98.

Smith, J. L., Carpenter, K. M., Amrheim, P. C., Brooks, A. C., Levin, D., Schreiber, E. A., . . . Nunes, E. V. (2012). Training substance abuse clinicians in motivational interviewing using live supervision via teleconferencing. *Journal of Consulting& Clinical Psychology, 80*, 450–464.

Son, E., & Ellis, M. V. (2013). A cross-cultural comparison of clinical supervision in South Korea and the United States. *Psychotherapy, 50*, 189–205.

Stoltenberg, C. D., & McNeill, B. W. (2010). *IDM supervision: An integrated developmental model for supervising counselors and therapists* (3rd ed.). San Francisco, CA: Jossey-Bass.

Stupart, Y., Rehfuss, M., & Parks-Savage, A. (2010). Counselor supervision in Jamaica: An initial exploration. *Journal of International Counselor Education, 2*, 74–95.

Szilagyi, A. (2013). *International clinical supervision: A cross-cultural perspective.* Opening plenary address given at the International Interdisciplinary Conference on Clinical Supervision, Adelphi University, Garden City, New York (June 13).

Tziner, A., Haccoun, R. R., & Kadish, A. (1991). Personal and situational characteristics influencing the effectiveness of transfer of training improvement strategies. *Journal of Occupational Psychology, 64*, 167–177.

Varvin, S., & Gerlach, A. (2011). The development of psychodynamic psychotherapy and psychoanalysis in China. *International Journal of Applied Psychoanalytic Studies, 8*, 261–267.

Vera, G., & Barreto, A. (2013). *On counseling and counseling supervision in Venezuela: Perspectives and current developments.* Presentation given at the International Interdisciplinary

Conference on Clinical Supervision, Adelphi University, Garden City, New York (June 14).

Wampold, B. E. & Holloway, E. L. (1997). Methodology, design and evaluation in psychotherapy supervision research. In C. E. Watkins (Ed.) *Handbook of psychotherapy supervision* (pp. 11–30). New York: Wiley.

Waskow, I. E., & Parloff, M. B. (1975). *Psychotherapy change measures.* Rockville, MD: National Institute of Mental Health.

Watkins, C. E., Jr. (1997). Some concluding thoughts about psychotherapy supervision. In C. E. Watkins Jr. (Ed.), *Handbook of psychotherapy supervision* (pp. 603–616). New York: Wiley.

Watkins, C. E., Jr. (2011a). The real relationship in psychotherapy supervision. *American Journal of Psychotherapy, 65,* 99–116.

Watkins, C. E., Jr. (2011b). Toward a tripartite vision of supervision for psychoanalysis and psychoanalytic psychotherapies: Alliance, transference-countertransference configuration, and real relationship. *The Psychoanalytic Review, 98,* 457–490.

Watkins, C. E., Jr. (2012a). Fortification strategies for supervisory relationship enhancement. *The Psychotherapy Bulletin, 47,* 46–50, 70–73.

Watkins, C. E., Jr. (2012b). Psychotherapy supervision in the new millennium: Competency-based, evidence-based, particularized, and energized. *Journal of Contemporary Psychotherapy, 42,* 193–203.

Watkins, C. E., Jr. (2013a). The beginnings of psychoanalytic supervision: The role of Max Eitingon. *American Journal of Psychoanalysis, 73,* 254–270.

Watkins, C. E., Jr. (2013b). The contemporary practice of effective psychoanalytic supervision. *Psychoanalytic Psychology, 30,* 300–328.

Watkins, C. E., Jr. (2013c). The learning alliance in psychoanalytic supervision: A fifty-year retrospective and prospective. *Psychoanalytic Psychology.* doi: 10.1037/a0034039

Watkins, C. E., Jr. (2013d). *The supervisory alliance: Fifty years and forty studies later.* Presentation given at the International Interdisciplinary Conference on Clinical Supervision, Adelphi University, Garden City, New York (June 13).

Watkins, C. E., Jr. (in press) On psychoanalytic supervision as signature pedagogy. *The Psychoanalytic Review.*

Watkins, C. E., Jr. (2014a). Psychoanalytic supervision in the new millennium: On pressing needs and impressing possibilities. *International Forum of Psychoanalysis* doi: 10.1080/0803706X.2013.779748.

Watkins, C. E., Jr. (2014b). The supervisory alliance as quintessential integrative variable. *Journal of Contemporary Psychotherapy* doi: 10.1007/s10879-013-9252-x.

Watkins, C. E., Jr. (2014c) The supervisory alliance: A half century of theory, practice, and research in critical perspective. *American Journal of Psychotherapy, 68,* 1–37.

Watkins, C. E., Jr., & Scaturo, D. J. (2013). Toward an integrative, learning-based model of psychotherapy supervision: Supervisory alliance, educational interventions, and supervisee learning/relearning. *Journal of Psychotherapy Integration, 23,* 75–95.

Young, C., Schulthess, P., Szyszkowitx, T., Oudijks, R., & Stabingis, A. (2013). The professional competencies of a European psychotherapist: An EAP project. *International Journal of Psychotherapy, 17,* 39–57.

Index

Note: Figures in *italics*, tables in **bold**, boxes marked with 'b'
Abbreviations used in subentries:
CLES – Clinical Learning Environment and Supervision
IAPT – Improving Access to Psychological Therapies
MFT – marriage and family therapy
REACTS – Rating of Experiential learning And Components of Teaching & Supervision

The Wiley International Handbook of Clinical Supervision, First Edition. Edited by C. Edward Watkins, Jr. and Derek L. Milne.

www.ingramcontent.com/pod-product-compliance
Lightning Source LLC
Chambersburg PA
CBHW081602160925
32635CB00005B/293